The Emerald International Handbook of Technology-Facilitated Violence and Abuse

The Emerald International Handbook of Technology-Facilitated Violence and Abuse

COMPILED AND EDITED BY

JANE BAILEY
University of Ottawa, Canada

ASHER FLYNN
Monash University, Australia

NICOLA HENRY
RMIT University, Australia

emerald PUBLISHING

United Kingdom – North America – Japan – India – Malaysia – China

Emerald Publishing Limited
Howard House, Wagon Lane, Bingley BD16 1WA, UK

First edition 2021

British Library Cataloguing in Publication Data
A catalogue record for this book is available from the British Library

ISBN: 978-1-83982-849-2 (Print)
ISBN: 978-1-83982-848-5 (Online)
ISBN: 978-1-83982-850-8 (Epub)

Printed and bound by CPI Group (UK) Ltd, Croydon, CR0 4YY

Open Access

The ebook edition of this title is Open Access and is freely available to read online.

ISOQAR certified Management System, awarded to Emerald for adherence to Environmental standard ISO 14001:2004.

ISOQAR REGISTERED

Certificate Number 1985
ISO 14001

INVESTOR IN PEOPLE

Table of Contents

Section 5 Intimate Partner Violence and Digital Coercive Control

Section 6 Legal Responses

List of Figures and Tables

Chapter 40

Chapter 5

Chapter 6

Chapter 12

Chapter 14

About the Editors and Contributors

Editors

Jane Bailey is a Full Professor at the University of Ottawa Faculty of Law (Common Law) in Canada. Jane's research focuses on technology's intersections with law and equality, with a particular current focus on technology-facilitated violence and its impacts on young people from marginalized communities. She has published and spoken locally, nationally, and internationally on a wide variety of technology-related topics, including "cyberbullying," online hate, gender-based technology-facilitated violence, and the discriminatory effects of corporate data collection practices and how those practices set young people up for conflict and harassment. She currently co-leads The eQuality Project, a seven-year Social Sciences and Humanities Research Council of Canada research initiative funded by a Cdn$2.5 million Partnership Grant. The Project involves an interdisciplinary group of researchers from Canada, the US, Hong Kong, and Finland, as well as over 20 community, governmental, educational, and youth organizations. It focuses on young people's experiences with privacy and equality in digitally networked environments. Jane leads the Project stream on technology-facilitated violence. She is a member of the New College of the Royal Society of Canada and the Women's Legal Education and Action Fund Committee on Gender-Based Technology-Facilitated Violence, was awarded the Ramon John Hnatyshyn Award for Law by the Canadian Bar Association, acted as lead counsel for an intervener before the Supreme Court of Canada on its first case dealing with the offense of voyeurism, and has been a visiting professor at RMIT, Hong Kong University, and the Universidad de Puerto Rico.

Dr Asher Flynn is an Associate Professor of Criminology at Monash University, a Group of Eight institution in Victoria, Australia. Asher's research utilizes a socio-legal framework to understand, critique, and transform legal policy and practice, with a particular focus on gendered and technology-facilitated violence and abuse. Asher has published widely and is lead researcher on several projects in the fields of AI-facilitated abuse, deepfakes, gendered violence, and image-based sexual abuse. Asher is the recipient of a number of prestigious national and international research fellowships including at the University of Durham, Pennsylvania State University, the University of Manchester, and the University of Warwick. She has advised the United Nations, Facebook, and the Australian Office of the eSafety Commissioner on policy and prevention of technology-facilitated violence and abuse and has received several awards for her research.

Nicola Henry is an Associate Professor and Vice-Chancellor's Principal Research Fellow in the Social and Global Studies Center at RMIT University (Melbourne, Australia). Nicola's research focuses on the prevalence, nature, and impacts of sexual violence, including legal and non-legal responses in Australian and international contexts. The goal of her work is to contribute to social, legal, and political change, deepen knowledge, and provide support to victim–survivors of violence. She has conducted numerous projects on image-based sexual abuse and technology-facilitated abuse which have led to significant legal and policy change in Australia. She is a member of the Office of the eSafety Commissioner's Expert Advisory Committee. She was Expert Advisor on the development of the eSafety Office's world-first image-based abuse portal as well as the award-winning eSafety Women: Online Training for Frontline Workers. Nicola has published widely in the sexual violence field and has been interviewed many times for television, radio, print, and online media.

Contributors

Moira Aikenhead is a PhD Candidate at the Peter A. Allard School of Law at the University of British Columbia, Canada. Her dissertation research explores the Canadian criminal response to technology-facilitated intimate partner violence through a feminist lens, and she has previously published research on Canada's nonconsensual distribution and voyeurism laws.

Sukaina Al-Nasrawi is a sustainable development expert at the United Nations ESCWA. She has a notable record of publications in the areas of technology for gender equality, digital divide, and smart sustainable cities, among others. Sukaina received research and professional awards including the United Nations Gold Award for Advancing Gender Equality and the Empowerment of Women. She holds a PhD in technology for development.

Briony E. Anderson is a graduate researcher in Criminology at the University of Melbourne, recently commencing her PhD candidature in 2020. Briony's thesis engages with privacy and anonymity in online space by considering the harm experience of doxxing.

Dr Kim Barker is Senior Lecturer in Law at the Open University (UK). Dr Barker's research focuses on internet regulation and intellectual property law. Her research focuses on the online regulation of platforms, with specific expertise in online abuses, online violence, and the legal responsibilities of internet actors.

Tabrina M. Bratton is a PhD student in the Department of Criminal Justice at the University of Arkansas at Little Rock. She received her Master's Degree in Criminal Justice. Tabrina's research interest includes public attitudes toward sexual and gender minority populations, policy processes, and technology-facilitated victimization.

Ella Broadbent is a Criminology Honors graduate, who has completed a thesis researching image-based sexual abuse. Her research interests include the role social media plays in facilitating violence and harm and how mixed methods and quantitative research design can enrich criminological scholarship.

Elena Cama is a Scientia PhD Candidate at UNSW Law in Sydney, Australia. She is a mixed methods researcher with a background in criminology, social science, and public health. Her PhD research focuses on digital communications technologies and the perpetration of sexual harms in online dating.

Professor Bronwyn Carlson is an Aboriginal scholar and Head of the Department of Indigenous Studies at Macquarie University. She is the recipient of three consecutive Australia Research Council grants that focus on Indigenous cultural, social, and political engagements on social media. Her current project explores Indigenous people's experiences of online conflict.

Anne Cheung is a Professor of Law at the University of Hong Kong whose research encompasses the areas of law and technology, freedom of expression, and privacy. Her most recent project concerns China's social credit system, and she is the co-editor of Privacy and Legal Issues in Cloud Computing (2015).

Sarai Chisala-Tempelhoff LLB (Hons) LLM is a Malawian human rights lawyer and legal researcher. She is the founder and Executive Director of the Gender and Justice Unit, an initiative that hones in on legal empowerment as a tool to bring about gender equality and social justice in Malawi.

Ben Colliver is a Lecturer in Criminology at Birmingham City University. His research interests include hate crime, queer studies, gender, and sexuality. He has recently published in the area of online hate speech. He is a member of the steering group of the British Society of Criminology Hate Crime Network.

Dr Elizabeth Coombs was Privacy Commissioner of New South Wales, Australia from 2011–2017 and held CEO positions and statutory appointments in Government. Based in Malta, Elizabeth works for the UN Special Rapporteur on the Right to Privacy, chairing the Taskforce "Privacy and Personality" and acting as a member of Health-Related Data; Corporations' Use of Personal Data, and Big Data–Open Data Taskforces.

Walter S. DeKeseredy is Anna Deane Carlson Endowed Chair of Social Sciences, Director of the Research Center on Violence, and Professor of Sociology at West Virginia University. He has published 26 books and over 100 refereed journal articles on topics such as woman abuse, rural criminology, and critical criminological theory.

Christopher Dietzel is a PhD candidate at McGill University. His doctoral research examines sexual consent related to dating app use and sexual violence against LGBTQ+ people.

Suzie Dunn is a PhD candidate and a Part-Time Professor at the University of Ottawa, Faculty of Law. Her research centers on the intersections of gender, equality, technology, and the law, with a specific focus the nonconsensual distribution of intimate images, deepfakes, and impersonation in digital spaces.

Dr Ryan Frazer is a settler scholar and cultural geographer. He recently completed his PhD, which drew on the work of Deleuze and Guattari to rethink geographies of care, volunteering, and refugee resettlement. He is currently Postdoctoral Research Fellow in Indigenous Studies, exploring Indigenous people's experiences of online conflict.

Chandell Gosse (she/her) is a PhD Candidate in Media Studies in the Faculty of Information and Media Studies at Western University in London, Ontario. Her research takes an interdisciplinary approach and sits most broadly at the intersection of feminism, digital culture, and anti-violence work. Find her on Twitter @ChandellEnid

Dr Elly Hanson is a Clinical Psychologist who focuses on the prevention of sexual abuse and reducing its impact. She has both academic and practice-based strands to her work, undertaking research, consultation, training and assessments, and working primarily with educators, law enforcement, social workers, survivors, and charities. Elly's recent research and writing has focused on online forces and dynamics conducive to sexual abuse.

Bridget Harris is an Australian Research Council DECRA Fellow based at Queensland University of Technology. Bridget researches on violence against women and spatiality; gender-based violence; domestic and family violence; and technology-facilitated violence, advocacy, and justice. Her edited collection (with Woodlock) examines Domestic Violence and Technology: Experiences, Perpetration, and Responses (Routledge).

Pam Hrick (JD, LLM) is a lawyer at Stockwoods LLP in Toronto, Canada. She maintains a broad practice that includes civil litigation, administrative law, criminal law, and constitution litigation. She regularly advises and represents survivors of sexual violence.

Heather K. Hudson is an Associate Professor in the Department of Health Sciences at the University of Central Arkansas. She received her PhD in Health Education from Southern Illinois University. Her research interests include human sexuality and technology, sexual communication and social media, and women's health issues.

Nchelem Kokomma Ichegbo is a Program Officer at Viable Knowledge Masters in Nigeria where she provides technical support to multiple projects. She is experienced in conducting literature reviews and collecting quantitative and qualitative data. She has interests in adapting technological innovations to public health and education.

Michael Gboyega Ilesanmi is a Senior Social Development Specialist and Social Safeguards Coordinator for the World Bank Nigeria Country Office, Abuja. Currently, he is co-leading the World Bank's operation on Women's Economic Empowerment in Nigeria and leads the Bank's GBV risk mitigation work in Nigeria.

Dr Emma A. Jane is an Associate Professor at UNSW Sydney. Her interdisciplinary research focuses on the political, economic, social, technological, legal, and environmental (PESTLE) causes and effects of emerging technology. Dr Jane's 10th book—Misogyny Online: A Short (and Brutish) History—was published by Sage in 2017.

Dr Olga Jurasz is a Senior Lecturer in Law at the Open University (UK). Dr Jurasz's research focuses on international law, human rights, and legal responses to violence against women (including online violence), specializing in feminist perspectives on law in these areas.

Dr Samantha Keene is a Lecturer at Criminology at the Institute of Criminology at Te Herenga Waka – Victoria University of Wellington. Dr Keene's research focuses on gendered experiences of crime, mainstream pornography and its effects, rough sex, and sexual violence.

Raine Liliefeldt is YWCA Canada's Director of Member Services and Development. She has over 16 years of experience in the nonprofit sector, was responsible for the federally-funded initiative Project Shift: Creating a Safer Digital World for Young Women, and oversees Lead Now, a national young women's leadership program.

Gisella Lopes Gomes Pinto Ferreira is a qualified lawyer in Brasil and has a degree in Law from UFMG. She holds a MPhil in Justice from Queensland University of Technology. Her thesis research explores the prevention of gendered violence in youth cohorts in Brasil.

Gabrielle L. Lory is a second-year PhD student at West Virginia University, specializing in criminology. Her research focuses on rural crime, violence against women, and restorative justice. She currently works as a Graduate Assistant in the Division of Diversity, Equity, and Inclusion and serves as co-editor of The Rural Criminologist newsletter.

Yee Man Louie is a PhD candidate at the Technology, Communication and Policy Lab, Digital Ethnography Research Center at RMIT University in Melbourne, Australia. Her current research focuses on the use of digital communication technologies, domestic violence, and the lived experiences of Chinese women in Melbourne.

Robert D. Lytle is an Assistant Professor in the Department of Criminal Justice at the University of Arkansas at Little Rock. He received his PhD in Criminology and Criminal Justice from the University of Nebraska – Omaha. Robert's research interests include criminal justice policy, corrections, and public attitudes about criminal justice.

Olusesan A. Makinde is the managing partner at Viable Knowledge Masters (VKM), a research and consulting company registered in Nigeria. He has researched the intersection between gender-based violence and social media in Nigeria.

Alison J. Marganski, PhD is Associate Professor and Director of Criminology at Le Moyne College in Syracuse, NY. Her research takes an interdisciplinary approach to studying violence (perpetration as well as victimization), including technologically facilitated violence, intimate partner violence, sexual violence, and mass murder, along with their respective solutions.

Olga Marques, PhD, is an Assistant Professor of Criminology and Justice at Ontario Tech University. Her teaching and research focuses on the construction, policing, and regulation of sexed, gendered, and raced bodies. She is also engaged in research on the impacts of incarceration, as well as Indigenous experiences of criminalization and victimization.

Lisa A. Melander, PhD, is an Associate Professor in the Department of Sociology, Anthropology, and Social Work at Kansas State University. Her primary research interests lie in the intersection of family and crime and include issues such as intimate partner violence, cyber aggression, and women's incarceration.

Neil Melhuish is Director of Policy and Research at Netsafe, New Zealand. He has worked on online safety issues since 2004.

Madeleine Novich, PhD is a Criminal Justice Professor at Manhattan College, USA. Her research focuses on the intersection of policing, procedural justice, and criminalized communities of color.

Emmanuel Olamijuwon is a Lecturer in the Department of Statistics and Demography at the University of Eswatini, Eswatini. He is also a PhD candidate in demography and population studies at the University of the Witwatersrand, South Africa. His current research examines opportunities for advancing sexual and reproductive health of young African adults in the digital age.

Dr Cheluchi Onyemelukwe is a lawyer, academic, and international consultant with expertise in gender law and policy, gender-based violence, international human rights, and health law and policy. She is Associate Professor of Law at Babcock University School of Law and Security Studies.

Dr Edgar Pacheco is a Research Analyst at Netsafe, New Zealand. His work focuses on online risks and harm as well as disability and higher education.

Eva PenzeyMoog is a user experience designer working to build out the field of "safety design." She works to make technology safe through centering the safety of survivors of domestic violence. Eva created the "Framework for Inclusive Safety" to help technologists create safe tech. Readers can learn more at www.inclusivesafety.com.

Dr Michael Salter is the Scientia Associate Professor of Criminology at the University of New South Wales, where he specializes in the study of complex trauma, gendered violence, and technology. He is an expert advisor to national and international online child protection agencies.

Sara Shayan is a lawyer practicing in Toronto, Ontario. She holds a Bachelor of Arts (Honors) in English Literature from the University of British Columbia and a JD from the University of Ottawa. The views and opinions expressed are those of the author and do not necessarily reflect the view of her employer.

Dr Danielle C. Slakoff is an Assistant Professor of Criminal Justice at California State University, Sacramento. Her research interests include media criminology and domestic violence. Danielle's work on women's issues within the criminal justice system can be found in Feminist Criminology, Sociology Compass, and Criminology, Criminal Justice, Law and Society.

Julia Slupska is a doctoral student at the Center for Doctoral Training in Cybersecurity and the Oxford Internet Institute. She researches how cybersecurity concepts and practices can address technologically mediated abuse, as well as how feminist theories and methodology—such as action research and the ethics of care—can improve cybersecurity.

Seonaid Stevenson-McCabe LLB (Hons) LLM is a Scottish lawyer and Lecturer in Law at Glasgow Caledonian University. Inspired by the rebellious lawyering movement founded by Gerald López, she is the co-founder of RebLaw Scotland, an organization which explores how law can be used as a tool for social justice.

Danielle M. Stoneberg is a PhD student in Sociology at West Virginia University. Her publications include articles in International Criminal Justice Review and Crime Prevention and Community Safety on topics such as drug use and policing in rural US communities and violence against women.

Leonie Maria Tanczer is Lecturer in International Security and Emerging Technologies at University College London's (UCL) Department of Science, Technology, Engineering and Public Policy (STEaPP). Her research focuses on questions related to internet security, and she is specifically interested in the intersection points of technology, security, and gender.

Kristen Thomasen is an Assistant Professor of Law, Robotics, and Society at the University of Windsor, Faculty of Law, and a PhD candidate at the University of Ottawa, Faculty of Law. Her research focuses on the legal, social, and ethical implications of robotic and autonomous machines, with particular focus on privacy and public spaces.

Chrissy Thompson holds a PhD in Criminology. Her doctoral research examined upskirting in Australia, and she has published on topics including media archeology, creepshots, viral justice, countersurveillance, and upskirting. Chrissy's research interests include understanding how crime intersects with technology, gender, and disability.

Elina Vaahensalo is a doctoral candidate in the field of digital culture at the University of Turku. Elina's chapter is based on her doctoral thesis that focuses on othering online discourse, polarization in internet cultures, and methods that can be applied to the study of online discussion cultures.

Dr Laura Vitis' research focuses on how technology is used to facilitate gendered, sexual, and domestic violence within the Global-South. Her work also examines the regulation of and resistance to technologically facilitated violence and youth sexting. In 2017, she co-edited a collection entitled Gender, Technology, and Violence for Routledge.

Ari Ezra Waldman is the John Marshall Harlan II Professor of Law and the Founding Director of the Innovation Center for Law and Technology at New York Law School. He earned a PhD in Sociology at Columbia University, a JD at Harvard Law School, and an AB, magna cum laude, at Harvard College.

Dr Alice Witt is a postdoctoral research fellow in the Digital Media Research Center, Faculty of Law at the Queensland University of Technology. Her research investigates the exercise of governing power in the digital age, focusing on the intersections of regulation, technology, and gender.

Mark A. Wood is a Lecturer in Criminology in the School of Humanities and Social Sciences at Deakin University. Most of Mark's research falls within the digital criminology sphere and examines intersections between technology, crime, and criminal justice. His first monograph, Antisocial Media, was published by Palgrave Macmillan in 2017.

Delanie Woodlock is a community researcher and adjunct lecturer at University of New England, Armidale, Australia and associate with the Research Center on Violence at West Virginia University. Her research interests include violence against women, domestic violence, and the medicalization of women's health.

Alyssa Zduniak is an English, Political Science, and Philosophy major at Manhattan College, USA. She previously presented research at the Undergraduate Woman's Philosophy Conference and the International Symposium on Lasallian Research. Alyssa will be graduating in the spring of 2020 and plans to pursue a PhD in English.

Acknowledgments

The creation of this Handbook is a manifestation of our ongoing desire to build international, intersectoral, and interdisciplinary collaboration in order to better understand and meaningfully address technology-facilitated violence and abuse. It would not have been possible without support from the following funding agencies:

- The Social Sciences and Humanities Research Council of Canada, which funds The eQuality Project (eQ), a 7-year partnership initiative co-led by Valerie Steeves and Jane Bailey. eQ brings together academics, policy makers, educators, and community organizations who are concerned about how our digitally networked environment affects the privacy and equality rights of young people; and
- The Research Grants Council of the Hong Kong Special Administrative Region, China (HKU 17623016), which funded "Tackling cyberbullying by enhancing privacy protection," a research project led by Dr Anne Cheung of the University of Hong Kong Faculty of Law. Funding from Dr Cheung's grant made it possible for this Handbook to be published as Open Access, ensuring that its contents are widely and freely available.

We wish to acknowledge and thank research assistants Taylor Bain, Jasmine Dong, Stefani Vasil, and Alice Witt, as well as Robert Porter (The eQ Project Manager) for their unflagging and dedicated efforts and support that were critical to seeing this Handbook through to completion. We also want to thank the Emerald Publishing team, in particular Jules Willan and Carys Morley, and the Digital Crime, Technology and Social Harms Series Editors, James Martin and Asher Flynn, for their ongoing support, responses to our numerous queries, and for their dedication to the research field of TFVA, which has helped result in an Open Access edition of this collection. Thanks also to the wonderful colleagues who generously donated their time to provide peer reviews of many of the chapters in this collection.

Jane wishes to personally thank her family for their unflinching patience, level-headedness, and amazing hugs. She is also deeply grateful to all of her eQ colleagues, including Drs Valerie Steeves, Jacquelyn Burkell, Priscilla Regan, and Leslie Regan Shade for always being willing to lend their wisdom, insights, expertise, and kind hearts when she needed them most. Thanks also to Angela

Cameron for being a wonderful colleague and friend and to Natasha Bakht, editor of the Canadian Journal of Women and the Law, for her help with obtaining the rights to republish the Bailey & Shayan chapter. And last, but not least, she wants to express her gratitude to her co-editors Nicola and Asher for working with her to bring the vision for this book to life in the face of all odds – notwithstanding the fact that an entire globe separates her from them and the uncertainties and tragedies arising from the arrival of a global pandemic midway through the process.

Asher wishes to thank her supportive and loving family, in particular, her amazing son Henry, who lights up this world and is going to make it a better place. She also wants to thank her colleagues and friends for their ongoing support, guidance and generosity – especially David Bright, Anastasia Powell, and Greg Stratton who have been the most wonderful lockdown companions throughout the uncertainty and difficult times we have experienced in 2020. Finally, she offers a big thank you to her co-editors – Jane and Nicola. Jane, thank you for your inclusive, supportive and understanding leadership style in keeping this collection moving forward. You are a generous and inspiring colleague.

Nicola: To my wonderful family: Mum, Dad, Justine, Emma, Matt, Alex, Mike, Emily, Isabel, Maya, Esther, Owen, Sylvie, Claire, and Ava, and to my aunties, uncles, and cousins, and to Brent's family – thank you for your support, love, and care. To my lovely friends, colleagues, and mentors: Nesam, Harriet, Kirstie, Rachel, Lea, Megan, Duncan, Sharyn, Jackie, Catherine, Ceridwen, Peta, Katherine, Suellen, Stef, Alice, Clare, Nicola, Angelica, Felicity, and Ascelin – thank you for your wisdom, humility, integrity, and generosity. To my co-editors: Jane and Asher – thank you for your amazing work on this collection, and a special thanks to Jane for doing such a great job in leading this. Finally, I would like to thank Brent and Frederick for providing me with a sublime sanctuary called home – thank you for always supporting me and believing in me.

Technology-Facilitated Violence and Abuse: International Perspectives and Experiences

Jane Bailey, Nicola Henry, and Asher Flynn

Abstract

While digital technologies have led to many important social and cultural advances worldwide, they also facilitate the perpetration of violence, abuse and harassment, known as technology-facilitated violence and abuse (TFVA). TFVA includes a spectrum of behaviors perpetrated online, offline, and through a range of technologies, including artificial intelligence, live-streaming, GPS tracking, and social media. This chapter provides an overview of TFVA, including a brief snapshot of existing quantitative and qualitative research relating to various forms of TFVA. It then discusses the aims and contributions of this book as a whole, before outlining five overarching themes arising from the contributions. The chapter concludes by mapping out the structure of the book.

Keywords: Technology-facilitated; violence and abuse; digital crime; intersectionality; violence; systemic discrimination and abuse

Introduction

Digital technologies have led to many important social and cultural changes worldwide, but they are also implicated in the facilitation of abusive behaviors. Technology-facilitated violence and abuse (TFVA) is an umbrella term used to describe the use of digital technologies to perpetrate interpersonal harassment, abuse, and violence, such as sexual violence (e.g., Powell & Henry, 2017), domestic and family violence (e.g., Douglas, Harris, & Dragiewicz, 2019;

The Emerald International Handbook of Technology-Facilitated Violence and Abuse, 1–17

doi:10.1108/978-1-83982-848-520211001

Fraser, Olsen, Lee, Southworth, & Tucker, 2010; Woodlock, 2017), prejudice-based hatred (e.g., Barnett, 2007; Citron, 2014; Perry & Olsson, 2009), and online othering (e.g., Lumsden & Harmer, 2019).

There are numerous examples of TFVA. These include (but are not limited to) technology-facilitated sexual assault (the use of digital devices or apps to facilitate in-person sexual assault); image-based sexual abuse (the nonconsensual taking, sharing, or threats to share intimate images); cyberstalking (surveillance, monitoring, repeated contact, and impersonation); unwelcome requests and sexual solicitation; image-based harassment (the sending of unwanted and unsolicited explicit images); hate speech; threats of rape and violence; restricting access to and use of technology for purposes of isolation and coercion; exposure to violent and abusive imagery (whether sexual or nonsexual); the creation, distribution, and possession of child sexual exploitation materials; cyberbullying; and the nonconsensual disclosure of personal information, also known as "doxxing." TFVA is carried out through text, images, and unwanted digitally-enabled or enhanced surveillance and monitoring, using a variety of devices and platforms from basic digital tools, such as texting, email, and social media, to more advanced technologies such as artificial intelligence (AI) (Flynn, 2019; Henry, Powell, & Flynn, 2018), GPS tracking (Wong, 2019), and drones (Thomasen, 2018).

TFVA arises in both public and private contexts across a spectrum of human relationships between strangers, acquaintances, friends, family members, and intimate partners (Citron, 2014). While a broad spectrum of people have experienced TFVA across different categories of age, sex, race, ethnicity, ability, sexuality, or socioeconomic status, TFVA is not simply a collection of random acts of hostility and animosity. It is a product of existing intersecting layers of structural and systemic inequalities (Southern & Harmer, 2019), such as misogyny (Henry, Flynn, & Powell, 2020), homophobia (Green, 2019), transphobia (Colliver, Coyle, & Silvestri, 2019), racism (Kerrigan, 2019), colonialism (Carlson, 2019), and ableism (Hall, 2019), with some forms disproportionately affecting children and young people (Powell & Henry, 2019; Quayle & Koukopoulos, 2018). Further, in the digital environment, corporate structuring and monitoring practices for the purposes of maximizing profit contribute to and shape TFVA, its proliferation, and its impacts (Dragiewicz et al., 2018).

This introduction provides an overview of existing quantitative and qualitative research relating to various forms of TFVA. It then discusses the aims and contributions of this Handbook, highlighting the breadth of the research included, before proceeding to focus on five overarching themes arising from these collected works. Finally, it maps out the sections within the book, each of which is preceded in the Handbook by its own introductory remarks.

Existing Research on TFVA

Quantitative Studies

While its presence and impacts span the globe, much of the existing published quantitative and qualitative research on TFVA is dominated by industrialized nations in the Global-North, such as Australia, the United States, and the United Kingdom. Some quantitative (survey-based) research has examined TFVA across a range of behaviors (e.g., Australia Institute, 2019; Pew Research Center, 2014; Powell & Henry, 2019). Others have focused on individual behaviors, for example, image-based sexual abuse (e.g., Citron, 2014; Lenhart, Ybarra, & Price-Feeney, 2016a; Henry et al., 2020; OeSC, 2017; Powell, Henry, & Flynn, 2018; Powell, Henry, Flynn, & Scott, 2019; Powell, Scott, Henry, & Flynn, 2020; Ruvalcaba & Eaton, 2019); digital dating abuse (e.g., Borrajo, Gámez-Guadix, Pereda, & Calvete 2015; Burke, Wallen, Vail-Smith, & Knox, 2011; Marganski & Melander, 2018; Martinez-Pecino & Durán, 2019; Ybarra, Price-Feeney, Lenhart, & Zickuhr, 2017); hate speech (e.g., OeSC, 2020); image-based harassment (e.g., Oswald, Lopes, Skoda, Hesse & Pederson, 2020); trolling (e.g., Akhtar & Morrison, 2019); online sexual harassment (e.g., Baumgartner, Valkenburg, & Peter, 2010; Douglass, Wright, Davis, & Lim, 2018; Powell & Henry, 2017); and cyberbullying (especially among youth – for a scoping review, see Brochado, Soares, & Fraga, 2016). Little quantitative research has investigated sexual assault victimization via online dating sites/apps or online rape threats (Powell & Henry, 2017; Rowse, Bolt, & Gaya, 2020), although a considerable amount of quantitative research has focused on online child sexual exploitation (e.g., Karayianni, Fanti, Diakidoy, Hadjicharamlambous, & Katsimicha, 2017).

With the exception of studies on digital dating abuse (e.g., Borrajo et al., 2015; Burke et al., 2011; Marganski & Melander, 2018; Martinez-Pecino & Durán, 2019; Ybarra et al., 2017), there is very little prevalence data on TFVA in the context of domestic and family violence (Messing, Bagwell-Gray, Brown, Kappas, & Durfee, 2020; Woodlock, 2017). Relatedly, little is known about the nexus or co-occurrence of TFVA with "in-person" experiences of sexual and domestic violence (Marganski & Melander, 2018) – also known as "poly-victimization" (Finkelhor, Ormrod, Turner, & Hamby, 2005). Studies on cyber-bullying show that victim-survivors are more likely to be also victims of offline bullying, such as abuse in the school yard (e.g., Hinduja & Patchin, 2008).

Qualitative Studies

A variety of qualitative studies have been conducted with "targets" (or victim-survivors) and frontline workers who support them in relation to cyberstalking (e.g., Dimond, Fiesler, & Bruckman, 2011; Weathers & Hopson, 2015); technology-facilitated domestic violence (Douglas et al., 2019; Dragiewicz et al., 2019; George & Harris, 2014; Harris & Woodlock, 2019; OeSC, 2019a; Woodlock, 2017); image-based sexual abuse (Amudsen, 2019; Bates, 2017; Henry, Flynn, & Powell, 2018; Henry et al., 2020; McGlynn et al., 2019, 2020; OeSC, 2017); image-based sexual harassment (Mandau, 2020); online sexual harassment; technology-facilitated sexual assault (Gillett, 2019); online hate (Lewis, Rowe, & Wiper, 2019; Smith, 2019); online child sexual exploitation (e.g., Gerwitz-Meydan, Walsh, Wolak, & Finkelhor, 2018; for an overview of studies see; DeMarco, Sharrock, Crowther, & Barnard, 2018); cyberbullying (especially in relation to children and youth – for an overview of studies see Dennehy et al., 2020); and TFVA more broadly (Henry & Powell, 2015; OeSC, 2019a, b; Powell & Henry, 2017). More research focusing on the experiences of Indigenous peoples; racial minorities; people with disabilities [but see: Alhaboby, al-Khateeb, Barnes, and Short (2016); Alhaboby, Barnes, Evans, and Short (2019)];

sex workers; lesbian, gay, bisexual, transgender, queer, and intersex (LGBTQI+) people; as well as those living in rural, regional, and remote areas is needed. Quantitative studies have shown that these groups (especially women within these groups) are more likely to experience TFVA and/or to experience more adverse impacts (e.g., Henry et al., 2020; Powell et al., 2019, 2020; OeSC, 2017, 2019a, b; Douglas et al., 2018; Lenhart, Ybarra, Zickuhr, & Price-Feeney, 2016b; Powell & Henry, 2019; Ybarra et al., 2017).

There have been relatively few qualitative studies of TFVA perpetrators and bystanders, although there are a number focused on offenders in the contexts of online child sexual exploitation and abuse (e.g., DeMarco et al., 2018), image-based sexual abuse against adults (e.g., Hall & Hearn, 2017; Henry & Flynn, 2019; OeSC, 2019c; Uhl et al., 2018); and online hate speech (e.g., Jane, 2014). Additionally, a number of qualitative studies have focused on perpetrator behaviors by examining content on online platforms, such as 4chan (Green, 2019), Reddit (Lumsden, 2019), Twitter (Megarry, 2014; Southern & Harmer, 2019), YouTube (Colliver et al., 2019), and Facebook (Scrivens & Amarasingam, 2020).

Research on Responses to TFVA

Often the empirical literature on TFVA also includes recommendations as to how best to respond to TFVA (see, e.g., Bailey, 2015; Harris, 2020; Henry, Flynn, & Powell, 2019; Powell et al., 2020). There is also, however, a significant literature focused primarily on proposing and/or analyzing the efficacy of one or more responses, including legal (criminal, civil, human rights, and regulatory), technological, and educational approaches, as well as improved support for TFVA targets and self-help initiatives undertaken by targets themselves.

In some cases, the analyses address TFVA generally (see, e.g., Bailey & Mathen, 2019; Dunn, Lalonde, & Bailey, 2017; Sheikh, 2018). In other cases, they focus on responses to specific forms of TFVA, including *image-based sexual abuse* [see, e.g., Citron & Franks, 2014 (focusing on criminal law); Dodge, 2019 (focusing on criminal law); Henry et al., 2020 (focusing on a range of legal and nonlegal responses); Powell & Henry, 2017 (focusing on digital citizenship)]; *online hate speech* [see, e.g., Bailey, 2010 (focusing on human rights–based legal responses); Citron, 2014 (focusing on a range of responses)]; *online harassment and trolling* [see, e.g., Bailey, 2017 (focusing on education policy); Citron, 2014; Pavan, 2017 (focusing on intermediary responsibility)]; *cyberbullying* [see, e.g., Hinduja, 2018 (focusing on building resilience)]; *technology-facilitated intimate partner violence* [see, e.g., Al-Alosi, 2020 (both considering technological responses); Harris, 2020; Tanczer, Lopez Neira, Parkin, Patel, & Danezis, 2018 (considering, among other things, improved security legislation)]; *online child sexual exploitation* [see, e.g., Bailey, 2007 (considering criminal law responses); Salter, 2018 (considering, among other things, therapeutic and legal responses)]; *online sexual harassment* [see, e.g., Jane, 2017; Vitis & Gilmour, 2017 (both focusing self-help/grassroots responses)]; and *abusive and offensive online content* [see, e.g., Bailey, 2018; Cheer, 2018; Schweppe, 2018 (all focusing primarily on criminal law responses)].

This Handbook

We imagined this collection as one that would contribute to the existing landscape in part by breaking away from geographic, sectoral, and disciplinary silos. To achieve this, we have brought together the work of a diverse range of contributors from 13 countries (Australia, Brasil, Canada, Eswatini, Finland, Hong Kong, Malawi, Malta, New Zealand, Nigeria, Scotland, the United Kingdom, and the United States) and seven different sectors (academia, ICT, nonprofit, consulting, policy, regulatory, and legal practice). Our academic contributions come from scholars in 11 different fields (communications/media studies; law; sociology; health; education; political studies; justice/criminology; behavioral studies; social, global, and cultural studies; digital ethics; and science and engineering), some of whom collaborated with contributors from different areas in the nonprofit sector (women's rights/gender equality, public health, development, privacy rights, and domestic violence). Our contributors report on research drawing on the lived experiences of TFVA targets in places around the globe from a wide range of social locations affected by categories such as gender, gender identity, age, sexual identity, race, and indigeneity, as well as from the on-the-ground advocates and community organizations that support them. They also present insights from academics and policy organizations actively engaged in developing meaningful responses for preventing and/or remedying the harms they inflict, as well as firsthand perspectives from TFVA perpetrators.

Our aim in bringing together this international, intersectoral, intersectional, and interdisciplinary group of contributors, whose work covers a wide spectrum of forms of TFVA, is to produce synergies that reinvigorate discussions of TFVA, encouraging opportunities for future collaboration, as well as insights from one area that could be applied to others. We also hope that in showcasing a range of legal, empirical, and theoretical research focused on the targets, support services, and perpetrators of TFVA, across a diverse range of social locations, as well as multiple strategies for addressing TFVA, this collection can contribute toward nuanced understandings of this complex phenomenon that can open up opportunities for developing meaningful multifaceted responses grounded in recognition of TFVA as both a product and producer of intersecting systems of power.

Research Contributions of this Handbook

This Handbook's empirical contributions include qualitative analyses of:

(1) Interviews and/or focus groups with:

- Men who have sex with men, and their understandings of "rape culture" on Grindr (Dietzel);
- Brasilian and Australian advocates working on technology-facilitated intimate partner abuse among youth (Lopes Gomes Pinto Ferreira);
- Canadian women who have experienced online abuse (Gosse);

- Women in remote, regional, and rural areas of Australia who have experienced digital coercive control (Harris & Woodlock, 2018);
- Australian women who have experienced online lateral violence from other women (Jane);
- New Zealand young heterosexual adults on their experiences of pleasure and harm relating to online pornography (Keene);
- Australian domestic violence practitioners on the experiences of their culturally and linguistically diverse women clients (Louie);
- Canadian sexual violence frontline professionals on their clients' experiences of nonconsensual disclosure of intimate images (Marques);
- US college students' understandings of the impacts of technologically shared images of racist police brutality (Novich & Zduniak);
- Singaporean frontline domestic violence, sexual violence, and LGBTQI+ support workers and the experiences of their clients (Vitis);

(2) Online content including:

- Counter-hegemonic responses to gendered violence on Twitter (Broadbent & Thompson);
- Transphobic comments on YouTube (Colliver);
- Digital platform policies to identify whether and how they address image-based sexual abuse (Henry & Witt);
- Discriminatory discussion threads posted on a Finnish discussion forum (Vaahensalo);
- Self-help efforts to address online child sexual exploitation (Salter & Hanson); and

(3) Existing research on:

- Doxxing (Anderson & Wood);
- Polyvictimization and TFVA (DeKeseredy, Lory, & Stoneberg); and
- TFVA against members of Indigenous communities (Bailey & Shayan; Carlson & Frazer).

This Handbook's empirical contributions also include quantitative analyses of:

(1) Young people's experiences of TFVA in sub-Saharan Africa (Makinde, Olamijuwon, Ichegbo, & Ilesanmi);
(2) Adult perpetrators of TFVA in New Zealand (Pacheco & Melhuish); and
(3) Gay and bisexual men's sharing and privacy-protection practices when using queer dating apps (Waldman).

Finally, this Handbook contributes to the literature relating to the spectrum of responses to TFVA, through analyses of:

(1) Theoretical and legal understandings of "violence" and the place of TFVA within them (Dunn);
(2) Legal responses to image and text-based abuse in the United Kingdom (Barker & Jurasz);

(3) International law instruments applicable to TFVA, particularly gender-based TFVA (Coombs);
(4) International and Arab region legal responses to gender-based TFVA (Al Nasrawi);
(5) Legal responses to image-based sexual abuse in Malawi and Scotland (Chisala-Templehoff & Stevenson);
(6) Judicial approaches to prosecution of (ex) intimate partners for nonconsensual distribution of intimate images in Canadian criminal law proceedings (Aikenhead);
(7) Legal approaches to privacy in the context of TFVA (Thomasen & Dunn);
(8) Legal approaches to doxxing in Hong Kong (Cheung);
(9) Benefits and limitations of responding to TFVA through statutory agencies (Hrick);
(10) Technology-based responses to TFVA (Marganski & Melander; PenzeyMoog & Slakoff; Slupska & Tanczer);
(11) Community-based/self-help/collaborative responses to TFVA (Broadbent & Thompson; Lytle, Hudson, & Bratton; Bailey & Liliefeldt); and
(12) Corporate responsibility for TFVA (Salter & Hanson; Henry & Witt).

Five Key Insights from this Handbook

While this collection yields a myriad of insights and possibilities for future engagement, below we highlight five overarching themes interwoven within this diverse group of contributions: (i) the importance of context; (ii) the need to define and redefine understandings of "violence"; (iii) the power of words and images; (iv) the need to think systemically; and (v) the need to employ a spectrum of legal responses that move beyond criminal law, as well as approaches beyond law altogether. Here we highlight aspects of each of these, leaving more detailed analyses of the content of each chapter for the introductions that precede each section of the collection.

The Importance of Context

The importance of taking context into account in order to better understand and respond to TFVA emerges from this collection in three main ways. The first relates to the critical role that contextuality plays in social science research focused on TFVA. For example, the chapters of Edgar Pacheco and Neil Melhuish, Olusean Makinde et al., and Lopes Gomes Pinto Ferreira, underscore the importance of supplementing quantitative findings with in-depth qualitative analyses in order to better understand and represent lived perspectives. These chapters raise questions about why those who perpetrate and experience behaviors often associated with TFVA fail to categorize them as forms of violence and abuse. There may be a variety of reasons to explain such quantitative findings. Perhaps survey respondents are uninformed or they are immersed in environments where violence is normalized. On the other hand, particular sorts of behavior (e.g., repeatedly texting someone during the day) could be part of otherwise harmless or even consensual practices. In these kinds of cases, supplemental qualitative research will often be a useful tool for better understanding the context in which listed behaviors are occurring, and concomitantly how to identify and meaningfully address those that are problematic. Further, as Bronwyn Carlson and Ryan Frazer point out, perspectives about "what counts" as a form of TFVA can be intimately interconnected with culture, thereby undermining the explanatory power of quantitative research based on standardized definitions with members of mainstream groups.

Second, context can and arguably should play a critical role in developing legal responses to TFVA. Anne Cheung's chapter, for example, illustrates the importance of sociopolitical context in differentiating legal responses to nonconsensually disclosing personal information about others online (doxxing) for the purposes of calling public authorities to account from doxxing for other motivations, such as sexual shaming and humiliation. Cheung's particular approach to doxxing in the Hong Kong context is consistent with Bree Anderson and Mark Wood's more general conclusion that doxxing should be understood as a typology of "interconnected motivations, expressions and experiences of harm." Seonaid Stevenson-McCabe's and Sarai Chisala-Templehoff's chapter emphasizes the role that context plays in determining whether a legal solution from one jurisdiction is likely to be workable in another. Kristen Thomasen's and Suzie Dunn's chapter centers the role of equality considerations in the legal interpretation and application of privacy principles, especially in cases involving the nonconsensual disclosure of intimate images, a form of privacy violation with particular consequences for women and members of LGBTQI+ communities that arise primarily from preexisting prejudices such as misogyny, homophobia, and transphobia.

Third, the chapters by Elena Cama, Chris Dietzel, and Moira Aikenhead remind us of the impact of preexisting rape cultures on understandings of and responses to TFVA. Cama and Dietzel's chapters connect sexually violent forms of TFVA on dating apps with pervasive myths and stereotypes about sexuality and gender that serve to normalize and excuse sexual violence harms. Similarly, Aikenhead's analysis of so-called "revenge porn" cases prosecuted under Canada's criminal prohibition on the nondisclosure of intimate images reveals the way that rape culture myths around women's sexuality lead to blaming targets for their own victimization and consequently manifest themselves in fact and in law.

Defining and Redefining "Violence"

Several chapters in the collection underscore the importance of grappling with preexisting conceptions of "violence" in order to understand how nonphysical technology-facilitated behaviors can and should be understood as "violence." Suzie Dunn's chapter emphasizes the role that conceptualizing TFVA as violence can play in communicating its social unacceptability (even with respect to actions that do not rise to the level of being illegal). Chandel Gosse's chapter further illustrates the complex ways in which the "online/offline" dichotomy works to minimize TFVA and in burdening TFVA targets to prove that the harms are "real." The chapters by Walter DeKeseredy, Danielle Stoneberg, and Gabrielle Lory, Bridget Harris and Delanie Woodlock, and Laura Vitis further challenge this false dichotomy by demonstrating the ways that TFVA can both emanate from and bleed into harmful *physical* interactions.

The Power of Words and Images

In digitally networked environments, words and images have power, yet false dichotomies, such as online/offline and real/virtual, work to obscure the real impacts of TFVA. The chapters by Kim Barker and Olga Jurasz (on the need for a legal response to online verbal assaults), Bridget Harris and Delanie Woodlock (on remote, regional, and rural women's experiences of digital coercive control), Emma Jane (on lateral violence between women in online spaces), and Laura Vitis (on TFVA in the context of intimate partner violence) highlight in particular the power of words as tools for exerting control over others in ways that undermine targets' dignity, security, and sense of self-worth, as well as their willingness to participate in public life. Ben Colliver (on anti-trans online discourse) and Elina Vaahensalo (on online othering) graphically illustrate in their chapters how words and discursive strategies are used as tools for re/making an "other" in an attempt to justify (or at least rationalize) violence and abuse.

In terms of the power of images, Olga Marques' chapter emphasizes the dignity and privacy harms arising from intimate images being circulated without consent because the images become a form of permanent remembering that freezes understandings and perceptions of the target at a particular point in time, not of their choosing. The chapters of Samantha Keene, and Madeleine Novich and Alyssa Zduniak highlight the differential effects of, respectively, sexually violent mainstream pornographic images and images of acts of police brutality on online spectators from different social locations, again revealing the power of images to cause harm.

Thinking Systemically: Corporations, the Role of the State, and Intersectionality

This collection also highlights the need to rethink individuated understandings of TFVA in favor of analyses that seek to understand and address TFVA as both a product and reflection of corporate, state, and discriminatory social systems. As the chapters of Nicola Henry and Alice Witt, and Michael Salter and Elly Hanson demonstrate, TFVA is perpetuated not just by "bad individuals," but also by the systems and practices of the technology companies that structure and facilitate online interactions. Ari Waldman's chapter builds upon these insights, highlighting the ways in which these structures can undermine gay and bisexual male dating app users' self-help strategies for avoiding TFVA by compromising their ability to maintain greater privacy. Bronwyn Carlson and Ryan Frazer's chapter demonstrates the harm done by research approaches that attempt to "standardize" conceptions such as "cyberbullying," noting the ways in which such homogenization fails to account for the lived realities of Indigenous peoples, whose experiences are shaped both by cultural traditions, as well as by often-intersecting "social forms of hate," including sexism, racism, homophobia, transphobia, and ableism. Jane Bailey and Sara Shayan's chapter reveals another outcome of taking a more systemic approach to TFVA. They highlight examples of both individual *and* state-based acts of TFVA targeting Indigenous peoples in Canada (with a particular focus on Indigenous women and girls), noting their intersecting colonialist, racist, and sexist underpinnings. Drawing on critical Indigenous scholarship, they argue Indigenous peoples are likely to have well-placed mistrust in colonial state-based responses to TFVA given the state's own involvement in perpetrating such acts.

Moving Beyond Law (Especially Criminal Law)

While a number of contributors call for improved laws for combatting TFVA, the theme of moving beyond law arises in two key ways. First, contributions such as those of Pam Hrick (focusing on administrative and regulatory bodies) and those by Elizabeth Coombs and Sukaina Al-Nasrawi (focusing on international human rights norms), while maintaining a focus on legal responses, help us to understand the roles that legal responses other than *criminal* law can play. Second, several contributions move beyond law completely to focus on technology-driven prevention of and responses to TFVA. Moving beyond state-based legal responses to TFVA is likely to be of particular relevance and import to members of marginalized communities that are disparately likely to be targeted by many forms of state violence (Palmater, 2016). While the chapters of Lopes Gomes Pinto Ferreira, Yee Man Louie, and Bridget Harris and Delanie Woodlock, highlight the particularly useful role that technological responses may play in serving isolated and socially marginalized targets of IPV, Alison Marganski and Lisa Melander, Eva PenzeyMoog and Danielle Slakoff, and Julia Slupska and Leonie Tanczer grapple with challenges and solutions for grounding technological design in targets' lived experiences. Finally, Ella Broadbent and Chrissy Thompson (counter-hegemonic tweets), Robert Lytle, Tabrina Bratton, and Heather Hudson (bystander intervention), Salter and Hanson (online self-help initiatives of child sexual exploitation survivors), and Jane Bailey and Raine Liliefeldt (multisector collaboration) focus on individual and collective strategies that can, in some instances, be understood as self-help strategies for seeking justice when formal legal channels are undesired, unavailable, and/or ineffective.

As discussed further in our Conclusion, the significance of bringing together diverse insights, experiences, and strategies for addressing TFVA and the underlying systemic drivers that inform it, have taken on renewed significance since we began this collection in 2019. The COVID-19 pandemic and the global outpouring of protests against highly publicized instances of anti-Black and other forms of racist violence and discrimination serve to remind us of the complex entanglements between our common humanity and the deep social, political, economic, technological, and geographic divisions between us. We hope that the collection of ideas and analyses presented here will contribute toward imagining a way forward.

The collection begins with contributions examining TFVA across a spectrum of behaviors. It then focuses more specifically on text-based harms before proceeding to image-based harms. Next, it considers TFVA in the relational contexts of dating apps and IPV. The final two sections focus on responses, beginning with legal approaches and ending with responses that move beyond law.

References

Akhtar, S., & Morrison, C. (2019). The prevalence and impact of online trolling of UK members of Parliament. *Computers in Human Behavior, 99*, 322–327. doi:10.1016/j.chb.2019.05.015

Al-Alosi, H. (2020). Fighting fire with fire: Exploring the potential of technology to help victims combat intimate partner violence. *Aggression and Violent Behavior, 52*, 101376. doi:10.1016/j.avb.2020.101376

Alhaboby, Z. A., al-Khateeb, H. M., Barnes, J., & Short, E. (2016). 'The language is disgusting and they refer to my disability': The cyberharassment of disabled people. *Disability & Society, 31*, 1138–1143. doi:10.1080/09687599.2016.1235313

Alhaboby, Z., Barnes, J., Evans, H., & Short, E. (2019). Cyber-victimization of people with chronic conditions and disabilities: A systematic review of scope and impact. *Trauma, Violence, & Abuse, 20*(3), 398–415. doi:10.1177/1524838017717743

Amundsen, R. (2019). 'The price of admission': On notions of risk and responsibility in women's sexting practices. In K. Lumsden & E. Harmer (Eds.), *Online othering: Exploring digital violence and discrimination on the Web* (pp. 145–164). Basingstoke: Palgrave Macmillan.

Australia Institute. (2019). *Trolls and polls: The economic costs of online harassment and cyberhate*. Retrieved from https://www.tai.org.au/content/trolls-and-polls-economic-costs-online-harassment-and-cyberhate

Bailey, J. (2007). Confronting collective harm: Technology's transformative impact on child pornography. *University of New Brunswick Law Journal, 56*, 65–102.

Bailey, J. (2010). Twenty years later Taylor still has it right: Section 13 of the CHRA's continuing contribution to equality. In S. McIntyre, & S. Rodgers (Eds.), *The Supreme Court of Canada and social justice: Commitment, retrenchment or retreat* (pp. 1–39). Markham, ON: Supreme Court Law Review and LexisNexis Canada.

Bailey, J. (2015). A perfect storm: How the online environment, social norms and law constrain girls' online lives. In J. E. Bailey & V. Steeves (Eds.), *eGirls, eCitizens: Putting technology, theory and policy into dialogue with girls' and young women's voices* (pp. 21–53). Ottawa, ON: University of Ottawa Press.

Bailey, J. (2017). From 'zero tolerance' to 'safe and accepting': Surveillance and equity implications of educational policy related to 'cyberbullying'. *Education and Law Journal, 26*, 146–162.

Bailey, J. (2018). *Abusive and offensive speech online: An overview of Canadian legal responses focusing on the criminal law framework*. London: UK Law Commission. Retrieved from https://s3-eu-west-2.amazonaws.com/lawcom-prod-storage-11jsxou24uy7q/uploads/2018/11/Canada-J-Bailey.pdf

Bailey, J., & Mathen, C. (2019). Technology-facilitated violence against women and girls: Assessing the Canadian criminal law response. *Canadian Bar Review*, *97*(3), 664.

Barnett, B. (2007). *Untangling the web of hate: Are online hate sites deserving of First Amendment protection?*. New York, NY: Cambria Press.

Bates, S. (2017). Revenge porn and mental health: A qualitative analysis of the mental health effects of revenge porn on female survivors. *Feminist Criminology*, *12*(1), 22–42.

Baumgartner, S. E., Valkenburg, P. M., & Peter, J. (2010). Unwanted online sexual solicitation and risky sexual online behavior across the lifespan. *Journal of Applied Developmental Psychology*, *31*(6), 439–447.

Borrajo, E., Gámez-Guadix, M., Pereda, N., & Calvete, E. (2015). The development and validation of the cyber dating abuse questionnaire among young couples. *Computers in Human Behavior*, *48*, 358–365.

Brochado, S., Soares, S., & Fraga, S. (2016). A scoping review of studies on cyberbullying prevalence among adolescents. *Trauma, Violence, & Abuse*, *18*(5), 523–531. doi:10.1177/1524838016641668

Burke, S. C., Wallen, M., Vail-Smith, K., & Knox, D. (2011). Using technology to control intimate partners: An exploratory study of college undergraduates. *Computers in Human Behavior*, *27*(3), 1162–1167.

Carlson, B. (2019). Disrupting the master narrative: Indigenous people and tweeting colonial history [online]. *Griffith Review*, *64*, 224–234. Retrieved from https://search.informit.com.au/documentSummary;dn=341995259289589;res=IELAPA->ISSN:1839-2954. [cited 13 June 20].

Cheer, U. (2018). *Abusive and offensive communications: The criminal law of New Zealand*. London: UK Law Commission. Retrieved from https://s3-eu-west-2.amazonaws.com/lawcom-prod-storage-11jsxou24uy7q/uploads/2018/11/New-Zealand-U-Cheer.pdf

Citron, D. K. (2014). *Hate crimes in cyberspace*. Boston, MA: Harvard University Press.

Citron, D., & Franks, M. A. (2014). Criminalizing revenge porn. *Wake Forest Law Review*, *49*, 345–392.

Colliver, B., Coyle, A., & Silvestri, M. (2019). The 'online othering' of transgender people in relation to 'gender neutral toilets'. In K. Lumsden & E. Harmer (Eds.), *Online othering: Exploring digital violence and discrimination on the Web* (pp. 215–238). Cham: Palgrave Macmillan.

DeMarco, J., Sharrock, S., Crowther, T., & Barnard, M. (2018). *Behaviour and characteristics of perpetrators of online-facilitated child sexual abuse and exploitation: A rapid evidence assessment. Prepared for independent inquiry into child sexual abuse*. London: NatCen Social Research.

Dennehy, R., Meaney, S., Walsh, K. A., Sinnott, C., Cronin, M., & Arensman, E. (2020). Young people's conceptualizations of the nature of cyberbullying: A systematic review and synthesis of qualitative research. *Aggression and Violent Behavior*, *51*, 101379. doi:10.1016/j.avb.2020.101379

Dimond, J., Fiesler, C., & Bruckman, A. (2011). Domestic violence and information communication technologies. *Interacting with Computers*, *23*(5), 413–421.

Dodge, A. (2019). Nudes are forever: Judicial interpretations of digital technology's impact on "revenge porn." *Canadian Journal of Law and Society*, *34*(1), 121–143.

Douglas, H., Harris, B., & Dragiewicz, M. (2019). Technology-facilitated domestic and family violence: Women's experiences. *British Journal of Criminology*, *59*(3), 551–570.

Douglass, C. H., Wright, C. J. C., Davis, A. C., & Lim, M. S. C. (2018). Correlates of in-person and technology-facilitated sexual harassment from an online survey among young Australians. *Sexual Health*, *15*(4), 361–365.

Dragiewicz, M., Burgess, J., Matamoros-Fernández, A., Salter, M., Suzor, N. P., Woodlock, D., & Harris, B. (2018). Technology facilitated coercive control: Domestic violence and the competing roles of digital media platforms. *Feminist Media Studies*, *18*(4), 609–625. doi:10.1080/14680777.2018.1447341

Dragiewicz, M., Harris, B., Woodlock, D., Salter, M., Easton, H., Lynch, A., … Milne, L. (2019). *Domestic violence and communication technology: Survivor experiences of intrusion, surveillance, and identity crime*. Sydney, NSW: The Australian Communications Consumer Action Network (ACCAN).

Dunn, S., Lalonde, J., & Bailey, J. (2017). Terms of silence: Addressing weaknesses in corporate and law enforcement responses to cyberviolence against girls. *Girlhood Studies*, *10*(2), 80–96.

Finkelhor, D., Ormrod, R. K., Turner, H. A., & Hamby, S. L. (2005). Measuring poly-victimization using the Juvenile Victimization Questionnaire. *Child Abuse & Neglect*, *29*(11), 1297–1312.

Flynn, A. (2019). 'Image-based abuse: The disturbing phenomenon of the "deep fake." *Monash Lens*, 12 March. Retrieved from https://lens.monash.edu/@politics-society/2019/03/12/1373665/image-based-abuse-deep-fake

Fraser, C., Olsen, E., Lee, K., Southworth, C., & Tucker, S. (2010). The new age of stalking: Technological implications for stalking. *Juvenile and Family Court Journal*, *61*(4), 39–55.

George, A., & Harris, B. (2014). *Landscapes of violence: Women surviving family violence in regional and rural Victoria*. Centre for Rural and Regional Law and Justice, Deakin University. Retrieved from https://www.deakin.edu.au/__data/assets/pdf_file/0003/287040/Landscapes-of-Violence-online-pdf-version.pdf

Gerwitz-Meydan, A., Walsh, W., Wolak, J., & Finkelhor, D. (2018). The complex experience of child pornography survivors. *Child Abuse & Neglect*, *80*, 238–248. doi:10.1016/j.chiabu.2018.03.031

Gillett, R. (2019). *Everyday violence: Women's experiences of intimate intrusions on Tinder*. Doctoral dissertation, Queensland University of Technology, Brisbane, QLD.

Green, A. (2019). Cucks, fags and useful idiots: The othering of dissenting white masculinities online. In K. Lumsden & E. Harmer (Eds.), *Online othering: Exploring digital violence and discrimination on the Web* (pp. 65–90). Cham: Palgrave Macmillan.

Hall, P. (2019). Disability hate speech: Interrogating the online/offline distinction. In K. Lumsden & E. Harmer (Eds.), *Online othering: Exploring digital violence and discrimination on the Web* (pp. 309–330). Cham: Palgrave Macmillan.

Hall, M., & Hearn, J. (2017). *Revenge pornography: Gender, sexuality and motivations*. Abingdon: Routledge.

Harris, B. (2020). *Technology, domestic and family violence: Perpetration, experiences and responses*. Brisbane: QUT Centre for Justice.

Harris, B., & Woodlock, D. (2018). Spaceless violence and advocacy: Technology-facilitated abuse, stalking and service provision in regional, rural and remote Australia. Canberra, ACT: Australian Institute of Criminology.

Harris, B. A., & Woodlock, D. (2019). Digital coercive control: Insights from two landmark domestic violence studies. *British Journal of Criminology*, *59*(3), 530–550.

Henry, N., & Flynn, A. (2019). Image-based sexual abuse: Online distribution channels and illicit communities of support. *Violence Against Women*, *25*(16), 1932–1955.

Henry, N., Flynn, A., & Powell, A. (2018). Policing image-based sexual abuse: Stakeholder perspectives. *Police Practice and Research: International Journal*, *19*(6), 565–581.

Henry, N., Flynn, A., & Powell, A. (2019). *Responding to revenge pornography: Prevalence, nature and impacts*. Canberra, ACT: Australian Research Council.

Henry, N., Flynn, A., & Powell, A. (2020). Technology-facilitated domestic and sexual violence: A review. *Violence Against Women*, *26*(15–16), 1828–1854.

Henry, N., McGlynn, C., Flynn, A., Johnson, K., Powell, A., & Scott, A. J. (2020). *Image-based sexual abuse: A study on the causes and consequences of non-consensual nude or sexual imagery*. London and New York, NY: Routledge.

Henry, N., & Powell, A. (2015). Beyond the "sext": Technology-facilitated sexual violence and harassment against adult women. *Australian and New Zealand Journal of Criminology*, *48*(1), 104–118.

Henry, N., Powell, A., & Flynn, A. (2018). AI can now create fake porn, making revenge porn even more complicated. *The Conversation*, 28 February 2018. Retrieved from https://theconversation.com/ai-can-now-create-fake-porn-making-revenge-porn-even-more-complicated-92267

Hinduja, S. (2018). *Cultivating resilience to prevent bullying and cyberbullying*. Cyberbullying Research Center. Retrieved from https://cyberbullying.org/cultivating-resilience-prevent-bullying-cyberbullying

Hinduja, S., & Patchin, J. W. (2008). Cyberbullying: An exploratory analysis of factors related to offending and victimization. *Deviant Behavior*, *29*(2), 129–156.

Jane, E. A. (2014). "Your a ugly, whorish, slut": Understanding e-bile. *Feminist Media Studies*, *14*(4), 531–546.

Jane, E. (2017). Feminist digilante responses to a slut-shaming on Facebook. *Social Media + Society*. doi:10.1177/2056305117705996

Karayianni, E., Fanti, K. A., Diakidoy, I.-A., Hadjicharalambous, M.-Z., & Katsimicha, E. (2017). Prevalence, contexts and correlates of child sexual abuse in Cyprus. *Child Abuse & Neglect*, *66*, 41–52. doi:10.1016/j.chiabu.2017.02.016

Kerrigan, N. (2019). Rural racism in the digital age. In K. Lumsden & E. Harmer (Eds.), *Online othering: Exploring digital violence and discrimination on the Web* (pp. 259–286). Cham: Palgrave Macmillan.

Lenhart, A., Ybarra, M., & Price-Feeney, M. (2016a). *Nonconsensual image sharing: One in 25 Americans has been a victim of "revenge porn."* New York, NY: Data & Society Research Institute. Retrieved from https://datasociety.net/pubs/oh/Nonconsensual_Image_Sharing_2016.pdf

Lenhart, A., Ybarra, M., Zickuhr, K., & Price-Feeney, M. (2016b). *Online harassment, digital abuse, and cyberstalking in America*. New York, NY: Data & Society Research Institute. Retrieved from https://www.datasociety.net/pubs/oh/Online_Harassment_2016.pdf

Lewis, R., Rowe, M., & Clare, W. (2019). Online/offline continuities: Exploring misogyny and hate in online abuse of feminists. In K. Lumsden & E. Harmer (Eds.), *Online othering: Exploring digital violence and discrimination on the Web* (pp. 121–143). Cham: Palgrave Macmillan.

Lumsden, K. (2019). "I want to kill you in front of your children" is not a threat. It's an expression of a desire: Discourses of online abuse, trolling and violence on r/MensRights. In K. Lumsden & E. Harmer (Eds.), *Online othering: Exploring digital violence and discrimination on the Web* (pp. 91–117). Cham: Palgrave Macmillan.

Lumsden, K., & Harmer, E. (Eds.) (2019). *Online othering: Exploring digital violence and discrimination on the Web*. Cham: Palgrave Macmillan.

Mandau, M. B. H. (2020). 'Directly in your face': A qualitative study on the sending and receiving of unsolicited 'dick pics' among young adults. *Sexuality & Culture*, *24*, 72–93. doi:10.1007/s12119-019-09626-2

Marganski, A., & Melander, L. (2018). Intimate partner violence victimization in the cyber and real world: Examining the extent of cyber aggression experiences and its association with in-person dating violence. *Journal of Interpersonal Violence*, *33*(7), 1071–1095.

McGlynn, C., Johnson, K., Rackley, E., Henry, N., Gavey, N., Powell, A., & Flynn, A. (2020). "It's torture for the soul": The harms of image-based sexual abuse. *Social & Legal Studies*, online first. doi:10.1177/0964663920947791

McGlynn, C., Rackley, E., Johnson, K., Henry, N., Flynn, A., Powell, A., … Scott, A. J. (2019). *Shattering lives and myths: A report on image-based sexual abuse*. Durham: University of Durham. Retrieved from https://www.researchgate.net/publication/339352950_Shattering_lives_and_myths_A_report_on_image-based_sexual_abuse/citations#fullTextFileContent

Megarry, J. (2014). Online incivility or sexual harassment? Conceptualising women's experiences in the digital age. *Women's Studies International Journal*, *47*, 46–55.

Messing, J., Bagwell-Gray, M., Brown, M. L., Kappas, A., & Durfee, A. (2020). Intersections of stalking and technology-based abuse: Emerging definitions, conceptualization, and measurement. *Journal of Family Violence*, 1–12.

Office of the eSafety Commissioner [OeSC]. (2017). *Image-based abuse national survey: Summary report*. Melbourne, VIC: OeSC. Retrieved from https://www.esafety.gov.au/sites/default/files/2019-07/Image-based-abuse-national-survey-summary-report-2017.pdf

Office of the eSafety Commissioner [OeSC]. (2019a). *eSafety for women from culturally and linguistically diverse backgrounds: Summary report*. Melbourne, VIC: OeSC. Retrieved from https://www.esafety.gov.au/sites/default/files/2019-07/summary-report-for-women-from-cald-backgrounds.pdf

Office of the eSafety Commissioner [OeSC]. (2019b). *Understanding the attitudes and motivations of adults who engage in image-based abuse: Summary report*. Melbourne, VIC: Social Research Centre. Retrieved from https://www.esafety.gov.au/sites/default/files/2019-

Office of the eSafety Commissioner [OeSC]. (2019c). *Online safety for Aboriginal and Torres Strait Islander women living in urban areas*. Melbourne, VIC: Social Research Centre. Retrieved from https://www.esafety.gov.au/sites/default/files/2019-10/Online%20safety%20for%20ATSI%20women%20living%20in%20urban%20areas.pdf

Office of the eSafety Commissioner [OeSC]. (2020). Online hate speech: Findings from Australia. New Zealand and Europe. Retrieved from https://www.esafety.gov.au/sites/default/files/2020-01/Hate%20speech-Report.pdf

Oswald, F., Lopes, A., Skoda, K., Hesse, C. L., & Pederson, C. L. (2020). I'll show you mine so you'll show me yours: Motivations and personality variables in photographic exhibitionism. *The Journal of Sex Research*, *57*(5), 597–609.

Palmater, P. (2016). Shining the light on the dark places: Addressing police racism and sexualized violence against Indigenous women and girls in the National Inquiry. *Canadian Journal of Women and the Law*, *28*(2), 253–284.

Pavan, E. (2017). Internet intermediaries and online gender-based violence. In L. Vitis, & M. Segrave (Eds.), *Gender, technology and violence* (pp. 62–78). London: Routledge.

Perry, B., & Olsson, P. (2009). Cyberhate: The globalization of hate. *Information and Communications Technology Law*, *18*(2), 185–199. doi:10.1080/13600830902814984

Pew Research Center. (2014). *Online harassment*. Retrieved from http://www.pewinternet.org/2014/10/22/online-harassment/

Powell, A., & Henry, N. (2017). *Sexual violence in a digital age*. London: Palgrave Macmillan.

Powell, A., & Henry, N. (2019). Technology-facilitated sexual violence victimization: Results from an online survey of Australian adults. *Journal of Interpersonal Violence*, *34*(17), 3637–3665.

Powell, A., Henry, N., & Flynn, A. (2018). Image-based sexual abuse. In W. S. DeKeseredy, & M. Dragiewicz (Eds.), *Routledge handbook of critical criminology* (2nd ed., pp. 305–315). Abingdon and New York, NY: Routledge.

Powell, A., Henry, N., Flynn, A., & Scott, A. J. (2019). Image-based sexual abuse: The extent, nature, and predictors of perpetration in a community sample of Australian residents. *Computers in Human Behavior*, *92*, 393–402.

Powell, A., Scott, A. J., Henry, N., & Flynn, A. (2020). *Image-based sexual abuse: An international study of victims and perpetrators*. Melbourne, VIC: RMIT University.

Quayle, E., & Koukopoulos, N. (2018). Deterrence of online child sexual abuse and exploitation, policing. *Journal of Policy Practice*, *13*(3), 345–362.

Rowse, J., Bolt, C., & Gaya, S. (2020). Swipe right: The emergence of dating-app facilitated sexual assault. A descriptive retrospective audit of forensic examination caseload in an Australian metropolitan service. *Forensic Science, Medicine and Pathology*, *16*, 71–77.

Ruvalcaba, Y., & Eaton, A. A. (2019). Nonconsensual pornography among US adults: A sexual scripts framework on victimization, perpetration, and health correlates for women and men. *Psychology of Violence*, *10*, 68–78. doi:10.1037/vio0000233

Salter, M. (2018). Child sexual abuse: Ethics and evidence. *Child Sexual Abuse Review*, *27*(3), 165–170.

Schweppe, J. (2018). *Abusive and offensive online communications: An Irish perspective*. London: UK Law Commission. Retrieved from https://s3-eu-west-2.amazonaws.com/lawcom-prod-storage-11jsxou24uy7q/uploads/2018/11/Ireland-J-Schweppe.pdf

Scrivens, R., & Amarasingam, A. (2020). Haters gonna "like": Exploring Canadian far-right extremism on Facebook. In M. Littler & B. Lee (Eds.), *Digital extremisms: Readings in violence, radicalisation and extremism in the online space* (pp. 63–89). Cham: Palgrave Macmillan.

Sheikh, M. M. R. (2018). Technology mediated violence against women in Bangladesh: Evidence from contemporary literature. In S. Sapna & S. Sharma (Eds.), *Gender equality through mainstreaming: Proceedings of international conference on gender equality through the strategy of gender mainstreaming*, Bengaluru (p. 198).

Smith, J. (2019). 'When I saw women being attacked it made me want to stand up and fight': Reporting, responding to, and resisting online misogyny. In K. Lumsden & E. Harmer (Eds.), *Online othering: Exploring digital violence and discrimination on the Web* (pp. 287–308). Cham: Palgrave Macmillan.

Southern, R., & Harmer, E. (2019). Othering political women: Online misogyny, racism and ableism towards women in public life. In K. Lumsden, & E. Harmer (Eds.), *Online othering: Exploring digital violence and discrimination on the Web* (pp. 187–213). Cham: Palgrave Macmillan.

Tanczer, L., Lopez Neira, I., Parkin, S., Patel, T., & George, D. (2018). Gender and IoT research report: The rise of the Internet of Things and implications for technology-facilitated abuse. London: STEaPP, PETRAS IoT Hub. Retrieved from https://www.ucl.ac.uk/research/domains/sites/research_domains/files/giot-report.pdf

Thomasen, K. (2018). Beyond airspace safety: A feminist perspective on drone privacy regulation. *Canadian Journal of Law and Technology*, *16*(2), 307–338.

Vitis, L., & Gilmour, F. (2017). Dick pics on blast: A woman's resistance to online sexual harassment using humour, art and Instagram. *Crime, Media, Culture*, *13*(3), 335–355.

Weathers, M. R., & Hopson, M. C. (2015). 'I define what hurts me': A co-cultural theoretical analysis of communication factors related to digital dating abuse. *Howard Journal of Communications*, *26*(1), 95–113.

Wong, R. (2019). *A guide for Canadian women experiencing technology-facilitated violence: Strategies for enhancing safety*. Vancouver, BC: BC Society of Transition Houses. Retrieved from https://bcsth.ca/wp-content/uploads/2019/03/BCSTH-A-guide-for-Canadian-women-experiencing-technology-facilitated-violence-2019-1.pdf

Woodlock, D. (2017). The abuse of technology in domestic violence and stalking. *Violence Against Women*, *23*(5), 584–602.

Ybarra, M., Price-Feeney, M., Lenhart, A., & Zickuhr, K. (2017). *Intimate partner digital abuse*. Data & Society Research Institute. Centre for Innovative Public Health Research. Retrieved from https://datasociety.net/pubs/oh/Intimate_Partner_Digital_Abuse_2017.pdf

Section 1
TFVA Across a Spectrum of Behaviors

Chapter 1

Introduction

Jane Bailey

As the introduction to this Handbook made clear, technology-facilitated violence and abuse (TFVA) includes a spectrum of behaviors carried out through a diverse range of digital technologies. The eight chapters in the book's first section focus on TFVA issues and experiences across that spectrum, creating a foundation for subsequent sections that focus on particular forms of TFVA.

The first two chapters by Suzie Dunn and Chandell Gosse set the stage for this section and, in many ways, for the collection as a whole, by grappling with some key underlying concepts and concerns, particularly the importance of language, and the deep interplay between so-called "online" and "offline" experiences of violence and abuse. Dunn's chapter addresses the not infrequently asked question of whether the term "violence" is actually applicable to the broad range of behaviors that this Handbook argues fall under the umbrella of TFVA. She examines this question from both sociopolitical and legal perspectives. In particular, she draws on feminist and critical race scholar approaches which, respectively, conceptualize sexual violence as falling on a continuum (Kelly, 1988) and identify systemic violence arising from often intersecting oppressions such as racism and misogyny (Matsuda, Lawrence, Delgado, & Crenshaw, 1993), as well as legal analysis of particular instances of TFVA in Canada and the European Union. Ultimately, Dunn argues that "violence" is an apt and necessary term for ensuring socio-cultural recognition and condemnation of harmful technology-facilitated behaviors.

Like Dunn's chapter, Gosse's chapter highlights the importance of language for ensuring more widespread recognition of the harms suffered by TFVA targets. In her chapter, she reports on findings from interviews she conducted with women who had been targets of TFVA. Her women participants' experiences help to illustrate the negative impacts of what she refers to as the "increasingly redundant distinctions between online and offline." Ultimately, she argues that the "digital dualism" of the online/offline distinction leads to the "treatment of offline life as *more real* than online life," thereby denying "women who experience online abuse the space they deserve to have the abuse seen, interpreted, and treated as *real and embodied.*"

The Emerald International Handbook of Technology-Facilitated Violence and Abuse, 21–23

doi:10.1108/978-1-83982-848-520211060

The next six chapters in this section engage with these insights in a variety of ways in the context of examining TFVA-related experiences within communities less frequently accounted for in the literature.

Walter S. DeKeseredy, Danielle M. Stoneberg, and Gabrielle L. Lory's chapter offers additional insights undercutting the online/offline distinction explored by Gosse. Their chapter examines the literature relating to the polyvictimization of North American women university/college students and considers the contribution of TFVA to these women's multiple victimization experiences. Noting emerging research demonstrating that TFVA has become "part and parcel of women's polyvictimization experiences at institutions of higher learning," they argue for comprehensive multi-pronged strategies that recognize the "co-occurrence of offline and online victimization," as part of a broader problem of male-to-female abuse on North American post-secondary campuses.

The chapters by Olusean Makinde, Emmanuel Olamijuwon, Nchelem Ichegbo, Cheluchi Onyemelukwe, and Michael Ilesanmi, and by Edgar Pacheco and Neil Melhuish report on the results of quantitative studies relating to a broad range of TFVA behaviors among two lesser studied communities. Makinde et al. report findings from their online survey of young people in sub Saharan Africa, a relatively understudied population in a geographic location where digital connectivity is an increasingly emphasized tool of economic growth and development. Among other things, their findings hint at the interconnection between "online" and "offline." For example, they suggest that their finding that the reporting of "gender-related abuse was much higher in women than several other forms of abuse," may be indicative of a "carry over to the digital space" of more broadly based patriarchal norms.

Pacheco and Melhuish's chapter details survey results relating to adult perpetrators of TFVA behaviors (e.g., unwanted sexual solicitations, etc.) in New Zealand. Given that much existing research focuses on targets of TFVA, as well as on young people (especially in the context of cyberbullying), their findings offer perspectives on TFVA from a different standpoint – that of the adult perpetrator. Better understanding the perspectives and motivations of perpetrators is likely to be an important component of developing meaningful, preventative approaches to TFVA. Like Makinde et al.'s chapter, aspects of Pacheco and Melhuish's chapter also speak to online/offline connections. For example, while almost half of their participants who had engaged in TFVA behaviors "indicated their actions occurred online only," significantly higher numbers of younger participants (aged 18–29 and 30–39) reported a connection between their online behavior and an offline or face-to-face situation.

The final two chapters in this section by Jane Bailey and Sara Shayan, and Bronwyn Carlson and Ryan Frazer focus on the experiences and effects of TFVA on Indigenous peoples – communities not often focused on in existing TFVA research. Both chapters illustrate the deep imbrication between "real/virtual" and "online/offline," highlighting how pre-existing systemic prejudices and cultural norms and practices are reflected in and re-entrenched through technologies. Bailey and Shayan's chapter discusses the impact of technology on the missing and murdered Indigenous women crisis in Canada, pointing not only to technology's use in perpetrating interpersonal violence and abuse against Indigenous women and girls, but also its use by the state to facilitate ongoing colonialist and misogynist abuses targeting Indigenous women, as well as Indigenous communities at large.

Carlson and Frazer's chapter focuses on cyberbullying and Indigenous peoples. They compellingly illustrate why "there are good reasons to assume that online conflict is different for Indigenous peoples because of diverse cultural practices and the broader political context of settler-colonialism." Their insights demonstrate the profoundly negative impacts of standardized scholarly approaches to cyberbullying on developing nuanced understandings of the ways in which cyberbullying is enacted and experienced. Noting that such approaches are "delimiting [scholarship's] ability to attend to social difference in online conflict," they "join calls for more theoretically rigorous, targeted, difference-sensitive studies into bullying."

References

Kelly, L. (1988). *Surviving sexual violence*. Cambridge: Polity Press.

Matsuda, M., Lawrence, C., Delgado, R., & Crenshaw, K. (1993). *Words that wound: Critical race theory, assaultive speech and the first amendment*. New York, NY: Routledge.

Chapter 2

Is it *Actually* Violence? Framing Technology-Facilitated Abuse as Violence

Suzie Dunn

Abstract

When discussing the term "technology-facilitated violence" (TFV) it is often asked: "Is it *actually* violence?" While international human rights standards, such as the United Nations' Convention on the Elimination of All Forms of Discrimination against Women (United Nations General Assembly, 1979), have long recognized emotional and psychological abuse as forms of violence, including many forms of technology-facilitated abuse (United Nations, 2018), law makers and the general public continue to grapple with the question of whether certain harmful technology-facilitated behaviors are actually forms of violence. This chapter explores this question in two parts. First, it reviews three theoretical concepts of violence and examines how these concepts apply to technology-facilitated behaviors. In doing so, this chapter aims to demonstrate how some harmful technology-facilitated behaviors fit under the greater conceptual umbrella of violence. Second, it examines two recent cases, one from the British Columbia Court of Appeal (BCCA) in Canada and a Romanian case from the European Court of Human Rights (ECtHR), that received attention for their legal determinations on whether to define harmful technology-facilitated behaviors as forms of violence or not. This chapter concludes with observations on why we should conceptualize certain technology-facilitated behaviors as forms of violence.

Keywords: Technology-facilitated violence; transgender; critical race theory; coercive control; continuum of violence; law

The Emerald International Handbook of Technology-Facilitated Violence and Abuse, 25–45

doi:10.1108/978-1-83982-848-520211002

Introduction: Words Matter

The words used to describe a phenomenon shape the legal and social understanding of that experience. A change in terminology around a particular behavior can in turn change the norms of that society. This was demonstrated in the 1970s when feminist advocates in North America began calling for the recognition of and end to sexual harassment (Backhouse, 2012a; Backhouse & Cohen, 1978; MacKinnon & Siegel, 2004). Prior to that time, much of what was redefined by these advocates as "sexual harassment" had previously been considered harmless flirtation or "boys being boys." In many situations, women were expected to take responsibility for provoking or encouraging men's sexual aggression toward them (Weiss, 2009). Unwanted sexual attention from men was something that might not have been viewed as entirely polite but should be tolerated by women, if not considered complimentary. At any rate, such behaviors were normalized and minimized.

Reframing unwanted sexual attention as sexual harassment altered the social acceptability of that behavior. This change in understanding did not come easily; in fact, many entrenched norms around gendered sexual expectations remain in place today, with some individuals continuing to brush off the harms of sexual harassment (Quinn, 2000). However, following the work of feminists who developed new terminology and reframed the issue, new laws that helped protect women from this harmful and discriminatory behavior were introduced. For example, in Canada, sexual harassment was recognized under human rights legislation as discrimination based on sex (Campbell, 2013). Due to the cultural changes that came along with the advocacy work undertaken by feminists and the shift in the legality of the behavior, people began to see sexual harassment as unacceptable and harmful. This altered the social and legal boundaries of what was considered sexually appropriate behavior (Balos, 2004). As this demonstrates, identifying and naming harms can have significant societal impacts.

At the present time, TFV is a relatively new phenomenon that is not well understood by general society. It faces the same challenges of tolerance and minimization that sexual harassment faced – and continues to face (Fairbairn, 2015). Scholars, legislators, advocates, and the general public are still grappling with what new behaviors such as online stalking, image-based sexual abuse, and harmful digital misrepresentations are and how they should be condemned or regulated, if at all (Henry et al., 2020; Powell & Henry, 2017). Even with some emerging laws that address certain forms of TFV, such as those that prohibit the nonconsensual distribution of intimate images, people continue to be blamed for the technology-facilitated abuse they experience (Henry et al., 2020; Waldman, 2019). For example, some abusers feel entitled to hack into women's online accounts in order to steal their nude photos to share on the internet (Massanari, 2017) or create simulated images of women engaging in sexual acts that they did not do using photoshop, deepfakes, and computer-generated images (Dunn, 2020). Women have been blamed for this type of abuse because they took sexualized images of themselves to begin with or for being celebrities with sexual allure (Marwick, 2017). Furthermore, feminists who have faced multiyear online campaigns against them, where groups of abusers have published their home addresses, created images of them being raped and beaten, threatened them with death and rape, and bombarded them with sexist and racist commentary, have been told they are overreacting when they complain and have had their experiences minimized by the public and the police (Jane, 2016; Kidd & Turner, 2016). They have been told it was just words and pictures on the internet and their fears were dismissed as an overreaction (Filipovic, 2007). In some cases, they have had to flee their homes, close their digital platforms, and cancel their events due to technology-facilitated attacks (Kidd & Turner, 2016). These instances, which were often rooted in sexism, caused them to feel fearful, and some targets of these attacks described their experiences as violence (Jane, 2016; Kidd & Turner, 2016). Yet, there remains uncertainty on where to draw the line between what aspects of these behaviors should be considered unacceptable or even violent.

These types of harmful behaviors are collectively known by a variety of names: TFV (Bailey & Mathen, 2017), cyberbullying (Bailey, 2016), trolling (Citron, 2014), online abuse (McGlynn & Rackley, 2017), cyberviolence (Peterson & Densley, 2017), digital harassment (Powell & Henry, 2017), technology-facilitated coercive control (Dragiewicz et al., 2018), symbolic violence (Barratt, 2018), and representational violence (Hall & Hearn, 2019), among others (Loise Backe, Lilleston, & McCleary-Sills, 2018). It can be difficult to determine what terms to use when a new phenomenon like this occurs or when advocates call for a new cultural understanding of an issue. This is particularly true if the new definition pushes back against entrenched stereotypes and systemic power structures. Even among those who support a new understanding, finding consensus on terminology is not an easy task for complex and nuanced concepts like TFV. More precise terminology is useful when examining specific behaviors such as image-based sexual abuse, doxing, and digital stalking (Loise Backe et al., 2018), but as an overarching term for behaviors that result in the harms described below, I argue that we should use "TFV."

"TFV" is preferred over "cyberviolence" because although it is a lengthier and less evocative term, it is a broader term that captures a wider range of technologies. The term "cyber" finds its roots in control and networked systems and was popularized in science fiction in the 1980s and 1990s by authors who described cyberspace as virtual or digitally connected spaces (Azmi & Kautsarina, 2019), such as in William Gibson's (1984) *Neuromancer*. Many forms of TFV occur in digital and networked spaces like the internet, but other forms of technology that are not connected to a network, such as some video or audio recording devices, are also used, making "technology" a more encompassing term. The term "cyber" also suggests a separate world in cyberspace, one that is distinct from the physical world (Azmi & Kautsarina, 2019). In our current society, our digital experiences are as much a relevant and integrated part of our everyday lives as our physical ones. Furthermore, for reasons described below, I argue that many of these abusive technology-facilitated behaviors are a form of violence that should be situated on the continuum of violence and, as such, should be broadly defined as "violence." To do otherwise risks minimizing the severity of these actions and fails to recognize their interconnectedness with other more familiar forms of violence.

Not recognizing these behaviors as violence may limit a person's access to legal protections and can reinforce social norms that view this harmful behavior as acceptable or causing minimal impact.

Old Meets New: Concepts of Violence in a Technological Era

To begin to understand the concept of TFV, it is worthwhile to first look at existing concepts of violence to consider some common characteristics of violent behavior, the systemic factors that contribute to violence, and the resulting harms caused by violence. As many forms of TFV are highly gendered and racialized (Amnesty International, 2018; McGlynn & Rackley, 2017), this chapter will rely on three concepts of violence that originate from gender-based and critical race theorists, including the continuum of violence (Kelly, 1988), coercive control (Stark, 2007), and critical race theory, which examines systemic violence (Matsuda, Lawrence, Delgado, & Crenshaw, 1993). These theories will be used to illuminate why certain technology-facilitated behaviors can (and should) be understood as violence.

In conceptualizing what is understood as TFV, this chapter adopts a broad understanding of violence that is not limited to criminal or otherwise legal definitions of violence, which themselves vary widely. There may be some instances where the legal understanding of violence should be limited to harmful physical contact and others where a broader definition that includes psychological and TFV will be appropriate. As such, not all forms of violence will reach a legal threshold (Bonnet, 2015), but all forms of this broader understanding of violence should be considered socially unacceptable. It is important to note that while the law plays a valuable role in shaping societal norms around which types of behavior are acceptable or not, the legal system has not always been a substantially effective or accessible tool to address violence (Backhouse, 2012b; Burgin & Flynn, 2019; Dunn, Lalonde, & Bailey, 2017). This is particularly true for communities that have been historically over-policed or under-protected due to systemic factors such as classism, racism, sexism, homophobia, and transphobia (Ashley, 2018a, 2018b; Matsuda, Lawerence, Delgado, & Crenshaw, 1993; Walcott, Foster, Campbell, & Seally, 2016). For some communities, the legal system itself has been a site of violence and criminal laws that are framed as protecting vulnerable members of society have resulted in disproportionate incarceration of their members (Delgado, 2014; Human Rights Watch, 2013). Due to this, we should not rely on legal institutions as the sole authorities to dictate the definition of violence and the solutions to it. Instead, a social and contextual understanding of what constitutes violence should be adopted to examine and critique the law's definition of violence and its enforcement of related laws. This chapter seeks to achieve this in its examination of two case studies.

As new concepts of violence like TFV emerge, the categorization of what is considered violent within a community can be contested (Fairbairn, 2015). It often requires advocacy and education within the community to shift cultural concepts of violence. This can be seen in the case of family violence that was once understood as legitimate family discipline, or that of marital rape that was once understood as an acceptable form of sexual interaction in a marriage, which are now understood as forms of violence (Balos, 2004; Koshan, 2017). One of the greatest challenges in conceptualizing harmful technology-facilitated behaviors as violence is the lack of physical contact between the target and the perpetrator in many of the cases. This is due to limited societal views of violence as only encompassing physical attacks; however, as will be examined below, violence can include a breadth of harmful behaviors that cannot be disentangled from physical abuse and may on their own be equally, if not more, debilitating for the survivor (Follingstad & Rogers, 2013). However, not every unwanted touch or unwelcome contact through technology will be considered violent nor should they be. We must avoid developing an understanding of violence that is so broad that it waters down the significance of violent behaviors or results in overly punitive measures for less consequential behaviors or acts of self-defense. In some cases, a single incident will be severe enough to be considered violence, such as threats of murder or rape, where in other cases, actions may only become violent due to their cumulative or coercive nature, such as unwanted text messages or cruel comments on a person's social media page (Bonnet, 2015; Dragiewicz et al., 2018). Social and legal understandings of violence may require a contextual analysis that takes into consideration situational and systemic factors, as well as the impacts of the behaviors and their connection to other acts of violence. Taking this into consideration, the following section will discuss how certain technology-facilitated behaviors can be captured in the folds of existing theoretical understandings of violence.

The Continuum of Violence: Interconnected Behaviors

Writing decades prior to the advent of social media and smartphones, feminist scholar Liz Kelly (1987) adopted a broad view of sexual violence against women, recognizing the interconnectivity between harmful physical, sexual, emotional, and psychological acts. After interviewing women with experiences of sexual violence, she found that discrete acts of physical and psychological attacks on women's sexual autonomy could not be understood as independent of each other, as they each played an overlapping role in controlling women's behavior. In her understanding of violence, Kelly (1987) focused on the overall impacts experienced by the survivor, describing how women reacted differently to various experiences of sexual coercion, both physical and psychological. Their reactions were influenced by the nature of the incident, the relationship between the parties, the amount of time over which the abuse occurred, and the feelings of fear induced by the incident. After listening to women's reactions to various behaviors, Kelly (1987) concluded that a hierarchy that places physical attacks at the top, as most serious, and emotional abuse at the bottom, as least serious, did not reflect the reality of women's lived experiences of sexual violence. Doing so minimized nonphysical harms caused by these behaviors. In her book, *Surviving Sexual Violence,* Kelly (1988) outlined her theory of the continuum of sexual violence.

She describes the ways in which actions like street harassment, coercive sex, and threats systemically limited women's sexual autonomy and contributed to their sexual domination. They caused women to feel a great deal of fear, and Kelly (1988) argued that these behaviors should not be overlooked because of the lack of physical damage to a woman's body. By focusing on the ways these intersecting harmful behaviors were a part of larger system that supported sexual violence against women, she included actions used to degrade, control, and cause fear in women within the conceptual parameters of sexual violence, both physical and psychological.

Kelly's (1987, 1988) work addressed the continuum of *sexual* violence, but the model of a continuum of violence has been adopted more generally by scholars such as Rashida Manjoo (2012), Emma Renold and Christine Barter (2005), and Kathy Sanders-Phillips (2009) who applied the continuum to all violence against women, violence experienced by youth in residential children's homes, and racialized youth, respectively. Other national and international bodies, including the United Nations, have adopted a similarly broad definition of violence that includes emotional and psychological violence and forms of TFV (Fairbairn, 2015).

The theory of a continuum of violence has been applied to technology-facilitated behaviors that share the underlying characteristics of coercing and controlling women, thus fitting within Kelly's (1987, 1988) concept of violence. Clare McGlynn, Erika Rackley, and Ruth Houghton (2017) drew on Kelly's continuum of violence when examining what they labeled the "continuum of image-based sexual abuse" (p. 1; see also, Henry et al., 2020). These authors situate image-based sexual abuse on a continuum with other forms of sexual violence. Image-based sexual abuse includes the creation or distribution of sexual images without consent, which captures things like the nonconsensual distribution of intimate images, upskirting, voyeurism, sexual deepfakes, digitally manipulated sexual images, images obtained via hacking, sextortion, images of sexual assault, and unsolicited dick pics (see e.g., Henry, Flynn, & Powell, 2018, 2019). These technology-facilitated behaviors are used to degrade women and control their sexual autonomy, resulting in significant harms. Women whose sexual images have been shared without consent have reported similar psychological impacts as survivors of sexual assault, including post-traumatic stress disorder, anxiety, depression, and suicidal thoughts (Bates, 2016), and some have drastically altered their behaviors in response to the misuse of their images (Powell, Henry & Flynn, 2018). In the case of shared images of sexual assault, Alexa Dodge (2016) found that the demeaning commentary that has accompanied these images normalizes and minimizes sexual violence against women and girls. Beyond sexual violence, many other forms of technology-facilitated behaviors have the effect of controlling or causing fear in women include stalkerware and death threats on digital platforms (Citron, 2014; Parson et al., 2019). These technology-facilitated behaviors are interconnected with other forms of physical, sexual, and psychological forms of violence as they share the underlying commonality of what Kelly (1987, 1988) conceptualized as violence. These behaviors are used to dominate, intimidate, and control the women who are targeted, negatively influencing their autonomy. Additionally, they are linked to a larger system of behaviors that influence societal norms that minimize and normalize violence.

Coercive Control: Beyond the Physical

Evan Stark's (2007) theory on coercive control demonstrates the ways that physical and psychological behaviors of one partner are used to break down the personality, self-worth, and agency of the other in an intimate partner violence relationship. This form of control relies on systemic inequalities such as gender inequality and employs ongoing behaviors that wear a person down over time. Its collective nature is the core of its severity, not any particular discrete physical act that causes injury. This can cause a level of invisibility to the harmful actions as it is difficult to spot the forest among the trees. It might seem unusual for a person to experience extreme fear for forgetting to text her partner at a specific time, but if failing to do so results in their partner relentlessly threatening and limiting her freedoms in their home for weeks afterward, it is a legitimate reason to be afraid. Women in abusive relationships can be controlled using physical force in combination with psychological abuse, but as noted by Anne Jones (2000), prolonged psychological abuse that leaves the woman in a state of fear and without control can be an equally effective form of abuse as physical attacks. As long as the perpetrator can destroy the will of his target, the behavior achieves its aims. The cumulative controlling effects of ongoing and repetitive attacks are part and parcel of the violence in those relationships, whether they are physical or not.

Heather Douglas, Bridget Harris, and Molly Dragiewicz (2019) have applied the theory of coercive control to TFV. In their study on the use of technology in domestic and family violence, they argue that some forms of technology-facilitated behaviors are "inextricably tied to" (p. 553) other forms of domestic and family violence and the systemic factors that contribute to their persistence. Douglas, Harris, and Dragiewicz (2019) identified isolation (through controlling digital communication), monitoring, stalking, image-based sexual abuse, social media–facilitated abuse, and online harassment as some of the more commonly reported forms of technology-facilitated behaviors they would categorize as coercive in violent relationships. Technology added to the feelings – and reality – of the perpetrator being ever-present and ever-threatening. In the case of stalkerware, Citizen Lab described this technology as having a "predator in your pocket" because it allows for an abusive partner to consistently monitor their spouse's movements and communications (Parsons et al., 2019). Ongoing tracking and excessive monitoring through technology can induce feelings of fear and a loss of autonomy in the same ways that physically controlling behaviors can. A simple buzz of a text may cause a person whose daily behaviors are being monitored by their abusive partner to feel legitimately fearful.

The use of this technology to dominate and control another person is another tool in the web of tactics employed by a violent perpetrator that can have a cumulative effect on the person targeted (Dragiewicz et al., 2018). The overarching effect of breaking down the agency in the person remains the same whatever tool the abuser uses. These harmful technology-facilitated behaviors can have a physical and psychological impact on the person targeted. Nicola Henry and Anastasia Powell (2015) have described reactions to technology-facilitated harms like these as embodied harms. They found that it is a myth that because the certain actions are not directed on the physical body or occur in digital spaces they have no effect on the physical body or social self. There are real psychological, physical, and social effects that impact a person's mental health, personal relationships, social position, and personal safety resulting from TFV. Creating bright lines between physical, psychological, and technology-facilitated behaviors when examining violent relationships would require a parsing of the cumulative behaviors that collectively lead to the loss of agency and feelings of domination by the person targeted. Creating these types of silos can dilute the severity of the overall experience and fails to recognize the physiological and psychological harms caused by all forms of violence.

Critical Race Theory: Systemic Violence

Critical race theory is foundational to understanding the ways words and images reinforce systemic factors, such as racism, sexism, and colonialism, that dehumanize particular groups and can be understood as a form of violence themselves (Jackman, 2002). Mari Matsuda, Charles Lawrence, Richard Delgado, and Kimberlé Crenshaw's (1993) book, *Words that Wound*, describe the inseparability of racism, hateful speech, and violence. They argue that racist speech and images can be a precursor to physical violence against people of color, such as inciting lynch mobs and contribute to normalizing physical and sexual violence against women of color. Racist speech and images can incite physical attacks, including violence by the state, as was raised as a concern in 2020 when a white woman in Central Park called the police falsely alleging that a Black man had threatened her physically (Bellafante, 2020), but they also dictate ideas of racial inferiority that make racial domination permissible and Black, Indigenous, and people of color (BIPOC) legitimate targets of physical attacks and social control (Walcott et al., 2016).

Understanding the ways in which words and images can be viewed as forms of systemic violence against BIPOC is valuable in conceptualizing many forms of harmful technology-facilitated behaviors as violence. For example, degrading images and speech are used in digital spaces to dehumanize, instill fear, and reinforce the subordination of BIPOC (Awan & Zempi, 2015; Nakamura, 2013), members of the LGBTQI community (Lenhart, Ybarra, Zickuhr, & Price-Feeney, 2016; Quodling, 2016; Stanko, 2005), women and girls (Duggan, 2014; Vera-Gray, 2016), and other equality-seeking groups (Bailey, 2007).

Amnesty International's (2018) #ToxicTwitter report found that being a woman of color in a leadership role online or speaking about race or gender online can trigger digital attacks that use threatening and discriminatory language and images. Some abusive Twitter users will seek out hashtags associated with equality issues and will encourage others to attack individuals promoting equality-focused campaigns. They use onslaughts of threatening, degrading, and violent comments, including death and rape threats, against individuals advocating for equality online. Other racist, sexist, and homophobic tropes are used during these online attacks to reinforce systemic power structures and can drive users who resist them off of digital platforms out of fear. Words and images like these cross over the line into violence when they create reasonable feelings of fear, reinforce the subordination of specific groups in ways that normalize violence against them, and dehumanize particular individuals or groups.

Manipulated images, decontextualized images, and images of violence play an important part in reinforcing the degradation of certain groups and normalizing violence against them. For example, after Black actor Leslie Jones starred in a new version of *Ghostbusters*, a campaign of individuals who were opposed to a Black woman starring in the film began trolling Jones with violent commentary and images that had racist and sexist undertones (Citron, 2019). The campaign was encouraged by conservative media commentator Milo Yiannopoulos, who was known for instigating online mob attacks against people he criticized (Silman, 2016).[1] Jones reported that she was sent doctored images that made it appear as though she had been ejaculated on, her website was hacked, her nude photos were stolen and posted online, photos of her personal identification documents were shared, and memes of a dead gorilla were posted on her website (Citron, 2019). These images violated her privacy and used racist and sexist tropes, along with other information, to make her feel fearful and to dehumanize her, thus fitting within the concept of violence described by the above critical race theorists.

Individuals like Leslie Jones may find themselves singled out for attacks, but many of these violent attacks are interconnected and led by discriminatory groups that organize in digital spaces. These abusers often find their homes in extremist alt-right, white supremist, homophobic, and misogynistic groups whose online messaging boards purposefully share discriminatory messages that dehumanize and encourage physical violence against equality-seeking groups (Baele, Brace, & Coan, 2019). Abusers' messages are often veiled under arguments for freedom of expression, conservative values, or described as jokes not to be taken seriously. However, much of the language and images on these boards actively reinforce the systemic dehumanization of certain groups of people (Conway, Scrivens, & Macnair, 2019).

In more extreme cases, multiple mass shootings have been linked to these online hate groups, one of which was live streamed on the internet. Several of the shooters have published racist and sexist manifestos on 8chan, which is an online forum that has been called a "cesspool of hate," where users have praised the mass killer's "high score" for the number of people killed (Conway et al., 2019, pp. 8 & 13). These spaces are used to recruit and radicalize their users and use memes, GIFs, and specialized jargon to reinforce their messages (Conway et al., 2019). Similar groups, such as Incels, have advocated for and celebrated physical violence against women and employ a similar pattern of shared images and language to reinforce their messages of violence. Incels have been connected to at least two mass killings where the killers have been upheld as heroes of the movement for murdering people in revenge for their lack of sexual access to women (Baele et al., 2019). What makes the words and images used by these groups violent is their ability to reinforce systemic discrimination that dehumanizes marginalized groups, normalizing or inciting real world attacks against them.

Technology-Facilitated Violence and the Law

This section will review two recent cases that addressed whether certain technologically facilitated behaviors could be legally recognized as violence. As noted in the previous section, the law should not be viewed as the primary source of how we understand violence. However, it plays an important role in shaping societal understandings of violence, and some courts have recently begun interpreting whether certain forms of harmful technology-facilitated behaviors should be understood as violence. The following two cases were chosen because they both address laws where emotional and psychological abuse is included in the definition of violence, making them broad enough to capture many forms of TFV. The first case, *AB v CD* (2020 BCCA 11),[2] involved a father sharing private information about his transgender son with fringe-conservative media websites that promote transphobic messaging. It was selected due to the large amount of media attention the case was given around the question of what could be considered family violence. The second case, *Buturugă v Romania* (2020), involved an intimate partner violence relationship where an allegedly abusive ex-husband accessed his ex-wife's computer documents and social media accounts without her consent. It was selected because it was one of the first cases out of the ECtHR that recognized technology-facilitated privacy invasions as a form of violence.

AB v CD

In a 2020 decision, *AB v CD*, the BCCA set aside a finding of family violence from a lower court in a case where a father, CD, had used social media platforms and provided interviews to online newspapers in which he misgendered his transgender son, AB, and shared private information about him. His online interviews exposed his son to substantial violent commentary and unwanted transphobic attention from the greater community. One of the questions before the court was whether CD's actions met the definition of family violence. Family violence under the British Columbia *Family Law Act* (2011) includes "psychological or emotional abuse of a family member" such as "intimidation, harassment, coercion or threats" and "unreasonable restrictions on, or prevention of, a family member's financial or personal autonomy" (s. 1).

AB was a teenage boy who was assigned female at birth. When he sought gender-affirming medical care, his doctors and his mother supported his decision to begin taking masculinizing hormones so his body would better match his gender identity. AB had been struggling with challenges related to his gender, including the stresses he felt about his body's "femaleness" and the bullying and harassment that accompanied it. He had attempted suicide in March 2018, in part, due to the stresses related to his gender identity. His mother was fearful that if AB did not get access to gender-affirming medical treatments he might attempt suicide again. With gender-affirming treatment, AB's doctor believed some of AB's stresses would be relieved, and that he would be less likely to be harassed by others, reducing his risk of suicide. However, AB's father, CD, did not engage with his son's medical team and did not support the decision. Instead, CD filed a claim in family court disputing AB's ability to make this medical decision without CD's consent and later instigated a public campaign that included speaking to online conservative media sites about his disapproval of his son's medical decision specifically and gender-affirming medical treatments for transgender youth more generally. The story was widely covered by both mainstream and fringe-conservative media sources.

During interviews with online fringe conservative media sites and in his court filings, CD misgendered his son, publicly rejecting his child's gender identity and name change. The two media sites of concern, *Culture Guard* and *The Federalist*, are fringe online conservative media sites who write articles opposing gender transitions, particularly those involving minors.[3] In those interviews, CD shared detailed personal and medical information about AB and trivialized AB's suicide attempt. The authors of the articles also misgendered AB and published unredacted copies of AB's medical documents that identified him. Court documents showed that comments on these stories included derogatory statements about AB, claiming he was mentally ill, encouraging his suicide, suggesting he be kicked out of his family home, suggesting he be disowned, and advocating for a "post birth abortion" of AB (*AB v CD and EF*, 2019 BCSC 604, para 33). The father, CD, expressed excitement about the media attention the story was getting and stated that he hoped that *Fox News* and *Breitbart* would pick up the story. *Brietbart* is an alt-right website known for spreading conspiracy theories and hiring provocative racist, sexist, and transphobic writers. Milo Yiannopoulos, the man credited for instigating the attacks on actor Leslie Jones, once worked there as a senior editor (Hunt, 2016). CD personally engaged in the comment sections on *Culture Guard*'s website, offered to speak as a keynote speaker at a *Culture Guard* event (which he later declined due to a court ordered publication ban), and posted commentary on social media sites. *Culture Guard* also raised funds for CD's legal costs related to the case (*AB v CD and EF*, 2019 BCSC 604).

In response to these acts, AB told the courts he was "terrified" that his father would go public with information that would identify AB, which could lead to "terrible bullying and violence" (2019 BCSC 604, para 32). AB was concerned about his physical and emotional safety around CD and felt scared to watch the interviews his father gave to *Culture Guard*. CD continued to engage online about his son's gender and medical decisions even after being cautioned by the courts that his behaviors were damaging to his son's well-being.

Lower lever courts (2019 BCSC 254 & 2019 BCSC 604) determined AB was a mature minor who was able to make decisions about his health without the consent of his father. A declaration was made that CD's behavior toward his son, including misgendering his son to third parties,[4] was a form of family violence and granted a protection order that restrained CD from sharing personal and medical information about AB with media outlets or on social media and required CD to refer to AB by his proper name and gender. The Court noted that CD's ongoing behavior put AB at risk of additional emotional and physical violence, including exposing AB to "degrading and violent public commentary" on social media (*AB v CD and EF*, 2019 BCSC 604, para 68) and putting AB at "a high risk of public exposure and acts of emotional or physical violence, in the form of bullying, harassment, threats and physical harm, including self-harm" (*AB v CD and EF*, 2019 BCSC 604, para 70). CD appealed the decision.

At the Court of Appeal, AB's ability to consent to his medical treatment was upheld, but the declaration that CD's actions were family violence and the protection order were set aside, largely due to procedural issues regarding which section of the *Family Law Act* (2011) was applied and what evidence was before the court (*AB v CD*, 2020 BCCA 11). The protection order was replaced with a conduct order (an order to manage behaviors that might frustrate the resolution of a family law dispute) that prohibited CD from providing information about AB's gender identity or medical information to third parties and requiring CD refer to AB as male and by his chosen name. On the question of violence, the majority of the Court of Appeal found that the father's refusal to acknowledge AB's gender was "clearly hurtful" to AB, but stated that there was insufficient evidence that CD intended to hurt his son (*AB v CD*, 2020 BCCA 11, para 171).

When considering the father's behaviour and the concept of family violence, the Court's (*AB v CD*, 2020 BCCA 11) focus on the father's intention was problematic, as the *Family Law Act's* (2011) definition of family violence does not specify that the psychological or emotional abuse needs to be intentional. However, there was evidence that CD's behaviors had emotionally and psychologically harmed AB, and his father had neglected to acknowledge that harm. The Court noted that CD did not engage with AB's medical team to better understand his son's medical decision and had not considered how AB would be negatively affected by his engagement with the public online forums that were advocating against young transgendered people's rights to make medical decisions related to their gender. The Court also noted that CD ignored the effect derogatory public comments would have on his son. Nonetheless, the Court of Appeal found that CD's actions were not emotional abuse amounting to family violence, but simply "misguided" and "irresponsible" behavior on the part of the father (*AB v CD*, 2020 BCCA 11, para 179).

Focusing on the intention of the abuser rather than the impact of the abused in this way has the potential to permit a great deal of abusers to avoid responsibility for their behavior (Jackman, 2002). Racist, sexist, and transphobic online commentators often claim to be protecting traditional values or are only making comments as jokes, but the impact for those targeted is consequential (Conway et al., 2019). To claim ignorance or a lack of intent to harm his son, CD should not have been able to rely on his own reckless disregard of the impact his online campaign would have on his son, particularly because the harms were well documented by the courts. While CD cannot be held responsible for the individual actions of others on the internet, his ongoing engagement with digital groups that were encouraging physical and social harm against his vulnerable son should have played a larger role in the analysis of the overall impact of CD's behavior. The Court's focus should have been on the actual impact his ongoing actions.

The *Family Law Act* (2011) specifically includes psychological and emotional abuse as a form of family violence, and TFV has been recognized as a form of family violence in other cases. However, when commenting on the legal understanding of family violence, the Court of Appeal in this case warned that "some caution should be exercised in identifying 'psychological or emotional abuse' as constituting 'family violence'" (*AB v CD*, 2020 BCCA 11, para 175). This is a troubling direction for the court to take as it minimizes the significant harms AB experienced from his father's technology-facilitated actions. *AB v CD* was not a case where the person's technology-facilitated actions – misgendering his child in public digital spaces known for dehumanizing transgender people – had a minimal emotional or psychological impact on the person targeted. AB provided evidence to the court that CD's ongoing behavior was causing AB to fear for his physical and emotional safety and was impacting his autonomy. CD's child was at risk of self-harm and had medical professionals who recognized the harms experienced due to transphobia by his father and the general public. The courts recognized that CD had made his son an "unwilling poster child" in a divisive public debate about transgender youth rights that made dehumanizing comments about his son and transgender people (*AB v CD and EF*, 2019 BCSC 604, para 69). Moreover, lower level courts in British Columbia have recognized forms of TFV as a form of family violence in the past. In previous cases, the courts found that excessive amounts of text messages and emails (*X v Y*, 2015; *M(MW) v K(JD)*, 2015) caused psychological or emotional harms amounting to family violence. The judgments in these cases did not focus on whether the abuser intended to harm the other person by their actions. Instead, in both cases, the abuser did not appreciate the full consequences of his behavior; however, the courts focused on the impact on the person being abused to determine if the technology-facilitated behavior was a form of family violence rather than the abuser's intention of his actions (*X v Y*, 2015; *M(MW) v K(JD)*, 2015).

Considering this, CD's behavior could be likened to critical race theories (Matsuda et al., 1993; Jackman, 2002) on violence where words and images are used to reinforce the systemic dehumanization of marginalized groups and risk inciting physical violence against them. Research has shown that transgender people are disproportionately at risk of discrimination, violence, and suicide (Ashley, 2018b). Due to the high levels of discrimination transgender people experience, Canada has recently recognized gender identity and expression under federal and provincial human rights legislation (e.g., Canadian Human Rights Act, 1985). As a transgender youth, AB was a member of group who experienced systemic discrimination. His father's actions were directly linked to AB's social location in this group, and CD was aware that AB had been harassed due to his gender identity and had attempted suicide in part due to challenges he faced having his proper gender recognized and affirmed. Yet, CD recklessly continued to make public statements rejecting his son's gender identity, engaging with transphobic media outlets, prioritizing his own agenda over the safety, and well-being of his child.

In sum, I would argue that the lower level courts' understanding of violence was more aligned with the concept of TFV outlined in this chapter than that of the Court of Appeal. In the lower court's decision, the "degrading and violent public commentary" was acknowledged as contributing to AB's fears, and it recognized that CD's behavior could incite emotional and physical violence against his son (*AB v CD and EF*, 2019 BCSC 604, para 68). In the future, it is important that courts look to the impact of technology-facilitated behaviors in controlling the targeted individual as well as whether systemic factors, like transphobia, are present in the cases where the definition of violence includes psychological harms and limitations on autonomy.

Buturugă v Romania

In early 2020, the ECtHR held that "cyberviolence" is a form of intimate partner violence and that Romanian authorities had a positive obligation to investigate an abusive partner's unauthorized access to his partner's computer and social media accounts as it related to her case of domestic violence (*Buturugă v Romania*). In *Buturugă v Romania* (2020), Gina-Aurelia Buturugă brought a complaint against the Romanian government for failing to adequately investigate complaints she made against her husband, who she alleged had physically assaulted her, threatened to kill her, and accessed her electronic documents and social media without consent, copying her private correspondence, photos, and other material. According to Buturugă, her husband, who is only named in the decision by his initials ("MV"), had physically abused her during their relationship. She stated that when they began discussing divorce in late 2013, the violence escalated to the point that her husband threatened to kill her by throwing her off the balcony to make it look as though she died by suicide. Several days later, MV allegedly hit Buturugă on the head and threatened to kill her with an axe. Buturugă visited the hospital where she required significant care and obtained a medical document that detailed her injuries.

According to Buturugă, the authorities failed to adequately investigate her claims and tried to convince her to withdraw her complaints of physical violence. When she later reported that MV had accessed her computer and social media without her consent, she asked the police to search their family computer to collect evidence that her husband had violated her privacy as a part of his pattern of abuse. However, she was told by the police that the privacy invasion was unrelated to the violence she reported. In 2014, MV violated a protection order that was put in place to protect Buturugă from violence by sending threats through a family member, chasing Buturugă down the street, and trying to convince her to drop the criminal charges. The police closed her case in early 2015, stating the threats against her were not serious enough to warrant investigation, there was no evidence that MV had been the one to cause her injuries (although the police did not investigate who else could have caused them), and the alleged violation of her privacy was irrelevant to the subject matter of the case. Buturugă unsuccessfully contested the decision in the Romanian courts.

Dissatisfied with the treatment of her case by the Romanian police and the courts, Buturugă filed a complaint with the ECtHR, arguing that the Romanian government had not properly investigated her case and had violated her right to be free from inhumane or degrading treatment and her right to privacy under the European Convention on Human Rights. After hearing the case, the ECtHR found Romania had a positive obligation to take reasonable measures to investigate Buturugă's claim as a form of domestic violence, including the unwanted access of her computer and social media accounts by her ex-husband. In its decision, the ECtHR found that the police had not adequately investigated who had caused Buturugă's injuries or the alleged privacy violations. Importantly, the Court noted that unauthorized access to someone's computer, digital surveillance, and the taking, storing, and manipulating of data and images were recognized forms of violence under both domestic and international law. Under Romanian law, family violence includes emotional harms, including hindering a woman from exercising her fundamental rights and liberties, such as her right to private life, as well as physical and sexual violence. The ECtHR found that technology-facilitated privacy invasions could be considered a form of violence.

This decision by the ECtHR recognizes the role of TFV in violent intimate partner relationships that fit within with some of the theories of violence discussed above. As noted by Evan Stark (2007) and Anne Jones (2000), psychological harms that make a person feel as though they are being surveilled and controlled can be as effective in dominating a person in a violent intimate partner relationship as physical violence. The Romanian police and courts failed to understand how MV breaking into his ex-wife's computer to access her digital content was part of a larger pattern of violence in their relationship that significantly impacted Buturugă's agency and autonomy. Entrenched norms of what "real" (i.e. physical) violence looks like likely influenced their decision. According to Buturugă, the police were encouraging her to drop the claims against her husband's physical abuse, and they neglected to include the privacy invasions in their investigation of his abuse, which suggests there may have been systemic factors at play that minimize gendered-based violence generally and TFV specifically. By separating the privacy invasion from the physical harms in their investigation, the police failed to see what McGlynn, Rackley, and Houghton (2017) described as the "commonalities between seemingly disparate phenomenon" that lie along the continuum of violence (p. 4).

In a violent intimate partner relationship, when an ex-partner who has been exhibiting controlling behaviors gains access to their ex's social media accounts and other personal digital files, it contributes to feelings of the partner being ever-present and controlling. The ECtHR made the decision in this case to ensure the harms caused by unauthorized access by an abusive partner to a person's digital content were not minimized. In the context of this relationship, which had a history of physical violence, threats, and harassment, it made sense that MV's nonconsensual access to Buturugă's digital information was a part of his pattern of control in this abusive relationship. This places TFV on the continuum of violence and acknowledges its role in violent coercive relationships, something that the ECtHR affirmed.

Conclusion

There is power in recognizing and naming violence, including psychological and TFV. As society and the courts make determinations on what violence is, it is critical that they avoid minimizing the effects of TFV. Like the early days of antisexual harassment advocacy, there is a need for a cultural shift around TFV. Naming something gives it clarity and helps people situate it within their cultural understanding of what behaviors are socially acceptable and which are not. In our current society, TFV needs to be recognized and condemned. We cannot rely solely on legal decisions, such as the two discussed above, to guide this understanding, however, legal definitions do help shape societal views on violence and can provide useful legal remedies. Additional efforts in education, advocacy, and changes to societal attitudes are needed so targets are not blamed for their victimization are also critical components to changing social views on TFV.

Building on the theories developed by critical race, feminist, and antiviolence scholars and advocates, this chapter argued that TFV can be recognized by looking for behaviors that control, dominate, and instill fear in the person targeted, particularly those behaviors that rely on existing systemic power structures to further dehumanize and limit the autonomy of a particular person or group. Understanding harmful technology-facilitated behaviors can be complex and may require examining the situational or systemic factors at play to assess whether it meets the threshold of violence. In *AB v CD* (2019 BCSC 1057, 2019 BCSC 254, 2019 BCSC 604, 2019 BCCA 256, 2019 BCCA 297, 2020 BCCA 11) and *Buturugă v Romania* (2020), systemic issues of transphobia and sexism, respectively, played a role in the TFV experienced. The publishing of private information online, misgendering a transgender youth on a digital platform, and accessing an ex-spouse's computer and social media without consent must be situated in larger patterns of systemic violence made to control, demean, and significantly limit the autonomy of the person targeted. This chapter argued that the Court of Appeal in *AB v CD* (2019 BCCA 256, 2019 BCCA 297, 2020 BCCA 11) was too limited in its assessment of violence, problematically relying on the intention of CD rather than the impact of his actions on AB. Whereas in *Buturugă v Romania*, the ECtHR was able to correctly situate MV's actions within the context of domestic violence. These are just two examples of the way courts can interpret TFV, but they illustrate two potential paths the courts may take in the future: one that minimizes TFV and one that illuminates it. In the future, we should look to the theories mentioned in this chapter to help us understand TFV and its place in our social and legal understanding of violence.

Notes

1. Milo Yiannopoulos is an alt-right public figure who was well known for his racist, homophobic, and sexist commentary online. His commentary was known to instigate harassment campaigns against the people he criticized. His account was permanently suspended from Twitter in 2016 due to his abusive and hateful commentary (Hunt, 2016).

2. See also: *AB v CD and EF*, 2019 BCSC 1057, 2019 BCSC 254, 2019 BCSC 604; *AB v CD*, 2019 BCCA 256, 2019 BCCA 297.
3. Each of these contain "transgender" sections, for example: https://www.culturguard.com/category/transgender/; https://thefederalist.com/tag/transgender/.
4. "Attempting to persuade AB to abandon treatment for gender dysphoria; addressing AB by his birth name; referring to AB as a girl or with female pronouns whether to him directly or to third parties; shall be considered to be family violence under s. 38 of the *Family Law Act*" (2019 BCSSC 254, para 70).

References

AB v CD. (2019). BCCA 256.

AB v CD. (2019). BCCA 297.

AB v CD. (2020). BCCA 11.

AB v CD and EF. (2019). BCSC 1057.

AB v CD and EF. (2019). BCSC 254.

AB v CD and EF. (2019). BCSC 604.

Amnesty International. (2018). *#ToxicTwitter*. London: Amnesty International.

Ashley, F. (2018a). Genderfucking non-disclosure: Sexual fraud, transgender bodies, and messy identities. *Dalhousie Law Journal*, *41*(2), 339–377.

Ashley, F. (2018b). Don't be so hateful: The insufficiency of anti-discrimination and hate crime laws in improving trans well-being. *University of Toronto Law Journal*, *68*, 1–36.

Awan, I., & Zempi, I. (2015). 'I will blow your face off': Virtual and physical world anti-Muslim hate crime. *British Journal of Criminology*, 1–10.

Azmi, R., & Kautsarina, K. (2019). Revisiting cyber definition. In *18th European Conference on Cyber Warfare and Security*.

Backhouse, C. (2012a). Sexual harassment: A feminist phrase that transformed the workplace. *Canadian Journal of Women and the Law*, *24*(2), 275–300.

Backhouse, C. (2012b). A feminist remedy for sexual assault: A quest for answers. In E. Sheehy (Ed.), *Sexual assault law in Canada* (pp. 725–739). Ottawa, ON: University of Ottawa Press.

Backhouse, C., & Cohen, L. (1978). *The secret oppression: Sexual harassment of working women*. Toronto, ON: Macmillan of Canada.

Baele, S. J., Brace, L., & Coan, T. G. (2019). From 'Incel' to 'saint': Analyzing the violent worldview behind the 2018 Toronto attack. *Terrorism and Political Violence*, 1–25.

Bailey, J. (2007). Confronting collective harm: Technology's transformative impact on child pornography. *University of New Brunswick Law Journal*, *56*, 65–102.

Bailey, J. (2016). *Canadian legal approaches to 'cyberbullying' and cyberviolence: An overview*. Ottawa Faculty of Law Working Paper No. 2016-37.

Bailey, J., & Mathen, C. (2017). *Technologically-facilitated violence against women and girls: If criminal law can respond, should It?* Ottawa Faculty of Law Working Paper No. 2017-44.

Balos, B. (2004). A man's home is his castle: How the law shelters domestic violence and sexual harassment. *Saint Louis University Public Law Review*, *23*(1), 77.

Barratt, S. A. (2018). Reinforcing sexism and misogyny: Social media, symbolic violence and the construction of femininity-as- fail. *Journal of International Women's Studies, 19*(3), 16–31.

Bates, S. (2016). Revenge porn and mental health: A qualitative analysis of the mental health effects of revenge porn on female survivors. *Feminist Criminology, 12*(1), 22.

Bellafante, G. (29 May 2020). Why Amy Cooper's use of 'African-American' stung. *New York Times.* Retrieved from https://www.nytimes.com/2020/05/29/nyregion/Amy-Cooper-Central-Park-racism.html

Bonnet, F. (2015). Intimate partner violence, gender, and criminalization: An overview of American debates. *Presses de Sciences, 2*(56), pp. 357–383.

Burgin, R., & Flynn, A. (2019). Women's behaviour as implied consent: Male "reasonableness" in Australian rape law. *Criminology and Criminal Justice.* doi: 10.1177/1748895819880953

Buturugă v. Romania. (2020). European Court of Human Rights, application no. 56867/15.

Campbell, D. A. (2013). *The evolution of sexual harassment case law in Canada.* Kingston, ON: Queen's University Industrial Relations Centre.

Canadian Human Rights Act. (1985). RSC. c H-6.

Citron, D. (2014). *Hate crimes in cyberspace.* Cambridge: Harvard University Press.

Citron, D. (2019). Sexual privacy. *The Yale Law Journal, 128*(7), 1870–1960.

Conway, M., Scrivens, R., & Macnair, L. (2019). *Right-wing extremists' persistent online presence: History and contemporary trends.* The Hague: International Centre for Counter-Terrorism.

Delgado, R. (2014). Law's violence: Derrick Bell's next article. *University of Pittsburgh Law Review, 75*, 435–455.

Dodge, A. (2016). Digitizing rape culture: Online sexual violence and the power of the digital photograph. *Crime, Media, Culture: An International Journal, 12*(1), 65–82.

Douglas, H., Harris, B. A., & Dragiewicz, M. (2019). Technology-facilitated domestic and family violence: Women's experiences. *British Journal of Criminology, 59*(3), 551–570.

Dragiewicz, M., Burgess, J., Matamoros-Fernández, A., Salter, M., Suzor, N., Woodlock, D., & Harris, B. (2018). Technology facilitated coercive control: Domestic violence and the competing roles of digital media platforms. *Feminist Media Studies*, 1–17.

Duggan, M. (2014). *Online harassment.* Washington, DC: Pew Research Center.

Dunn, S. (2020). Identity manipulation: Responding to advances in artificial intelligence and robotics. WeRobot 2020 conference paper (pp. 117-140).

Dunn, S., Lalonde, J., & Bailey, J. (2017). Terms of silence: Weaknesses in corporate and law enforcement responses to cyberviolence against girls. *Girlhood Studies, 10*(2), 80–96.

Fairbairn, J. (2015). Rape threats and revenge porn: Defining sexual violence in the digital age. In J. Bailey, & V. Steeves (Eds.), *eGirls, eCitizens: Putting technology, theory and policy into dialogue with girls' and young women's voices* (pp. 229–252). Ottawa, ON: University of Ottawa Press.

Family Law Act. (2011). *SBC.* c 25, Part 1 s 1, Part 9 s 183.

Filipovic, J. (2007). Blogging while female: How internet misogyny parallels real-world harassment. *Yale Journal of Law and Feminism, 19*(1), 295–304.

Follingstad, D., & Rogers, M. J. (2013). Validity concerns in the measurement of women's and men's report of intimate partner violence. *Sex Roles*, *69*(3), 149–167.
Gibson, W. (1984). *Neuromancer*. New York, NY: Ace Books.
Hall, M., & Hearn, J. (2019). Revenge pornography and manhood acts: A discourse analysis of perpetrators' accounts. *Journal of Gender Studies*, *28*(2), 158–170.
Henry, N., Flynn, A., & Powell, A. (2018). 'Policing image-based sexual abuse: Stakeholder perspectives'. *Police Practice and Research: An International Journal*, *19*(6), 565–581.
Henry, N., Flynn, A., & Powell, A. (2019). *Responding to revenge pornography: The scope, nature and impact of Australian criminal laws: A report to the criminology research council*. Canberra: Australian Institute of Criminology.
Henry, N., McGlynn, C., Flynn, A., Johnson, K., Powell, A., & Scott, A. J. (2020). *Image-based sexual abuse: A study on the causes and consequences of non-consensual nude or sexual imagery*. London, New York: Routledge.
Henry, N., & Powell, A. (2015). Embodied harms: Gender, shame, and technology-facilitated sexual violence. *Violence Against Women*, *21*(6), 758–779.
Human Rights Watch. (2013). *Those who take us away*. New York, NY: Human Rights Watch.
Hunt, E. (20 July 2016). Milo Yiannopoulos, rightwing writer, permanently banned from Twitter. *The Guardian*.
Jackman, M. R. (2002). Violence in social life. *Annual Review of Sociology*, *28*, 387−415.
Jane, E. A. (2016). Online misogyny and feminist digilantism. *Continuum*, *30*(3), 284–297.
Jones, A. (2000). *Next time, she'll be dead : Battering & how to stop it*. Boston, MA: Beacon Press.
Kelly, L. (1987). The continuum of sexual violence. In J. Hanmer, & M. Maynardm (Eds.), *Women, violence, and social control* (pp. 46–60). London: Macmillan Press.
Kelly, L. (1988). *Surviving sexual violence*. Cambridge: Polity Press.
Kidd, D., & Turner, A. J. (2016). The #GamerGate files: Misogyny in the media. In A. Novak, & I. El-Burki (Eds.), *Defining identity and the changing scope of culture in the digital age* (pp. 117–139). Hershey, PA: IGI Global.
Koshan, J. (2017). The judicial treatment of marital rape in Canada: A post-criminalisation case study. In M. Randall, J. Koshan, & P. Nyaundi (Eds.), *The right to say no marital rape and law reform in Canada, Ghana, Kenya and Malawi* (pp. 257–298). Portland, OR: Hart Publishing.
Lenhart, A., Ybarra, M., Zickuhr, K., & Price-Feeney, M. (2016). *Online harassment, digital abuse, and cyberstalking in America*. New York, NY: Data & Society.
Loise Backe, E., Lilleston, P., & McCleary-Sills, J. (2018). Networked individuals, gendered violence. *A literature review of cyberviolence*, *5*(3), 135–146.
MacKinnon, C., & Siegel, R. (2004). *Directions in sexual harassment law*. New Haven, CT: Yale University Press.
Manjoo, R. (2012). The continuum of violence against women and the challenges of effective redress. *International Human Rights Law Review*, *1*(1), 1–29.
Marwick, A. (2017). Scandal or sex crime gendered privacy and the celebrity nude photo leaks. *Ethics and Information Technology*, *19*(3), 177–191.

Massanari, A. (2017). #Gamergate and the fappening: How Reddit's algorithm, governance, and culture support toxic technocultures. *New Media & Society*, *19*(3), 329–346.

Matsuda, M., Lawerence, C., Delgado, R., & Crenshaw, K. (1993). *Words that wound: Critical race theory, assaultive speech, and the first amendment*. London: Routledge.

McGlynn, C., & Rackley, E. (2017). Image-based sexual abuse. *Oxford Journal of Legal Studies*, *37*(3), 534–561.

McGlynn, C., Rackley, E., & Houghton, R. (2017). Beyond 'revenge porn': The continuum of image-based sexual abuse. *Feminist Legal Studies*, *15*, 1–22.

M(MW) v K(JD). (2015). BCPC 315.

Nakamura, L. (2013). "It's a nigger in here! Kill the nigger!" User-generated media campaigns against racism, sexism, and homophobia in digital games. In K. Gates (Ed.), *The international encyclopeida of media studies VI: Media studies future* (pp. 1–15). Hoboken, NJ: Blackwell Publishing.

Parsons, P., Molnar, A., Dalek, J., Knockel, J., Kenyon, M., Haselton, B., & Deibert, R. (2019). *The predator in your pocket: A multidisciplinary assessment of the stalkerware application industry*. Toronto, ON: Citizenlab.

Peterson, J., & Densley, J. (2017). Cyber violence: What do we know and where do we go from here?. *Aggression and Violent Behavior*, *34*, 193–200.

Powell, A., & Henry, N. (2017). *Sexual violence in a digital age*. London: Palgrave Macmillan.

Powell, A., Henry, N., & Flynn, A. (2018). Image-based sexual abuse. In W. S. DeKeseredy, & M. Dragiewicz (Eds.), *Routledge handbook of critical criminology* (2nd ed., pp. 305–315). Abingdon and New York, NY: Routledge.

Quinn, B. (2000). The paradox of complaining: Law, humor, and harassment in the everyday work world. *Law & Social Inquiry*, *25*(4), 1151–1185.

Quodling, A. (2016). Platforms are eating society: Conflict and governance in digital spaces. In A. McCosker, S. Vivienne, & A. Johns (Eds.), *Negotiating digital citizenship: Control, contest and culture* (pp. 131–146). Lanham, MD: Rowman & Littlefield Publishers.

Renold, E., & Barter, C. (2005). Challenging the normalisation of violence in children's homes from young people's perspectives. In E. Stanko (Ed.), *The meanings of violence* (pp. 90–111). London: Routledge.

Sanders-Phillips, K. (2009). Racial discrimination: A continuum of violence exposure for children of color. *Clinical Child and Family Psychology Review*, *12*, 174–195.

Silman, A. (2016, August 24). A timeline of Leslie Jones's horrific online abuse. *The Cut*. Retrieved from https://www.thecut.com/2016/08/a-timeline-of-leslie-joness-horrific-online-abuse.html

Stanko, E. (Ed.). (2005). *The meanings of violence*. London: Routledge.

Stark, E. (2007). *Coercive control: The entrapment of women in personal life*. Oxford: Oxford University Press.

United Nations. (2018). HRC 38th, 18/06/2018. A/HRC/38/47, Report of the Special Rapporteur on violence against women, its causes and consequences on online violence against women and girls from a human rights perspective.

United Nations General Assembly. (1979). *Convention on the elimination of all forms of discrimination against women*. 18 December 1979, A/RES/34/180.

Vera-Gray, F. (2016). *Men's intrusion, women's embodiment: A critical analysis of street harassment*. New York, NY: Routledge.

Walcott, R., Foster, C., Campbell, M., & Seally, D. (2016). *Racial minority perspectives on violence: A report prepared for the review of the roots of youth violence*. Ontario, ON: Ministry of Children, Community and Social Services.

Waldman, A. E. (2019). Law, privacy, and online dating: 'Revenge porn' in gay online communities. *Law & Social Inquiry*, *44*(4), 987–1018.

Weiss, K. (2009). 'Boys will be boys' and other gendered accounts: An exploration of victims' excuses and justifications for unwanted sexual contact and coercion. *Violence Against Women*, *15*(7), 810–834.

X v Y. (2015). BCSC 336.

Chapter 3

"Not the Real World": Exploring Experiences of Online Abuse, Digital Dualism, and Ontological Labor

Chandell Gosse

Abstract

Online environments have become a central part of our social, private, and economic life. The term for this is "digital existence," characterized as a new epoch in mediated experience. Over the last decade, there has been a growing interest in how online abuse impacts one's digital existence. Drawing on 15 interviews with women, this chapter demonstrates a type of labor—which I call "ontological labor"—that women exercise when processing their own experiences of online abuse, and when sharing their experiences with others. Ontological labor is the process of overcoming a denial of experience. In the case of online abuse, this denial stems partly from the treatment of online and offline life as separate and opposing. This division is known as digital dualism, which I argue is a discourse that denies women the space to have their experiences of online abuse recognized as such.

Keywords: Digital dualism; ontology; embodiment; discourse; online abuse; harm

Introduction

Online environments, such as social media, online games, email, and instant messaging, have become a central part of our existence. They are a principal mode through which people experience their social, personal, and economic lives. The term for this is "digital existence" (Lagerkvist, 2019), which captures an

The Emerald International Handbook of Technology-Facilitated Violence and Abuse, 47–64

doi:10.1108/978-1-83982-848-520211003

important new epoch in mediated experience, but which also grows increasingly redundant as distinctions between the online and offline, the virtual and physical, collapse. In the last decade, much attention has been paid to the problems that technology-facilitated violence and abuse (TFVA for short, but henceforth referred to as "online abuse") raises for women's digital existence (Amnesty International, 2018; Barlow & Awan, 2016; Gosse & Burkell, 2020; Citron, 2014; Duggan, 2017; Hodson, Gosse, Veletsianos, & Houlden, 2018; Mantilla, 2015; Powell & Henry, 2017; West Coast LEAF, 2014). Despite the breadth of extant literature, online abuse remains a complex issue in need of further research.

This chapter aims to better understand experiences of online abuse in relation to digital existence by sharing findings from a set of interviews with 15 women. In particular, the central focus of this chapter is digital dualism, which is the process of making and thinking a distinction between online and offline life, experiences, spaces, and, most importantly for this study, harms (Jurgenson, 2011a). This distinction manifests in the treatment of offline life as *more real* than online life. The response to digital dualism is what I call "ontological labor," a form of effort exerted by women to convince others, and in some cases themselves, that the online abuse they experience, and the impact of that abuse, *is real*. This chapter also lends much needed evidence to the currently under-utilized concept and problem of digital dualism (Jurgenson, 2011a, b).

The first part of this chapter describes what digital dualism is, how distinctions between online and offline life have been addressed in academic literature, and ends with a description of how I use the term. The second part of this chapter focuses on findings from the interviews with women and offers an interpretation which demonstrates the impact of digital dualism vis-à-vis their experiences with online abuse. The final part of this chapter explores the concept of ontological labor and demonstrates how the women in this study engage in it.

Before moving forward, I want to note that it is necessary to differentiate linguistically between "online" and "offline" spaces in order to address the problem of digital dualism. By doing so, however, I am in some ways reinscribing the exact dichotomy I want to elide. There are, of course, reasons to use the language of "online" and "offline," particularly as they describe different modes of communication and mediation. So while this chapter relies on the argument that marking a distinction between online and offline makes almost no sense for many people whose lives and experiences in each are entwined, the fact remains that to talk about the enmeshed nature of experiences with and experiences without a screen, Wi-Fi connection, or device, we do require a reference point. I do not have a path out of this paradox, and so in this chapter, I rely on this linguistic distinction, but I wish to acknowledge it upfront so as not to undermine the arguments I make.

Digital Dualism

Media theorist Nathan Jurgenson (2011a,b) popularized the concept of "digital dualism" in a series of essays on *The Society Pages' Cyborgology* section. For Jurgenson (2011a), digital dualism is a bias that treats offline/physical life as *real* and online/digital life as virtual and somehow *less real*. Jurgenson points out that there is a strong and unflattering proclivity in the literature around digital culture that relies on the argument, more or less, that "the problem with social media is that people are trading the rich, physical, and *real* nature of face-to-face contact for the digital, virtual, and trivial quality of Facebook" (Jurgenson, 2011a, para. 6). The bias, in this case, is in the preferential treatment given to offline forms of communication, mediation, and interaction.

This bias also reinforces notions of online and offline life as separate and opposing. In the *Cyborgology* essays, Jurgenson (2011a) primarily critiques scholarly work and discussion for relying on such a tidy distinction between online and offline life. In particular, he critiques authors who continue to use now-outdated frameworks, such as Turkle's (1984) concept of the "second self," writing that "conceptually splitting so-called 'first' and 'second' selves creates a 'false binary' because 'people are enmeshing their physical and digital selves to the point where the distinction is becoming increasingly irrelevant'" (Jurgenson, 2011a, para. 5). This irrelevance is central to Jurgenson's critique, which he further develops – later describing digital dualism as not only a bias (2011a) but also a fallacy (2011b). Given the biased and fallacious nature of digital dualism, Jurgenson (2011a) advocates for an alternative perspective, which he calls "augmented reality" (para. 2). Augmented reality rests on the understanding that material reality and digital information influence and inform one another (Jurgenson, 2009).

Beyond Digital Dualism: IRL Fallacies, Embodiment, and Digital Ontology

Other scholars have articulated the limitations of conceptually separating online and offline spaces, but the concept of digital dualism has not yet been fully explored in academic literature. Instead, it is more common for scholars to engage with the concept of digital dualism without naming it as such. For example, Robinson (2015) writes about an "online-versus-'in real life' fallacy" (p. 80). In her article, she reflects on her experience with online abuse, which was an instance of "highly publicized violence against Black folks" (p. 80), and explains that her surprise over the adverse impacts the abuse caused was not a result of "two worlds [unexpectedly] colliding" (p. 80), but rather the very belief that there are two worlds (i.e., online and offline life) unraveling before her. Other important work that contributes to understanding the nuances involved with making and thinking a distinction between online and offline life include the use of embodiment theory by feminist scholars (Richard & Gray, 2018) and scholars who research TFVA (Powell & Henry, 2017), as well as scholars in the field of digital ontology (Lagerkvist, 2019; Schwartz, 2019).

Early internet research studies argued that a virtual presence can liberate individuals from the bodily constraints of gender, race, size, and ability/disability, to name only a few (Haraway, 1991; Turkle, 1984). This cyberutopian concept is a form of digital *dis*embodiment. Since then, feminist scholars have pushed back on this assumption and argued that the body – and bodily subjectivity – is central to the experience one has in online spaces (Pham, 2011; Richard & Gray, 2018). For example, as a way to nuance our understanding of how women operate online, Black cyberfeminists have adopted an intersectional framework that honors the complexity of identities "operating and existing in digital spaces" and argues that individuals cannot "rid bodily identifiers in any realm" (Richard & Gray, 2018, p. 121). Thinking specifically about the erasure of race, Pham (2011) compares the rhetoric of digital disembodiment to the "neoliberal racial agenda of color-blindness" (p. 3). Disconnecting the body from the user is not only impossible, but Pham further points out that such utopian conceptions of bodily liberation wrongly assume that "the disappearance of the body in cyberspace would effect the disappearance of the desire to consume difference" (p. 3). This is to say that collapsing, erasing, or pretending to collapse and erase identities such as race and gender does not prevent individuals from having differential experiences based on their identity and social locations, but instead "conflates or ignores intragroup differences" (Crenshaw, 1991, p. 1242) that are important to crafting open and equitable online spaces. Therefore, treating the body as necessarily tied to one's online experience provides room to think through the body as a site of power and struggle that shapes digital spaces.

Powell and Henry (2017) explain that embodiment theory has been underutilized particularly in cybercriminology. As a result, they advocate for an analytical framework that incorporates a theory of digital embodiment to better understand the consequences of drawing a dichotomy between online and offline life. For them, digital embodiment offers important avenues for thinking about the way digital life is lived through our bodies (Powell & Henry, 2017). Writing specifically about technology-facilitated sexual violence, they point out that dominant conceptions of violence and abuse as physical and bodily devalue online harms, many of which are "noncontact offenses" (Powell & Henry, 2017, p. 61). Digital embodiment, then, offers a connection between noncontact offenses and embodied harms.

Just as digital embodiment situates the body as central to the lived experience of digital culture, digital ontology demonstrates that vulnerability is a fundamental experience of being human whether that human experience is online or offline. It also recognizes that the philosophical tradition of ontology "has sought to eliminate or ignore the very embodied particularities that give vulnerability its shape and pull" (Schwartz, 2019, p. 82). This inclination to eliminate the body is heightened in socio-digital culture. Despite the appearance of being more technically connected than ever before, digital culture might actually be pulling us away from understanding ourselves as ontological beings who are interconnected with the world and with each other (Miller, 2019). Miller (2019) points out that the distanced and mediated nature of online interactions offers a new kind of omnipresent, metaphysical condition in time and space "which is beyond the body as we currently understand it" (p. 178).

In response to these inclinations, digital ontology repositions embodiment and vulnerability as central to any discussion about digital existence. Schwartz (2019) argues that digital existence is not at all disembodied, but instead creates new demands for care and "complex vulnerabilities" that require rethinking and reorienting our relationship to familiar binaries like "mind and machine or body and text" (p. 85). In fact, these complex vulnerabilities are omnipresent, no longer tied to time and space. As such, they give rise to new possibilities of what it means to experience embodied vulnerability (Lagerkvist, 2019).

A key argument within digital ontology is that online spaces and digital existence give rise to a misunderstanding of our ontological status that manifests as a "heightened impression of invulnerability in online social encounters with others" (Miller, 2019, p. 178). This misunderstanding is an important characteristic of digital dualism and, as I later show, a leading cause as to why the women in this study engage in ontological labor.

A Binary of Habit: A Habit Born of Discourse

The central concern in this chapter is not with expanding and nuancing the concept of digital dualism, though that work must be done to understand the consequences that emerge from it. My interest rather is in the fallout that stems from digital dualism. Establishing that pathway requires an understanding of how digital dualism operates. Jurgenson's description of digital dualism as a bias (2011a) and a fallacy (2011b) is an important contribution and central to conceptualizing what I later show is a harmful distinction. However, I expand on Jurgenson's original understanding of digital dualism and add that it is also a discourse that produces a habit, in addition to a bias and a fallacy. Acknowledging the discursive elements of digital dualism is important because it helps demonstrate how power is exercised through the language we use to talk about online and offline life (Butler, 1997; Fairclough, 1989).

More specifically, Jurgenson's critique focuses specifically on the way some scholars discuss online and offline spaces. In order to extrapolate this to a larger public, who likely thinks less deliberately about their choice of language and position on such a topic, it is necessary to expand on Jurgenson's concept of digital dualism to more clearly account for the casualness and naturalization – or the "habit of" – digital dualist thinking. Fairclough (1989) writes that when discursive practices – ways of speaking, thinking, and being – are regularly deployed, the beliefs that fuel them can become "common sense" (p. 77). While digital dualist thinking might not be intentional, the tendency to speak in these terms is catchy – it spreads and becomes part of the socio-digital fabric. And once repeated often enough it becomes an existing convention that governs and legitimizes social relations (Fairclough, 1989). With these additions to the concept of digital dualism in mind, the remainder of the chapter addresses two questions: How do participants experience digital dualism in relation to online abuse? And what are the implications of these experiences for digital existence?

Methods

While anyone can be subjected to online abuse, research shows that women are more likely than men to be targeted (Duggan, 2017) and that women experience "a wider variety of online abuse, including more serious violations" (Lenhart, Ybarra, Zickuhr, & Price-Feeney, 2016, p. 4). The aim of this study was to better understand women's experiences with digital dualism in relation to online abuse. As such, findings in this chapter come from a set of interviews with 15 women who had experienced online abuse.[1] Recruitment posters containing a link to an online screening tool were distributed throughout a medium-sized city in Canada and were shared on Twitter, Facebook, and through listservs from personal accounts and third-party organizations. An invitation to participate was extended to anyone who fit the study's inclusion criteria.[2] This process continued until clear themes began to emerge in the data, at which point recruitment stopped. The interviews took place from May to October 2018 over telephone and Skype. Each interview lasted between one and three hours and followed a semi-structured interview guide.

The majority of women in this study were from Canada (n = 13) and two were from the United States. They ranged between the ages of 21 and 44, with a mean age of 31. The experiences they discussed took place over a diverse range of online spaces including major social media sites like Facebook, Twitter, Instagram, and YouTube; email and text messaging services; dating platforms such as Tinder and Plenty of Fish; massive multiplayer online games like RuneScape and Star Wars Galaxies; personal blogs and forums such as Reddit and Tumblr; and older sites like MSN, ICQ, and MySpace. The types of abuse they experienced were far more wide-ranging than the sites on which they experienced them. For the safety and protection of the participants in this study, all names have been changed and cities, schools, and places of work have been removed.

Digital Dualism in Everyday Life: Findings

This section highlights interview data that were about "digital dualism." This includes any instance where participants mentioned a structural or conceptual separation between online and offline life. In total, the theme of digital dualism emerged in the data in three ways: as advice from others to turn off the computer, delete social media, and block users; as a denial of experiences *as real*; and as internalized by participants.

You Should Stop Using Social Media Altogether

A primary mode through which participants experienced the treatment of online and offline life as separate and opposing is in the advice they received from others when they shared their experiences of online abuse. For example, Ellie explained: "A big frustration for me is when I tell people about the problems I'm having and they say 'well, you should stop using social media altogether, you should delete your Instagram, you should delete your Facebook, you should just stop.'" For Ellie, this is not a possibility: "I hate when people say that to me. I'm like, this is my fucking job, like, I can't." Ellie made the point that even if she did "just stop," the consequences of not having an online presence would be disruptive and damaging to her career.

Another participant, Candice, expressed a similar sentiment, noting that the advice she received tended to overlook the fact that online interactions are embedded in offline social contexts:

> People are like, "why don't you turn it off [...] but like, if you have a shitty situation at work why don't you just stop? Leave your job,

> and never come back?" Like that's what people seem to kind of think, that you have total control.

Candice pointed out that online spaces are not necessarily independent from other aspects of people's lives, and that there is an unreasonable expectation that you can ignore online abuse – "that you have total control."

Abigail explained that in her experience people have also assumed that she had "total control." In her case, the assumption was coupled with the expectation that perpetrators of her abuse were unknown and anonymous, but as she pointed out, that is not always the case:

> The obvious response is always, well just block them. And that hasn't changed, it was true ten years ago and it's true now [... but] these interactions were embedded in social contexts, they weren't just like these random people that I could just block and never hear from again. It doesn't work like that.

Melody was also encouraged to "just block" her stalker when he began contacting her on different mobile apps:

> Originally [my friends] recommended that I just block him off everything, like including I block his number. And the reason I didn't do that was because I wanted to see what kind of messages he was sending so that I would have a record if I ever needed to report him or something.

Melody pointed out that blocking her stalker was not an option, despite her friends' recommendation, because doing so would limit her ability to keep a record of his harassing behavior and potentially her ability to report him and protect herself. This is a stark reminder of the inadequacy of advice to "get offline," because not seeing the abuse does not render the abuse any less harmful.

Having received the same advice so often has made some participants reluctant to seek support. For instance, Ellie explained: "There are some people I love and care about who I don't talk to about what's going on in my life because I don't want to hear them say, 'oh, just get offline.'"

These Aren't "Real Social Phenomena"

Participants in this study described encountering situations where the *very real* nature of their abuse was doubted, downplayed, or ignored. For example, during her undergraduate degree Maya wanted to write a paper exploring online abuse as a way to think through her own experiences. Her professor at the time rejected the topic, telling her that online abuse was not a "*real* social phenomena" and nothing she had described was "*real* and had happened because it hadn't happened in a face-to-face space." Her professor instead asked why she did not instead focus on "the elements of the virtual in face-to-face space."

The women I spoke to expressed the belief that online abuse is generally devalued and taken less seriously than other kinds of abuse, such as physical abuse. For instance, Maya sought therapy during the height of her abuse only to have those experiences dismissed:

> I would end up talking to counselors about this and there certainly was a lot of not understanding that stuff that goes on online can and will hurt you [...] [There was one] counselor, she listened, she was very nice. She still had the tendency to say "oh don't you think you're giving this person power?" So there was a little bit of victim-blaming going on where I think she still struggled to see anything experienced online as *real*.

At other times, she wanted – but was hesitant – to reach out:

> There's been times where I thought about calling a distress center just to be like, "I'm experiencing some stuff, like PTSD [...] and [it would be great] to be able to actually share that this was an online thing" and not have someone say like, "oh honey, don't you know that that's not *real*?"

Ellie explained that she was concerned that the onus would be on her to try to convince the therapist that the negative impact it has had on her is *real*: "[One reason for not seeking therapy] is that I think it would be more emotionally taxing for me to have to explain to someone what online abuse is." Expressing a similar sentiment, Fiona explained that the abuse itself left her with little energy to justify or explain the harm she had experienced. For this reason, Fiona did not seek support from law enforcement out of anticipation that her abuse would not be taken seriously: "At the time there was nothing [no laws or legal avenues of support]. And if I had to sit down with like, some 60-year-old cop and try to explain to him what Twitter was? Forget it." The concern here is twofold: first, that as targets of abuse you will have to explain (and re-explain) what online abuse is, how it manifests, and how it hurts; and second, after giving all of that emotional energy, you will be misunderstood or dismissed. This barrier to seeking support is amplified for certain communities where there is a history of state violence and tension with law enforcement.

The text-based and verbal nature of online abuse was also used as a way to deny women's experiences of harm. Fiona explained: "Online abuse is seen as something that is in the ether. Like it's just words. Actually, a couple of weeks ago I had a conversation about this with one of my coworkers. He doesn't think that words hurt." Maya explained that her therapist demonstrated the same attitude as Fiona's coworker, but focused on the online nature of those words – singling out the source of words as determinants of their impact: "Very often people's harsh words do become part of your self-talk [...] So [it was hurtful] for somebody who had the expertise to be able to say, yes, words matter. Oh, but not when they are said online."

While it might be relatively easy to shrug off the occasional insult, the repetition of injurious speech (Butler, 1997) is dangerous. As Maya explained:

> Human beings connect through conversation and we do tremendously great things, but we can [also] do really evil things [...]. People talk each other out of suicidal states, and they've talked each other into it. [...] I think when we discount that, we're literally discounting part of what it means to be human.

Such speech constructs subject through a process of "violating interpellation" (Butler, 1996, p. 204) that shapes and limits one's understanding of themselves. This process involves more than just the harmful language spoken in that moment – it also invokes "a community and history" (Butler, 1996, p. 204) of words and speakers which represent larger structures of limitation, oppression, and marginality. For example, Wendy, who described herself as able to dismiss much of what is said to her online, explained that the cumulative nature of online abuse "gets to you after a while."

The denial of online abuse as a *real* experience also came from perpetrators. Participants described how perpetrators shirked responsibility and downplayed the impact of their actions. For example, Trish explained that after confronting a man who shared her image without consent, the perpetrator became defensive: "He was like 'go think of something in the *real world*' and I was like, 'just because it's online doesn't mean it's not the *real world*'... he said something like 'stop telling yourself that' to get away with it." Reflecting on this problem, Lilly pointed out:

> It doesn't matter if they say it to your face or they say it to you online, you are damaged by this abuse, and you shouldn't be able to say "oh well it was just on Facebook" or hide behind the fact that you are on a keyboard.

Ellie described comments she has received in which perpetrators tried to deny her the space and context to understand their actions *as* violent or abusive by redirecting the harm: "One time a guy threatened to lock me up in Guantanamo, or like, one time they talked about flying me to Somalia so that I could experience what *real* violence was like."[3]

Perpetrators' belief that online abuse is less injurious and less consequential to those targeted is self-serving. It works to detract from the harm perpetrators cause and allows them to deflect responsibility. However, it also reflects a wider hierarchy of harm that has long circulated in offline spaces, where forms of abuse without physical markers are invisibilized and lack what little protection actually exits (Sims, 2008).

"Real Life," "Real World": Internalizing Discourses

The phrases "real world" and "real life" were frequently adopted by participants in this study (used by 13 out of 15 participants). Participants sometimes knowingly used the term. For example, Ellie said: "I think obviously online abuse is *real life*, you know, quote unquote 'real-life abuse,' because obviously online is *real life*." She also pointed out that she uses the language "'IRL [*in real life*] abuse' and 'digital abuse'" in gaming contexts. But most often participants unknowingly and casually used this language to mark a distinction between online and offline experiences. For example, Lilly used the term to point out that perpetrators of online abuse should face the same consequences as they would with other kinds of abuse: "I feel like they deserve to be treated just as if they had hurt me physically, like in *real life*." Jane used the term to talk about the limitations of escaping online abuse: "There's less control you can have online because there's no way of really running, you're running around within the construct of the internet, but in *real life* you can literally run anywhere." And Abigail used the term to point out that the comments said to her would likely not have been said offline: "I didn't know how to respond to it because I don't think he ever would have said those things to me in *real life*."

Although participants use the terms "real world" and "real life" to mark a difference between online and offline abuse, by virtue of their experience, many participants do not have the benefit of fully engaging with this online/offline divide. To use Robinson's (2015) point, online abuse unravels the perception that online life and offline life are distinct from one another. While participants might discursively engage with distinctions between online and offline life, their position as targets of online abuse pulls them away from fully engaging in this divide and instead returns them to a place where online life and offline life are completely enmeshed. This "returning" occurs in two ways: through the impact of abuse (i.e., the way experiences of online abuse permeate a target's emotions and embodied vulnerability) and through the content of the abuse they receive, which makes them think about "what […] it's like for [other] women in *real life*" (Candice). For example, Kate described being sent "booby traps" in the form of links to videos she was told to watch. When she followed the link it would lead to a woman being humiliated in a sexually violent way: "Even when someone would say like, Google 'goatse' or 'two girls one cup',[4] those were pictures of real people, right? Like in *real life* situations and so it always forced your hand to think about *real world* violence" (Kate).

Participants also drew on similarities between online and offline abuse to contextualize their experiences, for example, by comparing them to other instances of street harassment and catcalling. Lilly explained: "For me it falls under the same realm as when I was 16 and I'd walk down the street and people would grab my butt or catcall at me." Kate described online abuse as her first experience with verbal harassment:

> I remember my first catcall not being person to person, but just online [...] The graphic "I'm going to suck your tits and have sex with you and whatever," it actually predated the first time I was yelled at in public.

The offline abuse and harassment women are regularly subjected to acts as another reminder that there is no difference between the consequences and embodied impact of abuse online and abuse offline.

For Melody, the gravity of her situation began to sink in only once she labeled her abuser's behavior in relation to its offline counterpart: "He started messaging me on there and that's when I was like, that's just gone overboard, this is almost stalking, well I guess not almost, he's a cyberstalker, essentially." Like Melody, Ellie drew on the offline equivalent of the behavior to understand the significance and seriousness of her abuse:

> When someone makes a two-hour video about you, like, the *real life* equivalent of that is someone holding a lecture to a lecture hall of tens of thousands of people talking about how you're a horrible person and you need to be stopped.

Participants commonly connected the online abuse they encountered to other types of offline abuse that they have experienced. This is a reminder that online abuse is not a distinct and separate form of abuse, but instead is part of a spectrum, or continuum, of abuse and violence (Kelly, 1987). Drawing on this continuum, participants also relied on similarities between online and offline abuse as a way to justify and account for the harm they experienced.

Digital Dualism in Everyday Life: Interpretation

The separation of online and offline life came from participants themselves, the perpetrators of abuse, and from others with whom they shared their experiences. These findings are symptomatic of a culture that privileges face-to-face communication over digital communication (Jurgenson, 2011a) and where discursive practices of drawing a distinction between online and offline life govern and influence the way we speak, think, and act toward digital culture. For example, recommending that participants turn off their computer, sign out of social media, or remove themselves from online spaces, stems in large part from the digital dualist belief that online and offline life is separate and opposing. Specifically, digital dualism operates here in two ways: first, it implicitly treats targets of online abuse as less vulnerable; and second, it relies on digital disembodiment.

The type of advice participants received implies that individuals can stop the harm associated with abuse by simply cutting off communication. These strategies, however, cannot be realized because digital life is *real life* and you cannot just "sign out" of life. Furthermore, this type of advice demonstrates a misunderstanding of a core tenet to our ontological status: that we are profoundly vulnerable. It assumes that people are somehow less vulnerable as humans in online spaces and can thus easily protect themselves from harm and abuse. The consequence of normalizing this type of advice – or, of treating it as common sense (Fairclough, 1989) – is that it implants in individuals, and their support networks, a sense of false control over the repercussions of online abuse. This type of advice also assumes that the abuse, and the harm that it causes, can be turned off as easily as the devices themselves, as if the abuse is localized to the screen before us, rather than something that sits with us – that we carry affectively throughout our day.

Powell and Henry (2017) use Bourdieu's concept of symbolic violence to demonstrate how "dominant conception[s] of 'real' violence [...] hide or render invisible forms of non-physical violence" (p. 50). What they are pointing to here is a long history of physical abuse being considered more dangerous and certainly more worthy of attention than emotional, verbal, and psychological abuse. Online abuse has been treated in similar ways, which I argue is a product of digital dualist thinking. It also reflects wider attitudes toward gendered violence generally, where targets and victim-survivors are responsible for avoiding abuse and the harm they experience is erased or minimized. Online abuse becomes another example of these noncontact offenses and thus adopts a similar fate in terms of the (lack of) urgency and care it is given.

In particular, the textual basis through which much of the online abuse occurs is used against targets as a way to try and convince them that the abuse, and thus their feelings, is not legitimate.[5] Perpetrators also embody this digital dualist tendency and use it as a way to avoid responsibility and downplay the impact of their actions. In fact, perpetrators are susceptible to the same digital dualist habits as the families and friends' participants rely on for support. The difference, however, is that for perpetrators, drawing that distinction between offline as *real* and online as *un*real is overtly self-serving.

Despite perpetrators' attempts to downplay their abusive actions, participants were clear that what is said, shown, and shared online produces the same effect as it would if these actions occurred offline. However, digital existence is full of contradictions and many of the participants in this study continue to use language like "real life" or the "real world" despite an expressed concern for others doing and thinking the same thing.

The casualness with which participants used the language of the "real world" and "real life" demonstrates the power of digital dualist thinking. As Fairclough (1989) explains, when discursive practices are repeated enough, they begin acting like common sense. In other words, the use of this language – "real world" and "real life" – reflects a system of hegemonic domination that participants are simultaneously critical of and participating in.

Importantly, when participants use the phrase "in real life" they are not doing it to belittle experiences or downplay their abuse or emotions, and to be clear, their friends and family are not necessarily doing so either. Digital dualist frameworks are widely accepted and naturalized in socio-digital culture and the casualness and banality of this reference point – *the real world* – is indicative of this. It is, however, important to try and move beyond these casual references because the way we talk about the interconnectedness of online and offline life influences the way we treat and act toward said connection. A person's thoughts, actions, and choices are shaped by social conditions. Discursive practices, like those found in digital dualism, create social conditions that can too often limit possibilities for social existence (Butler, 1997), such as how individuals see themselves in relation to others and to the wider public sphere.

Ontological Labor

Citron (2009) writes that "the online harassment of women exemplifies twenty-first century behavior that profoundly harms women yet too often remains overlooked and even trivialized" (p. 373). Part of that trivialization stems from the digital dualist discourse that dismisses online spaces as merely virtual and *less real* and gives the "impression of a lack of embodied vulnerability" (Miller, 2019, p. 172).

But perhaps the most dangerous aspect of digital dualism is that those who tend to subscribe to the dichotomy fail to recognize that they do so. This is precisely Fairclough's (1989) point about the way discourse becomes naturalized, appearing as "common sense" and making the power relations enacted through it difficult to identify. In the case of digital dualism, the power relations prioritize the physical over the virtual and the atom over the digit. Without acknowledging the practice of digital dualism, or the power relations that give it strength, it is impossible for individuals to understand the harm it causes. It is "a violence which is wielded precisely inasmuch as one does not perceive it as such" (Bourdieu & Wacquant, 2004, p. 272).

When digital dualism is naturalized and invisibilized, it further erases the harm of online abuse because it hijacks an important process of recognition. Recognition is about being seen, heard, and having a framework to make meaning of and understand one's experience. As Langois (2014) points out, defining oneself and one's experiences involves an element of recognition that requires "patterns and rhythms of relationality" which are granted by others (p. 142). Drawing on Crossley (2001), Lumsden and Morgan (2017) explain that symbolic violence systematically denies some people a "degree of recognition enjoyed by others" and represents "the felt and/or lived suffering" of those who are "denied a basic level of recognition by their wider society" (p. 930). If digital dualism denies or hijacks recognition, then ontological labor is a response that encourages the process of recognition to continue and it necessitates the consideration of embodied vulnerability in online spaces. Ontological labor also has a deeply political and historical lineage that demonstrates women's struggle to have the violence and abuse they face taken seriously.

Ontological labor is the term I give to the process of overcoming what amounts to a denial of experience. The reactions and advice women receive about their online abuse – like being told to stop using social media altogether – and the way perpetrators claim they do not cause harm, for example, by telling women to "lighten up" because whatever said or shared was "just online," are evidence of this denial. Ontological labor, then, involves dismantling other people's perceptions of online spaces as *less real* and of online abuse as *less harmful.*

The practice of ontological labor is not exactly new. Women have long had their experiences of abuse rendered invisible, dismissed as unimportant, or had the onus of proof and persuasion rest solely with them (Price, 2005). If there is a difference between the ontological labor women engage in as a result of online abuse, it is one of circumstance and not of measure. Ontological labor is different from other forms of negation women face in social life. Unlike gaslighting, the process of emotionally manipulating someone into questioning their own sanity, the abuse women experience is not necessarily questioned, largely because textual and photographic evidence is abundant in these circumstances. In online abuse cases, it is the effect of/affect caused by the abuse which is called into question. In other words, ontological labor is not about trying to show that something occurred, it is about trying to show others that it had a *real* impact.

The need to engage in ontological labor stems from a complex set of factors: the trivialization of women's experiences, the treatment of noncontact offenses as less serious, and the common disbelief surrounding victim-survivors' experiences of violence and abuse, to name a few. These factors are compounded in online contexts by digital dualism. Focusing specifically on this online component, ontological labor then comes from (1) a widespread treatment and deep-seated understanding of online and offline life as separate and opposing; and (2) perceptions of vulnerability as primarily physical (which also involves a disconnect between social, physical, and psychical states of being). For the participants in this study, ontological labor is a gendered process performed in three key ways: demonstrating to others that one's online life is not distinct from their offline life; convincing others that words are hurtful; and constructing frameworks for exploring and understanding online abuse.

First, participants explain that being a target of online abuse means to be constantly demonstrating that online spaces are not distinct from other aspects of their lives. In Ellie's experience, she found she had to explain to people that social media is part of her job, and thus disconnecting is not that simple. In Candice and Abigail's experience, they found themselves having to reorient people's conception of online abuse so that it includes already established social relations; relations that cannot be neatly separated as either online or offline. This work is exhausting and requires that targets of online abuse take it upon themselves to convince others why their experiences matter.

Second, participants perform ontological labor in the work they do to convince others that online abuse causes (embodied) harm. This involves disregarding perpetrators' attempts to downplay or devalue the harm they cause and advocating for themselves by insisting that online abuse is *real*. This advocacy is quiet, and it emerges in conversations with friends, family, and therapists. Maya explained that she is practiced in trying to convince others that online abuse *is real*:

> So I'll tell them, "okay, it's not *real*?" [They say] "Right, nothing that happens online is *real*." And I'll ask them, "are you saying that in good faith?" [They say] "Well I mean if it was *real*, you would actually show that you were really suffering." "Ok […] so nothing that happens online is *real*?" [They say] "Correct." "Could you give me your credit card for a minute?" and then [they say] "woah, woah, woah!"

Third, participants' performance of ontological labor includes an effort to create a framework and a space to understand online abuse as such. As I have demonstrated, participants had a tendency to make sense of their experiences by pointing out the similarities they have with other forms of physical and/or offline abuse (e.g., when Ellie explained how outrageous the YouTube videos made about her are), or by relating them to their analogue counterparts (e.g., when Melody made sense of her experience by comparing cyberstalking with stalking more broadly). Participants were aware that some of the abuse they experienced would have been considered more serious and treated differently if it had occurred in an offline context. As mentioned earlier, physical abuse is treated as more serious than emotional and verbal forms of abuse, and emotional and verbal forms of abuse displayed online are further trivialized. Following this logic, it is understandable that participants try to show that one harm, online harm, is similar to other, offline harms that tend to carry more weight. The act of relating online abuse to other types of abuse, which have established frameworks for processing the transgression, is a fundamental aspect of ontological labor. Comparing online abuse with offline abuse is a way for participants to rationalize their feelings and contextualize the harm in ways that are familiar to them precisely because there is no common framework for understanding online abuse in its own right. In some ways, then, comparing different forms of abuse is a way to create a framework and carve out a social existence for online abuse.

Ontological labor also involves an enormous cognitive burden that comes from the emotional toll that retelling experiences of abuse – any kind of abuse – has on an individual. Couple that emotional exhaustion with the likelihood of not having one's abuse seen as abuse in the first place, and the strength of digital dualism as a barrier begins to take shape. While also adding to the labor women already perform to keep themselves safe (e.g., avoid walking alone, dress "with discretion," Gardner, 1990), this ontological negation and undermining of experience denies them permission from themselves or from others to feel the impact of such abuse. It is more important to understand that treating online and offline life as separate is itself a form of harm and barrier to support. Whether or not there is a difference between online and offline life, treating them as though there is no difference can help individuals, like the women in this study, feel supported throughout what is undoubtedly a difficult and harmful experience.

Not all women will experience ontological labor in the same way. Depending on their intersecting identities, their labor maybe be more onerous. As Sexwale (1994) explains, "although many forms of violence against women are common across the board, some forms and/or their incidence are strictly related to one's positioning in terms of the diversity of our realities" (p. 200). These same realities influence the level of ontological labor that targets engage in. Not only are the bodies we inhabit tied to the lives we live through online spaces, but when confronted with online abuse, those bodies become barriers to access in online and offline spaces: religion, race, sexuality, and gender become factors, among many others, that complicate support seeking and being believed.

Conclusion

This chapter expands on the original concept of digital dualism as a bias (Jurgenson, 2011a) and fallacy (Jurgenson, 2011b), and demonstrates the way it operates as a discourse and a habit. As a discursive practice, digital dualism denies women who experience online abuse the space they deserve to have that abuse seen, interpreted, and treated *as real* and embodied. For participants, this applies to other social media users (i.e., the perpetrators of abuse) and people and institutions on whom the women have leaned for support (such as therapists, friends, and family). Ontological labor, as a response to digital dualism, focuses on validating experiences of online abuse *as real* and requires women to go above and beyond already expected and practiced safety work to keep spaces of sociality – such as social media, mobile communication apps, and online game sites – accessible and safe. Hence collapsing the online/offline divide becomes an important step toward supporting targets of online abuse, because having the space and capacity to experience phenomena *as real* is a core element of one's existence, digital or otherwise.

Notes

1. This study was trans-inclusive. The digital and analogue recruitment posters for this study indicated that anyone who identified as a woman was welcome to participate. No further demographic information on gender was collected. Given the gendered nature of online abuse (Mantilla, 2015), further iterations of this project ought to include non-binary individuals, as well. For now, this remains a limitation of the project.
2. Participants were required to be 18 or older, identify as a woman, and have been the target of online abuse.
3. This comment points to the intersection of sexism, misogyny, and colonialism. In addition to the misogynistic intent and denial of harm embedded in this comment, there is also a reproduction of damaging stereotypes born out of colonial sexism, which assumes that women in the Global-South are treated worse than women in North America.
4. Goatse is an internet shock site that operated in the late 1990s and early 2000s. Two girls one cup is the nickname for a Brasilian fetish pornographic video that circulated widely in the mid 2000s.
5. Not all online abuse is text based, of course. Harms involving image-based abuse, control over the Internet of Things (IoT), and some forms of cyberstalking do not necessarily involve text.

References

Amnesty International. (2018). Toxic twitter: A toxic place for women. Retrieved from https://www.amnesty.org/en/latest/research/2018/03/online-violence-against-women-chapter-1/

Barlow, C., & Awan, I. (2016). You need to be sorted out with a knife: The attempted online silencing of women and people of Muslim faith within academia. *Social Media + Society*, *2*, 1–11.

Bourdieu, P., & Wacquant, L. (2004). Symbolic violence. In N. Scheper-Hughes & P. Bourgois (Eds.), *Violence in war and peace* (pp. 272–274). Oxford: Blackwell Publishing Ltd.

Butler, J. (1996). Burning acts: Injurious speech. *The University of Chicago Law School Roundtable*, *3*(1), 199–221.
Butler, J. (1997). *The psychic life of power*. Stanford, CA: Stanford University Press.
Citron, D. K. (2009). Law's expressive value in combating cyber gender harassment. *Michigan Law Review*, *108*, 373.
Citron, D. K. (2014). *Hate crimes in cyberspace*. Boston, MA: Harvard University Press.
Crenshaw, K. (1991). Mapping the margins: Intersectionality, identity politics, and violence against women of color. *Stanford Law Review*, *43*(6), 1241–1299.
Crossley, N. (2001). *Key concepts in critical social theory*. London: Sage.
Duggan, M. (2017). *Online harassment*. Pew Research Center, Internet & Technology. Retrieved from http://www.pewinternet.org/2017/07/11/online-harassment-2017/
Fairclough, N. (1989). *Language and power*. Essex: Addison Wesley Longman Ltd.
Gardner, B. G. (1990). Self conduct: Women, crime, and self in public places. *Social Problems*, *37*(3), 311–328.
Gosse, C., & Burkell, J. (2020). Politics and porn: How news media characterizes problems of deepfakes. *Critical Studies in Media Communication*, 37(5), 497–511.
Haraway, D. J. (1991). *Simians, cyborgs, and women: The reinvention of nature*. New York, NY: Routledge.
Hodson, J., Gosse, C., Veletsianos, G., & Houlden, S. (2018). "I get by with a little help from my friends": The ecological model and support for women scholars experiencing online harassment. *First Monday*, *23*(8), n.p.
Jurgenson, N. (2009). Toward theorizing an augmented reality. *Sociology Lens*. Retrieved from https://www.sociologylens.net/article-types/opinion/towards-theorizing-an-augmented-reality/4444
Jurgenson, N. (2011a). Digital dualism versus augmented reality. *The Society Pages: Cyborgology*. Retrieved from https://thesocietypages.org/cyborgology/2011/02/24/digital-dualism-versus-augmented-reality/
Jurgenson, N. (2011b). Digital dualism and the fallacy of web objectivity. *The Society Pages: Cyborgology*. Retrieved from https://thesocietypages.org/cyborgology/2011/09/13/digital-dualism-and-the-fallacy-of-web-objectivity/
Kelly, L. (1987). The continuum of sexual violence. In J. Hanmer & M. Maynard (Eds.), *Women, violence and social control* (pp. 46–60). London: Palgrave Macmillan.
Lagerkvist, A. (2019). Digital existence: An introduction. In A. Lagerkvist (Ed.), *Digital existence: Ontology, ethics and transcendence in digital culture* (pp. 1–26). New York, NY: Routledge.
Langois, G. (2014). *Meaning in the age of social media*. London: Palgrave Macmillan.
Lenhart, A., Ybarra, M., Zickuhr, K., & Price-Feeney, M. (2016). Online harassment, digital abuse, and cyberstalking in America. *Data & Society Research Institute and Center for Innovative Public Health Research Report*. Retrieved from https://www.datasociety.net/pubs/oh/Online_Harassment_2016.pdf
Lumsden, K., & Morgan, H. (2017). Media framing of trolling and online abuse: Silencing strategies, symbolic violence, and victim blaming. *Feminist Media Studies*, *17*(6), 926–940.
Mantilla, K. (2015). *Gendertrolling: How misogyny went viral*. Santa Barbara, CA: Praeger.

Miller, V. (2019). The ethics of digital being: Vulnerability, invulnerability, and 'dangerous surprises'. In A. Lagerkvist (Ed.), *Digital existence: Ontology, ethics, and transcendence in digital culture* (pp. 171–186). New York, NY: Routledge.

Pham, M. T. (2011). Blog ambition: Fashion feelings, and the political economy of the digital raced body. *Camera Obscura*, *26*(1), 1–37.

Powell, A., & Henry, N. (2017). *Sexual violence in a digital age*. London: Palgrave Macmillan.

Price, L. S. (2005). *Feminist frameworks: Building a theory of violence against women*. Black Point, NS: Fernwood Publishing.

Richard, G. T., & Gray, K. L. (2018). Gendered play, racialized reality: Black cyberfeminism, inclusive communities of practice, and the intersections of learning, socialization, and resilience in online gaming. *Frontiers: A Journal of Women Studies*, *39*(1), 112–148.

Robinson, Z. (2015). The IRL fallacy. *Contexts*, *14*(4), 80.

Schwartz, M. (2019). Thrownness, vulnerability, care: A feminist ontology for the digital age. In A. Lagerkvist (Ed.), *Digital existence: Ontology, ethics, and transcendence in digital culture* (pp. 81–99). New York, NY: Routledge.

Sexwale, B. M. M. (1994). Violence against women: Experiences of South African domestic workers. In H. Afshar & M. Maynard (Eds.), *The dynamics of 'race' and gender: Some feminist interventions* (pp. 196–221). London: Taylor & Francis.

Sims, C. D. L. (2008). Invisible wounds, invisible abuse: The exclusion of emotional abuse in newspaper articles. *Journal of Emotional Abuse*, *8*(4), 375–402.

Turkle, S. (1984). *The second self*. New York, NY: Simon & Schuster.

West Coast Leaf. (2014). Cyber misogyny report. Retrieved from http://www.westcoastleaf.org/our-work/cyber-misogyny/

Chapter 4

Polyvictimization in the Lives of North American Female University/College Students: The Contribution of Technology-Facilitated Abuse

Walter S. DeKeseredy, Danielle M. Stoneberg, and Gabrielle L. Lory

Abstract

Polyvictimization means looking at multiple victimizations of different kinds that one person has experienced. Virtually, all of the work in this field focuses on the effects of childhood trauma and victimization on currently distressed children, and empirical and theoretical work on the intertwining of adult female offline and online abuse experiences is in short supply. Recently, however, some scholars are starting to fill these research gaps by generating data showing that technology-facilitated violence and abuse are part and parcel of women's polyvictimization experiences at institutions of higher education. This chapter provides an in-depth review of the extant social scientific literature on the role technology-facilitated violence and abuse plays in the polyvictimization of female college/university students. In addition to proposing new ways of knowing, we suggest progressive policies and practices aimed at preventing polyvictimization on the college campus.

Keywords: Polyvictimization; Technology-facilitated abuse; gender-based violence; sexual violence on campus; sexual assault; online/offline overlap

The Emerald International Handbook of Technology-Facilitated Violence and Abuse, 65–81

doi:10.1108/978-1-83982-848-520211004

Introduction

Male-to-female abuse on North American university/college campuses is not a new social problem. This field of study started almost 65 years ago when Kirkpatrick and Kanin (1957) found that 20% of women in one US institution of higher education experienced attempted or completed rape in a one-year time period. At that juncture, their data garnered little, if any, attention from the academic community, policy makers, journalists, and the general public. It was not until the late 1980s that a new wave of feminist survey researchers uncovered similar alarmingly high rates of male physical and sexual assaults on female undergraduate students (e.g., DeKeseredy, 1988; Koss, Gidycz, & Wisniewski, 1987), and the issue of abuse against women on campuses started to get extensive publicity (DeKeseredy, 2017). Even so, despite the compelling results of two North American national surveys (see DeKeseredy & Schwartz, 1998; Koss et al., 1987), the legacy of university/college administrators ignoring the plight of survivors continued, and there was a major antifeminist backlash effort in the late 1980s and throughout the following decade (Schwartz, 2015).

The backlash continues today (see DeKeseredy, 2019), but some progressive tectonic shifts occurred in the early and middle part of the last decade in relation to woman abuse on campus. In the United States, due to the ongoing work of feminist coalitions, the formation of the White House Task Force to Protect Students from Sexual Assault in 2014, the widespread viewing of Kirby Dick's 2015 documentary *The Hunting Ground*, and the passage of the federal Sexual Violence Elimination Act (SaVE) in 2013, many people now view sexual assault and other crimes against female students as the "current problem of the day" on university/college campuses and their immediate surroundings (DeKeseredy, 2018a, p. 204). The same recognition of the issue can be seen in some parts of Canada. For instance, on October 28, 2016, the Quebec government announced spending $200 million (CAD) on a five-year strategy to prevent sexual violence and $500,000 of that amount went to resources and campaigns on postsecondary school campuses.

The antifeminist backlash against feminist empirical, theoretical, and policy work on male assaults on female postsecondary students will persevere. So will innovative, progressive scholarly contributions to the field; one of which is the study of how technology-facilitated abuse contributes to *polyvictimization* in the lives of North American female university/college students. This concept simply means looking at multiple victimizations of different kinds that one person has experienced (Mitchell, Segura, Jones, & Turner, 2018). There is a large literature on polyvictimization, but it focuses mainly on the extent to which multiple childhood victimizations can predict various problems in functioning in later childhood or adolescence (DeKeseredy, Schwartz, Nolan, Mastron, & Hall-Sanchez, 2019a; Dierkhising, Ford, Branson, Grasso, & Lee, 2019; Ford & Delker, 2019). Dozens of studies found that multiple victimizations can result in a variety of poor outcomes, be it youth crime, school failure, or any other psychological disturbance (Hamby et al., 2018; Musicaro et al., 2019; Wolfe, 2018). This can be the result of repeated episodes of the same behavior, such as sexual abuse or physical violence, or numerous victimizations, as some children are subject to a broad array of damaging behaviors.

Rigorous empirical and theoretical work on the intertwining of North American female university/college students' offline and online abusive experiences are scarce, but a small group of scholars are starting to address this research gap by uncovering data showing that technology-facilitated abuse is part and parcel of women's polyvictimization experiences at institutions of higher education. Following the approach taken by the contributors to White, Koss, and Kazdin's (2011) anthology *Violence Against Women and Children: Mapping the Terrain*, this chapter answers what White et al. (2011) refer to as "three seemingly simple questions": what do we know? how do we know it? and what are the next steps? (p. xx). In other words, the chapter provides an in-depth review of the extant empirical and theoretical literature on the role technology-facilitated abuse plays in the polyvictimization of female university/college students and suggests new avenues of inquiry. The first section reviews the work done by researchers in this field. The second section examines new directions in research, and the third section proposes a multipronged method of targeting the relationship between offline and online victimization.

Polyvictimization in the Lives of Female Postsecondary School Students: What Do We Know and How Do We Know It?

To date, polyvictimization researchers have not turned extensive attention to the abusive experiences of adults in general. Even when university/college-aged adults were studied, the main concern was the effect of childhood multiple victimizations on current behavior. For example, Alexander, Amerigo, and Harrelson (2018) found that polyvictimization was the best predictor of what they termed "risky sexual behavior" among postsecondary school women (p. 345), whereas Espelage, Hong, and Mebane (2016) and Holt et al. (2017) found childhood polyvictimization related to current psychological functioning among such students.

A major exception in the polyvictimization literature is elder abuse, where Hamby, Smith, Mitchell, and Turner (2016) recommend that new studies use the concept of polyvictimization to develop a broader understanding of the abused elderly. DeKeseredy et al. (2019a) also show that polyvictimization can be used to study adult problems. Using data derived from the Campus Quality of Life Survey (CQLS) recently administered at a large residential university in the South Atlantic region of the United States, the authors found that a variety of abusive behaviors touch many female students' lives and that many of these students suffer these victimizations multiple times. However, it is unclear from their findings whether offline assaults intertwine with those that are online because their composite measures of stalking and sexual harassment conflate in-person and electronic forms of victimization. In other words, they created two variables (one for stalking and one for sexual harassment) that combined offline and online forms of these two types of abuse.

This does not mean that CQLS data cannot be used to determine such intertwining. For example, DeKeseredy et al. (2019b) found that 21% (n = 633) of the total CQLS female sample (n = 3,271) received unwanted electronic sexual messages/images, including pornography. They also found that 18.2% (n = 551) experienced at least one of eight types of intimate physical violence, and 34% (n = 1,041) were targets of at least one of five variants of offline sexual assault. Moreover, female CQLS respondents who reported receiving these unwanted electronic sexual messages/images were 3.4 times more likely to state that they had been sexually assaulted offline than women who did not receive them. Additionally, women who reported getting these messages/images were twice more likely to report offline intimate physical violence as respondents who were not sent these media.

Thirty-four percent (n = 1,041) of the CQLS female respondents reported being targets of technology-facilitated stalking. Those respondents were 2.3 times more likely to report an offline sexual assault than women who were not victimized. As well, participants who reported electronic forms of stalking were 2.6 times more likely to report intimate physical violence than women who did not report stalking.

These findings are not surprising given the small but expanding base of university/college-based research which shows that female students' cyber victimization and in-person experiences of psychological, physical, and sexual abuse are related (Marganski & Melander, 2018; Marganski, Melander, & DeKeseredy, 2020; Reed, Tolman, & Ward, 2016; Sargent, Krauss, Jouriles, & McDonald, 2016). Nonetheless, except for studies done by DeKeseredy et al. (2019a) and DeKeseredy et al. (2019b), all the data on the linkage between cyber violence and the in-person victimization of college students come from surveys administered to convenience samples, and, thus, the data are not generalizable (Dragiewicz et al., 2019; Marganski & Melander, 2018). Another major limitation, one shared by the above two studies done by DeKeseredy and his colleagues, is that it is unclear which victimization (i.e., offline or online) occurred first (DeKeseredy & Rennison, 2019). Some researchers and practitioners contend that effective policy and program development requires knowing if technology-facilitated abusive behaviors are precursors to face-to-face abusive acts or if they occurred with or after them (Marganski & Melander, 2018).

What are the key determinants of the polyvictimization described here? So far, there are very few answers to this question. DeKeseredy et al. (2019a) found that one of the most powerful predictors is *negative peer support*, which is also strongly associated with image-based sexual abuse (DeKeseredy & Schwartz, 2016), another harm examined by those who study technology-facilitated violence and abuse. There are various definitions of negative peer support, but for the purpose of their study, DeKeseredy et al. (2019b) operationalized a revised rendition of DeKeseredy's (1988) definition of *male peer support* to refer to attachments to peers and the resources they provide that encourage and justify violence against women. DeKeseredy et al. (2019a) also used the same definition and operationalized it the same way in their study of polyvictimization.

Two types of negative peer support predicted digital victimization and both violence committed by an intimate partner and sexual assault: (1) *proabuse informational support* and (2) *attachments to abusive peers*. The former refers to guidance and advice that influence people to sexually, physically, and psychologically abuse their dating partners, and the latter is defined as having friends who sexually, physically, and psychologically victimize dating partners (DeKeseredy & Schwartz, 1998).

DeKeseredy et al. (2019b) found that female CQLS respondents who reported having both types of negative peer support were more than twice as likely to reveal that they had received unwanted sexual messages/images as those who did not report negative peer associations. Respondents who reported receiving proabuse informational support were 50% more likely to state that an intimate partner physically assaulted them. What is more, participants who reported attachments to abusive peers were 2.7 times more likely to report such violence.

Respondents who reported receiving proabuse informational support were two times more likely to report technology-facilitated stalking than female respondents who did not receive such support (DeKeseredy et al., 2019b). Respondents with attachment to abusive peers were nearly three times as likely to report technology-facilitated stalking than those who did not have these associations. Furthermore, respondents who reported receiving proabuse informational support were 50% more likely to state having been targeted by intimate physical violence. Similarly, participants who reported attachments to abusive peers were 2.7 times more likely to report such violence. The two types of negative peer support are key predictors of offline sexual assault. Still, the relationships reported here should not be interpreted as causal because it is unknown whether victimization or peer support came first.

More recently, Marganski et al.'s (2020) convenience sample data show that the following factors are significantly related to intimate partner polyvictimization (e.g., psychological, physical, sexual, and cyber): friends' and family members' perceptions of respondents' intimate relationships; family connectedness (e.g., dimensions of respondents' relationships with their families); respondents' attitudes about sex with their current intimate partner; and being in an exclusive relationship (e.g., neither partner is romantically pursuing other partners). DeKeseredy et al.'s (2019b) and Marganski et al.'s (2020) studies of technology-facilitated abuse in the contexts of offline types reveal that there is extensive polyvictimization among US university/college students, at least at two institutions of higher education. British radical feminist Liz Kelly (1987, 1988) would likely argue that the multiple abusive behaviors that these students experienced exist on a *continuum of sexual violence,* ranging from nonphysical acts like sexual harassment to physical acts such as rape. Although the idea of the continuum is often used to portray movement from least serious to most serious, for Kelly (1988), and those who follow in her footsteps (e.g., DeKeseredy et al., 2019a), all of these behaviors are serious and have a "basic common character" (p. 76). No behavior on the continuum is automatically considered more harmful than another, and, as Kelly (1988) states, women's experiences

> …shade into and out of a given category, such as sexual harassment, which includes looks, gestures and remarks as well as acts which may be defined as assault or rape. (p. 48)

In sum, the concepts of polyvictimization and the continuum of sexual violence help us focus attention on the cumulative effects of a broad range of highly injurious interrelated behaviors that women experience, many of which are both exempt from the coverage or scope of criminal law and simultaneously trivialized or minimized by the general public and the media (DeKeseredy & Rennison, 2019; McGlynn, Rackley, & Houghton, 2017). Researchers have devoted extensive energy to analyzing the long-term effects of specific instances of sexual harassment, sexual violence, stalking, physical assault, and other harms, or have analyzed repeated patterns of one of these, such as violence against a partner. Still, for many women, these forms of abuse "seep into one another" (DeKeseredy et al., 2019a; Ptacek, 2016; Wolfe, 2018).

Next Steps in Research

Six years ago, Henry and Powell (2015) noted that "as a result of the gender-blindness within studies of virtual or cyber criminality, the conceptualization of technology-mediated 'harm' against women remains significantly underdeveloped" (p. 764). At that time, there was a conspicuous absence of feminist empirical and theoretical work on technology-facilitated abuse. Documented by DeKeseredy and Schwartz (2016), researchers mainly examined the explanatory value of gender-blind perspectives (Reyns, Henson, & Holt, 2016), such as Cohen and Felson's (1979) routine activity theory and Gottfredson and Hirschi's (1990) general theory of crime. Now, a growing international cadre of scholars produces ample evidence of a strong relationship between gender and women's risk of being targeted by technology-facilitated abuse that cannot be adequately accounted for through the use of "male-stream" theories. Consider that one of the two polyvictimization studies reviewed here statistically supports Powell and Henry's (2017) claim that "peer support for sexual violence against women emerges as a particularly challenging and troubling feature of sexual violence in the digital age" (p. 5).

More research is required, including the collection of data that clarifies the temporal order of key variables. Again, it is unclear whether certain abusive behaviors are precursors to others or if they occurred with or after them (Marganski & Melander, 2018). More research on polyvictimization experiences is also necessary in other country contexts, as well as an international comparative study that includes students and members of the general public. We know there is extensive polyvictimization among US college students, but we do not know whether female members of the general population are likewise at higher or lower risk. As studies of adult polyvictimization are rare, these new empirical directions will help fill a major research gap.

The vast majority of quantitative studies conducted on campus are climate surveys that measure the victimization experiences of both men and women. As such, research on male perpetrators of woman abuse on and off campuses is scarce (DeKeseredy, 2020a; Wendt, 2016), and this type of work has, thus, provided "little context in which acts take place" (Dragiewicz et al., 2019, p. 11). As Foubert, Clark-Taylor, and Wall (2020) observe

> …the literature lacks a recent, clear understanding of the number of college men who commit… assault, the number of… assaults each perpetrator commits, and the relationship to traditional all male-campus groups such as fraternities and athletic groups. (p. 297)

If numerous female students experience polyvictimization, it is likely that many men engage in multiple assaults of different kinds, but there is no conclusive evidence to support this hypothesis at this juncture. Yet, Foubert et al.'s (2020) research reveals that many men enrolled at institutions of higher education in a Midwestern part of the United States committed multiple alcohol-related sexual assaults, which polyvictimization literature suggests is an indicator that they may also have committed multiple types of other assaults (i.e., physical, mental) on women.

Statistics on men not only give us data on the extent and distribution of *polyperpetration* but also shed light on causal factors, such as male peer support. Male peer support for various types of violence against women is ubiquitous and has a long history (DeKeseredy & Schwartz, 2013). Quantitative and qualitative research done to date is highly informative, but there is still much we do not know about the connection between proabuse peer dynamics and the intertwining of offline and online means of abusing women (DeKeseredy et al., 2019b). For instance, some men victimize women but do not communicate with abusive friends on a face-to-face basis (DeKeseredy & Olsson, 2011; DeKeseredy & Schwartz, 2016), and there may be other environments or places in which their peers influence them to abuse women, such as patriarchal online communities with members who never meet in person but often exchange written, audio, and visual communication with their peers (DeKeseredy & Corsianos, 2016; Dragiewicz, 2011; Kimmel, 2008; Salter, 2017). Hence, another essential question is whether peer support for polyperpetration is mainly offline, online, or a combination of both (DeKeseredy & Schwartz, 2016).

There are other major gaps in our knowledge of the polyvictimization of female postsecondary students. Besides additional quantitative work, in-depth interviews with women are needed to understand the impact of their repeated victimization. Interviews with male polyperpetrators are also sorely needed and will provide answers to the question "Why does he do that?" (Bancroft, 2002). Another understudied area is whether the concepts of polyvictimization and polyperpetration are relevant specifically to the lives of LGBTQI university/ college students.

Goodmark (2011) reminds us that, "When the first domestic violence and stalking laws were passed, no one could have foreseen how technology would facilitate abuse, stalking, and harassment" (p. 195). Documented by a growing number of studies, the co-occurrence of technology-facilitated abuse, in-person assaults, and other types of woman abuse is now in its endemic phase, possibly even worse than the widespread consumption of opioids and methamphetamine in West Virginia (DeKeseredy & Rennison, 2019). What is to be done? Most important of all are the responses by universities/colleges to this problem. Next, we turn to how these institutions of higher learning can enhance female students' health and safety.

Preventing and Responding to University/College Campus Polyvictimization

After many years of developing campus programming, responses to woman abuse remain "widely varied" (Wooten & Mitchell, 2016, p. 1), even though bystander intervention is now the "centerpiece" of violence against women prevention strategies at most North American institutions of higher education (Henson, Fisher, & Reyns, 2020, p. 506). Bystander intervention refers to people who

> ...by their very presence, have the potential to do nothing, to step in and diffuse a high-risk situation... or to make the situation worse by condoning a perpetrator's behavior... or being unsupportive in responding to a victim. (Banyard, 2011, p. 216)

In the United States, bystander intervention became the "gold standard" due to federal requirements to implement them as part of a broader sexual assault prevention strategy (Wooten & Mitchell, 2016). Bystander intervention programs attempt to increase the campus community's knowledge of various types of woman abuse, change students' acceptance of sexual assault and other types of violence, decrease rape myth acceptance, increase bystander intervention, and ultimately reduce the amount of sexual assault, interpersonal violence, and other such harms on college campuses (Henriksen, Mattick, & Fisher, 2016). Keep in mind, however, that bystander intervention in North American institutions of higher education prioritizes the prevention of offline rather than online abuse. Furthermore, as noted by Henson et al. (2020), "bystander intervention behaviors directed at online contexts are absent from both the online victimization and bystander intervention research" (p. 505).

Though bystander intervention was found to be an effective means of preventing both offline and online victimization (Henson et al., 2020), some cautionary notes are necessary. First, there is evidence of short-term effectiveness, but we know little about its long-term effects. Second, for bystander intervention to work during an online or offline attack, there must be a witness to the assault. Most acts of male-to-female abuse occur behind closed doors and not in public places. It is highly unlikely, then, that those physically victimized in private contexts and those who do not have online witnesses to their technology-facilitated abuse experiences will receive any type of intervention (DeKeseredy, 2018a; Henriksen et al., 2016; Hewitt & Beauregard, 2014).

Bystander intervention programs and most other campus-based prevention and intervention strategies are also "extremely heteronormative" (Wooten & Mitchell, 2016). Initiatives that meet the needs of sexual minorities are in short supply (DeKeseredy, 2018a; Ford & Soco-Marquez, 2016). What is more, violent and other types of assaults on members of the campus LGBTQI community must be addressed in the contexts in which LGBTQI lives are situated. Numerous LGBTQI survivors and offenders have experienced childhood abuse, partner violence, traumatic coming-out experiences, isolation, mental health problems, internalized homophobia, substance abuse, and a host of other problems (Ball, 2013; Guadalupe-Diaz, 2019; Messinger, 2017; Meyer, 2015).

This is not to say that bystander intervention training (both online and offline) should be abandoned. Rather, it should be used in conjunction with other strategies briefly discussed here, one of which is teaching students what White and Carmody (2018) refer to as *online citizenship*. This could entail senior students serving as mentors for junior students to model respectful and safe online communication. Of course, this type of mentoring should also be used to foster such communication in offline contexts. Senior campus administrators, too, need to contribute to this type of mentorship, and White and Carmody (2018) contend that this can be achieved by them rewarding students "who watch out for one another by telling their stories, awarding them honors and providing them with opportunities to develop and lead prevention programs" (p. 2304).

Training and education should always be major parts of any campus-based prevention strategy, and, in fact, the most widely supported intervention is some form of educational campaign. Not only does every researcher who has studied woman abuse in institutions of higher learning end up recommending educational interventions, but student and community groups who intensely study the harms covered in this chapter virtually always come to the conclusion that the first stop on the "road of change" is education. Generally, the argument goes, education campaigns are essential because without them, students will learn their "facts" from either gossip or the uninformed media (Bohmer & Parrot, 1993; Schwartz & DeKeseredy, 1997).

Since technology is constantly changing, university/college personnel responsible for education and program creation must constantly receive in-person training about new developments and trainers could "walk them through settings on their own devices, allowing them to ask questions in real time" (Dragiewicz et al., 2019, p. 37). It should also be noted that White and Carmody (2018) found that students prefer face-to-face education about preventing online victimization, but they want to be taught by their senior peers instead of university employees. As one of their respondents put it:

> I think too a lot of administration sometimes doesn't get that… no matter how we make it, the facts are still the facts and they waste a lot of money going and making brochures and pamphlets when they have all these students who have been here who could actually have these real conversations with the freshmen as soon as they get here. (White & Carmody, 2018, p. 2301)

Antipornography education is also essential for the following reasons. Every day, thousands of North American undergraduate and graduate students consume violent and racist internet pornography (DeKeseredy, 2020b). Nearly nine out of every ten men and one out of every three women aged 18–26 in the United States report accessing online porn (Lim, Carotte, & Hellard, 2016). As well, by age 17, 93% of boys and 62% of girls have been exposed to porn (Sabina, Wolak, & Finkelhor, 2008; Sun, Bridges, Johnson, & Ezzell, 2016). There are many harms associated with pornography, but violence against women is one of the most common (DeKeseredy, 2020b). Based on their own rich research experience and their review of the extant literature, Sun et al. (2016) note that "Research on pornography and violence against women in particular is long-standing, robust, and generally points to a positive association between the two…." (p. 1).

Violent and racist porn is definitely a component of the abuse of female university/college students (see DeKeseredy, 2020b), and many male students are graduates of what Bancroft (2002) coins as "the pornography school of sexuality" (p. 231). As Sun et al. (2016) recently discovered in their study of 487 male undergraduate students

> …the more pornography a man watches, the more likely he is to use it during sex, request particular pornographic sex acts of his partner, deliberately conjure images of pornography during sex to maintain arousal, and have concerns over his own sexual performance. (p. 983) (see also Keene, this volume)

Based on the above data, one would think that reducing and preventing pornography consumption would be a major goal of contemporary campus antiviolence programs. Yet, the harms done by porn are seldom addressed in these programs (DeKeseredy, 2018b). For campus educators and administrators, it is, then, essential to recognize that student consumption of porn is a widespread problem and will only get worse due to easy and free access to internet pornography. It is now time to demonstrate some progressive leadership by offering programs on gender issues that address porn in their schools. Many things can also be done on a personal level (Katz, 2006), such as talking to male students and male faculty in assemblies, classes, at sporting events, in faculty and staff training, and in private conversations. Additionally, university/college staff should employ the following strategies informed by the work of Thorne-Finch (1992, pp. 236–237) and Warshaw (1988, pp. 161–164): confront students, instructors, and athletic staff who speak positively about violent and dehumanizing pornography; confront students and staff who perpetuate rape myths; take every opportunity to speak out against porn and other symptoms of gender inequality; and create social media sites about the harms of pornography and how men and boys can work together to reduce the consumption, production, and distribution of hurtful sexual imagery.

The interventions proposed here constitute just the tip of the iceberg, and many more could be suggested. Regardless of which strategies are selected, faculty, staff, administrators, and students must be prepared to meet new challenges and develop new initiatives because woman abuse on campus is a "never ending and constantly evolving issue" (Ledwitz-Rigby, 1993, p. 93). This is particularly so in relation to digital technologies, as perpetrators are now "weaving technology into patterns of abuse" (Dragiewicz et al., 2019, p. 5). Undoubtedly, by the time you finish reading this chapter, there will be new electronic means of inflicting pain on people, and it is vital that university/college employees and students keep pace with the rapid spread of cyber harms such as those identified in this book.

The academic community still has much to learn about responding to and preventing polyvictimization, especially in the online contexts. No doubt, mistakes will be made, and there will be considerable resistance to change from "reinforcers of the status quo" (DeKeseredy, 2019). Nevertheless, again, one of the most important points to consider here is to avoid oversimplified solutions. Often, they do more harm than good and fail to address the many and complex sources of woman abuse in institutions of higher learning (Stark-Adamec, 1996a). What is required is a multiagency approach, one that involves the joint efforts of students, faculty, administrators, campus security, and many other members of the campus community. Woman abuse on campus, as well as other major expressions of gender inequality, cannot be stopped unless universities/colleges develop a collective responsibility to prevent it from occurring (Stark-Adamec, 1996b).

Conclusion

Many North Americans share a vision of universities/colleges as peaceful sanctuaries from the "real world." Institutions of higher education, too, are commonly seen as places where students, faculty, administrators, and support staff strive constantly to provide "practical solutions to the problems of the day" (Strong-Boag, 1996, p. 105). To some extent, these perceptions are correct. Yet, North American universities/colleges are also "hot spots" of male-to-female abuse as documented by decades of sound research. The burgeoning social scientific literature on the co-occurrence of offline and online victimization shows that things are getting worse. The research reported here, in fact, reveals that for many women "acts of abuse and violence are rarely singular, isolated events" (Wolfe, 2018, p. 833).

More studies of polyvictimization in the lives of female university/college students are sure to come, but it is also necessary to develop new, effective prevention and intervention initiatives. Experts on woman abuse collectively emphasize the importance of avoiding simplistic solutions and the value of a multipronged approach involving feminist digital activism, legal reforms, education and awareness programs, survivor support services, perpetrator re-education, and corporate efforts (Clevenger, 2016; DeKeseredy, Dragiewicz, & Schwartz, 2017; Hall & Hearn, 2018; Powell & Henry, 2017; Powell & Sugiura, 2019). There are other useful strategies to consider, but it is essential to always keep in mind that

> Ending abuse is not only about specialized services delivered by trained individuals. It is perhaps more importantly about "humdrum" cultural change in which everyone does things a little differently every day. (Klein, 2012, p. 127)

All members of university/college communities can play a key role in reducing women's experiences of polyvictimization.

Acknowledgment

The authors would like to thank Mackenzie Freeman for her assistance

References

Alexander, A. A., Amerigo, L. S., & Harrelson, M. E. (2018). Polyvictimization and sexual risk behaviors in college-aged women. *Criminal Justice Review*, *43*(3), 345–359. doi:10.1177/0734016818767727

Ball, M. (2013). Heteronormativity, homonormativity and violence. In K. Carrington, M. Ball, E. O'Brien, & J. Tauri (Eds.), *Crime, justice and social democracy: International perspectives* (pp. 186–199). New York, NY: Palgrave Macmillan.

Bancroft, L. (2002). *Why does he do that? Inside the minds of angry and controlling men*. New York, NY: Penguin.

Banyard, V. L. (2011). Who will help prevent sexual violence: Creating an ecological model of bystander intervention. *Psychology of Violence*, *1*(3), 216–229. doi: 10.1037/a0023739

Bohmer, C., & Parrot, A. (1993). *Sexual assault on campus: The problem and the solution*. New York, NY: Lexington.

Clevenger, S. (2016). Future directions. In J. N. Navarro, S. Clevenger, & C. D. Marcum (Eds.), *The intersection between intimate partner abuse, technology, and cybercrime: Examining the virtual enemy* (pp. 205–217). Durham, NC: Carolina Academic Press.

Cohen, L. E., & Felson, M. (1979). Social change and crime rate trends: A routine activity approach. *American Sociological Review*, *44*(4), 588–608. doi:10.2307/2094589

DeKeseredy, W. S. (1988). *Woman abuse in dating relationships: The role of male peer support*. Toronto, ON: Canadian Scholars' Press.

DeKeseredy, W. S. (2017). Explaining campus violence against women: Unhealthy masculinity and male peer support. In C. Kaukinen, M. Hughes Miller, & R. A. Powers (Eds.), *Addressing violence against women on college campuses* (pp. 65–77). Philadelphia, PA: Temple University Press.

DeKeseredy, W. S. (2018a). Sexual assault on the college campus. In P. Lussier, & E. Beauregard (Eds.), *Sexual offending: A criminological perspective* (pp. 204–219). New York, NY: Routledge.

DeKeseredy, W. S. (2018b). Confronting adult pornography. In W. S. DeKeseredy & M. Dragiewicz (Eds.), *Routledge handbook of critical criminology* (2nd ed., pp. 455–464). London: Routledge.

DeKeseredy, W. S. (2019). Defenders of freedom or perpetrators and facilitators of crimes? Beyond progressive retreatism in the Trump era. *Victims and Offenders*, *14*(8), 925–939. doi:10.1080/15564886.2019.1671282

DeKeseredy, W. S. (2020a). Enhancing feminist understandings of violence against women: Looking to the future. In S. Walklate, K. Fitz-Gibbon, J. Maher, & J. McCulloch (Eds.), *The Emerald handbook of feminism, criminology, and social change* (pp. 337–355). Bingley: Emerald Publishing Limited.

DeKeseredy, W. S. (2020b). *Understanding the harms of pornography: The contribution of social scientific knowledge*. Sterling, MA: Culture Reframed. Retrieved from https://www.culturereframed.org/wp-content/uploads/2020/02/CR_Harms_of_Porn_Report_2020.pdf

DeKeseredy, W. S., & Corsianos, M. (2016). *Violence against women in pornography*. London: Routledge.

DeKeseredy, W. S., Dragiewicz, M., & Schwartz, M. D. (2017). *Abusive endings: Separation and divorce violence against women*. Oakland, CA: University of California Press.

DeKeseredy, W. S., & Olsson, P. (2011). Adult pornography, male peer support, and violence against women: The contribution of the "dark side" of the Internet. In M. V. Vargas Martin, M. Garcia Ruiz, & A. Edwards (Eds.), *Technology for facilitating humanity and combating social deviations: Interdisciplinary perspectives* (pp. 34–50). Hershey, PA: IGI Global.

DeKeseredy, W. S., & Rennison, C. M. (2019). Key issues in the rape and sexual assault of adult women. In W. S. DeKeseredy, C. M. Rennison, & A. K. Hall-Sanchez (Eds.), *The Routledge international handbook of violence studies* (pp. 403–418). London: Routledge.

DeKeseredy, W. S., & Schwartz, M. D. (1998). *Woman abuse on campus: Results from the Canadian national survey*. Thousand Oaks, CA: Sage.

DeKeseredy, W. S., & Schwartz, M. D. (2013). *Male peer support & violence against women: The history & verification of a theory*. Boston, MA: Northeastern University Press.

DeKeseredy, W. S., & Schwartz, M. D. (2016). Thinking sociologically about image-based sexual abuse: The contribution of male peer support theory. *Sexualization, Media, & Society*, *2*, 1–8. doi:10.1177/2374623816684692

DeKeseredy, W. S., Schwartz, M. D., Nolan, J., Mastron, N., & Hall-Sanchez, A. (2019a). Polyvictimization and the continuum of sexual abuse at a college campus: Does negative peer support increase the likelihood of multiple victimizations? *British Journal of Criminology*, *59*(2), 276–295. doi:10.1093/bjc/azy036

DeKeseredy, W. S., Schwartz, M. D., Harris, B., Woodlock, D., Nolan, J., & Hall-Sanchez, A. (2019b, January-March). Technology-facilitated stalking and unwanted sexual messages/images in a college campus community: The role of negative peer support. *SAGE Open*, 1–12. doi:10.1177/2158244019828231

Dierkhising, C. B., Ford, J. D., Branson, C., Grasso, D. J., & Lee, R. (2019). Developmental timing of polyvictimization: Continuity, change, and association with adverse outcomes in adolescence. *Child Abuse & Neglect*, *87*, 40–50. doi: 10.1016/j.chiabu.2018.07.022.

Dragiewicz, M. (2011). *Equality with a vengeance: Men's rights groups, battered women, and antifeminist backlash*. Boston, MA: Northeastern University Press.

Dragiewicz, M., Harris, B., Woodlock, D., Salter, M., Easton, H., Lynch, A., & Milne, L. (2019). *Domestic violence and communication technology: Survivor experiences of instruction, surveillance, and identity crime*. Sydney: Australian Communications Consumer Action Network.

Espelage, D. L., Hong, J. S., & Mebane, S. (2016). Recollections of childhood bullying and multiple forms of victimization: Correlates with psychological functioning among college students. *Social Psychology of Education*, *19*(4), 715–728. doi: 10.1007/s11218-016-9352-z

Ford, J. D., & Delker, B. C. (Eds.). (2019). *Polyvictimization: Adverse impacts in childhood and across the lifespan*. London: Routledge.

Ford, J., & Soco-Marquez, J. G. (2016). Sexual assault victimization among straight, gay/lesbian, and bisexual college students. *Violence and Gender*, *3*(2), 107–115. doi: 10.1089/vio.2015.0030

Foubert, J. D., Clark-Taylor, A., & Wall, A. F. (2020). Is campus rape primarily a serial or one-time problem? Evidence from a multi-campus study. *Violence Against Women*, *26*(3–4), 296–311. doi:10.1177/1077801219833820

Goodmark, L. (2011). State, national, and international legal initiatives to address violence against women: A survey. In C. M. Renzetti, J. L. Edleson, & R. Kennedy Bergen (Eds.), *Sourcebook on violence against women* (2nd ed., pp. 191–208). Thousand Oaks, CA: Sage.

Gottfredson, M. R., & Hirschi, T. (1990). *A general theory of crime*. Stanford, CA: Stanford University Press.

Guadalupe-Diaz, X. L. (2019). *Transgressed: Intimate partner violence in transgender lives*. New York, NY: New York University Press.

Hall, M., & Hearn, J. (2018). *Revenge pornography: Gender, sexuality and motivations*. London: Routledge.

Hamby, S., Smith, A., Mitchell, K., & Turner, H. A. (2016). Poly-victimization and resilience portfolios: Trends in violence research that can enhance the understanding and prevention of elder abuse. *Journal of Elder Abuse & Neglect*, *28*(4–5), 217–234. doi:10.1080/08946566.2016.1232182

Hamby, S., Taylor, E., Jones, L., Mitchell, K., Turner, H. A., & Newlin, C. (2018). From poly-victimization to poly-strengths: Understanding the web of violence can transform research on youth violence and illuminate the path to prevention and resilience. *Journal of Interpersonal Violence*, *33*(5), 719–739. doi:10.1177/0886260517744847

Henriksen, C. B., Mattick, K. L., & Fisher, B. S. (2016). Mandatory bystander intervention training: Is the SaVE Act requirement the "right" program to reduce violence among college students?. In S. C. Wooten, & R. W. Mitchell (Eds.), *The crisis of campus sexual violence: Critical perspectives on prevention and response* (pp. 169–183). New York, NY: Routledge.

Henry, N., & Powell, A. (2015). Embodied harms: Gender, shame, and technology-facilitated sexual violence. *Violence Against Women*, *21*(6), 758–779. doi:10.1177/1077801215576581

Henson, B., Fisher, B. S., & Reyns, B. W. (2020). There is virtually no excuse: The frequency and predictors of college students' bystander intervention behaviors directed at online victimization. *Violence Against Women*, *26*(5), 505–527. doi: 10.1177/1077801219835050

Hewitt, A., & Beauregard, E. (2014). Sexual crime and place: The impact of the environmental context on sexual assault outcomes. *Journal of Criminal Justice*, *42*(5), 375–383. doi:10.1016/j.jcrimjus.2014.05.003

Holt, M. K., Felix, E., Grimm, R., Nylund-Gibson, K., Green, J. G., Poteat, V. P., & Zhang, C. (2017). A latent class analysis of past victimization exposures as predictors of college mental health. *Psychology of Violence*, *7*(4), 521–532. doi: 10.1037/vio0000068

Katz, J. (2006). *The macho paradox: Why some men hurt women and how all men can help*. Naperville, IL: Sourcebooks.

Kelly, L. (1987). The continuum of sexual violence. In J. Hanmer, & M. Maynard (Eds.), *Women, violence and social control* (pp. 46–60). Atlantic Highlands, NJ: Humanities Press International.

Kelly, L. (1988). *Surviving sexual violence*. Minneapolis, MN: University of Minnesota Press.

Kimmel, M. (2008). *Guyland: The perilous world where boys become men*. New York, NY: Harper.

Kirkpatrick, C., & Kanin, E. J. (1957). Male sex aggression on a university campus. *American Sociological Review*, *22*(1), 52–58. doi:10.2307/2088765

Klein, R. (2012). *Responding to intimate violence against women: The role of informal networks*. New York, NY: Cambridge University Press.

Koss, M. P., Gidycz, C., & Wisniewski, N. (1987). The scope of rape: Incidence and prevalence of sexual aggression and victimization in a national sample of higher education students. *Journal of Consulting and Clinical Psychology*, *55*(2), 162–170. doi:10.1037/0022-006X.55.2.162

Ledwitz-Rigby, F. (1993). An administrative approach to personal safety on campus: The role of a President's Advisory Committee on Women's Safety on Campus. *Journal of Human Justice*, *4*(2), 85–94. doi:10.1007/BF02619529

Lim, M. S. C., Carotte, E. R., & Hellard, M. E. (2016). The impact of pornography on gender-based violence, sexual health and well-being: What do we know?. *Journal of Epidemiology & Community Health*, *70*(1), 3–5. doi:10.1136/jech-2015-205453

Marganski, A., & Melander, L. (2018). Intimate partner violence victimization in the cyber and real world: Examining the extent of cyber aggression experiences and its association with in-person dating. *Journal of Interpersonal Violence*, *33*(7), 1071–1095. doi:10.1177/0886260515614283

Marganski, A., Melander, L., & DeKeseredy, W. S. (2020). *Patterns of intimate partner violence at a college campus: The contribution of victims' social support, sexual attitudes, and violence facilitators*. Manuscript submitted for publication.

McGlynn, C., Rackley, E., & Houghton, R. (2017). Beyond "revenge porn": The continuum of image-based sexual abuse. *Feminist Legal Studies*, *25*(1), 25–46. doi: 10.1007/s10691-017-9343-2

Messinger, A. M. (2017). *LGTBQ intimate partner violence: Lessons for policy, practice, and research*. Oakland, CA: University of California Press.

Meyer, D. (2015). *Violence against queer people: Race, class, gender, and the persistence of anti-LGBT discrimination*. London: Routledge.

Mitchell, K. J., Segura, A., Jones, L. M., & Turner, H. A. (2018). Poly-victimization and peer harassment involvement in a technological world. *Journal of Interpersonal Violence*, *33*(5), 762–788. doi:10.1177/0886260517744846

Musicaro, R. M., Spinazzola, J., Arvidson, J., Swaroop, S. R., Grace, L. G., Yarrow, A., & Ford, J. D. (2019). The complexity of adaptation to childhood polyvictimization in youth and young adults: Recommendations for multidisciplinary responders. *Trauma, Violence, & Abuse*, *20*(1), 81–98. doi:10.1177/1524838017692365

Powell, A., & Henry, N. (2017). *Sexual violence in a digital age*. London: Palgrave Macmillan.

Powell, A., & Sugiura, L. (2019). Resisting rape culture in digital society. In W. S. DeKeseredy, C. M. Rennison, & A. K. Hall-Sanchez (Eds.), *The Routledge international handbook of violence studies* (pp. 447–457). London: Routledge.

Ptacek, J. (2016). Rape and the continuum of sexual abuse in intimate relationships: Interviews with U.S. women from different social classes. In K. Yllo, & M. G. Torres (Eds.), *Marital rape: Consent, marriage, and social change in global context* (pp. 123–128). New York, NY: Oxford University Press.

Reed, L. A., Tolman, R. M., & Ward, M. (2016). Snooping and sexting: Digital media as a context for dating aggression and abuse among college students. *Violence Against Women*, *22*(13), 1556–1576. doi:10.1177/1077801216630143

Reyns, B. W., Henson, B., & Holt, T. (2016). Theoretical explanations of personal forms of online victimization. In J. N. Navarro, S. Clevenger, & C. D. Marcum (Eds.), *The intersection between intimate partner abuse, technology, and cybercrime: Examining the virtual enemy* (pp. 75–94). Durham, NC: Carolina University Press.

Sabina, C., Wolak, J., & Finkelhor, D. (2008). The nature and dynamics of Internet pornography exposure for youth. *CyberPsychology and Behavior*, *11*(6), 691–693. doi:10.1089/cpb.2007.0179

Salter, M. (2017). *Crime, justice and social media*. London: Routledge.

Sargent, K. S., Krauss, A., Jouriles, E. N., & McDonald, R. (2016). Cyber victimization, psychological intimate partner violence, and problematic mental health outcomes among first-year college students. *Cyberpsychology, Behavior, and Social Networking*, *19*(9), 545–550. doi:10.1089/cyber.2016.0115

Schwartz, M. D. (2015, September). Campus sexual assault and male peer support. *The Sociologist*. Retrieved from http://thesociologistdc.com/all-issues/campus-sexual-assault-and-male-peer-support/.

Schwartz, M. D., & DeKeseredy, W. S. (1997). *Sexual assault on the college campus: The role of male peer support*. Thousand Oaks, CA: Sage.

Stark-Adamec, C. (1996a). Collaboration and responsibility. In C. Stark-Adamec (Ed.), *Violence: A collective responsibility* (pp. 143–150). Ottawa, ON: Social Science Federation of Canada.

Stark-Adamec, C. (1996b). Violence and responsibility. In C. Stark-Adamec (Ed.), *Violence: A collective responsibility* (pp. 1–9). Ottawa, ON: Social Science Federation of Canada.

Strong-Boag, V. (1996). Too much is not enough: The paradox of power for feminist academics working with community feminists on issues related to violence. In C. Stark-Adamec (Ed.), *Violence: A collective responsibility* (pp. 105–115). Ottawa, ON: Social Science Federation of Canada.

Sun, C., Bridges, A., Johnson, J. A., & Ezzell, M. B. (2016). Pornography and the male sexual script: An analysis of consumption and sexual relations. *Archives of Sexual Behavior*, *45*, 983–994. doi:10.1007/s10508-014-0391-2

Thorne-Finch, R. (1992). *Ending the silence: The origins and treatment of male violence against women*. Toronto, ON: University of Toronto Press.

Warshaw, R. (1988). *I never called it rape*. New York, NY: Harper & Row.

Wendt, S. (2016). Intimate violence and abuse in Australian rural contexts. In J. F. Donnermeyer (Ed.), *The Routledge international handbook of rural criminology* (pp. 191–199). London: Routledge.

White, W. E., & Carmody, D. (2018). Preventing online victimization: College students' views on intervention and prevention. *Journal of Interpersonal Violence, 33*(14), 2291–2307. doi:10.1177/0886260515625501

White, J. W., Koss, M. P., & Kazdin, A. E. (Eds.). (2011). *Violence against women and children: Mapping the terrain.* Washington, DC: American Psychological Association.

Wolfe, D. A. (2018). Why polyvictimization matters. *Journal of Interpersonal Violence, 33*(5), 832–837. doi:10.1177/0886260517752215

Wooten, S. C., & Mitchell, R. W. (2016). Introduction. In S. C. Wooten, & R. W. Mitchell (Eds.), *The crisis of campus sexual violence: Critical perspectives on prevention and response* (pp. 1–11). New York, NY: Routledge.

Chapter 5

The Nature of Technology-Facilitated Violence and Abuse among Young Adults in Sub-Saharan Africa

Olusesan Ayodeji Makinde, Emmanuel Olamijuwon, Nchelem Kokomma Ichegbo, Cheluchi Onyemelukwe, and Michael Gboyega Ilesanmi

Abstract

Incidents of violence perpetrated through digital technology platforms or facilitated by these means have been reported, often in high-income countries. Very little scholarly attention has been given to the nature of technology-facilitated violence and abuse (TFVA) across sub-Saharan Africa (SSA) despite an explosion in the use of various technologies. We conducted a literature review to identify and harmonize available data relating to the types of TFVA taking place in SSA. This was followed by an online survey of young adults through the SHYad.NET forum to understand the nature of TFVA among young adults in SSA. Our literature review revealed various types of TFVA to be happening across SSA, including cyberbullying, cyberstalking, trolling, dating abuse, image-based sexual violence, sextortion, and revenge porn. The results of our online survey revealed that both young men and women experience TFVA, with the most commonly reported TFVA being receiving unwanted sexually explicit images, comments, emails, or text messages. Female respondents more often reported repeated and/or unwanted sexual requests online via email or text message while male respondents more often reported experiencing violent threats. Respondents used various means to cope with TFVA including blocking the abuser or deleting the abused profile on social media.

The Emerald International Handbook of Technology-Facilitated Violence and Abuse, 83–101

doi:10.1108/978-1-83982-848-520211005

Keywords: Adolescents; internet; social media; sub-Saharan Africa; mobile phones; violence

Introduction

The utilization of technology, including cell phones, cameras, internet-associated gadgets, personal computers, and social media, has become part of regular day-to-day activities (Douglas, Harris, & Dragiewicz, 2019; Gillwald, 2017; Henry & Powell, 2018; Simon, Goldberg, Aharonson-Daniel, Leykin, & Adini, 2014). These technologies are used for communicating and to carry out routine tasks. Africa's technology scene is fast-evolving, driven to a great extent by growth in cell phone penetration, which has become a significant tool for innovators beyond its basic use as a communication device. Today, Africa's continuous advancement in technology cannot be separated from the desire to solve its socioeconomic challenges (Eziakonwa, 2019). Cell phones brought new possibilities to Africa: connecting individuals and markets, and facilitating service delivery across the urban–rural divide (Aker & Mbiti, 2011).

The overwhelming importance of the internet to development and the economy in the current information age cannot be overemphasized. In 2016, access to the internet was deemed a human right by the United Nations and the intentional disruption of internet, a human rights violation (Howell & West, 2016). About 75% of respondents surveyed across 39 countries by Pew Research were found to either use the internet occasionally or own a smartphone (Poushter, Caldwell, & Chwe, 2018a). Unlike more developed parts of the world where internet access is almost universal and the growth in use has plateaued, internet use in sub-Saharan Africa (SSA)[1] has seen remarkable growth since 2013 (Silver & Johnson, 2018a). In SSA, 41% of respondents utilize the internet across six countries surveyed (Silver & Johnson, 2018a). Of these six countries, South Africa had the highest population with internet access, a median of 59%. This was followed by Senegal (46%), Nigeria (42%), Ghana (39%), Kenya (39%), and Tanzania (25%) (Silver & Johnson, 2018a). The majority of internet users in SSA go online for social communication purposes (Silver & Johnson, 2018a).

Paralleling the growth in use of the internet, the use of social media (such as Facebook, Instagram, and Twitter) has continued to see tremendous adoption in emerging and developing economies. The use of online social networking sites in these economies rose by 19% points from 34% to 53% between 2013 and 2018 (Poushter, Caldwell, & Chwe, 2018b). In 2010, Facebook was the most visited website in Africa with more than 17 million subscribers (André-Michel, 2010). The population accessing Facebook from Africa had ballooned to more than 139 million users a month by 2018, with the majority accessing it through their mobile devices (Shapshak, 2018). Social media has played important roles in sociopolitical discussions in the region such as during the "bring back our girls" campaign that was launched after more than 200 secondary school girls were kidnapped by Boko Haram insurgents in Nigeria (Peters, 2014). Twitter was used in coordinating the widespread condemnation and protests that followed to pressure the

Nigerian government to act (Fink, Schmidt, Barash, Cameron, & Macy, 2016). Twitter was also used for communication and coordination during the Westgate mall attack in Kenya, with researchers calling for a formal guideline on how to use these communication channels effectively in such emergency situations (Simon et al., 2014).

The internet has contributed to various facets of the economy in SSA, including education, health, agriculture, and communication (Silver & Johnson, 2018b; Tom-Aba et al., 2015). In Tanzania, mobile phones have been used as surveillance tools for managing data from a rabies outbreak (Mtema et al., 2016). Similarly, in Malawi, people living with HIV and AIDS receive text messages daily via mobile phones reminding them to take their medicines on schedule (Aker & Mbiti, 2011). In Nigeria, citizens can report domestic and sexual violence via phone calls or email (P.M. News, 2019), and in Ghana, farmers are able to find out the price of tomatoes in Accra, several kilometers away, via text message and decide whether it's worth ferrying their goods there for sale (Aker & Mbiti, 2011). Also in Niger, laborers are able to call friends in Benin Republic to find out about job opportunities ahead of traveling there (Aker & Mbiti, 2011).

African business owners are leveraging mobile phones to increase efficiency and delivery of services to consumers (Aker, 2010). The general availability of cell phones has paved the way for electronic banking (Donner & Tellez, 2008). Mobile payment systems have emerged as a reliable alternative payment platform for transactions, consistently reducing the market share of cash-based transactions in national economies that once relied absolutely on cash payments (Aker & Mbiti, 2011). Kenya launched M-PESA in 2007, "a mobile phone–based money transfer, financing, and microfinancing service to allow users to deposit, withdraw, transfer money and pay for goods and services" (Calvo, Morales, & Zikidis, 2017, p. 127). M-PESA allows branchless banking service whereby users can withdraw money from a network of agents that includes airtime resellers and retail outlets acting as banking agents (Jack & Suri, 2011). Between July 2016 and July 2017, 1.7 billion transactions were processed over M-PESA, totaling about 3.6 trillion shillings or 48.76% of the country's GDP (McGath, 2018). Thus, mobile technology has greatly affected the lives of the poor in Kenya and is noted to have lifted over 2% of households out of poverty (Suri & Jack, 2016).

Despite the many advantages of technology on a country's economy and populace (Silver & Johnson, 2018b), there are emerging negative consequences of the use of technology that require additional investigation on their dimensions and consequences, and possible action to mitigate their effect (Douglas et al., 2019). Technology-facilitated violence and abuse (TFVA) has emerged as one of these consequences and has been increasingly studied in developed countries that birthed and embraced the widespread use of information and communications technology (ICT) long before SSA countries.

The rapid growth in the adoption of various technologies across SSA increases the number of people at risk for TFVA. The use of the World Wide Web and cell phones exposes new opportunities for perpetrators of violence to abuse their targets. Across the world, the number of reported cases of cyberbullying has been on the rise (Burton & Mutongwizo, 2009). The unbound climes of the web equally make those accessing the internet from remote villages exposed to these risks. Hertz and David-Ferdon (2009) emphasize that the contemporary nature of electronic aggression limits the availability of information on the subject. However, available evidence is predominantly from the United States, Canada, the United Kingdom, Australia, and a few European countries.

Information relating to TFVA by race, ethnicity, gender, or location reveals TFVA's complexities. For example, although gender-based violence (GBV) is predominantly targeted at women, with at least one in three women having a lifetime experience of GBV (United Nations Population Fund, 2016), a large study conducted in Australia did not find significant differences between men's and women's reported experiences of TFVA (proportion of respondents who experienced at least one type of TFVA was 62.1% for women and 62.0% for men) (Powell & Henry, 2019), although variations were observed to exist across the different dimensions of TFVA investigated in the study.

Pockets of research have been conducted in various parts of SSA that describe what has been observed by researchers within their immediate environment. However, we are not aware of any study of TFVA that encompasses the whole of SSA. The purpose of this chapter is to examine the different types of TFVA that have been recorded in SSA, with a particular focus on young adults. The first section provides background information in the form of a review of the current literature on TFVA in SSA. The second section sets out the methodology we used in conducting an online survey of young adults in SSA relating to their experiences with TFVA. The third section sets out the results of our online survey and discusses connections between our findings and the existing literature. Our conclusion summarizes these results and suggests directions for future research and policy.

Literature Review

In our review of current literature on TFVA in SSA, we found various studies that highlighted a range of issues around the topic across specific countries. We have grouped the issues discussed by these studies into three categories: (1) cyberbullying, cyberstalking, and trolling; (2) digital dating abuse and electronic dating violence; and (3) image-based sexual abuse (IBSA), sextortion, and revenge porn. It is noteworthy that these have been categorized for convenience, and there is no clear line separating one category from the other.

Cyberbullying, Cyberstalking, and Trolling

Cyberbullying is "bullying which involves the use of ICT such as email, cell phone and text messages, instant messaging, defamatory personal websites, and defamatory online personal polling websites to support deliberate, repeated, and hostile behavior by an individual or group that is intended to harm others" (Belsey, 2005, cited in; Burton & Mutongwizo, 2009, p. 1). Cyberbullying has been widely reported across several countries in SSA including Botswana,

Ethiopia, Ghana, South Africa, Senegal, Nigeria, Uganda, and others (Madanda, Ngolobe, & Amuriat, 2009; Mooketsi, 2018; Mulisa & Getahun, 2018; Olumide, Adams, & Amodu, 2015b; Sall, 2017; Sam, Bruce, Agyemang, Amponsah, & Arkorful, 2019). In one study, more than 45% of 18- to 45-year-old female users of Facebook or Twitter in West and Central Africa reported having experienced some form of GBV on social media (Internet Sans Frontieres, 2019). In 2010, the UN estimated that 95% of online "aggressive behavior, harassment, abusive language and denigrating images in online spaces were aimed at women and came from partners or former male partners" (APC, 2010, para 2). Burton and Mutongwizo (2009) reported that in South Africa, young people experienced cyberaggression within and outside the school premises, although this was more pronounced outside the school environment (42.9% vs. 31.0%). Various studies have shown that in Nigeria, about 40% of young people had experienced some form of cyberbullying, though many of them were also perpetrators (Olumide, Adams, & Amodu, 2015a; Olumide et al., 2015b).

Cyberstalking involves the use of the internet or electronic devices to monitor a person's activity (Sissing, 2013), while internet trolling involves posting irritating comments, often to get others into an argument (Ansong, Takyi, Damoah, Ampomah, & Larkotey, 2013). These types of abuse have equally been reported in different countries in the region including Ghana, Uganda, South Africa, and Nigeria (Ansong et al., 2013; Madanda, Berna, & Amuriat, 2009; Punch Newspapers, 2020; Sissing, 2013). In Uganda, two women were murdered by their spouses after claiming they discovered romantic SMSs on their phones (APC, 2010; Madanda et al., 2009). In a recent incident reported in Nigeria, a woman was sentenced to death for killing her husband after finding nude pictures of another woman on his phone (Punch Newspapers, 2020).

Digital Dating Abuse and Electronic Dating Violence

Dating fraud is one of the most frequently discussed forms of TFVA in Africa. While Nigeria has been regularly accused of being the source of romance scams, leading such scams to be popularly referred to as "Nigerian scams," Edwards et al.'s (2018) analysis found several other African and non-African origins of such scams including Ghana, South Africa, Togo, Senegal, Ivory Coast, Kenya, Malaysia, the United Kingdom, the United States and Turkey. While most of the targets of the dating scams are women seeking companionship in developed countries, there are instances of men who are also tricked using various female profiles (Aransiola & Asindemade, 2011). The mode of operation of the dating scams often involves long-term engagements with victims who fall in love believing such to be a mutual feeling. Unfortunately, many of the victims are tricked into parting with huge sums of money before realizing they were being scammed. Victims of dating scams are left with scars that end up affecting their psychological health. The consequences of dating scams could go beyond emotional and financial losses. In one instance, someone being scammed was convinced to travel to meet her supposed boyfriend based in West Africa. In the course of her visit, she was kidnapped by the boyfriend's gang and held by the group for ransom (Edwards et al., 2018).

There is also evidence of severe physical and sexual violence arising from internet-facilitated dating and intimate relationships in Africa. Five cases of women who met their abusers on Facebook or were reunited with them through this channel after not being in contact for a while have been chronicled in Nigeria. Two of the victims were raped while the other three were victims of attempted rape (Makinde, Odimegwu, Abdulmalik, Babalola, & Fawole, 2016). One of the victims was murdered in the process while two others suffered severe physical violence. The victim who lost her life had traveled believing she was meeting with her boyfriend and his business partners based in Lagos (Idongesit, 2014). In another case, a young university undergraduate who first met with a young man on Facebook was pushed out of a third-floor apartment following an argument with him (Idongesit, 2014). While she did not die from her injuries, she suffered severe physical and life-changing injuries including a fractured pelvis (Idongesit, 2014).

Image-Based Sexual Abuse, Sextortion, and Revenge Porn

Technology-facilitated sexual violence (TFSV) is one form of TFVA. TFSV can include the use of technology to facilitate sexually violent physical encounters (as discussed above), as well as IBSA, sextortion, and revenge porn. IBSA is becoming a prevalent form of TFVA with the increasing availability of camera and video-enabled cell phones (Powell & Henry, 2019). Often, images and videos are made with the consent of everyone involved. However, when the relationship goes sour, one of those involved may threaten to use the image against the other unless the other person meets some specified requests. IBSA can take many forms including sextortion and "revenge porn" (McGlynn, Rackley, & Houghton, 2017). Sextortion is "the threatened dissemination of explicit, intimate, or embarrassing images of a sexual nature without consent, usually for the purpose of procuring additional images, sexual acts, money, or something else" (Patchin & Hinduja, 2018, p. 2). Revenge porn is "the nonconsensual distribution of private, sexual images by a malicious ex-partner" (McGlynn et al., 2017, p. 26). There have been documented incidents of sextortion and revenge porn in Malawi, Uganda, Senegal, Nigeria, and South Africa (Chisala-Tempelhoff & Kirya, 2016; Musoni, 2019; Sall, 2017). In Nigeria, a female university student was expelled after her boyfriend shared a sex video that they had both made at an earlier stage in their relationship (Vanguard News, 2019). Some research indicates that most of the denigrating sexual images available online feature women (APC, 2010).

Overall, there is relatively little research on TFVA generally or TFSV specifically in SSA. Only one identified study attempted to quantify the level of TFVA in the region, although its methodology was not adequately explained (Internet Sans Frontieres, 2019). Among available studies, various dimensions of TFVA have been recorded across the breadth of SSA, as outlined above, although incidents of TFVA and TFSV cannot be easily categorized as there is significant crossover among the various types. As a result, little is known about the nature and dimensions of TFVA and TFSV specifically in SSA as a whole, providing reason for additional investigation of these issues. Gaining a better understanding of these issues will be important for developing strategic advocacy, enactment of laws, and preventive action to respond to TFVA and TFSV in SSA.

Methodology

Study Design and Recruitment

We conducted an online survey between November 2019 and February 2020 in order to better understand experiences with various forms of TFVA (with a focus on TFSV) among young African adults between the ages of 18 and 34. Respondents were recruited primarily through a paid advertisement on Facebook. Our team also shared the link to the survey on personal social media profiles and early respondents were encouraged to share the survey link with their friends. The Facebook advertisement environment provides potential advertisers a unique opportunity to target users on the platform based on a set of socio-demographic characteristics (such as age, sex, education, location), interests, or behaviors. Leveraging this opportunity, we initially created an advertisement campaign targeting Facebook users who were living in any SSA country at the time of data collection, were between ages 18 and 34 years, and whose primary language on Facebook was English. However, in order to increase female participation, after observing initially low responses from women, we created another campaign targeting young female adults. Both advertisements ran throughout the period of data collection.

The Facebook advertisements were delivered on the news feed of users whose profile matched our inclusion criteria. The advertisement caption described the survey as exploring the use of technology and adverse experiences that could occur from its use. The Facebook advertisement included a link to the survey website (SHYad.NET). SHYad.NET is an online collaborative platform by and for young African adults and is actively managed by one of the authors (EO). The platform was developed in 2018 as a data collection network for monitoring the sexual and reproductive health changes in young African adults.

Detailed information about the survey was provided on the SHYad.NET website. Respondents were informed that participation in the survey was voluntary and they could skip any question they did not want to answer. The contact details of one of the authors was also provided on the survey, and respondents were informed that they could get in touch via email should they require additional information about the survey.

Instrument

We combined several approaches to delineate experiences and coping strategies of TFVA among young adults in SSA countries. Respondents were asked about four forms of TFVA, of which many focused on specific forms of TFSV, as shown in the list below:

- digital harassment;
- image-based abuse;
- sexual aggression and/or coercion; and
- gender-/sexuality-based harassment.[2]

The TFSV questions were adapted from a dichotomous scale with a 21-item measure of TFSV from a previous study conducted by Powell and Henry (2019). The TFSV scale covered four different thematic areas: digital sexual harassment, IBSA, sexual aggression and/or coercion, and gender- and/or sexuality-based hate speech. There were different questions that addressed each of these four themes. Four questions that related to intimate partner technology-facilitated violence in the original scale were modified to reflect technology-facilitated violence perpetrated by anyone. For example, "Partner gained access to your emails or other online accounts without permission" was revised to "Someone gained access to your emails or other online accounts without permission."

Furthermore, respondents who reported having experienced any of the listed behaviors were asked to provide an additional narration of the circumstances of such experience. The respondents who reported having experienced any of the listed behaviors were also asked to describe how upsetting the experience was for them and how they handled the situation (coping strategies). The descriptions provided by the respondents were reviewed and categorized based on themes.

Study Sample

A total of 581 responses were received on the survey website as of February 28, 2020. During data collection, respondents were first asked to indicate whether they consented to participating in the study or not. The survey was subsequently terminated for the respondents who did not consent to participate in the survey. The survey website tracked the number of attempts made by a user to complete the questionnaire. We identified a few instances of multiple attempts to complete the survey by some users. However, the majority of the multiple attempts involved respondents who did not initially consent to participate in the study during the first attempt but consented prior to participating subsequently. For a few respondents who responded more than once, we carefully identified and excluded all subsequent responses during data analysis. Due to ethical reasons regarding the sampling of minors, we excluded responses from adolescents under 18 years at the time of data collection. We also excluded survey responses with missing information on key demographic characteristics such as age, sex, country of residence, and religious affiliation. These criteria resulted in the exclusion of about 32% of responses from those who did not provide consent to participate in the study, were taking the survey more than once, or did not meet any of the criteria highlighted. Our final analytic sample for the study comprised 389 complete responses from young adults aged 18–34 years who were resident in SSA.

Ethical Considerations

Ethical approval to collect responses on sexual and reproductive health using SHYad.NET was obtained from the University of the Witwatersrand Human Research Ethics Committee (nonmedical) under research ethics number H19/02/25 prior to recruiting respondents.

Data Processing and Analysis

We assessed experiences with TFVA based on the respondent's self-reported experience of the listed behaviors. The results were further stratified by gender to compare differences in the experiences of men and women. We then tested the observed differences across gender using Chi-square. A qualitative text analysis of respondents' description of any of the listed experiences was also conducted to provide a contextual description and explanation of the quantitative analysis of TFVA. Quotes from these descriptions were extracted and used to provide additional clarity to observations. Finally, we examined how the respondents handled their personal experience of any of the listed behaviors. Their described experiences were recoded into categorical groups to allow for proportional analysis. All data processing, analysis, and visualizations were done using R statistical package. R is an open source robust statistical package that is rich in conducting visualizations and enables manipulation of charts produced through the application in various dimensions. Its strength in visualization made it helpful in the analysis.

Results and Discussion

Table 5.1 presents the summary of descriptive characteristics of the sample. The respondents were drawn from 22 countries with one-third of respondents resident in Nigeria (34%), 28% in Kenya, and about 6% in South Africa. The mean age of the respondents was 25 years (SD = 4.94 years). Respondents were mostly male (64%) and the majority (77%) had attained tertiary or higher education. More than three-quarters of the respondents were not married, although 43% were in a relationship. About 82% of the respondents were Christian and 14% were Muslim.

The high proportion of respondents from Nigeria, Kenya, and South Africa might have been influenced by the high penetration of internet in these countries (Silver & Johnson, 2018a). More educated and affluent people are known to participate in surveys than people with lower levels of education (Bhutta, 2012; Smith, 2008). As such, it was unsurprising that the majority of the respondents in this study had higher educational qualifications. Past research on using Facebook as a recruitment platform also suggests that the Facebook advertising platform

Table 5.1. Descriptive Characteristics of Respondents.

Sociodemographic Characteristics	N = 389
Age	24.8 (4.94)
Sex	
Female	140 (36.0%)
Male	249 (64.0%)
Education	
Tertiary	91 (23.4%)
Tertiary/Higher	298 (76.6%)
Country	
Ghana	27 (6.94%)
Kenya	108 (27.8%)
Nigeria	133 (34.2%)
South Africa	23 (5.91%)
Uganda	29 (7.46%)
Zambia	24 (6.17%)
Others	45 (11.6%)
Relationship Status	
Not married: not in relationship	148 (38.0%)
Not married: in a relationship	169 (43.4%)
Married or living with partner	65 (16.7%)
Formerly married	7 (1.80%)
Religious Affiliation	
Christian	318 (81.7%)
Muslim	53 (13.6%)
Others	10 (2.57%)
No religious affiliation	8 (2.06%)

tends to oversample better educated, young, and more active members (Rife, Cate, Kosinski, & Stillwell, 2016). This category of people may also have easier access to the internet than their peers with lower levels of education and income.

Reported Instances of Technology-Facilitated Violence and Abuse

Table 5.2 presents the distribution of self-reported experience of any of the listed behaviors by gender. About 89% of males and 82% of females reported experiencing at least one of the listed behaviors. While more male respondents reported

Table 5.2. Self-Reported Experience of Any Specific TFVA Among Respondents.

	Experience of TFVA	No Experience of Any TFVA	*p* Value
Sex			
Female	115 (82.1%)	25 (17.9%)	0.073
Male	222 (89.2%)	27 (10.8%)	

experiencing at least one of the listed behaviors, this difference was not statistically significant. This finding is similar to a study conducted in Australia that did not find an overall statistically significant difference across the proportion of men and women that had experienced at least one type of TFSV (Powell & Henry, 2019).

Type of Technology-Facilitated Violence and Abuse Experienced

Fig. 5.1 presents the most common types of TFVA that our respondents reported having experienced. The results show that unwanted sexually explicit images, comments, emails or text messages were the most common types of TFVA experienced by the respondents. More than half (56%) of the respondents (56% females, 56% males) reported receiving unwanted sexually explicit images, comments, or text messages. A 24-year-old male respondent from South Africa described his experience as follows:

> Someone unknown messaged me on Facebook and after I responded they started talking about sex and they (sent) nude pictures to me.

About 46% of the respondents reported receiving repeated and unwanted sexual requests online, via email or text message. We also found statistically significant evidence that female respondents (54%) reported this behavior more often than male respondents (42%) in the sample (χ^2 = 3.9283; *p*-value = 0.0475). Less than 10% of respondents (10% women and 9% men) reported having had an unwanted sexual experience with someone they met online. However, a 24-year-old female respondent from Uganda reported:

> A guy I met online and pretended to be knowing me forced me into sex once. When he was requesting another time (more than once) I refused.

Close to one-third of the respondents reported that someone had gained access to their emails or other online accounts without permission. Men (33%) more

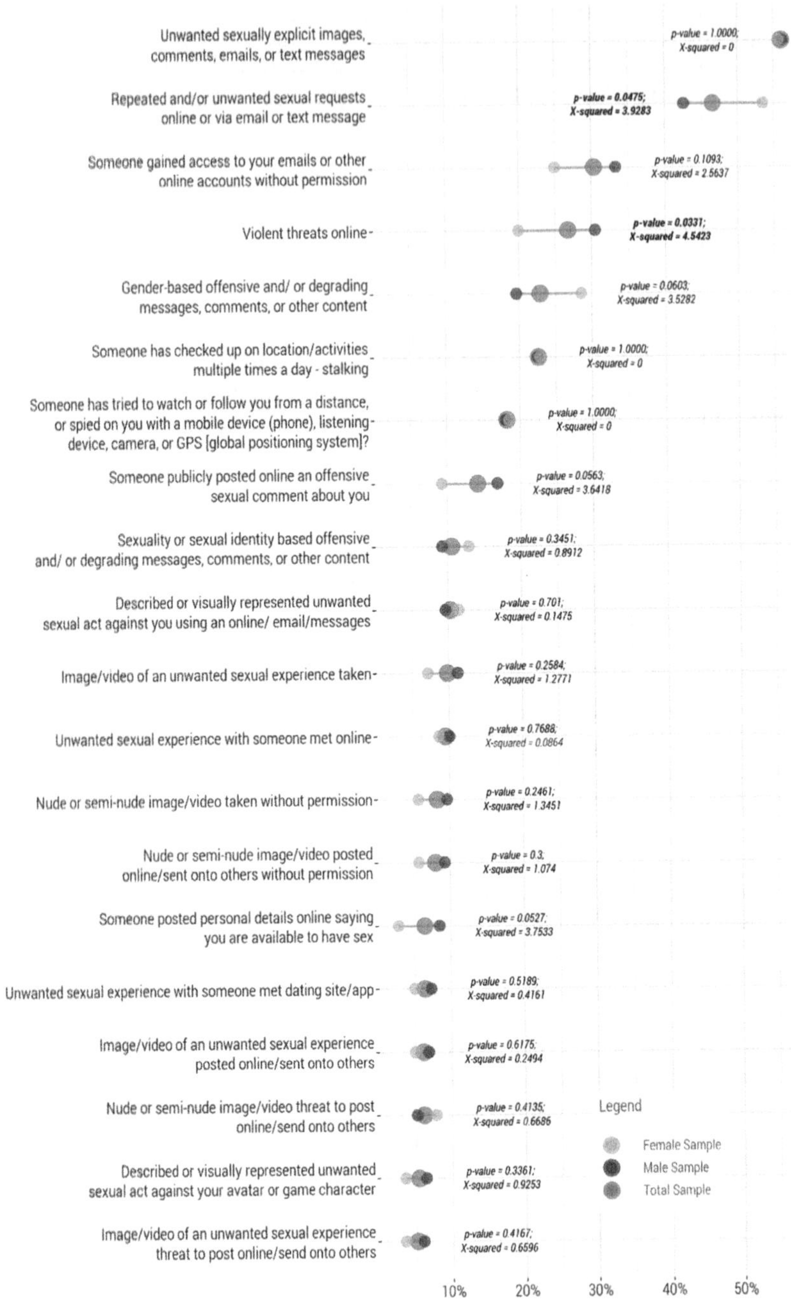

Fig. 5.1. Experiences of Various Dimensions of TFVA by Gender.

often reported this form of TFVA than women (25%). However, this difference was not statistically significant. A 31-year-old male Nigerian noted that:

> Someone hacked into my Facebook account and used the opportunity to request for financial assistance from my friends and family members.

About one-quarter (27%) of the respondents reported experiencing a violent threat online. We observed a statistically significant ($\chi^2 = 4.5423$; *p*-value = 0.0331) difference in the online experience of violent threats between males (33%) and females (25%). A 33-year old male respondent from Kenya reported the following:

> A fellow man was threatening to kill me and (was) sending abusive messages because he thought I was having (an) affair with her (his) wife.

Experiences of stalking (23%) and spying (18%) were also reported by the respondents. About one-fifth of respondents reported having had someone spy on them with a mobile device, listening device, camera, or GPS-enabled application. While we did not ask respondents whether the person stalking or spying on them was known to them, the concerning role that cyberstalking and tech-facilitated surveillance (e.g., by monitoring someone's phone messages) can play in intimate partner violence and homicide was graphically demonstrated in the murders of two Ugandan women discussed above (Madanda et al., 2009). And while studies of online stalking in other jurisdictions, such as Germany, indicate that victims are more likely to be women than men (Dreßing, Bailer, Anders, Wagner, & Gallas, 2014), our findings indicated no statistically significant difference between men and women.

Overall, women were less likely than men to report having experienced a number of the listed behaviors, including sharing an image or video of an unwanted sexual experience, someone posting an offensive sexual comment about them, and someone gaining access to their emails or other online accounts. However, more women (29%) reported having experienced gender-based offensive or degrading comments online than their male counterparts (20%), although this difference was not statistically significant. The higher frequency reported is similar to an earlier study that suggested that women in West and Central Africa were more likely than men to be targeted by gender-related abuses (Internet Sans Frontieres, 2019). In fact, in our study, gender-related abuse was much higher in women than several other forms of abuse (see Fig. 5.1). Thus, bias against the female population in gender-related abuse may be a carryover to the digital space of the patriarchal norms of African societies, which are more tolerant of men than women (Albertyn, 2009; Makinde, Onyemelukwe, Onigbanjo-Williams, Oyediran, & Odimegwu, 2017; Mudhai, Wright, & Musa, 2016).

Coping Strategies for Technology-Facilitated Violence and Abuse

As seen in Table 5.3, respondents who had experienced TFVA reported having used a number of strategies for coping with their experiences.

The most common approach for handling TFVA (which 32% of our respondents reported using) was reporting or employing the "block" option on the device, website, or app to avoid the perpetrator. For example, a 34-year-old female respondent from Nigeria reported the following:

> I always block the person or sometimes shut down the account and put a red flag on it.

Five percent of respondents reported attending a counseling session with a close associate – such as a family member, friend, teacher, or clergy person, while 12% of respondents apologized to their contacts and changed their passwords after their profiles had been used to transmit messages wrongfully (see Table 5.3). As a 28-year-old male respondent from Uganda puts it:

> I changed my Yahoo email password and emailed my contacts notifying them of (the) account having been hacked.

None of the respondents who had experienced one of the listed behaviors indicated that they had reported to the police or other security agencies for assistance. This might be a reflection of the gap in regulation of digital media in SSA and the limited action that internet users can take to seek redress when they have been violated online. An earlier study highlighted that the growth in ICT use in SSA has outpaced its regulatory framework, and this may have manifested in the strategies that respondents used to cope with abuse online (Chisala-Tempelhoff & Kirya, 2016). Similar challenges with policing IBSA have been reported in developed countries (Henry, Flynn, & Powell, 2018). Thus, survivors of TFVA may be left with few options to seek redress when violated.

Table 5.3. Coping Strategies by Respondents.

Description	**Number of Responses**	**Proportion**
I went for counseling/prayed	11	5%
I reported/blocked the offender	77	32%
I did not respond	44	19%
I deleted the account/messages	34	14%
I apologized because my account was hacked	28	12%
I took other actions	43	18%
Total	**237**	**100%**

Limitations

Although our study contributes to literature in diverse ways, it is not without limitations. First is that respondents were recruited online using a nonprobabilistic sampling process, and our sample size was small. As a result, findings are not generalizable to the entire population of young SSA adults. Nevertheless, we believe that our study paves the way for future work in this area. Furthermore, while the risk of multiple submissions by an individual is a common limitation of studies using online samples, our study minimized this possibility using cookies already installed on the SHYad.NET website. This helped us to log and identify multiple responses from a single device, which were subsequently addressed at analysis, as noted above. Finally, as is typical of quantitative methodologies, while our online survey results provide an overview, they invite many additional questions about the context in which the reported incidents arose, including the gender of the perpetrator, their relationship to the victim, whether the incidents were isolated or part of a pattern of behavior, and what their impact was on the victim. These are the sorts of questions that could be pursued in future qualitative research.

Conclusion

Though not generalizable, it is notable that the overwhelming majority of young adults in our sample reported having experienced at least one of the listed forms of behavior often associated with TFVA. This is in keeping with the very limited existing research that has been conducted on the distribution and types of TFVA across the region. The young people in our study indicated experiencing different types of TFVA, with the most common being a form of TFSV: receiving unwanted sexually explicit images, comments, emails, or text messages. Overall, the vast majority of both young men and women respondents reported experiencing at least one form of TFVA, with the women respondents experiencing more sexual requests online and gender-based offensive and/or degrading comments and men respondents experiencing more online threats of violence. In terms of coping mechanisms, the fact that respondents were most likely to use the block option or delete their profiles, coupled with the fact that none of them indicated having reported their experiences to the authorities, may be suggestive of a number of things. It may be that they did not perceive the incident to have been serious enough to merit reporting and/or that they did not believe reporting would lead to any meaningful response. Future qualitative research could be effective for exploring both of these tentative explanations. The latter explanation would be consistent with suggestions by others, such as Chisala-Tempelhoff and Kirya (2016) and Facebook's Mark Zuckerberg (BBC News, 2020), that there are gaps in the regulatory framework for addressing online aggression that need to be addressed. However, there is a need for additional research to appropriately quantify the magnitude of TFVA generally and TFSV specifically across countries in the region in order to provide the evidentiary basis necessary to pave the way for interventions that will limit the impact that these new forms of violence may cause. Meaningfully addressing TFVA is particularly important in SSA as technology becomes more and more implicated in people's lives, and increasingly central to plans for economic growth and development.

Notes

1. SSA is the part of the African continent that lies south of the Sahara.
2. More detailed examples of the specific types of behavior respondents were asked about are depicted in Fig. 5.1, which is included in our Findings section below.

References

Aker, J. C. (2010). Information from markets near and far: Mobile phones and agricultural markets in Niger. *American Economic Journal: Applied Economics*, *2*(3), 46–59.

Aker, J. C., & Mbiti, I. M. (2011). Mobile phones and economic development in Africa. *SSRN*. Retrieved from https://papers.ssrn.com/sol3/papers.cfm?abstract_id=1693963. Accessed on January 10, 2020.

Albertyn, C. (2009). 'The stubborn persistence of patriarchy'? Gender equality and cultural diversity in South Africa. *Constitutional Court Review*, *2*(1), 165–208.

André-Michel, E. (2010). A social media boom begins in Africa. *Africa Renewal*. Retrieved from https://www.un.org/africarenewal/magazine/december-2010/social-media-boom-begins-africa. Accessed on February 9, 2020.

Ansong, E. D., Takyi, T., Damoah, D., Ampomah, E. A., & Larkotey, W. (2013). Internet trolling in Ghana. *International Journal of Emerging Science and Engineering*, *2*(1), 42–43.

APC. (2010). *How technology is being used to perpetrate violence against women - and to fight it*. Johannesburg: APC.

Aransiola, J. O., & Asindemade, S. O. (2011). Understanding cybercrime perpetrators and the strategies they employ in Nigeria. *Cyberpsychology, Behavior, and Social Networking*, *14*(12), 759–763.

BBC News. (2020). Facebook boss calls for rules on harmful content. *BBC News*. February 15.

Belsey, B. (2005). *Fair play at school – fair play in society towards a school without bullying! A manual for teachers and head teachers*. Daphne Project. Retrieved from www.cyberbuying.ca/facts-st.html

Bhutta, C. B. (2012). Not by the book: Facebook as a sampling frame. *Sociological Methods & Research*, *41*(1), 57–88.

Burton, P., and Mutongwizo, T. (2009). Inescapable violence: Cyber bullying and electronic violence against young people in South Africa. *Centre for Justice and Crime Prevention*, *8*, 12.

Calvo, S., Morales, A., & Zikidis, Y. (2017). *Social and solidarity economy: The world's economy with a social face*. London: Taylor & Francis.

Chisala-Tempelhoff, S., & Kirya, M. T. (2016). Gender, law and revenge porn in sub-Saharan Africa: A review of Malawi and Uganda. *Palgrave Communications*, *2*, 16069.

Donner, J., & Tellez, A. (2008). Mobile banking and economic development: Linking adoption, impact, and use. *Asian Journal of Communication*, *18*, 318–332.

Douglas, H., Harris, B. A., & Dragiewicz, M. (2019). Technology-facilitated domestic and family violence: Women's experiences. *British Journal of Criminology*, *59*(3), 551–570.

Dreßing, H., Bailer, J., Anders, A., Wagner, H., & Gallas, C. (2014). Cyberstalking in a large sample of social network users: Prevalence, characteristics, and impact upon victims. *Cyberpsychology, Behavior, and Social Networking*, *17*(2), 61–67.

Edwards, M., Suarez-Tangil, G., Peersman, C., Stringhini, G., Rashid, A., & Whitty, M. (2018). The geography of online dating fraud. In *Workshop on technology and consumer protection (ConPro)* (Vol. 7). San Francisco, CA: IEEE.

Eziakonwa, A. (2019). Can investing in Africa's tech generation change the future of development? | UNDP in Africa. *UNDP*. Retrieved from https://www.africa.undp.org/content/rba/en/home/blog/2019/can-investing-in-africas-tech-generation-change-the-future-of-de.html. Accessed on January 13, 2020.

Fink, C., Schmidt, A., Barash, V., Cameron, C., & Macy, M. (2016). Complex contagions and the diffusion of popular twitter Hashtags in Nigeria. *Social Network Analysis and Mining*, *6*(1), 1–19.

Gillwald, A. (2017). *Internet use barriers and user strategies: Perspectives from Kenya, Nigeria, South Africa and Rwanda*. New York, NY: Mozilla Foundation.

Henry, N., Flynn, A., & Powell, A. (2018). Policing image-based sexual abuse: Stakeholder perspectives. *Police Practice and Research*, *19*(6), 565–581.

Henry, N., & Powell, A. (2018). Technology-facilitated sexual violence: A literature review of empirical research. *Trauma, Violence, & Abuse*, *19*(2), 195–208.

Hertz, M. F., & David-Ferdon, C. (2009). *Electronic media and youth violence: A CDC issue brief for educators and caregivers*. Atlanta, GA: Centerfor Disease Control and Prevention.

Howell, C., & West, D. M. (2016). *The internet as a human right*. Brookings. Retrieved from https://www.brookings.edu/blog/techtank/2016/11/07/the-internet-as-a-human-right/. Accessed on February 10, 2020.

Idongesit, E. (2014). Youths, social media and gender-based violence: An emerging trend in Nigeria. *International Journal of Economy, Management and Social Sciences*, *3*(1), 21–27.

Internet Sans Frontieres. (2019). #IWD2019: Online gender-based violence affects 45% of women on social media in West and Central Africa. *Internet Sans Frontières*. Retrieved from https://internetwithoutborders.org/iwd2019-online-gender-based-violence-affects-45-of-women-on-social-media-in-west-and-central-africa/. Accessed on February 10, 2020.

Jack, W., & Suri, T. (2011). *Mobile money: The Economics of M-PESA. w16721*. Cambridge, MA: National Bureau of Economic Research.

Madanda, A., Berna, N., & Amuriat, G. Z. (2009). *Uganda: Violence against women and information and communication technologies*. Johannesburg: Association for Progressive Communications (APC).

Makinde, O. A., Odimegwu, C. O., Abdulmalik, J. O., Babalola, S. O., & Fawole, O. I. (2016). Gender-based violence following social media acquaintance in Nigeria. *African Journal of Reproductive Health*, *20*(4), 67–76.

Makinde, O. A., Onyemelukwe, C., Onigbanjo-Williams, A., Oyediran, K. A., & Odimegwu, C. O. (2017). Rejection of the gender and equal opportunities bill in Nigeria: A setback for sustainable development goal five. *Gender in Management: An International Journal*, *32*(3), 234–240.

McGath, T. (2018). M-PESA: How Kenya revolutionized mobile payments. *Medium*. Retrieved from https://mag.n26.com/m-pesa-how-kenya-revolutionized-mobile-payments-56786bc09ef. Accessed on February 10, 2020.

McGlynn, C., Rackley, E., & Houghton, R. (2017). Beyond 'revenge porn': The continuum of image-based sexual abuse. *Feminist Legal Studies*, *25*(1), 25–46.

Mooketsi, B. (2018). An investigation on the prevalence of cyberbullying amongst undergraduate students in the University of Botswana. *Mosenodi Journal*, *21*(2), 44–54.

Mtema, Z., Changalucha, J., Cleaveland, S., Elias, M., Ferguson, H. M., Jo, E., … Hampson, K. (2016). Mobile phones as surveillance tools: Implementing and evaluating a large-scale intersectoral surveillance system for rabies in Tanzania. *PLoS Medicine*, *13*(4), e1002002.

Mudhai, O. F., Wright, B., & Musa, A. (2016). Gender and critical media-information literacy in the digital age: Kenya, South Africa and Nigeria. *Journal of African Media Studies*, *8*(3), 267–280.

Mulisa, F., & Getahun, D. A. (2018). Perceived benefits and risks of social media: Ethiopian secondary school students' perspectives. *Journal of Technology in Behavioral Science*, *3*(4), 294–300.

Musoni, M. (2019). The criminalization of 'revenge porn' in South Africa: Research. *Obiter*, *40*(1), 61–74.

Olumide, A. O., Adams, P., & Amodu, O. K. (2015a). International note: Awareness and context of cyber-harassment among secondary school students in Oyo state, Nigeria. *Journal of Adolescence*, *39*, 10–14.

Olumide, A. O., Adams, P., & Amodu, O. K. (2015b). Prevalence and correlates of the perpetration of cyberbullying among in-school adolescents in Oyo state, Nigeria. *International Journal of Adolescent Medicine and Health*, *28*(2), 183–191.

Patchin, J. W., & Hinduja, S. (2018). Sextortion among adolescents: Results from a national survey of US Youth. *Sexual Abuse*, *32*(1), 30–54. doi:10.1177/107906 3218800469

Peters, M. A. (2014). 'Western education is sinful': Boko Haram and the abduction of chibok schoolgirls. *Policy Futures in Education*, *12*(2), 186–190.

P.M. News. (2019). How to report sexual & child abuse, domestic violence in Nigeria. *P.M. News*. Retrieved from https://www.pmnewsnigeria.com/2019/06/28/how-to-report-sexual-child-abuse-domestic-violence-in-nigeria/. Accessed on January 20, 2020.

Poushter, J., Caldwell, B., & Chwe, H. (2018a). *Across 39 countries, three-quarters say they use the internet. Pew Research Center's Global Attitudes Project*. Retrieved from https://www.pewresearch.org/global/2018/06/19/across-39-countries-three-quarters-say-they-use-the-internet/. Accessed on February 9, 2020.

Poushter, J., Caldwell, B., & Chwe, H. (2018b). *Social media use continues to rise in developing countries. Pew Research Center's Global Attitudes Project*. Retrieved from https://www.pewresearch.org/global/2018/06/19/social-media-use-continues-to-rise-in-developing-countries-but-plateaus-across-developed-ones/. Accessed on February 9, 2020.

Powell, A., & Henry, N. (2019). Technology-facilitated sexual violence victimization: Results from an online survey of Australian adults. *Journal of Interpersonal Violence*, *34*(17), 3637–3665.

Punch Newspapers. (2020). Maryam Sanda sentenced to death for killing husband. *Punch Newspapers*. Retrieved from https://punchng.com/maryam-sanda-sentenced-to-death-for-killing-husband/. Accessed on February 12, 2020.

Rife, S. C., Cate, K. L., Kosinski, M., & Stillwell, D. (2016). Participant recruitment and data collection through Facebook: The role of personality factors. *International Journal of Social Research Methodology*, *19*(1), 69–83.

Sall, O. (2017). The impact of social and digital medias on Senegalese society. *Studies in Media and Communication*, *5*(2), 1–7.

Sam, D. L., Bruce, D., Agyemang, C. B., Amponsah, B., & Arkorful, H. (2019). Cyberbullying victimization among high school and university students in Ghana. *Deviant Behavior*, *40*(11), 1305–1321.

Shapshak, T. (2018). Almost all of Facebook's 139 million users in Africa are on mobile. *Forbes*. Retrieved from https://www.forbes.com/sites/tobyshapshak/2018/12/18/almost-all-of-facebooks-139m-users-in-africa-are-on-mobile/. Accessed on February 9, 2020.

Silver, L., & Johnson, C. (2018a). *Internet use growing across sub-Saharan Africa, but most are still offline. Pew Research Center's Global Attitudes Project*. Retrieved from https://www.pewresearch.org/global/2018/10/09/internet-use-is-growing-across-much-of-sub-saharan-africa-but-most-are-still-offline/. Accessed on February 9, 2020.

Silver, L., & Johnson, C. (2018b). *Sub-saharan Africans say internet use has positively impacted education, personal relationships and economy. Pew Research Center's Global Attitudes Project*. Retrieved from https://www.pewresearch.org/global/2018/10/09/sub-saharan-africans-say-internet-use-has-positively-impacted-education-personal-relationships-and-economy/. Accessed on February 9, 2020.

Simon, T., Goldberg, A., Aharonson-Daniel, L., Leykin, D., & Adini, B. (2014). Twitter in the cross fire—the use of social media in the Westgate mall terror attack in Kenya. *PloS One*, *9*(8), e104136.

Sissing, S. K. (2013). A criminological exploration of cyber stalking in South Africa. Ph.D. thesis. University of South Africa, Pretoria.

Smith, G. (2008). Does gender influence online survey participation?: A record-linkage analysis of university faculty online survey response behavior. ERIC Document Reproduction Service No. ED 501717.

Suri, T., & Jack, W. (2016). The long-run poverty and gender impacts of mobile money. *Science*, *354*(6317), 1288–1292.

Tom-Aba, D., Olaleye, A., Olayinka, A. T., Nguku, P., Waziri, N., Peter, A., … Shuaib, F. (2015). Innovative technological approach to ebola virus disease outbreak response in Nigeria using the open data kit and form hub technology. *PloS One*, *10*(6), e0131000.

United Nations Population Fund. (2016). *Gender-based violence*. UNFPA - United Nations Population Fund. Retrieved from http://www.unfpa.org/gender-based-violence. Accessed on February 11, 2016.

Vanguard News. (2019). Babcock university expels girl in viral sex tape video. *Vanguard News*. Retrieved from https://www.vanguardngr.com/2019/11/babcock-university-expels-girl-in-viral-sex-tape-video/. Accessed on February 10, 2020.

Chapter 6

The Face of Technology-Facilitated Aggression in New Zealand: Exploring Adult Aggressors' Behaviors

Edgar Pacheco and Neil Melhuish

Abstract

The nature and extent of adults' engagement in diverse manifestations of technology-facilitated aggression is not yet well understood. Most research has focused on victimization. When explored, engagement in online aggression and abuse has centered on children and young people, particularly in school and higher education settings. Drawing on nationally representative data from New Zealand adults aged 18 and over, this chapter explores the overall prevalence of online aggression with a focus on gender and age. Our findings support the need to also understand adult aggressors' behaviors to better address the distress and harm caused to targets through digital communications. The chapter discusses the implications of the results for policy and practice and proposes some directions for future research.

Keywords: Online harassment; perpetration; media and communication; online aggression; technology; quantitative research

Introduction

The Harmful Digital Communications Act 2015 (HDCA) is New Zealand's main legal response to online and technology-mediated abuses such as bullying, harassment, and intimidation. Its purpose is not only to deter, prevent, and mitigate harm caused through digital communications but also to provide those affected with a quick and efficient means of redress (Harmful Digital Communications Act

The Emerald International Handbook of Technology-Facilitated Violence and Abuse, 103–123

doi:10.1108/978-1-83982-848-520211006

[HDCA], 2015). The development of the HDCA (2015) became a legislative priority after the New Zealand Law Commission's 2012 review of the adequacy of existing legislation. Critically, this review concluded that abuse facilitated through digital technologies was emotionally more harmful than in the pre-digital era and that there were gaps in legal sanctions for perpetrators and in access to meaningful remedies for those experiencing such abuse (Law Commission, 2012).

The HDCA (2015) is based on 10 communications principles. Nine of the principles were derived from a range of pre-existing New Zealand laws, while one was new. The principles are intended to articulate these laws and rules in a form that is accessible to general internet users. In this sense, the HDCA (2015) states that a digital communication should not be, for example, threatening, intimidating, or menacing; should not be indecent or obscene; and should not make a false allegation. Together these principles provide a general framework for describing and identifying types of online abuse such as cyberbullying, cyberstalking, image-base sexual abuse, and online hate speech, among others.

In addition, the HDCA (2015) introduced some new legal responses to online aggression. One of these responses is the inception of civil court orders for a serious and/or repeated breach of the communication principles. It also introduced a criminal offense – sanctioned with fines and/or imprisonment – that makes it illegal to post a digital communication with the intention to cause harm or that actually causes harm to the victim (see HDCA, 2015). The HDCA (2015) defines harm as "serious emotional distress" (HDCA, 2015, p. 4). In a briefing to the New Zealand Parliament, the Ministry of Justice (2014) explained that serious emotional distress sets a relatively high threshold to ensure that subjective accounts of embarrassment, anxiety, worry, or outrage are not enough to trigger enforcement of the law.

Another key innovation of the HDCA (2015) is the establishment of the Approved Agency as part of the civil regime to be the first port of call for complaints and to assist New Zealand internet users in dealing with harm and distress caused through any form of digital communication. The Approved Agency does not have powers of sanction but uses advice, negotiation, mediation, and persuasion to resolve complaints. If the Approved Agency cannot resolve the complaint brought to it by an individual, then that person may apply to the courts for a civil order. As a result, the defendant might be required to take down or disable the material, desist from engaging in the behavior concerned, publish a correction or provide a right of reply, and/or publish an apology. In 2016, Netsafe (www.netsafe.org.nz) was appointed as the Approved Agency under the HDCA (2015). Netsafe is an incorporated society formed in 2001. Its designated role complements the educational, incident response, and advisory services it provides to New Zealand's internet users, government, and commercial and community organizations. Netsafe also generates research-based evidence that informs the development of its support services and online safety resources while helping to close the knowledge gap in New Zealand – the authors of this chapter are part of Netsafe's Policy and Research team.

From November 2016 to December 2019, Netsafe received 5,835 complaints from adults aged 18 years old and over (Netsafe, 2020). Of these, 62% were received from women, 36% from men, and 2% from people identifying as gender diverse. However, in 401 of these cases that Netsafe assessed as being the most serious – in terms of the breach of principles and potential to cause harm – the proportion of women making a complaint increased to 69% (with 31% men and 1% gender diverse). In relation to the ages of those who reported their complaint to Netsafe, 61% were 40 years old and under, rising to 67% in the most serious instances (Netsafe, 2020).

Meanwhile, since the inception of the HDCA (2015), figures from the justice system show that, until June 2019, a total of 253 people were charged with criminal offenses that fall under the umbrella of the HDCA principles. Of this number, 85% were males and 15% females, with similar proportions subsequently being convicted (88% male and 12% female). In relation to age, the data shows that 90% of those charged and convicted were aged 44 years or younger (Ministry of Justice, 2019). Data relating to civil claims under the HDCA (2015) are not currently publicly available.

The HDCA (2015) is a key legal instrument helping to address and sanction aggression and abuse online. However, a legislative response is not enough to prevent hurtful behaviors, reduce victimization, and mitigate harm. We suggest that research-based evidence to also support preventive interventions would significantly improve the safety of New Zealand internet users. However, research to date in the country has focused solely on victimization in the context of children and young people (Pacheco & Melhuish, 2018). Research-based evidence about the nature and extent of adults who engage in different forms of online aggression and their motivations for doing so is lacking in the country (see Background section for details). Creating new knowledge about adult perpetrators and victims can help to develop policy and programming to address and prevent matters of public concern in which digital technologies play a facilitative or mediating role, such as the live streaming video of the Christchurch terrorist attack and incidents of family and sexual violence in which technology is used to reproduce control and abuse. Research-based evidence can also help in developing contextually-appropriate interventions that distinguish between situations where individuals have consensually engaged with others in activities and exchanges (e.g., the sending of sexual images or making sexual advances) and situations where the behaviors are engaged in nonconsensually and/or were or ought to have been known to the perpetrator to have been unwelcome. Among other things, quantitative studies such as the one reported on here can play an important role in better understanding the sorts of context-specific inquiries that will need to be made in subsequent qualitative research.

In an effort to address the knowledge gap highlighted above, this chapter reports on aspects of the *Annual Population Survey* (APS), a quantitative study developed by Netsafe. The analysis presented here is guided by two underpinning research questions relating to APS data:

RQ1- What is the prevalence of engagement in technology-facilitated aggression (TFA) among adult New Zealanders in the prior year in the context of age and gender?

RQ2- What are the characteristics of TFA in relation to aggressors' motivations, their choice of the target(s), and whether their behavior was connected with a wider issue happening offline?

This chapter has been organized in the following way. It first summarizes available literature about adults and TFA in New Zealand and overseas, pointing out the research focus on victimization and young people, and the need to explore engagement in aggression based on key demographic variables. The chapter then describes the methodological approach, and the subsequent section deals with our study findings about the prevalence and extent of TFA. The last section discusses the implications of the findings for policy, practice, and research.

Background

Technology-Facilitated Aggression: Victimization in New Zealand

New Zealand research on diverse forms of aggression and abuse online is limited but growing. Similar to international trends, most studies have explored children and teenagers' experiences of online risks and harm, in large part, because of public concern (and news media's anxiety) around the dangers of technology (Pacheco & Melhuish, 2020). However, in recent years, researchers have turned their focus to adults as well. In this respect, some studies have looked at online harassment among New Zealand members of Parliament (Every-Palmer, Barry-Walsh, & Pathé, 2015), cyberbullying in the workplace in general (Gardner et al., 2016) or in more specific contexts such as within the health system (D'Souza, Catley, Tappin, & Forsyth, 2019; Minton, Birks, Cant, & Budden, 2018). While relevant, these studies do not provide measures matching the characteristics of the country's population as a whole.

Just a few large-scale quantitative studies exploring personal experiences of specific forms of online aggression and abuse among adults can be found in the New Zealand-based literature. One study explored the prevalence of cyberbullying with a focus on gender (Steiner-Fox et al., 2016), while another conducted by Netsafe looked at the extent of image-based sexual abuse (Pacheco, Melhuish, & Fiske, 2019). In addition, researchers have started reporting and analyzing annual measures of the incidence of online hate speech victimization and exposure (see Pacheco & Melhuish, 2019). Further, a 2017 study by Netsafe explored the prevalence and impact of harmful digital communications, finding that a third of adult New Zealanders received in the prior year at least one type of unwanted online content (Pacheco & Melhuish, 2018). Even with this increasing attention to adults, research has largely concentrated on victimization and the target's perceived impact of online aggression and abuse. Currently, to the best of our knowledge, there are no New Zealand-based data on the prevalence of adults' self-reported engagement in diverse forms of online aggression, also referred to here as technology-facilitated aggression (TFA). This knowledge gap limits the understanding of TFA and can hinder the impact of policy as well as the effective delivery of services and support to those who have been targeted.

People's Engagement in Technology-Facilitated Aggression

Notably, the paucity in New Zealand of quantitative inquiry on adults' engagement in TFA on the basis of representative data is in keeping with a similar pattern overseas (Henry, Flynn, & Powell, 2019; Henry & Powell, 2018; Jenaro, Flores, & Frías, 2018). At best, available research on specific aspects of TFA has largely centered on emerging adults and been small in scale. For instance, the few studies on cyberbullying "perpetration" have centered on tertiary students (see Barlett, Chamberlin, & Witkower, 2017; Bauman & Baldasare, 2015; Doane, Pearson, & Kelley, 2014) as researching this population group is more accessible for academics. Research on sexting, cyber dating, and cyberstalking has been similarly focused (see Borrajo, Gámez-Guadix, & Calvete, 2015; Deans & Bhogal, 2019; Gámez-Guadix, Almendros, Borrajo, & Calvete, 2015; Garcia et al., 2016). Relying on convenience sampling is a valid research approach (Bryman, 2008) and focusing on the experiences of young people in tertiary education also helps to understand the extent of TFA in a specific social setting. However, policy makers and practitioners also need research-based evidence that is closely aligned with the entire population group to answer emerging social science and policy questions such as those regarding engagement in TFA.

Further, the role of gender as a predictor of adults' engagement in TFA is not yet well understood. Some studies have found an association between gender and some forms of online aggression. For instance, in a nationwide Australian study, males (13.7%) were more likely to engage in image-based sexual abuse than females (7.4%) (see Henry et al., 2019). Similar trends have been reported in regard to cyber dating abuse and sexting among younger adults (see Deans & Bhogal, 2019; Morelli, Bianchi, Baiocco, Pezzuti, & Chirumbolo, 2016; Wick et al., 2017). Furthermore, an American study reported that, while men and women are equally likely to be harassed online, women have to deal with a wider and more serious variety of abuse online (Lenhart, Ybarra, Zickuhr, & Price-Feeney, 2016). However, others suggest that, compared to young men, young women are more likely to engage in controlling or monitoring online behaviors (see Bennett, Guran, Ramos, & Margolin, 2011; Burke, Wallen, Vail-Smith, & Knox, 2011). At the same time, some have found no strong link between gender and engagement in online aggression and abuse related to cyber dating (Borrajo et al., 2015) and interpersonal surveillance (Tokunaga, 2011). However, while Garcia et al.'s (2016) study on sexting and single adults in the United States (US) did not find a gender link among young people, it did so among older adults, with males being more likely to share a nude image than females.

Understanding the nature and extent of engagement in TFA is a critical component for effective online safety interventions. Recently, academics and the technology industry have been trying innovative approaches such as machine learning to detect and remove online aggression (BBC, 2019). Such computational approaches have a reactive role to deal with incidents. However, proactive responses are also needed, and they require research-based evidence to inform the development of interventions aimed at preventing the different forms of TFA and better understanding the circumstances in which adults engage in certain types of behaviors often associated with TFA.

Method

The findings for this chapter come from the APS, a self-report study which gathers data from New Zealanders aged 18 and over. It was developed by Netsafe based on its extensive operational experience in online safety, the

Communications Principles of the HDCA (2015), and in consultation with key stakeholders. The APS covers a range of topics regarding people's experiences of and attitudes toward unwanted digital communications and other online experiences as well as the potential harm they might cause.

Colmar Brunton, a research firm, was contracted to distribute the instrument via email between 4 and 26 June 2019 using independent online research panels for a population-based cross-sectional survey. Online surveys are increasingly used in the social sciences. They are less expensive and easier to administer than paper-based surveys. Moreover, online surveys are useful for exploratory research, particularly on topics regarding people's online activities and behaviors (Garcia et al., 2016; Henry & Talbot, 2019; Lenhart et al., 2016; Pacheco et al., 2019; Pacheco & Melhuish, 2017; Powell & Henry, 2019).

The sample was structured to be representative of the population in terms of age and gender. Data were weighted using key population targets drawn from New Zealand's 2013 Census data (Stats NZ, 2015). The maximum margin of error for the whole results is +/− 3.1% at 95% confidence. The response rate was 28%.

There were a total of 1,161 participants. Participants received an email with detailed information about the nature and purpose of the study and gave their consent to participate. Two email reminders were sent during fieldwork. Participants were also incentivized through a point-based reward system when they completed the survey. In terms of gender, females represented 51.7% of the total sample while males made up 47.9%. Only 0.4% of participants identified as gender diverse. Regarding age groups, participants were distributed as follows: 18–29 years old (20.9%), 30–39 years old (16.4%), 40–49 years old (18.9%), 50–59 years old (17.5%), 60–69 years old (13.6%), and 70 years old and older (12.6%).

For this chapter, only data regarding participants' self-reported engagement in behaviors often associated with TFA are presented and discussed. Descriptive statistics were used to present quantitative accounts or summaries of what the data show about the sample and the measures (Trochim & Donnelly, 2007) in the context of gender and age. Thus, broad patterns are discussed in the chapter only when findings are statistically significant.

Due to the sensitive nature of the research topic, the authors ensured that special attention was paid to research ethics at all stages of the study. Participants' informed consent was obtained after providing them with information about the purpose of the survey, what would be involved, and how collected data would be used and protected. The authors ensured that the Colmar Brunton Social Research Team administering the online survey followed ethical protocols to respect and protect participants' safety and rights to take part in and/or withdraw from the study. Moreover, contact information for support services, such as Netsafe's helpline, was also provided to the participants. In addition, the APS questionnaire was sensitively worded, cognitively tested, and piloted to identify any risk of causing distress to the participants.

Although this study provides new insights into adult New Zealanders' engagement in TFA, it has limitations that need to be mentioned. First, a potential issue relates to social desirability bias in the self-reported data provided by the participants (Bryman, 2008), meaning that some might not have disclosed their engagement in TFA and instead provided socially desirable answers. Second, despite surveying the sending of unwanted digital communications, some of the listed behaviors that participants were asked about may have taken place in consensual contexts where the behavior of the participant was not considered harmful (and perhaps was even welcomed) by the recipient (e.g., making a sexual advance, sending a sexual image). Since it can be difficult for quantitative instruments to delve deeply into context, future qualitative research could be beneficial for better understanding these contextual nuances. Third, although our gender measure allowed participants to identify themselves within the broad category of gender diverse, only 0.4% did so. Thus, arriving at statistically relevant conclusions for this sub-group was not possible. Fourth, a relatively small number of respondents reported engaging in listed behaviors, thereby limiting the possibility for broad generalizations about particular types of behavior within the population as a whole. Finally, as previously mentioned, data were weighted using the 2013 census data (Stats NZ, 2015). At the time of carrying out data processing and reporting, the 2018 census data were not yet available.

Findings

Engagement in Technology-Facilitated Aggression

To answer the first research question about engagement in TFA, participants were asked whether in the last 12 months they had undertaken a range of behaviors online toward someone else. These involved sending or sharing digital communications that (1) physically threatened someone, (2) attempted to get someone excluded from a friendship group, (3) tried to embarrass someone, (4) said offensive things about someone (e.g., the way they look, how they behave, or what they believe in), (5) posted or sent violent or sexual content, (6) made a false statement about someone's personal or professional life, (7) made a sexual advance toward someone (e.g., messages about sex, naked selfies, images, or video live stream), (8) regularly monitored someone's online activity in order to influence their behavior or thoughts, (9) shared intimate images or recordings of someone without their permission, (10) encouraged other people to send hurtful messages to someone else, or (11) tried to get someone to hurt themselves. The response options for each of these behaviors included: No, Yes – once, and Yes – more than once. The overall prevalence of TFA was obtained by aggregating the responses of participants who engaged at least in one of these behaviors.

In general, of all the participants (n = 1,161), over 1 in 10 (11.4%) disclosed having sent or shared at least one type of offensive or abusive digital communication to someone else (one or more times) in the last 12 months (Table 6.1). What is more, 2.5% reported posting hurtful content online only once while 8.9% did so more than one time. The study also found that, in regard to gender, males (16.5%) were more likely to engage in the listed behaviors compared to females (6.6%). Regarding age, sending or sharing an offensive digital communication

Table 6.1. Adult New Zealanders' Overall Engagement in TFA by Gender and Age.

	Sample	TFA Aggression
Male	556 (47.9%)	16.5%
Female	501 (51.7%)	6.6%
18–29	243 (20.9%)	19.8%
30–39	190 (16.4%)	19.4%
40–49	219 (18.95)	12.0%
50–59	203 (17.5%)	5.6%
60–69	158 (13.6%)	5.1%
70 or older	147 (12.6%)	1.5%
Total	**1,161**	**11.4%**

was more common among younger adults, particularly for those aged 18–29 (19.8%), followed by 30–39 and 40–49 years old, 19.4% and 12.0%, respectively.

Furthermore, our results also show which of the listed behaviors were more common among participants. In this respect, as Table 6.2 depicts, posting or sharing content that said offensive things (6%) was the most common form of TFA. Less common were sharing content that sought to embarrass someone, attempted to get someone excluded from a friendship group, was a sexual advance toward someone, was violent or sexual, or encouraged other people to send hurtful messages to someone (3% for each of them). Meanwhile, 2% was the rate for each of the remaining behaviors included in our typology of TFA. These included behaviors that monitored someone's online activity, physically threatened someone, shared intimate images or recordings without permission, was a false statement about someone's personal or professional life, and tried to get someone to hurt themselves.

Regarding gender, as previously mentioned, overall engagement in diverse manifestations of the listed behaviors was higher among males compared to females. Rates for some types were more significant statistically than others. For instance, 9% of males indicated to have posted offensive things about someone compared to 3% of females. Also, posting online content that attempted to get someone excluded from a friendship group was higher among males (6%) than females (1%). In terms of age, posting content that said offensive things about someone was more common among 18–29 and 40–49 years old, with rates at 8% for each of these age groups. Meanwhile, those aged 30–39 were more likely to send content online with the intention of getting someone excluded from a friendship group.

The Target of Technology-Facilitated Aggression

To explore the extent and nature of TFA, participants who indicated they had engaged in at least one of the listed behaviors in the prior year (n = 140) were

Table 6.2. Prevalence of Each Type of TFA by Gender and Age.

	Said Offensive Things About Someone	Tried to Embarrass Someone Online	Attempted to Get Someone Excluded from a Friendship Group	Was a Sexual Advance Toward Someone	Included Violent or Sexual Content	Encouraged Other People to Send Hurtful Messages to Someone Else	Involved Regularly Monitoring Someone's Online Activity	Physically Threatened Someone	Shared Intimate Images or Recordings Without Permission	Was a False Statement About Someone's Personal or Professional Life	Tried to Get Someone to Hurt Themselves	Was Harmful to Someone Else in Another Way
Male	48 (9%)	20 (4%)	35 (6%)	23 (4%)	26 (5%)	27 (5%)	15 (3%)	15 (3%)	21 (4%)	20 (4%)	22 (4%)	17 (3%)
Female	17 (3%)	13 (2%)	4 (1%)	9 (2%)	5 (1%)	5 (1%)	6 (1%)	5 (1%)	2 (–)	6 (1%)	4 (1%)	8 (1%)
18–29	20 (8%)	16 (7%)	9 (4%)	14 (6%)	9 (4%)	8 (3%)	6 (3%)	9 (4%)	9 (4%)	9 (4%)	7 (3%)	12 (5%)
30–39	20 (11%)	12 (6%)	25 (13%)	5 (2%)	11 (6%)	8 (4%)	9 (5%)	5 (3%)	9 (5%)	9 (5%)	9 (5%)	4 (2%)
40–49	19 (8%)	4 (2%)	1 (–)	9 (4%)	10 (4%)	11 (5%)	3 (1%)	1 (–)	2 (1%)	1 (1%)	9 (4%)	9 (4%)
50–59	6 (3%)	1 (–)	2 (1%)	4 (2%)	1 (–)	4 (2%)	–	6 (3%)	3 (2%)	4 (2%)	1 (1%)	1 (–)
60–69	–	1 (1%)	3 (2%)	–	1 (1%)	–	3 (2%)	–	–	3 (2%)	–	–
70-older	–	–	–	–	–	2 (1%)	–	–	–	–	–	–
Total	**65 (6%)**	**34 (3%)**	**40 (3%)**	**32 (3%)**	**32 (3%)**	**33 (3%)**	**21 (2%)**	**21 (2%)**	**22 (2%)**	**26 (2%)**	**27 (2%)**	**25 (2%)**

asked a follow-up question about who the target was. The response scale included: (a) a family member, (b) a friend, (c) a colleague/past colleague, (d) an acquaintance – someone who is part of their wider peer group, (e) other, and (f) none of the above.

As Table 6.3 depicts, 29% of targets were a friend, followed by a family member (20%). In addition, 13% of those targeted were strangers to the participants while 12% said they targeted a colleague or past colleague. In terms of gender, it was more common for males (33%) to target a friend compared to females (20%). In contrast, targeting a family member was more common among female participants (30%) than males (16%). Regarding age, 49% of participants aged 30–39 indicated having sent or shared an offensive communication to or with a friend, while 26% of those aged 18–29 did so too. Furthermore, young participants aged 18–29 (26%) were more likely to target a family member than their 30–39 years old peers (21%). Interestingly, targeting a stranger was more common among older adults aged 40 and over.

Reasons for Engaging in Technology-Facilitated Aggression

The survey also asked these participants about the main reason that motivated them to engage in the listed behaviors. To indicate their responses, participants were provided with the following items: (1) to embarrass the person, (2) to influence their behavior or thoughts, (3) to scare them, (4) to get revenge or get back at them, (5) for sexual pleasure, (6) for a joke, (7) to get money from them, (8) to get more images or videos from them, (9) other, and (10) don't know.

When asked about the reason for their behavior, just over a quarter (28%) of respondents (n = 140) said their communications were designed and sent as a joke (Table 6.4). The second most common reason was to influence their target's behavior or thoughts (14%). Less common reasons reported by the participants were to scare the target (8%), to embarrass them (6%), to get revenge (4%), or to get money from them (3%). While 19% said there were other reasons, 16% did not know the motivation behind their behavior. Interestingly, compared to males (23%), females (40%) were more likely to send an offensive communication as a joke. In contrast, for males it was more common to do so to influence their target's behavior or thoughts, to scare them, to embarrass them, and to get revenge. In terms of age, it is noticeable that for a significant proportion of participants aged 18–29 (61%) their behavior was intended as a joke. While a third of those aged 30–39 years old (33%) indicated not knowing what the motivation for their action was, 32% of those aged 40–49 reported that they sought to scare the target.

Channels Used for Technology-Facilitated Aggression

We were also interested in knowing what digital tools participants used to engage in the listed behaviors (Table 6.5). Our data indicate that for these respondents (n = 140), a phone text (39%) was the most common channel, followed by posting hurtful content on their own personal social media site (34%) and via email (20%).

Table 6.3. The Target of TFA by Gender and Age.

	Sample Size	Friend	Family Member	Stranger	Current/Past Colleague	Acquaintance	Other	None of These
Male	86	33%	16%	11%	18%	4%	–	18%
Female	51	20%	30%	17%	–	8%	2%	23%
18–29	58	32%	26%	10%	1%	8%	1%	21%
30–39	38	49%	21%	4%	18%	5%	–	3%
40–49	19	–	9%	19%	23%	4%	1%	44%
50–59	13	29%	2%	33%	1%	4%	–	31%
60–69	8	2%	42%	20%	33%	4%	–	–
70 or older	4	69%	–	–	19%	–	6%	5%
Total	**140**	**29%**	**20%**	**13%**	**12%**	**5%**	**1%**	**20%**

Table 6.4. Aggressors' Reasons for Engaging in TFA by Gender and Age.

	Sample Size	A Joke	To Influence Their Behavior or Thoughts	To Scare Them	To Embarrass the Person	To Get Revenge	To Get Money from Them	To Get More Image or Videos from Them	For Sexual Pleasure	Other	Don't Know
Male	86	23%	18%	11%	8%	5%	2%	2%	1%	11%	18%
Female	51	40%	5%	3%	–	1%	4%	–	1%	36%	10%
18–29	58	61%	9%	2%	4%	6%	–	5%	2%	2%	8%
30–39	38	10%	14%	2%	12%	1%	8%	–	1%	19%	33%
40–49	19	3%	6%	32%	–	5%	3%	–	1%	40%	10%
50–59	13	29%	13%	4%	–	–	1%	–	–	49%	5%
60–69	8	–	76%	–	13%	–	–	–	–	8%	2%
70–older	4	–	–	19%	–	–	–	–	–	6%	74%
Total	**140**	**28%**	**14%**	**8%**	**6%**	**4%**	**3%**	**2%**	**1%**	**19%**	**16%**

Table 6.5. Channels Used for TFA.

	Sample Size	Phone Text	Personal Social Media	Email	Others' Social Media	Dating Website/ App	Discussion Forum	Online Gaming	Other
Male	86	34%	44%	25%	8%	14%	8%	6%	8%
Female	51	50%	10%	9%	14%	3%	4%	1%	23%
18–29	58	50%	13%	9%	14%	10%	3%	8%	12%
30–39	38	48%	35%	33%	4%	24%	17%	–	14%
40–49	19	9%	41%	12%	17%	–	2%	6%	21%
50–59	13	53%	61%	47%	3%	3%	3%	–	–
60–69	8	8%	92%	4%	4%	–	–	–	4%
70–older	4	25%	6%	74%	–	–	5%	–	–
Total	**140**	**39%**	**34%**	**20%**	**10%**	**10%**	**6%**	**4%**	**12%**

Table 6.6. TFA as Part of a Wider Issue Happening Offline.

	Sample Size	**Yes**	**No - Only Online**	**Don't Know**
Male	86	26%	47%	27%
Female	51	20%	44%	36%
18–29	58	32%	38%	30%
30–39	38	23%	37%	40%
40–49	19	23%	63%	15%
50–59	13	4%	67%	29%
60–69	8	2%	63%	35%
70 or older	4	88%	6%	5%
Total	**140**	**24%**	**46%**	**30%**

Less common was the use of someone else's social media (10%) or a dating app (10%). For males who engaged in harmful online activities, it was much more common to post the content on their own social media site (44%). Other common channels were a phone text (34%) and email (25%). In contrast, half of the female participants who engaged in TFA said they sent a phone text. The second most common channel used was posting on other people's social media sites (14%) and then posting on their own social media site (10%). In terms of age, for both 18–29 (50%) and 30–39 years old participants (48%) engaging in one of the listed behaviors was more often done via phone text, while participants from older age groups tended to use their personal social media site to engage in the listed behaviors.

Technology-Facilitated Aggression as a Part of a Wider Issue Happening Offline

Table 6.6 presents results from a final question that explored whether engaging in the listed behaviors was related to a broader issue that was happening offline. We explained to participants that by "offline" we meant a situation occurring in a physical environment, such as through face-to-face interactions. Interestingly, nearly half of participants (46%) who engaged in the listed behaviors indicated that their actions occurred only online. Differences regarding gender were not significant, but in terms of age, younger adults, aged 18–29 and 30–39, reported a higher incidence of engagement in the listed behaviors connected with an offline situation.

Discussion and Conclusions

This empirical study sought to explore the extent of engagement in TFA among adult New Zealanders by examining engagement in a set of listed behaviors. It offers evidence about its prevalence based on nationally representative data. The study not only reveals that just over 1 in 10 participants (11.4%) admitted to having engaged in one or more of the listed behaviors in the past year, but also offers further insights about the nature of TFA and areas for further research, which are discussed below.

The Gendered Nature of Technology-Facilitated Aggression

The data show a higher rate of engagement in behaviors often associated with TFA, by 10 percentage points, among males (16.5%) compared to females (6.6%). This finding seems consistent with some prior research on the gendered nature of diverse forms of online aggression and abuse (see Deans & Bhogal, 2019; Henry et al., 2019; Morelli et al., 2016; Wick et al., 2017). Similarly, the finding is consistent with a pattern from New Zealand's justice system in which the number of men charged with criminal offenses under the HDCA (2015) is much higher than the number of women (Ministry of Justice, 2019). What is more, when looking at the main reasons behind engaging in behaviors often associated with TFA, males reported higher rates of motivations that, in general, sought to exert control over and coerce their target. For example, it was significantly more common for males to seek to influence their target's behavior/thoughts and to scare them. Males who engaged in the listed behaviors were also more likely to be trying to embarrass their target or to get revenge. Thus, in contrast to what some have suggested about women's monitoring behaviors (see Bennett et al., 2011; Burke et al., 2011), our results suggest that among adult New Zealanders, males' online aggression may be more likely to be intended for controlling and hurting their target. Although this study did not ask participants about their target's gender, research on online victimization (see Deans & Bhogal, 2019; Henry & Powell, 2018; Morelli et al., 2016; Wick et al., 2017) and Netsafe's operational experience (see the Introduction section in this chapter) suggests that in most forms of online aggression, women are more likely to be targeted.

The results also show the gender differences in the use of digital channels for TFA. While both males and females did not limit themselves to the use of one specific digital channel, aggregating results suggest that males tend to engage in the listed behaviors through platforms that, in most cases, are designed to be networked and/or public, such as social media sites, dating apps, discussion forums, and online gaming. For instance, it was much more common for males (44%) to post an unwanted communication on their personal social media compared to females (10%). In contrast, females who disclosed engagement in the listed behaviors preferred the use of digital channels that allow more personal and private communication. In this respect, for females (50%), it was more common to use a phone text to post an unwanted communication than males (34%). Considering the differing ways males and females use digital devices, participate in online activities, and engage with social media platforms (Pacheco & Melhuish, 2020), the findings suggest that the gendered pattern may extend to the use of digital channels for engagement in TFA.

Technology-Facilitated Aggression and Younger Adults

Another interesting finding is the link between age and engagement in behaviors often associated with TFA. As described in Table 6.1, our data reveal that such engagement was more common among young adults aged 18–29 and 30–39 (nearly 20% for each of these age groups), and that rates decreased progressively among older age groups. Prior research on adolescents shows that older teens tend to engage in risky online behaviors that might be potentially harmful such as sexting (Livingstone & Görzig, 2014; Pacheco & Melhuish, 2017). Our finding may provide some support for the conclusion that this pattern of risk taking online continues among younger adults.

Similarly, an unexpected finding relates to the role of fun-seeking in engagement in the listed behaviors among younger adults. Our results show that 61% of participants aged 18–29 who disclosed such engagement indicated their actions were intended as a joke, a rate far higher (by 33 percentage points) than the average responses gathered for this study (see Table 6.3). This finding suggests that, along with other social and psychological predictors, a tendency toward fun-seeking might be also a factor helping to explain younger adults' engagement in behaviors often associated with online aggression and abuse. The literature rarely looks at fun-seeking as a factor, and when it does so, it is in the context of children and cyberbullying (see Smith et al., 2008; Wong & McBride, 2018). However, a recent Netsafe empirical study on image-based sexual abuse among adults offers supporting evidence about the role of fun-seeking (Pacheco et al., 2019). The study revealed that 19% of targets believed their aggressor's main motivation was looking for fun, followed by seeking to get money from them (17%), and to get revenge (14%) (see Pacheco et al., 2019). Thus, future research should incorporate the role of fun-seeking as a factor helping to understand the nature of online aggression (Wong & McBride, 2018) and the extent of its link to the different behaviors associated with TFA not only among children but also the younger adult population. Furthermore, qualitative inquiry might shed light on the complexities of behaviors that are argued to be part of fun or play and their impact on targets' perceived harm. In addition, for practitioners, the implications of fun-seeking for potential harm should be included in the implementation of preventive interventions, in particular, educational and awareness programs.

Close Connections

A third interesting finding relates to those groups that were more commonly targeted by the listed behaviors. Surprisingly, half of participants indicated that the target was part of their close network of relationships, especially a friend (29%) or a family member (20%). This finding is surprising as it contrasts with prior New Zealand-based research regarding online victimization among adults. In this respect, a 2017 Netsafe study found that 36% of adult participants aged 18 and over believed they were targeted by a stranger—while rates for the person responsible being a friend or a family member were much lower (see Pacheco & Melhuish, 2018). This finding challenges the idea of the pervasiveness of "stranger danger" online which has been the focus of news media coverage as well as policy and law enforcement strategies, particularly for young people (Bailey, 2015; Pacheco & Melhuish, 2020). It also suggests a dissociation between what targets believe and/or know about who their online aggressor was and the self-reported accounts from those who admitted engagement in behaviors often associated with TFA. An explanation for this finding could be provided by the characteristics of digital communications. In this respect, aggressors may be taking advantage of the ease with which digital tools can facilitate anonymity or mask their real identity to target people familiar to them.

In addition, there seems to be a paradox regarding the role of close connections in the context of TFA and online risks, particularly among younger adults. On the one hand, research on children, for example, points out the supportive role of friends and family in managing online risks and harm. In this regard, Netsafe research shows, for example, that peer support becomes increasingly important among teens who deal with upsetting experiences online (Pacheco & Melhuish, 2020). On the other hand, however, this study shows that a close connection was also more likely to be the target of the listed behaviors – overall, 29% of participants who engaged in such behaviors targeted a friend and 20% a family member. Furthermore, as previously described in this chapter, the prevalence of targeting close connections is higher among younger adults, with males more likely to target a friend and females more likely to target a family member (see Table 6.2). Research on children shows some evidence about friends engaging in hurtful behaviors online against their close peers (Felmlee & Faris, 2016; Mishna, Wiener, & Pepler, 2008; Wei & Jonson-Reid, 2011) and what our data suggest is that this pattern continues among younger adults.

Future Directions

This study has collected relevant data on behaviors often associated with TFA in the context of the New Zealand adult population. However, despite its contribution, some aspects still need to be addressed in order to inform the development of comprehensive policies and effective interventions. First, we recommend annually monitoring not only the prevalence of adults' victimization but also engagement in TFA. Our operational and research experience at Netsafe shows that the incidence of some harmful behaviors online, such as hate speech, can change and affect people differently over time (Pacheco & Melhuish, 2019). Thus, gathering longitudinal data will help to understand evolving trends in engagement in TFA. Furthermore, quantitative research on the topic needs to include other variables such as those describing socio-economic and psychological characteristics of online aggressors. Further, qualitative inquiry is needed to learn about the context and views of those who engage in harmful online behaviors, including asking them about their target's gender or how specific digital tools (e.g., social media) are used to engage in online aggression. As previously mentioned, some qualitative work has been conducted but in the context of tertiary students. However, the line of inquiry needs to be expanded to other groups, considering people's sexual orientation or their intimate partner relationship status, for instance. Further, this approach would enable us to look more closely at the contexts that shape these experiences and that are out of reach in a quantitative study such as this. Qualitative inquiry would enable a richer look at TFA from the views of those who engage in online aggression and help to distinguish it from situations where what might appear to be aggressive behavior was actually part of a consensual or mutually-accepted form of exchange. Similarly, several questions remain to be answered such as to what extent engagement in TFA overlaps with experiences of victimization.

Acknowledgment

The research reported in this chapter was conducted by Netsafe with funding from the New Zealand Ministry of Justice.

References

Bailey, J. (2015). A perfect storm: How the online environment, social norms, and law shape girls' lives. In J. Bailey, & V. Steeves (Eds.), *eGirls, eCitizens* (pp. 21–53). Ottawa, ON: University of Ottawa Press. Retrieved from https://ruor.uottawa.ca/bitstream/10393/32376/1/9780776622590_WEB.pdf

Barlett, C., Chamberlin, K., & Witkower, Z. (2017). Predicting cyberbullying perpetration in emerging adults: A theoretical test of the Barlett gentile cyberbullying model. *Aggressive Behavior*, *43*(2), 147–154. doi:10.1002/ab.21670

Bauman, S., & Baldasare, A. (2015). Cyber aggression among college students: Demographic differences, predictors of distress, and the role of the university. *Journal of College Student Development*, *56*(4), 317–330. doi:10.1353/csd.2015.0039

BBC. (2019, September 18). New algorithms aim to stamp out abuse on Twitter. Retrieved from https://www.bbc.com/news/technology-49740135

Bennett, D. C., Guran, E. L., Ramos, M. C., & Margolin, G. (2011). College students' electronic victimization in friendships and dating relationships: Anticipated distress and associations with risky behaviors. *Violence & Victims*, *26*(4), 410–429. doi:10.1891/0886-6708.26.4.410

Borrajo, E., Gámez-Guadix, M., & Calvete, E. (2015). Cyber dating abuse: Prevalence, context, and relationship with offline dating aggression. *Psychological Reports*, *116*(2), 565–585. doi:10.2466/21.16.PR0.116k22w4

Bryman, A. (2008). *Social research methods* (3rd Ed.). New York, NY: Oxford University Press.

Burke, S. C., Wallen, M., Vail-Smith, K., & Knox, D. (2011). Using technology to control intimate partners: An exploratory study of college undergraduates. *Computers in Human Behavior*, *27*(3), 1162–1167. doi:10.1016/j.chb.2010.12.010

Deans, H., & Bhogal, M. S. (2019). Perpetrating cyber dating abuse: A brief report on the role of aggression, romantic jealousy and gender. *Current Psychology*, *38*(5), 1077–1082. doi:10.1007/s12144-017-9715-4

Doane, A. N., Pearson, M. R., & Kelley, M. L. (2014). Predictors of cyberbullying perpetration among college students: An application of the Theory of Reasoned Action. *Computers in Human Behavior*, *36*, 154–162. doi:10.1016/j.chb.2014.03.051

D'Souza, N., Catley, B., Tappin, D., & Forsyth, D. (2019). 'You live and breathe it…': Exploring experiences of workplace cyberbullying among New Zealand nurses. *Journal of Management and Organization*, 1–19. doi:10.1017/jmo.2019.71

Every-Palmer, S., Barry-Walsh, J., & Pathé, M. (2015). Harassment, stalking, threats and attacks targeting New Zealand politicians: A mental health issue. *Australian and New Zealand Journal of Psychiatry*, *49*(7), 634–641. doi:10.1177/0004867415583700

Felmlee, D., & Faris, R. (2016). Toxic ties: Networks of friendship, dating, and cyber victimization. *Social Psychology Quarterly*, *79*(3), 243–262. doi:10.1177/0190272516656585

Gámez-Guadix, M., Almendros, C., Borrajo, E., & Calvete, E. (2015). Prevalence and association of sexting and online sexual victimization among Spanish adults. *Sexuality Research and Social Policy*, *12*(2), 145–154. doi:10.1007/s13178-015-0186-9

Garcia, J. R., Gesselman, A. N., Siliman, S. A., Perry, B. L., Coe, K., & Fisher, H. E. (2016). Sexting among singles in the USA: Prevalence of sending, receiving, and sharing sexual messages and images. *Sexual Health*, *13*(5), 428–435. doi:10.1071/SH15240

Gardner, D., O'Driscoll, M., Cooper-Thomas, H., Roche, M., Bentley, T., Catley, B., & Trenberth, L. (2016). Predictors of workplace bullying and cyber-bullying in New Zealand. *International Journal of Environmental Research and Public Health*, *13*(5), 448. doi:10.3390/ijerph13050448

Harmful Digital Communications Act [HDCA]. (2015). Retrieved from http://www.legislation.govt.nz/act/public/2015/0063/latest/whole.html

Henry, N., Flynn, A., & Powell, A. (2019). Image-based sexual abuse: Victims and perpetrators. Retrieved from https://www.aic.gov.au/publications/tandi/tandi572. Accessed on February 28, 2020.

Henry, N., & Powell, A. (2018). Technology-facilitated sexual violence: A literature review of empirical research. *Trauma, Violence, & Abuse*, *19*(2), 195–208. doi: 10.1177/1524838016650189

Henry, C., & Talbot, H. (2019). The complexities of young New Zealanders' use and perceptions of pornography: A quantitative survey in context. *Porn Studies*, *6*(4), 391–410. doi:10.1080/23268743.2019.1656544

Jenaro, C., Flores, N., & Frías, C. P. (2018). Systematic review of empirical studies on cyberbullying in adults: What we know and what we should investigate. *Aggression and Violent Behavior*, *38*, 113–122. doi:10.1016/j.avb.2017.12.003

Law Commission. (2012). *Harmful digital communications: The adequacy of the current sanctions and remedies*. Wellington. Retrieved from http://www.lawcom.govt.nz/sites/default/files/projectAvailableFormats/NZLC MB3.pdf

Lenhart, A., Ybarra, M., Zickuhr, K., & Price-Feeney, M. (2016). *Online harassment, digital abuse, and cyberstalking in America*. Retrieved from https://datasociety.net/pubs/oh/Online_Harassment_2016.pdf. Accessed on March 30, 2017.

Livingstone, S., & Görzig, A. (2014). When adolescents receive sexual messages on the internet: Explaining experiences of risk and harm. *Computers in Human Behavior*, *33*, 8–15. doi:10.1016/j.chb.2013.12.021

Ministry of Justice. (2014). *Harmful digital communications bill – initial briefing*. Retrieved from https://www.parliament.nz/en/pb/sc/submissions-and-advice/document/50SCJE_ADV_00DBHOH_BILL12843_1_A381496/initial-briefing

Ministry of Justice. (2019). *Research & data: Data tables - harmful digital communication offenses*. Retrieved from https://www.justice.govt.nz/justice-sector-policy/research-data/justice-statistics/data-tables. Accessed on March 11, 2020.

Minton, C., Birks, M., Cant, R., & Budden, L. M. (2018). New Zealand nursing students' experience of bullying/harassment while on clinical placement: A cross-sectional survey. *Collegian*, *25*(6), 583–589. doi:10.1016/J.COLEGN.2018.06.003

Mishna, F., Wiener, J., & Pepler, D. (2008). Some of my best friends - experiences of bullying within friendships. *School Psychology International*, *29*(5), 549–573. doi:10.1177/0143034308099201

Morelli, M., Bianchi, D., Baiocco, R., Pezzuti, L., & Chirumbolo, A. (2016). Not-allowed sharing of sexts and dating violence from the perpetrator's perspective: The moderation role of sexism. *Computers in Human Behavior*, *56*, 163–169. doi:10.1016/j.chb.2015.11.047

Netsafe. (2020). Adult New Zealanders reporting online incidents to Netsafe. Unpublished raw data.

Pacheco, E., & Melhuish, N. (2017). Teens and "sexting" in New Zealand: Prevalence and attitudes. *SSRN Electronic Journal*, doi:10.2139/ssrn.3128598

Pacheco, E., & Melhuish, N. (2018). Harmful digital communications in New Zealand: Annual population survey 2017. *SSRN Electronic Journal*. doi:10.2139/ssrn.3128121

Pacheco, E., & Melhuish, N. (2019). Measuring trends in online hate speech victimisation and exposure, and attitudes in New Zealand. *SSRN Electronic Journal*. doi:10.2139/ssrn.3501977

Pacheco, E., & Melhuish, N. (2020). *New Zealand children's experiences of online risks and perceptions of harm. Evidence from Ngā taiohi matihiko o Aotearoa - New Zealand Kids Online*. Wellington: Netsafe. doi:10.31235/osf.io/qrhgv

Pacheco, E., Melhuish, N., & Fiske, J. (2019). Image-based sexual abuse: A snapshot of New Zealand adults' experiences. *SSRN Electronic Journal*. doi:10.2139/ssrn.3315984

Powell, A., & Henry, N. (2019). Technology-facilitated sexual violence victimization: Results from an online survey of Australian adults. *Journal of Interpersonal Violence*, *34*(17), 3637–3665. doi:10.1177/0886260516672055

Smith, P., Mahdavi, J., Carvalho, M., Fisher, S., Russell, S., & Tippett, N. (2008). Cyberbullying: Its nature and impact in secondary school pupils. *Journal of Child Psychology and Psychiatry*, *49*(4), 376–385. doi:10.1111/j.1469-7610.2007.01846.x

Stats NZ. (2015). *2013 census*. Retrieved from http://archive.stats.govt.nz/Census/2013-census.aspx#gsc.tab=0

Steiner-Fox, H. W., Dutt, S. J., Christiansen, S. J., Newton, H. J., Matika, C. M., Lindsay, C., & Stronge, S. (2016). Rates of cyberbullying among women and men in New Zealand in 2015. Retrieved from https://cdn.auckland.ac.nz/assets/psych/about/our-research/nzavs/Feedback Reports/NZAVS-Policy-Brief-Rate-of-Cyber-Bullying.pdf. Accessed on February 21, 2017.

Tokunaga, R. S. (2011). Social networking site or social surveillance site? Understanding the use of interpersonal electronic surveillance in romantic relationships. *Computers in Human Behavior*, *27*(2), 705–713. doi:10.1016/j.chb.2010.08.014

Trochim, W., & Donnelly, J. P. (2007). *Research methods knowledge base* (3rd ed.). Mason, OH: Thomson Custom Pub.

Wei, H.-S., & Jonson-Reid, M. (2011). Friends can hurt you: Examining the coexistence of friendship and bullying among early adolescents. *School Psychology International*, *32*(3), 244–262. doi:10.1177/0143034311402310

Wick, S. E., Nagoshi, C., Basham, R., Jordan, C., Kim, Y. K., Nguyen, A. P., & Lehmann, P. (2017). Patterns of cyber harassment and perpetration among college students in the United States: A test of routine activities theory. *International Journal of Cyber Criminology*, *11*(1), 24–38. doi:10.5281/zenodo.495770

Wong, N., & McBride, C. (2018). Fun over conscience: Fun-seeking tendencies in cyberbullying perpetration. *Computers in Human Behavior*, *86*, 319–329. doi: 10.1016/j.chb.2018.05.009

Chapter 7

The Missing and Murdered Indigenous Women Crisis: Technological Dimensions[#]*

Jane Bailey and Sara Shayan

Abstract

This article considers how digital technologies are informed by, and implicated in, the systematic and interlocking oppressions of colonialism,

[#]This chapter is an adapted version of an article originally published in a 2016 special issue of the *Canadian Journal of Women and the Law*. It has been reprinted in this Handbook with permission of the University of Toronto Press (http://utpjournals.press) © *Canadian Journal of Women and the Law* 2016. The 2016 special issue in which the original version appeared was focused on a then-forthcoming Canadian National Inquiry into Missing and Murdered Indigenous Women and Girls (NIMMIWG). The article was based primarily on the available Canadian literature at the time. It was intended to encourage the NIMMIWG to consider the technological dimensions of the crisis that has led to the deaths and disappearances of thousands of Indigenous women and girls in Canada. The NIMMIWG, which was besieged by controversy throughout its mandate (see e.g. Ward, 2019; Rabson, 2019), released its final report in 2019 (NIMMIW, 2019). The report itself was met with controversy because, among other things, it described (in our view accurately) the disappearances and murders of Indigenous women as a "Canadian genocide" (Barrera, 2019). Apart from several mentions of the use of social media as a tool for addressing the crisis (NIMMIW, 2019, Vol 1b, p. 158), and calls for improved internet access for Indigenous peoples (NIMMIW, 2019, Vol 1b, p. 186), the report did not contain any detailed analysis of other technological dimensions of the crisis. Given the lapse of time since the original article was published, this chapter must be read as a snapshot of the issues at the time it was originally written. As the other chapters in this Handbook demonstrate (in particular Carlson and Frazer's chapter), considerable additional research and scholarship in a number of areas relevant to the areas covered have been produced since the piece was originally published. We have attempted to flag some of this new material at relevant points throughout the document. Nonetheless, we believe that its intersectional approach and inclusion of state use of technologies of violence and surveillance against Indigenous and other equality-seeking communities continue to be important pieces of the puzzle in understanding and responding to technology-facilitated violence and abuse.

The Emerald International Handbook of Technology-Facilitated Violence and Abuse, 125–144

doi:10.1108/978-1-83982-848-520211007

misogyny, and racism, all of which have been identified as root causes of the missing and murdered Indigenous women crisis in Canada. The authors consider how technology can facilitate multiple forms of violence against women including stalking and intimate partner violence, human trafficking, pornography and child abuse images, and online hate and harassment and note instances where Indigenous women and girls may be particularly vulnerable. The authors also explore some of the complexities related to police use of technology for investigatory purposes, touching on police use of social media and DNA technology. Without simplistically blaming technology, the authors argue that technology interacts with multiple factors in the complex historical, socio-cultural environment that incubates the national crisis of missing and murdered Indigenous women and girls. The article concludes with related questions that may be considered at the impending national inquiry.

Keywords: Indigenous women and girls; online hate and harassment; human trafficking; state surveillance; DNA testing; sexual violence

Introduction

While violence against women (VAW) affects a broad spectrum of women and girls in Canada, Indigenous women and girls[1] are particularly vulnerable (Canadian Women's Foundation, 2014; UN CEDAW, 2015, p. 3). A conservative estimate suggests that there are more than 1,100 missing and murdered Indigenous women and girls in Canada (RCMP, 2014, p. 3).[2] Root causes of this crisis include interlocking systemic oppressions such as colonialism, misogyny, and racism. Meaningfully addressing VAW against Indigenous women and girls, then, means not limiting the conception of violence to individual acts but, rather, considering such violence in its broader social, historical, and colonial context. As a starting point, this requires acknowledging the ways that sexual violence is, as Sarah Deer (2009) writes, "deeply embedded in the colonial mindset" and "part and parcel of colonization" (p. 150).

Another body of emerging Canadian research focuses on the role that technology plays in VAW (e.g., Fairbairn, Bivens, & Dawson, 2013; Fairbairn,

*This article was first presented at the Canadian Feminist Alliance for International Action (FAFIA)/Native Women's Association of Canada (NWAC)/*Canadian Journal of Women and the Law* (*CJWL*) Symposium on Murders and Disappearances of Indigenous Women and Girls, which was held at the University of Ottawa on 30–31 January 2016. Thanks to FAFIA, the NWAC, and the CJWL for sponsoring the symposium and to Muriel Stanley Venne, President of the Institute for the Advancement of Aboriginal Women, for drawing her concerns around Project KARE to my attention at the symposium. Thanks also to the Social Sciences and Humanities Research Council for funding The eQuality Project, a seven-year partnership initiative, the work of which this article forms a part. Finally, thank you to two anonymous peer reviewers for their insightful comments and suggestions.

2015), including specific research that documents how digital communications technologies are used to facilitate the trafficking of Indigenous women and girls (UN, 2000, p. 41;[3] Sethi, 2007). Without simplistically blaming technology, this article suggests a need to explore the ways that technology interacts with other factors in the complex historical, socio-cultural environment that incubates the national crisis of missing and murdered Indigenous women and girls.

The first part of this article draws on feminist critiques that demonstrate how technology is culturally coded with existing forms of discrimination and, perhaps unsurprisingly, can intensify existing inequalities.[4] The second part focuses on digital communications technologies, exploring their role in both facilitating and responding to VAW. We consider existing research on human trafficking, online pornography and child sexual abuse images, and online hate and harassment, particularly as they relate to violence against Indigenous women and girls. We also consider how social media can be used for outreach, support, and community organizing as well as for facilitating access to the national inquiry and its processes. The third part of the article explores some of the complexities related to police use of technology for investigatory purposes, touching on police use of social media and DNA technology. The two sections in this part highlight, where possible, situations in which a focus on the particular technology identified fits within previously identified root causes of the crisis of missing and murdered Indigenous women and girls and supports or undermines reforms recommended by international human rights bodies, such as the UN Committee on the Elimination of Discrimination against Women (CEDAW). The conclusion suggests related questions that could be considered at the impending national inquiry.

Cultural Encoding of Technology

Feminist critics note that the institutions, practices, and artifacts of modern technology can reflect and reinforce stereotypes about women and other equality-seeking groups (Oldenziel, 2001; Wajcman, 2009). As Judy Wajcman (2009) notes, "different childhood exposure to technology, the prevalence of different role models, different forms of schooling, and the extreme gender segregation of the job market" all contribute to a mutual shaping of gender and technology that has ultimately led to a "taken-for-granted association of technology with men" (pp. 143–145). Furthermore, disparities of "wealth, power, agency, [and] sovereignty" in technological and scientific processes have entrenched stereotypes of women and minorities as passive consumers of technology rather than as agents of technological progress (Haraway & Goodeve, 1999, p. 157; Oldenziel, 2001, p. 128). These and other stereotypes can reinforce the unfounded belief that women and minorities are "technically incompetent or invisible in technical spheres" (Wajcman, 2009, p. 144).

Evaluating how technology can contribute to discrimination against Indigenous women and girls will require engaging with the "power relations of capitalism, nationalism, colonialism, and imperialism" that animate Western science and technology (Hill Collins, 2001, p. 278). Addressing barriers to technological access and agency in Indigenous communities also requires interrogating gendered and colonial understandings of technological competency, progress, and innovation.[5] Deconstructing the rhetoric of male mastery and control in technology, a domain often associated with the "tools of work and war," (Wajcman, 2009, p. 144) and considering how and why the technology sector can prove unwelcoming and even hostile to women and minorities will also prove particularly important for future equality projects (Subramaniam, 2003, p. 937).

Further work is needed to assess whether and how technological inequality may be implicated in technologically facilitated violence against Indigenous women and girls. In the interim, strategies for mitigating the effects of culturally encoded discrimination in technology may include advocating for increased access to high and higher-speed internet in Indigenous communities, evaluating the benefits and challenges of online Indigenous community building, and addressing critical skills gaps among vulnerable individuals and those who may be new to navigating online and digital spaces (First Nations Technology Council (FNTC), 2015). The Assembly of First Nations' e-community initiative and the First Nations Technology Council both offer examples of ongoing work in these critical areas, although increased federal funding for Indigenous technology projects is needed (FNTC, 2015). Perhaps most importantly, meaningfully addressing the root causes of discrimination and violence against Indigenous women and girls that constrain their right to participate as equals both online and offline is critical.

Violence Against Women and Digital Communications Technologies

In its 2015 report on missing and murdered Indigenous women, CEDAW stresses the need for Canada to take all forms of violence against Indigenous women seriously (para 210). In exploring the role of digital communications technologies in facilitating VAW, we have often relied on broader feminist work that "draws attention to the way that systems of gendered inequality enable and support physical, sexual and psychological violence against women and girls worldwide" while also recognizing the ways in which systemic forms of oppression such as racism, colonialism, and homophobia affect and inform such violence (Fairbairn, 2015, p. 231). Recognizing that sexual violence against Indigenous women and girls is a function of racism and sexism necessitates an intersectional analysis. As Pam Palmater (2016) writes,

> It is also important to note that violence against Indigenous women and girls is committed almost exclusively by men (Indigenous and non-Indigenous), which makes this a very gender-specific issue. This is about gendered, sexualized violence. Indigenous women and girls are victims because they are Indigenous and because they are female (p. 258).

In addition, meaningfully addressing violence against Indigenous women and girls also requires paying careful attention to the role of the state and state actors in creating conditions ripe for, and perpetuating, such violence. This means understanding such violence as a product of "colonialism, which has [among other things] pushed many Indigenous women to the margins of their own cultures and Canadian society as a whole" (Amnesty International, 2004, p. 8). It also means scrutinizing existing state policy and (in)action, as well as further proposed state interventions, as potential tools of patriarchy, racism, colonialism, and other forms of oppression (INCITE!, n.d.). For example, state policies around status, land holding, and rights of residence on reserves that are implicitly premised on sexist presumptions also frequently propagate heteronormativity (Simpson, 2014, pp. 13, 33) framed around "Anglo-American conceptions of family, home, desire, and personal identity" (Rifkin, 2011, p. 8).

We also suggest that there is a need to interrogate the role of technology in, and as a product of, this complex grid of interlocking oppressions that shape violence against Indigenous women and girls. In addition to international standards and definitions of VAW that are broad enough to include acts perpetrated through technology,[6] there is increasing evidence of national and international policy shifts toward specifically recognizing and addressing the role that technologies can and are playing (see e.g., APC, 2015; Government of Ontario, 2015; Status of Women Canada, 2013; Harris & Woodlock, this volume; Coombs, this volume; Henry & Witt, this volume). These shifts have led to initiatives focused on cyberviolence and its differential impacts on women and girls from diverse communities (see e.g., Fairbairn & Black, 2015; Estable & Meyer, 2015; Harris & Woodlock, this volume; Ferreira, this volume). More research is needed to understand the particular impacts of cyberviolence on Indigenous women and girls, particularly in the following four areas.

Stalking and Intimate Partner Violence

Digital communications technologies "complicate how women experience violence as well as how they are able to protect themselves" (Mason & Magnet, 2012, p. 107; see also Harris & Woodlock, this volume; and Louie, this volume). Survivors of VAW increasingly report being stalked through technological means, such as through global positioning systems, electronic records, web search engines, text messaging, and social media platforms that enhance abusers' ability to monitor their victims (Mason & Magnet, 2012, pp. 107–108; Southworth, 2005, p. 5; see also Harris & Woodlock, this volume). In 2013, SafetyNet Canada reported that 98% of surveyed Canadian anti-violence workers have indicated that they had "supported women and girls who have been threatened and/or intimidated via technology," while 72% provided support to women and girls whose online accounts had been hacked. As a result, anti-violence workers have serious concerns around privacy and confidentiality when communicating with women and girls using technology, and 84% discuss technology safety plans with women and girls, which might include the way that abusers can misuse technology (Safety Net Canada, 2013; see also Vitis, this volume; and Louie, this volume). While the degree to which Indigenous women and girls experience stalking by technological means is not well-documented (for further discussion of technology-facilitated violence against Indigenous peoples see Carlson & Frazer, this volume), as discussed in the next section of this chapter, there is evidence to suggest that those exploited by traffickers may be subject to technological surveillance and monitoring (Mason & Magnet, 2012, p. 107).

Human Trafficking

CEDAW has recommended that Canada "pay special attention to the needs and situation of aboriginal women in prostitution" and conduct studies to better understand and develop mechanisms for combatting trafficking of Aboriginal girls and women (CEDAW, 2015, para 217 (u)–(w)). Although the data about domestically trafficked persons are at best partial (Sethi, 2007, p. 58), other statistics, including those showing that Aboriginal girls and women are over-represented in prostitution (Sethi, 2007, p. 59; NWAC, 2014, pp. 8–9; CEDAW, 2015, para 98) and that 60% of sexually exploited youth are Aboriginal (Sethi, 2007, p. 59), help to shed light on the scope of the problem. Developing a better understanding and a concrete action plan for addressing the ways Indigenous women and girls are recruited into and kept in human trafficking will also require understanding the role of digital communications technologies in these processes.

Digital communications technologies, such as the internet and mobile devices, are used to facilitate human trafficking of young people in a variety of ways. Traffickers use the internet to recruit Indigenous girls, especially those in rural communities, often with promises of a job and the excitement of life in the city. Recruitment often proceeds with the goal of isolating young women from family and community, thus rendering them more vulnerable to being trafficked (Sethi, 2007, p. 60; Roos, 2013, pp. 21, 25). Traffickers also use the internet, including social media platforms such as Craigslist and Facebook to "advertise" sexually trafficked youth (NWAC, 2014, p. 56; BC Ministry of Public Safety, 2011, pp. 8–9), although it is now a crime in Canada to knowingly advertise the sexual services of others (*Criminal Code*, ss. 286.4, 286.5(1) (b)).[7] Traffickers communicate with trafficked youth using mobile technologies and track their activities by checking these young people's text message histories and phone logs (Thorn, 2015, pp. 17–31).

Clearly, technology is only one factor interacting with a variety of root causes that render Indigenous girls and women disproportionately vulnerable to human trafficking. Sethi (2007) identifies several root causes that must be addressed: the intergenerational impacts of colonization (including increased sexual abuse, violence, substance abuse, and suicide rates), a lack of awareness and acknowledgment of sexual exploitation, poverty, isolation, racism, gangs, gaps in services, and insufficient housing (pp. 61–65). International studies also demonstrate that being young, female, poor, socially or culturally excluded, and under-educated, as well as coming from "dysfunctional" families and having experiences with state institutions such as the child welfare system, increase vulnerability to being targeted by traffickers (NWAC, 2014, pp. 13–14). Furthermore, socio-economic marginalization, criminalization, systemic discrimination, child welfare institutional policies, vulnerability to prostitution and trafficking, colonialism, racism (including racial stereotyping by law enforcement institutions and officials), lack of safe transportation, and state failure to "address the prevalence of all forms of violence against aboriginal women" have all been identified as root causes of the missing and murdered Indigenous women crisis itself (CEDAW, 2015, para 102–131; BC Ministry of Public Safety, 2011, pp. 4–5).

In an increasingly technology-facilitated society, understanding the role that technology plays in relation to identified root causes of trafficking Indigenous women and girls and the crisis of missing and murdered Indigenous women and girls could play an important role in responding meaningfully. One might consider what role, if any, internet service providers are playing as well as the roles they can and should play[8] in addressing the use of their services for the purposes of human trafficking (particularly in light of recent *Criminal Code* amendments to prohibit knowingly selling the sexual services of others) and with respect to online pornography, hate, and harassment (*Criminal Code*, ss. 286.4, 286.5(1) (b)). As noted below, models for internet service provider responses already exist in other areas.

In the context of online child sexual exploitation, for example, Bell, Telus, Rogers, Shaw, MTS All stream, SaskTel, Vidéotron, and Aliant are part of the multi-sector Canadian Coalition against Internet Child Exploitation (CCAICE), along with the Royal Canadian Mounted Police's (RCMP) National Child Exploitation Coordination Center and the Department of Justice. The CCAICE's mandate is to "devise and implement an effective national strategy to help address the problem of online child sexual exploitation" (Canadian Center for Child Protection (a), n.d.). One of the CCAICE's undertakings is Cleanfeed Canada, an initiative that blocks "customer access to non-Canadian websites that are hosting child pornography" to "reduce Canadians' exposure to child abuse images and create a disincentive for those who access and distribute child pornography" (Canadian Center for Child Protection (b), n.d.).

In the context of alleged copyright infringement, the federal government has also encouraged voluntary initiatives by internet service providers. In 2015, federal legislation went into effect that "formalized a voluntary industry-based practice that has been in place for several years" (Office of Consumer Affairs, 2015). Pursuant to the Copyright Modernization Act (2012), copyright owners can send a notice of alleged infringement to the internet service provider of a user believed to be infringing copyright. The service provider is obliged to forward this notice to its customer and confirm to the copyright holder that this notice has been sent (Office of Consumer Affairs, 2015). Although the Act does not require a user to respond in any particular way, the system creates an incentive (whether rightly or wrongly) for users to remove allegedly infringing content.[9]

Impact of Online Pornography and Child Abuse Imagery

Some research suggests that the widespread dissemination of "hard-core, body-punishing sex in which women are demeaned and debased" should be understood as a legitimator of VAW (NWAC, 2014, citing; Dines, 2013). As a prime source of information for young people, messaging on the internet can shape young people's expectations of themselves and others and contribute to the conflation of sex with violence (Tankard Reist, 2016; see also Keene, this volume). Widespread availability of violent pornography may also facilitate the desensitization and increased interest in depictions of escalating levels of violence, including child sexual abuse (Bailey, 2007, p. 98). Moreover, online inculcation of youth with mainstream representations of thin, white, heterosexualized femininity can negatively affect girls' and young women's self-esteem and sense of belonging (Steeves, 2015, pp. 163–167). Research also suggests that these same representations often form the basis for peer harassment online, the consequences of which are discussed later in this chapter (Bailey, 2015, pp. 35–36). For these reasons, responses should not only target individual perpetrators but also focus on the impacts of commercial practices and online advertising that shape the online environments in which girls and women participate.

Online Hate and Harassment

CEDAW (2015) identified stereotyping as one of the root causes of the missing and murdered Indigenous women crisis, in part because stereotypes of Indigenous women that depict them as "prostitutes, transients or runaways … [living] high risk lifestyles" undermine public and law enforcement willingness to take these cases seriously (paras 137–140; see also MediaSmarts, n.d.; Jiwani & Young, 2006, pp. 898900). For this reason, CEDAW recommended that Canada adopt measures to address racism and sexism "with a view to eliminat[ing] negative stereotypes against aboriginal women" (205, para 219(b)). Racist and misogynist stereotypes familiar in offline spaces are also reflected in online spaces, sometimes with greater vitriol. Such vitriol is sometimes attributed to the apparent anonymity of online spaces as well as to the mob mentality that they can facilitate (Bailey, 2010, p. 24). Moreover, sexually violent online attacks, such as rape threats, are disproportionately targeted at women (Bailey, 2013, p. 723; Fairbairn, 2015, p. 230; West Coast LEAF, 2014, p. 5; Dunn, this volume). Indigenous persons in Canada and internationally are also targeted with extreme and hateful stereotyping and threats that can lead to withdrawal from online participation. In combination with other facts in extreme cases, such online abuses can lead to suicide (Angus, 2013; Carlson, Farrelly, Frazer, & Borthwick, 2015, pp. 2–3; Chapin, 2015; Oboler, 2012).

Online hatred for, and harassment of, Indigenous women and girls is grounded in interlocking oppressions, including colonialism, misogyny, racism, and homophobia (Jiwani & Young, 2006; Razack, 2000; Warman 2006; Warman 2006a; West Coast LEAF, 2014, pp. 68–69). These kinds of attacks can work to undermine the self-esteem and self-worth of Indigenous girls and women, contributing to an environment that can exacerbate vulnerability to other forms of victimization (NWAC, 2014, p. 19).[10] Research shows that being targeted by online hate and harassment (sometimes inaccurately mislabeled "cyberbullying"[11]) is associated with a variety of negative effects similar to those previously documented in relation to offline spaces, whether or not the target knows the perpetrator (Fairbairn, 2015, p. 234; Safety Net Canada, 2013a). Online hate and harassment can undermine self-esteem and lead to a lack of sense of belonging, depression, anxiety, fear of or withdrawal from public spaces, and, in extreme cases when combined with other kinds of factors, suicide (Bailey, 2014; Caltabiano & Torre, 2013, p. 31). Existing research showing how racism can undermine a sense of belonging and self-esteem in ways that facilitate the sexual trafficking of Indigenous women and girls (Sethi, 2007, p. 63), as well as research suggesting the prevalence of bullying in northern communities (Brownlee, Martin, Rawana, Harper, Mercier, Neckoway & Friesen, 2014, p. 45) and the potentially acute impacts of online harassment in smaller communities (Burkell & Saginur, 2015, pp. 146–152), underscores the need for further research to better understand the particular impacts of online hate and harassment on Indigenous women and girls.

It is also important to craft and implement measures that respond to online hate and harassment in ways that do not inadvertently disadvantage Indigenous women and girls by, for example, exposing them to greater risk of criminalization. Recent experiences relating to the nonconsensual distribution of intimate images and sexting suggest the need for restraint in using criminal law responses (particularly against youth), lest girls and young women, who are the primary targets of these offenses, be recast as the culprits under legal regimes originally designed to protect them (CBC News, 2015; Stillman, 2016). This is an especially important concern with respect to Indigenous women and girls who are disproportionately and increasingly criminalized in Canada[12] a stark reminder of the risks of relying on a criminal justice system that is rooted in racism, colonialism, and misogyny and that systematically over-criminalizes and under-protects Indigenous women and girls (Amnesty International, 2004; Palmater, 2016).

Outreach, Support, and Organization

CEDAW (2015) has recommended developing initiatives to address the devastating impacts of colonialism, racism, and misogyny by fostering Indigenous pride, self-esteem, and cultural identity. CEDAW (2015) has also encouraged measures to promote positive portrayals of Indigenous women in media and educational and public communications initiatives (para 219(d)). Furthermore, CEDAW and other organizations and researchers have strongly supported the development and distribution of meaningful awareness campaigns on a variety of issues, including procedures for reporting violence to the authorities as well as community capacity building to acknowledge and address issues of healthy relationships, sexual exploitation, and trafficking (including the recruiting tactics of traffickers) (CEDAW, 2015; Sethi, 2007, p. 67; NWAC, 2014, pp. 20–21; BC Ministry of Public Safety, 2011).

Digital communications technologies, such as the internet, can be used for outreach, support, organization, and education around the issues raised by CEDAW, the Native Women's Association of Canada (NWAC), and others (Cole, 2010, pp. 7, 120–121). Websites and social media platforms are already being used in positive ways[13] by public interest groups, community organizations, and governments to address issues of sexual exploitation,[14] stereotyping,[15] youth violence,[16] sexual health,[17] and Indigenous cultures, rights, and histories (including providing and raising awareness of culturally relevant services for Indigenous community members).[18] Ensuring that the information and services provided are grounded in experience and cognizant of the diversity of experience of Indigenous women and girls will be key to meaningfully building on these kinds of initiatives (NWAC, 2014, p. 44).

Accessibility of Inquiry and Its Processes[19]

CEDAW (2015) has recommended that Canada improve Indigenous women's access to justice, convene a national inquiry, and develop a national action plan (paras 167–72, 219(f), 220(a)–(b)). Digital communications technologies can and should be used to publicize and facilitate access to the impending inquiry, its goals, processes, and results for those for whom physical presence is not possible. Technologized participation should not become a substitute for physical presence, and it must be recognized that those living in very remote communities as well as in poorer sections of some urban centers may have restricted access to the internet (Bailey, Burkell, & Reynolds, 2013, p. 199). Keeping these limitations in mind, online communication relating to the inquiry, which should be translated into multiple languages, could still enhance the accessibility and transparency of the inquiry and its work. Technologically facilitated access, however, must also be tempered by respect for the dignity and integrity of families and victims, including the maintenance of the level of privacy and confidentiality they may desire in relation to their stories.

Police Use of Technology in Investigations

CEDAW (2015) has recommended a number of measures to improve policing and justice mechanisms to address the disproportionate number of unresolved cases of missing and murdered Indigenous women and girls (para 217). The police in particular, the RCMP use a variety of technologies in conducting investigations more generally. In this section, we focus on two of them: social media platforms and DNA collection programs.

The RCMP uses social media to raise public awareness and open a new space for tips related to unsolved cases. Whether technologically powered investigative tools such as the RCMP's #MMIW campaign will yield results in terms of locating missing women or solving unresolved murders remains to be seen (Tucker, 2015).[20] However, it has become an online point for raising awareness of the crisis, including commentary on pre-inquiry consultations (Tucker, 2015). Moreover, these sorts of initiatives could act as a signal to missing Indigenous girls and young women that they are important, which was a priority identified by front-line workers interviewed by the NWAC in 2014 (NWAC, 2014, pp. 54–55).

Specialized RCMP units across Canada have started to use DNA technology and voluntary DNA collection programs to investigate violence against Indigenous women and girls. Some DNA collection programs target vulnerable women themselves. For example, the Alberta RCMP's Project KARE was established in 2003 in response to unsolved murders in the Edmonton area (Alberta RCMP, 2015; Edmonton Journal, 2008; Ferris, 2014, p. 75; Who Cares, 2012). The RCMP's KARE/Pro-Active Team actively solicits hair samples, next-of-kin information, and other personal data from women it describes as being engaged in "vulnerable lifestyles" (Alberta RCMP, 2015). Many of the women enrolled with Project KARE are street-level sex workers who are recruited on strolls. Targeted women provide their DNA samples and personal information to plainclothes police teams in unmarked vans. Field officers build trust with project participants, offering women water and condoms and providing information about support services in the community. All women enrolled with Project KARE must sign a consent form that states that collected data will only be used to identify bodily remains or investigate crimes where the registrant has been victimized (Who Cares, 2012, 00h:13m:10s). These privacy assurances have likely contributed to Project KARE's high enrollment rates. Nonetheless, as Corporal Joe Verhaeghe of Alberta's Project KARE acknowledges in a documentary entitled *Who Cares*, proactive DNA collection "provides the police with information should [women] go missing.... but does not make them safer" (Who Cares, 2012, 01h:15m:10s).

RCMP units also collect voluntary DNA samples to assess and exonerate suspects in criminal investigations of violence against Indigenous women and girls (CBC News, 2013; Matas, 2011). For example, following the sexual assault and murder of 11-year-old Teresa Robinson, RCMP investigators requested DNA samples from all men living on the remote Garden Hill First Nations reserve in northeastern Manitoba (CBC News, 2016). Officers expected to register about 2,000 Indigenous men and boys aged 15–66 as part of the ongoing Garden Hill investigation. The project is the largest voluntary DNA collection operation in Manitoba and, when conducted, was estimated to be the largest voluntary DNA collection project conducted by the RCMP nationwide (Globe & Mail, 2016).

While voluntary DNA collection aids criminal investigations and can offer closure to grieving families, collection programs do not address the root causes of violence against Indigenous women and girls such as colonialism, misogyny, and racism. Furthermore, such programs divert attention away from harmful colonial practices by the state and the responsibility of the state to end violence against Indigenous women and girls. In this regard, Andrea Smith's (2015) description of the state's response to violence in native communities in the United States seems apt:

> [U]nder the guise of colonial paternalism, the state deems it necessary to carefully monitor and surveil the violence within native communities in order to once again save native peoples from themselves. Of course, in this constant "seeing" of violence within native communities, the state hides from view the fact that most such violence is a direct result of state policy. What must not get seen is the inherent violence of the state itself. (p. 30)[21]

Moreover, voluntary DNA collection programs raise important questions about the appropriate balance between police investigatory powers and the privacy rights of marginalized community members. The technological externalities of these programs merit critical evaluation (Magnet, 2011, p. 18). Further inquiry and RCMP transparency around these and other issues will be critical so long as voluntary DNA collection remains part of the RCMP's strategy for investigating violence against Indigenous women and girls.

Conclusion and Questions for Consideration

Digital communications technologies, such as the internet, interact with other socio-cultural and historical forces in ways that expose Indigenous women and girls to vulnerabilities recognized as the root causes of the missing and murdered Indigenous women crisis in Canada. While these and other technologies can be used as tools for addressing the crisis and the root causes underlying it, and for enhancing public access to the inquiry, they also raise serious issues related to the dignity and privacy of Indigenous women and girls and their communities that must also be taken into account. Most importantly, any analysis of, and response to, technology's impact on this crisis must recognize the interlocking effects of racism, sexism, and colonialism in the lives of Indigenous women and girls as well as the state's role in perpetuating this violence and its responsibility to end it.

To this end, questions that the inquiry might consider include:

- how are digital communications technologies being used to facilitate sexual trafficking of Indigenous girls and women, to disseminate violent pornography, and to distribute online hate and harassment aimed at Indigenous women and girls;
- how are internet service providers responding to these uses of their platforms and services;
- are the *Criminal Code* prohibitions on advertising the sexual services of others being enforced and, if so, how often and against whom;
- what further steps can be taken to diminish the use of digital communications technologies for these purposes;

- how can digital communications technologies be harnessed for the purposes of raising public awareness, education, and privacy-respectful investigation;
- how can the impending inquiry make use of digital communications technologies to expand access to its goals, processes, and results; and,
- with respect to the mass collection of DNA by law enforcement authorities:
    - should voluntary DNA collection remain part of the law enforcement strategy in investigating violence against Indigenous women and girls;
    - are voluntary DNA dragnets an effective investigation tool or do they detract resources from more community-respecting policing strategies better deserving of public trust (Vonn, n.d.);
    - how might voluntary DNA collection affect registrants in the future as the role and value of biometric data changes in Canada;
    - what safeguards are in place to prevent DNA and personal data from being mishandled or used in unrelated RCMP investigations[22]; and
    - how robust are consent provisions and how can subjects remove their data from RCMP indices?[23]

Notes

1. We have chosen to use the term "Indigenous women and girls" in this article to refer to women and girls who are part of the first peoples in Canada, including First Nations, the Inuit, and the Métis. Some research refers to Aboriginal women and girls, and where we quote from such research, we maintain these terms.
2. The RCMP statistics focus only on police-reported incidents. A lack of record keeping means that concrete statistics are difficult to find.
3. Article 3(a) of the Protocol to Prevent, Suppress and Punish Trafficking in Persons defines trafficking in persons as "the recruitment, transportation, transfer, harboring, or receipt of persons, by means of threat or use of force or other forms of coercion, of abduction or fraud, of deception, of abuse of power of a position of vulnerability or of the giving or receiving of benefits to achieve the consent of a person having control over other persons, for the purpose of exploitation," including sexual exploitation, forced labor, and slavery.
4. Thanks to an anonymous peer reviewer for this eloquent way of expressing this concern.
5. As Wajcman (2009) notes, "During the late nineteenth century, mechanical and civil engineering increasingly came to define what technology is, diminishing the significance of both artefacts and forms of knowledge associated with women. This was the result of the rise of engineers as an elite with exclusive rights to technical expertise" (p. 144). See also Oldenziel (2001), stating "What counts as technology or who is to be considered a technologist goes to the heart of contemporary feminist inquiry" (p. 128).
6. See e.g., Articles 1–2 of the *Declaration on the Elimination of All Forms of Violence against Women* (UN GAOR, 1993), which defines violence against women (VAW) to mean "any act of violence that results in, or is likely to result in, physical, sexual or psychological harm or suffering to women, including threats of such acts,

coercion or arbitrary deprivations of liberty, whether occurring in public or private life" and includes "physical, sexual and psychological violence within the family; child sexual abuse; dowry-related violence; marital rape; female genital mutilation; rape and sexual abuse; sexual harassment in the workplace and educational institutions; trafficking in women; and forced prostitution."

7. The provision makes it an offense to "knowingly [advertise] an offer to provide sexual services for consideration," although those who advertise their own services are immune from prosecution. While Department of Justice (2015) states it applies to intermediaries, Adam (2015) suggests that its application to a dating site is unclear.
8. For general discussions of technology company responsibility in relation to technology-facilitated violence, see Henry and Witt, this volume.
9. But for discussion of whether or not this incentive is based on a legitimate infringement claim, see Geist (2015).
10. NWAC (2014) refers to low self-esteem as one factor increasing vulnerability to trafficking, a factor compounded for Indigenous women and girls by poverty, lack of education, and colonial practices. For a general discussion of poly-victimization in the context of violence against women, see Broadbent & Thompson, this volume.
11. "Widespread use of the term 'cyberbullying' to describe a remarkable variety of situations and behaviours risks obscuring fundamental differences between those situations and behaviours. In particular, its application to situations of sexual, racial and other forms of online harassment can too easily eclipse underlying systemic structures of discrimination that expose members of particular groups to attack and violence" (Bailey, 2014, p. 663, n 2).
12. While Aboriginal women and men make up only around 3 percent of the adult population in Canada, in 2008–2009, 35% of women admitted to custody identified as an Aboriginal person. In the same year, Aboriginal girls accounted for 44% of admissions to open or secure custody and 34% of admissions to remand (Statistics Canada, 2011, pp. 36–37).
13. For further examples of the potentially positive role, technology can play in addressing violence against women and girls, see Harris & Woodlock, this volume; Lopes Gomes Pinto Ferreira, this volume; and Louie, this volume.
14. See e.g., Children of the Street Society http://www.childrenofthestreet.com.
15. See e.g., MediaSmarts, "Common Portrayals of Aboriginal People" http://mediasmarts.ca/diversity-media/aboriginal-people/common-portrayals-aboriginal-people.
16. See e.g., Youth Against Violence Line http://www.youthagainstviolenceline.com.
17. See e.g., Native Youth Sexual Health Network http://www.nativeyouthsexualhealth.com.
18. See e.g., Native Canadian Center of Toronto http://ncct.on.ca; Native Women's Association of Canada http://www.nwac.ca; Pauktuuitit: Inuit Women Canada http://pauktuutit.ca.
19. Digital technologies and platforms were in fact employed in a variety of ways by the National Inquiry during its hearings (NIMMIWG, 2019).
20. See #MMIW, Twitter https://twitter.com/hashtag/mmiw?ref_src=twsrc%5Egoogle%7Ctwcamp%5Eserp%7Ctwgr%5Ehashtag.

21. Since the original publication of the article reproduced in this chapter, we have become aware of controversy surrounding false claims to Cherokee heritage made by Andrea Smith. We mean no disrespect by including this quotation from Smith's work, which so precisely describes the situation we are attempting to address with respect to police use of DNA technology. We apologize for any hurt inclusion of this quotation may cause.
22. See Economic Action Plan, 2014 (creating five new DNA indices within the National DNA Data Bank for missing persons investigations and other humanitarian causes); Ducette, 2015 (reporting that a voluntary donors index (VDI) could launch as early as the spring of 2017); Public Safety Canada, 2014 (indicating that new DNA indices, including the VDI, would be subject to enhanced review and oversight procedures). In the meantime, it remains unclear where and how voluntarily provided DNA samples are currently indexed and stored.
23. See Rondinelli, 2003 (noting those who opt-out of voluntary DNA testing may have their genetic information nonetheless "covertly obtained by authorities," potentially by testing abandoned items, such as discarded food and coffee cups, for residual DNA (p. 24)); Vonn, n.d. (this "DNA dragnet catch-22" may undermine consent provisions of voluntary DNA collection programs and prevent subjects from meaningfully opting out).

References

Adam, A. (2015). Seeking arrangement: Is it a form of prostitution? *Global News*. January 27. Retrieved from http://globalnews.ca/news/1796393/seeking-arrangement-is-it-a-form-of-prostitution

Alberta RCMP. (2015, April 24). KARE/Pro-Active team. Ottawa, ON: RCMP. Retrieved from http://www.rcmp-grc.gc.ca/ab/community-communaute/mis-dis/kare/index-eng.htm

Amnesty International. (2004). Stolen sisters: A human rights response to discrimination and violence against Indigenous women in Canada. Retrieved from https://www.amnesty.ca/sites/default/files/amr200032004enstolensisters.pdf

Angus, C. (2013). Taking on the Trolls: Why the Online Race-Hatred Against First Nations? *Huffington Post*. July 16. Retrieved from http://www.huffingtonpost.ca/charlie-angus/aboriginal-online-commenters-_b_3600686.html

Association for Progressive Communications (APC). (2015). *Women's rights programme, technology-related Violence against women: A briefing paper*. Melville, APC. Retrieved from https://www.apc.org/en/system/files/HRC%2029%20VAW%20a%20briefing%20paper_FINAL_June%202015.pdf

Bailey, J. (2007). Confronting collective harm: Technology's transformative impact on child pornography. *University of New Brunswick Law Journal*, 5665.

Bailey, J. (2010). Twenty years later *Taylor* still has it right: Section 13 of the *CHRA*'s continuing contribution to equality. In S. McIntyre, & S. Rodgers (Eds.), *The Supreme Court of Canada and social justice: Commitment, retrenchment or retreat* (pp. 1–39). Markham, ON: Supreme Court Law Review & LexisNexis Canada.

Bailey, J. (2013). "Sexualized online bullying" through an equality lens: Missed opportunity in *AB v. Bragg*?. *McGill Law Journal*, *59*(3), 709.

Bailey, J. (2014). Time to unpack the juggernaut?: Reflections on the Canadian federal parliamentary debates on 'cyberbullying'. *Dalhousie Law Journal*, *37*(2), 61.

Bailey, J. (2015). A perfect storm: How the online environment, social norms and law constrain girls' online lives. In J. Bailey, & V. Steeves (Eds.), *eGirls, eCitizens: Putting technology, theory and policy into dialogue with girls' and young women's voices* (pp. 21–53). Ottawa, ON: University of Ottawa Press.

Bailey, J., Burkell, J., & Reynolds, G. (2013). Access to justice for all: Towards an 'Expansive Vision' of justice and technology, *The Windsor Yearbook of Access to Justice*, *31*(2), 181. Retrieved from http://ojs.uwindsor.ca/ojs/leddy/index.php/WYAJ/article/view/4419/3623

Barrera, J. (2019). *National inquiry calls murders and disappearances of Indigenous women a 'Canadian genocide'*. May 31. Retrieved from https://www.rcinet.ca/eye-on-the-arctic/2019/05/31/indigenous-women-canada-report-mmiwg/

BC Ministry of Public Safety and Solicitor General. (2011). *Stopping the sexual exploitation of children and youth*. Vancouver, BC: Victim Services and Crime Prevention. Retrieved from http://www2.gov.bc.ca/assets/gov/public-safety-and-emergency-services/crime-prevention/community-crime-prevention/publications/crime-prev-series2-sexual-exploitation-children-youth.pdf

Brownlee, K., Martin, J., Rawana, E., Harper, J., Mercier, M., Raymond, N., & Friesen, A. (2014). Bullying behaviour and victimization among aboriginal students within northwestern Ontario, *First Peoples Child and Family Review*, *9*(1), 38. Retrieved from http://journals.sfu.ca/fpcfr/index.php/FPCFR/article/view/225/215

Burkell, J., & Saginur, M. (2015). "She's just a small town girl, living in an online world": Differences and similarities between urban and rural girls' use of and views about online social networking. In J. Bailey, & V. Steeves (Eds.), *eGirls, eCitizens: Putting technology, theory and policy into dialogue with girls' and young women's voices* (pp. 129–152). Ottawa, ON: University of Ottawa Press.

Caltabiano, N., & Torre, S. (2013). Cyber-racism in schools. In N. Gopalkrishnan, & H. Babacan (Eds.), *Realities of Culture, colour and identity: Conference proceedings of the third international conference on racisms in the new world order, Cairns* (pp. 30–39). James Cook University, Cairns.

Canadian Centre for Child Protection (a). (n.d.). CCAICE. Cybertip.ca. Retrieved from https://www.cybertip.ca/app/en/projects-ccaice

Canadian Centre for Child Protection (b). (n.d.). Cleanfeed Canada. Cybertip.ca. Retrieved from https://www.cybertip.ca/app/en/projects-cleanfeed

Canadian Women's Foundation. (2014). Fact sheet: Moving women out of violence. Retrieved from http://www.canadianwomen.org/sites/canadianwomen.org/files/FactSheet-StopViolence-ACTIVE%20-%20May2015.pdf

Carlson, B., Farrelly, T., Ryan, F., & Borthwick, F. (2015). Mediating tragedy: Facebook, aboriginal peoples and suicide. *Australasian Journal of Information Systems*. *19*(1). Retrieved from http://ro.uow.edu.au/cgi/viewcontent.cgi?article=3222&context=lhapapers

CBC News. (2013). OPP accused of racially profiling Caribbean migrant workers, December 12. Retrieved from http://www.cbc.ca/news/canada/windsor/opp-accused-of-racially-profiling-caribbean-migrant-workers-1.2461844

CBC News. (2015). Victoria sexting teen given conditional discharge, April 27. Retrieved from http://www.cbc.ca/news/canada/british-columbia/victoria-sexting-teen-given-conditional-discharge-1.3050679

CBC News. (2016). Human rights advocate slams collection of DNA samples from men. *Boys in Manitoba First Nation*, February 4. Retrieved from http://www.cbc.ca/news/canada/manitoba/teresa-robinson-homicide-dna-samples-1.3433271

Chapin, A. (2015). CBC's racist comment sections spark debate over Canada's prejudice problem. *The Guardian*, December 4. Retrieved from http://www.theguardian.com/world/2015/dec/04/cbc-racist-comment-section-canada-prejudice-indigenous-people

Cole, Y. (2010). Marginalized Voices in a changing media environment: An analysis of aboriginal news strategies. MA thesis, Faculty of Public Affairs, Carleton University. Retrieved from https://curve.carleton.ca/system/files/etd/7cc5254e-0c57-4f5f-9c3d-905e600851d4/etd_pdf/4435774a5cd7a17fda86757be69dc99c/cole-marginalizedvoicesinachangingmediaenvironment.pdf[unpublished]

Copyright Modernization Act, SC 2012, c 20.

Criminal Code, RSC 1985, c C-45.

Deer, S. (2009). Decolonizing rape law: A native feminist synthesis of safety and sovereignty. *Wicazo Sa Review*, *24*(2), 149–167.

Department of Justice. (2015). Prostitution Criminal Law Reform: Bill C-36, the Protection of Communities and Exploited Persons Act: In force as of 6 December 2014 fact sheet. Ottawa, ON: Department of Justice. Retrieved from http://www.justice.gc.ca/eng/rp-pr/other-autre/c36fs_fi

Dines, G. (2013). How porn creates the John: Porn, trafficking and the social construction of masculinity. Unpublished. Lecture delivered at National Task Force on Trafficking of Women and Girls, Ottawa, November 19, 2013.

Ducette, J. (2015). Hope on the horizon: New DNA tools to support missing persons cases. *Gazette*, 77, p. 2. Retrieved from http://www.rcmp-grc.gc.ca/en/gazette/hope-horizon

Economic Action Plan 2014 Act No 2, SC 2014, c 39, s 232, Amending DNA Identification Act, SC 1998, c 37.

Edmonton Journal. (2008). Police want to expand DNA database. *Edmonton Journal*, June 30. Retrieved from http://www.canada.com/story_print.html?id=58e29be0-a94a-4d74-a663-25c5ac2d40ab

Estable, A. & Meyer, M. (2015). *Project shift: Needs assessment summary*. Toronto, ON: YWCA Canada. Retrieved from http://ywcacanada.ca/data/documents/00000460.pdf

Fairbairn, J. (2015). Rape threats and revenge porn: Defining sexual violence in the digital age. In J. Bailey, & V. Steeves (Eds.), *eGirls, eCitizens: Putting technology, theory and policy into dialogue with girls' and young women's voices* (pp. 229–252). Ottawa. ON: University of Ottawa Press.

Fairbairn, J., Bivens, R., & Dawson, M. (2013). *Sexual violence and social media: Building a Framework for prevention*. Ottawa, ON: Crime Prevention Ottawa & Ottawa Coalition to End Violence Against Women. Retrieved from http://www.octevaw-cocvff.ca/sites/default/files/pdf/sexual-violence-and-social-media.pdf

Fairbairn, J., & Black, D. (2015). *Cyberviolence against women & girls*. Ottawa. ON: Ottawa Coalition to End Violence Against Women. Retrieved from http://www.octevaw-cocvff.ca/sites/default/files/CyberViolenceReport_OCTEVAW.pdf

Ferris, S. (2014). *Street sex work and Canadian cities: Resisting a dangerous order*. Edmonton, AB: University of Alberta Press.

First Nations Technology Council (FNTC). (2015). Technology Council Annual Report 2014/2015. Vancouver, BC: FNTC. Retrieved from http://2015annualreport.technologycouncil.ca

Geist, M. (2015). The copyright notice flood: What to consider if you receive a copyright infringement notification. Michael Geist (blog), April 13. Retrieved from http://www.michaelgeist.ca/2015/04/the-copyright-notice-flood-what-to-consider-if-you-receive-a-copyright-infringement-notification

Globe & Mail. (2016). RCMP conduct huge DNA sweep in Manitoba in attempt to solve homicide. *Canadian Press*, February 9. Retrieved from http://www.theglobeandmail.com/news/national/rcmp-conduct-huge-dna-sweep-in-manitoba-in-attempt-to-solve-homicide/article28675233

Government of Ontario. (2015). *It's never okay: An action Plan to stop sexual Violence and harassment*. Toronto, ON: Queen's Printer for Ontario. Retrieved from https://dr6j45jk9xcmk.cloudfront.net/documents/4170/actionplan-itsneverokay.pdf

Haraway, D., & Goodeve, T. (1999). *How like a leaf: An interview with Donna Haraway*. New York, NY: Routledge.

Hill Collins, P. (2001). Moving beyond gender: Intersectionality and scientific knowledge. In M. M. Ferree, J. Lorber, & B. Hess (Eds.), *Revisioning gender* (pp. 261–284). Walnut Creek, CA: AltaMira Press.

INCITE! (n.d.). Dangerous intersections. Retrieved from https://incite-national.org/dangerous-intersections/

Jiwani, Y., & Young, M. L. (2006). Missing and murdered women: Reproducing marginality in discourse. *Canadian Journal of Communication*, *31*(4), 895.

Magnet, S. (2011). *When biometrics fail*. Durham, NC: Duke University Press.

Mason, C., & Magnet, S. (2012). Surveillance studies and violence against women. *Surveillance and Society*, *10*, 2–105.

Matas, R. (2011). RCMP demand DNA from Prince George Cab drivers. *Globe and Mail*, February 15. Retrieved from http://www.theglobeandmail.com/news/british-columbia/rcmp-demand-dna-from-prince-george-cab-drivers/article566486

MediaSmarts. (n.d.). Media portrayals of missing and murdered aboriginal women. Retrieved from http://mediasmarts.ca/diversity-media/aboriginal-people/media-portrayals-missing-and-murdered-aboriginal-women

National Inquiry into Missing and Murdered Indigenous Women and Girls. (2019). Reclaiming power and place: The final report of the national inquiry into missing and murdered Indigenous women and girls. Retrieved from https://www.mmiwg-ffada.ca/final-report/

Native Women's Association of Canada (NWAC) (2014). Sexual exploitation and trafficking of aboriginal women and girls: Literature review and key informant interviews: Final report. Ottawa, ON: NWAC. Retrieved from http://www.nwac.ca/wp-content/uploads/2015/05/2014_NWAC_Human_Trafficking_and_Sexual_Exploitation_Report.pdf

Oboler, A. (2012). Aboriginal memes & online hate report. Melbourne: Online Hate Prevention Institute. Retrieved from http://ohpi.org.au/reports/IR12-2-Aboriginal-Memes.pdf

Office of Consumer Affairs. (2015). *Notice and notice regime*. Ottawa, ON: Industry Canada. Retrieved from http://www.ic.gc.ca/eic/site/oca-bc.nsf/eng/ca02920.html

Oldenziel, R. (2001). Man the maker, woman the consumer: The conjunction junction revisited. In A. Creager, E. Lunbeck, & Londa Schiebingereds (Eds.), *Feminism in twentieth century science, technology, and medicine* (pp. 128–148). Chicago, IL: Chicago University Press.

Palmater, P. (2016). Shining light on the dark places: Addressing police racism and sexualized violence against Indigenous women and girls in the national inquiry. *Canadian Journal of Women and the Law*, *28*, 253.

Public Safety Canada. (2014, October 27). *Protecting privacy rights*. Ottawa, ON: PSC. Retrieved from http://news.gc.ca/web/article-en.do?nid=897099

Rabson, M. (2019). *Five things about the inquiry on murdered and missing Indigenous women and girls*. June 3. Retrieved from https://www.theglobeandmail.com/canada/article-five-things-about-the-inquiry-on-murdered-and-missing-indigenous-women-2/

Razack, S. (2000). Gendered racial violence and spatialized justice: The murder of Pamela George. *Canadian Journal of Law and Society*, *15*(2), 91.

Rifkin, M. (2011). *When did Indians become straight? Kinship, the history of sexuality, and native sovereignty*. London: Oxford University Press.

Rondinelli, V. (2003). The DNA dragnet: A modern day salem witch hunt. Criminal Reports (6th) *10*, 16.

Roos, H. (2013). Phase I: Service and capacity review for victims of sexual exploitation and human trafficking in Nunavut: Final report. Iqaluit, NU: Roos-Remillard Consulting Services. Retrieved from http://www.millennia2015.org/files/forms/306013894_0.5864069/Victims_of_sexual_exploitation.pdf

Royal Canadian Mounted Police (RCMP). (2014). *Missing and murdered aboriginal women: A national operational overview*. Catalogue no PS64-115/2014E-PDF. (focused only on police-reported incidents). Ottawa, ON: RCMP. Retrieved from http://www.rcmp-grc.gc.ca/pubs/mmaw-faapd-eng.pdf

Safety Net Canada. (2013a). Technology misuse and violence against women: Survey. Retrieved from http://bcsth.ca/sites/default/files/SNC/SNC_TechMisuse-Infograph2013-English.pdf

Safety Net Canada. (2013b). *Assessing technology in the context of violence against women & children: Examining benefits & risks*. Vancouver, BC: Safety Net Canada. Retrieved from http://www.bcsth.ca/sites/default/files/SNC/SNC_AssessingTech-VAWC-ES-2013.pdf

Sethi, A. (2007). Domestic sex trafficking of aboriginal girls in Canada: Issues and implications. *First Peoples Child and Family Review*, *3*(3), 57. Retrieved from http://journals.sfu.ca/fpcfr/index.php/FPCFR/article/view/50/88

Simpson, A. (2014). *Mohawk interruptus: Political life across the borders of settler states*. Durham, NC: Duke University Press.

Smith, A. (2015). Not-Seeing: State surveillance, settler colonialism, and gender violence. In R. Dubrofsky, & S. Magnet (Eds.), *Feminist surveillance studies* (pp. 21–38). Durham, NC: Duke University Press.

Southworth, Cindy. (2005). *A high-tech Twist on abuse: Technology, intimate partner stalking, and advocacy*. Saint Paul, MN: Violence Against Women Online Resources. Retrieved from http://www.mincava.umn.edu/documents/commissioned/stalkingandtech/stalkingandtech.pdf

Statistics Canada. (2011, April). Women and the criminal justice system. In T. H. Mahony (Ed.), *Catalogue no 89-503-X*. Ottawa, ON: Statistics Canada. Retrieved from http://www.statcan.gc.ca/pub/89-503-x/2010001/article/11416-eng.pdf

Status of Women Canada (SWC). (2013). *Cyber and sexual violence: Helping communities respond*. Ottawa, ON: SWC. Retrieved from http://www.swc-cfc.gc.ca/fun-fin/cfp-adp/2013-2/t1-eng.html

Steeves, V. (2015). "Pretty and just a little bit sexy I guess": Publicity, privacy and the pressure to perform 'appropriate' femininity in social media. In J. Bailey, & V. Steeves (Eds.), *eGirls, eCitizens: Putting technology, theory and policy into dialogue with girls' and young women's voices*. (pp. 153–174). Ottawa, ON: University of Ottawa Press.

Stillman, S. (2016). The list: When juveniles are found guilty of sexual misconduct, the sex-offender registry can be a life sentence, *The New Yorker*, March 14. Retrieved from http://www.newyorker.com/magazine/2016/03/14/when-kids-are-accused-of-sex-crimes

Subramaniam, B. (2003). A conversation on feminist science studies. *Signs*, *28*(3), 923.

Tankard Reist, M. (2016). Growing up in pornland: Girls have had it with porn conditioned boys. *ABC Religion and Ethics*, April 7. Retrieved from http://www.abc.net.au/religion/articles/2016/03/07/4420147.htm

Thorn, A. (2015). Report on the use of technology to recruit, Groom and sell domestic minor sex trafficking victims. Los Angeles, CA: Digital Defenders of Children. Retrieved from https://2715111qnwey246mkc1vzqg0-wpengine.netdna-ssl.com/wp-content/uploads/2015/02/Survivor_Survey_r5.pdf

Tucker, E. (2015). RCMP #MMIW campaign aims to bring home Canada's missing aboriginal women. *Global News*, October 8. Retrieved from http://globalnews.ca/news/2264152/rcmp-mmiw-campaign-aims-to-bring-home-canadas-missing-aboriginal-women

United Nations GAOR. (1993). Declaration on the elimination of all forms of violence against women. GA Res 48/104, 48th Sess, UN Doc A/RES/48/104. UNGAOR. Retrieved from https://documents-dds-ny.un.org/doc/UNDOC/GEN/N94/095/05/PDF/N9409505.pdf

United Nations GAOR. (2000). Protocol to prevent, Suppress and punish Trafficking in persons, especially Women and children, Supplementing the united Nations Convention against transnational organized crime. 55th Sess, Annex II, Agenda Item 2, UN Doc A/AC.254/34. UNGAOR. Retrieved from https://www.unodc.org/documents/treaties/UNTOC/Publications/TOC%20Convention/TOCebook-e.pdf

United Nations (UN), Committee on the Elimination of Discrimination against Women (CEDAW). (2015). Report of the inquiry concerning Canada of the CEDAW under article 8 of the optional protocol to the convention on the elimination of all forms of discrimination against women, UN Doc C/OP.8/CAN/1. CEDAW. Retrieved from http://tbinternet.ohchr.org/Treaties/CEDAW/Shared%20Documents/CAN/CEDAW_C_OP-8_CAN_1_7643_E.pdf

Vonn, M. (n.d.). Can a DNA dragnet undermine an investigation? A case study in Canada. *Forensic Genetics Policy Initiative*. Retrieved from http://dnapolicyinitiative.org/genewatch-forensic-dna/can-a-dna-dragnet-undermine-an-investigation-a-case-study-in-canada

Wajcman, J. (2009). Feminist theories of technology. *Cambridge Journal of Economics*, *34*(1), 143.

Ward, D. (2019). *Metis National Council says it's been left out of the national inquiry process and final report plans*. June 2. Retrieved from https://www.aptnnews.ca/national-news/metis-national-council-says-its-been-left-out-of-the-national-inquiry-process-and-final-report-plans/

Warman v Kouba. (2006). CHRT 50 (CanLII).

Warman v Western Canada for Us and Bahr (2006). CHRT 52 (CanLII).

West Coast Legal Education and Action Fund (LEAF). (2014). *#CyberMisogyny: Using and strengthening Canadian legal Responses to gendered Hate and harassment online*. Vancouver, BC: West Coast LEAF. Retrieved from http://www.westcoastleaf.org/wp-content/uploads/2014/10/2014-REPORT-CyberMisogyny.pdf

Who Cares. (2012). *DVD*. Edmonton, AB: National Film Board of Canada. Retrieved from https://vimeo.com/channels/1055773/140844739

Chapter 8

Attending to Difference in Indigenous People's Experiences of Cyberbullying: Toward a Research Agenda

Bronwyn Carlson and Ryan Frazer

Abstract

Broadly understood as repeated, intentional, and aggressive behaviors facilitated by digital technologies, cyberbullying has been identified as a significant public health concern in Australia. However, there have been critical debates about the theoretical and methodological assumptions of cyberbullying research. On the whole, this research has demonstrated an aversion to accounting for context, difference, and complexity. This insensitivity to difference is evident in the absence of nuanced accounts of Indigenous people's experiences of cyberbullying. In this chapter, we extend recent critiques of dominant approaches to cyberbullying research and argue for novel theoretical and methodological engagements with Indigenous people's experiences of cyberbullying. We review a range of literature that unpacks the many ways that social, cultural, and political life is different for Indigenous peoples. More specifically, we demonstrate there are good reasons to assume that online conflict is different for Indigenous peoples, due to diverse cultural practices and the broader political context of settler-colonialism. We argue that the standardization of scholarly approaches to cyberbullying is delimiting its ability to attend to social difference in online conflict, and we join calls for more theoretically rigorous, targeted, difference-sensitive studies into bullying.

Keywords: Indigenous; cyberbullying; social media; bullying; technology; violence

The Emerald International Handbook of Technology-Facilitated Violence and Abuse, 145–163

doi:10.1108/978-1-83982-848-520211008

Introduction

While new social technologies bring many benefits, they also "offer powerful, yet potentially damaging ways for young people to communicate and respond" (Nilan, Burgess, Hobbs, Threadgold, & Alexander, 2015, p. 2). Broadly understood as repeated, intentional aggressive behaviors facilitated by digital technology platforms, cyberbullying has emerged as one of the most prominent forms of digitally mediated harm. While often considered an extension of "traditional" forms of schoolyard bullying, cyberbullying has attracted additional concern because of the unique affordances of digital technologies. For example, in the online context, bullying can be enacted anonymously, producing a "disinhibition effect" on perpetrators (Walker, Craven, & Tokunga, 2013); it has been described as "non-stop bullying", in that it can pervade the previously "safe space" of the home (Mishna, Saini, & Solomon, 2009, p. 1224); and it can attract much larger audiences through connecting with extensive online networks.

Cyberbullying has recently been identified as a significant public health concern in Australia. A major 2014 report for the Australian Government Department of Communications concluded that some 20% of 8–17-year-olds experienced cyberbullying in the previous year (Spears, Keeley, Bates, & Katz, 2014, p. 2). A report by youth health organization ReachOut Australia (2018) found 380,000 young Australians were victims of cyberbullying in 2018. And a recent national survey found that 39% of Australians have experienced some form of cyber-hatred and violence, and that it has cost the Australian economy an estimated $3.7 billion (Australia Institute, 2019). Cyberbullying has been linked to a range of negative health outcomes, most seriously in the forms of depression, anxiety, and suicide ideation (Shohoudi Mojdehi, Leduc, Shohoudi Mojdehi, & Talwar, 2019). There are also significant social consequences, with victims and perpetrators being more likely to truant school, take leave from employment, and experience social estrangement more generally. Accordingly, cyberbullying has attracted significant attention from researchers, who have sought to accurately measure the rates, effects, and possible preventative measures of cyberbullying.

Recently, however, there have been critical debates about the theoretical and methodological assumptions of cyberbullying research. On the whole, this research has demonstrated an aversion to accounting for context, difference, and complexity. On one hand, there have been concerns that particular approaches to studying cyberbullying have become standardized and canonized, and their disciplinary histories and theoretical assumptions have become obscured in the process. A central issue has hinged on whether the concept of "cyberbullying" itself requires a clear, unambiguous, and consistently applied definition or whether it is too varied a social phenomenon to be fixed in such a way. On the other hand, cyberbullying researchers have tended to overlook important markers of social difference, generally conducting large-scale quantitative research that assumes a homogeneous, normalized, white subject; or, at best, differentiating participants only by age and binary sex.

This insensitivity to difference is evident in the absence of nuanced accounts of Indigenous people's experiences of cyberbullying, both in Australia and globally (Carlson & Frazer, 2018b). Internet technologies have been taken up enthusiastically by Indigenous peoples across Australia (Carlson & Frazer, 2018b). They have brought great benefits, such as overcoming difficulties in living across geographically distant communities, sustaining informal networks of care and support, and connecting with crucial knowledge, events, and opportunities. Researchers have shown these technologies are used in highly culturally specific ways, with a clear continuity between offline and online cultures (Carlson & Frazer, 2015).

However, they also present new dangers to Indigenous people's physical, emotional, and cultural safety. The rapid uptake of mobile technologies has seen, as noted by Indigenous scholar Peter Radoll (2012), "an increase in cyber-safety issues" (p. 11) in Indigenous communities – including exposure to racist violence, identity theft, and appropriation of sensitive cultural knowledge. Significantly, there is also evidence that, like many other minority groups, Indigenous peoples are disproportionately affected by cyberbullying (Kral, 2014, p. 181). Despite this, research to date has largely overlooked Indigenous people's experiences of cyberbullying. The small body of available research specifically on Indigenous cyberbullying – in Canada (Broll, Dunlop, & Crooks, 2018; Brownlee et al., 2014; Mobin, Feng, & Neudorf, 2017), the US (Samulski, 2014), and Australia (Carlson & Frazer, 2018a; Radoll, 2012; Vaarzon-Morel, 2014) – has yielded important insights, particularly in demonstrating that we cannot assume cyberbullying occurs at the same rate, for the same reasons, and with the same impacts, as for non-Indigenous peoples.

In this chapter, we extend recent critiques of dominant approaches to cyberbullying research and argue for novel theoretical and methodological engagements with Indigenous people's experiences of cyberbullying. It is structured in two major sections. In the first section, we unpack some of the major trends in current cyberbullying research, before attending to the growing chorus of critiques from qualitative researchers. We argue that the standardization of scholarly approaches to cyberbullying is delimiting its capacity to attend to social difference in online conflict; and we join calls for more theoretically rigorous, targeted, difference-sensitive studies into bullying.

Following this, in the second section, we review a range of literature that unpacks the many ways in which social, cultural, and political life is different for Indigenous peoples, specifically in relation to social conflict. On the one hand, we argue there are a range of cultural differences that mediate and shape interpersonal interactions, including cultures of kinship, communication, and conflict. On the other hand, we argue that Indigenous people's experiences of being online cannot be meaningfully separated from broader racial politics of settler-colonialism and its manifestation through disadvantage. To be Indigenous online, we argue, is to be already entangled within a violent, conflictual politics – for which research on online conflict has so far failed to account.

Finally, we close by outlining an initial agenda for research on Indigenous people's experiences of cyberbullying. In particular, we argue there are three major blind spots in cyberbullying research: their empirical focus, theoretical framings, and methodological approaches. Understanding cyberbullying as a discursive formation always embedded within a social, cultural, and political milieu, this chapter extends critical approaches to cyberbullying research and advances a politically and culturally nuanced approach to understanding cyberbullying.

Major Trends in Cyberbullying Research

Context-Insensitivity in Cyberbullying Research

Understanding the tensions in cyberbullying research requires an understanding of the academic field's historical and academic roots. To this end, in this first section, we offer a brief overview of the scholarly history of bullying and cyberbullying research, paying attention to its grounding in the field of developmental psychology, before moving on to recent critiques.

Scholarly interest in school bullying first emerged in the 1960s when researchers in Sweden began investigating what was initially called "mobbing" (Olweus, 2013) – broadly understood as repeated schoolyard aggression toward less powerful students. The field expanded significantly over the next few decades, as state and public concern around the possible negative effects of schoolyard bullying intensified. Bullying gradually became accepted as a significant, serious, and widespread public health concern. By and large, bullying research sought to better understand its prevalence and effects and sought to develop effective interventions.

Swedish scholar Dan Olweus has been a central figure in bullying research since the field's establishment. Before Olweus, researchers tended to focus on the broader contextual, group and social factors in bullying (see Canty, Stubbe, Steers, & Collings, 2016 for this academic history). Drawing on ideas from developmental psychology, however, Olweus's work shifted the focus to individual actors, analyzing their psychological traits and behaviors, and de-emphasizing any broader social and cultural context. The aim, for Olweus, was to predict and mitigate pathologically deviant bullying behavior (Canty et al., 2016). Through this work, Olweus (2013) produced the most influential definition of bullying, which is composed of three main criteria: (1) intentional aggressive behavior, (2) that involves an abuse of power, and (3) is repeated over time.

Cyberbullying emerged as a scholarly interest in 2000, where the term became used to describe seemingly new forms of aggressive behavior that were playing out on then-new digital technologies, particularly mobile phones and internet-capable computers. It soon became clear that these technologies had led to an evolution in the nature of peer-to-peer aggression (Hinduja & Patchin, 2010). At that time, there had been a series of high-profile deaths among teens who had experienced severe bullying through these new social technologies, and these events centered public, media, and state attention on these technologies' capacity to facilitate and proliferate harm on youth.

Researchers were quick to translate Olweus's generic conceptualization of "traditional" bullying into this new online context. Cyberbullying became understood "as a form of bullying, in line with other forms, such as verbal, physical and indirect/relational bullying" (Olweus & Limber, 2018, p. 141). While there is some disagreement around its exact definition, Kowalski, Giumetti, Schroeder, and Lattanner (2014) note that scholars generally emphasize four main elements: "(1) intentional aggressive behavior that (2) is carried out repeatedly, (3) occurs between a perpetrator and victim who are unequal in power, and (4) occurs through electronic technologies" (p. 1109). Over time, a more or less standard typology of cyberbullying forms emerged, including flaming, harassment, image-based sexual abuse, outing, exclusion, cyberstalking, and impersonation (Campbell, Cross, Spears, & Slee, 2010; Carlson & Frazer, 2018a; Henry et al., 2020).

Cyberbullying researchers, predominantly with backgrounds in behavioral psychology, health and education, have largely considered a uniform definition both desirable and necessary. Bauman (2015) argues that "research requires a precise and accepted definition that all can use" (p. 23) – what Olweus and Limber (2018) refer to as "concept validity". For these researchers, more or less universal agreement around what constitutes cyberbullying is necessary if we are to, first, measure the rates of cyberbullying perpetration and victimization; second, map rates of change across time, age, and location; and, third, identify effective interventions. By employing increasingly standardized definitions, these researchers have conducted large scale, quantitative, survey-driven studies that have sought validity, replicability, and comparability in cyberbullying research.

However, as we discuss in the following sections, the fast-growing body of cyberbullying research has also attracted significant criticism. In particular, there are disagreements among scholars about what actually constitutes "cyberbullying" and how it is best conceptualized in research. The gradual standardization of cyberbullying research has left it "typically blind to the relational nuances and complexities that characterize cyberbullying" (Nilan et al., 2015, p. 3). And as we will discuss in the chapter's second major section, this blindness is particularly acute when it comes to understanding cyberbullying toward and among Indigenous peoples.

Critiques of the Dominant Approach

While researchers have conducted excellent work in understanding the extent and effects of cyberbullying across a range of contexts, more recently, scholars from outside these more quantitative, positivist fields have posed critical questions around the implicit epistemological and ontological assumptions this research has made about what is, in practice, an extremely complex social phenomenon. The dominant approach – grounded in and inflected by the discipline of developmental psychology – has individualized and homogenized cyberbullying and related forms of online aggression, rather than understanding it as something alive and unstable, something that plays out in overlapping social fields, involving often ontologically ambiguous and differently positioned actors. These more critical researchers, generally from the social sciences, have argued that clear, rigid, axiomatized definitions can obscure the actual lived experiences, ideas, and motivations of people implicated in online conflict.

In this section, we outline four significant problems in dominant academic approaches to cyberbullying research, including (1) the problematic influence of its dominant definition, (2) its implicit assumption of cultural universalism, (3) the reproduction of a perpetrator–victim model, and (4) its implicit moral hierarchy.

The Standardization of Definitions

Over the last 10 years, a body of research has expressed concerns around "the power of prevailing definitions" of cyberbullying in research (Kofoed & Staksrud, 2019); a concern that popular definitions have a problematic influence on how researchers, policymakers, and young people themselves approach the issue. Definitions, as Canty et al. (2016) remind us, "are made not born" (p. 48); they have social, cultural, and academic histories that are often obscured through repeated use. Reflecting on the previous decade of research, Canty et al. (2016) argue that:

> … consistent *a priori* application of [Olweus's] definition has created an aura of authority and temporal stability that obscures its origin and development, its disciplinary paradigm and assumption, and evidence that the term "bullying" has multiple meanings and uses. (p. 48)

Kofoed and Staksrud (2019, p. 1007) heed Canty et al.'s (2016) warning and document the strange side effects of "definitional overlearning" in cyberbullying research, which can occur through anti-bullying efforts to educate children about bullying by providing them with existing models and definitions of bullying. This has produced "some puzzling side effects" (Kofoed & Staksrud, 2019, p. 1011), they observe, such as when students are surveyed and respond by telling researchers their definition is "wrong" because it doesn't match what they've already learnt elsewhere; or when students explain that they aren't "cyberbullying" because they only did it a single time – meaning it doesn't fit the official criteria. Their work demonstrates the ontological and social power definitions can have beyond academic circles, where children are taught the supposedly "right" definition of what constitutes cyberbullying. In these ways, the conventional definition leads to "artificial homogeneity," as Canty et al. (2016, p. 53) explain. Kofoed and Staksrud (2019) suggest current conceptualizations of cyberbullying are "inadequate in addressing the complexities of technologically mediated exclusionary processes" (p. 1007). Real situations, they argue, often exceed conventional understandings.

Difference Blindness and Cultural Imperialism

Second, by relying on a static, three-/four-pronged definition of bullying, which originated within a western social, cultural, and academic context, research has tended to be blind to important markers of social and cultural difference (Bodkin-Andrews, O'Rourke, Dillon, Craven, & Yeung, 2012; Coffin, Larson, & Cross, 2010). On the one hand, despite indications that minority populations experience higher rates of cyberbullying (Llorent, Ortega-Ruiz, & Zych, 2016), research has tended to be demographically limited (Broll et al., 2018; Mobin et al., 2017), focusing mainly on white, urban populations, differentiating research participants only by age and (binary) gender (Brownlee et al., 2014; Kowalski et al., 2014; Mobin et al., 2017). Consequently, it has largely overlooked non-majority populations, including ethnic, cultural, differently-abled, sexual, gender, and religious minorities. Likewise, demographic variables that cut along socioeconomic, geographical (urban, suburban, rural, etc.) and educational (state, private, religious, etc.) lines have also tended to be entirely overlooked.

Cyberbullying research has also tended to be geographically situated within white, majority world contexts – particularly North America and Europe. As Canty et al. (2016) note, "bullying" is a thoroughly Western concept, and correlates don't necessarily exist in other contexts (Smith, del Barrio, & Tokunga, 2015). Shohoudi Mojdehi et al.'s (2019) work has shown that there are significant cultural factors and "moral mechanisms" that shape how individuals experience and make sense of various forms of social conflict – such as differences between more "individualist" and more "collectivist" societies. In this context, Schott (2014) has questioned whether a cross-cultural definition of cyberbullying is even possible. By not acknowledging the social and cultural embeddedness of cyberbullying research, there is a danger of cultural imperialism – where an idea is taken and inappropriately imposed upon other cultural contexts (Canty et al., 2016).

Reified Subject Positions

Third, the dominant model of cyberbullying reifies fixed, individual subject positions. Based on Olweus's influential formulation, bullying is understood as a particular subset of "aggression," which relies on a basic perpetrator–victim binary (Kofoed & Ringrose, 2012). Kofoed and Ringrose (2012) note that in the vast majority of bullying research, then, there are a standard set of relatively fixed subjects: bully, victim, and bystander.

This reification of a standard, inflexible set of subject positions has major consequences for research and practice. As boyd (2014) explains, "by focusing on the perpetrator and protecting the victim, well-intentioned adults often fail to recognize the complexity of most conflicts" (p. 136). The victim–perpetrator dyad can obscure the more ambiguous and unstable elements of the cyberbullying event, overlooking other actors, practices, ideas, and objects involved. It also assumes the involvement only of *individual* actors. Bodkin-Andrews, O'Rourke, Dillon, Craven, and Yeung (2012) write that "most conceptualizations of bullying occur at the level of the individual, with little sensitivity to notions of cultural identity, broader community issues, socioeconomic and historical disadvantage or oppression" (p. 7). This individualist approach precludes the possibility of understanding more collective forms of hatred and bullying; including how social forms of hate – racism, sexism, homophobia, transphobia, ableism, and so on – can be entangled within particular cyberbullying events.

Consequently, rather than assuming a simple perpetrator–victim binary, smaller, more theoretically robust qualitative studies have shown that there are often many differently-positioned and ambivalently-motivated subjects entangled in the event of online conflict (Marwick & boyd, 2014). Things are much messier and more ambiguous and complex than quantitative studies tend to acknowledge.

The Moral Hierarchy

Finally, as Kofoed and Ringrose (2012) note, there is an implicit moral hierarchy baked into standard bullying analysis. The legacy of developmental psychological thinking in cyberbullying research is apparent in how bullying is understood as an individual pathology. The perpetrator–victim model carries moral assumptions: "if bullying is a subset of aggressive behavior, then bullies are aggressors," explains Schott (2014, p. 25). One set of behaviors is understood as "pathological violence," while much other "everyday cruelty" is considered "normal violence" (Ellwood & Davies, 2010; Kofoed & Ringrose, 2012) – and, as Ringrose and Renold (2010) have shown, there are often gendered, racialized, and sexualized aspects to this. There are two key points to be made here.

First, as research has repeatedly demonstrated, there is often a blurring of responsibility in online bullying. In practice, lines of fault and responsibility, the intentions of actors, the existence of violence and abuse are often ambiguous or morally ambivalent (Ellwood & Davies, 2010). In each actual case, it is often not clear who is the aggressor, who is the victim, and who wields power. Indeed, one of the defining marks of cyberbullying is its affordance of deniability – that it is often unclear who the perpetrator was, who "started" it, and what the intention of each actor was (Nilan et al., 2015). Online anonymity confuses clear culpability through plausible deniability – someone can always say it was someone else, or that they didn't "really" mean to hurt them (Mishna et al., 2009).

Second, and more generally, there needs to be a recognition that interpersonal conflict is often a normal and "healthy" part of sociality (boyd, 2014). Thornberg (2011) encourages researchers to look beyond the supposedly "pathological" behaviors of individuals and to instead try to understand bullying as a complex social phenomenon, involving a range of meanings, forces, desires, and practices. The dominant cyberbullying model precludes more nuanced understandings of how power, blame, intention, and agency are embedded within online conflicts. Rather than automatically assuming "bullies" to be bad, pathological, or even criminal actors, moral assumptions about social behaviors need to be understood and carefully contextualized (Shohoudi Mojdehi et al., 2019).

By and large, there appears to be an aversion to difference, complexity, and context in most cyberbullying research. By only taking into account the demographic variables of age and gender – and ignoring all other contextual factors – researchers have tended to produce relatively context-insensitive models of cyberbullying. These largely psychological and sociological studies, often drawing on standardized survey instruments, tend to individualize and homogenize participants, and in doing so, erase the social, cultural, political, and economic contexts in which cyberbullying occurs. The legacy of developmental psychology is one of a standardized, culturally-specific, and context-insensitive model of online conflict. The most critical research outlined above makes clear that there is room for research that thinks differently about cyberbullying, that draws on different understandings of "what counts" as cyberbullying, and is better equipped to attend to difference.

Considering Context in Indigenous People's Experiences of Cyberbullying

With a few important exceptions, Indigenous populations have not received adequate attention in cyberbullying research. This is despite a growing body of evidence that Indigenous peoples experience higher rates of cyberbullying across a diverse range of settler-colonial contexts, including Australia (Kral, 2014; Spears et al., 2014), Canada, and the US (Lemstra, Rogers, Thompson, Moraros, & Tempier, 2011; Samulski, 2014). This is a major shortcoming, as Indigenous peoples constitute a distinct social, cultural, and political population in settler nations, with wide-ranging consequences for how they engage with social media technologies.

In this second major section, we extend the above critiques of cyberbullying research by engaging with work across a range of disciplines – sociology, political economy, media studies, anthropology. Here we build on a literature review we were commissioned to produce by the Aboriginal Health & Medical Research Council of New South Wales, in which we argue that cyberbullying studies have – so far – failed to adequately engage with the cultural and political contexts in which Indigenous people are embedded through online conflict (see Carlson & Frazer, 2018a). On the one hand, we argue that researchers must acknowledge the importance of different cultural, social, and communicative formations in constituting how conflict arises and what role it plays within communities. On the other, we argue that, in understanding cyberbullying, research must attend to the broader context of settler-colonialism. In short, in this section we unpack some ways researchers can engage with the cultural and political contexts in which Indigenous peoples are embedded to better understand their experiences and meanings of cyberbullying.

Following this, in the chapter's final section, we suggest a number of pathways forward for cyberbullying research. We argue that research specifically on, by, and informed by, the ontological and epistemological frames of Indigenous people is needed, if we are to develop effective, relevant interventions for cyberbullying.

The Cultural Context of Cyberbullying

Encompassing hundreds of distinct nations and language groups across Australia, Indigenous populations hold myriad value systems, sets of norms, ontologies, and spiritual beliefs. Against western notions of the rational, discretely-bound and self-made individual, Indigenous ways of being and knowing tend to emphasize relations, connections, and collectivist notions of responsibility (Christie, 2005). These social and cultural differences are not set apart from the use of digital technologies but are entangled complexly within them – affecting both how these technologies can be used and what impact they have on Indigenous peoples and communities. While working to change social relations between people, social media technologies also have continuities with traditional communicative practices. Srinivasan (2013) notes, for instance, that mobile technologies tend to be "translated, adopted, and shaped as they move locally" – an observation that challenges the dominant "top-down" view of technology production and use (p. 207).

As discussed above, however, the vast majority of cyberbullying research is insensitive to these significant cultural contexts. Instead, by assuming a homogeneous – and generally white – population, research tends to ignore, reduce, and strip away these cultural differences. In this section, we draw on our prior research to point toward two key ways in which cultural difference affects online conflict (Carlson & Frazer, 2018a). First, we argue that systems of kinship and cultures of communication shape how Indigenous peoples engage with Internet technologies, which in turn affect the cause and mitigation of cyberbullying. Second, we argue that different peoples have different "cultures of conflict", which affect what is considered aggressive or pathological online behaviors. Thus, we argue, "what counts" as cyberbullying behavior should not be taken for granted by researchers.

Cultures of Kinship and Communication

Despite conflict being an essentially *social* phenomenon, cyberbullying research seldom recognizes that the use of digital communication technologies, such as social media, is a deeply cultural practice that both extends and alters broader social relations (Brownlee et al., 2014; Carlson & Frazer, 2018a; Kowalski et al., 2014). Broadly, Indigenous sociality is structured by specific relational forms, including clan membership, kinship structures, skin names, and moiety systems (Carlson & Frazer, 2018a, p. 14; Kral, 2014). These cultural modes of social relation shape one's place within and responsibility to others, including family, community, country, and knowledge.

These culturally specific forms of social relations have wide-ranging implications for cyberbullying research. First, cultural knowledges and practices directly inform how digital technologies are used. As Christie (2005) writes, "wherever Aboriginal people have their own computers they produce and make use of their own digital objects" (p. 61). In their research on mobile phone use among residents of a remote Aboriginal community, Vaarzon-Morel (2014) shows how the introduction of new communication technologies has both extended and transformed traditional social relations among community members. Our own work on Indigenous people's use of social media likewise reveals that online practices are directly informed by cultural knowledges and values, such as how information around Sorry Business (i.e., rules and responsibilities relating to death and dying) is managed, shared, and contained on Facebook (Carlson & Frazer, 2015).

Second, new communication technologies can lead to the transformation of traditional modes of communication and sociality (Carlson & Frazer, 2018a). Kral (2014) notes for instance that uptake of social media can "lead to intergenerational tensions as young people explore new patterns of behavior, and older people come to terms with new cultural challenges" (p. 171). In particular, they note that communities have expressed concerns that social media use has undermined traditional gerontocratic power structures, through which social relations are sustained and conflict is mediated. Indeed, as Rennie, Hogan, and Holcombe-James (2016) note, "some remote communities have gone so far as to reject the extension of mobile coverage because of cyber safety concerns" (p. 2).

Third, in contrast to the dominant emphasis on the self-made, atomized "individual" in Western social contexts, many Indigenous communities emphasize more collective and relational forms of selfhood (Carlson & Frazer, 2018a; Shodoudi Mojhedi et al., 2019). In their report on cyber-safety in remote Indigenous communities, Rennie, Yunkaporta, and Holcombe-James (2018) found that, even regarding online practices, "the individual is subsumed within the social, defined by kinship and clan membership" (p. 11). They found Aboriginal specific notions of privacy often do not correspond with mainstream populations; for instance, sharing mobile devices and mobile accounts was common. As a result, and as we have previously noted, "This more collective notion of the self means that cyberbullying incidents cannot always be considered as an isolated act between discrete individuals" (Carlson & Frazer, 2018a, p. 15). Instead, conflict online can be already embedded within and a continuation of longstanding acrimonious relations between whole families and communities.

Research on Indigenous youth's experience of "traditional" schoolyard bullying supports this argument. Coffin et al. (2010) show that bullying is not just an interpersonal relation, but is shaped by broader cultural practices and social relations. They argue that bullying is different in an Aboriginal context – motivated by different things (such as jealousy, family obligations), geographically differentiated (coastal and inland children reported different experiences), and bound up in different relations of responsibility. The students in their study often felt compelled to fight for their family – including cousins, distant relatives, and lifetime friends. Emery, Hayes, and Parlet's (1998) work on "racist bullying" likewise found there was strong evidence of in-group loyalty in the face of bullying; with Aboriginal students tending to look out for one another.

This more collective understanding of online conflict stands in contrast to the dominant framing in cyberbullying research, which sees conflict through the highly individualistic lens of the victim–perpetrator binary. Indigenous notions of agency and selfhood, which tend to emphasize relations between and responsibilities toward family, community, clan, and kin, need to be considered if the causes, effects, and mitigating factors of cyberbullying are to be adequately understood in these contexts.

Cultures of Conflict

As we discuss above, the concept of cyberbullying is deeply contested in recent literatures. There are crucial questions around whether "what counts" as cyberbullying specifically or conflict more broadly can be transplanted from one (predominantly white, Western) context to another. Considering cyberbullying is essentially a *social* practice, there is good reason to presume it will be socially heterogeneous.

On one hand, what researchers might consider a problematic form of interpersonal conflict, might be understood by others as legitimate and "normal" violence. As discussed in our prior work (Carlson & Frazer, 2018a, p. 15), interpersonal and social conflict is often considered a necessary, normal, and positive component of social relations. In the context of Ngaanyatjarra communities of Western Australia, Kral (2014) notes "public explosions of anger or frustration were a socially acceptable way of releasing tension in the Western Desert that enabled conflict between kin to be resolved… generally through ritualized payback, spearfights or 'yaarlpirri'" (p. 184). In Coffin's (2011) work on remote Aboriginal schools, schoolyard bullying was described by Aboriginal students as "something that Aboriginal people do" (p. 90). Finally, Rennie et al. (2018) suggest that, in Aboriginal communities, "physical conflict can be a reassertion of relatedness, even where it may fail to reinstate social order and may in fact have the opposite effect" (p. 8).

On the other hand, scholars have documented a range of culturally-specific forms of aggression and bullying, of which non-Indigenous researchers may not be aware. For instance, Vaarzon-Morel (2014) documents an escalating conflict between Warlpiri communities in which aggressors "uploaded photographs of deceased relatives of members of the opposite faction and defaced them with vitriolic comments" (p. 252) – a highly offensive practice that broke longstanding taboos around Sorry Business. Rennie et al. (2018) discuss a widespread practice across Aboriginal communities popularly referred to as "swearing," which they define as "almost akin to a curse, an indecent assault that must be answered with vigorous aggression" (p. 10). Finally, in Canada, research by Kentel and McHugh (2015) on Aboriginal people's participation in sport document a practice called "mean mugging," which involved staring at someone in a menacing way, intending to make the person feel bad about themselves.

Against Olweus's assertion that a clear, universal definition of cyberbullying is necessary and desirable, we can't assume that our own notions of conflict will always map neatly onto the peoples we study. Distinctions between "normal" and "pathological" violence are not clear cut, "natural," or universal. Rather, online conflict is always culturally mediated, determined, and normalized. By assuming we already know what cyberbullying and other "pathological violence" looks like, we risk incorrectly including behaviors that communities themselves wouldn't consider a problem, while overlooking forms of bullying that might have significant impacts on the individuals and communities involved.

This work makes clear that responses to, interventions for, and strategies to mitigate cyberbullying cannot be applied homogeneously across cultural groups (Carlson & Frazer, 2018a, p. 19). There are many differentiating factors that would, in many cases, make mainstream interventions ineffective or inappropriate in the context of Indigenous communities. As Broll et al. (2018) argue, "culturally-relevant programming is essential to meeting the needs of Indigenous adolescents" (p. 72). Likewise, Rennie et al. (2018) suggest that "conflict resolution […] in remote communities can be provided through traditional structures, by Indigenous organizations, or through mainstream legal services" (p. 30). However, these more context-sensitive approaches to understanding motivations for and mitigation of cyberbullying are precluded by the current dominant approach in research.

The Political Context of Cyberbullying

As we have previously noted, "Indigenous peoples occupy a unique political position both among mainstream populations and among other minority groups" in settler states (Carlson & Frazer, 2018a, p. 17). Most fundamentally, Indigenous peoples have, by definition, experienced colonization. While the vast social, cultural, and economic implications of colonization exceed the scope of this chapter, it is important to acknowledge that colonization comprises a significant part of the context in which Indigenous peoples engage with digital technologies (Carlson & Frazer, 2018a, p. 17).

In this section, we unpack some of the major political considerations in understanding Indigenous people's experiences of cyberbullying. We argue, first, that researchers must acknowledge the already-existing racial politics that underpin Indigenous–settler relations in Australia and seek to understand how this might instigate, facilitate, and mediate Indigenous peoples' experiences of online conflict. Second, we argue that researchers must attend to how settler power manifests materially through popular discourse, Indigenous disadvantage, and intergenerational trauma (Carlson & Frazer, 2018a, p. 17).

Settler-Colonialism and the Logic of Elimination

As we have previously argued (Carlson & Frazer, 2018a, p. 17), all accounts of bullying recognize it necessarily involves an imbalance and abuse of power. Slonje and Smith (2008), for instance, write that "bullying is a form of abuse that is based on an imbalance of power; it can be defined as a systematic abuse of power" (p. 147). Clearly, issues of power also matter in the context of relations between different ethnic, racial, and social groups. Scholarship from Indigenous studies, postcolonial theory, and settler-colonial studies has carefully analyzed the power relations that sustain settler-colonial societies. Settler-colonial scholar Patrick Wolfe (2006) argues that the political and logical foundation of all settler societies is the settler desire to "eliminate the native": those peoples whose ongoing existence rebukes the settler claim to land. He argues that for the settler state to be seen as right and legitimate, it needs to erase Indigenous people's prior (and therefore superior) claim to sovereignty – through physical, cultural, or epistemological elimination.

Existing cyberbullying research tends to overlook the fact that Indigenous people – in Australia and elsewhere – already live deeply entangled within these broader relations of power. Bodkin-Andrews et al. (2012) note that bullying research has, by and large, failed to engage with issues of race. They argue that racism research "has identified a wider cultural/identity-threat that bullying research … has largely ignored" (Bodkin-Andrews, 2012, p. 1). Bullying is about power and existing power dynamics between Indigenous and non-Indigenous peoples are likely to affect the frequency and forms of cyberbullying that occur.

While these broader political/power relations might seem far removed from issues of bullying – either offline or online – a growing body of literature has unpacked how Indigenous–settler relations play out in everyday encounters.

Settler-colonial studies understands colonialism as a continuing force in the present, effected through a range of settler institutions (the justice system, the welfare state, capitalist enterprise) and discursive arrangements that work to frame Indigenous people as the "lesser other."

These racial politics play out across a range of everyday social settings. For instance, racism is widespread in Australian schools, where many Indigenous students face direct and systemic forms of prejudice and discrimination (Emery, Hayes, & Parlet, 1998). Researchers have found bullying to be motivated by racial, ethnic and cultural differences, what Broll et al. (2018) describe generally as "ethnic bullying." The students in Emery et al.'s (1998) study articulated an understanding of racism "in terms of being devalued or disadvantaged on grounds of their race, color or culture" (p. 45). This work shows that Indigenous people are often targeted for abuse *because* they are Indigenous.

Additionally, as noted in our previous work (Carlson & Frazer, 2018a), these broader politics directly affect how victims, parents, and schools respond to bullying. Parents in Coffin et al.'s 2010 study of bullying of Aboriginal high school students explained that "teachers did not listen to Aboriginal students when they told them about bullying or that they did nothing to stop this." Meanwhile, the students in their study often responded by "separat[ing] oneself from non-Aboriginal children and [by being] as 'Aboriginal' as possible" (Coffin et al., 2010, p. 83). In Emery et al.'s (1998) research on bullying against Aboriginal students, they found students rarely told teachers about racist bullying, explaining they didn't seem to take their grievances seriously. "You get suspended if you hit someone," one student explained, "but nothing ever happens when people say racist things" (Emery et al., 1998, p. 54).

A growing body of work has also traced the ways that settler power is extended and racist violence enacted through social media technologies. Social media is a significant point of encounter between Indigenous peoples and settlers. Online, hate groups congregate, share racist materials, and organize attacks on others; Indigenous people are exposed to myriad forms of racist discourse and abuse. In some respects, then, social media can be understood as another avenue through which settler power can be affected and the "logic of elimination" might be realized. For these reasons, online interactions – even between two Indigenous users – are always mediated by broader, racial relations of settler power (Carlson & Frazer, 2020, p. 6).

Rather than understanding bullying as an individual pathology, a more context-sensitive approach can reveal these broader politics. As qualitative research on schoolyard bullying has shown, bullying is a practice through which a particular social and moral order is being sustained; that is, bullying both constrains and makes possible particular subject positions (Ellwood & Davies, 2010). As Kofoed and Ringrose (2012) argue, cyberbullying can be understood as "a set of discursive processes where certain subject positions are annulled, and deprived of intelligibility" (p. 8). In this way, the identification of difference, and its punishment through bullying, is involved in the creation and erasure of social categories. Understood in this way, the bullying of Indigenous peoples might be linked to the settler project of Indigenous elimination, in which Indigenous subjectivities are policed and deprived of intelligibility.

The Politics of Indigenous Disadvantage

Consequently, and as we have previously argued, cyberbullying research needs to consider the broader context of the material legacy of settler-colonization in Australia (Carlson & Frazer, 2018a). Indigenous disadvantage can be understood as "a systemic form of racism that manifests materially" (Carlson & Frazer, 2018a, p. 18), embedded within and arising from settler policies that removed Indigenous people from their land; stolen Indigenous children from families; suppressed Indigenous cultures, knowledges, and languages; and marginalized Indigenous citizens to the lowest social, educational, and economic rungs of settler society. As Mobin et al. (2017) have argued, in this context, we need to better understand how "intergenerational trauma and the after-effects of colonialism" play out through conflictual peer relations online (p. 479). Coffin et al. (2010), for instance, suggest that bullying behavior is affected by "the wider socio-economic context which, in this case, has been shaped by centuries of institutional racism toward Aboriginal Australians" (p. 85).

However, the vast majority of cyberbullying research – with its focus on individual, atomized actors – overlooks this significant social and political context. This is particularly troubling, as Broll et al. (2018) argue, that "given the plethora of evidence that colonization and forced assimilation policies have contributed to comparatively poorer mental health among Indigenous peoples" (p. 72). If we are to better attend to the cyberbullying experiences of Indigenous peoples and work toward effective interventions, the very real and significant material consequences of settler policy on Indigenous peoples need to be factored into research.

Toward a Research Agenda

In this paper, we have approached cyberbullying as a distinct discursive formation in both research and everyday life, which carries with it a set of often problematic built-in assumptions that require interrogation. Considering the shortcomings of standard cyberbullying research outlined in the first half of the chapter, we argue that scholars must move beyond quantitative, "top-down" approaches to research (Nilan et al., 2015), which rely on a static, reductive, moralized perpetrator–victim model that renders research insensitive to difference, context, and ambiguity – an issue that is particularly salient considering the absence of scholarly work on Indigenous people's experiences of cyberbullying.

To address this gap in knowledge, we call for rigorous, exploratory, qualitative research into diverse populations' experiences of cyberbullying. We need, as Thornberg (2011) argues, "theoretical and methodological pluralism" in cyberbullying research. The major strength of qualitative research is that it allows for re-theorizing and re-framing entire fields of study (Ellwood & Davies, 2010). By taking a more open, experimental and exploratory approach, we can produce what Kofoed and Ringrose (2012) describe as "complexity-sensitive knowledge of bullying" (p. 7). Rather than assuming to already know what constitutes bullying and seek only to then measure its prevalence and effects, researchers should ask more expansive questions, such as: what are the forces that lead to a bullying event? What are the social, cultural, material, affective, and historical factors at play? And how are these events mediated by technology, heterogeneous cultural knowledges, values and practices, and broader racial politics?

With this challenge in mind, and to close this chapter, we propose three potential pathways forward.

First, and most fundamentally, cyberbullying research needs to attend more closely to significant markers of social difference. While large-scale studies have produced critical knowledge around rates and effects of cyberbullying, too often they have failed to account for demographic and other social factors outside of age and gender. This "top-down" approach smooths over differences between participants within research populations, subsuming minority experiences within mainstream populations. As we demonstrated in the second half of the chapter, there are good reasons to assume that Indigenous people's understandings and experiences of cyberbullying diverge significantly from non-Indigenous peoples. These differences can only be attended to if they are intentionally approached as distinct research populations.

Second, there is a need to deconstruct and destabilize the standard academic discourse of cyberbullying. One way of approaching this task, as suggested by Canty et al. (2016), is to increase our vocabulary around online conflict. To this end, a range of scholars have mobilized alternative terms to approaching cyberbullying, including "drama" (Marwick & boyd, 2014) and "adversarial peer relations online" (Nilan et al., 2015, p. 1), or more morally neutral terms such as "networked publics" (boyd, 2014) or "online conflict." Rather than attempting to reduce a complex social phenomenon to something clear and rigid, Marwick and boyd (2014) found a lack of definitional clarity to be analytically illuminating; it increased their capacity to see other forms, effects, and causes of conflictual relations among social media users. The small body of qualitative work on Indigenous peoples' experiences of online conflict suggests there exist distinct, emic concepts already being used by participants to describe their online interactions, such as the "swearing" described by Rennie et al. (2018). A diverse conceptual arsenal will allow researchers to better embrace the messiness, ambiguity, and complexity of online conflict.

Finally, a commitment to "theoretical and methodological pluralism" should include Indigenous approaches to research. Indigenous scholars have developed a rich body of work elaborating Indigenous ontologies, epistemologies, and axiologies within social research – methodological approaches which tend to center the lived experiences and worldviews of Indigenous people themselves, rather than always already assuming they can be accurately captured within Western research paradigms (Moreton-Robinson & Walter, 2009; Nakata, 2007; Rigney, 1999; Tuiwai Smith, 2013). To this end, Coffin (2011) advocates a culture-centered approach to bullying research: a commitment to theories within the culture, an amplification of alternative voices, and a recognition of cultural context.

References

Australia Institute. (2019). *Trolls and polls –the economic costs of online harassment and cyberhate*. Retrieved from https://www.tai.org.au/content/trolls-and-polls-economic-costs-online-harassment-and-cyberhate. Accessed on March 20, 2020.

Bauman, S. (2015). Why it matters. In S. Bauman, D. Cross, & J. L. Walker (Eds.), *Principles of cyberbullying research: Definitions, measures, and methodology* (pp. 23–26). London: Routledge.

Bodkin-Andrews, G. H., O'Rourke, V., Dillon, A., Craven, R. G., & Yeung, A. S. (2012). Engaging the disengaged?: A longitudinal analysis of the relations between Indigenous and non-Indigenous Australian students' academic self-concept and disengagement. *Journal of Cognitive Education and Psychology*, *11*(2), 179–195.

boyd, d. (2014). *It's complicated: The social lives of networked teens*. New Haven, CT: Yale University Press.

Broll, R., Dunlop, C., & Crooks, C. V. (2018). Cyberbullying and internalizing difficulties among Indigenous adolescents in Canada: Beyond the effect of traditional bullying. *Journal of Child & Adolescent Trauma*, *11*(1), 71–79.

Brownlee, K., Martin, J., Rawana, E., Harper, J., Mercier, M., Neckoway, R., & Friesen, A. (2014). Bullying behaviour and victimization among aboriginal students within northwestern Ontario. *First Peoples Child & Family Review*, *9*(1), 38–52.

Campbell, M. A., Cross, d., Spears, B., & Slee, P. (2010). *Cyberbullying: Legal implications for schools* (Vol. 118). East Melbourne, VIC: The Centre for Strategic Education.

Canty, J., Stubbe, M., Steers, D., & Collings, S. (2016). The trouble with bullying–deconstructing the conventional definition of bullying for a child-centred investigation into children's use of social media. *Children & Society*, *30*(1), 48–58.

Carlson, B., & Frazer, R. (2015). "It's like going to a cemetery and lighting a candle": Aboriginal Australians, sorry business and social media. *AlterNative: An International Journal of Indigenous Peoples*, *11*(3), 211–224.

Carlson, B., & Frazer, R. (2018a). *Cyberbullying and Indigenous Australians: A review of the literature*. Sydney, NSW: Aboriginal Health and Medical Research Council of New South Wales and Macquarie University.

Carlson, B., & Frazer, R. (2018b). *Social media mob: Being Indigenous online*. Sydney, NSW: Macquarie University.

Carlson, B., & Frazer, R. (2020). The politics of (dis)trust in Indigenous help-seeking. In S. Maddison & S. Nakata (Eds.), *Questioning Indigenous-settler relations: Interdisciplinary perspectives* (pp. 87–106). Singapore: Springer Verlag.

Christie, M. (2005). Aboriginal knowledge traditions in digital environments. *The Australian Journal of Indigenous Education*, *34*, 61–66.

Coffin, J. (2011). "Make them stop it": What Aboriginalchildren and youth in Australia are saying about bullying. *First Peoples Child & Family Review*, *6*(1), 83–98.

Coffin, J., Larson, A., & Cross, D. (2010). Bullying in an Aboriginal context. *The Australian Journal of Indigenous Education*, *39*(1), 77–87.

Ellwood, C., & Davies, B. (2010). Violence and the moral order in contemporary schooling: A discursive analysis. *Qualitative Research in Psychology*, *7*(2), 85–98.

Emery, C., Hayes, R., & Parlet, M. (1998). Bullying of, and retaliation by, Aboriginal students in an Australian urban high school. *South Pacific Journal of Psychology*, *10*(2), 43–59. doi:10.1017/CBO9781107415324.004

Henry, N., McGlynn, C., Flynn, A., Johnson, K., Powell, A., & Scott, A. J. (2020). *Image-based sexual abuse: A study on the causes and consequences of non-consensual nude or sexual imagery*. London, NY: Routledge.

Hinduja, S., & Patchin, J. W. (2010). Bullying, cyberbullying, and suicide. *Archives of Suicide Research, 14*(3), 206–221.

Kentel, J. L., & McHugh, T. L. F. (2015). "Mean mugging": An exploration of young Aboriginal women's experiences of bullying in team sports. *Journal of Sport and Exercise Psychology, 37*(4), 367–378. doi:10.1123/jsep.2014-0291

Kofoed, J., & Ringrose, J. (2012). Travelling and sticky affects: Exploring teens and sexualized cyberbullying through a Butlerian-Deleuzian-Guattarian lens. *Discourse: Studies in the Cultural Politics of Education, 33*(1), 5–20.

Kofoed, J., & Staksrud, E. (2019). 'We always torment different people, so by definition, we are no bullies': The problem of definitions in cyberbullying research. *New Media & Society, 21*(4), 1006–1020.

Kowalski, R. M., Giumetti, G. W., Schroeder, A. N., & Lattanner, M. R. (2014). Bullying in the digital age: A critical review and meta-analysis of cyberbullying research among youth. *Psychological Bulletin, 140*(4), 1073.

Kral, I. (2014). Shifting perceptions, shifting identities: Communication technologies and the altered social, cultural and linguistic ecology in a remote Indigenous context. *The Australian Journal of Anthropology, 25*(2), 171–189.

Lemstra, M., Rogers, M., Thompson, A., Moraros, J., & Tempier, R. (2011). Prevalence and risk indicators of smoking among on-reserve First Nations youth. *Paediatrics and Child Health, 16*(10), e71–e77.

Llorent, V. J., Ortega-Ruiz, R., & Zych, I. (2016). Bullying and cyberbullying in minorities: Are they more vulnerable than the majority group?. *Frontiers in Psychology, 7*, 1507.

Marwick, A. E., & boyd, d. (2014). Networked privacy: How teenagers negotiate context in social media. *New Media & Society, 16*(7), 1051–1067.

Mishna, F., Saini, M., & Solomon, S. (2009). Ongoing and online: Children and youth's perceptions of cyber bullying. *Children and Youth Services Review, 31*(12), 1222–1228.

Mobin, A., Feng, C. X., & Neudorf, C. (2017). Cybervictimization among preadolescents in a community-based sample in Canada: Prevalence and predictors. *Canadian Journal of Public Health, 108*(5–6), e475–e481.

Moreton-Robinson, A., & Walter, M. (2009). Indigenous methodologies in social research. In Walter, M. (Ed.), *Social research methods* (pp. 95–109). Oxford: Oxford University Press.

Nakata, M. N. (2007). *Disciplining the savages, savaging the disciplines*. Canberra: Aboriginal Studies Press.

Nilan, P., Burgess, H., Hobbs, M., Threadgold, S., & Alexander, W. (2015). Youth, social media, and cyberbullying among Australian youth: "Sick friends." *Social Media & Society, 1*(2), 2056305115604848.

Olweus, D. (2013). School bullying: Development and some important challenges. *Annual Review of Clinical Psychology, 9*, 751–780.

Olweus, D., & Limber, S. P. (2018). Some problems with cyberbullying research. *Current Opinion in Psychology, 19*, 139–143.

Radoll, P. (2012). Cyber-safety and Indigenous youth. *Indigenous Law Bulletin, 8*(12), 11–14.

ReachOut. (2018). Cyberbullying a growing public health and safety issue for Australian families. Retrieved from https://about.au.reachout.com/cyberbullying-nd-australian-families/. Accessed on February 16, 2020.

Rennie, E., Hogan, E., & Holcombe-James, I. (2016). *Cyber safety in remote Aboriginal communities and towns: Report*. Melbourne, VIC: Digital Ethnography Research Centre, RMIT University.

Rennie, E., Yunkaporta, T., & Holcombe-James, I. (2018). *Cyber safety in remote Aboriginal communities: Final report*. Melbourne, VIC: Digital Ethnography Research Centre, RMIT University. Retrieved from https://apo.org.au/sites/default/files/resource-files/2018-06/apo-nid172076_1.pdf. Accessed on March 20, 2020.

Rigney, L. I. (1999). Internationalization of an Indigenous anticolonial cultural critique of research methodologies: A guide to indigenist research methodology and its principles. *Wicazo Sa Review*, *14*(2), 109–121.

Ringrose, J., & Renold, E. (2010). Normative cruelties and gender deviants: The performative effects of bully discourses for girls and boys in school. *British Educational Research Journal*, *36*(4), 573–596.

Samulski, E. T. (2014). *An exploratory study of cyberbullying among Native American Students at Humboldt State University*. Doctoral dissertation, Humboldt State University, Arcata, CA.

Schott, R. M. (2014). The social concept of bullying: Philosophical reflections on definitions. In R. M. Schott & D. M. Søndergaard (Eds.), *School bullying: New theories in context (ebook*., pp. 21–46). New York, NY: Cambridge University Press.

Shohoudi Mojdehi, A., Leduc, K., Shohoudi Mojdehi, A., & Talwar, V. (2019). Examining cross-cultural differences in youth's moral perceptions of cyberbullying. *Cyberpsychology, Behavior, and Social Networking*, *22*(4), 243–248.

Slonje, R., & Smith, P. K. (2008). Cyberbullying: Another main type of bullying?. *Scandinavian Journal of Psychology*, *49*(2), 147–154.

Smith, P., del Barrio, C., & Tokunga, R. S. (2015). Definitions of bullying and cyberbullying: How useful are the terms?. In S. Bauman D. Cross, & J. L. Walker (Eds.), *Principles of cyberbullying research: Definitions, measures, and methodology* (pp. 23–26). London: Routledge.

Spears, B., Keeley, M., Bates, S., & Katz, I. (2014). *Research on youth exposure to, and management of, cyberbullying incidents in Australia: Part A: Literature review on the estimated prevalence of cyberbullying involving Australian minors*. Sydney, NSW: Social Policy Research Centre.

Srinivasan, R. (2013). Re-thinking the cultural codes of new media: The question concerning ontology. *New Media and Society*, *15*(2), 203–223.

Thornberg, R. (2011). 'She's weird!'—the social construction of bullying in school: A review of qualitative research. *Children & Society*, *25*(4), 258–267.

Tuiwai Smith, L. T. (2013). *Decolonizing methodologies: Research and Indigenous peoples*. New York, NY: Zed Books Ltd.

Vaarzon-Morel, P. (2014). Pointing the phone: Transforming technologies and social relations among Warlpiri. *The Australian Journal of Anthropology*, *25*(2), 239–255.

Walker, J., Craven, R. G., & Tokunga, R. S. (2013). Introduction. In S. Bauman, D. Cross, & J. L. Walker (Eds.), *Principles of cyberbullying research: Definitions, measures, and methodology* (pp. 3–21). New York, NY: Routledge.

Wolfe, P. (2006). Settler colonialism and the elimination of the native. *Journal of Genocide Research*, *8*(4), 387–409.

Section 2
Text-Based Harms

Chapter 9

Introduction

Nicola Henry

The importance of language to our sense of self and our relationships with others makes us especially vulnerable to the injurious potential of speech, particularly "hate speech," which has been the subject of much political and polarizing debate, especially concerning questions of regulation in the form of hate speech or vilification laws. Although there is no universally agreed definition of "hate speech," critical race theorists Matsuda, Lawrence, Delgado, and Crenshaw (2018) define "assaultive speech" as "words that are used as weapons to ambush, terrorize, wound, humiliate, and degrade." The metaphor of physical injury for the harms of speech acts – the "wounds of words" (Matsuda et al., 2018) – was powerfully explored in Toni Morrison's (1993) Nobel Lecture, in which she claimed "Oppressive language does more than represent violence; it *is* violence" (emphasis added). Speech acts then both *cause* harm and *constitute* harm (see Barendt, 2019; Gelber & McNamara, 2016).

Speech harms can be cumulative, long-term, and generational, reinforcing and amplifying discriminatory attitudes and behaviors that treat the "other" as inferior and subordinate, and solidifying existing power relations (Matsuda et al., 2018; see also Calvert, 1997 for a discussion). Jeremy Waldron (2012) argues that hate speech undermines and compromises the dignity "of those at whom it is targeted, both in their own eyes and in the eyes of other members of society" (p. 5). The lived experiences of targets of hate speech attest to these consequential and constitutive harms, such as normalizing discriminatory attitudes and behaviors, as well as "subordination, silencing, fear, victimization, emotional symptoms, restrictions on freedom, lowering of self-esteem, maintenance of power imbalances, and undermining of human dignity" (Gelber & McNamara, 2016, p. 336).

In this section of the Handbook on "speech-based harms," the chapters by Kim Barker and Olga Jurasz, Emma Jane, Benjamin Colliver, Briony Anderson and Mark Wood, and Elina Vaahensalo, each take as their point of departure that

The Emerald International Handbook of Technology-Facilitated Violence and Abuse, 167–170

doi:10.1108/978-1-83982-848-520211061

words – in the form of online hate speech, doxxing, and other oppressive forms of online text or speech – cause wounds that are both physical and metaphysical, as well as individual and collective. Jane's chapter on "cyberhate" against women *by women* begins with a discussion of a "vicious attack" against a feminist colleague on Twitter. As Jane explains, online abuse leads to feelings of "hurt, fear, anger, and self-doubt," which are compounded by "despair, disbelief, and betrayal" when the targets discover that the assailants are women because they assume them to be "peers, friends, or allies." One participant in Jane's study described feeling like "she had been hit in the stomach by a baseball bat."

Barker and Jurasz focus their chapter on online text-based sexual abuse, which they define as "written, electronic communication containing threatening and/or disruptive and/or distressing content, such as … textual threats to kill, rape, or otherwise inflict harm on the recipient of such messages." Barker and Jurasz argue that text-based sexual abuse "has silencing effects on women and girls participating online and contributes to the creation of hostile spaces for women." They argue that the legal system has created "hierarchy of harm … in which more credence and gravitas are given to forms of online abuse involving photographic representations of the victim than textual – and frequently very violent – abuse." The resulting harms ranging from psychological to physical to democratic are frequently "shrugged off as less serious than offline," and seen as "'part and parcel' of what happens online."

Likewise, Colliver in his chapter describes a number of interconnected harms relating to transphobic online hate speech. In his study, he examined transphobic discourse in relation to YouTube videos concerning public toilet access and gender neutral toilets. He states that these speech acts reinforce rigid gendered stereotypes and binaries, as well as delegitimizing transpeople by invoking discourses of biological essentialism, functioning to "construct transgender people as a 'scientific absurdity.'"

Anderson and Wood focus their chapter on a newer form of speech harm, "doxxing," defined as "the intentional public release onto the internet of personal information about an individual by a third party, often with the intent to humiliate, threaten, intimidate, or punish the identified individual" (Douglas, 2016, p. 199). They characterize the harms of doxxing as a loss of the target's anonymity, obscurity, and legitimacy, with accompanying mental health effects (e.g., depression, anxiety), and in the case of "organizational doxxing," the loss of competitive advantage.

In addition to exploring the harms of speech acts online, a number of the authors in this section have sought to explore the underlying drivers of oppressive speech acts as a means through which to exert and maintain power over marginalized groups. Anderson and Wood explain that the act of doxxing may or may not involve malicious intention. They use the example of journalists and activists using doxxing to serve the public interest (see also Cheung, this volume), or as a result of carelessness or negligence (e.g., failing to anonymize a source). And yet they also discuss the more hostile forms of doxxing, which involve, for instance, releasing compromising information about a person to prove oneself within an online network of peers, or to extort financial benefits, force individuals or groups of people to remove themselves from an online forum or platform, or as a form of control or punishment (e.g., in the context of domestic and family violence).

None of the authors in this section of the Handbook treat oppressive speech acts in simplistic, individualistic terms. Colliver, for instance, in his exploration of the ways in which cisgender YouTube commenters construct and position themselves as victims of oppression and political correctness, argues that those who engage in transphobic online hate speech "provide links to one another, and expressly attempt to encourage both recruitment and discussion among like-minded people" (pp. 57-8).

Similarly, Vaahensalo's chapter explores community building through "online othering discourse" by analyzing the cacophony of "antisocial" and "cruel" comments on the Finish forum Suomi24. Vaahensalo argues that "othering" is a result of the social "mechanics of intersubjectivity" and "sociality" that work to reinforce notions of "us" and "them" and is "not always a conscious act of harassment." She notes too that "Othering, whether online or offline, is not always openly hostile or aggressive," but rather can range from "innocent concerns and fears to genuine and open hostility." This is an important point that highlights the insidious nature of less overt forms of discriminatory speech which are often downplayed as harmless expressions of free speech.

Jane too in her chapter examines the complex overlay of internalized misogyny and lateral violence as useful concepts for analyzing woman-to-woman online abuse. She argues that "subjugated peoples may lash out with displaced fury and frustration after internalizing and embodying dominant discourses and ideologies about their own groups." The abuse of women by women, therefore, is a product of a broader, systemic form of interlocking forms of inequality as well as patriarchal oppression. Jane, however, acknowledges that in attributing the causes of cyberhate to structural factors, such as patriarchy, it risks "eliding part or all of subjects' agency and responsibility for their actions." As such, individual traits such as psychopathy, Machiavellianism, and narcissism (or the "Dark Tetrad" as it is also known) must also be considered, alongside the "dark infrastructure" of digital platforms and their facilitation of "outrage and polarization."

References

Barendt, E. (2019). What is the harm of hate speech?. *Ethical Theory and Moral Practice*, 22, 539–553.

Calvert, C. (1997). Hate speech and its harms: A communication theory perspective. *Journal of Communication*, 47(1), 4–19.

Douglas, D. M. (2016). Doxing: A conceptual analysis. *Ethics and Information Technology*, 18(3), 199–210. doi:10.1007/s10676-016-9406-0

Gelber, K., & McNamara, L. (2016). Evidencing the harms of hate speech. *Social Identities*, 22(3), 324–341.

Matsuda, M. J., Lawrence, C. L., Delgado, R., & Crenshaw, K. W. (2018). *Words that wound: Critical race theory, assaultive speech, and the first amendment*. New York, NY: Routledge.

Morrison, T. (1993). Toni Morrison: Nobel lecture. Retrieved from https://www.nobelprize.org/prizes/literature/1993/morrison/lecture/
Waldron, J. (2012). *The harm in hate speech*. Cambridge, MA and London: Harvard University Press.

Chapter 10

"Feminism is Eating Itself": Women's Experiences and Perceptions of Lateral Violence Online

Emma A. Jane

Abstract

While a growing body of literature reveals the prevalence of men's harassment and abuse of women online, scant research has been conducted into women's attacks on each other in digital networked environments. This chapter responds to this research gap by analyzing data obtained from qualitative interviews with Australian women who have received at times extremely savage cyberhate they know or strongly suspect was sent by other women. Drawing on scholarly literature on historical intra-feminism schisms – specifically what have been dubbed the "mommy wars" and the "sex wars" – this chapter argues that the conceptual lenses of internalized misogyny and lateral violence are useful in their framing of internecine conflict within marginalized groups as diagnostic of broader, systemic oppression rather than being solely the fault of individual actors. These lenses, however, require multiple caveats and have many limitations. In conclusion, I canvas the possibility that the pressure women may feel to present a united front in the interests of feminist politics could itself be considered an outcome of patriarchal oppression (even if performing solidarity is politically expedient and/or essential). As such, there might come a time when openly renouncing discourses of sisterhood and feeling free to disagree with, and even dislike, other women might be considered markers of liberation.

Keywords: Cyberhate; misogyny; lateral violence; internalized misogyny; internalized oppression; feminism

---

The Emerald International Handbook of Technology-Facilitated Violence and Abuse, 171–188

doi:10.1108/978-1-83982-848-520211009

Introduction

As I was writing this chapter, a senior feminist colleague of mine was weathering a vicious attack on Twitter. A prestigious Australian university had invited her to give a talk on a polarizing, feminism- and gender-related topic, and in the days leading up to the event erroneous assumptions were being made about its content, accompanied by a storm of *ad hominem* bile. My colleague was called "clueless," was said to have had "zero training," and was accused of endorsing "eugenics" and "lobotomy." People said she hadn't "published shit" and needed to learn to "shut the fuck up" and to be "deplatformed."[1] Someone else posted a comment saying, "There is no way I could listen to this person's presentation without slapping them." My colleague was devastated. As a feminist scholar researching the ethics and unexpected consequences of emerging technology, she is familiar with the problem of misogyny online. What threw her on this occasion, however, was that most of her antagonists were women. Some were even senior academic colleagues who apparently had no qualms about attaching their real names, identities, and even institutional affiliations to their attempts to impugn her character and derail her presentation.

In recent years, a growing body of scholarly literature has revealed the ways in which large numbers of men around the world are making use of the affordances of media communications technology to abuse, threaten, harass, and stalk girls and women online (Citron, 2014; Jane, 2017; UN Broadband Commission, 2015). In contrast, very little research has been conducted on women's perpetration of these sorts of attacks against each other.[2] This chapter takes a small step toward addressing this lacuna. With the possible exception of intimate partner cyberstalking (IPCS)[3] and some dimensions of cyberbullying among youth populations,[4] woman-on-woman cyber violence is rare compared to that perpetrated by men against women.[5] When women *do* turn on each other online, however, they can be just as violent and threatening as men. As this chapter demonstrates, their attacks can include graphic slut-shaming and credible rape and death threats, as well as abuse, harassment, and stalking with offline as well as online dimensions.

How and why are women attacking each other online? Do these attacks differ from those involving male perpetrators? And is this phenomenon best understood within the prism of patriarchal oppression or are women among their own worst enemies? These are the problematics to which this chapter responds.

To address these research questions, in the first section I begin by explaining the methods, limitations, and definitions used in the larger study underpinning this chapter. In the second and third sections, I provide examples of the two most common themes of female-perpetrated abuse reported by the women in my interview cohort. These involved attacks about birth and motherhood, and attacks relating to sex and self-sexualization. In explicating these two genres of cyberhate, I show that each resonates with an historical, intra-feminist schism, namely, what have been dubbed the "mommy wars" and the "sex wars." Given that a large number of interviewees raised internalized oppression and lateral violence – concepts frequently deployed to explain peer-to-peer aggression in marginalized groups – as explanations for their experiences, the fourth section of the chapter is devoted to their take on these conceptual lenses. In the final section, I undertake my own appraisal of internalized misogyny and lateral violence. In a nutshell, my case is that these framings are helpful in their contextualization of individual instances of woman-on-woman cyberhate as involving "gendered constructions of self and internalized gender ideologies" (Homan, 2019, p. 494) that are diagnostic and constitutive of systemically discriminatory gender regimes. The framings do, however, have limitations and require caveats, particularly with regard to the need to recognize other factors, such as individuals' psychological states, as well as those heavily corporatized dimensions of online architectures which greatly amplify "outragification" and polarization. In conclusion, I reflect on the particularly painful sting women report feeling when they are attacked by other women, noting the stark challenges lateral cyber violence poses to feminism given that some of the most vicious assaults are perpetrated by attackers who claim to be acting in feminism's name. I argue that the pressure on, or necessity for, ideologically disparate women to get along with each other for the sake of feminism could itself be considered an outcome of oppression.

Definitions, Method, and Limitations

In this chapter, the general terms "gendered cyberhate" and "cyber violence against women and girls" ("cyber VAWG") are used to refer to a range of phenomena occurring at the gender-technology-violence nexus. These include sexually-graphic invective, rape, and death threats, image-based abuse (aka "revenge porn"), and impersonation. Following definitions furnished by bodies such as the United Nations (UN), my use of the term "violence" refers to "dehumanizing, aggressive, and harmful acts that are in turn physical, psychological, sexual, and exploitative" (UN Broadband Commission, 2015, p. 5). I use the term "target" rather than "victim" or "survivor" to avoid connotations of either helplessness or "forced heroism" (Sehgal, 2016). This chapter refers only to "female" and "male" actors, terms which I acknowledge exclude people who identify as other genders. This is because the broader research project on which this chapter draws on was restricted to interviewees who identified as female, and none of those interviewees reported being targeted by transgender or nonbinary antagonists.

Data for this chapter were drawn from the qualitative interview component of a large and ongoing research project concerned with mapping and studying the history, manifestations, nature, prevalence, causes, and impact of gendered cyberhate and misogyny online.[6] Interviews were conducted with 52 participants who were aged between 19 and 52,[7] and who were given the option of using their real names or pseudonyms.[8] Of these participants, six identified as belonging to the LGBTQI+ community (including one transgender woman), four identified as members of Australia's First Nations people, two identified as having Asian backgrounds, and two identified as Muslim.[9] For various reasons, many of the 14 women referred to in the previous sentence asked that these parts of their identities not be included or foregrounded in research outputs associated with the project, and I have respected this request in this chapter. While interviewees were not asked outright if they identified as feminists, 40 independently volunteered the fact that they were feminists during their interviews.

While the initial aim of this research was to examine misogynistic abuse and harassment perpetrated by men against women, the remit of the project was expanded after the first interviewee said she believed that a portion of the hateful and harassing material she had received had been sent by women. Queries about female-perpetrated attacks were subsequently added to the list of questions asked of all interviewees. A total of 36 out of the 52 interviewees said one or more of their attackers was female. Three members of this subgroup reported being attacked only or mostly by other women (in contrast to the other 33 women in this subgroup who said that, while they had been attacked by women, this occurred far less frequently than attacks by men).

Given that the anonymity and pseudonymity afforded by online environments can make it difficult, if not impossible, to be certain about people's offline identities and genders, the 11 case studies given particular attention in this chapter[10] refer only to scenarios in which interviewees were very confident their antagonists were women. This confidence was usually because perpetrators were already known personally to targets; inadvertently or deliberately disclosed some aspect of their real identities; and/or subsequently made themselves known to targets in offline contexts. For example, the colleague mentioned in the Introduction found herself face-to-face with her online attackers when they arrived in person as part of deplatforming protests against her talk. Ultimately, the relative ease with which gender can be obscured, ambiguous, or deliberately misrepresented online makes it impossible to identify the gender of perpetrators with Cartesian certainty. That said, my case is that this should not stand in the way of analyzing online violence from gendered perspectives. The fact that online actors are often anonymous and hard to identify and track down has historically been used as an excuse for various types of inaction (including the prosecution of scholarly research) in relation to gendered cyberhate (Jane, 2017, pp. 76–111). On my account, therefore, the risk of misgendering a perpetrator is the lesser evil to ignoring the various gendered dimensions of cyberhate altogether.

This study had a number of limitations. First, the data are drawn from qualitative research and are therefore unable to offer a reliable indication of prevalence. Second, while steps were taken to include women from a range of demographics, the recruitment techniques were not designed to obtain a representative population sample. Third, while this chapter is informed by international research findings, at the qualitative level, its focus is anglophone. Despite these limitations, however, the case studies furnished are extremely valuable in that they offer some of the first, rich descriptions of women's experiences and perceptions of lateral violence in digital environments.

Mothers Who Want Their Babies to Die

One of the two most dominant themes of hateful, female-perpetrated material directed at women in my interview cohort involved vitriol over issues relating to motherhood, such as home birth, breastfeeding, vaccination, discipline, and performing paid work after having children. These attacks comport with what has been referred to as the "mommy wars," a conflict which began in the late 1980s and initially focused on tension between working and stay-at-home mothers. Thanks to the advent of social media and the rise of what have been dubbed "mommy blogs," however, there now exists "animus between myriad parenting philosophies and choices" in which mothers are pitted against each other in a zero-sum battle where some mothers are winners and others are losers (Abetz & Moore, 2018, p. 275).

While some fathers have been observed weighing in on some parenting-related disputes online (Steiner & Bronstein, 2017), within my interview cohort, vicious attacks relating to motherhood were one of the few genres of cyberhate perpetrated by women that had distinct differences to that perpetrated by men. While members of various online men's rights groups often sent cyberhate impugning women's parenting, this was usually part of blanket criticisms of a perceived feminist agenda with regard to access to children after parental separation. Women's attacks on each other, in contrast, tended to focus on highly specific birth and parenting issues, in concert with venomous dismissals of women's physical appearances (the latter being a general feature of most cyberhate regardless of the gender of perpetrator or the putative reason for the attack).

Of the three interviewees who reported being attacked only or mostly by other women, two were castigated for what was perceived as bad mothering. Sally,[11] for instance, had received a large volume of extremely vitriolic cyberhate – all of which was sent by women, and most of which evinced an ideology of combative motherhood. At the time we spoke, the 32-year-old doula and blogger whose writing prompted an onslaught by female detractors who called Sally mentally ill, an irresponsible mother, and "unlady-like" because, as one woman put it in response to a photograph Sally had posted of herself breastfeeding, "ladies don't expose their tits for the world to see." Sally said much of the abuse seemed to involve a "toxic competition," in which women who chose to give birth in hospital were framed as "good" moms who wanted "their babies to live," whereas women who home-birthed like her were "bad" mothers who wanted "their babies to die." She also recalled that:

> There were a lot of comments about… just how revolting my body is… that it was fat, that my breasts were really large and floppy, that my areolas are huge, that I have lots of pubic hair and… should really get a Brasilian before I have a birth if I'm going to share birth photos…. One [woman said], "thanks for reminding me I need to wax before my next OB appointment."

While Sally was vilified for, among other things, breastfeeding too much (she and a friend "cross-nursed" each other's children) and for too long (she was still nursing her children when they were two years old), another interviewee, Jacinta Tynan, was attacked by women online because she was perceived as not breastfeeding enough. Like Sally, most of Jacinta's online attackers were female. These women (wrongly) accused the 45-year-old television reporter and news anchor of "chuck[ing]" her baby on to bottled formula milk so she could return to work, and condemned her for being a bad mother because her television appearances suggested she had time to go to the hairdresser, which, as Jacinta pointed out in her interview, was simply part of her work requirements.

While women frequently criticized Jacinta for looking too attractive, they also vilified her for not looking attractive enough at a time when her face and body had changed due to a pregnancy Jacinta had not made public, claiming the mere sight of her induced nausea. Jacinta – who went into labor with her first child while onscreen reading the news – was also subjected to a "blast of online bullying," most of it by women, after writing an opinion piece about finding motherhood more enjoyable and easier than she had anticipated. On this occasion, she received about 2,000 hateful comments "absolutely tearing shreds off" her. Some commentators wished illness on her son and infertility on her. Others accused her of "setting the cause back" for women with postnatal depression, a charge Jacinta found particularly hurtful because she had experienced depression herself.

In this example, a public declaration about enjoying motherhood is framed by other women as taboo because it is seen as erasing or underplaying the experiences of those struggling as mothers. A similar zero-sum framing – but one relating to remarks about finding motherhood *difficult* – is evident in the experiences of the 26-year-old Australian blogger Annie Nolan, who became the target of a mob "pile on" after posting a photograph of her two-year-old twins with what were intended to be funny statements written on the back of two large envelopes. These statements took the form of a series of answers to questions strangers frequently asked Annie about her twins, including "conceived by f***ing," "born via c-section," and "yes, my hands are full (sometimes with two glasses of wine just to get through)." After uploading the photo to her blog's public Facebook page, the post went viral and was viewed more than two million times over two days. As a result, Annie was inundated with abuse and death threats, including messages from women sending photographs of their dead children and the urns of their cremated babies, alongside accusations that she was a terrible mother and was ungrateful that her children were alive.

A similarly vicious attack was launched at Catherine Hughes, a 28-year-old businesswoman who became a vaccination advocate after her four-week-old son, Riley, died of pneumonia as a result of contracting whooping cough. In the 24 hours after his death, Catherine and her husband created a Facebook page to honor the memory of their son, to encourage vaccination, and to field intense media interest in the story. The page was shared widely and provoked a tsunami of hateful messages from "anti-vaxxers" – including many women – who sent messages such as: "fuck you," "go grieve in private," "you'll have the blood of other babies on your hands," "Riley was a hoax," "this didn't happen," "you're being paid by Big Pharma," "vaccines don't work," "it was god's will," "survival of the fittest," and "if you'd tried… alternative therapy, your child would still be alive."

In addition to the cruel and extremely caustic nature of the comments directed at targets, the case studies furnished in this section illustrate a stark lose/lose dynamic, in that mothers were attacked and bullied by other women online regardless of the nature of their birth- and parenting-related choices and experiences, and regardless of whether they were perceived as either subscribing to or subverting stereotypical norms around feminine appearance. As I will demonstrate in the next section, similar patterns were evident in woman-on-woman cyberhate with thematic content relating to sex.

Ugly Sluts and "Attention Whores"

The second, dominant theme of female-perpetrated abuse experienced by women in my interview cohort concerned issues relating to sex and self-sexualization practices. Messages were frequently couched in the rhetoric of "slut-shaming" – that is, the embarrassment, insult, or denigration of girls and women "for their real or extrapolated sexual behavior, including for dressing in sexual ways, having sexual feelings and/or exploring and exhibiting them" (Chemaly, 2012, para 2). While this was sometimes linked to the fact that targets worked or were perceived as working in the sex industry, targets were also called variations of "you're a fat, ugly, slut" by women who had taken exception to targets' writing, profession, music, clothing, domestic violence activism, views on Middle Eastern politics, skin color, religion, and so on. Like abuse about women's appearances, the deployment of slut-shaming as an all-purpose admonition had much in common with male-perpetrated cyberhate against women, as did the more general lack of discernible links between the propositional content of hateful messages and those aspects of targets perpetrators ostensibly found objectionable.

A key difference in slut-shaming perpetrated by women compared to that perpetrated by men lay in the fact that women often simultaneously berated targets for failing to engage in enough or the right sort of feminism. Exhortations to feminism, combined with sex-related bullying, resonate with some of the nastier in-fighting around what have been dubbed the "feminist sex wars." These date back to divisions within feminism – originating in the late 1960s – with regard to how women should "best undo patriarchal definitions of women's 'proper' sexual expression," and originally manifested in debates around sexual orientation and sexual practices (Showden, 2016, p. 1). New, intra-feminist tensions around sex have since emerged in response to factors such as the availability of pornography online, the so-called "pornification" of culture, and the frequency with which female internet users engage in self-sexualization practices on platforms such as Instagram. Bitter intra-feminist fighting also continues about whether, for instance, sex work, pornography, and BDSM[12] sex practices are best understood as violence against women or a "sex-positive" feminist practice (Showden, 2016, p. 1), as well as around transgender-related issues. Kate Toone (2018), for instance, argues that trans-exclusionary radical feminist (TERF) and sex worker–exclusionary radical feminist (SWERF) separatist politics have resulted in "extreme whorephobia, erasure, and lateral violence" against queer sex workers like herself (p. 110).

Zahra Stardust, 32, a (recently graduated) PhD student who had had a long career in many sectors of the sex industry, including striptease, pole dancing, burlesque, brothel work, mistressing, and pornography, had received "consistent harassment" online from both men and women. Men tended to display a toxic sense of entitlement to sexual encounters, while women antagonists usually expressed anti-pornography hostility. For instance, a media article describing Zahra as a "feminist stripper" prompted Facebook comments from women such as "Feminist strip tease, give me a fucking break – it's an oxymoron," and "feminism is about developing high order ability so that one doesn't have to rely on materialism or sexuality to survive." Zahra spoke of her immense fatigue at feeling a feminist obligation to constantly respond to ugly and unkind messages from other women who demonstrated "no ethic of care" for sex workers.

While Zahra had a large number of female antagonists attacking her online, Christa Hughes received severe abuse and harassment from just one woman. The 44-year-old feminist singer, circus performer, and comedian was attacked, harassed, and stalked online and offline by a woman who used five different pseudonyms, sometimes claiming she was a representative of the "Australian Women's Movement." Repeatedly calling Christa names such as "slag" and "cunt," this woman accused Christa of being "pro-rape" and of performing songs that caused women to be raped. She then threatened that Christa herself would be raped as punishment. A typical example of the multiple messages this woman sent over a period of years read:

> It's me again, you little fucking cocksucker. When we get hold of you, you little fucking prick teaser, we're going to fuck you senseless. We're going to tie you to a fucking tree and fuck you front and back. Then we're going to fuck your sisters and maybe your mum.... We know where you fucking live.... You're gone, baby, we'll get you. I'm going to stick my carrot[13] so [far] up your fucking little yuppie cunt, it'll probably fucking kill you.... When you fucking least expect it, we'll be there... we fucking swear we fucking mean it.

The woman also hacked Christa's email and impersonated her in order to send abusive messages to various musical artists, recording companies, music writers, and media outlets, as well as delivering notes to other residents of Christa's apartment block warning that Christa was a thief, liar, and cheat. When Christa reported the woman to authorities, police said they could not act "until something happens," raising the possibility that this woman's criminal actions were regarded as not being particularly serious and as not posing a credible threat because she was female.

Accusations of being a "bad feminist" were also directed at Elinor Lloyd-Philipps, a 28-year-old office worker who ran a website where she blogged about and sold retro and vintage undergarments, with a focus on body pride and plus-sized garments. Of the dozens of abusive and harassing messages she received daily, Elinor said about 20% came from women who claimed she was "slutting around" with their husbands, "damaging people's bodies by forcing them to wear old-fashioned underwear," promoting "torture devices... invented by men," and/or "pressuring plus-sized or obese women to change their bodies." Women also frequently wrote to Elinor chastising her about the "flaws" in her body, saying she looked like someone's grandmother and should put her "disgusting... arse away."

Similar messages were sent to Jackie McMillan, a live performer and the public face of a Sydney fetish club she co-founded in 1993. At the time of our interview, Jackie, 41, was also doing media work for an organization advocating for the rights of sex workers and was receiving a great deal of abuse from other women, most of whom she identified as belonging to morally conservative organizations and/or "anti-sex-work" feminist factions. Yet, rather than engaging predominantly with Jackie's opinions and politics, most women focused hatefully on her body size and aesthetics:

> I had a really aggressive young woman come and tell me I was a fat, ugly, slut because she believes in free speech.... Lots of people call you an idiot or say that you have no idea. Then it goes to fat insults if you don't back down. And I don't usually back down.

One woman who identified herself a political conservative sent Jackie a number of "aggressive" and "violent" messages calling her a "fat cow" and "sauerkraut" before suggesting Jackie would end up like Amanda Todd – the 15-year-old Canadian student who took her own life after being bullied online. Jackie took this as a veiled threat and said she found the comment "haunting."

Female-perpetrated cyberhate with sex-related themes often accused targets of having secured a job or having achieved some other form of professional success because they had engaged in sexual favors with men in power. On other occasions, targets were attacked because they were perceived as being intimately involved with perpetrators' friends or former romantic partners. Sarah Connor, 32, an award-winning hip-hop artist and lawyer, developed anxiety issues, including shortness of breath and feeling sick and light-headed before live music performances, after being attacked by other women associated with the music industry (alongside other antagonists). One woman contacted a person she thought Sarah was romantically involved with, saying:

> I've heard you're involved with Sarah. You do know she's like the biggest slut in the hip-hop scene? You really should be careful getting involved with her because I thought you were smarter than that and you'll just end up with a bad reputation as well.

Beth,[14] a 37-year-old therapist working in a freelance capacity as a photographer, identified sexual competitiveness as a theme in much of the hateful material she had received from other women. While Beth was expected to dress in – and post selfies of herself wearing – club-wear when she photographed nightclub events, these invariably provoked a large volume of cyberhate from women, many of whom Beth had encountered socially or while working, who sent messages such as "Why the fuck would you post this picture? Doesn't your boyfriend give you enough attention? ... Are you an attention whore or something?"

During our interview, Beth invoked the "crab syndrome" – a metaphor used as an analogy for the dysfunctional lateral violence that can occur among members of oppressed communities (Lateroute, 2007) – to explain why she thought women were attacking her so violently online:

> [We're like] crabs… all being held by patriarchy at the bottom of the bucket. As soon as one crab is successful and gets to the top of the bucket, the other crabs are trying to pull it back down again because they don't like the idea that one's getting to the top.

As I will explain in the next section, a lateral violence framing was volunteered by multiple interviewees as part of their explanatory narratives for the female-perpetrated cyberhate they had experienced, and, for the most part, offers a useful lens for making sense of the phenomenon under discussion.

Internalized Misogyny and Lateral Violence

Lateral violence – also known as "horizontal violence" – refers to peer-on-peer violence in marginalized groups such as Indigenous cultures (Gooda, 2011; Korff, 2019) and LGBTQI+ communities (Kelly, 2017; Toone, 2018; Vivienne, 2017), as well as more generally among women (Daly, 1978; Moane, 2000; Trott, 2017). As a conceptual framing, it recognizes that subjugated peoples may lash out with displaced fury and frustration after internalizing and embodying dominant discourses and ideologies about their own groups, even and especially if these work against the interests of individual subjects as well as against the interests of the larger groups to which they belong. These may take the form of the damaging slurs and falsehoods constantly directed at them by their oppressors (Bailey, 2019, p. 5); discourses and ideologies relating to, for instance, gender hierarchy and subordination; and/or ideology-driven norms that seem commonsensical or "natural" – such as "good mothers stay at home with their babies" or "good girls don't enjoy sex."

When internalized oppression manifests, it may take the form of physical violence, as well as malicious gossiping, shaming and undermining, backstabbing, social exclusion, scapegoating, bullying, and organizational conflict (Gooda, 2011; Korff, 2019). Rather than confronting the system that oppresses them, subjugated peoples may direct their dissatisfaction inward toward themselves and/or outward toward their peers – or toward those even less powerful than themselves (Korff, 2019). A vicious cycle can develop in that, if violence or other forms of conflict and antisocial behavior emerge, the oppressor may then label and stereotype the oppressed "for the responses that they have been set up to make," which then becomes "a self-fulfilling prophecy" (Lateroute, 2007, p. 289). This chimes with the phenomenon known as "stereotype threat," which recognizes that strong, negative, societal views may not only be internalized by targets but may actually affect their behavior (Barker & Jane, 2016, p. 314).

Of my interviewees who had been attacked by other women online, almost all volunteered some take on internalized misogyny and/or lateral violence as an explanation for this aggression. Jacinta, for instance, saw women's attacks on her as stemming from a comprehensive and systemic lack of support for mothers, suggesting that the consequent stress, isolation, and hardship resulted in attacks on other women perceived as having better circumstances. Caitlin Roper, an interviewee who was a member of the morally-conservative Australian women's group Collective Shout, nominated internalized misogyny as the reason the abuse she received from women was so similar to the abuse she received from men. Jackie – at the opposite end of the political spectrum to Caitlin – raised similar concerns:

> I've seen feminism really demonized.... The... movement is in crisis but I think that's [because there's] so much pressure from outside. [Feminism] is... eating itself in places.... It's that misogyny that we've taken on board as women.

Sally's take on the issues was equally blunt:

> It comes from... trying to survive patriarchy. You've got to cut down that bitch so that you're not cut down.... Patriarchy sets women up against each other.... It's really hard to be a woman and I think it's getting harder and... we're competing even more.

Discussion

On my account, the use of internalized misogyny and lateral violence as conceptual lenses for unpacking women's attacks on each other online is useful for understanding internecine conflict within marginalized groups as diagnostic of broader, systemic oppression, rather than focusing solely or predominantly on individual interactions in the hunt for explanations and blameworthy actors. In the context of cyberhate, these lenses also help explain some key similarities and differences between the attacks perpetrated by men against women and those perpetuated by women against each other, while also showing that both these types of cyberhate are gendered in a way that keeps women socially and politically subjugated.

For instance, internalized misogyny and lateral violence might explain why sex-related cyberhate perpetuated by women had so many striking similarities with that generated by men with regard to content, idiomatic usage, and context (or, in relation to slut- and appearance-shaming, *lack* of context). Given that shaming and blaming women for DNA-level deficiency is the lingua franca of patriarchy, it is revealing, but unfortunately not surprising, that women are calling each other "fat," "ugly," "slutty," and "stupid" online using almost identical locutions as those deployed by men. It seems feasible that these lines of attack are chosen because antagonists have been conditioned to accept the "logic" of judging women against these overlapping yet contradictory sets of "key performance indicators," and are aware of the power of these words to wound – quite possibly because they have previously been wounded by them personally.

With regards to abuse with thematic content relating to birth and parenting, it is surely no coincidence that these hostilities focus on the domestic sphere which – despite many decades of feminist activism – is still widely regarded as a woman's natural domain. Research in 2014, for instance, revealed that 58% of 18-year-old high school seniors in the United States thought the best kind of family was one in which the man was the outside "achiever" and the woman took care of the home (a rise of 16% from two decades earlier when only 42% of high school seniors held this belief) (Anderson, 2017, para 3). It is possible, therefore, that bitter wars wage over these issues because many women still regard the home as one of the few spheres of life that is their domain, a place they may achieve a degree of power and prestige, and where their knowledge is valued in a way it might not be valued elsewhere.

So long as we are conditioned to believe or accept that the most significant things about ourselves are our choices and circumstances with regard to birth and parenting, the impulse to fiercely defend our own approaches and to attack others whose parenting practices differ from our own is likely to remain powerful. Such dynamics are eminently understandable. Yet, continuing to expend so much time and emotional labor arguing about individual parenting without questioning the larger, embedded assumption that parenting is primarily or exclusively women's business may well detract from or even stymie big picture feminist activism. It also risks further reifying gendered ideologies. As Sally puts it: "Where are the dads competing over [this] shit?"

Despite the usefulness of the lenses of internalized misogyny and lateral violence, however, my conclusions are that they do require some caveats when applied to sex and gender. Given that lateral violence framings are most commonly used to analyze contexts involving Indigenous peoples (see e.g., Freeman & Lee, 2007; Gooda, 2011; Korff, 2019; Lateroute, 2007), care must be taken to avoid conflating issues relating to gender and race. Similarly, the term "lateral" should be deployed with caution to avoid problematically flattening or homogenizing individual women's contexts, as well as the intersectional oppression suffered by, for example, women who are also of color, queer, differently-abled, and/or Muslim, and so on.

Diagnoses of internalized misogyny and lateral violence also risk eliding part or all of subjects' agency and responsibility for their actions. In the context of feminism, these framings could be taken to infer, at best, an absence or dearth of self-reflection and/or self-determination (because women are incarnating pernicious stereotypes that are oppressive both to themselves as individuals and to women overall) or, at worst, a type of brainwashing (in which women are being manipulated as hapless victims). It is also potentially politically disingenuous because it conveniently permits the *a priori* dismissal of other people's dissenting positions as merely the products of manipulation or delusion. Indeed, accusing other women of speaking and acting out of internalized misogyny might *itself* be a form of lateral violence. It is revealing, for instance, that some of my morally conservative feminist interviewees were strident in their claims that sex-positive feminists were suffering from internalized misogyny, and vice versa.

Another concern is that focusing solely on issues relating to gender oppression and feminist politics risks missing those aspects of cyberhate better understood as being produced by the architectures of the internet. For instance, Tristan Harris and Aza Raskin (2020) argue that online hate speech should not be considered a mirror that reflects the sorts of things people have always said behind closed doors. Instead, they argue that contemporary social problems such as cyberhate are the result of "dark infrastructure" (rather than "dark patterns" or bad actors), that have been generated by business models that do not just facilitate but *rely* on the amplification of outrage and polarization (Harris & Raskin, 2020). Also cogent here is Kerry Carrington's (2013) observation that rises in young women's offline violence in Western nations – much of which appears to be directed at friends or peers – correlate with a rise in social online networking that normalizes, rewards, and incites girls' fights (pp. 65 & 67). For instance, there have been steep rises in the number of online searches for videos of girls physically fighting with other girls, with these rates vastly exceeding comparable searches for boys fighting boys (Carrington, 2013, p. 69).

The central focus of this chapter has explicated woman-on-woman attacks online in terms of overarching structural forces in forms such as patriarchy, neoliberalism, social fragmentation, capitalism, and heteronormativity. It is important, however, to acknowledge the intersection of these structural forces with perpetrators' individual traits, in terms of, for example, insecurity, jealousy, competitiveness, personal and/or professional rivalry, narcissism, mental illness, thrill-seeking, boredom, cruelty, and/or a desire for "bragging rights" (Carrington, 2013, p. 70).[15] With regard to work in psychology, for instance, we might consider the role played by what is known as the "Dark Tetrad"; that is, the personality traits of Machiavellianism, narcissism, psychopathy, and sadism. In their research into IPCS, for instance, Melissa Smoker and Evita March (2017) found that women were significantly more likely than men to engage in IPCS, and that all Dark Tetrad traits were significant predictors of this behavior (p. 393).

To reflect the role commercialized infrastructure plays in relation to digital ills such as hate speech online, Harris and Raskin (2020) use the slogan: "It's not the people. It's the pipes." With regard to this chapter's discussion of woman-on-woman cyberhate, we might amend this to "it's not *just* the people but also the pipes and the patriarchy" to better capture the complex interplay of individual psychologies, mob dynamics, corporatized technological architectures and business models, *and* systemic gender inequity that facilitate and amplify all forms of contemporary gendered cyberhate, including women-perpetrated forms.

Conclusion: Et Tu Brutè?

As I was proofreading and fact-checking the final version of this chapter before submission, I contacted the feminist colleague mentioned in the introduction to reconfirm her willingness to share an anonymized version of her cyberhate experience and to double check whether "devastated" was too strong a word to characterize her feelings about being attacked by other women on Twitter. Her reply was that, if anything, this word was not strong enough:

> I had what I think would be described as two nervous breakdowns in the 12 hours leading up to the talk, and I couldn't sleep the night prior because of the extreme abuse. What is that expression from *A Clockwork Orange*? Ultraviolence? That's what it felt like to me.

Finding oneself at the epicenter of a mob attack online is invariably a harrowing experience. Yet, as my colleague discovered, it can be especially wounding to discover our assailants are those we had assumed were peers, friends, or allies. Many of the women interviewed for this chapter concurred, saying that when their online aggressors were women, the hurt, fear, anger, self-doubt, and sense of vulnerability they usually experienced during cyberhate onslaughts perpetrated by men were compounded by feelings of despair, disbelief, and betrayal, as well as a sense of pessimism about the threat these types of brutal, internecine conflicts posed to the broader feminist project. Some interviewees were even changing, reducing, or ceasing their feminist commentary and activism online. Sally, for instance, said that five years after starting her blogs, she was giving up writing in an attempt to escape "the comment wars." She made this decision after receiving – on her birthday – a message from a woman who wrote, "I hope that your daughter dies so she doesn't have to grow up with a mum like you." Sally said she felt like she had been hit in the stomach by a baseball bat. She wondered why another woman hated her "so much that she didn't want me dead, she wanted my child dead."

While lateral cyber violence is extremely concerning in light of its capacity to harm individual women as well as the feminist movement more broadly, in this chapter I have deliberately chosen not to attempt to propose potential solutions to the problems under discussion with a simplistic appeal that we all just settle our differences and get along. As the history of the feminist movement shows all too acutely, pleas for unity and/or attempts to paper over deep, intra-feminist fault lines with the rhetoric of solidarity and sisterhood have not proved helpful or realistic.

Further, the pressure women might feel to present a united front or even to *like* one another, could itself be considered an outcome of patriarchal oppression. Under patriarchy, we are categorized and oppressed purely on the basis of this one trait, even though individually our differences are tremendous and intractable, incorporating but also extending well beyond those diversities, oppositions, and asymmetries that fall under the umbrella of intersectionalism. Feminism has a long history of schisms and internecine disputes, most obviously in relation to debates between generations (for example, between second- and third-wave feminists), and around intersectionalism (in terms of the ongoing – and well-founded – critique that the dominant feminisms are White, privileged, and Western). At the same time, given the stark injustices caused by systemic gender inequity at the global level, there is a great deal at stake and urgent incentive to take action. Much recent scholarship on the upsurge of rage in Western feminism (see e.g., Banet-Weiser, 2018; Chemaly, 2018; Traister, 2018), for example, urges intersectional collectivist action.[16]

Yet, involvement in a collective feminist effort means we are likely to experience intense pressure to align ourselves with and work alongside folk we might otherwise find personally unlikeable or even ideologically abhorrent. My contention is that the ideal/expectation/imperative that all women could and should be comrades – or at least to publicly perform comradeship – is *itself* unfair and oppressive. From a feminist perspective, presenting as a harmonious coalition is certainly politically pragmatic and possibly even politically essential. Yet calls for, or prescriptions of, sisterhood may have the unintended effect of contributing to essentialist framings of women as identic and fungible. They may also cause additional layers of suffering in that, in addition to the personal unpleasantness of experiencing conflict with another woman, women who find themselves involved in such conflict may feel they are letting the larger feminist team down.

It is an understatement to say that this is a complex problem with no easy solutions. Women's savage attacks on each other – both online and elsewhere – present a new front of what has long been a painful and politically fraught dilemma for feminism. This is especially true given the prevalence of what could be categorized as a form of feminist or pseudo-feminist policing around who should be permitted to do and say what in the name of feminism, and the arguably unfair (if politically expedient) expectation that women settle or conceal their differences in the interests of the movement. My hope, however, is that the case studies furnished and issues raised in this chapter will at least help lay the foundations for future research into, and candid conversations about, the pressing need for feminism to find novel ways to accommodate the radical diversity of its members in order to muster enough social and political solidarity necessary to effect structural change.

Notes

1. "Deplatforming" refers to attempts to stop a political opponent from having access to virtual and online venues to communicate their viewpoints.
2. As discussed below, most research in this area has focused on women's attacks on each other's birth choices and parenting practices via "mommy blogs" (see e.g., Abetz & Moore, 2018; Akass, 2012; Lehto, 2019; Steiner & Bronstein, 2017). While parenting-related disputes are an important subsector of woman-on-woman attacks online, they offer only a limited view of a much larger problem.
3. While research on cyberstalking is limited and has resulted in inconclusive findings on gender distribution vis-à-vis perpetrators (Ahlgrim & Terrance, 2018, p. 5), Melissa Smoker and Evita March's (2017) study of cyberstalking against former and current intimate partners suggests it is women and not men who are more likely to engage in these behaviors, possibly in an effort to attain intimacy (p. 393).
4. While some studies suggest girls are more likely than boys to be both the perpetrators and victims of cyberbullying in youth populations (Carrington, 2013, p. 69), more recent meta-analyses of cross-national data indicate a preponderance of male perpetrators in instances of both traditional and online bullying (Smith, López-Castro, Robinson, & Görzigc, 2019, p. 38). That said, a decrease in the male:female ratio has been observed in mid-adolescence, possibly related to online bullying (Smith et al., 2019, p. 33).

5. According to the United Nations Broadband Commission (2015), 73% of women and girls have encountered some form of online violence, with women being 27 times more likely to be abused online than men and 61% of online harassers being male (p. 2 & 15). Powell, Henry, and Flynn (2018) have also shown that the majority of perpetrators of image-based sexual abuse are male, particularly if the victim is female (p. 309). Research into cyberbullying among youth populations, meanwhile, suggests that on average girls are "significantly and appreciably" more likely to be online victims, than boys (Smith et al., 2019, p. 37). After many years of digital ethnography in trolling subcultures, Whitney Phillips (2015) also maintains that the vast majority of trolls are likely to be relatively privileged White males (p. 42).
6. The two main selection criteria for participation in the interview component of this project were self-identification as female; and first-hand experience of technology-facilitated hate, abuse, and/or harassment. Subjects were recruited via a range of techniques and interviews were conducted in 2015 through 2017. Interviews were conducted in person and/or via Skype, and NVivo software was used to code interview transcripts using approaches from grounded theory. The study was approved by the University of New South Wales Human Research Ethics Committee and funded through an Australian Research Council (ARC) Discovery Early Career Researcher Award (DE150100670).
7. This chapter refers to the age of subjects at the time they were interviewed.
8. This was at the request of participants and was ultimately approved by the UNSW Sydney Human Research Ethics Committee. I have indicated throughout this chapter when pseudonyms have been used.
9. Please note that not all interviewees wished to answer questions about their sexual orientation and cultural backgrounds.
10. While only 11 case studies are directly cited in this chapter, my analysis and findings are informed by all the interviews conducted, as well as by the larger research project of which these interviewees were a part.
11. Sally is a pseudonym.
12. "BDSM" refers to sex practices incorporating bondage and discipline, and/or sadism and masochism.
13. This referred to one of Christa's original songs called "Carrot Day."
14. "Beth" is a pseudonym.
15. As I have argued previously, a type of "recreational nastiness" has become a key form of entertainment and mode of engagement online (Jane, 2017, p. 22).
16. Banet-Weiser (2018), for instance, argues that contemporary, internetized "popular rage" is not sufficient and must be transfigured into "a powerful rage, an intersectional, collective rage, directed at a racist and sexist structure" (p. 185).

References

Abetz, J. & Moore, J. (2018). "Welcome to the mommy wars, ladies": Making sense of the ideology of combative mothering in mommy blogs. *Communication, Culture & Critique*, *11*(2), 265–281. doi:10.1093/ccc/tcy008

Ahlgrim, B., & Terrance, C. (2018). Perceptions of cyberstalking: Impact of perpetrator gender and cyberstalker/victim relationship. *Journal of Interpersonal Violence*, 1–20. doi:10.1177/0886260518784590

Akass, K. (2012). Motherhood and myth-making: Despatches from the frontline of the US mommy wars. *Feminist Media Studies*, *12*(1), 137–141. doi:10.1080/14680777.2011.640005

Anderson, J. (2017, March 31). Are millennials more likely than their parents to think women's place is in the home? *Quartz*. Retrieved from https://qz.com/

Bailey, K. A. (2019). Indigenous students: Resilient and empowered in the midst of racism and lateral violence. *Ethnic and Racial Studies*, *43*(6), 1032–1051. doi:10.1080/01419870.2019.1626015

Banet-Weiser, S. (2018). *Empowered: Popular feminism and popular misogyny*. Durham, NC and London: Duke University Press.

Barker, C., & Jane, E. A. (2016). *Cultural studies: Theory and practice* (5th ed.). Los Angeles, CA: Sage.

Carrington, K. (2013). Girls and violence: The case for a feminist theory of female violence. *International Journal for Crime, Justice and Social Democracy*, *2*(2), 63–79. doi:10.5204/ijcjsd.v2i2.101

Chemaly, S. (2012, March 9). A slut manifesto. *Huffpost*. Retrieved from https://www.huffpost.com

Chemaly, S. (2018). *Rage becomes her: The power of women's anger*. London; New York, NY; Sydney, NSW; Toronto, ON; New Delhi: Simon & Schuster.

Citron, D. K. (2014). *Hate crimes in cyberspace*. Cambridge, MA and London: Harvard University Press.

Daly, M. (1978). *Gyn/Ecology: The metaethics of radical feminism*. Boston, MA: Beacon Press.

Freeman, B., & Lee, B. (2007). Towards an Aboriginal model of community healing. *Native Social Work*, *6*, 97–120. Retrieved from https://www.collectionscanada.gc.ca/obj/thesescanada/vol2/OSUL/TC-OSUL-396.pdf

Gooda, M. (2011). *Lateral violence in Aboriginal and Torres strait Islander communities - Social justice report 2011*. Retrieved from https://www.humanrights.gov.au/our-work/chapter-2-lateral-violence-aboriginal-and-torres-strait-islander-communitiessocial

Harris, T. & Raskin, A. (2020, January 30). Mr. Harris goes to Washington [Audio podcast]. *Your Undivided Attention*. Retrieved from https://humanetech.com/podcast/

Homan, P. (2019). Structural sexism and health in the United States: A new perspective on health inequality and the gender system. *American Sociological Review*, *84*(3), 486–516. doi:10.1177/0003122419848723

Jane, E. A. (2017). *Misogyny online: A short (and brutish) history*. Los Angeles, CA; London; New Delhi: Sage.

Kelly, C. (2017, March 23). Racists, sexist, bigots—can Australia's queer community really call itself inclusive? *SBS*. Retrieved from https://www.sbs.com.au

Korff, J. (2019, February 8). Bullying & lateral violence. *Creative Spirits*. Retrieved from https://www.creativespirits.info/aboriginalculture/people/bullying-lateral-violence

Lateroute, B. (2007). The ole crab story: Analysis of a personal experience in colonialism and antiracism theory. *Canadian Journal of Native Education*, *30*(2), 289–304. Retrieved from https://iportal.usask.ca/index.php?sid=538872931&id=14421&t=self_identify

Lehto, M. (2019). Bad is the new good: Negotiating bad motherhood in Finnish mommy blogs. *Feminist Media Studies*, *20*(5), 657–671. doi:10.1080/14680777.2019.1642224

Moane, G. (2000). Psychic liberation: Feminist practices for transformation among Irish women. In S. L. Hoagland & M. Frye (Eds.), *Feminist interpretations of mary daly* (pp. 389–417). University Park, PA: Pennsylvania State University Press.

Phillips, W. (2015). *This is why we can't have nice things: Mapping the relationship between online trolling and mainstream culture*. Cambridge, MA and London: The MIT Press.

Powell, A., Henry, N., & Flynn, A. (2018). Image-based sexual abuse. In W. S. DeKeseredy & M. Dragiewicz (Eds.), *Routledge handbook of critical criminology* (2nd ed., pp. 305–315). Abingdon and New York, NY: Routledge.

Sehgal, P. (2016, May 3). The forced heroism of the "survivor." *The New York Times*. Retrieved from https://www.nytimes.com/

Showden, C. R. (2016). Feminist sex wars. In N. Naples, R. C. Hoogland, M. Wickramasinghe & W. C. A. Wong (Eds.), *The Wiley Blackwell encyclopedia of gender and sexuality studies*. Hoboken, NJ: John Wiley & Sons, Ltd. doi:10.1002/9781118663219

Smith, P. K., López-Castro, L., Robinson, S., & Görzigc, A. (2019). Consistency of gender differences in bullying in cross-cultural surveys. *Aggression and Violent Behavior*, *45*, 33–40. doi:10.1016/j.avb.2018.04.006

Smoker, M., & March, E. (2017). Predicting perpetration of intimate partner cyberstalking: Gender and the Dark Tetrad. *Computers in Human Behavior*, *72*, 390–396. doi:10.1016/j.chb.2017.03.012

Steiner, L. & Bronstein, C. (2017). Leave a comment: Mommyblogs and the everyday struggle to reclaim parenthood. *Feminist Media Studies*, *17*(1), 59–76. doi:10.1080/14680777.2017.1261840

The United Nations Broadband Commission for Digital Development Working Group on Broadband and Gender. (2015). Cyber violence against women and girls: A world-wide wake-up call. Retrieved from http://www.unwomen.org/~/media/headquarters/attachments/sections/library/publications/2015/cyber_violence_gender%20report.pdf

Toone, K. (2018, November). Come back for us: A critical reflection on the shared history of queers and sex workers and our need for solidarity. *Hecate*, *44*(1), 110–121. Retrieved from https://search-proquest-com.proxy.bib.uottawa.ca/docview/2339839585?accountid=14701

Traister, R. (2018). *Good and mad: The revolutionary power of women's anger*. London: Simon & Schuster.

Trott, V. (2017). Connected feminists: Foregrounding the interpersonal in connective action. *Australian Journal of Political Science*, *53*(3), 1–14. doi:10.1080/10361146.2017.1416583

Vivienne, S. (2017). "I will not hate myself because you cannot accept me": Problematizing empowerment and gender-diverse selfies. *Popular Communication*, *15*(2), 126–140. doi:10.1080/15405702.2016.1269906

Chapter 11

Claiming Victimhood: Victims of the "Transgender Agenda"

Ben Colliver

Abstract

Transgender people have received substantial attention in recent years, with gender identity being a focal point of online debate. Transgender identities are central to discussions relating to sex-segregated spaces and activities, such as public toilets, prisons, and sports participation. The introduction of "gender-neutral" spaces has received criticism because some argue that there is an increased risk of sexual violence against women and children. However, little is known about the implications that these constructions have for whom is able to claim a "victim status." In this chapter, I provide a critical analysis of the techniques used by individuals to align themselves with a "victim status." These claims are presented and contextualized within varying notions of victimization, from being victims of political correctness to victims of a more aggressive minority community. This feeds into an inherently transphobic discourse that is difficult to challenge without facing accusations of perpetuating an individual's "victimhood." Transphobic rhetoric is most commonly expressed through constructing transgender people as "unnatural," "sinful," or as experiencing a "mental health issue." This chapter argues that the denial of transphobia and simultaneous claims of victimization made by the dominant, cisgender majority are intrinsically linked.

Keywords: Transgender; victimhood; discourse analysis; transphobia; gender neutral; sex-segregated; cisgender

Introduction

Transgender identities have attracted significant academic, political, and social attention in recent years. Indeed, there is an ever-growing body of research that

The Emerald International Handbook of Technology-Facilitated Violence and Abuse, 189–204

doi:10.1108/978-1-83982-848-520211014

explores issues relating to, and affecting, transgender communities (Pearce, 2018; Roen, 2001; Shuster, 2017). Transgender identities are also the subject of discussion, "debate," and de-legitimization across various social media platforms including YouTube, Twitter, and Facebook (Colliver, Coyle, & Silvestri, 2019). While it is acknowledged that transgender people have long existed within and across societies globally (Jamel, 2018), it is only more recently in the United Kingdom that such intense public visibility has been centered upon issues affecting transgender communities.

The structural visibility has meant that the lives of transgender people have come under public scrutiny. Simultaneously to this increasing structural visibility, the United Kingdom has seen an annual increase in hate crime targeting transgender people (Home Office, 2019). In an online context, progressive protections and formal acknowledgment of transgender people are regularly contested on a number of apparent binary "trade-offs," including "sex vs gender," and "science vs subjectivity." As will be demonstrated in this chapter, it is common for individuals to claim that their "sex-based" rights are diminishing in light of "gender-based" rights. Yet, the ways in which cisgender people claim victimhood has not yet attracted significant academic attention. Instead, research into "claiming victimhood" has primarily focused on racial oppression (King, 2015; Kolber, 2017) and "men's rights" movements (Coston & Kimmel, 2013; Girard, 2009).

The term "transgender" has been defined in a number of different ways, offering different levels of inclusivity of identities, experiences, and expressions that fall outside contemporary Western gender binaries (Davidson, 2007). In this chapter, the terms "transgender" and "trans" will be used interchangeably and are defined as denoting:

> A range of gender experiences, subjectivities and presentations that fall across, between or beyond stable categories of "man" and "woman". "Transgender" includes gender identities that have, more traditionally, been described as "transsexual", and a diversity of genders that call into question an assumed relationship between gender identity and presentation and the "sexed" body. (Hines, 2010, p. 1)

The term "cisgender" describes a person whose gender identity aligns with the sex they were assigned at birth. The use and implications of this term have been contested as a result of the enforcement of another socially constructed binary (Jamel, 2018). Despite the complexities associated with this term, it is used within this chapter as a useful identity marker and to challenge dominant representations of both cisgender and trans people.

This chapter draws on a discourse analysis of 1,756 online comments made in response to YouTube videos regarding transgender people's access to public toilets, and more specifically, the implementation of "gender-neutral" toilets. Existing literature shows that public toilets can be sites of anxiety, policing, and abuse for trans people (Browne, 2004; Faktor, 2011). Public toilets often receive such high levels of attention as they are conceptualized as being the ultimate gender-segregated space (Doan, 2010). Access to a number of sex-segregated spaces, including public toilets, fitting rooms, changing room, prisons, and hospital wards has gained significant social and political attention in recent years and are often core to the debates relating to "sex-based" vs "gender-based" rights. Gender-neutral spaces have been engaged with both politically and socially. Within the United Kingdom, media attention has been paid to the introduction, or discussion, of gender-neutral toilets in a range of public spaces including schools, restaurants, and train stations (Davidson, 2019; Middleton, 2019; Noor, 2019). This has coincided with online debate on social media platforms regarding the implementation of and access to gender-neutral toilets.

This chapter seeks to challenge the dominant framework that allows for cisgender identities to remain uninterrogated. While my previous research has identified the ways in which transgender people are constructed in an online context (Colliver et al., 2019), this chapter seeks to present the ways in which cisgender people construct themselves online, more specifically in relation to transgender people.[1] This chapter responds to the gap in academic research by providing a critical expose of the ways in which "they," the transgender "other," and "us," the cisgender majority are constructed as being in constant opposition in the quest for a greater level of "rights." The chapter explores the ways in which "victimhood" is worked up and constructed on social media platforms. It will be argued that any progression for transgender people in relation to human rights, protective legislation, and acknowledgment is constructed in direct opposition, and ultimately, at the cost of, cisgender people's rights.

The rise of the internet, and in particular, social media has seen a rise in text posted online which may be considered problematic for a number of reasons, including the anonymity of online interactions. A growing body of literature has been developed recently that considers the similarities and differences between online and offline hate speech (Awan & Zempi, 2016; Brown, 2018). It is vital to address transphobia and hate speech more broadly in an online context as this can have very practical offline implications if these views (re)gain unchallenged political traction. These implications include the legitimization of transphobic hate crime and an uncontested call for a rollback of protective legislation. As a result, the need to address issues of discrimination, prejudice, and violence that transgender people face can be minimized and deflected. Addressing prejudicial and discriminatory speech in an online context is important as research has shown that those who engage in these behaviors "provide links to one another, and expressly attempt to encourage both recruitment and discussion among like-minded people" (Sunstein, 2007, pp. 57, 58). The analysis of text and talk from online platforms provides an opportunity to move away from attitudinal scales, which are often decontextualized within the life of the participants and provides a more subjective overview of the ways in which people construct minority groups. The analysis of naturally occurring text and talk demonstrates that views vary depending upon the function of the text at that point in time. Talk and text is therefore contextual, situational, and relational (Potter & Wetherell, 1987). It is important to note that it is not the intention of this chapter to judge the authenticity of claims made, nor to "debate" the authenticity or existence of transgender people. Despite the data presented in this chapter, this work is firmly grounded in the position that transgender people are valid and authentic.

Method

The data and analysis presented in this chapter are taken from a larger research project that examines "everyday" experiences of discrimination, abuse, and hate crime targeting transgender people (Colliver et al., 2019). Ethical approval was received from Kingston University in November 2016. The data used within this chapter formed part of a larger online element of the research project that explored the ways in which transgender people were constructed in an online context in relation to videos that focused on "gender-neutral" toilets. The dataset consisted of 1,756 comments posted by YouTube users on 10 randomly-sampled videos that were identified using the search term "gender-neutral toilets."

All videos were sampled on May 1, 2017, and a total of 431 videos were collated. A number of inclusion criteria were set that determined whether videos were eligible to be sampled, including the relevance of the video content to the topic, not being a duplicate of another video, and having had elicited a minimum of five user comments from viewers. After the inclusion criteria were applied, 100 videos were identified as suitable for the study. All videos were assigned a number, and an online random number generator was then used to select a manageable sample of 10 videos. Similar sampling methods have been used in other online studies exploring narratives of international travel described in online personal blogs (Snee, 2013). Despite the wider research project having a focus on the United Kingdom, the online element of the study was not restricted to UK videos to be able to explore the globalization of online communities. It is important to note, however, that the specific geographical location of each commenter could not be established.

Three videos featured news coverage from the United States, of President Obama's instruction to schools to allow transgender students to access the toilet that aligned with their gender identity. One video featured a short clip from the *Jimmy Kimmel Live* show which featured US citizens being asked to comment on gender-neutral toilets, more specifically, their opinion on potential visual indicators that a toilet was "gender neutral." One video featured a transgender woman who resides in the United States asking members of the public if they would have concerns over sharing a public toilet with her, before disclosing her trans identity. The other five videos were face-to-camera videos, three of which were produced by cisgender people (two from the United Kingdom and one from the United States) and two produced by transgender people (one from the United Kingdom and one from the United States) sharing opinions on "gender-neutral" toilets.

The dataset was subjected to critical discursive psychology, a form of discourse analysis (see Coyle, 2016 for an overview of this approach). This form of analysis is strongly grounded within a social constructionist philosophy and assimilates with the epistemological stance of the wider research study. This particular type of analysis has also been used effectively in other research exploring prejudice and discrimination (Goodman & Burke, 2010a, 2010b; Reisigl & Wodak, 2001). In this chapter, the focus is on what is *accomplished* by comments posted in response to the sampled YouTube videos. As such, the analysis is centered around the text's action orientation, meaning the data are not analyzed or interpreted in a manner that speculates or attempts to establish the motivation or intentions of the commenter. In particular, the analysis seeks to identify some of the key discursive resources that are drawn upon to construct and position cisgender people as the victims of a "transgender agenda." The excerpts presented are verbatim from YouTube, so all spelling and grammatical errors remain, as does the use of italics and upper-case letters.

Thematic Overview

A central theme developed from the data was "gender-neutral toilets as sites of sexual danger," and notions of sexual danger formed a fundamental part of the case that was put forward against the implementation of gender-neutral toilets. In particular, male sexuality was constructed as uncontrollable, animalistic, and overpowering, and commenters regularly drew upon graphic descriptions of sexual violence to contextualize their claims of risk. Child imagery was routinely invoked and functioned to transform a logistical issue into a moral debate. Comparisons were made and distinctions were drawn between public and private spaces in the construction of gender-neutral toilets to emphasize the inherent risk associated with these spaces. These specific constructions that were regularly mobilized problematize gender-neutral toilets in socially recognizable ways. In doing so, these constructions function to sustain the status-quo of sex-segregated toilets while reinforcing gendered stereotypes and norms of male dominance.

The second theme developed from the data related to "the de-legitimization of trans people," and these constructions often occurred simultaneously to the construction of gender-neutral toilets as sites of sexual danger (see Colliver et al., 2019 for a detailed analysis). A variety of motifs were drawn upon to achieve this de-legitimization, including commenters invoking notions of science, biological essentialism, and "naturalness." These notions functioned to construct transgender people as a "scientific absurdity," and clearly establish boundaries between the significant "natural" majority – cisgender people – and the "unnatural" minority – transgender people. These claims also provided a foundation for transgender people to be de-legitimized through claims of religious morality.

Another significant motif that was drawn upon by YouTube users was that of "mental health," and recurrent claims were made that "transgenderism" is a "mental illness." Finally, conspiracy-like claims were made that wider societal structures and institutions are responsible for the emergence of a new "trend" of "transgender" as a category. Social media is regularly discussed, and a significant amount of responsibility is assigned for the emergence of transgender people.

Claiming Victimhood: Gender Neutral Toilets as Undermining the Rights of Cisgender People

The discursive resources that are used within talk and text that constructs trans people in negative, problematic, and challenging ways is a growing area of interest within academia (Colliver et al., 2019). However, little attention has been paid to the ways in which cisgender people construct the risk that they deem to be associated with gender-neutral toilets and the self-identification of one's gender. Attitudinal studies toward transgender and gender non-conforming people have found correlations between negative or discriminatory attitudes alongside age and gender, with some studies reporting higher levels of negative attitudes in women and older people (Hill & Willoughby, 2005; Tee & Hegarty, 2006). On the other hand, some studies have founder higher negative attitudes toward transgender and gender non-conforming people among men (Norton & Herek, 2013). However, it is not clear whether attitudes toward transgender people change when specifically looking at transgender women, of whom the focus of much debate around public toilets is focused.

Doan (2010, p. 635) suggests that transgender people experience a "special kind of tyranny – the tyranny of gender – that arises when people dare to challenge the hegemonic expectations for appropriately gendered behavior in Western society." When people challenge hegemonic expectations of gender, they also challenge deeply engrained ideas around which bodies belong in which spaces. This may be most intensely felt within public spaces segregated by gender in which others are able to apply, and attempt to enforce cisnormative standards relating to gender expression and presentation. The level of gender-policing in these spaces may be intensified as a result of the spatial structure of public toilets which facilitates monitoring and surveillance (Cavanagh, 2010). Bodies and spaces "simultanesously (re)create one another," and there are implications for how we navigate the spaces we occupy (Nash, 2010, p. 588). This chapter focuses on the ways in which cisgender commenters construct and position themselves as victims, which often surfaced through three sub-themes: "Victims of a political agenda"; "loss of rights, privacy, and safety"; and "the end of the world," each of which is discussed below. It is argued throughout this chapter that these claims of victimization are intrinsically linked to the denial of transphobia and function to negate any requirement for a change in societal provisions for minority communities.

Victims of a Political Agenda

A recurrent theme developed from the data was the concept of victimhood in relation to political correctness and wider political structures that seek to oppress the dominant majority. It has been argued that making claims of structural oppression is key for the "in-group" to maintain a positive moral group identity (Sullivan, Landau, Branscombe, & Rothschild, 2012). In this sense, making claims of structural and political oppression serve to construct the dominant majority as innocent and powerless in the face of structures that are more powerful. This type of victimhood was evident in the data sampled, in which "transphobia" is constructed as a politically correct term, functioning to limit the freedom of the dominant majority. In these discussions, the construction of transphobia as a politically correct term also serves to refute accusations of transphobia, while simultaneously claiming a victim status.

> No one is afraid of gays. Homophobia and transphobia are made up terms used to bully people into a specific way of thinking. In reality those perversions are a mental disorder but the script has been flipped and now anyone who doesn't agree with those mental disorders must have a mental disorder or a "phobia" of them. (This comment was made in response to other YouTube users debating whether children would be safe in gender neutral toilets.)

> Awww we are bigots because we don't want men in the ladies restroom lmao? Fuck off sicko. (This comment was made in response to a previous comment which suggested a separate bathroom should be made for bigots.)

In the extracts presented above, transphobia is constructed as a socio-political term. The use of inverted commas around the word "phobia" in the first comment and the direct claim that "homophobia and transphobia are made up terms" function to deny responsibility, accountability, or even the existence of discriminatory views. As a result, the commenter is positioned as the victim of "political correctness," while simultaneously de-legitimizing gender and sexual minorities through claims of mental health and "perversion." While the second comment does not construct transphobia as non-existent, it does construct the label "bigot" as assigned unfairly. The use of an acronym (lmao) to suggest extreme laughter within a rhetorical question also functions to maximize the absurdity of these labels and minimize the accusations of bigotry and the label that has been assigned by another YouTube user.

Not only are cisgender people constructed as victims of "political correctness" but also other YouTube users construct themselves as victims within the context of a wider, intentional political agenda. Commenters claim that issues of gender-neutral facilities and adjustments that may potentially ease the access for transgender people in public places are intentionally pushed by politicians and the media to mask the "real" issues that affect the dominant, cisgender majority. As a result, cisgender people are constructed as victims of a political system which fails to tend to their needs.

> Wait, between all this shit, are we fucking fixing the economy? (This was a direct response to the video commented on.)

> We the people are given a "Toy" to play with while bigger things happen … (This was a direct response to the video commented on.)

> To me this whole thing just seems like a distraction from all the real problems in this country. (This was a direct response to the video commented on.)

> The trans issue is way overblown, they are a small minority (Like less than 1% of our population) it seems like a huge expense nationally for us all to create bathrooms for them. (This was a direct response to the video commented on.)

The first three comments presented above highlight the "problems" that are not being attended to as a result of a political focus on gender-neutral toilets. In the first comment, a specific example is given and framed within a rhetorical question. The use of a rhetorical question within this comment functions to negate the need for any response. As such, the economy is firmly established as in need of "fixing." In both the second and third comments, gender-neutral toilets are constructed as a side issue, unworthy of attention, and therefore a trivial matter. While both comments allude to more pressing "issues," neither comment specifies any particular issue that is deemed to be more important. However, the general allusion to more significant "issues" that countries face functions to construct the dominant majority as victims of a failing political system. In the final comment, the dominant, cisgender majority are constructed as victims owing to the economic and financial implications associated with implementing gender-neutral toilets. These adjustments are constructed as unnecessary, and the commenter quantifies the transgender population which reinforces the unreasonableness of these adjustments.

Loss of Rights, Privacy, and Safety

Within the data, gender-neutral toilets were also worked up and constructed as presenting a "trade-off" in relation to the rights, privacy, and safety between transgender and cisgender people. This was presented in ways that position cisgender people as the victims of this trade-off and claims were often made that the implementation of gender-neutral toilets will result in diminished rights and safety for the dominant, cisgender majority.

> I just think with this issue you need to decide who's comfort level you are willing to side with is it a) the trans-gendered person who feels more comfortable in the opposite sexes bathroom or B) the female in the FEMALE bathroom who feels uncomfortable with MALES in the female bathroom...everyone has different comfort levels, so please keep that in mind. (This was a direct response to the video being commented on.)

> We all have a right to be comfortable in a public bathroom facility. I don't see why hundreds of people who identify as the gender they were born should be uncomfortable just so very few transgender people can use the bathroom that they want to. (This was a direct response to the video being commented on. One other YouTube user responded and compared gender-neutral toilets to pornography and that people will eventually get used to it.)

> The argument you make should apply to the others as well that have a choice in how they want to live their life. Last I checked if someone that doesn't want a sex change its their decision and their rights are just as important as a transgender. (This was in response to another comment which suggested if someone is transgender it is their choice, and if people don't like it, it is their problem.)

The first comment constructs a "trade-off" in relation to rights and safety, in which one must decide whose rights are most important. The use of the phrase "opposite sex" and the capitalization of the words "Females" and "Males" functions to reinforce a rigid gender binary, de-legitimizes those who identify outside of that binary, and de-legitimizes the authenticity of "claimed" transgender identities. The de-legitimization of transgender people is crucial in raising the "worthy" victim status of cisgender people. The quantification of people in the second comment also functions to raise the "worthy" victim status of cisgender communities, as it highlights the significantly larger population of people who may be potentially harmed as a result of the implementation of gender-neutral toilets. However, this comment is also contradictory in nature, as it begins by claiming that "we all have a right" to be comfortable, yet the comment constructs comfortability as a significantly more fundamental right of cisgender people. In the final comment, "worthy" victim status is worked up by emphasizing the role of free-will, autonomy, and choice in the decision trans individuals make.

The role of choice in transgender people's lives functions to decrease the "worthiness" of them as victims, as they are constructed as freely choosing to be in this particular position. The use of the phrase "a transgender" also functions to dehumanize transgender people, contributing to their inauthenticity as victims. In the three comments above, cisgender people are constructed as "victims" of advancing transgender equality. Similar techniques have been found in a study of "white victimhood" in which white people are threatened by racial equality movements (Wilkins, Hirsch, Kaiser, & Inkles; 2017).

The concept of privacy was also key in commenters exploring the "trade-off" between safety and rights. Anderson (2009, p. 91) argues that "anxieties about privacy violations while using a toilet are profoundly strong in Western culture." Therefore, it is unsurprising that notions of privacy were present within the data.

> For me it has nothing to do with trans people or the issue with weirdos in the bathroom. It's hard enough trying to shit with women in the bathroom. It's a lack of privacy. (This was made in direct response to the video being commented on.)
>
> Why should I have to sacrifice my privacy and comfort just for the sake of 1% of the population? (One YouTube user replied asking how their privacy is sacrificed, to which they responded "Because I'm not really comfortable going to the bathroom with the opposite sex.")

The issue of privacy is framed in a similar manner to that of safety and rights, as a "trade-off." This is most evident in the second comment in which the commenter claims they would have to "sacrifice" their privacy to accommodate the needs of transgender people. This is also followed by a quantification of the transgender community to further highlight how it is the privacy of the overwhelming cisgender majority that will be sacrificed. On the contrary, the loss of privacy is constructed in a significantly more mundane way in the first comment, referring to the process of excretion and positioning this bodily function as the key reason for their anxiety regarding gender-neutral toilets.

It is clear that the implementation of gender-neutral toilets is constructed as undermining the rights of cisgender people. In a similar way that claims of "white victimhood" were made in King's (2015) study, claims of "cisgender victimhood" are present in this study and create a protective barrier of needing to directly address cisnormativity and therefore gender norms and the gender binary are maintained.

Beyond reasons of safety and privacy, themes of men's convenience were positioned as a key reason against the implementation of gender-neutral toilets. Gender-neutral toilets are therefore constructed as inconvenient for men, representing a loss of practicality.

> Don't install urinals? They help things move faster. No ways. (That seems discriminatory.) (This comment was in direct response to another YouTube user who suggested not installing urinals would address issues of privacy in gender-neutral toilets.)

> I'm against unisex bathrooms. I don't know what women do in public bathrooms that leads to the long queues in front of them, and I don't care. But I don't want to have to queue because women are apparently unable to get rid of their body secretions in a time-efficient manner. (This comment was made in direct response to the video being commented on.)

Male convenience is not a new concept. Greed (1995) found that in relation to public toilets, the convenience afforded to men was significantly higher than that afforded to women, and this was evident through the provision of two-thirds more public facilities. Further to inconvenience, the victim status of men is explicitly discussed in the first comment in which the commenter claims to be a victim of discrimination. This clearly highlights the victimization that cisgender people, particularly cisgender men, will experience as a result of gender-neutral toilets being implemented. In claiming discrimination, access to urinals is constructed as a fundamental right for men, and the implementation of gender-neutral toilets an infringement upon this fundament right. In the second comment, there is also a construction of "difference" between men and women, with men being the main victims as a result of a loss of convenience.

Finally, in relation to a loss of rights, the gains of the broader lesbian, gay, bisexual, trans, queer and intersex (LGBTQI) movement are often highlighted to position the dominant majority as accommodating, which is necessary to facilitate a discriminatory comment. Furthermore, victim status is also established through constructing the broader LGBTQI community as demanding, unfair, and "bullies." Constructing the LGBTQI community in this way, positions the cisgender community as victims.

> LGBTQ = BULLIES. (This comment was in direct response to the video being commented on.)

> They talk about they being bullied, but sometimes when the victim gets lots of power they can end up becoming the bully they hate so much. So congrats LGBT and Liberals you became what you hated so much. (This comment was in direct response to the video being commented on.)
>
> Some people suggested a Transgender bathroom. The LGBT didn't want it. They just want what they want. No negotiations. (This comment was in response to another YouTube user who claimed there should be a separate "transgender bathroom.")
>
> They want to annoy us. A Transgendered restroom would've been better cause that they they're not violating our space, but no. Only restroom I'll be using is in my house. (This comment was made in direct response to comment three above.)

A key part of establishing a "victim identity" is constructing a suitable offender. This is established in all of the comments presented above. In the first comment, the LGBTQI community is constructed as bullies. This comment is homogenizing, in that the comment does not function to differentiate between groups of people. As such, a clear offender is constructed. Widely accepted tropes surround the "abused" becoming the "abuser" is drawn upon to construct LGBTQI people, and "liberal" people more broadly as offending against cisgender, conservative people. Although largely accepted, these claims have been proven to be unfounded (Leach, Stewart, & Smallbone, 2016). The final two comments construct LGBTQI communities as irritating, boisterous, and demanding. The use of the phrase "no negotiations" functions to construct these communities as unfair and unresponsive to compromise. In addition, the use of the word "violating" serves to construct a clear incident of victimization that cisgender communities experience. Through implication, this constructs cisgender communities as victims of this unfairness, building up their identity as "victims." Similar findings have been found in the study of men's rights movements, in which women who are perceived to be feminist are constructed as vicious and aggressive (Coston & Kimmel, 2013). In studies of the men's rights movements, men as the dominant group are often framed as in need of protection from women (Girard, 2009). A similar rhetoric was found in these data in which cisgender people are constructed as needing protection, and a "safe space" away from transgender people.

The End of the World

In light of the ways "victimhood" was developed within the data, slippery slope arguments are then developed, ultimately functioning to highlight the extreme harms facing cisgender communities if the "righteous" do not intervene. The result is that "the end of world" is constructed as imminent if cisgender communities do not unite and prevent the progression of transgender equality and rights. This is most common throughout the data in extreme case formulations, in which extreme harm is speculated and predicted.

> Marrying animals and then ultimately dead people are next! Watch! (This comment was made in direct response to the video being commented on.)

> If we lie to 'transsexuals' to make them feel better, who is the next group we have to lie to: animal sex lovers, pedophiles, necrophiliacs. Just how far down that rabbit hole do we want to go as a society. (This comment was made in direct response to the video being commented on.)

In the comments presented above, specific reference is made to socially unacceptable practices, such as bestiality, pedophilia, and necrophilia. By drawing upon socially unacceptable practices, transgender identities are conflated with these concepts, while also constructing the existence and acceptance of transgender people as a pathway into moral social decline. In the first comment, a catalog of absurdity is established through claims of necrophilia and bestiality. Pomerantz (1984) argues that "extreme case" examples are drawn upon when attempts are made to justify a conclusion. Within this construction of "societal decline," transgender people are also de-legitimized through the use of inverted commas around the word "transsexuals." The function of the inverted commas is to present transgender people as inauthentic.

However, as can be seen below, some commenters accentuate this moral social decline even further. Within these slippery slope arguments, apocalyptic claims are developed which prophesize the end of the world because of increasing trans equality.

> Societal rot. We are on a very dangerous path. (This comment was made in direct response to the video being commented on.)

> I can't wait to see when this place burns like Sodom and Gomorrah. (This comment was made in direct response to the video being commented on.)

> These laws are feminism and LGBTQ run amuk, but, let it go down. It will be the great undoing of them all. When you begin to get into this level of confusion, you know you're at the end. Let it burn. It's time. (This comment was made in direct response to the video being commented on.)

The "end of the world" rhetoric that is present within these comments is framed in various different ways. In the first comment, the "end of the world" is constructed subtly, through implication. The use of the phrase "on a very dangerous path" functions to allow the reader to construct the outcome, but through using the word "dangerous" signifies that the outcome is inevitably negative. The "end of the world" is much more explicit in the second comment where religious rhetoric is used to create an apocalyptic image through the story of Sodom and Gomorrah (mentioned in the Hebrew Bible and in the Christian New Testament). Within this passage, inhabitants are commonly assumed to have been destroyed because of homosexuality and other depravities, sins, and vices. The use of this rhetoric is central in condemning transgender communities, while also constructing an "end of the world" argument.

In the final comment, the "end of the world" is directly associated with gains made by LGBTQI communities. Unlike the other comments, the end of the world has already been occurred. This ultimately serves to heighten the sense of urgency for cisgender communities to intervene and regain societal control. Similar rhetorics have been found in the construction of homosexuality (Cragun, Williams, & Sumerau, 2015) and in this sense, transgender people are constructed as a social issue which forecasts the definitive obliteration of civil society. In this framing, cisgender people are constructed as the victims of a less social morality and civility. As such, transgender people are legitimate targets for abuse, discrimination, and oppression through the constructed risk they present to a wider societal moral decline.

Conclusion

This chapter identified the discursive themes that are used to construct and position cisgender people as "victims" in relation to gender-neutral bathrooms. The themes manifested in various ways, but most significantly cisgender people were constructed as victims of political correctness, a wider political agenda and victims of depreciating rights and privacy. The implications of these constructions culminate in an "end of the world" rhetoric in which significant and extreme harms will be experienced by cisgender people as a result of continuing transgender equality. These significant harms are framed within notions of severe moral decline. As such, transgender people are "othered" and problematized as those who are responsible for the harms cisgender communities face and are therefore positioned as offenders.

At times, similar rhetoric is drawn upon by YouTube users that have historically been invoked in the construction of homosexuality and heterosexuality (see e.g., Baker, 2004; Perone, 2014). In this sense, we are not witnessing anything new or innovative, rather a recycling of socially recognizable motifs in the construction of cisgender people as victims. It also becomes evident throughout this chapter that claims of victim status highlight how the construction of "the self" as a victim is often achieved within a collective framework, in which entire communities are positioned as victims, emphasizing the otherness of the minority group. It is argued that claiming a victim position is key in successfully opposing the implementation of gender-neutral toilets, while simultaneously deflecting claims of transphobia, bigotry, and hatred.

It is key to address transphobia in an online context as research has demonstrated the detrimental impact that online abuse can have on those targeted (Awan & Zempi, 2016). The online construction of cisgender people as victims has significant, practical, and real-life consequences in the context of gaining political traction and therefore minimizing the need to address incidents of transphobia. To develop effective ways to challenge and combat transphobia and discrimination against transgender people, it is vital to identify barriers that exist in identifying incidents of transphobia. As such, understanding the discursive resources that are drawn upon to construct cisgender populations as victims of a wider political and social agenda is key. In this chapter, I have outlined that claiming a victim position is central in minimizing and deflecting accusations of transphobia. I hope to have made a contribution to understanding the discursive resources that are drawn upon to frame cisgender communities as victims that can be used in future research to develop effective interventions.

Note

1. It is important to note that there is no one specific construction of "cisgender." Constructions of privileges or oppressions claimed to be experienced by cisgender people are dependent upon other social factors and characteristics including sexuality, race, and class. What it means to be cisgender and the assumed privileges associated with this identity are context dependant.

References

Anderson, J. (2009). Bodily privacy, toilets, and sex discrimination: The problem of 'manhood' in a women's prison. In O. Gershenson and B. Penner (Eds.), *Ladies and gents: Public toilets and gender* (pp. 90–104). Philadelphia, PA: Temple University Press.

Awan, I. & Zempi, I. (2016). The affinity between online and offline anti-Muslim hate crime: Dynamics and impacts. *Aggression and Violent Behavior*, *27*, 1–8.

Baker, P. (2004). 'Unnatural acts': Discourses of homosexuality within the House of Lords debates on gay male law reform. *Journal of Sociolinguistics*, *8*(1), 88–106.

Brown, A. (2018). What is so special about online (as compared to offline) hate speech? *Ethnicities*, *18*(3), 297–326.

Browne, K. (2004). Genderism and the bathroom problem: (Re)materialising sexed sites, (re)creating sexed bodies. *Gender, Place & Culture*, *11*(3), 331–346.

Cavanagh, S. (2010). *Queering bathrooms: Gender, sexuality, and the hygienic imagination*. Toronto, ON: University of Toronto Press.

Colliver, B., Coyle, A., & Silvestri, M. (2019). The online 'othering' of transgender and non-binary people. In K. Lumsden & E. Harmer (Eds.), *Online othering: Exploring the dark side of the web* (pp. 215–238). London: Palgrave Macmillan.

Coston, B. & Kimmel, M. (2013). White men as the new victims: Reverse discrimination cases and the men's rights movement. *Nevada Law Journal*, *13*(2), 368–385.

Coyle, A. (2016). Discourse analysis. In E. Lyons & A. Coyle (Eds.), *Analysing qualitative data in psychology* (2nd ed., pp. 160–181). London: SAGE.

Cragun, R., Williams, E., & Sumerau, J. (2015). From sodomy to sympathy: LDS elites' discursive construction of homosexuality over time. *Journal for the Scientific Study of Religion*, *54*(2), 291–310.

Davidson, M. (2007). Seeking refuge under the umbrella: Inclusion, exclusion, and organizing within the category Transgender. *Sexuality Research and Social Policy*, *4*(4), 60–80.

Davidson, G. (2019). Mixed sex loos in Scottish schools break regulations, warn campaigner. *The Scotsman*, September, 1. Retrieved from https://www.scotsman.com/news/politics/mixed-sex-loos-in-scottish-schools-break-regulations-warn-campaigners-1-4995254. Accessed on September 23, 2019.

Doan, P. (2010). The tyranny of gendered spaces: Reflections from beyond the gender dichotomy. *Gender, Place & Culture*, *17*, 635–654.

Faktor, A. (2011). Access and exclusion: Public toilets as sites of insecurity for gender and sexual minorities in North America. *Journal of Human Security*, *7*(3), 10–22.

Girard, A. (2009). Backlash or equality? The influence of men's and women's rights discourses on domestic violence legislation in Ontario. *Violence Against Women*, *15*(1), 5–23.

Goodman, S. & Burke, S. (2010a). 'Oh you don't want asylum seekers, oh you're just racist':A discursive analysis of discussions about whether it's racist to oppose asylum seeking. *Discourse & Society*, *21*(3), 325–340.

Goodman, S. & Burke, S. (2010b). Discursive deracialization in talk about asylum seeking. *Journal of Community & Applied Social Psychology*, *21*(2), 111–123.

Greed, C. (1995). Public toilet provision for women in Britain: An investigation of discrimination against urination. *Women's Studies International Forum*, *18*(5), 573–584.

Hill, D. B. & Willoughby, B. L. B. (2005). The development and validation of the genderism and transphobia scale. *Sex Roles*, *53*(7–8), 531–544.

Hines, S. (2010). Introduction. In S. Hines & T. Sanger (Eds.), *Transgender identities: Towards a social analysis of gender diversity* (pp. 1–22). New York, NY: Routledge.

Home Office. (2019). *Hate crime: England and Wales, 2018/19*. London: Home Office.

Jamel, J. (2018). *Transphobic hate crime*. London: Palgrave Macmillan.

King, M. (2015). The 'knockout game': Moral panic and the politics of white victimhood. *Race & Class*, *56*(4), 85–94.

Kolber, J. (2017). Having it both ways: White denial of racial salience while claiming oppression. *Sociology Compass*, *11*(2), 1–9.

Leach, C., Stewart, A., & Smallbone, S. (2016). Testing the sexually abused-sexual abuser hypothesis: A prospective longitudinal birth cohort study. *Child Abuse & Neglect*, *51*, 144–153.

Middleton, L. (2019). Outrage of TfL poster which suggests female toilets are becoming gender neutral. *METRO*, August 21, 2019. Retrieved from https://metro.co.uk/2019/08/21/outrage-tfl-poster-suggests-female-toilets-becoming-gender-neutral-10607395/. Accessed on September 23, 2019.

Nash, C. (2010). Trans geographies, embodiment and experience. *Gender, Place & Culture*, *17*(5), 579–595.

Noor, P. (2019). Wagamama to make its toilets gender-neutral. *The Guardian*, May 31, 2019. Retrieved from https://www.theguardian.com/society/2019/may/31/wagamama-toilets-gender-neutral. Accessed on September 23, 2019.

Norton, A. T. & Herek, G. M. (2013). Heterosexuals' attitudes toward transgender people: Findings from a national probability sample of US adults. *Sex Roles*, *68*(11–12), 738–753.

Pearce, R. (2018). *Understanding trans health: Discourse, power and possibility*. Bristol: Policy Press.

Perone, A. (2014). The social construction of mental illness for lesbian, gay, bisexual, and transgender persons in the United States. *Qualitative Social Work*, *13*(6), 766–771.

Pomerantz, A. (1984). Giving a source a basis: The practice in conversation of telling "how I know". *Journal of Pragmatics*, *8*, 607–625.

Potter, J. & Wetherell, M. (1987). *Discourse and social psychology: Beyond attitudes and behaviour*. London: Sage.

Reisigl, M. & Wodak, R. (2001). *Discourse and discrimination: Rhetorics of racism and antisemitism*. London: Routledge.

Roen, K. (2001). Transgender theory and embodiment: The risk of racial marginalisation. *Journal of Gender Studies*, *10*(3), 253–263.

Shuster, S. (2017). Punctuating accountability: How discursive aggression regulates transgender people. *Gender & Society*, *31*(4), 481–502.

Snee, H. (2013). Making ethical decisions in an online context: Reflections on using blogs to explore narratives of experience. *Methodological Innovations Online*, *8*(2), 52–67.

Sullivan, D., Landau, M., Branscombe, N. & Rothschild, Z. (2012). Competitive victimhood as a response to accusations of ingroup harm doing. *Journal of Personality and Social Psychology*, *102*(4), 778–795.

Sunstein, C. (2007). *Republic.com 2.0*. Princeton, NJ: Princeton University Press.

Tee, N. & Hegarty, P. (2006). Predicting opposition to the civil rights of trans persons in the United Kingdom. *Journal of Community & Applied Social Psychology*, *16*(1), 70–80.

Wilkins, C., Hirsch, A., Kaiser, C. & Inkles, M. (2017). The threat of racial progress and the self-protective nature of perceiving anti-White bias. *Group Processes & Intergroup Relations*, *20*(6), 801–812.

Chapter 12

Doxxing: A Scoping Review and Typology

Briony Anderson and Mark A. Wood

Abstract

This chapter examines the phenomenon of doxxing: the practice of publishing private, proprietary, or personally identifying information on the internet, usually with malicious intent. Undertaking a scoping review of research into doxxing, we develop a typology of this form of technology-facilitated violence (TFV) that expands understandings of doxxing, its forms and its harms, beyond a taciturn discussion of privacy and harassment online. Building on David M. Douglas's typology of doxxing, our typology considers two key dimensions of doxxing: the form of loss experienced by the victim and the perpetrator's motivation(s) for undertaking this form of TFV. Through examining the extant literature on doxxing, we identify seven mutually non-exclusive motivations for this form of TFV: extortion, silencing, retribution, controlling, reputation-building, unintentional, and doxxing in the public interest. We conclude by identifying future areas for interdisciplinary research into doxxing that brings criminology into conversation with the insights of media-focused disciplines.

Keywords: Doxxing; Technology-facilitated violence; anonymity; privacy; personally identifying information; informational privacy

Introduction

Doxxing, a neologism derived from the hacker culture slang of "dropping dox [documents]," has been used to describe a range of acts in which private, proprietary, or personally identifying information is published on the internet against a party's wishes, usually with malicious intent. To assist researchers in distinguishing between the different forms doxxing may take, in this chapter, we undertake a scoping review of research into doxxing and develop a typology of this form of technology-facilitated violence (TFV).

The Emerald International Handbook of Technology-Facilitated Violence and Abuse, 205–226

doi:10.1108/978-1-83982-848-520211015

Our scoping review reveals that the majority of studies that have examined doxxing focus on its use either within specific fora, such as cryptomarkets (Bancroft & Scott Reid, 2017) and hacker communities (Serracino-Inglott, 2013), or against specific groups, such as white supremacists (Colton, Holmes, & Walwema, 2017). Furthermore, our review identifies seven mutually non-exclusive motivations for doxxing: *extortion*, *silencing*, *retribution*, *controlling*, *reputation-building*, *unintentional*, and *doxxing in the public interest*. These various motivations represent the first dimension of our doxxing typology. The second dimension we consider is the form of loss faced by victims of doxxing, and here we build upon David M. Douglas's (2016) compelling typological work on the phenomenon. As we hope to demonstrate, the intersections between these motivations for doxxing and the subsequent losses experienced by its victims are paramount in understanding harms associated with this form of TFVA.

Our chapter begins by reviewing Douglas's (2016) typology of doxxing, the most sophisticated typological accounting of the phenomenon to date. After detailing the methodology employed to undertake our review, we discuss our findings in three substantial sections. Drawing on Sayer's (1999) distinction between extensive and intensive research, we have divided our review into (1) extensive studies of doxxing, which examine common patterns and characteristics of doxxing; (2) intensive studies of doxxing, which examine how doxxing works within particular cases, communities, and circumstances; and (3) legal studies of doxxing, which examine legal precedent in responding to doxxing. This division, in part, reflects key methodological differences in the studies reviewed. The extensive studies of doxxing (n = 5) reviewed employed quantitative methods, namely large-scale cross-sectional surveys (n = 2; 40%), content analysis (n = 2; 40%), and software testing (n = 1; 20%). Moreover, they attempted to generate generalizable knowledge on different dimensions of doxxing. By contrast, the intensive studies of doxxing (n = 13) employed qualitative methods, namely interviews (n = 3; 23%), content analysis (n = 4; 31%), focus groups (n = 1; 8%), participant observation (n = 2; 15%) and discourse analysis (n = 3; 23%), or they represented purely theoretical treatments of doxxing (n = 3; 23%).

Douglas's Typology of Doxxing

Douglas (2016) offers the most sophisticated typological treatment of the nature and forms of doxxing. At its core, Douglas defines doxxing as "the intentional public release onto the internet of personal information about an individual by a third party, often with the intent to humiliate, threaten, intimidate, or punish the identified individual" (2016, p. 199). Within this definition, he distinguishes between three forms of doxxing: (1) deanonymizing doxxing; (2) targeting doxxing; and (3) delegitimizing doxxing. In each of the three forms of doxxing, Douglas (2016) identifies the individual targeted as being faced with a loss or damage to different things. In the case of deanonymizing doxxing, the target is faced with the loss of their anonymity, either in a professional or personal capacity. In the case of targeting doxxing, the target faces the loss of their obscurity, for example, through having their home address revealed online. And in the case of delegitimizing doxxing, the target faces a loss of credibility, for example, through a doxxer releasing evidence that they have engaged in willful deception or 'immoral' activity.

In conceptualizing these different forms of doxxing, Douglas (2016) draws upon Gary Marx's (1999) typology of the seven forms of *identity knowledge*: information that, if known, precludes the perfect anonymity of an individual. Marx's concept is particularly useful in conceptualizing doxxing because, as Douglas (2016) notes, it removes "some degree of anonymity from a specific person" (p. 200). For this reason, Douglas (2016) suggests that we understand doxxing as the act of publicly releasing a type of identity knowledge about an individual, which acts to establish a "verifiable connection" between one or more other types of identity knowledge about the individual (p. 201).

One important part of Douglas's definition is that it entails the *intentional* public release of personal information. This intentional release of information need not be undertaken with malicious intent. For example, journalists publicly outing the identities of an individual's pseudonym in stories represents doxxing, even when there is no intent of wrongdoing. But for Douglas, accidentally "outing" an individual on the internet through unintentionally releasing personal information does not represent doxxing. In other words, while doxxing may represent one form of outing individuals online, the two terms are not synonymous. According to Douglas (2016), doxxing is also not synonymous with blackmail, defamation and gossip, though it may represent a technique of blackmail (p. 202). Unlike gossip, doxxing trades in identity knowledge as opposed to "suggestion, hearsay [or] innuendo" (Douglas, 2016, p. 202). As Douglas (2016) cogently observes, the difference between doxxing and gossip is "the difference between communicating information *about* someone and communicating information *of* someone" (p. 202).

Methodology

The articles presented in this scoping review were obtained using two electronic research databases: Web of Science and Google Scholar. Articles and conference papers were primarily located using the search terms: "doxing," "doxxing," "dox," and "doxxed." However, to locate articles that discussed the phenomenon of doxxing without using the term, we also searched for: "publication of personal details," "publish personal details," and "exposing personal information," in combination with the terms "malicious," "threaten," "harass," "abuse," and "intimidate." Finally, a snowballing approach was employed to locate relevant articles by scanning the reference lists of each article identified.

Studies were included in the review if they met two eligibility criteria: (1) they discussed the nonconsensual disclosure of personally identifying information on the internet (i.e., doxxing); and (2) they examined the phenomenon at length, as opposed to merely in-passing. These broad inclusion criteria enabled us to include articles that, while not focusing primarily or wholly on doxxing, detailed the phenomenon at length in relation to other issues such as online hacktivism (Heemsbergen, 2016) or intimate partner violence (Fish & Follis, 2016). Articles published in languages other than English were excluded from the review.

Titles, abstracts, and keywords were screened to identify clear inclusions. In cases where we were unsure of an article's eligibility, we analyzed how the terms "doxing"/"doxxing," "doxed," or "dox" were used in context. Our initial searches returned 48 results on Google Scholar and 10 results on Web of Science. Three additional articles were located through a snowball technique for an initial total of 61 papers. Following a preliminary analysis, 29 papers were excluded as they mentioned doxxing only in-passing, leaving 32 articles, which are the focus of this chapter.

Results

As we found, the academic literature on doxxing is relatively new. Despite the term dating back to the mid-1990s, we identified no academic articles published before 2010 that employed the term in the sense explored here. Indeed, the earliest reference to the term in academic literature that we identified appears in Phillips's (2011) article on RIP Trolling (the organized practice of targeting social media memorial pages with abusive or harmful content). The overwhelming majority of the articles identified in our scoping review dated from the mid-2010s onwards, with most articles being published between 2017 and 2018. Few articles had doxxing as their primary focus. More frequently, doxxing was discussed alongside other practices, as a technique of politically motivated harassment (Colton et al., 2017; Fish & Follis, 2016; Massanari, 2015, 2018), as a form of intimate partner violence (Freed et al., 2018), or as a contestation of privacy rights (Corbridge, 2018; MacAllister, 2017) (Fig 12.1).

As noted above, we identified seven mutually non-exclusive motivations for doxxing in the literature: *extortion*, *silencing*, *retribution*, *controlling*, *reputation-building*, *unintentional*, and *public interest*. *Extortion doxxing* or "doxtortion" entails

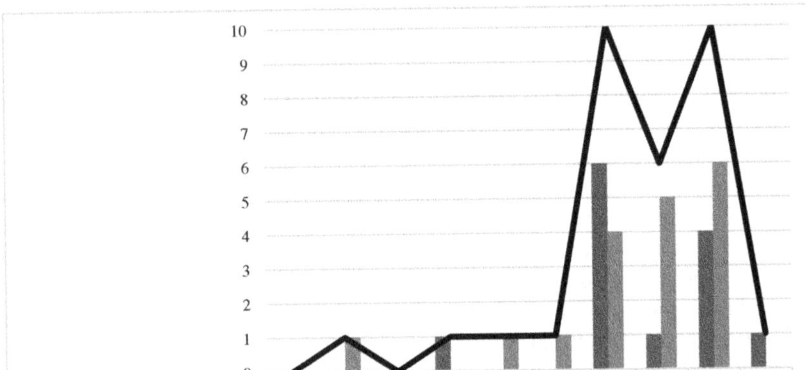

	2010	2011	2012	2013	2014	2015	2016	2017	2018	2019
Doxing primary focus	0	0	0	1	0	0	6	1	4	1
Doxing discussed at length	0	1	0	0	1	1	4	5	6	0
Total articles	0	1	0	1	1	1	10	6	10	1

Fig. 12.1. Combined Line/Bar Graph Showing the Number of Doxxing-Related Studies Published per Year between 2010–2019.

releasing or threatening to release compromising information about an individual online to extort (usually) financial benefits from them. *Silencing doxxing* involves leveraging doxxing, or the threat of doxxing, to remove an individual from an online forum. *Retribution doxxing* is doxxing motivated specifically by a desire to "punish" an individual. As detailed in the studies discussed below, retribution doxxing may represent a technique of targeted harassment employed against individuals holding opposing political views. However, it may also take the form of informal justice-seeking actions (see Salter, 2013; Wood, Rose, & Thompson, 2019), wherein victims of crime seek justice beyond the formal justice system through publishing personally identifiable information online about their perpetrator's actions.

Controlling doxxing is used to control an individual's behavior. As such, it may represent a measure of technology-facilitated coercive control, often employed in concert with other iterations of intimate partner violence (Douglas, Harris, & Dragiewicz, 2019). Often coinciding with one or more of the other motivations we identified, *reputation-building doxxing* serves to grant entry or clout within a group or subculture through, for example, demonstrating skill within a hacker forum. Unlike the forms of doxxing outlined above, *unintentional doxxing* is not undertaken with malicious intent but rather results from carelessness or negligence on the part of the perpetrator. Unintentional doxxing may, for example, result from journalists failing to protect the anonymity or obscurity of their sources. Lastly, *public interest doxxing* is motivated by a belief that the release of personally identifiable or proprietary information will promote the welfare or well-being of the general public (see Cheung, this volume). Public interest doxxing may take numerous forms, including as a mechanism for holding governments, institutions, and public figures accountable, as well as a mechanism for issuing public safety announcements through, for example, releasing personally identifiable information about predatory Tinder dates.

As detailed in Table 12.1, most of these motivations can underpin more than one of the three forms of doxxing identified by Douglas (2016), leading to a variety of subcategories. However, our review of the literature also indicates that the forms of loss that may be faced by doxxing victims are not exhausted by the three forms anonymity, obscurity, and legitimacy identified by Douglas. Specifically, Douglas's original typology faces challenges when we consider the case of corporate or organizational doxxing: doxxing that targets an organization rather than an individual (Khanna, Zavarsky, & Lindskog, 2016). As we detail below, the existence of corporate doxxing necessitates the addition of a fourth form of potential loss faced by doxxing victims, *competitive advantage* over other corporations or organizations. This prompts a fourth variety of doxxing, *disadvantaging doxxing*, which may be underpinned by a variety of motivations.

Extensive Studies of Doxxing

To date, only a few studies have examined the demographic characteristics of doxxing perpetrators and victims (Chen, Chan, & Cheung, 2018; Chen, Cheung, & Chan, 2019). Drawing on a random sample of 2,120 secondary school students

Table 12.1. A Typology of Doxxing.

	Form of Information Published	**Personal Identifiable Information**			**Proprietary Information**
	Loss experienced by the victim	**Loss of anonymity (Deanonymizing doxxing)**	**Loss of obscurity (Targeting doxxing)**	**Loss of legitimacy (Delegitimizing doxxing)**	**Loss of competitive advantage (Disadvantaging doxxing)**
Motivation	**Extortion**	**Deanonymizing doxtortion** • Acquisitive doxxing extortion.	**Targeting doxtortion**	**Delegitimizing doxtortion** • Doxware-facilitated doxtortion. • Sexual extortion/ doxtortion.	**Disadvantaging doxtortion** • Corporate doxtortion (Khanna et al., 2016).
	Silencing	**Deanonymizing doxxing to silence** (Massanari, 2018; Jones, 2016). • Doxxing as a political silencing technique (Massanari, 2018).	**Targeting doxxing to silence** (Jones, 2016; Massanari, 2018). • "Swatting" a member of a marginalized community (Binder, 2018).	**Delegitimizing** doxxing **to silence** • Gamergate Zoe Quinn case: rumors of unprofessionalism imbued with sexist and derogatory comment (McIntyre, 2016).	

	Controlling	**Deanonymizing doxxing to control** (Bancroft & Scott Reid, 2017; Fish & Follis, 2016; Heemsbergen, 2016; Marwick, 2013).	**Targeting doxxing to control** (Freed et al., 2018). • Doxxing as a form of intimate partner violence (Freed et al., 2018).	**Delegitimizing doxxing to control** (Freed et al., 2018). • Threats of doxxing as a technique of coercive control (Freed et al., 2018).	
Motivation	**Retribution**	**Retributive deanonymizing doxxing** (Coleman, 2014; Colton et al., 2017; Corbridge, 2018; MacAllister, 2017; Marwick, 2013; McNealy, 2017; Serracino-Inglott, 2013; Snyder et al., 2017) • Stalking and other malicious harassment; see *Wilkinson v Downton* (Corbridge, 2018).	**Retributive targeting doxxing** (Marshak, 2017; Snyder et al., 2017)	**Retributive delegitimizing doxxing** (Chen et al., 2018, 2019; Snyder et al., 2017). • Threat to professional reputation e.g., the case of Dr Quinn (Pittman, 2018). • Nonconsensual sharing of sexual imagery.	**Retributive disadvantaging doxxing**

Table 12.1. *(Continued)*

	Form of Information Published	Personal Identifiable Information			Proprietary Information
	Loss experienced by the victim	**Loss of anonymity (Deanonymizing doxxing)**	**Loss of obscurity (Targeting doxxing)**	**Loss of legitimacy (Delegitimizing doxxing)**	**Loss of competitive advantage (Disadvantaging doxxing)**
		• Online hate campaigns; Brianna Wu case (MacAllister, 2017).			
	Reputation-building	**Deanonymizing doxxing for reputation-building** (Massanari, 2018; Snyder et al., 2017). • Doxxing as a vehicle for obtaining social capital within hacker subculture (Snyder et al., 2017).	**Targeting doxxing for reputation-building** (Massanari, 2018; Snyder et al., 2017).	**Delegitimizing doxxing for reputation-building** (Massanari, 2018; Snyder et al., 2017).	**Disadvantaging doxxing for reputation-building**
Motivation	**Public interest**	**Deanonymizing doxxing in the public interest** (Coleman, 2014; Colton et al., 2017).	**Targeting doxxing in the public interest**	**Delegitimizing doxxing in the public interest** (Oldberg, 2016). • Snowden NSA leaks as a form of	**Disadvantaging doxxing in the public interest**

	• Citizen journalists deploying Twitter and other platforms to identify attendees of a white supremacist rally.		"organisational doxxing" (Oldberg, 2016).	
Unintentional	**Unintended deanonymizing doxxing** (McNealy, 2017). • Journalistic doxxing of anonymous sources (McNealy, 2017).	**Unintended targeting doxxing** (McNealy, 2017). • Journalistic doxxing of individuals (McNealy, 2017).	**Unintended delegitimizing doxxing** (Chen et al., 2018, 2019).	**Unintended disadvantaging doxxing**

in Hong Kong, the first article published by Chan and colleagues reports on a cross-sectional survey of doxxing victimization, as well as the age, gender, and education-level demographics of doxxing victims and perpetrators. Chen et al.'s (2018) regression analysis found positive correlations between depression, anxiety, and stress, and the doxxing of most forms of personal information. Furthermore, they found strong positive correlations between the doxxing of mobile phone numbers and depression and anxiety among victims. The disclosure of phone numbers provides an example of our category of *retributive targeting doxxing*: doxxing underpinned by a perpetrator's motivation to punish a victim through facilitating harassment against them. Furthermore, Chen et al.'s (2018) study indicates that women are more likely to be victims of doxxing than men, with victimization prevalence for all but one type of information (Hong Kong ID number) higher among female students (p. 4). In the same study, 50.7% of respondents indicated that they had been doxxed by a classmate, 30.3% had been targeted by an individual in the same grade, 25.7% by a friend outside of school, and 24.6% by a parent or family member (Chen et al., 2018). Only 4.1% indicated that they had been doxxed by a stranger (Chen et al., 2018). This suggests that the interpersonal relationship between the victim and perpetrator is one of familiarity, which casts doxxing as a technique of social harassment, rather than random harassment of a stranger.

In a second article stemming from this study, Chen et al. (2019) examine adolescents' intentions when doxxing their peers. In doing so, Chen et al. (2019) distinguish between what they term social doxxing defined as "obtain[ing] social information" but not releasing it about a person they liked and hostile doxxing, which is collecting and releasing personal information with malicious intent (p. 1). Here, however, we identify several definitional concerns about the category of "social doxxing." Namely, given that the notion of social doxxing proposed by Chen et al. (2019) does not involve the *releasing* of personal information by perpetrators, does this constitute doxxing at all? We argue that it does not. Rather, what Chen et al. (2019) describe as social doxxing more accurately represents what Andrejevic (2004) has termed "lateral surveillance." There are two reasons for this: first, it involves *public* rather than *private* information which conflicts with Chen et al.'s (2019) acknowledgment that the target information of doxxing "can be any personal, private, or sensitive information" (p. 2) and second, it does not involve the release of this information.

Given social doxxing arguably falls outside the definitional boundaries of doxxing, we focus here on Chen et al.'s (2019) findings relating to hostile doxxing. Although Chen et al. (2019) did not find gender a statistically significant predictor of perpetrating hostile doxxing, the young males sampled in their study were more likely than the young women to target "personally identifiable and physical location information" (p. 11). Given the expansive definition of doxxing employed within this research includes "social information" that is publicly self-disclosed by individuals, this finding *indicates* that what is generally understood as doxxing (the public release of personally identifiable and other private information) is a gendered phenomenon in both its perpetration and victimology.

Whereas Chen et al. (2018) and Chen et al.'s (2019) study of doxxing drew upon a cross-sectional survey approach, Snyder, Doerfler, Kanich, and McCoy (2017) adopt a naturalistic approach to examining doxxing rates, employing a specialized web crawler to collect data on doxxing files uploaded to three websites associated with doxxing: Pastebin, 4Chan, and 8Chan. This approach produced several findings contrasting with those of Chen et al. (2018) and Chen et al. (2019). For example, Snyder et al. (2017) found that victims of doxxing were overwhelmingly male and a significant number were active in a gamer community (p. 432). However, we would suggest that this may be a product of Snyder et al.'s (2017) focus on files uploaded to Pastebin, 4Chan, and 8Chan, rather than a generalizable finding. Indeed, Snyder et al.'s (2017) somewhat questionable assertion that there "appears to be few dox files that appear elsewhere that do not also appear on pastebin.com, 4chan.org, and 8ch.net" (p. 434) contrasts with Chan et al.'s (2018) finding that it was instant messenger applications and mainstream social networking sites that were the most prevalent platforms used to perpetrate doxxing. This hypothesis is given further credence by the fact that two of the other main "communities" targeted by doxxing on these sites were hackers (a key community associated with 4Chan and 8Chan) and celebrities; a demographic that has been targeted by hack-facilitated doxxing (Snyder et al., 2017). This discrepancy further indicates that Snyder et al. (2017) focused on a particular subset of doxxing incidents, rather than doxxing more generally, which, as a number of the studies discussed below indicate, is often quotidian in nature and not necessarily classified as doxxing by its perpetrators.

Through their analysis, Snyder et al. (2017) identify four general motivations for doxxing: (1) *competitive*: demonstrating superior abilities within a subculture; (2) *revenge*: doxxing in retribution to a perceived harm committed against the perpetrator; (3) *justice*: doxxing someone in response to them committing an act perceived to be immoral or unfair; and (4) *political*: doxxing in the service of a goal larger than targeting a single individual. As the intensive studies discussed in the next section demonstrate, these four motivations are very much ideal types and are far from exhaustive, with doxxing also being employed for the purpose of coercion and control, among other things (Dragiewicz et al., 2018; Freed et al., 2018). Although we question Synder et al.'s (2017) distinction between revenge and justice, (given that both are underpinned by a retributive conception of justice), three key motivations for doxxing can be extracted from their typology: *reputation building* (analogous with Synder et al.'s competitive motivation), *retribution*, and *public interest* doxxing (analogous with their political motivation category) (p. 1).

Unlike the three papers detailed above, the final two articles broadly reporting on extensive studies of doxxing examine *responses* to doxxing. The first of these, Fiesler et al.'s (2018) study of the community rules governing subreddits within the social media site Reddit, provides an indication of the prevalence of anti-doxxing rules on the site. Analyzing a dataset of 100,000 subreddits, Fiesler et al. (2018) found that, of the 23,752 subreddits that had rules, only 128 (0.54%) had rules specifically prohibiting doxxing. However, it is worth contextualizing this finding by noting that posting "personal and confidential information" (i.e., doxxing) is prohibited in Reddit's (2019) Content Policy. This may explain, in part, why few of the subreddits Fiesler et al. (2018) examined banned the behavior.

The four papers examined so far in this section pertain to personal doxxing, that is, doxxing targeting an individual. Khanna et al.'s (2016) study, however, focuses on responses to *organizational* or *corporate doxxing*: releasing organizational secrets and sensitive proprietary information (see Oldberg, 2016). In their analysis, Khanna et al. (2016) examine tools used to undertake organizational doxxing attacks, most notably Maltego Chlorine CE 3.6.0, a forensics and intelligence program that gathers information from open sources. Identifying key limitations in Maltego Chlorine CE 3.6.0 as a doxxing tool, Khanna et al. (2016) suggest a number of countermeasures that organizations may employ to prevent doxxing attacks. These include employing the very tools of organizational doxxers used against companies and conducting information privacy audits through websites such as Pipl, which can trace the source of information on the internet.

Although Khanna et al. (2016) do not systematically compare and contrast corporate doxxing to doxxing targeting individuals, their analysis demonstrates two key ways in which the former may differ from the latter. Namely, corporate doxxing often differs from doxxing targeting individuals in that it (1) often involves the release of proprietary information rather than personally identifiable information; and (2) the form of loss faced by the victim is often an economic loss of competitive advantage against other corporations, as opposed to a loss of anonymity, obscurity, or legitimacy. When the form of loss is competitive advantage through the release of proprietary information, we might term such doxxing *disadvantaging doxxing*. In proposing this category, it is important to qualify that disadvantaging doxxing is not synonymous with corporate/organizational doxxing, for corporations can be the victim of both disadvantaging and delegitimizing doxxing. Moreover, that this can occur suggests that, contra Douglas, delegitimizing doxxing can be underpinned by a disclosure of either personally identifying information or proprietary information. The release of sensitive confidential information about a corporation's waste (mis)management may, for example, lead to backlash against the corporation, and consequently, economic losses as a result of boycotts. However, this economic loss is rooted in the corporation's loss of legitimacy, rather than in a loss of trade-secrets, and thus should be categorized as delegitimizing doxxing.

Intensive Studies of Doxxing

Doxxing in Forums Characterized by Social Community Anonymity

A considerable portion of the literature examining doxxing concerns its use within populations and communities characterized by strategic internet-facilitated anonymity, namely, hacker collectives and subcultures (Coleman, 2014; Fish & Follis, 2016), webcam models (Jones, 2016), darknet cryptomarkets (Bancroft & Scott Reid, 2017), and internet news story commenters (McNealy, 2017). In internet fora, where anonymity affords users protection, such as hacker subcultures and darknet cryptomarkets, doxxing may be employed as a technique to "out" individuals who break rules or to ensure compliance with a community's norms (Bancroft & Scott Reid, 2017). As Bancroft and Scott Reid's (2017) interviews with cryptomarket users demonstrated, cryptomarket users may use the threat of doxxing for disciplining vendors who scam buyers (p. 504). In some situations, the motivation for deanonymizing individuals in these fora was retribution, falling within the category of *retributive deanonymizing doxxing*. In other situations reported in the literature, however, the motivation for deanonymizing other users was instead a bid to control behavior–what we term *deanonymizing doxxing to control*. A vendor may, for example, be "partially doxxed" through publicly releasing part of their phone number to demonstrate the doxxer's knowledge of the number, without releasing it in its entirety and opening them up to abuse (Bancroft & Scott Reid, 2017, p. 504). Such threats of doxxing would often, however, elicit a very negative response from other users. Given that in such fora "anonymising [is] both practical and a moral norm" (Bancroft & Scott Reid, 2017, p. 504), doxxing can be viewed as a threat to social community anonymity, evoking a similar response to the practice of "snitching."

While doxxing use within hacker and hacktivist subcultures has primarily been examined in relation to doxxes carried out against out-group members, doxxing also represents a strategy employed against fellow hackers (Fish & Follis, 2016; Serracino-Inglott, 2013). Writing on the hacktivist collective "Anonymous," for example, Serracino-Inglott (2013) states that "Being 'doxxed'... is perhaps the worst form of humiliation that can befall an Anon [member of Anonymous], and the community uses 'doxxing' as a form of internal discipline/punishment" (pp. 219–220). This "outing" of hackers' identities again falls under the category of *deanonymizing doxxing to control*.

Like cryptomarket vendors, hacktivists often seek to maintain anonymity on the internet to avoid law enforcement detection. Effective information management is, therefore, key to maintaining a hacktivist identity (Fish & Follis, 2016). For this reason, Fish and Follis (2016) argue that "outing" hacktivists through doxxing represents a technique for opening them up to forms of subjection: the "broader process of subordination and subject creation that [emerge] in relation to dominating institutions of power" (p. 3282). A similar line of argument is offered in Heemsbergen's (2016) analysis of doxxing as a form of control. Drawing on Brighenti's (2010) visibilities theory, Heemsbergen (2016) discusses the doxxing of hacktivists as one example of *visibilities of control*: techniques that invoke the "purposeful and contextual asymmetrisation and hierarchisation of visibilities" for the purposes of (social) control (Brighenti, 2010, p. 148).

Law-enforcement-related detection or subjection are not, however, the only motivations for doxxing members of anonymous internet communities. Nor is such doxxing employed solely in anonymous forums characterized by illicit activities. As Jones (2016) details in a study of the adult webcam model industry, doxxing is also employed in forums characterized by anonymity to harass members engaging in legal pursuits. Within the adult webcam model industry, as Jones (2016) explains, doxxing represents a key strategy employed to harass models. For this reason, the models Jones (2016) studied took stringent measures to prevent doxxing, such as keeping up-to-date firewall and virus protection to avoid hacking of personal information, turning off smartphone geotagging, using a separate work phone, and manufacturing a cam-girl identity (pp. 243–245).

Such doxxing may fall under a number of our categories. For example, when used to facilitate further harassment of a model, we might categorize the doxxing as *retributive targeting doxxing*. When used with the specific aim to remove a model from a forum, we might instead speak of *targeting doxxing to silence*.

Examining a very different population characterized by social community anonymity, McNealy (2017) describes "media doxxing," in which news media outlets dox either a source or commenter on news articles (p. 283). This may fall into one of two of our categories: *deanonymizing doxxing in the public interest* when a journalist deliberately "outs" a source citing public interest and *unintentional deanonymizing doxxing* when an individual through accident or negligence deanonymizes a person. It is worth qualifying here, however, that where the boundaries lie between journalistic reporting and doxxing is a contested issue (see Garber, 2014), and as Grey Ellis (2017) notes, we should be wary of conflating the two.

Doxxing as Digilantism and Technology-Facilitated Coercive Control

Much of the media attention doxxing has received has concerned its use by activists and other individuals for politically motivated goals. Doxxing, as Bowles (2017) describes, has become "a mainstream tool in the culture wars," while numerous news articles have examined its use by members of the alt-right (Faruqi, 2019; Grey Ellis, 2017) and Antifa (Mohammed, 2017). It is perhaps unsurprising then that a considerable portion of the small academic literature examining doxxing has similarly addressed this issue. Regardless of the politics espoused by its perpetrators, when used for political ends, doxxing represents a form of what scholars have termed "digilantism";

> …politically motivated (or putatively politically motivated) practices outside of the state that are designed to punish or bring others to account, in response to a perceived or actual dearth of institutional remedies. (Jane, 2017, p. 3)

In a socio-technical analysis of the #Gamergate controversy, Massanari (2015) examines doxxing as one technique deployed by what she terms "toxic technocultures." Such toxic technocultures, Massanari (2015) argues, are "unique in their leveraging of sociotechnical platforms as both a channel of coordination and harassment and [in their] seemingly leaderless, amorphous quality" (p. 333). Within such toxic technocultures, doxxing can represent a coordinated technique of harassment employed in response to an issue members have united against. Such doxxing can represent what we term *targeting doxxing to silence* and *delegitimizing doxxing to silence*, for it aims to "silence" or remove individuals from social media through launching coordinated harassment and/or shaming campaigns. Moreover, within such technocultures, successfully obtaining private information about a perceived "opponent" offers a vehicle for members to demonstrate technological prowess; what we term *targeting doxxing for reputation-building*.

Importantly, as Massanari's (2015) analysis demonstrates, toxic technocultures that sanction doxxing can be supported by the very design and polices of social media platforms themselves (336). This is on account of their "platform politics": "the assemblage of design, policies, and norms that encourage certain kinds of cultures and behaviors to coalesce on platforms while implicitly discouraging others" (Massanari, 2015, p. 336). Furthermore, as Massanari (2018) explores in her article on the risks and ethics of researching "alt-right" movements, researchers studying White ethnonationalist, fascist, and misogynistic communities themselves face the risk of being doxxed. Researching the alt-right, in short, can result in academics, as well as their family, friends, and professional networks, becoming targets of the "alt-right gaze" and its attendant techniques of harassment and doxxing (Massanari, 2018, p. 4).

In news media discourse, doxxing has been associated with members of the alt-right, fueled, in part by Reddit banning the r/altright subreddit for doxxing (Coldewey, 2017). It would be incorrect, however, to characterize doxxing as a weapon solely wielded by right-leaning groups. Although doxxing has been regarded as one of the alt-right's weapons of choice, the technique has also been employed *against* members of this group, as well as individuals who engage in trolling (Phillips, 2011) or identify as white supremacists (Colton et al., 2017; Mohammed, 2017). Marwick (2013), for example, explores the use of doxxing as a regulatory mechanism, targeting individuals who perpetrate hate speech on the internet anonymously or pseudonymously – a further example of what we term *deanonymizing doxxing to control*. Here, Marwick (2013) considers doxxing narrowly as an act of unmasking anonymous transgressors and considers it closely aligned with the logic of online shaming (p. 15). Yet, as Marwick (2013) notes, the use of doxxing as a regulatory mechanism is extremely vexed, for the technique "is as frequently used to further online sexism as to prevent it" (p. 14). Furthermore, it is important to qualify here that while certain forms of doxxing may follow a similar logic to online shaming, the two are not synonymous, as the aim of shaming victims is not a necessary condition of doxxing. At this point, it should be noted that no scholarship to our knowledge has considered the application of doxxing as a technique of community safety, as commonly deployed on Twitter to warn other users of "dodgy Tinder dates" or sexual assailants in a community. This phenomenon could be an exemplar of *deanonymizing doxxing in the public interest* and warrants further research attention.

As this and the preceding section have detailed, the overwhelming majority of academic research into doxxing have examined its use within the context of political, activist, and transgressive communities. However, doxxing victimization and perpetration is far from limited to political, activist/hacktivist, hacker, and cryptomarket circles. As Freed et al.'s (2018) study of technology-facilitated intimate partner violence reveals, doxxing may be readily employed as a technique of intimate partner abuse in at least three different forms. First, in an example of what we term *delegitimizing doxxing to control*, a perpetrator may threaten to release personal information shared confidentially with them (for example, sexual orientation or HIV status). Alternatively, abusers may release such information to family, friends, and employers of the victim. And finally, in an example of either *targeting doxxing to control* or *retributive targeting doxxing*, abusers may distribute personal information about a victim to facilitate abuse by others. In the latter instance, perpetrators might, for example, create fake internet profiles that present the victim as a sex worker, leading them to be harassed by individuals seeking sexual services (Freed et al., 2018; see also; MacAllister, 2017). Owing to its use as a technique of intimate partner violence, scholars such as Dragiewicz et al. (2018) have recently proposed labeling it, along with acts such as monitoring a partner's email and stalking their Global Positioning System data, as a form of "technology-facilitated coercive control."

Jurisdictional Interpretations of Privacy and Doxxing

Although scholarly works placing doxxing within legal frameworks are scant, substantial literature about the legal definitions, rulings, and contestations of the right to privacy exists. As a breach of privacy and a technique of harassment, doxxing is aligned with these literatures, while testing the thresholds of meaning held by traditional notions of privacy. Assessing the jurisdictional interpretations of privacy in Australia, the United States and the European Union, this section will reflect on legal remedies for doxxing articulated in existing studies.

While most of the legal articles included some consideration of legal responses and remedies, Corbridge (2018) and McIntyre (2016) offer the most sustained engagement with possible legal reparations for doxxing offenses. Drawing on legislation in the Australian context, Corbridge (2018) argues that there is sufficient legal precedent to address doxxing as a harassment harm, using the South Australian Criminal Code as an exemplar. In South Australia, doxxing can be punished by up to three years in prison as a stalking offense in cases where the victim has been doxxed more than twice by a perpetrator (*Criminal Law Consolidation Act*, 1935, s. 19AA(1) (a) (ivb)). This response has several shortcomings. In the case of viral doxxing campaigns, a victim might receive hundreds of breaches of personally identifiable information, all from different users/perpetrators. This raises the question: how can the legal condition of "two or more" instances of doxxing be satisfied when the victim suffers hundreds of singular breaches of their privacy? To address this, Corbridge (2018) argues for an expansion of powers granted in the Australian Constitution to include a new statutory cause of action: "serious invasion of privacy," taking the form of a tort (p. 1). Corbridge (2018) puts forward that this approach will disregard the US propensity to lean "towards protecting freedom of information," and instead will emulate the EU's robust consideration of privacy and data protection (p. 3).

In contrast, McIntyre's (2016) work is largely critical of current legal understandings of doxxing as a form of harassment. Addressing doxxing in the US context, McIntyre's (2016) work criticizes the response of the criminal law as contingent on the outcomes of doxxing rather than the initial breach of privacy. In the United States, charges can only be laid if the doxxing leads to the facilitation of stalking and only within specific states (McIntyre, 2016, p. 118). McIntyre (2016) also highlights that "legal" doxxing–that is, information that was published in an open access online forum before the doxxing–cannot be prosecuted as a criminal act. US interpretations of the harm of doxxing are commonly conflated with challenges to free speech rights, resulting in convoluted and circular claims of the right "to" dox. Highlighting that many statutes only apply to abuse that is "communicated directly to the victim," McIntyre (2016) exposes a key oversight in the existing US legal precedent (p. 120). While harassment offenses have historically been "events" that directly affect the victim, doxxing is a harm that both directly and tacitly affects its victim, as it combines the real risk of present-day privacy breaches with the future risk of ongoing breaches. McIntyre (2016) also offers a critique of tort remedies, finding that the tort of public disclosure of private facts is inhibited by dated definitions of "private" information, lacking the specificity of online contexts to be functionally useful as a remedy. Indeed, this is a common critique that contemporary legal responses "lack the vocabulary" to distinguish between harassment in "online" and "offline" spaces (Marshak, 2017, p. 502).

In the US context, this "lack of vocabulary" is underpinned by First Amendment considerations, which significantly impede doxxing cases from being prosecuted. Binder's (2018) article discusses the ruling of *Elonis v United States (2015)*, in which the "true threat" exception to protected speech is tested: if the doxxing resulted in "expression of an intent to commit an act of unlawful violence," then the speech is not protected by the First Amendment and can be actioned under federal anti-threat statutes (p. 63). Bizarrely, the Supreme Court held that the "true threat" exception only exists if the doxxer "subjectively views their actions as threatening," with no regard for victim perspectives (Binder, 2018, p. 63). MacAllister (2017) continues this US-centric critique in her work, examining the "true threat" exception to the First Amendment in doxxing cases. Differentiating between "intent to commit unlawful violence" and the "conditional" threats, MacAllister (2017) couches doxxing as a type of speech that is not protected by the First Amendment and can therefore be feasibly brought before a court as an offense (p. 2565). However, MacAllister (2017) also problematizes the inability to hold US internet service providers liable in cases of doxxing because of the protections afforded by the *Communications Decency Act* (1996).[1] As explored in the legal articles discussed above, legal remedies for doxxing remain unclear and provide limited consideration of victim's experiences compared to the free speech considerations of perpetrators.

In contrast to the US's prohibitive treatment of privacy as a secondary right to freedom of speech, more affirmative conceptions of individuals' right to privacy can be found in England, as well as in the *European Convention of Human Rights*. Nicole Moreham (2014), for example, shifts away from the proprietary framings of privacy by distinguishing "informational privacy" as the "misuse of private information," from "physical privacy" as "unwanted sensory access" (p. 353). In this framing of privacy, the subject can choose "the extent to which he or she is accessed by others" (2014, p. 352), echoing Corbridge's (2018) call for law to protect informational self-determination. While traditional English legal approaches treat breaches of privacy as the exchange of information, Article 8 of the *European Convention of Human Rights* broadens legal considerations of "private life" (Moreham, 2014, p. 356). Namely, Article 8 adds nuance to considerations of privacy breaches being an imposition on the right to not be surveilled, peeped at, or infiltrated in the private domain. Importantly, Article 8 must be balanced against the perpetrator's Article 10 right to freedom of expression (Moreham, 2014, p. 359), – a key departure from the US approach, as it brings freedom of speech and privacy into *conversation with each other*. Moreham (2014) notes that an expansion of legal language to include the "right to be free from unjustified surveillance, search and recording" would clarify modern privacy problems by treating online profiles as defensibly private, or at least a sphere of limited access (p. 358). This would bring a cause of action against users who abuse this access and use online space to mediate breaches of privacy. Although this expansion of legal language is yet to occur, the UK jurisdiction is poised to be a world leader in the modernization of privacy as a legal right. Such an approach might have considerable implications for the prosecution of doxxing as a breach of individual privacy rights.

Conclusions

The phenomenon of doxxing has gradually been addressed in research examining TFV, where it has often been attached to more generic discussions of online harassment and blackmailing practices. With the notable exception of the reviewed legal studies of doxxing, few studies of doxxing have taken an applied research approach in offering recommendations for reducing harm to victims or developing prevention programs. There is, therefore, a need for policy-geared research into doxxing that extends beyond juridical responses to the phenomenon, for example, research examining doxxing victims' specific reporting needs.

Relatedly, as our review demonstrates, much of the literature on doxxing emanates not from criminology, but rather from ethics, and media and communications studies. This comparative lack of criminological research into doxxing has several consequences. For one, little research to date has examined doxxing with a specific view to its causes. To our knowledge, no study to date has focused on non-demographic predictors of individuals perpetrating doxxing, nor sought to apply or develop crime causation theories that explain different forms of this comparatively under-researched form of TFV. Of course, this is not to make a case for criminological parochialism in examining the causes of doxxing; given its mediated nature, there is much to be gained by taking an interdisciplinary approach drawing on the insights of a range of technology-focused disciplines. We therefore suggest that future research into the causes of doxxing brings criminological theory into conversation with media studies and other disciplines that engage extensively with digital technologies. Furthermore, in noting the need for further research into the causes of doxxing, it is important to issue a caveat: doxxing, like any other crime or social harm is polygenetic–it may be caused by a number of mechanisms. There can be no general theory explaining the causes of doxxing, however, criminological theory can offer transferable accounts on the mechanisms that underpin doxxing events.

In scoping out the current legal interpretations of doxxing, key gaps in the literature have emerged. Presently, legal critiques of doxxing are approached through traditional definitions and conceptualizations of privacy and harassment. As it stands, doxxing is ambiguous in the eyes of the law: it is neither a breach of privacy nor a technique of harassment, but an assemblage of both. By treating harassment and the loss of privacy as discrete outcomes of doxxing, rather than synonymous and intertwined experiences, the legal literature may miss an opportunity to robustly engage with doxxing as a unique form of TFV.

In developing our typology, we stress that it is one of ideal types. Acts of doxxing may be underpinned by multiple motivations, meaning that we must be mindful in applying the types we propose here. Moreover, while our typology considers two of the central dimensions of doxxing the (loss or form of damage faced by the victim, and the perpetrator's motivations) there are other key dimensions worth considering. Future typographical work may, for example, consider the personal information acquisition techniques employed by doxxing perpetrators, such as whether the personal information is obtained consensually or through coercion, hacking, or malware. One such example is doxxing extortion, or "doxtortion," which involves blackmailing or coercing a victim under the threat of releasing personally identifiable information. Doxtortion highlights the need to expand investigations of doxxing beyond the release of documents to encompass the threat of releasing private documents about another person. When undertaken by "doxware" or "leakware" that enables the doxtortion to be carried out by a malware program, doxtortion further complicates the notion of agent responsibility, replacing the "doxxer" with a software that threatens to publish a user's private data (Nadir & Bakhshi, 2018). This illustrates the complexity of this harm, which cannot be reduced to its human actors (see Powell, Stratton, & Cameron, 2018; Wood, 2020). By conceptualizing doxxing using a typology that interconnects motivations, expressions, and experiences of harm, it is our hope that future research will make complex and nuanced connections between the direct and tacit harms of doxxing.

Note

1. The *Communications Decency Act* (1996) outlines the rights and responsibilities of internet service providers in the United States. It primarily outlines anti-obscenity and child pornography provisions, while also detailing that internet service providers cannot be deemed "publishers" of material and are therefore exempt from liability for hate speech and harassment on their platforms.

References

Andrejevic, M. (2004). The work of watching one another: Lateral surveillance, risk, and governance. *Surveillance and Society*, *2*(4), 479–497. doi:10.24908/ss.v2i4.3359

Bancroft, A., & Scott Reid, P. (2017). Challenging the techno-politics of anonymity: The case of cryptomarket users. *Information, Communication & Society*, *20*(4), 497–512. doi:10.1080/1369118X.2016.1187643

Binder, N. (2018). From the message board to the front door: Addressing the offline consequences of race- and gender-based doxxing and swatting. *Suffolk University Law Review*, *51*(1), 55–76. Retrieved from https://heinonline.org/HOL/LandingPage?handle=hein.journals/sufflr51&div=7&id=&page=

Bowles, N. (2017). How 'doxxing' became a mainstream tool in the culture wars. *The New York Times*. Retrieved from https://www.nytimes.com/

Brighenti, A. M. (2010). *Visibility in social theory and social research*. London: Palgrave.

Chen, Q., Chan, K., & Cheung, A. (2018). Doxing victimization and emotional problems among secondary school students in Hong Kong. *International Journal of Environmental Research and Public Health*, *15*(12), 2665–2673. doi:10.3390/ijerph15122665

Chen, M., Cheung, A. S. Y., & Chan, K. L. (2019). Doxing: What adolescents look for and their intentions. *International Journal of Environmental Research and Public Health*, *16*(2), 1–14. doi:10.3390/ijerph16020218

Coldewey, D. (2017). Reddit bans r/altright over doxing. *Tech Crunch*. Retrieved from https://techcrunch.com/2017/02/01/reddit-bans-raltright-over-doxing/

Coleman, G. (2014). *Hacker, hoaxer, whistleblower, spy: The many faces of anonymous*. London: Verso.

Colton, J. S., Holmes, S., & Walwema, J. (2017). From noobguides to# OpKKK: Ethics of anonymous' tactical technical communication. *Technical Communication Quarterly*, *26*(1), 59–75. doi:10.1080/10572252.2016.1257743

Corbridge, Å. (2018). Responding to doxing in Australia: Towards a right to informational self-determination. *UniSA Student Law Review*, *3*, 1–28. Retrieved from https://ojs.unisa.edu.au/index.php/uslr/article/view/1489

Douglas, D. M. (2016). Doxing: A conceptual analysis. *Ethics and Information Technology*, *18*(3), 199–210. Retrieved from https://link.springer.com/article/10.1007/s10676-016-9406-0

Douglas, H., Harris, B. A., & Dragiewicz, M. (2019). Technology-facilitated domestic and family violence: Women's experiences. *The British Journal of Criminology*, *59*(3), 551–570. doi:10.1093/bjc/azy068

Dragiewicz, M., Burgess, J., Matamoros-Fernández, A., Salter, M., Suzor, N. P., Woodlock, D., & Harris, B. (2018). Technology facilitated coercive control: Domestic violence and the competing roles of digital media platforms. *Feminist Media Studies*, *18*(4), 609–625. doi:10.1080/14680777.2018.1447341

Faruqi, O. (2019). 'We're watching you': Why doxxing is the new weapon of choice for cyber bullies and trolls. *ABC News*. Retrieved from: https://www.abc.net.au

Fiesler, C., Jiang, J., McCann, J., Frye, K., & Brubaker, J. R. (2018). Reddit rules! Characterizing an ecosystem of governance. Twelfth International AAAI Conference on Web and Social Media. Retrieved from https://aaai.org/ocs/index.php/ICWSM/ICWSM18/paper/view/17898/16998

Fish, A., & Follis, L. (2016). Gagged and doxed: Hacktivism's self-incrimination complex. *International Journal of Communication*, *10*, 3281–3300. Retrieved from https://ijoc.org/index.php/ijoc/article/view/5386

Freed, D., Palmer, J., Minchala, D., Levy, K., Ristenpart, T., & Dell, N. (2018, April). "A stalker's paradise": How intimate partner abusers exploit technology. In *Proceedings of the 2018 CHI conference on human factors in computing systems* (p. 1–13). Montreal: ACM. doi:10.1145/3173574.3174241

Garber, M. (2014, March 6). Doxing: An etymology. *The Atlantic*. Retrieved from www.theatlantic.com

Grey Ellis, E. (2017). Whatever your side, doxing is a perilous form of justice. *Wired*. Retrieved from https://www.wired.com/

Heemsbergen, L. (2016). From radical transparency to radical disclosure: Reconfiguring (in) voluntary transparency through the management of visibilities. *International Journal of Communication*, *10*, 138–151. Retrieved from https://ijoc.org/index.php/ijoc/article/view/4413

Jane, E. A. (2017). Feminist digilante responses to a slut-shaming on Facebook. *Social Media+ Society*, *3*(2), 1–10. doi:10.1177/2056305117705996

Jones, A. (2016). "I get paid to have orgasms": Adult webcam models' negotiation of pleasure and danger. *Signs: Journal of Women in Culture and Society*, *42*(1), 227–256. Retrieved from https://www.journals.uchicago.edu/doi/10.1086/686758?mobileUi=0&

Khanna, P., Zavarsky, P., & Lindskog, D. (2016). Experimental analysis of tools used for doxing and proposed new transforms to help organizations protect against doxing attacks. *Procedia Computer Science*, *94*, 459–464. doi:10.1016/j.procs.2016.08.071

MacAllister, J. M. (2017). The doxing dilemma: Seeking a remedy for the malicious publication of personal information. *Fordham Law Review*, *85*(5), 2451. Retrieved from https://ir.lawnet.fordham.edu/cgi/viewcontent.cgi?article=5370&context=flr

Marshak, E. (2017). Online harassment: A legislative solution. *Harvard Journal on Legislation*, *54*, 503. Retrieved from https://harvardjol.com/wp-content/uploads/sites/17/2017/05/HLL205.pdf

Marwick, A. (2013, October). There's no justice like angry mob justice: Regulating hate speech through internet vigilantism. In *Selected Papers of Internet Research* (Vol. 14). Denver, CO: AoIR.

Marx, G. T. (1999). What's in a name? Some reflections on the sociology of anonymity. *The Information Society*, *15*(2), 99–112. doi:10.1080/019722499128565

Massanari, A. (2015). #Gamergate and the Fappening: How Reddit's algorithm, governance, and culture support toxic technocultures. *New Media & Society*, *19*(3), 329–346. doi:10.1177/1461444815608807

Massanari, A. L. (2018). Rethinking research ethics, power, and the risk of visibility in the era of the "alt-right" gaze. *Social Media+ Society*, *4*(2). doi:10.1177/2056305118768302

McIntyre, V. (2016). Do (x) you really want to hurt me: Adapting IIED as a solution to doxing by reshaping intent. *Tulane Journal of Technology & Intellectual Property*, *19*, 111–134. Retrieved from https://journals.tulane.edu/TIP/article/view/2667

McNealy, J. (2017). Readers react negatively to disclosure of poster's identity. *Newspaper Research Journal*, *38*(3), 282–292. doi:10.1177/0739532917722977

Mohammed, F. (2017) Is doxxing the right way to fight the "alt-right?" *JSTOR Daily*. Retrieved from https://daily.jstor.org/is-doxxing-the-right-way-to-fight-the-alt-right/

Moreham, N. A. (2014). Beyond information: Physical privacy in English law. *The Cambridge Law Journal*, *73*(2), 350–377. doi:10.1017/S0008197314000427

Nadir, I., & Bakhshi, T. (2018, March). Contemporary cybercrime: A taxonomy of ransomware threats & mitigation techniques. In *2018 International Conference on Computing, Mathematics and Engineering Technologies (iCoMET)* (pp. 1–7). Pakistan: IEEE.

Oldberg, C. J. (2016). Organizational doxing: Disaster on the doorstep. *Colorado Technology Law Journal, 15*, 181–206. Retrieved from https://ctlj.colorado.edu/wp-content/uploads/2017/01/8-Oldberg-12.25.16_FINAL_PDF-A.pdf

Phillips, W. (2011). LOLing at tragedy: Facebook trolls, memorial pages and resistance to grief online. *First Monday, 16*(12), 1. Retrieved from https://firstmonday.org/article/view/3168/3115

Pittman, J. (2018). Privacy in the age of doxxing. *Southern Journal of Business and Ethics, 10*, 53–58.

Powell, A., Stratton, G., & Cameron, R. (2018). *Digital criminology: Crime and justice in digital society*. London: Routledge.

Reddit. (2019). Reddit content policy, *Reddit*. Retrieved from https://www.redditinc.com/policies/content-policy

Salter, M. (2013). Justice and revenge in online counter-publics: Emerging responses to sexual violence in the age of social media. *Crime, Media, Culture, 9*(3), 225–242. doi:10.1177/1741659013493918

Sayer, A. (1999). *Realism and social science*. London: Sage.

Serracino-Inglott, P. (2013). Is it OK to be an anonymous? *Ethics & Global Politics, 6*(4), 217–244. doi:10.3402/egp.v6i4.22527

Snyder, P., Doerfler, P., Kanich, C., & McCoy, D. (2017). Fifteen minutes of unwanted fame: Detecting and characterizing doxing. In *Proceedings of the 2017 internet measurement conference* (pp. 432–444), London: ACM.

Wood, M. A. (2020). Rethinking how technologies harm. *The British Journal of Criminology*. doi:10.1093/bjc/azaa098

Wood, M. A., Rose, E., & Thompson, C. (2019). Viral justice? Online justice-seeking, intimate partner violence and affective contagion. *Theoretical Criminology, 23*(3), 375–393. doi:10.1177/1362480617750507

Chapter 13

Creating the Other in Online Interaction: Othering Online Discourse Theory

Elina Vaahensalo

Abstract

The growth of online communities and social media has led to a growing need for methods, concepts, and tools for researching online cultures. Particular attention should be paid to polarizing online discussion cultures and dynamics that increase inequality in online environments. Social media has enormous potential to create good, but in order to unlock its full potential, we also need to examine the mechanisms keeping these spaces monotonous, homogenous, and even hostile toward some groups. With this need in mind, I have developed the concept and theory of othering online discourse (OOD).

This chapter introduces and defines the concept of OOD and explains the key characteristics and different attributes of OOD in relation to other concepts that deal with disruptive and discriminatory behavior in online spaces. The attributes of OOD are demonstrated drawing on examples gathered from the Finnish Suomi24 (Finland24) forum.

Keywords: Othering; internet culture; online discussion; discursive; exclusion; anonymity; online community

Introduction

Nowadays, people looking for information are almost completely dependent on the internet. Various groups and communities are formed in online environments and social media discourses play a large role in that process. In addition to the potential for widespread distribution, online conversations, ideas, and discourses can be powerful and meaningful. The downside is that easy access to both information and communications makes the dissemination of ideas easier and hate

The Emerald International Handbook of Technology-Facilitated Violence and Abuse, 227–246

doi:10.1108/978-1-83982-848-520211016

speech and fake information find their way more stealthily to the hands of internet users (Citron, 2014; Meddaugh & Kay, 2009; Weaver, 2013).

With the growing popularity of social media, inequality and discrimination in online spaces has received increasing attention. However, well-known and frequently used concepts like hate speech, cyberbullying, online misogyny, and online racism are often either impractically vague or impractically narrow to describe the complex ways in which "othering" speech unfolds in online contexts. The problem with the concept of hate speech, for instance, is that it is not confined to online environments, which means that the concept does not take into account the specific characteristics of online interaction, which range from complete anonymity to the different power structures that affect online communities. Hate speech is a multipurpose umbrella term used to describe expressions of hate and hostility regardless of the environment in which they occur. Public speeches, political demonstrations, radio broadcasts, and blog posts can all be defined as hate speech (Waldron, 2012, p. 34; Walker, 1994). The concept of hate speech has also become increasingly commonplace in everyday speech, which has led to subjective perceptions of what hate speech constitutes. Ruotsalainen (2018) states that hate speech has become a rhetorical trope and a populistic tool, which is often used to obscure the actual matter discussed. She notes that hate speech has become a "floating signifier, which avoids strict definition" and is "emptied" from its history and its connotation with racism (Ruotsalainen, 2018, p. 226). Waldron (2012, p. 1,601) further notes that hate speech is often misunderstood as "thinking" rather than communicating, and thus freedom of speech advocates argue that restrictions on speech (including hate speech) is tantamount to censoring thought and freedom of expression. On the other hand, conceptual narrowness is encountered especially when online discourse is examined from the perspective of racism or misogyny. While both concepts are important tools for examining inequality, researchers need concepts that are not limited to race, ethnicity, nationality, or gender. Discourses against inclusion also rely on, for example, socioeconomic background and age.

To address these conceptual and terminological deficiencies, I created the concept and theory of "othering online discourse" (OOD) that can be used to examine polarizing online interaction as a combination of public identity speech and online gatekeeping. By identity speech, I mean expressions of one's identity via online interaction. Especially in anonymous online conversations, identity is often showcased by describing traits and opinions that are hoped to ignite a sense of sameness and social cohesion (see, e.g., Chayko, 2002; Litt & Hargittai, 2016). In this chapter, I argue first that these same dynamics can produce not only sameness, but also otherness and exclusion. Second, I argue that by combining elements from concepts such as hate speech, online racism, and online misogyny, one can create a tool that allows a flexible view on discursive exclusion in online spaces. With the help of the OOD theory, I seek to demonstrate how othering and discursive exclusivity are created from different starting points, by different discursive means, and for different purposes.

In this chapter, I define the concept of OOD, explain the key characteristics of OOD, and demonstrate the flexibility of the theory by introducing different kinds of attributes of OOD that can be used to analyze, describe, and decode any kind of online interaction. To demonstrate the attributes, I provide examples gathered from the Finnish Suomi24 (Finland24) forum. In the Finnish media, Suomi24 is often referred to as an antisocial and cruel environment that hosts a community of online bullies (Vaahensalo, 2018). The same rhetoric is frequently used to describe other anonymous online environments such as the infamous imageboard 4chan or the content rating website Reddit (Arntfield, 2015; ElSherief, Kulkarni, Nguyen, Wang, & Belding, 2018; Miller, 2015; Vainikka, 2018). However, while othering behavior in online environments is often an unpleasant, hostile, and antisocial phenomenon, its power lies specifically in its sociality: "othering" discourses are produced in a public environment for the purpose of others seeing it and interacting with it. Interaction in online environments also needs to be seen in its own original context. In some online communities, generally disapproved behavior may well have the effect of fostering a sense of community.

In the first section of the chapter, I review the concepts of otherness and othering in relation to the study of online discussions and social media. In the second section, I explain further what kind of online space Suomi24 forum is. I also clarify how I gathered the examples of OOD, and what kind of methods I used for constructing the theory and concept of OOD. In the third section, I review the different ethical issues that define the research of hostile online discussion as well as the utilization of the concept of otherness in research. The fourth section of the chapter is dedicated for the more extensive definition of the concept of OOD and the key characteristics that differentiate OOD from other concepts that deal with discriminatory behavior in online spaces. In the final section of the chapter, I examine the attributes of OOD that are demonstrated with different quotations collected from the Suomi24 forum. These attributes describe how online othering relates to the topic of the discussion, what kind of repercussions othering can have, and how it will appear to the reader.

A Theory of Othering

The concept of otherness refers to the dichotomy between the self and the other; between the "us" and the "them." Ideas of similarity and sameness are used to construct the idea of "us," but simultaneously conceptions of difference are used to construct "them" (Bauman & May, 2004, pp. 30–35). "The other" can be seen as a building block for the self, self-image, and identity. Okolie (2003) states that identity has little meaning by its own. Identity and a sense of self are thus acquired and claimed by defining the other. Consequences of claiming identities usually reflect an imbalance of power, since groups do not have equal powers to define both self and the other (Okolie, 2003, p. 2). That is why otherness is often determined or dictated by those who are in a position of power (Jensen, 2011; Miles, 1989; Pickering, 2001). By referring to position of power, I do not necessarily mean a position of literal political power. The power play of othering operates especially through production of culture, knowledge, and representations (Hall, 1997). For example, in anonymous online discussions, power usually falls into the hands of those who support norms of maleness and whiteness (Phillips, 2019). Popularity, social cohesion, and power are more easily available in anonymous online environments if participants reproduce widely accepted norms.

The process of othering is a key part of the OOD theory. Othering is a process where individuals are classified into the hierarchical groups of "them" and "us." This often happens by stigmatizing and simplifying differences. Hence, the self or the "us" gives itself identity by setting itself apart from the other (Staszak, 2008, p. 2). One motivation for establishing these kinds of twofold categories is to achieve a sense of social belonging by excluding the undesired and the other. This process produces imbalanced narratives, where some identities are marked as superior and some inferior (Jensen, 2011). Robert Miles (1989, p. 61) points out that by classifying an individual or group of people as the other, the classifier also defines the criteria for how themselves come to be represented. Through this asymmetric process, the superior maintains their position and at the same time seeks to control the formation of the identity of the inferior group.

According to Jensen (2011), the history of the concept of otherness can be roughly divided into three stages, through which the concept has evolved and taken shape in the research literature. The first step can be seen in G.W.F. Hegel's conception of the master–slave dialectic presented in the *Phenomenology of Spirit* published in 1807. In Hegel's theory, the juxtaposition toward the other constitutes the self. Simone de Beauvoir (1997) has universalized the theory in relation to both gender and other hierarchical social differences, with men being regarded as the norm and women as the "other." The next stage can be found in the post-colonial writing of literary scholar Edward Said (1995), who theorized about how the West created orientalist images of the strange, exotic, and above all, of the "other" East. A third stage is exemplified by psychoanalyst Jacques Lacan's (1966) theory on the "little other" (the mirrored/projected self/ego) and the "big Other" (the non-self "other"). According to Lacan (1966), the "big Other" is the symbolic order through which language, discourse, and interaction play a significant role in the formation of self, identity, and the construction of reality (pp. 93–100).

The formation of identity in the dialogue between self and the other shows that the mind and identity are formed as part of an interactive and intersubjective process (Benjamin, 1990). According to Patrick Jemmer (2010, p. 22), the act of othering and the unequal and asymmetric relationship between the self and the other might even be seen as a natural and unavoidable result of social mechanics of intersubjectivity. This phenomenon is, of course, also reflected in online environments, where people negotiate hierarchies, positions of power, and the identities that settle into them. Intersubjectivity is a process of sharing experiences and emotions, and it is inevitably reflected in online discussions as well. Comments on a discussion thread are produced in relation to previous comments, allowing participants to express their interpretations of each other's thoughts and the topic of discussion.

Stuart Hall (2003) argues that globalization has led people to look at their own cultural identity and its relationship to other cultures. The internet has been one of the most powerful engines of globalization, enabling new encounters and visibility for many marginalized groups. Collisions with "new" types of identities may well be one of the reasons why some participants in online conversations have a strong need to underline the superiority of their own identity and emphasize what represents the desired norm. On the other hand, it should also be noted that discriminatory discourses are not a new phenomenon in online environments. Networks have been used to disseminate hate and prejudice even before the widely popular social media platforms like Twitter or Facebook (see, e.g., Back, 2002; Massanari, 2017; Phillips, 2019). However, online communication has become more commonplace and, as a result, the handling of social and political issues in social media has become more widespread and, above all, more visible.

Suomi24 Forum as an Anonymous Community of Communities

Suomi24 forum is one of Finland's largest online topic-centric discussion forums and one of the largest non-English online discussion forums in the world. The site has operated under the same name since 2000 and was originally established in 1998. Suomi24 allows users to engage in discussion anonymously, without registration. The topics vary from everyday life to politics. The number of subforums in Suomi24 has varied over time but over a 20-year period, it has ranged from 20 to 30. Under those subforums, there are even more specialized and defined subcategories, the number of which can at best be up to several thousand. In a way, Suomi24 is a community of smaller communities. Users of Suomi24 cannot create subcategories themselves, but the administrators take user suggestions into consideration when creating new categories (Lagus, Ruckenstein, Pantzar, & Ylisiurua, 2016, p. 6; Suominen, Saarikoski, & Vaahensalo, 2019, pp. 11–15).

Suomi24 is an open, anonymous, and low-threshold forum intended for "all Finns" to participate in. However, the ideal of equal participation cannot be achieved if the forum is used to disseminate hate. Anonymous discussion is often more uninhibited and open (Papacharissi, 2004, p. 267; Suler, 2004, pp. 321–322). Massanari (2017, p. 331) suggests that when the threshold of participation is low and the interaction is anonymous – or pseudonymous – the interactions tend to feature elements of play that might not be as visible or common in social media spaces that enforce "real name" participation. The openness of the Suomi24 forum makes it an interesting subject for research because all forms of disruptive behavior in online communication benefits from technologies that make it easier to engage in confrontations and disseminate discriminatory ideas.

Method

In this study, I collected examples to demonstrate the different attributes of OOD from 66 discussion threads from six different subcategories in Suomi24. The topics for these six categories were patriotism; developing countries and development aid; poverty; world affairs; trans people; and Romani people. Most of these subcategories have a specific topic or they are targeted to a specific kind of users, but the world affairs forum is a general forum for discussion that deals with both domestic and international news.

I approached the concept of OOD by layering different qualitative methods that acknowledge the social, cultural, and technological dimensions of OOD. This combination of methods can also be called triangulation, according to its broader definition (Denzin, 1978; Jick, 1979). The methodological tools for this research were concept analysis; practices of online ethnography; and critical discourse analysis.

First, concept analysis is an activity where concepts and their characteristics are clarified and described (Nuopponen, 2010). The definition of OOD was done by applying an eight-step concept analysis model (Puusa, 2008), based on the model originally presented by John Wilson (1963). These eight steps consist of identifying the origin of the concept; setting goals for analysis; specifying different interpretations and uses of the concept; identifying the defining characteristics of the concept; developing a model case of the concept; reviewing related concepts; describing the attendants and consequences of the concept; and naming empirical referents. In particular, the most critical role in defining OOD was differentiating it from other similar concepts, such as online racism, cyberbullying, and hate speech.

OOD is a concept mainly for research use, but the phenomenon itself does not exist as a mere concept and it cannot be definitively defined without the study of the actual online discussions. Therefore, the second approach utilized in this study was an online ethnographic approach which facilitated the observing and collecting of examples of OOD. Observing online discussion and collecting data do not necessarily fall completely within the definition of online ethnographic research, especially if the researcher does not interact with the forum participants that are being observed. Hine (2015, pp. 157–161) describes this kind of approach as an unobtrusive method that utilizes generalized ethnographic strategies without any actual interaction. Especially in a media ethnographic-focused study, the researcher's participation is not perceived solely as an interaction with the informants. In digital environments such as an online forum, the visitor is rarely a mere observer. The visitor interacts with the site through the user interface and by clicking on links and using search engines. All these acts and interactions leave a digital footprint that affects the observation of the discussions and the data collection (Laaksonen et al., 2017; Sumiala, 2012).

The third tool used in this study was critical discourse analysis. Critical discourse analysis is not a method in itself but serves as a framework through which different power relations and language-supported social practices are explored (Wodak, 1999). In this case, critical discourse analysis is a tool for addressing the often subtle nature of OOD. Nikolas Coupland (2010, p. 247) points out that othering may not be noticeable from the "surface" of the text. Occasionally, speech that is intended to be divisive is indirect, and in order to comprehend it, it is necessary to understand the social context of the speech. Discourse analysis is not just a superficial analysis of text, but also an analysis of contexts and interactions (Fairclough, 2003; Van Dijk, 2000). Because of the indirect and potentially subtle nature of othering discourse, a discourse analytical perspective helps to contextualize online interactions. Comments posted online can be taken out of context and viewed as stand-alone texts, but then the communication between separate texts might be ignored.

The Ethics of Studying Hateful Online Discourse

The ethics of studying hateful online interaction can be divided into two different main issues: How to protect the privacy of subjects participating the online discussion; and how to address the explicit and hostile comments in the discussion threads.

Guidelines for online research have been provided by, among others, the Association of Internet Researchers (AoIR). The guidelines take into account the intricacies of online research, such as assessing possible harm to the subject. In cases of web-based forums, such as Suomi24, AoIR guidelines advise to take notice of the expectations for privacy and publicity in that forum and whether the participants would consider the information shared sensitive. According to the guidelines, it is also important to recognize personally identifiable information in the potential data and address risks to individual privacy accordingly (Markham & Buchanan, 2012, p. 11). In the case of the Suomi24 forum, the discussions are public and accessible to everyone. It is important to remember that publicity does not make any data just "free game," which could be uncritically gathered for use (Zimmer, 2018). However, the publicity of the forum is known to the users themselves, and partly for this reason discussions often take place behind unregistered nicknames. Due to the public nature of the discussions and the anonymity of the commenters, the consent of the users contained in the data has not been collected in this study. Comments in their original context are intended to be anonymous and visible for all internet users, and commenters have not participated in the discussions under their own names or otherwise personally identifiable information. I have also made sure that among the comments collected, there is not identifiable, sensitive, or private information and no individuals are recognizable in the examples presented in this chapter. The discussion material collected is originally in Finnish, and translating the comments into English has also acted as anonymization.

While protecting forum participants is an important ethical component of this research, one must also be aware of the problems that arise from using the concept of otherness. Criticism has been directed specifically toward the potentially simplifying effect of the concepts of othering and otherness (Gingrich, 2004; Jensen, 2011, p. 66). Utilizing these concepts often requires a usage of different kinds of social categories and that in turn may highlight intragroup differences and asymmetry even further. Unreflective use of social categories can lead to harmful oversimplification and overgeneralization (Dervin, 2015, pp. 7–8; Gillespie, Howarth, & Cornish, 2012, pp. 399–400). Another significant pitfall in the study of otherness is the reproduction of racializing or other possibly offensive discourses. By examining discriminatory discourses, the researcher might give a voice to hateful discourses that do not deserve to be heard.

However, dismantling hateful dynamics in online communities is impossible if the dark side of internet communication is left in the shadows. Jane (2014), who has explored hostile misogynist rhetoric on the internet, suggests that explicit online hate needs to be explored and made visible because only in that way can their widespread impact be truly understood (see also Jane, this volume). Jane (2014) also states that the anonymous producers of hateful discourses are likely to benefit from the fact that the most violent side of social media is often considered too detestable to be repeated in an academic context. In this chapter, I similarly highlight how blatantly violent OOD can be and in that way also make visible the destructive effect it can have on equality in online spaces, drawing on explicit examples of OOD.

Definition and Key Characteristics of Othering Online Discourse

OOD is a social process of online interaction and is often about exploiting public visibility of an online space to define and reinforce the polarizing dichotomy between "us" and "them." OOD is also a way to express whose participation in the conversation is wanted and whose is unwanted. By deeming someone's participation as unwanted, producers of othering discourses strive to create spaces that accept the presence and visibility of only certain types of identities.

As a phenomenon, OOD aligns and intertwines with the broad framing of "internet culture," that Phillips (2019) describes as a discursive category that often reproduces the norms of whiteness and maleness. Phillips argues that by reproducing these norms in the forms of racist and misogynistic content, internet culture has restricted participation to online interactions only for those who have, in one way or another, accepted these norms. From this viewpoint, OOD can be seen as a form of internet gatekeeping that strives to hold on to these norms and as its worst, dehumanizes groups that may not be in an equal position to defend themselves. In this section, I have listed seven key characteristics that differentiate OOD from other similar concepts.

Not a Monologue

OOD occurs in conversations and situations that are open for commenting. One-way individual texts (such as blog posts, news texts, or online videos) can also have an othering effect, but they are not able to communicate with their recipients in the same way as comments made in an online forum or a social media platform. This distinguishes OOD from, among other things, the concept of hate speech, which, in its multidimensionality, can occur both in interactional and individual texts.

As I stated earlier, OOD is about sociality. In some online spaces, even the most incivil othering and adherence to hateful narratives conform to communal norms (Vainikka, 2018; Watt, Lea, & Spears, 2002, p. 73). For instance, incivil correspondence among online forum participants takes the form of a back-and-forth banter in which commenters compete with each other to see who can create the cruelest way to describe the other (see, e.g., Jane, 2014, p. 560). At their worst, communally shared hateful narratives and norms can even propagate behaviors that are ultimately exploitative or violent (see, e.g., Quayle, Vaughan, & Taylor, 2006).

A Public Forum

Participants of OOD are aware of the interactivity and publicity of the conversation. Not all online conversations are truly interactive, but a comment posted on a discussion forum is by definition intended to be part of social interaction. By publicity, I mean in this case that the interaction is visible and open to an audience. Some online communities meet in more closed spaces that require registration to participate. Othering discourses are not limited to social media spaces that are open for everyone regardless of registration. However, hateful discourses naturally gain a wider audience, if they can be found by everyone.

Arguments about Humanity

Othering discourses are particularly present in discussions that concern identities and humanity in general. This does not mean that OOD is not to be found in discussions circulating around, for example, cars, pets, or travel. However, it is clear that prejudiced ideas about identities are brought up in forums where the topics of the discussions deal prominently with identity, humanity, and the policies affecting them (Hmielowski, Hutchens, & Cicchirillo, 2014, p. 1,197; Papacharissi, 2004, p. 278). The topic of the discussion does not need to be particularly flammable but an emotive or polarizing topic that emphasizes some kind of conflict can easily create a cycle of othering in which one's own "normative" identity and opinions are defended by pushing down the supposed other (see, e.g., Coffey & Woolworth, 2004, p. 12).

An Intersectional Phenomenon

Dynamics of online interaction needs to be looked at with concepts that are not restricted by gender or ethnicity. As a framework, intersectionality helps to reveal how power works in diffuse through the creation of overlapping identity categories (see, e.g., Cho, Crenshaw, & McCall, 2013). Just as in real life, countless marginalized groups are affected by online discrimination and harmful power structures. A variety of different aspects of identity and social status influence how people are talked about and how people are encountered in social media. The diversity of online othering has been acknowledged in many studies of online racism and hate speech (Atton, 2006; Back, 2002; Baumgarten, 2017). It is therefore important that research of online discrimination and technology-facilitated violence can also be approached with concepts that take into account the intersectionality of online discrimination.

It is About Groups

Cyberbullying or online bullying is targeted and often focused on individuals or groups whose members are individually identifiable. This also applies to hate speech, which can also be directed at individuals. The definition of cyberbullying also emphasizes the repetition of harassment, which makes the activity very personal and deliberate (Hinduja & Patchin, 2010, p. 206). Cyberbullying and personally directed hate speech can meet the definition of OOD if the bullying is justified with group characteristics, such as ethnicity, gender, nationality, or socioeconomic background. As a general rule, OOD is about generalization and categorization instead of personal harassment.

Subtle and Cloaked

Othering, whether online or offline, is not always openly hostile or aggressive. Stereotypical views and comments of the other can range from innocent concerns and fears to genuine and open hostility (Pickering, 2001, p. 71). Teun A. Van Dijk (2000) describes a subtle form of discriminatory speech as "new" racism which is typically not overtly violent or hostile. Often described as "merely speech," this kind of racism pervades everyday life from ordinary conversations to television shows and schoolbooks and is just as effective in marginalizing groups of people (Van Dijk, 2000, p. 34).

The sometimes subtle nature of racism is also acknowledged in the framework of critical race theory. Critical race theory recognizes that racism is deeply rooted in the fabric and system of societies (Delgado, Stefancic, & Harris, 2017). OOD draws on this view of deeply rooted discrimination since power relations established in society are also reflected in online interactions. Humor is also used to convey stereotyping and marginalizing ideas (see, e.g., Coupland, 2010, p. 254; Hughey & Daniels, 2013, pp. 334–335; Malmqvist, 2015, pp. 748–749.) At times, it is also common for different hostile groups to seek credibility by using more subtle language and referring to terms such as "community" and "identity" rather than hardcore racist terminology (Atton, 2006, p. 576).

A Discursive Counterbalance

Massanari (2017) describes discriminatory and hostile cultures that are distributed via social media, with the term "toxic technocultures" (p. 330). These cultures often rely on harassment, pushing against ideas of diversity and othering of marginalized groups (Massanari, 2017). OOD could be seen as part of the process of forming such hostile cultures and communities, but OOD is also part of group formation in online communities that may not meet Massanari's (2017) definition of "toxic technocultures." OOD is not always a conscious act of harassment and can also be used as an act of resistance against such toxic cultures. Sometimes OOD is utilized to place typically normative communities and master narratives – cis people, straight men, or upper-middle-class people, for example – in a subordinate position. In these cases, OOD is used to subvert and reclaim the experience of otherness (see, e.g., McKenna & Chughtai, 2020; Mehra, Merkel, & Bishop, 2004; Staszak, 2008, p. 2).

Attributes of Othering Online Discourse: Orientation and Usage

Different attributes of OOD can be divided into two categories: orientation and usage. Orientation describes how OOD relates to the topic and the imagined audience of the discussion. Usage refers to the repercussions that othering can have or how it will appear to the reader (see Fig. 13.1). The two categories also work in relation to each other. The consequences of othering and how they appear to the reader are often determined by the topic of the discussion or the imagined audience.

In this case, the definition of the imagined audience is based on the topic of the forum. For example, in a forum dedicated to the topic of patriotism, patriotic anti-immigration commenters can be seen to belong to the imagined audience, but similarly proponents of multiculturalism represent the "outsiders." In a forum for transgender people, transgender people naturally represent the imagined audience while cis-gendered represent outsiders. In a topic-oriented forum, such as Suomi24, the imagined audience is usually more clearly defined, while in social media platforms, such as Facebook and Twitter, the imagined audience is much

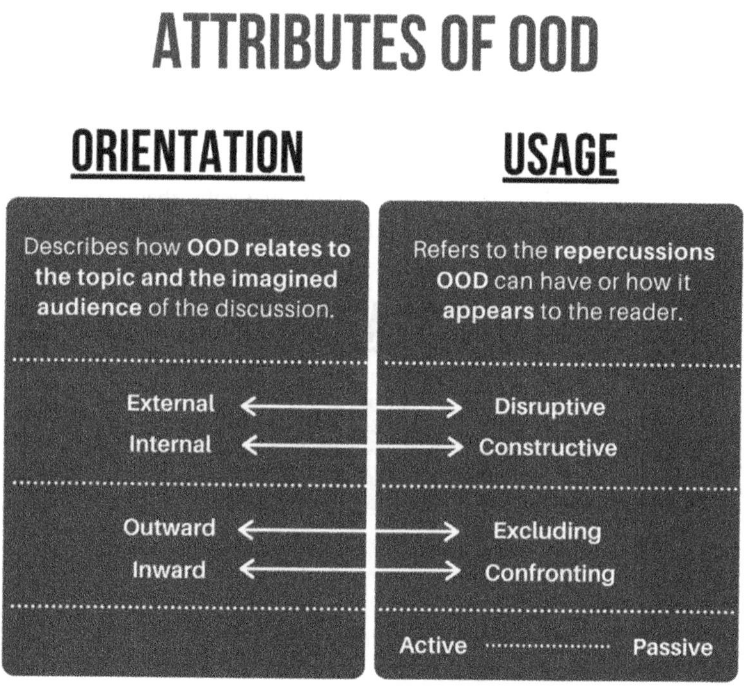

Fig. 13.1. Attributes of Othering Online Discourse (OOD) Can Be Divided Based on How the Discourses Relate to the Topic and Imagined Audience of the Discussion or How the Discourses Appear to the Reader. *Source:* Figure created by the author.

more ambiguous (Cook & Teasley, 2011; Litt & Hargittai, 2016; Marwick & boyd, 2014). If the OOD theory were applied to data collected from Facebook or Twitter, the researcher should be aware that definitions of the imagined audience rely heavily on their own interpretation.

Orientation of Othering Online Discourse

There are four types of orientation of OOD in relation to the topic and the audience of the discussion: external and internal; and inward and outward (see Fig. 13.2). External and internal discourses describe whether the producer of othering discourses is possibly part of the imagined audience of the forum or whether they come from outside. Inward and outward discourses, in turn, refer to the target of the othering: Inward othering is targeted to the imagined audience, and outward othering, outside the audience. Defining the boundary between outsiders and insiders may be next to impossible just by analyzing the discussion data. However, identifying the difference between internal and external discourses helps to outline the different starting points from which OOD is produced and what kind of power relations OOD creates. Positive representation of the imagined audience is more often better received, and discourses that strengthen the social cohesion of the imagined audience are more likely to resonate within the participants of the forum.

Usage of Othering Online Discourse

In addition to the previously listed orientations of OOD, there are roughly six different usages of othering: disruptive and constructive; excluding and confronting;

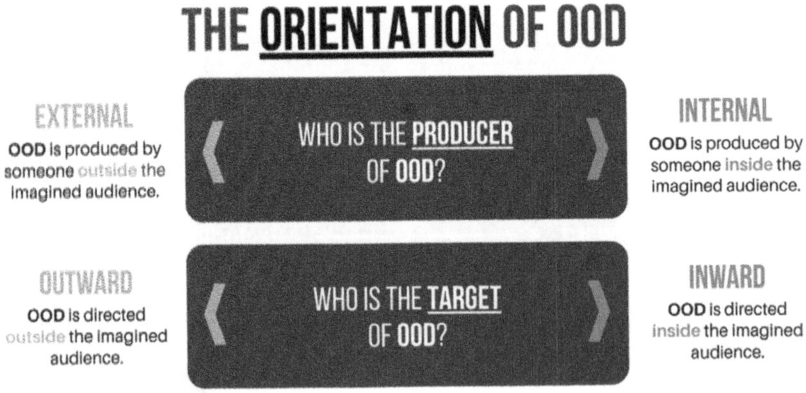

Fig. 13.2. The Orientations of Othering Online Discourse (OOD) Explore the Relationship between the Producer or the Target of OOD and the Imagined Audience of the Discussion.
Source: Figure created by the author.

and active and passive (see Fig. 13.3). Constructive and disruptive othering refers to whether the commenter conforms to the norms maintained by the imagined audience or whether they discursively oppose those norms. Excluding and confronting othering describe whether the target of the othering discourses is explicitly excluded from the interaction or instead explicitly addressed by the producer of the discourse. By active or passive othering, I mean whether the comment is explicitly and openly offensive or whether the discourses are more discrete and subtle in nature.

Examples of Orientation and Usage

Internal othering discourses are produced by commenters that are part of the imagined audience. Below is an excerpt from a conversation collected from the patriotism subcategory in Suomi24 forum:

> … Shit talk! Europeans are being fucked again. Somalis are the most homogeneous people in Africa, all belonging to the same ethnic group. Yes, they are divided into different clans. However, is it not better that they do what they have always done? By that I mean killing each other there in the Horn of Africa instead of coming here to murder and rape us. (Suomi24 forum, July 29, 2004)

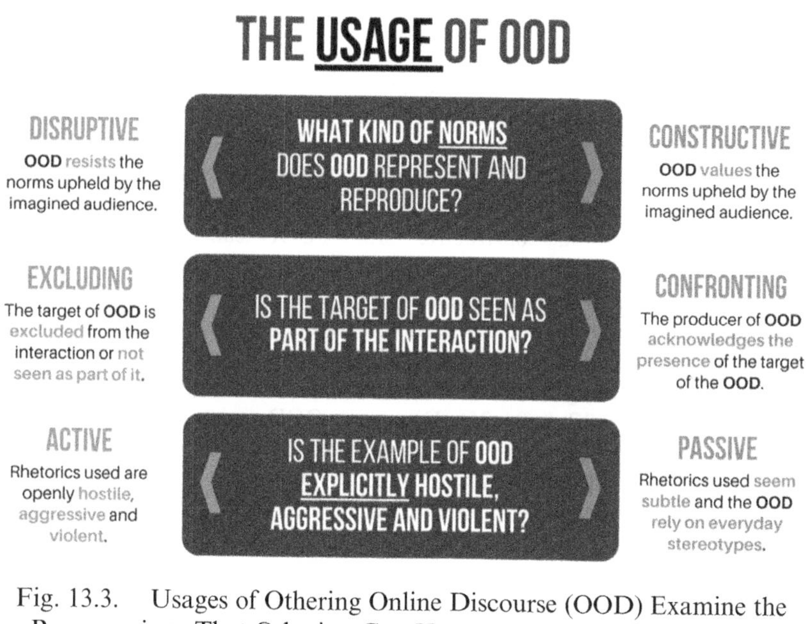

Fig. 13.3. Usages of Othering Online Discourse (OOD) Examine the Repercussions That Othering Can Have or How It Will Appear to the Reader. *Source:* Figure created by the author.

Based on the comment, it is reasonable to assume that the author identifies themselves as a white patriot and thus belongs to the imagined audience of the forum. It is also typical that internal othering discourses in openly aggressive, racist discussion threads include few divergent opinions and the comments consist mainly of conforming to previous threads. This is not uncommon in anonymous online interaction as it is not easy to disagree with the comments made, even in faceless and low-threshold online conversations (Mikal, Rice, Kent, & Uchino, 2014). Internal othering discourses are typically produced for like-minded readers, and they are often constructive in nature. In other words, instead of dichotomy, the purpose of these internal othering discourses is to strengthen internal social cohesion and commonly shared norms of the forum. The constructive and positive effect of comments is therefore limited to within the group, as when taken out of context, the content of the comments can be vile and far from helpful.

External othering discourses come from outside the imagined audience. If the forum is meant, for example, for people inflicted by poverty, external othering discourses are produced by people who do not identify themselves poor, as in this example:

> As far as I know, it takes two to make children. Don't have more children than you can afford to support! I myself have only one child and my salary is about 5200 euros a month. I pay almost two tons of tax on it, and this tax money is used to support social welfare parasites. (Suomi24 forum, March 27, 2010)

The comment above is taken from a discussion forum on poverty and a discussion thread about a single mother's financial distress. Once again, it is impossible to say how the author identifies themselves. However, according to the comment, the author clearly places themselves above people who live on social welfare, and thus othering discourses come from outside the imagined audience. I have previously pointed out that OOD is often a group formation promoting action in some forums that foster a culture of hate and bigotry. As shown in the example above, in addition to its constructive nature, OOD can also be deliberately disruptive – especially when the commenter comes from outside the imagined audience. The above commenter emphasizes their superiority, and in no way seeks to find common ground with other users. This kind of disruptive action may also take the form of trolling, whereby the commenter may seek to shock and entertain themselves by disrupting the flow of the conversation (Hardaker, 2010, p. 238; Phillips, 2015, pp. 3, 17 & 24–25). Disruptive OOD resists the norms that are upheld by the imagined audience. For example, if the forum's shared norms encourage inclusion and diversity, disruptive OOD opposes inclusion.

When the discourse is *inward*, othering is directed to the imagined audience of the forum:

> Poor people cannot have any relationships at all. No woman wants a poor man. I'm always alone and depressed because I'm always alone. (Suomi24 forum, September 30, 2015)

While the commenter above acknowledges they are part of the discussion's imagined audience, they also direct their othering comment on that audience. The commenter positions themselves outside the cultural norm, where a financially high status is believed to help in finding a companion. In this example, sense of community is built through shared experience of otherness and opposing the cultural master-narrative (see, e.g., Vainikka, 2018). This kind of inward and internal OOD may foster a communal experience of otherness and can work as a form of peer support. When the othering discourses are inward and thus comments are explicitly targeted to the imagined audience of the forum, the comments are confronting.

In turn, *outward* discourse is directed to someone outside the imagined audience of the discussion. This may mean, for example, that in a forum for trans people, othering discourses are directed at cis-gendered people:

> Cis men seem to be more phobic than women. Men are always on average more phobic/conservative in everything – our culture even requires it. After all, you are no man at all if you don't drink beer, watch hockey, and hate gays. (Suomi24 forum, May 18, 2010)

As can be seen from the example above, norms of whiteness, straightness, and maleness can also be turned upside down in groups meant for marginalized identities. In these cases, the master-narrative that favors cis men is set to a subordinate position. Instead of just peer support, this kind of outward OOD can create a sense of empowerment in a group that shares experiences of otherness. The way the commenter above addresses cis men can also be seen as *excluding* othering. Excluding othering means that the commenter explicitly expresses their desire to keep the "other" out of the conversation or the commenter expresses an assumption that the other is not involved in the discussion.

Maria Ruotsalainen (2018, p. 226) has mapped the use of the term hate speech in Finnish public discourse and has found that hate speech typically reduces the other to the role of mere object instead of seeing the other as a subject. This finding aligns with these examples of confronting and excluding OOD. Regardless of whether the discourses are confronting or excluding, the other often remains merely as a static object that is described through stereotypes and inferiority.

By *passive* othering, I mean that its producer does not necessarily deliberately seek to offend. A person who produces passive othering can use very subtle – but still harmful – stereotypes. The feelings and emotions described in passive othering may refer to feelings such as fear, frustration, suspicion, or anxiety. By *active* othering I am referring in particular to comments that explicitly refer to violence, hatred, or inferiority of the other – just like in this example:

> When it comes to an accident, a plane crash or a shipwreck, or even a natural disaster, most people feel some compassion for the victims. But when it comes to a ship carrying refugees, I feel only joy in the accident. The more victims, the more joyful I feel. (Suomi24 forum, April 20, 2015)

While the commentator above describes the feelings of joy, the comment itself contains much more destructive emotions since the comment openly wishes for the death of refugees.

These attributes can work as a way to describe the othering qualities of dialogue and also as a way to decode the process of OOD in a discussion thread. They help to illuminate the social aspects of OOD and demonstrate how a single dialogue, thread, or comment can work in many ways and still contain characteristics that contribute to social injustice, discrimination, bigotry, and even violence

Conclusion

In summary, OOD is a phenomenon that is social, intersectional, and discursively diverse. OOD often exploits the public nature of online spaces to create a sense of community based on marginalization and harmful stereotypes. There is an inherent duality in the sociality of OOD. In some cases, by producing othering discourse, commenters invite like-minded people to ostracize the "other" and create social cohesion based on discrimination. In other cases, OOD takes a much more disruptive form, where othering discourses are used to disagree and possibly troll the imagined audience of the conversation. OOD can also be seen as a form of internet gatekeeping that, at its worst, dehumanizes groups that don't fit to a narrowly defined norm of whiteness and maleness. Sometimes this discursive gatekeeping takes a form of empowerment and rebellion. In those cases, the narratives against inclusion and diversity are set to an inferior position and seen as the other. At the heart of the OOD theory is the idea that while public online discussions are a powerful medium to convey identity speech and they can help to construct sameness and group identities, they can also produce inequality, hostility, marginalization, and the experience of otherness.

In this chapter, I demonstrated that by combining elements from concepts dealing with inequality and discursive exclusivity, it is possible to develop a theory that is flexible enough to examine different kinds of online othering discourses. With the examples of othering discourses, I demonstrated the attributes of OOD and showed how discursive exclusivity is created from different starting points, by different discursive means, and for different purposes. In addition to the theoretical core of OOD, the concept also has a practical side. OOD theory and especially its attributes can be utilized as an analysis model to decode and contextualize online discussion data. The attributes of OOD help to understand the relationships between the producer of othering, the target of othering, the possible purpose of the othering, and the online space that hosts the discourses. Considering these different contexts is important when identifying and, above all, preventing technology-facilitated hatred and violence.

References

Arntfield, M. (2015). Towards a cybervictimology: Cyberbullying, routine activities theory, and the anti-sociality of social media. *Canadian Journal of Communication*, *40*(3), 371–388.

Atton, C. (2006). Far-right media on the internet: Culture, discourse and power. *New Media & Society*, *8*(4), 573–587.

Back, L. (2002). Aryans reading Adorno: Cyber-culture and twenty-first-century racism. *Ethnic and Racial Studies*, *25*(4), 628–651.

Bauman, Z., & May, T. (2004). *Thinking sociologically* (2nd ed.). Hoboken, NJ: Blackwell Publishing Ltd.

Baumgarten, N. (2017). Othering practice in a right-wing extremist online forum. *language@Internet*, *14*(1). Retrieved from https://www.languageatinternet.org/articles/2017/baumgarten

Benjamin, J. (1990). An outline of intersubjectivity: The development of recognition. *Psychoanalytic Psychology*, *7*, 33–46.

Chayko, M. (2002). *Connecting: How we form social bonds and communities in the internet age*. New York, NY: State University of New York Press.

Cho, S., Crenshaw, K., & McCall, L. (2013). Toward a field of intersectionality studies: Theory, applications, and praxis. *Signs*, *38*(4), 785–810.

Citron, D. K. (2014). *Hate crimes in cyberspace*. Hoboken, NJ: Harvard University Press.

Coffey, B., & Woolworth, S. (2004). "Destroy the scum, and then neuter their families": The web forum as a vehicle for community discourse?. *The Social Science Journal*, *41*(1), 1–14.

Cook, E. C., & Teasley, S. D. (2011). Beyond promotion and protection: Creators, audiences and common ground in user-generated media. In *Proceedings of the 2011 iConference* (pp. 41–47).

Coupland, N. (2010). "Other" representation. In J. Jaspers, J. Verschueren, & J. O. Östman (Eds.), *Society and language use* (Vol. 7, pp. 241–260). Amsterdam: John Benjamins Publishing.

De Beauvoir, S. (1997). *The second sex*. London: Vintage [first published in French in 1949].

Delgado, R., Stefancic, J., & Harris, A. (2017). *Critical race theory: An introduction* (3rd ed..). New York, NY: New York University Press.

Denzin, N. K. (1978). *The research act: A theoretical introduction to sociological methods* (2nd ed.). New York, NY: McGraw-Hill.

Dervin, F. (2015). Discourses of othering. In K. Tracy, C. Ilie & T. Sandel (Eds.), *The international encyclopedia of language and social interaction* (pp. 447–456). New York, NY: John Wiley & Sons.

ElSherief, M., Kulkarni, V., Nguyen, D., Wang, W. Y., & Belding, E. (2018). Hate lingo: A target-based linguistic analysis of hate speech in social media. In *Twelfth International AAAI Conference on Web and Social Media*.

Fairclough, N. (2003). *Analysing discourse: Textual analysis for social research*. London & New York: Routledge.

Gillespie, A., Howarth, C. S., & Cornish, F. (2012). Four problems for researchers using social categories. *Culture & Psychology*, *18*(3), 391–402.

Gingrich, A. (2004). Conceptualizing identities. In G. Bauman and A. Gingrich (Eds.), *Grammars of identity/alterity –A structural approach* (pp. 3–17). Oxford: BergHahn.

Hall, S. (1997). The centrality of culture: Notes on the cultural revolutions of our time. In K. Thompson (Ed.), *Media and cultural regulation* (pp. 207–238). London: Sage.

Hall, S. (2003). Kulttuuri, paikka, identiteetti. In M. Lehtonen & O. Löytty (Eds.), *Erilaisuus* (pp. 85–128). Tampere: Vastapaino.

Hardaker, C. (2010). Trolling in asynchronous computer-mediated communication: From user discussions to academic definitions. *Journal of Politeness Research: Language, Behavior, Culture*, *6*(2), 215–242.

Hinduja, S., & Patchin, J. W. (2010). Bullying, cyberbullying, and suicide. *Archives of Suicide Research*, *14*(3), 206–221.

Hine, C. (2015). *Ethnography for the internet: Embedded, embodied and everyday*. London: Bloomsbury Publishing Plc.

Hmielowski, J. D., Hutchens, M. J., & Cicchirillo, V. J. (2014). Living in an age of online incivility: Examining the conditional indirect effects of online discussion on political flaming. *Information, Communication & Society*, *17*(10), 1196–1211.

Hughey, M. W., & Daniels, J. (2013). Racist comments at online news sites: A methodological dilemma for discourse analysis. *Media, Culture & Society*, *35*(3), 332–347.

Jane, E. (2014). 'Back to the kitchen, cunt': Speaking the unspeakable about online misogyny. *Continuum: Journal of Media & Cultural Studies*, *28*(4), 558–570.

Jemmer, P. (2010). The O(the)r (O)the(r). In P. Jemmer (Ed.), *Engage Newcastle* (Vol. 1, pp. 7–39). Newcastle: Newcastle Philosophy Society.

Jensen, S. Q. (2011). Othering, identity formation and agency. *Qualitative Studies*, *2*(2), 63–78.

Jick, T. D. (1979). Mixing qualitative and quantitative methods: Triangulation in action. *Administrative Science Quarterly*, *24*(4), 602–611.

Laaksonen, S. M., Nelimarkka, M., Tuokko, M., Marttila, M., Kekkonen, A., & Villi, M. (2017). Working the fields of big data: Using big-data-augmented online ethnography to study candidate–candidate interaction at election time. *Journal of Information Technology & Politics*, *14*(2), 110–131.

Lacan, J. (1966). *Écrits*. Paris: Le Seuil.

Lagus, K. H., Ruckenstein, M. S., Pantzar, M., & Ylisiurua, M. J. (2016). *SUOMI24: Muodonantoa aineistolle*. Helsinki: University of Helsinki.

Litt, E., & Hargittai, E. (2016). The imagined audience on social network sites. *Social Media+ Society*, *2*(1), doi:10.1177/2056305116633482

Malmqvist, K. (2015). Satire, racist humour and the power of (un) laughter: On the restrained nature of Swedish online racist discourse targeting EU-migrants begging for money. *Discourse & Society*, *26*(6), 733–753.

Markham, A., & Buchanan, E. (2012). Ethical decision-making and internet research: Version 2.0. recommendations from the AoIR ethics working committee. Retrieved from aoir.org/reports/ethics2.pdf.

Marwick, A. E., & Boyd, D. (2014). Networked privacy: How teenagers negotiate context in social media. *New Media & Society*, *16*(7), 1051–1067.

Massanari, A. (2017). #Gamergate and the Fappening: How Reddit's algorithm, governance, and culture support toxic technocultures. *New Media & Society*, *19*(3), 329–346.

McKenna, B., & Chughtai, H. (2020). Resistance and sexuality in virtual worlds: An LGBT perspective. *Computers in Human Behavior*, *105*, 106199.

Meddaugh, P. M., & Kay, J. (2009). Hate speech or "reasonable racism?" The other in Stormfront. *Journal of Mass Media Ethics*, *24*(4), 251–268.

Mehra, B., Merkel, C., & Bishop, A. P. (2004). The internet for empowerment of minority and marginalized users. *New Media & Society*, *6*(6), 781–802.

Mikal, J. P., Rice, R. E., Kent, R. G., & Uchino, B. N. (2014). Common voice: Analysis of behavior modification and content convergence in a popular online community. *Computers in Human Behavior*, *35*, 506–515.

Miles, R. (1989). *Racism*. London: Routledge.

Miller, T. (2015, December 17). Social or antisocial media? *APPS Policy Forum*. Retrieved from https://www.policyforum.net/social-or-anti-social-media/

Nuopponen, A. (2010). Methods of concept analysis-a comparative study. *LSP Journal-Language for special purposes, professional communication, knowledge management and cognition*, *1*(1), 2–14.

Okolie, A. (2003). Introduction to the special issue – identity: Now you don't see it; now you do. *Identity*, *3*(1), 1–7.

Papacharissi, Z. (2004). Democracy online: Civility, politeness, and the democratic potential of online political discussion groups. *New Media & Society*, *6*(2), 259–283.

Phillips, W. (2015). *This is why we can't have nice things: Mapping the relationship between online trolling and mainstream culture*. Cambridge, MA: The MIT Press.

Phillips, W. (2019). It wasn't just the trolls: Early internet culture,"fun," and the fires of exclusionary laughter. *Social Media + Society*, *5*(3), doi:10.1177/2056305119849493

Pickering, M. (2001). *Stereotyping: The politics of representation*. Basingstoke: Palgrave.

Puusa, A. (2008). Käsiteanalyysi tutkimusmenetelmänä. *Premissi*, *4*(2008), 36–43.

Quayle, E., Vaughan, M., & Taylor, M. (2006). Sex offenders, internet child abuse images and emotional avoidance: The importance of values. *Aggression and Violent Behavior*, *11*(1), 1–11.

Ruotsalainen, M. (2018). Tracing the concept of hate speech in Finland. *Nykykulttuurin tutkimuskeskuksen julkaisuja*, *122*, 213–230.

Said, E. (1995). *Orientalism*. London: Penguin Books [first published in 1978].

Staszak, J. (2008). Other/otherness. In R. Kitchin & N. Thrift (Eds.), *International encyclopedia of human geography* (pp. 43–47). London: Elsevier.

Suler, J. (2004). The online disinhibition effect. *CyberPsychology and Behavior*, *7*(3), 321–326.

Sumiala, J. (2012). *Media and ritual: Death, community and everyday life*. London: Routledge.

Suominen, J., Saarikoski, P., & Vaahensalo, E. (2019). *Digitaalisia kohtaamisia: Verkkokeskustelut BBS-purkeista sosiaaliseen mediaan*. Helsinki: Gaudeamus.

Vaahensalo, E. (2018). Keskustelufoorumit mediainhokkeina–Suositut suomenkieliset keskustelufoorumit mediassa. *Wider screen*, *3*(2018). Retrieved from http://widerscreen.fi/numerot/2018-3/keskustelufoorumit-mediainhokkeina-suositut-suomenkieliset-keskustelufoorumit-mediassa/

Vainikka, E. (2018). The anti-social network: Precarious life in online conversations of the socially withdrawn. *European Journal of Cultural Studies*. doi:10.1177/1367549418810075

Van Dijk, T. A. (2000). New (s) racism: A discourse analytical approach. *Ethnic minorities and the media*, *37*, 33–49.

Waldron, J. (2012). *The harm in hate speech*. Cambridge, MA: Harvard University Press.

Walker, S. (1994). *Hate speech: The history of an American controversy*. Lincoln: University of Nebraska Press.

Watt, S., Lea, M., & Spears, R. (2002). How social is internet communication? A reappraisal of bandwidth and anatomy effects. In S. Woolgar (Ed.), *Virtual society?: Technology, cyberbole, reality* (pp. 61–77). New York: Oxford University Press.

Weaver, S. (2013). A rhetorical discourse analysis of online anti-Muslim and anti-Semitic jokes. *Ethnic and Racial Studies*, *36*(3), 483–499.

Wilson, J. (1963). *Thinking with concepts*. Cambridge: Cambridge University Press.

Wodak, R. (1999). Critical discourse analysis at the end of the 20th century. *Research on Language and Social Interaction*, *32*(1–2), 185–193.

Zimmer, M. (2018). Addressing conceptual gaps in big data research ethics: An application of contextual integrity. *Social Media+ Society*, *4*(2). Retrieved from https://journals.sagepub.com/doi/full/10.1177/2056305118768300

Chapter 14

Text-Based (Sexual) Abuse and Online Violence Against Women: Toward Law Reform?

Kim Barker and Olga Jurasz

Abstract

The ideal of an open, all-inclusive, and participatory internet has been undermined by the rise of gender-based and misogynistic abuse on social media platforms. Limited progress has been made at supranational and national levels in addressing this issue, and where steps have been taken to combat online violence against women (OVAW), they are typically limited to legislative developments addressing image-based sexual abuse. As such, harms associated with image-based abuse have gained recognition in law while harms caused by text-based abuse (TBA) have not been conceptualized in an equivalent manner.

This chapter critically outlines the lack of judicial consideration given to online harms in British courts, identifying a range of harms arising from TBAs which currently are not recognized by the criminal justice system. We refer to non-traditional harms recognized in cases heard before the British courts, assessing these in light of traditionally recognized harms in established legal authorities. This chapter emphasizes the connection between the harms suffered and the recognition of impact on the victims, demonstrated through specific case studies. Through this assessment, this chapter advocates for greater recognition of online harms within the legal system – especially those which take the forms of misogynistic and/or gendered TBA.

Keywords: Text-based sexual abuse; online harms; online violence against women (OVAW); online misogyny; gender equality; digital rights; misogyny

The Emerald International Handbook of Technology-Facilitated Violence and Abuse, 247–264

doi:10.1108/978-1-83982-848-520211017

Introduction

The ideal of an open, all-inclusive, and participatory internet has been undermined by the rise of gender-based and misogynistic abuse on social media platforms. In June 2018, the United Nations Special Rapporteur on Violence Against Women presented a thematic report to the UN Human Rights Council on online violence against women (OVAW), in which she noted that

> Despite the benefits and empowering potential of the internet and [information and communications technology (ICT)], women and girls across the world have increasingly voiced their concern at harmful, sexist, misogynistic and violent content and behaviour online. (UN, 2018, p. 5)

OVAW has indeed grown in prevalence especially on social media platforms and has an everyday impact on women and girls who participate online, be it in a private or professional capacity. In the United Kingdom, despite the increase in public focus and campaigning on this issue (Change.org, 2020; Mason, Davies, & Bakare, 2020), as well as the Government's attempts to address online harms more generally (UK Government, 2019), little has been done to address OVAW through the legal system in a comprehensive, holistic, and gender-sensitive manner. Instead, a fragmented and ad hoc approach to addressing OVAW has been deployed, resulting in the emergence of a legal framework and proposals for further law reform (e.g., UK Government, 2019), which demonstrates a narrow understanding of the phenomenon of OVAW, the real and continuing impact it has on its victims, as well as the limited and old-fashioned conceptualization of harms resulting from online abuse (Barker & Jurasz, 2019c). Typically, reform proposals that focus on the online abuse suffered by women tend to place the emphasis on selected aspects of OVAW. For example, when it involves image-based sexual abuse (IBSA) or when it is committed in domestic violence/intimate partner violence contexts. These proposals also largely exclude a gender-focused analysis of the responsibilities of platform providers (Barker & Jurasz, 2020c). Equally, the proposals for reform addressing online harms (not only those suffered by women) do not engage with a full spectrum of OVAW and exclude gendered and non-traditional harms resulting from it. Instead, they engage with selected and politically appealing aspects of online abuse and online harms, such as the protection of children (to the exclusion of the fact that children and adolescents perpetrate online abuse too), or place a disproportionate focus on cases where online abuse results in physical harms such as suicide (Mason et al., 2020; UK Government, 2019).

However, one of the key exclusions within the proposed legal frameworks both domestically and internationally is the continuous omission of online, gendered text-based abuse (TBA) and the harms arising from it (Barker & Jurasz, 2019a, 2020c). Despite the prevalence of this form of online abuse directed at women and girls, TBA has not been conceptualized or enshrined in the domestic laws in the United Kingdom and harms arising from it have not been afforded a thorough and modern judicial consideration. This chapter outlines the problems, such as omission causes, and advocates for the inclusion of a TBA as a distinct category. Such recognition would give credence to the harmful impact such abuses have on those subjected to them – something also missing from the current paradigm and redress mechanisms.

The chapter begins by offering an overview of text-based (sexual) abuse (TB(S)A) and its correlation to the much more widely known phenomenon of IBSA. The discussion then moves on to assess the harms caused by TBA, outlining their wide-ranging impact, especially upon prominent women, before exploring the misperceptions that pervade these harms leading to their lack of capture by the legal and judicial systems. The argument concludes by highlighting that a failure to capture TBA, and a failure to address the harms caused by such behaviors, is a failure to prioritize digital equality. This chapter argues for increased recognition of, and redress for, TB(S)As within the legal system to ensure digital and participatory rights for women.

Text-Based (Sexual) Abuse

TBA can be defined as "written, electronic communication containing threatening and/or disruptive and/or distressing content, such as, e.g. textual threats to kill, rape, or otherwise inflict harm on the recipient of such messages" (Barker & Jurasz, 2019a, p. xiv). Further examples of TBA can include hateful posts or tweets online, and textual content aimed to degrade or distress the recipient. TBA is frequently directed against women participating online and can take sexualized forms, including sexualized messages and threats. In such instances, TBA becomes text-based sexual abuse (TB(S)A). However, both sexualized and non-sexualized forms of TBA amount to OVAW. TB(S)A can also amount to online hate speech if the content of the message demonstrated prejudice because of a person's specific characteristics, such as race, religion, or gender. That said, while hate crime and hate speech are closely related, the concept of online hate speech is much broader than the legal categorization of hate crime – in case of the latter, there is a requirement for an underlying criminal act to be committed and motivated by hostility or prejudice against a person's (or persons') characteristic or perceived characteristic (Barker & Jurasz, 2019a; CPS, 2017).

TB(S)A is demonstrative of the persisting gender inequalities that are mirrored in online environments. It is also an indicator of the persistent normalization of violence against women within modern societies – be it in its physical, structural, or symbolic forms – and the reluctance of the legal system to adequately address gendered harms suffered by women, including prevention, and adequate reparation. Instead, the exclusion of TB(S)A from the legal framework on OVAW and online harms reinforces the existing status quo, whereby the harms suffered by women are not adequately addressed in the legal system, the gender-based and wide-ranging aspects of harms involved in TBA/TB(S)A are largely missing, and victims are left without adequate recourse to justice and reparation. The prevalence of TB(S)A has repercussions not only at an individual but also a collective level. For example, the hypervisibility of TB(S)A and gender-based forms of TBA on social media platforms legitimises the social acceptance of violence against women, and the perpetuation of gender discrimination and inequalities. Paradoxically, the hypervisibility of TB(S)A leads to a growing absence of women from public/online spaces and the invisibility of their voices within those spaces. As such, TB(S)A has silencing effects on women and girls participating online and contributes to the creation of hostile spaces for women.

This is a significant concern from the perspective of ensuring non-discrimination and equality of participation as TB(S)A leads many women and girls to effectively withdraw from participating online and in public life (Barker & Jurasz, 2019b; Barker & Jurasz, 2019d). For instance, the UK Girlguiding Girls' Attitudes Survey (2016) showed that 49% of the 1,600 surveyed girls aged 11–16 and 44% of young women aged 17–21 felt unable to express their views in an online environment (pp. 17–19). The impact of online TBA on women's participation online and in public life was also evidenced in the responses of women politicians who were subjected to online abuse in the lead up to the UK 2017 General Election (Dhordia, 2017), which pointed toward an extremely high volume of online abuse affecting women's participation and expressing themselves online. This has not been confined to the 2017 General Election. In the 2019 General Election, 18 of the 50 Members of Parliament (MPs) standing down were female, and several attributed their departure to the abuse and harassment suffered while in elected office (Barker & Jurasz, 2020a; Oppenheim, 2019). As such, TB(S)A affects women's rights to full and equal participation in public and political life, the ensuring of which is also an international obligation of states that are parties to the 1979 UN Convention on Elimination of All Forms of Discrimination Against Women (CEDAW). Under Article 7 of CEDAW, states are obliged to take steps to prevent and eliminate discrimination of women in public and political life and to ensure their equal participation. While this obligation was articulated over 40 years ago (and therefore before the rise of social media and the internet), its contemporary interpretation ought to extend to online spaces as a primary location of modern day political and public life (Barker & Jurasz, 2019c, p. 5).

Text-Based Sexual Abuse versus Image-Based Sexual Abuse

Despite the widespread and everyday nature of TB(S)A and its harrowing impact on victims, the law in the United Kingdom (and many other jurisdictions worldwide) has not been reformed to address this pressing issue. This stands in stark contrast with the attitude of legislators in the United Kingdom and in selected overseas jurisdictions toward addressing a different type of OVAW – image-based sexual abuse (IBSA). IBSA, which involves the nonconsensual creation and distribution of private sexual images (McGlynn & Rackley, 2017), has been the subject of speedy legal reform in the United Kingdom and also in other jurisdictions, such as Australia, Canada, France, Israel, and Japan (Flynn & Henry, 2019).[1] The introduction of new laws tackling IBSA (or, the problematic term, "revenge pornography") has become a legislative priority which is rarely seen in legal reforms aimed at addressing sexual abuse or other forms of gender-based violence. Although new legal provisions dealing with IBSA have attracted some criticism from academic commentators (e.g., Henry et al., 2020; McGlynn & Rackley, 2015; Powell, Scott, Henry, & Flynn, 2020), the provisions nonetheless signified a remarkable progress in addressing a modern form of violence that is perpetrated typically using the internet or otherwise facilitated by communications technology.

While harms associated with IBSA have gained recognition in law (leading to expeditious law reforms and an increase in accountability), harms caused by TBA have not been conceptualized in an equivalent manner, nor given the same attention. The juxtaposition of the prompt IBSA reforms with the lethargic response of the legal system to TB(S)A raises questions about the ultimate hierarchy of harms within the legal system and the visibility of non-image based gendered violence.

Both IBSA and TB(S)A while involving somewhat different acts lead to a number of harms in online and offline contexts. Harms associated with IBSA have been categorized to include wide ranging consequences, both for the individual (e.g., the violation of a person's dignity, privacy, and physical integrity) and broader society, including cultural harms (McGlynn & Rackley, 2017). Powell and Henry (2017) also note emotional distress, reputational harms, loss of job opportunities and when IBSA happens in the context of domestic violence/IPV nonconsensual acts (pp. 137, 138) as likely implications of IBSA. As we demonstrate later in this chapter, many of the harms associated with IBSA also happen when TB(S)A is committed. However, unlike IBSA, the victims are left without appropriate channels of redress because of severe shortcomings in the legal system which do not capture this particular form of online abuse. Although TB(S)A can be directed against both men and women (by both men and women alike[2]), TB(S)A directed against women typically takes sexualized and gender-based forms which are rarely addressed within the existing laws, nor by the key actors in the justice system.

The IBSA-TB(S)A dualism created by the contrasting approach of the legal and justice system toward these two forms of online abuse, if unaddressed, leads to the perpetuation of gender inequalities within the law. The unequal approach of the legislators toward IBSA as compared to TB(S)A results in the creation of a hierarchy of harms within the legal system, in which more credence and gravitas are given to forms of online abuse involving photographic representations of the victim than textual and frequently very violent abuse. By maintaining such a status quo through legislative inaction, the legal system creates a self-reinforcing but false perception that IBSA is more harmful and serious than non-image based (sexual) abuse. As such, the legislative gap results in non-image-based forms of abuse and violence against women remaining invisible within the legal system. This contributes to the erasure of the full narrative of OVAW from the legal system, coupled with a resulting lack of reliable data capturing the prevalence of TB(S)A. Ultimately this results in very limited accountability and redress for these violent acts. In turn, TB(S)A becomes a normalized form of OVAW and women's experiences of it remain on the periphery of the legal and justice systems.

Text-Based Sexual Abuse Harms: An Early Assessment

The early assessment of the treatment of online harms – especially those associated with TB(S)A – in British courts shows very slow progress toward an understanding of these modern behaviors and their consequences. Notably, in the few cases that actually involved TB(S)A and/or TBA directed against women, there is a remarkable absence of gender analysis of TB(S)A and harms in the judgments. The judgments also lack substantive judicial reasoning on the broader harmfulness of online TB(S)A – especially in relation to promoting and normalizing violence against and abuse of women and girls, as well as, where applicable, promoting the hatred of women and/or inciting violence against women through misogynistic TBA. The 2014 case of *R v Nimmo and Sorley* – the first judgment in England & Wales marking a successful prosecution for TB(S)A – is an early exemplar of such shortcomings, despite some notable steps in recognizing and beginning to conceptualize non-traditional harms.[3]

Nimmo and Sorley (2014) dealt with online abuse in the form of abusive, threatening, and violent tweets sent by the defendants to the feminist campaigner Caroline Criado-Perez and Stella Creasy MP in relation to their involvement in the campaign to bring more women onto the Bank of England banknotes in 2013 (Barker & Jurasz, 2019a). The sentencing remarks of Judge Riddle have made a significant contribution in that they highlighted the issue of the transference of harms between online and offline worlds. For example, Judge Riddle commented that the harm, while serious, was "entirely predictable," and was exacerbated by the manner in which the threats and harassment were communicated online, at all hours, and promising physical harm, too (*R v Nimmo and Sorley*, 2014, p. 2). Riddle identified these as indicators of aggravating features in the sentencing considerations especially because, "[t]he victims had no way of knowing how dangerous the people making the threats were" (*R v Nimmo and Sorley*, 2014, p. 3). Riddle's remarks also focused on the anonymity of the perpetrators as a factor heightening the victims' fear for their personal safety, as well as outlining several non-traditional harms, such as the economic and residential consequences of online TBA and the severe psychological impact on the victims. Riddle stated that, "the effects of the harassment [they] received have been life-changing" (*R v Nimmo and Sorley*, 2014, p. 2). However, none of the judicial remarks engaged with the sexualized and violent nature of many of the tweets received by Criado-Perez and Creasy, nor elaborated on how the visibility of such content promotes (O)VAW and normalizes such forms of gendered abuse and violence within society.

Similarly, the 2017 judgment and sentencing comments in *R v Viscount St Davids* – a case dealing with extreme online abuse suffered by the anti-Brexit campaigner Gina Miller – lack the gender analysis of TB(S)A received by Miller, and its impact. Miller was subjected to racist, sexist, and misogynistic abuse, yet the judgment focused only on the racist aspect most likely because of the aggravation based on race that resulted in a harsher sentence for the perpetrator (*R v Viscount St Davids,* Sentencing Comments, para 30).[4] As such, the intersectional nature of Miller's TBA was rendered invisible in the official legal documents concerning the case, therefore only partially providing an accurate record of the nature, the extent, and the impact of the overwhelming amount of the abuse received. For instance, Miller received messages stating that the "Jo Cox killing would be good for you" (Anthony, 2018) – such messages suggesting that the Jo Cox murder is being used as a symbolic point of reference for the extreme acts of violence targeting women. The harmful nature of such tweets and the socio-cultural harms they perpetuate have not been thus far addressed, nor condemned by the legal system, overlooking incitement to VAW. Despite a number of social campaigns against VAW and the "in principle" commitment to tackling VAW by the Government and agencies of the justice system, these everyday, symbolic acts of violence continue to be inflicted upon women on social media.

While not addressing gender, Judge Arbuthnot made an important recognition in her sentencing remarks in *R v Viscount St Davids* (2017) when noting that the public profile of the victim does not justify such "warped behaviour" (para 3) being directed at them. This is significant, especially in light of proposals in the United Kingdom to afford higher levels of protection to politicians (UK Government, 2018) and high-profile individuals (Barker & Jurasz, 2020b). As we argue elsewhere (Barker & Jurasz, 2017)

> ...the profile of the alleged victim should be entirely irrelevant in terms of the alleged abuse received – the harm and the impact of the harm should be the determining features in tackling issues of online abuse. (p. 15)

It is equally important to recognize that online abuse is not only a matter concerning celebrities and politicians. As Miller's case evidences, the extreme levels of abuse can be – and are – frequently directed at women involved in high-profile legal proceedings, and cause harms not only to the individual, but which also undermine democratic values and fundamental rights. The harmful impact of online abuse, especially TBA, on the latter was explicitly recognized by the then President of the UK Supreme Court, Lord Neuberger, at the opening of the Article 50 appeal case brought by Gina Miller. While making the court order to ban the names of former claimants in the proceedings, prohibiting the publication of the home address of Gina Miller and other parties, and prohibiting publication of any information which could identify the interested parties in the proceedings, Lord Neuberger stated:

> We have made this order largely because various individuals have received threats of serious violence and unpleasant abuse in emails and other electronic communications. Threatening and abusing people because they are exercising their fundamental right to go to court undermines the rule of law. Anyone who communicates such threats or abuse should be aware that there are legal powers designed to ensure that access to the courts is available to everyone (Scottish Legal News, 2016).

Given the overwhelming absence of substantive judicial reasoning concerning social, democratic, and participatory harms associated with online abuse and TB(S)A, Lord Neuberger's statement (although not a part of the *Miller* judgment) provides a significant recognition of the impact of online TBA on the rule of law, as well as on one's fundamental rights. It is nonetheless regrettable that similar recognition has not been made in relation to the impact of TBA on the normalization and promotion of (O)VAW.

Misperceiving Text-Based (Sexual) Abuse: Time to Capture Its Harmful Impact?

In addressing the phenomenon of TB(S)A, the approach that has been witnessed to date is one that focuses on the ability of various and disparate legal provisions to capture behaviors (not harms) that amount to TB(S)A conduct. The essential weakness of this attitude is one that permeates misperceptions about the behaviors, the motivations behind such behaviors, and the harm inflicted by allowing this to go unchecked, unchallenged, and uncaptured. For instance, in tackling TB(S)A that includes rape and sexualized death threats as in *Nimmo and Sorley* (2014), the predominant legal response in England and Wales is to address this through the criminal law provisions dealing with the misuse of a public communications network through section 127 of the *Communications Act* 2003. In such convictions, and in those of *R v Nunn* (2014) that followed, no consideration nor criminal charge was levied in respect of the more serious criminal behavior of making threats to kill (Barker, 2018). The inaction in tackling these behaviors through the criminal law is broadly reflective of the wider perception that none of this is "serious" and resides purely "online" (Barker & Jurasz, 2020c). This attitude was particularly evident in the response of the local police when Stella Creasy MP initially reported the abusive and threatening tweets to her local police via Twitter. In their response, the police indicated that she would need to report the issue if it was not an overreaction (Barnett, 2014). By extension, responses indicating that such behaviors are trivial imply that there are no significant repercussions, and it is therefore acceptable to engage in such activity. This perpetuates the misperception that TB(S)A is not a "real" problem, and when compared to IBSA also not a visible one.

The conceptions of TBAs have been frequently shrugged off as less serious than offline and are "part and parcel" of what happens online (Barker & Jurasz, 2014), including by the actors in the criminal justice system (Holt, Lee, Liggett, Holt, & Bossler, 2019). Such an attitude – as noted in early reports of what amounts to the trivilization of TBSA – perpetuates the idea that such behaviours are to be expected. Given the significant impact that reported threats and harassment can cause those subjected to it, there is growing recognition of the harmful and long-lasting impact and increasing prevalence of TB(S)A. The Inter-Parliamentary Union in 2018 highlighted that 85.2% of the women parliamentarians surveyed have been subjected to some form of psychological violence – an overwhelming majority of those surveyed, and more disappointingly, an increase from 81.8% just two years earlier (Inter-Parliamentary Union, 2016). Similarly, Amnesty International highlighted the scope of the problem in 2017 (Dhordia, 2017), and Tim Berners-Lee – the founding father of the internet – reiterated on the 31st birthday of the internet's creation that it remains an incredibly hostile environment for women (Berners-Lee & Berners-Lee, 2020). All of these indicators demonstrate a lingering notion that TB(S)A is not "real," is not harmful, and does not require attention. This comes almost a decade on from the Gamergate fiasco,[5] which first saw Zoe Quinn, and then Anita Sarkeesian, raise widely the topic of the online abuse of women, something which Sarkeesian (quoted in Webber, 2017), says is "very easily done and there are very few consequences for it" (para 5; see also Barker & Jurasz, 2014). The notion that TB(S)A is not harmful persists, and is not changing despite the increased attention that the phenomenon receives – awareness raising does not lead to redress nor reform, and instead often confuses the legal landscape (Barker & Jurasz, 2020d) and to date, little meaningful action has been taken to challenge the idea that persistent volumes of TB(S)A lead to harms not traditionally conceptualized in law.

The transferability and intrusiveness of TB(S)A is also something that is frequently misperceived – with suggestions to "mute" or "hide" tweets (and by extension the TB(S)A)) not uncommon, and encouraged, in particular by Twitter itself (Cuthbertson, 2019). Given the "always on" nature of digital life, TB(S)A is a personal, pervasive, and intrusive issue that is not something that can be left outside of our homes. While there have been few prosecutions for the high-profile abuses suffered by prominent women, TB(S)A is much more widespread, and much more encompassing in its impact. For instance, while courts have given judicial recognition to reputational harms that can manifest themselves in civil suits – such as the harmful and defamatory impact of tweets in *Monroe v Hopkins* (2017), no such recognition has been forthcoming in a criminal context for similarly abusive tweets. Indeed, in Monroe (2017), the court found that there had been "serious harm" inflicted on the claimant

> …on the straightforward basis that the tweets complained of have a tendency to cause harm to [Ms. Monroe's] reputation in the eyes of third parties, of a kind that would be serious to her (para 70)

If serious harm can be recognized in reputational circumstances in civil law cases, there is clear precedent for the recognition of the harmful impact TB(S)A can have. This, along with other (legally) recognized harms, suggests that there remains a mental block on the recognition of the general harm that can be caused by TB(S)A. For instance, while there is no specific judicial recognition given to TB(S)A as a hate crime, the harm caused by disablist abuse is recognized by the hate crime framework in England and Wales. Again though, no recognition of the online aspect of this has been judicially considered, and not beyond the hate crime perspective.

TB(S)A also makes a stark distinction between the recognition of physical harms, such as assault, and the digital equivalents. Where physical harms have been forthcoming, such as the murder of Jo Cox, there is clear capturing of the harm by the legal system. Yet, where there is a real text-based *threat* of physical harm – which could in itself be sufficient to give rise to criminal charges – this receives much less attention when the threat is communicated electronically, again indicating that TBSA is still considered to be something of a lesser element in the legal conceptions of harm.

As Table 14.1 demonstrates, TB(S)A invades homes, social groups, families, and non-work interactions. It is a continuous barrage of abuse that causes ongoing impacts; something Jess Phillips MP (2018) has made very clear when she indicated that its invasiveness can catch you off-guard because it is unexpected in the "warmth and safety" (p. 208) of the family home. This point is also recognized by former MPs Heidi Allen and Nicky Morgan in their decisions to stand down from front-line politics. What is perhaps the most harmful aspect of this – but which goes almost unrecognized by the existing legal structures – is the expectation that prominent and visible women – especially online – will be subjected to TB(S)A because, "any publicity will come with a whole load of abuse" (Phillips, 2017, p. 217). The enduring harm that perpetuates has significant psychological impacts – on both the victims and those who witness the abuse, reiterating the dangers of engaging online, but also the risks associated with being engaged digitally. Harm to bystanders, and harms to other "followers" of the target, are harms that are not categorized nor recognized by the courts in respect of TB(S)A either. These harms signal to women that they are not welcome online, and their opinions are dismissed, shouted down, or manipulated. This is not, of course, confined purely to online spaces, with such behaviors replicating the shutting down of women's voices in many offline spaces, too (Vera-Gray, 2016).

Table 14.1. Harms Arising from Text-Based (Sexual) Abuse.

Type of Harm[a]	**Impact**	**Victim**	**Context**
Residential	Extra security measures, panic button installed in the home.	Stella Creasy MP	Campaign to include more women on the Bank of England banknotes (2014).
Economical	Money and time spent on ensuring to be as untrackable as possible.	Caroline Criado-Perez	Campaign to include more women on the Bank of England banknotes (2014).
Emotional	Long-term personality changes; feelings of panic, fear, and horror; distress.	Caroline Criado-Perez	As above.

Table 14.1. *(Continued)*

Type of Harm[a]	Impact	Victim	Context
Physical	Online abuse; violent threats; assassination in her constituency in June 2016.	Jo Cox MP	Jo Cox was a Labour politician who was an outspoken feminist and who stood up to online abuse, and violence against female politicians. She campaigned for greater social equality and identified as a remainer in the lead up to the 2016 Brexit referendum.
Social	The invasiveness of "always on" mobile devices, allowing the intrusion of text-based sexual abuse into family and social life.	Jess Phillips MP	Jess Phillips first received tranches of rape threats when wrapping presents for her children in her home.
Reputational	Regularly subjected to abuse that alleges she is too ugly to be raped, with repeated slurs regarding her sexuality.	Mhairi Black (S)MP	In one of her speeches in Parliament, Black used the word cunt four times when reading out examples of the online abuse she receives.
Intersectional	Extreme racist and misogynistic abuse; distress; fear for security of herself and her family, resulting in employing security detail.	Gina Miller	Campaign to stop Brexit (2016–2017), leading the case which led to the Parliament voting on triggering Article 50 of the EU Treaty.
Democratic	As above. Broader impact of the online text-based abuse on democratic values and the rule of law (as suggested by Lord Neuberger).	Gina Miller	As above.

Table 14.1. *(Continued)*

Type of Harm[a]	Impact	Victim	Context
Disablist	Disablist online abuse because of Asperger's syndrome; comparisons between Thunberg and the Nazi Propaganda; portrayal as "deeply disturbed"; death threats and death wishes (e.g., Arron Banks's tweets in August 2019); cartoon portraying Thunberg being sexually assaulted.	Greta Thunberg	Campaigning for addressing climate change at a local and global level.
Ageism	Sexist and ageist abuse (e.g., a sexist tweet from a French philosopher Bernard Pivot)[b]; comparisons to a "little brat," "prophetess in shorts," "deeply disturbed teen."	Greta Thunberg	As above.

[a]Two other categories of harm which are pervasive and affect *all* of the individuals listed in this table are psychological harm, and emotional distress. For instance, Joanna Cherry QC (S)MP, Nicky Morgan, and Aileen Campbell MSP in particular have outlined the severe impact that TBSA has had on their lives.

[b]"In my generation, the boys were looking for the little Swedes who had the reputation of being less stuck than the French girls. I imagine our astonishment, our fear, if we had approached a Greta Thunberg" (@bernardpivot1, 25 September 2019, 7.38 a.m.: Dans ma génération, les garçons recherchaient les petites Suédoises qui avaient la réputation d'être moins coincées que les petites Françaises. J'imagine notre étonnement, notre trouille, si nous avions approché une Greta Thunberg…). Translation by the authors.

With an unchanging perception of TB(S)A, the inevitable consequences are also perpetuated in their impact and spread of harm. To protect themselves – especially where the criminal justice system has proven unwilling or unable to act against the perpetrators – women subjected to TB(S)A are opting out of online visibility and online interactions (Barker & Jurasz, 2020b). Inaction underlines the social harms (Table 14.1) that come from making online spaces more hostile to women than to other groups. This is, in itself, a further harmful response to the original harm – but one which manifests its impact more widely than with an individual victim. In a democratic, modern society, the internet is a source of information but also access to networks, interactions, family, friends, and work. By essentially being driven to online invisibility through online hostility and TB(S)A, women are disengaging as a means of self-protection first, and a response second, resulting in social, democratic, and reputational harms, too. This is damaging not just to the participatory rights of the victims themselves, but to society more broadly, where visible women with powerful messages are forced into self-silencing. This damages wider societal debates and interactions, particularly relating to topics of interest to other women.

Consequently, where the criminal justice system fails to protect women from TBSA, the original harm from the threats and abuse persists, manifesting itself in democratic, social, and participatory harms (see Table 14.1). This is particularly evident through the – unfortunately increasingly frequent – examples of the UK General Election in 2019, and the forthcoming Scottish Parliament Election of 2021, where a number of high-profile women politicians – including former government ministers (Oppenheim, 2019) – have opted, or are opting, out of seeking re-election because of the impact of TB(S)A, especially trolling and online abuse (Barker & Jurasz, 2020b; McLaughlin, 2020; Paton, 2020). Not only are these women victims of crime, but they are also victims of participatory and democratic silencing – harms very evident but not (yet) judicially recognized in this context. Disappointingly, given the UK Government's (2019) commitment to addressing online harms, none of these harms have been specifically listed nor explicitly discussed in the Online Harms White Paper (which lists 23 types of online harm (p. 31)), which further evidences that such harmful online behaviors should be recognizable but are not a priority for the legislative reform agenda. The lackluster reaction of the Government in this respect reflects the manifestation of silencing and continues to contribute to the production of a system which excludes women, and the voices of women. This active silencing – arguably necessary as a mechanism of self-care by victims in the absence of other responses is the realization of gender stereotyping moving from the offline to the online, reflecting the transference of harm moving from online TB(S)A to offline lives.

Beyond this, omitting to recognize and address TB(S)A fails to appreciate fully the core elements of digital democracy, and the protections that are required. Selective inaction for TB(S)A compared with – for example – offline public order offenses,[6] sends a clear signal that online criminality will go unpunished and unprosecuted. Not only does this undermine the equality that the internet (purportedly) offers but also it weakens the usefulness of a virtual common space for – otherwise impossible – gatherings, solidarity, and protests for change, such as the Arab Awakening[7] (Barker & Baghdady, 2017). This is broadly reflective of a much larger problem in that the existing mechanisms – including reporting – are designed to mask, rather than tackle, the problem of TB(S)A itself. This approach, through technical tools such as muting and blocking (Arthur & Kiss, 2013), suggests that the problem is one that is not really a "big deal" and is really just a form of social "banter," rather than anything more menacing, despite the clear *mens rea* that is presented in the sending of the threatening and abusive communications. Given that the threats are clear statements as to the intention of the sender, the (mis)perceptions of TB(S)A are even more difficult to justify. That said, the existing criminal law framework does not make provision for addressing online forms of gender-based violence such as TB(S)A and is steadfast in its insistence that those behaviors are captured by existing legislative provisions (Communications Select Committee, 2014–2015), despite arguments that this is not the case (Barker & Jurasz, 2019a).

Conclusion: Text-Based Sexual Abuse as Digital Equality?

The participatory harm of TB(S)A is significant in a number of ways, both in terms of silencing women as victims, but also as a representation to other women of the target they will become should they dare to step up, speak out, and use the internet as a platform for debate and engagement. This in turn leads to a reduction in the volume and quality of voices online, especially those in politics, and democracy more broadly, which is significantly lessened. The internet has been battling on this point for 31 years and is still a place that is hostile to and for women (Berners-Lee & Berners-Lee, 2020). These harms culminate in a much broader social harm whereby interactions and opportunities are lost, but also where the ability to socialize and network online are compromised. This is tantamount to the silencing and exclusion of not only individuals but also groups, and entire sectors of society, reinforcing gender inequality in the digital arena. It is also evident of the intersectional discrimination (Table 14.1) that is prevalent in the context of the harms suffered by prominent women online.

All of these non-traditional harms contribute to a much broader, and more problematic, further harm; that of the bystander. The misperception and the inability to address the original problem appropriately causes other, non-direct harms, especially to those to whom it is visible. In other instances, dealing with problematic tweets, including *Monroe v Hopkins* (2017), senior courts have shown the capability to assess non-traditional harms, particularly serious harm to reputation or, as in *Chambers v DPP* (2012) when (joke) tweets were posted threatening to bomb airports for canceled flights, the harm to the wider public. Clearly there is a distinction between threatening communications that may amount to the disruption of travel plans and multiple victims of physical harms – where action was swiftly taken, and prosecution followed – and, the TBSA received by women that results in the relocation of families, panic button installations, and personal security recruitment, but where little action is taken without repeated requests for assistance.

Misperceptions, and a failure to capture the harmful impact of TB(S)A mean that it is a phenomenon which goes largely unchecked. Other areas, including IBSA, have seen legal responses fast tracked to address the harms they cause, though these have not been without criticism in their capacity to fully address the harms or lived experiences of IBSA victims, particularly in England and Wales (see McGlynn & Rackley, 2015; Powell et al., 2020). The inequality of treatment between these two related phenomena reinforces the message that disparity, vitriol, and abuse is an expectation and a natural consequence for women and girls participating online.

To protect participatory rights, and tackle TB(S)A, urgent reforms are needed. These reforms need to spread beyond the alteration or introduction of legislative provisions – the law itself cannot (and should not) be charged with tackling the phenomenon. The legal system needs to pay direct attention to the issue, rather than suggesting (again) that the existing law is capable of addressing the issue; it must capture TB(S)A specifically within the online harms landscape as a matter of urgency, and before the internet becomes a place entirely too hostile to women. TB(S)A is a pressing issue for the digital era, but also for digital equality.

Notes

1. France: Digital Republic Law 2016; Israel: Prevention of Sexual Harassment Law, 5758-1998, amended in 2014; Canada: section 162.1 Criminal Code (amended through Bill C-13 *Protecting Canadians from Online Harm Act* 2015); Japan: Shiji Seiteki Gazou Kiroku No Teikyotō Niyoru Higai No Boushi Nikansuru Hōritsu [Act on Prevention of Victimization Resulting from Provision of Private Sexual Image], Law No. 126 of 2014; England and Wales: section 33 Criminal Justice and Courts Act 2015; Scotland: Part 1, s2 Abusive Behavior and Sexual Harm Act 2016; Northern Ireland: Part 3, section 51 Justice Act (Northern Ireland) 2016.
2. For instance, the Daily Mail columnist, Katie Hopkins, sent a tweet to journalist Laurie Penny that referred to Penny as a woman of ISIS and also implied she is subjected to sexual violence perpetrated against women by ISIS members. The tweet and the context in which it was sent was outlined in *Monroe v Hopkins* (2017): "Hopkins tweeted a photograph of the vandalised war memorial, and a link to @PennyRed's tweet of 8:04 p.m. with these observations: '@PennyRed thinks this is OK. Burn her passport, bulk buy her lube & make her a woman of ISIS.'" (para 14).
3. Here, we define non-traditional harms as harms which have not been recognized in the legislation nor in judicial statements (for instance, participatory harms). We list a number of non-traditional harms, together with specific examples, in Table 14.1.
4. Given that neither sex nor gender is protected as a characteristic in the hate crime framework of England and Wales, there is no statutory aggravation based on either sex or gender.
5. Gamergate is the catch-all term for the vicious online hate, trolling, and harassment campaigns conducted largely through the use of hashtags, and which arose in light of the release of game Depression Quest by Zoe Quinn in 2013. The dichotomy between fans and critics highlights the contrast between the traditional preserves of online gamers, and the newer era of gamers. The orchestrated and anonymous "campaign" known now as Gamergate extends to include targeting prominent feminist media critics, as well as independent game developers.

6. Under the Public Order Act 1986 (POA), offenses usually require the perpetrator and the victim (or another who could be similarly affected) to be in the physical proximity of the abusive behavior – something quite distinct from the online environment in which TBSA is directed at women and – yet prosecutions under the POA provisions are frequent and numerous.
7. Alternatively known as the Arab Spring, a series of pro-democracy and anti-government protests, demonstrations, rebellions, uprisings, and mass gatherings in the Middle East, and Northern Africa in 2010 and 2011.

References

Anthony, A. (2018, August 19). Gina Miller: I was absolutely shocked, I didn't know those attitudes still existed. *The Observer*. Retrieved from https://www.theguardian.com

Arthur, C., & Kiss, J. (2013, July 29). Twitter abuse: What can be done to stop trolling? *The Guardian*. Retrieved from https://www.theguardian.com

Barker, K. (2018). R v Nimmo and Sorley (2014). In E. Rackley, & R. Auchmuty (Eds.), *Women's legal landmarks: Celebrating 100 years of women and law in the UK and Ireland* (pp. 608–610). Oxford: Hart.

Barker, K., & Baghdady, C. (2017). Building online hybrid identities. In N. Lemay-Herbert, & R. Freedman (Eds.), *Hybridity: Law, culture and development* (pp. 218–234). London, New York, NY: Routledge.

Barker, K., & Jurasz, O. (2014). Gender, human rights and cybercrime: Are virtual worlds really that different? In M. Asimow, K. Brown, & D. Papke (Eds.), *Law and popular culture: International perspectives*. Newcastle upon Tyne: Cambridge Scholars Publishing.

Barker, K., & Jurasz, O. (2017, November). Submission of evidence on online violence against women to the UN special rapporteur on violence against women, its causes and consequences, Dr Dubravka Šimonović. Retrieved from http://oro.open.ac.uk/52611/

Barker, K., & Jurasz, O. (2019a). *Online misogyny as a hate crime: A challenge for legal regulation?* London, New York:Routledge.

Barker, K., & Jurasz, O. (2019b). Online misogyny: A challenge for digital feminism? *Journal of International Affairs*, *72*(2), 95–113.

Barker, K., & Jurasz, O. (2019c, June). Online harms white paper consultation response (on file with authors).

Barker, K., & Jurasz, O. (2019d). Online violence against women: Addressing the responsibility gap? [Blog post]. *LSE WPS*. Retrieved from https://blogs.lse.ac.uk/wps/2019/08/23/online-violence-against-women-addressing-the-responsibility-gap/

Barker, K., & Jurasz, O. (2020a). Gendered misinformation & online violence against women in politics: Capturing legal responsibility? *CoInform*. Retrieved from https://coinform.eu/gendered-misinformation-online-violence-against-women-in-politics-capturing-legal-responsibility/

Barker, K., & Jurasz, O. (2020b). Online harms and Caroline's law – What's the direction for law reform? *OU News*. Retrieved from http://www.open.ac.uk/research/news/online-harms-and-carolines-law%E2%80%93whats-direction-law-reform

Barker, K., & Jurasz, O. (2020c). Online violence against women as an obstacle to gender equality: A critical view from Europe. *European Equality Law Review, 1*, 47–60.

Barker, K., & Jurasz, O. (2020d, March 26). Why misogyny and hate crime reforms need more than slick campaigns. *The Conversation*. Retrieved from https://theconversation.com/why-misogyny-and-hate-crime-reforms-need-more-than-slick-campaigns-134265#comment_2180791

Barnett, E. (2014, September 29). Stella Creasy hits out at police over Twitter troll case failures. *The Telegraph*. Retrieved from https://www.telegraph.co.uk

Berners-Lee, T., & Berners-Lee, R. (2020, March 12). Why the web needs to work for women and girls. *Web Foundation*. Retrieved from https://webfoundation.org/2020/03/web-birthday-31/

Chambers v DPP. (2012). EWHC 2157.

Change.org. (2020). Caroline's law. Retrieved from https://www.change.org/p/instagram-make-social-media-a-safer-place

Communications Select Committee. (2014–2015). Social media and criminal offences. (HL Paper 37). Retrieved from http://www.publications.parliament.uk/pa/ld201415/ldselect/ldcomuni/37/3704.htm

CPS. (2017). Hate crime. Retrieved from www.cps.gov.uk/hate-crime

Cuthbertson, A. (2019, March 1). Twitter reveals new 'hide tweet' feature to let users moderate replies. *The Independent*. Retrieved from https://www.independent.co.uk/life-style/gadgets-and-tech/news/twitter-new-feature-hide-tweet-update-moderate-replies-a8803301.html

Dhordia, A. (2017, September 3). Unsocial media: Tracking twitter abuse against women MPs. *Medium*. Retrieved from https://medium.com/@AmnestyInsights/unsocial-media-tracking-twitter-abuse-against-women-mps-fc28aeca498a

Flynn, A., & Henry, N.. (2019). Image-based sexual abuse: An Australian reflection. *Women and Criminal Justice,* online first, doi:10.1080/08974554.2019.1646190

Girlguiding. (2016). Girls' Attitudes Survey 2016. Retrieved from www.girlguiding.org.uk/globalassets/docs-and-resources/research-and-campaigns/girls-attitudes- survey-2016.pdf

Henry, N., McGlynn, C., Flynn, A., Johnson, K., Powell, A., & Scott, A. J. (2020). *Image-based sexual abuse: A study on the causes and consequences of non-consensual nude or sexual imagery*. London, New York: Routledge.

Holt, T. J., Lee, J. R., Liggett, R., Holt, K. M., & Bossler, A. (2019). Examining perceptions of online harassment among constables in England and Wales. *International Journal of Cybersecurity Intelligence & Cybercrime, 2*(1), 24–39.

Inter-Parliamentary Union. (2016, October). Sexism, harassment, and violence against women parliamentarians. *Issues Brief*. Retrieved from https://www.ipu.org/resources/publications/issue-briefs/2016-10/sexism-harassment-and-violence-against-women-parliamentarians

Inter-Parliamentary Union. (2018, October). Sexism, harassment and violence against women in parliaments in Europe. *Issues Brief*. Retrieved from https://www.ipu.org/resources/publications/issue-briefs/2018-10/sexism-harassment-and-violence-against-women-in-parliaments-in-europe

Mason, R., Davies, H. J., & Bakare, L. (2020, February 17). No 10 calls on social media firms to act after Caroline Flack death. *The Guardian*. Retrieved from https://www.theguardian.com

McGlynn, C., & Rackley, E. (2015, October 29). More than just 'revenge porn': Tackling the misuse of private sexual images. *The Holyrood.* Retrieved from https://www.holyrood.com/comment/view,more-than-just-revenge-porn-tackling-the-misuse-of-private-sexual-images_6029.htm

McGlynn, C., & Rackley, E. (2017). Image-based sexual abuse. *Oxford Journal of Legal Studies*, *37*(3), 534–561.

McLaughlin, M. (2020, March 9). Quitting MSPs blame online trolls and long hours. *Sunday Times*. Retrieved from https://www.thetimes.co.uk

Monroe v Hopkins. (2017). EWHC 433 (QB).

Oppenheim, M. (2019, October 31). General Election: Women MPs standing down over 'horrific abuse' campaigners warn. *The Independent*. Retrieved from https://www.independent.co.uk

Paton, C. (2020, March 15). Vitriol is driving women out of politics says finance minister Kate Forbes. *Sunday Times*. Retrieved from https://www.thetimes.co.uk

Phillips, J. (2017). *Everywoman: One woman's truth about speaking the truth*. London: Hutchinson.

Powell, A., & Henry, N. (2017). *Sexual violence in a digital age*. Basingstoke: Palgrave Macmillan.

Powell, A., Scott, A. J., Henry, N., & Flynn, A. (2020). *Image-based sexual abuse: An international study of victims and perpetrators. Summary report*. Melbourne: RMIT University.

R v Nimmo and Sorley. (2014, January 24). Westminster Magistrates' Court.

R v Viscount St Davids. (2017, July 11). Westminster Magistrates' Court.

R v Nunn. (2014, September 29). City of London Magistrates' Court.

Scottish Legal News. (2016, December 5). Lord Neuberger warns against publication of parties' details in Article 50 case and emphasises role of Supreme Court. Retrieved from https://www.scottishlegal.com/article/lord-neuberger-warns-against-publication-of-parties-details-in-article-50-case-and-emphasises-role-of-supreme-court

UK Government. (2018, February 6). PM speech on standards in public life.Retrieved from https://www.gov.uk/government/speeches/pm-speech-on-standards-in-public-life-6-february-2018. Accessed on February 6, 2018.

UK Government. (2019, April). Online harms white paper (CP 57). Retrieved from https://assets.publishing.service.gov.uk/government/uploads/system/uploads/attachment_data/file/793360/Online_Harms_White_Paper.pdf

United Nations Human Rights Council. (2018, June 18). Report of the Special Rapporteur on violence against women, its causes and consequences on online violence against women and girls from a human rights perspective, A/HRC/38/47. Retrieved from https://www.ohchr.org/EN/HRBodies/HRC/RegularSessions/Session38/Documents/A_HRC_38_47_EN.docx

Vera-Gray, F. (2016). Men's stranger intrusions: Rethinking street harassment. *Women's Studies International Forum*, *58*, 9–17.

Webber, J. (2017, October 16). Anita Sarkeesian: 'It's frustrating to be known as the woman who survived #Gamergate'. *The Guardian*. Retrieved from https://www.theguardian.com

Section 3
Image-Based Harms

Chapter 15

Introduction

Nicola Henry

The original idea around the development of the internet in the 1960s was that machines would "talk to each other" in exchanging messages, data, and programs (Leiner et al., 2009). Several decades later the era of the "interactive web"(or Web 2.0) has ushered in user-generated content, social networking, and cloud technology, making the visual image – photo, animation, and video – a staple of digital communications, epitomized by content hosting sites, social media, multimedia messaging, video chat, live-streaming, and online gaming. Digital technologies have facilitated a unique means through which to communicate and exchange information both textually and visually, and are an important medium for curiosity, pleasure, spectacle, and political activism. And yet images can also be harmful, not only for those depicted in the image but also for those who are exposed to the viewing of those images. Key components of harm – particularly in the digital era – relate to the permanence, accessibility, and spread of images on a global scale.

This section of the Handbook focuses on image-based harms, which we define as the creation or dissemination of images that denigrate and subjugate the person depicted in the image, or which expose the viewer to vicarious affect or trauma. While several chapters in this Handbook discuss the legal, social, or psychological implications of image-based harms, the three chapters in this section on image-based harms are based on original empirical research on three important issues: exposure to abhorrent violent material; pornography use and exposure; and image-based sexual abuse.

First in relation to exposure to abhorrent violent material, there have been growing media reports of social media content moderators experiencing post-traumatic stress disorder (PTSD) in their day-to-day work (see e.g., Boran, 2020); of the harmful exposure of law enforcement personnel to child sexual abuse material (see e.g., Vedelago, 2020); and of individual users viewing acts of violence online either in real time or after the fact (see e.g., Lungumbu, 2020). After the Christchurch mosque shootings in New Zealand, which were live-streamed by the gunman on March 15, 2019, the Australian Government passed legislation which gives the Australian eSafety Commissioner powers to

The Emerald International Handbook of Technology-Facilitated Violence and Abuse, 267–270

doi:10.1108/978-1-83982-848-520211062

issue take-down notices to digital platforms that host abhorrent violent material (AVM), with failure to do so potentially resulting in criminal prosecution. AVM is defined in the legislation as "audio, visual, or audio-visual material recorded of extreme violent acts," which includes terrorist acts involving serious physical harm or death, murder or attempted murder of another person, torture, rape, or kidnapping involving violence (*Criminal Code Amendment (Sharing of Abhorrent Violent Material) Act 2019*).

Despite the growing attention to this issue, as well as accompanying legislative reform, there remains little scholarly attention to the short- or long-term impacts of viewing this type of content. In their chapter, Madeleine Novich and Alyssa Zduniak address this gap by examining the ways in which images of police violence shape perceptions of police, as well as the harms that exposure causes individual users of social media. Drawing on 19 interviews with a diverse sample of urban male and female college students, Novich and Zduniak found that participants of color were more adversely affected than white participants in terms of forming negative perceptions of police and experiencing emotional distress and fear of victimization. Although Novich and Zduniak acknowledge that the publication and circulation of violent imagery is also a political tool designed to garner awareness, outrage, and action, they argue that images of police brutality "affirm what minority communities have experienced for decades"; that is, they further entrench deeply held fears of victimization. They argue that for people of color, viewing images of police brutality restricts their social mobility and behavior and leads to "a traumatic impact on the brain … brain dysregulation, stress, PTSD, and self-destructive behavior." These harms have been recently discussed in relation to the video that went viral in May 2020 of a white Minneapolis police officer's murder of African American man George Floyd. According to BBC journalist Sandrine Lungumbu (2020), "It is mentally and physically draining for me to watch yet another unarmed black man dying under arrest at the hands of another white police officer."

While the vicarious effects of exposure to violent online content is a relatively new issue, the debate about the harms of pornography on adults and young people has been at the forefront of the feminist agenda for the past four decades. In relation to adults, for instance, Andrea Dworkin (1985) argued that pornography subordinates women, creating a sexual dynamic which normalizes sexual violence as sex "the putting-down of women, the suppression of women, and ultimately the brutalization of women" (p. 9). In relation to the effects of pornography on children, Michael Flood (2009) contends that these are likely to be: "emotional disturbance, sexual knowledge and liberalised attitudes, shifts in sexual behaviour, and sexist and objectifying understandings" (p. 384). He adds that for boys and young men, "the use of pornography may exacerbate violence-supportive social norms and encourage their participation in sexual abuse" (Flood, 2009, p. 384).

Samantha Keene begins her chapter on the impacts of pornography with a succinct summary of the long-standing pornography harms debate. While Keene argues that much mainstream pornography is "infused with themes of male dominance, aggression, and female subservience," and that pornography plays a key role in the development of normative sexual scripts and the endorsement of violence against women and girls, her conclusions about the harms and pleasures of pornography are far more nuanced. She draws inspiration from "critical porn studies," which seeks to move beyond the pro- and anti-pornography dichotomy that focuses on "harms and their impacts or possibilities for legislative interventions or prohibitions" (Smith & Attwood, 2014, p. 7), and instead "draw[s] on insights from disciplines that acknowledge the complexity of culture and are aware of the shifts and continuities in the ways that sex and media are constructed historically" (Smith & Attwood, 2014, p. 11).

Based on interviews conducted with 24 heterosexual adults living in Aotearoa/New Zealand about their pornography use, Keene argues that empirical studies can help to contribute to a critical understanding of "the complex ways that pornography is experienced by viewers and their partners." She found that although both male and female participants were reflexive of the misogynistic representations of sex, gender, and sexuality in mainstream heterosexual pornography, men tended to be more concerned about their own sexual performances, whereas women's experiences were shaped by how their intimate partners related to them sexually, which in some cases included sexual coercion or sexual assault.

The third and final chapter in this section, by Olga Marques, focuses on image-based sexual abuse, also known as "nonconsensual pornography" (see e.g., Citron & Franks, 2014; Henry et al., 2020; McGlynn & Rackley, 2017), which refers to the nonconsensual taking or sharing of nude or sexual images, including threats to share images. Image-based sexual abuse began to receive attention in the early 2010s when the term "revenge porn" came into popular usage with media reports of websites that hosted nonconsensual nude or sexual images of musicians, sportspersons, and celebrities, as well as nonconsensual intimate images of "ordinary" people, often accompanied by their personal details, such as their name, occupation, geographical location, and social media handle.

As Marques notes, there is a lack of empirical research with sexual violence service providers on the topic of image-based sexual abuse. She conducted interviews with 10 frontline professionals to garner their perspective on the nature and harms. She argues that the sharing of images compounds the harms to sexual violence survivors by "adding a virtual – and indelible – 'permanent remembering' of the violence." Marques argues that the trauma of the threat that the images can be discovered and seen at any time without warning "becomes part of the crisis that frontline professionals must also address."

The chapters in this section are a timely reminder of the enduring power of images that survive and linger in both space and time, which can have significant implications for both the subjects of the image as well as the spectators.

References

Boran, M. (2020, February 27). Life as a Facebook moderator: 'People are awful. This is what my job has taught me.' *The Irish Times*. Retrieved from https://www.irishtimes.com/

Citron, D., & Franks, M. (2014). Criminalizing revenge porn. *Wake Forest Law Review*, *49*, 345–391. doi:10.1177/1557085117698752

Dworkin, A. (1985). Against the male flood: Censorship, pornography, and equality. *Harvard Women's Law Journal*, *8*, 1–29.

Flood, M. (2009). The harms of pornography exposure among children and young people. *Child Abuse Review*, *18*, 384–400.

Henry, N., McGlynn, C., Flynn, A., Johnson, K., Powell, A., & Scott, A. J. (2020). *Image-based sexual abuse: A study on the causes and consequences of non-consensual nude or sexual imagery*. London and New York, NY: Routledge.

Leiner, B. M., Cerf, V. G., Clark, D. D., Kahn, R. E., Kleinrock, L., Lynch, D. C., … Wolff, S. (2009). A brief history of the Internet. *ACM SIGCOMM - Computer Communication Review*, *39*(5), 22–31.

Lungumbu, S. (2020, June 7). George Floyd killing: Why I decided not to watch the video. *BBC World Service*. Retrieved from https://www.bbc.com/news/world-us-canada-52942105

McGlynn, C., & Rackley, E. (2017). Image-based sexual abuse. *Oxford Journal of Legal Studies*, *37*(3), 534–561.

Smith, C., & Attwood, F. (2014). Anti/pro/critical porn studies. *Porn Studies*, *1*(1–2), 7–23. doi:10.1080/23268743.2014.887364

Vedelago, C. (2020, June 19). 'Clarity of purpose': How child abuse investigators cope with their job. *The Age*. Retrieved from https://www.theage.com.au/national/victoria/clarity-of-purpose-how-child-abuse-investigators-cope-with-their-job-20200619-p554e3.html

Chapter 16

Violence Trending: How Socially Transmitted Content of Police Misconduct Impacts Reactions toward Police Among American Youth

Madeleine Novich and Alyssa Zduniak

Abstract

Videos of police abuse are often spread through technology, raising questions around how perceptions of police are impacted by these images, especially for 18–24-year-olds who are constantly "logged on." Limited research investigates the impact of social media on attitudes toward police accounting for age and race. The present study utilizes 19 in-depth interviews with a diverse sample of urban college students who regularly use social media in order to understand how they have been impacted by this content. The findings suggest the necessity of using an intersectional framework to understand the impact of tech-witnessed violence. While no gender differences were uncovered, racial differences did surface. White participants described being minimally influenced by videos of police misconduct, rationalizing it as a "few bad apples." In contrast, participants of color, except those with family members in law enforcement, described being negatively impacted. Viral content contributed to negative opinions of police, emotional distress, and fears of victimization. Ultimately, videos of police brutality do not impact young populations equally. Instead, they are comparatively more harmful to young people of color who spend more time on social media, can envision themselves as the victims, and experience feelings of fear, despair, and anger after watching these videos.

Keywords: Policing; police misconduct; social media and race; digital violence; perceptions of law enforcement; abhorrent violent behavior

The Emerald International Handbook of Technology-Facilitated Violence and Abuse, 271–288

doi:10.1108/978-1-83982-848-520211020

Introduction

Attitudes and reactions toward police are complex and result from various factors including gender (Brown & Benedict, 2002), race (Brunson, 2007; Gau & Brunson, 2007), and age (Brunson, 2007; Flexon, Lurigio, & Greenleaf, 2009). Firsthand and vicarious encounters with police are also impactful in shaping attitudes (Papachristos, Braga, & Hureau, 2012; Rosenbaum, Schuck, Costello, Hawkins, & Ring, 2005; Tyler, 2006; Weitzer, 2002). Contemporary literature demonstrates that face-to-face encounters can have profound effects on an individual's opinion of law enforcement, especially if the interaction is marred by perceptions of biased, disrespectful, indifferent, and untrustworthy officers (Novich & Hunt, 2016; see also Tyler, 2006).

Emerging evidence suggests that vicarious experiences shared by family and friends through social networks can also shape one's perspective of and response to police (Dowler & Zawilski, 2007; Lim, 2015; Papachristos et al., 2012). There has been growing concern and awareness of police misconduct and brutality as a result of viral social media (Tynes, Willis, Stewart, & Hamilton, 2019). Research demonstrates that media functions as a key mechanism for shaping attitudes toward police (Dowler & Zawilski, 2007) and, perhaps more concerning, witnessing officer-initiated abhorrent violent behavior (AVB) causes psychological trauma, depression, and posttraumatic stress among viewers who can identify with the victim (Tynes et al., 2019). Police misconduct shared through social media may be more harmful to young people of color when compared with their white counterparts because they invest more time and energy into social media, and social media increases their ability to witness misconduct against people of their racial and ethnic background. Conversely, social media provides young people of color a platform to express themselves and raise concerns relating to their marginalized social experience (Grasmuck, Martin, & Zhoa, 2009; Lee, 2011). It is therefore important to investigate perceptions of and responses to police using an intersectional framework that accounts for race, age, and social media usage.

In response, this chapter is premised on a study that utilizes interviews with a racially diverse sample of college-aged participants and examines if and how their perceptions and feelings toward police are impacted by social media and videos of police violence transmitted via technology. The chapter will first provide an overview of current literature on attitudes toward police. The second section will describe the methodological strategies employed in the study, and the third section will present the findings. Finally, the chapter will end with a discussion of how the salient findings, which are that participants of color are disproportionately negatively impacted by violent police videos, fit into the broader context of contemporary empirical research.

Literature Review

Attitudes Toward the Police

There are many factors that contribute to an individual's attitude toward police. Extensive research indicates that race and ethnicity are a significant predictor in determining attitudes toward police (Brown & Benedict, 2002; Brunson, 2007; Gau & Brunson, 2007; Novich & Hunt, 2016). In America, people of color, especially young Black and Latino men, have more negative views of the police when compared with white men (Brown & Benedict, 2002; Cheurprakobkit, 2000; Weitzer & Tuch, 1999). This is likely due to minority populations experiencing greater levels of poor officer treatment, including discriminatory and aggressive police behavior (Brown & Benedict, 2002; Fratello, Rengifo, & Trone, 2013; Novich & Hunt, 2016; Weitzer & Tuch, 1999).

Attitudes toward police also appear to be influenced by gender, whereby females tend to hold more favorable opinions of police when compared with male counterparts (Weitzer & Tuch, 1999). However, American women of color generally view police more negatively when compared with white women (Brick, Taylor, & Esbensen, 2009; Hurst, McDermott, & Thomas, 2005). Age is also significant, with young people more likely to view police less favorably than older people (Cheurprakobkit, 2000; Hurst, Frank, & Browning, 2000a). This may be due to the increased probability of a young person being stopped by the police than an older one or the tendency of older residents to desire safety in their community, which law enforcement can provide (Brown & Benedict, 2002; Lee, Lim, & Lee, 2015; Lim, 2015).

Overall, young populations hold strong opinions about police (Brick et al., 2009; Brunson, 2007; Flexon et al., 2009; Leiber, Nalla, & Farnworth, 1998) and these attitudes are profoundly impacted by direct experiences with law enforcement (Brick et al., 2009; Flexon et al., 2009; Leiber et al., 1998; Novich & Hunt, 2016; Rosenbaum et al., 2005). Encounters where individuals perceive police as dishonest or untrustworthy, or feel stripped of their agency, negatively impact perceptions of police legitimacy (see Tyler, 2006). However, personal relationships can mitigate negative responses, especially for individuals that have a personal connection to a law enforcement officer (Lee et al., 2015; Lim, 2015).

Impact of Social Media on Perceptions of Police

Emerging evidence suggests that attitudes toward law enforcement are also formed via vicarious experiences from family, friends, and community members (Brunson, 2007; Hurst, Frank, & Browning, 2000b; Papachristos et al., 2012; Rosenbaum et al., 2005; Weitzer, 2002; Wu, 2013). Most citizens in the population have an opinion on law enforcement, despite the fact that "[four] out of [five] Americans do not have direct contact with police officers during any given year" (Rosenbaum et al., 2005, p. 360). Opinions about police are likely formed as a result of experiences witnessed or learned about from family, friends, or posts on their social networks (Papachristos et al., 2012). There are several theoretical frameworks that may explain the impact of socially transmitted videos of police behavior on perceptions of law enforcement. Research suggests that media is "decoded" or understood differently depending on the unique background of each viewer (see Hall, 1980, p. 107). The different groups of viewers, of which there are many, may understand media differently depending on an individual's self, gender, family, class, nation, race/ethnicity, sexual orientation, and age (Fiske, 1986; Hall, 1980).

In terms of age, social networking platforms may create a social modeling atmosphere for young people. These platforms are where young people learn through observing others, especially those they hold in esteem, and follow suit (see Lim, 2015). Premised on Bandura's (1962) imitation theory, research suggests that there are three kinds of social modeling: live (an individual demonstrating a certain behavior in real time); verbal (descriptions or explanations of a particular behavior); and symbolic (real or fictional characters found in media, books, or online). "Symbolic" personas, both real and fake, offer a behavioral model through secondary sources like social media, television, and literature (Lim, 2015, p. 675). Social media sites like Facebook and Instagram create easy access to symbolic models since friends, family, and groups can post videos and caption them so that the "correct" opinion can be easily obtained while scrolling through a feed. Due to their more persistent uses of these sites, young people may be more impacted by highly publicized events. With regards to police specifically, research suggests that young people's reactions may be significantly impacted if those highlighted virtual events focus on procedural injustice, police misconduct, and AVB on behalf of police (Reisig & Correia, 1997; Tynes et al., 2019; Weitzer, 2002).

Indeed, people are negatively impacted by witnessing AVB and/or traumatic events online (TEO) (Feinstein, Audet, & Waknine, 2014; Holman, Garfin, & Silver, 2013; Tynes et al., 2019). Seeing graphic footage of extreme violence can evoke involuntary memories (Clark, Holmes, Woolrich, & Mackay, 2016) or can cause acute stress, posttraumatic stress disorder (PTSD), and depression, especially if such footage is viewed frequently (Feinstein et al., 2014; Holman et al., 2013). While people of all backgrounds are no doubt harmed, witnessing socially transmitted AVB perpetrated by police may be more harmful for populations of color. Not only does the footage contribute to negative attitudes toward law enforcement (Weitzer, 2002), but also it may cause individual and community-spread psychological trauma (Tynes et al., 2019).

Social media posts that showcase police in a negative light affirm what minority communities have experienced for decades (Aymer, 2016; Bonilla & Rosa, 2015; Bryant-Davis, Adams, Alejandre, & Gray, 2017). Children of traditionally marginalized ethnicities are raised to fear and expect police harassment, and this fear limits their mobility and informs social behavior (Bryant-Davis et al., 2017). Social media featuring police misconduct solidifies these feelings of "fear, despair, and anxiety," which has a traumatic impact on the brain and can lead to brain dysregulation, stress, PTSD, and self-destructive behavior (Bryant-Davis et al., 2017, p. 855). Further, this type of content raises fears of victimization among social media consumers of color (Callanan, 2012; Dowler, 2003; Kohm, Waid-Lindberg, Weinrath, Shelley, & Dobbs, 2012). Higher levels of fear are found in the African American community and are generated when the violence portrayed through the media source is in the same geographical area as the individual viewing the content (Callanan, 2012; Dowler, 2003; Kohm et al., 2012). Additionally, Tynes et al. (2019) examined the impact of witnessing viral videos of race-related police killings of unarmed citizens among youth of color and found that viewing AVB that was directed at one's own racial/ethnic group was related to an increase in PTSD and depression. The researchers also raised concerns that, given how easily transmitted this content is among peers, the negative impact may contribute to community-wide mental health problems.

Racial differences may be further exacerbated if the individuals are "logged on" often. Contemporary research suggests that people of color are heavy consumers of media content of police misconduct and are more likely to believe it is frequently occurring (Dowler & Zawilski, 2007; Tynes et al., 2019). Additionally, research suggests that people of color interact with social media differently than their white counterparts (Chan, 2017; Grasmuck et al., 2009; Lee, 2011). People of color invest more time and energy into networking platforms because of the opportunity it creates to be heard and to connect with others of similar racial backgrounds. On social media, users can consume information through posts, determine its relevance to their own experience, and further develop their understanding of their racial identity (Chan, 2017; Grasmuck et al., 2009).

How responses toward police are formed is complex and requires an intersectional framework. Age and race can play an important role, as does first-hand and vicarious encounters with law enforcement. Social media and the transmission of police violence through social networks is increasingly of interest to researchers, especially when examining young people of color. In response, this study utilizes interviews with young, heavy social media users to investigate how technologically transmitted videos of police misconduct may impact their reactions toward officers. Paying close attention to racial differences, this investigation attempts to narrow the scholarly understanding of how social media may influence their feelings about police.

Methodology

The qualitative data were collected from September to November 2018 on an urban college campus as part of a semester-long undergraduate Research Methods course. These interviews solicited feedback on participants' experience with and attitudes toward police, social media usage, and the impact of video content on opinions of law enforcement. The data included 19 participants: men (53%, n = 10) and women (47%, n = 9). The largest ethnic group was Latinx (42%, n = 8), followed by white (37%, n = 7), Asian (11%, n = 2), and African Americans (11%, n = 2). The target age range was 18–24 years, given that this age group consumes social media at higher rates and visit more platforms than other age groups (see Smith & Anderson, 2018). The participants indicated that they used one or more popular social media sites including Facebook, Twitter, and YouTube.

The interviews were conducted in English, typically lasted 30 minutes, and took place in various campus locations. No compensation was provided. The data were digitally recorded, transcribed verbatim, redacted, and anonymized. The interviews were semistructured and included open-ended questions concerning the participants' opinion of police, experiences with content about police shared on social media, and if and how they believed social media impacted their perceptions of police. Each interview was read repeatedly and was systematically inductively coded. The analysis was refined using narrative analysis, where long narratives of personal experiences were organized sequentially and broken down into coded categories salient to the current investigation (Presser & Sandberg, 2015), as well as progressive focusing, which was the ongoing evaluation of relationships between themes, trends, and concepts throughout the entire coding and analysis process (Chambliss & Schutt, 2016). The data were arranged on matrices to ensure that patterns, comparisons, and deviant cases could be assessed thoroughly (Maxwell, 1996) and all cases were included (Silverman, 2006).

There were several limitations. The interviews were conducted by different individuals so the follow-up questions were not standardized. The research used a college-aged population, which is often viewed as a convenience sample, not representative of the larger society, and can produce findings that may not be generalizable. However, this population was the intended target because this age group is most active on social media compared with other age groups (Arceneaux & Dinu, 2018; Chan, 2017; Lee, 2011; see also Smith & Anderson, 2018). Also, the sample size may be considered small, raising concerns of generalizability. However, the smaller sample size allowed for a more nuanced inquiry which can enhance the validity of in-depth investigations (Crouch & McKenzie, 2006). Finally, the research is based on US-centric data where police and populations of color, of whom are ethnic minorities, have a unique history of tension and violence. As such, the findings may not be applicable to other nations that do not share similar historical challenges. Despite these limitations, the impact of abhorrent violent police behavior was discussed repeatedly by participants, often without prompting, providing a rich qualitative data source for this investigation.

Findings

Attitudes toward the Police: The Racial Divide

Opinions about police are complicated and formed as a result of many factors (see Brown & Benedict, 2002). As one Latina aptly noted, "I would say [my attitude toward police] is a sum of a lot of things." Attitudes toward police can be shaped by face-to-face interactions (Tyler, 2002), television and fictional media (Donovan & Klahm, 2015), opinions from family and friends, and vicarious experiences of police behavior, including stories shared between friends and family and videos of police transmitted through news and social media (Brown & Benedict, 2002; Reisig & Correia, 1997; Weitzer & Tuch, 1999). However, the relative influence of each factor is not wholly understood and may impact individuals differently. This may be especially so with regard to people of different racial and ethnic backgrounds.

As consistent with previous research, the majority of the participants of color expressed negative opinions about police compared to their white counterparts (Brown & Benedict, 2002; Cheurprakobkit, 2000; Weitzer & Tuch, 1999). In all, 9 of 12 participants of color described the police in an unfavorable way. One Latino male student stated, "I don't like the cops." The majority (6 of 9) of participants that expressed negative opinions of the police indicated they distrusted the police and/or viewed police as criminal justice actors who abused their authority and harmed civilians. One Latino male stated, "I don't agree with how the police abuse their power and treat people." The issue of power surfaced among several participants. For example, one Latino male believed the asymmetrical power dynamic between officers and citizens gave police the right to be disrespectful and harmful, a conclusion based on a personal experience:

> I'm not the biggest fan of the police...they let their power get to their head...when they put that uniform on, they are a different person. I feel like it gives them too much power and authority...it gives them the right to disrespect us.... I've had times where I would hop the train and one of 'em handcuffed me so bad I had a mark on my wrist all day.

For three participants, negative opinions about law enforcement stemmed from the belief that the police were "racist." A Black female, for instance, described the police as "prejudiced," basing her opinion on racially motivated incidents she witnessed. While her attitude toward police was premised on vicarious experiences, two participants indicated their opinion was shaped by first-hand encounters with police. One Latino male, for example, lamented that he "never had a positive experience" with police and described feeling "uncomfortable" around law enforcement, especially "white officers."

While these narratives reflect the majority of the participants of color, three participants of color expressed positive opinions about the police. One explained he was former military and had a positive encounter with the military police. Two others indicated that they had family members who were in law enforcement. One Latina woman succinctly explained, "I come from a family of ... cops so I like them." Despite these outliers, the findings reflect extensive research that populations of color have negative attitudes toward police, especially when compared with their white counterparts.

Consistent with previous research, the white participants had generally more favorable attitudes toward the police. Overall, four of the seven[1] white participants described law enforcement favorably, indicating they trusted them, "appreciate what they do," and generally felt they were "good" people who did their job well. One white female stated, "I like the police... I trust them to do their job and to protect the citizens of this country. To be unbiased members of the community." Similarly, a white male noted, "I believe most police officers are good and do their job the way they should." Like the two participants of color with relatives in law enforcement, one white female explained that she had family members that were officers and expressed that she had "a strong personal connection to law enforcement."

There were two outliers who expressed negative attitudes toward the police. These cases appeared to have serious extenuating circumstances of experiencing or witnessing extreme violence. One white female, for example, indicated she had multiple negative encounters including one where she was sexually assaulted by an officer. Aside from these two, the attitudes toward the police were clearly delineated along racial lines where white participants' perceptions were more favorable than the participants of color.

The Impact of Videos Seen on Social Media

Social media for many is a source of news and a means to transmit popular culture, social justice content, and information on trending topics between friends, family, and trusted networks. This includes viral videos of police misconduct. Indeed, every participant confirmed they used social media (19 of 19), and most (18 of 19) reported seeing videos of police through their various social networks. This included positive videos, where police were described as doing something kind or helpful, and negative videos, where police were described as doing something harmful against civilians. The slight majority (n = 11[2] of 19) of participants described only having seen negative videos of police. The remaining participants (7 of 19) described viewing both types of videos.

Limited Impact: Videos Focus on "Bad Apples"

For 10 of the 19 participants, social media was described as having a minimal impact on their opinions about police. This was true for five of the seven white participants as they indicated that content shared on social media did not significantly contribute to their attitudes toward law enforcement. This sentiment was also expressed by six of the seven participants who held favorable opinions toward law enforcement. Nearly all (six of the seven) of the study participants who held positive opinions about police indicated that social media and videos of police misconduct did not factor into their opinion. This was also true for the two participants who held a neutral opinion of the police.[3] Instead, most maintained their positive perspective and seemingly believed that the video displays of poor police behavior were misrepresentative or a result of the media's inappropriate focus on "bad apples." "Bad apples" are defined as the few officers that are problematic, prone to racism, and/or abuse their authority (Nhan, 2019). The officers featured in these videos are viewed as being an inaccurate depiction of police and therefore not a valid reason to change one's opinion. As one white student explained, "[Social media] won't have an effect on my opinion. Cops in general are good people but when they get reported on in the media, it focuses on one 'bad apple,' which exist, but there are way more good cops." Another white male stated the same, despite witnessing extreme violence:

> You can [see videos of] police officers giving CPR to little kids, to a police officer shooting a guy who turns out to be unarmed. Anytime somebody loses their life regardless of what the reason

> is, it's always unfortunate because that's someone son or daughter…[but] I try not to be too reactionary because one video can't change your whole mindset, it's sort of like the "bad apple" analogy.

These narratives indicate that videos shared on social media, even ones of intense violence, may not shift an individual's orientation toward police.

Instead, the participants that were minimally impacted by social media often described seeing social media that reflected or validated current attitudes toward police. This was found to be the case for participants who held positive and neutral opinions toward the police and also applied to a small number of cases of negative attitudes toward the police. This finding suggests that social media may be a mechanism for reinforcing attitudes already formed, especially among those who are more favorable toward police. As one white male who described himself as having neutral feelings toward the police stated, "I think [social media] does validate what I have to say because I see good videos of police, I also see police officers shooting unarmed individuals. I think that it validates how I already feel about police officers most of the time." Likewise, a white woman, who was generally supportive of the police, reflected on the impact of social media. While she admitted it expanded on her knowledge about police misconduct, it primarily reinforced her previously held opinions:

> I never thought about the possibility of there being a bad police officer until I saw it on social media, but I know that they are not all like that... [Social media] reaffirmed what I already knew. But after seeing all those brutal videos…I know there are "bad apples."

These findings suggest that social media may not have the ability to change opinions among some populations, including white individuals who are supportive of law enforcement. Given this is in opposition to what was the participants of color reported, this finding indicates that the impact of social media may be less impactful and less harmful for white youth when compared with young people of color.

Videos Can Shape Opinions: "Videos Impacted the Way I Think About Police"
For 8 of the 19 participants, videos of violent police behavior were described as contributing to their opinions of police and causing feelings of fear and distress. Among these eight, seven held unfavorable attitudes about police and all were participants of color. While not described as being the sole determinant for their attitudes, social media, and specifically videos of police violence, was explicitly mentioned as a contributing factor in how their perspectives and reactions toward police were formed.

For seven of these eight participants,[4] seeing negative videos, such as shootings and wrongful deaths, raised concerns of serious police misconduct, corruption, and racism, a lack of trust, and fear of victimization. One Latina believed that officers have excessive power and when combined with racism can lead to "murder" or the unjustified killing of innocents:

> There was a video of a man that got shot at a gas station…he wasn't doing anything, he was just getting gas, when this cop came over, and…the guy in the driver's seat went into the glove department to get his driver's license, [and] when he reached down, the cop just shot him. [The officer] said that he thought [the victim] was getting a gun…even though he had asked him for the insurance stuff. It seemed senseless, and like he had no reason to even touch his gun. The guy had his hands up, it wasn't like he was rushing to get into the glove compartment. That just seemed completely harmless and straight up murder…. It's a system that's corrupt.

Likewise, one Latino male noted, "You don't ever see anything positive about the police on social media. Like what I see is always people like bashing them or videos of cops like over exercising their power." He specifically recalled one video that stood out most in his memory, commonly known as the "2015 Texas Pool Party" where Dajerria Becton, a 15-year-old Black female who was wearing a swimsuit, was violently restrained by a white police officer, corporal Eric Casebolt. This video contributed to his lack of trust in police, especially for white officers:

> I saw this video of these girls from Texas…they went to some pool party…it got shut down…and one of the cops put every single [youth of color] on the ground and he was on top of some girl and she was Black. For like five minutes with his knee on her neck and she wasn't even doing anything. She was just trying to have a conversation and ask him why he was doing what he was doing and he was going crazy on her…. I draw a difference between White police officers and minority police officers…. I just don't trust [White officers].

The Asian female in the study also referenced this video. She described how the graphic, racially motivated and disproportionate use of force on the frightened Black teenager caused her emotional distress:

> We watched this video…. It was like a pool party and Black people were invited to [the] party…. Someone called the cops [and] basically the cops came and made the Black people leave. This cop who was White, he was like middle aged, he was sitting on a young girl in her bikini restraining her. She was like half naked and scared. I started tearing up because she wasn't doing anything, she was just asking him to get off and he was just on her.

These negative videos highlighted, according to her, that officers "are not doing what they are supposed to be doing," and this was impactful because "you can see racism is real." Similarly, one Latino male felt these videos of extreme violence were so disturbing that they made him nauseous and influenced how he felt about the police:

> There was this one video where there was this White cop basically sitting on top of this Black guy.... [The officer] thought the Black guy was gonna take something out his pockets and [the officer] just started shooting him point blank in the chest. It's the most gruesome thing I've seen really. It's sick to me and I hate even thinking about it.... I see things on social media everyday really that's related to police and most of it is in a negative way.... These videos are important. We see 'em every day and they kind of shape our thinking.

Furthermore, several participants of color indicated that the videos resulted in fear of victimization. Three participants described witnessing videos of police misconduct against people of color and being afraid of the police for themselves or their relatives. For example, one Latina woman raised concerns of personal sexual victimization after learning about an officer allegedly targeting and raping women of color in her city:

> I think [news of police misconduct] does impact me when it is relative to my location. Like when I see stories or videos of cop interactions in [home state] or New York.... It is scary to me because it could potentially happen to me. There was this police officer in New York last year that was going around and raping women.... This was really frightening to me because he was targeting women of color.

Along similar lines, the Black woman, who noted that she had "seen a lot of [videos on] police brutality on minorities, specifically African Americans," stated that she was frightened on behalf of her male relatives after witnessing the footage of Eric Garner's arrest. In 2014, Eric Garner died when a New York Police Department officer, Daniel Panteleo, placed him in a chokehold during arrest despite Garner stating, "I can't breathe" 11 times. Garner died shortly thereafter as a result of the chokehold and his positioning during the altercation. The video of his detainment went viral and sparked protests, demonstrations, and "die-ins," where protestors simulate being dead, all over America. The Black female described the video:

> The police accused Eric Garner of selling cigarettes...he said he was not, and the police continued to arrest him anyway, even putting him in a chokehold, and he was not struggling or resisting at all until the police did that, and Eric Garner even

> said to the police that he couldn't breathe while he was being held in a chokehold but the police still continued.... He started coughing and suffocating because of that.

She explained that it was profound because she could envision something like that happening to her family members, especially if they left the safety of their neighborhood:

> [The] Eric Garner video... made me...feel unsafe. Not me specifically, but for my male relatives... God forbid my Dad or Grandpa goes outside of [urban hometown]. I would fear for their safety more than if they were [in urban hometown].

The Black male in the study echoed a similar concern after seeing the Sandra Bland video. Sandra Bland, a 28-year-old African American, was arrested during a pretext traffic stop. The arrest showed the officer threatening her with a taser and forcing her to the ground while she screamed. Sandra Bland died in custody by suicide via hanging. However, her cause of death was disputed and sparked nationwide protests. The young man noted that the video of her arrest made him scared that he would become a victim due to his race and the long history of tension between people of color and law enforcement:

> It was a video on Sandra Bland [that had the biggest impression on me] and how she was a black teacher that got pulled over by a police officer and it got a little out of hand and she got arrested. While in jail for three days, she was found dead and it was so-called suicide.... This video made me feel fearful because it was someone of my own race that it happened to and with past history, people from my racial background don't have the best relationships with authorities.

These findings suggest that videos can not only impact perceptions of police but also cause negative emotional, physical, and mental reactions from viewers. Videos of police misconduct may be especially important among populations of color who may become fearful of being personally subjected to racially motivated police violence.

While videos of police behavior can contribute to one's holistic perception of police, it is important to note that there was a range of relative impacts. For some, the videos were deeply profound, like the Black female who found the negative videos so powerful she changed her previously held positive opinions about police:

> I always had that positive image [of] and encounters with police officers, but knowing how history goes and what has been happening lately in the news, my opinion of the police has begun to lean more toward a negative light.... The more

> negative encounters, like the ones I've seen on social media and the news have more of an impact on me and my opinion.

For others, although videos were important, the relative impact was described as less impactful than face-to-face encounters. Several participants (5 of the 19) directly indicated that their in-person interactions with police were more meaningful in shaping their opinions than what they witnessed on social media. This was especially so if the face-to-face encounters were negative, as was the case with four of the five participants. One Latino male stated, "We are always on social media so that's maybe where I get my feelings but most of it comes from my face-to-face encounters." This sentiment was echoed by several others as well, including another Latino male who stated, "I feel that my personal experiences are stronger influences, but social media does give you more information and brings awareness to issues around the world." Despite this, however, these findings suggest that videos of police behavior can shape opinions about law enforcement, although the relative impact may range from profoundly influential to somewhat influential. Further, the videos may be especially meaningful for individuals of color because they can raise concerns of police brutality, abuse of authority, racism, distrust, trauma, and fear of victimization.

Discussion

Reactions toward police derive from a complex mixture of identity, experience, and socialization. Consistent with extensive literature, the research conducted in this study shows that the influence of parents, friends, face-to-face encounters, vicarious experiences, and social media contributes to the development of young people's perspectives of law enforcement (see Brown & Benedict, 2002). In line with previous American studies, evidence shows that perspectives of police differ among racial and ethnic identities. The participants of color in this study, except those who had family in law enforcement, generally held negative views of police (Brunson, 2007; Gau & Brunson, 2007). These participants described disliking the police due to perceptions of them being racist, untrustworthy, and abusing their power (Fratello et al., 2013). On the contrary, white participants, except for the two that had particularly egregious face-to-face encounters, expressed more favorable opinions of law enforcement (Brown & Benedict, 2002). The white participants were generally appreciative of police officers' work and perceived them as good, hard working people. This research shows that race and ethnicity can impact perceptions of law enforcement (Brunson, 2007; Fiske, 1986; Gau & Brunson, 2007; Novich & Hunt, 2016), with Black participants more likely to have the most negative views, their white counterparts the most positive, and other ethnic identities falling in the middle (Brown & Benedict, 2002; Cheurprakobkit, 2000; Rosenbaum et al., 2005). While these findings support previous work, the examination of social media offers innovative evidence on how different populations synthesize police content shared through their social networks.

Although the research yielded limited gender discrepancies, possibly due to sample limitations, clear racial differences surfaced. Participants of all ethnoracial identities in the study referred to viral videos that they remembered seeing, indicating the ability of this content to reach different populations. However, a majority of the white participants indicated that social media had a limited impact on their perceptions of police and tended to rationalize videos of police misconduct by isolating these incidents to a few "bad apples" that do not represent the whole. Many white participants appeared to use positive social media to validate preexisting positive opinions, while dismissing negative content as biased or out of context. The content shared on social media did not seem to have a significant impact on the formation of white participants' attitudes toward police.

This was a stark contrast to the participants of color (Weitzer, 2002) who "decoded" trending police violence differently than their white counterparts (Fiske, 1986; Hall, 1980). The witnessing of AVB and/or TEO directly contributed to negative attitudes toward police and raised concerns of abuse of authority, distrust, and excessive use of power. These data suggest that negative videos can have detrimental consequences on perceived police legitimacy (Novich & Hunt, 2016; Tyler, 2006). This was the case even among those who had positive face-to-face encounters with police. This is significant because previous research has suggested that face-to-face encounters are most important when forming opinions of police (see Tyler, 2006). The research suggests that this may not always be the case among young people of color.

Moreover, the witnessing of AVB and TEO had serious negative consequences for participants of color. The findings suggest that the AVB and TEO may be a form of tech-facilitated abuse due to the emotional manipulation of viewers. Not only did several study participants easily recall memories of AVB and TEO, which is linked to acute stress (Clark et al., 2016), but also AVB and TEO engendered extreme distress (i.e., the viewer started crying), feelings of nauseated disgust, and anxiety – reactions associated with poor mental health (Feinstein et al., 2014; Holman et al., 2013). Further, the racially motivated police violence witnessed by participants was applied to real-world expectations whereby they personally identified with the victims and raised concerns of fear of victimization for themselves, family members, and/or friends (see Tynes et al., 2019). This contributed to heightened levels of stress and trauma (see Bryant-Davis et al., 2017; Tynes et al., 2019). These reactions may be further exacerbated given the "daily" frequency in which participants reported seeing AVB and TEO in their feeds (see Feinstein et al., 2014; Holman et al., 2013). Of additional concern is the widespread community consequences (Tynes et al., 2019). Given how readily shared AVB is among family and friends, which may be rationalized as a way of inspiring social awareness and a desire for justice, whenever it is forwarded the harm spreads and makes each person unknowingly complicit in disseminating technology-facilitated abuse.

The evidence in the present study indicates young people of color interpret shared content differently than their white counterparts. Young people of color are not only more sensitive to the material (Lim, 2015) but also raise more concerns of police legitimacy (Novich & Hunt, 2016) and experience greater levels of trauma, fear, concerns of victimization, and anger (Bryant-Davis et al., 2017; Tynes et al., 2019). As such, this study highlights the need for police departments, especially those working with diverse populations, to implement workshops like procedural justice training which focus on establishing respect through courteous interpersonal treatment (Tyler, 2006). These practices may help reduce violent police behavior while simultaneously improving perceptions of legitimacy and relationships with young communities of color (Novich & Hunt, 2016).

Second, this research also demonstrates the need for police departments to take immediate action following the circulation of AVB videos in order to mitigate trauma, emotional distress, and concerns of victimization. This may come in the form of providing mental health support to the communities directly impacted and police leadership taking accountability for officer misconduct. This may be a critical way in which police can improve public support and acknowledge harm caused. Ultimately, this research has shown the disproportionate emotional and psychological impact of AVB showcasing police violence on young people of color. For a world constantly "logged on," therein lies a responsibility to recognize social media's influence on police-community relationships and its ability to enable widespread technologically facilitated abuse. Recognizing this responsibility is especially necessary in order to understand those who are inordinately impacted by viral content and calls to attention the critical need to put practices into place that mitigate the subsequent harm.

Notes

1. One white male described himself as "neutral" regarding his opinion about police and was not placed in either the positive or negative category.
2. One student reported seeing a video where the police were being disrespected. This was considered a negative police video. The other 10 described negative videos as police misconduct.
3. Two students of color who held negative opinions about police also indicated that social media had a limited impact on their perceptions of police. For one, as will be further discussed in detail, face-to-face encounters were more impactful than social media.
4. One Latino male noted how his opinion of police changed to be less negative and more neutral as a result of witnessing videos of officers engaging in positive and helpful behavior.

References

Arceneaux, P. C., & Dinu, L. F. (2018). The social mediated age of information: Twitter and Instagram as tools for information dissemination in higher education. *New Media & Society*, *20*(11), 4155–4176. doi:10.1177/1461444818768259

Aymer, S. R. (2016). "I can't breathe": A case study—helping black men cope with race-related trauma stemming from police killing and brutality. *Journal of Human Behavior in the Social Environment*, *26*(3–4), 367–376. doi:10.1080/10911359.2015.1132828

Bandura, A. (1962). Social learning through imitation. In M. R. Jones (Ed.), *Nebraska symposium on motivation* (pp. 211–274). Lincoln, NE: University of Nebraska Press.

Bonilla, Y., & Rosa, J. (2015). #Ferguson: Digital protest, hashtag ethnography, and the racial politics of social media in the United States. *American Ethnologist*, *42*(1), 4–17. doi:10.1111/amet.12112

Brick, B. T., Taylor, T. J., & Esbensen, F. (2009). Juvenile attitudes toward the police: The importance of subcultural involvement and community ties. *Journal of Criminal Justice*, *37*(5), 488–495. doi:10.1016/j.jcrimjus.2009.07.009

Brown, B., & Benedict, W. R. (2002). Perceptions of the police. *Policing: An International Journal of Police Strategies & Management*, *25*(3), 543–580. Retrieved from http://www.observatoriodeseguranca.org/files/p543.pdf

Brunson, R. K. (2007). "Police don't like Black people": African-American young mens' accumulated police experiences. *Criminology & Public Policy*, *6*(1), 71–101. doi:10.1111/j.1745-9133.2007.00423.x

Bryant-Davis, T., Adams, T., Alejandre, A., & Gray, A. A. (2017). The trauma lens of police violence against racial and ethnic minorities. *Journal of Social Issues*, *73*(4), 852–871. doi:10.1111/josi.12251

Callanan, V. J. (2012). Media consumption, perceptions of crime risk and fear of crime: Examining race/ethnic differences. *Sociological Perspectives*, *55*(1), 93–115. doi: 10.1525/sop.2012.55.1.93

Chambliss, D. F., & Schutt, R. K. (2016). *Making sense of the social world: Methods of investigation*. Thousand Oaks, CA: Sage Publications, Inc.

Chan, J. (2017). Racial identity in online spaces: Social media's impact on students of color. *Journal of Student Affairs Research and Practice*, *54*(2), 163174. doi:10.1080/19496591.2017.1284672

Cheurprakobkit, S. (2000). Police-citizen contact and police performance: Attitudinal differences between Hispanics and non-Hispanics. *Journal of Criminal Justice*, *28*(4), 325–336. doi:10.1016/S0047-2352(00)00042-8

Clark, I. A., Holmes, E. A., Woolrich, M. W., & Mackay, C. E. (2016). Intrusive memories to traumatic footage: The neural basis of their encoding and involuntary recall. *Psychological Medicine*, *46*(3), 505–518. doi:10.1017/S0033291715002007

Crouch, M., & McKenzie, H. (2006). The logic of small samples in interview-based qualitative research. *Social Science Information*, *45*(4), 483–499. doi:10.1177/0539018406069584

Donovan, K. M., & Klahm, C. F. (2015). The role of entertainment media in perceptions of police use of force. *Criminal Justice and Behavior*, *42*(12), 1261–1281. doi:10.1177/0093854815604180

Dowler, K. (2003). Media consumption and public attitudes toward crime and justice: Relationship between fear of crime, punitive attitudes, and perceived police effectiveness. *Journal of Criminal Justice and Popular Culture*, *10*(2), 109–126. Retrieved from https://www.researchgate.net/publication/285675137_Media_consumption_and_public_attitudes_toward_crime_and_justice_The_relationship_between_fear_of_crime_punitive_attitudes_and_perceived_police_effectiveness

Dowler, K., & Zawilski, V. (2007). Public perceptions of police misconduct and discrimination: Examining the impact of media consumption. *Journal of Criminal Justice*, *35*(2), 193–203. doi:10.1016/j.jcrimjus.2007.01.006

Feinstein, A., Audet, B., & Waknine, E. (2014). Witnessing images of extreme violence: A psychological study of journalists in the newsroom. *JRSM Open*, *5*(8), 1–7.

Fiske, J. (1986). Television: Polysemy and popularity. *Critical Studies in Mass Communication*, *3*, 391–408. doi:10.1080/15295038609366672

Flexon, J. L., Lurigio, A. J., & Greenleaf, R. G. (2009). Exploring the dimensions of trust in the police among Chicago juveniles. *Journal of Criminal Justice*, *37*(2), 180–189. doi:10.1016/j.jcrimjus.2009.02.006

Fratello, J., Rengifo, A., & Trone, J. (2013). *Coming of age with stop and frisk: Experiences, self-perceptions, and public safety implications:* Summary Report. New York, NY: Vera Institute of Justice. Retrieved from http://www.vera.org/stop-and-frisk-summary-report

Gau, J., & Brunson, R. (2007). Procedural injustice, lost legitimacy, and self-help: Young males' adaptations to perceived unfairness in urban policing tactics. *Journal of Contemporary Criminal Justice*, *3*(2), 132–150.

Grasmuck, S., Martin, J., & Zhoa, S. (2009). Ethno-racial identity displays on Facebook. *Journal of Computer-Mediated Communication*, *15*(1), 158–188. doi:10.1111/j.1083-6101.2009.01498.x

Hall, S. (1980). *Culture, media and language*. London: Hutchinson. doi:10.4324/9780203381182

Holman, E. A., Garfin, D. R., & Silver, R. C. (2013). Media's role in broadcasting acute stress following the Boston Marathon bombings. *Proceedings of the National Academy of Sciences*, *111*(1), 93–98. doi:10.1073/pnas.1316265110

Hurst, Y. G., Frank, J., & Browning, S. L. (2000a). How kids view cops: The nature of juvenile attitudes toward the police. *Journal of Criminal Justice*, *28*(3), 189–202. doi:10.1016/S0047-2352(00)00035-0

Hurst, Y. G., Frank, J., & Browning, S. (2000b). The attitudes of juveniles toward the police: A comparison of black and white youth. *Policing: An International Journal of Police Strategies & Management*, *23*, 37–53. doi:10.1108/13639510010314607

Hurst, Y. G., McDermott, M. J., & Thomas, D. L. (2005). The attitudes of girls toward the police: Differences by race. *Policing: An International Journal of Police Strategies & Management*, *28*(4), 578–593. doi:10.1108/13639510510628677

Kohm, S. A., Waid-Lindberg, C. A., Weinrath, M., Shelley, T. O., & Dobbs, R. R. (2012). The impact of media on fear of crime among university students: A cross-national comparison. *Canadian Journal of Criminology and Criminal Justice*, *54*(1), 67–100. doi:10.3138/cjccj.2011.E.01

Lee, E. B. (2011). Young, Black, and connected: Facebook usage among African American college students. *Journal of Black Studies*, *43*(3), 336–354. doi:10.1177/0021934711425044

Lee, J., Lim, H., & Lee, H. (2015). Differential social distance and confidence in the police. *International Journal of Police Science & Management*, *17*(3), 147–154. doi:10.1177/1461355715596305

Leiber, M. J., Nalla, M. K., & Farnworth, M. (1998). Explaining juveniles' attitudes toward the police. *Justice Quarterly*, *15*(1), 151–174. doi:10.1080/07418829800093671

Lim, H. (2015). Social modeling effects on perception of the police: Focus on indirect police contact experience among college students. *Policing: An International Journal of Police Strategies & Management*, *38*(4), 675–689. doi:10.1108/PIJPSM-02-2015-0018

Maxwell, J. A. (1996). *Qualitative research design: An interactive approach*. Thousand Oaks, CA: Sage Publications, Inc.

Nhan, J. (2019). *Issues and controversies in policing today*. Lanham, MD: Rowman & Littlefield.

Novich, M., & Hunt, G. (2016). "Get off me": Perceptions of disrespectful police behaviour among ethnic minority youth gang members. *Drugs: Education, Prevention and Policy*, *24*(3), 248–255. doi:10.1080/09687637.2016.1239697

Papachristos, A. V., Braga, A. A., & Hureau, D. M. (2012). Social networks and the risk of gunshot injury. *Journal of Urban Health*, *89*(6), 992–1003. doi:10.1007/s11524-012-9703-9

Presser, L., & Sandberg, S. (2015). *Narrative criminology understanding stories of crime*. New York, NY: NYU Press.

Reisig, M. D., & Correia, M. E. (1997). Public evaluations of police performance: An analysis across three levels of policing. *Policing: An International Journal of Police Strategies and Management*, *20*(2), 311–325. doi:10.1108/13639519710169153

Rosenbaum, D. P., Schuck, A. M., Costello, S. K., Hawkins, D. F., & Ring, M. K. (2005). Attitudes toward the police: The effects of direct and vicarious experience. *Police Quarterly*, *8*(3), 343–365. doi:10.1177/1098611104271085

Silverman, D. (2006). *Interpreting qualitative data: Methods for analysing talk, text and interaction*. London: Sage Publications.

Smith, A., & Anderson, M. (2018). *Social media use 2018: Demographics and statistics*. Washington, DC: Pew Research Center.

Tyler, T. R. (2002). A national survey for monitoring police legitimacy. *Justice Research and Policy*, *4*(1–2), 71–86. doi:10.3818/JRP.4.1.2002.71

Tyler, T. R. (2006). *Why people obey the law*. Princeton, NJ: Princeton University Press.

Tynes, B. M., Willis, H. A., Stewart, A. M., & Hamilton, M. W. (2019). Race-related traumatic events online and mental health among adolescents of color. *Journal of Adolescent Health*, *65*(3), 371–377. doi:10.1016/j.jadohealth.2019.03.006

Weitzer, R. (2002). Incidents of police misconduct and public opinion. *Journal of Criminal Justice*, *30*(5), 397–408. doi:10.1016/S0047-2352(02)00150-2

Weitzer, R., & Tuch, S. A. (1999). Race, class, and perceptions of discrimination by the police. *Crime & Delinquency*, *45*(4), 494–507. doi:10.1177/0011128799045004006

Wu, Y. (2013). Race/ethnicity and perceptions of police: A comparison of White, Black, Asian, and Hispanic Americans. *Policing and Society*, *24*(2), 135–157. doi:10.1080/10439463.2013.784288

Chapter 17

Just Fantasy? Online Pornography's Contribution to Experiences of Harm

Samantha Keene

Abstract

Mainstream pornography is popular, freely accessible, and infused with themes of male dominance, aggression, and female subservience. Through depicting sex in these ways, mainstream pornography has the potential to influence the further development of harmful sexual scripts that condone or endorse violence against women and girls. These concerns warrant the adoption of a harms-based perspective in critical examinations of pornography's influence on sexual experiences. This chapter reports on findings from interviews with 24 heterosexual emerging adults living in Aotearoa/New Zealand about how pornography has impacted their lives. Despite a shared awareness among participants of mainstream pornography's misogynistic tendencies, and the potential for harm from those displays, men's and women's experiences were profoundly gendered. Men's reported experiences were often associated with concerns about their own sexual behaviors, performances, and/or abilities. Conversely, women's experiences were often shaped by how pornography had affected the way that men related to them sexually. Their experiences included instances of sexual coercion and assault which were not reported by the men. These findings signal the need for a gendered lens, situated within a broader harms-based perspective, in examinations of pornography's influence.

Keywords: Pornography; relationships; violence against women; internet; gender; sexual scripts

Introduction

Pornography is a topic that incites debate, controversy, and angst in community, political, and academic circles. Research on pornography is often imbued with

The Emerald International Handbook of Technology-Facilitated Violence and Abuse, 289–308

doi:10.1108/978-1-83982-848-520211021

moralistic evaluations, strong personal opinions (Böhm, Franz, Dekker, & Matthiesen, 2015), and it remains a contentious issue for academics due to the difficulties involved in establishing casual links between pornography and sexual violence (Vera-Gray & McGlynn, 2020). Pornography has been central to much feminist scholarship and activism due to its potential contribution to gendered harms, in particular its role in influencing harmful sexual attitudes, behaviors, and perpetuating violence against women and girls. Early feminist anti-pornography scholarship located pornography – and the associated sex industry – as situated within a patriarchal structure of men's control of, and violence against, women (Brownmiller, 1975; Dworkin, 1981; Dworkin & MacKinnon, 1988). These critiques focused on its rampant misogyny and violent portrayals of heterosexual relations. Feminist scholar Andrea Dworkin (1981) identified male power as intrinsic to pornography and defined it as:

> ...the graphic, sexually explicit subordination of women in pictures and/or words that also includes women presented dehumanized as sexual objects, things, or commodities; or women presented as sexual objects who experience sexual pleasure in being raped; or women presented as sexual objects tied up or cut up or mutilated or bruised or physically hurt; or women presented in postures or positions of sexual submission, servility, or display. (p. xxxiii)

Feminist scholars drew links between pornography and women's experiences of sexual violence, leading Robin Morgan (1980) to conclude that "pornography is the theory; rape is the practice" (p. 139). Strong objections to pornography encouraged efforts to censor it, seeing it as "the preferred solution to the pornography problem" (Bronstein, 2011, p. 328). However, many feminist activists and scholars were critical of the anti-pornography position. Calls for censorship were considered by some as an attempt to minimize and suppress women's sexuality (Duggan, Hunter, & Vance, 1995; Rubin, 1984; Vance, 1984). Lisa Duggan (1995) argued that the anti-censorship position set out to "counter antiporn accounts of 'pornography' as a unified (patriarchal) discourse with a singular (misogynistic) impact" (p. 7), thereby recognizing the potential for alternative readings of pornography, especially those which prioritize women's pleasurable experiences and alternative and transgressive works (Attwood, 2005).

While the division in perspectives on pornography is often characterized by anti/pro-pornography positions, some scholars suggest that such binary distinctions and framing stifle the possibility for understanding the complexities and nuances in the debates through critical readings of pornography and its influence (Smith & Attwood, 2014). Though anti-pornography feminism thrusts a focus on pornography as sexual domination, and pro-pornography feminism situates it as a more complex force in women's lives, some scholars argue that "sexuality cannot be viewed solely as sexual domination" but at the same time cannot be understood as "unproblematically a site of unmodified pleasure and agency," thereby making it necessary to understand sexuality – and therefore pornography – "as a terrain of struggle and contradiction" (Cossman & Bell, 1997, p. 22).

The divide in feminist perspectives on pornography continues today, however, with many scholars occupying either anti-pornography or "porn-sympathetic" positions. Indeed, as Karaian (2005) notes

> …as long as there exists burning desire, the flames of passion, and their representation in one form or another, both the bonfire that is the pornography debate, and feminists, will roar on. (p. 133)

Boyle (2014) contends that porn-sympathetic scholarship often focuses on the genre's peripheries, such as feminist or queer pornography, thereby "ignoring or sidelining important feminist questions about violence and inequality while advocating a more hedonistic world-view linked to sexual practice" (p. 229). A harms-based approach to pornography remains dominant in the field of pornography studies, and many contemporary critiques continue to focus on the misogyny, aggression, racism, and gender inequity which is inherent in much mainstream pornography (Boyle, 2010; DeKeseredy & Corsianos, 2016; Jensen, 2007).

Shifts in the content of mainstream pornography, in conjunction with its increased accessibility and popularity, provide the foundation for ongoing academic attention to pornography and its potential contribution to harms. The aim of this chapter is to explore how internet pornography has influenced the lives of a sample of heterosexual emerging adults living in Aotearoa/New Zealand. This chapter begins with an examination of the changing content of internet pornography. It demonstrates how mainstream pornography routinely displays misogynistic and aggressive behaviors which are markedly gendered, in that women are overwhelmingly the receivers of such acts. It then considers these behaviors through the lens of sexual script theory and posits how the portrayal of such behaviors in pornography can contribute to harmful experiences for both individuals and their partners. Following this, the chapter provides an overview of the study and participants, before moving to present participants' perspectives on the content of pornography. While acknowledging that pornography can be experienced both positively and negatively by viewers, this chapter focuses on the negative impacts reported by participants in detail. In so doing, it differentiates between how these negative experiences were discussed by men and women both individually and in their intimate relationships. Ultimately, this chapter concludes that attention must be paid to men's and women's differential experiences of harm. It affirms the need for a harms-based approach to understanding mainstream pornography's influence on people's lives.

The Changing Nature of Internet Pornography

As a genre, pornography has a decades-long history and has been immensely popular in both magazine and video formats. Pornography refers to:

> …visual depictions that are intended to sexually arouse the viewer, such as still photos, magazines, adult cable television channels, or

> VHS movies. Today, pornography is more likely to mean online video; and in the future, technological changes may again shift how these visual depictions are delivered to the consumer. (Tarrant, 2016, p. 3)

Men's pornographic magazines emerged in the 1960s and were the dominant way that men engaged with the genre at this time. By 1972, popular men's magazine *Playboy* recorded a circulation rate of over 7 million copies per month, making magazine sales responsible for half of company revenue and most of the company's net income (Gunelius, 2009). In the 1990s, and owing to technological advances, pornography transformed from the glossy pages of *Playboy* to both VHS and DVD formats. The dynamic evolution of the video pornography industry in the mid-1990s saw adult pornography generating revenue of $3.1 billion dollars from rentals and sales (Dines, 1998). Today, pornography is now almost completely accessed online. Internet pornography is increasingly accessible, with entire "tube" sites now dedicated to pornography. Tube sites follow a similar platform to websites such as YouTube, where content can be uploaded and engaged with by viewers across the globe (Tarrant, 2016).

Mainstream pornography is immensely popular, much more than *Playboy* was at its peak in the 1970s. Mainstream pornography refers to the most common genres and representations of sex in internet pornography, operating within hegemonic norms of gender, sexuality, and commerce (Sostar & Sullivan, 2017). For instance, visits to the most popular site, Pornhub, totaled over 42 billion in 2019 alone, averaging 115 million visits per day (Pornhub, 2019). During the global COVID-19 pandemic, Pornhub offered viewers free membership to "premium" content to encourage social distancing, with Pornhub reporting a nearly 25% increase in daily traffic following the announcement (Pornhub, 2020a). The landing page of Pornhub's website shows that at the time of writing there are 11,821,291 videos available to view (Pornhub, 2020b). Pornhub is one of thousands, perhaps millions, of websites dedicated to pornographic content. The sheer volume of content available suggests there is massive viewer demand for the genre.

Reliable data regarding the revenues of pornography websites is difficult to locate due to the multifaceted nature of the internet industry and the range of activities included under the porn umbrella. Revenue estimates for pornography websites are also wildly varied. Tarrant (2016) suggests that an "often-repeated figure is that people spend $3,000 every second on internet porn; another is that industry revenues surpass earnings by Microsoft, Google, Amazon, eBay, Yahoo, Apple, and Netflix combined" (p. 42). The pervasiveness of internet pornography websites suggests that pornographic magazines have been surpassed – perhaps even buried – by the very industry they inspired.

Alongside the shifts in the way pornography is produced has been a dramatic shift in content. Today's pornography is a world removed from the images that previously graced the pages of *Playboy* magazine, with Jackson Katz (2006) arguing that people of a certain age who associate pornography with *Playboy* magazine imagery would be shocked by the brutality inherent in mainstream content. DeKeseredy and Corsianos (2016) argue that mainstream pornography frequently depicts behaviors such as heterosexual anal sex, double penetrations, double anal, double vaginal, and ass-to-mouth sequences which are infused with themes of male dominance and female subservience. They conclude that mainstream pornography is inherently misogynistic as "the most common images that overwhelmingly cater to a straight male audience are images of women always ready for sex, always willing to please, and always sexually satisfied" (DeKeseredy & Corsianos, 2016, p. 11). That said, female subservience is not always featured in the pornographic script.

Moreover, sexualized images often intersect with racialized and classist stereotypes regarding women's sexuality. In pornography, women of color are often depicted as "animalistic" (Mayall & Russell, 1993; Walker, 1980), or as bound and restrained, linking directly back to the history of slavery (Amoah, 1997). Amoah (1997) argues that depicting women of color as insatiable serves to reinforce the notion that she needs to be "restrained for her own good, and the white slave master was doing her a favor by enslaving her" (p. 211). Such racialized and sexualized stereotypes have powerful implications, as they can ultimately culminate in Black women's experiences of sexual violence being viewed as less important or less credible (Crenshaw, 1991).

Previous content analyses of internet pornography report that aggression (Fritz & Paul, 2017; Shor, 2019), sexual violence (Gossett & Byrne, 2002), degradation (Gorman, Monk-Turner, & Fish, 2010), gender inequalities (Klaassen & Peter, 2015; Vannier, Currie, & O'Sullivan, 2014), and racism (Shor & Golriz, 2019; Zhou & Paul, 2016) are frequently found in mainstream content. In a recent analysis of age, aggression, and pleasure in 172 videos available on Pornhub, it was reported that 43% of videos included visible depictions of aggression, 15.1% included nonconsensual aggression, and that female performers were more likely to respond pleasurably to aggressive behaviors (Shor, 2019). The author concludes that these videos promoted and endorsed aggression and degradation, thereby reinforcing problematic ideas about young women's sexuality (Shor, 2019).

Ultimately, today's pornography presents an assemblage of easy-to-access, misogynistic, and hostile depictions of heterosexual relationships that are freely available online with the click of a button. Presenting pornography in this way runs the risk of normalizing such practices for viewers, particularly in the absence of comprehensively delivered, holistic relationship and sexuality education. In light of these concerns, sexual script theory is often used as an overarching framework for understanding the effects of pornography (Bridges, Sun, Ezzell, & Johnson, 2016; Marshall, Miller, & Bouffard, 2018). Sexual script theory is commonly used within feminist writing on sexuality and rape (Frith, 2013). It contends that sexual acts follow a script that is influenced by our social and learned interactions (Simon & Gagnon, 1986). Sexual scripts are "cultural messages which define what counts as sex, how to recognize sexual situations, and what to do in sexual encounters" (Frith, 2013, p. 100). Pornography's "formulaic" depiction of sex (Young, 2014) often prioritizes masculine sexual pleasure and structures the way sexual pleasure is enacted and visualized, enforcing an essentialist gender ideology in online depictions (van Doorn, 2010).

Theoretically, then, these depictions can operate as a key cultural site for influencing the development, acquisition, and activation of sexual scripts in sexual encounters (Wright, 2011). Known as the "3AM model" of media sexual socialization, it suggests that pornography can provide viewers with

> ...sexual scripts they were unaware of (acquisition), prime sexual scripts they were already aware of (activation) and can encourage the utilization of sexual scripts (application) by portraying them as normative, acceptable, and rewarding. (Wright, 2013, p. 319)

Previous research has demonstrated how pornography can contribute to experiences of harm. Much of the concern about pornography and its harmful influence relates to children or young people's engagement with the genre (Flood, 2010; Peter & Valkenburg, 2016); however, concerns have also been raised about adult usage. Research with men has suggested that pornography can play a pivotal role in the development of hostile attitudes or sexually aggressive behaviors among some men (Hald, Malamuth, & Lange, 2013; Malamuth, Addison, & Koss, 2000; Malamuth, Hald, & Koss, 2012). For instance, a 2010 meta-analysis of nonexperimental studies reported a positive association between the viewing of pornography and attitudes which support violence against women, especially when viewers engage with sexually violent content (Hald, Malamuth, & Yuen, 2010). Survey data show that viewing pornography can influence men's sexual scripts as they are more likely to use pornography during sex, request specific sexual acts of a partner, or deliberately fantasize about pornography during sex to maintain their own arousal (Sun, Bridges, Johnson, & Ezzell, 2016). Qualitative research with male viewers also suggests that a common practice in pornography – ejaculation on a woman's face – can serve as a powerful model for men's offline sexual encounters (Sun, Ezzell, & Kendall, 2017). More recently, research has also demonstrated the way that viewing pornography can become compulsive for viewers (Duffy, Dawson, & das Nair, 2016; Sniewski, Farvid, & Carter, 2018), and that this can result in unrealistic expectations of sex and sexuality for some men (Sniewski & Farvid, 2020).

Research with women suggests that many are concerned about pornography's influence on men's attitudes and behaviors (Gurevich et al., 2017; Shaw, 1999), which is a realized fear for women who report pornography being linked to their sexually abusive experiences (Bergen & Bogle, 2000; DeKeseredy & Hall-Sanchez, 2017, 2018). In relationships, research suggests pornography is more likely to have negative effects on relationship quality, sexual satisfaction, and self-esteem for women (Bergner & Bridges, 2002; Bridges, Bergner, & Hesson-McInnis, 2003; Schneider, 2000; Stewart & Szymanski, 2012; Tylka & Kroon Van Diest, 2015). Research also suggests that women feel pressured to embrace pornography in intimate relationships (Benjamin & Tlusten, 2010; Resch & Alderson, 2014).

In light of the range of negative effects that pornography can have on intimate relationships, there is a surprising lack of critical criminological perspectives on adult pornography (DeKeseredy, 2015). Much more insight is needed which examines the gendered dynamics and complexities of adult pornography, especially in intimate relationships. The empirical study described below contributes to understandings of adult pornography and the complex ways that pornography is experienced by viewers and their partners. The analysis provides a critical insight into the way that mainstream pornography influenced the lives of a sample of emerging adults living in Aotearoa/New Zealand. It explores how men and women differentially experience harms attributed to pornography both on an individual and relational level, such as feeling "addicted" to pornography, experiences of sexual harm, and relationship distress and instability.

The Study

The data which inform this chapter are drawn from a doctoral project involving semi-structured interviews with 24 emerging adults living in Aotearoa/New Zealand. The project was an exploratory study of the pleasures and pains of pornography for individuals and their partners. It was conducted in a country where little is known about the effects of adult men's and women's engagement with pornography, despite high levels of engagement by both genders.[1] Ethical approval for this research was sought and provided from the author's institution prior to data collection.

The study was open to participants who felt that pornography had either positive and/or negative influences on their lives. The research was restricted to self-identifying heterosexual men and women between the ages of 18 and 30, thereby understood as being in "emerging adulthood."[2] The rationale for only recruiting heterosexual participants was because the study was focused on heterosexual pornography and because the researcher identifies as heterosexual and would therefore be an "outsider" doing research in other communities. Although the research was limited to self-identifying heterosexuals, a small number (n = 3) identified as bisexual during the course of interviews.[3] Future research on queer experiences with, and of, pornography would be a welcome addition to the wider pornography literature.

In total, a self-selected sample of 24 participants (13 men and 11 women) participated in this research via one-on-one, face-to-face interviews at locations across the North Island of Aotearoa/New Zealand. Participants were recruited via Facebook and Twitter pages dedicated to the project, as well as local advertising in bathrooms at tertiary institutions. Recruitment flyers invited participants who were keen to talk about pornography and who felt that pornography had affected their lives in either positive or negative ways. Demographically, participants were diverse in terms of age, ethnicity, educational background, and relationship status. Participants in this research were aged between 18 and 30, with a median age of 24 years. Participants in this study were given the opportunity to self-identify their ethnicity, with New Zealand European/Pākehā (n = 15), Caucasian/White (n = 4), Māori (n = 6), European (n = 1), Chinese (n = 1), Australian (n = 1), and Italian (n = 1) backgrounds reported by participants.[4] Participants reported a range of relationship statuses, including single (n = 5), nonmonogamous/friends with benefits/casual (n = 3), currently de-facto partnered (n = 13), engaged (n = 1), and married (n = 2).

The small-scale nature of this study, in conjunction with its voluntary and self-selecting nature, limits the generalizability of the findings reported beyond the cohort. While gathering generalizable data was not the purpose of the project, there is likely some bias within the sample. It is possible that participants who volunteered to take part were more comfortable or forthright speaking about pornography generally, or that participants were more likely to report negative effects or concerns about their own, or their partners' use, of pornography, given the dominance of a harms-based perspective on pornography in wider society. That said, the data which inform this chapter provide a unique insight into a range of diverse experiences with pornography, with many supporting prior findings reported in the literature.

The Content of Mainstream Pornography: Participants' Perspectives

Virtually all participants in this research who viewed pornography described it as content which fits within a definition of mainstream pornography; that is, it was largely heterosexual, involving cisgender performers, and which was freely available on tube sites, with Pornhub being the primary site for viewing content. Many participants described pornography as a genre which conformed to normative ideas about gendered bodies, sex, and power. Further, many participants recognized that depictions of aggression and/or degradation were frequently portrayed in content on tube sites. In light of this, many participants thought "amateur" content depicting sex between "real" partners was more authentic. However, the concept of "authenticity" in pornography can be contentious, as amateur pornography is still designed to serve the imagined consumer, traditionally men, with commercial wishes and expectations (Ashley, 2016).

Much of the content that participants described viewing included bodies which conformed to Western standards of beauty. Participants frequently spoke about how women's bodies in professionally produced, studio pornography were "plastic" or "fake" and conformed to a *Playboy*-esque stereotype. In defining the stereotype, Tom, 28, summed this up as "very white. Very blonde. Very fake." Men's bodies were not immune to Western ideals of attractiveness in professional pornography, with some male participants referring to male bodies in pornography as "masculine," "ripped," "jacked," and able to perform like a "sexual machine."

Many participants were critical of pornography, suggesting it did not depict "real" sex; rather, it was "scripted," "fake," "unrealistic," "plastic," "superficial," and "glossy." Intimacy – or lack thereof – also featured in some participants' descriptions of sex in internet pornography. Rach, 27, felt pornography presented a "very unrealistic picture of a healthy, intimate relationship with someone you love," especially in professional pornography which Cameron, 24, felt lacked "any kissing or any caressing or any intimate touch." It was suggested by one participant that intimacy-based content was "niche" and not found on mainstream sites. Tina, 21, felt that the sex depicted in pornography was hard "like bang, bang, bang" and lacked "warmth." Internet pornography was also described as infused with power imbalances and gender inequality. Women performers were described as "submissive" and not "in control." Matt, 19, suggested that sex in internet pornography was oriented around the "wants of the male." Aggression in pornography was ever-present, especially in heterosexual pornography which was "dominance-based," "demeaning to women," "male-focused," "misogynistic," "derogatory," and "borderline violent." Many participants accepted that much pornography was scripted, and therefore unrealistic, but some concerns were also expressed about the welfare of female performers in pornography, especially in "harder" or more aggressive genres.

The Potential for Harm: Participants' Views on the Harms of Pornography

Given the frequency of aggressive and misogynistic depictions, many participants in this study were aware of pornography's harmful potential, both for themselves and for others. Pornography was understood by several men as something that could be "bad" or "dangerous," with Chris, 20, suggesting that

> ...there is the dominant narrative about how it can ruin your view of women and sex itself. And there's definitely room for that. I feel like it's definitely a danger.

Further, overexposure to pornography was seen by Derek, 25, as something which contributed to "womanizing" ideas among young men, and Matt, 19, felt that while he could distinguish between pornography and fantasy, he could see "a lot of men not seeing through that at all. Especially if that's the only exposure that they have to sex, is through pornography." Pete, 25, was worried about the "societal impact" of pornography, and George, 25, felt that critical conversations about pornography's role in informing rape culture were overdue. The idea that pornography could be bad was nestled alongside the view that pornography could also be "very good" or "fine" when viewers were "balanced," had a "healthy view," or the "right education" about what they were viewing in pornography.

Women's fears about pornography related to female performer's safety, but also their own safety in their offline relations with men. Many expressed a strong aversion to aggressive pornography, and several women were anxious about whether such videos depicted real experiences of violence or aggression. Holly, 25, enjoyed pornography as a genre, but hated "real demeaning, aggressive porn toward women" because "yeah it could be fake but it could be real." Carly, 24, suggested that heterosexual pornography had "dirty talking and a lot of like derogatory speak to women" which she hoped was merely a portrayal and not a real reflection of how the female performer was being treated, indicating a shared concern for other women's safety in pornography. This commentary echoes previous findings that suggest women's ability to experience pleasure from pornography is regulated by whether they can alleviate concerns about the treatment of female actresses and empathize with them (Gurevich et al., 2017; Parvez, 2006).

Gurevich et al. (2017) suggest that many women fear the way that men interpret and understand pornography, primarily due to how it may influence their attitudes and behaviors in offline sexual encounters. Ultimately, they conclude that these fears are a central dilemma for women and an inevitable pain associated with pornography's pleasures. This was true for a number of women in this study. In mainstream pornography, women are unlikely to respond negatively to targeted acts of aggression from men (Bridges, Wosnitzer, Scharrer, Sun, & Liberman, 2010; Shor, 2019), and Tara, 20, worried that women's pleasurable – yet scripted – responses to some acts, such as aggression, "might translate to be normal for some people." Concerns about men's "forceful" nature in pornography were raised, and Jasmine, 18, felt that pornography "convinces guys that it's okay to like treat a girl in a certain way." Further, Jasmine, 18, suggested that viewing pornography turns off your morals, which could encourage men to perpetrate sexually coercive behaviors:

> I don't know, what I've noticed is that when you're turned on and you're watching porn it's normal, it's like enjoyable, but then when you're not and you watch it, it seems kind of like disgusting… It's kind of like your morals when you're not turned on are there but when you are it's like a natural instinct to like switch it off or something. I don't know, I just noticed that and I was thinking that maybe that ties into like when guys sexually assault someone, maybe it just like switches off in their head or something?

While participants in this research had a shared awareness of pornography's capacity to contribute to offline harm, men's and women's reported experiences of harm differed substantially. In discussing how pornography had influenced their lives, both men and women reported a range of positive and negative impacts. In discussing how pornography could be positively experienced, participants described pornography as an important outlet for sexual arousal and pleasure, and most used it as a masturbatory aid. Carly, 24, described viewing pornography as "a means to an end," and Lilith, 23, reported that watching porn meant an orgasm was able to be achieved through "not much effort." Others described viewing pornography with a partner as a playful way of enhancing intimacy in the couple relationship. Luke, 28, said that he had "been with partners that have enjoyed watching porn while we've had sex," and Nadia, 26, reported that she and her partner would view pornography together while they had sex and "it wasn't something that was really given a second thought."

Conversely, the negative impacts reported by participants were many, particularly those reported by women. The discussion below focuses on those reported negative effects. While there were some similarities in experiences between the genders, the negative offline harms reported by men largely related to their own sexual functioning or their attitudes toward sex. In contrast, many of the negative harms reported by women related to how men used pornography and subsequently treated them in sexual encounters and/or relationships. This next section examines how men and women experienced offline, gendered harms because of their own, or others', use of pornography.

Experiences of Offline Harm: Participants' Experiences

Speaking openly about viewing pornography can be challenging as it remains a distinctly private practice. First in relation to men, Kimmel (2005) suggests that men are fearful that being open about their concerns about pornography exposes them to other men as less than "real men." However, several men in this study reported that pornography had affected their lives. Pornography was recognized as a force which could affect men's sexual behaviors with their intimate partners, but also their attitudes toward women. Kevin, 25, suggested viewing pornography had "influenced" his sexual behaviors and normalized particular practices – namely anal sex and deep throating – which became something for him to "strive" for in his offline sexual relationships. He reflected that he had not initially considered the influence of pornography to be negative on his experiences of intimacy until his partner raised the issue and he agreed "100 percent she's got a point." Pete, 25, queried whether his early exposure to pornography, in conjunction with extensive use as an adult, had had a negative effect on his life. He accepted that it "probably has had a really significant impact on my approach to sexuality," contributing to his sexual promiscuity, adventurousness, and sexual objectification of women.

Alongside these negative attitudinal effects, several men self-identified as "addicted" to pornography which resulted in a range of negative effects. Pornography addiction has attracted a wave of media attention in recent years, and while many scholars accept pornography addiction as a real issue, others question its existence or clinical utility as a label (Ley, 2018; Ley, Prause, & Finn, 2014). Several men in this study reported that their compulsive use of pornography had been, or was currently, harmful or problematic in their lives. Most of these men felt unable to talk to others, such as friends or partners, about their concerns about pornography and its impacts. Kevin, 25, indicated that "the conversation never gets that far" in real life, but that there might be "more discussion in online forums where people are anonymous and can talk about their interests free from being judged." That said, the men in this study reported a range of negative effects, including impaired sexual functioning, relationships ending, religious conflict, negative self-esteem, and altered perceptions of the world around them.

Jack, 21, attributed his erectile dysfunction issues to his compulsive use of pornography, and 25-year old George's use of pornography was at odds with his religious values and his relationship with God. Ethan, 23, felt "guilty" about viewing pornography because his partner perceived it as akin to cheating, and he reported he was "less concerned about consent" when he was unable to manage his compulsive pornography viewing. Ethan felt that his use of pornography made him feel reclusive because he prioritized viewing pornography over socializing with friends. Chris, 20, recognized the time loss associated with his viewing, noting that

> ...if it wasn't for the difficulty in stopping if I so desired, I would consider it as an analogous time waster to playing video games. Except with that added danger of warped perceptions if you weren't careful.

Nathan, 28, expressed concern about managing his pornography use in the future. Nathan did not outwardly disclose the type of pornography that he viewed, but he was consciously aware that his pornography viewing was a sign of a bigger problem within himself. He reflected that "for the moment, porn's fine. But if I don't deal with it soon then it might not be that great for me."

In the same way that speaking about pornography was difficult for men, many women in this study felt that it was even more difficult for them to be open about viewing pornography due to their gender. Although women's levels of engagement with pornography have increased in recent years (Smith, Barker, & Attwood, 2015), their engagement with the genre remains heavily stigmatized. This relates to the shame associated with women's viewing of pornography, but also because it contravenes ideas about how women should behave sexually (Neville, 2018). Much like the men included in this study, many of the women reported a range of negative impacts that they attributed to either their own, or their partners', use of internet pornography. These effects varied across women in the study, but included effects on their sense of self and internal identity, on intimacy and security in heterosexual relationships, on sexual behaviors and preferences, and the way that they were perceived – and treated – by others, especially male partners.

Several women described how they understood men's use of pornography to have affected their sexual experiences, especially experiences of sexual harm. Naomi, 26, said her ex-partner used pornography to coerce her into losing her virginity:

> I did feel like I was getting groomed. You know for him to do that he would, you know if I'd sort of say things like I'd like to wait until this point in time, because I had no idea of what I wanted to do, and he'd get quite mad and he'd like pick up his laptop, try and find something porn related to watch and he'd go into the toilet and come back and sort of like sulk for a while. I guess that was sort of like my first experience. I guess in order to like push me along a bit, then he'd start watching it in bed... he'd try and make me feel shit for not doing it so he had to find other ways.

His use of pornography meant she "felt like I had a lot to live up to and that this was the epitome of like the perfect woman." She also felt inadequate as a partner and pressured to do things such as wear "garish" lingerie as she wanted to "live up to his expectation of what sexual activity should look like." Twenty-one-year old Tina's previous sexual partner used to send her videos of "quite dom/sub porn which kind of instead of being nice it was more of just women being used as an object." This affected her self-esteem and made her feel like she was only "there for him… it wasn't anything to do with me." Miranda, 28, said her ex-partner was heavily interested in "kinky" sex and he encouraged her to view this type of pornography. In order "to please him" she then pushed herself "into doing these kinds of things as well," despite this being at odds with her own sexual preferences or pleasures. Tara, 20, recalled her ex-partner used to push her head down a lot during oral sex, despite her resistance and refusal for rough oral sex. Holly, 25, thought her partner's use of pornography contributed to "how he fucks" and his preference for "skullfucking"[5] her during oral sex, despite this not being enjoyable for her as it reminded her of her previous work in the sex industry.

One woman also felt that her partner's knowledge about her use of pornography, and her preference for "rough sex," came with "real-life consequences." Jasmine, 18, said that her ex-partner was fascinated by threesomes and she suspected he viewed this in pornography as well. He assumed because she was into "rough sex" that she would be "into having sex with other people" and attempted to coerce her into a threesome with her friend while she was drunk. Ultimately, she suggested that women's openness about viewing pornography encouraged men to assume "maybe you're a bit of a like a slut or you're keen for sex," signaling the pervasiveness of sexual double standards which see men heralded for their sexual conquests and engagements and women shunned for their own (Farvid & Braun, 2017; Farvid, Braun, & Rowney, 2017).

As previously discussed, several men reported that they felt addicted to pornography, while several women reported that their partners were addicted. Rach, 27, and Izzy, 30, for instance, were in relationships with "addicted" male partners which negatively affected intimacy, trust, self-esteem, body confidence, and overall relationship stability. Both women reported that it was difficult to talk openly with their friends and family what they were experiencing in their relationships, as others do not view pornography addiction seriously. Izzy's partner tried to "introduce things from the porn into our sex lives," which made her feel "awful" as she did not identify as a dominatrix and he expected her to degrade him. Rach's partner's use made her fearful for leaving their daughter alone with him, knowing that she could encounter pornography on his phone at any time. Rach reported that she used to find "soiled items of clothing and hand towels" in her home and there was "a pattern to how he treated me before and after" viewing pornography. His use affected her "confidence in intimacy" because he would view pornography then come to bed and use her for "finishing," leaving her feeling like a "fill-in." Both Rach and Izzy reported that they were unable to talk about their partner's use of pornography with others because of the "judgment" around it, and for fear of others thinking they were responsible for their partner's addiction due to their sexual inadequacy as a partner. Rach's mother encouraged her to lose weight to be more desirable for her partner, implying that she was somehow responsible for her partner's decision to compulsively view pornography. Rach reflected that her mother encouraged her to "do yourself up a bit and be more attractive" to stop her partner viewing pornography, which amplified the distress she was feeling in the relationship.

As these excerpts show, a male partner's use of pornography can have serious detrimental effects on intimate relationships which differed from those reported by men, indicating the need for continued investigation into the gendered nature of these impacts.

Conclusion

In line with certain feminist critiques, participants in this study recognized that mainstream content was overwhelmingly one-sided and aggressive, conforming to normative ideas about bodies, sex, gender, and power. Mainstream pornography's portrayals of heterosexual sex are regularly infused with themes of male dominance, male power, and female sexual subservience. These gendered power relations ultimately essentialize ideas about masculine sexual prowess and female sexual availability. These depictions are hosted on free pornography websites which provide a seemingly endless menu of sexually explicit content for a hungry audience of viewers. The demand for mainstream pornography is unprecedented, with porn producers continually creating new content to meet consumer demand and preferences. In turn, the audience engages with this content at levels that far surpass the circulation rates ever reported by popular men's magazines such as *Playboy*. Staggering levels of pornography use are reported by sites such as Pornhub, and these rates continue to increase on an annual basis.

In light of internet pornography's immense popularity and in conjunction with its potential to contribute to the development, acquisition, and activation of sexual scripts in viewers (Wright, 2011), we are right to be concerned about how these depictions may affect those who view pornography, and those in relationships with people who do. While pornography can be a powerful sexual aid, a site for sexual pleasure, and a playful addition to couple relationships, the excerpts included in this chapter demonstrate how harmful pornography can also be for men and women. From compulsive viewing of pornography to experiences of sexual coercion, these harms varied between men and women and thereby affirm the need for a gendered lens when conceptualizing and understanding the harms of pornography both for individuals and for those in relationships. In the absence of a utopian world without free and easy access to hardcore, misogynistic content online, it is critical that we continue to apply a gendered lens to our understandings about pornography from a harms-based paradigm. In so doing, these understandings provide a solid foundation for developing effective and holistic relationships and sexual education for adolescents, and for informing future violence prevention efforts which enhance users' safety and well-being in an increasingly digitally-mediated world.

Notes

1. Pornhub insights data suggest that women make up 35% of New Zealand's pornography audience (Pornhub, 2020c).

2. The concept of emerging adulthood is understood as a developmental period characterized by the exploration of life and love in a variety of ways, especially romantic love (Arnett, 2015). Emerging adulthood is also often characterized by the frequent use of pornography (Coyne, Padilla-Walker, & Howard, 2015), and concerns have been raised about emerging adults' susceptibility to the influences of sexually explicit material (Braithwaite, Coulson, Keddington, & Fincham, 2015; Carroll et al., 2008).
3. Interviews were transcribed verbatim and are presented as such throughout this chapter. All participants have been given a pseudonym to ensure anonymity, and pseudonyms accompanied with the age of the participant are used throughout this chapter for individualized quotes.
4. Some participants identified with multiple ethnicities, so the numbers presented here do not add to 24 in total.
5. "Skullfucking" is a commonly used term to describe forcefully penetrating someone's mouth.

References

Amoah, J. D. (1997). Back on the auction block: A discussion of Black women and pornography. *National Black Law Journal, 14*(2), 204–221.

Arnett, J. (2015). *Emerging adulthood: The winding road from the late teens through the twenties.* (2nd ed.). New York, NY: Oxford University Press.

Ashley, V. (2016). Porn – artifice – performance – and the problem of authenticity. *Porn Studies, 3*(2), 187–190. doi:10.1080/23268743.2016.1184481

Attwood, F. (2005). What do people do with porn? Qualitative research into the comsumption, use, and experience of pornography and other sexually explicit media. *Sexuality & Culture, 9*(2), 65–86. doi:10.1007/s12119-005-1008-7

Benjamin, O., & Tlusten, D. (2010). Intimacy and/or degradation: Heterosexual images of togetherness and women's embracement of pornography. *Sexualities, 13*(5), 599–623. doi:10.1177/1363460710376492

Bergen, R. K., & Bogle, K. A. (2000). Exploring the connection between pornography and sexual violence. *Violence & Victims, 15*(3), 227–234.

Bergner, R. M., & Bridges, A. J. (2002). The significance of heavy pornography involvement for romantic partners: Research and clinical implications. *Journal of Sex & Marital Therapy, 28*(3), 193–206. doi:10.1080/009262302760328235

Böhm, M., Franz, P., Dekker, A., & Matthiesen, S. (2015). Desire and dilemma – gender differences in German students' consumption of pornography. *Porn Studies, 2*(1), 76–92. doi:10.1080/23268743.2014.984923

Boyle, K. (2010). Introduction: Everyday pornography. In K. Boyle (Ed.), *Everyday pornography* (pp. 1–14). Abingdon, OX: Routledge.

Boyle, K. (2014). Feminism and pornography. In M. Evans, C. Hemmings, M. Henry, H. Johnstone, S. Madhok, A. Plomien, & S. Wearing (Eds.), *The SAGE handbook of feminist theory* (pp. 215–232). London: SAGE Publications Ltd.

Braithwaite, S. R., Coulson, G., Keddington, K., & Fincham, F. D. (2015). The influence of pornography on sexual scripts and hooking up among emerging adults in college. *Archives of Sexual Behavior, 44*, 111–123.

Bridges, A. J., Bergner, R. M., & Hesson-McInnis, M. (2003). Romantic partners' use of pornography: Its significance for women. *Journal of Sex & Marital Therapy*, *29*(1), 1–14.

Bridges, A. J., Sun, C. F., Ezzell, M. B., & Johnson, J. (2016). Sexual scripts and the sexual behavior of men and women who use pornography. *Sexualization, Media, & Society*, *2*(4). doi:10.1177/2374623816668275

Bridges, A., Wosnitzer, R., Scharrer, E., Sun, C., & Liberman, R. (2010). Aggression and sexual behavior in best-selling pornography videos: A content analysis update. *Violence Against Women*, *16*(10), 1065–1085. doi:10.1177/1077801210382866

Bronstein, C. (2011). *Battling pornography: The American feminist anti-pornography movement, 1976–1986*. New York, NY: Cambridge University Press.

Brownmiller, S. (1975). *Against our will: Men, women and rape*. New York, NY: Simon & Schuster.

Carroll, J. S., Padilla-Walker, L. M., Nelson, L. J., Olson, C. D., McNamara Barry, C., & Madsen, S. D. (2008). Generation XXX: Pornography acceptance and use among emerging adults. *Journal of Adolescent Research*, *23*(1), 6–30. doi:10.1177/0743558407306348

Cossman, B., & Bell, S. (1997). Introduction. In B. Cossman, S. Bell, L. Gotell, & B. Ross (Eds.), *Bad attitudes(s) on trial: Pornography, feminism, and the Butler decision* (pp. 3–47). Toronto, ON: University of Toronto Press.

Coyne, S. M., Padilla-Walker, L. M., & Howard, E. (2015). Media uses in emerging adulthood. In J. J. Arnett (Ed.), *The Oxford handbook of emerging adulthood* (pp. 349–363). New York, NY: Oxford University Press.

Crenshaw, K. (1991). Mapping the margins: Intersectionality, identity politics, and violence against women of color. *Stanford Law Review*, *43*(6), 1241–1299. doi:10.2307/1229039

DeKeseredy, W. S. (2015). Critical criminological understandings of adult pornography and woman abuse: New progressive directions in research and theory. *International Journal for Crime Justice and Social Democracy*, *4*(4), 4–21. doi:10.5204/ijcjsd.v3i2.184

DeKeseredy, W., & Corsianos, M. (2016). *Violence against women in pornography*. New York, NY: Routledge.

DeKeseredy, W. S., & Hall-Sanchez, A. (2017). Adult pornography and violence against women in the heartland: Results from a rural southeast Ohio study. *Violence Against Women*, *23*(7), 830–849. doi:10.1177/1077801216648795

DeKeseredy, W., & Hall-Sanchez, A. (2018). Thinking critically about contemporary adult pornography and woman abuse. In W. DeKeseredy, & M. Dragiewicz (Eds.), *Routledge handbook of critical criminology*. (2nd ed., pp. 280–294). New York, NY: Routledge.

Dines, G. (1998). Dirty business: Playboy magazine and the mainstreaming of pornography. In G. Dines, R. Jensen, & A. Russo (Eds.), *Pornography: The production and consumption of inequality* (pp. 37–64). New York, NY: Routledge.

van Doorn, N. (2010). Keeping it real: User-generated pornography, gender reification, and visual pleasure. *Convergence: The International Journal of Research Into New Media Technologies*, *16*(4), 411–430. doi:10.1177/1354856510375144

Duffy, A., Dawson, D. L., & das Nair, R. (2016). Pornography addiction in adults: A systematic review of definitions and reported impact. *The Journal of Sexual Medicine*, *13*(5), 760–777. doi:10.1016/j.jsxm.2016.03.002

Duggan, L. (1995). Introduction. In L. Duggan, & N. D. Hunter (Eds.), *Sex wars: Sexual dissent and political culture* (pp. 1–14). New York, NY: Routledge.

Duggan, L., Hunter, N. D., & Vance, C. S. (1995). False promises: Feminist anti-pornography legislation. In L. Duggan, & N. D. Hunter (Eds.), *Sex wars: Sexual dissent and political culture* (pp. 43–67). New York, NY: Routledge.

Dworkin, A. (1981). *Pornography: Men possessing women*. New York, NY: Penguin Group.

Dworkin, A., & MacKinnon, C. A. (1988). *Pornography and civil rights: A new day for women's equality*. Minneapolis, MN: Organizing Against Pornography.

Farvid, P., & Braun, V. (2017). Unpacking the "pleasures" and "pains" of heterosexual casual sex: Beyond singular understandings. *The Journal of Sex Research, 54*(1), 73–90. doi:10.1080/00224499.2016.1143442

Farvid, P., Braun, V., & Rowney, C. (2017). 'No girl wants to be called a slut!': Women, heterosexual casual sex and the sexual double standard. *Journal of Gender Studies, 26*(5), 544–560. doi:10.1080/09589236.2016.1150818

Flood, M. (2010). Young men using pornography. In K. Boyle (Ed.), *Everyday pornography* (pp. 164–178). London: Routledge.

Frith, H. (2013). Sexual scripts, sexual refusals and rape. In M. Horvath, & J. Brown (Eds.), *Rape: Challenging contemporary thinking* (pp. 99–124). Abingdon: Routledge.

Fritz, N., & Paul, B. (2017). From orgasms to spanking: A content analysis of the agentic and objectifying sexual scripts in feminist, for women and mainstream pornography. *Sex Roles, 77*, 639–652.

Gorman, S., Monk-Turner, E., & Fish, J. N. (2010). Free adult internet websites: How prevalent are degrading acts? *Gender Issues, 27*, 131–145.

Gossett, J. L., & Byrne, S. (2002). "Click here": A content analysis of internet rape sites. *Gender & Society, 16*(5), 689–709. doi:10.2307/3081955

Gunelius, S. (2009). *Building brand value the Playboy way*. Basingstoke: Palgrave Macmillan.

Gurevich, M., Brown-Bowers, A., Cosma, S., Vasilovsky, A. T., Leedham, U., & Cormier, N. (2017). Sexually progressive and proficient: Pornographic syntax and postfeminist fantasies. *Sexualities, 20*(5–6), 558–584. doi:10.1177/1363460716665785

Hald, G. M., Malamuth, N. N., & Lange, T. (2013). Pornography and sexist attitudes among heterosexuals. *Journal of Communication, 63*(4), 638–660. doi:10.1111/jcom.12037

Hald, G. M., Malamuth, N. M., & Yuen, C. (2010). Pornography and attitudes supporting violence against women: Revisiting the relationship in nonexperimental studies. *Aggressive Behavior, 36*(1), 14–20. doi:10.1002/ab.20328

Jensen, R. (2007). *Getting off: Pornography and the end of masculinity*. Cambridge, MA: South End Press.

Karaian, L. (2005). Troubling the definition of pornography: Little Sisters, a new defining moment in feminists' engagement with the law? *Canadian Journal of Women and the Law, 17*(1), 117.

Katz, J. (2006). *The macho paradox: Why some men hurt women and how all men can help*. Naperville, IL: Sourcebooks, Inc.

Kimmel, M. (2005). *The gender of desire: Essays on male sexuality*. Albany, NY: State University of New York Press.

Klaassen, M. J. E., & Peter, J. (2015). Gender (in)equality in internet pornography: A content analysis of popular pornographic internet videos. *The Journal of Sex Research, 52*(7), 721–735. doi:10.1080/00224499.2014.976781

Ley, D. (2018). The pseudoscience behind public health crisis legislation. *Porn Studies, 5*(2), 208–212.

Ley, D., Prause, N., & Finn, P. (2014). The emperor has no clothes: A review of the 'pornography addiction' model. *Current Sexual Health Reports, 6*, 94–105.

Malamuth, N. M., Addison, T., & Koss, M. (2000). Pornography and sexual aggression: Are there reliable effects and can we understand them? *Annual Review of Sex Research, 11*, 26–91.

Malamuth, N. M., Hald, G. M., & Koss, M. (2012). Pornography, individual differences in risk and men's acceptance of violence against women in a representative sample. *Sex Roles, 66*(7–8), 427–439.

Marshall, E. A., Miller, H. A., & Bouffard, J. A. (2018). Bridging the theoretical gap: Using sexual script theory to explain the relationship between pornography use and sexual coercion. *Journal of Interpersonal Violence*. doi:10.1177/0886260518795170

Mayall, A., & Russell, D. E. H. (1993). Racism in pornography. *Feminism & Psychology, 3*(2), 275–281. doi:10.1177/0959353593032023.

Morgan, R. (1980). Theory and practice: Pornography and rape. In L. Lederer (Ed.), *Take back the night: Women on pornography* (pp. 134–140). New York, NY: William Morrow.

Neville, L. (2018). *Girls who like boys who like boys: Women and gay male pornography and erotica*. Cham: Springer Nature Switzerland AG.

Parvez, Z. F. (2006). The labor of pleasure: How perceptions of emotional labor impact women's enjoyment of pornography. *Gender & Society, 20*(5), 605–631. doi: 10.1177/0891243206291109

Peter, J., & Valkenburg, P. M. (2016). Adolescents and pornography: A review of 20 years of research. *The Journal of Sex Research, 53*(4–5), 509–531. doi:10.1080/00224499.2016.1143441

Pornhub. (2019). Year in review. Retrieved from https://www.pornhub.com/insights/2019-year-in-review.

Pornhub. (2020a). Coronavirus traffic update. Retrieved from https://www.pornhub.com/insights/coronavirus-update-april-14. Accessed on April 14, 2020.

Pornhub. (2020b). Landing page. Retrieved from www.pornhub.com. Accessed on April 28, 2020.

Pornhub. (2020c). Pornhub & New Zealand. Retrieved from https://www.pornhub.com/insights/pornhub-new-zealand. Accessed on 28 April, 2020.

Resch, M. N., & Alderson, K. G. (2014). Female partners of men who use pornography: Are honesty and mutual use associated with relationship satisfaction? *Journal of Sex & Marital Therapy, 40*(5), 410–424. doi:10.1080/0092623X.2012.751077

Rubin, G. (1984). Thinking sex: Notes for a radical theory of the politics of sexuality. In C. S. Vance (Ed.), *Pleasure and danger: Exploring female sexuality* (pp. 267–312). New York, NY: Routledge.

Schneider, J. P. (2000). Effects of cybersex addiction on the family: Results of a survey. *Sexual Addiction & Compulsivity, 7*(1–2), 31–58. doi:10.1080/10720160008400206

Shaw, S. M. (1999). Men's leisure and women's lives: The impact of pornography on women. *Leisure Studies, 18*(3), 197–212. doi:10.1080/026143699374925

Shor, E. (2019). Age, aggression, and pleasure in popular online pornographic videos. *Violence Against Women, 25*(8), 1018–1036. doi:10.1177/1077801218804101

Shor, E., & Golriz, G. (2019). Gender, race, and aggression in mainstream pornography. *Archives of Sexual Behavior, 48*, 739–751. doi:10.1007/s10508-018-1304-6

Simon, W., & Gagnon, J. H. (1986). Sexual scripts: Permanence and change. *Archives of Sexual Behavior, 15*(2), 97–120.

Smith, C., & Attwood, F. (2014). Anti/pro/critical porn studies. *Porn Studies, 1*(1–2), 7–23. doi:10.1080/23268743.2014.887364

Smith, C., Barker, M., & Attwood, F. (2015). Why do people watch porn? Results from PornResearch.Org. In L. T. Comella, & Shira (Eds.), *New views on pornography: Sexuality, politics, and the law* (pp. 277–296). Santa Barbara, CA: ABC-CLIO, LLC.

Sniewski, L., & Farvid, P. (2020). Hidden in shame: Heterosexual men's experiences of self-perceived problematic pornography use. *Psychology of Men & Masculinities, 21*(2), 201–212. doi:10.1037/men0000232

Sniewski, L., Farvid, P., & Carter, P. (2018). The assessment and treatment of adult heterosexual men with self-perceived problematic pornography use: A review. *Addictive Behaviors, 77*, 217–224. doi:10.1016/j.addbeh.2017.10.010

Sostar, T., & Sullivan, R. (2017). The money shot in feminist queer and mainstream pornographies. In T. Miller (Ed.), *The Routledge companion to global popular culture* (pp. 197–206). New York, NY: Routledge.

Stewart, D. N., & Szymanski, D. M. (2012). Young adult women's reports of their male romantic partner's pornography use as a correlate of their self-esteem, relationship quality, and sexual satisfaction. *Sex Roles, 67*(5), 257–271. doi:10.1007/s11199-012-0164-0

Sun, C., Bridges, A., Johnson, J. A., & Ezzell, M. B. (2016). Pornography and the male sexual script: An analysis of consumption and sexual relations. *Archives of Sexual Behavior, 45*(4), 983–994. doi:10.1007/s10508-014-0391-2

Sun, C., Ezzell, M., & Kendall, O. (2017). Naked aggression: The meaning and practice of ejaculation on a woman's face. *Violence Against Women, 23*(14), 1710–1729.

Tarrant, S. (2016). *The pornography industry: What everyone needs to know*. New York, NY: Oxford University Press.

Tylka, T., & Kroon Van Diest, A. M. (2015). You looking at her "hot" body may not be "cool" for me: Integrating male partners' pornography use into objectification theory for women. *Psychology of Women Quarterly, 39*(1), 67–84. doi:10.1177/0361684314521784

Vance, C. S. (1984). Pleasure and danger: Towards a politics of sexuality. In C. S. Vance (Ed.), *Pleasure and danger: Exploring female sexuality* (pp. 1–27). London: Routledge.

Vannier, S. A., Currie, A. B., & O'Sullivan, L. F. (2014). Schoolgirls and soccer moms: A content analysis of free "teen" and "MILF" online pornography. *The Journal of Sex Research, 51*(3), 253–264. doi:10.1080/00224499.2013.829795

Vera-Gray, F., & McGlynn, C. (2020). Regulating pornography: Developments in evidence, theory and law. In C. Ashford, & A. Maine (Eds.), *Research handbook on gender, sexuality and the law* (pp. 471–483). Cheltingham: Edwar Elgar Publishing, Ltd. Retrieved from https://www.elgaronline.com/view/edcoll/9781788111140/9781788111140.00044.xml

Walker, A. (1980). Coming apart. In L. Lederer (Ed.), *Take back the night: Women on pornography* (pp. 84–93). New York, NY: William Morrow.

Wright, P. J. (2011). Mass media effects on youth sexual behavior assessing the claim for causality. *Annals of the International Communication Association*, *35*(1), 343–385. doi:10.1080/23808985.2011.11679121

Wright, P. J. (2013). Internet pornography exposure and women's attitude towards extramarital sex: An exploratory study. *Communication Studies*, *64*(3), 315–336. doi:10.1080/10510974.2012.755643

Young, M. (2014). Authenticity and its role within feminist pornography. *Porn Studies*, *1*(1–2), 186–188. doi:10.1080/23268743.2014.888250

Zhou, Y., & Paul, B. (2016). Lotus Blossom or dragon lady: A content analysis of 'Asian women' online pornography. *Sexuality & Culture*, *20*(4), 1083–1100. doi: 10.1007/s12119-016-9375-9

Chapter 18

Intimate Image Dissemination and Consent in a Digital Age: Perspectives from the Front Line

Olga Marques

Abstract

Media attention on nonconsensual intimate image dissemination has led to the relatively recent proliferation of academic research on the topic. This literature has focused on many areas including victimization and perpetration prevalence rates, coerced sexting, legal and/or criminal contexts, sexual violence in digital spaces, gendered constructions of blame and risk, and legal analysis of high-profile cases and legislation. Despite this research, several gaps exist, including a lack of empirical research with service providers. Informed by in-depth interviews with 10 sexual violence frontline professionals in Southern Ontario (Canada), this chapter focuses on their perspectives of the additive role of technology. With respect to nonconsensual intimate image dissemination, technology acts as a digital "layer" that operates in addition to the commission of physical acts of sexual violence, and compounds the harms experienced by the victim by adding a virtual – and indelible – "permanent remembering" of the violence. Nuancing the contours of consent in a digital age, this chapter concludes by considering what consent means in a technological context.

Keywords: Nonconsensual intimate image dissemination; consent; permanent remembering; sexual violence; frontline workers; barriers to legal system

Introduction

Public outrage, particularly by women students, was garnered following reports that a revenge pornography website[1] was targeting universities (Green, 2018). In

The Emerald International Handbook of Technology-Facilitated Violence and Abuse, 309–328

doi:10.1108/978-1-83982-848-520211022

2018, the website, which had entries for several Canadian universities in the Greater Toronto Area (GTA), stated that it specialized in the "trade, sale, and distribution of sexually explicit images and videos of women, without their consent."[2] Users could view images and videos, leave comments, and request more images of particular women, offering money in exchange. Images were shared through a temporary file-storing service that deleted personal information, such as IP addresses, 48 hours after uploading. In April 2018, after Dutch police shut down the site (Liptak, 2018), reader comments on news message boards as well as social media responses were polarized by those lauding police efforts, and those blaming the women themselves. Most telling among these responses were those that suggested the futility of shutting down such websites, including a reader comment posted to the Liptak (2018) news report by @thewhitesand that stated: "One door closes, another opens. [Redacted] will resurface under a new name in no time," (April 29, 2018), as well as a single (and since deleted) tweet by @satancow, the only tweet ever posted by this account at the time: "#[redacted] #youcannotwin You may stop one, but will only give rise to another. Good luck stopping us all" (May 15, 2018). The fact that a website focused on posting nude images of women without their consent or knowledge was able to exist and be supported solidifies the urgency of further understanding the harms and implications of nonconsensual intimate image dissemination.

Extant media attention to nonconsensual intimate image dissemination, often colloquially and problematically referred to as "revenge pornography" (see e.g., McGlynn, Rackley, & Houghton, 2017; Powell, Henry, & Flynn, 2018), has led to the relatively recent emergence of academic research on the topic. Existing research has largely focused on ascertaining victimization and perpetration prevalence rates (e.g., Branch, Hilinski-Rosick, Johnson, & Solano, 2017; Eaton, Jacobs, & Ruvalcaba, 2018; Henry et al., 2020; Powell, Henry, Flynn, & Scott, 2019; Powell, Scott, Flynn, & Henry, 2020), coerced sexting (e.g., Lee & Crofts, 2015; Wolak, Finkelhor, Walsh, & Treitman, 2018), the legal and/or criminal context (Bloom, 2014; Flynn & Henry, 2019; Slane, 2013; Slane & Langlois, 2018), sexual violence in digital spaces (e.g., Fairbairn, 2015; Powell & Henry, 2017), gendered constructions of blame and risk (e.g., Karaian, 2014; Starr & Lavis, 2018), and legal analysis of specific high-profile cases and legislation (e.g., Henry, Flynn, & Powell, 2019; Penney, 2016). Despite this, several research gaps exist. For instance, empirical research focusing exclusively on the experiences of survivors is lacking (see Bates, 2017; Henry et al., 2020; McGlynn et al., 2019, 2020; Walker & Sleath, 2017 for exceptions). While much research has focused on prevalence rates of nonconsensual intimate image sharing, few have attended to the motivations of perpetrators (see Henry et al., 2020; Powell et al., 2019; Walker & Sleath, 2017 for exceptions). In addition, there exists a lack of empirical research on nonconsensual intimate image dissemination, which focuses on the perspectives of sexual violence service providers (see Henry, Flynn, & Powell, 2018 for exception).

This chapter seeks to contribute to the existing knowledge on the issue of nonconsensual intimate image dissemination by focusing on professionals' perspectives and understandings of the additive role that technology plays in the harms and impacts of sexual violence. This chapter focuses on intimate image/

video dissemination as a digital "layer" that operates in addition to the commission of physical acts of sexual violence, and which compounds the harms experienced by the victim by adding a virtual – and indelible – "permanent remembering" (Mayer-Schönberger, 2009, p. 127) of the violence (see also Henry et al., 2020; McGlynn et al., 2019, 2020). The permanency of images, as well as the trauma associated with the "threat" that images/videos can be released at any time in the future, without warning, becomes part of the crisis that frontline professionals must address in their responses. This chapter concludes by considering what consent means in a technological context. Here, I seek to nuance the contours of consent in a digital age, extending beyond the theoretical frameworks of cyberbullying or risk management proffered in existing literature, and engage with the discussions highlighted by the research participants as they grapple with this question.

Research Overview

In-depth, semi-structured qualitative interviews were conducted with 10 professionals working in various capacities employed in organizations that provide counseling and support services to women victims of sexual assault and violence generally, in a large suburban regional area in Southern Ontario, Canada.[3] These professionals included executive directors, program managers, counsellors, and nurses. Interviews were conducted in the respondents' private offices, recorded, and transcribed. Interview length ranged from 35 minutes to 1 hour.

The overall purpose of this research was twofold. First, to discover, describe, and understand the perspectives of frontline sexual violence support professionals on the topic of nonconsensual intimate image dissemination. Second, to explore generalized accounts of the contexts and situations where this act/crime is perpetrated, how client disclosures are navigated, as well as the supports/counseling currently available and offered. The interview questions were designed to address these research purposes.

The research itself focused on organizations, and not what individual professionals may or may not do in individual practice. No identifying information about clients was shared, and the following statement was highlighted in the Letter of Informed Consent: "Participants are responsible for ensuring that anything they discuss within the interviews does not violate the terms of their licensing and confidentiality which must be maintained in their practice." In order to further protect the identity of clients, all identifying organizational information was anonymized, or redacted and replaced with general descriptors. In this chapter, only the generalized job titles of the interview respondents (e.g., manager) are used.

While victimization research continues to find high overall incidence rates of sexual violence, it remains one of the most underreported of the violent crimes (Beres, Crow, & Gotell, 2009; Chon, 2014; Patterson, Greeson, & Campbell, 2009). There exists much research on barriers to formal police reporting, including feelings of shame, guilt, and/or embarrassment; fear of not being believed; perceived responsibility for the assault; and notions that the victimization did not reflect stereotypical characterizations of sexual assault (cf. Chon, 2014; Flynn, 2015; Patterson et al., 2009; Sable, Danis, Mauzy, & Gallagher, 2006). Of course, while individuals who experience unwanted sexual violence may not be reporting to the police, research suggests they may be disclosing to and seeking out counseling and emotional support from other service providers, such as community clinics, private mental health professionals, or speciality agencies such as rape crisis centers (Campbell, 2006). In Ontario, Canada, the 42 sexual assault centers combined receive an estimated 50,000 crisis calls annually (Rushowy, 2020). Research on sexual violence support services as well as disclosure and reporting rates and/or barriers are important to understanding the broader context in which victimization by nonconsensual intimate image dissemination is situated. McGlynn et al. (2017) argue that this type of sexual violence "should be understood as just one form of a range of gendered, sexualized forms of abuse which have common characteristics forming what we have conceptualized as the 'continuum of image-based sexual abuse'" (p. 26).

Questioning whether or not independent rape crisis centers play a unique role in their communities for survivors of sexual violence and the community at large, O'Sullivan and Carlton (2001) argue that they do:

> ...independent centres were the only ones that advanced inclusive definitions of sexual assault, incorporated cultural concerns in assessing their services and outreach, used volunteers as community educators, and targeted community education to young people and males. Second, embedded centres, particularly ones within domestic violence programs, seem to underserve sexual assault victims in the community. [...] The staff members and volunteers of the independent centres focus solely on sexual assault. They read the sexual assault literature. Their clients have all been affected by sexual assault. When they speak at schools, community gatherings, and in-service training sessions, they talk about sexual assault. They observe how people respond to sexual violence, and they reflect on what they see and hear. They try to be more inclusive and to understand variations in their client population, that is, who is likely to never contact them, who calls only once, and who uses and benefits from available services (p. 356).

Given their position within society and research indicating that community service providers are more likely to hear disclosures of sexual violence than formal reporting institutions like the police, it is important to understand how frontline service, support, and counseling providers are navigating the new virtual terrain. This is particularly so, given the types of challenges this can raise, considering that "nonconsensual pornography did not exist on such a broad scale even five years ago" (Bates, 2017, p. 25), and images can initially be obtained through consensual sharing between parties with the expectation they will not be distributed outside those parameters (Bates, 2017).

This chapter relies heavily on Mayer-Schönberger's (2009) concept of "permanent remembering," a term introduced in the book *Delete: The Virtue of Forgetting in the Digital Age*. Tracing the history of memory – the basis of human knowledge – Mayer-Schönberger (2009) questions the implications of permanent digital memory. While critiques might suggest that a key benefit of digital technology is that it compensates for the inability of the human mind to remember everything, Mayer-Schönberger (2009) argues that this benefit should not be at the expense of the valuable capacity to forget. The consequences, it is argued, of not being able to leave our pasts behind, is a more unforgiving future. In the same way that Jeremy Bentham conceptualized prison as an all-seeing and ever-present panopticon where prisoners are watched, it can be argued that this panopticon now extends to society more broadly across time and cyberspace. As Mayer-Schönberger (2009, p. 127) asserts, "At the interface of power and time, permanent remembering creates the specter of a spatial and temporal panopticon, in which everybody may constantly be tempted to self-censor." As a result of the knowledge of the permanency of digital traces, risk management language is deployed cautioning us to be cognizant of our digital footprint, as well as about what, where, and for whom, we post virtually.

While Mayer-Schönberger (2009) does not speak specifically about sexual violence or nonconsensual intimate image dissemination or the ramifications of "permanent remembering" for victims of these crimes, these ideas can – and should – be extended to this area (see Henry et al., 2020; McGlynn et al., 2019). The questions posed of digital memory, the inability to forget, and the self-policing and censorship surrounding this virtual panopticon provide an analytic entry point to contextualize the accounts of sexual violence support and/or counseling professionals, and situate the experiences of those who seek support after having their intimate images and videos nonconsensually disseminated.

Digital Layer Lends to "Permanent Remembering"

The sexual violence professionals interviewed for this study had much to say regarding the ways in which victimization by nonconsensual intimate image dissemination is disclosed within their respective organizations. The contexts in which this victimization occurs varied. Some participants described examples where images were initially shared consensually within the confines of a relationship then subsequently released. Others mentioned images being "stolen" from devices or manipulated. Some participants reported victims were coerced to take images, and others described acts of sexual violence being recorded and disseminated. However, what was evident throughout the interviews was the additional layer of trauma, support, and healing that this type of victimization necessitated. As one nurse described:

> I don't know if there is a lot of education around what the ramifications are, and when it is no longer a loving relationship or fun anymore. And we do know victims when they found out later that pictures where taken … maybe a picture was shown to

> them, or their friend sends them a picture saying "is this you?" And they didn't even know a picture was taken because they were sleeping. Or it can be a consensual relationship, but the person took a picture of them sleeping. The picture was not taken under consent, and then they are feeling violated.

Since nonconsensual intimate image dissemination is technologically facilitated and exists through digital spaces, this poses an additional layer that counsellors and support providers must navigate. Throughout the interviews, all respondents spoke to the permanency of these images and how part of their service or counseling practice related to working through associated feelings of (at least partial) self-responsibilization, as well as the practicalities of dealing with the virtual world. All respondents reported that clients had different sorts of questions and concerns related to being victimized in this way. For instance, an executive director stated:

> … they are wanting to address the feelings associated with that. Feelings of powerlessness, of shame, of feeling victimized sexually, sexually interfered with or violence in some way. Even though it is virtual as opposed to physical. Dealing with the practicalities of "What can I do?" "What are my options?" With youth, when they have shared those images, they are not necessarily wanting to get that person into trouble. Or maybe they are, but they aren't because of the implications of that for them socially. So it's not always super easy to navigate.

Mayer-Schönberger (2009, p. 127) writes that:

> [C]omprehensive digital remembering collapses history, impairing our judgement and our capacity to act in time. It denies us humans the chance to evolve, develop, and learn, leaving us helplessly oscillating between two equally troubling options: a permanent past and an ignorant present.

This is a poignant statement when related to the effects of nonconsensual intimate image dissemination. The pictures or videos circulating virtually are permanent vestiges of broken trust and acts of violence. While therapeutic support, and even legal intervention, may assist in an individual's ability to cope, survive, and thrive *post* physical acts of sexual violence, the permanency associated with digital spaces results in a *post* that is ambiguous. Is there even a *post* when images and videos are virtual? As a victim/survivor in McGlynn et al.'s (2019, p. 7) study of 60 victims across Australia, New Zealand, and the United Kingdom observed:

> Maybe you could have something happen to you that was traumatic, but you don't have to necessarily feel like you're

> defined by it for the rest of your life. But with this, there's such a level of permanence which affects everything … especially if it's impossible now to take photos down, especially if it's impossible to stop the dissemination of the images … There will never be a day in my entire lifetime that all of the images of me could ever be deleted.

This space of uncertainty is also captured in my interviews by a counselor who claimed:

> … the impact of something like this cannot be just devastating, but can be lifelong. This is the kind of thing that one potentially carries with them for the rest of their lives. And if you add to that the additional fear that other people will find out, and the image of them is floating out there in cyber world, that's also terrifying. Because you are waiting for the "ball to drop" sort of thing. …The impact of that alone is quite devastating, because anybody can find out. So now they are trying to deal with something that has happened to them, while also simultaneously having been exposed sort of to the world.

This reiterates Mayer-Schönberger (2009) statement that we become "helpless" to a past that is permanent and to a present – and even a future – that we cannot anticipate.

Within the context of nonconsensual intimate image dissemination, the sexual violence does not cease. The threat of revictimization by the same act will always be present. As one executive director observed:

> …you are not just dealing with the original assault, you are also dealing with all of these other fears and shame and, you know, everything that can come out of that. It doesn't go away. When something is on the internet or shared on social media, and you haven't put it up there, you don't have the control to take it down. It is there forever. How do you deal with that? How do you deal with the possibility of it coming up over and over in your life? It's hard to get closure that way.

As the popular idiom "forgive and forget" suggests, in order to make the decision to move past any given act, incident, or event that caused harm, a modicum of not remembering is required. This does not mean that harms are excused or forgotten, nor does it mean that the individual is in denial, but rather that a decision is made to work through, and potentially let go of feelings of resentment, so that the traumatic event does not become central to one's identity, or poorly incorporated into one's broader autobiographical memory (cf. Burkell, 2016; Ehlers & Clark, 2000). Therapeutically working through associations that trigger memories of traumatic events and/or induce emotional responses, and coming up with coping strategies is often part of professional practice; however, the virtual nature of nonconsensual intimate image dissemination poses challenges in identifying these associations. As a nurse described to me:

> It's very difficult because there is no, there is no reconciliation for that. How do you fix that? You can't. So it is then something that the victims have to think about for the rest of their lives. That there are images out there that they have no control over, and there is no way of eliminating them forever.

Mayer-Schönberger (2009) highlights the important role that forgetting has played throughout history, indicating that "[s]ince the beginning of time, for us humans, forgetting has been the norm and remembering the exception" (p. 2). Digital and virtual technology has turned this dynamic around, in that "forgetting has become the exception, and remembering the default" (p. 2). Providing examples of adults who have suffered repercussions (e.g., job loss, public shaming) when memories resurfaced online from incidents or mistakes of their youth, Mayer-Schönberger (2009, p. 3) asks, "Do we want a future that is forever unforgiving because it is unforgetting?" The response to this question may vary depending on the group or topic in question, particularly during current times characterized by the hashtags #cancelculture or #calloutculture[4] (Romano, 2019). But it important to question: What can the future look like for individuals whose victimization is indelibly etched in the virtual world?

Compounding of Trauma

Across the interviews, a key theme emerged surrounding the potential consequences of the digital traces of victimization that are left behind and how these digital traces serve to compound the trauma that is already being experienced. While the previous section spoke to the digital layer of trauma, and how acts of sexual violence experienced physically are also re-experienced virtually, the additive trauma and/or potential consequences incurred as a result of having intimate images disseminated nonconsensually online extend well beyond this.

Considerations were made within the interviews to consequences to personal safety, potential judgment, as well as impacts to future job opportunities. As one executive director described:

> It's hard enough that they're dealing with the trauma, after the sexual assault, but then dealing with the possibility of their image being shared with god knows who, you know, whether it is in their own country, in another country, are people going to see it? What effect is that going to have on you down the road? What assumptions might be made about you because of that? Are there people that are going to judge you, you know, who may not realize that this was not consensual? … Just dealing with those initial fears. Fears around your own security, your own safety.

> What if somebody sees it and then they track her down? Being approached on social media. Would somebody try to reach out to her friends? Her family? Share information about this?

Another executive director similarly reflected:

> It's not just the consequence of "well this person betrayed my trust," it's the trauma that you know victims or survivors of this endure. It's ongoing. This is now out in the world, and we don't know who's hand it's in. And we don't know where it is. And if you are looking for a job later on, and how this would perpetually impact your life. And that's a deep trauma that we have to constantly process with the client that we support. In terms of how they are feeling, and the embarrassment, the shame; there's so many therapeutic pieces that needs to be addressed.

That virtual spaces and digital memory offers a permanent and – for corporations, governments, and even law enforcement – a "usable" record of any given individual's deeds, misdeeds, actions, opinions, preferences, and so forth, is something that warrants much consideration. Individuals and societies will be altered as we move toward a lived reality where all of our digital transactions leave permanent digital traces; a dystopian future where our digital pasts may constrain our presents (Mayer-Schönberger, 2009). While some may neglect to grasp the scope of the issue of "permanent remembering," others may cling to the notion that they have "nothing to hide," and only those who contravened against societal norms will be affected. The public vitriol, shaming, and threats against Melissa Petro,[5] for instance, and the subsequent loss of her teaching job after she wrote an op-ed about her brief time as a sex worker when she was 19, evinces that we must seriously consider what digital recall means for our lives. Petro (2017) continues to write that years after the publication of this op-ed, and despite being employed in many other fields, her work in the sex industry continues to surface virtually as her main identifier.

Morality, value, and worth continue to be tied to women's sexual passivity, while women who are actively sexual, particularly in nonsocially normative ways, are slut-shamed, victim-blamed, and responsibilized for any harms incurred (Marques & Rinaldi, 2020). This suggests there are particular gendered realities and consequences to "permanent remembering" that must be considered.

Digital memory creates an illusion that we know someone's character, denies the possibility of change, and stymies decision-making and critical thought, as we have somehow come to believe that digital records are comprehensive accounts and complete. We have media reports of the impacts of digital memory for individuals who actively either posted accounts, videos, or images online, or at the very least, actively and consensually engaged in the acts or words depicted. However, we must reflect upon the impacts for individuals who have had images or videos nonconsensually disseminated – particularly in the case of intimate images and/or videos of women and teenage girls.

Research exists on victim-blaming and rape myth acceptance generally, which serves to both responsibilize female victims for sexual violence incurred against them and minimize the realities of the scope of sexual violence (cf. Bailey, 2015; Edwards, Turchik, Dardis, Reynolds, & Gidycz, 2011). As a result of rape myth acceptance, we are seeing calls for teenage girls and women to just *not* take intimate images and/or videos because, as Starr and Lavis (2018) indicate, "a victim of revenge porn may be viewed as responsible for taking and sending an image to someone in the first place" (p. 428; see also, Henry et al., 2019; Powell et al., 2018, 2020). It is without a doubt that the digital ways in which we are engaging with sexuality and sexual practice, as well as the virtual nature of the nonconsensual intimate image dissemination, pose interesting questions related to consent and what consent looks like in a technological context, which I explore below.

Consent in the Technological Context

Consent is the defining criteria when measuring what constitutes sexual violence within law, research, and interpersonal interactions (Burgin & Flynn, 2019; Humphreys, 2007). However, there exists much conversation within the literature about what consent means, and what it can mean when decontextualized from conversations about hetero-patriarchal constructions of normative – and thus good and moral – sexual practice; the pleasures of sex and not just its dangers and consequences; and the shackles of constructs such as virginity, purity, and women's marital duty (Marques & Rinaldi, 2020). This is all to suggest that while definitions of sexual consent are inscribed by law (for example, s. 273.1(1) of the *Criminal Code* of Canada) and guidelines for organizations with respect to collection and disclosure of personal information in a privacy context exist (for example, Office of the Privacy Commissioner of Canada, 2018), in interpersonal and relational practice, consent is much more nuanced.

While much scholarly and activist attention has advocated for affirmative consent – the knowing and voluntary assent to sexual activity throughout all stages of a sexual interaction, also known as the "enthusiastic yes" – much media-led conversation has been leveled against its "plain unworkability" (see for instance, McArdle, 2019). For example, Burgin and Flynn (2019) found that in practice, gendered narratives of implied consent – a perpetrator's subjective interpretation of a woman's ordinary behavior as indicative of her consent to sex – endure in sexual assault trials. It is no wonder that consent, particularly consent within the context of digital technology, was a significant topic of discussion during the interviews.

All research participants had much to say with respect to consent, how the contours of consent – what it is, what it means, and how it is articulated – become more malleable and unclear when an act of sexual violence takes places virtually, and when, in nonconsensual intimate image dissemination, the initial image may have been shared consensually. Within the context of taken and subsequently shared pictures and videos, the meaning of consent and the revocation of consent become blurred. These nuances are captured by the following counselor's comments:

> What is consent and do you waive consent when you send a photo? Like that's something that could be part of an act, is that consent waived? Is that something people need to know about? But again, that still should not give the right to someone to share it. But that risk is always there. And even if that individual doesn't share it, something can get stuck in the communication, in the middle. So it's not always necessarily the person you sent it to that did it, but someone that was in between that line of technology that got access to it.

A nurse similarly claimed:

> If you don't really understand what your actions are, then you are really not in a position to give consent. And if you don't understand the risks of taking nude pictures of yourself and sending them out, then you are not really consenting to it, even though you are doing it. Even though consent is fluid, you can consent one minute and not the next. You can stop the sex act in the middle of it if you don't like it or if it's making you uncomfortable. But, once that send button is done on those pictures, you can't rescind your consent. And even if you do, it doesn't really matter, it's gone. It's out there. So it doesn't really matter what you consent to or not. You might have regrets the next day, or 30 friends point fingers at you and laugh, it's too late now to consent.

All participants raised the notion that consent in a technological context must extend to the potential foreseen and unforeseen consequences of the digital social sphere. In other words, consent does not just begin and end with taking an image and sharing it, but to the digital memory of those images. As a program manager described:

> I don't think that young people understand that just because they have an image that other people should be able to share it. I feel like they don't understand what consent even means. That consent is a clear "yeah, I am putting this out there to share." And that even if you are sharing with your group of friends who you approved, doesn't mean that they should be able to share that with their friends, and with their friends. I don't think they understand that. I just don't think that young people even always understand what consent means. That they have the right to clearly say "yes" or "no" for anything want, and it is not just for physical acts, but acts that happen through technology.

There is no denying that many of us live at least part of our lives on online platforms and use technology to facilitate sharing and communication within relationships. For youth, the digitization of their lives and experiences has always existed and is "normal." As a result, many interview participants – especially those who worked with youth – spoke about the challenges of teaching youth that online spaces are neither "safe" nor private to their own social worlds. For instance, a counselor observed:

> I think the internet can be a very scary place and I am not too sure if enough teaching is being done around what is safe and what isn't safe. What can be posted and what shouldn't be posted. I think the innocence is that, you know, I can send my boyfriend this picture and it goes to my boyfriend. And as soon as there is that falling out, or power and control concerns come into play, and now it gets sent forward to whoever it may be. So videos, anything, and not realizing what the final outcome could look like just from sending a picture, or a message, or a video.

When describing consent, several participants were clear that we should be careful to not allow fears of digital memory to inculcate victim-blaming through discourses of risk management, or bring back regressive and sex-negative ideas about "appropriate" sexual conduct, especially appropriate sexual conduct for women and teenage girls. Corporeal agency still exists. Instead, we should attend to better educating ourselves as to what consent is, what consent means, and to the realities of lack of ownership over redistribution and future dissemination once content is shared digitally. This is reflected in this executive director's comments:

> It's your right to share your pictures, your body to who you consent to do that to, and that doesn't give them the right to share it once it's their possession. But on the other side, once you give it to someone, you have no control about what they did with it, right? ... Educating young people about the nuances of consent. I think they are learning the wrong information. They are learning "yes means yes" and "no means no," and that's not really the true definition of consent. It can't be given under pressure, has to be ongoing, there are so many elements. I think young people need to understand what could happen if they send this to someone. That it could possibly be sent out. Without blaming them, without making them feel like it's their fault. But that a potential consequence of sharing, is that it is no longer under your control. It is in the world, and it could go into other people's hands that you didn't intend it to go to.

While research and laws are attempting to keep pace with cyber-criminality and cyber-victimization, it is important to ensure that individuals engaging in their regular everyday lives are considered. This can be seen in research that being a perpetrator or victim of nonconsensual intimate image dissemination is outside of some people's thought processes. Rather, they are focused on expressing their sexuality and engaging relationally with others using digital tools, and in accordance with social constructions of appropriately gendered sexual expressions, roles, and expectations (Lee & Crofts, 2015; Marques & Rinaldi, 2020). More nuanced understandings of consent, what it means, and what it looks like are required – even more so when applied to the digital world.

The Search for Solutions

In accounting for individual consequences as a result of digital remembering (e.g., individuals who failed to get hired or were terminated when records of their past emerged online), historically tracing the history of human forgetting, and documenting the rise of technologies that allow for "permanent remembering," Mayer-Schönberger (2009) outlines six potential solutions to the problem. Some of these draw on digital rights management, privacy laws, and the passage – and enforcement – of regulatory and legal measures. One solution that is a common fixture in current online risk management strategies is digital abstinence. Digital abstinence suggests that individuals themselves play a central role in the compilation of their own digital image. Mayer-Schönberger (2009, p. 129) argues, "If one abstains from putting personal information online, one does not have to fear the consequences of an enduring digital memory – neither loss of control and power over information, nor being exposed to the digital panopticon or impaired reasoning."

To those well versed in sexual violence and rape myth acceptance literature, digital abstinence may sound familiar to the "she was walking at night by herself," "she is promiscuous," and "she was asking to be raped in that outfit" statements that evince victim-blaming rhetoric (see also, Flynn, 2015). If you do not want to be sexually victimized, just do not allow yourself to be victimized. If you do not want people to see your intimate images, just do not take them. Anything short of this abstinence renders you, as this rhetoric suggests, responsibilized and culpable (Powell et al., 2013, 2018). Of course, digital abstinence or victim-blaming rhetoric fails to account for how relationships have been technologized, relieves the onus of responsibility on the person who perpetrated the harm, and ignores that disseminated intimate images and videos may not have always been initially created in contexts of full consent (see Henry et al., 2020; Powell et al., 2020). As noted previously, Mayer-Schönberger (2009) is not writing specifically about violence, so the six potential solutions or responses outlined do not consider the impacts to victims of digitally perpetrated violence. However, Mayer-Schönberger (2009) also does not advocate digital abstinence (which is virtually impossible in current Western societies), nor to the other solutions outlined. Instead, the solution he proposes is to impose expiration dates on every single piece of information that is online – from emails, search terms, online purchase histories, pictures, to files on our hard drives. While this does not yet exist, he calls for the creation of simple interfaces to allow the user to specify what the data expiry date should be. While an analysis of this proposed solution is beyond the scope of this chapter, it begs the importance of working toward creative solutions that consider the impacts on victims of digitally perpetrated violence and do not focus solely on more laws and more regulations which do not serve to address the social contexts in which gender-based sexual violence arises and persists.

On March 10, 2015, the Protecting Canadians from Online Crime Act amended the *Criminal Code* of Canada. Included provisions are: (1) making criminal the nonconsensual distribution of intimate images, (2) empowering courts to order the removal of such images from the internet, (3) permitting the forfeiture of the devices used in the commission of the offense, and (4 reimbursing victims for costs incurred as a result of removing the images from the internet and elsewhere (Government of Canada, 2015). Despite the fact that it is been five years since the sharing of intimate images or videos without consent became a crime in Canada, police continue to receive thousands of complaints from individuals whose images have been posted or circulated (Allen, 2019). This suggests a disconnect between rendering an act criminal, its policing of it, lived experiences surrounding the role of digital technologies in sexual relationships, as well as broader public understandings of sexual harm and sexual privacy. This is to say that disclosures of nonconsensual intimate image dissemination will likely also increase to community support services and specialized rape crisis centers. Given that sexual violence offenses are among the least formally reported (Beres et al., 2009; Chon, 2014; Patterson et al., 2009), and when they are, existing research dictates experiences of revictimization or inadequate law enforcement response (cf. Chon, 2014; Flynn, 2015; Patterson et al., 2009; Sable et al., 2006), it is likely that these community and specialized supports are more likely to hear about these offenses. Attending to the practicalities of what such supports should look like, and what types of clinical or therapeutic strategies are the most efficacious in attending to the various issues and concerns associated with being victimized in this manner, should be a central focus for community service providers.

While Mayer-Schönberger (2009) does not write specifically about sexual or gender-based violence, extending his analysis to this area forces us to ask what the impacts of "permanent remembering" might be for those whose sexual victimization was in whole, or in part, facilitated digitally and disseminated virtually. As more people continue to engage with technology to facilitate communication and engage with others, a more cogent analysis of the impacts of the permanence of digital memory and the inability to forget is necessary. Such analysis must extend beyond debates over privacy in cyberspace or even cyberbullying. To be clear, nonconsensual intimate image dissemination is not *only* an issue of (sexual) privacy or bullying (through coercion or manipulation), although it can comprise both these types of harm. Above all, however, it is an issue of violence – more specifically, gender-based violence (McGlynn et al., 2017). Attending to the gendered component of sexual violence, particularly the gendered nature of nonconsensual intimate image dissemination, is also of central concern, however challenging. As Beres (2009, p. 159) notes:

> At a policy and discursive level, we are witnessing the decontextualization of "crime" from social conditions and power relations that contribute to the widespread problem of sexual violence. While committed to "a get tough on crime agenda," the Harper Conservative government cut the budget of Status of Women Canada by 40%, removed the word "equality" from its mandate and fundamentally altered the funding criteria for women's organizations, making research and activities related to activism ineligible for funding.

Research suggests that nonconsensual dissemination of intimate images for the purposes of revenge occurs across heterosexual and same-sex couples is perpetrated by both males and females, and includes both males and females as its targets (Starr & Lavis, 2018). Despite this, we cannot discount the compendium of literature that speaks to how sexual violence disproportionately affects girls and women in scope, impact, and societal consequences, as a result of gendered hierarchies, social locations, and role expectations (Henry et al., 2020; McGlynn et al., 2017). Addressing the problems and challenges of the virtual world – and potential solutions – necessitates an intersectional analysis. This type of analysis not only attends to gender, but also to other intersecting aspects of an individual's social and political identity that positions them in the interstices of power oppression. As Armstrong, Gleckman-Krut, and Johnson (2018, p. 99) note, "sexual violence reproduces inequalities of gender, race/ethnicity, class, age, sexuality, ability status, citizenship, and nationality." As such, more research on the harms of nonconsensual intimate image dissemination, particularly that which is nuanced by an intersectional analysis, will provide insight into the types of solutions and best service provision practices required in order to not replicate the silencing and narrow focus "by some antisexual violence activism [that] fails women of color and other marginalized groups" (Armstrong et al., 2018, p. 99).

Conclusion

Relying on Mayer-Schönberger's (2009) concept of "permanent remembering," this chapter explored professionals' perspectives and understandings of the additive role that technology plays in the harms and impacts of sexual violence. The nonconsensual dissemination of intimate images and videos acts as a digital "layer" operating in addition to the commission of physical acts of sexual violence. This serves to layer, or compound, the harms experienced by the victim by adding a virtual – and indelible – "permanent remembering" of the act of violence. Violence here is a broad term, which speaks to an array of contexts in which such images are produced and shared. This ranges from images that were initially shared within the confines of a consensual sexual exchange and then nonconsensually distributed to physically perpetrated sexual assaults that were recorded and distributed virtually; to a myriad of contexts in between, such as being manipulated or coerced to take or share images. In addition to providing therapeutic and/or practical supports to survivors of physical acts of sexual violence, the permanency of images, as well as the trauma associated with the "threat" that images/videos can be released at any time in the future without warning, becomes part of the crisis that frontline professionals must also address.

Given that definitions of consent are central in legal determinations of sexual violence, and educational and awareness campaigns are focused on ongoing and enthusiastic positive consent as evinced by the slogan "yes means yes," nuancing the contours of consent in a technological context is of great importance. The ways in which digital and other technologies are used in sexual relationships; the additive role of, and considerations surrounding, navigating technology in sexual consent decision-making; the digital layering of harms; and the risks of digital "permanent remembering" must be attended to in educational and awareness contexts, in support and service practices, but also within the legal and criminal context. The harms of nonconsensual intimate image dissemination can be conceptualized under many frameworks, including cyberbullying (e.g., blackmail, humiliation, extortion, threat), privacy violation, criminal code infractions, and socio-legal analysis. However, as McGlynn et al. (2017) caution, we must be attentive to the uneven gendered scope, impacts, and consequences of sexual violence.

When looking to potential solutions, we must ensure that we recognize the normative discourses embedded in our understandings of sex, sexual conduct, and sexed gender roles and interactions. That the colloquialism "revenge pornography," for instance, is frequently used suggests an uncritical reflection to the ways in which the vocabularies of women's sexuality and women's sexual conduct are framed by patriarchal, heteronormative, and phallocentric narratives of gender, gender roles, sex, and sexual conduct. That nonconsensual nude images of women are referred to as revenge pornography suggests that women's nude bodies are always pornographic, and that the central issue of concern is the nudity or sex (e.g., leading to questions of why women took and shared the images in the first place) – and not the actual acts of harm and violence perpetrated (e.g., the violation of sexual privacy, trust, and engaging in sexual conduct without consent). This in turn leads to, for instance, calls for digital abstinence, and subsequent risk management strategies that serve to curtail or constrain the sexual conduct of individuals (generally teenage girls and women), responsibilizing individuals for the initial image-making, and centralizing the images themselves as problematic or the harm. As Mayer-Schönberger (2009) suggests, digital abstinence is virtually incongruent with how technology is embedded in our everyday lives, both professionally and personally. When thinking through the necessary support strategies and services available to victims of this type of sexual violence, as well as the ways that we legislate technologically facilitated sexual violence, we must unravel the complex ways that technology and digital spaces reveal the manifold layers of consent and the narratives or discourses embedded in our education, awareness, policing, or law-making.

Notes

1. Although the website was stated to have been shut down in April 2018, it is currently operational, with new posts as of May 2020. In addition, an archive of images dated from 2018 and 2019 still remains on the website. Given that there is no indication that consent was obtained prior to the images being shared online, the website name will not be publicized in this chapter.
2. The website now indicates that it is "an adult image board where anyone can share porn images and write comments anonymously." It also has posted four rules: "1. Do not post any images containing minors, or questionable content that may contain minors under the age of 18! (This includes nonnude images); 2. Do not post or request personal information ('dox'); 3. The posting of any external links (URLs) is strictly forbidden, this also includes private trading (giving out your user id for offsite contact); 4. You will not upload, post, discuss, request, or link to anything that violates international law."
3. The research was approved by the Research Ethics Board at Ontario Tech University in Ontario, Canada, REB #15000.
4. #cancelculture is a variant of #calloutculture. They are both a form of online shaming and describe a boycott – or a call to boycott – someone who has shared a controversial or offensive opinion or has engaged in behavior that is controversial or questioned. As Romano (2019) explains: "A celebrity or other public figure does or says something offensive. A public backlash, often fueled by politically progressive social media, ensues. Then comes the calls to cancel the person – that is, to effectively end their career or revoke their cultural cachet, whether through boycotts of their work or disciplinary action from an employer."
5. In 2010, while Melissa Petro was working as a public school teacher in New York, she was outed by the *New York Post* as a former sex worker. Petro herself had written a column for *Huffington Post* about her experiences selling sexual services through the "erotic services" section of Craigslist.com, an online classifieds site. She was forced to resign, not after her initial column, but after other newspapers started reporting on her, calling her "stripper teaching" in headlines. Parents and commentators remarked on her lack of "morals," "values," and "decency" required of the "higher" standards that are expected of teachers and questioned her ability to be a "role model" and her "suitability" to work with children.

References

Allen, B. (2019). Revenge porn and sext crimes: Canada sees more than 5,000 police cases as law marks 5 years. *CBC News*. Retrieved from https://www.cbc.ca/news/canada/saskatchewan/reveng-porn-and-sext-crimes-canada-sees-more-than-5-000-police-cases-as-law-marks-5-years-1.5405118

Armstrong, E. A., Gleckman-Krut, M., & Johnson, L. (2018). Silence, power, and inequality: An intersectional approach to sexual violence. *Annual Review of Sociology*, *44*, 99–122.

Bailey, J. (2015). A perfect storm: How the online environment, social norms, and law shapes girls' lives. In J. Bailey & V. Steeves (Eds.), *eGirls, eCitizens: Putting technology, theory and policy into dialogue with girls' and young women's voices* (pp. 21–53). Ottawa, ON: University of Ottawa Press.

Bates, S. (2017). Revenge porn and mental health: A qualitative analysis of the mental health effects of revenge porn on female survivors. *Feminist Criminology*, *12*(1), 22–42.

Beres, M. A., Crow, B., & Gotell, L. (2009). The perils of institutionalization in neoliberal times: Results of a national survey of Canadian sexual assault and rape crisis centres. *Canadian Journal of Sociology*, *34*(1), 135–163.

Bloom, S. (2014). No vengeance for 'revenge porn' victims: Unraveling why this latest female-centric, intimate-partner offence is still legal, and why we should criminalize it. *Fordham Urban Law Journal*, *42*, 233–289.

Branch, K., Hilinski-Rosick, C., Johnson, E., & Solano, G. (2017). Revenge porn victimization of college students in the United States: An exploratory analysis. *International Journal of Cyber Criminology*, *11*(1), 128–142.

Burgin, R., & Flynn, A. (2019). Women's behavior as implied consent: Male "reasonableness" in Australian rape law. *Criminology and Criminal Justice*. doi: 10.1177/1748895819880953

Burkell, J. A. (2016). Remembering me: Big data, individual identity, and the psychological necessity of forgetting. *Ethics and Information Technology*, *18*(1), 17–23.

Campbell, R. (2006). Rape survivors' experiences with the legal and medical systems. Do rape victim advocates male a difference?. *Violence Against Women*, *12*(1), 30–45.

Chon, D. S. (2014). Policing reporting by sexual assault victims in Western and non-Western countries. *Journal of Family Violence*, *29*(8), 859–868.

Eaton, A. A., Jacobs, H., & Ruvalcaba, Y. (2018). 2017 nationwide online study of non-consensual porn victimization and perpetration: A summary report. Retrieved from https://www.cybercivilrights.org/

Edwards, K. M., Turchik, J. A., Dardis, C. M., Reynolds, N., & Gidycz, C. A. (2011). Rape myths: History, individual and institutional-level presence, and implications for change. *Sex Roles*, *65*, 761–773.

Ehlers, A., & Clark, D. M. (2000). A cognitive model of posttraumatic stress disorder. *Behaviour Research and Therapy*, *38*, 319–345.

Fairbairn, J. (2015). Rape threats and revenge porn: Defining sexual violence in the digital age. In J. Bailey, & V. Steeves (Eds.), *eGirls, eCitizens: Putting technology, theory and policy into dialogue with girls' and young women's voices.* (pp. 229–252). Ottawa, ON: University of Ottawa Press.

Flynn, A. (2015). Sexual violence and innovative responses to justice: Interrupting the recognisable narratives. In A. Powell, N. Henry, & A. Flynn (Eds.), *Rape justice: Beyond the criminal law* (pp. 92–111). Basingstoke: Palgrave Macmillan.

Flynn, A., & Henry, N. (2019). Image-based sexual abuse: An Australian reflection. *Women and Criminal Justice*. doi:10.1080/08974454.2019.1646190

Government of Canada. (2015). Protecting Canadians from Online Crime Act. Department of Justice. Retrieved from https://www.canada.ca/en/news/archive/2015/04/protecting-canadians-online-crime-act-.html

Green, D. (2018, February 20). Revenge porn sites targets Canadian university students. *The Phoenix*. Retrieved from http://www.thephoenixnews.com/2018/02/revenge-porn-site-targets-canadian-university-students/

Henry, N., Flynn, A., & Powell, A. (2018). Policing image-based sexual abuse: Stakeholder perspectives. *Police Practice and Research: An International Journal, 19*(6), 565–581.

Henry, N., Flynn, A., & Powell, A. (2019). *Responding to revenge pornography: The scope, nature and impact of Australian criminal laws: A report to the criminology research council.* Canberra, ACT: Australian Institute of Criminology.

Henry, N., McGlynn, C., Flynn, A., Johnson, K., Powell, A., & Scott, A. J. (2020). *Image-based sexual abuse: A study on the causes and consequences of non-consensual nude or sexual imagery*. London and New York, NY: Routledge.

Humphreys, T. (2007). Perceptions of sexual consent: The impact of relationship history and gender. *The Journal of Sex Research, 44*(4), 307–315.

Karaian, L. (2014). Policing 'sexting': Responsibilization, respectability and sexual subjectivity in child protection/crime prevention responses to teenager' digital sexual expression. *Theoretical Criminology, 18*(3), 282–299.

Lee, M., & Crofts, T. (2015). Gender, pressure, coercion and pleasure: Untangling motivations for sexting between young people. *British Journal of Criminology, 55*, 454–473.

Liptak, A. (2018, April 29). Dutch police have shut down Anon-IB in the course of a revenge porn investigation. *The Verge*. Retrieved from https://www.theverge.com/2018/4/29/17299020/anon-ib-the-netherlands-dutch-police-revenge-porn-shut-down

Marques, O., & Rinaldi, J. (2020, July). The politics of consent and the problem with focusing on violence. In G. C. Becker, & A. T. Dionne (Eds.), *Rape culture 101: Programming change* (pp. 128–147). Brantford, ON: Demeter.

Mayer-Schönberger, V. (2009). *Delete: The virtue of forgetting in the digital age.* Princeton, NJ: Princeton University Press.

McArdle, M. (2019, August 13). The problem with making 'yes means yes' the standard for sexual assault. *The Washington Post*. Retrieved from https://www.washingtonpost.com/opinions/why-rape-laws-have-historically-relied-on-no-means-no-not-yes-means-yes/2019/08/13/cfeff8de-be0f-11e9-a5c6-1e74f7ec4a93_story.html

McGlynn, C., Rackley, E., & Houghton, R. (2017). Beyond 'revenge porn': The continuum of image-based sexual abuse. *Feminist Legal Studies, 25*(1), 25–46.

McGlynn, C., Rackley, E., Johnson, K., Henry, N., Gavey, N., Flynn, A., & Powell, A. (2020). "It's torture for the soul: The harms of image-based sexual abuse". *Social & Legal Studies*, online first, doi:10.1177/0964663920947791

McGlynn, C., Rackley, E., Johnson, K., Henry, N., Flynn, A., Powell, A., … Scott, A. (2019). Shattering lives and myths: A report on image-based sexual abuse. Retrieved from https://claremcglynn.files.wordpress.com/2019/06/shattering-lives-and-myths-final.pdf

Office of the Privacy Commissioner of Canada. (2018, May). *Guidelines for obtaining meaningful consent.* Retrieved from https://www.priv.gc.ca/en/privacy-topics/collecting-personal-information/consent/gl_omc_201805/#_seven

O'Sullivan, E., & Carlton, A. (2001). Victim services, community outreach, and contemporary rape crisis centres: A comparison of independent and multiservice centres. *Journal of Interpersonal Violence, 16*(4), 343–360.

Patterson, D., Greeson, M., & Campbell, R. (2009). Understanding rape survivors' decisions not to seek social systems help. *Health & Social Work, 34*(2), 127–136.

Penney, R. (2016). The rhetoric of the mistake in adult narratives of youth sexuality: The case of Amanda Todd. *Feminist Media Studies, 16*(4), 710–725.

Petro, M. (2017). The "hooker teacher" tells all. In D. M. Halperin & T. Hoppe (Eds.), *The war on sex* (pp. 291–296). London: Duke University Press.

Powell, A., & Henry, N. (2017). *Sexual violence in a digital age*. London: Palgrave Macmillan.

Powell, A., Henry, N., & Flynn, A. (2018). Image-based sexual abuse. In W. S. DeKeseredy & M. Dragiewicz (Eds.), *Routledge handbook of critical criminology* (2nd ed., pp. 305–315). Abingdon and New York, NY: Routledge.

Powell, A., Henry, N., Flynn, A., & Henderson, E. (2013). Meanings of "Sex" and "Consent" and the Impact of Rape Law Reform in Victoria, Australia. *Griffith Law Review*, *22*(2), 456–480.

Powell, A., Henry, N., Flynn, A., & Scott, A. J. (2019). Image-based sexual abuse: The extent, nature, and predictors of perpetration in a community sample of Australian adults. *Computers in Human Behavior*, *92*, 393–402.

Powell, A., Scott, A. J., Flynn, A., & Henry, N. (2020). *Image-based sexual abuse: An international study of victims and perpetrators. Summary report*. Melbourne, VIC: RMIT University.

Romano, A. (2019, December 30). Why we can't stop fighting about cancel culture. *Vox*. Retrieved from https://www.vox.com/culture/2019/12/30/20879720/what-is-cancel-culture-explained-history-debate

RSC. (1985, c C-46). Canadian criminal code.

Rushowy, K. (2020, February 18). Ontario's rape crisis centres worry additional funding won't continue beyond March. *Toronto Star*. Retrieved from https://www.thestar.com/politics/provincial/2020/02/18/ontarios-rape-crisis-centres-worry-additional-funding-wont-continue-beyond-march.html

Sable, M. R., Danis, F., Mauzy, D. L., & Gallagher, S. K. (2006). Barriers to reporting sexual assault for women and men: Perspectives of college students. *Journal of American College Health*, *55*(3), 157–162.

Slane, A. (2013). Sexing and the law in Canada. *The Canadian Journal of Human Sexuality*, *22*, 117–122.

Slane, A., & Langlois, G. (2018). Debunking the myth of 'not my bad': Sexual images, consent, and online host responsibilities in Canada. *Canadian Journal of Women and the Law*, *30*(1), 42–81.

Starr, T. S., & Lavis, T. (2018). Perceptions of revenge pornography and victim blame. *International Journal of Cyber Criminology*, *12*(2), 427–438.

Walker, K., & Sleath, E. (2017). A systematic review of the current knowledge regarding revenge pornography and non-consensual sharing of sexually explicit media. *Aggression and Violent Behavior*, *36*, 9–24.

Wolak, J., Finkelhor, D., Walsh, W., & Treitman, L. (2018). Sextortion of minors: Characteristics and dynamics. *Journal of Adolescent Health*, *62*, 72–79.

Section 4
Dating Applications

Chapter 19

Introduction

Asher Flynn

As digital technologies continue to develop, so too does our reliance on them as ways to communicate and connect with each other. This engagement through technology has become central to many of our social and dating lives, providing us with a way to digitally express intimacy to another person through chat and imagery. Within this context, the creation of a range of applications and websites that seek to bring people together have become more common and a socially acceptable way to seek out connection, intimacy, sex, romance, and companionship. As Ari Waldman reflects in his chapter, for more marginalized populations, digital dating applications have also provided an outlet for "expressions of sexual and romantic freedom after decades of marginalization." However, such services have also been used to perpetrate harm, including image-based sexual abuse, sexual assault, and sexual harassment, among other abusive behaviors.

In this section, we bring together three chapters that examine the lived experiences of those who have been subjected to abusive behaviors on, or facilitated by, dating applications, as well as considering the socio-cultural norms, values, and practices that perpetuate a rape culture within these intimate settings.

In his chapter, Chris Dietzel provides voices to men who have sex with men (MSM), exploring their understandings and experiences of rape culture through the use of dating applications like Grindr. In doing so, he explores how a rape culture manifests in key ways in-application interactions, for example, unwanted sexual messages and imagery, and in-person encounters, for example, sexual assault. Elena Cama similarly considers how socio-cultural and sexual norms that reflect a rape culture underpin dating applications, and her chapter considers the ways in which this may facilitate, normalize, and excuse sexual harms. In particular, Cama reflects on how this may play out in the context of the normalization of male sexual aggression and female passivity, as well as the myths, victim-blaming, and policing of women's behavior that both minimizes and excuses men's violence.

The research on technology-facilitated violence and abuse both within and beyond the dating applications context has largely focused on the experiences of

The Emerald International Handbook of Technology-Facilitated Violence and Abuse, 331–332

doi:10.1108/978-1-83982-848-520211063

cisgender women perpetrated by cisgender men. As Cama explains in her chapter, this results in the privileging of white, able-bodied, middle class women's experiences, and the erasing and silencing of the violence experiences of those whose victimization "is multilayered on the basis of a combination of factors, including gender, sexuality, race, and/or disability." In his chapter, Waldman similarly describes how the pressures and norms surrounding digital dating pose unique and risky experiences including "privacy invasions, exploitation, extortion, and harassment" for marginalized populations, particularly for women and sexual minorities.

In this section, we recognize this gap in knowledge and respond to it by seeking to explore the experiences of people with diverse gender and sexual identities in using dating applications and experiencing sexual harms to consider how these may differ from heteronormative experiences. As Cama claims, "by 'queering' understandings of dating app usage … we may be able to more meaningfully explore how these discourses feature in and are potentially differently mobilized and navigated in non-heterosexual dating cultures." This is particularly important as Waldman discusses the evidence of the frequent use of such applications among the sexually and gender diverse communities, comparative to heterosexual users.

The chapters in this section also provide an insight into the ways that gender and sexually diverse people face similar experiences to other marginalized groups, where there are powerful discourses, rape myths, and stereotypes that act to silence and discredit experiences of sexual harm. The impacts of which, Dietzel observes, "reduce people to sexual objects."

Further to considering the role of rape culture, Waldman explores how dating applications, particularly those that are designed for gay and bisexual men, socially construct and build in norms that create pressures on users both to share intimate and private information, for example, sexual imagery or descriptions, or as Dietzel found, to participate in sexual activity creating a murky or gray interaction, where the acts are unwanted, but are not defined as either consensual or nonconsensual. As Jadyn (32-year-old black, gay, male) a participant in Dietzel's study reflected of the MSM dating application culture, "it's a sort of social obligation gun-being-held-to-my-head and I feel like I'm doing something that I don't actually want to do."

Chapter 20

Understanding Experiences of Sexual Harms Facilitated through Dating and Hook Up Apps among Women and Girls

Elena Cama

Abstract

In recent years, the use of dating and hook up apps has become an increasingly socially acceptable and commonly used method of seeking romantic and sexual partners. This has seen a corresponding rise in media and crime reports of sexual harms facilitated through these services, including sexual harassment, unsolicited sexual imagery, and sexual assault. Emerging empirical research shows that experiences of sexual harms in this context are common and predominantly impact women and girls. The aim of this chapter is to examine the sociocultural and sexual norms that underpin online dating and which perpetuate a "rape culture" within which sexual harms become both possible and normalized. This chapter also considers how the discourses that minimize and legitimize sexual harms are encoded within the responses undertaken by dating and hook up apps to sexual harms. It is argued that together these norms and discourses may act to facilitate and/or prevent sexual harms, and may normalize and excuse these harms when they occur.

Keywords: Online dating; rape culture; sexual harms; technology-facilitated sexual violence; hook up apps; gender-based sexual violence

Introduction

The proliferation of mobile dating and hook up apps for seeking romantic and/or sexual partners has radically altered the way that people negotiate sex and intimacy. Although it is difficult to determine the number of people using dating and hook up apps, data indicate that use of these platforms is common.

The Emerald International Handbook of Technology-Facilitated Violence and Abuse, 333–350

doi:10.1108/978-1-83982-848-520211025

Approximately 30% of US adults report that they have ever used a dating app or site (Pew Research Center, 2020). One of the most popular apps, Tinder, has approximately 57 million users worldwide, 10 million active daily users, and around 1.6 billion daily swipes (Iqbal, 2019; Smith, 2020).

Following Byron and Albury's (2018) work, "dating and hook up apps" in this chapter refers to mobile applications that offer opportunities for service users to seek dates, love, sex, or romance. "Hook up" refers to the increasingly normative practice among adults of engaging in sexual encounters (including, but not limited to, sexual intercourse) where there is no expectation of dating or forming a romantic relationship (Garcia, Reiber, Massey, & Merriwether, 2012). While the term "hook up app" may primarily refer to users' motivations for seeking casual sexual encounters using mobile apps, in practice there are a wide range of reasons why people use these platforms, including socializing and friendship, relational ambitions, sex, ease of communication, validation of self-worth, self-esteem enhancement, and fun and entertainment (Bryant & Sheldon, 2017; Sumter, Vandenbosch, & Ligtenberg, 2017).

The focus in public health research on sexual health and other "risks" (e.g., sexual risk behaviors and sexually transmissible infections) in relation to dating and hook up app use has been criticized for failing to consider the broader affordances these apps offer for negotiating and engaging in sex and intimacy (Byron & Albury, 2018). However, alongside the potential benefits of dating and hook up apps, it is also clear that these platforms have served as sites for the perpetration or facilitation of sexual harms, such as the sending of unsolicited or unwanted sexual imagery and contact-based sexual offenses. Although there is a broader literature base on people's experiences and the impacts of digital harms (Powell & Henry, 2017, 2019), examination of the nature and impacts of harms within online dating remains understudied and warrants urgent attention.

In this chapter, I examine the sociocultural and sexual norms that underpin online dating, and which perpetuate the norms, values, and practices that underlie "rape culture." I discuss how these norms may be embedded within the responses undertaken by dating and hook up apps to sexual harms. Together these may act to facilitate and/or prevent sexual harms, as well as normalize and excuse these harms when they occur. I first briefly outline the literature on sexual harms perpetrated or facilitated via dating and hook up apps and websites, then turn to the sociocultural and sexual norms that underpin online dating and which perpetuate rape culture. This is followed by an examination of the ways in which these norms are embedded within dating and hook up app responses to sexual harms, and how these apps may facilitate and/or prevent sexual harms from occurring. While this chapter focuses on women's and girls' experiences of sexual harms, I end this chapter with a call to "queer" sexual violence by rejecting cis-sexist, heteronormative discourses of sexuality and gender which perpetuate rape culture, and embracing alternative narratives of experiences of sexual harms.

Sexual Harms in Online Dating

Online dating has its origins in personal ads placed in newspapers from the late 1600s (Lee, 2016). The first online dating website, Kiss.com, launched in 1994, and the first mobile app, Grindr, launched in 2009 (Jackson, 2018; Lee, 2016). Despite dating apps and websites being available for more than two decades, it is only more recently that researchers have begun to examine experiences of sexual harms in the context of modern dating platforms. In this chapter, "sexual harms" refer to a complex array of unwanted sexual behaviors that people may experience as harmful, including, but not limited to, those that are perpetrated or mediated via digital communications technologies. This approach is influenced by the work of feminist scholars who reject linear, hierarchical conceptualizations of harm and move instead toward continuum-based approaches to women's safety and experiences of sexual harms (Kelly, 1987, 1988, 2012; Stanko, 1985, 1990). This approach also recognizes the diverse range of harms that may be experienced and demonstrates how the categories that are typically used to define sexual harms are not discrete, but rather overlap in their nature and impacts (Kelly, 1987, 1988, 2012; Stanko, 1985, 1990).

Sexual harms in dating and hook up app contexts may include, but are by no means limited to, unwanted requests for sex, unwanted sexual comments, unsolicited sexual imagery or video, image-based sexual abuse, and contact-based harms. Sexual harms intersect with other identity markers and reinforce social asymmetries, such as race, class, sexuality, and disability. Thus, the term "sexual harms" may also include harms that are not necessarily "sexual" in nature, but which nevertheless reproduce gendered power relations (Kelly, 1988). More broadly, data indicate that experiences of sexual harms perpetrated or facilitated via digital communications technologies, commonly referred to as "technology-facilitated sexual violence," are common (Powell & Henry, 2017, 2019; Powell, Scott, Flynn, & Henry, 2020). While both men and women experience these types of harms, research suggests that the nature and impacts of these experiences are gendered in nature. For example, men are more likely to be perpetrators of these harms, and women report greater impacts resulting from their experiences of these harms, such as feelings of distress and fears for their physical safety (Powell & Henry, 2017, 2019).

Available research indicates that such experiences in the context of online dating are common. Gillett's (2019) doctoral research on women's experiences of everyday violence on Tinder is the most comprehensive examination of the range of sexual harms experienced by women and girls via dating platforms. Her findings highlight the continuum of experiences that women face, including unwanted requests for sex, attacks on gender and sexuality, unsolicited sexual images, possessive and controlling messages, and physical intrusions in face-to-face interactions, including those that would meet legal definitions of sexual assault. To date, much of the available literature has focused on women's experiences of sexual harassment, including the receipt of unsolicited sexual images of men's genitals, popularly termed "dick pics" (e.g., Douglass, Wright, Davis, & Lim, 2018; Shaw, 2016; Vitis & Gilmour, 2016). Survey data suggest that this practice is common, with one US survey by Match.com finding that almost half of men reported sending a picture of their penis to a potential partner and nearly half of women reported receiving one without asking for it (Match, 2017). A survey of Australians aged 16–29 years found that among the 535 participants who had used a dating app in the previous year, 57% had experienced sexual harassment[1] in this context (Douglass et al., 2018).

There have also been reports of physical sexual harms facilitated through dating and hook up apps, such as in initial face-to-face meetings (National Crime Agency, 2016; Powell & Henry, 2017; Rowse, Bolt, & Gaya, 2020). Data from the UK National Crime Agency (2016) indicate that the number of serious sexual assaults initiated as a result of online dating increased sixfold between 2009 and 2014, with the majority of victims being female. Although there are no similar data on trends in Australia, some comparative work has found that 9% of Australian adults and 10% of UK adults had reported that they have had an unwanted sexual experience with someone they had met via a dating app or website (Powell & Henry, 2017). Finally, survey data among 1,244 US women found that 31% had been sexually assaulted or raped by someone they had met through a dating website (Flynn, Cousins, & Picciani, 2019).

"The Cultural Scaffolding of Rape": How "Rape Culture" Shapes Our Understandings of Sexual Harms in Online Dating

The concept of "rape culture" is a useful lens through which to examine sexual harms occurring in the context of online dating. The ways in which victim-survivors understand and respond to their personal experiences of sexual harms are largely contingent upon the social, cultural, political, and temporal context within which these experiences occur (Kelly, Burton, & Regan, 1996). Therefore, it is useful to examine the norms, values, and practices that underpin the context in which these harms occur, and that may be creating an environment within which sexual harms become both possible and tolerated. The term "rape culture" was first articulated by feminists in the 1970s and has experienced a resurgence in popularity in more recent years in the wake of various feminist movements calling out and challenging rape culture (e.g., the #MeToo Movement). Rape culture refers to a "complex set of beliefs that encourages male sexual aggression and supports violence against women" (Buchwald, Fletcher, & Roth, 2005, p. xi). Within this culture, "sexual violence against women is implicitly and explicitly condoned, excused, tolerated, and normalized" (Powell, 2015, p. 575), and these beliefs are embedded to varying degrees within language, sociocultural and political practices, laws, and institutions (Powell & Henry, 2014). While rape culture arguably applies globally, there are differences in its manifestation in distinctive sociocultural, legal, political, and temporal contexts (Mendes, Ringrose, & Keller, 2019), and this chapter largely focuses on conceptualizations and manifestations of the concept in the Global-North.

There are two connected features that help to foster a rape culture and create and sustain the conditions for sexual harms: (1) heteronormative discourses of sex and gender that normalize male sexual aggression and female passivity; and (2) rape myths and jokes, victim-blaming, the policing of women's bodies and behaviors, and other discourses that serve to minimize, legitimize, and excuse men's violence (Gavey, 2005; Keller, Mendes, & Ringrose, 2016; Sills et al., 2016). Scholarship on rape culture critiques assumptions that sexual violence is perpetrated by deviant individuals and instead highlights the ways that these harms are linked to or enabled by everyday sociocultural norms, values, and practices (Gavey, 2005; Sills et al., 2016). These two interconnected features and how they manifest in dating and hook up apps will be discussed in turn below.

Heteronormative Discourses of Sex and Gender

Gavey (2005) has explored the ways that "everyday taken-for-granted normative forms of heterosexuality work as a cultural scaffolding for rape" (p. 2). She suggests that normative discourses of sex and gender set up the preconditions for sexual violence by providing implicit templates for heterosex that position women's sexuality (or rather, asexuality) as passive and men's sexuality as aggressive and in need of sexual release ("male sexual drive" discourse). These discourses produce cultural meanings of sex and desire, which differentially impact men and women. Such discourses can potentially have the effect of constraining or compromising women's choices in heterosexual relationships, such that women have limited agency to pursue their own desires as their actions are premised on either meeting or denying men's desires (i.e., acting as "gate-keepers" of sex; see Gavey, 2005).

In her work, Gavey (2005) presents examples of unwanted sexual encounters that women experience in the absence of the use of physical force. For example, in interviews, women described having unwanted sex with their male partners for the purposes of maintaining a heterosexual relationship due to feelings of obligation or pressure. This is not to suggest that these forms of heterosex are rape. Rather, the norms surrounding heterosex can produce ambiguity about whether interactions are consensual or nonconsensual, and arguably authorize, legitimize, and trivialize sexual encounters that are not always distinguishable from dominant, or indeed legal, understandings of "rape" (Fileborn, 2016). These norms result in what Gavey (2005) notes is a "complex gray area between what we might think of as mutually consenting sex, on the one hand, and rape or sexual coercion on the other" (p. 128). While the concept of a gray area has been subject to critique (Hardcastle cited by Sebag-Montefiore, 2020), it may better capture those experiences that do not constitute rape (according to both normative and legal definitions), but which may be harmful, such as receiving unsolicited sexual imagery (i.e., "dick pics") via dating and hook up apps.

Drawing from Gavey's (2005) work, the normative heterosexual scripts that underpin online dating (and indeed, dating more broadly) may help to set up the preconditions for sexual harms experienced by women and girls, as well as normalize and excuse it when it occurs. Culturally produced meanings of sex and desire may influence the motivations and practices of dating and hook up app use by heterosexual men and women. For example, men are more likely to use Tinder for seeking casual sex (Sumter et al., 2017), while women are more likely to use it to seek long-term relationships, friendship, or for validation (Ranzini & Lutz, 2017).

Research indicates that women are much less likely to initiate conversations on Tinder compared to men but are more likely to receive messages (Timmermans & Courtois, 2018). These practices potentially support discourses that position men as active pursuers of sex. On the other hand, women may be more selective in their choice of men on Tinder in order to avoid those only interested in sexual encounters (Timmermans & Courtois, 2018). For example, some women indicate on their dating profiles that casual sex is not an option in an attempt to prevent unwanted sexual requests before they occur (Chan, 2018). Women may also be required to interpret and respond to men's indications about their desires for sex on these platforms (Chan, 2018). If men have expectations that women will place obstacles in the way of their sexual gratification as an indication of lack of consent (Cense, Bay-Cheng, & van Dijk, 2019), these practices of filtering out male partners and proactively avoiding sex are demonstrative of discourses of heterosex that position women as gatekeepers of sex.

While creating the possibility for nonconsensual or coercive experiences to occur, these norms simultaneously result in many experiences being labeled as "just sex," as they do not fit within dominant rape scripts. Rape scripts refer to the template for how sexual violence is viewed to typically proceed, including beliefs about who experiences sexual violence, the relationship between the victim and the perpetrator, the use of a weapon, the steps that typically women should take in order to prevent an assault (such as explicit nonconsent, wearing modest clothing, and not drinking alcohol), and how victims should respond to or be affected by the experience (Ryan, 2011). Encounters that do not conform to these normative scripts are often not perceived as meeting the threshold for inclusion as a form of sexual violence. That our normative understandings of sexual violence are framed in dichotomous terms (either an experience is "rape" or it is "not rape," and "violence" or "not violence") (Hindes & Fileborn, 2019) means that experiences that are ambiguous or fall somewhere in between (or outside) may be more often discounted. This is exemplified by sexual harms that include the use of violence in an otherwise consensual sexual encounter and those that are not characterized by the use of physical violence. For example, media reports refer to women's experiences of stealthing[2] in face-to-face interactions with men they have met on dating and hook up apps, with some noting that victims may be uncertain about whether these experiences constitute "rape" in the absence of physical violence (e.g., Triple J Hack, 2017). As another example, while the sending of unsolicited "dick pics" – a practice commonly associated with dating and hook up apps – is not an act of physical violence, women nevertheless may feel "visually assaulted" after receiving them (Segran & Truong, 2016). Therefore, given that normative understandings of violence tend to be limited to the use of physical force and the explicit expression of nonconsent, interactions which do not conform to these understandings may be dismissed and potentially normalized (Gillett, 2018).

Discourses that Serve to Minimize, Legitimize, and Excuse Men's Violence

In addition to the ways that everyday norms, actions, and values enable sexual violence, Gavey (2005) was interested in the ways that these attitudes and behaviors also serve to legitimate breaches of sexual boundaries when harms do occur. These include a complex interplay of victim-blaming, rape myths and jokes, and the regulation of women's bodies (e.g., slut-shaming[3]). Where a victim's experience does not play out according to the expected script, this experience may be dismissed (including by the victim) (Gillett, 2019), and the victim may be blamed for what happened. Because dating and hook up apps are used by some women for the purposes of seeking casual sex, their experiences of sexual harms may be dismissed as "just sex," and they may be blamed for actions perceived to have been taken which put them at risk. This could include blame for behaviors that are a normative part of using dating and hook up apps to meet prospective partners, such as consumption of alcohol in face-to-face interactions and engaging in casual sex.

Dating and hook up apps are sexualized spaces, often with explicit purposes of facilitating "hook ups," yet some women are condemned for using the platforms according to their intended function (Chan, 2018; Jane, 2017), reflecting the sexual double standard[4] that continues to exist in dating contexts (Jane, 2017; Sales, 2015). Some women dismiss their own experiences of intrusive behaviors by arguing that men have different motivations for using the apps than they do (Gillett, 2019). For instance, heterosexual women explain that these experiences occur because men are using these apps for the purposes of casual sex (Gillett, 2019), with both heterosexual and queer women justifying these experiences as inextricable from using dating and hook up apps (Duguay, Burgess, & Suzor, 2020; Gillett, 2019). These findings are illustrative of assumptions of men's urgent, uncontrollable sex drive, which women must manage, as well as the discourses that continue to perpetuate victim-blaming and minimize sexual harms. There is no research examining slut-shaming and victim-blaming for women who experience sexual harms facilitated or perpetrated via dating platforms. However, other researchers have pointed to slut-shaming as an expression of victim-blaming of women who engage in digitally-mediated sexualized practices, such as the sending of sexual or sexually suggestive images or videos (Shariff & DeMartini, 2015).

The sexual harms experienced by women and girls in dating and hook up app contexts do not occur in isolation of the broader harms experienced by women and girls in public and private spaces. Some women report that they expect to experience these harms both due to the sexualized nature of the apps and because they have experienced these harms in other contexts (Gillett, 2019). While online dating may be governed by its own set of norms and values, these do not operate in isolation from the sociocultural template governing social and sexual relations in society more broadly (Fileborn, 2016; Gavey, 2005). Instead, these are contexts in which sexual interaction is both normative and acceptable and therefore present an "intensification of the higher-level scaffolds" whereby the performance of sexuality may be exaggerated (Fileborn, 2016, p. 122).

Technological Constraints and Affordances of Dating and Hook Up Apps

While some researchers have pointed out the potential for social media platforms to be used as spaces to challenge rape culture (Rentschler, 2014), very few researchers have explored the ways that platforms may perpetuate rape culture. In this section, I consider how rape culture, particularly the discourses that minimize and legitimize sexual harms, is encoded within the responses undertaken by dating and hook up apps to sexual harms. I also consider the opportunities afforded by these apps for women to prevent and respond to sexual harms.

Judy Wajcman's (2002) "technofeminist" framework "conceive[d] of a two-way mutually shaping relationship between gender and technology in which technology is both a source and consequence of gender relations and vice versa" (p. 356). Technology is a "socio-technical" issue; that is, it is shaped by the social relationships within which it is produced and used. Adopting Wajcman's framework, sociocultural norms and values are programmed into technologies like dating and hook up apps (Bivens & Hoque, 2018) and these technologies are encoded with gendered meanings which shape both their design and use. For example, the enforcement of rigid binary gender identification (i.e., male or female) on the dating apps Tinder and Bumble demonstrates the ways that gendered meanings can be encoded within technology. These practices serve no technological function, but instead act to limit the ways users can authentically present their gender identities to others (MacLeod & McArthur, 2018).

The sociocultural and sexual norms that help to foster a rape culture are embedded within institutions to varying degrees. For dating and hook up apps, discourses that act to minimize, legitimize, and excuse sexual harms are key examples of the manifestations of a rape culture. Despite the "strong stance" supposedly taken by many of the dating and hook up apps in relation to harassment and abuse, these platforms have been criticized for failing to take action to prevent and respond to sexual harms (Duguay et al., 2020; Flynn et al., 2019; Picciani, 2020; see also Henry & Witt, this volume). For example, in 2017 Tinder introduced "Reactions" as an antiharassment tool for women users, consisting of a set of animated responses permitting them to virtually throw a martini or sarcastically eye roll at another user. Arguably, this tool places responsibility on women to counter harmful behavior. It blurs the boundaries between flirting and abuse, has no tangible consequences for perpetrators, and ultimately serves to normalize, minimize, and trivialize experiences of harms perpetrated via the platform (Davies, 2017; Duguay et al., 2020).

Few platforms undertake background screening of users, and those that do are monetarily incentivized via paid subscriptions (Flynn et al., 2019). The majority of perpetrators of contact-based sexual offenses facilitated via dating and hook apps have no prior criminal record (National Crime Agency, 2016), thus platforms may be limited in their ability to prevent sexual harms from occurring. Further, reporting tools on platforms can be obscure and nondescript (Duguay et al., 2020). Even where women have reported experiences of sexual assault to these platforms, many of these women report that the platforms do not even respond, let alone act on these reports (Picciani, 2020). The ease of creating dating and hook up app profiles means that users who are temporarily or permanently banned from using the platform can create alternative profiles through which to perpetrate harms.

Social norms also influence the uptake, enforcement, and effectiveness of policies and the ways that users understand the culture of the platform. Perceptions of a "hook up culture" (Sales, 2015), or "culture of sexting," may result in users not reporting harmful behavior when it occurs (Duguay et al., 2020, p. 242) and dismissing these experiences as "just sex." The framing of platforms like Tinder in this way could also influence the way that users engage with the app and with other people, in the sense that its connection to casual sexual encounters carries expectations for users to engage in such conduct (Duguay et al., 2020; Gillett, 2019). One woman described the pressures of having sex with men she had met through the app, stating, "well I met him on Tinder, this is what they expect" (Gillett, 2019, p. 149). If women are reporting expectations of experiencing unwanted sexual attention as well as engaging in sexual encounters they would not otherwise want (Duguay et al., 2020; Gillett, 2019), these apps may facilitate those "gray area" interactions that can neither be considered consensual nor nonconsensual, but nonetheless are unwanted. Given that women's motivations for using apps are less likely to be focused on sexual gratification (Ranzini & Lutz, 2017), the design and marketing of apps for "hook ups" primarily services male user motivations and so are encoded with the same heteronormative discourses that govern dating more broadly.

While potentially constraining women's movement within digital spaces, technologies may simultaneously afford various opportunities. Technology is neither inherently patriarchal nor inherently liberating for women, but rather leaves "space for women's agency in transforming technologies" (Wajcman, 2004, p. 7), such as by reinterpreting technologies for political organizing or creating new feminist communities. These platforms may also possess features that help prevent or respond to sexual harms. For instance, platforms have a range of policies, guidelines, and reporting tools aimed at regulating harmful behavior.

"Unmatching," blocking, and reporting users are options that can help users to respond to unwanted communications. In 2019, the app Bumble launched new software to automatically blur "dick pics" and other graphic images, enabling users to make a choice as to whether or not they wish to view the image, block the user, or report the user to the app (Holmes, 2019). Communication within dating and hook up apps is recorded, and apps may require user identification, both of which could be used to support reports of harmful behavior both to the platform and other authorities (Duguay, 2017). However, the extent of the uptake or effectiveness of these mechanisms has been debated (Duguay et al., 2020; Picciani, 2020). For example, queer women speculate that reports to Tinder are rare due to the nondescript nature of the reporting button, and do not appear to be either technologically or socially enforced in any case (Duguay et al., 2020). As Waldman (2019) notes in the context of queer dating apps, while platforms may have near identical policies toward unwanted sexual behaviors, the differences may lie in design and enforcement, with some platforms having more intuitive reporting tools and being more responsive than others.

An additional affordance of dating and hook up apps is the ability to undertake filtering processes and safety work with potential dates in online communications prior to meeting up face-to-face (Cama, 2019; Couch & Liamputtong, 2008).

For example, women report utilizing a range of filtering and safety strategies when meeting someone from a dating or hook up app, including checking social media pages, meeting in a neutral public place, telling other people about the date (e.g., location), and having an exit strategy in case the date does not go well (Cama, 2019). However, these strategies place the burden for mitigating the risk of experiencing harm on women. The relative anonymity afforded by these apps may simultaneously provide opportunities for the perpetration of harmful behavior, while also providing women with opportunities to resist these harms. For example, women may feel emboldened to resist, reject, or call out men's sexist comments and unwanted requests for sex, as they may not have the same concerns for retaliation and physical safety that they would otherwise have in a face-to-face interaction (Dhillon & Bakaya, 2014).

While dating and hook up apps may act as sites for the perpetration or facilitation of a range of sexual harms, they may also be used to subvert the same heteronormative discourses that help to perpetuate these harms. For example, some women use these platforms to disrupt discourses that assume women's supposed (a)sexuality and passive role in sex (Chan, 2018). For queer women, digital spaces may connect them with the LGBTQI+ community and help them to develop a sense of identity, helping to counter the negative effects of stigma and discrimination (Craig & McInroy, 2014). The dating app Dattch, later renamed Her, was developed for women who are attracted to women, under the assumption that the rapid hook up affordances of apps like Grindr and Tinder do not work for queer women (Murray & Ankerson, 2016). The dating app Bumble was founded with the stated aim of subverting the heteronormative gender roles and sexual scripts in modern dating by ensuring that women always make the first contact with prospective male partners (Bivens & Hoque, 2018). However, Bivens and Hoque (2018) suggest that the norm that men should ask women out on a date reasserts itself after the initial contact, indicating that the extent to which these design practices can achieve their stated feminist goals is questionable (p. 450). Finally, feminist activists are co-opting other social media platforms to resist, reject, and call out men's perpetration of sexual harms via dating and hook up apps and in-person interactions (e.g., Bye Felipe, Tinder Nightmares). Not only do these act as a consciousness-raising tool in relation to gendered forms of violence and inequality, they also act as sites for people seeking social support following their own experiences of these harms.

"Queering" Sexual Violence: Toward an Intersectional Understanding of Sexual Harms

Research on sexual violence largely focuses on the perpetration of cisgender men's violence against cisgender women, privileging the voices of White, able-bodied, middle-class women who experience sexual harms. Such a focus erases and silences the experiences of people whose experience of violence is multilayered on the basis of a combination of factors, including gender, sexuality, race, and/or disability (Hackworth, 2018). Ethnically diverse people, and gender and sexuality diverse people, are significantly more likely to experience digitally-mediated sexual harms, including harassment based on their gender and/or sexuality (Powell, Scott, Flynn, & Henry, 2020; Powell, Scott, & Henry, 2020), and this applies in the context of dating and hook up apps and websites (Albury et al., 2019; Douglass et al., 2018). Same-sex attracted people report concerns about physical safety and nonconsensual experiences with people they have met online (Albury & Byron, 2016; Bauermeister, Giguere, Carballo-Diéguez, Ventuneac, & Eisenberg, 2010; Corriero & Tong, 2016). Further, research suggests that there are high rates of experiences of nonconsensual distribution of sexual images among gay and bisexual men (Waldman, 2019; see also Dietzel, this volume). Much of the available research fails to capture the nuances of sexual harms experienced by people with other marginalized identities (Hackworth, 2018; Patterson, 2016). This chapter has thus far been predominantly focused on cisgender men's perpetration of harms against cisgender women. However, I will briefly note here the ways that rape culture harms those whose identities are situated outside heteronormative identities and whose experiences do not necessarily comply with "typical" rape scripts.

The dominant discourses of heterosex and sexual harms also function in specific ways to frame discourses of queer sexuality and violence (Mortimer, Powell, & Sandy, 2019). This acts to silence and render invisible the experiences of people who do not occupy heteronormative identities (Serisier, 2007). If the experiences of sexual harms among queer communities, people of culturally and linguistically diverse backgrounds, people living with disabilities, and other marginalized identities continue to be silenced, this perpetuates the myths and stereotypes that contribute to and perpetuate a rape culture. Mortimer et al.'s (2019) work highlights that heteronormative ideas about sex inform "typical" rape scripts, and assume the involvement of an "active" aggressive male against a "passive" victimized woman. This excludes the experiences of gender and sexuality diverse people and may restrict their capacity to access and identify with the language and concepts required to understand and articulate their experiences.

Heteronormative discourses relating to men's sex drive similarly result in sexual coercion among gay men being regarded as "unthinkable" or "oxymoronic" (Braun, Schmidt, Gavey, & Fenaughty, 2009, p. 337). For example, as one gay male describes of unwanted experiences on dating apps, "gay male guys are, you know, everybody thinks that we always want sex" (Dietzel, this volume). In the context of dating and hook up app use, these discourses can result in gender and sexuality diverse people not identifying harmful experiences as constituting violence (Girshick, 2002); instead, rape culture positions these experiences as "just sex" (Gavey, 2005; see also Dietzel, this volume). As one participant in Dietzel's (this volume) research notes:

> It's this weird fucked-up dynamic of when you are going through with something when you don't really want to. … In a sense, you are consenting, because you're like, "I am going forward. No one is holding a gun to my head or whatever." But it's a sort of social obligation gun-being-held-to-my-head and I feel like I'm doing something that I don't actually want to do. (p. 359)

Patterson (2016) encourages a shift to "queer" sexual violence, in the political sense of the term "queer." This involves a rejection of mainstream ideas on sexuality and gender, to move us beyond dominant narratives around sexual violence, and to examine the stories of those whose survivorhood does not follow "normal" or predictable narratives or trajectories of harm. Patterson (2016) states that "until we… acknowledge that all genders experience and perpetrate violence, we will be working on only a small piece of the larger puzzle" (p. 11). The lack of a strong body of conceptual work on alternative narratives of sexual harms, including those experienced by gender and sexuality diverse people, presents an opportunity for future research on dating and hook up apps to embrace alternative voices and stories within the survivor movement. This will necessarily include examination of sexual harms in all their "complexities and 'messiness'" (Fileborn & Phillips, 2019, p. 100), opening up the possibilities for our understandings of these harms and including those experiences that are minimized and normalized within popular culture, and which not all people necessarily experience as harmful (Vera-Gray, 2016). As just one example, "dick pics" may be a normative part of the culture of dating online for many gay and bisexual men (Alvear, 2017; Dietzel, this volume). Thus, while we need to recognize the ways in which sharing images may feature as a wanted exchange for some, we must also remain sensitive to the ways that these norms, including assumptions about men's sexuality, may be used to dismiss or trivialize the perspectives of those who experience receiving such images as distressing and harmful.

Conclusion

This chapter has attempted to contribute to a more nuanced understanding of the broad range of "sexual harms" perpetrated or facilitated via dating and hook up apps. The values and norms which underpin this highly sexualized context represent an intensification of the broader social template and can act to minimize, excuse, and condone men's violence against women. These norms are embedded within the design of the apps themselves, with many apps designed and marketed for the purposes of casual sex. Given that women commonly report using these apps for purposes other than casual sex, the sociocultural and sexual norms embedded within apps may constrain and limit the choices that women have to pursue their own desires. Many of the harms experienced in dating and hook up app contexts occur online or in the absence of physical force, and therefore these norms may also act to legitimize and dismiss harmful experiences as "just sex," where they do not fit within dominant rape narratives.

Further, limited reporting options and a lack of action taken by platforms in responding to sexual harms are illustrative of a culture within which harms are tolerated and excused. The introduction of features by platforms, which place the burden on users to respond to harmful experiences and trivializes experiences where physical forms of harm are absent, is particularly demonstrative of this point. While limiting the ability of women and girls to safely negotiate intimacy via these platforms, these apps may potentially afford women and girls with opportunities to resist and subvert heteronormative discourses and sexual harms. By "queering" understandings of dating app usage and sexual harms, we may be able to more meaningfully explore how these discourses feature in and are potentially differently mobilized and navigated in nonheterosexual dating cultures.

Notes

1. Sexual harassment was broadly defined as "any unwanted sexual attention/harassment including cat-calling, comments on appearance, getting 'hit on', touching, staring, receiving sexual pictures/texts, stalking or any other form of unwanted attention from strangers or people you know" (Douglass et al., 2018, p. 362).
2. "Stealthing" refers to the nonconsensual removal of a condom during what is an otherwise consensual sexual encounter (Chesser & Zahra, 2019).
3. Slut-shaming refers to "the act of criticizing women or girls for their real or presumed sexuality or sexual activity, as well as for looking or behaving in ways that are believed to transgress sexual norms" (Karaian, 2014, p. 296).
4. The term "sexual double standard" describes how men and women's engagement in sexual behaviors are held to different standards – women are expected to engage in digitally-mediated sexual practices by men, yet are morally condemned and slut-shamed when they do, while men are not subject to the same judgements (Ringrose, Harvey, Gill, & Livingstone, 2013).

References

Albury, K., & Byron, P. (2016). Safe on my phone? Same-sex attracted young people's negotiations of intimacy, visibility, and risk on digital hook-up apps. *Social Media + Society*, *2*(4), 1–10. doi:10.1177/2056305116672887

Albury, K., Byron, P., McCosker, A., Pym, T., Walshe, J., Race, K., & Dietzel, C. (2019). *Safety, risk and wellbeing on dating apps: Final report*. Melbourne, VIC: Swinburne University of Technology.

Alvear, M. (2017). 83 percent of gay men have sent a dick pic on dating apps, says survey. *Huff Post*. Retrieved from https://huffpost.com

Bauermeister, J. A., Giguere, R., Carballo-Diéguez, A., Ventuneac, A., & Eisenberg, A. (2010). Perceived risks and protective strategies employed by young men who have sex with men (YMSM) when seeking online sexual partners. *Journal of Health Communication*, *15*(6), 679–690. doi:10.1080/10810730.2010.499597

Bivens, R., & Hoque, A. (2018). Programming sex, gender, and sexuality: Infrastructural failures in 'feminist' dating app Bumble. *Canadian Journal of Communication*, *43*(3), 441–459. doi:10.22230/cjc.2019v44n3a3375

Braun, V., Schmidt, J., Gavey, N., & Fenaughty, J. (2009). Sexual coercion among gay and bisexual men in Aotearoa/New Zealand. *Journal of Homosexuality*, *56*(3), 336–360. doi:10.1080/00918360902728764

Bryant, K., & Sheldon, P. (2017). Cyber dating in the age of mobile apps: Understanding motives, attitudes, and characteristics of users. *American Communication Journal*, *19*(2), 1–15. Retrieved from https://pdfs.semanticscholar.org/c32e/d8d871edc872b7793891c2bf9e1184421080.pdf

Buchwald, E., Fletcher, P., & Roth, M. (2005). *Transforming a rape culture (revised)*. Minneapolis, MN: Milkweed Editions.

Byron, P., & Albury, K. (2018). "There are literally no rules when it comes to these things": Ethical practice and the use of dating/hook-up apps. In A. S. Dobson, B. Robards, & N. Carah (Eds.), *Digital intimate publics and social media* (pp. 213–229). Cham: Palgrave Macmillan.

Cama, E. (2019, December). The nature and impacts of technology-facilitated sexual violence in online dating. Paper Presented at the 32nd Annual Australian and New Zealand Society of Criminology Conference, Perth, WA.

Cense, M., Bay-Cheng, L., & van Dijk, L. (2019). 'Do I score points if I say "no"?': Negotiating sexual boundaries in a changing normative landscape. *Journal of Gender-Based Violence*, *2*(2), 277–291. doi:10.1332/239868018x15266373560443

Chan, L. S. (2018). Liberating or disciplining? A technofeminist analysis of the use of dating apps among women in urban China. *Communication, Culture and Critique*, *11*(2), 298–314. doi:10.1093/ccc/tcy004

Chesser, B., & Zahra, A. (2019). Stealthing: A criminal offence?. *Current Issues in Criminal Justice*, *31*(2), 217–235. doi:10.1080/10345329.2019.1604474

Corriero, E. F., & Tong, S. T. (2016). Managing uncertainty in mobile dating applications: Goals, concerns of use, and information seeking in Grindr. *Mobile Media and Communication*, *4*(1), 121–141. doi:10.1177/2050157915614872

Couch, D., & Liamputtong, P. (2008). Online dating and mating: The use of the internet to meet sexual partners. *Qualitative Health Research*, *18*(2), 268–279. doi: 10.1177/1049732307312832

Craig, S. L., & McInroy, L. (2014). You can form a part of yourself online: The influence of new media on identity development and coming out for LGBTQ youth. *Journal of Gay & Lesbian Mental Health*, *18*(1), 95–109. doi:10.1080/19359705.2013.777007

Davies, H. J. (2017, October 9). Does Tinder's Menprovement initiative do enough to protect women?. *The Guardian*. Retrieved from https://www.theguardian.com

Dhillon, M., & Bakaya, S. (2014). Street harassment: A qualitative study of the experiences of young women in Delhi. *SAGE Open*, *4*(3), 1–11. doi:10.1177/2158244014543786

Douglass, C. H., Wright, C. J. C., Davis, A. C., & Lim, M. S. C. (2018). Correlates of in-person and technology-facilitated sexual harassment from an online survey among young Australians. *Sexual Health*, *15*(4), 361–365. doi:10.1071/SH17208

Duguay, S. (2017). Dressing up Tinderella: Interrogating authenticity claims on the mobile dating app Tinder. *Information, Communication & Society*, *20*(3), 351–367. doi:10.1080/1369118X.2016.1168471

Duguay, S., Burgess, J., & Suzor, N. (2020). Queer women's experiences of patchwork platform governance on Tinder, Instagram, and Vine. *Convergence*, *26*, 237–252. doi:10.1177/1354856518781530

Fileborn, B. (2016). *Reclaiming the night-time economy: Unwanted sexual attention in pubs and clubs*. London: Palgrave Macmillan.

Fileborn, B., & Phillips, N. (2019). From 'me too' to 'too far'? Contesting the boundaries of sexual violence in contemporary activism. In B. Fileborn & R. Loney-Howes (Eds.), *#MeToo and the politics of social change* (pp. 99–115). Cham: Palgrave Macmillan.

Flynn, H., Cousins, K., & Picciani, E. N. (2019). *Tinder lets known sex offenders use the app. It's not the only one*. ProPublica. Retrieved from https://www.propublica.org
Garcia, J. R., Reiber, C., Massey, S. G., & Merriwether, A. M. (2012). Sexual hookup culture: A review. *Review of General Psychology, 16*(2), 161–176. doi:10.1037/a0027911
Gavey, N. (2005). *Just sex? The cultural scaffolding of rape*. East Sussex: Routledge.
Gillett, R. (2018). Intimate intrusions online: Studying the normalisation of abuse in dating apps. *Women's Studies International Forum, 69*, 212–219. doi:10.1016/j.wsif.2018.04.005
Gillett, R. (2019). *Everyday violence: Women's experiences of intimate intrusions on Tinder*. Brisbane: Queensland University of Technology.
Girshick, L. B. (2002). No sugar, no spice: Reflections on research on woman-to-woman sexual violence. *Violence Against Women, 8*(12), 1500–1520. doi:10.1177/107780102237967
Hackworth, L. (2018). Limitations of "just gender": The need for an intersectional reframing of online harassment discourse and research. In J. R. Vickery, & T. Everbach (Eds.), *Mediating misogyny: Gender, technology and harassment* (pp. 51–70). Cham: Palgrave Macmillan.
Hindes, S., & Fileborn, B. (2019). "Girl power gone wrong": #MeToo, Aziz Ansari, and media reporting of (grey area) sexual violence. *Feminist Media Studies, 20*, 1–18. doi:10.1080/14680777.2019.1606843
Holmes, A. R. (2019). Bumble to launch software that blurs dick pics and graphic images. *Metro*. Retrieved from https://metro.co.uk
Iqbal, M. (2019). Tinder revenue and usage statistics (2018). Retrieved from https://www.businessofapps.com/data/tinder-statistics/
Jackson, K. C. (2018). *A brief history of online dating*. Retrieved from https://swipe-life.tinder.com/post/a-brief-history-of-online-dating
Jane, E. A. (2017). Feminist digilante responses to a slut-shaming on Facebook. *Social Media + Society, 3*(2), 1–10. doi:10.1177/2056305117705996
Karaian, L. (2014). Policing 'sexting': Responsibilization, respectability and sexual subjectivity in child protection/crime prevention responses to teenagers' digital sexual expression. *Theoretical Criminology, 18*(3), 282–299. doi:10.1177/1362480613504331
Keller, J., Mendes, K., & Ringrose, J. (2016). Speaking 'unspeakable things:' documenting digital feminist responses to rape culture. *Journal of Gender Studies, 27*, 1–15. doi:10.1080/09589236.2016.1211511
Kelly, L. (1987). The continuum of sexual violence. In J. Hanmer & M. Maynard (Eds.), *Women, violence and social control* (pp. 46–60). London: Macmillan Press.
Kelly, L. (1988). *Surviving sexual violence*. Minneapolis, MN: University of Minnesota Press.
Kelly, L. (2012). Standing the test of time? Reflections on the concept of the continuum of sexual violence. In J. M. Brown & S. L. Walklate (Eds.), *Handbook of sexual violence* (Vol. xvii–xxvi). Oxon: Routledge.
Kelly, L., Burton, S., & Regan, L. (1996). Beyond victim or survivor: Sexual violence, identity and feminist theory and practice. In L. Adkins & V. Merchant (Eds.), *Sexualizing the social: Power and the organization of sexuality* (pp. 77–101). New York, NY: St Martin's Press.

Lee, S. (2016). The history of online dating from 1695 to now. *Huff Post*. Retrieved from https://www.huffpost.com

MacLeod, C., & McArthur, V. (2018). The construction of gender in dating apps: An interface analysis of Tinder and Bumble. *Feminist Media Studies*. doi:10.1080/14680777.2018.1494618

Match. (2017). *Singles in America*. Retrieved from https://www.singlesinamerica.com/2017/

Mendes, K., Ringrose, J., & Keller, J. (2019). *Digital feminist activism : Girls and women fight back against rape culture*. New York, NY: Oxford University Press.

Mortimer, S., Powell, A., & Sandy, L. (2019). 'Typical scripts' and their silences: Exploring myths about sexual violence and LGBTQ people from the perspectives of support workers. *Current Issues in Criminal Justice*, *31*(3), 333–348. doi:10.1080/10345329.2019.1639287

Murray, S., & Ankerson, M. S. (2016). Lez takes time: Designing lesbian contact in geosocial networking apps. *Critical Studies in Media Communication*, *33*(1), 53–69. doi:10.1080/15295036.2015.1133921

National Crime Agency. (2016). *Emerging new threat in online dating: Initial trends in internet dating-initiated serious sexual assaults*. London: National Crime Agency.

Patterson, J. (Ed.). (2016). *Queering sexual violence*. Riverdale, NY: Riverdale Avenue Books.

Pew Research Center. (2020). *The virtues and downsides of online dating*. Retrieved from https://www.pewresearch.org/internet/wp-content/uploads/sites/9/2020/02/PI_2020.02.06_online-dating_REPORT.pdf

Picciani, E. N. (2020). *He sexually assaulted her after they met on Bumble. Then she saw him on Tinder. Then Hinge*. ProPublica. Retrieved from https://www.propublica.org

Powell, A. (2015). Seeking rape justice: Formal and informal responses to sexual violence through technosocial counterpublics. *Theoretical Criminology*, *19*(4), 1–35. doi:10.1177/1362480615576271

Powell, A., & Henry, N. (2014). Framing sexual violence prevention: What does it mean to challenge a rape culture?. In N. Henry & A. Powell (Eds.), *Preventing sexual violence: Interdisciplinary approaches to overcoming a rape culture* (pp. 1–21). London: Palgrave Macmillan.

Powell, A., & Henry, N. (2017). *Sexual violence in a digital age*. London: Palgrave Macmillan.

Powell, A., & Henry, N. (2019). Technology-facilitated sexual violence victimization: Results from an online survey of Australian adults. *Journal of Interpersonal Violence*, *34*, 3637–3665. doi:10.1177/0886260516672055

Powell, A., Scott, A. J., & Henry, N. (2020). Digital harassment and abuse: Experiences of sexuality and gender minority adults. *European Journal of Criminology*, *17*(2), 199–223. doi:10.1177/1477370818788006

Powell, A., Scott, A. J., Flynn, A., & Henry, N. (2020). *Image-based sexual abuse: An international study of victims and perpetrators*. Melbourne: RMIT University. Retrieved from https://www.researchgate.net/publication/339488012_Image-based_sexual_abuse_An_international_study_of_victims_and_perpetrators

Ranzini, G., & Lutz, C. (2017). Love at first swipe? Explaining Tinder self-presentation and motives. *Mobile Media & Communication*, *5*(1), 80–101. doi:10.1177/2050157916664559

Rentschler, C. (2014). Rape culture and the feminist politics of social media. *Girlhood Studies*. *7*(1), 65–82. doi:10.3167/ghs.2014.070106

Ringrose, J., Harvey, L., Gill, R., & Livingstone, S. (2013). Teen girls, sexual double standards and 'sexting': Gendered value in digital image exchange. *Feminist Theory*, *14*(3), 305–323. doi:10.1177/1464700113499853

Rowse, J., Bolt, C., & Gaya, S. (2020). Swipe right: The emergence of dating-app facilitated sexual assault. A descriptive retrospective audit of forensic examination caseload in an Australian metropolitan service. *Forensic Science, Medicine and Pathology*, *16*, 71–77. doi:10.1007/s12024-019-00201-7

Ryan, K. M. (2011). The relationship between rape myths and sexual scripts: The social construction of rape. *Sex Roles*, *65*(11), 774–782. doi:10.1007/s11199-011-0033-2

Sales, N. J. (2015). Tinder and the dawn of the "dating apocalypse." *Vanity Fair*. Retrieved from https://www.vanityfair.com

Sebag-Montefiore, C. (2020). Sophie hardcastle on finding her voice after sexual violence: "We do scream deep down." *The Guardian*. Retrieved from https://www.theguardian.com

Segran, E., & Truong, K. (2016). Why do men send dick pics - 10 men explain. *Refinery 29*. Retrieved from https://www.refinery29.com

Serisier, T. (2007). Speaking out against rape: Feminist (her)stories and anti-rape politics. *Lilith: A Feminist History Journal*, *16*, 84–95. Retrieved from https://pure.qub.ac.uk/en/publications/speaking-out-against-rape-feminist-herstories-and-anti-rape-polit

Shariff, S., & DeMartini, A. (2015). Defining the legal lines: eGirls and intimate images. In J. Bailey & V. Steeves (Eds.), *eGirls, eCitizens* (pp. 281–305). Ottawa, ON: The University of Ottawa Press.

Shaw, F. (2016). "Bitch I said hi": The Bye Felipe campaign and discursive activism in mobile dating apps. *Social Media + Society*, *2*(4), 1–10. doi:10.1177/2056305116672889

Sills, S., Pickens, C., Beach, K., Jones, L., Calder-Dawe, O., Benton-Greig, P., & Gavey, N. (2016). Rape culture and social media: Young critics and a feminist counterpublic. *Feminist Media Studies*, *16*(6), 935–951. doi:10.1080/14680777.2015.1137962

Smith, C. (2020). 50 interesting Tinder statistics and facts | by the numbers. Retrieved from https://expandedramblings.com/index.php/tinder-statistics/

Stanko, E. (1985). *Intimate intrusions: Women's experience of male violence*. London: Routledge & Kegan Paul Ltd.

Stanko, E. (1990). *Everyday violence: How women and men experience sexual and physical danger*. London: Pandora Press.

Sumter, S. R., Vandenbosch, L., & Ligtenberg, L. (2017). Love me Tinder: Untangling emerging adults' motivations for using the dating application Tinder. *Telematics and Informatics*, *34*(1), 67–78. doi:10.1016/j.tele.2016.04.009

Timmermans, E., & Courtois, C. (2018). From swiping to casual sex and/or committed relationships: Exploring the experiences of Tinder users. *The Information Society*, *34*(2), 59–70. doi:10.1080/01972243.2017.1414093

Triple J Hack. (2017). Manipulation, abuse, deceit: How I learnt about 'stealthing' from a Tinder date. *ABC*. Retrieved from https://www.abc.net.au/triplej/programs/hack/manipulation-abuse-deceitl-how-i-learnt-about-stealthing/8480696

Vera-Gray, F. (2016). Men's stranger intrusions: Rethinking street harassment. *Women's Studies International Forum*, *58*, 9–17. doi:10.1016/j.wsif.2016.04.001

Vitis, L., & Gilmour, F. (2016). Dick pics on blast: A woman's resistance to online sexual harassment using humour, art and Instagram. *Crime, Media, Culture*, *13*(3), 335–355. doi:10.1177/1741659016652445

Wajcman, J. (2002). Addressing technological change: The challenge to social theory. *Current Sociology*, *50*(3), 347–363. doi:10.1177/0011392102050003004

Wajcman, J. (2004). *Technofeminism*. Cambridge: Polity Press.

Waldman, A. E. (2019). Law, privacy, and online dating: "Revenge porn" in gay online communities. *Law & Social Inquiry*, *44*(4), 987–1018. doi:10.1017/lsi.2018.29

Chapter 21

"That's Straight-Up Rape Culture": Manifestations of Rape Culture on Grindr

Christopher Dietzel

Abstract

Rape culture, described as when "violence is seen as sexy and sexuality as violent" (Buchwald, Fletcher, & Roth, 1993, p. vii), exists online and offline (Henry & Powell, 2014). Much of the research on rape culture focuses on the experiences of heterosexual women, and few studies have explored rape culture in the context of dating apps. This chapter explores how men who have sex with men (MSM) understand and experience rape culture through their use of Grindr and similar dating apps. A thematic analysis of interviews with 25 MSM dating app users revealed problematic user behavior as well as unwanted sexual messages and images as common manifestations of rape culture on dating apps. Participants explained that rape culture extends beyond in-app interactions to in-person encounters, as evident by incidents of sexual violence that several participants had experienced and one participant had committed. Participants were unsure about the extent to which MSM dating apps facilitate rape culture but asserted that some apps enable rape culture more than others. This chapter demonstrates the importance of investigating sexual violence against people of diverse gender and sexual identities to ensure their experiences are not minimized, ignored, or rendered invisible.

Keywords: Rape culture; sexual violence; dating apps; gay; queer; MSM

Introduction

During the 1970s, second-wave feminists began critiquing myths about women and sexual violence and introduced the term "rape culture" to articulate how society normalizes and condones sexual violence (Brownmiller, 1975). Since then,

The Emerald International Handbook of Technology-Facilitated Violence and Abuse, 351–368

doi:10.1108/978-1-83982-848-520211026

scholars, activists, and others have conceptualized rape culture as "the social, cultural, and structural discourses and practices in which sexual violence is tolerated, accepted, eroticized, minimized and trivialized" (Henry & Powell, 2014, p. 2). In a rape culture, there are blurred lines around consent, male sexual aggression is accepted and encouraged, and victims are blamed for the violence they have suffered (Phipps, Ringrose, Renold, & Jackson, 2018; Sills et al., 2016). Perpetrators are excused, and sexual violence is rendered acceptable, attractive, and inevitable (Keller, Mendes, & Ringrose, 2018; Smith, 2004).

One of the most cited definitions of rape culture comes from Buchwald, Fletcher, and Roth (1993, p. vii) in their book, *Transforming A Rape Culture*:

> It is a complex set of beliefs that encourages male sexual aggression and supports violence against women. It is a society where violence is seen as sexy and sexuality as violent. In a rape culture women perceive a continuum of threatened violence that ranges from sexual remarks to sexual touching to rape itself. A rape culture condones physical and emotional terrorism against women as the norm.

Consistent with other authors, Buchwald et al. (1993) describe rape culture as the ideologies and systems that have normalized and condoned sexual violence. They explain that sexual violence exists on a continuum that includes harassment, coercion, threats, and emotional and physical harm (see also Kelly, 1988). This notion of rape culture, however, presents a challenge when considering the systems and practices that trivialize and perpetuate sexual violence against people of diverse genders and sexualities, such as men who have sex with men (MSM), women who have sex with women, and trans and gender diverse people. Problematizing – or queering – rape culture in this way exposes the fact that rape culture is a heteronormative concept framed as sexual violence that men perpetrate against women. When we conceptualize rape culture in heteronormative terms, MSM are implicated without being affected. MSM participate in systems and practices that normalize and condone sexual violence against women but are not recognized as targets of such violence. However, if we consider rape culture in broader terms – without restricting the normalization and condonation of sexual violence in society to people of a particular gender or sexuality – then the concept can also apply to MSM.

It is not within the scope of this chapter to scrutinize the various definitions of rape culture or to propose a new conceptualization sensitive to people of diverse genders and sexualities. Rather, I have adopted Shariff's (2017, p. 56) definition of rape culture: "the way in which sexist societal attitudes and language tacitly condone, minimize and/or normalize sexual violence, mostly against women, but also against other genders through institutions, communities and individuals" (p. 56).

This aim of this chapter is to explore how MSM understand and experience rape culture through their use of Grindr and similar dating apps. There are several reasons why it is useful to investigate these experiences. First, MSM are avid users of dating apps. Grindr, the most popular of the MSM dating apps (Badal, Stryker, DeLuca, & Purcell, 2018), recently reported that it has 3.8 million daily active users worldwide (Clement, 2019). Second, MSM dating apps are highly sexualized spaces (Race, 2015), and MSM may feel pressured or expected to engage in sexual activity even if they do not want to (Gavey, Schmidt, Braun, Fenaughty, & Eremin, 2009; Klesse, 2016). Third, MSM may dismiss or trivialize their experiences with sexual violence because of the assumption that men always want sex (Hollway, 1998). Although MSM dating apps are highly sexualized spaces, MSM actually use the apps for a variety of reasons, including to socialize and pass the time (Albury et al., 2019). This means that MSM may presume all dating app users want to engage in sexual activities even though some users may not be interested in anything sexual, thereby creating the possibility for unwanted sexual advances. Lastly, there are high rates of sexual violence against MSM (Rothman, Exner, & Baughman, 2011), and MSM dating app users are concerned about experiencing sexual violence through their use of dating apps (Corriero & Tong, 2016). Thus, in order to investigate manifestations of rape culture against MSM, it is beneficial to explore their experiences with dating apps.

This chapter presents findings from an empirical study conducted with 25 MSM dating app users. Applying thematic analysis to the interview data, I found that participants talked about a variety of user behaviors indicative of rape culture, including imposing, aggressive, assumptive, and coercive behavior. Participants identified unwanted sexual messages and unwanted sexual images as two common manifestations of rape culture on dating apps and discussed how rape culture extends from in-app interactions to in-person encounters. Several participants disclosed that they had experienced sexual violence from MSM dating app users and one participant admitted that he had committed an act of sexual violence. Participants also reflected on the ways in which apps facilitate rape culture, though there was not consensus among participants regarding the extent to which dating app companies should be held accountable. I discuss the challenges in addressing rape culture and sexual violence against MSM, while also considering the sexual norms of MSM communities and the unique positionality of MSM as perpetrators and victims of sexual violence. The chapter closes with a call to (re)conceptualize rape culture so that definitions and understandings take into consideration the unique experiences of people with diverse gender and sexual identities.

Manifestations of Rape Culture

Rape culture manifests across society, including in law, medicine, education, and media (Dietzel, 2019; Phillips, 2016; Shariff, Dietzel, & Jaswal, 2017). Institutions such as these excuse perpetrators, fail to offer adequate support or resources to survivors, and contribute to social structures that perpetuate gender inequality and violence (Buchwald et al., 1993; Burt, 1980; Henry & Powell, 2014). These macrolevel manifestations illustrate how sexual violence has been condoned and trivialized in society, further evident by the high rates of sexual violence against women and MSM (Cotter & Savage, 2019; Rothman et al., 2011). However, rape culture is also present at the microlevel, such as when individuals blame victims for the sexual violence they have suffered or make jokes about sexual assault and rape (Henry & Powell, 2014). Of course, these manifestations reflect societal structures, gendered power relations, inequality, and social ideologies that condone and trivialize sexual violence against women.

Rape culture also manifests online. In some cases, rape culture is reproduced in virtual spaces; people in online communities perpetuate rape myths and trivialize sexual violence (Phipps et al., 2018; Stubbs-Richardson, Rader, & Cosby, 2018). In other cases, technology creates new problems, such as the nonconsensual distribution of intimate images and videos (Powell, Henry, & Flynn, 2018). Although most of the research investigating rape culture online has focused on the experiences of heterosexual women and girls (e.g., Henry & Powell, 2014; Keller et al., 2018), these studies still offer a valuable starting point to explore how rape culture can manifest in the experiences of MSM. Like women (see Cama, this volume), MSM are targets of male sexual aggression, can be exploited and coerced into engaging in unwanted sexual acts, are often blamed for the sexual violence a perpetrator has committed against them, and may not be believed or taken seriously when they disclose or report an incident of sexual violence (Braun, Schmidt, Gavey, & Fenaughty, 2009; Davies, 2002; Gavey, 2005). Similar to women, MSM face rape myths and stereotypes that serve to silence their experiences of sexual violence (Mortimer, Powell, & Sandy, 2019). Moreover, concerning manifestations of rape culture online, women and MSM both experience high rates of technology-facilitated sexual violence (Powell, Scott, Flynn, & Henry, 2020).

Technology-facilitated sexual violence (TFSV) is an umbrella term that refers to a range of behaviors in which technology is "used to facilitate both virtual and face-to-face sexually based harms" (Henry & Powell, 2016, p. 1). TFSV includes image-based sexual abuse, psychological violence, sexual harassment, coercion, cyberstalking, threats, hate speech, and the use of digital technologies to commit sexual violence in person (Henry & Powell, 2014). One example is online sexual harassment, or cyber-sexual harassment, which refers to unwanted or unwelcome behavior of a sexual nature (Biber, Doverspike, Baznik, Cober, & Ritter, 2002; Ritter, 2014; Schenk, 2008), including unwanted sexual attention and uninvited sexual advances (Van Royen, Vandebosch, & Poels, 2015). People may also use an online space to make threats of sexual violence against someone and then share their personal details in an effort to encourage others to commit violence against them (Fairbairn, 2015; Powell & Henry, 2017).

One of the most common experiences of TFSV is image-based sexual abuse (IBSA). IBSA is "the nonconsensual creation of nude or sexual images, the nonconsensual distribution of those intimate images, and the threat of distributing intimate images" (Powell et al., 2018, p. 306). Sometimes referred to as "revenge porn," IBSA occurs when a perpetrator seeks status, money, retribution, or personal enjoyment (Powell et al., 2018). IBSA refers to a range of behaviors, including voyeurism (i.e., sharing sexual images for sexual pleasure), sextortion (i.e., trying to obtain money, sexual images, or sexual acts by threatening the dissemination of sexual images), and sexual assault image sharing (i.e., distributing images or videos of a victim of sexual assault or rape) (see Powell & Henry, 2017).

Research has shown that MSM experience high rates of IBSA compared to heterosexual people. Henry, Powell, and Flynn (2017) found that 39% of MSM reported being victims of IBSA compared to 21% of heterosexual people. Some research has estimated that MSM dating app users are more than twice as likely as the general population to experience IBSA (Waldman, 2019), though other research suggests MSM may suffer IBSA at a rate five to six times higher than heterosexual people (Lenhart, Ybarra, & Price-Feeney, 2016). In a recent study, Powell et al. (2020) found that over half of MSM have experienced IBSA.

It should be noted that men are more likely than women to be perpetrators of IBSA (Powell et al., 2020). This finding holds true for MSM. Henry et al. (2017) found that 80% of MSM who had experienced IBSA reported that the abuse was perpetrated by another man. Similarly, in a study by Garcia, Gesselman, and Siliman (2016), MSM were more than twice as likely to distribute another person's sexual image without their consent. These findings suggest that MSM occupy a unique position relative to IBSA: although they experience high rates of victimization, they are also frequently perpetrators.

In addition to online sexual harassment, IBSA, online threats, and other sexually aggressive behaviors online, another manifestation of TFSV is the use of dating apps to perpetrate a sexual assault in person (Fairbairn, 2015; Powell & Henry, 2017). In their investigation of sexual assaults related to dating app use, Rowse, Bolt, and Gaya (2020) found that 14% of alleged sexual assaults happened after meeting someone from a dating app; over 50% occurred at the perpetrator's private residence; and, in over 80% of cases, the assault was committed the first time the dating app users met in person. Although Rowse et al.'s (2020) study did not include statistics on MSM, there are reports of men experiencing sexual assault from someone they met through online dating (see National Crime Agency, 2016).

TFSV is a concern for MSM dating app users. In a study on perceived risks related to dating app use, Albury and Byron (2016) noted that same sex attracted individuals were more worried about sexual predators and nonconsensual sexual relations than sexual health. Bauermeister, Giguere, Carballo-Dieguez, Ventuneac, and Eisenberg (2010) found that about half of MSM worry about their physical safety when meeting someone online, and more than one in 10 are specifically concerned about forced sex and rape. Similarly, Corriero and Tong (2016) reported that fears of sexual violence – such as harassment, physical harm, and rape – are common among MSM dating app users. These concerns are not unfounded. Waldman's (2019) study found that MSM have experienced harassment, catfishing, sextortion, and IBSA through their use of dating apps.

Method

The data presented in this chapter comes from a qualitative research project examining the experiences of MSM dating app users. Semi-structured interviews were conducted with 25 MSM dating app users in Autumn 2017 in Montreal, Canada. Participants were required to identify as an MSM dating app user and be at least 18 years old. Participants were recruited for three months using snowball sampling and flyers posted at a large Canadian university and in Montreal's gay neighborhood.

Following Blackwell, Birnholtz, and Abbott's (2015) approach for collecting data, participants were offered three interview options – in person, by telephone, or via an online chat – and were encouraged to choose the option best suited to their desired level of comfort, accessibility, and anonymity. The majority of participants chose to interview in person (n = 19), although a few interviewed by telephone (n = 3) and online chat (n = 3). Each interview lasted about one hour and was conducted in either English or French (with French interview data later translated into English).

All participants self-identified as MSM dating app users, with 24 identifying their gender as male and one identifying as gender-fluid. Most participants identified as gay, though two identified as queer and one identified as bisexual. No participants identified as transgender. Participants' ages ranged from 18 to 62 years. While the majority of participants identified as White (n = 14), participants also identified as Middle Eastern (n = 3), Hispanic (n = 3), Multiracial (n = 3), Asian (n = 1), and Black (n = 1). Pseudonyms are used throughout the chapter in order to protect participants' identities. The most used MSM dating app among participants was Grindr (n = 23), though many participants also used other apps and websites, including Tinder, Scruff, Hornet, and OkCupid. Participants reported that they mainly used the apps to seek sex, meet people, and find dates or relationships.

In the interviews, I asked participants about their experiences with dating apps, including any unwanted sexual interactions they may have had while interacting with other MSM online or in person. I also asked participants if, and how, rape culture manifests on Grindr. Participants were not provided with a definition of rape culture, nor were they corrected if their definition did not align with the definition I adopted for this research. I thematically analyzed the data following Braun and Clarke's (2006) approach. Thematic analysis "is a method for identifying, analyzing and reporting patterns (themes) within data" such that "it minimally organizes and describes [a] data set in (rich) detail" (Braun & Clarke, 2006, p. 79).

Findings

Participants said that MSM dating app users regularly imposed their sexual desires on other users and presumed another user's consent without asking. According to Michael (18, gay, male, White), "they don't know or care if the other person is attracted to them… if the other person is even looking for a sexual relationship." Ang (36, gay, male, Asian) similarly felt that users "assume that they have the right to do everything that they want." Robert (23, gay, male, White) figured this was because app users share common sexual identities: "gay guys are, you know, everybody thinks that we always want sex."

Participants talked about how MSM presume what another dating app user wants because of the information available on their profile. Robert (23, gay, male, White) explained that "if your profile says, 'looking for hookup' of course you're going to think, 'Oh, he wants naked pictures.'" Jadyn (32, gay, male, Black) gave another example: "someone may put on their profile that they're 100% a power bottom and someone just automatically messages them and is like, 'Oh yeah, you like to take it up on the ass or get gang banged.'"

Some participants discussed race and ethnicity in relation to rape culture. Charlie (24, gay, male, White) identified the fetishization of racialized MSM dating app users as one of its manifestations. Jadyn (32, gay, male, Black) talked about a user profiling him because he is Black: "he hits me up, and we start talking a little bit, and he went on to say, 'You look like you'd be a great rapist.'"

A few participants talked about situations in which MSM dating app users had pressured them or tried to persuade them into engaging in a sexual activity, even if they said they were not interested. As Nicolas (62, gay, male, Multiracial) explained, "they think that they'll be able to convince you, that you're almost playing hard to get, as if it's a game." Alexandre (25, gay, male, White) found that "some people can't understand that you're not interested in them and keep insisting." Similarly, Mason (26, bisexual, male, Multiracial) said some users do not take "no" for an answer: "if they're insisting and you made it very clear that you're not interested, that could probably be one way that rape culture could manifest itself on Grindr."

Participants were not always on the receiving end of this behavior. Some participants admitted that they may have interacted with other users in problematic ways. Gabriel (21, gay, male, White), for example, reflected on why other users had blocked him on the apps: "I imagine that I might have been insistent." Similarly, Robert (23, gay, male, White) said, "I may have been pushy one or two times with someone." Jadyn (32, gay, male, Black) also recognized that his behavior could have been an issue sometimes: "maybe I was the one who was being persistent or maybe I said something that was not savory or classy or… I mean, we're not perfect, right?"

The two most commonly mentioned experiences of rape culture on MSM dating apps include unwanted sexual messages and unwanted sexual images. As Oscar (22, gay, male, White) explained: "that's its manifestation on Grindr, when there's been no consent or there's been no context to go further sexually by text or images." Below I discuss participants' experiences with messages and images and also explore how rape culture extends from apps to in-person encounters. This section closes with reflections on the ways in which apps facilitate rape culture.

Messages

Participants talked about MSM dating app users who impose themselves on unwilling, uninterested recipients by sending "aggressive" and "invasive" messages. Jadyn (32, gay, male, Black) gave the following example: "the first message, you open up to a guy who is like, 'I want to take you, grab you by the hair, and fuck you hard in the ass.'" Charlie (24, gay, male, White) said these messages "might make you feel threatened for your physical safety or for your own personal integrity," while Noah (28, gay, male, White) described them as "degrading" but "normalized in the gay male world."

Skyler (28, queer, male, White), who had experienced this "super pushy" and "violent" behavior from users despite not giving any indication he was interested in them, explained that these messages imply "someone is purely meant for someone else's sexual gratification." Elijah (18, gay, male, White) said these messages reduce people to sexual objects: "you're not necessarily treating them like a person, you're just treating them as someone to have sex with." Talking about how he felt when he received such messages, Nicolas (62, gay, male, Multiracial) said, "it's almost like being violated right off the bat."

Images

Participants said it was common for MSM dating app users to save and share other users' sexual images without their consent. Oscar (22, gay, male, White) had exchanged photos with a casual sex partner and found his photos shared on Facebook. Noah (28, gay, male, White) had a sexual partner from years ago who saved and shared his photos and only became aware of it when a friend approached him at the gym and informed him that the person was distributing photos of his penis online. Both Jadyn (32, gay, male, Black) and Charlie (24, gay, male, White) reported that in the weeks prior to their interviews, numerous local MSM dating app users had their photos posted on an anonymous Tumblr account. Said Charlie (24, gay, male, White): "someone made a Montreal Tumblr blog where they were messaging all these people and getting their pictures and their dick pics, and they posted them all on this Tumblr."

Charlie (24, gay, male, White) and Theo (20, gay, gender-fluid, Multiracial) referred to the nonconsensual dissemination of sexual photos as "revenge porn." Charlie (24, gay, male, White) explained that revenge porn is "a form of sexual assault" and "a huge part of rape culture." Theo (20, gay, gender-fluid, Multiracial) agreed that this was a clear example of rape culture from MSM dating apps: "the sharing of pictures without someone's consent – that's straight-up rape culture."

Participants were concerned about the consequences that dissemination could have on their lives and careers. Ravi (28, gay, male, Middle Eastern) stated he and his friends do not trust anyone on Grindr out of concerns for their sexual photos being leaked. Ang (36, gay, male, Asian) agreed: "Given the fact that I am in the profession I am, I'm really reluctant to take such pictures. Anything that can get out could have devastating consequences." Mason (26, bisexual, male, Multiracial) and William (25, gay, male, White) also discussed the ease at which sexual photos can become public and explained that an MSM dating app user could extort another person by using their photos as blackmail.

Participants identified unwanted sexual photos, such as unsolicited "dick pics," as a manifestation of rape culture on MSM dating apps. Oscar (22, gay, male, White) and William (25, gay, male, White) explained it was common for people to assume that other users want to receive these photos, even without "any indication of wanting them." Toby (20, gay, male, White) found "an unsolicited nude" problematic because "I can see that causing harm to someone who doesn't want to see it." Some participants admitted that they had sent unsolicited dick pics to other MSM dating app users: "If I'm really horny," said Elijah (18, gay, male, White), "sometimes I'll send one of those."

Robert (23, gay, male, White) described rape culture on MSM dating apps in terms of feeling coerced or pressured to reciprocate in sharing sexual photos, whether or not he had wanted to receive them from someone else. He explained, "you feel like you have to send a picture just because you received one. So that's part of the definition, I think, that applies to Grindr."

From Apps to In-Person Encounters

Participants emphasized that rape culture extended beyond their interactions on MSM dating apps to interactions they had in person. For example, participants talked about users who did not respect personal boundaries. Michael (18, gay, male, White) said there was a user who had stalked him online and used the social media accounts connected to his dating app profile to find and contact his friends. Nicolas (62, gay, male, Multiracial) expressed concern about users taking advantage of the geo-locating function of dating apps to pinpoint where he lived. Skyler (28, queer, male, White) said he felt uncomfortable when people found him in real life and gave the example of receiving a message from someone who said they had seen him on the street: "I think they're trying to be flirty, but it's a little bit creepy."

Participants talked about feeling pressured to follow through on a proposed sexual activity when they met an MSM dating app user in person. For example, Toby (20, gay, male, White) explained that users might feel obligated to have sex because of the amount of time they spent arranging and preparing for a sexual encounter. Toby (20, gay, male, White) commented that, "there's such an expectation, like if you traveled to get here, if you douched as a bottom, if you shaved or whatever, it's [sex] very much expected." Karam (46, gay, male, Middle Eastern) similarly spoke about feeling compelled to have sex, even if he was no longer interested in the user: "I wouldn't call that rape, but I would definitely start lumping it in." Jadyn (32, gay, male, Black) described the situation as such:

> It's this weird fucked-up dynamic of when you are going through with something when you don't really want to and you're like, "I need to get this over with." In a sense, you are consenting, because you're like, "I am going forward. No one is holding a gun to my head or whatever." But it's a sort of social obligation gun-being-held-to-my-head and I feel like I'm doing something that I don't actually want to do.

Participants also discussed feeling passive and complaisant, and experiencing situations where they agreed to engage in an unwanted sexual activity. Robert (23, gay, male, White) recounted a time when he conceded to having sex because of how badly the other person wanted it. Pierre (22, gay, male, White) said there were a few times when an MSM dating app user he was giving oral sex expected him to deep throat even though "the consent wasn't there." Elijah (18, gay, male, White) said he had been "taken advantage of" when he was younger because he would "just roll with things" and give "a hesitant 'yes' not a solid 'yes.'" Logan (18, gay, male, White) admitted that there were times he "regretted having sex with someone" even though the sexual interaction was "not bad enough for me to stop." Joe (31, gay, male, White) had this experience:

> There was one man who came – and I like soft sensual sex and he liked really rough sex – and he just jammed it in there. And I thought, "I do not like that." But instead of extricating myself from the situation, I just sat and finished and let him be on his way. And that made me uncomfortable because there was a point in the situation when I was no longer consenting, but it was still happening. And I didn't feel comfortable enough to stop it from happening.

A few participants gave examples of sexual violence they had experienced from MSM dating app users. Hugo (23, queer, male, Hispanic) recounted a time when he was forced to give a blow job. Charlie (24, gay, male, White) talked about a user he had invited to his house to have sex with but was too aggressive and would not take "no" for an answer: "It actually ended with me almost calling the cops." Ravi (28, gay, male, Middle Eastern) gave the example of a user who seemed fine online but when they met in person, turned out to be a "wild sex animal" who tried to bite him and force him into having sex. Luis (43, gay, male, Hispanic) discussed two situations in which casual sex partners prioritized their sexual interests over his comfort, safety, and wellbeing: "I have been raped twice as a result of the recklessness of people and the dismissiveness, the lack of respect for an already-agreed-upon conversation." In one instance, Luis (43, gay, male, Hispanic) and an MSM dating app user had messaged and agreed about what they would and would not do during sex. When they met in person, however, the user disregarded their agreement and penetrated Luis without his consent.

As explained above, some MSM dating app users make assumptions about other users based on their profiles, which can lead to sexually violent behavior. Noah (28, gay, male, White), for example, had a casual sex partner who he thought liked rough sex, so he choked him. After they hooked up, Noah (28, gay, male, White) discovered that this partner did not like being choked and immediately apologized, but said that experience "kind of traumatized" him.

Reflections on the Ways in Which Apps Facilitate Rape Culture

Participants felt that rape culture manifests more on some MSM dating apps than others. William (25, gay, male, White) explained that because any user can contact any other user on Grindr, it is "more likely" to experience an unwanted interaction on Grindr than on Tinder. Elijah (18, gay, male, White) similarly asserted that it is "easier" for rape culture to manifest on Grindr than Tinder because "on Tinder you have to give them the opportunity first – you both have to swipe right."

However, there was a lack of consensus among participants regarding the extent to which MSM dating apps facilitate rape culture. Some participants felt that the apps were responsible. Diego (35, gay, male, Hispanic) said the design of MSM dating apps and the affordances of the internet, such as the ability to operate anonymously online, provide a "shield" for users to act however they want without any consequences. Ang (36, gay, male, Asian) asserted that the culture of the apps encouraged sexual violence: "For such applications, the base goal is fast encounters. So, when you go for fast encounters, you're not necessarily going to have the time to cover all the angles of what you consent to and what you don't."

Other participants felt that rape culture on MSM dating apps was a reflection of societal norms. Toby (20, gay, male, White) said, "I wouldn't vilify Grindr. I think it's just the platform that we see rape culture occurring because of the society and the norms that we live in." Similarly, Luis (43, gay, male, Hispanic) explained that even though apps may be the venue through which rape culture occurs, sexual violence is not the fault of apps, but is caused by "utmost selfishness of a human being."

One participant held both perspectives. Although Dion (37, gay, male, Middle Eastern) felt that rape culture was made "easier" by MSM dating apps, he did not blame them for the sexual violence MSM may experience:

> Grindr would be the facilitator, but not really the culprit.... As a hook-up app, you might go and meet a stranger in a sexual setting and this person might do things to you, or you do things to them, that is not consensual and it's just part of rape culture.

Discussion

When considering how rape culture manifests on MSM dating apps, participants said rape culture appeared through the messages and images they received from other users. They spoke about being sent violent comments and unsolicited nude photos. These examples are not surprising because, by the very nature of being online, people's behavior is limited to specific virtual actions and interactions. Messages and images are the main ways that individuals communicate and connect with one another online. The aggressive, dominating, presumptive, and unwanted behavior that comes about through users' messages and images indicates the presence of rape culture on MSM dating apps.

Participants discussed situations where rape culture extended beyond their online interactions with MSM dating app users. They gave numerous examples of technology-based sexual violence, including image-based sexual abuse, harassment, stalking, coercion, threats, and sexual assault. These results align with previous research, which has similarly found that TFSV spans across people's online and offline interactions (Henry & Powell, 2014; Powell & Henry, 2017).

Participants also explained that incidents of TFSV were emotionally traumatizing, physically violent, and could negatively impact their lives and careers. Again, these results support previous research that has documented the detrimental effects of TFSV on people's safety, health, and wellbeing (Scarduzio, Sheff, & Smith, 2018), including emotional and physical harm (Fairbairn, 2015; Henry & Powell, 2016), as well as consequences on their jobs and relationships (Citron & Franks, 2014).

The online and in-person manifestations of rape culture participants described relative to their use of MSM dating apps demonstrate that rape culture is not limited to a space or context; rape culture is present throughout society. This was further evident as participants considered the extent to which apps facilitate rape culture. The socio-cultural societal norms that people embody, practice, and perpetuate mean that rape culture can manifest wherever people are: online, in person, and across these spaces. Technology does not create a separate world in which rape culture can manifest; rather, it extends and expands upon the experiences people have in physical space (boyd, 2010; Mowlabocus, 2010).

This notion was reflected in participants' comments about the extent to which MSM dating apps facilitate rape culture. As Toby (20, gay, male, White) explained, dating apps are "the platform[s] that we see rape culture occurring because of the society and the norms that we live in." Even though participants disagreed about whether the affordances of MSM dating apps made it was easier for rape culture to manifest, participants recognized that MSM dating app users' behaviors were indicative of larger socio-cultural issues present in society.

MSM dating apps occupy a unique position in the lives of MSM because they can help address everyday manifestations of rape culture. For example, MSM dating apps offer users the ability to block and report users who engage in "bad behavior" (Grindr, 2020a). In 2019, Grindr added options for users to indicate on their profile if, or to what extent, they are open to receiving "NSFW [Not Safe For Work] Pics" from other users and where they prefer to meet another app user, such as "My Place," "Your Place," "Bar," "Coffee Shop," or "Restaurant" (Grindr, 2020b). While there is a need for researchers to investigate the effectiveness of these in-app features, their presence suggests that MSM dating app companies are cognizant of the sexual violence that can happen through their platforms and feel at least some sense of responsibility to help their users tackle such problems.

One challenge in addressing rape culture against MSM is understanding that MSM can be both victims and perpetrators of sexual violence. This finding was reflected in the experiences of participants who described, in their interactions online and in person, situations where they had been both victims and perpetrators of sexual violence. MSM occupy a unique position in society as they possess both majority and minority identities. As men, MSM are endowed with power and privilege, but as queer people with non-normative sexual and gender identities, MSM may also be marginalized: "This person might do things to you, or you might to things to them, that is not consensual and it's just part of rape culture," explained Dion (37, gay, male, Middle Eastern).

Participants spoke to this duality as they discussed the sexual norms of MSM communities, specifically as they asserted that gay men "always want sex" and that unwanted sexual advances are "normalized in the gay male world." These comments reflect Hollway's (1998, p. 63) male sexual drive discourse, which "sees men as sexually insatiable and male sexuality as naturally an uncontrollable drive." When applied to the context of MSM dating apps, this means MSM dating app users may feel pressured to consent or follow through with a sexual activity, even when they are uninterested. It also suggests that MSM may assume other dating app users are always open to sexual advances, that other users always want to engage in sexual activity, and subsequently, that other users always consent.

However, as evident in the data, MSM can also be targets of sexual violence. Participants spoke of societal assumptions about them, such as always wanting sex, and about the pressure to engage in a sexual activity, in both their online and offline interactions with other MSM. On apps, participants asserted that users "assume they have the right to do whatever they want," such as send sexual messages and photos to a recipient without "any indication of wanting them." Participants discussed feeling pressured to engage in sexual acts with MSM on dating apps, such as feeling obliged "to send a picture just because you received one." When interacting with MSM dating app users in person, participants similarly explained that sexual activity was "expected," and described it as "a sort of social obligation" that they "didn't feel comfortable enough to stop it from happening," even when it was "not a solid 'yes'" (see also Cama, this volume). Whether on apps or in person, MSM dating app users may presume the consent of other users and may expect themselves, and others, to engage in a sexual act, even when feeling coerced or disinterested (Gavey et al., 2009; Klesse, 2016).

Sexual violence comes in many forms (Kelly, 1988) yet men, and MSM in particular, do not always identify themselves as victims or survivors of sexual violence (Braun et al., 2009; Davies, 2002). Further, rape myths perpetuate stereotypes and assumptions about sexual violence against people of diverse gender and sexual identities in ways that further obfuscate MSM experiences with rape culture (Mortimer et al., 2019). Whether intentionally or unintentionally, MSM dating app users may also contribute to the trivialization and denial of rape culture against MSM and queer people.

Dion's (37, gay, male, Middle Eastern) comment that "this person might do things to you, or you might to things to them, that is not consensual and it's just part of rape culture" not only highlights the unique positionality of MSM but also dismisses the sexual aggression, harm, and violence MSM dating app users commit against one another. Similarly, other participants seemed to accept sexual violence as banal and unavoidable, including Noah (28, gay, male, White) who said this behavior was "normalized in the gay male world." Comments such as these minimize and invisibilize sexual violence against MSM and also frame rape culture against MSM as "inevitable" (Keller et al., 2018; Smith, 2004).

In a rape culture, a person's body exists only as a source of sexual pleasure for another person, such that the body is objectified and, in the cases of racialized people, fetishized (Smith, 2004). These ideologies were also reflected in participants' experiences, including for Skyler (28, queer, male, White) who explained that receiving messages made him feel like a sexual object, "purely meant for someone else's sexual gratification." However, it is important to note that rape culture does not affect everyone similarly. Racialized people face higher rates of sexual violence than white people (Black et al., 2011), and racialized MSM experience additional oppression and victimization that white MSM do not (Meyer, 2012). My findings similarly suggest that racialized MSM dating app users are uniquely targeted in rape culture. It would be valuable for future research to investigate issues of sexual consent and sexual violence specific to racialized MSM dating app users.

There are other limitations in this study that future research could address. Since this chapter focused on manifestations of rape culture against MSM, future studies could explore and develop a conceptualization of rape culture sensitive to people of diverse genders and sexualities. Similarly, a future study could examine how factors like culture, country of origin, and language affect MSM perceptions of, and experiences with, rape culture online and in person. Because participants were not given an "official" definition of rape culture, they may have held different or conflicting understandings. Furthermore, since men may not perceive of themselves as victims or survivors of sexual violence (Braun et al., 2009; Davies, 2002), some participants may have experienced sexual violence but did not identify it as such, or did not consider it as a manifestation of rape culture. Future research could present MSM with a definition of rape culture and a variety of scenarios to examine if, and how, they connect sexual violence with rape culture. Lastly, it would be beneficial for future research to take a quantitative or mixed methods research approach to explore potential connections between rape culture and different variables, such as MSM identities (e.g., age, sexual position, relationship status), sexual practices (e.g., condom use, drug and alcohol consumption), and app-related behaviors (e.g., profile image, profile content, years of usage, frequency of use).

Conclusion

Rape culture, described as when "violence is seen as sexy and sexuality as violent" (Buchwald et al., 1993, p. vii), manifests for MSM in a variety of ways on dating apps and in person. This chapter has documented rape culture related to the use of MSM dating apps and highlighted the range of sexually violent behaviors present in online and offline spaces and across those spaces. While this research is helpful as scholars increasingly explore rape culture against people of diverse genders and sexualities, these findings largely support current understandings of rape culture: sexual violence is tolerated and normalized in society (Henry & Powell, 2014); male sexual aggression is expected and condoned (Keller et al., 2018; Smith, 2004); perpetrators of sexual violence are excused (Phipps et al., 2018; Sills et al., 2016); men's consent is presumed (Hollway, 1998); bodies are objectified and fetishized (Smith, 2004); and racialized people experience additional victimization (Meyer, 2012).

If we continue to focus on heterosexual people's experiences with rape culture, the experiences of people outside of those identities risk being minimized, silenced, and rendered invisible. This can result in people who have suffered sexual violence failing to identify their own experiences as such because of a lack of awareness, representation, and understanding. Particularly in relation to connections facilitated by technology, there is an urgent need to understand how sexual violence manifests in and across online spaces and in-person spaces. It is crucial for research to continue to explore rape culture, sexual violence, and the lived experiences of sexually diverse and gender diverse people so we, as a society, can develop better theoretical and empirical understandings of these problems and work toward safe, healthy, and consensual sexual relationships for everyone in practice.

References

Albury, K., & Byron, P. (2016). Safe on my phone? Same-sex attracted young people's negotiations of intimacy, visibility, and risk on digital hook-up apps. *Social Media + Society*, *2*(4), 1–10. doi:10.1177/2056305116672887

Albury, K., Byron, P., McCosker, A., Pym, T., Walshe, J., Race, K., … Dietzel, C. (2019). Safety, risk and wellbeing on dating apps: Final report. Retrieved from https://apo.org.au/sites/default/files/resource-files/2019-12/apo-nid268156.pdf

Badal, H. J., Stryker, J. E., DeLuca, N., & Purcell, D. W. (2018). Swipe right: Dating website and app use among men who have sex with men. *AIDS and Behavior*, *22*(4), 1265–1272. doi:10.1007/s10461-017-1882-7

Bauermeister, J. A., Giguere, R., Carballo-Dieguez, A., Ventuneac, A., & Eisenberg, A. (2010). Perceived risks and protective strategies employed by young men who have sex with men (YMSM) when seeking online sexual partners. *Journal of Health Communication*, *15*(6), 679–690. doi:10.1080/10810730.2010.499597

Biber, J. K., Doverspike, D., Baznik, D., Cober, A., & Ritter, B. A. (2002). Sexual harassment in online communications: Effects of gender and discourse medium. *CyberPsychology & Behavior*, *5*(1), 33–42. doi:10.1089/109493102753685863

Black, M. C., Basile, K. C., Breiding, M. J., Smith, S. G., Walters, M. L., Merrick, M. T., … Stevens, M. R. (2011). The national intimate partner and sexual violence survey (NISVS): 2010 summary report. Retrieved from https://www.cdc.gov/violenceprevention/pdf/nisvs_report2010-a.pdf

Blackwell, C., Birnholtz, J., & Abbott, C. (2015). Seeing and being seen: Co-situation and impression formation using Grindr, a location-aware gay dating app. *New Media & Society*, *17*(7), 1117–1136.

boyd, d. (2010). Social network sites as networked publics: Affordances, dynamics, and implications. In Z. Papacharissi (Ed.), *A networked self* (pp. 47–66). New York, NY: Routledge.

Braun, V., & Clarke, V. (2006). Using thematic analysis in psychology. *Qualitative Research in Psychology*, *3*(2), 77–101. doi:10.1191/1478088706QP063OA

Braun, V., Schmidt, J., Gavey, N., & Fenaughty, J. (2009). Sexual coercion among gay and bisexual men in Aotearoa/New Zealand. *Journal of Homosexuality*, *56*(3), 336–360. doi:10.1080/00918360902728764

Brownmiller, S. (1975). *Against our will: Men, women and rape.* New York, NY: Simon & Schuster.

Buchwald, E., Fletcher, P. R., & Roth, M. (Eds.) (1993). *Transforming a rape culture.* Minneapolis, MN: Milkweed Editions.

Burt, M. R. (1980). Cultural myths and supports for rape. *Journal of Personality and Social Psychology, 38*(2), 217–230. doi:10.1111/j.1471-6402.2010.01596

Citron, D. K., & Franks, M. A. (2014). Criminalizing revenge porn. *Wake Forest Law Review, 49*, 345. Retrieved from https://heinonline-org.ezproxy.lib.rmit.edu.au/HOL/Page?handle=hein.journals/wflr49&div=15&g_sent=1&casa_token=&collection=journals

Clement, J. (2019). Number of Grindr daily and monthly active users worldwide as of August 2018. Retrieved from https://www.statista.com/statistics/719621/grindr-user-number/

Corriero, E. F., & Tong, S. T. (2016). Managing uncertainty in mobile dating applications: Goals, concerns of use, and information seeking in Grindr. *Mobile Media & Communication, 4*(1), 121–141. doi:10.1177/2050157915614872

Cotter, A., & Savage, L. (2019). Gender-based violence and unwanted sexual behaviour in Canada, 2018: Initial findings from the survey of safety in public and private spaces. Retrieved from https://www150.statcan.gc.ca/n1/pub/85-002-x/2019001/article/00017-eng.htm

Davies, M. (2002). Male sexual assault victims: A selective review of the literature and implications for support services. *Aggression and Violent Behavior, 7*(3), 203–214. doi:10.1016/S1359-1789(00)00043-4

Dietzel, C. (2019). Rape culture and universities: Examining the perspectives of men who have sex with men. In M. Bergeron, E. Paquette, S. Ricci, C. Rousseau, & M. St Hilaire (Eds.), *Actes du symposium canadien sur la violence sexuelle dans les milieux d'enseignement supérieur. Proceedings of the Canadian symposium on sexual violence in post-secondary education institutions* (pp. 69–73). Montréal, QC: Université du Québec à Montréal (UQAM).

Fairbairn, J. (2015). Rape threats and revenge porn: Defining sexual violence in the digital age. In J. Bailey & V. Steeves (Eds.), *eGirls, eCitizens: Putting technology, theory and policy into dialogue with girls' and young women's voices* (pp. 229–252). Ottawa, ON: University of Ottawa Press.

Garcia, J. R., Gesselman, A. N., Siliman, S. A., Perry, B. L., Coe, K., & Fisher, H. E. (2016). Sexting among singles in the USA: Prevalence of sending, receiving, and sharing sexual messages and images. *Sexual Health, 13*(5), 428–435. doi:10.1071/SH15240

Gavey, N. (2005). *Just sex? The cultural scaffolding of rape.* London: Routledge.

Gavey, N., Schmidt, J., Braun, V., Fenaughty, J., & Eremin, M. (2009). Unsafe, unwanted: Sexual coercion as a barrier to safer sex among men who have sex with men. *Journal of Health Psychology, 14*(7), 1021–1026. doi:10.1177/1359105309342307

Grindr. (2020a). Blocking and reporting users. Retrieved from https://help.grindr.com/hc/en-us/articles/217763127-Blocking-and-Reporting-Users

Grindr. (2020b). What are the fields NSFW and meet at?. Retrieved from https://help.grindr.com/hc/en-us/articles/360026423034-What-Are-The-Fields-NSFW-And-Meet-At-

Henry, N., & Powell, A. (2014). *Preventing sexual violence: Interdisciplinary approaches to overcoming a rape culture.* London: Palgrave Macmillan.

Henry, N., & Powell, A. (2016). Technology-facilitated sexual violence: A literature review of empirical research. *Trauma, Violence, & Abuse, 19*(2), 195–208. doi: 10.1177/1524838016650189

Henry, N., Powell, A., & Flynn, A. (2017). Not just 'revenge pornography': Australians' experiences of image-based abuse: A summary report. Retrieved from https://www.rmit.edu.au/content/dam/rmit/documents/college-of-design-and-social-context/schools/global-urban-and-social-studies/revenge_porn_report_2017.pdf

Hollway, W. (1998). Gender difference and the production of subjectivity. In J. Henriques, W. Hollway, C. Urwin, C. Venn, & V. Walkerdine (Eds.), *Changing the subject: Psychology, social regulation and subjectivity* (pp. 223–261). London: Methuen.

Keller, J., Mendes, K., & Ringrose, J. (2018). Speaking 'unspeakable things': Documenting digital feminist responses to rape culture. *Journal of Gender Studies, 27*(1), 22–36. doi:10.1080/09589236.2016.1211511

Kelly, L. (1988). *Surviving sexual violence*. London: John Wiley & Sons.

Klesse, C. (2016). *The spectre of promiscuity: Gay male and bisexual non-monogamies and polyamories*. New York, NY: Routledge.

Lenhart, A., Ybarra, M., & Price-Feeney, M. (2016). Nonconsensual image sharing: One in 25 Americans has been a victim of 'revenge porn'. Retrieved from https://datasociety.net/pubs/oh/Nonconsensual_Image_Sharing_2016.pdf

Meyer, D. (2012). An intersectional analysis of lesbian, gay, bisexual, and transgender (LGBT) people's evaluations of anti-queer violence. *Gender & Society, 26*(6), 849–873. doi:10.1177/0891243212461299

Mortimer, S., Powell, A., & Sandy, L. (2019). 'Typical scripts' and their silences: Exploring myths about sexual violence and LGBTQ people from the perspectives of support workers. *Current Issues in Criminal Justice, 31*(3), 333–348. doi:10.1080/10345329.2019.1639287

Mowlabocus, S. (2010). *Gaydar culture: Gay men, technology and embodiment in the digital age*. Abingdon: Routledge.

National Crime Agency. (2016). Emerging new threat in online dating: Initial trends in internet dating-initiated serious sexual assaults. Retrieved from https://www.west-info.eu/online-dating-safety-advice/file-7/

Phillips, N. D. (2016). *Beyond blurred lines: Rape culture in popular media*. Lanham, MD: Rowman & Littlefield.

Phipps, A., Ringrose, J., Renold, E., & Jackson, C. (2018). Rape culture, lad culture and everyday sexism: Researching, conceptualizing and politicizing new mediations of gender and sexual violence. *Journal of Gender Studies, 27*(1), 1–8. doi: 10.1080/09589236.2016.1266792

Powell, A., & Henry, N. (Eds.), (2017). *Sexual violence in a digital age*. London: Palgrave Macmillan.

Powell, A., Henry, N., & Flynn, A. (2018). Image-based sexual abuse. In W. S. DeKeseredy & M. Dragiewicz (Eds.), *Routledge handbook of critical criminology* (2nd ed., pp. 305–315). Abingdon and New York, NY: Routledge.

Powell, A., Scott, A., Flynn, A., & Henry, N. (2020). Image-based sexual abuse: An international study of victims and perpetrators. Retrieved from https://www.researchgate.net/publication/339488012_Image-based_sexual_abuse_An_international_study_of_victims_and_perpetrators

Race, K. (2015). Speculative pragmatism and intimate arrangements: Online hook-up devices in gay life. *Culture, Health & Sexuality*, *17*(4), 496–511. doi:10.1080/13691058.2014.930181

Ritter, B. A. (2014). Deviant behavior in computer-mediated communication: Development and validation of a measure of cybersexual harassment. *Journal of Computer-Mediated Communication*, *19*(2), 197–214. doi:10.1111/jcc4.12039

Rothman, E. F., Exner, D., & Baughman, A. L. (2011). The prevalence of sexual assault against people who identify as gay, lesbian, or bisexual in the United States: A systematic review. *Trauma, Violence, & Abuse*, *12*(2), 55–66. doi:10.1177/1524838010390707

Rowse, J., Bolt, C., & Gaya, S. (2020). Swipe right: The emergence of dating-app facilitated sexual assault. A descriptive retrospective audit of forensic examination caseload in an Australian metropolitan service. *Forensic Science, Medicine and Pathology*, *16*, 71–77. doi:10.1007/s12024-019-00201-7

Scarduzio, J. A., Sheff, S. E., & Smith, M. (2018). Coping and sexual harassment: How victims cope across multiple settings. *Archives of Sexual Behavior*, *47*(2), 327–340. doi:10.1007/s10508-017-1065-7

Schenk, S. (2008). Cyber-sexual harassment: The development of the cyber-sexual experiences questionnaire. *McNair Scholars Journal*, *12*(1), 82–91. Retrieved from https://scholarworks.gvsu.edu/mcnair/vol12/iss1/8/

Shariff, S. (2017). Navigating the minefield of sexual violence policy in expanding "university contexts." *Education Law Journal*, *27*(1), 39–58. Retrieved from http://ezproxy.its.rmit.edu.au/login?url=https://search-proquest-com.ezproxy.lib.rmit.edu.au/docview/1983613562?accountid=13552

Shariff, S., Dietzel, C., & Jaswal, N. (Eds.). (2017). Navigating the minefield: Responding to legal and educational dilemmas in addressing sexual violence in universities [Special Issue]. *Education & Law Journal*, *27*(1).

Sills, S., Pickens, C., Beach, K., Jones, L., Calder-Dawe, O., Benton-Greig, P., & Gavey, N. (2016). Rape culture and social media: Young critics and a feminist counterpublic. *Feminist Media Studies*, *16*(6), 935–951. doi:10.1080/14680777.2015.1137962

Smith, M. (2004). *Encyclopedia of rape*. Westport, CT: Greenwood Press.

Stubbs-Richardson, M., Rader, N. E., & Cosby, A. G. (2018). Tweeting rape culture: Examining portrayals of victim blaming in discussions of sexual assault cases on Twitter. *Feminism & Psychology*, *28*(1), 90–108. doi:10.1177/0959353517715874

Van Royen, K., Vandebosch, H., & Poels, K. (2015). Severe sexual harassment on social networking sites: Belgian adolescents' views. *Journal of Children and Media*, *9*(4), 472–491. doi:10.1080/17482798.2015.1089301

Waldman, A. E. (2019). Law, privacy, and online dating: "Revenge porn" in gay online communities. *Law & Social Inquiry*, *44*(4), 987–1018. doi:10.1017/lsi.2018.29

Chapter 22

Navigating Privacy on Gay-Oriented Mobile Dating Applications*

Ari Ezra Waldman

Abstract

Mobile dating apps are widely used in the queer community. Whether for sexual exploration or dating, mobile and geosocial dating apps facilitate connection. But they also bring attendant privacy risks. This chapter is based on original research about the ways gay and bisexual men navigate their privacy on geosocial dating apps geared toward the LGBTQI community. It argues that, contrary to the conventional wisdom that people who share semi-nude or nude photos do not care about their privacy, gay and bisexual users of geosocial dating apps care very much about their privacy and engage in complex, overlapping privacy navigation techniques when sharing photos. They share semi-nude and nude photos for a variety of reasons, but generally do so only after building organic trust with another person. Because trust can easily break down without supportive institutions, this chapter argues that law and design must help individuals protect their privacy on geosocial dating apps.

Keywords: LGBTQI; cyberharassment; privacy; trust; platform design; social networks; online dating

Introduction

Sharing personal information has always been an integral part of social life, binding us together in productive and healthy ways (Derlega, Metts, Petronio,

---

*Portions of this chapter are based on previously published work: Waldman, A. (2019). Law, privacy, and online dating: 'Revenge porn' in gay online communities. *Law & Social Inquiry*, 44(4), 987–1018.

The Emerald International Handbook of Technology-Facilitated Violence and Abuse, 369–381

doi:10.1108/978-1-83982-848-520211027

& Margulis, 1993). At the same time, sharing creates privacy and safety risks, especially for marginalized populations. The moment we share something, we lose control over it. We run the risk of its wider dissemination. We are vulnerable to those who have information about us, especially when that information is stigmatizing, out of context, and potentially harmful (Richards & Hartzog, 2016). And yet, we still share. This is not because we do not care about our privacy; we care a great deal. We share personal information using complex privacy navigation techniques that develop organic trust within communities (boyd, 2014; Waldman, 2018a).

This chapter is about the privacy and safety risks faced by members of the LGBTQI community who use online social networks, particularly dating applications and platforms, and the ways in which LGBTQI persons navigate their privacy in a digital environment with strong and persistent norms of disclosure. I will make two arguments, one descriptive and one normative. The descriptive argument is that individuals engage in complex privacy self-navigation on queer-oriented geosocial dating applications to build and maintain organic trust norms that protect themselves from some privacy risks. In particular, gay and bisexual men anonymize photos, develop a rapport through conversation, engage reciprocal sharing and mutual surveillance, and rely on identity-based familiarity in an attempt to organically build trust and enhance safety. My normative argument is that self-navigation will always be insufficient, and that norms of trust in online social spaces require support from endogenous design and exogenous law to make those spaces safe for sharing.

This chapter proceeds in four parts. Part I explores the powerful disclosure norms in geosocial dating applications, particularly those that cater to gay and bisexual men. These norms are both designed-in and socially constructed, and they create strong pressures to share intimate information. Part II discusses the privacy risks that come with disclosure. Given that the focus of this chapter is on gay and bisexual experiences, this Part shows how sharing in the online dating context poses unique challenges to marginalized populations. Part III describes how users navigate their privacy in a disclosure-heavy environment. Finally, Part IV argues that the organic trust users are trying to create is insufficient to protect privacy online. Law and design must help.

The Disclosure Norms of Geosocial Dating Applications

Online social networks and mobile applications are multifactor information-sharing environments (Goffman, 1959). We disclose voluminous personal information on social networks like Facebook not just our "likes," but everything Facebook can learn from that engagement. Geosocial dating platforms are a widely used subset of online social networks (Anderson, Vogels, & Turner, 2020) and they require or strongly encourage the disclosure and exchange of highly intimate information, including sexual interests, HIV status, and, at times, graphic or revealing images. Put another way, geosocial dating applications operate with powerful norms of disclosure generated in three ways: design requirements, design nudges, and social practice.

Design Requirements

Platform designers require that users share certain information. Grindr, the popular gay-oriented geosocial application, requires an email address and other information on the backend. As a geosocial application, it also requires location information; it incorporates geolocation technology (hence the portmanteau "geosocial") to not only identify potential matches nearby but also to tell users their relative proximity to those matches "Dave is 1,500 feet away," for example. Some applications require at least one photograph; most require that all users are above a certain age. Disclosure requirements serve several purposes, some technical, some social, and some both. For example, platforms may require a valid email address or phone number for both verification and two-factor authorization. Those disclosure mandates stem from how the technology works. Dating platforms may also require users to select a gender identity and/or sexual orientation, allowing them to match users. The same is true for zip codes, the disclosure of which allows geosocial applications to function and meet users' expectations.

Design Nudges

"Nudges" refer to any aspect of "choice architecture," or the context in which people make decisions, can "alter people's behavior in a predictable way without forbidding any options," like how grouping expensive cereals at eye-level and relegating the cheaper ones below encourages a more expensive purchase (Thaler & Sunstein, 2008, p. 6). Nudges are subtle yet powerful, triggering any number of cognitive biases that make disclosure more likely (Mathur et al., 2019; Waldman, 2019c). Dating applications, especially those that purport to match compatible people, nudge users to disclose personal information to receive extra benefits from the platform. OkCupid (n.d.), for example, "ask[s] interesting questions to get to know [users] on a deeper level" and encourages users to answer as many questions as possible to improve their matches. Users answer questions about detailed and deeply personal questions: "If a partner asked you to have sex in a sex shop booth with others watching, would you?" or "How does the idea of being slapped hard in the face during sex make you feel?" or "Have you ever gone on a rampant sex spree while depressed?" (Donovan, 2012). Answering these questions is optional, but the platform pushes what it calls a "super-smart algorithm" that matches compatible users based on the answers. This implies that the more answers users provide, the better their match should be. Although there is reason to question the need for all these data points (Dressel & Farid, 2018; Salganik, 2019), the pressure to disclose remains.

The design of geosocial applications nudges users to share personal and intimate images, which are the currencies of these platforms. Sometimes presented in a grid based on proximity or as a single picture that fills most of the smartphone screen, photos are the first and sometimes only thing other users see about other users, thus creating pressure to upload at least one image. Although all platforms allow users to add information to their profiles including name, age, and physical characteristics, pictures are at the center of these profiles, as is sharing pictures over and above the profile image. Beyond the first picture, platforms are designed to allow users to upload at least six photos, with some including space for hundreds of images.

Social Practice

According to the Pew Research Center, 71% of online daters said it was important or very important to them that others' profiles included at least one photo of themselves (Anderson et al., 2020). Wide majorities also want to see complete profiles, filled with information that is at once intimate, but also necessary to set expectations. Gay and bisexual men want to know others' HIV status, sexual interests, and professional and educational backgrounds. They also want to see more than one photo, with at least one study arguing that representation through imagery was an important part of identity-formation on Grindr (Blackwell, Birnholtz, & Abbott 2014). This demand creates strong disclosure norms that put pressure on users to share intimate information and ultimately put their privacy at risk.

In previous research, I showed how the social practice of LGBTQI-oriented dating applications includes the expectation of sharing intimate photos (Waldman, 2019a). That study, which includes surveys and ethnography, suggested that for many gay and bisexual men, "if you don't share photos, you can't really participate" (p. 997). One respondent noted that "there's an expectation; gays want to see what you're offering" (p. 997). Another stated that "[s] haring photos seems to be essential to maintaining interest. I wish it weren't the case, but whatever" (p. 997). Although many gay and bisexual men share intimate photos for other reasons, such as body positivity and sexual exploration, other factors remain powerful, including the verification of identity and security, and the expectation to share and prevailing norms of disclosure. Put another way, any one individual may experience pressure to share personal information or intimate photos. The pervasiveness of that pressure makes disclosure a social fact of queer-oriented dating applications; the norm exists independent of any particular request for a photo.

With Disclosure Comes Privacy Risk

It is axiomatic that disclosing personal information to others online puts us at risk of privacy invasions, exploitation, extortion, and harassment. This is particularly true for women, sexual minorities, and other marginalized populations (Burkell & Bailey, 2018; Citron, 2014). Interactive digital technologies amplify those risks. Information is easy and cheap to store, disseminate, and leverage. Online interactions erode traditional in-person social norms by dehumanizing and flattening the identities of other individuals. Digital technologies, therefore, lower social barriers that hold hateful and harassing conduct at bay, and in so doing, amplify and entrench the power dynamics that already exist in society (Citron, 2009).

With respect to LGBTQI-oriented geosocial dating applications, concerns about privacy invasions, harassment, and stalking are neither theoretical nor idle. These platforms have already exposed their users to major privacy breaches. Grindr shared its users' HIV status with third parties for years (Ghorayshi & Ray, 2018). Farnden, Martini, and Choo (2015) found that Grindr sends all profile images unencrypted across its network. User locations are also sent from devices to the Grindr server with country and city data, as well as exact longitude and latitude of the users. The researchers noted that combining this information with a timestamp could allow someone to track users in real space. This information has been used in violent homophobic attacks. For example, people have used Grindr to murder and torture gay men in the United States, Canada, and across the world, especially in countries that criminalize homosexuality and sodomy (Carroll, 2019; Fitzsimmons, 2020; Tracy, 2020). On Badoo, which is identical to the Blendr application, Farnden et al. (2015) were able to collect profile names, chat histories, nearby users, profile information, and device information. On Tinder, the most popular dating application in the United States, researchers retrieved exact user locations, profile images, and all message history. The potential dissemination of this kind of information could uniquely harm queer populations, especially those in need of the protection of anonymity or in the closet (Stern, 2016).

Despite these risks, individuals who identify as gay and bisexual frequently use these applications and share information to meet others who share their identities. According to one study, dating application users who identified as heterosexual opened their applications eight times per week and used them for 71 seconds at a time (Grov et al., 2014). Gay and bisexual men, on the other hand, averaged 22 times per week for 96 seconds at a time. Grindr reported that in 2013, more than one million users logged in to the application every day and sent more than seven million messages and two million photos (Grov et al., 2014). There may be several reasons for this, not the least of which is that digital spaces offer social opportunities when stigma and discrimination make face-to-face interaction difficult. Social engagements on these applications are also expressions of sexual and romantic freedom after decades of marginalization. Some even argue that they facilitate a form of self-pornography and eroticism (Tziallas, 2015). Whatever the reason, it is clear that gay and bisexual individuals use these applications frequently (Anderson et al., 2020) and share a significant amount of personal information as a result. Because everything that we share may be recorded, retained, screenshotted, and saved, this puts us at risk for cyberharassment, exploitation, so-called "revenge porn" (more appropriately termed "nonconsensual pornography" because it involves the nonconsensual sharing of someone else's identifiable intimate or graphic images or videos and is not necessarily done out of a desire for revenge), and technology-facilitated intimate partner violence, among myriad other abuses.

Privacy Self-Help

Gay and bisexual users of geosocial dating applications face strong pressures to disclose intimate information and images. Because doing so involves some risk, users go to great lengths to protect their privacy. This is not just true of members of the LGBTQI community. As Sarah Heath (2015) has shown, women and girls leverage "controls initiated by users to protect and maintain their security online" (p. 362). The goal of these measures is to create and maintain norms of trust that can help ameliorate the risks of disclosure.

Previously, I surveyed 834 gay and bisexual men who used geosocial dating applications and engaged a subset of respondents in semi-structured interviews pursuant to their consent. Some findings from that study, particularly about the frequency with which nonconsensual pornography affects gay and bisexual men on these applications, have been published elsewhere (Waldman, 2019a). I demonstrated that 87.4% of gay and bisexual men have shared "graphic, explicit, or nude photos or videos" of themselves on geosocial dating applications, while 93.4% have shared "shirtless or otherwise revealing" photos (Waldman, 2019a, p. 996). But that disclosure is not random. It happens in the context of specific norms and expectations. Exactly 82.6% of survey respondents either agreed or strongly agreed with the statement: "Sharing photos is pretty much a necessary part of the process of meeting people on these applications." That means the users in this survey felt the pressures of disclosure norms. At the same time, 89.7% share images with the expectation that they will not be shared further, which means their sharing takes place in a context of expectations of trust, discretion, and confidentiality (Richards & Hartzog, 2016; Waldman, 2019a).

Users create those expectations by engaging in, primarily, four privacy self-help techniques: anonymizing photos; developing a rapport through conversation; reciprocal sharing and mutual surveillance; and identity-based familiarity. Together, these strategies are aimed at building organic trust norms to mitigate the risks posed by the powerful norms of disclosure that have become social facts of these dating applications.

Anonymization

Many users upload or send intimate images without their faces or without identifying characteristics, at least initially. Or, they will send identifiable non-intimate pictures, but only cropped explicit photos. Or, they will only send photos that they "wouldn't be embarrassed by if [they] were made public" (Waldman, 2019a, p. 998). This strategy reduces the risk of harm if the pictures are shared or posted online because identifiable nude photos are prime weapons in the perpetuation of nonconsensual pornography, extortion, and other forms of cyberexploitation (see Citron & Franks, 2014; Henry et al., 2020; Powell, Henry, & Flynn, 2018). This particular strategy navigates the design nudge to share photos, which are the first parts of profiles other users see. And it is a popular one. Over a period of two weeks in 2017, I logged onto Grindr and Scruff, two geo-social dating applications geared toward gay and bisexual men, once per day and categorized the first 40 photos visible on my feed for each application. Excluding repeat accounts or duplicate photos (105), the total number of photos in the sample was 455. Of those, 68.8% were anonymized or de-identified.

People share anonymized photos for several reasons. The most common explanation for this provided by the 24 individuals that consented to be interviewed for this project was privacy through compartmentalization. Even if particular users had nothing to hide, they wanted a "strict separation between my Grindr life and my work life," per one respondent's formulation. The second most popular rationale was that users wanted to share sexualized photos of themselves and, as one reported, "didn't want that to get around." Both explanations are based on conceptualizations of privacy well-recognized in the scholarly literatures, including privacy as intimacy and separation from others (Waldman, 2018a).

Rapport Development

Online dating sites foster initial communication between potential romantic partners. Studies have shown that some online daters engage in long pre-meeting communications, but Whitty and Carr (2006) found that most online daters arranged to meet in person within one week of their initial online encounter. However, Ramirez and Zhang (2007) and Ramirez and Wang (2008) found that the amount of time and online communication between those who met online helped determine outcomes when they met offline. That is, although many but certainly not all people may not want to engage in an endless online back and forth, especially where sex rather than long term dating is involved, more opportunities to develop a rapport with someone online gave online daters a better sense of whether any offline meeting would be successful. Gay and bisexual men experience this on geosocial dating applications as well, choosing to use chat features to develop a rapport with others before sharing intimate information. Many gay and bisexual men only share photos, graphic or otherwise, after "chatting with the other person" (Waldman, 2019a, p. 998) for some time ranging from a few hours to a few weeks sufficient to "develop a rapport" (Waldman, 2019a, p. 998) or, as Jared S. responded in my previous study, "feel somewhat comfortable with the other person" (Waldman, 2019a, p. 998). As another anonymous respondent noted, "you begin to trust the person and let your guard down" (Waldman, 2019a, p. 998)

A rapport with another person, even one we have only recently met, is a signal of sharing values, worldviews, and ultimately trust. Although sociologists have long suggested that trust usually comes from long interactions with others, trust in the form of expectations of continued adherence to norms can develop between relative strangers (Waldman, 2018a). That is at least one goal of online engagements before meeting in person.

Reciprocity

Some gay and bisexual men only share intimate photos after another user has shared with them, maintaining power in a social exchange for as long as possible and relying on reciprocity and mutual vulnerability to reduce the likelihood of bad behavior (Berg, Dickhaut, & McCabe,1995; Brin, 1999; Kahan, 2003). As Ben Z. noted in my previous study, "reciprocity is the norm, but I like to be the one to reciprocate. It makes me feel more comfortable because the other person has already put himself out there. He's more at risk than I am, right?" (Waldman, 2019a, p. 999). Then, after reciprocation, users rely on a form of mutually assured surveillance. As one study participant noted, "I'm sharing photos of myself, some with my shirt off that I wouldn't necessarily want to get home to nana. But, so is he. He's in it just as deep as I am" (Waldman, 2019a, p. 999).

Familiar Identity

Some rely on the comfort and familiarity in an application's exclusive queerness. Stephen P. noted in my previous study: "[Y]ou go on Grindr and you trust that everyone realizes we're all in this together. We're all gay, all of us looking for companionship" (Waldman, 2019a). John H. noted, unintentionally echoing Max Weber's (1946) argument that a common religion allowed for trustworthy contracting in the early American republic and Talcott Parsons' (1978) argument that cultural similarity inspires trust, that "someone who is also gay, also about the same age, also single, also lonely, also looking for the same thing you're looking for, just seems less likely to hurt you than someone else who doesn't share the same personal narrative" (Waldman, 2019a, p. 999). Not all of these mitigation strategies are successful. But their use suggests a high level of privacy sophistication in an environment with powerful disclosure norms (Waldman, 2019a).

Self-Help isn't Sufficient

These strategies make users *feel* safer. They create and try to maintain a sense of trust among social actors, and trust is an essential piece of the privacy puzzle (Richards & Hartzog, 2016; Waldman, 2018a). But these strategies cannot create safe social spaces on their own. Indeed, nonconsensual pornography is rampant on LGBTQI-oriented geosocial dating applications. According to the Data & Society Research Institute, 7% of lesbian, gay, and bisexual internet users say someone has shared their intimate images without their consent (Lenhart, Ybarra, & Price-Feeney, 2016; see also; Powell, Henry, Flynn, & Scott, 2019; Powell, Scott, Henry, & Flynn, 2020). Among gay and bisexual men who use geosocial dating applications, that number jumps to nearly 15% (Waldman, 2019a). There is also powerful anecdotal evidence. In May 2017, two North Carolina high school students created a fake profile on Grindr, the popular gay-oriented geosocial application. They solicited nude photographs from one of their teachers and distributed the pictures throughout the school. The teacher was first suspended and then transferred elsewhere in the district (Towle, 2017). Matthew Herrick, an openly gay man living in New York City, alleged in a lawsuit that an ex-boyfriend stole his intimate images, impersonated him on an application, shared his photos with other men, and ultimately sent 1,100 of those men to Herrick's home and workplace looking for sex (O'Brien, 2017; Herrick v. Grindr, 2018).

Norms of trust require the assistance of privacy- and safety-enhancing design and privacy-protective law to counter the powerful norms of disclosure and ameliorate the vulnerabilities those norms create (Waldman, 2019b). These elements endogenous design of the social environment and exogenous law providing protections to individuals, constraints on platforms, and opportunities for justice are what make other social spaces safe for sharing. Scholars have long recognized that law and endogenous design work together to guide and constrain activities in digital spaces (Bailey & Steeves, 2015; Reidenberg, 1997). And we see this everywhere, both offline and online. The privacy of Alcoholics Anonymous meetings is protected by norms buttressed by organization rules and the courts, which protect expectations of confidentiality. Attorney-client relationships are based on trust, but that trust is protected and supported by ethical rules as well as legal regimes that punish lawyers who betray their clients' confidences. Even co-workers are more likely to share when they trust their teammates, but the trust that others will not work against the team or share their secrets is buttressed by both internal corporate rules and the law of trade secrets (Waldman, 2019b). These social institutions make social spaces safe in the offline context. There is no reason why they cannot be leveraged to protect online spaces as well.

Rather than operate to enhance and support trust norms on digital platforms like geosocial dating applications, technology design and the law do the opposite: they collect data from users, make it difficult to protect privacy and safety, and provide no legal incentive for companies to take necessary pro-privacy action. As Woodrow Hartzog (2018) has deftly described, digital platforms are designed as information extraction machines, passively gathering data on our behavior and nudging us to disclose more than we otherwise might. They leverage so-called "dark patterns" or design tricks that manipulate us into granting consent or giving up information (Mathur et al., 2019). And the law does not stop them. Regulators have never taken a close look at the ways in which technology design influences our behavior (Hartzog, 2018). And, in the United States, a federal law known as the Communications Decency Act Section 230 has been interpreted by the federal courts to grant broad immunity to technology companies for the tortious conduct of third parties on their platforms. That broad immunity takes away any legal incentive companies have to make their platforms safer, more privacy protective, and less welcoming to opportunists, mischief makers, and criminals (Citron & Wittes, 2017; Sylvain, 2018).

There are, therefore, specific steps platforms and policymakers can take to change this status quo. On the technical side, geosocial platforms can change their defaults to minimize information sharing with third parties, requiring users to take the affirmative step of opting in. Safety by design could involve ephemeral messaging for intimate images, access restrictions, streamlined takedown procedures, and frictionless tagging of profiles that spew hate, engage in harassment, and violate other terms of use (Hartzog, 2018). Privacy advocates can even be collocated with technical designers to provide them real-time insight on privacy issues as they come up (Waldman, 2018b).

Law can reorient the relationship between users and platforms by statutorily creating duties of care, loyalty, and confidentiality by which platforms must abide. Technology companies running techno-social platforms should be considered information fiduciaries for the same reasons that doctors, lawyers, and investment advisers are considered traditional fiduciaries. We are vulnerable to them because they know everything about us. We are dependent on them because of the services they provide and the expertise they bring to those services. And they hold themselves out as sufficiently trustworthy to gain our business (Balkin, 2016). The notion of an information fiduciary would, as a practical matter, mean that platforms cannot abuse their users by extracting intimate information and nonconsensual pornography, for example, would be a violation of a duty of loyalty. Alongside a duty of loyalty, duties of care and confidentiality would impose specific requirements of reasonable security and limited disclosure to third parties in accordance with user expectations. Some of these ideas have been included in proposals for new privacy and data protection laws in the United States, but the prospects for approval are, as of this writing, slim.

Section 230 of the Communications Decency Act must be amended. It is difficult to see why a digital platform would, outside of market pressures, take steps to protect their users from harm without a legal incentive. Those market pressures, if they exist, do not seem to be working now. As such, legal changes are necessary. Olivier Sylvain (2018) suggests Congress maintain Section 230s immunity but create an explicit exception from immunity for civil rights violations. Policymakers have called for additional exceptions, in addition to those enacted recently by the Stop Enabling Sex Traffickers Act (SESTA), which exempted from Section 230 any platform knowingly hosting sex trafficking content (Brody & Nix, 2000; Cole, 2018). But these kinds of piecemeal approaches are flawed. Sylvain's well-intentioned proposal creates a hierarchy of harms, which is not only worrisome per se but also subject to misuse and misinterpretation by the federal courts. SESTA, again though well-intentioned, predicates liability on knowledge, which has the perverse incentive of encouraging ignorance or overinclusive content moderation to eliminate all sex-related content. Instead of these approaches, Andrea Slane and Ganaele Langlois (2018) have proposed a tiered system of liability. Those platforms that invite and welcome illegal conduct like nonconsensual pornography should be held directly liable as publishers of illegal conduct. Other platforms that do not directly traffic in harassment and exploitation, but are at high risk of doing so, like the amateur pornography industry, should be required to verify that all participants are of age. And those platforms, like Facebook, that operate digital spaces of user generated content at scale, should be required to respond to user complaints of nonconsensual pornography. Citron and Wittes (2017) suggest making Section 230 immunity contingent on good faith and reasonable content moderation: only those who make a good faith effort to remove harassing, unlawful, and tortious content would be able to take advantage of the immunity, leaving the otherwise "bad Samaritans" with a strong legal incentive to do something about the safety and privacy problems on their platforms.

Conclusion

In the end, no social spaces, online or offline, can always be safe. Life involves risk, and so do disclosures, social networking, online dating, and the conveniences of modem life. But privacy and safety remain relevant. Privacy, expectations of confidentiality and discretion, as well as relief from hate and harassment, are all necessary for identity formation, intellectual freedom, and equality. Marginalized populations also bear a disproportionate burden of the hate and harassment and thus experience the greatest harms while being unable to exercise their rights as free citizens. Techno-social spaces do not have to be like this. Many of us want to engage on these platforms, and take significant steps to protect ourselves as best we can. But we cannot do this alone. Design and law can play guiding and expressive roles in support of enhancing trust, safety, and privacy.

References

Anderson, M., Vogels, E., & Turner, E. (2020). *The virtues and downsides of online dating*. Pew Research Center. Retrieved from https://www.pewresearch.org/internet/2020/02/06/the-virtues-and-downsides-of-online-dating/

Bailey, J., & Steeves, V. (2015). Introduction. In J. Bailey & V. Steeves (Eds.), *eGirls, eCitizens: Putting technology, theory and policy into dialogue with girls' and young women's voices* (pp. 1–20). Ottawa, CA: University of Ottawa Press.

Balkin, J. (2016). Information fiduciaries and the first amendment. *University of California, Davis Law Review*, *49*(4), 1183–1234.

Berg, J., Dickhaut, J., & McCabe, K. (1995). Trust, reciprocity, and social history. *Games and Economic Behavior*, *10*(1), 122–142.

Blackwell, C., Binrholz, J., & Abbott, C. (2014). Seeing and being seen: Co-situation and impression formation using Grindr, a location-aware gay dating app. *New Media & Society*, *17*(7), 1117–1136.

Boyd, D. (2014). *It's complicated: The social lives of networked teens*. New Haven, CT: Yale University Press.

Brin, D. (1999). *The transparent society*. New York, NY: Basic Books.

Brody, B., & Nix, N. (2000). *Lindsey Graham proposal could expose apple, Facebook to lawsuits*. Bloomberg. Retrieved from https://www.bloomberg.com/news/articles/2020-01-30/lindsey-graham-proposal-could-expose-apple-facebook-to-lawsuits

Burkell, J., & Bailey, J. (2018). Equality at stake: Connecting the privacy/vulnerability cycle to the debate about publicly accessible online court records. *Canadian Journal of Comparative and Contemporary Law*, *4*, 1–46.

Carroll, O. (2019). Gay hunters: How criminal gangs lure men on dating apps before extorting cash and beating them. *Independent UK*. Retrieved from https://www.independent.co.uk/news/world/europe/gay-hunters-russia-moscow-apps-gangs-homophobia-a8865376.html

Citron, D. K. (2009). Cyber civil rights. *Boston University Law Review*, *89*, 61–125.

Citron, D. K. (2014). *Hate crimes in cyberspace*. Cambridge, MA: Harvard University Press.

Citron, D. K., & Franks, M. A. (2014). Criminalizing revenge porn. *Wake Forest Law Review*, *49*, 345–391.

Citron, D. K., & Wittes, B. (2017). The internet will not break: Denying bad Samaritans section 230 immunity. *Fordham Law Review*, *86*(2), 401–423.

Cole, S. (2018). Senator suggests the Internet needs a FOSTA/SESTA for drug trafficking. *Vice*. Retrieved from https://www.vice.com/en_us/article/8xbwvp/joe-manchin-fosta-sesta-law-for-drug-trafficking-senate-intelligence-committee-hearing

Derlega, V. J., Metts, S., Petronio, S., & Margulis, S. T. (1993). *Self-disclosure*. Newbury Park, CA: Sage.

Donovan, B. (2012). A tour of the sex questions on OkCupid. *Thought Catalog*. Retrieved from https://thoughtcatalog.com/brian-donovan/2012/09/a-tour-of-the-sex-questions-on-okcupid/

Dressel, J., & Farid, H. (2018). The accuracy, fairness, and limits of predicting recidivism. *Science Advances, 4*, 1–5. Retrieved from https://advances.sciencemag.org/content/4/1/eaao5580/tab-pdf

Farnden, J., Martini, B., & Choo, K. R. (2015). Privacy risks in mobile dating apps. In *Proceedings of the 21st Americas conference on information systems (AMCIS 2015)*, Fajardo (pp. 1–16).

Fitzsimmons, T. (2020). Michigan man charged in Grindr slaying. *NBC News*. Retrieved from https://www.nbcnews.com/feature/nbc-out/michigan-man-charged-grindr-slaying-n1109596. Accessed on April 30, 2020.

Ghorayshi, A., & Ray, D. (2018). Grindr is letting other companies see user HIV status and location data. *BuzzFeed*. Retrieved from https://www.buzzfeednews.com/article/azeenghorayshi/grindr-hiv-status-privacy. Accessed on March 20, 2020.

Goffman, E. (1959). *The presentation of self in everyday life*. New York, NY: Doubleday.

Grov, C., Breslow, A. S., & Newcomb, M. E., (2014). Gay and bisexual men's use of the internet: Research from the 1990s through 2013. *The Journal of Sex Research, 51*(4), 390–409.

Herrick V. Grindr. (2018, January 25). Opinion and order, 17-CV-932 (VEC) (S.D.N.Y.).

Hartzog, W. (2018). *Privacy's blueprint: The battle to control the design of new technologies*. Cambridge, MA: Harvard University Press.

Heath, S. (2015). Security and insecurity online: Perspectives from girls and young women. In J. Bailey & V. Steeves (Eds.), *eGirls, eCitizens: Putting technology, theory and policy into dialogue with girls' and young women's voices* (pp. 361–384). Ottawa, CA: University of Ottawa Press.

Henry, N., McGlynn, C., Flynn, A., Johnson, K., Powell, A., & Scott, A. J. (2020). *Image-based sexual abuse: A study on the causes and consequences of non-consensual nude or sexual imagery*. London and New York, NY: Routledge.

Kahan, D. M. (2003). The logic of reciprocity: Trust, collective action, and the law. *Michigan Law Review, 102*(1), 71–103.

Lenhart, A., Ybarra, M., & Price-Feeney, M. (2016). Nonconsensual image sharing: One in 25 Americans has been a victim of "revenge porn." Retrieved from https://datasociety.net/pubs/oh/Nonconsensual_Image_Sharing_2016.pdf

Mathur, A., Acar, G., Friedman, M. J., Lucherini, E., Mayer, J., Chetty, M., & Narayanan, A. (2019). Dark patterns at scale: Findings from a crawl of 11K shopping websites. Retrieved from https://arxiv.org/pdf/1907.07032.pdf. Accessed on March 20, 2020.

OkCupid. (n.d.). Retrieved from www.okcupid.com. Accessed on March 20, 2020.

O'Brien, S. A. (2017). 1,100 strangers showed up at his home for sex. He blames Grindr. Retrieved from http://money.cnn.com/2017/04/14/technology/grindr-lawsuit/index.html. Accessed on March 20, 2020.

Parsons, T. (1978). *Action theory and the human condition*. New York, NY: Free Press.

Powell, A., Henry, N., & Flynn, A. (2018). Image-based sexual abuse. In W. S. DeKeseredy & M. Dragiewicz (Eds.), *Routledge handbook of critical criminology* (2nd ed., pp. 305–315). Abingdon and New York, NY: Routledge.

Powell, A., Henry, N., Flynn, A., & Scott, A. J. (2019). Image-based sexual abuse: The extent, nature, and predictors of perpetration in a community sample of Australian adults. *Computers in Human Behavior*, *92*, 393–402.

Powell, A., Scott, A. J., Henry, N., & Flynn, A. (2020). *Image-based sexual abuse: An international study of victims and perpetrators. Summary report*. Melbourne, VIC: RMIT University.

Ramirez, A., Jr., & Wang, Z. (2008). When online meets offline: An expectancy violations theory perspective on modality switching. *Journal of Communication*, *58*(1), 20–39.

Ramirez, A., Jr., & Zhang, S. (2007). When online meets offline: The effect of modality switching on relational communication. *Communication Monographs*, *74*, 287–310.

Reidenberg, J. (1997). Lex informatica: The formulation of information policy rules through technology. *Texas Law Review*, *76*, 553–593.

Richards, N., & Hartzog, W. (2016). Taking trust seriously in privacy law. *Stanford Technology Law Review*, *19*, 431–472.

Salganik, M. (2019). Measuring the predictability of life outcomes with a scientific mass collaboration. Presentation at Princeton University, Center for Information Technology Policy, September 17, 2019. Retrieved from https://cloud.swivl.com/v/8da7d538a3d9aa1972e3e5d5e38509df

Slane, A., & Langlois, G. (2018). Debunking the myth of "not my bad": Sexual images, consent, and online host responsibilities in Canada. *Canadian Journal of Women and the Law*, *30*, 42–81.

Stern, M. J. (2016). This Daily Beast Grindr stunt is sleazy, dangerous, and wildly unethical. *Slate*. Retrieved from https://slate.com/technology/2016/08/the-daily-beasts-olympics-grindr-stunt-is-dangerous-and-unethical.html. Accessed on March 20, 2020.

Sylvain, O. (2018). Intermediary design duties. *Connecticut Law Review*, *50*, 203–277.

Thaler, R. H., & Sunstein, C. (2008). *Nudge: Improving decisions about health, wealth, and happiness*. New Haven, CT: Yale University Press.

Towle, A. (2017). Two NC high school students catfished gay teacher for nude photos on Grindr, and passed them around. *Towleroad*. Retrieved from http://www.towleroad.com/2017/05/catfish-teacher/. Accessed on March 20, 2020.

Tracy, M. (2020). Moroccans use Grindr location data to out, target gay men. *Gay City News*. Retrieved from https://www.gaycitynews.com/moroccans-use-grindr-location-data-to-out-target-gay-men/

Tziallas, E. (2015). Gamified eroticism: Gay male 'social networking' applications and self-pornography. *Sexuality & Culture*, *19*(4), 759–775.

Waldman, A. (2018a). *Privacy as trust: Information privacy in an information age*. New York, NY: Cambridge University Press.

Waldman, A. (2018b). Designing without privacy. *Houston Law Review*, *55*, 659–727.

Waldman, A. (2019a). Law, privacy, and online dating: 'Revenge porn' in gay online communities. *Law & Social Inquiry*, *44*(4), 987–1010.

Waldman, A. (2019b). Safe social spaces. *Washington University Law Review*, *96*, 1537–1579.

Waldman, A. (2019c). Cognitive biases, dark patterns, and the 'privacy paradox.' *Current Opinion in Psychology*, *31*, 105–109.

Weber, M. (1946). *Essays in sociology*. Oxford: Oxford University Press.

Whitty, M. T., & Carr, A. N. (2006). *Cyberspace romance: The psychology of online relationships*. Basingstoke: Palgrave Macmillan.

Section 5
Intimate Partner Violence and Digital Coercive Control

Chapter 23

Introduction

Jane Bailey

The four chapters in this section focus on technology-facilitated violence and abuse (TFVA) in the contexts of domestic and family violence, as well as between intimate partners. Together, they provide rich insights from survivors and from the advocates and practitioners who support them. They highlight the double-edged sword of technology in both perpetuating and combatting these forms of TFVA, as well as the necessity of taking an intersectional approach to gender-based violence. As Crenshaw (1991) so ably demonstrated, failure to take into account the impacts of intersecting forms of oppression on women experiencing violence is likely to result in policy and services that fail to meet the needs of women from the most marginalized communities, such as immigrant and refugee women, as well as racialized and Indigenous women, and women living in remote and rural areas. From an international perspective, the Global-North's domination in published research has meant that the narratives and experiences of women in the Global-South have received too little consideration on the world stage (Barberet & Carrington, 2018). The chapters in this section help to address some of the existing gaps in the literature by giving voice to the lived experiences of women living in remote areas of Australia (Bridget Harris & Delanie Woodlock), and those of advocates and practitioners supporting women experiencing domestic violence in Singapore (Laura Vitis), young women experiencing intimate partner violence (IPV) in Brasil and Australia (Lopes Gomes Pinto Ferreira), and culturally and linguistically diverse women in Australia (Yee Man Louie).

The section opens with Harris and Woodlock's chapter that acknowledges how the spacelessness of digital coercive control allows IPV perpetrators to create an overwhelming sense of omnipotence, but also emphasizes the continuing relevance of spatiality. Harris and Woodlock conducted individual interviews and a focus group with Aboriginal and non-Aboriginal women living in rural areas of New South Wales, Queensland, and Victoria (31% of whom were born outside of Australia). Their findings highlight both the significance of intersectionality in research in this area, as well as the double-edged sword of digital technology in

The Emerald International Handbook of Technology-Facilitated Violence and Abuse, 385–386

doi:10.1108/978-1-83982-848-520211064

the fight against IPV. While technology played a role in amplifying (ex) intimate partners' coercive control over their participants because of their remote locations, it was also sometimes their only point of connectivity with the outside world.

Vitis' chapter addresses the gap in the existing empirical research on TFVA against women in South East Asia by providing insights from interviews with frontline workers about the ways technology is shaping the dating, domestic, and family violence experiences of women in Singapore. Vitis' results support the need to include TFVA in future quantitative surveys in Singapore and for further qualitative research with women survivors of TFVA to gain a better understanding of the role of technology in Singaporean women's experiences of violence. She argues that research grounded in lived experience could play a crucial role in formulating meaningful policy responses.

Lopes Gomes Pinto Ferreira' chapter also reports on findings from interviews of those working on the front lines to address IPV. In this case, however, the advocates are based in the Global-South – Brasil and Australia – and their work focuses on IPV and young people. Approaching her research through a Southern Feminist framework, the results of Lopes Gomes Pinto Ferreira' interviews with 14 Brasilian and five Australian advocates emphasize both the negative and positive roles played by technology in the context of IPV among youth. Noting other findings suggesting a normalization of IPV in young people's relationships, as well as their own observations of the use of technology to perpetrate IPV among the young people they work with, Lopes Gomes Pinto Ferreira' participants also identify the important role that social media, websites, and/or online games can play in raising awareness about healthy relationships and signs of IPV among this highly digitally connected population.

Finally, Louie's chapter helps to address the gap in the domestic violence literature with respect to the experiences of culturally and linguistically diverse women. Her interviews with 13 domestic violence practitioners from a variety of sectors who had experiences working with culturally and linguistically diverse women, specifically provide insights with respect to victim-survivors of Chinese descent, with eight of her participants having worked with women in this demographic. Louie's results demonstrate both the importance of intersectionality, as well as the double-edged sword of technology in the domestic violence context. Similar to the research participants reported on in other chapters in this section, Louie's participants confirm the role of technology as both a facilitator of and a response to IPV. However, they also note the importance of ensuring the accessibility of technology-based responses in terms of meeting the linguistic needs of victim-survivors and using the platforms they are most likely to access.

References

Barberet, R. & Carrington, K. (2018). Globalizing feminist criminology: Gendered violence during peace and war. In K. Carrington, R. Hogg, J. Scott & M. Sozzo (Eds.), *The Palgrave Handbook of Criminology and the Global South* (pp. 821–845). London: Palgrave Macmillan.

Crenshaw, K. (1991). Mapping the margins: Intersectionality, identity politics, and violence against women of color. *Stanford Law Review*, *43*(6), 1241–1299.

Chapter 24

Digital Coercive Control and Spatiality: Rural, Regional, and Remote Women's Experience

Bridget Harris and Delanie Woodlock

Abstract

Technology increasingly features in intimate relationships and is used by domestic violence perpetrators to enact harm. In this chapter, we propose a theoretical and practical framework for technology-facilitated harms in heterosexual relationships which we characterize as *digital coercive control*. Here, we include behaviors which can be classified as abuse and stalking and also individualized tactics which are less easy to categorize, but evoke fear and restrict the freedoms of a particular woman. Drawing on their knowledge of a victim/survivor's experiences and, in the context of patterns and dynamics of abuse, digital coercive control strategies are personalized by perpetrators and extend and exacerbate "real-world" violence.

Digital coercive control is unique because of its spacelessness and the ease, speed, and identity-shielding which technology affords. Victim/survivors describe how perpetrator use of technology creates a sense of omnipresence and omnipotence which can deter women from exiting violent relationships and weakens the (already tenuous) notion that abuse can be "escaped." We contend that the ways that digital coercive control shifts temporal and geographic boundaries warrant attention. However, spatiality more broadly cannot be overlooked. The place and shape in which victim/survivors and perpetrators reside will shape both experiences of and response to violence. In this chapter, we explore these ideas, reporting on findings from a study on digital coercive control in regional, rural, and remote Australia. We adopt a feminist research methodology in regard to our ethos, research processes, analysis, and the outputs and outcomes of our project. Women's voices are

The Emerald International Handbook of Technology-Facilitated Violence and Abuse, 387–406

doi:10.1108/978-1-83982-848-520211030

foreground in this approach and the emphasis is on how research can be used to inform, guide, and develop responses to domestic violence.

Keywords: Digital coercive control; technology-facilitated coercive control; domestic violence; rurality; violence against women; spatiality

Introduction

Technology increasingly features in intimate relationships and is used by domestic violence perpetrators to enact harm. Advocate and practitioner knowledge of this issue is growing, but thus far the literature has largely focused on dating violence in teen and adolescent settings, examining different phenomena in each study and not always using a gendered lens. Often these investigations fail to distinguish between perpetrator types (friends, acquaintances, partners) or consider the broader dynamic in which online (and also offline) harms are enacted. In this chapter, we propose a theoretical and practical framework for technology-facilitated harms in heterosexual relationships which we characterize as *digital coercive control*. Here, we include behaviors which can be classified as abuse and stalking and also individualized tactics, which are less easy to categorize, but evoke fear and restrict the freedoms of a particular woman. Drawing on their knowledge of a victim/survivor's experiences and in the context of patterns and dynamics of abuse, digital coercive control strategies are personalized by perpetrators and extend and exacerbate "real-world" violence.

Digital coercive control is unique because of its *spacelessness* and the ease, speed, and identity-shielding which technology affords. Victim/survivors describe how perpetrator use of technology creates a sense of omnipresence and omnipotence, which can deter women from exiting violent relationships and weakens the (already tenuous) notion that abuse can be "escaped." We contend that the ways that digital coercive control shifts temporal and geographic boundaries warrant attention. However, spatiality more broadly cannot be overlooked. The place and shape in which victim/survivors and perpetrators reside will shape both experiences of and response to violence. In this chapter, we explore these ideas, reporting on findings from a study on digital coercive control in regional, rural, and remote Australia. We adopt a feminist research methodology in regard to our ethos, research processes, analysis, and the outputs and outcomes of our project. Women's voices are foreground in this approach and the emphasis is on how research can be used to inform, guide, and develop responses to domestic violence.

The behaviors we discuss are not exclusive to heterosexual relationships, although we emphasize that, recognizing patterns in victimization and perpetration, our work has focused on examination of female victim/survivors and male abusers.

We begin with a review of related literature, with a focus on intimate partner violence, and the key concepts of digital coercive control, and spacelessness and spatiality. We then provide necessary background explaining what led us to undertake the study we report on in this chapter. Next, we set out our research approach and methods before moving on to report on our findings, discussing them in the context of the existing literature, highlighting themes related to digital coercive control; low versus high-tech abuse; gendered and sexualized shaming; monitoring and surveillance; spacelessness and post-separation violence; technology as a tool for breaking isolation, rurality and patriarchal gender roles; and networking of abuse using family and friends. In conclusion, we call for future scholarly investigation and policy and practice developing relating to intimate partner violence that considers spatiality, not only in terms of the spacelessness of digital media and devices but also the influence of place and space more generally.

Overview of Related Literature and Key Concepts

Investigating Intimate Partner Violence

The bulk of literature on technology-facilitated violence in intimate relationships centers on "electronic (or cyber) dating violence." Sometimes the focus is purely on electronic channels, though there may be consideration of how "online" violence intersects with "offline" dating violence (see, for instance, Barter et al., 2017; Borrajo, Gámez-Guadix, & Calvete, 2015a; Draucker & Martsolf, 2010; Marganski & Melander, 2018; Temple et al., 2016; Zweig, Dank, Yahner, & Lachman, 2013). Often a quantitative methodology and system of analysis is adopted which draws on surveys or questionnaires of high school or college/university students (Cutbush, Williams, Miller, Gibbs, & Clinton-Sherrod, 2018; Harris & Woodlock, 2019). Potentially, such approaches can provide insight into prevalence rates, too, although there has been extensive variation in rates recorded. Proportionally lower or mid-range levels have been observed by some (12% by Hinduja & Patchin, 2011; 26% by Zweig et al., 2013; 32.2%–53% by Reed, Tolman, & Ward, 2017; 40% by Barter et al., 2017, in their respective studies) and higher levels in others (93% by Leisring & Giumetti, 2014). Essentially, these variations in prevalence rates can be attributed to differences in framework, such as the phenomena examined as well as measurement and theoretical processes.

Reviews of electronic dating violence have undoubtedly yielded useful data, both in regard to the role of technology in young people's intimate interactions and the ways that intrusion, harassment, aggression, abuse, and stalking can be performed in these settings. However, in some investigations, the relationships between parties are not necessarily restricted to dating partners, but may also include friends (Bennett, Guran, Ramos, & Margolin, 2011) and other behaviors, such as cyberbullying (Cutbush & Williams, 2016). There is some debate among scholars as to whether or not there is a sex symmetry or asymmetry of cyber partner violence. We (Harris & Woodlock, 2019) are concerned with the "gender blindness" of the literature. However, Borrajo, Gámez-Guadix, and Calvete (2015b) maintain that studies generally show that men and women perpetrate different types of cyber aggression and that the women experience more harmful effects in victimization. We contend that, where the dynamics, patterns and context of violence are not foreground, sex differences in the type, intention, and impacts of acts are obscured (Harris, 2018; Harris & Woodlock, 2019, see also Dragiewicz et al., 2018). Some measurement scales may include "false positives" for violence (Dragiewicz, 2009; Hamby & Turner, 2013) or fail to distinguish patterns of control and coercion – which underscores domestic violence – from incidents of situational couple violence.

Young people are certainly heavy adopters of technology, yet by generally drawing from a school or college/university cohort, scholars have inadvertently reinforced myths that older persons do *not* experience technology-facilitated violence in relationships (George & Harris, 2014). Here, we note that, while much can be learned from works on digital dating violence, this is not always characterized as interpersonal violence and there are likely significant lifestyle contrasts between the age cohorts. For instance, middle or high schoolers (and indeed college/university students) are less likely to reside together, share children, or have connected finances. Our own work, which focuses specifically on adult women's victimization by domestic violence, has found an average age in the early-mid 30s and affirmed that older women (above the age of 50) also report experiencing image-based sexual abuse and other forms of technology-facilitated domestic violence (Harris & Woodlock, in press; Woodlock, 2013, 2017). Literature on perpetrator use of technology in the context of domestic violence is limited, but growing, and driven both by advocates and academics (Dimond, Fiesler, & Bruckman, 2011; Fraser, Olsen, Lee, Southworth, & Tucker, 2010; Hand, Chung, & Peters, 2009; Mason & Magnet, 2012; Southworth, Dawson, Fraser, & Tucker, 2005). Domestic violence agencies and civil societies (such as the United Nations and also organizations such as Take Back the Tech) broadly have also shaped research, policy, and practice agendas (Harris, Dragiewicz, & Woodlock, 2021).

Digital Coercive Control

Digital media can provide channels to enact, extend, and exacerbate other forms of abuse (such as economic, psychological, or sexual abuse). In-person stalking may be accompanied by cyberstalking (technology-facilitated monitoring of a victim/survivor's movements, activities, or communications [George & Harris, 2014]). Additionally, abusers may impair an authorized function or cause an unauthorized function on a device. Victim/survivors also report incidents of "doxing": when their private and identifying information is published without their consent. Technology can provide vehicles for abusers to impersonate real people (or create profiles of fake people) or engage in identity theft, in efforts to intimidate, harass, or defraud targets (Douglas, Harris, & Dragiewicz, 2019; Dragiewicz et al., 2018; Harris, 2020; Harris & Woodlock, in press). These acts can be accomplished through access to a victim/survivors' actual or virtual properties and achieved through force, coercion, deception, or stealth (Dragiewicz et al., 2019). This is not an unchanging list. Technologies and strategies of perpetration will evolve as will, ideally, recognition and responses to such harms.

Some of the aforementioned presentations can be identified, categorized, and regulated under various laws, such as those pertaining to domestic violence, stalking, image-based sexual abuse, or cyber offenses. However, the same behaviors performed by perpetrators in abusive relationships can also be present and innocuous in nonabusive relationships. Checking locations of an intimate partner, or sending frequent text messages, for instance, can be deemed harmless or harmful depending on the dynamics of the relationship (Dragiewicz et al., 2019). Similarly, while video phone calls can enable connections between parents and children in families without domestic violence, we have heard accounts of perpetrators encouraging children to turn on video functions in efforts to locate a woman's residence and gain information about entrance points and security in a refuge (Dragiewicz et al., 2019; Harris & Woodlock, in press). Moreover, abusers have knowledge of a victim/survivor's personal history, experiences, and health of a victim/survivor, and so their strategies are individualized. Women might be sent messages that may not be viewed as offensive or abusive by an outsider, but might evoke fear and unrest because of the terms or incidents mentioned or because the time at which contact was made has a certain meaning for them (Woodlock, 2013).

Ultimately, we contend that "the relational and individual features of technology-facilitated domestic violence mean that it cannot be easily or absolutely cataloged" (Harris & Woodlock, in press). To capture the use of devices and digital media to stalk, harass, threaten, and abuse partners (or ex-partners and direct or collateral victims, such as children), we propose that the phrase (and term) *digital coercive control* be adopted (Harris & Woodlock, 2019; Dragiewicz et al., 2018 suggest "technology-facilitated coercive control"). This term identifies "the method (digital), intent (coercive behavior), and impact (control of an ex/partner)" and positions harm in a broader setting of sex-based inequality (Harris & Woodlock, 2019, p. 533). The concept of "coercive control" is central here (see also Havard & Lefevre, 2020; Woodlock, 2013, 2017), which is a gendered theory. Essentially, theorists maintain that men use coercive control violence in efforts to exploit, maintain, and reinforce their status and power (Douglas et al., 2019; Harris & Woodlock, 2019; Hester, 2010; Stark, 2007). Though there is debate about how applicable coercive control may be for some victim/survivor experiences (such as in LGBTIQ+ relationships, Harris & Woodlock, in press), we emphasize that we see this as an intersectional approach and that the dynamics, distribution, and outcomes of violence are also shaped by racism, xenophobia, and homophobia (Stark & Hester, 2019).

Though Stark (2007) did not pioneer the concept of coercive control, his work has been most influential in academic study and practical application (Douglas et al., 2019). Stark's (2007, 2012) model encompasses spatially diffuse modes (like "spaceless" digital channels) and a range of perpetrator tactics (such as isolation, intimidation, threats, degradation, gaslighting, monitoring, and stalking), including those not generally classed as "serious" forms of violence (Harris, 2018). While advocates often appreciate that technology-facilitated abuse has extensive impacts on victim/survivors' sense of well-being and security, criminal justice agents have, in the past, suggested these harms are less serious and distinct from other forms of abuse (George & Harris, 2014). We see digital coercive control as typically part of women's broader experience of violence and highlight the pattern as opposed to using an "incident" centric model of abuse (Stark, 2007; Woodlock, 2013). Digital coercive control specifically (and coercive control more broadly) creates a condition of "entrapment" and "unfreedom", which constrains women's "space for action" (Kelly, 2003).

Spacelessness and Spatiality

Digital coercive control is an extension of violence enacted through more traditional, "offline" channels (Harris & Woodlock, 2019). However, there are unique features of technology which warrant attention. Temporal boundaries have been shifted as digital media has afforded instantaneous communication. Scholars and civil societies have wondered if the ease and immediacy of messaging and the absence of face-to-face contact (of some channels) may result in senders exhibiting little empathy for recipients or dissociating from the effects of the message they are sending (Gray, 2012; see also Amnesty International, 2018). The spacelessness of technology, too, is transformative. While access points (devices) exist in the "real-world," social media accounts, digital profiles and alike are not bound to any geographic location. Thus, victim/survivors can be exposed to digital coercive control anywhere and anytime they use digital media (Harris, 2018; Woodlock, 2013, 2017). This is exacerbated by the "context collapse": the blurring of public and private, professional and personal lives on social media (Davis & Jurgenson, 2014). As the different domains become intermeshed, violence is increasingly not confined to certain domains. Thus, even abuse in the domestic sphere which was long shrouded by a "veil of privacy" (Fineman, 1994) is by no means enacted only in "private" digital spaces (Vickery & Everbach, 2018). Abusers, for instance, mount campaigns on social media platforms in efforts to publicly shame and humiliate victim/survivors and post intimate images and videos without consent on internet sites (George & Harris, 2014; Harris & Woodlock, 2019; Woodlock, 2013).

Domestic violence abusers capitalize on temporal and spaceless features of technology to erode boundaries and create a sense of omnipresence and omnipotence (Woodlock, 2017). This can include, for instance, high volumes of contact such as seemingly unending abusive text or email messages and posts on social media and constantly monitoring the activities, movements, and correspondence of victim/survivors using technology (Woodlock, 2013). As noted above, such practices create a condition of entrapment and unfreedom (Stark, 2007) and can be a deterrent to help-seeking and attempting to exit a violent relationship (Dimond et al., 2011; Hand et al., 2009). Our heavy utilization and reliance on technology (in providing education, employment, leisure, social, and civic engagement opportunities) ensures that it is difficult for victim/survivors to escape exposure to digital coercive control. There has been some recognition in the existing literature of spatiality in these regards, but little exploration of how the place and space in which digital coercive control is enacted can shape victim/survivor experiences of and responses to such abuse (Harris, 2016; Harris & Woodlock, 2019; Harris & Woodlock, in press).

Background to Our Study

Our study evolved from previous work we conducted in this field. Woodlock's (2013; 2017) SmartSafe project was one of the first investigations, globally, to survey victim/survivors and support workers about the use of technology in abusive relationships. She documented how, via digital channels and devices, abusers sought to control, intimidate, and isolate women. Woodlock's research provided insights into impacts of and trends in perpetration and areas to knowledge-build in the Australian domestic violence sector (such as in safety planning processes). At the time there was scant scholarship on this topic. Some literature made reference to perpetrators using technology though this was not their focus. A study by George and Harris (2014) on victim/survivor's experiences of family violence in regional and rural Victoria (Australia) reported that technology-facilitated abuse and stalking had particular impacts on the well-being and safety of women in nonmetropolitan areas. They also highlighted the innovative digital strategies of advocates, offering opportunities to overcome geographic and social barriers to help-seeking, with limited resource investment. This was the first study to explore sociospatial impacts of violence in regard to technology-facilitated abuse, stalking, and advocacy, although not their main area of inquiry. Moving forward, we (Woodlock and Harris) decided to jointly develop a project that would advance our understanding of how technology shapes experiences of and responses to domestic violence in different places and spaces (Harris & Woodlock, in press).

Our research project *Spaceless Violence and Advocacy: Technology-Facilitated Abuse, Stalking and Service Provision in Australia* examined women's experiences of digital coercive control in regional, rural, and remote Australia (centering on the most heavily populated jurisdictions of Australia, the states of New South Wales [NSW], Victoria, and Queensland). We recognized that, compared to urban victim/survivors, those in nonurban locations face exacerbated barriers when seeking assistance (DeKeseredy & Schwartz, 2009; George & Harris, 2014; Hogg & Carrington, 2006). Abusers often capitalize on and seek to extend geographic and social isolation, including through technology (Farhall, Harris, & Woodlock, 2020). Risk in rural locations can be elevated by the sheer distance between a victim/survivor's residence and first responders. Consequently, what would be a serious assault in a metropolitan zone can quickly become a homicide in a nonmetropolitan zone (Harris, 2018; Lanier & Maume, 2009). In these settings, technology has the potential to contribute to the abuse and danger victim/survivors face (Harris, 2016). However, we emphasize that technology also can potentially bolster and provide new borderless avenues for help-seeking, the provision of assistance and services to victim/survivors, and regulation of violence (see also Harris, 2016; Harris et al., 2021). There is evidence that, in some rural or remote places, women have greater uptake of technology (for personal and professional purposes) than men (Hay & Pearce, 2014) and that Indigenous people are high adapters of technology (Carlson, 2013). This is significant, particularly as Indigenous women are overrepresented as victims/survivors of domestic and family violence (see Our Watch, 2018) and because there are indications that rates of domestic and family violence are highest in (at least some) regional and rural areas (see Dillon, Hussain, & Loxton, 2015; George & Harris, 2014).

Research Approach and Methods

We used feminist research methods in our project as this approach is centered on providing an insight into women's experiences as they understand them. Using feminist methods means that the researchers are concerned with not only the methods used and how appropriate they are for the topic but also with the research process and ethics (Burman, Batchelor, & Brown, 2001). The outcome of the research is also of importance when using feminist methods, with an obligation that the outputs and outcomes are for, not just about, those that are participating in a project. Ethical feminist research practice is seen as work that "will get to places and audiences where it might help further the social good" (Sprague, 2005, p. 224). Reflecting on and integrating these principles into our study, our aim was that the product of our work would be shared with community organizations that work directly with victim/survivors. Our findings would also inform training for domestic violence advocates and practitioners.

Our project used semistructured interviews as the main research method. Interviews provide an insight into women's experiences that have often been marginalized, and as such are central to feminist research methods (Reinharz, 1992). As in-depth interviewing usually works with small sample sizes, feminist interviewing aims to gain deep understanding into women's experiences, and the findings may not necessarily be able to be generalized to larger populations (Hesse-Biber, 2007). We wanted to understand the meaning that women made of the use of technology in violence they were subjected to, and if they felt that where they lived shaped their experiences. Consequently, we cannot draw generalizations about how many women in rural, regional, and remote locations in Australia are subjected to technology abuse, but our findings can advance understandings about how technology is used in domestic violence and how geographical space and place impact these experiences.

Recruitment

We partnered with Women's Legal Service (NSW), a community legal center which provides free information, education, and representation for women, as well as engaging in law reform and campaigning for women's rights and protections. The agency had also worked with Woodlock previously on the issue of technology and domestic violence (Woodlock, 2015). Through their facilitation we made contact with women's services throughout rural NSW, Queensland, and Victoria, to recruit victim/survivors who had been subjected to the use of technology in domestic violence.

Recruiting women who were connected to domestic violence support services ensured that our participants had support from a service throughout the process; they were able to discuss risks before the interview and debrief with staff afterward. This approach has limitations, as the majority of women who are subjected to domestic violence do not seek formal support. Therefore, the participants only included women who had recognized the abuse they were subjected to was domestic violence, or someone else they had contact with (such as family, friends, or professionals), prompted them to seek support. Relying on services to assist with the recruitment processes also puts added pressure on domestic violence services, which are already under considerable strain, and we found it an uncomfortable process to send reminders and prompts to organizations.

Interview Process and Demographics

We conducted individual interviews with 13 women and one focus group with two women. Our participants ranged in age from 25 to 50, with an average age of 33. While this correlates with the average age of women impacted by domestic violence, it is older than the high school and university aged cohorts that are largely focused on in relation to electronic dating violence. When asked about their cultural background, the majority of participants said they were Australian (69%) and within this group 15% identified as Aboriginal. There were 31% who said they were born overseas, with 15% from New Zealand, 8% from South America, and 8% from Asia. All women were subjected to abuse from a male former intimate partner.

Interviews were conducted in person as well as via the telephone depending on the participant's preference. The in-person interviews were held at the support service offices. One focus group was also held at a support service office. Prior to their participation, women were given plain language information about the project and had time to discuss the risks and benefits with the support services, as well as with the researchers. The interviews and focus group that were conducted at the support service offices were attended by both researchers, with one taking the lead and the other researcher offering support. For the interviews that were conducted via the phone, contact was first made via the support service who explained the research to the participant and then with her permission, forwarded her details to the researchers, as well as outlining any safe contact protocols. These included sending a text message before calling the phone so that the participant recognized our numbers. All participants received a $50 gift card to acknowledge their contribution and time. We also gave a donation to services that assisted us in recognition of their time and the effort that went into finding participants for our research. The interviews and focus group were recorded, with participant consent, and transcripts were subsequently prepared. Pseudonyms were assigned to participants in the transcripts in order to protect their confidentiality.

Analysis and Interpretation of Findings

The transcripts from our 13 interviews and one focus group were coded using thematic analysis, and we used NVivo to assist with categorization (King & Horrocks, 2010; Saldaña, 2012). We applied the system of thematic analysis outlined by King and Horrocks (2010), first coding the interviews descriptively, using codes such as "GPS used to track" and "Contact with police." Then we applied interpretive coding to the findings, where meaning was interpreted according to the research question. Interpretive codes included "Technology used to control" and "Victim-blaming by police." Both researchers read and coded the transcripts separately, using double coding to increase the trustworthiness of the analysis. Our codes and themes were then compared and contrasted, and we worked together in the development of a thematic structure of descriptive and interpretive codes. We then collaborated on the final stage of thematic analysis which is to define overarching themes (King & Horrocks, 2010). These overarching themes include "The use of technology by perpetrators is often not taken seriously as a form of abuse" and that "Technology is used alongside other forms of abuse."

Findings

Digital Coercive Control

Victim/survivors in our study detailed the way that technology was incorporated into perpetrating coercive and controlling tactics, often extending and exacerbating other forms of (offline) abuse (Harris & Woodlock, in press). Digital coercive control occurred alongside other forms of harm such as sexual violence, physical abuse, and nonfatal strangulation. For many victim/survivors, digital coercive control began during the relationship and was largely characterized by abusive text messages, monitoring via apps and GPS devices, and image-base sexual abuse. Technology had a heavy presence in their lives and abusers' reach and contact was extensive. Women talked about feeling as though they were exposed to harm anywhere and at any time and being constantly under surveillance. Kira described her abuser making "constant [contact]. I wouldn't be surprised if there was a hundred [texts and emails] a day. It was very, very frequent." Likewise, Louise was sent a raft of messages – "10 in a row" – before she had a chance to respond, and

> ...full on harassment with phone calls all the time... at four o'clock in the morning – phone call after phone call and if I'd tell him to stop, like there would be [no] chance [that] he would.

Earlier in relationships, women might feel that such contact was romantic or demonstrated their devotion. As Claire explained:

> [It was] little things that I kind of mistook as, oh, he's very caring, [but it] was obviously the beginning of the grooming and the controlling and the forward behaviors that I ended up accepting actually, as someone caring for me.

Abusers often framed their behaviors as helpful or positive. Maya's ex would routinely open her email inbox and "clean up" her emails for her. He linked his phone number to her email account because, he said, she was forgetful, and he could help retrieve her account if she lost her password. Women also talked about how their abusers would demand to have passwords on children's devices too, "to keep her [our daughter] safe." As Fiona explained, these can be claims and concerns all parents have, but the context of her relationship meant his access to her devices and, her children's devices, was problematic:

> I've got a friend who's got a tracking device on her son (he hurt himself from riding) and he said 'just look me up, where I am, if you're worried', you know? She's a great woman, right? So she's got his best interests. But in a DV [domestic violence] situation, it's completely different.

Low-Tech vs High-Tech Methods

Navarro (2015) notes that abusers can use "low-tech" methods (which do not require specialized knowledge) or "high-tech" methods (drawing on advanced knowledge). Women in our study believed that perpetrators mainly drew on low-tech strategies and skill sets. However, it can be hard to discern exactly what avenues perpetrators engage. Sometimes perpetrators delighted in women being forewarned they had control of devices or accounts, creating a (perhaps inflated) sense of perpetrator omnipresence and omnipotence. Abusers also sought to hide their activities (see also Dragiewicz et al., 2019; Harris & Woodlock, 2019). Many women suspected that perpetrators engage in covert strategies and applications they had not discovered, which was a source of great anxiety. Fiona stressed that "there are some things you will never know about, with technology." Complicating the issue, domestic relationships involve the sharing of intimate knowledge, account ownership and access, and unique relational dynamics that enable insider threats to digital security (Freed et al., 2018, see also Dragiewicz et al., 2019). While we appreciate that some abusers may be more tech-savvy than others or use high-tech approaches and apps (like spwyare, screenloggers, or keyloggers), abusers are also well positioned to guess or locate account information and can also use stealth, deception, and force to accomplish their goals (Harris, 2020). As our participants acknowledged, there was information (such as about their location) that could have been either gleaned from high-tech channels (like GPS tracking devices, hidden in their property) or low-tech channels (such as location-enabled features on devices, like "find my friends" apps).

Gendered and Sexualized Shaming and Humiliation

Abuse and harassment were often gendered and sexualized and technology was used in attempts to shame and humiliate women. Six of the thirteen women we consulted were subjected to image-based sexual abuse. Some women talked about images or videos being created with consent but numerous women, upon reflection during interviews, mentioned feeling manipulated, pressured, or coerced by abusers. Our participants also described feeling unease knowing perpetrators had possession of images or videos. Shelly lamented that her ex refused to delete "inappropriate photos" of her and

> …he brings up that he has these photos, and he's tried to use them as an emotional tool as well. Just saying "I've got a whole memory stick full of photos, if you want to get smart, I'll post them."

Three women were aware that their abuser had publicly shared images or videos of them.

In text and social media communications "name-calling" like "slut" was common "[i]f he didn't get his own way" (Fiona), as were attacks on women's sexuality. Threats of rape and sexual assault were widely reported, too, like messages that said "I deserved to be raped because I needed somebody to straighten me out" (Kira). Filipovic (2007) and Jane (2014) report that sexual violence can be presented as "corrective" to perceived "transgressions" from gender roles: here, we might think about expectations of female passivity and men's expectations of dominance. Menacing terms and expressions could evoke anxiety and pain in all of our participants. For those who had previous histories of sexual violence, these words had particular meanings and consequences. Cody's ex was well aware she had been sexually abused as a child. During their relationship he referred to and blamed her for this victimization. Post-separation he knew that adopting slurs she associated with her past and mentioning names of family members would trigger her memory and trauma. Natalie's ex shared information about her sexual history with her mother, family, and friends, over the phone. As Woodlock (2017) and Logan, Shannon, and Walker (2005) explain, perpetrators use technology and their knowledge of women's fears and personal history to torment women, to deter them from leaving, and to show they have power beyond the private sphere.

Monitoring and Surveillance

Perpetrators used access to our participants' accounts and devices to monitor their communications, activities, and movements. Some set up or gifted phones, tablets, or computers on shared plans which allowed them to follow women's use. Others would view billing information. Women were not always aware of men's oversight. Fiona recalled how, at the time, she did not know that her abuser was examining her message and call histories:

> He would say it in a way that [was off-the-cuff] so I didn't realize he was actually looking at the phone bill. I didn't realize he was checking how long and how often I would call certain people and would remark "oh you talk to such-and-such for [a while] every day, don't you?" I'd say "no, I don't"…. He said "yeah, you do."

Several abusers informed women they were using (GPS) tracking mechanisms. Natalie's ex told a friend of hers he was using technology to find her:

> He'd just appear. I'd be in some random supermarket and he'd just be behind me, or I'd be in some bushy area… he'd just appear in random places… just behind me.

As a consequence, she felt like he could turn up at any time: "I just had the nervous tic of looking over my shoulder every five seconds."

Spacelessness and Continued Violence Post-Separation

The accounts of our participants challenged myths surrounding domestic violence, including that violence can be easily escaped and that violence ends post-separation, as has been well established in the literature (see, for instance, DeKeseredy, Dragiewicz, & Schwartz, 2017; DeKeseredy & Schwartz, 2009). For many, digital coercive control escalated (especially in regard to cyberstalking); at the very least, it did not subside, post-separation. Thus, the notion of "'feeling safe' from an abuser no longer has the same geographic and spatial boundaries it once did" (Hand et al., 2009, n.p.; see also Dimond et al., 2011; Fraser et al., 2010). These harms are spaceless which means "[t]here wasn't ever a break from it… you can't actually escape it," as Kira says, "every other type of abuse, I was able to…it just ended at some point." However, the space in which the woman and perpetrators are based matters.

Impact of Social and Geographic Features on Visibility

Social and geographic features of regional, rural, and remote locations shaped experiences of abuse and barriers that our participants encountered when seeking help and responding to violence. They described how, living in small communities, they felt more visible. They were more likely to be known to services and agencies when disclosing violence and seeking assistance and so were confronted with "going public" with private violence (see also George & Harris, 2014). Victim/survivors who identified as Indigenous, culturally or linguistically diverse, or those who had previously come into contact with the criminal justice system described feeling especially visible.

Technology as a Tool for Breaking Isolation

Though women in our study engaged with support workers and practitioners in their geographic area, we note that, for rural women, technology can provide confidential channels beyond their community to respond to violence. In that way, technology was a lifeline for many of our participants, especially those who were geographically and/or socially isolated. Perpetrators sought to extend their isolation while they lived together, for instance, by moving their family to remote farms, destroying their relationships with others, and restricting their access to technology. For those who did not have social networks in the area, including newly arrived women (and those on temporary visas), technology offered key channels to maintain links with friends and family. Digital media could also offer further employment and education channels, which was vital, as rural communities had less opportunities than in urban communities. Our participants' experiences demonstrate the ways in which technology can be a source of empowerment, in enabling women to access resources and build capabilities to exit relationships and gain independence (see also Louie, this volume).

Rurality and Patriarchal Gender Roles

In essence, rurality brought forward barriers into our participants' lives. A wealth of literature has documented how geographic, social, and ideological structures and features in rural places can foster and facilitate violence (Farhall et al., 2020; see also Bosch & Bergen, 2006; Loxton, Hussain, & Schofield, 2003). In our study, as with our previous studies (see George & Harris, 2014; Harris, 2016), victim/survivors described their communities as conservative or conducive to violence, because of localized gender roles and patriarchal values. As Hogg and Carrington (2006, p. 180) argue, gender in rural communities can have unique meanings and presentations:

> The social organisation of masculinity in these rural social sites is constructed more narrowly around heteronormative conceptions of masculinity that subordinate others through practices of domination that have historically relied on the exercise of violence.

Rural hegemonic masculinity has been observed by scholars, internationally (in New Zealand, by Campbell, 2000; South Africa, by Jewkes et al., 2006; the United States, by DeKeseredy & Schwartz, 2009; United Kingdom, by Hey, 1986; Whitehead, 1976 as cited in Harris & Woodlock, in press).

In small, close-knit communities, women can be ostracized or demonized when disclosing abuse, particularly when "traditional" patriarchal, gender, and family values are present (George & Harris, 2014; Hornosty & Doherty, 2002; Wendt, 2009). Speaking to this, Kira, reflecting on her past victimization (as a child in the family setting and, being sexually assaulted as a child and adolescent and, as an adult, subjected to domestic violence) noted:

> I grew up in a small community… once one [person] started [engaging in violence] it was kind of a trend where all the males in the community would just, I guess, jump on board, if that makes sense?

Informal support networks can be reluctant to assist victim/survivors or intervene to prevent violence, especially where perpetrators are well-known and regarded (National Rural Crime Network, 2019; Neilson & Renou, 2015). Claire's ex "went around the streets telling people that I'm crazy" and his version of events spread quickly, because of the small size community. Claire went on to explain: "he [my abuser] is established – he knows people and he's well-liked ... He's in a boy's club and knows lots of people." She talked about, in contrast, feeling alone. Here, we can consider how abuser allies and perpetrator peer support networks (see DeKeseredy, 1990; DeKeseredy & Schwartz, 2016) are shaped by rurality, facilitating not only violence but also women's isolation.

DeKeseredy and Schwartz proposed that "abusive patriarchal men" may have like-minded allies who develop, exchange, and reinforce values and beliefs that support violence and provide resources and guidance that essentially "allows men to feel normal and justified when committing violence against current and former intimate partners" (2016, p. 4). Numerous participants spoke about these structures which underscored what we termed "proxy perpetrators." This can include persons within their abuser's social network who elect to engage in digital coercive control.

Engagement of Family and Friends in Networks of Abuse

Family members or friends may, for instance, contribute to negative social media campaigns attacking a victim/survivor, send demeaning messages to her, or use technology to stalk her movements, without prompting from the perpetrator (see also George & Harris, 2014). We include, in this category, persons who unwillingly or unknowingly facilitate perpetration, such as children (see also Dragiewicz et al., 2019).

Children were also manipulated into facilitating abuse of our participants. When Shelly blocked her ex on social media, he reached out to her daughter, claiming he wanted to watch her play sports and "she felt excited that he wanted to watch, so she gave him all the details [that helped him find me]." Other family members and friends appeared to be actively commissioned by an abuser, enlisted to harass or watch a woman using digital channels (see Bosch & Bergen, 2006; Dutton & Goodman, 2005; Murray et al., 2019). One woman, Kira, told us that friends of her ex would inform him of her whereabouts and activities. When she blocked his number, others provided their phones or digital profiles so he could contact her and "continue to harass me through [their accounts]." It was difficult for her to know if he was also using tracking devices to monitor her movements. These networks of abuse exacerbated the vulnerabilities of rural women.

Conclusion

Moving forward, we advocate for further studies of technology in the context of domestic violence which examine how victim/survivors, perpetrators, and advocates use technology. Technology shifts temporal and geographic boundaries and so will impact experiences of violence and abuse, as well as the responses that follow. We call for future scholarly investigation and policy and practice development to consider spatiality, examining not only the spacelessness of digital media and devices but also the influence of place and space. The metropole has, overwhelmingly, been the focus of studies in this arena. This is a knowledge deficit that must be addressed: barriers and risk to regional, rural, and remote women can not only be exacerbated but also potentially overcome (or at least abated) through technology.

References

Amnesty International. (2018). *Toxic Twitter: Violence and abuse against women online*. London. Amnesty International.

Barter, C., Stanley, N., Wood, M., Lanau, A., Aghtaie, N., Larkins, C., & Øverlien, C. (2017). Young people's online and face-to-face experiences of interpersonal violence and their subjective impact across five European countries. *Psychology of Violence*, *7*(3), 375–384.

Bennett, C. C., Guran, E. L., Ramos, M. C., & Margolin, G. (2011). College students' electronic victimization in friendships and dating relationships: Anticipated distress and associations with risky behaviours. *Violence & Victims*, *26*(4), 410–429.

Borrajo, E., Gámez-Guadix, M., & Calvete, E. (2015a). Cyber dating abuse: Prevalence, context, and relationship with offline dating aggression. *Psychological Reports*, *116*(2), 565–585.

Borrajo, E., Gámez-Guadix, M., & Calvete, E. (2015b). Justification beliefs of violence, myths about love and cyber dating abuse. *Psicothema*, *27*(4), 327–333.

Bosch, K., & Bergen, M. B. (2006). The influence of supportive and nonsupportive persons in helping rural women in abusive partner relationships become free from abuse. *Journal of Family Violence*, *21*(5), 311–320.

Burman, M. J., Batchelor, S. A., & Brown, J. A. (2001). Researching girls and violence: Facing the dilemmas of fieldwork. *British Journal of Criminology*, *41*(2), 443–459.

Campbell, H. (2000). The glass phallus: Pub(lic) masculinity and drinking in rural New Zealand. *Rural Sociology*, *65*, 562–581.

Carlson, B. (2013). The 'new frontier': Emergent Indigenous identities and social media. In M. Harris, M. Nakata, & B. Carlson (Eds.), *The politics of identity: Emerging indigeneity* (pp. 147–168). Sydney: University of Technology Sydney E-Press.

Cutbush, S., & Williams, J. (2016). Teen dating violence, sexual harassment, and bullying among middle school youth: Examining measurement invariance by gender. *Journal of Research on Adolescence*, *26*(4), 918–926.

Cutbush, S., Williams, J., Miller, S., Gibbs, D., & Clinton-Sherrod, M. (2018). Longitudinal patterns of electronic teen dating violence among middle school students. *Journal of Interpersonal Violence*. doi:10.1177/0886260518758326

Davis, J. L., & Jurgenson, N. (2014). Context collapse: Theorising context collusions and collisions. *Information, Communication & Society*, *17*(4), 476–485.

DeKeseredy, W. S. (1990). Male peer support and woman abuse: The current state of knowledge. *Sociological Focus*, *23*(2), 129–139.

DeKeseredy, W. S., Dragiewicz, M., & Schwartz, M. D. (2017). *Abusive endings: Separation and divorce violence against women*. Oakland, CA: University of California Press.

DeKeseredy, W. S., & Schwartz, M. D. (2009). *Dangerous exits: Escaping abusive relationships in rural America*. New Brunswick, NJ: Rutgers University Press.

DeKeseredy, W. S., & Schwartz, M. D. (2016). Thinking sociologically about image-based sexual abuse: The contribution of male peer support theory. *Sexualization, Media & Society*, *2*(4), 1–8.

Dillon, G., Hussain, R., & Loxton, D. (2015). Intimate partner violence in the young cohort of the Australian longitudinal study on women's health: Urban/rural comparisons and demographic associations. *Advances in Mental Health*, *13*(1), 18–29.

Dimond, J. P., Fiesler, C., & Bruckman, A. S. (2011). Domestic violence and information technologies. *Interacting with Computers*, *29*, 413–431.

Douglas, H., Harris, B. A., & Dragiewicz, M. (2019). Technology-facilitated domestic and family violence: Women's experiences. *British Journal of Criminology*, *59*(3), 551–570.

Dragiewicz, M. (2009). Why sex and gender matter in domestic violence research and advocacy. In E. Stark, & E. Buzawa (Eds.), *Violence against women in families and relationships: Volume 3, Criminal Justice and the Law* (pp. 201–215). Santa Barbara, CA: Praeger.

Dragiewicz, M., Burgess, J., Matamoros-Fernández, A., Salter, M., Suzor, N. P., Woodlock, D., & Harris, B. (2018). Technology-facilitated coercive control: Domestic violence and the competing role of digital media platforms. *Feminist Media Studies*, *18*(4), 609–625.

Dragiewicz, M., Harris, B., Woodlock, D., Salter, M., Easton, H., Lynch, A., … Milne, L. (2019). *Domestic violence and communication technology: Survivor experiences of intrusion, surveillance, and identity crime*. Sydney: The Australian Communications Consumer Action Network.

Draucker, C. B., & Martsolf, D. S. (2010). The role of electronic communication technology in adolescent dating violence. *Journal of Child and Adolescent Psychiatric Nursing*, *23*(3), 133–142.

Dutton, M. A., & Goodman, L. A. (2005). Coercion in intimate partner violence: Towards a new conceptualization. *Sex Roles*, *52*(11–12), 743–756.

Farhall, K., Harris, B., & Woodlock, D. (2020). The impact of rurality on women's 'space for action' in domestic violence. Findings from a meta-synthesis. *International Journal of Rural Criminology*, *5*(2), 181–203.

Filipovic, J. (2007). Blogging while female: Hoe internet misogyny parallels 'real world' harassment. *Yale Journal of Law and Feminism*, *19*, 295–303.

Fineman, M. A. (1994). Preface. In M. A. Fineman, & R. Mykitiuk (Eds.), *The public nature of private violence: The discovery of domestic abuse* (pp. xi–xvii). New York, NY: Routledge.

Fraser, C., Olsen, E., Lee, K., Southworth, C., & Tucker, S. (2010). The new age of stalking: Technological implications for stalking. *Juvenile and Family Court Journal*, *61*, 39–55.

Freed, D., Palmer, J., Michala, D., Levy, K., Ristenpart, T., & Dell, N. (2018). A stalker's paradise: How intimate partner abusers exploit technology. Presented at the IEEE Symposium on Security and Privacy (Oakland 2018), Oakland, ACM Press (pp. 1–13).

George, A., & Harris, B. (2014). *Landscapes of violence: Women surviving family violence in regional and rural Victoria*. Geelong: Deakin University.

Gray, K. L. (2012). Deviant bodies, stigmatized identities, and racist acts: Examining the experiences of African-African gamers in Xbox Live. *New Review in Hypermedia and Multimedia, 18*(4). 261–271.

Hamby, S., & Turner, H. (2013). Measuring teen dating violence in males and females: Insights from the national survey of children's exposure to violence. *Psychology of Violence, 3*, 323–339.

Hand, T., Chung, D., & Peters, M. (2009). *The use of information and communication technologies to coerce and control in domestic violence and following separation*. Sydney: Australian Domestic and Family Violence Clearinghouse.

Harris, B. (2016). Violent landscapes: A spatial study of family violence. In A. Harkness, B. Harris, & D. Baker (Eds.), *Locating crime in context and place: Perspectives in regional and rural Victoria* (pp. 70–84). Sydney: The Federation Press.

Harris, B. (2018). Spacelessness, spatiality and intimate partner violence: Technology-facilitated abuse, stalking and justice. In K. Fitz-Gibbon, S. Walklate, J. McCulloch, & J. M. Maher (Eds.), *Intimate partner violence, risk and security: Securing women's lives in a global world* (pp. 52–70). London: Routledge.

Harris, B. (2020). *Technology, domestic and family violence: Perpetration, experiences and responses*. Brisbane: Queensland University of Technology, Centre for Justice.

Harris, B., Dragiewicz, M., & Woodlock, D. (2021). Positive uses of technology to address domestic violence. In J. Blaustein, K. Fitz-Gibbon, N. W. Pino, & R. White (Eds.), *Emerald handbook of crime, justice and sustainable development*. (pp. 295–313) Bingley: Emerald Publishing Limited.

Harris, B., & Woodlock, D. (2019). Digital coercive control: Insights from two landmark domestic violence studies. *British Journal of Criminology, 59*(3), 530–550.

Harris, B., & Woodlock, D. (in press). *Spaceless violence and advocacy: Technology-facilitated abuse, stalking and service provision*. Canberra: Australian Institute of Criminology.

Havard, T., & Lefevre, M. (2020). Beyond the power and control wheel: How abusive men manipulate mobile phone technologies to facilitate coercive control. *Journal of Gender-Based Violence*. doi:10.1332/239868020X15850131608789

Hay, R., & Pearce, P. (2014). Technology adoption by rural women in Queensland, Australia: Women driving technology from the homestead for the paddock. *Journal of Rural Studies, 36*, 318–327.

Hesse-Biber, S. N. (2007). The practices of feminist in-depth interviewing. In S. N. Hesse-Biber (Ed.), *Feminist research practice: A primer* (pp. 233–263). Thousand Oaks, CA: SAGE Publications.

Hester, M. (2010). Gender and sexuality. In C. Itzin, A. Taket, & S. Barter-Godfrey (Eds.), *Domestic and sexual violence and abuse: Tackling the health and mental health effects* (pp. 99–131). London: Routledge.

Hey, V. (1986). *Patriarchy and pub culture*. London: Tavistock.

Hinduja, S., & Patchin, J. W. (2011). Electronic dating violence: A brief guide for educators and parents. United States of America: Cyberbullying Research Centre.

Hogg, R., & Carrington, K. (2006). *Policing the rural crisis*. Sydney: The Federation Press.

Hornosty, J., & Doherty, D. (2002). Responding to wife abuse in farm and rural communities: Searching for solutions that work. Paper presented at The rural Canada: Moving forward or left behind? A national conference, Regina, Canada.

Jane, E. A. (2014). 'Back to the kitchen, cunt': Speaking the unspeakable about online misogyny. *Continuum: Journal of Media & Cultural Studies*, *28*(4), 558–570.

Jewkes, R., Dunkle, K., Koss, M. P., Levin, J. B., Nduna, M., Jama, N., & Sikweyiyam, Y. (2006). Rape perpetration by young, rural South African men: Prevalence, patterns, and risk factors. *Social Science & Medicine*, *63*, 2949–2961.

Kelly, L. (2003). The wrong debate: Reflections on why force is not the key issue with respect to trafficking in women for sexual exploitation. *Feminist Review*, *73*, 139–144.

King, N., & Horrocks, C. (2010). *Interviews in qualitative research*. Thousand Oaks, CA: SAGE.

Lanier, C., & Maume, M. O. (2009). Intimate partner violence and social isolation across the rural/urban divide. *Violence Against Women*, *15*, 1311–1330.

Leisring, P. A., & Giumetti, G. W. (2014). Sticks and stones may break my bones, but abusive text messages also hurt: Development and validation of the Cyber Psychological Abuse scale. *Partner Abuse*, *5*(3), 323–341.

Logan, T. K., Shannon, L., & Walker, R. (2005). Stalking victimization in the context of intimate partner violence. *Violence Against Women*, *11*(7), 876–911.

Loxton, D., Hussain, R., & Schofield, M. (2003). Women's experiences of domestic abuse in rural and remote Australia. Paper presented at the 7th National Rural Health Conference, Hobart, Australia.

Marganski, A., & Melander, L. (2018). Intimate partner violence victimization in the cyber and real world: Examining the extent of cyber aggression experiences and its association with in-person dating violence. *Journal of Interpersonal Violence*, *33*(7), 1071–1095.

Mason, C., & Magnet, S. (2012). Surveillance studies and violence against women. *Surveillance and Society*, *10*, 105–118.

Murray, L., Warr, D., Chen, J., Block, K., Murdolo, A., Quiazon, R., … Vaughan, C. (2019). Between 'here' and 'there': Family violence against immigrant and refugee women in urban and rural Southern Australia. *Gender, Place & Culture*, *26*(1), 91–110.

National Rural Crime Network. (2019). Captive and controlled: Domestic abuse in rural areas. National Rural Crime Network.

Navarro, J. (2015). Cyberabuse and cyberstalking. In J. N. Navarro, S. Clevenger, & C. D. Marcum (Eds.), *The intersection between intimate partner abuse, technology, and cybercrime: Examining the virtual enemy* (pp. 125–140). Durham, NC: Carolina Academic Press.

Neilson, C., & Renou, B. (2015). *Will somebody listen to me? Insight, actions and hope for women experiencing family violence in regional Victoria*. Bendigo, VIC: Loddon Campaspe Community Legal Centre.

Our Watch. (2018). *Changing the picture: A national resource to support the prevention of violence against Aboriginal and Torres strait Islander women and their children*. Melbourne: Our Watch.

Reed, L. A., Tolman, R. M., & Ward, L. M. (2017). Gender matters: Experiences and consequences of digital dating abuse victimization in adolescent dating relationships. *Journal of Adolescence*, *59*, 79–89.

Reinharz, S. (1992). *Feminist methods in social research*. Oxford: Oxford University Press.

Saldaña, J. (2012). *The coding manual for qualitative researchers*. Thousand Oaks, CA: SAGE Publications.

Southworth, C., Dawson, S., Fraser, C., & Tucker, S. (2005). A high-tech twist on abuse: Technology, intimate partner stalking, and advocacy. *Violence Against Women Online Resources*. Retrieved from http://nnedv.org/downloads/SafetyNet/NNEDV_HighTechTwist_PaperAndApxA_English08.pdf

Sprague, J. (2005). *Feminist methodologies for critical researchers: Bridging differences*. Alta Mira: Rowmman & Littlefield.

Stark, E. (2007). *Coercive control: The entrapment of women in personal life*. Oxford: Oxford Unversity Press.

Stark, E. (2012). Looking beyond domestic violence: Policing coercive control. *Journal of Police Crisis Negotiations*, *12*, 199–217.

Stark, E., & Hester, M. (2019). Coercive control: Update and review. *Violence Against Women*, *25*(1), 81–104.

Temple, J. R., Choi, H. J., Brem, M., Wolford-Clevenger, C., Stuart, G. L., Peskin, F. M., & Elmquist, J. (2016). The temporal association between traditional and cyber dating abuse among adolescents. *Journal of Youth and Adolescence*, *45*, 340–349.

Vickery, J. R., & Everbach, T. (2018). The persistency of misogyny: From the streets, to our screens, to the White House. In J. R. Vickery, & T. Everbach (Eds.), *Mediating misogyny: Gender, technology and harassment* (pp. 1–27). Cham: Palgrave.

Wendt, S. (2009). *Domestic violence in rural Australia*. Sydney: The Federation Press.

Whitehead, A. (1976). Sexual antagonisms in Herefordshire. In D. Barker, & S. Allen (Eds.), *Dependence and exploitation in work and marriage* (pp. 169–203). London: Longman.

Woodlock, D. (2013). *Technology-facilitated stalking: Findings and recommendations from the SmartSafe project*. Carlton, VIC: Domestic Violence Resource Centre Victoria.

Woodlock, D. (2015). *Recharge: Women's technology safety, legal resources, research and training*. Collingwood: Women's Legal Service NSW, Domestic Violence Resource Centre Victirua and WESNET. Retrieved from https://www.dvrcv.org.au/sites/default/files/ReCharge_0.pdf

Woodlock, D. (2017). The abuse of technology in domestic violence and stalking. *Violence Against Women*, *23*(5), 584–602.

Zweig, J. M., Dank, M., Yahner, J., & Lachman, P. (2013). The rate of cyber dating abuse among teens and how it relates to other forms of teen dating violence. *Journal of Youth and Adolescence*, *42*, 1063–1077.

Chapter 25

Technology-Facilitated Violence Against Women in Singapore: Key Considerations

Laura Vitis

Abstract

Technology-facilitated violence against women (TFVW) is readily becoming a key site of analysis for feminist criminologists. The scholarship in this area has identified online sexual harassment, contact-based harassment, image-based abuse, and gender-based cyberhate – among others – as key manifestations of TFVW. It has also unpacked the legal strategies available to women seeking formal justice outcomes. However, much of the existing empirical scholarship has been produced within countries like the United States, United Kingdom, and Australia, and there has been limited research on this phenomenon within South East Asia. As such, this chapter maps how technology is shaping Singaporean women's experiences of gendered, sexual, and domestic violence. To do so, it draws upon findings from a research project which examined TFVW in Singapore by utilizing semistructured interviews with frontline workers in the fields of domestic and sexual violence and LGBT services. Drawing from Dragiewicz et al.'s (2018) work on technology-facilitated coercive control (TFCC), I argue that victims-survivors of dating, domestic, and family violence need to be provided with support that is TFCC informed and technically guided. I also suggest that further research is needed to fully understand the prevalence and nature of TFVW in the Singaporean context.

Keywords: Surveillance; Technology-facilitated violence against women; technology-facilitated coercive control; coercive control; Singapore; domestic violence

The Emerald International Handbook of Technology-Facilitated Violence and Abuse, 407–425

doi:10.1108/978-1-83982-848-520211031

Introduction

Technology-facilitated violence against women (TFVW) has become a key site of analysis for feminist criminologists. The scholarship in this area has identified online sexual harassment, contact-based harassment, image-based abuse (IBA), and gender-based cyberhate – among others – as key manifestations of TFVW (Dragiewicz et al., 2019; Jane, 2017; Powell, Henry, Flynn, & Scott, 2019). It has also explored the legal strategies available to women seeking formal justice outcomes. However, much of the existing empirical scholarship has been produced within countries like the United States, United Kingdom, and Australia, and there has been comparatively less research on this phenomenon in South East Asia. This is a key gap considering the important role that the legislative, service sector, and sociopolitical landscape plays in both support provision and help-seeking. This chapter examines how technology has shaped Singaporean women's experiences of dating, domestic, and family violence. It begins by outlining what is known about TFVW in the Singaporean context and the criminal and civil mechanisms available for redress. The chapter then draws upon findings from a research project which examined TFVW in Singapore, utilizing semistructured interviews with frontline workers in the fields of domestic and sexual violence and LGBT support. Drawing from Dragiewicz et al.'s (2018) work on technology-facilitated coercive control (TFCC), I explore the modalities of TFCC reported in these accounts and argue that tech-abuse training should be provided to frontline workers to ensure that more well-known forms of TFVW, such as "camera sexual voyeurism (CSV),"[1] do not obscure the other forms located within the domestic or intimate partner context. I also argue that victims-survivors of dating, domestic, and family violence need to be provided with support that is TFCC informed and technically guided.

Technology and Violence Against Women

As noted throughout this collection, feminist scholars, researchers, and advocates have highlighted how contemporary technologies are woven into women's experiences of violence. Importantly, researchers have brought to the fore the diverse modalities of abuse and their distribution across women's lifeworlds. Research into IBA, for instance, has shown how strangers, intimate partners, ex-partners, acquaintances, and networks have nonconsensually produced, possessed, altered, distributed, and threatened to distribute women's intimate images for the purposes of harm, humiliation, profit, and control (Henry, Powell, & Flynn, 2017; Powell et al., 2019; Vitis, 2020a). This literature has also highlighted how women are subject to unsolicited pictures of men's genitals across various mediated contexts (Hayes & Dragiewicz, 2018). More broadly, gender-based invective, harassment, dismissal, and criticism have become embedded in women's participation in online spaces (Jane, 2017). For example, recent research with Australian female Tinder users showed that they routinely experienced the following: sexualized messages; hostility; appearance judgment; possessive/controlling messages; and unsolicited nude images on the platform (Gillet, 2019). Gillet's (2019) work noted that sexual double standards and gendered invective are used to both justify and sustain this harassment. This finding is affirmed by Thompson's (2018, p. 83) analysis of Tinder

Nightmares and ByeFelipe,[2] which found that when sexualization was challenged, men deployed sexual double standards to justify their behavior. This included assertions that dating apps are "… transactional space[s] for sex where women are to be used as a 'free' source of sex" and women who use dating apps invite sexualization (Thompson, 2018, p. 83).

One of the many contributions of this body of work is that it demonstrates how technologies have further despatialized violence against women (VAW) by separating it from physical space (Harris & Woodlock, 2019). Concomitantly, it has shown that online harassment and abuse targeted at women and those "othered" within social spaces serves to

> (re)draw boundaries in, around, and between virtual spaces... which shape the rules and norms concerning which individuals and groups are endowed with status and legitimated to participate in these spaces, and those who are not. (Harmer & Lumsden, 2019, p. 13)

Jane's (2017) examination of Australian journalists' experiences of gender-based cyberhate and subsequent self-censorship demonstrates how harassment "mutes" women's public presence (p. 54). This was also affirmed in Gillet's (2019) research which found that participants decided to withdraw from Tinder and/or delete their accounts "… to mitigate intimate intrusions in a context where they were likely to occur" (p. 92). Therefore, these different forms of abuse also reterritorialize social spaces and entrench sociopolitical hierarchies (Harmer & Lumsden, 2019).

These observations are prominent in the contemporary domestic violence literature, which highlights how digital and internet technologies are embedded within practices of coercive control in ways that compromise women's ability to seek freedom from violence and render abusers "omnipresent" (Dragiewicz et al., 2019; Southworth, Finn, Dawson, Fraser, & Tucker, 2007). Indeed, Dragiewicz et al. (2018) have developed the term "technology-facilitated coercive control" (TFCC) to describe the "technological and relational aspects of patterns of abuse against intimate partners" (p. 69). Their research has shown that abusers use communication and internet technologies[3] to infiltrate women's spaces of autonomy, control at a distance, and reduce women's opportunities to separate and sever contact (Dragiewicz et al., 2018). Abusers use these technologies to enact control during separation by unsettling women's ability to create "safe distances" and spaces (Bruton & Tyson, 2017; Hand, Chung, & Peters, 2009; Maher, McCulloch, & Fitz-Gibbon, 2017; State of Victoria, 2016, p. 17). Moreover, this literature suggests that certain elements of TFCC, like stalking, tracking, and restricting phone usage, are key risk factors for intimate partner homicide (Domestic and Family Violence Death Review, 2017).

As is evident from this brief overview, it is important to remain alert to the wider landscape of TFVW to fully encapsulate the ubiquity of these practices across women's lifeworlds and their imbrication with sociopolitical subjectivities. As such, this chapter aims to continue the project of this wider body of literature by exploring the role of technology in women's experiences of dating, domestic, and family violence in Singapore. In the following sections, I map the current literature on Singaporean women's experiences of TFVW, including the legislative landscape within which they are situated. I also address some of the gaps on the relationship between domestic violence, coercive control, and technology in this burgeoning field.

Technology-Facilitated Violence Against Women in the Singaporean Context

Research into women's experiences of domestic violence in the Singaporean context has included limited large-scale prevalence studies and small studies that rely on service data and police statistics (Chan, 2013, p. 329). For example, Bouhours, Chan, Bong, and Anderson (2013) conducted the International Violence Against Women Survey in Singapore. In the survey, 6.1% of Singaporean women reported they had experienced physical or sexual violence from an intimate partner in their lifetime. Around 2% of women reported either physical or sexual violence in a current relationship. Additionally, 22.4% of women reported controlling behaviors by an intimate partner (e.g., angry if she speaks to other men, insists on knowing where and with whom she is, limits contacts with her family and friends, tracks her whereabouts, suspicious of her being unfaithful), and 7.1% reported emotionally abusive behaviors by an intimate partner (e.g., damages/destroys her property, harms/threatens to harm her children, threatened to kill himself, threatens to kill her, harms/threats to harm others close to her, threatens to hurt her or her children if she leaves him).

Within these wider studies there has been no exploration to date of the ways in which technology shapes VAW. Despite this, recent research, court/news reports, and reports from a local women's organization demonstrate that IBA, such as CSV and threats to distribute intimate images, has become a prominent issue in Singapore (AWARE, 2019a; Vitis, 2020a). Since 2004, men across Singapore have been prosecuted for using phones and spy cameras to record underneath women's clothes in public spaces like Mass Rapid Transit (MRT) stations and shopping centers (Vitis, 2020). This practice, referred to as "upskirting,"[4] has also been recognized by Singaporean police, who have reported a rise in "insult of modesty" cases,[5] from 571 in 2013 to 629 in 2016 (Chong, 2015). The prominence of IBA has been affirmed in Vitis, Joseph, and Mahadevan's (2017) review of case file data from the Sexual Assault Care Centre (SACC), which found that in 2016, 18% of client reports involved the use of technology to either facilitate or record violence. Of these 60 cases, 29 involved IBA incidents including the nonconsensual distribution of intimate images; threats to distribute intimate images; and CSV (Vitis, 2020a). Additionally, in 2019, the SACC found that of the 124 client reports involving technology, more than 50% involved IBA (AWARE, 2019a).

Public recognition of IBA came to the fore in 2019 with media coverage of several key IBA cases. In April 2019, the media reported that Monica Baey – a student at the National University of Singapore (NUS) – was filmed in the

University's residential showers by a fellow student. This case circulated widely in the media after Baey took to Instagram to expose the perpetrator and call into question the police's decision to give him a warning and the University's decision to suspend him for a semester (Ang, 2019a). After these posts, her case gained a large online following and local news coverage. Moreover, students at NUS objected to the University's response to the case and NUS subsequently altered its policies on investigating sexual harassment on campus (Ang, 2019a).

The wider scale of the problem was further affirmed in a recent AsiaOne investigation which found that men were using private Telegram group chats entitled "SharingIsCaring" and "SG Nasi Lemak" to circulate nonconsensual and voyeuristic images of women and girls riding public transport, including voyeuristic images of children in school uniforms (Ang, 2019b). The proliferation of nonconsensual image sharing between men was also shored up by recent reports that CSV or "upskirting" images were being disseminated on popular Singaporean countercultural message board forums like Sam's forum (Alkhatib, 2019). This wider practice is evident in the disclaimers on Sam's forum private image exchange threads, which explicitly dissuade users from sharing "snipe" images (a term for CSV or "upskirt" images) while inviting them to "trade pix of [their] sexcapades with, wives, girlfriends & broads" (Sam's Forum, 2020). Although these varying sources of information on IBA cannot provide an overall sense of prevalence, taken together, they do indicate the ways in which IBA is shaping women's experiences of sexual violence and public space in Singapore.

As has been established throughout this collection, TFVW comprises varying modalities and IBA constitutes just one (important) modality within this continuum. For example, in the SACC's review of its 2016 case files, contact-based harassment was one of the main forms of TFVW reported by clients (Vitis, Joseph, & Mahadevan, 2017). Contact-based harassment involved the use of communication technologies to facilitate unwanted sexual contact and included behaviors such as sending explicit, coercive, and sexually harassing messages and posting negative comments on social media. In these cases, perpetrators were employers, colleagues, strangers, teachers, and unknown persons (Vitis et al., 2017).

The public discourse on TFVW has featured IBA prominently because of high volume media coverage of CSV cases perpetrated by strangers in public spaces (Vitis, 2020b). While it is greatly important that these forms of IBA are addressed, it is also important to recognize how technology shapes other, more hidden, forms of abuse. As my own (Vitis, 2020a, p. 27) research into IBA in Singapore found, several cases took place in the private sphere. This research found that in cases where perpetrators threatened to distribute intimate images, they would threaten to share these images with family members. Additionally, threats or coercion often occurred in more hidden contexts like the workplace or in contexts where perpetrators used citizenship status to leverage their harassment. Therefore, as the wider literature on TFVW shows, it is crucial to foreground the continuum of violence, in order to highlight how technology comes to shape women's everyday experiences of violence/harassment.

There are several reasons why it is important to examine the wider patterns of TFVW in the Singaporean context. First, this research can address gaps in the literature and counter the hierarchies of feminist knowledge that privilege the experiences of western or northern women (Carrington, Bull, & Vitis, 2020; Mohanty, 2012). Secondly, despite media reports, public outrage, and evidence from local women's groups (AWARE, 2019a; Vitis, 2020a; Vitis et al., 2017), "gendering" TFVW is complex. This is particularly evident in the media/online discourse on IBA. For instance, my examination of the *Straits Times'* coverage of "upskirting" cases found that while "upskirting" was roundly condemned, the media discourse did not contextualize CSV in relation to VAW (Vitis, 2020). Similarly, research examining public responses to the Monica Baey case on popular online message boards has shown that while there was widespread condemnation of the perpetrator, there was less overt recognition of this case as part of the wider continuum of sexual VAW (Vitis, Naegler, & Ahmad Salehin, 2019).

The gendered dimensions of women's experiences of TFVW can be occluded by such conflations and absences. For example, in my study (Vitis, 2020a), I found that threats to distribute intimate images were used as a tool of sexual assault and coercion. Vitis et al.'s (2017) research into TFVW in the SACC also found that contact-based harassment was imbricated within sexual harassment in the workplace. Moreover, at AWARE's recent panel session on technology-facilitated sexual violence, clients reported that perpetrators had threatened to distribute intimate images taken during consensual sexual encounters and engaged in CSV while stalking them (Tan, 2019). This demonstrates how women's various experiences of TFVW intersect with wider patterns of sexual violence, workplace harassment, dating violence, and coercive control (Dragiewicz et al., 2019).

Relatedly, Association of Women for Action and Research (AWARE) has reported that victims of threats to distribute intimate images and CSV have refrained from going to police because they have been told by others that they are to blame for what happened (Tan, 2019, p. 15). Therefore, the gendered myths that have long surrounded sexual violence continue to constrain women's decisions to come forward, tell friends, family, and police, and seek freedom from violence. These examples demonstrate the importance of research which emphasizes the location of TFVW along the continuum of sexual violence and its imbrication within women's lifeworlds.

Legislative Landscape

Until very recently, IBA (both the nonconsensual production and distribution of intimate images) has been dealt with under a range of laws in Singapore. Prior to January 2020, sexual voyeurism cases were prosecuted under the "insult of modesty" offense. This is a nonphysical sexual harassment offense which defines prohibited behaviors as instances where a person says:

> any word, makes any sound or gesture, or exhibits any object, intending that such word or sound shall be heard, or that such

> gesture or object shall be seen by such woman, or intrudes upon the privacy of such woman. (Penal Code 2008 Rev. Ed., section 509)

Additionally, those who have been found possessing or sharing images have been charged with making, distributing, or possessing an obscene film (Films Act 1998 Rev. Ed., section 29.1, 29.3, 30.1).[6] Also, in 2014, the Protection from Harassment Act (POHA) 2014, extended the substantive definition of harassing behavior to include electronic means and provided more comprehensive protection orders for victims outside intimate relationships (Goh & Yip, 2014). As such, victims are potentially able to obtain a protection order from the courts, after their images have been shared without consent.

There are clear limits with this legislation. While sexual voyeurism cases have been prosecuted under the insult of modesty offense (c.f. Chong, 2017), it is overly broad and does not address the varying modalities of IBA, such as the distribution of intimate images without consent, or threats to distribute intimate images without consent. It is also a nonarrestable offense and as such police are unable to arrest without a warrant, and the victim must first make a Magistrate's complaint prior to police intervention, which can act as a deterrent to reporting. Additionally, the offenses under the Films Act 1998 are used to target the production and distribution of "pornography." While this has been used in successful prosecutions, it punishes perpetrators for "obscenity," not for violating women's consent, bodily autonomy, or privacy. This also has the potential to conflate the nonconsensual production and use of these images with consensual pornography.

Parliament has recently reformed the penal code to better address acts of technology-facilitated violence. In February 2019, the Criminal Law Reform Bill 2019 was introduced into Parliament. This bill created several IBA offenses, including a voyeurism offense which prohibits observing or recording someone in a private act/their genitals or underwear (Criminal Law Reform Bill 2019, section 377). It also prohibits viewing or possessing voyeuristic images (Criminal Law Reform Bill 2019, section 377BD) and distributing or threatening to distribute intimate images without consent (Criminal Law Reform Bill 2019, section 377BE). One of the aims of the Criminal Law Reform Bill 2019 was to clearly recognize different forms of IBA as unique offenses. As the Minister for Home Affairs Mr. K. Shanmugam noted in the second reading of the bill:

> The current laws, in my view, do not adequately address the range of offenses involving voyeuristic recordings, and the distribution of such material on the Internet. We propose to introduce specific offenses involving "voyeurism" which will define the offending behavior, and provide for adequate punishments.... (Ministry of Home Affairs, 2019, p. 88)

Additionally, the Protection from Harassment (POHA) (Amendment) Act 2019 enhanced penalties for people who commit harassment in the context of an intimate relationship (both dating and married) and included making breaches of Protection Orders arrestable offenses where there is evidence of hurt, intimidation, or continued harassment (Protection from Harassment Amendment Act 2019, section 8B-C). It also implemented a specialist Protection from Harassment Court to manage POHA matters (Protection from Harassment Amendment Act 2019, section 16). These laws came into effect on January 1, 2020 and are a welcome change in terms of recognizing the rise of IBA behaviors, such as CSV (including "upskirting" and "downblousing"). Moreover, the criminalization of both the distribution of intimate images and threats to distribute intimate images also recognizes two modalities of IBA which have been raised as concerns by the SACC and within research (AWARE, 2019a; Vitis, 2020a). As such, they demonstrate the important roles that public condemnation, activism, and media reporting play in relation to legislative reform.

However, there are still questions about how and whether other modalities of abuse are recognized in current legislative protections, particularly in the context of family violence. In Singapore, family violence is defined within the Women's Charter (1961). The Charter defines nonphysical violence as "wrongfully confining or restraining a family member against his will" or "causing continual harassment with intent to cause or knowing that it is likely to cause anguish to a family member" (Women's Charter, 1961, section 64). The first provision makes no mention of nonphysical restraint as a result of contact-based harassment or surveillance, and the second emphasis on "intention" could also be refuted by abusers who use embedded technologies as part of their patterns of coercive control. Alternatively, contact-based harassment can easily be dismissed due to the social normalization of high-volume contact and the heteronormative acceptance of relationship surveillance (Levy, 2015). The term "continual harassment" could be applied to the range of abuses described above; however, the lack of clarity in relation to TFVW or TFCC (Dragiewicz et al., 2018) may complicate this. Therefore, while the Criminal Law Reform Bill 2019 explicitly recognizes the rise of IBA, it is also important to recognize the role that technologies have played within the varying and complex relations of domestic and family violence.

Technology and Dating, Domestic, and Family Violence in Singapore

As noted above, there has been limited research that has examined how technologies have shaped women's experiences of domestic violence in Singapore. In the interest of adding to this knowledge, in this section, I report findings from a research project which examined the role of technology in Singaporean women's experiences of dating, domestic, and family violence. This project involved semistructured interviews with 14 frontline workers in the fields of domestic violence, sexual violence, and LGBT support. Participants were identified and contacted through publicly available email addresses located on their organization's website. Participants were then interviewed at their places of employment and interviews focused on their observations of the role of technology in their clients' experiences of dating, domestic, and family violence. After data collection, I conducted a thematic analysis of their responses. In line with the international domestic violence literature (Dragiewicz et al., 2019; Harris & Woodlock, 2019; Woodlock, 2013), frontline workers reported three main modalities of tech abuse: contact-based harassment; surveillance; and IBA. They also noted connections between these modalities and coercive and controlling behaviors.

Contact-Based Harassment

One of the most common forms of tech abuse reported by workers was contact-based harassment. This included cases where perpetrators would use phones – mostly WhatsApp or SMS – to send abusive, insulting, controlling, or harassing messages. Participants noted that despite a complex technological landscape, the "standard" communication devices like phones were used far more commonly to harass and control during abusive relationships. These messages were identified as being both persistent and unwanted and involved gendered invective, threats, and in some cases threats to kill:

> ... I think the most common one would be through texting. To harass or even to threaten the victims.... There... could be repeated texts or calling and all these thing. It puts the receiver, the victims at a very unease mental states... the husband, because he will be texting the wife. Scolding, abusive language. Very harsh and [unclear] to the wife. (Participant C)

These accounts indicated that repeated, unwanted, and abusive messages were additional mechanisms through which perpetrators could enact abuse in high volume. One of the contexts in which contact-based harassment occurred was at separation. For example, workers reported that abusive messaging became apparent after a client took out a Personal Protection Order (PPO) and had attempted to separate or sought a divorce. This highlights what Dimond, Fiesler, and Bruckman (2011) describe as the technological "web of entanglement" (p. 419) and affirms international scholarship which has found that high volume/abusive messages are a common tactic used to reassert control and contact during separation (Dragiewicz et al., 2019; Woodlock, 2013). While in many cases messages were used to facilitate contact between perpetrator and victim-survivor, there were other cases where the perpetrator would engage in networked contact-based harassment. This was achieved by either enlisting extended members of the victim-survivor's direct community to harass on his behalf or threatening to expose or humiliate them within that community. For example, in one case, the perpetrator was blocked by the victim-survivor and in response he began threatening to contact her immediate circle of friends and family in order to humiliate or embarrass her. This aligns with other research which has shown that individual or networked contact-based harassment is facilitated through communication technologies and a technosocial landscape which enables networked social connections and collapses boundaries of space and time (NNEDV, 2014).

Surveillance

One of the most prominent modalities of abuse reported was the use of surveillance technologies to exert control. Participants discussed four types of surveillance. The first type was overt camera surveillance in the home. In these cases, abusers overtly installed cameras in the house to record spouses and family members. This footage was either passively recorded or actively reviewed by abusers and then used to issue correction at a distance. Second, participants discussed covert surveillance, involving the hidden installation or use of recording devices in the home, and third is the movement surveillance, where perpetrators used repeated messaging or the GPS capabilities on phone applications to restrict women's movement outside the home (Vitis, 2020b). One example was provided by a participant who articulated how apps with GPS capabilities were used for the purposes of control:

> So situations where a couple is in a relationship where there's certainly controlling behaviors. So using of – I had to learn this from my client – certain apps that are GPS linked. So going on those apps and basically knowing where your partner is because you know what profile they're using. They're knowing that okay they're on and they're there and they're supposed to be somewhere else but they're there instead.... (Participant H)

The fourth type of surveillance was social surveillance. In these cases, the perpetrator would intrude women's devices, social media accounts, or emails or restrict access to communication devices in order to monitor and control who they were in contact with (Vitis, 2020b). Dragiewicz et al. (2019) argue that these experiences can be explained in relation to the wider inclusion of technology into forms of coercive control, as abusers increasingly rely on the surveillant affordances of digital media to both gain access to and exert control over women's lifeworlds. This was affirmed within these accounts which showed that technologies were used to create surveillant assemblages to restrict women's freedom and autonomy within their homes, social networks, and/or the public sphere. Importantly, these assemblages are supported by the rising consumer spyware industry and the affordable and accessible integration of surveillance into everyday devices (Harkin, Molnar, & Vowles, 2020).

Image-Based Abuse

Workers did not indicate that IBA was prominent, although they were able to identify cases where IBA had taken place. One worker suggested that it was not common for husbands to take and store photos of their wives in Singapore. Another worker attributed this to Singapore being a conservative country and suggested that clients were not technologically proficient enough for such practices:

> No, I think Singapore is quite conservative in the sense where they don't take videos of, yes, maybe they're not that sophisticated… in terms of thinking of take photos of, I don't know, sexual intimacy, or cultural kind of sensitive things. I think either they don't, I don't know, I think the mind of Singaporeans maybe, I don't know, maybe they're not so exposed to ideas like that. (Participant D)

Despite this, four workers spoke about incidents where boyfriends, husbands, or ex-husbands nonconsensually shared intimate images of their wives, girlfriends, or ex-wives with third parties. One participant noted that her client's partner shared her intimate images with an acquaintance on a chat room. Another worker described her wider professional experience in the school context, where boys had nonconsensually shared consensually obtained intimate images of girls with other boys as an accepted standard of dating and breaking up. The use of images for homosocial bonding, attaining status (Ringrose & Harvey, 2015), or "doing masculinity" (DeKeseredy & Schwartz, 2016, p. 3) was also noted by other participants. For example, one worker described a case at her workplace where a young woman reported that her boyfriend shared her intimate images with his friends:

> The intentions initially wasn't – it wasn't to threaten the relationship. There was a friendly share with a close group of friends… the boyfriend didn't really practice discretion with his group of friends…. She only heard it from her friend who received that photo. Of course, she felt quite thrown off guard. (Participant M)

This reflects Ringrose and Harvey's (2015) finding that in school/peer contexts, boys "… can gain value and reputational reward from possessing images of esteemed girls' bodies and the implication of sexual services from girls" (p. 214). It also indicates how images are used within homosocial contexts as a way of sustaining relationships between men or boys. Furthermore, it accords with recent reports that men and boys are using online sites or private chat groups to nonconsensually share nude images of Singaporean women with peers.

Images were also used as a way of sustaining control in an abusive relationship, particularly at separation. In one case, a client's husband gave his current partner access to a hard drive where her nude images were stored. In another, a woman's husband shared her intimate images with her new partner in order to seek revenge:

> So, he warned him that "this is the kind of woman that you are going to marry – if you're eventually going to marry – and I felt being betrayed by her," that kind of thing. So, he's like, in a way

> like blackmailing.... It's that warning him that "are you sure you want to get, you want to marry her in the future?" "She has been my wife and she's doing all this kind of thing behind my back – the mistress having an affair with you." (Participant F)

This aligns with research into both domestic violence and IBA which has shown that separation is a common context for men to circulate intimate images without consent for the purpose of harming or humiliating women, as part of a narrative of "pay back" (Bruton & Tyson, 2017; State of Victoria, 2016). Therefore, while some workers claimed that this practice was not commonplace in Singapore, the casual ways in which men shared these images, coupled with wider reports of IBA in the community, raise questions about whether this assessment is accurate, particularly considering the varied nature of these reports which include peer sharing in schools, peer sharing online, and instrumental and coercive use of images.

Training and Support

None of the 14 participants I spoke to discussed receiving training on TFVW or TFCC. In some cases, they noted that they had limited knowledge of the nature, deployment, and impacts of TFCC. For example, one participant reflected on a client whose husband installed cameras in the home:

> If I recall, I was probably a lot more interested in the physical line that's being perpetrated. I didn't ask about how it felt being – having cameras watching you all the time. Maybe it was a part, I didn't ask, I felt, I suspected, I didn't, we didn't know what to do with that. I felt as if I ask her questions, because I kind of know where, what you could do with it. I think I, I probably felt as helpless as well, I suspect. (Participant K)

Moreover, some reported that they learned about tech abuse from their clients. For example, one worker stated that she found out from a client that apps were GPS linked and could enable abusers to stalk their partners at a distance. Another participant reported that they were uncertain as to how the abuser had managed to track their client via their devices:

> I had this client where the husband had control of the wife's WhatsApp messages. He somehow was tracking it via his laptop. I don't know how he did it, but this was what the client told me. Whoever she sends a text message, whoever she calls or whatever, husband is aware and also whereabouts. (Participant E)

TFCC training for police and support staff is crucial. Without appropriate training, workers in these fields may not recognize the range of technologies being used, their interrelationship with coercive control, and how to advise women on appropriate safety planning (Dragiewicz et al., 2019). For example, when coercive and controlling behaviors are reported, police may lack the knowledge required to check devices or advise victim-survivors on how to adequately record evidence (Dragiewicz et al., 2019). The onus is then placed upon the victim-survivor to gather complex device-based evidence without technical support (Dorozenko & Chung, 2018). These knowledge gaps are then carried through to the courts where victim-survivors report that the true seriousness of TFCC is not adequately recognized (Dragiewicz et al., 2019).

Similarly, service providers have acknowledged that face-to-face training, which provides up-to-date information on the various technologies being deployed by abusers and how to conduct device checks, is important (Dragiewicz et al., 2019). For example, a review of WESNET's[7] "Safer technology for women training" found that workers who completed the training felt more confident in advising clients on how to address contact-based harassment (Dorozenko & Chung, 2018). They were also better able to identify the different modalities of tech abuse and implement relevant safety strategies (Dorozenko & Chung, 2018). Importantly, this evaluation highlighted that, without training, workers may rely on "common sense" strategies (such as blocking) to protect women from stalking and abuse; however, this may further compromise their safety (Dorozenko & Chung, 2018). This is a key issue, as research with practitioners has shown that strategies which prioritize restricting contact via devices or changing numbers do not fully address the problem (Harris & Woodlock, 2019).

What was evident, however, was that women coming to these services had developed their own safety strategies that allowed them to maintain some autonomy while simultaneously managing the abuser's controlling behaviors:

> She mentioned that usually she will delete all this information or whatever calls that she makes out before going back home. Also, when we contact her or message her, she will delete. (Participant E)

> Then eventually the husband kept checking her phone, and then she eventually registered another phone, another line secretly. She keeps the phone somewhere else. (Participant F)

> She told me that she can't deal with the text messages, she just blocks them, so she's able to then restrict these messages by blocking him totally, even blocking her husband from texting her, from messaging her, even from email. She's able to block all access of contacts with the husband. (Participant D)

Similarly, Dragiewicz et al. (2019) found that women were best placed to assess their own safety, and this may mean staying in contact with the perpetrator via controlled devices. However, limited formal training for workers raises important questions about the pressure placed on victims-survivors to develop the technological skills required to both understand the dynamics of TFCC and create tech-inclusive safety strategies (Harris & Woodlock, 2019).

Conclusion

This research makes no claims about the prevalence of TFCC; however, the types of abuses reported by workers accord with findings from outside Singapore which have shown that TFCC is a key issue for victim-survivors of domestic and family violence (Dragiewicz et al., 2019; Woodlock, 2013). As such, these findings suggest that the next large-scale survey of VAW in Singapore includes these technological modalities in order to obtain a more accurate understanding of the prevalence of TFVW and TFCC in the Singaporean context. These findings also demonstrate the need for qualitative research which draws directly from the insights of victims-survivors. The current Singaporean research on domestic violence and TFVW, mine included, has focused on service data and interviews with service providers. As such, it is important that contemporary empirical scholarship includes both large-scale surveys to highlight the prevalence of this problem, in addition to in-depth interviews with victims-survivors to better understand the impact of communication, digital, and internet technologies on their experiences of violence. This is of particular importance during this period of legislative reform in Singapore. In order to assess the impacts of the recently implemented IBA offenses (Criminal Law Reform Bill, 2019) and changes emerging from the Protect from Harassment (Amendment) Act 2019, research which draws upon the experiences of victims-survivors of TFVW who have pursued these formal avenues of intervention is required. This work is needed to ensure that the experiences of victims-survivors guide current and future law reform, prevention strategies, and service responses.

As noted above, these abuses have come to the public's attention through media reporting, protest, and political support for including (some) instances of IBA in the Criminal Law Reform Bill 2019. This political engagement demonstrates some awareness of tech-based abuses. However, to fully realize the extent of VAW and the role of technology in that violence, these abuses need to be recognized as part of the patterns of gendered, sexual, domestic, intimate partner, and family violence (Vitis, 2020a). Without this, it will be difficult to uncover the complexities of controlling behavior in domestic violence or address women and girls' experiences of violence in the everyday. This work is already underway. AWARE has recently launched their Alt-Ctrl program, which aims to provide a platform for community members to develop projects which address tech and gender violence and includes prevention, policing, and pathways to justice (AWARE, 2019b). However, there are additional avenues to consider. More consultation is needed with workers to map knowledge and knowledge gaps in order to develop appropriate training programs. On February 17, 2020, the Ministry of Home Affairs and the Ministry of Social and Family Development announced a new task force which will respond to family violence by setting up a dedicated hotline and placing social workers in all police divisions to assess victims and refer them to relevant agencies (CNA, 2020). It is important to ensure that TFCC and tech abuse training for police and frontline workers is on the agenda for this task force. These efforts could also be supported by ensuring the community is aware of the relationships between technology and coercive control. This could be expressed by updating public service announcements developed by the National Family Violence Networking System, which provide descriptions of dating, domestic, and family violence without mentioning the role of technology (NFVNS, 2018).

Notes

1. Camera sexual voyeurism (CSV) is the use of camera devices to record intimate images of another person without their consent, for instance, taking images up a woman's skirt or shorts, or down her top, or planting a hidden camera to record a person in private spaces.
2. Tinder Nightmares and ByeFelipe are Instagram accounts that repost women's experiences of negative or objectionable behavior on dating applications.
3. While TFCC is diverse, the following behaviors are prominent manifestations: contact-based harassment (repeated, unwanted use of communication, digital and internet technologies for contact); IBA (the nonconsensual, production, possession, and dissemination of intimate images or threats to disseminate intimate images); and surveillance (the use of varying technologies to monitor) (Dragiewicz et al., 2019).
4. "Upskirting" is only one example of camera technology being used to record without consent. In order to capture other acts, I use the term "camera sexual voyeurism" (CSV).
5. An "insult of modesty" offense is defined as sexual harassment, which includes CSV.
6. This carries a prison term ranging from 2 years for making an obscene film to 6 months for possessing a single obscene film.
7. WESNET is the national peak body for specialist women's domestic violence services in Australia.

References

Alkhatib, S. (2019, March 28). Man linked with Sammyboy Forum jailed for filming women in toilet. *The Straits Times*. Retrieved from https://www.straitstimes.com/singapore/

Ang, J. (2019a, April 26). Exclusive interview: Posting my story on Instagram about NUS Peeping Tom was last resort, says Monica Baey. *The Straits Times*. Retrieved from https://www.straitstimes.com/singapore/

Ang, L. (2019b, October 20). Police looking into another Telegram chat group allegedly circulating obscene materials. *The Straits Times*. Retrieved from https://www.straitstimes.com/singapore/

AWARE. (2019a). A recap: Taking ctrl, finding alt 2019. Retrieved from https://www.aware.org.sg/2019/11/a-recap-taking-ctrl-finding-alt-2019/

AWARE. (2019b). Taking ctrl, finding alt contest. Retrieved from https://www.aware.org.sg/tfsvcontest/

Bouhours, B., Chan, W.C., Bong, B., & Anderson, S. (2013). International violence against women survey: Final report on Singapore. Retrieved from https://ssrn.com/abstract=2337291

Bruton, C., & Tyson, D. (2017). Leaving violent men: A study of women's experiences of separation in Victoria, Australia. *Australian and New Zealand Journal of Criminology*, *51*(3), 339–354. doi:10.1177/0004865817746711

Carrington, K., Bull, M., & Vitis, L. (2020). Gender-based violence: Case studies from the Global South. In S. Walklate, K. Fitz-Gibbon, J. Maher, & J. McCulloch (Eds.), *The Emerald handbook of feminism, criminology and social change* (pp. 373–394). Bingley: Emerald Publishing Limited.

Chan, W. C. (2013). Violence against women in Singapore: Initial data from the International Violence Against Women Survey. In J. Liu, B. Hebenton, & S. Jou (Eds.), *Handbook of Asian criminology* (pp. 329–342). New York, NY: Springer.

Chong, E. (2015, December 23). Jail for taking upskirt videos of 21 women. *The Straits Times*. Retrieved from https://www.straitstimes.com/singapore/

Chong, E. (2017, September 28). Ex-bank officer jailed 24 weeks for taking upskirt videos of strangers and colleague. *The Straits Times*. Retrieved from https://www.straitstimes.com/singapore/

CNA. (2020, February 17). MHA, MSF set up joint task force to tackle family violence. *Channel News Asia*. Retrieved from https://www.youtube.com/watch?v=NYPa3OBGg1Y

Criminal Law Reform Bill. (2019). Section 377BD, 377BE. Retrieved from https://sso.agc.gov.sg/Bills-Supp/6-2019/Published/20190211?DocDate=20190211

DeKeseredy, W., & Schwartz, M. (2016). Thinking sociologically about image-based sexual abuse: The contribution of male peer support theory. *Sexualization, Media, & Society*, *2*(4), 1–8. doi:10.1177/2374623816684692

Dimond, J., Fiesler, C., & Bruckman, A. (2011). Domestic violence and information communication technologies. *Interacting with Computers*, *23*(5), 412–421. doi:10.1016/j.intcom.2011.04.006

Domestic and Family Violence Death Review and Advisory Board. (2017). Domestic and Family Violence Death Review and Advisory Board: 2016/17 annual report. Retrieved from https://www.courts.qld.gov.au/__data/assets/pdf_file/0003/541947/domestic-and-family-violence-death-review-and-advisory-board-annual-report-2016-17.pdf

Dorozenko, D., & Chung, D. (2018). Research and evaluation of the safer technology for women training and the safe connections program. Retrieved from https://wesnet.org.au/wp-content/uploads/sites/3/2019/10/Safe-Connections-Evaluation_Telstra-Report_-Final.pdf

Dragiewicz, M., Burgess, J., Matamoros-Fernández, A., Salter, M., Suzor, N. P., Woodlock, D., & Harris, B. (2018). Technology facilitated coercive control: Domestic violence and the competing roles of digital media platforms. *Feminist Media Studies*, *18*(4), 609–625. doi:10.1080/14680777.2018.1447341

Dragiewicz, M., Harris, B., Woodlock, D., Salter, M., Easton, H., Lynch, A., & Milne, L. (2019). Domestic violence and communication technology: Survivor experiences of intrusion, surveillance and identity crime. Retrieved from https://accan.org.au/grants/completed-grants/1429-domestic-violence-and-communication-technology-victim-experiences-of-intrusion-surveillance-and-identity-theft

Films Act 1998 Rev. Ed., section 29.1, 29.3, 30.1. Retrieved from https://sso.agc.gov.sg/Act/FA1981

Gillet, R. (2019). Everyday violence: Women's experiences of intimate intrusions on tinder. Doctoral dissertation, Queensland University of Technology. Retrieved from https://eprints.qut.edu.au/131121/

Goh, Y., & Yip, M. (2014). The Protection from Harassment Act 2014: Legislative comment. *Singapore Academy of Law Journal*, *26*, 703–726. Retrieved from ssrn.com/abstract=2531196

Hand, T., Chung, D., & Peters, M. (2009). The use of information and communication technologies to coerce and control in domestic violence and following separation. *Australian Domestic & Family Violence Clearinghouse*, Paper 6. Retrieved from https://research-repository.uwa.edu.au/en/publications/the-use-of-information-and-communication-technologies-to-coerce-a

Harkin, D., Molnar, A., & Vowles, E. (2020). The commodification of mobile phone surveillance: An analysis of the consumer spyware industry. *Crime, Media, Culture: An International Journal*, *16*(1), 33–60. doi:10.1177/1741659018820562

Harmer, E., & Lumsden, K. (2019). Online othering: An introduction. In K. Lumsden, & E. Harmer (Eds.), *Online othering* (pp. 1–33). Cham: Springer International Publishing.

Harris, B. A., & Woodlock, D. (2019). Digital coercive control: Insights from two landmark domestic violence studies. *British Journal of Criminology*, *59*(3), 530–550. doi:10.1093/bjc/azy052

Hayes, R. M., & Dragiewicz, M. (2018). Unsolicited dick pics: Erotica, exhibitionism or entitlement? *Women's Studies International Forum*, *71*, 114–120. doi:10.1016/j.wsif.2018.07.001

Henry, N., Powell, A., & Flynn, A. (2017). Not just 'revenge pornography': Australians experiences of image-based abuse: A summary report. Retrieved from https://www.rmit.edu.au/content/dam/rmit/documents/college-of-design-and-social-context/schools/global-urban-and-social-studies/revenge_porn_report_2017.pdf

Jane, E. (2017). Feminist flight and fight responses to gendered cyberhate. In M. Segrave, & L. Vitis (Eds.), *Gender, technology and violence* (pp. 45–61). London: Routledge.

Levy, K. (2015). Intimate surveillance. *Idaho Law Review*, *51*(3), 679–694. Retrieved from https://heinonline-org.ezproxy.lib.rmit.edu.au/HOL/Page?lname=&public=false&collection=journals&handle=hein.journals/idlr51&men_hide=false&men_tab=toc&kind=&page=679

Maher, J. M., McCulloch, J., & Fitz-Gibbon, K. (2017). New forms of gendered surveillance? Intersections of technology and family violence. In M. Segrave, & L. Vitis (Eds.), *Gender, technology and violence* (pp. 14–27). London: Routledge.

Ministry of Home Affairs. (2019). Second reading of Criminal Law Reform Bill. Speech by Mr. K Shanmugam. Minister for Home Affairs and Minister for Law. Retrieved from https://www.mha.gov.sg/newsroom/in-parliament/parliamentary-speeches/news/second-reading-of-criminal-law-reform-bill-speech-by-mr-k-shanmugam-minister-for-home-affairs-and-minister-for-law

Mohanty, C. (2012). Under Western eyes: Feminist scholarship and colonial discourses. In M. G. Durham, & D. M. Kellner (Eds.), *Media and cultural studies: Key works* (pp. 347–364). Malden, MA: Wiley-Blackwell.

NFVNS. (2018). What is family violence. The national family violence networking system. Retrieved from https://www.msf.gov.sg/breakthesilence/SitePages/Home_Family.aspx?family=1

NNEDV. (2014). *A glimpse from the field: How abusers are misusing technology*. Washington, DC: Safety Net Technology Safety Survey. Retrieved from https://static1.squarespace.com/static/51dc 541ce4b03ebab8c5c88c/t/54e3d1b6e4b08500fcb455a0/1424216502058/NNEDV_Glimpse+ From+the+Field+-+2014.pd

Penal Code 2008 Rev. Ed., section 509. Retrieved from https://sso.agc.gov.sg/Act/PC1871?

Powell, A., Henry, N., Flynn, A., & Scott, A. (2019). Image-based sexual abuse: The extent, nature, and predictors of perpetration in a community sample of Australian residents. *Computers in Human Behavior*, *92*, 393–402. doi:10.1016/j.chb.2018.11.009.

Protection from Harassment (Amendment) Act 2019. Retrieved from https://sso.agc.gov.sghttps://sso.agc.gov.sg/Acts-Supp/17-2019/Published/20190610?DocDate=20190610&ViewType=Within#:~:text=The%20long%20title%20to%20the,and%20to%20provide%20for%20the

Ringrose, J., & Harvey, L. (2015). Boobs, back-off, six packs and bits: Mediated body parts, gendered reward, and sexual shame in teens' sexting images. *Continuum*, *29*(2), 205–217. doi:10.1080/10304312.2015.1022952.

Sam's Forum. (2020). Sam's Forum: Where REAL people discuss what REALLY matters in their lives. Retrieved from www.samsimply.rocks

Southworth, C., Finn, J., Dawson, S., Fraser, C., & Tucker, S. (2007). Intimate partner violence, technology, and stalking. *Violence Against Women*, *13*(8), 842–856. doi:10.1177/1077801207302045.

State of Victoria. (2016). Royal Commission into Family Violence: Summary and recommendations (Parl Paper No 132). Retrieved from http://rcfv.archive.royalcommission.vic.gov.au/MediaLibraries/RCFamilyViolence/Reports/RCFV_Full_Report_Interactive.pdf

Tan, T. M. (2019, November 25). Tech-enabled sexual violence cases almost triple since 2016, says Aware. *The Straits Times*. Retrieved from https://www.straitstimes.com/singapore/

Thompson, L. (2018). "I can be your Tinder nightmare": Harassment and misogyny in the online sexual marketplace. *Feminism & Psychology*, *28*(1), 69–89. doi:10.1177/0959353517720226.

Vitis, L. (2020a). Private, hidden and obscured: Image based sexual abuse in Singapore. *Asian Journal of Criminology*, *15*(1), 25–43. doi:10.1007/s11417-019-09293-0.

Vitis, L. (2020b). Surveillance in the city: The role of surveillance in women's experiences of domestic violence in Singapore, perspectives from frontline workers. Unpublished Work.

Vitis, L. (2020). Media representations of camera sexual voyeurism in Singapore: A medicalised, externalised and community problem. *Feminist Media Studies. Online First*. doi:10.1080/14680777.2020.1810095

Vitis, L., Joseph, A., & Mahadevan, D. (2017). Technology and sexual violence: SACC summary report. Retrieved from https://www.aware.org.sg/wp-content/uploads/SACC-TFSVH-Report-Final-report.pdf

Vitis, L., Naegler, L., & Ahmad Salehin, M. S. (2019). The Challenges of online networked ethnographic: Researching image based abuse online. Paper presentation. The American Society of Criminology Conference, San Francisco, CA.

Women's Charter 1961 section 64. Retrieved from https://sso.agc.gov.sg/Act/WC1961

Woodlock, D. (2013, Spring/Summer). The rise of technology-based stalking. *DVRCV Advocate*, *2*, 4–7.

Chapter 26

Technology as Both a Facilitator of and Response to Youth Intimate Partner Violence: Perspectives from Advocates in the Global-South

Gisella Lopes Gomes Pinto Ferreira

Abstract

Much of the research on intimate partner violence focuses on adults, and little of it emanates from the Global-South. The study reported upon in this chapter is aimed at addressing these gaps. Adopting a Southern Feminist Framework, it discusses findings from interviews with Brasilian and Australian advocates working on prevention of youth IPV. Participants from both countries noted disturbing instances of digital coercive control among the youth with whom they work, as well as underlying factors such as gender-based discrimination that simultaneously contribute to the prevalence of such behaviors, as well as their normalization among young people. However, they also emphasized the positive role that technology can play in distributing educational programming that reaches young people where they are and circumvents conservative agendas that in some cases keep education about gender discrimination and healthy relationships out of schools.

Keywords: Technology-facilitated abuse and stalking; young people; Global-South; Brasil; Australia; prevention

Introduction

Scholarly and government research suggests that, generally, young people are the age cohort most susceptible to intimate partner violence (IPV) but lack

The Emerald International Handbook of Technology-Facilitated Violence and Abuse, 427–446

doi:10.1108/978-1-83982-848-520211032

understanding of how IPV manifests and can be addressed (Australian Institute of Health and Welfare, 2018; Fórum Brasileiro de Segurança Pública, 2019; Murta et al., 2019). Normalization or naturalization of abuse can also be a barrier (Murta et al., 2019). There are profound health-related and social impacts for young people because this time of life is often when people engage in their first intimate relationship, and prior experience of abuse can affect later relationships (Murta et al., 2019). Evidence suggests that the presence of technology in relationships is increasing, and with it the use of technology to enact IPV (Politoff et al., 2019; UN General Assembly, 2018). In this vein, King-Ries (2011) claims that teenagers are particularly vulnerable, as they "pervasively use and incorporate technology in their intimate relationships" and so "tend to believe that what is happening [the abuse and stalking] to themselves and their peers is normal" (p. 155).

Given the role of technology in friendship networks and dating practices, the immediate and future consequences of youth IPV and young people's higher risk of this type of violence, it is imperative that we investigate how abuse and stalking are perpetrated using technology, which may also be a channel for preventing IPV. In this vein, it is fundamental to talk with advocates. Historically, advocates' and feminist movements' hard work prompted shifts in policy and prevention, yet they are often overlooked in academic studies (Flood, 2019; Harris, Dragiewicz, & Woodlock, 2020). This chapter aims to address this gap in the literature by drawing on interviews conducted with Brasilian and Australian advocates. It adopts the concept of Digital Coercive Control (DCC) (defined as "the use of devices and digital media to stalk, harass, threaten and abuse partners or ex-partners [Harris & Woodlock, 2019, p. 533])" to examine how IPV is perpetrated among youth groups based on the perspectives of the advocates interviewed. In their research on DCC, Harris and Woodlock (2019) use Stark's work on coercive control (2007) focused on adults. However, this concept is also relevant in the youth context because it highlights how this violence is enacted, and its motivation and consequences (Harris & Woodlock, 2019; Taylor, Murphy-Graham, & Lauro, 2019). This chapter also explores how technology has been used by advocates to prevent youth DCC, and the benefits and limitations of such.

The chapter begins with an overview of previous research relating to youth and IPV before turning to discuss the methodology used in my study of advocates in Brasil[1] and Australia. It then discusses the results of my study in light of previous research findings before concluding with suggestions for future research that focuses on gaining a better understanding of and preventing technology-facilitated IPV (TFIPV) among youth.

Previous Research

Young people are the age group most vulnerable to IPV; however, most research to date has targeted adult IPV (Taylor et al., 2017). The existing research on youth IPV comes predominantly from North America (Murta, dos Santos, Martins, & de Oliveira, 2013; Rodríguez Domínguez, Pérez-Moreno, & Durán, 2020). There is a relatively small body of literature in the Global-South. In Brasil, these studies are mostly concerned with the prevalence of youth IPV, and they frequently do not mention youth experiences of DCC (Beserra et al., 2015). There are a few exceptions including the work of Oliveira, Assis, Njaine, and Oliveira (2011), Instituto Avon/Data Popular (2014), Énois I Inteligência Jovem, Instituto Vladimir Herzog, & Instituto Patrícia Galvão (2015) and more recently Campeiz (2018) and Taylor et al. (2017, 2019). There are a few studies in Brasil focused on the prevention of IPV and gender-based violence more broadly among youth, for example, the work of Murta et al. (2013, 2019, 2020), Taylor et al. (2017) and Viza, Sartori, & Zanello (2017). In Australia, youth IPV was addressed in prevention research, including the work of Flood (2019) guiding the engagement of men and boys for preventing violence against women and girls. Additional examples include the research of Pascua, Khokhar, Saeed, Uwineza, and Taukolo (2019) and Struthers, Parmenter, and Tilbury (2019) focused on preventing violence in relationships through peer education, and "also referring to related programs such as sexual violence prevention programs, image-based abuse, and on-line abuse prevention programs" (Pascua et al., 2019, p. 2); The Line (2017) social marketing campaigns targeting young people and promoting healthy, respectful, and consensual relationships; Senior, Helmer and Chenhall's (2017) work on Indigenous young women's perceptions of IPV; Mackenzie and Mackay's report on young country women's perceptions of IPV (2019); and research focused on youth attitudes toward violence against women (Politoff et al., 2019).

While there are particularities based on country, region, and group, the existing research demonstrates that in general, technology plays a crucial role in youth intimate relationships as it is heavily used by youth to engage in relationships, and also to perpetrate DCC, including tracking and monitoring their partners and their digital accounts. These controlling behaviors are often mistaken by youth as signs of love, caring, and jealousy (Campeiz, 2018; Taylor et al., 2017). Brasilian and Australian research indicates that often other forms of online violence such as image-based abuse (IBA) accompany DCC, particularly after the end (or the attempt to end) a relationship (Henry, McGlynn, Flynn, Johnson, Powell, & Scott, 2020; Henry, Powell, & Flynn, 2017; Oliveira et al., 2011). The threat of IBA was also referred to as a means used by boys to force girls to remain in a relationship (Oliveira et al., 2011). Furthermore, the co-occurrence of family violence and IPV was also noted, as well as the fact that previous experience of abuse during childhood and adolescence can be a predictor of experiencing IPV in adult life too (Taylor et al., 2017; Ávila, 2017).

Brasilian and Australian studies highlight that young people face barriers to help-seeking, feeling ashamed, or lacking knowledge about support services (Soares, Lopes, & Njaine, 2013; Tarzia, Iyer, Thrower, & Hegarty, 2017). In this context, preventative use of technology can deliver useful widespread outcomes, by providing information and support in platforms where youth anonymity is ensured and free of judgment (Tarzia et al., 2017). Yet, there is limited research focused on the prevention of youth IPV via technological means (Tarzia et al., 2017). Many of the existing Brasilian and Australian prevention initiatives are face-to-face and based in schools which are often regarded as more effective (Flood, 2019). However, a few technology-based prevention initiatives have been documented. These include the construction of websites and a computer-tailored intervention to prevent youth IPV (Murta et al., 2020; Woodlock, 2017), chatbots to raise awareness about sexting and IBA among youth (UNICEF, 2019), and social marketing campaigns (The Line, 2017). There are other initiatives involving artificial intelligence, like the chatbots MAIA (Microsoft News Center Brasil, 2020) and Isa.bot (Cosmobots, n.d). These chatbots were launched in 2020 and 2019, respectively, which might explain the lack of published research regarding their development. A number of authors have recognized the potential of technology for preventing youth IPV and stressed the importance of engaging with young people themselves to develop initiatives designed to address their needs (Murta et al., 2020).

Methodology

Southern Feminist Framework

To date, the majority of the research on the prevention of youth IPV comes from North America (Daff, Mcewan, & Luebbers, 2018; Murta et al., 2013). Thus, much of the global economy of knowledge in this area is imposed by the metropole (North) onto the periphery (South), disregarding the differences between these geographic areas and restricting the potential of "possible projects of knowledge" (Connell, 2014, p. 216). This chapter uses southern theory (Connell, 2007) and southern criminology (Carrington, Hogg, & Sozzo, 2016) to address this knowledge deficit by drawing upon interviews with key advocates from Australia and Brasil who are engaged in the prevention of youth IPV. Advocates are the key responders to IPV, and their work has made IPV visible to the public; yet they are often overlooked in research (Harris et al., 2020). This chapter contributes toward filling this gap by giving voice to advocates from Brasil and Australia – countries that, despite their differences, share a violent history of colonialism, geological formation, geographic location, and a significant university system (Connell, Pearse, Collyer, Maia, & Morrell, 2018) being part of what Connell (2013) refers to as the Southern tier. It acknowledges the need to include voices from the Global-South, and thereby to democratize the production of knowledge and redress the Anglo-Saxon dominance of language (Carrington et al., 2016; Faraldo-Cabana, 2018).

The southern feminist framework combines southern criminology (Carrington et al., 2016) with a feminist research methodology (Bandeira, 2014). Gender inequality is a central focus of feminist research methodology. Considerable research suggests that heterosexual IPV is gendered, with women disproportionately represented as victim/survivors and men as perpetrators (Bancroft, 2002; Fitz-Gibbon, Walklate, McCulloch, & Maher, 2018). Research suggesting symmetry between the sexes in youth IPV (e.g., Strauss, 2004; Wolfe et al., 2001) has been criticized for using methods that fail to capture the violent context, dynamics of power and control, and acts of self-defense typically present in IPV (DeKeseredy & Schwartz, 1998; Dobash & Dobash, 1995), and for failing to take into account youth experiences with IPV (Daff et al., 2018; Minayo, Assis, & Njaine, 2011). The United Nations Broadband Commission (2015) highlighted that young women aged 18–24 years are at heightened risk of exposure to all forms of TFVA, which supports a gendered understanding of young women's and girls' experiences of DCC. Furthermore, an intersectional lens is needed to fully comprehend youth IPV, encompassing age, class, race, ethnicity, and colonialism along with gender. While some dynamics of IPV in heterosexual relationships can apply to same-sex relationships, the latter has unique features which deserve attention, but are not the focus of this study (Bancroft, 2002; Our Watch, 2017).

Methodology

This qualitative and exploratory research draws from 14 interviews conducted with Brasilian advocates between June and July 2019 and five interviews conducted with Australian advocates between July 2019 and February 2020 to answer the following research questions: how is technology used to perpetrate abuse and stalking in young people aged 12–18 and how it can be used to address youth IPV from an advocate's perspective? Ethics approval was granted by the QUT Human Research Ethics Advisory Team (No. 1900000344). Participants were offered anonymity. Although most agreed to be identified, to protect their confidentiality, as well as the confidentiality of the youth they serve, all are referred to without identifying information in this chapter.

The greater number of Brasilian advocates (14) compared to Australian advocates (5) in the study helps to redress the over-representation of Australian advocates in existing related research. The participants were selected using purposive and snowball sampling which targeted advocates from peak organizations involved in youth IPV prevention in both countries. This sampling strategy was chosen to ensure that the most relevant participants were included, resulting in rich data and outcomes. Of the 14 participants from Brasil, nine were involved in the legal/justice sector, two were researchers/consultants, and three worked for anti-violence organizations. Of the five participants from Australia, four worked for anti-violence organizations, and one was a researcher.

All interviews were recorded and transcribed, and the transcripts were examined using thematic analysis. This procedure involved categorizing the emerging themes from my reflective journals and tables of data and importing the interviews into NVivo for further analysis and coding (Bazeley & Jackson, 2013; Bryman, 2016).

Focusing on the perspectives of Brasilian and Australian advocates involved in youth IPV prevention helps to fill the gap in evidence from the Global-South and contributes to knowledge in the relatively new and understudied area of TFIPV among youth. Although the study did not engage with young people to gain their firsthand perspectives, the participating advocates' direct work with youth and/or in IPV prevention among youth offers rich insights relevant to TFIPV among youth and its prevention. Furthermore, these advocates may be in a better position to identify and report IPV than young people for whom IPV may be normalized (King-Ries, 2011). Thus, it provides relevant perspectives about youth experiences of TFIPV and technology use in prevention from key responders' eyes. As a qualitative study of key informants, while the results reported here are informative, they are not generalizable.

Results and Discussion

Brasilian and Australian Landscapes of Digital Coercive Control

Youth (15–24 years) are globally the most connected cohort group, as 71% are online (UNICEF, 2017). Most participants in this study agreed with the literature from the Global-South that young people are particularly vulnerable to DCC because this is a formative time when they are often engaging in their first intimate relationships and developing an identity (Politoff et al., 2019). Participants outlined behaviors that are covered by the DCC concept, including IBA and controlling behaviors. The majority of advocates raised concerns about the practice of and responses to sexting in youth intimate relationships. While most participants indicated that in their experience girls are at higher risk of IBA, this chapter focuses on the distinct forms of DCC described by participants, as research is scarce in this field. These include the use of technology by young people to exert power and control, as well as patterns of violence such as stalking.

Politoff et al. (2019) identified that, overall, young Australians (aged 16–24 years) understand that domestic violence encompasses physical and non-physical forms of violence, but that young men have less understanding of non-physical forms than do young women. Their data reveal that 79% of young men and 93% of young women in Australia identified "repeatedly keeps track of location, calls or activities through a mobile phone or other devices without consent" (stalking) as forms of violence (Politoff et al., 2019, pp. 19–20). By contrast, Énois et al.'s 2015 study indicates that, in Brasil, 55% of girls aged 14–24 years had experienced their male partners checking – or trying to check – their phones, social media, and email; yet only 64% of these respondents identified this controlling behavior as a violent act. While these studies seem to suggest that Australian youth more readily identify controlling behaviors as abusive than do young Brasilians, there may be other explanations for the difference in results. The most prominent difference between the Brasilian and Australian evidence may be that the latter has often focused on youth knowledge of and attitudes toward gender-based violence against women (Politoff et al., 2019), while the former has focused on prevalence and examining young people's personal experiences of IPV (Énois et al., 2015; Instituto Avon/Data Popular, 2014). Therefore, it is not possible to conclude from these studies whether there is a significant difference between the overall understanding of violence among youth from both countries, or if in general young people might be downplaying these violent acts when they are the targets of them.

Overall, young Australians seem to identify digital controlling behaviors as a form of domestic violence; yet recent data highlights a decline in the understanding of domestic violence as gendered among young people compared to data from previous years (Politoff et al., 2019). One of my Australian participants who was from an anti-violence organization expressed their concern over this evidence:

> we're really concerned with [the data] in Australia that shows up for young people and adults is that the understanding that domestic violence is gendered is reducing. So, less people are understanding [that] domestic violence is most regularly perpetrated by men. At the same time that more people are more knowledgeable about the types of violence.

A similar trend can be seen in Brasil. Results from a study by the Instituto Avon/Data Popular (2014) highlighted that 96% of young Brasilians are against machismo. However, one participant from the Brasilian legal sector noted that many of these young people affirmed *machista* belief[2] in their intimate relationships by perpetrating and normalizing a wide range of DCC behaviors, including tracking their partners through mobile phones and social media. This evidence from both countries raises key concerns, as denying and normalizing the drivers of gender-based violence create a barrier to effective prevention of such violence.

Many of my participants suggested that young people in Brasil often normalize monitoring, tracking, and stalking via mobile devices, primarily using applications like WhatsApp, and social media such as Instagram, Facebook, and Snapchat. They also conveyed their concern about the speed and level of use of WhatsApp among young Brasilians. Several times participants reported this application as a means used by boys to monitor/track their girlfriends through messages or video calls, demanding that their partners show them where they are and who they are with – behaviors explicitly demonstrative of patterns of power and control according to my participants, but not according to young people themselves. Access to a partner's mobile device and accounts without the partner's consent or knowledge through WhatsApp Web and hidden applications that permit the perpetrator to find their partner's location, listen to them and visualize their steps were also discussed in the interviews.

In contrast, two participants from the Australian anti-violence sector noted that in their experience, the use of WhatsApp is not very popular among young Australians, with its use primarily limited to communications with family overseas or workgroups. One of these advocates explained that Facebook, Instagram, Snapchat, Twitter, and YouTube are the most frequently used social media by young people in Australia – platforms also mentioned by the Brasilian advocates. Another Australian participant from the anti-violence sector expressed the view that apps like Snapchat can facilitate stalking as they have a "feature that automatically showed your location to people that use them." Both an Australian anti-violence sector participant and a Brasilian legal sector participant conveyed their impression that Facebook was not as popular as it had once been among youth in both countries. These observations contrasted with the Office of the eSafety Commissioner (2018) report indicating that Facebook was one of the most used platforms by Australian teens (aged 13–17 years). The data for the eSafety Commissioner report was collected in 2017, and the rapid development of technologies and changes in youth preferences might be reflected in the perspectives of my participants, indicating that Facebook is less popular now compared to 2017.

The digital era fosters a culture of surveillance, inviting us all to control and to be controlled. As a result, some have argued that greater control might be "normative" in young people's relationships (Flach & Deslandes, 2019; Harris & Woodlock, 2019). In this regard, a recent study by Flach and Deslandes (2019) identified 40 applications designed to enable people to monitor their partners within Android and iOS operating systems. These authors' discourse analysis of these applications revealed the same dichotomy identified by the literature and by 12 of the 14 participants in this study, which equates tracking and control with caring and love. In this vein, Taylor et al. (2019) argue that controlling behaviors via technological means is present in the intimate relationships of most young Brasilians and that their overt use might indicate "collaboration" between partners as a strategy to prevent escalation of conflicts involving fears of infidelity and jealousy. In keeping with this analysis, one Brasilian participant from the legal sector emphasized that a common practice among young Brasilians is to create a shared account on social media as soon as they start dating as a way to keep track of each other (see also Campeiz, 2018). This participant explained that at first glance, this practice reflects an understanding of reciprocal control. However, she emphasized that it is commonly a means by which boys exert control over girls. Similarly, eight other participants from both countries highlighted their impressions that male partners often perpetrate DCC against their female partners. Three Brasilian participants also reported hearing of instances when boys had promised to give their girlfriend their password, but then did not; or sometimes where boys kept their contacts in hidden folders or outside the platforms their female partners could access.

The scarcity of examples of healthier relationships might hinder young people's identification of what is acceptable or not (Taylor et al., 2019). Taylor et al. (2019) indicate that, while many young Brasilians do not identify control as abuse, they often said they did not like it. There is limited research on how young people might be developing unhealthy technological norms within their intimate relationships and whether and how these norms might be perceived as distinct from the behaviors understood as truly abusive (Harris & Woodlock, 2019). While this area requires further investigation, participants in my study saw digital controlling behaviors as problematic. One Australian participant from an anti-violence organization, for example, noted that technology "can increase the frequency and intensity of violence in some ways (…) [and] the stalking, and the harassment, and the mind games." Two other Brasilian participants from the legal sector further noted that such behaviors can sometimes escalate into physical violence and femicide, which is consistent with research findings relating to adults (Harris & Woodlock, 2019; Taylor et al., 2019). Furthermore, three Brasilian participants identified as an aggravating factor the fact that digital technologies make the abuse and violence omnipresent. What Harris and Woodlock (2019) characterized as the spaceless nature of DCC, one Brasilian legal sector participant described as giving perpetrators "an almost totalitarian control of others' life and privacy space."

Both my Brasilian and Australian participants emphasized the significance of society's rigid gender stereotypes that normalize male control and female submission, as well as the understanding of DCC as a reflection of jealousy and therefore acceptable. Furthermore, five Brasilian participants expressed the view that the media also plays a crucial role in reinforcing these stereotypes by romanticizing control and stalking as desirable and positive signs within a relationship, increasing the tolerance of DCC and therefore the harm inflicted on girls who experience it. Participants from both countries expressed the view that this normalization blurs the line between what is acceptable and what is abusive, highlighting the need for greater attention on prevention initiatives. Their views in this regard are aligned with research findings such as that of Taylor and colleagues (2019). In this vein, one Australian participant from the anti-violence sector explained that education plays a fundamental role in prevention:

> It's definitely crucial that young people are taught, from a young age, what is acceptable and what isn't acceptable. What crosses the line and is harmful, because sometimes it isn't just that easy in say—in black and white. Sometimes it's very grey.

While violence, abuse, and stalking have been enacted via digital technology, my participants highlighted that such technology can also be used to prevent youth IPV. The next section explores participants' perspectives on the use of technology to prevent violence, examining its potential benefits and limitations.

Preventing Youth Intimate Partner Violence through Technology in the Global-South: Benefits and Challenges

Participants argued that technology could be used as a means to educate, prevent, and respond to youth IPV, by spreading a message of gender equality and respectful relationships. Most participants indicated that they use social media, websites, and/or online games not only to promote their initiatives and research but also to raise awareness and engage young people (see also, for example, R4Respect, Pascua et al., 2019; Struthers et al., 2019). The broad reach to young people was my participants' most cited advantage of using technology for prevention, considering the high use of technology by youth and the ease of updating and adapting digital content (see also Murta et al., 2020; Tarzia et al., 2017). One Australian participant highlighted these advantages:

> we can reach teenagers where they are. So, the fact that we can advertise, for example, in an online gaming platform, that that's where young men are, is really useful. Because we know that a lot of young people, but particularly young men, don't seek out this information.

This participant observed that technology "allows you to speak directly to young people without a mediator in between." This implies a major benefit: that reaching young people in digital spaces overcomes the obstacles faced in trying to reach them in other spaces, such as schools (in Brasil) or through certain digital platforms (in Australia) to which advocates often face barriers in gaining access. For example, one participant noted that in Australia, because the subject of IPV is considered sensitive, there are restrictions on any discussion of it on specific platforms, regardless of whether or not such discussion relates to prevention. Hence, the creation of advocates' own platforms is crucial. In this vein, The Line (2017) and other social marketing campaigns developed by Our Watch in Australia are seen as effective examples, with one participant from the research sector noting that they aim "to change the norms that shape dating violence, and that shape sexual violence among children and young people," and are well-tested and well-developed. At the same time, this participant believed that these campaigns could be improved as they do not pay "enough attention to how masculinity, for example, shapes some men's use of partner violence and dating violence."

In Brasil, two participants noted that the focus of public campaigns on IPV has predominantly been on encouraging women to report violence (see also Ávila, 2017) rather than on targeting the underlying causes of violence. One Brasilian participant from the consulting/research sector outlined that the police discourse was necessary in the past to encourage society to acknowledge violence against women as a serious issue. However, in her view, Brasilian society still does not understand the severity of this violence, and the justice system is not the only pathway for addressing gendered violence. She suggested, for example, that the Resource Center for Women in Situations of Violence could provide women with broader support, including information and psychological and social assistance. This observation is consistent with Tarzia et al.'s (2017) findings based on interviews with young Australian women, which affirmed that websites and applications should provide them not only with information regarding IPV but also how to contact support services and take further action. Consequently, campaigns should also encompass this approach to address young women's needs. The campaigns highlighted by the Brasilian and Australian participants differed regarding the moment at which intervention should take place – that is, before (Australia) or after the occurrence of the violence (Brasil). While all interventions are important, other research highlights the key importance of primary prevention (before the violence has happened) for young people (Flood, 2019).

Two of the Brasilian participants highlighted the development of artificial intelligence to assist young women in abusive relationships and enable them to discuss online violence, through chatbots like MAIA and Isa.bot. According to them, these bots play an essential role in support and prevention, given that girls and young women often do not seek help, and that these forums maintain their privacy and confidentiality and make no judgment about their story. However, it is important to check the privacy policies of technologies such as these to be certain about what is being done with user data. For example, according to the privacy policies of MAIA, the chatbot does not ask for any identifiable or personal information of users. It considers the users' anonymity fundamental, which is the reason why the content of the chat will not be stored (Microsoft News Center Brasil, 2020). By contrast, the Isa.bot policy indicates that the personal data provided by users can be collected and will be accessed exclusively by the team who provides support to women experiencing violence and might be used for research (Cosmobots, n.d).

The perspective that technology can be useful because it keeps users' anonymity and does not judge them is also found in the literature (Tarzia et al., 2017; UNICEF, 2019). In this regard, one Brasilian participant, along with Microsoft and other partners, developed MAIA (the Portuguese acronym for "my artificial intelligence friend"). Similarly, another Brasilian participant, in collaboration with her university research team developed a computer-tailored intervention hosted by a website called SOS Dating (Grupo de Estudos em Prevenção e Promoção de Saúde no Ciclo de Vida, n.d), which consists of four online sessions tailored to the participant's profile, including their sex, relationship type, knowledge of violence, and support network (see Murta et al., 2020). She believes that this initiative has the potential to be very successful because it provides customized advice to users rather than the one-size-fits-all advice generally offered on such platforms:

> According to the literature on customized computerized interventions, they are more effective than interventions that are generalist, which is the same intervention for everyone. So, more identification, more memory and more behavior change would be expected. I don't know if we are going to achieve all this because the phenomenon is complex (…) But if we can at least get people to start looking for help, I will be more satisfied, it's already a result.

While one might argue that customization raises privacy concerns, this participant's research team ensures that all data is kept confidential and that only they will be able to use information shared by users, who will never be identified.

One Brasilian participant from the consulting sector highlighted that applications like *Juntas* (meaning "together" in Portuguese Geledés, 2014) could be seen as an important tool, particularly in the context of distrust of police (and perhaps in the context of a lack of knowledge about whether we should be trusting technology):

> You can insert the contacts of some people you know, your sister, your friend, people close to you that you can contact in a situation of violence. It's also a nice thing because you're not relying only on the police service that might not answer to you, right?

Notwithstanding a certain level of community mistrust in the police, participants from both Brasil and Australia raised as important the availability and use of government-based applications for women who have been granted domestic violence orders (DVOs), as they provide a pathway to quickly contact the police via the application's emergency button in case of a threat. Several Brasilian states and the Federal District have adopted similar applications

(Governo do Distrito Federal, 2017). One Brasilian participant suggested that this initiative is more useful for adult women, although young women can also access this service if they hold a DVO. While the restriction on the use of these government applications to DVO holders seems to be related to capacity building, this limitation excludes the majority of young and adult women experiencing IPV, as IPV is usually under-reported. Consequently, they will not have a DVO or access to the government application (Observatório da Mulher Contra a Violência et al., 2018).

Regarding the use of applications and bots, Brasilian participants flagged ethical and evaluation concerns. For example, one Brasilian participant outlined the risks these applications can pose to users, describing a situation in which, if these disguised applications that enable contact with police services are discovered by a woman/girl's abusive male partner, the violence can escalate dramatically. In relation to bots, this participant reflected:

> we are talking about a robot giving advice, so one of the things we need to be sure of is if that advice and the result of this conversation of a girl interacting with a robot will not put her at risk (…) [and] how we can use [the] data and intelligence that the robot is accumulating without violating the girl's privacy, this is also something that we still don't have very clear (…) But it's happening (…) and we will not be able to stay very far from this, we will have to monitor it, but we are not doing this.

Most participants from both countries highlighted the lack of funding and human resources as primary barriers to the development of prevention strategies in general and those involving technology in particular. This obstacle impacts the effectiveness and duration of implementation of the strategies developed by advocates. In this regard, one Brasilian participant explained that she has been developing a computer-tailored intervention for almost five years and highlighted the complexity of this intervention, which demands qualitative studies and testing, revealing the amount of work and human and financial resources needed to implement this intervention. She also emphasized that the website would only be available for six months because this is the period for which they could pay for use of the software license, which is Dutch – demonstrating the dependency on tools from the Global-North. Illustrating how limited funding can impact strategies, this participant outlined that if she had more funding, her team could work on developing its own national software, making this website available permanently. Similarly, a participant in Australia noted that

> often funding for these sorts of initiatives is really short term. But we know that we need ongoing work in order to make real change. So the funding environment can be a real limitation or challenge to maximize [prevention initiatives].

While both the existing literature and my participants highlight the elevated use of the internet by young people, participants were also concerned about the needs of marginalized groups who have limited or no access to the internet or even mobile phones and of illiterate people – representing the digital divide. One Brasilian participant explained that applications connecting people with police services, for example, would not work in areas where no internet or mobile phones are available, which is a reality for many people in Brasil. Likewise, she noted that such applications would not work effectively in remote and rural areas of the country with the internet because by the time the police arrive at these areas, women and girls might already be dead. She outlined her concerns as follows:

> I think it is a policy that we have to think about more because we adopt, there are a multitude of these applications. Apps are sold as easy and accessible, but is it accessible to whom? Who has 24-hour access to mobile internet? It's an expensive service, women who live on the outskirts who suffer violence cannot depend on an application on their cell phones, they don't have it all the time as we have it. So, we develop big projects and make huge publicity that they save lives, but we save the life of [small] parts [of the population] right? Of small parts of the population.

In relation to the above concerns, Brasilian and Australian participants emphasized the importance of developing strategies tailored to marginalized groups and the need to adopt multiple strategies to prevent youth IPV (see also Mackenzie & Mackay, 2019). In this regard, it is fundamental to embrace an intersectional approach that recognizes all of the factors that, along with gender, increase the vulnerability of women to violence. Participants from Brasil noted, for example, how class and education can limit one's access to digital strategies, while other research shows how age, race, ethnicity, and colonialism place Black women in Brasil and Indigenous women in Australia at a higher risk of gendered violence (Carneiro, 2016; Our Watch, 2018). Hence, participants from both countries emphasized that it is vital to meet the needs of these groups and reach young people in the spaces in which they interact, beyond the internet.

In addition to access concerns, are concerns about whether and, if so, how well existing programming has been evaluated. With few exceptions, such as the program H evaluation of Promundo Brasil (Promundo, n.d), there is a significant lack of evaluation of primary prevention policies in Brasil. Indeed, the literature highlights that this field requires greater attention (Flood, 2019). One Australian participant suggested that Australian advocates who have more experience in this field and have produced evidence could assist Brasilian advocates with best practices for conducting evaluations of programs (see also Flood & Kendrick, 2012; Our Watch, 2016; Pascua et al., 2019; Struthers et al., 2019). Nonetheless, despite significant efforts in the field of primary prevention in the Australian context, more work is needed in the evaluation space because from one Australian participant's perspective, program evaluations are usually

> short term, so you can only show very short-term change. Which basically means you can't track significant behaviour change, and you can't track perpetration.

Furthermore, one Australian participant noted that the evaluations conducted in Australia to date have mainly targeted school-based programs rather than initiatives involving technology. In a similar vein, Harris et al. (2020) highlighted that technology initiatives, such as chatbots, "are relatively new and are rarely evaluated." Thus, there is also a need to build evaluation tools to assess strategies based on digital technologies.

Both my Brasilian and Australian participants expressed an interest in, as one Brasilian participant put it, "how social media is used to create movements and communities." For example, four of the Brasilian participants spoke of how they have been engaging teenagers to produce short films and publish them on YouTube to raise awareness about violence against women and girls. By assessing the students' engagement with this initiative and the quality of the content and videos produced, these Brasilian participants perceived this strategy as successful and concluded that the benefits of using technology are thus evident. Some participants from both countries noted that the benefits overcome the setbacks because they can connect directly with young people as they are usually hyperconnected.

Finally, both Brasilian and Australian participants outlined how technology can be used to resist a gender backlash. In this vein, technology can reach young people who have not had access to school-based education programs around gender-based violence because of fundamentalist and conservative resistance from religious and political groups. In this regard, in both Australia and Brasil, participants reported that conservative agendas have been obstructing their work. In Brasil, one participant noted that some advocates have been avoiding talking about gender directly, particularly since this word was removed from the country's National Plan of Education in 2014, placing advocates, educators, and students at risk. In Australia, a feminist and gendered perspective seems to be stronger than in Brasil; however, resistance in the school setting was also noted by Australian participants. For example, one Australian participant described how a teacher, while discussing violence and healthy relationships in the classroom, told their students that "men experience domestic violence at the same rate as women" highlighting the types of barriers to addressing the problem, and the need to work with a whole-of-school approach. Messages about respectful relationships and gender equality need to be aligned and reinforced at all levels of society and in all spaces. In the meantime, technology could be a means to reach youth in both countries and to challenge the ongoing backlash.

Conclusion

This chapter has discussed advocates' perspectives on how technology is used by young Brasilians and Australians to enact DCC, and outlined the leading platforms used by youth to interact with each other and to perpetrate violence. It has also revealed how advocates in both countries have been incorporating technology into their own work and the work of others around the prevention of youth IPV, and considered the associated advantages and challenges. The main benefits of using technology to address youth IPV are the broad reach of technology, talking to young people where they are, and overcoming barriers imposed by conservative agendas and policies to access young people in physical and digital spaces, addressing youth barriers to help-seeking by preserving their anonymity, the ease to update and adapt the content, and the possibility to build and contact private networks in case of emergency (particularly important due to police mistrust). The main challenges identified are the lack of financial and human resources to create technology strategies, concerns of privacy, and lack of evaluation. The global production of knowledge is often driven by research undertaken in the English-speaking countries in the Global-North (Connell, 2007). This study challenges this global dominance. While the findings presented in this chapter are intended to inform the creation of preventive approaches to youth IPV in Brasil and Australia, the findings may well be relevant for other countries. There is no question that prevention initiatives should be tailored to each country according to the needs of its diverse population, but listening to contributions from countries which are often unheard and marginalized in the global economy of knowledge, can certainly generate new insights.

This study highlights the need to incorporate a gender perspective into initiatives to prevent youth IPV in both countries and to develop pathways to resist the gender backlash present – albeit to different degrees – in both countries.

A greater acknowledgment of youth IPV is needed, as most research targets adult IPV, and most research into youth DCC has focused on IBA rather than other forms of violence. Thus, future research should engage young people directly, exploring young people's needs and firsthand accounts of DCC experiences to inform prevention and evaluate prevention initiatives involving technology. Finally, countries need to prioritize IPV prevention and address the lack of funding in this area to allow advocates to develop medium-to long-term initiatives (and evaluations) that can promote real change around ending IPV against women and girls.

Acknowledgment

Thank you to Professor Jane Bailey and Sahana Sarkar for your feedback, and Dr Bridget Harris, Dr Laura Vitis, and Professor Kerry Carrington for their support and guidance on the chapter. Thank you to QUT Faculty of Law Research Scholarship for funding this research.

Notes

1. Inspired by Connell, Brasil is spelled with and "s" as in its national language, resisting Anglophone dominance (2014).
2. This refers to beliefs based on *machismo* "the belief that women should be subordinate to the needs and desires of their male partners, taking care of them,

providing them pleasure (either as wives or partners or as approached in predatory fashion by men who would not consider marrying them), and bearing their children" (Wilson, 2014, p. 4).

References

Australian Institute of Health and Welfare. (2018). Family, domestic and sexual violence in Australia. Retrieved from https://www.aihw.gov.au/getmedia/d1a8d479-a39a-48c1-bbe2-4b27c7a321e0/aihw-fdv-02.pdf.aspx?inline=true

Ávila, T. P. d. (2017). Políticas públicas de prevenção primária à violência contra a mulher: Lições da experiência australiana. *Revista Gênero*, *17*(2), 95–125. doi: 10.22409/rg.v17i2.944

Bancroft, L. (2002). *Why does he do that?: Inside the minds of angry and controlling men*. New York, NY: Putnam.

Bandeira, L. (2014). Violência de gênero: A construção de um campo teórico e de investigação. *Sociedade e Estado*, *29*(2), 449–469. doi:10.1590/S0102-69922014000200008

Bazeley, P., & Jackson, K. (2013). *Qualitative data analysis with NVivo*. (2nd ed.). London: SAGE.

Beserra, M. A., Leitão, M. N. C., Fernandes, M. I. D., Scatena, L., Vidinha, T. S. S., Silva, L. M. P., & Ferriane, M. G. C. (2015). Prevalence of dating violence among adolescents from Brazilian public schools of Recife/PE – Brazil. *Revista de Enfermagem Referência*, *7*, 91–99. doi:10.12707/RIV15006

Bryman, A. (2016). *Social research methods*. (5th ed.). Oxford: Oxford University Press.

Campeiz, A. B. (2018). *A violência nas relações de intimidade entre os adolescentes sob a perspectiva do Paradigma da Complexidade*. Masters dissertation, Universidade de São Paulo.

Carneiro, S. (2016). Mulheres negras na educação: Desafios para a sociedade brasileira. In D. Carreira, C. Vianna, I. Leão, S. Unbehaum, Carneiro, & S. Cavasin (Eds.), *Gênero e educação: Fortalecendo uma agenda para as políticas educacionais* (pp. 121–185). Rio de Janeiro: Henrich Boll. Retrieved from http://acaoeducativa.org.br/blog/publicacoes/porque-discutir-genero-na-escola/

Carrington, K., Hogg, R., & Sozzo, M. (2016). Southern criminology. *British Journal of Criminology*, *56*(1), 1–20. doi:10.1093/bjc/azv08

Connell, R. (2007). *Southern theory: The global dynamics of knowledge in social science*. Crows Nest: Allen & Unwin.

Connell, R. (2013). The shores of the Southern Ocean: Steps toward a world sociology of modernity, with Australian examples. In S. Arjomand & E. Reis (Eds.), *Worlds of difference* (pp. 58–72). Los Angeles, CA: SAGE. doi:10.4135/9781446288641.n4

Connell, R. (2014). Using southern theory: Decolonising social thought in theory, research and application. *Planning Theory*, *13*(2), 210–223. doi:10.1177/1473095213499216

Connell, R., Pearse, R., Collyer, F., Maia, J., & Morrell, R. (2018). Re-making the global economy of knowledge: Do new fields of research change the structure of North-South relations? *British Journal of Sociology*, *69*(3), 738–757. doi:10.1111/1468-4446.12294

Cosmobots. (n.d.). ISA.bot. Retrieved from https://www.isabot.org/#block-13769

Daff, E., Mcewan, T., & Luebbers, S. (2018). Australian adolescents' experiences of aggression and abuse by intimate partners. *Journal of Interpersonal Violence*, 1–24. doi:10.1177/0886260518801936

DeKeseredy, W. S., & Schwartz, M. D. (1998). *Measuring the extent of woman abuse in intimate heterosexual relationships: A critique of the conflict tactics scales*. Harrisburg, PA: US Department of Justice Violence Against Women Grants Office Electronic Resources.

Dobash, R., & Dobash, R. (1995). Reflections on findings from the violence against women Survey. *Canadian Journal of Criminology*, *37*(3), 457–504. Retrieved from http://search.proquest.com/docview/216100452/

Énois I Inteligência Jovem, Instituto Vladimir HerzogInstituto Patrícia Galvão. (2015). #meninapodetudo: Machismo e violência contra a mulher. Retrieved from https://dossies.agenciapatriciagalvao.org.br/dados-e-fontes/pesquisa/meninapodetudo-machismo-e-violencia-contra-a-mulher-enois-inteligencia-joveminstituto-vladimir-herzoginstituto-patricia-galvao-2015/

Faraldo-Cabana, P. (2018). Research excellence and Anglophone dominance: The case of law, criminology and social science. In K. Carrington, R. Hogg, & M. Sozzo (Eds.), *The Palgrave handbook of criminology and the Global South* (pp. 163–181). Cham: Springer International Publishing. doi:10.1007/978-3-319-65021-0_9

Fitz-Gibbon, K., Walklate, S., McCulloch, J., & Maher, J. (Eds.). (2018). *Intimate partner violence, risk and security: Securing women's lives in a Global world* (pp. 1–15). Oxon: Routledge. Retrieved from https://ebookcentral.proquest.com

Flach, R., & Deslandes, S. (2019). Cyber dating abuse or proof of love? The use of apps for surveillance and control in affective-sexual relations. *Cadernos de Saúde Pública*, *35*(1), e00060118. doi:10.1590/0102-311x00060118

Flood, M. (2019). *Engaging men and boys in violence prevention*. New York, NY: Palgrave Macmillan US. doi:10.1057/978-1-137-44208-6

Flood, M., & Kendrick, V. (2012). *LOVEBiTES: An evaluation of the LOVEBiTES and respectful relationships programs in a Sydney school*. Wollongong: University of Wollongong. Retrieved from https://ro.uow.edu.au/cgi/viewcontent.cgi?article=2969&context=artspapers

Fórum Brasileiro de Segurança Pública. (2019). Visível e invisível – a vitimização de mulheres no Brasil. (2a edição). Retrieved from http://www.forumseguranca.org.br/wp-content/uploads/2019/02/relatoriopesquisa-2019-v6.pdf

Geledés (2014). Juntas no enfrentamento à violência contra as mulheres. Retrieved from https://juntas.geledes.org.br/

Governo do Distrito Federal. (2017). Aplicativo viva flor. Retrieved from http://www.brasilia.df.gov.br/aplicativo-viva-flor/

Grupo de Estudos em Prevenção e Promoção de Saúde no Ciclo de Vida. (n. d). SOS namoro. Retrieved from http://sosnamoro.geppsvida.com.br/

Harris, B., Dragiewicz, M., & Woodlock, D. (2020). Technology, domestic violence advocacy and the sustainable development goals. In J. Blaustein, K. Fitz-Gibbon, N. W. Pino, & R. White (Eds.), *Emerald handbook of crime, justice and sustainable development* (pp. 295–313). Bingley: Emerald Publishing Limited.

Harris, B., & Woodlock, D. (2019). Digital coercive control: Insights from two landmark domestic violence studies. *British Journal of Criminology*, *59*(3), 530–550. doi:10.1093/bjc/azy052

Henry, N., McGlynn, C., Flynn, A., Johnston, K., Powell, A., & Scott, A. J. (2020). *Image-based sexual abuse: A study on the causes and consequences of non-consensual nude or sexual imagery*. London, New York: Routledge.

Henry, N., Powell, A., & Flynn, A. (2017). Not just 'revenge pornography': Australians' experiences of ImageBased abuse. A Summary Report. RMIT University, Melbourne.

Instituto Avon/Data Popular. (2014). Violência contra a mulher: o jovem está ligado?. Retrieved from https://dossies.agenciapatriciagalvao.org.br/dados-e-fontes/pesquisa/violencia-contra-a-mulher-o-jovem-esta-ligado-data-popular-instituto-avon-2014/

King-Ries, A. (2011). Teens, technology, and cyberstalking: The domestic violence wave of the future? *Texas Journal of Women and the Law*, *20*(2), 131–164. Retrieved from http://search.proquest.com/docview/902629166/

Mackenzie, C., & Mackay, T. (2019). *'I just wanted to keep my boyfriend happy': Young country women's perceptions of intimate partner violence*. Adelaide: The Australian Alliance for Social Enterprise. University of South Australia.

Microsoft News Center Brasil. (2020). Chatbot Maia é lançada para ajudar na conscientização de meninas sobre relacionamentos abusivos. Retrieved from https://news.microsoft.com/pt-br/chatbot-maia-e-lancada-para-ajudar-na-conscientizacao-de-meninas-sobre-relacionamentos-abusivos/

Minayo, M. S. C., Assis, S. G., & Njaine, K. (2011). Amor e violência: Um paradoxo das relações de namoro e do'ficar' entre jovens brasileiros. doi:10.7476/9788575413852

Murta, S. G., de Oliveira Parada, P., da Silva Meneses, S., Medeiros, J. V. V., Balbino, A., Rodrigues, M. C., & de Vries, H. (2020). Dating SOS: A systematic and theory-based development of a web-based tailored intervention to prevent dating violence among Brazilian youth. *BMC Public Health*, *20*(1), 1–14.

Murta, S. G., dos Santos, B. R. P., Martins, C. P. S., & de Oliveira, B. (2013). Prevenção primária à violência no namoro: Uma revisão de literatura. *Contextos clínicos*, *6*(2), 117–131.

Murta, S. G., Pires, M. R. P., Tavares, A. S., Cordeiro, M. A., Teixeira, E. G., & Adorno, N. (2019). Intimidade e apego no namoro: Implicações de estudos de caso para prevenção à violência. *Contextos Clínicos*, *12*(1), 204–225.

Observatório da Mulher Contra a Violência, Instituto de Pesquisa DataSenadoSecretaria da Transparencia. (2018). Panorama da violência contra as mulheres no Brasil: Indicadores nacionais e estaduais. Retrieved from http://www.senado.gov.br/institucional/datasenado/omv/indicadores/relatorios/BR-2018.pdf

Office of the eSafety Commissioner. (2018). State of play: Youth, kids and digital dangers. Retrieved from https://www.esafety.gov.au/about the-office/research-library

Oliveira, Q. B. M., Assis, S. G. d., Njaine, K., & Oliveira, R. C. d. (2011). Violências nas relações afetivo-sexuais. In M. C. S. Minayo, S. G. Assis, & K. Njaine (Eds.), *Amor e violência: Um paradoxo das relações de namoro e do'ficar' entre jovens brasileiros* (pp. 45–54). doi:10.7476/9788575413852

Our Watch. (2016). Final evaluation report: Technical appendix A – evaluation design and tools. Retrieved from https://www.ourwatch.org.au/getmedia/97ec4f00-e277-4c17-ae48-553d7cae68bb/RRE_Technical-Appendices-A-Final.pdf.aspx

Our Watch. (2017). Primary prevention of family violence against people from LGBTI communities. Retrieved from https://www.ourwatch.org.au/resource/primary-prevention-of-family-violence-against-people-from-lgbtiq-communities-an-analysis-of-existing-research

Our Watch. (2018). *Changing the picture: A national resource to support the prevention of violence against Aboriginal and Torres Strait Islander women and their children.* Melbourne: Our Watch.

Pascua, R., Khokhar, B., Saeed, N., Uwineza, J., & Taukolo, A. (2019). *R4Respect. Respectful relationships peer education guide.* Logan, Queensland: YFS Ltd.

Politoff, V., Crabbe, M., Honey, N., Mannix, S., Mickle, J., Morgan, & Webster, K. (2019). *Young Australians' attitudes to violence against women and gender equality: Findings from the 2017 National Community Attitudes towards Violence against Women Survey (NCAS) (ANROWS insights, issue 01/2019)*. Sydney: ANROWS.

Promundo. (n. d). Program H. Retrieved from https://promundoglobal.org/programs/program-h/

Rodríguez Domínguez, C., Pérez-Moreno, P. J., & Durán, M. (2020). Cyber dating violence: A review of its research methodology. *Anales de Psicología, 36*(2), 200–209.

Senior, K., Helmer, J., & Chenhall, R. (2017). 'As long as he's coming home to me': Vulnerability, jealousy and violence in young people's relationships in remote, rural and regional Australia. *Health Sociology Review, 26*(2), 204–218.

Soares, J. D. S. F., Lopes, M. J. M., & Njaine, K. (2013). Violência nos relacionamentos afetivo-sexuais entre adolescentes de Porto Alegre, Rio Grande do Sul, Brasil: Busca de ajuda e rede de apoio. *Cadernos de Saúde Pública, 29*, 1121–1130.

Stark, E. (2007). *Coercive control: How men entrap women in personal life*. New York, NY: Oxford University Press.

Straus, M. (2004). Cross-cultural reliability and validity of the revised conflict tactics scales: A study of university student dating couples in 17 nations. *Cross-Cultural Research, 38*(4), 407–432. doi:10.1177/1069397104269543

Struthers, K., Parmenter, N., & Tilbury, C. (2019). Young people as agents of change in preventing violence against women. Research Report, 02/2019. ANROWS, Sydney, NSW.

Tarzia, L., Iyer, D., Thrower, E., & Hegarty, K. (2017). "Technology doesn't judge you": Young Australian women's views on using the internet and Smartphones to address intimate partner violence. *Journal of Technology in Human Services, 35*(3), 199–218.

Taylor, A., Lauro, G., Murphy-Graham, E., Pacheco, T., Pacheco Montoya, D., & Araújo, D. (2017). Adolescent relationship violence in Brazil and Honduras. Retrieved from https://promundoglobal.org/resources/adolescent-relationship-violence-brazil-honduras/?lang=english

Taylor, A. Y., Murphy-Graham, E., & Lauro, G. (2019). Conceptualizing controlling behaviors in adolescent and youth intimate partner relationships. *Partner abuse, 10*(2), 137–163.

The Line. (2017). Tracking change: Snapshot evaluation findings for the line campaign 2015 to 2017. Retrieved from https://www.ourwatch.org.au/resource/tracking-change-snapshot-evaluation-findings-for-the-line-campaign-2015-to-2017/

UN Broadband Commission. (2015). Cyber violence against women and girls. Retrieved from https://www.unwomen.org/~/media/headquarters/attachments/sections/library/publications/2015/cyber_violence_gender%20report.pdf?v=1&d=20150924T154259

UN General Assembly. (2018). Report of the Special Rapporteur on violence against women, its causes and consequences on online violence against women and girls from a human rights perspective. Retrieved from https://digitallibrary.un.org/record/1641160?ln=en

UNICEF. (2017). The state of the world's children 2017: Children in a digital world. Retrieved from https://www.unicef.org/publications/index_101992.html

UNICEF. (2019). Projeto Caretas. Retrieved from https://www.unicef.org/brazil/projeto-caretas

Viza, B., Sartori, M. C., & Zanello, V. (Eds.). (2017). *Maria da Penha vai à escola: Educar para prevenir e coibir a violência doméstica e familiar contra a mulher*. Brasília: TJDFT. Retrieved from https://www.tjdft.jus.br/informacoes/cidadania/centro-judiciario-mulher/documentos-e-links/e-book-maria-da-penha-vai-a-escola

Wilson, T. D. (2014). Violence against women in Latin America. *Latin American Perspectives*, *41*(1), 3–18. doi:10.1177/0094582X13492143

Wolfe, D. A., Scott, K., Reitzel-Jaffe, D., Wekerle, C., Grasley, C., & Straatman, A. L. (2001). Development and validation of the conflict in adolescent dating relationships inventory. *Psychological Assessment*, *13*(2), 277–293.

Woodlock, D. (2017). The abuse of technology in domestic violence and stalking. *Violence Against Women*, *23*(5), 584–602.

Chapter 27

Technology-Facilitated Domestic Abuse and Culturally and Linguistically Diverse Women in Victoria, Australia

Yee Man Louie

Abstract

The rapid advancement of technology poses many social challenges including the emerging issue of technology-facilitated abuse (TFA) and violence. In Australia, women from culturally and linguistically diverse (CALD) backgrounds are found to be more vulnerable to domestic violence (DV) and abuse, including TFA. This chapter presents a snapshot of CALD women's technology-facilitated domestic abuse (TFDA) experiences in Melbourne through the eyes of a small group of DV practitioners. Findings show CALD women experience TFA similar to that of the mainstream, with tracking and monitoring through the use of smartphone and social media most common. Their migration and financial status, and language and digital literacy can increase their vulnerability to TFDA, making their experience more complicated. Appropriate digital services and resources together with face-to-face support services can be a way forward. Further research should focus on better understanding CALD women's perceptions of and responses to TFDA and explore ways to improve engagement with and use of community media channels/platforms.

Keywords: Domestic violence; coercive control; migrant women; social policy; digital technologies; cyberstalking intimate partner

Introduction[1]

Domestic violence (DV[2]) is the most common form of violence against women and is often perpetrated by women's current or former intimate partners (Cox,

The Emerald International Handbook of Technology-Facilitated Violence and Abuse, 447–467

doi:10.1108/978-1-83982-848-520211033

2016). As technology advances and changes, so do the methods and tactics for committing DV. Technology has changed all of our lives, sometimes for better and sometimes for worse. Women who are victim-survivors of DV are no exception. In recent years, perpetrators increasingly use a range of internet-connected devices such as smartphones, smart cameras, watches, toys, and tablets to carry out abusive acts against their (ex-)partners (Southworth, Finn, Dawson, Fraser, & Tucker, 2007; Women's Health East, 2018; Woodlock, 2013, 2015). In addition, women from culturally and linguistically diverse (CALD[3]) backgrounds have been identified as a vulnerable group to this new form of abuse. In this chapter, I refer to this form of technology-facilitated abuse (TFA) in the context of DV as technology-facilitated domestic abuse (TFDA). TFDA denotes the use of digital technologies to control, coerce, intimidate, humiliate, stalk, or harass an intimate partner (usually a female) both during a relationship and after separation (Hand, Chung, & Peters, 2009; Maher, McCulloch, & Fitz-Gibbon, 2017).

In many ways, the advancement of communications technology has disrupted the restrictions of time and space in our everyday interactions with others. For DV victim-survivors, the seemingly boundless spatial and temporal dimensions of ubiquitous computing[4] extend coercive control and significantly impact victim-survivor experiences of and response to DV (Harris, 2018; Mason & Magnet, 2012; Stark, 2007). Moreover, the impact of emotional and psychological abuse caused by TFDA is equally, if not more, damaging than physical violence (Hand et al., 2009; Sackett & Saunders, 1999), sometimes affecting victim-survivors long after they have left their abusive relationships.

Amid the emerging issue of TFDA, we are also witnessing the increased use of digital technologies for prevention of and intervention in DV (Meurn, 2012; Tarzia, Iyer, Thrower, & Hegarty, 2017). For example, the installation of internet-connected surveillance devices or duress alarms, or the use of smartphone safety apps that purport to keep women safer (Davenport, Richey, & Westbrook, 2008; Mason & Magnet, 2012). Seemingly, online platforms can also provide positive information for advocacy purposes, while social media can offer victim-survivors a safe place to discuss their experiences and to seek help (United Nations, 2005). The use of technology in fighting DV is particularly relevant at the time of writing this chapter, since many parts of the world are in lockdown during the COVID-19 outbreak, and the risk of DV is escalating (Foster & Fletcher, 2020; Peterman et al., 2020; UN Women, 2020). In my hometown of Melbourne, many DV agencies have suspended their face-to-face services to exercise social distancing, but are tapping into innovative ways of working online so women can continue to access services and be supported safely[5] (UN Women, 2020).

However, reliance on technology raises a number of concerns for DV victim-survivors. For example, the trading off of privacy for safety (Mason & Magnet, 2012); putting the onus on women to keep themselves safe (Freed et al., 2018; Mason & Magnet, 2012); and barriers to accessibility, usability, and visibility of online resources (Davenport et al., 2008; Hand et al., 2009) especially for women from minority and Indigenous groups (WESNET The Women's Services Network, 2019).

So, on one hand, perpetrators can use internet-enabled devices to extend surveillance and coercive control on their intimate (ex-)partner, while on the other, victim-survivors can use digital technology for information and support to help them find safety, and immediate access to emergency services. The relationship between technology and DV is indeed complex and intriguing. Could technology be both friend and foe for women who are experiencing or have experienced DV?

Emerging research continues to expand our understanding of the nature, impact, theoretical frameworks, and women's experiences of TFDA. There is evidence suggesting that women from CALD backgrounds are one of the groups most at risk of TFDA (Douglas, Harris, & Dragiewicz, 2019; WESNET The Women's Services Network, 2019; Woodlock, 2015) and that they face particular barriers in seeking support for TFDA (Office of the eSafety Commissioner, 2019; WESNET The Women's Services Network, 2019). While there is a growing literature that reflects the complexity facing this group of women, CALD women with limited or no English are in general under-represented in DV studies and support services but overrepresented in the DV crisis system (Crenshaw, 1991; George & Harris, 2014; InTouch, 2010).

Much remains unknown about CALD women's experiences of DV in the digital age. How is technology being used against them? How is it being used to assist them? What are some of the challenges? Identifying and addressing the experiences of DV, including this new form of abuse, and CALD women's needs (particularly those who seldom seek help) is therefore essential. This chapter contributes toward responding to these questions by drawing on research findings from a small-scale qualitative study I conducted in 2018 with DV practitioners in Melbourne, Australia. It begins by providing the research context and background, including an overview of the limited existing research on TFDA in Australia. It then presents the methodology used in the study before turning to discuss my findings. It concludes by emphasizing the need for further studies relating to the role of technology both in facilitating and responding to CALD women's experiences of DV.

Background

Domestic Violence: The Australian Context

DV came into the public limelight in Australia following political activist work by radical feminists in the 1970s (Theobald, Murray, & Smart, 2017). Prior to that, DV was treated as a private family matter between husband and wife, and physical violence, mostly perpetrated by husbands, was treated as acceptable and warranting little external intervention (Dobash & Dobash, 1980; Murray & Powell, 2009). This second wave of feminism foregrounded gender-inequality as the core of the problem, and we saw the emergence of community-based refuges providing women's crisis accommodation (Murray, 2002). The ethos of many of these refuges was for women to take control and to leave their abusive relationship. In the 1980s, concerns over the specific needs of women from different cultural and linguistic backgrounds not being met led to the establishment of a number of CALD-specific refuges and social services in Victoria (Theobald et al., 2017). In recent years, state and national governments in Australia undertook several significant policy initiatives, including the *National Plan to Reduce Violence against Women and their Children 2010–2022* (COAG, 2011), to tackle DV in a more coordinated way. Prior to this, DV was not recognized as a significant social issue warranting significant funding for primary prevention campaigns, research evaluation, and national amelioration efforts.

In the state of Victoria, where my research took place, the first ever Minister for Prevention of Domestic Violence was appointed in 2014, who then oversaw the Victorian Royal Commission into Family Violence (VRCFV)[6] in 2015 (Richardson, 2014). The VRCFV made a total of 227 recommendations with a number of them directly concerning people from CALD communities (e.g., recommendation no. 157 on improving the use of interpreters in family violence-related matters [State of Victoria, 2016b, p. 87]).

With the changing landscapes of DV due to the rise of online coercive control perpetrated by intimate partner abusers, TFDA further complicates policy and legal responses (Douglas & Burdon, 2018). For example, the Victorian criminal justice system has expanded several policies and laws to protect women who are harmed by TFA behaviors such as matters concerning image-based abuse.[7] The VRCFV recommendations and other policy and law developments offered a welcome change, but whether they fully address the unique, diverse, and complex lived experiences of women from CALD communities without essentializing CALD women's experiences is debatable (Ghafournia & Easteal, 2018).

The Nature and Prevalence of Technology-Facilitated Domestic Abuse in Australia

TFA comes in many forms, which includes harassment, threats, stalking, monitoring, hate speech, hacking, identify theft, online stalking, and image-based sexual abuse through digital technologies and can occur between strangers or between intimate (ex-)partners (Henry & Powell, 2014; Women's Health East, 2018). This chapter, however, focuses on TFA between intimate (ex-)partners – TFDA, which centers on coercive control and power dynamics, and a sustained pattern of abuse and threat. TFDA extends offline domestic abusive behaviors into online spaces (Harris, 2018), and in some instances (e.g., covert monitoring) affected women may not even know that it is occurring (WESNET The Women's Services Network, 2019). It thus causes women to feel powerless and unable to be completely free from the perpetrators' presence (Dimond, Fiesler, & Bruckman, 2011), making this form of abuse more pervasive, relentless, and damaging (Hand et al., 2009).

National data capturing the prevalence of TFDA is not currently available, but there are indicators that it is very common. The Personal Safety Survey (PSS) provides the most up-to-date prevalence estimates of all forms of interpersonal violence in Australia at a national level, including an in-depth look at intimate (ex-)partner emotional abuse[8] (ABS, 2017a; DVRCV, 2019). The latest PSS found approximately one in four (23%, or 2.2 million) women have experienced emotional abuse from an intimate (ex-)partner (ABS, 2017a). Many of these women were subjected to socially controlling and isolating behaviors including restrictions on phone or internet use, tracking via GPS, and monitoring through social media (DVRCV, 2019), which resemble TFDA behaviors.

The landmark Australian SmartSafe research (SmartSafe) was the first study investigating TFDA. It found TFDA is a significant emerging issue in Victoria, with women[9] reporting their abusers were using a range of mobile technologies to stalk, control, and monitor them from a distance, both during relationships and after separation (Woodlock, 2013). The second SmartSafe survey of DV practitioners from around Australia found nearly every respondent had had clients who had experienced TFDA (Woodlock, 2015). In addition, the trend of perpetrators using smartphones, mobile phones, and Facebook for TFDA continued, with the use of GPS for tracking on the rise (Woodlock, 2015).

The PSS, the two SmartSafe studies, and other international studies indicate TFDA is prevalent and a worldwide phenomenon (Laxton, 2014; Southworth et al., 2007; United Nations Broadband Commission, 2015). However, few studies have been conducted among different or specific CALD communities, and the true extent of TFDA among CALD women remains unknown.

Culturally and Linguistically Diverse Women and Technology-Facilitated Domestic Abuse

Although CALD women have been identified as more vulnerable to experiencing TFDA (Douglas et al., 2019; Woodlock, 2015), there is very little published research on their lived experience. The Office of the eSafety Commissioner's 2019 qualitative study was the first published research to address this gap. It found CALD women share similar experiences of TFDA with other women including being harassed; having their physical movement, phone usage, and other online activity closely monitored and tracked via internet-enabled devices such as smartphones; gaslighting; and having limiting access to technology. CALD women reported being blackmailed or punished by perpetrators sharing or threatening to share with their family sexual, degrading, or hysterical images or videos of them (Office of the eSafety Commissioner, 2019). There were several cases of CALD women who were subjected to culturally specific threats. For example, perpetrators threatened women with deportation to keep them quiet about the abuse, mobilizing extended family overseas and in Australia to harass and send death threats to coerce them to stay. Some of the threats made by the perpetrators and other family members were in the targeted women's first language, creating additional hurdles to prosecution (Office of the eSafety Commissioner, 2019).

The Women's Services Network (WESNET) (2019) conducted a study with DV practitioners to explore how TFDA occurs among Aboriginal and Torres

Strait Islander (ATSI) and CALD women survivors of DV. The study found the type of TFDA experienced by CALD women tends to involve basic technologies; however, technology exacerbated social isolation and limited their help-seeking options (WESNET The Women's Services Network, 2019). The study also found that TFDA is not often recognized as abuse by survivors, and addressing it is often not a priority for them or practitioners (WESNET The Women's Services Network, 2019).

Existing research adds important information about an under-researched group and emerging issue. It suggests CALD women's experiences of TFDA are more complex (Office of the eSafety Commissioner, 2019; WESNET The Women's Services Network, 2019). This could be due to a wide range of intersecting factors such as a lack of technology skills and access, low English literacy, and barriers to accessing information and services (WESNET The Women's Services Network, 2019).

Technology-Based Responses to Domestic Violence

Australian governments and DV support services increasingly recognize the role played by digital technologies in supporting and empowering DV victim-survivors (Carter, 2015; Dragiewicz et al., 2019; State of Victoria, 2016a; Tarzia et al., 2017). A recent review of technology-assisted services showed every year thousands of Australians access telephone and online communications (e.g., helplines, websites, and mobile applications) to seek support relating to DV, family, and sexual violence (Australian Institute Health and Welfare, 2019). For example, mobile web apps such as "Ask Izzy" enable users to search and find support services, and online and phone counseling services like "1800RESPECT" (AIHW, 2019, pp. 39–40). Additionally, free phone apps like "Arc" enables women to collect evidence of family violence by keeping track of perpetrators' abusive behaviors (DVRCV, 2019).

The Social Shaping Technology (SST) field posits that technology is socially shaped by the way society adopts and uses it to achieve desired outcomes (Dixon et al., 2014). With our everyday lives increasingly mediated by digital technologies, it is not surprising then to see suggested uses of communication technologies such as social media overcome language and literacy barriers that exist in some CALD communities, and ethnic radio and other multicultural media being used to reinforce anti-violence against women campaign messages (Department of Social Services, 2015). Indeed, one international study found women living in households with multiple information and communications technology (ICT) ownership (particularly mobile phones or computers) were more likely to reject justifications for wife beating (Cardoso & Sorenson, 2017, p. 1179). Furthermore, having access to affordable internet service with the ability to perform a range of activities online confidently is integral to digital inclusion, and ultimately social and economic participation (Thomas et al., 2019). However, household ownership does not necessarily equate to access (Cardoso & Sorenson, 2017) and available digital resources may not be linguistically or readily accessible for CALD women. In addition, those who are nonusers of the internet are more likely to miss out on the advantages and assistance that digital technology can offer (Thomas et al., 2019). This is particularly so for CALD women who have their access and usage controlled, restricted or monitored due to TFDA.

Methodology

This chapter discusses findings from stage one of a two-stage research project. The first stage of the research examined DV practitioners' perspectives of TFDA and CALD women, and the use of digital technologies for prevention and intervention. The second stage explored the lived experience of DV victim-survivors who are of Chinese descent. The overall project aims to investigate how digital technologies affect the experiences of, and responses to, DV among Chinese immigrant women living in Melbourne, Victoria.

Sampling Technique

Stage one harnessed the experiences and knowledge of DV practitioners who have worked or are working closely with CALD women, including women of Chinese descent. They were recruited via purposive sampling as my goal was to sample participants who have the relevant experience and are informed about the emerging issue of TFDA (Bryman, 2012; Neuman, 1997). I also used snowball sampling techniques to help overcome the difficulties that can arise when conducting research on sensitive issues such as DV (Bryman, 2012). It begins small, with one or a few people, and then spreads out based on links to the initial recruits (Neuman, 1997). However, the downside of using a non–probability sampling approach means findings from the research will not likely be representative of all DV practitioners (Bryman, 2012).

The research received ethics approval from RMIT Human Research Ethics Committee (HREC) in 2018 for stage one and in 2019 for stage two.

Recruitment

All stage one participants were drawn from a database of specialized DV agencies in Victoria, which was composed by searching the internet and through personal knowledge of existing services. Cold calls were made to these agencies to ascertain their interests and to explain the purpose of the study. When interest was shown, the agency was sent a Plain Language Statement and Consent (PLSC) via email for their further consideration. When they could not be reached via phone, an email invitation was sent to their advertised contact email together with a copy of the PLSC. Further contacts were added to the database by word-of-mouth either through agency staff whom I spoke with on the phone or from recruited participants.

In total, 42 agencies were contacted either via email or phone calls. The initial interaction with agencies revealed that not many of them had supported a lot of Chinese or CALD women, therefore they kindly declined. Some declined citing lack of time or resources, or that they were already involved, or had been asked to participate in other research. Ultimately, out of the 13 DV practitioners from seven agencies, five participated in a group interview, and eight were individually interviewed in phase one of the research. They included 12 women and one man, with six working in refuges, two working in specialist family violence services, one from a counseling and health care service, one from a social welfare service, two from a women's health service, and one from a statewide anti-violence agency. Between them, they provided a range of support service including but not limited to intake and assessment, crisis and outreach response, intensive case management, prevention and promotion, and counseling.

All interviewees had experience working with CALD women, and eight of them had worked directly with victim-survivors of Chinese descent. Seven of the 13 DV practitioners are bi-lingual, speaking either Mandarin or Cantonese or both, and two are bi-cultural practitioners employed to work specifically with Chinese communities with whom they share similar cultural experiences and understandings.

All the participants were informed about the aim of the study, and the relevance of their participation for the study. All participants provided written or verbal informed consent. On average, each semi-structured interview lasted approximately 52 minutes and was audio-recorded. Interview transcripts were imported to the NVivo software program for content and thematic data analysis. Data collected included the agency's services, participants' perspectives of CALD women's experiences of DV including the occurrence of TFA, and implications of technology on their clients' lives. The participant names used in this chapter are pseudonyms.

Since only DV practitioners were engaged in stage one and not victim-survivors, this is a noted limitation of this chapter. Moreover, the outcome of my research cannot be generalized due to the small sample size, and by focusing on a specific ethnic group I acknowledge the research excludes many women from diverse backgrounds. People of Chinese ancestry are heterogenous, and Chinese migration and settlement in Australia has a long history and is growing. Nonetheless, the study generated richer in-depth qualitative data relating to a hard-to-reach and under-researched group.

Results and Discussion

Technology-Facilitated Domestic Abuse and Culturally and Linguistically Diverse Women in Victoria

TFDA is an emerging and rising issue among Australian women (Cox, 2016; Hand et al., 2009; Woodlock, 2013, 2015). In my interviews with DV practitioners, they told me most CALD women they worked with experienced physical, financial, emotional, and sexual abuse, and some of the abusive behaviors concerned the misuse of technology. The most common TFDA my participants reported CALD women having experienced was tracking and monitoring through the use of digital communication media.

Surveillance and Stalking
One of the practitioners described some of the TFDA activities she had seen in her clients from CALD backgrounds:

> So, well going through the phone pretty much to check her, cos some women [are] probably a new migrant here, the perp will sign up the phone plan for her, essentially the phone is under his name, so he has access to all the history records, who she's been talking to, how much time she spent on the phone today, what is in [it,] you know like calling who, who she called and then he has all the access to that so he can log on [and ask], "why [do] you spend so much time talking to blah blah".... Or some of them, they think, the other common things that stop her from seeing [or] calling the family overseas or you know, yeah it could be like physically stop [ping] her from going home or pretty much like [being] verbally aggressive after she made the contact [and] all [this] stuff, argu[ing] and all that. (Alex, Specialist family violence service)

Many practitioners revealed cases of CALD women either being monitored or stalked by smartphone, GPS, social media, or email. For example, Anna, who worked at a specialist family violence service, told me one of her clients was convinced that her ex had been physically stalking her, or he had someone tracking her. However, upon examining the woman's iPhone she found all the location services were turned on and believed the tracking was most likely through the "Find my iPhone" application via the linked iCloud account. She also reported another case where a camera was installed and linked to a perpetrator's mobile phone and on a router. However, in the majority of the cases reported by my participants perpetrators tended to use low tech:

> ... it's actually less likely that there'll be spyware or [a] hidden app on someone's phone [and more likely perpetrators using details from]... say geo-tagging on a photo [posted on Facebook for example] or if you have find my iPhone on your phone. So, things like that, they're actually... more likely to occur rather than... [a] bug on their phone. (Grace, Statewide anti-violence agency)

Most participants reported CALD women they worked with experienced TFDA through smartphones and their applications. This included perpetrators who had installed tracking apps on the women's mobile phones, switching on the location services of the mobile, or other installed social media apps. Other times legitimate software such as "Find my iPhone" or other location services were switched on by the women themselves, without thinking of the potential consequences. These findings are in keeping with previous research that has shown by far the most popular way of tracking by perpetrators are through low-tech techniques like smartphone tracking and social media (Freed et al., 2018;

Mason & Magnet, 2012; Woodlock, 2015). The use of children's digital devices to do the spying, monitoring, and tracking (Southworth et al., 2007; Women's Health East, 2018) was less common, with only one participant citing a case she had worked on where the abuser located the woman via their children's iPad:

> [k]ids were playing [on] their iPad and the iPad location was also on and you know [the] family photo-sharing iCloud is there as well, so [the] perpetrator actually found the mum in a caravan.... [The] mum [was] being supported by one of the women's refuge[s], and ah she was hiding basically overnight with the kids in the caravan, but the perpetrator found her. (Claire, Refuge)

Harassment and Threats

Mobile communication technology allows instant messaging and contact with others, permitting TFDA perpetrators to extend their coercive control beyond spatial and temporal dimensions, further terrorizing and disempowering DV victim-survivors (Harris, 2018; Mason & Magnet, 2012; Stark, 2007). My research participants reported that social media, messaging platforms, and emails were commonly used by perpetrators to harm, humiliate, and threaten their CALD clients. Jack, a bilingual and bi-cultural practitioner, reported a few cases involving social media and phone technology harassment of his clients both during and after the abusive relationships. His account below illustrated how gaslighting increased his client's anxiety:

> The abuses were mainly through all sort[s] of technology, electronic technology. So, she was concerned about [her] email getting monitored, strange things happened on email like change[s to] settings that she was not aware of. And things like she can't send email[s] and things like that. Email, phone... I think she was creating [a] new account every now and then. (Jack, Social welfare services)

Bethany, also a bilingual and bi-cultural practitioner, shared with me how damaging persistent abusive messages had made her client feel powerless:

> [Perpetrators] try to send messages or threatening messages through WeChat or SMS, yeah to make the victims feel very unsafe.... I have come across a client who... just kept receiving the messages from the perpetrator. She tried to block him, but she couldn't do it because she's worried that if she blocks him, he'd [take] revenge.... "If I block him, he might try to find me and or [have] some other people find me, and I will be in danger so I cannot." (Bethany, Counseling & health care service)

Some abusers wrote threatening messages in a language other than English to disguise the seriousness. Eva, a refuge worker, shared a disturbing case where her client's abuser "would write [threatening text] in Vietnamese" and sent visual images of "dead babies" saying he was worried "this would be our baby" and accusing her client of being "a bad mother."

These findings are in keeping with other research showing how TFDA erodes women's sense of safety (Hand et al., 2009; Harris, 2018), and instils in them fear and pressure, amplifying emotional and psychological abuse through the omnipresence of abusers even when a woman has left the relationship (Mason & Magnet, 2012; Sackett & Saunders, 1999; Stark, 2007). The impact of absolute control and power, in the most extreme case, can result in total submission, rendering use of digital surveillance tools unnecessary, as Eva observed:

> But they haven't generally said that [being stalked by technology has] been their experience. I mean yeah, it's more messages and things, checking where she is or he always know where she is, is the other thing, it's often not much of a social life happening for the woman. So, perhaps that hasn't even been necessary a lot of the time. (Eva, Refuge)

Vulnerability to Technology-Facilitated Domestic Abuse

Prior research has shown perpetrators deliberately restricting CALD women's access to technology to further isolate them (WESNET The Women's Services Network, 2019; Woodlock, 2015), and many of my participants noted similar tactics. Participants said perpetrators would manipulate their CALD clients' social location such as their migration and financial status, gender role beliefs, English language proficiency, and digital literacy skills. As Grace succinctly put it:

> I think what can make it harder for migrant women is that… you could have your phone taken off you or monitored and controlled by the perpetrator. So for example one client, she has come from an Asian country, married an Australian man, she didn't have fluent English, she wasn't well connected, she didn't have her bank account so [she was] financially dependent on the perpetrator, … he wouldn't provide her a phone, he wouldn't allow her to have a phone. So, it's very hard for her then to contact anyone or be connected at all. (Grace, Statewide anti-violence agency)

Many participants also said women tended to minimize their DV experience. One participant explained for newly arrived women this could be due to juggling multiple priorities in their new life in Australia:

> I think a lot of the women from, well the one[s] I've seen, they are usually trying to settling down in Australia. So, I think at that stage they are also working on, you know, stabilizing their

> financial income, trying to find a house or if they are trying to develop further in their career.... I think they don't have time to, you know, and sometime[s] there're also conflicts going on so there is living stress and there's also family stress or I guess relationship stress, and it really takes out a lot of their attention. (Jack, Social welfare services)

Others reported that abusers would threaten women with deportation or cancellation of immigration sponsorship. This added pressure for them to stay, especially if they had children. As Mei, a refuge worker, said, women's migration status gave perpetrators one more tactic to control them through threats. Citizenship status aside, Anna said some women are willing to give up everything for their children: "... you can have a very well-educated person, [but] I think at the end of the day, it also comes down to that sort of traditional belief of what a mother's role is." Participants reported that many women would sacrifice their own safety and well-being in exchange for their children's.

Joan, also a worker from a refuge, explained that many CALD women at her refuge did not have ownership of their smartphones and phone accounts. These phones and accounts were often given to them by their partners who owned and set up both the account and device. This was very challenging, especially for new migrants:

> So then for someone who maybe doesn't have any English... who doesn't actually maybe know the country or the area they're living in, doesn't have friends maybe, doesn't know... who to go to for help. Thinking about how that person might then get her own phone, or access the computer, it's such an insurmountable challenge. (Grace, Statewide anti-violence agency)

Technology-Based Responses to Domestic Violence

Most of my participants agreed that technology has the potential to assist and to empower CALD women DV victim-survivors. Many of my participants saw the benefits of using technology for educating the community about DV. For example, Claire (a refuge worker) who had worked closely with CALD women from Sri Lanka, India and East Asia noted:

> I found particularly there are barriers as well because women are restricted to make or go to those information sessions or mix with the people.... So, there is a big difference for the CALD women and the Australian culture of domestic violence through self-regulation. But to me it would be the best option [for] media, television, [and] radio [to] talk about more and more with the different language(s) like (the) Chinese language, Mandarin, or any [other non-English] languages. So that might be... helpful to reach that information to the woman.

In keeping with findings in prior research (Cardoso & Sorenson, 2017; Department of Social Services, 2015), the use of traditional communication channels and online platforms could complement each other to promote agencies' services and establish rapport with the target community:

> Yeah, technology, hm so the main way we engage with our clients is by WeChat, also we use… radio, we use radio, we use newspaper, … we send email, email is also technology. Basically, if you want to promote your service everything is about technology. (Bethany, Counseling & health care service)

Tapping into what the CALD communities use in terms of communication and media platforms can also be crucial to promote change and raise awareness of DV (Dixon et al., 2014). Many CALD women, especially newly arrived migrant women or those who have little English, prefer to communicate in their own language according to many participants. They use digital platforms that they are familiar with; as pointed out by Anna: "it's always through like whatever that, the community uses." In my participants' experience, remaining online is particularly important to women as the digital platform can be the only channel for them to maintain contact with their friends and families in other countries.

Having a support network can also break the social isolation so often experienced by CALD women DV victim-survivors. Some of my participants advocate the use of online forums or online peer support groups for information sharing, social connection, and support. For example, WeChat can be utilized when services work with the Chinese community:

> So when… family violence happens they don't know where and how to seek help. But I reckon even for these women, WeChat would be a platform they have daily access to. I, I can't think [of] any people who don't have access to the platform these days…as long as she has [a] smart phone, I think WeChat would be the platform… (Martha, Women's health service)

Besides social connection and support, there is potential for online forums to be utilized for prevention and early intervention. Many of my participants agreed that if women can access relevant resources and support to identify DV earlier, it might actually help to prevent a situation before it is too late:

> … if the woman… can find a way to communicate even… [if] it's like an online chatroom they can just access that and then talk to someone in their language and then they can sort of identify the family violence earlier than later, that might actually help overall to prevent, [or] stop them in the middle way, … not just, until like wait, escalate, and then incident happen. (Alex, Special family violence service)

The use of a tech-based response to DV can also reach women who otherwise cannot be reached. It may be more sustainable, allowing service providers and clients to stay connected without much managed space and resources. Some participants also suggested that women may be able to interact with workers via phone or Skype calls when they cannot access services in person.

Technology also has the potential to keep women and their children safe from violence in their own home, if it is safe to do so, as Eva postulated:

> We see how hard it is for women to start all over again. We absolutely would like them to be able to return home if that's an option [installing CCTV, personal alarms, locks and security doors] .... [N]ot every perpetrator would abide the order obviously, if, however, he does have a fear of the police [and] then would abide by the order… then yes, because we do want the kids to stay in their schools and women to keep their support network. (Eva, Refuge)

Opportunity also exists to use smartphones to document evidence of DV (DVRCV, 2019). Some of my participants reported CALD women using their smartphones to capture breaches of court orders and incidents of DV.

Overall, from my participants' perspectives, digital technologies can be a lifeline for CALD women TFDA victim-survivors and can potentially help them to obtain information and/or help maintain a social support/network, and lessen social isolation. Nonetheless, all participants stressed that face-to-face service delivery remains critical when working with DV victim-survivors.

Challenges for Culturally and Linguistically Diverse Women re: Technology-Based Responses to Domestic Violence

Although using technology to combat DV seems promising, previous research has found barriers to accessibility, usability, and visibility of online resources (Davenport et al., 2008; Hand et al., 2009). Many participants suggested CALD women face some challenges in this regard.

English Proficiency. My participants identified language barriers as the number one issue affecting CALD women's experience of TFDA, both in terms of being targeted by technology and in terms of using technology to respond to abuse. Many participants explained that when English is not your first language, life-saving actions such as calling triple zero (000) or communicating with workers can become a daunting task. As such, a few participants said some clients are more willing to disclose to them because they speak the same language. But when women's phone settings were in a language other than English, some participants found it difficult to conduct safety checks. Below is Anna's experience helping Chinese speaking clients:

> And then adding to that is… everything [video on how to perform safety check] is in English…. [S]ometimes I struggle with that too because if I were to explain how to turn off certain settings to a client, the client wants to speak Mandarin, I don't know how to explain in Mandarin either because my phone is in English, I know the settings in English, I don't know the settings in Mandarin. (Anna, Specialist family service)

Even assisting clients to transfer data to a safer phone can be a difficult task as Joan (a refuge worker) explained:

> [y]ou know, you have to know how to set it up, even if it's the CALD woman who doesn't speak the language so that's another barrier because you know, you need to go through their, her phone to transfer the number. Maybe those numbers are not even in English they are in another language so you can see the multiple layers of the barriers of assisting….

Further, some observed that due to language barriers many of their CALD clients did not access mainstream services, and therefore were unaware of mainstream DV campaigns. Some also noted that even if technology could be used to capture evidence of abusive acts, if they were not in English, such recordings might not be accepted as admissible evidence in court. Such recordings could be translated, but translation costs may deter victim-survivors and/or agencies working with them from doing so:

> …they have evidence on their phone… but the problem is a lot of these are in Mandarin. And to submit it to the police, they would have to have it translated. Cos sometimes the police kind of go "It's all in Mandarin I don't know." They're not supposed to know, they [are] supposed to kind of go "what is this?" But they don't always take that as evidence because it's all in Mandarin… they do run into the trouble of everything being Mandarin. And then to have it translated it would cost money. (Anna, Specialist family service)

Digital Literacy. Another challenge noted by some of my participants related to women's lack of confidence in using IT or their low level of IT skills:

> Some [CALD women] often… don't, they don't even know where to find the location setting. They don't even know how to turn it off on their phones…. [A]t every intake we do a safety planning with the women…. We always tell them to turn it off, the location, tell them how to get it, how to go to the setting[s] and turn [it] off…. (Alex, Specialist family violence service)

Most participants observed that many of their CALD clients did not know how to access resources online. Even when women were aware of online resources or safety apps, some participants expressed concern that some clients would not be able to utilize them. None of my participants noted or recalled their CALD clients ever using any existing safety apps when they came to their services. Mei explained the fact that a majority of these apps are in English could be a deterrent since "they don't have the language skills to access it." Di, another refuge worker believed "it's beyond them" since they would not have the knowledge and digital skills to search for and download these sorts of safety apps. From my participants' perspectives, when women experience TFDA, having the confidence and skills to use their smartphones could help to ensure safety and facilitate access to support services, and take advantage of being digitally included (Thomas et al., 2019).

Conclusion

This chapter provides a very basic snapshot of TFDA and CALD women based on the experiences of several DV practitioners in Victoria, Australia. In my participants' experience, CALD women commonly experience tracking and monitoring through the use of smartphones and social media. Further, CALD women's migration and financial status, and language and digital literacy can impact and increase their vulnerability to TFDA, making their experience of TFDA more complicated. Coercive control of a woman's use of and access to a smartphone and other mobile communication technology can limit their capacity to seek help or leave and prevent them from being digitally included.

Findings from stage one of my research are consistent with the literature that notes the complexity of the issue of TFDA. Technology can compound the coercive nature of DV to exacerbate risk and further disempower CALD women victim-survivors of TFDA. Yet, despite the devastating impact of TFDA on its victim-survivors, many participants revealed technology can also have positive effects for their CALD clients. Technology-based responses such as safety apps, online resources, and social online counseling services provide vital information, social connection, and emotional support, which can be a critical lifeline for many.

Based on my participants' experiences, for CALD women, providing culturally and linguistically appropriate digital services and resources to complement existing face-to-face mainstream and CALD-specific support services can be a way forward. To succeed it would require collaboration and coordination of the entire community, including CALD women victim-survivors, and all levels of government to ameliorate the immense issue of DV. Furthermore, policy and service delivery need to be equitable and meet the needs of all victim-survivors, including those who are underrepresented and more marginalized. Many participants acknowledged building rapport with CALD women victim-survivors and establishing long-term relationships with the community as crucial.

There is an urgent need to better understand how women experience TFDA and their responses to it, including their access to, use, and ownership of technology. This is especially so for women from CALD backgrounds. Far too often, their voices, their wisdom, and their agency are not being heard in responding to and recovering from DV. If we are to achieve the vision of the VRCFV of a more responsive and culturally appropriate mainstream universal/specialist service, identifying and addressing the needs and lived realities of CALD women is critical. Research on the areas of TFDA and the CALD community is sparse. Future research should focus on better understanding CALD women's perceptions of and responses to TFDA, their relationship with digital communication media, and on exploring ways to improve engagement and utilize community media channels/platforms. The full potential of utilizing digital technologies in the intricate prevention and intervention space is yet to be realized. It is hoped that the results of my study will contribute toward satisfying some of that need.

Notes

1. The author acknowledges her research participants and all those who have worked and are working tirelessly in their effort to eradicate all forms of violence against women.
2. Also known as intimate partner violence (IPV) and family violence (FV) in Australia. DV and FV are the terms that tend to be used most by professionals working in the VAW fields and the broader community.
3. The term CALD is frequently used to distinguish ethnic minority communities from the mainstream community. The CALD population in Australia is mainly defined by country of birth, language spoken, and cultural diversity (Sawrikar & Katz, 2009).
4. Also known as "ubicomp," ubiquitous computing "embeds computer technology in our everyday environment, providing a human with information services and applications through any device over different kinds of networks" and "can be seen as prerequisite for pervasive computing that emphasizes mobile data access and the mechanisms needed for supporting a community of nomadic users" (Niemelä & Latvakoski, 2004, p. 71).
5. See Saferfamilies.org (n.d.) for some examples of online resources during the COVID-19 pandemic and the government announcement of $5M toward new technology for family violence organizations in Victoria (Premier of Victoria, 2020).
6. The final VRCFV report was tabled into the Victorian Parliament in 2016, and the Victorian government has committed to implement all 227 recommendations. As of December 31, 2019, the Victorian government has implemented 154 recommendations (see vic.gov, n.d.).
7. See Summary Offences Act 1966 (Vic) section 41DV: distribution of intimate image intentionally without consent carries a maximum penalty of seven years imprisonment.
8. The PSS refers to emotional abuse caused by a set of behaviors or actions characterized in nature by their intent to manipulate, control, isolate, or intimidate the person they are aimed at (see the ABS (2017b) Personal Safety Survey, Australia: User Guide, 2016 for detailed background to the Survey).
9. The majority of the SmartSafe online survey victim-survivor participants self-identified as Anglo.

References

ABS. (2017a). *Personal Safety, Australia, 2016 cat no. 4906.0*. Canberra: ABS.

ABS. (2017b). Personal safety survey, Australia: User Guide, 2016. Retrieved from https://www.abs.gov.au/AUSSTATS/abs@.nsf/Lookup/4906.0.55.003Main+Features12016?OpenDocument

AIHW. (2019). *Family, domestic and sexual violence in Australia: Continuing the national story 2019*. Canberra: Australian Institute of Health and Welfare (AIHW).

Bryman, A. (2012). *Social research methods*. (4th ed.) Oxford: Oxford University Press.

Cardoso, L. F., & Sorenson, S. B. (2017). Violence against women and household ownership of radios, computers, and phones in 20 countries. *American Journal of Public Health*, *107*(7), 1175–1181. doi:10.2105/AJPH.2017.303808

Carter, J. S. (2015). Card helps curb 'national emergency' of domestic violence. RN Afternoons presented by Michael Mackenzie. Retrieved from http://www.abc.net.au/radionational/programs/rnafternoons/safety-card-helps-curb-domestic-violence-national-emergency/6481238

COAG. (2011). *National plan to reduce violence against women and their children 2010-2022*. Canberra: Council of Australian Governments (COAG).

Cox, P. (2016). Violence against women in Australia: Additional analysis of the Australian Bureau of Statistics' personal safety survey, 2012. ARNOWS Horizons: 01.01/2016 Rev. ed. ANROWS, Sydney.

Crenshaw, K. W. (1991). Mapping the margins: Intersectionality, identity politics, and violence against women of color. *Stanford Law Review*, *43*(6), 1241–1299. doi:10.2307/1229039

Davenport, D. D., Richey, J., & Westbrook, L. (2008). E-government access to social service information: State web resources for domestic violence survivors. *Journal of the American Society for Information Science and Technology*, *59*(6), 903–915. doi:10.1002/asi.20787

Department of Social Services. (2015). *Hearing her voice: Report from the kitchen table conversations with culturally and linguistically diverse women on violence against women and their children*. Canberra: Commonwealth of Australia.

Dimond, J. P., Fiesler, C., & Bruckman, A. S. (2011). Domestic violence and information communication technologies. *Interacting with Computers*, *23*(5), 413–421. doi:10.1016/j.intcom.2011.04.006

Dixon, L. J., Correa, T., Straubhaar, J., Covarrubias, L., Graber, D., Spence, J., & Rojas, V. (2014). Gendered space: The digital divide between male and female users in internet public access sites. *Journal of Computer-Mediated Communication*, *19*(4), 991–1009. doi:10.1111/jcc4.12088

Dobash, R. E., & Dobash, R. (1980). *Violence against wives: A case against the patriarchy*. London: Open Books.

Douglas, H., & Burdon, M. (2018). Legal responses to non-consensual smartphone recordings in the context of domestic and family violence. *University of New South Wales Law Journal*, *41*(1), 157–184.

Douglas, H., Harris, B., & Dragiewicz, M. (2019). Migrant women are particularly vulnerable to technology-facilitated domestic abuse. *The Conversation*, *Vol. 1*, February. Retrieved from https://eprints.qut.edu.au/131201/2/131201.pdf

Dragiewicz, M., Harris, B., Woodlock, D., Salter, M., Easton, H., Lynch, A., & Milne, L. (2019). *Domestic violence and communication technology: Survivor experiences of intrusion, surveillance, and identity crime*. Sydney: Australian Communications Consumer Action Network.

DVRCV. (2019). *Arc smartphone app*. Melbourne: Domestic Violence Resources Centre Victoria. Retrieved from https://www.dvrcv.org.au/knowledge-centre/our-blog/arc-smartphone-app Viewed on November 13, 2020.

Foster, H., & Fletcher, A. (2020). Impact of COVID-19 on women and children experiencing domestic and family violence and frontline domestic and family violence services: Summary report. Women's Safety Nsw, Sydney.

Freed, D., Palmer, J., Minchala, D., Levy, K., Ristenpart, T., & Dell, N. (2018). "A stalker's paradise": How intimate partner abusers exploit technology. Paper presented at the Proceedings of the 2018 CHI Conference on Human Factors in Computing Systems, Montreal QC. doi:10.1145/3173574.3174241

George, A., & Harris, B. (2014). *Landscapes of violence: Women surviving family violence in regional and rural Victoria*. Melbourne: Deaking University School of Law's Centre for Rural and Regional Law and Justice.

Ghafournia, N., & Easteal, P. (2018). Are immigrant women visible in Australian domestic violence reports that potentially influence policy? *Laws*, *7*(4). doi:10.3390/laws7040032

Hand, T., Chung, D., & Peters, M. (2009). The use of information and communication technologies to coerce and control in DV and following separation. In *Australian domestic and family violence clearinghouse stakeholder paper* (*Vol. 6*, pp. 1–15) Sydney: University of New South Wales and Australian Government. Retrieved from https://advocacy4oromia.files.wordpress.com/2015/03/stakeholderpaper_6.pdf on 19/03/2017

Harris, B. (2018). Spacelessness, spatiality and intimate partner violence: Technology-facilitated abuse, stalking and justice administration. In K. Fitz-Gibbon, S. Walklate, J. McCulloch, & J. Maher (Eds.), *Intimate partner violence, risk and security: Securing women's lives in a global world*. (1st ed., *Vol. 1*, pp. 52–70). Milton: Routledge.

Henry, N., & Powell, A. (2014). Beyond the 'sext': Technology-facilitated sexual violence and harassment against adult women. *Australian and New Zealand Journal of Criminology*, *48*(1), 104–118. doi:10.1177/0004865814524218

InTouch. (2010). *"I lived in fear because I knew nothing" barriers to the justice system faced by CALD women experiencing family violence*. Melbourne: InTouch Inc. Multicultural Centre Against Family Violence.

Laxton, C. (2014). *Virtual world, real fear: A women's aid report into online abuse, harassment and stalking*. Bristol: Women's Aid Federation of England.

Maher, J., McCulloch, J., & Fitz-Gibbon, K. (2017). New forms of gendered surveillance? Intersections of technology and family violence. In M. Segrave & L. Vitis (Eds.), *Gender, technology and violence* (pp. 14–27). Milton: Taylor & Francis.

Mason, C., & Magnet, S. (2012). Surveillance studies and violence against women. *Surveillance and Society*, *10*(2), 105–118.

Meurn, C. (2012). The role of information and communications technologies in violence prevention. In K. M. Blakeslee, D. M. Patel, & M. A. Simon (Eds.), *Communications and technology for violence prevention: Workshop summary*. Washington, DC: The National Academies Press.

Murray, S. (2002). *More than refuge: Changing responses to domestic violence*. Perth: University of Western Australia (UWA) Publishing.

Murray, S., & Powell, A. (2009). "What's the problem?" Australian public policy constructions of domestic and family violence. *Violence Against Women, 15*(5), 532–552.

Neuman, W. L. (1997). *Social research methods: Qualitative and quantitative approaches* (3rd ed.). Boston, MA: Allyn & Bacon.

Niemelä, E., & Latvakoski, J. (2004). Survey of requirements and solutions for ubiquitous software. Paper presented at the Proceedings of the 3rd International Conference on Mobile and Ubiquitous Multimedia, College Park, Maryland. doi: 10.1145/1052380.1052391

Office of the eSafety Commissioner. (2019). *eSafety for women from culturally and linguistically diverse backgrounds*. Canberra: Office of the eSafety Commissioner.

Peterman, A., Potts, A., O'Donnell, M., Thompson, K., Shah, N., Oertelt-Prigione, S., & van Gelder, N. (2020). *Pandemics and violence against women and children*. Washington, DC: Center for Global Development. Retrieved from https://www.cgdev.org/sites/default/files/pandemics-and-vawg-april2.pdf

Premier of Victoria. (2020). *A safe place to escape family violence during coronavirus*. [Press release]. Retrieved from https://www.premier.vic.gov.au/a-safe-place-to-escape-family-violence-during-coronavirus/

Richardson, F. (2014). *Measuring the toll: Family violence index*. Melbourne: State of Victoria.

Sackett, L. A., & Saunders, D. G. (1999). The impact of different forms of psychological abuse on battered women. *Violence & Victims, 14*(1), 1–13.

Saferfamillies.org. (n.d.). Retrieved from https://www.saferfamilies.org.au/covid19-resources

Sawrikar, P., & Katz, I. (2009). *How useful is the term 'Culturally and Linguistically Diverse' (CALD) in Australian research, practice, and policy discourse?* Sydney: Social Policy Research Centre.

Southworth, C., Finn, J., Dawson, S., Fraser, C., & Tucker, S. (2007). Intimate partner violence, technology, and stalking. *Violence Against Women, 13*(8), 842–856. doi:10.1177/1077801207302045

Stark, E. (2007). *Coercive control: How men entrap women in personal life*. New York, NY: Oxford University Press.

State of Victoria. (2016a). Royal commission into family violence: Report and recommendations. Vol. V, Parl Paper No 132 (2014-16). Melbourne: Victorian Government Printer.

State of Victoria. (2016b). Royal commission into family violence: Summary and recommendations. Parl Paper No 132 (2014-16). Melbourne: Victorian Government Printer.

Summary Offences Act 1966 (Vic), § 41. Retrived from https://www.legislation.vic.gov.au/in-force/acts/summary-offences-act-1966/132 Accessed on April 6, 2020.

Tarzia, L., Iyer, D., Thrower, E., & Hegarty, K. (2017). "Technology doesn't judge you": Young Australian women's views on using the internet and smartphones to address intimate partner violence. *Journal of Technology in Human Services, 35*(3), 199–218. doi:10.1080/15228835.2017.1350616

Theobald, J., Murray, S., & Smart, J. (2017). *From the margins to the mainstream: The domestic violence services movement in Victoria, Australia* (pp. 1974–2016) VIC: Melbourne University Press.

Thomas, J., Barraket, J., Wilson, C., Rennie, E., Ewing, S., & MacDonald, T. (2019). Measuring Australia's digital divide: The Australian digital inclusion index 2019. doi:10.25916/5d6478f373869

UN Women. (2020). COVID-19 and ending violence against women and girls In United Nations Entity for Gender Equality and the Empowerment of Women (UN Women). Retrieved from https://www.unwomen.org/en/digital-library/publications/2020/04/issue-brief-covid-19-and-ending-violence-against-women-and-girls#view

United Nations. (2005). *Gender equality and the empowerment of women through ICT*. New York, NY: United Nations.

United Nations Broadband Commission. (2015). Cyber violence against women and girls: A world-wide wake-up call. Retrieved from http://www.unwomen.org/en/news/stories/2015/9/cyber-violence-report-press-release

Vic.gov. (n.d.). The 227 family violence recommendations. Retrieved from https://www.vic.gov.au/family-violence-recommendations

WESNET The Women's Services Network. (2019). Supporting survivors of technology-facilitated abuse from Aboriginal and or Torress Strait Islandr, and/or culturally and linguistically diverse communities: National Listening Tour, Report. WESNET The Women's Services Network, Canberra.

Women's Health East. (2018). *Women online: The intersection of technology, gender and sexism*. Melbourne: WHE.

Woodlock, D. (2013). *Technology-facilitated stalking: Findings and recommendations from the SmartSafe project*. Collingwood: Domestic Violence Resource Centre Victoria.

Woodlock, D. (2015). *ReCharge: Women's technology safety, legal resources, research and training*. Collingwood: Women's Legal Service NSW, Domestic Violence Resource Centre Victoria and WESNET.

Section 6
Legal Responses

Chapter 28

Introduction

Jane Bailey

The seven chapters in this section examine legal responses to technology-facilitated violence and abuse (TFVA) generally, but also with respect to specific forms, including the nonconsensual disclosure of intimate images (NDII) and other privacy-invasive tactics such as voyeurism and doxxing. The section moves from consideration of the international human rights and obligations at play, toward a specific call to address legislative gaps between those guaranteed rights and existing legislative measures in the Arab region and in Malawi. The remainder of the chapters in the section remind us of the integral tie between the desirability and efficacy of legal responses, and the broader socio-political context in which they are situated. Simply put, this broader context can play a central role in determining whether domestic legal responses are actually likely to work to protect the internationally recognized human rights of TFVA targets.

Drawing on social science findings relating to TFVA generally, as well as the gendered dimensions arising from those findings, Elizabeth Coombs explores some of the ways in which various forms of TFVA violate internationally protected human rights to privacy, and to freedom from violence (particularly gender-based violence). Pointing to the obligations on nation states to take steps to protect their citizens' enjoyment of these rights, Coombs highlights states' obligations to ensure that private corporate actors operate in ways that respect them.

Sukaina Al Nasrawi's chapter builds on the international human rights framework outlined by Coombs, in this case, highlighting more specifically the applicable obligations for members of Arab nations to take action to address gender-based TFVA. She then provides a comprehensive analysis of existing legal responses within those nations, and identifies gaps between those responses and these nations' international human rights obligations. Ultimately, Al Nasrawi calls for new legislative initiatives aimed at filling those gaps.

The final five chapters in the section move beyond the question of whether additional legal responses are needed to consider how various aspects of context affect the efficacy of those responses. These explorations of the role of context in

The Emerald International Handbook of Technology-Facilitated Violence and Abuse, 471–473

doi:10.1108/978-1-83982-848-520211065

determining legislative efficacy begin with Sarai Chisala-Templehoff and Seonaid Stevenson-McCabe's comparison of legislative responses to NDII in Malawi and Scotland. The authors chronicle the lack of an explicit legal prohibition on NDII in Malawi and the successful campaign that led to creation of such an offense in Scotland. However, they caution that the absence of a strong feminist movement to push for the creation of such an offense in Malawi may impede its passage there. Moreover, they note that even if a legal prohibition on NDII were created in Malawi, its efficacy could be limited by the absence of an informed and engaged police force and a risk of misuse against targeted women in an effort to enforce discriminatory tropes of chastity and propriety.

Next, Moira Aikenhead examines the degree to which the surrounding context of rape culture is reflected in the facts of reported cases relating to criminal prosecution of NDII in Canada, and in the reasons for judgment in those cases. Her analysis focuses on all reported decisions in which Canada's criminal prohibition on NDII was used to prosecute instances of "revenge porn" – the nonconsensual sharing of intimate images by a current or ex-intimate partner. The cases examined by Aikenhead support an understanding of "revenge porn" as a serious form of communal, gendered intimate partner violence (IPV) that is particularly harmful, because of the kind of myths and stereotypes about women's sexuality identified by Chisala-Templehoff and Stevenson-McCabe. Furthermore, she finds that victim-blaming and other patterns arising from a rape culture context may also be informing Canadian judicial assessments of such violence.

Kristen Thomasen and Suzie Dunn's chapter demonstrates the impact of context on the efficacy of legal responses to TFVA, with a particular focus on the disparately negative implications of privacy-invasive attacks, especially in light of the growing prevalence of drones and sexualized deepfakes. The authors focus on the Supreme Court of Canada's analysis of privacy in *R v Jarvis* (a voyeurism case in which a high-school teacher surreptitiously recorded images of the breasts of female students on a pen camera). Demonstrating how the Court's failure to explicitly factor the gendered context of such crimes into the analysis is likely to undermine the efficacy of legislative responses to gender-based privacy violations, they call for an evolution of normative and legal conceptions of privacy, an evolution they predict will become increasingly urgent as drone and deepfake technologies proliferate.

Like Thomasen and Dunn's chapter, Anne Cheung's chapter also focuses on a privacy-invasive form of TFVA – the nonconsensual release of personal information, known as "doxxing," and its uses in the particular socio-political context of mass protests against abuses of state power in Hong Kong. After examining several cases in which injunctions have been issued to prevent the release of personal information about law enforcement officials who refused to identify themselves while policing these protests, as well as journalists involved in reporting on the protests, Cheung argues for a contextually sensitive legal analysis of doxxing. In particular, she advocates for a defense to doxxing that is tailored to allow for the nonconsensual release of personal information about police officers that is necessary to hold the state publicly accountable for abuse of power, particularly in socio-political contexts pervaded by well-grounded and widely held concerns about the abuse of state authority.

Finally, Pam Hrick's chapter shifts away the primarily *criminal* legal responses to TFVA focused on in this section of the Handbook toward statutorily created administrative bodies. In particular, she assesses the capacity of agencies such as the Office of the eSafety Commissioner in Australia, NetSafe in New Zealand, and the Cyberscan Unit and Canadian Center for Child Protection in Canada to effectively respond to TFVA against women. In this chapter, she identifies the needs and priorities of TFVA survivors as being the relevant context to be taken into account. Drawing on the literature focused on survivor-centered approaches to violence against women, Hrick argues that these sorts of administrative bodies hold some promise for meaningfully addressing TFVA against women, where their approaches are intersectional, provide multiple options that allow survivors to choose their own course of action, ensure that survivors are treated with dignity and respect, center prevention as a key goal, and are grounded in research, evidence, and the first-hand perspectives of survivors themselves.

publicly accountable for abuse of power, particularly [illegible] motivated by well-grounded and widely held concerns about the abuse of state authority.

[illegible]

Chapter 29

Human Rights, Privacy Rights, and Technology-Facilitated Violence

Elizabeth Coombs

Abstract

This chapter examines technology-facilitated violence from the perspective of international human rights law. It explores current research relating to technology-facilitated violence and then highlights the international human rights instruments that are triggered by the various forms of such violence. Ultimately, it focuses upon international human rights to privacy and to freedom from violence (especially gender-based violence) and the obligations on State and Nonstate actors to address violations of these rights. It argues that adoption of a human rights perspective on technology-facilitated violence better enables us to hold State and Nonstate actors to account in finding meaningful ways to address violence in all of its forms.

Keywords: Gender-based violence; international human rights; privacy; corporate responsibility; state obligations; technology-facilitated violence and abuse

Introduction

Violence is among the leading causes of death worldwide for people aged 15–44 years. Each year, 1.4 million people lose their lives to violence and many more are injured and left with physical, sexual, reproductive, and mental health problems (WHO, 2017). Violence cuts across generations, nationalities, communities, and societies, takes many forms, and is facilitated by technology.

While new information communication technologies are enabling learning, creativity, and social connections; reducing isolation; communicating ideas, news, and activism; providing employment and business opportunities; and enabling

The Emerald International Handbook of Technology-Facilitated Violence and Abuse, 475–491

doi:10.1108/978-1-83982-848-520211036

transactions, financing, and services, they also enable covert commercial monitoring and data harvesting; surveillance in public and private places; hate speech and disinformation; privacy infringements; and violence and abuse. These negative uses of technologies facilitate polarization of societies and violations of human rights (UN Digital Co-operation, 2019). Further, distinctive features of information communication technologies such as portability, reach, and speed deliver maximum impact for technology-facilitated violence and abuse (TFVA) (Hall & Hearn, 2017).

Numerous international human rights instruments guarantee, among other things, rights to privacy, and freedom from violence and abuse, and impose obligations on States to honor and protect those rights, and in some cases, to ensure that Nonstate actors such as corporations, respect them as well. The United Nations (UN) Human Rights Council and the General Assembly have confirmed that "the same rights that people have offline must also be protected online" (United Nations General Assembly [UNGA], 2018; United Nations Human Rights Council [UNHRC], 2016). This chapter brings together some current research on TFVA with applicable international human rights instruments and argues that the international human rights framework can and should be brought to bear in assessing both State and Nonstate actors' actions and inactions relating to TFVA. The first section highlights relevant research on TFVA, particularly its forms, discriminatory patterns, and impacts. The second section provides an overview of applicable aspects of the international human rights framework as it relates to State and Nonstate actors, ultimately focusing specifically on the rights to privacy protection and to freedom from gender-based[1] violence such as that directed at women and individuals of diverse gender orientations, identity, and sex characteristics.

TFVA: Definition, Forms, Discriminatory Patterns, and Impacts

There are different views of what constitutes "violence" (see Dunn, this volume). The definition used here is "the intentional use of physical force or power, threatened or actual, against oneself, another person, or against a group or community, that either results in or has a high likelihood of resulting in injury, death, psychological harm, maldevelopment, or deprivation" (Krug, Dahlberg, Mercy, Zwi, & Lozano, 2002). The term TFVA refers to violence carried out using technologies such as the internet and/or mobile devices (European Institute for Gender Equality [EIGE], 2020; International Center for Research on Women [ICRW], 2018).

Violence is more than interpersonal incidents between individuals. The social, political, and economic dimensions of violence cannot be ignored. This definition expands the narrow view of violence to include actions arising from power relationships. It captures acts of omission, such as States' failure to act, in addition to acts of commission, and encompasses violence against groups committed for social, political, and/or economic reasons (Krug et al., 2002). Importantly, it enables the proposition that human rights – as a protection against abuse – are a necessary dimension of discussions of violence, including TFVA.

The diversity of digital technologies enables TFVA to take many forms. For example, social networking sites and global positioning systems facilitate cyberstalking behavior by making it easier for perpetrators to monitor the activities and whereabouts of their targets, and to repeatedly communicate with them via email, instant messages, voicemails, and texts. Spyware is now cheaper and more readily available. Abusers are installing spyware apps on phones to track location, monitor communications, and exert control. Not only are there several hundred spyware apps but also numerous tools with legitimate purposes which can be easily repurposed for spying (Chatterjee et al., 2018; Parsons et al., 2019). Phone control and child monitoring apps enable remote control of phone settings, such as GPS or Wi-Fi, provide access to location, SMS content, call logs (sometimes recordings), media content, app usage, internet activity logs, keylogging, plus, in some cases, the sending of notifications when the monitored phone leaves a set geofence or calls certain numbers. Where these "dual-use" apps are built into the phone's operating system, they can be impossible to remove (Chatterjee et al., 2018). Websites, email, and texts are commonly used in online child sexual exploitation (West Coast LEAF, 2014). The geolocation features of dating apps, such as Grindr, have been reported to be used to lure, entrap, and abuse gay and transgender users (Article 19, 2018; see also Dietzel, this volume; Waldman, this volume). Smart home devices enable new ways to control and harass (Bowles, 2018; UCL IoT, 2019). Technological devices designed to prevent sexual violence can also be hacked or used by perpetrators to track or stalk (Harris, 2019). Other technologies, such as virtual assistants, have been found lacking in their responses to requests for assistance with violence (Radhakrishnan, 2018).

Social media platforms, text and messaging apps, email and online gaming sites, phones, and phone messaging apps are commonly used facilitators of online harassment which often spans multiple online venues. One US study, for example, found that 41% of respondents had been personally subjected to online harassing behaviors, and 66% witnessed others being harassed (PEW, 2017, p. 3). In that study, harassing behavior ranged from offensive name-calling to intentional embarrassment, physical threats, stalking, and sexual harassment, with 26% of adult respondents having had false information posted about them online and 9% experiencing mental or emotional stress as a result (PEW 2017, p. 58). Since apps and platforms are most often created and operated by Nonstate actors, it is unsurprising that 79% of respondents to the PEW (2017) survey felt online services had a responsibility to intervene when harassing behavior occurred on their platforms, while only 15% said these services should not be held responsible for the behavior and content posted by users (p. 46).

Deeply disturbing gender-based online infringements of privacy have led to violence and discrimination in online and offline spheres, in private and public settings, and across physical and national boundaries (UNSRP, 2019, Annex 2). Research such as PEW's 2017 survey which showed online harassment was especially prevalent in the lives of younger adults (67% of 18–29-year olds) (p. 5) also suggests that women and young people (especially young women) may be particularly affected by TFVA. In terms of TFVA prevalence, a Fundamental Rights Agency (FRA) (2014) survey of 28 European countries found 11% of women received unwanted and offensive sexually explicit emails or SMS messages or intrusive, inappropriate advances on social media, and 14% of women received offensive or threatening messages or phone calls repeatedly from the same person (pp. 81, 104). Cyberstalking by text messages, email, or the internet particularly affected young women with 4% of all 18–29 year olds having experienced cyber-stalking in the preceding 12 months (FRA, 2014, p. 87). Fears of gender-based violence affected women's freedom of movement with 53% of all women avoiding certain places for fear of being physically or sexually assaulted (FRA, 2014, p. 109) and 7% closed their social network account in response to stalking (FRA, 2014, p. 90). Recent research has highlighted abusive behavior directed at LGB social media users (PEW, 2020).

The greater prevalence of TFVA in younger age groups, with sexualized TFVA particularly directed at younger women, is supported by research from other parts of the world including developing countries. Over 60% of poor urban women and men in developing countries aged 18–24 years using the internet reported being abused online in a 2016 study (African Development Bank Group, 2016, p. 1; see also Makinde et al., this volume). The African Development Bank Group's (2016) research in Kenya found abuse spanned personal hate speech, intimate image abuse, online intimidation, trolling, and cyberbullying, with the majority of victims being women. The consequences included 25% exiting the platform and a majority avoiding engaging with strangers online (p. 2). Research from Brasil and other parts of Latin America reveals similar findings (CODING RIGHTS; INTERNETLAB, 2017).

Age and gender may also affect the experience and impact of TFVA. Those reporting severe experiences of harassment in the 2017 PEW survey, for example, were more likely to say personal characteristics, such as gender or race/ethnicity, triggered the harassment, and to report they deleted their profile or changed their username, ceased attending certain offline places, or contacted law enforcement. Women were twice as likely as men to say they had been targeted as a result of their gender (11% vs. 5%) (PEW, 2017, p. 5). Men, however, were around twice as likely as women to say they had been harassed as a result of their political views (19%:10%) (PEW, 2017, p. 5). And while men were somewhat more likely to report experiencing any form of harassing behavior online (44% of men and 37% of women), women, especially young women, encountered sexualized forms of abuse at much higher rates (although slightly more men than women reported incidents of nonconsensual distribution of intimate images) (PEW, 2017, p. 7). Twenty one percent of women aged 18 to 29 reported being sexually harassed online, more than double that of men in the same age group (9%), and roughly half (53%) reported receiving explicit images without consent (PEW, 2017, p. 5). Among the youngest adults (ages 18–24), women were more than three times as likely to be sexually harassed online (20%:6% men) (PEW, 2017, p. 5).

In the PEW (2017) study, women were especially likely to report being deeply impacted by harassment with 35% reporting their most recent experience as either "extremely" or "very" upsetting, more than double the men who said the same (16%) (p. 5). Witnessing harassment of others saw 27% refraining from posting online and 13% stopped using an online service after witnessing other users engage in harassing behaviors. This "chilling effect" especially affected women aged 18 to 29 with 45% not posting something online after witnessing the harassment of others

(PEW, 2017, p. 36). Unsurprisingly, women, particularly young women (ages 18–29), were more likely than men to see online harassment as a major problem (PEW, 2017).

Gender-based violence directed at groups such as feminists, Human Rights Defenders, journalists, gender diverse individuals, and activists on social media platforms such as Twitter have led many of members of these communities to censor their postings, limit their interactions, and even leave Twitter completely (Bailey & Mathen, 2019; CODING RIGHTS; INTERNETLAB, 2017; Privacy International, 2017; Valente, 2018; Varon, 2017; Zuckerberg, 2018; Amnesty International, 2018a, b). Research relating to other websites and dating apps also suggests gendered and homophobic patterns of TFVA, with young women reporting threats of physical harm at roughly twice the rate of men of the same age, and higher rates of abusive behavior being reported by LGB users (PEW, 2020).

While research relating to individual experiences with TFVA is crucial to understanding its shape and dimensions, it is also critical to recognize the ways in which systemic factors and patterns, such as misogyny, act as underlying societal drivers of violence. New technologies, for example, facilitate creation of networks supporting a collective subculture of male dominance conducive to gender-based violence (Henry & Powell, 2015). This subculture both reflects and amplifies "backlash attitudes" that have surfaced in recent years leaving gender rights advocates, including Human Rights Defenders, increasingly subjected to online and offline violence (Pavone, 2018; UN Women, 2015; UNIESOGI, 2019; Women Against Violence Europe [WAVE], 2017). It is a subculture that espouses binary gender norms and views such as "biological differences between women and men result in specific gender roles" and "women perpetrate domestic violence at the same rate and gravity as men" (FRA, 2017, p. 21).

These are more than isolated or random incidents of cyberbullying. Patriarchal and white supremist ideology has appropriated online, the literature and history of ancient Greece and Rome, along with the artifacts, texts, and historic figures evocative of this era, to promote and lend cultural weight to reactionary visions of ideal white masculinity (Zuckerberg, 2018). These ideologies promote divisive and discriminatory views about gender, and proponents have targeted women and activists advocating online gender equality and gender inclusive policies (Hall & Hearn, 2017; Tomkinson, Attwell, & Harper, 2020; UNIESOGI, 2018; Zuckerberg, 2018). And it is effective – one of the main reasons deterring women from engaging in politics and public life is the level of abuse and violence directed toward them because of their gender and their increased presence (Inter-Parliamentary Union and the Parliamentary Assembly of the Council of Europe, 2018). The extreme forms of online abuse and the invasion of the personal and familial privacy inflicted upon high-profile women not only discourage girls and women from participating in politics but also adversely affect gender representation in democratic institutions (Australian Women Against Violence Alliance [AWAVA], 2018). The ideological nature of the more extremely violent online rhetoric of some groups such as "Incels," has been assessed as "an emerging domestic terrorism threat as current adherents demonstrate marked acts or threats of violence in furtherance of their social grievance" – a threat that "could soon match, or potentially eclipse, the level of lethalness demonstrated by other domestic terrorism types" (Texas Department of Public Safety, 2020, p. 3).

This snapshot of some current research on TFVA (in addition to detailed TFVA findings in this volume) helps to frame TFVA as a phenomenon carried out through a wide variety of technologies and platforms typically provided by Nonstate actors with sometimes serious repercussions for individuals' privacy, safety, physical and emotional well-being, and engagement in both personal and public life. The consequences of TFVA include: physical and mental health issues; chilling of self-expression; restrictions on freedom of movement and association; suicides; inability to work and participate in social, cultural, and political life; damage to reputation and careers; curtailment of education; homelessness; reduced opportunities for creativity and self-expression; and inability to find redress (UN Women, 2020a, b; Al-Alosi, 2017; Australian Institute of Health and Welfare [AIHW], 2019; Bailey, Steeves, & Dunn, 2017; FRA, 2014, 2017; Solove, 2004; UNSRVAW, 2018a, b; UNIESOGI, 2019; UNSRP, 2019; UNSRFOE, 2018; PEW, 2017, 2020).

The cost of violence is known to be high, and highest to the individuals and communities affected, but also to economies and societies. The chilling effect of TFVA produces a loss of confidence of individuals to share ideas and to assemble, undermining societies and democracy (Bailey et al., 2017; Franklin, 2018). And while financial and economic costings specifically for TFVA are unavailable, it has been reported that women experiencing violence earn less than those who had never been abused, and those severely abused earn even less again (World Bank Group, 2014). In Australia, a country of some 25.5 million people, the cost to the economy in 2015–16 was estimated at $AU22 billion (KPMG, 2016).

For all of these reasons, TFVA and all forms of violence must be taken seriously as a human rights concern, one that triggers international obligations relating to both State and Nonstate actors.

TFVA and the International Human Rights Framework: State and Nonstate Actors

The wide variety of forms and effects of TFVA discussed above affect an equally wide variety of internationally protected human rights, including (as depicted in Table 29.1) rights to privacy, freedom of movement, freedom of expression, and freedom of assembly to name a few, as well as rights relating to freedom from violence. Given space constraints, however, the balance of this section focuses on two: the right to privacy and rights relating to freedom from violence (and related protections against discrimination), in relation to both State and Nonstate actors.

Table 29.1. Relating Technology-Facilitated Violence and Abuse Harms to Human Rights Instruments.

Harms Reported	Research	Human Rights Instrument
Reputational damage	PEW (2017)	UDHR Art. 12 (UN General Assembly, 1948); ICCPR Art. 17 (UN General Assembly, 1966) relating to the right to privacy
Avoided certain places Ceased attending certain offline places	FRA (2014) PEW (2017)	UDHR Art. 13 (UN, 1948); ICCPR (UN General Assembly, 1966) Art. 12 relating to the right to freedom of movement
Stopped using an online service Deleted their profile or changed their username Refrained from posting something online	African Development Bank Group, 2016; FRA, 2014; PEW, 2017 PEW (2017) PEW (2017)	UDHR Art. 19 (UN, 1948): ICCPR Art. 19 (UN General Assembly, 1966) relating to the right to freedom of opinion and expression, through any media
Exited the platform Avoided engaging with strangers online	African Development Bank Group, 2016; FRA, 2014; PEW, 2017 African Development Bank Group (2016)	UDHR Art. 20 (UN, 1948); ICCPR Art. 22 (UN General Assembly, 1966); CEDAW Art. 13 (UN General Assembly, 1993) relating to freedom of peaceful assembly and association, and participation in all aspects of cultural life

The Right to Privacy

The groundwork for respect of privacy as a human right tied to the right to free development of personality, and the role privacy plays in allowing the enjoyment of other human rights is laid out in Article 12 of the Universal Declaration on Human Rights (UDHR):

> No one shall be subjected to arbitrary interference with his privacy, family, home or correspondence, nor to attacks upon his honour

> and reputation. Everyone has the right to the protection of the law against such interference or attacks. (UN General Assembly, 1948, Art. 12)

The language of Article 12 creates a broad legal right to privacy and casts that right as an essential element of human dignity, autonomy, and the democratic process:

> [Privacy] is directly tied to our sense of identity and dignity, and it is the umbrella that enables us to enjoy our other human rights. Privacy is by definition a commitment to the human over the technical. (Steeves, 2017)

While not an absolute right, the right to privacy is essential to the free development of an individual's personality. It is a right that derives from and conditions the innate dignity of the person and applies in both public and private spheres. Privacy also protects against violence and discrimination that stunt personal and societal development and is particularly important for those vulnerable due to their gender. In some countries, for example, members of LGBTQI + communities are subject to higher degrees of surveillance, and fake accounts on dating apps and social media platforms have been reported to be used by State and Nonstate actors to lure gay men, expose, entrap, and arrest them or subject them to cruel and degrading treatment or extortion (UNSRP, 2019).

As human rights are inalienable, indivisible, and interrelated, when TFVA violates one right such as privacy, it can undermine other human rights such as freedom of association and expression.

The ultimate objective of human rights is the recognition of the inherent dignity and the equal and inalienable rights of all members of the human family (Santos-Pais, 1999). Every person is entitled to the human rights and freedoms enshrined in international human rights law. But intersectionality and gender for instance, mean for some, the protection of privacy rights is particularly connected to freedom from violence and discrimination, placing a specific onus upon State and Nonstate actors to secure the right to privacy. The lack of action by both has left many with the belief that online gender-based privacy incursions, no matter how abusive or potentially dangerous, are tolerated if not condoned (UNSRP, 2019).

In essence, gender-based privacy infringements are a systemic form of denial of human rights, discriminatory in nature and frequently perpetuating unequal social, economic, cultural, and political structures (UNSRP, 2019). Their discriminatory harms extend beyond individuals to impact society as a whole. As information technologies become an integral part of our lives, the harms arising from technology-facilitated infringements of privacy such as cyberstalking, and technological surveillance and monitoring are not trivial matters for individuals, communities, or society.

Protections Against Violence and Discrimination

Like protections for privacy, protections against violence and discrimination are contained in universally accepted human rights standards, from the UDHR to the almost universally ratified Convention on the Rights of the Child (UN General

Assembly, 1989),[2] as well as in other nonbinding international covenants and agreements that relate to State and Nonstate actors.

The UDHR Article 3 states that "Everyone has the right to life, liberty, and security of person" (UN General Assembly, 1948) and other UN conventions, such as the International Covenant on Civil and Political Rights (ICCPR) (UN General Assembly, 1966), and the International Covenant on Economic, Social, and Cultural Rights (1966), the Convention on the Elimination of all Forms of Racial Discrimination (UN General Assembly, 1965), and the Convention against Torture and other Cruel, Inhuman, or Degrading Treatment or Punishment (UN General Assembly, 1984), also guarantee rights to freedom from violence and discrimination (UN Office of the High Commissioner Human Rights, 2020). These conventions apply universally and are not open to arbitrary interpretation. While predating the digital era, their intent and inherent values remain applicable as confirmed by the UN Human Rights Council and the UN General Assembly affirmations that human rights apply online not just offline (UNGA 2018; UNHRC, 2016).

In addition to legally binding instruments, there are UN human rights declarations relating to gender-based violence, and most explicitly to violence directed toward women, for example, the Declaration on the Elimination of Violence Against Women (UN General Assembly, 1993)[3] and intergovernmental documents, standards, and norms that address violence against women and girls. The 1995 Beijing Declaration and Plan of Action adopted by the Fourth World Conference on Women[4] established strategic objectives in relation to understanding, preventing, and eliminating violence against women.[5] The legally binding framework on women's rights and protections against violence is provided by the Convention on the Elimination of All Forms of Discrimination against Women (CEDAW) (UN General Assembly, 1993)[6] and General Recommendations Nos. 19 and 35, and regional instruments on violence against women. The past 25 years of jurisprudence developed by the CEDAW Committee connects violence against women with discrimination prohibited under Article 1[7] and recognizes intersecting forms of discrimination that increase some women's vulnerability to violence and interfere with their enjoyment of human rights.[8]

The 1993 World Conference on Human Rights recognized violence against women as a human rights violation. A variety of regional instruments reflect this recognition. The regional Inter-American Convention on the Prevention, Punishment, and Eradication of Violence against Women (Belem do Paraá Convention) adopted in 1994 was the world's first binding international treaty to recognize violence against women as a violation of human rights. It has been widely ratified, with only two member states of the Organization of American States (Canada and the United States), not parties. Similarly, the Council of Europe's Istanbul Convention adopted in 2011 and applicable to all victims of domestic violence, including men, children, and the elderly, provides that "violence against women is understood as a violation of human rights and a form of discrimination against women" (Art. 3). The Protocol to the African Charter on Human and Peoples' Rights on the Rights of Women in Africa (Maputo Protocol adopted 2003, in force 2005) (African Union, 2003) also imposes legally binding obligations on ratifying States for combatting violence against women.

Protections Against Violence and Discrimination by Nonstate Actors

Gender-based rights to protection from violence and discrimination also intersect with international obligations relating to business, reflecting the fact that women and girls generally experience adverse impacts of business activities differently and often disproportionately compared to men and boys (UNHRC, 2016). The responsibility for States' regulation of business enterprises' activities entailing violence against women is established under the "due diligence obligation" of States through the Declaration on the Elimination of Violence Against Women (UN General Assembly, 1993) Article 4(c) and CEDAW General Recommendation No. 35. These importantly link human rights obligations to the acts of Non-state actors (UNOHCHR, 2020). The due diligence obligation means States have a duty to take positive action to prevent and protect against violence, including that committed by corporations, and their products and services (UNB-Tech, 2019). The failure of a State to take all appropriate measures to prevent acts of gender-based violence tacitly permits or encourages such acts and constitutes a human rights violation.

The UN Guiding Principles (UNGP) for business-related human rights impacts reinforce States' international human rights obligations to protect against human rights abuse by third parties, including business enterprises (UN Working Group on the Issue of Human Rights and Transnational Corporations and other Business Enterprises, 2019). A central premise of the UNGP is that companies should avoid infringing on the human rights of others and should address adverse human rights impacts with which they are involved (UNB-Tech, 2019). The gender dimension is addressed in Guidance accompanying these "Guiding Principles."

Additionally, two of the UN's 2030 Sustainable Development Goals (SDGs) (UN General Assembly, 2015) are particularly relevant to TFVA. SDG 5 is to "achieve gender equality and empower all women and girls" with SDG5 (b), explicitly positioning technologies to empower women. SDG 16 addresses violence more broadly with SDG 16.1 aiming to "significantly reduce all forms of violence and related deaths everywhere."[9] Regionally, the Istanbul Convention (Art. 17) requires State parties to encourage the private sector, particularly the information technology sector and the media, to address the issue of violence against women (Council of Europe, 2016).[10]

Addressing obligations relating to the private sector is particularly important in the context of gender-based TFVA since, as noted above, TFVA is conducted using digital technologies and platforms predominately supplied by private sector technology companies. As the UN Special Rapporteur on violence against women (2018a) stated:

> … the use of ICTs without the provision of a proper human rights-based protection of women's rights and against gender-based violence of women, could even widen sex and gender-based discrimination and increase violence against women and girls in the whole society. (Thematic report, para 6)

Relevantly to TFVA, the Special Rapporteur noted "most States still fail to recognize violence against women in digital spaces as a 'real' form of violence" (UNSRVAW, 2018a).

TFVA expresses and maintains unequal power relations between perpetrators and victims. It also depends upon the unequal relationship between platform providers and their users which characterizes the business models of the titans of the digital economy. To date, the operations of these companies have been largely unregulated (see Henry & Witt, this volume). Increasingly, however, questions are being raised around the operations of social media giants, particularly the regulation of the content of their sites (UK Parliament, 2019), the commercial surveillance at the heart of their business model (Zuboff, 2019), and the management of personal information (Australian Competition and Consumer Commission [ACCC], 2018, 2019; Norwegian Consumer Council, 2016, 2020). As the analysis of Henry and Witt (this volume) makes evident, relying upon big tech to self-regulate has proven problematic. Regulation will be essential to establishing big tech companies' corporate responsibility to the people and societies from whom they make their vast profits (Rushe, 2020) and to upholding human rights.[11]

In view of the power of digital platforms and the increasing reliance upon them by individuals, economies, and democracies globally, their impact upon fundamental human rights cannot be ignored. There is a critical need for action on human rights compliance by private companies as they develop and deploy digital technologies – a need especially pressing for social media companies (UNDC, 2019). The principle of due diligence requires States to ensure respect for the international rights framework that prohibits gender-based violence (UNSRVAW, 2018b) and protects privacy (Steeves, 2017; UNSRP, 2019, 2020).

Supporting and utilizing the human rights framework is pressing as is embedding digital technologies in commitments to human rights and the rule of law. Technology is constantly evolving, and there is an increasing array of technologies that can be, and are being, used to stalk, intimidate, humiliate, abuse, and violate human rights. Public and international scrutiny of States' and private actors' actions and inaction to prevent violence, including TFVA, is essential.

Conclusion

Violence, whether offline or online, is a destructive attack upon human dignity which effectively deprives individuals of their fundamental human rights, restricts the free development of personality, and perpetuates gender-based inequalities – not just of women and girls but also of gender diverse individuals. Violence and its pernicious effects are matters that States have legal and moral obligations to address, as articulated in numerous international and regional human rights instruments, and as called upon by UN experts such as the Special Rapporteur on violence against women; the Special Rapporteur on the right to privacy and the Independent Expert on sexual orientation and gender identity, among others. The common theme is the urgent need to fully apply human rights standards to gender-based violence whether online or offline.

While the international and regional instruments signed and ratified by Member States of the UN have not eradicated violence, the values, humanity, and principles captured within their Articles provide the foundations for addressing TFVA in all its forms. These instruments also provide a measure against which to assess States' and Nonstate actors' actions and failure to act. These foundations and the benchmark they provide are not to be discounted. TFVA is not a simple issue that can be fixed by a few codes of conduct and some technological solutions. A human rights standpoint enables us to hold States to account for their responses to TFVA, and their acquittal of their due diligence obligations to protect our rights to be free from violence.

Notes

1. All references to "gender" should be read as inclusive of cisnormativity, sexual orientation, gender identity, gender expression, and sex characteristics and the social norms attributed to biological characteristics.
2. The United States has not ratified the Convention on the Rights of the Child.
3. General Assembly resolution 48/104, 20 December 1993. Other examples include General Assembly resolution 65/228 2010 adopting the "Updated Model Strategies and Practical Measures on the Elimination of Violence against Women in the Field of Crime Prevention and Criminal Justice" (UN General Assembly, 2011).
4. Beijing Declaration, adopted at the 16th plenary meeting, on 15 September 1995 (para 14).
5. Beijing Declaration (Annex I) and Platform for Action (Annex II), Chapter IV, Section D. Violence Against Women (paras 112–130, p. 48).
6. Adopted in 1979, instituted in 1981, and adopted by 189 countries.
7. The Convention on the Elimination of All Forms of Discrimination against Women and its Optional Protocol do not explicitly cover violence against women.
8. General Recommendation No. 28, which calls upon states to legally recognize and act upon intersecting forms of discrimination and their compounding negative effect.
9. See https://www.un.org/sustainabledevelopment/development-agenda/for Sustainable Development Goal information.
10. Nonbinding standards give detailed recommendations for putting Article 17 into practice.
11. This responsibility is distinct from issues of legal liability and enforcement defined largely by national law provisions in relevant jurisdictions.

References

Australian Competition and Consumer Commission [ACCC]. (2018). Digital platforms inquiry: Preliminary report. December 2018 [PDF file]. Retrieved from https://www.accc.gov.au/system/files/ACCC%20Digital%20Platforms%20Inquiry%20-%20Preliminary%20Report.pdf

Australian Competition and Consumer Commission [ACCC]. (2019). Digital platforms inquiry: Final report. June 2019 [PDF file]. Retrieved from https://www.accc.gov.au/system/files/Digital%20platforms%20inquiry%20-%20final%20report.pdf

African Development Bank Group. (2016). Minding the gaps: Identifying Strategies to address gender-based cyber violence in Kenya, policy brief [PDF file]. Retrieved from https://www.afdb.org/fileadmin/uploads/afdb/Documents/Generic-Documents/Policy_Brief_on_Gender_Based_Cyber_Violence_in_Kenya.pdf

African Union. (2003). *Protocol to the African charter on human and people's rights on the rights of women in Africa.* Addis Ababa: African Union.

Australian Institute of Health and Welfare [AIHW]. (2019). *Family, domestic and sexual violence in Australia: Continuing the national story.* [PDF file]. Retrieved from https://www.aihw.gov.au/getmedia/b0037b2d-a651-4abf-9f7b-00a85e3de528/aihw-fdv3-FDSV-in-Australia-2019.pdf.aspx?inline=true

Al-Alosi, H. (2017). Cyber-violence: Digital abuse in the context of domestic violence. *University of New South Wales Law Journal, 40*(4), 1573–1603.

Amnesty International. (2018a). Toxic Twitter—a toxic place for women. [PDF file]. Retrieved from https://www.amnesty.org/en/latest/research/2018/03/online-violence-against-women-chapter-1/

Amnesty International. (2018b). Troll patrol findings. Retrieved from https://decoders.amnesty.org/projects/troll-patrol/findings

Article 19. (2018). LGBTQ ONLINE summary report: Apps, arrests and abuse in Egypt, Lebanon and Iran. [PDF file]. Retrieved from https://www.article19.org/wp-content/uploads/2018/02/LGBTQ-Apps-Arrest-and-Abuse-report_22.2.18.pdf

Australian Women Against Violence Alliance [AWAVA]. (2018). Submission on the gender perspectives on privacy. Retrieved from https://awava.org.au/2018/10/02/submissions/submission-on-the-gender-perspectives-on-privacy?doing_wp_cron=1582376179.5971219539642333984375

Bailey, J., & Mathen, C. (2019). Technology-facilitated violence against women & girls: Assessing the Canadian criminal law response.Retrieved from https://commentary.canlii.org/w/canlii/2019CanLIIDocs3806#!fragment/zoupio-_Tocpdf_bk_1/BQCwhgziBcwMYgK4DsDWszIQewE4BUBTADwBdoAvbRABwEtsBaAfX2zhoBMAzZgI1TMAjAEoANMmylCEAIqJCuAJ7QA5KrERCYXAnmKV6zdt0gAynlIAhFQCUAogBl7ANQCCAOQDC9saTB80KTsIiJAA

Bailey, J., Steeves, V., & Dunn, S. (2017). Submission to the special Rapporteur on violence against women Re: Regulating online violence and harassment against women. [PDF file]. Retrieved from http://www.equalityproject.ca/wp-content/uploads/2017/12/Bailey-Steeves-Dunn-Submission-27-Sep-2017.pdf

Bowles, N. (2018). Thermostats, locks and lights: Digital tools of domestic abuse. Retrieved from https://www.nytimes.com/2018/06/23/technology/smart-home-devices-domestic-abuse.html?smid=tw-nytimes&smtyp=cur

Chatterjee, R., Doerfler, P., Orgad, H., Havron, S., Palmer, J., Freed, D., & Ristenpart, T. (2018). The spyware used in intimate partner violence. Retrieved from https://nyuscholars.nyu.edu/en/publications/the-spyware-used-in-intimate-partner-violence

CODING RIGHTS; INTERNETLAB. (2017). *Online gender-based violence: Diagnosis, solutions and challenges.* Retrieved from https://www.internetlab.org.br/en/inequalities-and-identities/organizations-release-report-on-online-gender-based-violence-that-will-assist-discussions-at-the-un/

Council of Europe. (2011) Council of Europe Convention on preventing and combating violence against women and domestic violence (Istanbul Convention).

Council of Europe. (2016). Encouraging the participation of the private sector and the media in the prevention of violence against women: Article 17 of the Istanbul Convention. [PDF file]. Retrieved from https://rm.coe.int/16805970bd

European Institute for Gender Equality [EIGE]. (2020). *Cyber violence against women and girls.* Retrieved from https://eige.europa.eu/thesaurus/terms/1484

European Union Agency for Fundamental Rights [FRA]. (2014). *Violence against women: An EU-wide survey. Results at a glance*. Retrieved from https://fra.europa.eu/en/publication/2014/violence-against-women-eu-wide-survey-results-glance

European Union Agency for Fundamental Rights [FRA]. (2017). Challenges to women's human rights in the EU: Gender discrimination, sexist hate speech and gender-based violence against women and girls. Retrieved from http://fra.europa.eu/en/publication/2017/colloq-womens-rights

Franklin, M. (2018). Internet policy politics—a Q&A with Marianne Franklin. Retrieved from https://policyreview.info/articles/news/internet-policy-politics-qa-marianne-franklin/1349

Hall, M., & Hearn, J. (2017). Revenge pornography and manhood acts: A discourse analysis of perpetrators' accounts December 2017. *Journal of Gender Studies*, *28*(2), 158–170.

Harris, B. (2019). Anti-rape devices may have their uses, but they don't address the ultimate problem. Retrieved from https://theconversation.com/anti-rape-devices-may-have-their-uses-but-they-dont-address-the-ultimate-problem-123011

Henry, N., & Powell, A. (2015). Embodied harms: Gender, shame, and technology-facilitated sexual violence. *Violence Against Women*, *21*(6), 758–779.

International Center for Research on Women [ICRW]. (2018). *Defining and measuring technology-facilitated gender-based violence*. [PDF file]. Retrieved from https://www.icrw.org/wp-content/uploads/2019/03/ICRW_TFGBVMarketing_Brief_v4_WebReady.pdf

Inter-Parliamentary Union and the Parliamentary Assembly of the Council of Europe. (2018). Sexism, harassment and violence against women in parliaments in Europe. Retrieved from https://www.ipu.org/resources/publications/issue-briefs/2018-10/sexism-harassment-and-violence-against-women-in-parliaments-in-europe

KPMG. (2016). The cost of violence against women and their children in Australia. [PDF file]. Retrieved from https://www.dss.gov.au/sites/default/files/documents/08_2016/the_cost_of_violence_against_women_and_their_children_in_australia_-_summary_report_may_2016.pdf

Krug, E. G., Dahlberg, J. A., Mercy, J. A., Zwi, A. B., & Lozano, R. (2002). World report on violence and health. [PDF file]. Retrieved from https://apps.who.int/iris/bitstream/handle/10665/42495/9241545615_eng.pdf;jsessionid=66F745B1B8A51446CCF483F0010AEAE7?sequence=1

Norwegian Consumer Council. (2016). Appfail report—threats to consumers in mobile apps. Retrieved from https://www.forbrukerradet.no/undersokelse/2015/appfail-threats-to-consumers-in-mobile-apps/

Norwegian Consumer Council. (2020). *Out of control: How consumers are exploited by the online advertising industry*. Retrieved from https://www.forbrukerradet.no/out-of-control/

Organization of American States. (1994). *Inter-American convention on the prevention, punishment and eradication of violence against women ("Convention of Belem do Para")*. Washington, DC: Organization of American States.

Parsons, C., Molnar, A., Dalek, J., Knockel, J., Kenyon, M., Haselton, B., & Deibert, R. (2019). The predator in your pocket A multidisciplinary assessment of the stalkerware application industry, citizenlab. Retrieved from https://citizenlab.ca/2019/06/the-predator-in-your-pocket-a-multidisciplinary-assessment-of-the-stalkerware-application-industry/

Pavone, G. (2018). In parliaments across Europe women face alarming levels of sexism, harassment and violence. Retrieved from https://www.europeandatajournalism.eu/eng/News/Data-news/In-parliaments-across-Europe-women-face-alarming-levels-of-sexism-harassment-and-violence

PEW Research Center. (2017). *Online harassment 2017*. Retrieved from https://www.pewresearch.org/internet/2017/07/11/online-harassment-2017/

PEW Research Center. (2020). *The virtues and downsides of online dating*. February 6th. Retrieved from https://www.pewresearch.org/internet/2020/02/06/the-virtues-and-downsides-of-online-dating/

Privacy International. (2017). *Social media intelligence*. Retrieved from https://privacyinternational.org/explainer/55/social-media-intelligence

Radhakrishnan, R. (2018). Are smart-device based virtual assistants capable of assisting with gender based violence concerns in India?. [PDF file]. Retrieved from https://itforchange.net/e-vaw/wp-content/uploads/2018/01/Are-Smart-Device-Based-Virtual-Assistants-Capable-of-Assisting-with-Gender-Based-Violence-Concerns-in-India-1.pdf

Rushe, D. (2020). $15bn a year: YouTube reveals its ad revenues for the first time. Retrieved from https://www.theguardian.com/technology/2020/feb/03/youtube-ad-revenue-google-alphabet-shares

Santos-Pais, M. (1999). *A human rights conceptual framework for UNICEF*. Retrieved from https://www.unicef-irc.org/publications/2-a-human-rights-conceptual-framework-for-unicef.html

Solove, D. J. (2004). *The digital person, technology and privacy in the digital age*. (GWU Law School Public Law Research Paper 2017-5). Retrieved from https://scholarship.law.gwu.edu/cgi/viewcontent.cgi?article=2501&context=faculty_publications

Steeves, V. (2017). Foreword to EDPL, the future of privacy. *European Data Protection Law Review*, *3*(4), 438–440.

Texas Department of Public Safety. (2020). *Texas domestic terrorism threat assessment*. [PDF file]. Retrieved from https://www.dps.texas.gov/director_staff/media_and_communications/2020/txTerrorThreatAssessment.pdf

Tomkinson, S., Attwell, K., & Harper, T. (2020). 'Incel' Violence is a form of extremism. It's time we treated it as a security threat. Retrieved from https://theconversation.com/incel-violence-is-a-form-of-extremism-its-time-we-treated-it-as-a-security-threat-138536

UCL IoT. (2019). Written submission to the online harms white paper consultation. [PDF file]. Retrieved from https://www.ucl.ac.uk/steapp/sites/steapp/files/online_harms_white_paper_consultation_response_giot_june_2019_final.pdf

UK Parliament. (2019). Disinformation and 'fake news': Final report published. Retrieved from https://www.parliament.uk/business/committees/committees-a-z/commons-select/digital-culture-media-and-sport-committee/news/fake-news-report-published-17-19/

UN General Assembly. (1948). *Universal declaration of human rights (217 [III] A)*. Paris.

UN General Assembly. (1965). *International convention on the elimination of all forms of racial discrimination*. United Nations, Treaty Series, Vol. 660, p. 195.

UN General Assembly. (1966). *International covenant on Civil and political rights*. United Nations, Treaty Series, Vol. 999, p. 171.

UN General Assembly. (1984). *Convention against torture and other cruel, inhuman or degrading treatment or punishment*. United Nations, Treaty Series, Vol. 1465, p. 85.

UN General Assembly. (1989). *Convention on the rights of the child.* United Nations, Treaty Series, Vol. 1577, p. 3.

UN General Assembly. (1993). *Declaration on the elimination of violence against women, A/RES/48/104.*

UN General Assembly. (2011). Resolution adopted by the general assembly at its sixty-fifth session. Strengthening crime prevention and criminal justice responses to violence against women. Updated model strategies and practical measures on the elimination of violence against women in the field of crime prevention and criminal justice. 31 March 2011, A/RES/65/228.

UN General Assembly. (2015). *Transforming our world: The 2030 Agenda for sustainable development, A/RES/70/1.* Retrieved from https://www.un.org/sustainabledevelopment/development-agenda/

UN Office of the High Commissioner Human Rights. (2020). *International standards and regional instruments.* Retrieved from https://www.ohchr.org/EN/Issues/Women/SRWomen/Pages/InternationalStandards.aspx

UN Women. (2015). The Beijing declaration and platform for action turns 20. [PDF file]. Retrieved from https://sustainabledevelopment.un.org/content/documents/1776The%20Beijing%20Declaration%20and%20Platform%20for%20Action%20turns%2020.pdf

UN Women. (2020a). Ending violence against women. Retrieved from https://www.unwomen.org/en/what-we-do/ending-violence-against-women

UN Women. (2020b). *Creating safe public spaces.* Retrieved from https://www.unwomen.org/en/what-we-do/ending-violence-against-women/creating-safe-public-spaces

UN Working Group on the Issue of Human Rights and Transnational Corporations and other Business Enterprises. (2019). Report to Human Rights Council. [PDF file]. Retrieved from https://documents-dds-ny.un.org/doc/UNDOC/GEN/G19/146/08/PDF/G1914608.pdf?OpenElement

UNB-Tech, United Nations Human Rights Business and Human Rights in Technology Project (2019). Applying the UN Guiding Principles on business and human rights to digital technologies. [PDF file]. Retrieved from https://www.ohchr.org/Documents/Issues/Business/B-Tech/B_%20Tech_Project_revised_scoping_final.pdf

UN Digital Co-operation [UNDC]. (2019). The age of digital interdependence. Report of the UN secretary-general's high-level panel on digital cooperation. [PDF file]. Retrieved from https://www.un.org/en/pdfs/DigitalCooperation-report-for%20web.pdf

United Nations General Assembly [UNGA]. (2018). Resolution adopted December 2018, 'the right to privacy in the digital age', A/RES/73/179. Retrieved from https://undocs.org/en/A/RES/73/179

United Nations Human Rights Council [UNHRC]. (2016). *The promotion, protection and enjoyment of human rights on the internet.* Retrieved from https://www.ohchr.org/EN/HRBodies/HRC/RegularSessions/Session32/Pages/ResDecStat.aspx

UNIESOGI, United Nations Independent Expert on protection against violence and discrimination based on sexual orientation and gender identity. (2018). Report to the Human Rights Council. Retrieved from https://documents-dds-ny.un.org/doc/UNDOC/GEN/G18/132/12/PDF/G1813212.pdf?OpenElement

UNIESOGI, United Nations Independent Expert on protection against violence and discrimination based on sexual orientation and gender identity. (2019). Report to General Assembly, A/74/181. Retrieved from https://undocs.org/A/74/181

United Nations. (1948). *Universal declaration of human rights.* (217 [III] A) [PDF file]. Retrieved from https://www.ohchr.org/EN/UDHR/Documents/UDHR_Translations/eng.pdf

UNOHCHR, Office of the High Commissioner for Human Rights. (2020). *Violence against women.* Retrieved from https://www.ohchr.org/EN/Issues/Women/WRGS/Pages/VAW.aspx

UNSRFOE, United Nations Special Rapporteur on the promotion and protection of the right to freedom of opinion and expression. (2018). Retrieved from https://documents-dds-ny.un.org/doc/UNDOC/GEN/G18/096/72/PDF/G1809672.pdf?OpenElement

UNSRP, United Nations Special Rapporteur on the right to privacy. (2019). *Annex 2: The human right to privacy: A gender perspective.* [PDF file]. Retrieved from https://www.ohchr.org/Documents/Issues/Privacy/SR_Privacy/2019_HRC_Annex2_GenderReport.pdf

UNSRP, United Nations Special Rapporteur on the right to privacy. (2020). Report to the Human Rights Council. Retrieved from https://www.ohchr.org/EN/Issues/Privacy/SR/Pages/AnnualReports.aspx

UNSRVAW, United Nations Special Rapporteur on violence against women its causes and consequences. (2018a). *Statement to Human Rights Council.* Retrieved from https://www.ohchr.org/en/NewsEvents/Pages/DisplayNews.aspx?NewsID=23235&LangID=E

UNSRVAW, United Nations Special Rapporteur on violence against women its causes and consequences. (2018b). Report to the Human Rights Council, A/HRC/38/47. Retrieved from https://digitallibrary.un.org/record/1641160?ln=en

Valente, M. (2018). Do we need new laws to address non-consensual circulation of intimate images: The case of Brazil. Retrieved from https://www.genderit.org/articles/do-we-need-new-laws-address-non-consensual-circulation-intimate-images-case-brazil

Varon, J. (2017). Chupadados: The data sucker—the hidden faces of our beloved technologies. Retrieved from https://www.codingrights.org/3-2/

Women Against Violence Europe [WAVE]. (2017). Country report 2017. [PDF file]. Retrieved from http://fileserver.wave-network.org/researchreports/WAVE_CR_2017.pdf

West Coast LEAF. (2014). #Cybermisogyny using and strengthening Canadian legal responses to gendered hate and harassment. Online [PDF file]. Retrieved from http://www.westcoastleaf.org/wp-content/uploads/2014/10/2014-REPORT-CyberMisogyny.pdf.s

WHO, World Health Organisation. (2017). *Violence against women key facts.* Retrieved from https://www.who.int/news-room/fact-sheets/detail/violence-against-women

World Bank Group. (2014). Voice and agency empowering women and girls for shared prosperity. [PDF file]. Retrieved from https://www.worldbank.org/content/dam/Worldbank/document/Gender/Voice_and_agency_LOWRES.pdf

Zuboff, S. (2019). *The age of surveillance capitalism: The fight for a human future at the new frontier of power.* New York, NY: Public Affairs.

Zuckerberg, D. (2018). *Not all dead white men. Classics and misogyny in the digital age.* Boston, MA: Harvard University Press.

Chapter 30

Combating Cyber Violence Against Women and Girls: An Overview of the Legislative and Policy Reforms in the Arab Region*

Sukaina Al-Nasrawi

Abstract

Violence against women and girls is globally prevalent. Overcoming it is a prerequisite for attaining gender equality and achieving sustainable development. The United Nation's 2030 Agenda for Sustainable Development considers technology as a means to combat violence against women and girls, and there is ample evidence on the positive impact of technology in combating violence. At the same time, however, technology can promote and perpetrate new forms of violence. Research shows that more than 70% of women and girls online are exposed to forms of cyber violence. Most of these cases remain unreported.

This chapter argues that technology contributes to increasing cyber violence against women and girls which in turn leads to severe social and economic implications affecting them. It also argues that legislative and policy reforms can limit this type of violence while enabling women and girls to leverage technology for empowerment. It highlights cases of cyber violence in the Arab region and provides an overview of applicable legislative frameworks. The chapter concludes with recommended policy reforms and measures to strengthen and harmonize efforts to combat cyber violence against women and girls in the Arab region.

*This chapter presents the opinion of the author solely. The United Nations Economic and Social Commission for Western Asia (UN ESCWA) does not represent or endorse any advice, opinion, statement, or information provided.

The Emerald International Handbook of Technology-Facilitated Violence and Abuse, 493–512

doi:10.1108/978-1-83982-848-520211037

Keywords: Violence against women and girls; cyberviolence; sustainable development; Arab region; legislation; policy reform; technology

Introduction

Combating violence against women and girls (VAWG) is a prerequisite for achieving gender equality, which is pivotal for sustainable development. VAWG can be physical, sexual, emotional, and/or economic and can happen everywhere – peaceful countries, countries in conflict, physical spaces, and digital contexts (UN Women, 2020a). Violence constitutes one of the main barriers for women and girls affecting their ability to enjoy fundamental rights and freedoms (United Nations-GA, 2019). Countries need to take appropriate measures to combat this by enacting dedicated laws, policies, strategies, and programs.

Research indicates that technology is used to facilitate violence, abuse, and harassment against women and girls. One in three women worldwide face violence and more than 70% of women online have been exposed to some form of cyber violence (Cyber VAWG) (UN-BC-DDWGBG, 2015). Groups of women, including human rights defenders, women in politics, journalists, bloggers, and women with disabilities, are particularly targeted by technology-facilitated violence (OHCHR, 2018). In times of COVID-19, even more women and girls have been subjected to online violence in the form of physical threats, sexual harassment, stalking, "zoom bombing," and trolling (UN Women, 2020b).

International human rights frameworks on VAWG recognize that technology is not only being used to perpetrate violence but is also a key tool for combating forms of VAWG. Arab countries have committed to these frameworks in some way. This chapter aims to show that while technology plays a critical role in achieving gender equality and sustainable development, it fosters existing forms of violence and creates new ones. This chapter also highlights the need for legislative and policy reforms addressing VAWG in both physical and virtual spaces and suggests ways forward to ensure that strategies in the Arab region for addressing VAWG generally and technology-facilitated VAWG specifically keep pace with international legal frameworks that combat VAWG and technology-facilitated abuse.

The first section of the chapter explores the diverse ways in which technology is used to facilitate VAWG, including during the COVID-19 pandemic period. The second section considers possible means to transform these negatives into methods for combatting VAWG. The third section overviews the international frameworks on VAWG and those related to technology-facilitated abuse and highlights the gaps that exist in legal frameworks addressing VAWG and cybercrime in the Arab region. The chapter concludes with recommendations for governments and relevant stakeholders on how to address negatives of technology to further VAWG and turn it into a positive means to combat the pandemic of violence.

Technology as a Tool to Perpetrate Violence Against Women and Girls in the Arab Region

Sexual violence and domestic violence are two of the most common forms of VAWG (Eltigani, 2019). According to the World Health Organization, one in every three women worldwide has experienced physical and/or sexual violence by a male partner (WHO, 2013). Also, about 7% of women aged 15 and older have experienced sexual violence by a non-partner, with wide variations by region (García-Moreno et al., 2013). In the East Mediterranean region, which encompasses most of the Arab states, the percentage of ever-partnered women facing physical or sexual violence reached around 37% in 2017 (UN ESCWA, 2017). Sexual harassment is also a widespread issue in the Arab region as evidenced by the 2018/2019 survey conducted by the Arab Barometer (Bouhlila, 2019). The survey indicated that sexual harassment was most common in Egypt (44%) and Sudan (38%) and less reported in Libya (20%) and Tunisia (15%) (Bouhlila, 2019, p. 4).

Technology-facilitated violence is common, and cyber VAWG can take many forms, including hate speech, hacking, identity theft, online stalking, trafficking, and sex trade (UN-BC-DDWGBG, 2015). The United Nations (UN) report "Cyber Violence Against Women and Girls: A Worldwide Wake-Up Call" called for a global wake-up to combat cyber violence, including cyber VAWG, and labeled it as a systemic concern given the global spread of technology, including in the Arab region. The report notes that globally 73% of women have endured cyber violence, and that women are 27 times more likely than men to be harassed online (UN-BC-DDWGBG, 2015).

Many cases of cyber VAWG were recently under the spotlight in the Arab region, but the scarcity of data makes it difficult to understand the nuances of this phenomenon. More than half of young people surveyed in Jordan were bullied online at least once (UNICEF, 2020). As well, the Arab Center for the Development of Social Media and the Swedish "Kvinna till Kvinna Foundation" studied gender-based violence in Palestinian communities through social networks and the internet. The results were based on quantitative and qualitative data. A total of six focus groups were held in the Gaza Strip, the West Bank, Jerusalem, Haifa, and the Galilee. Additionally, a face-to-face poll included more than 1,200 Palestinian women between the ages of 15 and 35 throughout historic Palestine. One of the main outcomes of this research was that a third of young Palestinian women experienced online sexual harassment (Odeh, 2018).

In Morocco, data were collected via the second National Survey on the prevalence of violence against women in the 12 regions of the Kingdom. 13,543 women aged 18–64 out of an estimated total of 10,937,433 adult females in Morocco were surveyed between January 2 and March 10, 2019. The results of the National Survey showed that violence against women stood at 54% in 2018, and more than 13% of the women surveyed had experienced online abuse. Of these, 30% were aged 18–25 years, and 46% held advanced university degrees (MFSESD, 2019).

In Egypt, females were highly exposed to cyber violence, with a recent study showing 41.6% of the 356 female participants experienced cyber violence during 2019 (Hassan, Khalifa, Desouky, Salem, & Ali, 2020). Up to 45.3% of respondents reported multiple instances of exposure to online violence. In 92.6% of cases, the offender was unknown to survivors. The study results indicated the most common forms of violence as follows: 41.2% had received images or symbols with sexual content; 26.4% had received insulting emails or messages; 25.7% had received offensive or humiliating posts or comments; 21.6% had received indecent or violent images that humiliated women; and 20.3% had received infected files through emails. Most of the victims (76.9%) experienced psychological effects in the form of anger, worry, and fear. Blocking the offender was the most common response. Furthermore, none of the cases surveyed were reported to the police (Hassan et al., 2020, p. 2), which could be for numerous reasons (Gracia, 2004); for example, victims may fear damage to their reputation through police reporting and publicization or lack awareness of laws condemning cyber violence (Lewis, Rowe, & Wiper, 2017), which are discussed further below.

The status of cyber violence worsened during COVID-19, the first major pandemic of the social-media age (Vox, 2020). Despite the existing digital gender divide which is at its highest in the Arab region, women and girls started using the internet more frequently during the global pandemic (ITU, 2020). During lockdown, quarantine measures and self-isolation policies led to an increased use of the internet. Women, men, girls, and boys turned to the internet for work, school, and social activities (UN Women, 2020b). This increase was tightly coupled with an increase in cyber violence, particularly for users with limited digital skills (UNODC, 2020). Given that the Arab region has the highest digital gender divide (ITU, 2020), Arab women and girls are at a higher risk for these forms of violence.

Technology as a Tool to Combat Violence Against Women and Girls in the Arab Region

Technology has a dual effect when it comes to combatting VAWG and achieving gender equality. On one hand, as the data discussed above indicate, it can propagate existing forms of VAWG and even create new ones. On the other hand, if properly used, technology becomes core to achieving gender equality. The examples below, though not exclusive, show the role that technology can play in breaking the cycle of VAWG.

There is a growing number of technological interventions used in the Arab region for combating VAWG. In some instances, technology is used to raise awareness of harassment in public spaces, map safe areas, advocate for safe services, report unsafe areas, and track women and girls to take action when needed (Al-Nasrawi, 2019). In Egypt, for instance, a real time violence mapping tool called HarassMap (HarassMap, 2020) receives reports of sexual harassment through SMS messages. These reports are uploaded in real time to an online map which monitors where sexual harassment is happening in Cairo through hotspots.

These hotspots indicate to women and girls areas to avoid in order to ensure their safety. This use of technology is timely as a high percentage of women have been exposed to sexual harassment in the country. In 2013, according to research undertaken by UN Women (2013), 99% of Egyptian girls and women surveyed reported experiencing some form of sexual harassment in their lifetime (UN Women, 2013). Today, sexual harassment is still considered a major problem in Egypt (Promundo & UN Women, 2017).

Another example from Egypt is "StreetPal" (StreetPal, 2018), an application for women and girls to raise awareness about sexual harassment. The application empowers women and girls to take a stand against harassment and provides them with an array of options, such as sending a short text or email to a trusted person to report harassment or safety issues. The application also includes a map that could be used by women and girls to reach the nearest police station or hospital in case medical care is required. Moreover, the application can make audio recordings to be used as evidence if needed. It also provides psychological support and a library of information about sexual harassment.

In Morocco, technology is used to address sexual violence and harassment of women in public spaces through the "Finemchi" application (Finemchi, 2020). This application proposes safe places for women and girls to visit based on reviews and ratings provided by users on how female-friendly the places are. The technology helps women and girls avoid places where harassment might happen and make safe decisions related to their movements. It also encourages owners of businesses or identified hot spots to take necessary measures to enhance their safety rating.

Another example is "Securella" (Richter, 2018), a mobile application also developed in Morocco. Securella alerts women about unsecure or dangerous streets. The application exposes users to a network of participating restaurants and shops, so they can call for help with a wearable device and be located through a Global Positioning System. These places are labeled as "Securella places" (Vodafone, 2017). The application enables users to trigger an "alarm" when they feel at risk. Users can benefit from the application not only by triggering the safety alarm but also by being connected to agents for immediate intervention if in danger. Agents could be police, friends, or even members of the Securella places network. It is important to note that technology-enabled initiatives that involve tracking also create their own privacy and surveillance problems for women and girls should the devices or collected data fall into the wrong hands.

In Tunisia, "SafeNes" (WomenYSK, 2018) is a mobile application aimed at raising awareness for VAWG and connecting survivors with specialized non-governmental organizations. It provides a means to pinpoint VAWG and identify a person that users entrust to track their movements when they are in a place that makes them feel anxious or unsafe. The application also provides users with self-defense tutorial videos and information about legal procedures following a sexual harassment report.

To benefit from technology-enabled initiatives, women and girls need to be connected. In the Arab region, 36.9% females compared to 46.2% males currently have access to and use the internet (Badran, 2017). If this digital gender gap persists, women and girls will not only be prevented from benefiting from technology-enabled anti-violence initiatives, they will also be at a serious disadvantage in acquiring digital skills and literacy, learning about and exercising their rights, and accessing economic opportunities that could lead to bridging the gender gap and fostering the achievement of gender equality in the Arab region. Being connected is a must for women's empowerment, especially in our current knowledge society. However, being connected is tightly related to a bundle of challenges. Telephones, computers, and the internet can be used to harm women and girls, and these harmful actions can push women and girls to step back from technology completely, further contributing to gender inequality in the region.

International Frameworks and National Legal and Policy Reforms for Addressing Offline and Online Violence Against Women and Girls

The false dichotomy between VAWG (offline) and cyber VAWG (online) underestimates the harms of cyber VAWG and characterizes victims' experiences as incidents rather than repeated behavioral patterns. Research indicates that the perpetrator of offline VAWG often repeats the acts online with the same victims (EIGE, 2017). Therefore, a mutually reinforcing relationship between combating offline and online VAWG exists. Accordingly, general laws against VAWG may also be of assistance in combatting technology-facilitated VAWG. One of the main entry points to combating the pandemic of offline and technology-facilitated VAWG is through top-down changes introduced by governments and political leaders enacting the appropriate legislative and policy reforms. This section reviews the progress and challenges of gender justice and equality before the law, both in relation to VAWG and to women's and girls' access to and use of technology. It will first provide an overview of the relevant international human rights frameworks, and second, it will overview the status of national legislative and policy reforms in the Arab region focused on domestic violence, sexual harassment, and cybercrime.

International Frameworks

In 1979, the UN General Assembly adopted the Convention on the Elimination of All Forms of Discrimination against Women (CEDAW), which entered into force as an international treaty in 1981 (OHCHR, n.d.). In 1992, the CEDAW's general recommendation 19 (Article 1) noted that discrimination includes VAWG, which made preventing and addressing VAWG an obligation for ratifying states. In 2017, that general recommendation was updated by general recommendation 35, which established the prohibition of VAWG as a norm for international law. Moreover, in 1995, the Fourth World Conference on Women witnessed the adoption of the Beijing Declaration and Platform for Action, which addressed, through paragraph 113, VAWG and its different forms and proposed actions for governments to consider.

In 2015, countries around the world, including all Arab countries, adopted the 2030 Agenda for Sustainable Development (2030 Agenda) which recognized the impact of VAWG on the well-being of women and girls through its various Sustainable Development Goals. Specifically, this was addressed through Goal 5 on gender equality, Goal 16 on peaceful and inclusive societies, and Goal 11 on sustainable cities and communities. In addition, the UN General Assembly gave sexual harassment special attention by issuing the first resolution on the issue, numbered 73/148, adopted in January 2019 (United Nations-GA, 2019). This resolution called for increasing the focus on preventing and eliminating all forms of VAWG, including sexual harassment, as a barrier to gender equality, the empowerment of all women and girls, and the full realization of their human rights globally and in the Arab region.

Access to technology has become a necessity for the economic well-being of all people and is increasingly regarded as a fundamental human right (EIGE, 2017). The role of technology in achieving gender equality has been highlighted in international forums and global development agendas for decades. The Fourth World Conference on Women in Beijing in 1995 was the first to recognize the critical impact of Information and Communication Technologies (ICTs) on achieving women's empowerment and gender equality. Also, in 2003, ICTs were regarded as offering opportunities for the full engagement of women in society by the World Summit on the Information Society (WSIS). This was reiterated in 2005 and in WSIS+10 in 2015. At the level of the UN Commission on the Status of Women, the role of ICTs was clearly stated in its 55th and 57th sessions. ICTs' positive role has gained increasing consideration and was more recently highlighted in the 2030 Agenda as a means of implementing Goal 5 on gender equality, including two targets specifically focused on VAWG and on sexual harassment of women and girls in public spaces.

In 2018, the UN Special Rapporteur on Violence against Women (VAW) further extended the concept of the intersections of violence and highlighted online violence and its different forms from a human rights perspective. For instance, there are many shared risk factors between VAW and Violence against Children (VAC). Child abuse and VAW often occur in parallel in the same household, both types of violence are often supported by social norms, and seeking help is often discouraged (Guedes, Garcia-Moreno, & Colombini, 2016). The Special Rapporteur noted the intersectional nature of health, economic, and criminal justice service costs (UN ESCWA, 2019), as well as the worsening of VAWG in full or in part because of the use of ICTs such as phones, internet, social media platforms, email, and other means. The Special Rapporteur noted that although technology is internationally recognized to achieve gender equality and sustainable development, it must be used with care (OHCHR, 2018). The positive impact of technology should be harnessed to combat VAWG, but its exacerbating impact on violence and the potential creation of new forms of violence should be addressed in parallel.

National Legislative and Policy Reforms

Despite these international frameworks and efforts that countries are exerting to combat VAWG (formulating sound policies, enacting and enforcing legislation and reforms, enhancing services, and encouraging technology-enabled initiatives), more needs to be done. Overcoming VAWG in physical and digital contexts, as well as ensuring women's and girls' access to technology, are prerequisites for attaining gender equality and achieving sustainable development. The discussion below demonstrates some of the related gaps in national laws in the Arab region.

Tables 30.1 and 30.2 include data reported for 82% of the countries in the Arab region (18 out of 22 countries). The missing countries are Comoros, Kuwait, Mauritania, and the United Arab Emirates. Whether a country has a law or not for a specific reported category of VAWG is indicated by "Yes," "No," and "Partly." "Yes" indicates that the country has a law which calls for gender equality and/or protection from gender-based violence and is substantially compliant with international standards; "No" indicates that the law does not focus on gender equality and/or there is no or minimal protection from gender-based violence; "Partly" denotes that some gender justice aspects of the law have been addressed, but important gender inequalities remain. General laws against VAWG may also be beneficial in combating technology-facilitated VAWG in these areas because existing laws may also be applied to technology-facilitated instances and because technology-facilitated instances of VAWG are often connected with physical in-person VAWG.

Domestic Violence Laws

Six Arab countries out of 18 (33%) have enacted laws specifically addressing domestic violence: Bahrain, Jordan, Lebanon, Morocco, Saudi Arabia, and Tunisia. Algeria and Iraq have partial laws. In Algeria, domestic violence was criminalized by Law No. 15–19 of December 30, 2015 amending the Penal Code, but there is no law on domestic violence prevention measures, such as protection orders. In Iraq, there is no federal domestic violence law, but the Iraqi Kurdistan region is protected by their local law to combat domestic violence. Table 30.1 overviews the status of laws of domestic violence in the Arab region by country.

Sexual Harassment Laws

Nine countries out of 18 (50%) have enacted laws addressing sexual harassment: Algeria, Egypt, Iraq, Morocco, Qatar, Saudi Arabia, Somalia, Sudan, and Tunisia. The remaining countries have partial laws to address the issue. For instance, Bahrain does not have a sexual harassment law, but has other instruments that penalize sexual offenses in the workplace context and has criminalized acts of immorality and assault in their Penal Code. In Oman, there is no specific sexual harassment law, but VAWG, which falls under this category, is criminalized under Article 266 of the Penal Code. The same applies to Palestine, which criminalizes unwanted sexual conduct including sexual harassment through Article 305 of the Penal Code. Table 30.2 describes the status of sexual harassment laws in the Arab region by country.

Table 30.1. The Status of Domestic Violence Laws in the Arab Region.

	Existence of Domestic Violence Law	Detailed Description
Algeria	**Partly**	Domestic violence was criminalized by Law No. 15–19 of December 30, 2015 amending the Penal Code. Penalties for some Penal Code offenses involving spouses were increased. However, there is no law on domestic violence prevention measures, such as protection orders.
Bahrain	**Yes**	Women and girls are protected by the Law on Protection against Domestic Violence, Law No. 17 of 2015. The Law does not specifically include marital rape.
Djibouti	**No**	Djibouti has no domestic violence legislation.
Egypt	**No**	There is no law on domestic violence. Some domestic violence offenses may be punishable under the Penal Code and Law No. 6 of 1998, but only if the act exceeds the accepted limits of discipline decided by the judge and if the injuries are apparent when filing the complaint at the police station.
Iraq	**Partly**	Women and girls in Iraqi Kurdistan Region (IKR) are protected by the Law to Combat Domestic Violence in IKR, Law No. 8 of 2011. There is no federal domestic violence law. Article 41 of the Iraqi Penal Code of 1969 states that the punishment of a wife by her husband is the exercise of a legal right.
Jordan	**Yes**	Women and girls are protected by the Law on Protection from Domestic Violence, No. 15 of 2017. The law does not provide a definition of domestic violence crimes.
Lebanon	**Yes**	Women and girls are protected by the Law on Protection of Women and other Family Members from Domestic Violence, Law No. 293 of 2014. The

Table 30.1. *(Continued)*

	Existence of Domestic Violence Law	Detailed Description
		Law does not include marital rape. A Bill that proposes amendments to improve the Law has been drafted but is yet to be considered by Parliament.
Libya	**No**	Libya has no domestic violence legislation.
Morocco	**Yes**	Women and girls are protected by the Law on Combating all Forms of Violence against Women, Law No. 103–13. However, it does not include marital rape or provide a definition of domestic violence.
Oman	**No**	Oman has no domestic violence legislation.
Palestine	**No**	Palestine has no domestic violence legislation.
Qatar	**No**	Qatar has no domestic violence legislation.
Saudi Arabia	**Yes**	Women and girls are protected by the Law on Protection from Abuse 2013. It creates criminal penalties for acts of domestic violence and establishes a process for people to lodge complaints and receive protection. The law does not include marital rape.
Somalia	**No**	Somalia has no domestic violence legislation.
Sudan	**No**	Sudan has no domestic violence legislation.
Syria	**No**	Syria has no domestic violence legislation.
Tunisia	**Yes**	Women and girls are protected by the Law on Eliminating Violence against Women, No. 58 of 2017.
Yemen	**No**	Yemen has no domestic violence legislation.

Source: Compiled from the Country Profiles on "Gender Justice and Equality before the Law" developed by UN ESCWA, UN Women, UNFPA and UNDP, 2019.

Table 30.2. The Status of Sexual Harassment Laws in the Arab Region.

	Existence of Sexual Harassment Law	Detailed Description
Algeria	**Yes**	Sexual harassment is criminalized by Articles 333 bis and 341 bis of the Penal Code.
Bahrain	**Partly**	Although there is no sexual harassment offense in the Labor Law No. 36 of 2012, workplace sexual harassment of government employees is penalized by the Civil Service Law. The Penal Code also criminalizes acts of immorality and assault (Articles 344 and beyond of the Penal Code).
Djibouti	**Partly**	Penal Code offenses may cover some forms of sexual harassment. Articles 430–431 of the Penal Code criminalize public insult with penalties of six months' imprisonment and a fine.
Egypt	**Yes**	Law No. 50 of 2014 amended the Penal Code (Articles 306 bis(a) and 306 bis(b)) to introduce penalties for sexual harassment, including imprisonment.
Iraq	**Yes**	Sexual harassment in the workplace is prohibited by the Labor Law. Some forms of sexual harassment are prohibited by Articles 400 and 402 of the Penal Code. These offenses include committing an immodest act, making indecent advances, or assaulting a woman in a public place in an immodest manner.
Jordan	**Partly**	Sexual harassment can be punished as the offense of unwanted sexual contact under Articles 305 and 306 of the Penal Code. However, the scope of the law is unclear and online harassment is not addressed. Penalties are increased if the perpetrator is an employer or supervisor.

Table 30.2. *(Continued)*

	Existence of Sexual Harassment Law	Detailed Description
Lebanon	**Partly**	The Labor Code does not prohibit workplace sexual harassment. The Penal Code includes the punishment of some indecent acts to which the description of sexual harassment may apply, including Articles 385, 507, 519, and 532.
Libya	**Partly**	Article 12 of the Labor Relations Law prohibits employees from performing or inciting acts of sexual harassment. Articles 368–398 of the Penal Code criminalize physical and sexual assaults in public.
Morocco	**Yes**	Article 503 of the Penal Code criminalizes sexual harassment.
Oman	**Partly**	Although there is no specific sexual harassment offense, indecent acts or gestures against women and girls are criminalized by Article 266 of the Penal Code.
Palestine	**Partly**	Sexual harassment is not criminalized by the Labor Code. Article 305 of the Penal Code criminalizes unwanted sexual conduct, which covers some types of sexual harassment.
Qatar	**Yes**	Offensive remarks, sounds, or gestures against women and girls are criminalized by Article 291 of the Penal Code.
Saudi Arabia	**Yes**	Sexual harassment was criminalized in 2018. The law defines "harassment" as any word, act, or sign with a sexual connotation by a person to any other person that harms their body or modesty by any means, including through modern technology.

Table 30.2. *(Continued)*

	Existence of Sexual Harassment Law	Detailed Description
Somalia	**Yes**	Article 24 of the Provisional Constitution prohibits sexual abuse in the workplace. The Puntland Sexual Offences Act 2016 prohibits sexual harassment.
Sudan	**Yes**	Article 151 of the Criminal Act was amended in 2015 to criminalize acts of sexual harassment.
Syria	**Partly**	There is no specific sexual harassment offense in the Penal Code or Labor Law. However, according to the Penal Code, criminal conduct includes indecent touching.
Tunisia	**Yes**	Article 226 of the Penal Code prohibits sexual harassment.
Yemen	**Partly**	There is no specific offense of sexual harassment. Some types of harassment may fall under the crimes of committing disgraceful acts against women and girls, which are punishable under Articles 273 and 275 of the Penal Code.

Source: Compiled from the Country Profiles on "Gender Justice and Equality before the Law" developed by UN ESCWA, UN Women, UNFPA and UNDP, 2019.

In summary, among the listed Arab countries, 33% of countries have domestic violence laws, and 50% have sexual harassment laws. A thorough analysis of these laws indicates that technology is not considered, except for the law enacted in Saudi Arabia in 2018, which defines "harassment" as any word, act, or sign with a sexual connotation by a person to any other person that harms their body or modesty by any means, including through modern technology. Moreover, none of these countries have introduced specific legislation to address the problem of technology facilitated abuse. This is alarming and requires immediate action from governments in the region.

For a comprehensive analysis of the status of laws impacting offline and online VAWG, the following subsection overviews the status of cybercrime laws in the Arab region.

Cybercrime Laws

Cybercrime has witnessed a rapid growth in the connected world we are living in. Though there is no agreed-upon standardized definition for the term "cybercrime," it is commonly defined as "any activity in which computers or networks are a tool, a target, or a place of criminal activity" (ITU-D., 2009). International and regional instruments refer to cybercrime as "a set of conducts or a collection of acts, making it an umbrella term rather than assigning a single definition" (Council of Europe, 2020a, 2020b). Cybercrime can be divided into two main categories: crimes that target networks or devices, and crimes that use devices to participate in criminal activities such as cyberstalking and identity theft (Panda Security, 2019). Enacting laws to combat cybercrime, including cyber VAWG, assists in tackling this growing issue.

The Council of Europe Convention on Cybercrime, also called the Budapest Convention, was opened for signature in 2001 and is globally considered the most relevant international instrument on cybercrime. Signatory States ratifying the Budapest Convention commit to harmonizing their laws, enhancing cybercrime investigative techniques, and increasing international cooperation between other States. As of March 2020, there were 64 signatory States to the Convention, among which only three states signed without subsequent ratification, and no Arab States signed (Council of Europe, 2020a, 2020b).

The adoption of cybercrime legislation in the Arab region varies between countries. Currently, 138 countries, including 13 Arab countries, have enacted cybercrime laws. The remaining nine Arab countries either applied general laws to fight cybercrime or did not take any measures. Therefore, only 60% of Arab countries have enacted laws to combat cybercrime, cyber VAWG inclusive. The United Arab Emirates was the first country in the region to adopt such a law with Cybercrime Law No. 2 in February 2006. In 2007, Saudi Arabia issued a cybercrime law named "the Information Technology Crime System." This was followed by Sudan, Alegria, Jordan, Oman, Syria, Bahrain, Qatar, Kuwait, Mauritania, Egypt, and Palestine (Shqair, 2019). Table 30.3 overviews the status of existing cybercrime laws in the Arab region with a description for each country.

As mentioned, technology is now globally recognized as a means for achieving gender equality and sustainable development. However, in order to exploit the potential of technology in empowering women and girls in the region, eliminating cyber VAWG through immediate, multidimensional, and comprehensive action becomes a key priority. This requires a legal framework substantiated by relevant policies and programs with a follow-up and monitoring mechanism. The Arab region can fill the gap in the legal framework needed to combat VAWG and give particular consideration to technology-facilitated violence, especially given the escalation of this form of violence during the COVID-19 pandemic. This can only happen if the efforts of various related stakeholders, including governments, civil society, and internet intermediaries are concerted. VAWG is a human rights breach and a pandemic that technology can spread further if governments and relevant stakeholders do not take immediate actions.

Table 30.3. The Status of Cybercrime Laws in the Arab Region.

	Existence of Cybercrime Laws	Detailed Description
Algeria	**Yes**	Law No. 09–04 of August 5, 2009 containing specific rules on the prevention and fight against information technologies and communications crimes.
Bahrain	**Yes**	Law No. 60 of 2014 concerning information and communications technology crimes.
Comoros	**No**	Comoros does not have specific criminal legislation pertaining to cybercrime
Djibouti	**No**	Laws on the information and communications technology and the postal and telecommunication sectors; law on protection of copyright and penal code.
Egypt	**Yes**	Law No. 17 of August 2018 concerning Anti-Cyber and Information Technology Crimes
Iraq	**No**	A draft law was prepared and then revoked in 2013.
Jordan	**Yes**	Law issued in 2010 as a temporary one and then became permanent in 2015 Information Systems Crime Law no. 30 of 2010.
Kuwait	**Yes**	Law No. (63) issued in 2015 on Combating Information Technology Crimes.
Lebanon	**No**	Lebanon does not have specific criminal legislation pertaining to cybercrime.
Libya	**No**	Libya does not have specific legislation pertaining to cybercrime. However, Libya is

Table 30.3. *(Continued)*

	Existence of Cybercrime Laws	Detailed Description
		currently drafting new legislations on cyber-activities.
Morocco	No	Legislation on cybercrime has been enacted through the Penal Code
Oman	Yes	Royal Decree No 12/2011 issued the Cyber Crime Law in 2011
Palestine	Yes	Law issued in 2018.
Qatar	Yes	Law No (14) issued in 2014 on Promulgating the Cybercrime Prevention Law.
Saudi Arabia	Yes	Anti-Cyber Crime Law, Royal Decree No. M/17, March 26, 2007.
Somalia	No	Somalia does not currently have any officially recognized national legislation pertaining to cybercrime but there is a work in progress.
Sudan	Yes	Law issued in 2007 and then amended in 2018.
Syria	Yes	Law No. 17/2012 Organizing Online Communication and eCrime Prevention.
Tunisia	No	Cybercrime Bill, 2014.
United Arab Emirates	Yes	Federal Decree-Law No. (5) of 2012 on Combating Cybercrimes.
Yemen	No	Draft Law on Combating Electronic Crime

Source: Compiled from the International Telecommunication Union's country profiles on CyberWelness, 2013; UNCTAD Cybercrime legislation worldwide database (https://unctad.org/en/Pages/DTL/STI_and_ICTs/ICT4D-Legislation/eCom-Cybercrime-Laws.aspx) and https://arij.net/wp-content/uploads/2019/12/Policy-Paper-Cyber-Crime-Laws-in-the-Arab-World-ARIJ-1.pdf.

Conclusion

Different factors will underpin and guide future policy reforms and measures to strengthen and harmonize efforts geared toward combating offline and online VAWG in the Arab region. Governments in the region need to implement a national prevalence survey on cyber VAWG to design evidence-based policies and programs. Violence prevention initiatives should engage men and boys to help transform gender power imbalances that reinforce VAWG and should be tailored to address gender discrimination and break social norms that normalize violence. Moreover, implementing a national anti-cyber VAWG program that ensures inclusive engagement of women, men, girls, and boys to counteract this growing phenomenon will further contribute to positive change.

Governments should ratify the Budapest Convention on Cybercrime and enact laws to protect women and girls from all types of cyber VAWG. By strengthening specialized protocols and codes of conduct for law enforcement officials governments play a critical role in breaking the cycle of technology facilitated VAWG. They play a major role in informing internet users about these protocols, where to report cases of technology facilitated VAWG, and in times of pandemics such as COVID-19, inform users how to access essential services online. Also, to combat sexual exploitation, governments should strengthen existing directives on addressing sexual exploitation online and highlight good practices that effectively address technologyfacilitated VAWG to inform a range of stakeholders.

Civil society organizations also play a central role in combatting VAWG. They can raise awareness and help women advocates, educators, and internet users to identify and report technology-facilitated violence. They can also provide tools and resources needed for women and girls to report online violence and produce simple communication materials that demonstrate its harmful impact especially on high-risk groups of women and girls. By promoting an intersectional understanding and approach to communities who experience multiple forms of oppressions and harassment online, as part of the continuum of violence, civil society can prevent the further spread of online VAWG.

Internet intermediaries also play an important role in combatting VAWG. They should always set clear commitments to safeguarding women and girls in online spaces and provide accessible and transparent reporting procedures for technology-facilitated VAWG. Among many actions, internet intermediaries should invest in education campaigns on preventing online VAWG and promoting human rights and digital security for all (see Henry & Witt, this volume).

These suggested actions and initiatives require the engagement of all relevant stakeholders. Fostering public-private partnerships could ensure that governance structures, strategies, investments, technology sectors, access, and skills development are inclusive and gender-responsive. Ensuring an enabling environment for these multi-stakeholder collaborations remains a precondition for harvesting their added value in combating VAWG.

References

Al-Nasrawi, S. (2019). *Technology as a tool to make cities safe and combat violence against women* (pp. 1–13). Beirut: United Nations Economic and Social Commission for Western Asia.

Badran, M. (2017). *Achieving gender equality in the Arab region amidst the changing world of work* (pp. 1–16). Geneva: International Labor Organization (ILO).

Bouhlila, D. (2019). *Sexual harassment and domestic violence in the Middle East and North Africa* (pp. 1–42). Tunis: University of Tunis El Manar.

Council of Europe. (2020a). Details of Treaty No.185 - Convention on Cybercrime. Retrieved from http://www.coe.int/en/web/conventions/full-list/-/conventions/treaty/185. Accessed on March 15, 2020.

Council of Europe. (2020b). Chart of signatures and ratification of Treaty 185 - Convention on Cybercrime. Retrieved from https://www.coe.int/en/web/conventions/full-list/-/conventions/treaty/185/signatures?p_auth=fM7PZIXX. Accessed on March 8, 2020.

EIGE. (2017). *Cyber violence against women and girls*. Retrieved from https://eige.europa.eu/publications/cyber-violence-against-women-and-girls. Accessed on May 01, 2020.

Eltigani, N. (2019, November 25). Three prevalent forms of violence against women in the Arab world. Retrieved from https://infotimes.org/three-prevalent-forms-of-violence-against-women-in-the-arab-world/. Accessed on March 1, 2020.

Finemchi. (2020). *Maroc, Vie Pratique et Évènements*. Retrieved from https://finemchi.com/. Accessed on March 14, 2020.

García-Moreno, C., Pallitto, C., Devries, K., Stöckl, H., Watts, C., & Abrahams, N. (2013). *Global and regional estimates of violence against women: Prevalence and health effects of intimate partner violence and non-partner sexual violence*. Geneva: World Health Organization.

Gracia, E. (2004). Unreported cases of domestic violence against women: Towards an epidemiology of social silence, tolerance, and inhibition. *Journal of Epidemiol Community Health*, *58*, 536–537. doi:10.1136/jech.2003.019604

Guedes, A., Bott, S., Garcia-Moreno, C., & Colombini, M. (2016). Bridging the gaps: A global review of intersections of violence against women and violence against children. *Global Health Action*, *9*(1). doi:10.3402/gha.v9.31516

HarassMap. (2020). Stop sexual harassment. Retrieved from https://harassmap.org/en/. Accessed on February 2, 2020.

Hassan, F. M., Khalifa, F. N., Desouky, E. D. E., Salem, M. R., & Ali, M. M. (2020). Cyber violence pattern and related factors: Online survey of females in Egypt. *Egyptian Journal of Forensic Sciences*, *10*(1), 1–7. doi:10.1186/s41935-020-0180-0

ITU. (2020). *The digital gender gap is growing fast in developing countries*. Geneva: International Telecommunication Union (ITU). Retrieved from https://itu.foleon.com/itu/measuring-digital-development/gender-gap/. Accessed on May 20, 2020.

ITU-D. (2009). *Understanding cybercrime: A guide for developing countries* (pp. 1–225). Geneva: International Telecommunication Union (ITU).

Lewis, R., Rowe, M., & Wiper, C. (2017). Online abuse of feminists as an emerging form of violence against women and girls. *The British Journal of Criminology*, *57*(6), 1462–1481. doi:10.1093/bjc/azw073

MFSESD. (2019). The second national study on the prevalence of violence against women in Morocco. The Ministry of Family, Solidarity, Equality and Social Development (MFSESD). Retrieved from http://www.social.gov.ma. Accessed on April 19, 2020.

Odeh, S. (2018). *Gender-based violence against Palestinian: Women in virtual space* (pp. 1–25). Stockholm: Kvinna till Kvinna.

OHCHR. (2018). Report of the Special Rapporteur on violence against women, its causes and consequences on online violence against women and girls from a human rights perspective. Retrieved from https://www.ohchr.org/EN/Issues/women/SRWomen/Pages/SRWomenIndex.aspx. Accessed on May 28, 2020.

OHCHR. (n.d.). Convention on the Elimination of All Forms of Discrimination Against Women. Retrieved from https://www.ohchr.org/EN/ProfessionalInterest/Pages/CEDAW.aspx. Accessed on January 10, 2020.

Panda Security. (2019, March 13). Types of cybercrime. Retrieved from https://www.pandasecurity.com/mediacenter/panda-security/types-of-cybercrime/. Accessed on January 15, 2020.

Promundo & UN Women. (2017). Understanding masculinities. Retrieved April 20, 2020, from https://promundoglobal.org/wp-content/uploads/2017/05/IMAGES-MENA-Multi-Country-Report-EN-16May2017-web.pdf

Richter, C. (2018, October 2). Securella – When security meets Cinderella. Retrieved from https://www.vodafone-institut.de/f-lane/securella-security-meets-cinderella/. Accessed on January 28, 2020.

Shqair, Y. (2019). Cybercrime laws in the Arab region focused on Jordan, UAE and Egypt (pp. 1–56). Arab Reporters for Investigative Journalism (ARIJ) with the support of the Friedrich Naumann Foundation for Freedom. Retrieved from https://en.arij.net/wp-content/uploads/sites/3/2019/12/Cyber-Crime-Laws-in-the-Arab-world-Policy-paper-by-ARIJ.pdf. Accessed on November 22, 2020.

StreetPal (2018, May 3). Streetpal App: Building a community to help you face sexual harassment. Retrieved from https://egyptinnovate.com/en/success-stories/streetpal-app-building-community-help-you-face-sexual-harassment. Accessed on March 1, 2020.

UN Broadband Commission for Digital Development Working Group on Broadband and Gender (UN-BC-DDWGBG). (2015). Cyber violence against women and girls: A worldwide wake up call (pp. 1–70). Retrieved from https://www.unwomen.org/~/media/headquarters/attachments/sections/library/publications/2015/cyber_violence_gender%20report.pdf?v=1&d=20150924T154259. Accessed on November 22, 2020.

UN ESCWA. (2017). Status of Arab women report 2017 violence against women: What is at stake?. Retrieved from https://www.unescwa.org/sites/www.unescwa.org/files/publications/files/arab-women-report-violence-against-women-english.pdf. Accessed on April 18, 2020.

UN ESCWA. (2019). *Guidelines to estimate the economic cost of domestic violence in the Arab region*. Beirut: United Nations Economic and Social Commission for Western Asia (UN ESCWA). Retrieved from https://www.unescwa.org/publications/guidelines-estimate-economic-cost-domestic-violence-arab-region. Accessed on April, 18, 2020.

UN Women. (2020a). *Convention on the Elimination of All Forms of Discrimination Against Women*. New York, NY: United Nations Entity for Gender Equality and the Empowerment of Women (UN Women). Retrieved from http://www.un.org/womenwatch/daw/cedaw/. Accessed on February 2, 2020.

UN Women. (2020b). *COVID-19 Response: Online and ICT facilitated violence against women and girls during COVID-19*. New York, NY: United Nations Entity for Gender Equality and the Empowerment of Women (UN Women). Retrieved from https://www.unwomen.org/-/media/headquarters/attachments/sections/library/publications/2020/brief-online-and-ict-facilitated-violence-against-women-and-girls-during-covid-19-en.pdf?la=en&vs=2519. Accessed on May 30, 2020.

UN Women, Demographic Centre in Egypt, Egyptian National Planning Institute, Safe Cities in Cairo, European Union (2013). Study on ways and methods to eliminate sexual harassment in Egypt. Retrieved from https://web.law.columbia.edu/sites/default/files/microsites/gender-sexuality/un_womensexual-harassment-study-egypt-final-en.pdf. Accessed on April 20,2020.

UNICEF. (2020, February 10). *Cyberbullying: What is it and how to stop it*. Retrieved from https://www.unicef.org/jordan/stories/cyberbullying-what-it-and-how-stop-it. Accessed on March 5, 2020.

United Nations General Assembly (United Nations-GA). (2019). Intensification of efforts to prevent and eliminate all forms of violence against women and girls: Sexual harassment. Retrieved from https://undocs.org/A/res/73/148

UNODC. (2020). Cybercrime and COVID19: Risks and responses. UNODC Cybercrime and Anti-money Laundering section. Retrieved from https://www.unodc.org/documents/Advocacy-Section/UNODC_-_CYBERCRIME_AND_COVID19_-_Risks_and_Responses_v1.2_-_14-04-2020_-_CMLS-COVID19-CYBER1_-_UNCLASSIFIED_BRANDED.pdf. Accessed on November 22, 2020.

Vodafone. (2017). Securella – When security meets Cinderella. Vodafone Institute for Society and Communication. Retrieved from https://www.vodafone-institut.de/f-lane/securella-security-meets-cinderella/. Accessed on April 20, 2020.

Vox. (2020). *How coronavirus took over social media*. Retrieved from https://www.vox.com/recode/2020/3/12/21175570/coronavirus-covid-19-social-media-twitter-facebook-google. Accessed on May 20, 2020.

WHO. (2013). *Global and regional estimates of violence against women: Prevalence and health effects of intimate partner violence and non-partner sexual violence*. Geneva: World Health Organization.

WomenYSK. (2018, February 20). Tunisian youth activist working to make women and girls feel safe in public spaces. Retrieved from https://women-youshouldknow.net/tunisian-activist-women-girls-feel-safe/. Accessed on January 14, 2020.

Chapter 31

Image-Based Sexual Abuse: A Comparative Analysis of Criminal Law Approaches in Scotland and Malawi

Seonaid Stevenson-McCabe and Sarai Chisala-Tempelhoff

Abstract

Technology-facilitated violence and abuse including image-based sexual abuse (IBSA) is a phenomenon affecting women and girls around the world. Abusers misuse technology to attack victims and threaten their safety, privacy, and dignity. This abuse is gendered and a form of domestic and sexual violence. In this article, the authors compare criminal law approaches to tackling IBSA in Scotland and Malawi. We critically analyze the legislative landscape in both countries, with a view to assessing the potential for victims to seek and obtain redress for IBSA. We assess the role criminal law has to play in each jurisdiction while acknowledging the limits of criminal law alone in terms of providing redress.

Keywords: Image-based sexual abuse; law; Scotland; Malawi; feminism; domestic and sexual violence

Introduction[1]

The criminal law is often perceived as a crucial tool in combating technology-facilitated violence and abuse (TFVA). In recent years, there has been an increased focus on criminalizing TFVA, with numerous jurisdictions attempting to regulate the digital domain.[2] In this research, we discuss the criminal legislative landscapes in Scotland and Malawi relating to one particular form of TFVA: image-based sexual abuse (IBSA).

The Emerald International Handbook of Technology-Facilitated Violence and Abuse, 513–532

doi:10.1108/978-1-83982-848-520211038

While often colloquially referred to as "revenge porn," the literature in this area has provided detailed explanations as to why the term is inappropriate (see, e.g., Gosse, this volume; McGlynn & Rackley, 2016). The terminology adopted in this research is that of IBSA, as developed by McGlynn and Rackley, to mean the "non-consensual creation and/or distribution of private sexual images" (see, e.g., McGlynn & Rackley, 2016, Image-based sexual abuse section, para 1; McGlynn & Rackley, 2017, p. 536).

IBSA operates as a broad term which captures a range of connected practices and which emphasizes the abusive nature of these behaviors (McGlynn & Rackley, 2016). As noted by McGlynn and Rackley (2016, Image-based sexual abuse section, para 1):

> The non-consensual creation and/or distribution of private, sexual images is a serious harm often resulting in considerable mental and physical injuries. It is a form of harassment and often part of a pattern of coercive, domestic abuse. It is also a breach of the fundamental rights to privacy, dignity, and sexual autonomy, with women (and victims are mostly women) being forced offline and blamed or targeted for expressing themselves sexually through imagery.

This analysis of IBSA accurately captures some of the experiences of women and girls in Scotland and Malawi. In Scotland, the long-term impact on women and girls, including anxiety, self-harm, and suicide has been recognized by Scottish Women's Aid (BBC News, 2017, para 19), and it is understood that this behavior often forms part of a wider pattern of abuse (Scottish Parliament, 2015, para 24). In the Malawian context, victims have not only been forced offline but have fled the country as a result of the shame associated with IBSA (Chisala-Tempelhoff & Kirya, 2016, p. 3). Equally, we find McGlynn, Rackley, and Houghton's (2017; McGlynn & Rackley, 2016, Image-based sexual abuse section, para 2) approach to locating IBSA as part of the "continuum of sexual violence" useful. Recognising that IBSA shares characteristics with other sexual offenses can help to ensure that appropriate legal safeguards and support networks are made available to victims everywhere (McGlynn & Rackley, 2016, para 2), including in Scotland and Malawi.

In 2018, the Scottish and Malawian Governments entered into The Global Goals Partnership Agreement which encourages collaboration between their respective Governments (The Republic of Malawi and Scotland, 2018). With reference to gender equality, the Agreement notes that the Parties intend to work together "to formulate, enforce and implement laws and policies related to gender-based violence" (Republic of Malawi and Scotland, 2018, Annex, Global Goal 5, para 6). We have been working collaboratively in recent years to discuss the challenges IBSA presents for women and girls and those working to support them in our respective nations. While we acknowledge that IBSA can impact on people of any gender, those most likely to be victims in Scotland and Malawi are women and girls (see, e.g., Chisala-Tempelhoff & Kirya, 2016, p. 2; Scottish Parliament Justice Committee, 2016, para 44). It is therefore hoped that this research advances the discussion on seeking redress for IBSA, while supporting the shared Governmental objective to collaborate in the implementation of laws and policies related to gender-based violence.

Both Scotland and Malawi have criminal legislation which can be used to tackle IBSA.[3] Yet neither legal system is providing a comprehensive solution. In this chapter, we highlight the potential for the criminal law in each country to provide redress, while acknowledging the importance of wider civic campaigning and education. We begin by addressing the potential for criminal prosecution in Malawi and then turn to assess the successes and shortcomings of Scotland's approach to IBSA. In conclusion, we highlight the inherent shortcomings of existing criminal law responses and the risks of attempting to "transplant" the legislative approach from one jurisdiction into another without examining important contextual differences. Finally, we emphasize the importance of public education and multi-sector collaboration as part of a multi-pronged strategy for responding to IBSA.

Malawi: Potential for Prosecution

Malawi has several legislative provisions which could be used to protect victims of IBSA. The *Constitution of the Republic of Malawi* (1994) protects rights at the core of tackling IBSA, including rights to privacy, equality, dignity, and the rights of women (Chisala, 2019b, para 3). Since the entry into force of the Constitution in 1994, legislation has progressively been introduced to enhance gender equality, promote the rights of women, and allow for the prosecution of gender-based violence, including IBSA. However, to fully understand the legislative context in which IBSA could be tackled using this recent, progressive legislation, it is also crucial to understand the ways in which criminal law provisions are currently being used to silence, control and shame women and girls. In some ways, the very body of laws put in place to purportedly protect women has been used to prosecute women in deeply gendered ways.

One such provision is section 137 of the *Malawi Penal Code* (1930) (Chisala, 2019b, para 10). Section 137 creates the offense of "insulting the modesty of a woman" which provides that:

> Whoever, intending to insult the modesty of any woman, utters any word, makes any sound or gesture or exhibits any object intending that such word or sound shall be heard, or that such gesture or object shall be seen, by such woman or intrudes upon the privacy of such woman, shall be guilty of a misdemeanour and shall be liable to imprisonment for one year. (*Malawi Penal Code*, 1930, section 137 (3))

While the language of the provision is clearly archaic, rooted in the patriarchal concept of female "modesty" (Chisala, 2019a), it is conceivable that IBSA could be prosecuted under this provision; intimate images being an "object" which "intrude upon the privacy" of a woman. In a recent IBSA case, a group of men were charged with insulting the modesty of a woman, among other offenses (Chisala, 2019a, para 10). This charge was made in response to an attack on a young woman, referred to here as "VK."[4] In 2019, VK was attacked while wearing clothing supporting a political party. Supporters of an opposing party filmed her while forcibly removing her clothes. This video was shared widely. The incident triggered national uproar and demonstrations, which ultimately led to the perpetrators being charged with insulting the modesty of a woman, robbery, and use of force (Chisala, 2019a).

However, the offense of insulting the modesty of a woman cannot consistently provide appropriate redress for victims of IBSA. In practice, this provision has also been weaponized against human rights defenders, particularly the women it purports to protect. A recent, concerning, example of this involves Beatrice Mateyo, the Executive Director of the Coalition for the Empowerment of Women and Girls (Chisala, 2019a). Mateyo was arrested in 2017 for involvement in a feminist protest. During the protest, she carried a placard which stated "kubadwa ndi nyini si tchimo, my pussy my pride" (loosely translated into English to mean "to be born with a vagina is not a crime/sin, my pussy my pride"). Mateyo herself was arrested and charged with insulting the modesty of a woman.[5] The Mateyo example is significant in that it demonstrates the dangers of imprecise criminal legislation. As the Penal Code currently stands, it is not unimaginable that a victim of IBSA may themselves be prosecuted under this provision (Chisala, 2019b, para 12).

The Mateyo example also illustrates wider, societal issues which are at play in Malawi in relation to IBSA. While the incident involving VK was widely condemned, including by the President and the media (Khamula, 2019), the response to Mateyo's case was more divided (Chisala, 2019a, para 11; Simango, 2017, para 4). In Malawi, there remains a desire to regulate female sexuality and to shame women themselves for perceived immodest behavior (Chisala, 2019a; Chisala-Tempelhoff & Kirya, 2016, pp. 3–4). Understanding this wider societal view is crucial to understanding the apparent failures of the existing criminal law in providing redress to victims of IBSA.

Nevertheless, as noted above, in recent years, more progressive legislation has been introduced which may be more appropriate in terms of protecting victims of IBSA. In particular, the *Gender Equality Act* 2013 presents some opportunity to protect victims of IBSA (Chisala, 2019b, paras 4–6; Chisala-Tempelhoff & Kirya, 2016, p. 5). Section 5 of the Act states that "a person shall not commit, engage in, subject another person to, or encourage the commission of any harmful practice" (*Gender Equality Act*, 2013). Section 3 of the Act defines a harmful practice as a:

> ...social, cultural or religious practice which, on account of sex, gender or marital status does or is likely to (a) undermine the dignity, health or liberty of any person; or (b) result in physical, sexual, emotional, or psychological harm to any person. (*Gender Equality Act*, 2013)

Further, section 6 of the Act provides that:

> …a person commits an act of sexual harassment if he or she engages in any form of unwanted verbal, non-verbal or physical conduct of a sexual nature in circumstances in which a reasonable person, having regard to all the circumstances, would have anticipated that the other person would be offended, humiliated or intimidated. (*Gender Equality Act*, 2013)

An offense under these sections is punishable by a fine of one million Kwacha (approximately £1,050 GBP) and a term of imprisonment of five years. While IBSA was not at the forefront of the drafters' minds in writing these provisions, it is conceivable that they could be expansively interpreted to prosecute IBSA (Chisala-Tempelhoff & Kirya, 2016, p. 5). The focus on the harm caused to the individual is particularly pertinent in terms of McGlynn and Rackley's (2016, Image-based sexual abuse section, para 1) aforementioned definition of IBSA.

However, to date there have been no IBSA prosecutions under the *Gender Equality Act* 2013. Indeed, it is unclear if there have been any sexual harassment prosecutions whatsoever under the Act. The first high-profile prosecution was the case of Eric Aniva, who was prosecuted under the harmful practices provisions of section 5 for his role in conducting "sexual cleansing rituals" of women and girls in Nsanje (BBC News, 2016, para 10). However, this case provides very little by way of instruction on the possibility of using the legislation to protect victims of IBSA, particularly as it was decided in the Magistrates' Court and, as such, has no binding legal effect on other courts. It is, therefore, unclear how the law will be interpreted in the future. Furthermore, as with the offense of insulting the modesty of a woman, there is concern that if the provision was used to respond to an incident of IBSA, the victim could be prosecuted for engaging in the creation of their own intimate images.

The most pertinent piece of Malawian legislation in terms of prosecuting IBSA is the *Electronic Transactions and Cyber Security Act 2016* (the 2016 Act) (Chisala, 2019b, para 8). The 2016 Act is a broad piece of legislation which attempts to regulate cyber-crime and data protection. However, in section 3(b), one of the stated objectives of the Act is also "to ensure that information and communication technology users are protected from undesirable impacts of information and communication technology, including the spread of pornographic material, cyber-crime and digital fraud" (2016 Act).

The 2016 Act is evidently not a specific piece of IBSA legislation. Aside from a provision concerning child pornography, the Act does not explicitly refer to IBSA. Nonetheless, it does prohibit cyber harassment, cyber stalking, and offensive communication under which IBSA can potentially be prosecuted. For example, section 87 prohibits "offensive communication," stating that "any person who willfully and repeatedly uses electronic communication to disturb or attempt to disturb the peace, quietness or right of privacy of any person" commits a misdemeanor (2016 Act). As noted by McGlynn and Rackley (2016, Image-based sexual abuse section, p. 1), IBSA clearly "disturbs" the right of privacy of the victim (see, e.g., Bailey & Mathen, 2019, p. 677; Dickson, 2016, p. 56). However, the requirement for repeated behavior is problematic. Furthermore, the provision is troubling because although it potentially lends itself to criminalizing IBSA, it could also be used to criminalize speech critical of the Government (Freedom House, 2019, section C2, para 2).

Section 86 of the 2016 Act prohibits cyber harassment, which focuses on anyone who uses a computer system and:

> …continues (a) making any request, suggestion or proposal which is obscene, lewd, lascivious or indecent; or (b) threatening to inflict injury or physical harm to the person or property of any person; or (c) knowingly permits any electronic communications device to be used for any of the above-mentioned purposes. (2016 Act)

As with section 87, this provision could potentially be used to tackle IBSA, particularly in relation to those threatening to release intimate images, although the requirement for "continuing" behavior is once again unhelpful (2016 Act). Equally, the use of the language of obscenity and the focus on requests, suggestions, or proposals which are "obscene, lewd, lascivious or indecent" is problematic (2016 Act, s. 86). This language focuses once more on archaic notions of modesty that, like other provisions discussed above, could expose IBSA victims to prosecution.

Section 88 of the 2016 Act prohibits cyber stalking, which could also be invoked to prosecute IBSA. Under this provision, any person who "willfully, maliciously and repeatedly uses electronic communication to harass another person and makes a threat with the intent to instill reasonable fear in that person for his or her safety" commits an offense known as cyber stalking (2016 Act, s. 88). Section 88 would be useful in circumstances where repeated threats have been issued to disclose intimate images. In the Scottish context, it has been noted that threats can be a form of control in IBSA offenses (Brindley, 2015, para 3). However, the provision's efficacy is limited by the repeated behavior requirement. Furthermore, the provision could be open for abusive prosecution of vulnerable persons. For example, in 2020, a woman was prosecuted under section 88 for allegedly spreading "fake news" because she had posted a message to a WhatsApp group stating the FDH Bank was collecting information on citizens and passing this information to the Government (Nyasa Times, 2020, para 1). She was ultimately convicted of cyberstalking and given an 18 month suspended sentence and a fine of MWK 500,000 (Nyasa Times, 2020). This prosecution is concerning for a variety of reasons, not least in relation to freedom of speech. In terms of IBSA, this case demonstrates the potential use of the legislation to protect the powerful, rather than victims of misogynistic abuse.

Perhaps the most significant innovation of the 2016 Act is the takedown notification system. Section 30 details the responsibilities of intermediary service providers to takedown content that is unlawful or violates rights. Similarly, under section 96, anyone who is affected by a criminal offense may lodge a complaint with the Malawi Communications Regulatory Authority (MACRA) which then has the power to undertake investigations.

In theory, the creation of these offenses should mean that MACRA and the police are able to tackle IBSA. Unfortunately, however, the authors are not aware of any IBSA investigations to date under this legislation. Indeed, recent reports involving the online abuse of women, which could have been prosecuted under the Act, appear not to have been fully investigated.

In 2018, over 200 women had their phone numbers leaked into a WhatsApp group by a Malawian man, where they were labeled "the easiest young women/girls to sleep with or to have a good time" (Phiri, 2020, Public shaming and harassment on and offline section, para 1). These women received messages sexually harassing them, including pictures of male genitalia. While not an IBSA specific offense, this case was an opportunity to test the ability of the 2016 Act to protect women in online spaces. The victims reported the incident to the police. However, one of the victims noted that the police declined to investigate, stating that:

> … this was a violation against a group of people; therefore, it needed several victims to come forward and accuse the young man for the case to be registered. Once the police turned me down and demanded a group report or no justice, most young women dropped off. (Phiri, 2020, Attempted collective response section, para 3)

It is concerning to hear this victim's account, which suggests the police shifted the focus to the victims themselves, requiring them to present evidence. This is particularly disappointing given the extensive evidence available in the public domain in this instance.

Women who are victims of IBSA offenses are often subjected to intense societal shaming (Chisala-Tempelhoff & Kirya, 2016, pp. 3–7) and are ill-equipped to press for prosecution. A complaint in the aforementioned WhatsApp case was also lodged by the Young Feminists Network with the Malawi Human Rights Commission, although there has been no response to date (Chisala-Tempelhoff, 2020, Reporting remains a challenge section, para 2). It is unsurprising that the victim concluded from this experience that "[t]he police make it difficult for victims of online violence to report" (Phiri, 2020, Attempted collective response section, para 6). Examples such as this may indicate a wider problem with police responsiveness to digital offenses against women in Malawi. Prosecutorial guidelines and extensive training are required if we are to ensure that cyber-laws are enforced to protect women in online spaces generally, as well as used to tackle IBSA specifically.

From this brief overview, it can reasonably be concluded that IBSA is not currently being addressed through the existing Malawian criminal law. Older, archaic pieces of legislation can be weaponized against women and other human rights defenders. Equally, more modern pieces of legislation which have the potential to protect victims of IBSA are not used to that effect. It is therefore tempting to suggest that specific IBSA legislation, such as that recently introduced in Scotland, may help address this issue. To assess the viability of this proposition, the benefits of the Scottish legislation are explored below. However, throughout this analysis, it is vital to recognize the wider social issues at play, including societal shaming concerning female sexuality and potential reluctance from the authorities to investigate online offenses. As will be explored in the Scottish context, these challenges cannot be solved through legislation alone.

Scotland: Success and Shortcomings

In Scotland, section 2 of the *Abusive Behavior and Sexual Harm (Scotland) Act 2016* (the 2016 Act) creates the offense of disclosing, or threatening to disclose, an intimate photograph or film. Before the Act came into force, Scotland's legislative landscape resembled Malawi's in that a variety of different offenses were potentially applicable to IBSA.[6] While these offenses continue to be available, the 2016 Act specifically focuses on the offense of disclosure of intimate images.

In the Policy Memorandum which accompanied the Bill it was noted that

> ...in the absence of an offense specifically concerned with the sharing of intimate images the exact scope of the law in this area can be seen by many as being unclear. (Scottish Parliament, 2015, para 26)

It was also noted that victims may not be aware that they were, in fact, victims of a criminal offense and that, even in those cases which did result in successful prosecutions, victims may not feel that their particular experiences were reflected in a prosecution based on the existing criminal law (Scottish Parliament, 2015, para 26). Equally, there were concerns that the legislative position before the 2016 Act made it difficult to strategically analyze and address the wider patterns of IBSA in Scotland, with it being suggested that "a piecemeal approach involving prosecutions under different statutes does not even allow for accurate collation of statistics to track the rise in the number of offenses" (Mawdsley, 2014, p. 5). Accordingly, creation of a discrete criminal offense was considered necessary.

This thinking did not take place in a Parliamentary vacuum.[7] Indeed, Rackley (2019) has noted that the 2016 Act was a "legal landmark" in terms of women's rights, with campaigning by women's rights organizations being crucial in the process. In 2013, Scottish Women's Aid launched their campaign to end "revenge porn" which included the creation of dedicated websites.[8] The websites provided a safe space for women who had been victims of IBSA to share their experiences and a space for others to display their support. The sites also offered advice to victims. The wider Scottish Women's Aid campaign involved training for civil servants and roundtables with legal experts (Hutchinson, 2013b, para 2) as well as a Parliamentary debate which received cross-party support (Scottish Parliament, 2013). As part of an extensive media campaign, Ellie Hutchinson of Scottish Women's Aid directly tackled the victim-shaming which often dominated public discourse at the time, noting that:

> One of the most consistent questions that women are asked is "why did you send/take those pictures?" To me, this is just a variation on the "why does she stay" theme, with added shaming around female sexuality. It places all the responsibility on the victim rather than the perpetrator.... The question we really need to be asking (and answering) is not "why did you do it?", but "why does he think it's ok?" (Hutchinson, 2013a, paras 5–6)

The campaign also acknowledged that the young people who tended to be the victims of these offenses experienced "a particular kind of disbelief and minimizing" (Hutchinson, 2013b, para 5) with those in authority failing to acknowledge the significance of online crimes. This reframing of the narrative around IBSA, focusing on the need for education, and prevention and to encourage women to come forward, was significant in tackling IBSA in Scotland.

Following commencement of the campaign, discussions began to take place as to whether the existing law was adequate (see, e.g., Rose, 2013; Whitelaw, 2014). In March 2015, the Government launched a consultation seeking views on the creation of a new criminal offense (Scottish Government, 2015). It is important to note that, while the manner in which the consultation process was conducted was not without its critics (Chalmers, 2015, p. 400) a resounding majority (99%) of those who responded agreed that a specific offense should be created (Scottish Parliament, 2015, para 38). This consensus that disclosure of intimate images was a discrete criminal offense requiring clear regulation was in many ways remarkable given that the public awareness campaign was launched only two years previously. With regards to raising awareness of IBSA and emphasizing the criminality of this behavior, this campaigning appears to have been successful. As mentioned above, Rackley (2019, p. 643) has praised the work of Scottish Women's Aid in particular, noting that the 2016 Act is "a clear example of the power of sustained and collective feminist campaigning." The central role that this campaigning played in Scotland should be kept in mind when drawing comparisons between the Scottish and Malawian contexts, given that no similar IBSA campaign has as yet emerged in Malawi. Section 2 of the Act entered into force on July 3, 2017 alongside a media campaign entitled "Not Yours to Share."[9]

Section 2 of the 2016 Act has three core requirements to prove an offense. Firstly, a person ("person A") discloses or threatens to disclose, a photograph or film which shows, or appears to show, another person ("person B") in an intimate situation (2016 Act). Secondly, A must intend to cause B fear, alarm, or distress, or be reckless as to whether this is the case (2016 Act). Finally, the photograph or film must not have previously been disclosed to the public by B or with B's consent (2016 Act). In this context, disclosure occurs if a photograph or film, "or any data or other thing which is capable of being converted into it" is given, shown or made available to someone other than person B (2016 Act, s. 2).

Section 3 defines an "intimate situation" as being one where the person is engaging or participating in, or present during, an act which a reasonable person would consider to be a sexual act and which is not of a kind ordinarily done in public; or if the person's genitals, buttocks, or breasts are exposed or covered only with underwear (2016 Act). Available defenses under section 2(3) include that person B consented to the disclosure or that person A reasonably believed that B consented to the disclosure (2016 Act). The maximum penalty on summary conviction is 12 months in prison or a fine not exceeding the statutory maximum (or both) or, on conviction on indictment, to five years in prison or a fine (or both) (2016 Act, s. 2(7)).

There are a number of positive aspects of the offense. For example, *mens rea* is constituted through either intention or recklessness. This may be contrasted, for example, with the equivalent legislation in England and Wales. Section 33 of the *Criminal Justice and Courts Act 2015* does not criminalize reckless behavior. The inclusion of recklessness recognizes the wide range of circumstances in which disclosure may occur. A perpetrator may, of course, intend to cause their victim fear, alarm, or distress, as is seen in paradigmatic "revenge porn" cases. However, it is also important to recognize the wider nature of the offense and understand that there will be cases where this intention is not present and the perpetrator is reckless as to whether they cause fear, alarm, or distress. It is important that victims in these circumstances are also protected.

Another positive element of the Scottish framework is the offense's application both to actual disclosure *and* to the threat of such disclosure. The inclusion of threats is important in recognizing that IBSA can form part of a wider pattern of domestic abuse. Sharing their experience in evidence to Parliament on the Bill, Rape Crisis Scotland explained that

> [t]hreats to share images of this nature are often used following the ending of a relationship, or as a way of coercing someone to do something they do not wish to do. (Brindley, 2015, para 3)

The equivalent legislation in England and Wales does not include threats and instead requires actual disclosure. Pegg (2018) has noted "there are potential difficulties with this omission," (p. 517) explaining:

> In October 2017 Daniel Stainton was convicted of blackmail and disclosing private sexual images after he threatened three women with the disclosure of the intimate images the women had shared with him. The money Stainton extorted from one of his victims ensured the offense of blackmail could be made out, but to rely on blackmail to police this behaviour is to assume that perpetrators will be looking to make a gain in money or other property. (Pegg, 2018, p. 517)

It is therefore clear that the inclusion of threats to disclose was crucial in terms of ensuring that the full extent of IBSA was capable of prosecution in Scotland.

Furthermore, it is important that the section 3(2) of the Act specifically provides that films or photographs that have been altered in any way are included within the scope of the offense. In doing so, the Act ensures that a wide range of IBSA is captured. As noted by McGlynn and Rackley (2015, para 5.3) in their evidence provided to the Scottish Parliament's Justice Committee, "[t]he harm to a victim's dignity, and the harm which comes from images going viral, is the same whether or not the image is an 'original' or altered."

In many ways, therefore, the legislation itself can be said to be exemplary, wide-ranging yet nuanced in its drafting. However, to understand the impact of the legislation it is, of course, essential to understand how it is operating in practice. The first successful prosecution came shortly after section 2 came into force. The Crown Office & Procurator Fiscal Service released a statement emphasizing that "victims are in no way responsible just because they may have consented to an image being taken" (Crown Office & Procurator Fiscal Service, 2017, para 10). It was hoped that this early prosecution would reassure victims that the criminal justice system could provide adequate redress.

The recent case of *Shanks v Procurator Fiscal, Glasgow* [2018] SAC (Crim) 18 confirms the severity with which this behavior is to be treated. Shanks had threatened to disclose intimate images of the complainer to her children. The Sheriff Appeal Court noted that, considering the maximum sentencing available under the Act, it is "clear that Parliament views these offenses extremely seriously" and that

> …an individual who has entrusted a partner with an intimate image is entitled to a reasonable expectation that the court will deal severely with those who perpetrate this type of offense. (*Shanks v Procurator Fiscal, Glasgow* [2018] SAC (Crim) 18 para 3)

This case emphasizes the abusive nature of this offense and demonstrates that the judicial system will treat seriously threats to disclose, even without actual disclosure.

However, it is important to acknowledge the limitations of the Scottish legislation. Statistics provide a crucial insight into the effectiveness of the new regime. Section 2 came into force in July 2017, and 421 new crimes of disclosing or threatening to disclose an intimate image were recorded in the period July 3, 2017 to March 2018 (Scottish Government, 2019, p. 36). In 2018–2019, the first full reporting year in which section 2 was in force, 596 crimes were recorded (Scottish Government, 2019, p. 36). To fully understand these statistics, it is necessary to delve beyond the recording rate.

In March 2018, BBC Scotland published data they had obtained through a series of freedom of information requests made to Police Scotland (Ellison, 2018). Between July and December 2017, 225 complaints were reported to the Police but only 89 were detected (Ellison, 2018, para 2). The BBC explains that detected in this context means "that an accused has been identified, and that a report may be referred to the Crown Office or the Scottish Children's Reporter for consideration" (Ellison, 2018, Women victims section, para 3). The low proportion of detected cases raised concerns. Glasgow Women's Aid stated they were "disappointed" by these statistics, particularly given that "it must be extremely difficult to come forward and extremely demoralising if the complaint does not progress" (Ellison, 2018, How was "revenge porn" distributed section, para 4). In response, Police Scotland stated that these investigations were often "very complex" and that they would "encourage victims to come forward early which will better enable us to get evidence from any devices, or provide support to them, and advise how best to minimise impact" while also noting that there may also be an issue of under-reporting due to the shame surrounding the offense (Ellison, 2018, Police won't judge you section, para 3).

More recent data suggests that detection remains an issue.[10] In 2018–2019, 596 crimes were recorded but only 44.5% were detected (Police Scotland, 2019, p. 5). The data for 1 April to December 31, 2019 shows 478 crimes had been recorded by the end of the third quarter, and that the detection rate is 46.7% (Police Scotland, 2020, p. 5). To compare these figures to other sexual crimes, the detection rate for rape is 51.6% and for taking, distributing, and possessing indecent photos of children is 94.9% (Police Scotland, 2020, p. 5). The detection rate for intimate image sharing is the lowest rate for all sexual crimes (Police Scotland, 2020, p. 5). This suggests that there are clear challenges in police detection for these offenses and, ultimately, prosecution. Accordingly, it would seem that even IBSA specific legislation leaves much to be desired in terms of providing redress.

Conclusion: Inherent Limitations of Criminal Law and Need for a Multi-Pronged Approach

Having examined the criminal legislative landscapes in both countries, it is clear that neither legal system is responding perfectly to IBSA. While the problems in each nation are rooted in distinct local contexts, there are core commonalities in terms of the challenges presented in successfully policing and prosecuting IBSA.

Scotland's 2016 Act is, in many ways, an excellent example of criminal legislation responding to IBSA. In particular, the comprehensive drafting, which allows for the inclusion of a broad spectrum of IBSA (including the threat to disclose intimate images), is to be commended. In being an IBSA specific provision, the legislation avoids some of the unintended consequences inherent in the existing Malawian legislation, where archaic and imprecise offenses can be used to turn victims into accused (Chisala, 2019b, para 12). Equally, section 2 of Scotland's 2016 Act clearly articulates that IBSA is a criminal offense, alleviating any confusion on this point.

This raises the question as to whether a further, IBSA specific offense may be beneficial in Malawi. In our view, the answer to this question, at this time, is "no." The current Malawian criminal law clearly has limitations and is undeniably imperfect. However, there is some potential to use existing legislation to tackle IBSA through "nuanced" interpretation (Chisala-Tempelhoff & Kirya, 2016, p. 8).[11] Specific IBSA legislation may ultimately prove helpful in Malawi but it is crucial to remember that Scotland's 2016 Act was born of a lengthy public education and media campaign by feminist activists (Rackley, 2019, p. 643) and was introduced with overwhelming support for a specific IBSA offense. It is vital to engage with this wider context in order to understand what can be learned from the Scottish experience. Even against this backdrop of campaigning and consensus, detection rates in Scotland remain worryingly low. In the local Malawian context, introducing further legislation at this time risks futility.

To understand why this is the case, it is helpful to recall our earlier reference to the Constitution of Malawi and the rights protected therein. While these rights are protected by the Constitution, the reality of being able to enforce these rights is, in practice, challenging. Copies of the Constitution are not widely available to the public. They are also often not available to the police and other justice actors including magistrates. There are some versions of the Constitution and key gender-related laws which have been translated into local languages other than English, but these are neither widely available nor easily accessible. Lack of public accessibility is typical of significant swathes of Malawian legislation. Efforts to digitize Malawian legal resources are ongoing. For example, the Gender and Justice Unit[12] hosts MalawiLII.org, part of a broader effort to ensure online availability of Malawian legislation and case law. However, public engagement with the law remains low. Furthermore, the digital divide in Malawi is significant in this context. It is estimated that in 2017, only 13.78% of the population had internet access (International Telecommunications Union, 2019). This restricts the ability of the public to engage with new offenses as they are created. Even where complete versions of legislation are readily available, they tend to be in a format that is difficult for the wider population to consume. Data from 2015 demonstrate that Malawi has low literacy rates and these rates are significantly lower when disaggregated by gender (UNESCO, 2019a; 2019b). Women lag far behind. Work is ongoing to counter these issues.[13] Nevertheless, it is important to acknowledge that much remains to be done in terms of ensuring access to justice for women and girls. While these issues of accessibility are, of course, wider than IBSA offenses, they illustrate the challenges associated with creating an effective criminal offense in this context.

Equally, it is important to recognize the wider social context in which these crimes are occurring in Malawi. Social condemnation of the victims of IBSA is widespread, as "the public largely scorns and shames the female victims, women whose lives are already irreparably changed" (Chisala-Tempelhoff & Kirya, 2016, p. 4). As demonstrated in the Mateyo example discussed above, there remains a strong social stigma surrounding female sexuality, and a culture of shame is pervasive. As noted by Chisala-Tempelhoff and Kirya (2016, p. 3), "[w]omen who are perceived as deviating from this norm, for example, by 'allowing' themselves to be photographed naked, are derided and chastised in the court of public opinion." This is, of course, not unique to Malawi; victim shaming in IBSA cases is a global phenomenon which has also been recognized in the Scottish context (see, e.g., Hutchinson, 2013a). However, it is crucial to understand the prevalence of these attitudes in Malawi to understand how IBSA can effectively be challenged and prosecuted. Our previous discussion about the *Electronic Transactions and Cyber Security Act* and potential police and prosecutorial reluctance alludes to a wider societal minimization of online offenses such as IBSA.

It is also important to acknowledge the wider issues concerning reliance on the criminal law in this context (Chisala-Tempelhoff, 2020, Is the law enough section, para 4). The criminal law is often used against the vulnerable and therefore cannot be treated as a comprehensive solution for IBSA victims. Again, this analysis is not unique to the Scottish and Malawian criminal justice systems. In the Canadian context, Bailey and Mathen (2019, pp. 666, 668, 695) have noted that criminal law has a disproportionate impact on minority and marginalized groups. They also note that

> ...the kind of long-term social transformation that will be necessary to eradicate the sorts of GBV evident in cases of TFVAWG far exceeds the capacity of a reactive and punitive criminal law system. (Bailey & Mathen, 2019, p. 695)

Over-reliance on the criminal law therefore can be harmful and we need to ensure that criminal law is only one thread in a wider tapestry of responses. As noted by Bailey and Mathen (2019, p. 695), "In many cases, survivors will have good reason to take a different approach." One such reason victims may pursue a "different approach" is the length of time it takes to receive a criminal justice response. As Dickson (2016, p. 51) has argued with reference to the Australian legal system, a swift response is essential in IBSA cases where removal of the images is particularly important in terms of protecting victims from ongoing abuse. As Dickson (2016, p. 52) notes

> ...the criminal law does not provide victims with an efficient and accessible means for obtaining the removal of revenge pornography from the internet. While criminal laws are important, they are not sufficient in isolation.

It is therefore vital that any responses to tackling IBSA in Malawi and in Scotland do not rely solely on the criminal justice system.

For these reasons, we expect that Malawi's existing criminal legislation will continue to yield unsatisfactory results and further legislation risks becoming yet another a paper tiger without wider civic campaigning. Therefore, we would suggest that the focus in Malawi, at this time, ought to be on campaigning, community engagement, and training of front-line services to raise awareness of IBSA. Such an approach would be in keeping with Rackley's (2019) observations about the vital role that the Women's Aid campaigning played in Scotland before the introduction of IBSA legislation.

To return to the present Scottish landscape, it is equally clear that public legal education and training of front-line services have a continuing role to play if we are to see effective use of the new criminal law. In the words of the First Minister in 2018, when asked about the lack of prosecution

> ...while putting laws in place is important, making sure that these laws can effectively be used is what matters most and I think these statistics tell us that there is still work to be done on this important issue. (The Scotsman, 2018, para 10)

In terms of the "work" now to be done, we need to focus on how to ensure IBSA offenses are prosecuted under Scotland's 2016 Act. Police Scotland has stated that investigations are "very complex" (Ellison, 2018, Police won't judge you section, para 1). A helpful starting point could potentially be reviewing the particular difficulties officers encounter with a view to increasing detection rates. Similarly, while public legal education to date has been significant, maintaining this momentum and distributing high-quality resources throughout Scotland is likely to be essential to encouraging reporting and continued de-stigmatization of IBSA.

Ultimately, we owe the victims of IBSA, in Scotland and in Malawi, a nuanced response which invokes the power of the criminal law while also recognizing the need for wider civil society engagement. Tackling IBSA in both Scotland and Malawi will require a societal shift driven by continual, strategic campaigning, and collaboration across sectors. As lawyers, we must therefore engage with the importance of public legal education and cross-sector partnerships to deliver justice in the fullest sense.

Notes

1. The authors would like to thank Eleanor Livingston LLB (Hons) for her insightful research and work on earlier drafts. Her support has been invaluable, and we are greatly indebted to her. The authors would also like to thank Wangari Mwenda LLB for research support in the Malawian context and both Chikondi Mandala (Legal Research Associate, Gender and Justice Unit Malawi) and Maria Fletcher (Senior Lecturer, University of Glasgow) for their comments and support. Any errors are those of the authors.
2. Specifically, in relation to IBSA, jurisdictions including England and Wales; Germany; and States across the US have created offenses. See, Scottish Government (2015, pp. 16-17) for a brief discussion of these jurisdictions.
3. In this chapter, the authors focus on legislation which creates IBSA offenses. It should be noted that there are other Malawian laws which may be relevant in this context which are not discussed, including obscenity provisions in the Malawi Penal Code (1930) and the Prevention of Domestic Violence Act 2006. For further information and discussion of these pieces of legislation, please refer to Chisala-Tempelhoff and Kirya (2016) and Chisala (2019b). Similarly, the authors acknowledge that civil law mechanisms are available in our respective domestic jurisdictions although an analysis of these remedies is outside the scope of this discussion.
4. While the victim in this incident has been named widely in Malawian media, we have chosen to refer to her only by her initials.
5. The case is ongoing. Mateyo is represented by the Women Lawyers Association of Malawi, who have submitted that the offense is inappropriately broad and, supported by the Southern Africa Litigation Center, are seeking to challenge the law through a public interest litigation (Chisala, 2019a).
6. For a non-exhaustive list of relevant available offenses before the 2016 Act, see, Scottish Parliament (2015, para 25).

7. Discussions around specific IBSA offenses were taking place across the jurisdictions of the United Kingdom at this time. Scotland has a distinct legal system from England and Wales, but it is important to note that England and Wales introduced an IBSA offense in 2015 through the Criminal Justice and Courts Act 2015. For a discussion of the parallel journeys toward the creation of IBSA offenses in both Scotland and England and Wales, see, Rackley (2019).
8. Scottish Women's Aid created the site "Stop Revenge Porn Scotland" (available at https://stoprevengepornscotland.wordpress.com/) to share information in relation to revenge porn and highlight the ways in which they could support victims. Separately, a Flickr site was also created (available at https://www.flickr.com/photos/scottish-womensaid/sets/72157634479421774/) to allow individuals to share messages of support.
9. "Not Yours to Share" is a Scottish Government campaign which was created in partnership with Police Scotland, the Crown Office, and a variety of third sector organizations. The website (available at http://notyourstoshare.scot/) assisted individuals in understanding how the new law would operate.
10. It is important to understand that the statistics referred to here are from Police Management Information Quarterly Reports. The data used in these reports are provisional and do not constitute official statistics. The reports make clear that the official statistics produced by the Scottish Government should be relied on when drawing longer term trend comparisons. However, given that the 2018–2019 National Statistics do not offer information on detections and the 2019–2020 official statistics are not yet available, we refer here to the Police Management Information Statistics, while noting the caveats contained therein.
11. Chisala-Tempelhoff and Kirya (2016, p. 8) have previously advocated for "specific legislation or a nuanced interpretation of existing laws" in the Malawian context. While it is submitted herein that further legislation may risk futility in the present climate, and a nuanced interpretation of the existing law is therefore preferable, it is acknowledged that specific legislation may be beneficial in the future.
12. An organization which was founded by one of the authors.
13. For example, the Malawian Gender and Justice Unit has researched women's ability to access civil justice and developed simplified versions of critical legislative provisions accompanied by detailed process charts to bridge the gap between women and the justice solutions promised by legislation (see, Gender and Justice Unit, 2019).

References and Resources

Bailey, J. & Mathen, C. (2019). Technology-facilitated violence against women & girls assessing the Canadian criminal law response. *The Canadian Bar Review, 97*(3), 664–696. Retrieved from https://cbr.cba.org/index.php/cbr/article/view/4562

BBC News. (2016, November 22). Malawi 'hyena man' Eric Aniva sentenced to two years hard labour. *BBC News*. Retrieved from https://www.bbc.co.uk/news/world-africa-38063345

BBC News. (2017, July, 3). New 'revenge porn' law comes into force in Scotland. *BBC News*. Retrieved from https://www.bbc.co.uk/news/uk-scotland-40473912

BBC News. (2020, January 6). Number seeking advice over revenge porn doubles. *BBC News*. Retrieved from https://www.bbc.co.uk/news/uk-scotland-50998325

Brindley, S. (2015). Written submission from Rape Crisis Scotland to the Scottish Parliament Justice Committee on the Abusive Behaviour and Sexual Harm (Scotland) Bill. Retrieved from http://www.parliament.scot/S4_JusticeCommittee/Inquiries/ABSH9._Rape_Crisis_Scotland.pdf

Brown, J. (2018). 'Revenge porn' and the actio iniuriarum: Using 'old law' to solve 'new problems'. *Legal Studies*, *38*, 396–410. doi:10.1017/lst.2018.8

Brown, G. (2019). Voyeurism by "observing" and "recording" the complainer – the decision in KT v PF. *Falkirk Green's Criminal Law Bulletin*, *157*, 5–7.

Chalmers, J. (2015). Criminal law reform in Scotland. *Edinburgh Law Review*, *19*(3), 399–403. doi:10.3366/elr.2015.0302

Chisala, S. (2019a, May 9). Insulting the Modesty of a Woman" and the push by the women's movement in Malawi. [Web log post]. Retrieved from https://africanfeminism.com/insulting-the-modesty-of-a-woman-and-the-push-by-the-womens-movement-in-malawi/

Chisala, S. (2019b, 15 August). Malawi: Criminal law responses to non-consensual distribution of intimate images. [Web log post]. Retrieved from https://www.uofgschooloflaw.com/blog/2019/8/14/malawi-criminal-law-responses-to-non-consensual-distribution-of-intimate-images

Chisala-Tempelhoff, S. (2020, June 4). Accessing justice for image-based sexual abuse: A challenge for victims in Malawi. [Web log post]. Retrieved from https://africanfeminism.com/accessing-justice-for-image-based-sexual-abuse-a-challenge-for-victims-in-malawi/

Chisala-Tempelhoff, S., & Kirya, M. T. (2016). Gender, law and revenge porn in Sub-Saharan Africa: A review of Malawi and Uganda. *Palgrave Communications*, *2*, 16069. doi:10.1057/palcomms.2016.69

Cowan, S. (2019). Sense and sensibilities: A feminist critique of legal interventions against sexual violence. *Edinburgh Law Review*, *23*(1), 22–51. doi:10.2139/ssrn.3429595

Crofts, T., & Kirchengast, T. (2019). A ladder approach to criminalizing revenge pornography. *Journal of Criminal Law*, *83*(1), 87–103. doi:10.1177/0022018318814361

Crown Office & Procurator Fiscal Service. (2017, September 4). First 'intimate images' conviction under new legislation. [Web log post]. Retrieved from https://www.copfs.gov.uk/media-site/media-releases/1594-first-intimate-images-conviction-under-new-legislation

Dickson, A. (2016). 'Revenge Porn': A Victim Focused Response. *UniSA Student Law Review*, *2*, 42–69. doi:10.21913/USLRunisaslr.v2i0.1357

Ellison, M. (2018, March 6). Less than half revenge porn cases passed to prosecutors. *BBC News*. Retrieved from https://www.bbc.co.uk/news/uk-scotland-42689607

Freedom House. (2019). Freedom on the net 2019: Malawi. Retrieved from https://freedomhouse.org/country/malawi/freedom-net/2019#footnote4_6fnynzz

Gender and Justice Unit. (2019). *The civil justice needs booklet*. Retrieved from http://www.genderandjustice.org/wp-content/uploads/2019/12/The-GJU-Civil-Justice-Needs-Booklet-2019.pdf

Hutchinson, E. (2013a, August 5). Stop revenge porn. [Web log post] Retrieved from https://thefword.org.uk/2013/08/stop_revenge_porn/

Hutchinson, E. (2013b, October 5). We need to talk about revenge porn. *New Statesman*. Retrieved from https://www.newstatesman.com/politics/2013/10/we-need-talk-about-revenge-porn

International Telecommunication Union. (2019). Percentage of individuals using the internet. Retrieved from https://www.itu.int/en/ITU-D/Statistics/Documents/statistics/2019/Individuals_Internet_2000-2018_Dec2019.xls

Kettles, L. (2015). Written submission from the Scottish Women's Convention to the Scottish Parliament Justice Committee on the Abusive Behaviour and Sexual Harm (Scotland) Bill. Retrieved from https://www.parliament.scot/S4_JusticeCommittee/Inquiries/ABSH4._SWC.pdf

Khamula, O. (2019, January 24). Court refuses bail to UTM woman undressing suspects: Case adjourned to Feb 6. Court refuses bail to UTM woman undressing suspects: Case adjourned to Feb 6. *Nyasa Times*. Retrieved from https://www.nyasatimes.com/court-refuses-bail-to-utm-woman-undressing-suspects-case-adjourned-to-feb-6/

Mawdsley, G. (2014, December). "Hell hath no fury like a person scorned": Considering the offence of "revenge porn". *Green's Criminal Law Bulletin*, *132*, 2–4.

McGlynn, C., & Rackley, E. (2015). Written submission from Professor Clare McGlynn (Durham University) and Professor Erika Rackley (University of Birmingham) to the Scottish Parliament Justice Committee on the Abusive Behaviour and Sexual Harm (Scotland) Bill. Retrieved from https://www.parliament.scot/S4_JusticeCommittee/Inquiries/ABSH3._McGlynn_and_Rackley.pdf

McGlynn, C., & Rackley, E. (2016, February 15). Not 'revenge porn', but abuse: let's call it image-based sexual abuse. [Web log post] Retrieved from https://inherentlyhuman.wordpress.com/2016/02/15/not-revenge-porn-but-abuse-lets-call-it-image-based-sexual-abuse/

McGlynn, C., & Rackley, E. (2017). Image based sexual abuse. *Oxford Journal of Legal Studies*, *37*(3), 534–561 doi:10.1093/ojls/gqw033

McGlynn, C., Rackley, E., & Houghton, R. (2017). Beyond 'revenge porn': The continuum of image-based sexual abuse, *Feminist Legal Studies*, *25*, 25–46. doi: 10.1007/s10691-017-9343-2

McGlynn, C., & Westmarland, N. (2019). Kaleidoscopic justice: Sexual violence and victim-survivors' Perceptions of justice. *Social & Legal Studies*, *28*(2), 179–201. doi: 10.1177/0964663918761200

Nyasa Times. (2020, April 17). Blantyre woman convicted for spreading fake news against FDH Bank on Whats App. *Nyasa Times*. retrieved from https://www.nyasatimes.com/blantyre-woman-convicted-for-spreading-fake-news-against-fdh-bank-on-whatsapp/

Pegg, S. (2018). A matter of privacy or abuse? Revenge porn in the law. *Criminal Law Review*, *7*, 512–530.

Phiri, B. (2020, June 1). How leaking of my contact data triggered an avalanche of online abuse. [Web log post]. Retrieved from https://africanfeminism.com/how-leaking-of-my-contact-data-triggered-an-avalanche-of-online-abuse/

Police Scotland. (2019). Management Information: Force Report: Quarter 4 2018/2019. Retrieved from https://www.scotland.police.uk/spa-media/ixxlpvxe/management-info-report-q4-2018-19.pdf

Police Scotland. (2020). Management Information: Force report: Quarter 3 2019/2020. Retrieved from https://www.scotland.police.uk/spa-media/ffypnwyw/force-mi-q3.pdf

Rackley, E. (2019). Section 2 of the Abusive Behaviour and Sexual Harm (Scotland) Act 2016. In E. Rackley, & R. Auchmuty (Eds.), *Women's legal landmarks: Celebrating the history of women and law in the UK and Ireland* (pp. 637–643). Oxford: Hart Publishing. doi:10.5040/9781782259800.ch-001

Rose, G. (2013, September 28). Crackdown promised over online revenge porn videos. *The Scotsman*. Retrieved from https://www.scotsman.com/news/politics/crack-down-promised-over-online-revenge-porn-videos-1559797

Scottish Government. (2015). Equally Safe – Reforming the criminal law to address domestic abuse and sexual offences consultation paper. Retrieved from https://www2.gov.scot/Resource/0047/00473932.pdf

Scottish Government, National Statistics Publication for Scotland. (2019). Recorded Crime in Scotland 2018 – 2019. Retrieved from https://www.gov.scot/publications/recorded-crime-scotland-2018-19/

Scottish Parliament. (2013, September 11). End revenge porn debate. Retrieved from https://www.theyworkforyou.com/sp/?id=2013-09-11.22.0

Scottish Parliament. (2015). Policy Memorandum Abusive Behaviour and Sexual Harm (Scotland) Bill. Retrieved from https://www.parliament.scot/S4_Bills/Abusive%20Behaviour%20and%20Sexual%20Harm%20(Scotland)%20Bill/SPBill81PMS042015.pdf

Scottish Parliament Justice Committee. (2016). Stage 1 Report on the Abusive Behaviour and Sexual Harm (Scotland) Bill (SP paper 885.1 2nd report, 2016 (Session 4)). Retrieved from https://www.parliament.scot/S4_JusticeCommittee/Reports/JS042016R02Rev.pdf

Simango, W. (2017, 14 September). Woman arrested for protesting against gender based violence. *Malawi 24*. Retrieved from https://malawi24.com/2017/09/14/woman-arrested-protesting-gender-based-violence/

The Republic of Malawi and Scotland. (2018). Global Goals Partnership Agreement. Retrieved from https://www.gov.scot/publications/global-goals-partnership-agreement-between-scotland-and-malawi/

The Scotsman. (2018, March 8). First Minister 'concerned' by revenge porn detection rate. *The Scotsman*. Retrieved from https://www.scotsman.com/news/politics/first-minister-concerned-revenge-porn-detection-rate-330278

The World Bank. (2015). Country at a Glance – Malawi. Retrieved from https://datatopics.worldbank.org/education/country/malawi

The World Bank. (2018). Individuals using the Internet (% of population). Retrieved from https://data.worldbank.org/indicator/IT.NET.USER.ZS?end=2018&most_recent_value_desc=true&start=1960

UNESCO Institute for Statistics. (2019a). Adult Literacy rate, population, 15+ years, female (%). Retrieved from http://data.uis.unesco.org/index.aspx?queryid=121

UNESCO Institute for Statistics. (2019b). Adult Literacy rate, population, 15+ years, male (%). Retrieved from http://data.uis.unesco.org/index.aspx?queryid=121

Whitelaw, J. (2014, April 10). Call for internet revenge porn legislation. *The Scotsman*. Retrieved from https://www.scotsman.com/news/politics/call-internet-revenge-porn-legislation-1540012

Case law and legislation

Abusive Behaviour and Sexual Harm (Scotland) Act 2016
Criminal Justice and Courts Act 2015
Electronic Transactions and Cyber Security Act 2016
Gender Equality Act 2013
Malawi Penal Code 1930 (consolidated 2014, December 31)
Prevention of Domestic Violence Act 2006
Shanks v Procurator Fiscal, Glasgow [2018] SAC (Crim) 18
The Constitution of the Republic of Malawi. (1994).

Chapter 32

Revenge Pornography and Rape Culture in Canada's Nonconsensual Distribution Case Law

Moira Aikenhead

Abstract

Canada criminalized the nonconsensual distribution of intimate images in 2014. Lawmakers and commentators noted that this new offense would fill a legislative gap in relation to "revenge pornography," which entails individuals (typically men) sharing intimate images of their ex-partners (typically women) online in an attempt to seek revenge or cause them harm. Feminist writers and activists categorize revenge pornography as a symptom and consequence of "rape culture," in which sexual violence is routinely trivialized and viewed as acceptable or entertaining, and women are blamed for their sexual victimization. In this chapter, I analyze Canada's burgeoning revenge pornography case law and find that these cases support an understanding of revenge pornography as a serious form of communal, gendered, intimate partner violence, which is extremely effective at harming victims because of broader rape culture. While Canadian judges are taking revenge pornography seriously, there is some indication from the case law that they are at risk of relying on gendered reasoning and assumptions previously observed by feminists in sexual assault jurisprudence, which may have the result of bolstering rape culture, rather than contesting it.

Keywords: Revenge pornography; rape culture; nonconsensual distribution; gender violence; intimate partner violence; Canadian criminal law

The Emerald International Handbook of Technology-Facilitated Violence and Abuse, 533–553

doi:10.1108/978-1-83982-848-520211039

Introduction

Revenge pornography is a form of technology-facilitated violence that has attracted significant attention from the public, the media, and governments in recent years. It is perpetrated primarily by men against women, with significant repercussions for female victims' social, professional, and psychological well-being. Revenge pornography is both a symptom and consequence of rape culture, in which sexual violence is excused and legitimized. In this chapter, I demonstrate that the Canadian case law regarding nonconsensual distribution of intimate images (NCD) supports an understanding of revenge pornography as a manifestation of rape culture. The burgeoning case law indicates judges are taking revenge pornography seriously, emphasizing denunciation and deterrence in sentencing offenders for this behavior. Nevertheless, some troubling trends are emerging that echo concerns previously raised by feminist legal scholars in the context of sexual assault case law.

In the first section of this chapter, I define "revenge pornography" and detail Canada's legal response to this phenomenon, the *Criminal Code* offense of NCD. I review the work of previous authors who have highlighted the ways image-based abuse, such as revenge pornography, forms part of the broader rape culture. In the second section of this chapter, I analyze the Canadian nonconsensual distribution case law involving revenge pornography, highlighting the ways the facts of these cases reflect rape culture. I explore how the cases of revenge pornography appearing in Canadian courts paint a picture of revenge pornography as a highly gendered, communal form of sexual violence where victims suffer significant repercussions as a result of gendered double-standards regarding male and female heterosexuality. Throughout this section, I examine the factors sentencing judges are relying on to determine the seriousness of an instance of revenge pornography, as well as judicial analysis of victims' credibility in the few available reasons for judgment at trial, and highlight areas where judges are at risk of relying on problematic reasoning and assumptions previously identified by feminist legal scholars in the context of sexual assault.

"Revenge Pornography"

Definition

"Revenge pornography," as it is commonly understood, involves a person (typically a man) posting nude or sexual images of a former romantic partner online in an effort to punish that person for infidelity, terminating the relationship, or some other perceived wrongdoing. The images may have been created with the consent or active participation of the victim, or they may have been obtained via coercion or surreptitious recording. The term "revenge pornography" is controversial, and has been rejected by many on the basis that it reduces the severe harms of this behavior to the narrative of a scorned ex-partner, improperly implies offenders are motivated solely by vengeance, and casts images that were not created for public consumption as "pornography" (Maddocks, 2018).

Alternative labels, including "nonconsensual pornography" and "image-based abuse," have been proposed, however such terms inevitably encompass a broader range of behavior than I am concerned with in this chapter, the intentional NCD of a current or former partner. I believe it is crucial that revenge pornography is understood as a form of intimate partner violence, which has historically been viewed as "private" or non-criminal in Western societies (Minaker, 2001). Revenge pornography is often a type of separation abuse intended to block a partner's leaving, retaliate for their departure, or forcibly end a separation (Mahoney, 1991). The nonconsensual sharing of intimate images of a current or former partner is a distinct form of intimate partner violence, requiring examination separate from the nonconsensual sharing of intimate images more generally. I acknowledge "revenge pornography" is something of a misnomer for this behavior, for the reasons outlined above. However, as this is the term most frequently used in media and governmental discourses around the phenomenon of nonconsensual distribution of partners' intimate images, I use it throughout this chapter to refer to this specific form of technology-facilitated sexual violence.

Canada's Legal Response – Section 162.1 of the Criminal Code

Men nonconsensually sharing intimate recordings and images of female partners obtained during the course of a romantic relationship is not a new phenomenon (Citron & Franks, 2014; Maddocks, 2018; Salter & Crofts, 2015). The growing ubiquity of smartphones with built-in cameras and internet access in the past decade has, however, greatly increased the average person's ability to engage in this behavior. By 2013, the phenomenon of online revenge pornography was receiving worldwide attention and had been criminalized in several countries and US states. In Canada, then Justice Minister Peter MacKay named revenge pornography as one of the targets of the Conservative Government's "anti-cyberbullying" legislation, the *Protecting Canadians from Online Crime Act* (Canada, 2013–2015). This legislation created new *Criminal Code* (*Code*) provisions intended to combat NCD, which read as follows:

> 162.1 (1) Everyone who knowingly publishes, distributes, transmits, sells, makes available or advertises an intimate image of a person knowing that the person depicted in the image did not give their consent to that conduct, or being reckless as to whether or not that person gave their consent to that conduct, is guilty
>
> (a) of an indictable offense and liable to imprisonment for a term of not more than five years; or
> (b) of an offense punishable on summary conviction.

An "intimate image" is defined in section 162.1(2) of the *Code* as "a visual recording of a person made by any means including a photographic, film, or video recording":

> (a) in which the person is nude, is exposing his or her genital organs or anal region or her breasts or is engaged in explicit sexual activity;
> (b) in respect of which, at the time of the recording, there were circumstances that gave rise to a reasonable expectation of privacy; and
> (c) in respect of which the person depicted retains a reasonable expectation of privacy at the time the offense is committed.

All revenge pornography involves NCD, however not every case of NCD is an instance of revenge pornography. Revenge pornography is a specific form of gendered, intimate partner violence, and manifestation of rape culture, as will be examined throughout this chapter.

Revenge Pornography as a Manifestation of Rape Culture

The popularity of revenge pornography on both "mainstream" and niche pornography websites is a symptom of modern Western society's broader "rape culture," in which sexual violence against women and persons who do not conform to heterosexist norms of masculinity and femininity is routinely "excused, legitimized and viewed as inevitable" (Smith, 2004, as cited in Dodge, 2016, p. 67; Dietzel, this volume). Revenge pornography is a form of gender violence as it depends on the gender identities of the parties (Merry, 2009). There is ongoing debate about the extent to which intimate partner violence is a gendered phenomenon, however there is broad consensus among researchers that women are overwhelmingly victims of sexual intimate partner violence in heterosexual relationships (Johnson, Holmes, & Johnson, 2016). Recent research indicates that men perpetrate image-based sexual abuse more frequently than women (Powell, Scott, Flynn, & Henry, 2020; Ruvalcaba & Eaton, 2019), the vast majority of images on revenge pornography websites depict women (Cyber Civil Rights Initiative, 2014, as cited in; Henry & Powell, 2018, p. 202; Franks, 2017), and women suffer unique and distinctly damaging consequences as a result of their gender when they are targeted for revenge pornography (Bates, 2017; Citron, 2019; Powell et al., 2020).

Revenge pornography is popular not because it depicts women nude or engaged in sexual activity, but because of its nonconsensual nature. Viewers seek out revenge pornography images specifically because they believe the women depicted did not consent to the image's distribution (Franks, 2017; Slane & Langlois, 2018). Research indicates that female revenge pornography victims experience harms similar to those suffered by victims of sexual assault (Bates, 2017), however many individuals who view revenge pornography images may not consider them to be particularly harmful. Under rape culture, viewing women's naked bodies or sexual activity without their consent is frequently understood as an acceptable pornographic preference, and form of entertainment (Dodge, 2016; Franks, 2017). The result is that victims may experience the extremely harmful, gendered, consequences of revenge pornography intended by their current or former partners, while at the same time attracting little sympathy and having their victimization extended by the numerous individuals who circulate and consume their intimate images.

Revenge pornography is a communal form of violence. To have its intended impact on the victim, there must be a receptive audience for the images. Rape culture is fostered in online environments where the sexualized abuse and harassment of women and girls is tolerated or encouraged, and where victims are viewed as responsible for their victimization (Fairbairn, 2015). Male peer support theory holds that patriarchal men situated in rape culture will have their values and beliefs reinforced by male friends with similar beliefs, allowing them to feel normal and justified in abusing their female intimate partners (DeKeseredy & Schwartz, 2016). The ease with which men holding such views can be located online has allowed abusive men to find large audiences to consume and participate in their partners' victimization and has allowed for the proliferation of materials depicting this abuse (DeKeseredy & Schwartz, 2016). Many pornography websites allow users to comment on videos and images, and such comments frequently direct disgust and shame toward the women depicted, and admiration toward the male poster (Dodge, 2016; Langlois & Slane, 2017). When men include their victim's name or other identifying information in a posting, they can ensure she will be a target for contact and surveillance by strangers, both online and offline (Langlois & Slane, 2017).

As with other crimes of sexual violence, rape culture results in victims of revenge pornography having their actions scrutinized and criticized, while the (male) offender's behavior is understood as predictable and inevitable, if not acceptable (Powell & Henry, 2017; Salter & Crofts, 2015). Members of the general public may blame revenge pornography victims for having consented to the recording of such images in the first place, as victims of sexual violence have traditionally been blamed for behaving provocatively, or not exercising sufficient caution to avoid victimization (Gotell, 2006). Revenge pornography is a means by which men situated in rape culture can harm their current or former partners by instrumentalizing the gendered double standard that punishes women for perceived promiscuity, while rewarding men for the same behavior (Salter & Crofts, 2015). As a result, female victims frequently suffer significant social or reputational repercussions as a result of their partners nonconsensually sharing their intimate images.

Methodology: Examining Revenge Pornography within Canada's Nonconsensual Distribution Case Law

In this chapter, I review all available English-language criminal law decisions involving charges under section 162.1 of the *Code,* in which the intimate images depict the accused's current or former intimate partner. The data set does not include cases of revenge pornography that took place before the enactment of section 162.1, or where NCD charges were not pursued. Furthermore, it does not include cases of revenge pornography prosecuted pursuant to other sections of the *Code,* such as its child pornography provisions, as I am particularly interested in how the NCD legislation is being interpreted and applied with respect to a specific behavior it was enacted to target.

I located the decisions in my data set by noting-up section 162.1 of the *Code* on both Westlaw and Quicklaw online databases, and reviewing all English-language decisions citing that section. For each decision I located, I reviewed any potentially relevant cases cited in the text and noted-up each decision to locate additional relevant cases. Finally, I conducted searches on both Westlaw and Quicklaw for the terms "revenge porn," "revenge pornography," and "intimate image," and added all additional relevant decisions to the data set. I completed my search for case law on February 12, 2020, and thus the data set is current up to that date.

Results: Evidence of Revenge Pornography as Rape Culture in Canada's Nonconsensual Distribution Case Law

I located 33 cases involving NCD charges, consisting of 37 individual decisions (for example, the case *R v MR* (2017) consists of two decisions: trial reasons and reasons for sentence). Over 80% of all NCD cases, (27 of 33), met my criteria for "revenge pornography," as they involved individuals accused of distributing intimate images of their current or former intimate partners. I excluded one of these cases from the data set, *R v Tunney* (2018), as the only available decision was a ruling on an application which did not include a clear description of the facts, or any judicial commentary regarding NCD. The data set therefore consists of 26 revenge pornography cases, made up of 30 individual decisions (see Table 31.1).

Judges in all 21 sentencing decisions emphasized denunciation and deterrence as the primary sentencing objectives in cases of NCD. Leach J. in *R v JB* (2018), for example, noted that denunciation and deterrence must be more pronounced in cases of NCD than the similar offenses of voyeurism and criminal harassment in order to properly reflect Parliament's intention to address NCD in a targeted and serious manner (para 55). The high rate of prison sentences outlined in Table 31.1 indicates judges are treating NCD as a serious offense. In general, facts that corresponded with longer terms of imprisonment in the data set cases included: intimate images obtained by surreptitious or nonconsensual recording; widespread or public dissemination of images; and "explicit" sexual images or recordings. I will discuss each of these factors, and their relevance to understanding revenge pornography as a manifestation of rape culture, in more detail throughout this chapter.

Table 31.1. Data Set Decisions and Outcomes.

Case	Associated Decision(s)	Outcome	Sentence re: Nonconsensual Distribution of Intimate Images
R v AB	Sentencing	Guilty plea	Conditional sentence (Two months)
R v AC	Sentencing	Guilty plea	Five months
R v BS	Sentencing	Guilty plea	Three months (intermittent)
R v Calpito	Sentencing	Guilty plea	Conditional discharge
R v CRD	Trial	Acquittal	NA
R v Greene	Sentencing	Guilty plea	Five months
R v JB	Sentencing	Guilty plea	Conditional sentence (16 months)
R v JR	Sentencing	Guilty plea	60 days
R v JS (AB)	Sentencing	Guilty plea	

Table 31.1. *(Continued)*

Case	Associated Decision(s)	Outcome	Sentence re: Nonconsensual Distribution of Intimate Images
			Suspended sentence (Two years)
R v JS (ON)	Sentencing	Guilty plea	18 months
R v JTB	Sentencing	Guilty plea	Four years
R v Ly	Sentencing	Guilty plea	Four years (Three counts of NCD)
R v MR	Trial; Sentencing	Conviction	Five months
R v MTB	Sentencing	Conviction	Five months
R v Newby	Sentencing	Guilty plea	90 days (intermittent)
R v NM	Sentencing	Guilty plea	12 months
R v NN	Sentencing	Guilty plea	30 days (intermittent)
R v OK	Trial	Conviction	(unavailable)
R v PSD	Sentencing	Guilty plea	Suspended Sentence (Two years)
R v Ruby	Trial; Sentencing	Conviction	21 days
R v Sobh	Trial	Acquittal	NA
R v TD	Sentencing	Guilty plea	90 days
R v Trinchi	Application; Sentencing; Appeal	Acquittal (on NCD charges)	NA
R v Tsang	Motion	Acquittal	NA
R v Verner	Trial	Conviction	(unavailable)
R v Wilson	Sentencing	Conviction	Six months

Note: Offenders were frequently sentenced to terms of probation. Probation terms have not been included in the above table as they apply to the global sentence, while the sentences listed above apply only to the NCD charges.

Gender Violence

Every published Canadian decision involving charges of NCD that met the definition of "revenge pornography" involved a male accused and a female victim. Some offenders were described as harboring negative attitudes toward a number of their female ex-partners, or women in general (*R v BS*, 2019; *R v JTB*, 2018; *R v MTB*, 2019). Offenders posted sexist and vulgar titles, descriptions, and comments alongside their partners' intimate images in a number of cases, often referring to them as "sluts" (*R v AC*, 2017; *R v JS* (ON), 2018; *R v JTB*, 2018; *R v TD*, 2018). There were no instances of revenge pornography in the context of LGBTQ relationships in the reported NCD case law, however this does not mean that NCD is not occurring in the context of same-sex partnerships. Indeed some studies indicate that LGBTQ persons face disproportionately high rates of image-based sexual abuse (see Dietzel, this volume; Powell et al., 2020). The lack of reported decisions involving LGBTQ persons could be reflective of warranted distrust of law enforcement and unwillingness to report violent incidents to police in the LGBTQ community (see Dario, Fradella, & Verhagen, 2020).

As Galiatsatos J. Q. C. notes in *R v AB* (2020), there is a discernible trend in the Canadian NCD case law of male, first-time offenders (para 76). In the 22 cases where judges discussed whether the accused had a criminal record, the accused had no record in 15, a minor record in three, and a more extensive record in four. That so many accused were first-time offenders cannot be attributed to their generally being youthful. While the accused's age was not noted in every decision, the accused was 30 or older in 11 of the 18 cases where age was discussed. It is possible that NCD is a common first offense given the ease with which it can be committed, as camera-equipped digital technologies are now ubiquitous (Dodge, 2019). Furthermore, some offenders may not view this behavior as particularly deviant or harmful, given the prevalence and popularity of online revenge pornography images under rape culture (DeKeseredy & Schwartz, 2016). For example, in a series of interviews with perpetrators of image-based abuse, Flynn and Henry found that many viewed these offenses as "untroubling and normative within a context of male bonding and homosociality" (cited in Powell et al., 2020, p. 6).

A number of judges noted that engaging in revenge pornography may be tempting for men in possession of intimate images of their partners, such that this behavior must be denounced in clear terms. Shandler J. in *R v Ly* (2016) noted that general deterrence may be particularly relevant to prevent "like-minded individuals with intimate recordings of ex-partners in their possession who are otherwise ordinarily law-abiding people" from engaging in revenge pornography (at para 45). Two sentencing judges determined periods of incarceration were necessary in part because house arrest might be considered a small price to pay for an "aggrieved spouse" or a person "considering humiliating a former partner on the internet," as compared with the benefit of taking revenge on a former spouse (*R v JR*, 2018, p. 34; *R v AC*, 2017, para 66). Such reasoning belies a belief that it may be difficult for an "average" man to resist sharing his former partner's intimate images, particularly if the relationship ended badly, such as through his ex-partner's infidelity (*R v JR*, 2018, pp. 33–34). Feminists have criticized the persistence of such narratives in relation to intimate partner violence, where acts of violence are frequently characterized as "crimes of passion" borne out of volatile relationships and intense emotions, despite more often forming part of a long-term pattern of abuse and control (Fairbairn & Dawson, 2013).

The most commonly cited motive for revenge pornography was to humiliate the victim, and indeed victims in many cases testified that they were humiliated or embarrassed by the offender posting their intimate images (*R v Calpito*, 2017; *R v JTB*, 2018; *R v Ly*, 2016; *R v Newby*, 2018; *R v NN*, 2019; *R v TD*, 2018; *R v Trinchi*, 2016 (trial and sentencing), 2019). Victims' experiences of humiliation and shame as a result of revenge pornography are consistent with other forms of gendered sexual violence. Within rape culture, female victims are understood by society as wholly or partly to blame for the sexual violence committed against them, and victims often internalize this shame (Bates, 2017; Citron & Franks, 2014; Dodge, 2016).

The consequences experienced by men and women as a result of having their intimate images nonconsensually shared are likely to diverge on gendered lines, based on the differential expectations and understandings of male and female heterosexuality under rape culture. While there were no male victims in the data set cases to use as a comparator, female victims in the data set cases suffered significant harms beyond humiliation and embarrassment. In *R v TD* (2018), the victim described losing relationships with friends who viewed the images, while in two cases, *R v MTB* (2019) and *R v NM* (2019), victims had to upend multiple aspects of their lives, including moving and changing jobs. Other victims suffered negative impacts on their educational or professional lives, including the images being sent to or viewed by their current employers, or fears that this would occur (*R v AC*, 2017; *R v BS*, 2019; *R v Calpito*, 2017; *R v JB*, 2018; *R v JTB*, 2018; *R v Ly*, 2016; *R v MR* (trial), 2017; *R v NN*, 2019; *R v Newby*, 2018). Numerous victims expressed warranted fear for their physical safety as a result of offenders' actions, as will be discussed further below. Rape culture results in female victims experiencing far-reaching social, professional, and emotional repercussions as a result of revenge pornography, in addition to the significant harms to their privacy, dignity, and sexual autonomy occasioned by the initial nonconsensual distribution.

A final aspect of case law that may reflect the gendered nature of revenge pornography is the impact of the "explicitness" of intimate images on sentencing. Cases involving images depicting sexual activity, or focusing on the victim's genitals or anus, generally attracted harsher sentences than cases where the victim was "merely" nude. The three cases where accused were granted a conditional discharge or suspended sentence involved such "non-explicit" images (*R v Calpito*, 2017; *R v JS (AB)*, 2019; *R v PSD*, 2016). The longest sentence imposed in a case involving non-explicit intimate images was 90 days imprisonment (*R v TD*, 2018).

The impact of the explicitness of intimate images on sentencing likely reflects a judicial understanding that explicit images constitute a greater violation of privacy when they are nonconsensually shared. In a number of cases, judges emphasized that the primary purpose of the NCD provisions is to protect privacy (see *R v AC*, 2017; *R v JB*, 2018; *R v JS* (AB), 2019). Legal conceptions of privacy are controversial from a feminist perspective, as "privacy" historically shielded abusive male partners from legal scrutiny (MacKinnon, 1987), and the legal privacy rights extended to women traditionally reflected certain raced and classed notions of feminine "modesty" (Bailey, 2008, p. 285; Gotell, 2006, p. 747). For example, Gotell (2006) found that Canadian judges considering applications for the admission of sexual history evidence sometimes emphasized the potential for victims' "humiliation" and "embarrassment," which they "based upon a scale of sexual activity in which evidence of sexual intercourse is viewed as the most serious threat to privacy" (p. 768). In the data set cases, two judges expressly found the fact that the images (which depicted close-ups of victims' genitals) could not have been more "private" (*R v JB*, 2018, para 44) or "intimate" (*R v JTB*, 2018, para 97) to be an aggravating factor on sentencing.

The privacy harms of revenge pornography are significant, and it is unsurprising that judges emphasized this aspect of the offense in their reasons. Judges should ensure, however, that their reasons do not support an understanding of privacy based on gendered notions of modesty, shame, and concealment in relation to sexual activity. Understanding the sharing of explicit intimate images as a greater violation of privacy can be consistent with an equality-preserving account of privacy if framed within the broader context of the significant, gendered consequences female victims suffer as a result of NCD in an unequal society, rather than because intimate images of women are inherently humiliating or embarrassing. The former interpretation contests patriarchy and rape culture, while the latter upholds it. Thus, in discussing victims' right to privacy in the context of revenge pornography, judges should characterize the implications for victims' privacy in relation to their dignity, sexual autonomy, and equality (Bailey, 2008; Citron, 2019). While a number of judges noted the violation of dignity inherent in NCD in their reasons (*R v AC*, 2017; *R v JB*, 2018; *R v JS* (AB), 2019; *R v JS* (ON); *R v JTB*, 2018; *R v Newby*, 2018), none characterized it as a violation of victims' (or women's and girls' generally) right to gender equality.

The data set cases strongly support an understanding of revenge pornography as form of gendered sexual violence bolstered by rape culture. "Ordinary" men without criminal records are the overwhelming perpetrators, indicating that these offenders may not view NCD as a serious act of violence, or that the ease with which they can use their female partners' intimate images to cause them harm is too "tempting" to pass up. Revenge pornography victims experience shame, humiliation, and other significant repercussions as a result of gendered double-standards around sexuality. Judges in the data set cases treated revenge pornography as a serious offense, worthy of denunciation and deterrence; however, it was not always clear whether their reasons for doing so reflected an understanding of women's sexuality as inherently shameful, or was grounded in respect for victims' dignity, autonomy, and right to equality.

Communal Violence

The data set cases were fairly evenly split between those involving broad public or semi-public dissemination of intimate images, and more limited, targeted distribution. Of the 22 cases in which offenders were found or pleaded guilty, intimate images were posted on publicly accessible pornography, dating, or sexual service websites in 10, disseminated on social media in four, and sent directly to an individual or small group of recipients (for example, via text message or e-mail) in 10. Some cases involved multiple forms of distribution.

Images posted on public pornography websites have enormous potential audiences. In *R v JS* (ON) (2018), the victim's intimate images had been viewed over 10,000 times at the time of judgment, and in *R v TD* (2018), the victim's images were viewed by "at least 7,000 people" (para 1). While any images posted online have the potential to exist permanently on the internet or on individuals' hard drives, intimate images of women and girls will often be downloaded, saved, and redistributed at a particularly high rate (see Clancy, Klettke, & Hallford, 2019; UN Broadband Commission, 2015), as rape culture casts these images as acceptable sources of titillation and entertainment.

Broader dissemination tended to correspond with lengthier sentences in the data set cases. A number of judges directly linked the number of people who viewed intimate images with the seriousness of the privacy breach (*R v AC*, 2017; *R v JS* (AB), 2019; *R v JTB*, 2018; *R v TD*, 2018). For example, Justice Rahman in *R v AC* (2017) noted that "[t]he more people to whom the image is exposed, the greater the invasion of privacy and the greater the harm caused to the victim" (para 20). Other judges grappled with whether it is "worse" to have one's intimate images distributed widely to anonymous strangers, or narrowly to known individuals. In *R v JB* (2018), for example, the offender posted intimate images of the victim to a fake Facebook profile he created under her name. Many of the victim's close friends and family members accepted friend requests from this fake account. Leach J. found that this targeted distribution was intended to maximize the victim's degradation and embarrassment (para 44). He noted, however, that known individuals were less likely to redistribute the images, which decreased the harmful nature of the distribution (para 60).

The judge in *R v AB* (2020) made a similar observation, noting that the offender's choice to distribute an intimate image to a female friend of the victim reduced the likelihood the image would be distributed further (para 110). In many cases, targeted distribution may indeed result in intimate images not being viewed as many times or by as many people as images that are posted publicly. Nevertheless, judges should not lose sight of the fact that once an image has been distributed digitally to even a single individual, a significant risk remains that that image will be posted publicly online at some point in the future. Furthermore, under rape culture, friends, family, or acquaintances of victims may blame the victim for the offender's NCD and actively participate in their victimization. In *R v Newby* (2018), for example, the offender distributed intimate images to two individuals who had known his ex-partner for long periods of time. One of these recipients questioned why the offender was sharing the images (to which the offender replied it was because the victim "didn't swallow lol" (*R v Newby*, 2018, Appendix, para 15)), but did not otherwise object or express concern for the victim. Rather, he noted that the victim could "be a huge bitch lol" and was "super slutty," musing that she "must have fucked up big time" for the offender to be sharing the images (*R v Newby*, 2018, Appendix, para 15). The recipient's comments in *R v Newby* (2018) are reflective of rape culture, as he used the victim's intimate images as a means for bonding with a male peer and blamed the victim for the offender's actions (DeKeseredy & Schwartz, 2016; Dodge, 2016).

Dodge (2019) notes that the

> ...impact of a digital image shared with a few people known to the victim will not necessarily cause less harm than an image shared with hundreds of people on a pornography site. (p. 134)

Victims in the data set cases suffered significant harms regardless of whether images were distributed broadly, or in a narrow, targeted manner. Victims who had their images distributed publicly did not generally report greater embarrassment or humiliation, however they did in some cases express heightened fear for their safety as a result of the distribution. Offenders included victims' names or other identifying information alongside their intimate images on publicly accessible websites in 11 cases, sometimes indicating the victims were escorts or sex workers. Unknown men contacted many of these women. In *R v JTB* (2018), Leach J. noted that since the arrest of the offender over a year previously, strangers continued to actively use the photos and information posted by the offender to track down and contact the victim online. The victim stated that she had reason to fear not only the offender but also all those unknown individuals who viewed the images, and who continued to contact her seeking to fulfill the "rape fantasy" the offender claimed she was seeking in the fake online profile (para 97). Victims received sexualized messages from strangers via social media (*R v AC*, 2017; *R v TD*, 2018), and in one case, a victim received over 300 calls and messages in response to a fake advertisement the offender created using her intimate images on the "escort" section of Backpage.com indicating she was "into anything" (*R v JS* (ON), 2018, para 10).

Rape culture ensures that when women's personal information is posted online alongside their intimate images, a certain number of men will feel entitled to contact and harass them. While in some cases the men contacting the victims in the data set cases likely believed they were responding to legitimate postings authored by the women themselves, victims' reported reactions to these communications indicated they often felt threatened or degraded. Victims may experience large-scale dissemination of intimate images as particularly harmful not necessarily because it is more embarrassing, but because it increases the possibility that they will come across men in their daily lives who have viewed their intimate images, or that such men will attempt to locate them, representing a significant risk to their safety and psychological well-being.

Rape culture creates conditions where revenge pornography victims will experience significant shame regardless of whether images are shared with known or unknown individuals, as any recipients are likely to draw negative conclusions about the victim as a result of viewing her images. Widespread distribution results not only in humiliation but also substantial fear for many victims who must live with the reality that individuals they meet in their daily lives could have viewed their images and will view them as appropriate targets for sexualized behaviors or communications. Judges should determine the seriousness or harmful nature of an instance of revenge pornography based on the actual impact on the victim's psychological, emotional, social, and professional well-being, where these impacts are known. In addition, they should consider the communal harms of revenge pornography as an offense of gendered, sexual, intimate partner violence. Assumptions about the inherent harms of NCD should be informed by a broad conception of sexual privacy premised on equality, as discussed previously, rather than understanding the harms of breaches of privacy primarily in terms of humiliation or embarrassment.

Victim Blaming

Men who disseminate ex-partners' intimate images can be confident not only that they will find a receptive audience for those images but also that those who view them will likely direct some measure of blame toward the victim. A woman who agrees to have her intimate images recorded may be understood as complicit in her own victimization, and as such not truly worthy of concern or empathy. Feminists have long highlighted the ways the media, the public, and legal system actors cast women as responsible for the sexual violence committed against them (Gotell, 2007; Randall, 2010). While judicial victim-blaming can be overt, such as former Judge Robin Camp's questioning why a sexual assault victim "couldn't… just keep [her] knees together" (Canadian Judicial Council, 2016, para 135), it may also be subtle. Such subtle blaming occurs where judges reach conclusions that imply women were not sufficiently cautious or did not take adequate steps to ensure they would not be victimized (Gotell, 2007). A victim may be viewed as less credible as a result of her "poor choices," a finding that is extremely harmful in the context of sexual assault cases, which often do not involve direct evidence and therefore turn on parties' credibility (Koshan, 2017, p. 265). The data set indicates that revenge pornography cases will similarly rarely involve direct (i.e., eyewitness or forensic) evidence of a perpetrator's identity, and thus victims' credibility may be central in these cases as well.

The four data set cases in which an accused was not convicted of NCD lacked any direct evidence as to the perpetrator's identity. In *R v Tsang* (2019), the victim's intimate images were uploaded to an anonymous revenge pornography website, and while the victim testified she only ever shared those images with the accused, Quigley J. granted the defense's motion for a directed verdict on the basis that the Crown failed to adduce evidence it was the accused who uploaded the images. In *R v Trinchi* (2016 (trial and sentencing), 2019), the victim's intimate images were distributed through an anonymous e-mail account, and the trial judge acquitted the accused based on evidence that one of the accused's girlfriends had the motive, opportunity, and propensity to distribute the intimate images, which left him with a reasonable doubt that it was the accused who distributed the images.

The other two data set cases resulting in acquittals involved complainants who had shared their own intimate images before the alleged nonconsensual distribution. In *R v CRD* (2019), the complainant testified that while she may have sent some of the intimate images that were later nonconsensually distributed to multiple individuals, one was sent exclusively to the accused. She testified that she did not remember that the accused was the sole recipient of that image until one to two days after she learned of the distribution. Cheverie J. noted

> [w]hile I found [the complainant] to be generally credible, I found it unusual that it would take her a day and a half to two days to conclude she sent [the image] exclusively to C.R.D.

He ultimately found that the circumstantial evidence did not exclude the possibility that all of the images were sent to someone other than the accused, and as such was left with reasonable doubt as to the identity of the perpetrator.

In *R v Sobh* (2018), the complainant consented to the accused producing and distributing a number of her intimate images, and in some instances, she distributed these images online herself. She claimed that she did not consent to the accused disseminating intimate images in which she was depicted having sex, as opposed to nude, including the two images which were the subject of the NCD charges. The two contested images depicted the complainant at nude resorts having sex with men Bondy J. made a point of noting she had met one to three hours before the photos were taken (paras 25 and 27). Bondy J. found the complainant was not a reliable or credible witness for a variety of reasons related to her evasiveness, inconsistency, and possible fabrication or misrepresentation of certain evidence (paras 173–228). He did not state that the complainant's choices to engage in sex in public spaces, allow this sexual activity to be recorded, or distribute her own intimate recordings negatively impacted her credibility. Bondy J. did, however, find her credibility was undermined by the fact that she initially testified that she only shared intimate images with two individuals other than the accused, but later conceded she "maybe" shared images with other individuals named by defense counsel (para 198). While she maintained that she did not share the images that were the subject of the charges with anyone other than the accused, Bondy J. expressed difficulty believing the complainant "could not recall who she had sent photos of herself to, yet could recall with certainty what images had been sent to those people" (para 199).

The complainants in both *R v CRD* (2019) and *R v Sobh* (2018) had their credibility questioned in part because judges doubted their ability to accurately recall who they had shared the contested images with, having previously shared intimate images with individuals other than the accused. Once again, there were a number of serious issues with the complainant's testimony in *R v Sobh* (2018), in particular, such that a finding she was not a credible witness was likely warranted. It is not necessarily problematic that judges question complainants who have previously distributed their own intimate images regarding who received those images. Indeed this will be a crucial issue when the identity of the perpetrator is contested. Judges must ensure that in doing so, however, they do not allow value judgments regarding victims' lifestyles and choices regarding their intimate images color their thinking about victims' credibility in general.

The data set cases for which there are reasons for judgment at trial and accused were convicted each involved additional circumstantial evidence substantiating the victim's version of events. In *R v Ruby* (2018, 2019), Flynn P. J. C. found the circumstantial evidence, which included copies of text messages in which the offender apologized for posting the images, was sufficient to establish guilt. In *R v OK* (2019), the accused asserted that the victim posted her own intimate images to the pornography website Pornhub. The judge rejected this theory, noting that the victim's version of events was bolstered by transcripts of abusive Facebook messages the accused sent to the victim around the time the images were posted, and emails between the victim and Pornhub in which she implored the website to remove the images. In *R v MR* (2017), Felix J. rejected the defense's theory that a hacker distributed the victim's intimate images, based in part on the fact the images were sent to a very specific group of individuals close to the victim, and text message evidence indicating the accused "possessed peculiar information concerning the timing and content of the dissemination emails" ((trial), para 124). The data set cases indicate that if offenders do not engage in additional communications implicating themselves in distributing the images, charges of NCD may be difficult to prove in cases of revenge pornography. This is particularly troubling if one understands revenge pornography as an act of sexual violence, as corroborating evidence is explicitly not required for a conviction on sexual assault charges, thanks to significant feminist legal reform efforts (Cunliffe, 2012; *Code,* 1985, s. 274).

Seven of the data set cases had facts that created little risk of victim blaming, as the intimate images were initially obtained without victims' consent. These cases resulted in the harshest sentences in the data set. Offenders took screenshots of what were intended to be live or fleeting online sexualized interactions with victims in three cases (*R v CRD*, 2019; *R v Ly*, 2016; *R v Trinchi,* 2016 (trial and sentencing), 2019). In *R v Trinchi* (2016 (trial and sentencing), 2019), while the offender was acquitted of NCD at trial, the Ontario Court of Appeal upheld the trial judge's finding that capturing a permanent image from a live, online sexual encounter met the definition of voyeurism in the *Code,* given the significant harms that can result from recording a permanent image as opposed to mere observation. In two cases, *R v JS* (ON) (2018) and *R v Verner* (2017), offenders used hidden cameras to surreptitiously record consensual sexual activity with their partners, and subsequently distributed those recordings. In *R v PSD* (2016), the offender pulled down his partner's shirt to expose her breasts and took a photograph with his phone, which he immediately texted to two friends. Finally, in the particularly egregious case of *R v NM* (2019), the offender created numerous recordings of himself sexually assaulting his partner while she was unconscious, often using weapons and in one instance abusing the couple's pet dog in the process. The offender edited these recordings, set them to music, and posted them on pornography websites with vulgar titles. Each of these cases attracted lengthy prison sentences, apart from *R v PSD* (2016). In that case, the judge appeared to rely on problematic narratives around intimate partner violence, noting the offender was "very frustrated and angered by seemingly mixed signals" from the victim, and that the distribution was a "rash decision," such that the circumstances of the NCD were less egregious than other cases (*R v PSD,* 2016, paras 12–13).

While NCD involving images that were captured nonconsensually is extremely serious, and should attract a harsh sentence, an inverse conclusion that the non-consensual distribution of consensually created images is less serious or harmful should be avoided. Section 162.1 of the *Code* is intended to address the harms inherent in having one's intimate images *distributed* without consent. The non-consensual recording of intimate images in some cases may be addressed through corresponding voyeurism charges. Judges must ensure that by emphasizing the harmful nature of nonconsensual recording, they are not attributing blame to victims who consensually participate in the creation of intimate images, or who distribute those images themselves.

Overall, sentencing judges in the data set cases did a good job of emphasizing that victims having consented to the recording of intimate images is not a mitigating factor, and indeed, Justice Ghosh in *R v JS* (ON) (2018) noted that reaching such conclusions "engages retrograde thinking surrounding the interplay of sex, privacy, consent and control" (para 36; also see *R v BS*, 2019). Some sentencing judges did, however, use their reasons to caution victims or people in general (in reality, women) about producing intimate images. Justice West addressed the victim in *R v NN* (2019) in his oral reasons for sentence, stating that she should not let the NCD define her, but that the offender's actions should

> ...have an impact on how you conduct yourself in the future because while you might think initially you can trust someone with everything, even the most intimate things about yourself, certain things probably should never be shared, like intimate photographs. (p. 52)

Galiatsatos J. Q. C. noted in *R v AB* (2020) that many couples, particularly young couples, were now making intimate recordings "without first pausing to consider the future consequences" (para 8). The judge in that case also reached the problematic conclusion that because the recipient of the images already had them in their possession at the time of the NCD, this neutralized the harms of the offender's actions as the victim could "hardly suggest that her privacy was tarnished *by the accused* if the recipient of the video already had possession of it" (*R v AB,* 2020, para 116). While Galiatsatos J. Q. C. noted that the victim had the right to control access to her intimate images (*R v AB,* 2020, para 115), the effect of locating the harmful nature of the NCD in whether a recipient has already viewed or possessed the images is inconsistent with an understanding of privacy as grounded in dignity, equality, and sexual autonomy (Aikenhead, 2018).

The case law data set represents an extremely small sample, including only six reasons for judgment at trial. However, these few cases indicate that charges of NCD may be more difficult to prove where women have previously distributed their own intimate images (whether or not these are the intimate images in question), and where there is no corroborating evidence, which will often take the form of communications authored by the accused themselves. Judges in two decisions indicated they viewed the creation of intimate images as an inherently risky behavior that should be avoided, despite the fact that it is the nonconsensual distribution of these images that is the source of their harm. Each of these findings are problematic in the context of broader rape culture in which women's accounts of sexual violence are frequently cast in doubt, and their choices regarding their sexual lives are understood as contributing to their own victimization.

Conclusion

The early Canadian case law involving instances of revenge pornography prosecuted pursuant to section 162.1 of the *Code* support an understanding of revenge pornography as a manifestation of rape culture. Every case in my data set involved a male accused and female victim. The offenders often had no previous criminal record, indicating these men may not consider nonconsensual distribution to be a harmful act of sexual violence or found the ease with which they could cause significant harm to their former partners too tempting to pass up. Victims in the cases suffered serious consequences. Individuals both known and unknown to victims participated in and extended the violence of revenge pornography, and victims were subjected to shame, humiliation, and more tangible professional, educational, and social consequences as a result of offenders' actions.

Overall, judges emphasized the serious and harmful nature of NCD, consistently naming denunciation and deterrence as primary sentencing objectives, and often sentencing offenders to periods of incarceration. Certain findings in the data set cases, however, raise some red flags from a feminist perspective. Judges must ensure that in emphasizing the privacy harms inherent in revenge pornography, they are not directly or indirectly implying that women's intimate images are inherently shameful and humiliating, but rather account for the broader context of rape culture and gender inequality that allows women's intimate images to be weaponized against them. The few available reasons for judgment at trial indicate that corroborating evidence may be necessary to ground a conviction, and that a woman's choice to distribute her own intimate images might have negative implications for judicial assessment of her credibility. While judges generally emphasized that a victim's choice to participate in an intimate recording in no way lessened the serious nature of NCD, the particularly harsh sentences in cases involving surreptitiously recorded images, and occasional judicial commentary regarding the risky nature of creating and sharing intimate images, indicate that judgments about victims' choices may be coloring judicial attitudes toward revenge pornography victims. Judges in revenge pornography cases must ensure they are not relying on myths and stereotypes informed by broader rape culture, which feminist legal reformers have identified and problematized in the context of sexual assault.

References

Aikenhead, M. (2018). Non-consensual disclosure of intimate images as a crime of gender-based violence. *Canadian Journal of Women and the Law*, *30*, 117–143. doi: 10.3138/cjwl.30.1.117

Bailey, J. (2008). Towards an equality-enhancing conception of privacy. *Dalhousie Law Journal*, *31*(2), 267–309. Retrieved from https://papers.ssrn.com/sol3/papers.cfm?abstract_id=2281447.

Bates, S. (2017). Revenge porn and mental health: A qualitative analysis of the mental health effects of revenge porn on female survivors. *Feminist Criminology*, *12*(1), 22–42. doi:10.1177/1557085116654565

Canada. Parliament. House of Commons. (2013–2015). *Debates (41st Parliament, 2nd Session, Vol. 147*, No. 25). Ottawa, ON: Canadian Government Publishing.

Canadian Judicial Council. (2016). In the matter of an inquiry pursuant to s. 63(1) of the Judges Act regarding the Honourable Justice Robin Camp: Report and Recommendation of the Inquiry Committee to the Canadian Judicial Council. Ottawa: Canadian Judicial Council.

Citron, D. K. (2019). Sexual privacy. *The Yale Law Journal*, *128*(7), 1870–1960. Retrieved from https://www.yalelawjournal.org/article/sexual-privacy

Citron, D. K., & Franks, M. A. (2014). Criminalizing revenge porn. *Wake Forest Law Review*, *49*, 345–391. Retrieved from https://papers.ssrn.com/sol3/papers.cfm?abstract_id=2368946

Clancy, E. A., Klettke, B., & Hallford, D. J. (2019). The dark side of sexting – Factors predicting the dissemination of sexts. *Computers in Human Behavior*, *92*, 266–272. doi:10.1016/j.chb.2018.11.023

Criminal Code, RSC 1985, c. C-46.

Cunliffe, E. (2012). Sexual assault cases in the Supreme Court of Canada: Losing sight of substantive equality? *Supreme Court Law Review*, *57*(2), 295–316. Retrieved from https://digitalcommons.osgoode.yorku.ca/sclr/vol57/iss1/13

Cyber Civil Rights Initiative. (2014). Effects of revenge porn survey. Retrieved from http://www.endrevengeporn.org

Dario, L. M., Fradella, H. F., Verhagen, M., & Parry, M. M. (2020). Assessing LGBT people's perceptions of police legitimacy. *Journal of Homosexuality*, *67*(7), 885–915. doi:10.1080/00918369.2018.1560127

DeKeseredy, W. S., & Schwartz, M. D. (2016). Thinking sociologically about image-based sexual abuse: The contribution of male peer support theory. *Sexualization, Media, & Society*, *2*(4), 1–8. doi:10.1177/2374623816684692

Dodge, A. (2016). Digitizing rape culture: Online sexual violence and the power of the digital photograph. *Crime, Media, Culture: An International Journal*, *12*(1), 65–82. doi:10.1177/1741659015601173

Dodge, A. (2019). Nudes are forever: Judicial interpretations of digital technology's impact on "revenge porn". *Canadian Journal of Law and Society*, *34*(1), 121–143. doi:10.1017/cls.2019.4

Fairbairn, J. (2015). Rape threats and revenge porn: Defining sexual violence in the digital age. In J. Bailey, & V. Steeves (Eds.), *eGirls, eCitizens: Putting technology, theory and policy into dialogue with girls' and young women's voices* (pp. 229–252). Ottawa, ON: University of Ottawa Press.

Fairbairn, J., & Dawson, M. (2013). Canadian news coverage of intimate partner homicide: Analyzing changes over time. *Feminist Criminology*, *8*(3), 147–176. doi:10.1177/1557085113480824

Franks, M. A. (2017). "Revenge porn" reform: A view from the front lines. *Florida Law Review*, *69*(5), 1251–1337. Retrieved from https://papers.ssrn.com/sol3/papers.cfm?abstract_id=2853789

Gotell, L. (2006). When privacy is not enough: Sexual assault complainants, sexual history evidence and the disclosure of personal records. *Alberta Law Review*, *43*, 743–778. doi:10.29173/alr1504

Gotell, L. (2007). The discursive disappearance of sexual violence: Feminist law reform, judicial resistance, and neo-liberal sexual citizenship. In D. E. Chunn, S. Boyd, & H. Lessard (Eds.), *Reaction and resistance: Feminism, law and social change* (pp. 127–153). Vancouver, BO: UBC Press.

Henry, N., & Powell, A. (2018). Technology-facilitated sexual violence: A literature review of empirical research. *Trauma, Violence, & Abuse*, *19*(2), 195–208. doi:10.1177/1524838016650189

Johnson, N. L., Holmes, S. C., & Johnson, D. M. (2016). It is and it is not: The importance of context when exploring gender differences in perpetration of physical partner violence. *Journal of Family Violence*, *31*(8), 999–1003. doi:10.1007/s10896-016-9858-3

Koshan, J. (2017). The judicial treatment of marital rape in Canada: A post-criminalisation case study. In M. Randall, J. Koshan, & P. Nyaundi (Eds.), *The right to say no: Marital rape and law reform in Canada, Ghana, Kenya & Malawi* (pp. 257–298). Oxford: Hart Publishing.

Langlois, G., & Slane, A. (2017). Economies of reputation: The case of revenge porn. *Communication and Critical/Cultural Studies*, *14*(2), 120–138. doi:10.1080/14791420.2016.1273534

MacKinnon, C. A. (1987). *Feminism unmodified: Discourses on life and the law*. Cambridge, MA: Harvard University Press.

Maddocks, S. (2018). From non-consensual pornography to image-based sexual abuse: Charting the course of a problem with many names. *Australian Feminist Studies*, *33*(97), 345–361. doi:10.1080/08164649.2018.1542592

Mahoney, M. R. (1991). Legal images of battered women: Redefining the issue of separation. *Michigan Law Review*, *90*(1), 1–94. Retrieved from https://repository.law.umich.edu/mlr/vol90/iss1/2/

Merry, S. E. (2009). *Gender violence: A cultural perspective*. Chichester: Wiley-Blackwell.

Minaker, J. C. (2001). Evaluating criminal justice responses to intimate abuse through the lens of women's needs. *Canadian Journal of Women and the Law*, *13*, 74–106.

Powell, A., & Henry, N. (2017). *Sexual violence in a digital age*. London: Palgrave Macmillan.

Powell, A., Scott, A., Flynn, A., & Henry, N. (2020). *Image-based sexual abuse: An international study of victims and perpetrators*. Clayton: Monash University. doi:10.13140/RG.2.2.35166.59209

Randall, M. (2010). Sexual assault law, credibility, and "ideal victims": Consent, resistance, and victim blaming. *Canadian Journal of Women and the Law*, *22*(2), 397–433. Retrieved from https://papers.ssrn.com/sol3/papers.cfm?abstract_id=1742077

Ruvalcaba, Y., & Eaton, A. A. (2019). Nonconsensual pornography among U.S. adults: A sexual scripts framework on victimization, perpetration, and health correlates for women and men. *Psychology of Violence*, *10*(1), 68–78. doi:10.1037/vio0000233

Salter, M., & Crofts, T. (2015). Responding to revenge porn: Challenges to online legal impunity. In L. Comella, & S. Tarrant (Eds.), *New views on pornography: Sexuality, politics, and the law* (pp. 233–253). Santa Barbara, CA: Praeger.

Slane, A., & Langlois, G. (2018). Debunking the myth of "not my bad": Sexual images, consent, and online host responsibilities in Canada. *Canadian Journal of Women and the Law*, *30*(1), 42–81. doi:10.3138/cjwl.30.1.42

Smith, M. (2004). *Encyclopedia of rape*. Westport, CT: Greenwood Press.

UN Broadband Commission for Digital Development Working Group on Broadband and Gender. (2015). *Cyber violence against women and girls: A world-wide wake-up call*. Geneva: Broadband Commission for Sustainable Development. Retrieved from https://en.unesco.org/sites/default/files/genderreport2015final.pdf

APPENDIX: DATA SET CASES

R v AB, 2020 QCCQ 260

R v AC, 2017 ONCJ 317

R v BS, 2019 MBPC 26

R v Calpito, 2017 ONCJ 129

R v CRD, 2019 PESC 30

R v Greene, [2018] NJ No 95; 2018 Carswell Nfld 101

R v JB, 2018 ONSC 4726

R v JR, 2018 ONCJ 851

R v JS (AB), 2019 ABPC 134

R v JS (ON), 2018 ONCJ 82

R v JTB, 2018 ONSC 2422; [2018] ON No 7196

R v Ly, [2016] OJ No 7196

R v MR (trial), 2017 ONCJ 558

R v MR (sentencing), 2017 ONCJ 943

R v MTB, 2019 BCPC 77

R v Newby, [2018] OJ No 6279

R v NM, [2019] OJ No 6238

R v NN, 2019 ONCJ 512

R v OK, 2019 ONCJ 804

R v PSD, 2016 BCPC 400

R v Ruby (trial), [2018] NJ No 407

R v Ruby (sentencing), [2019] NJ No 155

R v Sobh, 2018 ONSC 2299; [2018] OJ No 1921

R v TD, 2018 ABPC 232

R v Trinchi (application), 2016 ONSC 2537

R v Trinchi (sentencing), 2016 ONSC 6586

R v Trinchi (appeal), 2019 ONCA 356

R v Tsang, 2019 ONSC 3235

R v Tunney, 2018 ONSC 961

R v Verner, 2017 ONCJ 415

R v Wilson, [2019] OJ No 2059

Chapter 33

Reasonable Expectations of Privacy in an Era of Drones and Deepfakes: Expanding the Supreme Court of Canada's Decision in *R v Jarvis*

Kristen Thomasen and Suzie Dunn

Abstract

Perpetrators of technology-facilitated gender-based violence are taking advantage of increasingly automated and sophisticated privacy-invasive tools to carry out their abuse. Whether this be monitoring movements through stalkerware, using drones to nonconsensually film or harass, or manipulating and distributing intimate images online such as deepfakes and creepshots, invasions of privacy have become a significant form of gender-based violence. Accordingly, our normative and legal concepts of privacy must evolve to counter the harms arising from this misuse of new technology. Canada's Supreme Court recently addressed technology-facilitated violations of privacy in the context of voyeurism in *R v Jarvis (2019)*. The discussion of privacy in this decision appears to be a good first step toward a more equitable conceptualization of privacy protection. Building on existing privacy theories, this chapter examines what the reasoning in Jarvis might mean for "reasonable expectations of privacy" in other areas of law, and how this concept might be interpreted in response to gender-based technology-facilitated violence. The authors argue the courts in Canada and elsewhere must take the analysis in Jarvis further to fully realize a notion of privacy that protects the autonomy, dignity, and liberty of all.

Keywords: Reasonable expectation of privacy; equality; R v Jarvis; deepfakes; drones; stalkerware

---

The Emerald International Handbook of Technology-Facilitated Violence and Abuse, 555–576

doi:10.1108/978-1-83982-848-520211040

Introduction

Advances in technology over the past several decades have changed our understandings of what is considered "private" in relation to both location and information (Bailey, 2009; Scassa, 2010). Technologies such as drones, stalkerware, and hidden cameras have impacted our expectations of privacy. Traditional approaches to privacy law that drew a bright line between private and public spaces – a conceptual division that has not historically benefitted women (Allen, 1988) and has been rejected by many privacy scholars (Nissenbaum, 2010) – are further broken down by what we describe in the first section of this chapter as "technologies of exposure and control." These technologies provide third-party access to once private realms and allow for the unwarranted gathering and sharing of private information in ways never seen before (Dodge, 2016; Khoo, Robertson, & Deibert, 2019). As privacy norms shift to incorporate these new technologies, it is important to acknowledge the ways in which privacy norms have and continue to neglect the interests of women and other marginalized groups (Bailey, 2014). As noted by Anita Allen (1988), women have had too much of the wrong type of privacy (requiring them to be modest in public or risk inviting privacy invasions, such as sexual harassment), and not enough of the right type of privacy (some privacy norms failed to protect women from gender-based violence in the private sphere, such as intimate partner violence, which was considered a private affair not deserving of state or outside intervention). Gendered privacy norms meant that experiences of domestic violence, workplace and street harassment, voyeurism, and stalking of women long went un- or under-protected in law (Balos, 2004).

Gendered privacy invasions have evolved in the digital era. Unfortunately, perpetrators of technology-facilitated gender-based violence are taking advantage of privacy-invasive tools that are increasingly sophisticated and user-friendly to carry out their abuse (Bailey & Mathen, 2019; Powell & Henry, 2017). Today, we grapple with issues of whether it is appropriate to take sexualized photos of women in public without their knowledge, dox[1] them without consent using facial recognition technology (FRT), replicate their images through technology in sexist ways, or trace their activities using tracking software or drones. Accordingly, our normative and legal concepts of privacy must evolve to counter the gender-based harms arising from this misuse of new technology. This evolution must include the court's assessment of when a person can reasonably expect privacy against the use of these emerging technologies.

Oftentimes in the Canadian legal system, legal protection of privacy interests and remedies for invasions of privacy are framed around the concept of a "reasonable expectation of privacy" (REP). This concept of REP can serve as a legal threshold that a person claiming protection must establish. Generally, to assess a claimant's REP, courts will consider the context of an alleged privacy invasion to determine whether an imagined "reasonable person" would have expected privacy in those circumstances. This may include considering factors such as the location of the invasion, what was accessed, why it was accessed, how it was accessed, who accessed it, and/or the privacy interests in whatever was accessed. The most substantial REP jurisprudence in Canada emerges from Section 8 of the *Charter of Rights and Freedoms* (1982), which prohibits sanctionless state searches that interfere with one's REP, such as warrantless police searches (McGill & Kerr, 2012). However, REP is also significant when assessing whether other laws prohibit gender-based privacy intrusions, or where a survivor of such intrusions can seek compensation or another remedy (Aikenhead, 2018). For instance, Canada's voyeurism and nonconsensual distribution of intimate image offenses (*Criminal Code*, 1985, ss. 162 & 162.1) require an analysis of a claimant's REP in order to convict. Analysis of a plaintiff's expectation of privacy also arises in civil claims for invasion of privacy, and for the nonconsensual distribution of intimate images (e.g., *Jane Doe 72511 v Morgan*, 2018; *Intimate Images Protection Act*, 2018). Further, REP guides an analysis of whether police interview records, therapy records, or other intimate records related to a sexual assault complainant must be provided to an accused in a sexual assault criminal trial, engaging the complainant's privacy interests as well as the retraumatizing experience of a sexual assault trial (*R v Mills*, 1999; see also Gotell, 2006). In all of these cases, the REP concept is the conceptual hurdle to the legal system's denunciation of gendered privacy invasions.

When the courts address these privacy issues, we argue that they must consider equality as a guiding factor in the REP analysis in order to recognize and refute sexist and other discriminatory privacy norms that could otherwise be replicated alongside these new technologies (Aikenhead, 2018; Bailey, 2008). Canada's Supreme Court recently addressed technology-facilitated violations of privacy in the context of criminal voyeurism in *R v Jarvis* (2019). In this decision, the court listed several factors that could be relevant in a REP analysis under the voyeurism offense; however, it did not note equality as a specific factor. This was despite the case's relevant equality issues related to the gender and age of the complainant, and the arguement by two intervenors that equality should be a relevant factor in the REP analysis. This decision appears to be a good first step toward a more equitable conceptualization of privacy protection (Bailey, 2020). However, we argue that neglecting to explicitly acknowledge equality as a distinct factor in the REP analysis was a missed opportunity. Including equality in the REP analysis is a necessary next step in the advancement of REP jurisprudence.

To provide a technological context to our privacy discussion, the first section of this chapter introduces examples of privacy-invasive technologies of exposure and control, highlighting the ways in which technology can be used for gender-based abuse. The chapter then moves on to a summary of *R v Jarvis* examining the REP framework it established. The subsequent section builds on previous privacy scholarship to discuss why and how equality could be considered when assessing expectations of privacy, particularly in response to the ways in which technologies of exposure and control are used to specifically invade the privacy of women and other equality-seeking groups. The chapter concludes with a summary of how the contextual approach to privacy in *Jarvis* (2019) must extend even further to address new technology-facilitated ways of exposing and controlling one another that have significant equality impacts for privacy-marginalized groups, including women.

While the *Jarvis* (2019) decision arises out of a criminal law proceeding, we recognize that the criminal justice system is not necessarily a substantially effective or appropriate mechanism for addressing sexual and gender-based violence, like voyeurism, from the perspective of survivors, offenders, or society as a whole. Nevertheless, what the Supreme Court of Canada (SCC) has to say about privacy in general, and the nonconsensual collection and use of intimate images specifically, sets social norms. It is therefore important to examine these aspects of the decision, while simultaneously considering how we as a society can better respond to sexual violence (Thomasen & Dunn, 2019).

The Technological Landscape

Digital technologies are becoming increasingly sophisticated, compact, affordable, and user-friendly, changing the landscape of accessible tools that can be used to invade another person's privacy (Citron, 2019; Khoo et al., 2019). While these new tools often have beneficial social uses, they can also be used in privacy-invasive ways that target equality-seeking groups. In fact, some are specifically designed and marketed with the intention to invade people's privacy, including targeting women. Stalkerware has been advertised as a "girlfriend tracking" application (Parsons et al., 2019, p. 69), and facial recognition tools have been promoted to help people match strangers they find attractive in public places with their social media accounts, regardless of whether that person is interested in being identified (Royakkers, Timmer, & KoolRinie van Est, 2018; Walker, 2016). In this section, we define and look at examples of two groups of technology that we have termed "technologies of exposure" and "technologies of control" to explore the ways that technology shifts the ability of people to invade other people's privacy, thus impacting societal expectations of privacy. These groupings are not meant to be mutually exclusive, but rather allow us to focus on the new privacy-invasive capabilities that these technologies bring with them. We will highlight some of the ways these technologies are used to expose and/or control women and other equality-seeking groups.

Technologies of Exposure

Technologies of exposure are technologies that can be used to identify, share, publish, create, or decontextualize information about another person that they might not want discovered or used in a particular context.[2] This section reviews several current examples of technologies of exposure that have facilitated gendered privacy intrusions, including the use of FRT to identify women without their consent (Brinckerhoff, 2018); social network platforms used to dox women (Rothrock, 2016); deepfake videos (Chesney & Citron, 2019); and creepshots (Laidlaw, 2017). The examples cited in this section help demonstrate how these technologies are specifically, though certainly not exclusively, targeted against women. Abusers of this technology expose women's information to intentionally draw unwanted attention to them, sometimes encouraging groups of people to collectively harass the exposed individual (Citron, 2014). They typically draw attention to women in ways that sexualize their everyday activities, shame them for engaging in sexual activity, or threaten them for transgressing patriarchal gender norms (Hargreaves, 2014; Henry & Flynn, 2019; McGlynn, Rackley, & Houghton, 2017). Decontextualized information further reinforces sexist ideas about women, such as publishing collections of images on "revenge porn" or creepshot sites that suggest women deserve to be sexually objectified and criticized, and that men are entitled to view and sexualize images of their bodies without their consent (Dunn & Petricone-Westwood, 2018; Henry & Flynn, 2019). This can cause women to disengage from digital spaces, puts them at risk of harassment and violence, and creates additional burdens for women who feel the need to modify their self-expression to avoid being exposed (Powell & Henry, 2017), as is discussed at further length in the next subsection on technologies of control.

Facial Recognition and Doxing

FRT uses biometric data to map a person's facial structure to identify the individual by matching data points from their image to previous images of them (Introna & Nissenbaum, 2011). Many facial recognition systems have been notoriously unreliable, particularly with respect to accurately identifying people of color, and women of color more specifically, as the data sets used in these programs have not included a wide diversity of images of these groups of people to learn from (Buolamwini & Gebru, 2018; Grother, Ngan, & Hanaoka, 2019). Nevertheless, some designers boast statistically significant accuracy rates in identifying the targeted person (Lippman, Cassimatis, & Renn, 2019). Disturbingly, this technology has been used to identify and dox women who appear in sexual content online. Both individual hobbyists and organized groups have used FRT for this purpose. For example, many sex workers choose not to associate their real names or contact information with their online sexual content for privacy or safety reasons (Nelson, 2019). In 2016, there were media reports that a group in Russia used a facial recognition app, FindFace, to create a database that matched images of female escorts and pornography actors with their social media profiles (Rothrock, 2016). Once matched with their social media information, the group shared the women's sexual content with their family and social media contacts, and publicly posted their identifying information and contact information, encouraging others to harass the women (Rothrock, 2016). In May 2019, a computer programmer, Li Xu, published a post on Weibo claiming he had used FRT to identify over 100,000 women from adult pornography videos by cross-referencing their images with images he had scraped from social media sites. The stated purpose of his program was to allow men to find out if their girlfriends had ever been featured in sexual content online (Dickson, 2019). Neither Xu nor the FindFace group used this technology to expose the men featured in the sexual content.

Sex workers are not alone in being targeted for appearing in sexual content online by technologies of exposure. Some users of websites hosting so-called "revenge pornography," child pornography, or sexual exploitation content identify and reveal the names and contact information of the people in these images (Powell & Henry, 2017; Powell, Henry, & Flynn, 2018). Young women who were coerced into being featured in the popular GirlsDoPorn videos were often doxed in the comments section of the videos once they were published on PornHub without their consent. The women featured in these films were typically promised that the videos would not be posted on the internet. Once viewers identified the cities and towns the women lived in, they would share the sexual content with members of that community and harass the women featured in the films (Cole, 2019). This causes fear in the women who were doxed and encourages mob harassment (Citron, 2014), which is closely connected to issues of control discussed below, in particular, the intended and practical silencing of women's contributions online.

Deepfakes

The term "deepfake" refers to the use of "deep learning," or machine learning techniques, to create "fake" images or videos of people. This is done using an artificial intelligence technique that maps out the details of a person's face in order to superimpose that person's face onto the face of another person in a video (Chesney & Citron, 2019). Deepfakes have gained recent attention out of concerns that malicious actors could use this technique to create disruptive fake political videos (Caldera, 2019). However, a recent report by Deeptrace Labs found that 96% of all deepfake videos were pornographic and nonconsensual videos made of women (Ajder, Patrini, Cavalli, & Cullen, 2019). While this technique can also be used in ways unrelated to gender and gender-based abuse, creating an opportunity for new forms of reputational and dignitary abuse (as a woman's face can be superimposed on any number of base videos, not just sexual ones), these videos most often bring unwanted sexual attention to the targeted women and can negatively impact their sexual autonomy by presenting them in sexual scenarios in which they did not participate (Flynn, 2019; Henry et al., 2020).

Discrete Camera Technology

Discrete and high-resolution cameras constitute a technologies of exposure when used for gender-based privacy invasions colloquially called "creepshots" (Burns, 2018). Creepshots are photos taken using cameras, sometimes hidden in everyday objects such as pens or shoes. These cameras are concealed so that they can be used to take pictures of women's bodies without their consent or awareness while they are out in public. The women in the images are typically clothed, but the images are focused on their bodies in a sexualized manner and can be posted online along with other sexual commentary (Tran, 2015). Some photos are taken up a woman's skirt or down her blouse, known as "upskirting" or "down-blousing" (Flynn & Henry, 2019; McGlynn, Rakley, & Houghton, 2017). It is not just the camera technology that allows for creepshots, but the ability to share the images with a larger audience online. The images on creepshot websites, forums, and hashtags are almost exclusively focused on women (Thompson & Wood, 2018). In Canada, a man hosted a "CanadaCreeps" Twitter page where he had over 17,000 followers and posted images of women and girls to the account who were photographed without their knowledge while walking in public (Laidlaw, 2017). Research has shown that the allure of creepshots includes taking the image of a woman without her noticing, and then consuming it without her consent (Burns, 2018; Oliver, 2016). This is made easier through technological improvements that increase the resolution and decrease the size of cameras, making them more discreet and operable at greater distances, fueling this form of privacy intrusion. These exposure concerns also arise in relation to drone technology, discussed below as a technology of control.

Technologies of Control

Technologies of control are those that can be used to monitor, track, or observe the conduct and activities of a person in ways intended to either cause that person to self-regulate their behavior or permit someone else to control or affect their behavior, such that they do not feel free to do as they please. Studies have shown that surveillance technologies can cause a person to alter or self-censor their behaviors if they believe they are being watched (Manokha, 2018). Much has been written about the panoptic effect of technology – where the feeling of being observed (sometimes even without actually being observed) limits one's sense of freedom to act, move, or speak as they would otherwise (e.g., Koskela, 2000; Koskela, 2002a). Surveillance technologies that monitor, track, follow, and report back to another contribute to different forms of self-regulation or avoidance of different spaces and the sense of an external exertion of control over how the targeted individual conducts their daily life. These technologies can also build on the disempowering effects of unwanted exposure by subjecting individuals on an *ongoing* basis to monitoring and potential subsequent exposure, or the sense thereof. Surveillance technologies like drones and spyware/stalkerware make monitoring – or even just the perception of it – easier to carry out, and in some cases these technologies permit fully automated monitoring. Similar to the targeting by technologies of exposure noted in the previous section, technologies of control are often specifically targeted toward women and other equality-seeking groups (Bailey, 2020; Gilliard, 2020; Waldman, 2019; see also Anderson, 2015). The following subsections discuss two examples of emerging technologies of control that will challenge the way privacy expectations are currently understood by Canadian precedents: drones and stalkerware.

Public Space Drone Surveillance

Countless examples of the use of drone technology to spy on and harass women in public spaces have made media headlines in recent years, to the point of becoming a notable (and overly simplistic) media trope (Kaminski, 2013; Thomasen, 2018).

Drone technology is becoming increasingly accessible on the consumer market in terms of availability and cost. Because a drone operates remotely from its pilot – with ranges commonly up to several hundred meters – the technology can overcome not only physical barriers like fences and walls but also normative barriers, like expectations that a person will not take photographs in a particular location, or stare at someone for too long. Drone technology has been used to film or photograph women on their balconies, in backyards, on public beaches, and at public pools. Instances of drones being used to stalk, intimidate, and harass women have been cited in different countries (see examples in Thomasen, 2018). These encounters can affect how targeted individuals are able to freely access, use, and enjoy public and publicly visible spaces, risking inequitable exclusion from or enjoyment of these spaces.

The features of drone technology – including its remote operation, aerial overhead nature, and increasing commercial availability – give it the potential to exacerbate existing privacy-invasive experiences of unwanted monitoring and photography, street harassment, and intimidation, in terms of both the frequency and the quality of the experience (Davis, 1994; Koskela, 2000, 2002b; Thompson, 1993; Vera-Gray, 2016). Footage collected by a drone can take on a further invasive quality when posted and shared online, leading to exposure concerns such as those discussed in the sections above.

Spyware/Stalkerware

Commercially available applications of spyware can be installed on mobile devices and used to illicitly track the location of, and gather information from, a device and share it with another person (Parsons et al., 2019). Spyware can be used for a range of malicious surveillance activities, but numerous investigations have revealed a gendered dimension to the use of spyware. Citizen Lab recently released two reports on stalkerware (spyware used for the purpose of surveillance in contexts of intimate partner violence). The reports, among other things, emphasize the frequent use of different spyware apps in the context of intimate partner violence, often targeted at spying on women specifically (Parsons et al., 2019), and assess legal and policy responses to this technology (Khoo et al., 2019). The reports emphasize the ways in which this technology can be used (and in some cases, is specifically designed) to exert control and power over another individual. As the authors explain:

> Spyware has a wide range of capabilities, including pervasive monitoring of text and chat messages, recording phone logs, tracking social media posts, logging website visits, activating a GPS system, registering keystrokes, and even activating phones' microphones and cameras, as well as sometimes blocking incoming phone calls. These capabilities can afford dramatic powers and control over an individual's everyday life. And when this software is used abusively, it can operate as a predator in a person's pocket, magnifying the pervasive surveillance of the spyware operator.

> Intimate partner violence, abuse, and harassment is routinely linked with efforts to monitor and control a targeted person. As new technologies have seeped into everyday life, aggressors have adopted and repurposed them to terrorize, control, and manipulate their current and former partners. (Parsons et al., 2019, p. 25)

This technology, like the ones discussed above, is not the reason that control and monitoring occurs in intimate partner relationships and elsewhere, but it alters the ease and secrecy of collection, and the quantity and quality of monitoring in ways that are poorly restricted by the current legal system. These new technologies also do not create or cause gendered violence, but emerging technologies do make such exposure and control easier to carry out, expanding and potentially deepening the range of privacy intrusions experienced by women and other equality-seeking groups.

Each of the above technologies generates new sociolegal challenges and exacerbates gendered and systemic privacy challenges, to which legal and other institutions must adjust and respond. We argue that one crucial component of this response will be for courts to recognize the ways in which privacy invasions can reflect inequality, and to incorporate an analysis of this reality into the legal protections of privacy. In particular, into the concept of REP which serves as a threshold for obtaining legal recourse.

Technology and Equality-conscious Assessments of Privacy Expectations

The above section demonstrates how emerging technologies have been used to, or in some cases are explicitly designed to, permit gender-based invasions of privacy. These technologies exacerbate systemic privacy challenges by increasing the quantity and changing the quality of intrusions and by taking advantage of weaknesses in legal protection. The selective targeting of women in these examples is central to understanding how equality and privacy issues intersect. In other words, some groups are more targeted for privacy invasions and less protected by law because legal protections were not historically developed to respond to their privacy experiences. Accordingly, new theoretical approaches are needed to better address this disparity. We need approaches that take equality into account, particularly when considering the legal understanding of a REP. Several privacy laws that require a REP analysis, including those prohibiting voyeurism and nonconsensual distribution of intimate images, were enacted in Canada specifically in response to privacy violations that typically target vulnerable groups, including women and children (Bailey, 2020; Department of Justice, 2002; Department of Justice, 2013), yet do not explicitly address equality. The introduction of these laws helps protect against gender-based privacy invasions (Bailey, 2016; Dunn & Petricone-Westwood, 2018). However, we argue that although the courts are moving toward a contextual approach that could support an equality analysis (Bailey, 2020), the gendered and equality impacts of these invasions are not sufficiently addressed in the courts' privacy analysis as it stands.

The SCC recently considered the privacy-invasive nature of technology-facilitated voyeurism in *R v Jarvis* (2019). The next subsection outlines the SCC's decision. While the decision had many positive features, it neglected to explicitly consider equality as a factor in the privacy analysis. The following subsection discusses why this is a problem and outlines some theoretical approaches that could help decision-makers integrate equality into the REP analysis in the future.

R v Jarvis: Reasonable Expectation of Privacy Analysis

The criminal voyeurism appeal in *R v Jarvis* (2019) asked the SCC to consider whether young women had a REP in the semipublic place of their high school. Ryan Jarvis, a teacher, had been using a camera hidden in a pen to secretly take photos of his female students while they were on school property, for his personal sexual use. Dozens of videos found on the device focused predominantly on his female students' breasts and upper bodies.[3] One of his female colleagues was also the focus of his recordings.

Jarvis was charged with voyeurism under a *Criminal Code* provision that hinges on whether the complainants had a REP in the circumstances in which they were recorded. At the trial level, Jarvis was acquitted, as the court did not conclusively find the images were taken for a sexual purpose. The Ontario Court of Appeal upheld the acquittal, however, this time on the basis that the young women did not have a REP. This assessment was based on the fact that the girls were in a semipublic space in their school at the time of the recording; that there were CCTV security cameras in the school and students were aware they were being filmed by those cameras; and the girls' bodies were available for public gaze because they were not completely concealed by conservative clothing. That decision was overturned by the SCC, which recognized the privacy expectations of the women filmed by Jarvis.

The majority of the SCC recognized that privacy expectations are not solely predicated on whether the girls were in a public or a private space, finding instead that the determination must be based on a variety of contextual factors. The relative privacy of the space was only one factor to consider among many. Chief Justice Wagner, for the majority, noted a nonexhaustive list of nine factors relevant to assessing the complainants', and any future complainant's, REP under the voyeurism offense, including:

- The location the person was in when she[4] was observed or recorded;
- The nature of the impugned conduct, that is, whether it consisted of observation or recording;
- Awareness of or consent to potential observation or recording;
- The manner in which the observation or recording was done;
- The subject matter or content of the observation or recording;

- Any rules, regulations, or policies that governed the observation or recording in question;
- The relationship between the person who was observed or recorded and the person who did the observing or recording;
- The purpose for which the observation or recording was done; and
- The personal attributes of the person who was observed or recorded (*R v Jarvis*, 2019).

Applying these factors, the majority of the Court found that the complainants in this case did have a REP against being secretly recorded by their teacher for a sexual purpose, even though they were in a semipublic place. In particular, the majority emphasized that Jarvis's use of technology to collect sustained, focused, and long-lasting images engaged the students' reasonable expectations of privacy in the semipublic spaces of their high school.

At the SCC hearing, two interveners argued that equality should be a factor in the REP analysis given the gendered dynamic at issue in this case and in voyeurism more generally, putting the Court on notice that equality could be a relevant issue to address in the REP analysis (CIPPIC, 2019; LEAF, 2019). In the end, the Court did not list equality as a factor to consider, nor did it specifically address the gendered nature of the privacy invasion at issue in this case. As previously noted by Moira Aikenhead (2018) and Jane Bailey (2020), while this decision moves the REP analysis closer to an equality-focused approach to privacy, it was a missed opportunity to include equality in the analysis, leaving a critical gap in Canadian privacy jurisprudence.

Equality

As demonstrated in the previous sections, the development and use of privacy-invasive technologies are not neutral. Technology, like the camera pen used by Jarvis or drones used to photograph women, have disparate impacts on equality-seeking groups who are uniquely targeted (Thomasen, 2018). Not only are women the primary targets of creepshots (Burns, 2018) and deepfakes, technology like stalkerware has been overtly marketed to surreptitiously invade women's privacy and monitor their private moments, communications, and life choices (Parsons et al., 2019). Women with intersecting marginalities are further targeted by invasive technologies. LGBTQI people have had their sexual orientation or birth sex "outed" and exposed to homophobic social groups in ways that put them at risk (Ashley, 2018; Waldman, 2019). Racialized women activists have been stalked and tracked online due to their race and gender, including by governments and law enforcement (Amnesty International, 2018; Office of the Privacy Commissioner of Canada, 2013). When private or identifying information is published online, it has been paired with derogatory sexist, racist, and homophobic commentary and images (Jane, 2014). These privacy invasions are specifically tied to equality factors such as gender, sexuality, and race. This discriminatory targeting and marketing, combined with the challenges that targets face in having protective laws applied or enforced, results in inequality that must be addressed by the legal system (Citron, 2019; Dunn, Lalonde, & Bailey, 2017; Khoo et al., 2019). Without directly recognizing this inequality, the legal system risks neglecting discriminatory norms that impact equality-seeking groups' autonomy and signaling that important equality factors in privacy are not worth directly addressing.

Inequality in privacy is nothing new, modern technologies only reemphasize the need to acknowledge equality when considering REP. Privacy norms, and the laws that protect them, illuminate the ways in which dominant groups have controlled who benefits from privacy protection – or the lack thereof. Whether it be legally permissive male access to women's bodies (Koshan, 2017), institutionally sanctioned homophobic invasion of LBGTQI spaces (Bérubé, 2003), or colonial surveillance of Indigenous, Black, and racialized people (Browne, 2015; Choudry, 2019; Crosby & Monaghan, 2018; Magnet, 2011; Tulloch, 2018), examining *whose* privacy is protected and whose is permissibly breached, both historically and currently, exposes the lived impacts of privacy norms on equality-seeking groups.

In order to properly address systemic and substantive equality issues related to privacy, legal decision-makers must explicitly inform privacy law-making and enforcement with equality in mind. Without considering equality, the law only grants permeable protection to those vulnerable to intrusions due to their social location. On the surface, it would seem that the SCC considered some factors that could be affiliated with equality in their REP analysis in *Jarvis* (2019). Factors such as the personal attributes of the individual targeted or her relationship to the perpetrator could be used to address some of the power imbalances that are rooted in inequality. In fact, the Court recognized the girls' youth as a factor that contributed to their REP. However, the Court was surprisingly quiet on how their gender influenced their REP, despite the highly gendered nature of this crime. As noted by Jane Bailey (2020), neglecting equality leaves the burden on future victims to weave an equality argument into the REP analysis within the current factors. If equality had been explicitly recognized as a factor relevant to REP, we believe the Court would need to actively examine whether the claimants were members of an equality-seeking group and how that may impact their experience of privacy and their REP. This recognition and analysis from the Court would go a long way in countering discriminatory privacy norms.

Integrating Equality into the Reasonable Expectation of Privacy Analysis

The SCC's decision in *Jarvis* (2019) was a clear step forward in addressing many concerns regarding the advancement of technology and its impact on privacy norms (Thomasen & Dunn, 2019). The Court acknowledged how a recording device allows for a level of scrutiny and permanence that is fundamentally different than human observation and permits repetitive viewing. The recording device also allows for the potential redistribution of the images in question. Beyond the important recognition that technology changes the REP analysis, the Court also recognized the role that the relationship between the person using technology to invade privacy and the person targeted plays in the REP analysis, as well as the personal attributes of the person targeted (*R v Jarvis*, 2019). These factors can be used to understand some of the issues of power and vulnerability that affect privacy invasions. The Court in *Jarvis* (2019) noted the power imbalance between the teacher and his students and the vulnerability of the young people filmed. However, while these factors may provide space for courts to recognize the effect of inequalities between the specific parties in a particular case, the factors as they stand now do not go far enough to ensure systemic inequalities will be addressed in the REP analysis. This was a significant gap in the REP framework set out by the SCC.

In this section, we examine some of the ways the court could have incorporated equality into the decision in *Jarvis* (2019). Drawing on several privacy theories, we highlight a selection of equality issues that were central to this case and argue that including these considerations would have led to a more fulsome decision that could better address substantive equality in this case and future cases. We suggest that acknowledging equality in the REP analysis by actively examining the intersecting social locations of the individual(s) targeted, the challenges women and other equality-seeking groups face in remaining obscure, and the ways that inequality affects the capacity to trust would encourage an analysis that more adequately addresses privacy in the technological age.

First, by incorporating equality into the analysis, courts would be expected to recognize the ways in which an individual's social location will influence their experiences of privacy. The Court in *Jarvis* (2019) included the personal attributes of the claimants in the list of factors to consider in the voyeurism REP analysis, something that could allow equality factors like age and gender to be addressed. This "personal attributes" factor creates space for an equality-based argument from claimants, but it does not go far enough. It does not require courts to address equality considerations directly and explicitly. Ideally, courts would take an intersectional approach to acknowledge the ways in which gender and other sites of oppression can change the quality and quantity of privacy intrusions, and accordingly strengthen one's REP.

For instance, in applying this factor in *Jarvis* (2019), the Court noted the young age of the claimants and the particular vulnerability of young people. However, the claimants were not specifically targeted or made vulnerable solely because they were *young* people. No young boys were the focus of Jarvis's films. Furthermore, it is often overlooked that Jarvis not only filmed his young female students but also filmed an adult female colleague, suggesting youth alone was not the reason for his focus. The social location in terms of *both* the age and gender of the complainants was relevant in this case, as was pointed out by two interveners. Yet gender was not noted as a relevant personal attribute of the claimants by the Court, even though all shared the same gender. Had the Court been expected to look to equality factors, we argue that both age and gender would likely have been addressed, and importantly, the analysis of Jarvis's conduct would have more fully reflected the claimants' lived experiences and expectations of privacy – enhancing their REP against this use of technology that deepens (and creates a permanent record of) existing social vulnerabilities.[5]

For the courts to ensure equal protection of privacy interests, judges must resist any formalist application of the law and recognize that because different groups of people have different lived experiences of privacy, protection needs to respond to, rather than overlook, those differences. Anita Allen (1988, 2010) has found that women, people of color, and LGBTQI people have not historically benefited from privacy norms and laws in the same ways as cisgender white men (see also Allen & Mack, 1991). Certain groups face repetitive and sometimes daily privacy invasions as part of their reality. As women and girls experience more regular invasions of privacy, there is a cumulative effect in addition to the specific effect of each invasion. Street harassment, digital stalking, doxing, and the decontextualization of their sexuality can cause women to avoid certain behaviors or spaces in anticipation of privacy invasions (Henry et al., 2020). This denies women the respite, anonymity, and self-exploration that others might enjoy in physical and digital public spaces (Allen, 2000; Citron, 2019).

Inequitable privacy norms can be seen in the ways in which others, particularly those in dominant groups, might feel entitled to invade a woman's privacy by inquiring about or touching her body, questioning the legitimacy of her gender or sexual expression, commenting on her in digital spaces, or tracking her movements through public space, depending on her intersecting social locations. A pregnant Indigenous ciswoman (Ridgen, 2020) may experience privacy-related interactions differently than a transgender lesbian (Ashley, 2018), or a woman experiencing a long-term disability (*Milner v Manufacturers Life Insurance Company,* 2005), though all should be entitled to equal legal protection for their REP, even if what is necessary and reasonable differs based on circumstances and identity factors.[6]

The specificity and regularity of privacy invasions can cause many women and girls to have a heightened awareness that their privacy may be unfairly invaded. Overlooking that reality obscures an essential part of the harm women experience, including the reasons why they may have a different sense of what is "reasonable" in regards to their privacy and the role the courts should play in correcting these societal harms.

In the case of *Jarvis* (2019), the young girls Jarvis filmed faced higher risks of having their images taken and sexualized in general due to the societal hypersexualization and fetishization of young women's and teen girls' bodies, as we have seen is the case in voyeuristic creepshots (Burns, 2018). If the REP analysis is meant to be based in the circumstances of the case, the scope of these circumstances must expand to address systemic realities. Courts must recognize how inequality contributes to the normalization of certain types of intrusion and condemn discriminatory privacy norms as "unreasonable" in their REP analysis. This should be the case regardless of who is carrying out the intrusion – be it the state, a company, or a private individual.

Second, building on the recognition of differing privacy experiences between equality-seeking groups, courts also need to recognize the ways in which circumstantially dominant groups (i.e., the members of this group might change depending on the circumstances) can rely on normative privacy protections that are not always available to minority groups, and fill in those gaps with law. Woodrow Hartzog (2018) has defined the concept of "obscurity" as

> …the notion that when our activities or information are unlikely to be found, seen or remembered, it is, to some degree, safe. People calculate risk every day based on how obscure they are or are likely to be. (p. 108)

Women's, girls', and many transgender people's bodies do not remain obscure in the same way cis-men's and boys' do, and as such they are not able to take the same kinds of risks in regards to their sexual and gender expression (Ashley, 2018; Dodge, 2016). For example, women are much more likely to be policed for their sexual conduct on digital platforms (Powell & Henry, 2017), targeted by sexual deepfakes (Chesney & Citron, 2019), doxed if they are sex workers (Rothrock, 2016), and experience violence due to the outing of their transfeminine gender identity (Ashley, 2018).

A person's social location can draw unwanted attention toward them, as was the case for the girls and woman in *Jarvis* (2019). Due to their gender, they could not benefit from obscurity in the ways that the men and boys in the school were able to. Incidents like these can influence how girls and women in the future perceive privacy in their schools and workplaces, diminishing the benefits they have in these spaces as their expectations of these types of privacy invasions are heightened (even though they should not *reasonably* have to expect such targeting). In addition, where technology makes intrusive conduct easier or allows conduct to become more deeply intrusive, it undermines one's expectations that physical and normative barriers will protect against different types of invasions (Hartzog, 2018). This can be seen in the increasing ease of surveillance and control of women that accompanies increasingly automated and remote technologies like drones and spyware apps that provide access to once private spaces and information (Khoo et al., 2019; Thomasen, 2018). Technologies like Jarvis's camera pen overcome the practical barriers that would otherwise prevent his long-term visual access to the complainants' bodies.

The SCC introduced the idea of privacy by obscurity into its *Jarvis* (2019) factors by emphasizing the differences between human observation and a recording. Obscurity that might exist in human forgetfulness or the fleeting nature of an interaction is lost when the interaction is recorded and becomes storable and sharable. Yet, if equality had been recognized, the Court could have taken notice of who is more likely to be captured by these technologies by voyeurs, not just how these technologies change the observation. Canadian case law clearly demonstrates that women and girls are less likely to benefit from obscurity when it comes to voyeuristic recordings as they are the primary targets of voyeurs (Bailey, 2020). Women and girls walking in public for everyday reasons or engaging in normal activities in private spaces are more likely to have their photos surreptitiously taken by people who want to collect and share photos of women they find sexually attractive (Burns, 2018). As such, a woman's ability to remain obscure is limited in a way that the obscurity of a man in the same situation is not. Of course, men's obscurity might be affected by their social locations in other ways, as is the case of men on gay dating apps (Waldman, 2019), or Black men targeted for greater police scrutiny in public spaces (OHRC, 2018), a reality that similarly must be accounted for in the REP analysis. This amplified scrutiny can be better accounted for in the REP analysis through, among other things, a recognition of the ways in which certain people gain privacy protection through obscurity that those in equality-seeking groups may not. Members of equality-seeking groups should nevertheless be entitled to reasonably expect the same amount of privacy protection as others. The REP analysis should fill any practical gaps in obscurity created by invasive technologies, recognizing that everyone should be entitled to reasonably expect the same amount of privacy by obscurity, even if in practice those experiences differ.

Finally, by considering the relationship between the parties as a factor in the *Jarvis* (2019) REP analysis, the SCC implicitly acknowledged that trust can serve as an important mechanism for expecting privacy when sharing information or space with others (Hartzog, 2018; Richards & Hartzog, 2017; Waldman, 2018). This relationship factor allows for a consideration of what a claimant should reasonably be able to expect, for instance, in what should be a trusting relationship between students and a teacher. Recognizing the importance of trust in this relationship helps to mitigate the vulnerability and power imbalance that can arise when sharing information or space in the context of such a relationship (Waldman, 2018). However, similar to obscurity, the Court could have taken this analysis a step further and recognized the ways in which trust, as a mechanism for subjectively experiencing privacy, is inequitably distributed in society. Due to the gendered nature of the common misuses of invasive technologies, such as Jarvis's use of a hidden camera, and systemic gendered norms, such as the societal hypersexualization of teen girls' bodies, women and girls may have legitimate reasons to be less trusting in certain circumstances, even in what should be relationships of trust (Powell & Henry, 2017). The court in its REP analysis should be prepared to supplement the interpersonal trust that individuals are able to rely upon in their lived experiences, even where claimants lose out due to their social location. In fact, one of the students filmed by Jarvis has since reported that she now lives in fear of people she thinks may be taking photos of her (Dodge, 2020). Her day-to-day expectation of privacy through trust has been undermined as a result of her experience. The courts must nevertheless assure that her equal access to legal protection of her privacy, including through trust, remains intact.

The Court's reasoning in *Jarvis* (2019) lays important precedential groundwork to justify further nuancing of REP analyses, both under the voyeurism offense and hopefully in other areas of the law as well. We argue that equality should be explicitly incorporated as a guiding factor in the REP analysis in order to prompt courts to consider the systemic conditions that impact claimants' expectations and experiences of privacy.

Conclusion

The technologies of exposure and control highlighted in this chapter reveal some of the equality issues that arise when considering a person's REP. With gendered privacy violations on the rise, it is time for the courts to consider equality in their REP analysis. While the SCC decision in *Jarvis* (2019) took positive steps toward a REP analysis that addresses privacy issues in an era of modern technology, it did not go far enough. Gendered privacy invasions have shaped the introduction of privacy laws in Canada, including laws prohibiting the nonconsensual distribution of intimate images and voyeurism, but the equality factor has yet to be adequately addressed by legislators and the courts. For privacy laws to be effective at addressing the realities of deepfakes, creepshots, drones, and stalkerware, the courts must explicitly examine the ways these technologies impact equality-seeking groups.

In this chapter, we highlighted how women and other equality-seeking groups may not share equal benefits from obscurity and have legitimate trust concerns that impact their privacy experiences due to their social location. Courts need to recognize this reality. Including equality in the REP analysis would not only provide a more fulsome understanding of the privacy questions before the courts, but decisions that address equality would assist in denouncing privacy norms that rely on discriminatory standards to minimize the severity of certain types of invasions. Excluding equality from the REP analysis minimizes the lived experiences of members of equality-seeking groups and misses a key contextual factor in the REP analysis. For our laws to truly address privacy breaches in modern society, equality must be a factor.

Notes

1. Doxing is the unwanted publication of private or identifying information, such as a person's name, address, and contact information.
2. For an understanding of contextual integrity in relation to privacy, see Nissenbaum (2010).
3. Madison Woodburn, one of the complainants in this case, fought to lift a publication ban that prevented her from speaking firsthand about her experiences throughout the criminal investigation and court proceedings (Dodge, 2020).
4. It is worth noting that the SCC used female-gendered pronouns when referring to the neutral singular person throughout the decision, and its hypotheticals exclusively featured women or girls as the victims, suggesting that the Court may have been alert to the gendered impacts of the voyeurism offense.
5. No details were provided about other social identity factors about the claimants and we recognize there may have been other equality issues at stake here that could have been addressed.
6. The privacy rights and interests of Indigenous women in Canada have too long been overlooked in Canadian colonial state policies. For example, pregnant Indigenous women are statistically more likely to have their births reported to social services through a "birth alert" system that flags their files to social services, increasing the chances that their child will be taken into state care at birth.

Additionally, Canadian criminal and privacy law fail to account for the dignitary interests and privacy expectations of transgender individuals in the ways they do cis individuals. Transgender people who want to choose when to disclose their status as a transgender person may be forced to disclose due to heteronormative and transphobic concerns of gender fraud. Further, privacy law has been permissive of intense public space scrutiny of individuals who claim insurance benefits for workplace injuries and long-term disabilities. These are just some examples of the ways a person's social location and status in an equality-seeking group will affect the privacy norms surrounding them and what sort of intrusions the courts determine they should expect.

References

Aikenhead, M. (2018). A 'reasonable' expectation of sexual privacy in the digital age. *Dalhousie Law Journal, 59*(2), 273–300.

Ajder, H., Patrini, G., Cavalli, F., & Cullen, L. (2019). *The state of deepfakes: Landscape, threats, and impact*. Amsterdam: Deeptrace.

Allen, A. (1988). *Uneasy access: Privacy for women in a free society*. Totawa, NJ: Rowan & Littlefield.

Allen, A. (2000). Gender and privacy in cyberspace. *Stanford Law Review, 52*, 1175–1200.

Allen, A. (2010). Privacy torts: Unreliable remedies for LGBT plaintiffs. *California Law Review, 98*(6), 1711–1764.

Allen, A., & Mack, E. (1991). How privacy got its gender. *Northern Illinois University Law Review, 10*, 441–478.

Amnesty International. (2018). *#ToxicTwitter*. London: Amnesty International.

Anderson, E. (2015). The white space. *Sociology of Race and Ethnicity, 1*(1), 10–21.

Ashley, F. (2018). Genderfucking non-disclosure: Sexual fraud, transgender bodies, and messy identities. *Dalhousie Law Journal, 41*(2), 339–377.

Bailey, J. (2008). Towards and equality-enhancing conception of privacy. *Dalhousie Law Journal, 31*(2), 267–311.

Bailey, J. (2009). Life in the fish bowl: Feminist interrogations of webcamming. In I. Kerr, V. Steeves, & C. Lucock (Eds.), *Lessons from the identity trail : Anonymity, privacy and identity in a networked society* (pp. 283–301). Oxford: Oxford University Press.

Bailey, J. (2014). 'Sexualized online bullying' through an equality lens: Missed opportunity in AB v. Bragg?. *McGill Law Journal, 59*(3), 709–740.

Bailey, J. (2016). *Canadian legal approaches to 'cyberbullying' and cyberviolence: An overview*. Ottawa Faculty of Law Working Paper No. 2016-37.

Bailey, J. (2020). Implicitly feminist? The Supreme Court of Canada's decision in R v Jarvis. *Canadian Journal of Women and the Law, 32*(1), 196–220.

Bailey, J., & Mathen, C. (2019). Technology-facilitated violence against women & girls: Assessing the Canadian criminal response. *Ontario Bar Review, 97*(3), 664–696.

Balos, B. (2004). A man's home is his castle: How the law shelters domestic violence and sexual harassment. *Saint Louis University Public Law Review, 23*(1), 77–105.

Bérubé, A. (2003). Resorts for sex perverts: A history of gay bathhouses. *Journal of Homosexuality, 44*(3/4), 33–53.

Brinckerhoff, R. (2018). Social network or social nightmare: How California courts can prevent Facebook's frightening foray into facial recognition technology from haunting consumer privacy rights forever. *Federal Communications Law Journal, 70*, 105–156.

Browne, S. (2015). *Dark matters: On the surveillance of blackness*. Durham, NC: Duke University Press.

Buolamwini, J., & Gebru, T. (2018). Gender shades: Intersectional accuracy disparities in commercial gender classification. *Proceedings of Machine Learning Research, 81*(1), 1–15.

Burns, A. (2018). Creepshots and power: Covert sexualised photography, online communities and the maintenance of gender inequality. In M. Bohr, & B. Sliwinska (Eds.), *The evolution of the image: Political action and the digital self* (pp. 27–40). New York, NY: Routledge.

Caldera, E. (2019). Reject the evidence of your eyes and ears: Deepfakes and the law of virtual replicants. *Seton Hall Law Review, 50*(1), 177–205.

Canadian Charter of Rights and Freedoms, s 8, Part 1 of the Constitution Act, 1982, being Schedule B to the Canada Act 1982 (UK). (1982), c 11.

Chesney, R., & Citron, D. (2019). Deep fakes: A looming challenge for privacy, democracy, and national security. *California Law Review, 107*, 1753–1819.

Choudry, A. (2019). *Activists and the Surveillance State: Learning from Repression*. London: Pluto Press.

CIPPIC. (2019). R v Jarvis, 2019 SCC 10, Factum of the intervenor Samuelson-Glushko Canadian Internet Policy and Public Interest Clinic. Retrieved from https://www.scc-csc.ca/WebDocuments-DocumentsWeb/37833/FM030_Intervener_Samuelson-Glushko-Canadian-Internet-Policy-and-Public-Interest-Clinic.pdf

Citron, D. (2014). *Hate crimes in cyberspace*. Cambridge, MA: Harvard University Press.

Citron, D. (2019). Sexual privacy. *The Yale Law Journal, 128*(7), 1870–1960.

Cole, S. (2019, October 16). 'Girls Do Porn' was a crime ring, not a porn site, industry experts say. *Motherboard.*

Criminal Code, RSC 1985, c C-46, s 318(1)(a), ss 162 & 162.1.

Crosby, A., & Monaghan, J. (2018). *Policing Indigenous movements: Dissent and the security state*. Winnipeg, MB: Fernwood Publishing.

Davis, D. (1994). The harm that has no name: Street harassment, embodiment, and African American Women. *UCLA Women's Law Journal, 4*, 133–178.

Department of Justice. (2002). Voyeurism as a criminal offence: A consultation paper. Department of Justice Canada.

Department of Justice. (2013). Cyberbullying and the non-consensual distribution of intimate images. Department of Justice. Canada. CCSO Cybercrime Working Group.

Dickson, E. (2019, May 31). How facial recognition technology could bring a slut-shaming nightmare. *Rolling Stone*.

Dodge, A. (2016). Digitizing rape culture: Online sexual violence and the power of the digital photograph. *Crime, Media, Culture: An International Journal, 12*(1), 65–82.

Dodge, A. (2020). This voyeurism case changed Canadian privacy laws. It also changed this victim's life. *CBC News*. Retrieved from https://www.cbc.ca

Dunn, S., Lalonde, J., & Bailey, J. (2017). Terms of silence: Weaknesses in corporate and law enforcement responses to cyberviolence against girls. *Girlhood Studies, 10*(2), 80–96.

Dunn, S., & Petricone-Westwood, A. (2018). More than 'revenge porn': Civil remedies for the non-consensual distribution of intimate images. CCLA 38th Civil Litigation Conference publication.

Flynn, A. (2019). Image-based abuse: The disturbing phenomenon of the "deep fake". *Monash Lens*, March 12.

Flynn, A., & Henry, N. (2019). Image-based sexual abuse: An Australian reflection. *Women & Criminal Justice*.

Gilliard, C. (2020, January 9). *Caught in the spotlight*. Urban Omnibus.

Gotell, L. (2006). When privacy is not enough: Sexual assault complainants, sexual history evidence and the disclosure of personal records.(Canada). *Alberta Law Review, 43*(3), 743–778.

Grother, P., Ngan, M., & Hanaoka, K. (2019). *Face recognition vendor test (FRVT). Part 3: Demographic effects*. NISTIR 8280. Washington, DC: National Institute of Standards and Technology, US Department of Commerce.

Hargreaves, S. (2014). Jones-ing' for a solution: Commercial street surveillance and privacy torts in Canada. *Laws, 3*(3), 388–409.

Hartzog, W. (2018). *Privacy's blueprint the battle to control the design of new technologies*. Cambridge, MA: Harvard University Press.

Henry, N., & Flynn, A. (2019). Image-based sexual abuse: Online distribution channels and illicit communities of support. *Violence Against Women*.

Henry, N., McGlynn, C., Powell, A., Scott, A. J., Johnson, K., & Flynn, A. (2020). *Image-based sexual abuse: A study on the causes and consequences of non-consensual nude or sexual imagery*. New York, NY: Routledge.

Intimate Images Protection Act, RSNL 2018, c I-22.

Introna, L., & Nissenbaum, H. (2011). *Facial recognition technology: A survey of policy and implementation issues. Lancaster University management school*. Working Paper 49012.

Jane, E. (2014). 'You're a ugly, whorish, slut': Understanding e-bile. *Feminist Media Studies, 14*(4), 531–546.

Jane Doe 72511 v Morgan, 2018. ONSC 6607.

Kaminski, M. (2013). Drone federalism: Civilian drones and the things they carry. *California Law Review, 4*, 57–74.

Khoo, C., Robertson, K., & Deibert, R. (2019). *Installing fear: A Canadian legal and policy analysis of using, developing, and selling smartphone spyware and stalkerware applications*. Toronto, ON: Citizen Lab.

Koshan, J. (2017). The judicial treatment of marital rape in Canada: A post-criminalisation case study. In M. Randall, J. Koshan, & P. Nyaundi (Eds.), *The right to say no marital rape and law reform in Canada, Ghana, Kenya and Malawi* (pp. 257–298). Portland, OR: Hart Publishing.

Koskela, H. (2000). 'The gaze without eyes': Video-surveillance and the changing nature of urban space. *Progress in Human Geography, 24*(2), 243–265.

Koskela, H. (2002a). 'Cam era': The contemporary urban panopticon. *Surveillance and Society, 1*(3), 292–313.

Koskela, H. (2002b). Video surveillance, gender, and the safety of public urban space: 'Peeping Tom' goes high-tech? *Urban Geography, 23*, 257–278.

Laidlaw, E. (2017, July 6). 'CanadaCreep' case highlights need for better privacy laws. *The Canadian Press*. Retrieved from https://theconversation.com/canadacreep-case-highlights-need-for-better-privacy-laws-79983

LEAF. (2019). R v Jarvis, 2019 SCC 10, Factum of the intervenor women's legal education and action Fund. Retrieved from https://www.scc-csc.ca/WebDocuments-DocumentsWeb/37833/FM050_Intervener_Women's-Legal-Education-and-Action-Fund-Inc..pdf

Lippman, J., Cassimatis, N., & Renn, A. (2019). *Clearview AI Accuracy Test Report*. American Civil Liberties Union.

Magnet, S. (2011). *When biometrics fail: Gender, race, and the technology of identity*. Durham, NC: Duke University Press.

Manokha, I. (2018). Surveillance, panopticism, and self-discipline in the digital age. *Surveillance and Society*, *16*(2), 219–237.

McGill, J., & Kerr, I. (2012). Reduction to absurdity: Reasonable expectations of privacy and the need for digital enlightenment. *Digital Enlightenment Yearbook*, 199–217.

McGlynn, C., Rakley, E., & Houghton, R. (2017). Beyond 'revenge porn': The continuum of image-based sexual abuse. *Feminist Legal Studies*, *15*, 25–46.

Milner v Manufacturers Life Insurance Company. 2005. BCSC 1661.

Nelson, S. (2019). Sex work and social media: Policy, identity, and privacy in networked publics and counterpublics. *Journal of the Cultural Studies Association*, *8*(1).

Nissenbaum, H. (2010). *Privacy in context: Technology, policy, and the integrity of social life*. Stanford, CA: Stanford Law Books.

Office of the Privacy Commissioner of Canada. (2013). *Aboriginal Affairs and Northern Development Canada wrongly collects information from First Nations activist's personal Facebook page*. Ottawa, ON: Office of the Privacy Commissioner of Canada.

Oliver, K. (2016). Rape as spectator sport and creepshot entertainment: Social media and the valorization of lack of consent. *American Studies Journal*, 61.

Ontario Human Rights Commission. (2018) A Collective Impact: Interim report on the inquiry into racial profiling and racial discrimination of Black persons by the Toronto Police Service. Retrieved from http://www.ohrc.on.ca/en/public-interest-inquiry-racial-profiling-and-discrimination-toronto-police-service/collective-impact-interim-report-inquiry-racial-profiling-and-racial-discrimination-black

Parsons, P., Molnar, A., Dalek, J., Knockel, J., Kenyon, M., Haselton, B., & Deibert, R. (2019). *The predator in your pocket: A multidisciplinary assessment of the stalkerware application industry*. Toronto, ON: Citizenlab.

Powell, A., & Henry, N. (2017). *Sexual violence in a digital age*. London: Palgrave Macmillan.

Powell, A., Henry, N., & Flynn, A. (2018). Image-based sexual abuse. In W. S. DeKeseredy, & M. Dragiewicz (Eds.), *Routledge handbook of critical criminology* (2nd ed., pp. 305–315). Abingdon and New York, NY: Routledge.

Richards, N., & Hartzog, W. (2017). Privacy's trust gap: A review. *The Yale Law Journal*, *126*, 1180–1224.

Ridgen, M. (2020, January 30). Province of Manitoba to end birth alerts. *APTN*. Retrieved from https://www.aptnnews.ca/national-news/province-of-manitoba-to-end-birth-alerts/

R v Jarvis, 2019. SCC 10.

R v Mills. (1999). 3 SCR 668.

Rothrock, K. (2016, April 26). Facial recognition service becomes a weapon against Russian porn actresses. *ArsTecnica.* Retrieved from https://arstechnica.com/tech-policy/2016/04/facial-recognition-service-becomes-a-weapon-against-russian-porn-actresses/

Royakkers, L., Timmer, J., & KoolRinie van Est, L. (2018). Societal and ethical issues of digitization. *Ethics and Information Technology*, *20*(2), 127–142.

Scassa, T. (2010). Information privacy in public space: Location data, data protection and the reasonable expectation of privacy. *Canadian Journal of Law and Technology*, *7*(1 & 2), 193–220.

Thomasen, K. (2018). Beyond airspace safety: A feminist perspective on drone privacy regulation. *Canadian Journal of Law and Technology*, *16*, 307–338.

Thomasen, K., & Dunn, S. (2019, February 25). Court ruling on voyeurism could have broad social impact. *IRPP Policy Options.* Retrieved from https://policy-options.irpp.org/magazines/february-2019/court-ruling-voyeurism-broad-social-impact/

Thompson, D. (1993). 'The woman in the street': Reclaiming the public space from sexual harassment. *Yale Journal of Law and Feminism*, *2*, 313–348.

Thompson, C., & Wood, M. (2018). A media archeology of the creepshot. *Feminist Media Studies*, *18*(4), 560–574.

Tran, M. (2015). Combatting gender privilege and recognizing a woman's right to privacy in public spaces: Arguments to criminalize catcalling and creepshots. *Hastings Women's Law Journal*, *26*(2), 185–206.

Tulloch, M. (2018). *Report of the independent street checks review*. Toronto, ON: Queen's Printer for Ontario.

Vera-Gray, F. (2016). Men's stranger intrusions: Rethinking street harassment. *Women's Studies International Forum*, *58*, 9–17.

Waldman, A. E. (2018). *Privacy as trust-Information privacy for an information age*. Cambridge: Cambridge University Press.

Waldman, A. E. (2019). Law, privacy, and online dating: 'Revenge porn' in gay online communities. *Law & Social Inquiry*, *44*(4), 987–1018.

Walker, S. (2016, May 17). Face recognition app taking Russia by storm may bring end to public anonymity. *The Guardian*.

Chapter 34

Doxing and the Challenge to Legal Regulation: When Personal Data Become a Weapon

Anne Cheung

Abstract

Doxing refers to the intentional public release by a third party of personal data without consent, often with the intent to humiliate, intimidate, harass, or punish the individual concerned. Intuitively, it is tempting to condemn doxing as a crude form of cyber violence that weaponizes personal data. When it is used as a strategy of resistance by the powerless to hold the powerful accountable, however, a more nuanced understanding is called for. This chapter focuses on the doxing phenomenon in Hong Kong, where doxing incidents against police officers and their family members have skyrocketed since 2019 (a 75-fold increase over 2018). It contends that doxing for political purposes is closely related to digital vigilantism, signifying a loss of confidence in the ruling authority and a yearning for an alternative form of justice. The chapter therefore argues that public interest should be recognized as a legal defense in doxing cases when those discharging or entrusted with public duty are the targets. Equally, it is important to confine the categories of personal data disclosed to information necessary to reveal the alleged wrongdoer or wrongdoing. Only in this way can a fair balance be struck between privacy, freedom of expression, and public interest.

Keywords: Doxing; injunction; privacy; public interest; personal data; Hong Kong

The Emerald International Handbook of Technology-Facilitated Violence and Abuse, 577–594

doi:10.1108/978-1-83982-848-520211041

Introduction

It is often said that personal data are the new oil and currency of modern economies (The Economist, 2017). However, personal data can also become a digital weapon, as evidenced by the phenomenon of doxing, which can easily escalate into technology-facilitated harassment. Doxing is generally defined as the intentional public release on the internet of personal data that can be used to identify or locate an individual without their consent. It is often done with the intent to humiliate, threaten, intimidate, or punish the identified individual (Douglas, 2016, p. 199). Once personal data have been released on and circulated via the internet, they are extremely difficult to erase. This "low-tech, high-harm" form of privacy violation often brings about immense disruption and anxiety, and sometimes even the risk of physical harm or other grave consequences (NYU Tandon School of Engineering, 2017, para 1). There are thus pressing calls for legal intervention and regulation.

On its face, there seem to be overwhelming reasons to denounce doxing completely as a toxic practice and a form of technology-facilitated violence and abuse (TFVA). Although it undoubtedly has a dark side, doxing – or the unauthorized disclosure of personal data – has also become an important tactic for those engaged in social action. For example, netizens used doxing to expose the identity of police officers who had allegedly used excessive force against peaceful demonstrators during Occupy Wall Street (Tenold, 2018), and the hacker group known as Anonymous released the personal data of KKK members as part of the fight against racism (Woolf, 2015). Doxing is seen by some as the "democratization of force," a resistance tactic, and a political tool to expose and shame wrongdoers (Tenold, 2018, para 14). Trottier (2019) observed that doxing for political purposes is closely affiliated with the notion of digital vigilantism, that is, netizens taking the law into their own hands in the name of justice.

This chapter focuses on doxing as a tactic of political action and resistance, arguing that doxing to increase the transparency of the government or to bring to light newsworthy information of public interest serves an important checks and balances function in society, especially in political contexts where public power is widely perceived to have gone awry (Trottier, 2019, p. 6). Situated in the context of ongoing protests in Hong Kong, which kicked off in June 2019, the chapter advocates for a more nuanced approach to doxing, taking the position that doxing that serves the primary aim of deanonymizing those discharging or entrusted with public duty to establish their identity and hold them accountable for their wrongdoing, warrants different considerations from doxing in other contexts. Provided that the personal data disclosed in these kinds of circumstances are confined to the information necessary to reveal the alleged wrongdoers or their wrongdoing, without releasing personal data of family members, a public interest defense should be available.

This chapter uses Hong Kong as a case study to examine doxing, not as a general phenomenon, but as a specific form of calling public officials to account for their alleged wrongdoing. It first discusses literature relating to doxing in the pursuit of justice. Next, it provides background about the context in which doxing has occurred in Hong Kong. It then turns to consider the ways in which doxing was raised in three cases before the Hong Kong Court, analyzing the significance in each case by examining who applied for injunctive relief, against whom the order was granted, and the scope of the order granted. Finding that the Court overreached, the chapter then focuses on articulating the justification for and parameters of a proposed public interest defense that would allow for a better balancing of the competing interests at stake when doxing is used to call public officials to account. It concludes by recognizing that, although doxing can be a form of TFVA, there may be limited contexts in which its use can be justified.

Doxing and the Pursuit of Justice

"Doxing" (or sometimes "doxxing") comes from an alternative spelling of the abbreviation of documents, i.e., "docs," prevalent in the hacker world. It originally referred to documenting, compiling, uncovering, and/or releasing personal data on an individual or group on the internet. The term was first used in the 1990s in the context of hackers doxing a rival hacker (Cooper, 2019). Over the years, doxing has evolved into a practice that a group of netizens engages in in a coordinated or spontaneous manner. It often takes the form of the crowdsourcing of information, with available personal data gathered and published by a number of netizens, resulting in a "dossier" on the targeted individuals. When netizens mobilize to cyber-hunt perceived wrongdoers, a vast amount of personal data is exposed, which can easily escalate into harassment, sometimes of innocent parties, as seen in the aftermath of the Boston Marathon bombing in 2013 when a university student who had been wrongly identified by netizens as a culprit was harassed and committed suicide shortly after being doxed (Lee, 2013).

In a study of over 5,500 online text files associated with doxing, a group of US scholars found that more than 90% included the victim's address, 61% included a phone number, 53% included an e-mail address, and 51% included information on family members (Snyder, Doerfler, Kanich, & McCoy, 2017). When such identifying information is disclosed, doxing can easily lead to in-person harassment, stalking, and vilification. Despite the negative connotations of doxing, the same study showed the most common reason for doxing to be seeking justice against something that was seen to be immoral or unfair to a third party (68%), with doxing targets including both individuals who had allegedly cheated others in online forums and law enforcement officers (Snyder et al., 2017).

In fact, malicious intent is not a prerequisite for doxing. Often, doxing is used as a tool of protest to increase transparency and expose wrongdoing, which is analogous to whistleblowing that reveals wrongdoing within an organization (Douglas, 2016, pp. 200 & 206). Yet, as the exposure is not done by insiders, it makes sense for MacAllister (2017) to characterize the act as "doxing for political purposes" (p. 2454) to mark its distinction from doxing for purely malicious purposes such as revenge, harassment, or stalking. Trottier (2019) further identifies doxing as a form of digital vigilantism whereby individuals aim to achieve justice by relying on digital media to denounce and shame those deemed to have transgressed legal or moral boundaries. Nevertheless, it is a form of private justice that is both extra-state and extra-legal (Trottier, 2017, p. 61). Trottier (2017) warns that digital vigilantism not only renders a targeted individual visible and subject to monitoring; it is often a sign that the public is losing confidence in the state's ability to manage crime and losing faith in the police and criminal justice (p. 62). It may even foreshadow a crisis of legitimacy in the state.

Doxing in the Context of Hong Kong Protests

Hong Kong provides fertile ground for digital vigilantism: since June 2019, public confidence in the police has reached an all-time low, and the city has been wracked by political protests that saw hundreds marching in the streets and multiple incidents of police violence (CNN, 2020). The turmoil was initially sparked by a proposed extradition bill that would have allowed criminal suspects to be extradited to mainland China under certain circumstances, triggering fears that anyone present in Hong Kong would be at risk of an unfair trial or even violent treatment in the mainland (BBC News, 2019; see also Fugitive Offenders and Mutual Legal Assistance in Criminal Matters Legislation (Amendment) Bill, 2019). Numerous rounds of protest have seen tear gas, plastic bullets, and water cannons wielded against protestors by the police (Amnesty International, 2019a), with a journalist and a voluntary health worker left partially blinded after being hit in the eye by police projectiles (Graham-Harrison, Kuo, & Yu, 2019; Kilpatrick, 2019). In another incident, a teenage protestor was shot in the chest at close range (Graham-Harrison et al., 2019), and there are many reports of the police resorting to arbitrary arrests and unnecessary violence against protesters (Amnesty International, 2019b). In a public opinion poll conducted in October 2019, nearly 70% of the more than 800 respondents were in favor of restructuring the police force, and over half gave the police a grade of zero (Lee, 2019). For their part, protestors have also escalated the violence, hurling bricks and petrol bombs at police officers and police stations (Lo & Mok, 2020).

As the city has been dragged deeper and deeper into political conflict, doxing is increasingly being used as a tactic, largely against police officers alleged to have engaged in abusive tactics (Privacy Commissioner for Personal Data, Hong Kong [PCPD], 2020a), although journalists and protesters critical of government and law enforcement policies and tactics have also been targeted (Chan & Blundy, 2019).

According to the Office of the PCPD (2020a), there were 4,400 doxing-related complaints between June 14, 2019 and January 10, 2020, involving 17 online social media platforms and nearly 3,000 web links, which represents a 75-fold increase over 2018.[1] Of the 4,400 complaints, 36% concerned police officers or their family members, 4% concerned government officials or public servants, 30% concerned members of the public who had expressed views in support of the government or the police, 10% concerned citizens who had made online comments against the government or police, and 20% concerned protestors. During this period, eight people have thus far been arrested for contravening section 64(2) of the Personal Data Privacy Ordinance in disclosing any personal data about another individual without their consent and if the disclosure causes psychological harm (PCPD, 2020a). In November 2020, a telecommunication technician became the first person to be convicted of doxing – violating section 64(2) of the PDPO – for obtaining and disclosing the personal data of police officers and their family members without consent (*HKSAR v Chan King Hei* (2020)). The defendant was sentenced to imprisonment for 18 months (PCPD, 2020b).

Doxing of the police is believed to have begun after police officers stopped displaying identifying badge numbers on their uniforms while dealing with the protests (Hale, 2019), prompting protesters to attempt to identify the individual officers concerned through other means, including doxing, which soon extended to officers' family members. It is not only the police who have been targeted. Journalists and protesters have also been doxed by the pro-authorities camp (Hale, 2019). In one instance, police officers went so far as to hold up the identity cards and press passes of journalists in front of a live-streaming camera during a stop and search operation (Leung, 2020). The doxing perpetrated by the pro-authorities camp is also apparently much more organized than that by protestors. For example, a site called HK Leaks, which targets pro-democracy leaders, protesters, and journalists, is registered anonymously on a Russian server and is promoted by powerful groups with links to China's ruling Communist Party (Chan & Blundy, 2019).

Doxing engaged in by the opposing sides has turned the internet into a new and dramatic form of political theater played out for all to see, opening up new mobilizing strategies for participants at both ends of the political spectrum (Lustbader & Gullapalli, 2019). Although doxing has been used as a tool by both the antigovernment and pro-authorities camps, the nature of that use is very different. Doxing by the former constitutes a citizen-led intervention, largely against the police and government officials. It is an attempt by the powerless to voice their disapproval of the actions of the powerful, to police the police whose power has gone unchecked. Like the military, the police force is a state institution that has monopolized the legitimate use of violence. Lashing out against the police represents anger, dissatisfaction, and frustration with asymmetrical power relations and abuses of power. Moreover, as representatives of the state authority, the police have borne the brunt of public anger in demonstrations against the extradition bill and during the long fight for democracy in Hong Kong. From this perspective, doxing is closely affiliated with digital vigilantism, a form of collective digital resistance, which appeals to the established norm of holding authorities accountable. The presumed connection between the pro-authorities camp and the state, in contrast, has rendered doxing by the former a weapon for silencing dissenting voices, and the death threats against journalists uttered on the sites an ugly means of intimidation. Further, in using doxing as a tactic against protesters, the pro-authorities camp has illustrated that doxing for political purposes is no longer a tool used solely by the self-proclaimed righteous to expose wrongdoers; it is a tool that is available to everyone and can be used against anyone. Arguably, in drawing moral equivalence between doxing as a powerful tool in the fight for democracy and doxing as a potent weapon for punishing troublemakers, the pro-authorities camp has reminded us of the repugnant nature of doxing and stopped ethical protesters from celebrating its use. In other words, doxing has been used as a tool of the powerful and its capacity for use by the powerless has been limited.

Doxing, in the context of social action, invokes the complex dynamics of social power and the exercise of free speech, as well as the differing responsibilities of individuals and the government. Not only has personal data become weaponized, but the "weaponized visibility" of targeted victims has emerged as an object for monitoring and control (Trottier, 2017, pp. 65–66). What remains critical is to determine whether, and if so when, doxing could be justified.

Doxing before the Hong Kong Court

In October 2019, the Hong Kong court finally made its judicial stance on doxing known by granting three interim injunction orders. The first concerned an action brought by *Apple Daily*, a widely circulated local newspaper. The Court granted an interim injunction restraining anyone from disclosing or publishing the personal details of *Apple Daily* staff or helping anyone to do so (HC 1741/2019, cited in *Junior Police Officers' Association*, 2019a, HKCA, para 20). At least 18 of the paper's journalists had been doxed on a Russia-hosted website that sought "to know who these people are and why [they are] messing up Hong Kong" (Lau & Ng, 2019). As a written judgment is not available for this case, analysis of judicial reasoning related to doxing can only be carried out for the two other injunction cases.

The second doxing case was brought by the Junior Police Officers' Association and heard by the Hong Kong Court of Appeal (HKCA) (2019a). In *Junior Police Officers' Association of the Hong Kong Police Force v Electoral Affairs Commission and others* (2019a) (the decision on substantive merits of the case was later heard and will be referred as *Junior Police Officers' Association*, 2020a),[2] the HKCA overturned a lower court ruling and granted an interim injunction prohibiting the electoral registers showing the names of the registered electors together with their principal residential address (i.e., the linked information) in the district council polls in November 2019. The challenge was based on the rights to privacy under article 14 of the Hong Kong Bill of Rights (HKBOR) and the right to vote under article 26 of the Basic Law. The court emphasized that it is only the disclosure of that linked information, which would facilitate the doxing of police officers' family members, that was being restricted and further noted that more than 2,000 police officers and family members had been subject to doxing between June and October 2019 (*Junior Police Officers' Association*, 2019a, HKCA, paras 3–4 & 51). The HKCA defined "doxing" as the "extensive leaking of personal information and cyberbullying on the internet and various social and other media" (*Junior Police Officers' Association*, 2019a, para 4).

In dealing with interim injunctions in public law, the Hong Kong court generally applies the well-established principles governing civil cases laid down in the English landmark case of *American Cyanamid Co. (No. 1) v Ethicon Ltd.* (1975),[3] albeit with certain necessary modifications (*Junior Police Officers' Association*, 2019a, HKCA, para 14).[4] One main modification pertains to the question of balance of convenience,[5] with the Hong Kong court adopting a wider view than just the interests of the immediate parties to the application to take the public interest into account. First, the HKCA took the view that the interests of the great majority of the police force (85% of which the plaintiff represented) were at stake (*Junior Police Officers' Association*, 2019a). There was cogent evidence to show that police officers and their families had been subjected to doxing, accompanied by harassment, intimidation, and serious threats against personal safety (*Junior Police Officers' Association*, 2019a, HKCA, para 18). The HKCA condemned doxing as a "hideous practice, as [a] weapon to cause harm to individuals and target groups" (*Junior Police Officers' Association*, 2019a, para 19). The Court considered that the possibility of identifying a police officer's residential address through the register's list was not a "fanciful risk" (*Junior Police Officers' Association*, 2019a, HKCA, para 31). Second, the Court further stated doxing seriously endangers our society as a whole for it will instill a chilling effect on our society when many are intimidated into silence for fear of being victimized by doxing (*Junior Police Officers' Association*, 2019a, HKCA). Third, with respect to the issue of balance, the HKCA's decision is grounded in the protection of privacy, although the court did not go into detail concerning the nature and scope of the privacy interest involved (*Junior Police Officers' Association*, 2019a). Finally, the court ruled that there was a wider public interest at stake in safeguarding the integrity of the then upcoming district council election. In an attempt to strike a balance between privacy and public access to the Final Register, the HKCA decided to allow only validly nominated candidates and their political parties to have access to the linked information therein (*Junior Police Officers' Association*, 2019a, para 51).

The third relevant application for an interim injunction was in *Secretary for Justice and Commissioner of Police v Persons Unlawfully and Wilfully Conducting Themselves in any of the Acts Prohibited under Paragraph 1(a), (b) or (c) of the Indorsement of Claim* (2019a) (hereinafter referred as *Secretary for Justice and Commissioner of Police*).[6] Justice Chow of the Hong Kong Court of First Instance (HKCFI) granted the interim injunction that prohibited "using, publishing, communicating or disclosing to any other person the personal data" of any police officers and/or their family members intended or likely to intimidate, molest, harass, threaten, pester, or interfere with them (*Secretary for Justice and Commissioner of Police*, 2019a, para 1).[7] Personal data included but were not limited to the name, job title, residential address, office address, school address, e-mail address, date of birth, telephone number, identity card number or identification number on any official identity document, Facebook account ID, and license plate number of any police officer and/or their family members, as well as photographs thereof. The application of the continuation of the interim injunction was later heard and granted by Justice Coleman, who added a journalism exemption to balance government accountability, privacy, and freedom of the press (*Secretary for Justice and Commissioner of Police,* 2019b). This was in response to the Hong Kong Journalists Association's application for the order to be varied to exclude "news activity" from the prohibition. As the reasoning behind Justice Chow's initial granting of the interim injunction is unavailable, we focus here on the judgment delivered by Justice Coleman.[8]

Justice Coleman first ruled that the applicant had demonstrated that what the defendant did was threatening, and in fact intended, to cause imminent and substantial harm. He then stated that he was satisfied that widespread doxing activities had created a state of affairs in society that endangered the lives, safety, health, property, or comfort of the public, which constituted a public nuisance (*Secretary for Justice and Commissioner of Police,* 2019b, para 39). In addition, doxing activities and the resulting harassment and intimidation had caused intimidation or fear of harm (*Secretary for Justice and Commissioner of Police,* 2019b, para 40). Further, the damage caused by public nuisance and intimidation was not quantifiable, and an award of damages could not be an adequate remedy (*Secretary for Justice and Commissioner of Police,* 2019b, para 41). Finally, as to the test of balance of convenience, Justice Coleman concluded that it was strongly in favor of granting the injunction (*Secretary for Justice and Commissioner of Police,* 2019b, para 45). In weighing the different interests at stake, he acknowledged that the right to freedom of expression had to be considered together with the rights of police officers and their family members to respect and privacy, and with the need to maintain public order (*Secretary for Justice and Commissioner of Police,* 2019b, para 43). On balance, he was prepared to amend the injunction order to exclude news activity, as it was never the court's intention to "stifle genuine and lawful journalistic activities" (*Secretary for Justice and Commissioner of Police,* 2019b, para 68). In summary, "real journalists" would be entitled to report personal information about police officers in order to carry out the valuable watchdog role of the press, but "fake journalists" whose activities amounted to nuisance, harassment, or intimidation would not and should be punished for doing so (*Secretary for Justice and Commissioner of Police,* 2019b, paras 68–70).

At this point, it is worth examining the three court decisions by probing three queries: who applied for the interim injunction order concerned; against whom was the order granted; and what was the order's scope? The answers to these questions enable us to better understand the dynamics of doxing in a political context when the authorities have resorted to legislative measures to suppress attempts to call for accountability. It also lends support to the need for a public interest defense to the offense of doxing.

Who Applied for the Interim Injunction?

An application for the granting of an injunction order can be filed by any party. In the three aforementioned decisions, the applications were made by a newspaper to protect its journalists, by the Junior Police Officers' Association on behalf of the majority of the Hong Kong Police Force, by the Commissioner of Police on his own behalf and that of all police officers, and by the Secretary for Justice on behalf of the public at large. In this battle over doxing, it is obvious what interests the first three applicants represented and what parties they wished to protect. However, the interests pursued by the Secretary for Justice and the role that she played were not entirely clear or convincing. In other words, who constituted the public at large and whose interests was the Secretary seeking to protect?

In *Secretary for Justice and Commissioner of Police* (2019b), Justice Coleman noted that the Secretary for Justice had brought the application in her role as "guardian of the public" (para 26). He also acknowledged that many would "see some irony in the invocation of that role," and question whether the Secretary for

Justice was in fact "protecting only, or primarily, police officers and their families" (*Secretary for Justice and Commissioner of Police,* 2019b, para 27). Further, he took judicial notice of the concern raised by a significant number of people that some police officers had failed to protect the public or even on occasion made victims of some members of the public (*Secretary for Justice and Commissioner of Police,* 2019b, para 27). Nevertheless, Justice Coleman was equally quick to add that he could not presume that the Secretary for Justice had not been taking appropriate and necessary follow-up measures concerning allegations of improper conduct, regardless of how slow the process might seem to be (*Secretary for Justice and Commissioner of Police,* 2019b, para 28). In addition, he relied on *Junior Police Officers' Association* (2019a) to emphasize that doxing's effects extend far beyond its immediate targets to exert a harmful effect on society as a whole. Finally, he cautioned that "two wrongs do not make a right," referring directly to the allegation and perception that even if some members of the police force have "conducted themselves in a way which does no credit to the force," doxing can never be justified (*Secretary for Justice and Commissioner of Police,* 2019b, para 32). Overall, Justice Coleman's decision is to be applauded for recognizing the political crisis in which Hong Kong is embroiled and honestly confronting the political overtones of the legal issue he had been asked to resolve (*Secretary for Justice and Commissioner of Police,* 2019b, paras 34–35).

Yet, it is in treading exactly this line of logic that one finds little solace or faith in the Secretary for Justice or even in the Hong Kong court system. Although the doxing and harassment of police officers and their family members (which represent 36% of doxing complaints made to the Privacy Commissioner) have to be condemned, their interests are already represented by the Junior Police Association and the Commissioner of Police. In contrast, the protesters and members of the public who have been doxed for expressing views critical of the police and government (30% of total doxing complaints) (PCPD, 2020a) have no representation. The powerless have no means or knowledge to start legal proceedings. Sadly, as custodian of the public interest, the Secretary for Justice has chosen only to side with the police force as the injunction order was effective only to protect the police officers and their family members. In parallel, while recognizing the frustration of the public, a high court judge asked the public to be patient and to put up with the allegedly nonprofessional conduct of the police until a better solution can be devised.

Against Whom was the Order Granted?

Of the three decisions discussed, only the second named a specific defendant, namely, the Electoral Affairs Commission (and others). The other two decisions were, in effect, being brought against anyone anywhere in the world. Justice Coleman remarked that the identification of defendants on a writ or injunction order without naming any individual had been approved in previous cases (*Secretary for Justice and Commissioner of Police,* 2019b, para 7). He further noted that while it is a fundamental principle of justice to ensure that a person is not made subject to the jurisdiction of the court without having such notice of proceedings as would enable them to be heard, he was satisfied that the description adopted to identify the defendant had met this requirement, as the mode of service could reasonably give rise to an expectation that the proceedings would come to the relevant person's attention (*Secretary for Justice and Commissioner of Police*, 2019b, para 7).

Justice Coleman's reasoning was unfortunately made without any reference, and is in direct contradiction, to the UK Supreme Court's decision in *Cameron v Liverpool Victoria Insurance* (2019), which is of high persuasive value.[9] Here, the Supreme Court's reasoning on the requirements of justice is of particular pertinence to the issue of injunction orders against unnamed parties.

The plaintiff in *Cameron v Liverpool Victoria Insurance* (2019) had been injured in a car accident caused by a hit-and-run driver who could not be identified. The issue at stake was whether legal action can be brought against an unnamed and unidentifiable defendant (*Cameron v Liverpool Victoria Insurance*, 2019, paras 1 & 12). In delivering the leading judgment of a unanimous court, Lord Sumption gave a definitively negative answer and overruled previous judgments that allowed such a practice (*Cameron v Liverpool Victoria Insurance*, 2019, para 21). Although he admitted that English law has permitted actions, including injunctions, against unnamed wrongdoers, with specific reference to such jurisdiction being regularly invoked in the context of abuse of the internet, "the powerful tool for anonymous wrongdoing," Lord Sumption drew a distinction between two categories of unnamed defendants (*Cameron v Liverpool Victoria Insurance*, 2019, para 11). The first category comprises anonymous defendants who are identifiable but whose names are unknown, such as squatters occupying a property who are identifiable by their location, whereas the second comprises defendants who are not only anonymous but cannot be identified. In the first category, the defendant is described in a way that makes it possible in principle to locate or communicate with him or her and to determine without further inquiry whether he or she is the person described in the claim form, whereas in the second category they are not described in an identifiable manner (*Cameron v Liverpool Victoria Insurance*, 2019, para 13). Lord Sumption pointed out that the fundamental principle of natural justice requires that a court give a litigant notice of the proceedings against them to enable the litigant to be heard (*Cameron v Liverpool Victoria Insurance*, 2019, para 17). In Lord Sumption's opinion, giving notice is vital to determine the balance of rights between the litigants, and afford them an opportunity to substantially present their case before the court (*Cameron v Liverpool Victoria Insurance*, 2019, para 17). He emphasized that effective notice must be served to bring the proceedings to the attention of the defendant, which was the long-standing practice of common law courts before statutory rules of procedure were introduced, and one of the foundations of English litigation procedure for centuries (*Cameron v Liverpool Victoria Insurance*, 2019, paras 18 & 21). Accordingly, Lord Sumption considered previous judgments allowing unnamed and unidentifiable defendants to be sued to be unequivocally wrong (*Cameron v Liverpool Victoria Insurance*, 2019, para 21).

Lord Sumption explained that an unknown person cannot be identified "simply by referring to something that he has done in the past," and thus naming the defendant as a person driving a vehicle that collided with another vehicle on a particular date does not identify anyone (*Cameron v Liverpool Victoria Insurance*, 2019, para 16). He added that although the publicity attending to such proceedings sometimes makes it possible to speculate that the wrongdoer knows about the proceedings, service is an act of the court, and it "cannot be enough that the wrongdoer himself knows who he is" (*Cameron v Liverpool Victoria Insurance*, 2019, para 16). These legal principles are equally applicable to the Hong Kong context.

First, the great emphasis that *Cameron v Liverpool Victoria Insurance* (2019) places on the natural justice principle may well cast doubt on the recent, and increasingly common, practice in Hong Kong of naming unknown defendants by way of a description of their conduct. Doubt may also arise over whether the Hong Kong court had the jurisdiction to grant the recent injunction orders prohibiting doxing against unnamed and unidentifiable defendants by way of a general description of their past or even future conduct, a description that could actually be applicable to the public at large. Allowing such defendants to be sued violates the principle that justice in legal proceedings must be available to both sides (*Cameron v Liverpool Victoria Insurance*, 2019, para 17). Second, in describing the defendants as "[p]ersons unlawfully and wilfully conducting themselves in any of the acts prohibited" under the injunction order (*Secretary for Justice and Commissioner of Police*, 2019b), the HKCFI risked covering persons who had perpetrated no such acts in the past, and so would have no interest in opposing the injunction application, thereby rendering them liable for contempt of court for acts performed in the future. This broad attempt to capture "any" potential defendant amounts to the court making a new law applicable to the public at large that prohibits the doxing of police officers and their family members. Finally, in addition to trespassing the legislative role, it is also doubtful whether the HKCFI has struck the right balance between the various rights involved without the benefit of public consultation and the meticulous law drafting procedures associated with legislation. As injunction orders are granted in civil cases, and thus any breach thereof can be enforced only at the instigation of the plaintiff, the HKCFI's decision risks allowing plaintiffs unchecked discretion to engage in selective enforcement of said legislation.

What was the Scope of the Order Granted?

Doxing involves a direct conflict between one person's freedom of expression and another's right to privacy, both of which are constitutionally protected in Hong Kong.[10] To resolve the conflict, the court has to strike a balance between the two rights, which calls for an examination of the nature of personal data.

In the action brought by *Apple Daily*, the HKCFI prohibited the disclosure of personal details on the 18 journalists concerned. In a similar vein, in *Secretary for Justice and Commissioner of Police* (2019a, 2019b), the HKCFI prohibited the disclosure of *any* personal data on *any* police officers or their family members that was intended or likely to intimidate, molest, harass, threaten, or pester them (emphasis added). As noted above, the personal data concerned were expansive, including even job titles and e-mail addresses. In marked contrast, the subject matter of the injunction order in *Junior Police Officers' Association* (2019a) is much narrower: the public still has access to the names of registered electors and their principal residential addresses as separate data, rather than as linked-up data (HKCA, para 46). The HKCA was concerned that linked information could be misused for doxing and could have a chilling or deterrent effect such that some individuals would be reluctant to register as electors to exercise their right to vote (*Junior Police Officers' Association*, 2019a, para 53).

Location data, one's home address in particular, are undeniably private. Knowing a targeted person's address allows others to encounter them in person and observe their target's movements, habits, physical appearance, and characteristics (Douglas, 2016). Still, to safeguard the integrity of the then imminent district council election, and to ensure an open, fair, and honest election, the linked information concerned would remain available to all validly nominated candidates and their political parties (*Junior Police Officers' Association*, 2019a, HKCA, paras 33 & 40). The HKCA's approach was consistent with and in direct correlation with its definition of doxing, that is, the extensive leaking of personal information *and* cyberbullying on the internet and various social and other media (emphasis added) (*Junior Police Officers' Association* 2019a, para 4). There must be a close connection between the type of personal data leaked and the subsequent forms of misuse and harm, constituting "the worst and [most] reprehensible forms of intrusion of the privacy of the individuals concerned" (*Junior Police Officers' Association*, 2019a, HKCA, para 18).

Shortly after delivering the interim injunction order, the HKCA was asked to rule on the substantive merits of the same case in *Junior Police Officers' Association* (2020a). The issue concerns whether making available the linked information for public inspection would have violated the registered voters' right to privacy and the right to vote. The HKCA reiterated that a fair balance has to be struck between the voters' rights and societal benefit of making known the linked information (*Junior Police Officers' Association*, 2020a). It ruled that the injunction order has to be relaxed to allow candidates, the press, and political parties to have access to the linked information (*Junior Police Officers' Association*, 2020a, HKCA, para 104). At the same time, the electoral authorities should have limited discretion to restrict inspection of the linked information for those voters who have valid safety concerns (*Junior Police Officers' Association*, 2020a, para 108). Substantive hearing of the case also reveals the limitations of an interim injunction application where merits of substantive arguments cannot be fully articulated, resulting in premature and unjustified curtailment of rights of the parties.

In comparison, the other two judgments – *Apple Daily* and *Secretary for Justice and Commissioner of Police* (2019a, 2019b) – are hearings on interim injunction applications without any follow-up hearings on the substantive merits of the case (given the absence of the unnamed defendants). The interim injunction orders granted were broad and vague in terms of the personal data covered. Both orders covered the names, job titles, and office addresses of the protected class of persons in question. Although Justice Coleman in the latter case referred explicitly to the need to balance freedom of expression with the right to privacy (*Secretary for Justice and Commissioner of Police,* 2019b, paras 31, 43, & 44), he did not examine the nature of the personal data involved. He made no attempt to explain why names, job titles, and office addresses, particularly those of police officers, who should be accountable to the public, should not be disclosed. While it is only fair and just that the personal data of their family members should not be disclosed without consent, for they are unrelated to the exercise of public duty, the court's prohibition on the disclosure of any personal data on police officers is questionable indeed. Although the injunction order specifies that it is disclosure coupled with an intention to intimidate, molest, harass, threaten, or pester – or the likelihood of intimidation, molestation, harassment, threats, or pestering occurring – that is objectionable, a number of uncertainties remain unresolved: namely, the standard of likelihood has not been determined, and the legal meaning of "pester" is undefined. Previous judgments have referred to harassment and pestering as interchangeable legal concepts (see *A (HK)* Ltd *and Another v Yeung Yuk Sing and Others,* 2017; *Secretary for Justice v Cheung Kai Yin,* 2016). What Justice Coleman conducted was a preliminary sketch of the balancing test, not an application of the doctrine of proportionality to which he referred (*Secretary for Justice and Commissioner of Police,* 2019, para 44). The nature and form of the exercise of the rights concerned and risks to public order have yet to be delineated (Arai-Takahashi, 2013). We turn now to consider how creation of a public interest defense to doxing might be framed to achieve an acceptable democratic balance.

The Public Interest Defense

In his study of doxing, political philosopher David Douglas (2016) argued that doxing may be justified in cases where the aim is to reveal wrongdoing so as to serve the public interest and the personal data disclosed are confined to that sufficient to reveal the wrongdoing (p. 199). Particular instances of the public interest he had in mind are allegations of legal wrongdoing and establishing a person's identity for the social benefit of making them accountable for offensive behavior (Douglas, 2016, pp. 207–208). At the same time, Douglas (2016) recognized that doxing could turn into the private enforcement of public law and develop into a run-away form of vigilantism (p. 208). In his view, therefore, deanonymizing doxing for the purpose of establishing the identity of a formerly anonymous individual and delegitimizing it for the purpose of contradicting an individual's credibility may both be justified, although the revelation of the specific details of an individual's circumstances that are usually private, obscure, or obfuscated (e.g., his or her home address) is never permissible, as it increases the risk of physical harm to that individual (Douglas, 2016, p. 206).

Further developing Douglas's (2016) argument, I contend that public interest should be introduced as a legal defense for doxing. The disclosure of the personal data of anyone discharging or entrusted with public duty, including politicians, government officials, and police officers, for the purpose of establishing their identity and holding them accountable for alleged legal wrongdoings should be allowed. Other than abuse of power, the category of wrongdoings justifying disclosure of public officials' personal data should include situations where police officers refuse to show their police identity and warrant card, which is a breach of the Police General Orders.[11] However, the personal data disclosed should be confined to data establishing the identity of the individual concerned and relating directly to the alleged wrongdoing. A good example of such a restriction can be found in the Texas Penal Code, under which there is a rebuttable presumption that a person is interfering with a peace officer if he or she intentionally disseminates the home address, home telephone number, or social security number of the officer concerned or of one of the officer's family members (found in section 38.15(d) (1)). The category of personal data prohibited from disclosure is specific and narrow and, rightly, bears no relation to the officer's discharge of duty or public interest. However, neither this Texas provision nor legislative instruments in Hong Kong clearly articulate a general public interest defense to disclosure of personal data. Singapore perhaps comes closest to articulating such a defense. In 2019, Singapore amended its *Protection from Harassment Act* (*POHA*) to criminalize the act of doxing. Although an accused can defend publication of identifying information about a targeted person on the basis that their conduct was reasonable (*POHA*, 2019, ss. 3, 5, & 6), what reasonable conduct would entail is unclear.

In Hong Kong, it is an offense to disclose any personal data about an individual without their consent if the disclosure causes psychological harm (section 64(2) of the Personal Data Privacy Ordinance [PDPO]). Public interest is a defense only for news workers (section 64(d) PDPO). Proposals have been made to reform the PDPO to tackle doxing, and there have also been suggestions for introducing legislative amendments to specifically address doxing and confer on the Privacy Commissioner statutory powers to request the removal of doxing content from social media platforms or websites, as well as the powers to carry out criminal investigations and prosecutions (Legislative Council Panel on Constitutional Affairs Review of the Personal Data (Privacy) Ordinance, 2020). The focus of the current debate is preoccupied with the need to enlarge the scope of offenses to criminalize the act of doxing. However, it is contended here that a public interest defense should also be considered in any future amendment of the law concerned. While doxing is a form of TFVA, we need to consider who is being exposed, what personal data are being revealed, and why that revelation is taking place. When doxing is carried out for the purpose of exposing the wrongful deeds of those discharging or entrusted with public duty, it is a signal that the public is losing confidence in the ability of established institutions to deliver justice.

Conclusion

Doxing is a complicated and complicating phenomenon and a form of TFVA. However, not all instances of doxing should be treated the same. In contrast with the instances of doxing reported on by Anderson and Wood in this volume, the prevalent trend of doxing against police officers by netizens at this turbulent time in Hong Kong's history reflects a deep yearning for social and legal reform. What might otherwise appear to be a blatant form of user-led data privacy violation and an extreme form of expression may in Hong Kong's case reflect acute awareness, and even anguish, that those entrusted with public duty are abusing their powers unchecked. Doxing for public interest, from this perspective, constitutes an endeavor to renegotiate what is considered acceptable within a given social and legal context.

Nevertheless, regardless of its cause, doxing remains a contested practice. Whatever the purported purpose, there will always be the lurking question of whether doxing, as an attempt to hold public authorities to account, is the best way to exact social justice. Doxing has serious implications, not least the real risk of physical and psychological harm to targeted individuals. This chapter argues that in political contexts such as the current one in Hong Kong, establishing a public interest defense to doxing would help to strike a better balance between public accountability and privacy. If personal data are a weapon of visibility, what we need is a fair and regulated system of visibility and invisibility.

Postscript

Judges in Hong Kong who were perceived as sympathetic to police and the authorities have become targets of doxing. In November 2020, the HKCFI granted and extended an injunction order restraining unlawful and wilful doxing against judges, any judicial officers, and their family members (Secretary for Justice v Persons Unlawfully and Wilfully Conducting Themselves in Any of the Acts Prohibited under Paragraph 1(a), (b) or (c) of the Indorsement of Claim (2020).

Acknowledgments

The work described in this chapter was fully supported by the General Research Fund (GRF) from the Research Grants Council of the Hong Kong Special Administrative Region (HKU 17623016).

Notes

1. The number of complaints increased markedly, from 57 in 2018 to 4,370 in 2020 (PCPD, 2020a).
2. *Junior Police Officers' Association* (2019, HKCA), reversing the lower court's (*Junior Police Officers' Association*, 2019, HKCFI) decision. Application for judicial review dealing with substantive arguments was heard before the HKCFI on 8 April 2020 (*Junior Police Officers' Association*, 2020), which was partially affirmed by the HKCA (*Junior Police Officers' Association*, 2020).
3. Namely, to decide (1) whether there is a serious issue to be tried in the action (i.e., the claim must not be frivolous or vexatious and must have prospect of success); (2) whether the plaintiff would be adequately compensated by an award of damages for any loss caused by a refusal to grant an interlocutory injunction if they were to succeed at trial; (3) if damages would not be an adequate remedy to the plaintiff, whether, if the injunction were granted, the defendant would be adequately compensated under the plaintiff's undertaking as to damages; and (4) if damages would not be adequate, whether the balance of convenience lies in favor of granting or refusing the interim injunction sought.
4. Relying on the judgment of *Re Leung Chung Hang Sixtus & Another* (2018).
5. In considering the balance of convenience, the Court has to decide whether the cost and inconvenience caused by granting an interlocutory injunction could be

outweighed by the benefits and justice for the applicant. The Hong Kong court must also take into account the interests of the general public in the balancing test (*Turbo Top Ltd v Lee Cheuk Yan*, 2013).

6. Judgment issued on 25 October 2019, amended and reamended on 28 October and 1 November 2019. Further, on 10 December 2019, the Court amended the interim injunction order such that Special Constables would also be protected (Hong Kong Police Force, 2019).
7. The reference to "interfere" was removed by Justice Coleman in a subsequent application for the continuation of the interim injunction as the word was "insufficiently precise" (*Secretary for Justice and Commissioner of Police*, 2019b, para 48).
8. The association applied as a party who may be affected by the injunction order but not as a named defendant nor other party to the action (*Secretary for Justice and Commissioner of Police*, 2019b, paras 9–10). News activity is defined under section 61(3) of the Personal Data (Privacy) Ordinance (Cap. 486).
9. Article 84 of the Basic Law.
10. Freedom of expression is guaranteed by article 16 of the HKBOR while right to privacy by article 14 of the same document.
11. The relevant provision of the Hong Kong Police General Orders is not available to the public. Reference to this requirement can be found at the Independent Police Complaints Council (2012) Special Report (para 2.13.11).

References

A (HK) Ltd and Another v Yeung Yuk Sing and Others. (2017). HKCFI 1926.

American Cyanamid Co. (No. 1) v Ethicon Ltd. (1975). UKHL 1.

Amnesty International. (2019a, June 21). Evidence of Hong Kong police violence verified. *Amnesty International [News release]*. Retrieved from https://www.amnesty.org/en/latest/news/2019/06/hong-kong-police-violence-verified/

Amnesty International. (2019b, September 19). New evidence of shocking police abuses against Hong Kong protesters. *Amnesty International [News release]*. Retrieved from https://www.amnesty.org/en/latest/news/2019/09/hong-kong-arbitrary-arrests-brutal-beatings-and-torture-in-police-detention-revealed/

Arai-Takahashi, Y. (2013). Proportionality (chapter 19). In *Oxford handbook of international human rights law*. Retrieved from https://www.oxfordhandbooks.com/view/10.1093/law/9780199640133.001.0001/law-9780199640133-e-20

BBC News (2019, October 14). Hong Kong protests explained in 100 and 500 words. BBC News. Retrieved from https://www.bbc.com/news/world-asia-china-49317695

Cameron v Liverpool Victoria Insurance. (2019). UKSC 6.

Chan, E., & Blundy, R. (2019, November 1). "Bulletproof" China-backed doxxing site attacks Hong Kong's democracy activists. *Hong Kong Free Press*. Retrieved from https://www.hongkongfp.com/2019/11/01/bulletproof-china-backed-doxxing-site-attacks-hong-kongs-democracy-activists/

CNN. (2020). Hong Kong protests. Retrieved from https://edition.cnn.com/specials/asia/hong-kong-protests-intl-hnk

Cooper, S. (2019, March 28). What is doxxing (with examples) and how do you avoid it. *Comparitech*. Retrieved from https://www.comparitech.com/blog/vpn-privacy/what-is-doxxing-how-to-avoid/

Douglas, D. M. (2016). Doxing: A conceptual analysis. *Ethics and Information Technology*, *18*(3), 199–210. doi:10.1007/s10676-016-9406-0

Fugitive Offenders and Mutual Legal Assistance in Criminal Matters Legislation (Amendment) Bill. (2019). Retrieved from https://www.legco.gov.hk/yr18-19/english/bills/brief/b201903291_brf.pdf

Graham-Harrison, E., Kuo, L., & Yu, V. (2019, October 6). A battle for the soul of the city: Why violence has spiralled in the Hong Kong protests. *The Guardian*. Retrieved from https://www.theguardian.com/world/2019/oct/06/a-battle-for-the-soul-of-the-city-why-violence-has-spiralled-in-the-hong-kong-protests

Hale, E. (2019, September 20). Hong Kong protests: Tech war opens up with doxxing of protesters and police. *The Guardian*. Retrieved from https://www.theguardian.com/world/2019/sep/20/hong-kong-protests-tech-war-opens-up-with-doxxing-of-protesters-and-police

HKSAR v Chan King Kei. (2020). [2020] HKDC 1020 (in Chinese).

Hong Kong Police Force, HKSAR. (2019, December 11). Interim injunction order of the high court (HCA 1957/2019) – doxxing and harassment against police officers, special constables and their families. *Hong Kong Police Force [News release]*. Retrieved from https://www.police.gov.hk/ppp_en/03_police_message/iio_1957.html

Independent Police Complaints Council, HKSAR. (2012). Final report on complaint cases arising from the visit by the Vice Premier Mr Li Keqiang. Retrieved from https://www.ipcc.gov.hk/doc/en/report/Other/Report_f_en.pdf

Junior Police Officers' Association of the Hong Kong Police Force v Electoral Affairs Commission and others. (2019a). [2019] HKCA 1197.

Junior Police Officers' Association of the Hong Kong Police Force v Electoral Affairs Commission and others. (2019b). [2019] HKCFI 2628.

Junior Police Officers' Association of the Hong Kong Police Force v Electoral Affairs Commission and others. (2020a). [2020] HKCA 352.

Junior Police Officers' Association of the Hong Kong Police Force v Electoral Affairs Commission and others. (2020b). [2020] HKCFI 554.

Kilpatrick, R. H. (2019, August 16). "An eye for an eye": Hong Kong protests get figurehead in woman injured by police. *The Guardian*. Retrieved from https://www.theguardian.com/world/2019/aug/16/an-eye-for-an-eye-hong-kong-protests-get-figurehead-in-woman-injured-by-police

Lau, C., & Ng, K. (2019, September 20). Hong Kong newspaper gets injunction against reporters' doxxing. *South China Morning Post*. Retrieved from https://www.scmp.com/news/hong-kong/law-and-crime/article/3029573/hong-kong-newspaper-apply-daily-gets-injunction

Lee, D. (2013, April 19). Boston: Internet detectives get it wrong. *BBC News*. Retrieved from https://www.bbc.com/news/technology-22214511

Lee, F. L. F. (2019, October 16). Our research in Hong Kong reveals what people really think of the protesters – and the police. *The Independent*. Retrieved from https://www.independent.co.uk/voices/hong-kong-protests-police-violence-public-opinion-polling-support-a9158061.html

Legislative Council Panel on Constitutional Affairs Review of the Personal Data (Privacy) Ordinance. (2020, 20 January). LC Paper No. CB (2)512/19–20(03).

Leung, C. (2020, January 22). Police officers 'warned' for mishandling reporters' personal data. *South China Morning Post*. Retrieved from https://www.scmp.com/news/hong-kong/law-and-crime/article/3047073/police-officers-received-verbal-warnings-holding

Lo, C., & Mok, D. (2020, January 29). Hong Kong protests: Radicals in bomb threat against police living quarters. *South China Morning Post*. Retrieved from https://

www.scmp.com/news/hong-kong/law-and-crime/article/3048133/hong-kong-protests-petrol-bombs-thrown-kwai-chung
Lustbader, S., & Gullapalli, V. (2019, January 15). The ethics of doxing and the politics of public shaming. *The Appeal*. Retrieved from https://theappeal.org/the-ethics-of-doxing-and-the-politics-of-public-shaming/
MacAllister, J. M. (2017). The doxing dilemma: Seeking a remedy for the malicious publication of personal information. *Fordham Law Review*, *85*(5), 2451–2483.
NYU Tandon School of Engineering. (2017, November 7). First large-scale doxing study reveals motivations and targets for cyber bullying. *ScienceDaily*. Retrieved from https://www.sciencedaily.com/releases/2017/11/171107122918.htm
Privacy Commissioner for Personal Data, Hong Kong [PCPD]. (2020a, January 12). Privacy commissioner responds to public concern about disclosure of a reporter's personal data [Media Statement]. Retrieved from https://www.pcpd.org.hk//english/news_events/media_statements/press_20200108.html
Privacy Commissioner for Personal Data, Hong Kong [PCPD]. (2020b, November 3). First doxxing case sentenced for contravention of PDPO privacy commissioner urges the public not to flout the law [Media Statement]. Retrieved from https://www.pcpd.org.hk/english/media/media_statements/press_20201103.html
Protection from Harassment (Amendment) Act, 17 October 2019, with effect on 1 January 2020.
Re Leung Chung Hang Sixtus & Another. (2018). HKCFI 1869.
Secretary for Justice and Commissioner of Police v Persons Unlawfully and Wilfully Conducting Themselves in any of the Acts Prohibited under Paragraph 1(a), (b) or (c) of the Indorsement of Claim. (2019a). [2019] HCA1957/2019.
Secretary for Justice and Commissioner of Police v Persons Unlawfully and Wilfully Conducting Themselves in any of the Acts Prohibited under Paragraph 1(a), (b) or (c) of the Indorsement of Claim. (2019b). [2019] HKCFI 2773.
Secretary for Justice v Persons Unlawfully and Wilfully Conducting Themselves in Any of the Acts Prohibited under Paragraph 1(a), (b) or (c) of the Indorsement of Claim. (2020). [2020] HKCFI 2785.
Secretary for Justice v Cheung Kai Yin. (2016). HKCA 457.
Snyder, P., Doerfler, P., Kanich, C., & McCoy, D. (2017). Fifteen minutes of unwanted fame: Detecting and characterizing doxing. In *Proceedings of the 2017 Internet Measurement Conference*, London (pp. 432–444). doi:10.1145/3131365.3131385
Tenold, V. (2018, July 26). To doxx a racist. *The New Republic*. Retrieved from https://newrepublic.com/article/150159/doxx-racist
The Economist. (2017, May 6). The world's most valuable resource is no longer oil, but data Retrieved from https://www.economist.com/leaders/2017/05/06/the-worlds-most-valuable-resource-is-no-longer-oil-but-data.
Trottier, D. (2017). Digital vigilantism as weaponisation of visibility. *Philosophy & Technology*, *30*(1), 55–72. doi:10.1007/s13347-016-0216-4
Trottier, D. (2019). Denunciation and doxing: Towards a conceptual model of digital vigilantism. *Global Crime*, *21*, 1–17. doi:10.1080/17440572.2019.1591952
Turbo Top Ltd v Lee Cheuk Yan. (2013). HKCFI 723.
Woolf, N. (2015, November 6). Anonymous leaks identities of 350 alleged Ku Klux Klan members. *The Guardian*. Retrieved from https://www.theguardian.com/technology/2015/nov/06/anonymous-ku-klux-klan-name-leak

Chapter 35

The Potential of Centralized and Statutorily Empowered Bodies to Advance a Survivor-Centered Approach to Technology-Facilitated Violence Against Women

Pam Hrick

Abstract

As the means and harms of technology-facilitated violence have become more evident, some governments have taken steps to create or empower centralized bodies with statutory mandates as part of an effort to combat it. This chapter argues that these bodies have the potential to meaningfully further a survivor-centered approach to combatting technology-facilitated violence against women – one that places their experiences, rights, wishes, and needs at its core. It further argues that governments should consider integrating them into a broader holistic response to this conduct.

An overview is provided of the operations of New Zealand's Netsafe, the eSafety Commissioner in Australia, Nova Scotia's Cyberscan Unit, and the Canadian Centre for Child Protection in Manitoba. These types of centralized bodies have demonstrated an ability to advance survivor-centered approaches to technology-facilitated violence against women through direct involvement in resolving instances of violence, education, and research. However, these bodies are not a panacea. This chapter outlines critiques of their operations and the challenges they face in maximizing their effectiveness.

Notwithstanding these challenges and critiques, governments should consider creating such bodies or empowering existing bodies with a statutory mandate as one aspect of a broader response to combatting

The Emerald International Handbook of Technology-Facilitated Violence and Abuse, 595–615

doi:10.1108/978-1-83982-848-520211043

technology-facilitated violence against women. Some proposed best practices to maximize their effectiveness are identified.

Keywords: Technology-facilitated violence; survivor-centered responses; gender-based violence; cyberviolence; government responses to technology-facilitated violence; government agencies; image-based abuse

Introduction

Gender-based violence is not a new phenomenon. However, with the proliferation of digital technology have come additional ways in which such violence can be committed. As the means and harms of technology-facilitated violence have become more evident, some governments have taken steps to create or empower centralized bodies with statutory mandates as part of an effort to combat it. This chapter argues that these bodies have the potential to meaningfully further a survivor-centered approach to combatting technology-facilitated violence against women and that governments should consider integrating them into a broader holistic response to this conduct.

This chapter begins by providing my working definition of technology-facilitated violence against women and argues that meaningfully responding to its significant harms requires a holistic and survivor-centered approach – one that places the experiences, rights, wishes, and needs of survivors at its core. Drawing on existing feminist literature and internationally adopted standards on "survivor-centered" approaches to domestic and sexual violence, several foundational elements of a "survivor-centered" approach to technology-facilitated violence against women are elucidated: intersectionality, choice, dignity and respect, prevention, and research.

The chapter then turns to examining the emerging trend of governments creating or funding centralized bodies with statutory mandates to address technology-facilitated violence. An overview is provided of the operations of New Zealand's Netsafe, the eSafety Commissioner in Australia, Nova Scotia's Cyberscan Unit, and the Canadian Centre for Child Protection in Manitoba. These types of centralized bodies have demonstrated an ability to advance survivor-centered approaches to technology-facilitated violence against women through education, research, and direct involvement in resolving instances of violence. However, these bodies are not a panacea. Drawing from their experiences, I outline critiques of their operations and the challenges they face in maximizing their effectiveness.

Notwithstanding these challenges and critiques, I conclude by arguing that governments should consider creating such bodies or empowering existing bodies with a statutory mandate as one aspect of a broader response to combatting technology-facilitated violence against women. Some proposed best practices to maximize their effectiveness are identified.

The Need for a Survivor-Centered Approach to Technology-Facilitated Violence Against Women

This chapter uses "technology-facilitated violence against women" to describe a broad range of conduct targeting women, defined as individuals who self-identify as such.[1] This conduct includes cyber harassment or stalking, monitoring or surveillance, image-based abuse (creating, distributing, or threatening to distribute intimate images without consent), impersonation, doxing (publishing private or identifying information online without consent), and deep fakes (digital falsification of images, video, and audio to simulate participation in pornography) (Chesney & Citron, 2019; Wong, 2019; Woodlock, 2017). This type of conduct disproportionately targets and impacts women, among other marginalized groups (Bailey, 2013; Bailey & Mathen, 2019; Powell & Henry, 2019), with women of color, women with precarious status, women with disabilities, women whose first language is not English, and Indigenous women being particularly vulnerable (e.g., Woodlock, 2015). This chapter refers to an individual who commits technology-facilitated violence as a "perpetrator" and to the target of that violence as a "survivor," although various other terms are used in the literature, including "responsible person," "victim," and "victim-survivor."

Technology-facilitated violence can lead to real harms to real women (Powell & Henry, 2017, p. 62),[2] including well-documented harms to their privacy, security, autonomy, and equality interests (e.g., Marganski & Melander, 2018; Powell & Henry, 2017). However, law and society have tended to trivialize technology-facilitated violence as a form of gender-based violence and blame women for bringing this abuse on themselves (e.g., Citron, 2014). This response is arguably linked not just to how we have historically responded to violence against women, but to the belief that harms caused by "online" conduct are less serious than those caused by "offline" conduct (Powell & Henry, 2017, p. 66; Citron, 2014, p. 102; see also Gosse, this volume). This has led to responses that minimize the former and that tend to place responsibility for mitigating or avoiding those harms on survivors.

The serious harms caused by technology-facilitated violence against women, as a form of gender-based violence rooted in misogyny, call for an effective survivor-centered approach to combatting it. "Survivor-centered" has been defined as meaning "that the survivor, not the advocate, guides the intervention, in both what needs are to be met and how to go about meeting them" (Allen, Larsen, Trotter, & Sullivan, 2013). The concept of survivor-centered approaches (sometimes referred to as "victim-centered" or "survivor-centric" responses) has been explored in feminist approaches to domestic violence and sexual violence (e.g., Goodman & Epstein, 2008; Nova Scotia Provincial Sexual Violence Prevention Committee, 2019; UN Women Virtual Knowledge Centre to End Violence Against Women and Girls, 2011; Spangler & Brandl, 2007). It has also been advocated in the context of post-conflict mechanisms of transitional justice, such as truth commissions and prosecutions (e.g., Soueid, Willhoite, & Sovcik, 2017).

In conceptualizing a survivor-centered approach to domestic violence, Goodman and Epstein (2008) emphasize the imperative to honor the differences in domestic violence survivors' particular needs by creating opportunities for them to be heard and to play an active role in shaping the assistance they receive (the principle of "voice"); to recognize the importance of their relationships and community ties (the principle of "community"); and, in expanding resources available to them, to focus on those whose socioeconomic status limits their opportunities to be safe (the principle of "economic empowerment") (pp. 90 and 135). Survivors and their needs differ based on many factors, including mental and physical well-being; religious, ethnic, and cultural background; immigration status; sexual orientation; embeddedness in social networks; and socio-economic status (Goodman & Epstein, 2008). Important to a survivor-centered approach is ensuring the survivor is able to control the decisions that affect her life (Goodman & Epstein, 2008).

The United Nations has also encouraged a survivor-centered approach to violence against women, meaning that all those engaged in related programming should "prioritize the rights, needs, and wishes of the survivor" (UN Women Virtual Knowledge Centre to End Violence Against Women and Girls, 2011, para 1; see also UN High Commissioner for Refugees, 2016; UN Security Council, 2019). Training materials produced by the UN High Commissioner for Refugees (2016) describe "a survivor-centered approach" as "recogniz[ing] the fact that each person is unique, reacts differently to [sexual and gender-based violence] and has different needs" and as "promot[ing] respect for the survivors' rights by placing them at the centre of the support system" (Module 2, p. 16). In the context of health-care provision, survivors' rights enumerated by the UN Women Virtual Knowledge Centre to End Violence Against Women and Girls (2011) are the rights to:

- be treated with dignity and respect instead of being exposed to victim-blaming attitudes;
- choose the course of action in dealing with the violence instead of being powerless;
- privacy and confidentiality instead of exposure;
- non-discrimination instead of discrimination based on gender, age, race/ ethnicity, ability, sexual orientation, HIV status, or any other characteristic; and
- receive comprehensive information to help her make her own decision instead of being told what to do.

These principles have also been invoked in the context of providing guidance on the development of survivor-centered sexual violence policies and responses in the context of post-secondary institutions (Nova Scotia Provincial Sexual Violence Prevention Committee, 2019).

In the context of transitional justice, Soueid et al. (2017) have described some of the most important components of a survivor-centered approach: gender-sensitive mechanisms that empower women in the society; incorporating cultural sensitivities that allow ethnic, racial, and religious minorities to meaningfully participate; providing social, medical, psychological, and other rehabilitative services; and ensuring access to effective legal representation.

Drawing from this context-specific existing feminist literature and guidance, this chapter proposes that there are several foundational aspects of a holistic survivor-centered approach to technology-based violence against women.

First, a survivor-centered approach is intersectional. Women are not a monolithic group. Women who also identify as racialized, Indigenous, trans, disabled, and/or immigrant (among other identities) will often experience technology-facilitated violence and its harms in diverse ways. The same holds true for women who live in predominantly English-speaking societies, but who do not speak English, as well as women who live in remote communities (see Woodlock & Harris, this volume). Women who exist at these and other intersections may also face different barriers to accessing information about technology-facilitated violence (see Woodlock & Harris, this volume). Recognizing the diversity of women and the extent to which their needs and experiences are likely to diverge based on social location is necessary to an effective survivor-centered approach.

Second, this approach permits and empowers survivors to choose their own course of action in addressing their individual experience of violence. This requires that multiple courses of action be available to survivors to address technology-facilitated violence in the manner in which they deem most appropriate. By way of example, a woman experiencing violence perpetrated by a former partner may want this conduct to stop, but may not want the perpetrator to be criminalized. Having a broad range of options available to a survivor is not only appropriate in light of the unique insight she may have into how the perpetrator might react and what is best for her safety, but it also provides an appropriate way to try to return control of the situation to the survivor. Related to this is the need to ensure survivors are actually informed about these various courses of action so that they may choose the one that is best suited to their own needs and wishes.

Third, a survivor-centered approach seeks to ensure that survivors are treated with dignity and respect, rather than blamed for the violence they have experienced. This principle should underlie the development and delivery of both services and information related to technology-facilitated violence against women. Goodman and Epstein (2008) have highlighted the need to better educate communities about ways to assist survivors of domestic violence and to "reach out to community leaders in religious institutions, health care agencies, educational institutions, workplaces, and other community settings to transform these places into supportive environments" for survivors (pp. 121 and 123).

Fourth, a survivor-centered approach incorporates prevention as a key goal. Reducing instances of technology-facilitated violence, and therefore reducing the number of survivors who need to rely on services and supports to address this conduct, should be prioritized. The burden of prevention should not be placed on survivors; rather, it should be a collective responsibility that encourages a cultural shift in attitudes toward technology-facilitated violence specifically and gender-based violence more generally, including through public education and the education of those who perpetrate this violence or may do so in the future.

Fifth, the implementation of a survivor-centered approach is informed by research, evidence, and the perspectives of survivors. Research is crucial to understanding the nature and impacts of recent and emerging forms of technology-facilitated violence against women. Understanding the experiences of survivors who are subjected to this conduct as well as their specific needs must inform the preventative, informational, and remedial aspects of a survivor-centered approach.

The Potential of Centralized and Statutorily Empowered Bodies to Advance a Survivor-Centered Approach

In recent years, several national and sub-national governments have taken steps to create centralized agencies or entrust a designated organization with a statutory mandate to address various aspects of technology-facilitated violence. This section provides an overview of several of these entities and the ways in which they have demonstrated their potential to further a survivor-centered response to technology-facilitated violence. However, this potential is not limitless. They are susceptible to a number of challenges and critiques, which are also explored.

The Proliferation of Centralized and Statutorily Empowered Bodies

In New Zealand, the idea to bestow upon an organization a statutory mandate related to technology-facilitated violence was raised in an August 2012 report of its Law Commission, recommending the government adopt a suite of reforms to address harmful digital communications. Among the recommended reforms was to designate an "approved agency" to receive and attempt to resolve complaints related to harmful online communications (Law Commission, 2012, p. 110). The impetus for this designation, which the Law Commission (2012) recommended pairing with an independent tribunal, was to enhance access to justice and respond to submissions of key stakeholders that "New Zealand users need access to a complaints body that is accessible and that has some teeth to negotiate with global entities" (Law Commission, 2012, pp. 100, 104, and 134). The Law Commission (2012) recognized that "[m]any complaints will be much better handled by less formal means: by techniques of mediation, negotiation and persuasion" (p. 128). It also identified education, research, and policy oversight as needed general functions for an "approved agency" (Law Commission, 2012, p. 130). The Law Commission (2012) recommended that Netsafe, an independent non-profit organization founded in 1998, be designated the "approved agency," as it was already partly funded by government, performed many of these tasks, and had an established relationship with offshore operations such as Google and Facebook (Law Commission, 2012, p. 130; see also Pacheco & Melhuish, this volume).

In late 2013, the New Zealand government introduced what would eventually become the Harmful Digital Communications Act, 2015 (HDCA). The legislation's purposes are to deter, prevent, and mitigate harm caused to individuals by digital communications, and to provide survivors with a quick and efficient means of redress (HDCA, 2015, s. 3). In June 2016, the government appointed Netsafe as the "approved agency" under the HDCA (Government of New Zealand, 2016). Netsafe's legislative mandate includes receiving and assessing complaints about harm caused to individuals by digital communications; investigating complaints; using advice, negotiation, mediation, and persuasion (as appropriate) to resolve complaints; establishing and maintaining relationships with domestic and foreign service providers, online content hosts, and agencies (as appropriate) to achieve the HDCA's purposes; and providing education and advice on policies for online safety and conduct on the internet (HDCA, 2015, s. 8(1) (a)–(c), (e)). While New Zealand did not implement the Law Commission's recommendation for an independent tribunal, the HDCA does require that a complaint about a harmful digital communication first be made to Netsafe before an individual applies to the District Court for certain enumerated civil remedies such as a takedown order (HDCA, 2015, ss. 12(1), 18, and 19). Netsafe itself has no authority to order the takedown of harmful communications.

Shortly after the HDCA was introduced, the Australian government issued a consultation paper on enhancing online safety for children as part of a September 2013 election commitment to establish a "Children's e-Safety Commissioner" (Government of Australia, 2014, p. 5). This proposal was part of a larger commitment to enhance the online safety of children, with a view to ensuring that content and cyber-bullying concerns were handled faster; that children could quickly access assistance with online safety concerns; that criminal laws relating to cyberbullying were appropriate and effective; and that there was clear and expert leadership in online safety (Government of Australia, 2014). Pointing to the New Zealand example, the Australian government recognized "the need for an accessible and centralized point of contact to deal with online safety" (Government of Australia, 2014, p. 5).

Australia considered following New Zealand's model of designating a non-governmental organization to act as the Commissioner. However, it ultimately established the Office of the Children's eSafety Commissioner under the *Enhancing Online Safety for Children Act 2015* in July 2015 as an independent statutory office within the Australian Communications and Media Authority (Office of the eSafety Commissioner [Commissioner], 2015). Notwithstanding the Commissioner's child-focused mandate, in 2016, it launched eSafetyWomen "to help empower and encourage women to take control of the technology in their lives" in response to an "increase in the use of technology to control, stalk and abuse Australian women" (Office of the eSafety Commissioner, 2016). The Commissioner's governing legislation was amended in 2017 to re-establish its title as the Enhancing Online Safety Act 2015 (EOS Act), to rename the Office, and to reflect that the Office's mandate extends beyond the ambit of children (Reichert, 2017).

Today, the Office of the eSafety Commissioner is "the only government agency in the world solely dedicated to the online safety of its citizens" (Office of the eSafety Commissioner, 2019, p. 3). The Commissioner's legislative functions include collecting, analyzing, interpreting, and disseminating information relating to online safety for Australians; supporting, encouraging, conducting, accrediting, and evaluating educational, promotional, and community awareness programs relevant to online safety for Australians; supporting, encouraging, conducting, and evaluating research about online safety for Australians; publishing reports and papers relating to online safety for Australians; administering a complaints system for cyberbullying against children; and administering a complaints and objections system for the nonconsensual sharing of intimate images (EOS Act, ss. 15(1) (e), (f), (h), (i), 18, and 19A).

Around the same time that New Zealand and Australia took action, at the sub-national level, two Canadian provinces created legislative mandates for agencies to address some forms of technology-facilitated violence, including violence that disproportionately impacts women.

On April 25, 2013, Nova Scotia's provincial government introduced legislation intended "to better protect victims and hold cyberbullies accountable for their harmful behaviour" (Nova Scotia, n.d., p. 1). The *Cyber-Safety Act* was introduced in the wake of the suicide death of 17-year-old Nova Scotian Rehtaeh Parsons on April 7, 2013, after she was subjected to acts of sexual violence, image-based abuse, and cyber-harassment (CBC News, 2013). The legislation created CyberScan, a unit within the Public Safety Division of the provincial Department of Justice. The unit consisted of a director and investigators whose authority included receiving and investigating complaints about cyberbullying from anyone in the province, attempting to resolve the complaint by agreement or informal action, writing a warning letter to the perpetrator, and filing protection orders (Nova Scotia House of Assembly, 2013, p. 1483; Cyber-Safety Act, 2013, s. 26A–26G). The legislation received Royal Assent just over two weeks later on May 10, 2013.

However, on December 10, 2015, the *Cyber-Safety Act* was struck down in its entirety as an unconstitutional incursion on freedom of expression (the definition of "cyberbullying" was ruled to be too broad) and liberty interests (because failure to comply with a protection order under the Act could lead to imprisonment) (*Crouch v. Snell,* 2015). In 2017, this legislation was replaced by the *Intimate Images and Cyber-Protection Act* (IICPA), a purpose of which is to "provide assistance to Nova Scotians in responding to non-consensual sharing of intimate images and cyber-bullying" (IICPA, 2017, s. 2(c)). Under the IICPA (2017), CyberScan's narrowed mandate includes providing public information and education regarding harmful online conduct; providing support and assistance to survivors of nonconsensual distribution of intimate images and cyber-bullying, including with respect to the criminal justice system and civil proceedings under the legislation; and providing voluntary dispute-resolution services, including advice, negotiation, mediation, and restorative justice approaches concerning harmful online conduct (IICPA, 2017, ss. 12(1) (a), (c)–(f); Nova Scotia, 2018).

Finally, on June 9, 2015, Manitoba's provincial government introduced *The Intimate Image Protection Act* (IIPA). Regarding the factors motivating the legislation, the Minister of Justice cited the death of Parsons and several other young women in similar circumstances, as well as the desire of survivors for help in getting intimate images removed without always having to go to court (Legislative Assembly of Manitoba, 2015). In January 2016, the Canadian Centre for Child Protection (C3P) was designated as the "authorized agency" to provide certain services and supports under the legislation to individuals whose intimate images have been or may be shared without their consent (*Intimate Image Protection Act Regulation*, s. 2). The C3P is "a national charity dedicated to the personal safety of all children" and its purposes relate primarily to reducing the sexual abuse and exploitation of children (Canadian Centre for Child Protection [C3P], 2019). To that end, it administers a tip line for reporting child sexual abuse and exploitation of children online, as well as various intervention, prevention, and education services to the Canadian public (C3P, 2019).

Advancing a Survivor-Centered Approach to Technology-Facilitated Violence Against Women

In and of itself, establishing or recognizing a centralized and statutorily empowered body to address technology-facilitated violence has certain survivor-centered benefits. It signals that the government takes this conduct seriously and condemns it, which can contribute to preventing this conduct and messaging that survivors ought to be treated with dignity and respect, rather than being blamed for it. It can also provide a single entry point for survivors to seek redress, thereby facilitating access to justice and available remedial options, empowering them to pursue the remedy they judge to be best suited to their circumstances. Furthermore, legislative empowerment creates a more permanent authority to address this conduct than a mere funding commitment to a non-government entity, meaning that a change in government is less likely to impact the availability of services and supports to survivors.

Broadly categorized, there are at least three additional ways in which centralized bodies with statutory mandates have demonstrated their potential to further a survivor-centered response to technology-facilitated violence against women: direct service-provision to resolve instances of violence; delivering education and information on technology-facilitated violence; and conducting research on the forms and harms of technology-facilitated violence against women.

Direct Involvement in Resolving Instances of Technology-Facilitated Violence

Particularly in relation to the nonconsensual distribution of intimate images, existing statutorily empowered bodies have been able to provide services related directly to assisting survivors in addressing instances of technology-facilitated violence.

Legislative amendments in 2018 empowered Australia's eSafety Commissioner to address image-based abuse, defined as nonconsensual sharing of intimate images or threatening to share intimate images without consent (Office of the eSafety Commissioner, 2019). It has implemented a "world-first government-led reporting service for victims of image-based abuse" through which it received 950 reports in 2018–2019, leading to the removal of material from over 1,700 locations online during that period (Office of the eSafety Commissioner, 2019). This represented a 90% success rate for removal, notwithstanding most material being hosted overseas (Office of the eSafety Commissioner, 2019). A civil penalties scheme, which allows the Commissioner's office to issue warnings, infringement notices, removal notices, or fines to those who post or threaten to post the content, as well as the host site, provides significant leverage in targeting and remedying this abuse on behalf of survivors (Office of the eSafety Commissioner, 2019). The Office has previously attributed its success in part to its close working relationship with social media partners and online platforms to ensure quick removal of material (Office of the eSafety Commissioner, 2018a).

The Commissioner is also mandated to administer a cyberbullying reporting regime for Australian children under 18 years of age, which endows her with powers to take remedial steps similar to those she possesses to address image-based abuse. Although the Commissioner does not have the same enforcement powers to address cyberbullying against adults, she does offer support to assist in attempting to resolve concerns (Office of the eSafety Commissioner, n.d.).

In New Zealand, Netsafe provides a free and confidential online service, as well as a helpline, for reporting harmful content, online abuse and bullying, and illegal content (Netsafe, n.d.). Where a report relates to the organization's mandate under the HDCA, Netsafe is empowered to assist in resolving the report, which may include liaising with website hosts, internet service providers, and other content hosts (whether in New Zealand or abroad) to request that impugned content be taken down or moderated (Netsafe, 2019c; HDCA, 2015, s. 25(1)). In resolving reports related to harmful digital content, Netsafe does not advocate for or favor anyone involved in the incident (Netsafe, 2019a). Rather, it assesses whether the report falls within the scope of the HDCA and the extent of the serious emotional distress, then develops a resolution plan to remove or reduce the alleged harm, which may include giving advice and using persuasion, negotiation, and mediation to resolve the issue (Netsafe, 2019a).

In Manitoba, the C3P is authorized under the IIPA (2015) to assist any person targeted by the nonconsensual distribution or threatened distribution of intimate images by receiving requests for assistance; provide information or assistance to enable a person to have their intimate images returned, destroyed, deleted, or removed from the internet or any other place where they may be viewed by others; provide information or assistance that may facilitate the resolution of a dispute between a person depicted in an intimate image and a person who may be in possession of the image or who may have distributed the image; and provide information about the legal remedies and protections available [including a civil action created by the IIPA (C3P, 2016)] where there has been a nonconsensual distribution of an intimate image or where there is a concern that an intimate image is about to be distributed without consent (IIPA, 2015, ss. 3–4; Intimate Image Protection Regulation, 2016, ss. 2–3).

If the identity of a person in possession of an intimate image is known and the C3P has reason to believe the person has distributed or will distribute the image without consent, it may send a written notice to the person that states the person depicted in the image does not consent to its distribution that includes a summary of the legal consequences that may result from its nonconsensual distribution (IIPA, 2015, s. 8). It appears, however, that the C3P may interpret this mandate to be limited to "[a]ssist[ing] with language to reach out to the individual who shared (or may share) the intimate image" (C3P, 2016, January 18). It will also "[p]rovide instructions on getting content removed from online sites or social media" (C3P, 2016). The C3P may also assist a person who made a request for assistance to make a request to police (IIPA, 2015, s. 9). The C3P reported in 2018 that since 2016, 1,300 people in Manitoba had used its online resources to seek help on this issue and 50 people (nearly half of them adults) had sought help directly from its staff (Kubinec, 2018).

In Nova Scotia, individuals who have experienced cyberbullying (which includes harassment, threats, impersonation, and revealing personal facts or confidential information using electronic communication) or nonconsensual distribution of intimate images can contact CyberScan for assistance in resolving a dispute (Cyberscan, n.d.). Staff may contact the person who distributed the intimate images or engaged in cyberbullying to try to resolve the matter informally using restorative practices or other approaches (Cyberscan, n.d.).

To various extents, these mandates to directly engage in dispute resolution further a survivor-centered approach to technology-facilitated violence. They contribute to increasing survivors' choices to meaningfully address at least some forms of technology-facilitated violence without needing to resort to potentially costly, complex, and emotionally draining civil or criminal legal processes. Moreover, some conduct that causes harm may fall below thresholds for civil or criminal prosecution. Extra-legal remedial measures such as mediation and negotiation can also ensure that harmful digital content or conduct is addressed in a more expeditious manner than would be the case in the legal system. This type of approach has the potential to promote treating survivors with dignity and respect in addressing the violence they have encountered.

Education and Information Distribution

Centralized and statutorily empowered bodies also have a demonstrated ability to advance a survivor-centered approach by providing education and distributing information related to technology-facilitated violence to survivors, frontline workers, the broader public, and law enforcement.

To at least some extent, each of the centralized agencies examined in this chapter educates and provides information to survivors on the options available to them if they experience forms of technology-facilitated violence. By way of example, CyberScan has produced a guide on the provincial *Intimate Images and Cyber-Protection Act*, including the definitions of cyberbullying and nonconsensual distribution of intimate images, what assistance CyberScan can provide, and how to obtain a cyber-protection order under the legislation to address this conduct (Cyberscan, n.d.). It is important that survivors be educated about their potential avenues of recourse when they experience this conduct and in some cases, there is also a need to inform survivors that the conduct they have experienced is, in fact, abusive and in many cases illegal (e.g., Woodlock, 2017). Netsafe also provides guidance on what constitutes image-based abuse, its illegality, and what to do if someone experiences it (Netsafe, 2018).

Although the fault for committing technology-facilitated violence always lies with the perpetrator, educating women about how best to protect themselves against technology-facilitated abuse is also important to enhancing women's safety and is responsive to their expressed needs. In the context of intimate partner violence, one study found that survivors identified their own lack of understanding of technology as compared to that of their partners as a factor that made them more vulnerable to abuse (Douglas, Harris, & Dragiewicz, 2019). In another study, survivors reported wanting to learn about technology and expressed a desire for better tools and trainings to increase their awareness and education regarding technology (Freed et al., 2017).

To this end, in 2016, the Office of the eSafety Commissioner launched eSafetyWomen as part of the Australian government's "Women's Safety Package to Stop the Violence" (Office of the eSafety Commissioner, 2018b, para 6). The program "empower[s] Australian women to manage technology risks and abuse" (Office of the eSafety Commissioner, 2019, p. 215). Through the program, the Office has developed how-to videos to provide guidance on privacy and security features of popular platforms and devices, as well as a personal technology check-up and virtual tours of technologies commonly found in homes, in cars, and on mobile devices (Office of the eSafety Commissioner, 2019). A range of guides have been released in 12 community languages, responding to research that demonstrated women from culturally and linguistically diverse communities face barriers in seeking support (Office of the eSafety Commissioner, 2019; see also Louie, this volume). Netsafe has similarly developed guidance on how to "stay safe online," though this is not specifically targeted to women (Netsafe, 2020).

Centralized bodies have also demonstrated a potential to educate and provide information to frontline service providers, who have expressed a desire for more and better technology-focused training (Freed et al., 2017). In their study, Freed et al. (2017) concluded that there is "a deep and urgent need for better information and training when it comes to technology and abuse – both for clients and professionals" (p. 18). In an example of filling this need, Australia's Office of the eSafety Commissioner delivered face-to-face training through eSafety Women on how technology-facilitated violence manifests and what action can be taken to more than 3,400 frontline workers in 2018–2019, while more than 1,900 frontline workers became registered users of the Office's online training (Office of the eSafety Commissioner, 2019).

Education of the broader public is also an important aspect of operations of these centralized bodies. In the context of image-based abuse, Flynn and Henry (2019) have emphasized the importance of educational campaigns to raise awareness of the causes, harms, and impacts of this conduct; to promote proactive and safe bystander interventions to challenge problematic behaviors and attitudes; and to address cultures of nonconsensual dissemination of intimate images and victim-blaming that excuse perpetrator behavior and prevent survivors from seeking help.

These centralized bodies have demonstrated their capacity to engage in this type of productive public education. In New Zealand, the Ministry of Education has an agreement with Netsafe to provide online safety services to schools (Netsafe, 2019a). Australia's Office of the eSafety Commissioner also provides online safety education for youth (Office of the eSafety Commissioner, 2019). In addition, it considers its specific responsibilities to include supporting, encouraging, and conducting educational, promotional, training, and community awareness programs that are relevant to online safety for people at risk of family or domestic violence (Office of the eSafety Commissioner, 2019). As part of its own efforts to address image-based abuse, the C3P has collaborated with the

Winnipeg Police Service on a campaign to inform youth that help is available if their intimate image is being shared (C3P, 2019). It has also run a public awareness campaign "on the consequences of sharing someone else's nudes without their consent" which "reached hundreds of thousands of Canadians through bus stop ads, in-mall videos, as well as a pre-show video on 16 Landmark Cinema movie screens across Manitoba" (C3P, 2019, p. 52).

Finally, at least one of the aforementioned centralized agencies engages with law enforcement to provide tailored training on issues related to technology-facilitated violence against women. The Office of the eSafety Commissioner offers evidence-based, targeted advice to law enforcement on issues including cyber abuse, image-based abuse, and other technology-facilitated abuse (Office of the eSafety Commissioner, n.d.; Office of the eSafety Commissioner, 2019). The importance of training law enforcement relates both to effective enforcement of existing laws as well as ensuring survivors see the justice system as a forum in which they can seek redress. Ultimately, perceptions of law enforcement attitudes impact survivors' willingness to report abuse, as "they fear being blamed for having taken or shared an intimate photo" or perhaps for sharing their cell phone password with the perpetrator of the violence (Powell & Henry, 2017, p. 203).

To the extent that centralized and statutorily empowered bodies engage in these types of education and information-distribution initiatives, they have a demonstrated potential to advance a survivor-centered approach to technology-facilitated violence against women. These efforts can arm survivors with information about what constitutes technology-facilitated violence, how to safeguard themselves against it, and how to address it when it occurs. This can empower survivors with more choices about how to confront this conduct, while also giving them certain tools they have indicated they would like to assist in preventing this sort of abuse while recognizing that responsibility for this conduct always lies with the perpetrator. Education of frontline service providers further contributes to ensuring survivors are aware of the choices available to them and are supported in accessing them with dignity and respect. In the case of the eSafety Commissioner, providing guides in multiple languages is an important measure to render information more accessible to a broader range of survivors, embodying an intersectional approach that recognizes survivors at certain social locations may experience linguistic barriers to accessing information. Public education plays an important role in encouraging a culture shift that condemns, rather than trivializes or normalizes, technology-facilitated violence, thereby contributing to preventing this conduct and ensuring survivors are treated with dignity and respect in its wake. Finally, educating and partnering with law enforcement can help ensure survivors are treated with dignity and respect when they determine that engaging with the criminal justice system is the right choice for them.

Conducting Research on Issues Related to Technology-Facilitated Violence

Centralized agencies have also demonstrated they can play an important role in advancing a survivor-centered approach through conducting and commissioning research related to technology-facilitated violence against women. This can inform a broader understanding of its prevalence and impact, as well as specific educational and remedial responses.

Australia's eSafety Commissioner "produce[s] world-leading research into online safety issues" which "provide valuable insights for key stakeholders working in this space, while also boosting the evidence base that informs [its] service and program delivery and targeted communities" (Office of the eSafety Commissioner, 2019, p. 195). In 2017–2018, the Office released numerous research reports, including a national survey summary report on image-based abuse and a qualitative research summary report on image-based abuse (Office of the eSafety Commissioner, 2019, p. 133). In September 2019, it published new research aimed at understanding the beliefs, attitudes, and motivations of adults who commit image-based abuse. This research suggests that image-based abuse is normalized and that few perpetrators are aware their behavior is illegal, while recommending possible strategies aimed at helping to improve the visibility of image-based abuse (Mortreux, Kellard, Henry, & Flynn, 2019). Qualitative research published in October 2019 on online safety for Aboriginal and Torres Strait Islander women living in urban areas identified social and system barriers to seeking support for technology-facilitated abuse, as well as service provider recommendations for addressing those barriers (Office of the eSafety Commissioner, 2019). Similar research has been conducted about the experiences of women from culturally and linguistically diverse backgrounds with technology-facilitated violence (Office of the eSafety Commissioner, 2019).

Netsafe also produces and funds this type of research. In 2019 it released a report called "Image-based sexual abuse: A snapshot of New Zealand adults' experiences" (Netsafe, 2019b). Among other things, the organization has funded a research project exploring public attitudes toward image-based abuse and documentary shorts telling stories about cyber-bullying, internet safety, and image-based abuse (Netsafe, 2019a). Netsafe representatives Edgar Pacheco and Neil Melhuish have also contributed Chapter 6 to this volume focused on recent findings relating to adult perpetration of technology-facilitated violence.

A well-developed body of research and evidence in which to ground services and initiatives is essential to a survivor-centered approach. Research on the experiences and perspectives of diverse communities can ensure that the development of services is intersectional and responsive to the needs of survivors at a range of social locations. It can also inform effective approaches to prevention. For example, the above-mentioned research on perpetrators can inform improved education efforts aimed at preventing individuals from becoming perpetrators.

Critiques and Challenges

Notwithstanding centralized agencies' demonstrated potential to advance a survivor-centered response to technology-facilitated violence against women, this potential is not limitless. They are both susceptible to legitimate critiques and must be prepared to confront certain inherent challenges.

Centralized agencies are not a panacea, nor can they be expected to be ubiquitous in their activities and services. The independent review of Australia's EOS Act noted the need for the eSafety Commissioner to work across sectors, including with non-governmental organizations, to collaborate on education initiatives, as well as to avoid overlap and duplication of efforts (Briggs, 2018). The existence of a centralized agency does not negate the vital role that community-based frontline service providers, for example, play in addressing technology-facilitated violence and providing ongoing support to survivors. This role is particularly important for members of racialized or Indigenous communities, who have been frequently victimized by the state (e.g., Bobo & Thompson, 2006; Fast & Collin-Vézina, 2010) and may be skeptical of state-based responses. In this regard, centralized agencies should be seen as a complementary component of a broader survivor-centered approach to effectively addressing technology-facilitated violence against women.

The effectiveness of these bodies in combatting this problem is also linked to the extent to which their mandate expressly includes technology-facilitated violence against women and their funding to do so. For example, it is not a coincidence that the depth and breadth of work done by the eSafety Commissioner (whose statutory mandate and funding is expressly linked in many ways to violence against women) in this field far outstrips that done by C3P (whose statutory mandate is much narrower and whose primary corporate objectives relate to child protection).

Concerning inherent challenges, tensions between the proposed mandate of a centralized agency and freedom of expression were raised in the lead-up to adopting enabling legislation in Australia (Government of Australia, 2014) and New Zealand (Law Commission, 2012). Nova Scotia's statute was struck down for unconstitutionally infringing rights to free speech (*Crouch v. Snell,* 2015). This highlights the extent to which legislators and agencies exercising legislative authority in this area must be conscious of acting in ways that respect applicable speech protections while effectively addressing instances of technology-facilitated violence.

The critiques and challenges considered here are not exhaustive. Further research and analysis about both the benefits and limitations of these bodies (particularly from the perspectives of the survivors whom they are supposed to serve) is warranted. However, the work of the bodies discussed in this chapter offers promising evidence of their potential to advance, even if imperfectly, a survivor-centered approach.

Best Practices for Centralized and Statutorily Empowered Bodies

Centralized and statutorily empowered bodies merit careful consideration by governments as one aspect of a broader survivor-centered approach to technology-facilitated violence against women. The experiences of these bodies suggest a number of best practices to consider in creating or empowering such a body.

- *An express mandate to address technology-facilitated violence against women*: At least initially, many of the bodies discussed in this chapter were designed for and had as their primary focus combatting the abuse of children online. An explicit mandate to address the abuse of women and the ways in which the body is empowered to address it (e.g., through education, research, and intervention in resolving disputes) will help ensure the body's focus remains on this work.
- *Survivor-centered by design*: While this chapter identifies and evaluates these bodies against indicia of a survivor-centered approach to technology-facilitated violence against women, none appear to have been designed with this explicitly in mind. Integrating a survivor-centered approach in the design of such bodies and/or their mandates will help ensure their effectiveness in contributing to this project is maximized. For example, in its submissions on Australia's current review of online safety laws, the Australian Women Against Violence Alliance recommends that an intersectional gender lens be embedded in policy and legislation aimed at responding to online abuse (Andrew, 2020, p. 4). Governments can also ensure women with experience in the field of gender-based technology-facilitated violence are involved in designing the body and/or its mandate.
- *Adequate funding relative to agency mandate*: In multiple contexts, the need has been expressed to adequately fund centralized agencies to properly carry out the statutory mandates given to them (Briggs, 2018; Law Commission, 2012; Legislative Assembly of Manitoba, 2015). Ensuring that agencies are properly funded is relevant to ensuring they are able to advance a survivor-centered approach.
- *Regular review of statutory mandate and operations*: Provision is made in most of these bodies' enabling statutes for a review a certain period of time after it has come into effect (EOS Act, s. 107; IIPA, 2015, s. 17; IICPA, 2017, s. 14). Conducting a review of the statutory scheme, as well as ensuring formal or informal review of the agency's operations informed by survivors' experiences with it, provides a mechanism to measure the extent to which an agency is advancing a survivor-centered approach. The statutory review conducted under the EOS Act has led the government to propose an expanded role for the Commissioner.
- *Ensuring relationships with external organizations*: As stated above, centralized and statutorily empowered bodies are not a panacea. Where such bodies exist, it is important that they maintain relationships and collaborate with, among others, expert frontline service organizations for the benefit of survivors. An instructive example is the eSafety Commissioner's collaboration with WESNET (Australia's peak women's advocacy body working on behalf of women and children who have experienced or are experiencing domestic or family violence) on training materials rolled out at the time of the launch of eSafety Women (Office of the eSafety Commissioner, 2016).

Maintaining and leveraging relationships with technology and social media organizations is also essential to advancing survivors' interests. For example, the Office of the eSafety Commissioner has cited its productive working relationship with these companies as a key reason for its ability to get harmful material quickly removed from certain platforms (Office of the eSafety Commissioner, 2018a). At the same time, corporate mandates must be kept in check so as not to overshadow input from grassroots women's organizations or to effectively usurp the body's own authority.

These best practices are not exhaustive, but are intended to provide some foundational guidance for governments to consider in potentially designing or empowering a body with a statutory mandate to address technology-facilitated violence against women.

Conclusion

Technology-facilitated violence against women is a form of gender-based violence that causes significant and varied harms. These harms necessitate a survivor-centered approach to this conduct whose foundational aspects include intersectionality, choice, dignity and respect, prevention, and research.

Centralized bodies with legislative mandates in several jurisdictions around the world have shown a promising potential to advance this approach to the benefit of survivors, women, and society more broadly, through direct engagement in resolving incidents of violence, education, and research. While not a cure-all for this scourge of gender-based violence, their demonstrated benefits suggest that they merit careful consideration by governments as part of a holistic approach to effectively combat technology-facilitated violence against women.

Acknowledgments

I would like to thank Jane Bailey and Suzanne Dunn, both of the University of Ottawa, for reviewing and providing helpful comments on drafts of this chapter.

Notes

1. Many women exist at the intersection of multiple identities, including trans women, women of color, and immigrant women. This chapter acknowledges that these intersecting identities impact the extent to which women may be targeted by this conduct and the severity of the harms it causes.
2. While Powell and Henry (2017, 2019) write specifically of "technology-facilitated sexual violence," the same observation applies to conduct falling within the scope

of "technology-facilitated violence against women," as that term is used in this chapter.

References

Allen, N., Larsen, S., Trotter, J., & Sullivan, C. (2013). Exploring the core service delivery processes of an evidence-based community advocacy program for women with abusive partners. *Journal of Community Psychology*, *41*(1), 1–18. doi:10.1002/jcop.21502

Andrew, M. (2020, February 19). Submission on the review of online safety laws. *Australian Women Against Violence Alliance*. Retrieved from https://www.communications.gov.au/sites/default/files/submissions/consultation_on_a_new_online_safety_act_-_submission_-_australian_women_against_violence_alliance.pdf

Bailey, J. (2013). 'Sexualized online bullying' through an equality lens: Missed opportunity in *AB v. Bragg?*. *McGill Law Journal*, *59*(3), 709–737. doi:10.7202/1025142ar

Bailey, J., & Mathen, C. (2019). Technology-facilitated violence against women and Girls: Assessing the Canadian criminal law response. *The Canadian Bar Review*, *97*(3), 664–696. Retrieved from https://cbr.cba.org/index.php/cbr/article/view/4562

Bobo, L. D., & Thompson, V. (2006). Unfair by design: The war on drugs, race, and the legitimacy of the criminal justice system. *Social Research: International Quarterly*, *73*(2), 445–472. Retrieved from https://muse.jhu.edu/article/527464/pdf

Briggs, L. (2018). Report of the statutory review of the enhancing online safety act 2015 and the review of schedules 5 and 7 to the broadcasting services act 1992 (online content scheme). *Commonwealth of Australia*. Retrieved from https://www.communications.gov.au/publications/report-statutory-review-enhancing-online-safety-act-2015-and-review-schedules-5-and-7-broadcasting

Canadian Centre for Child Protection. (2016, January 18). Statement: Canadian centre working with the Manitoba government to help Manitobans take back control of their image. Retrieved from https://www.cybertip.ca/app/en/media_release_201601_statement_ncdii. Accessed on May 7, 2020.

Canadian Centre for Child Protection. (2019). The power of eleven: 2018-19 social value report. Retrieved from https://www.protectchildren.ca/pdfs/C3P_SocialValueReport_2018-2019_en.pdf

CBC News. (2013, August 7). N.S. cyberbullying legislation allows victims to sue. Retrieved from https://www.cbc.ca/news/canada/nova-scotia/n-s-cyberbullying-legislation-allows-victims-to-sue-1.1307338. Accessed on June 8, 2020.

Chesney, B., & Citron, D. (2019). Deep fakes: A looming challenge for privacy, democracy, and national security. *California Law Review*, *107*(6), 1753–1820. doi: 10.15779/Z38RV0D15J

Citron, D. (2014). *Hate crimes in cyberspace*. Cambridge, MA: Harvard University Press.

Crouch v. Snell. (2015). NSSC 340.

Cyber-safety Act. (2013). S.N.S., c. 2.

CyberScan. (n.d.). What you need to know about the intimate images & cyber-protection act. Retrieved from https://novascotia.ca/cyberscan/documents/What%20You%20Need%20To%20Know%20about%20the%20Intimate%20Images%20and%20Cyber-Protection%20Act.pdf

Douglas, H., Harris, B., & Dragiewicz, M. (2019). Technology-facilitated domestic and family violence: Women's experiences. *The British Journal of Criminology*, *59*(3), 551–570. doi:10.1093/bjc/azy068

Enhancing Online Safety Act 2015 (Cth).

Fast, E., & Collin-Vézina, D. (2010). Historical trauma, race-based trauma, and resilience of Indigenous peoples: A literature review. *First Peoples Child & Family Review*, *5*(1), 126–136.

Flynn, A., & Henry, N. (2019). Image-based sexual abuse: An Australian reflection. *Women & Criminal Justice*, 1–14. doi:10.1080/08974454.2019.1646190

Freed, D., Palmer, J., Minchala, D., Levy, K., Ristenpart, T., & Dell, N. (2017). Digital technologies and intimate partner violence: A qualitative analysis with multiple stakeholders. *PACM: Human-Computer Interaction: Computer-Supported Cooperative Work and Social Computing (CSCW)*, 1(No. 2), 46. doi:10.1145/3134681

Goodman, L., & Epstein, D. (2008). *Listening to battered women: A survivor-centered approach to advocacy*. Washington, DC: American Psychological Association.

Government of Australia. (2014). Enhancing online safety for children: Public consultation on key election commitments, January 2014.

Government of New Zealand. (2016, June 1). NetSafe appointed to cyberbullying role. Retrieved from https://www.beehive.govt.nz/release/netsafe-appointed-cyber-bullying-role

Harmful Digital Communications Act 2015.

Intimate Images and Cyber-Protection Act, S.N.S. 2017, c. 7.

Intimate Image Protection Regulation, Man. Reg. 3/2016, ss. 2–3.

Kubinec, V. (2018, April 27). More than 1,300 Manitobans seek help after intimate images shared. *CBC News*. Retrieved from https://www.cbc.ca/news/canada/manitoba/revenge-porn-help-online-1.4637615

Law Commission. (August 2012). Harmful Digital Communications: The adequacy of the current sanctions and remedies. Wellington: Ministerial Briefing Paper. Retrieved from https://www.lawcom.govt.nz/sites/default/files/projectAvailableFormats/NZLC%20MB3.pdf

Legislative Assembly of Manitoba. (2015, March 26). Hansard debates and proceedings of the Legislative Assembly of Manitoba. Retrieved from https://www.gov.mb.ca/legislature/hansard/40th_4th/hansardpdf/71.pdf

Marganski, A., & Melander, L. (2018). Intimate partner violence victimization in the cyber and real world: Examining the extent of cyber aggression experiences and its association with in-person dating violence. *Journal of Interpersonal Violence*, *33*(7), 1071–1095. doi:10.1177/0886260515614283

Mortreux, C., Kellard, M., Henry, N., & Flynn, A. (2019). Understanding the attitudes and motivations of adults who engage in image-based abuse. *eSafety*

Commissioner. Retrieved from https://www.esafety.gov.au/sites/default/files/2019-10/Research_Report_IBA_Perp_Motivations.pdf

Netsafe. (2018, March 20). What is image based abuse?. Retrieved from https://www.netsafe.org.nz/image-based-abuse/

Netsafe. (2019a). Annual report 2018/2019. Retrieved from https://www.netsafe.org.nz/wp-content/uploads/2019/12/2019-Annual-Report-R174WEB-1.pdf

Netsafe. (2019b). Image-based sexual abuse: A snapshot of New Zealand adults' experiences. Retrieved from https://www.netsafe.org.nz/wp-content/uploads/2019/01/IBSA-report-2019_Final.pdf

Netsafe. (2019c, July 1). What is the HDCA?. Retrieved from https://www.netsafe.org.nz/what-is-the-hdca/. Accessed on May 7, 2020.

Netsafe. (2020, April 17). Staying safe online: Quick reference guide. Retrieved from https://www.netsafe.org.nz/staying-safe-online/

Netsafe. (n.d.). Make a report. Retrieved from https://report.netsafe.org.nz/hc/en-au/requests/new. Accessed on May 7, 2020.

Nova Scotia House of Assembly. (2013, April 26). Hansard debates and proceedings of the house of assembly. Retrieved from https://nslegislature.ca/legislative-business/hansard-debates/assembly-61-session-5/house_13apr26

Nova Scotia. (2018, July 5). Intimate images and cyber-protection legislation proclaimed. Retrieved from https://novascotia.ca/news/release/?id=20180705004

Nova Scotia. (n.d.). Cyber-safety act. Retrieved from https://novascotia.ca/just/global_docs/Cyberbullying_EN.pdf. Accessed on May 7, 2020.

Nova Scotia Provincial Sexual Violence Prevention Committee. (2019). Guidelines and recommendations for Nova Scotia universities and the Nova Scotia Community College: Development of survivor-centric sexual violence policies and responses. Retrieved from https://novascotia.ca/lae/pubs/docs/development-of-survivor-centric-sexual-violence-policies-guidelines-for-universities-nscc.pdf

Office of the eSafety Commissioner. (2015, January 7). Children's eSafety Commissioner launches cyberbullying complaints scheme. Retrieved from https://www.esafety.gov.au/about-us/newsroom/childrens-esafety-commissioner-launches-cyberbullying-complaints-scheme. Accessed on May 7, 2020.

Office of the eSafety Commissioner. (2016). Giving women tech tools to take control. Retrieved from https://www.esafety.gov.au/about-us/newsroom/giving-women-tech-tools-take-control

Office of the eSafety Commissioner. (2018a). Annual report: 2017-2018. Retrieved from https://www.esafety.gov.au/sites/default/files/2019-07/ACMA_OeSC_AR2017_18.pdf

Office of the eSafety Commissioner. (2018b, October 10). Acclaimed program empowers and protects victims of domestic violence. Retrieved from https://www.esafety.gov.au/about-us/newsroom/acclaimed-program-empowers-and-protects-victims-domestic-violence

Office of the eSafety Commissioner. (2019). Annual report 2018-2019. Retrieved from https://www.esafety.gov.au/sites/default/files/2019-10/ACMA_and_eSafety_annual_reports_2018_19.pdf

Office of the eSafety Commissioner. (n.d.). Law Enforcement: Presentations about online safety tailored for law enforcement workers. Retrieved from https://www.esafety.gov.au/educators/training-for-professionals/law-enforcement

Powell, A., & Henry, N. (2017). *Sexual violence in a digital age*. Melbourne, VIC: Macmillan Publishers.

Powell, A., & Henry, N. (2019). Technology-facilitated sexual violence victimization: Results from an online survey of Australian adults. *Journal of Interpersonal Violence*, *34*(17), 3637–3665. doi:10.1177/0886260516672055

Reichert, C. (2017, June 20). Australian Parliament passes eSafety expansion Bill. *ZDNet*. Retrieved from https://www.zdnet.com/

Soueid, M., Willhoite, A., & Sovcik, A. E. (2017). The survivor-centered approach to transitional justice: Why trauma-informed handling of witness testimony is a necessary component. *George Washington International Law Review*, *50*(1), 125–180.

Spangler, D., & Brandl, B. (2007). Abuse in later life: Power and control dynamics and a victim-centered response. *Journal of the American Psychiatric Nurses Association*, *12*(6), 322–331. doi:10.1177/1078390306298878

The Intimate Image Protection Act. (2015). C.C.S.M. c. 187.

UN High Commissioner for Refugees. (2016). SGBV prevention and response: Training package. Retrieved from https://www.unhcr.org/publications/manuals/583577ed4/sgbv-prevention-response-training-package.html

UN Security Council. (2019). Security Council Resolution 2467. Adopted on April 23, 2019. Retrieved from https://www.securitycouncilreport.org/atf/cf/%7B65BFCF9B-6D27-4E9C-8CD3-CF6E4FF96FF9%7D/s_res_2467.pdf

UN Women Virtual Knowledge Centre to End Violence Against Women and Girls. (2011, February 25). Survivor-centered approach. Retrieved from http://www.endvawnow.org/en/articles/652-survivor-centred-approach.html

Wong, R. (2019). A guide for Canadian women experiencing technology-facilitated violence: Strategies for Enhancing Safety. *BC Society of Transition Houses*. Retrieved from https://bcsth.ca/wp-content/uploads/2019/03/BCSTH-A-guide-for-Canadian-women-experiencing-technology-facilitated-violence-2019-1.pdf

Woodlock, D. (2015). ReCharge: Women's technology safety, legal resources, research and training. *Women's Legal Service NSW, Domestic Violence Resource Centre Victoria and WESNET, Collingwood*. Retrieved from https://www.dvrcv.org.au/sites/default/files/ReCharge_0.pdf

Woodlock, D. (2017). The abuse of technology in domestic violence and stalking. *Violence Against Women*, *23*(5), 584–602. doi:10.1177/1077801216646277

Powell, A., & Henry, N. (2017). *Sexual violence in a digital age*. Melbourne, VIC: Macmillan Publishers.
Powell, A., & Henry, N. (2016). Technology-facilitated sexual violence [illegible]
[illegible]
Reichert, [illegible]
[illegible]

Section 7
Responses Beyond Law

Chapter 36

Introduction

Asher Flynn

As the previous section has shown, legal responses to technology-facilitated violence and abuse (TFVA) are mixed and varied in their effectiveness. While legal responses are vital in holding perpetrators to account for their behavior and in sending a clear message to the community, laws alone are not sufficient to prevent, challenge, and respond to the growing problem of TFVA. As Alison Marganski and Lisa Melander observe in their chapter, approximately three-quarters of women and girls have experienced or been exposed to online violence, which highlights the importance of identifying "inclusive" responses that "stretch beyond traditional design to dismantle problematic norms." Julia Slupska and Leonie Tanczer similarly report that around three-quarters (72%) of people accessing the UK's largest domestic violence charity (Refuge) experience this abuse through technology. As the chapters in this section explore, preventing and responding to TFVA requires a multifaceted and collaborative approach that incorporates criminal and civil justice laws, prevention education, as well as technological and other societal/community approaches.

In this section, we bring together eight chapters that explore options, methods, techniques, and avenues beyond the law in dealing with TFVA. In some chapters, the authors consider how technology can be used to combat and protect against TFVA, exploring innovative ways to prevent and respond to these abusive behaviors, including tech design and multifaceted collaborations. In other chapters, authors consider how victim–survivors and their support networks have sought to reach beyond traditional "justice" responses when their needs and interests are not being met; for example, in seeking informal justice through hashtag activism campaigns, naming and shaming perpetrators, and organizing rallies or demonstrations to highlight the extent of abuse and failings of traditional legal responses.

In their chapter, for example, Ella Broadbent and Chrissy Thompson explore the notion of informal justice beyond the law and what they refer to as the "assembly of counter-publics by girls and women on social media to contest social exclusion and subordination." An example they provide is when technology is used by victims, such as through "name and shame tactics, to ensure that behavior of abusers is not

The Emerald International Handbook of Technology-Facilitated Violence and Abuse, 619–622

doi:10.1108/978-1-83982-848-520211066

excused and to contest the inadequacy of institutional responses to sexual violence." Using a unique combination of applied thematic analysis and social network analysis, they examine a high-profile case of image-based sexual abuse that occurred in Australia, exploring the altered discourses that appeared on social media, specifically Twitter, in support of the victim and condemning the actions of the perpetrator. They consider how informal justice seeking responses gain traction and can counter "hegemonic discourses" and disrupt "the neutral narrative" of events, ultimately producing "a more favored and balanced consideration of the harms to the victim."

Marganski and Melander's chapter further considers the ways in which technology can be both a "weapon and a shield" in the context of violence against women and girls. They argue that any attempted solutions to TFVA"must engage various actors – including marginalized and oppressed persons ... not only victims/survivors and victim advocates, but also tech companies, healthcare providers, legal/criminal justice personnel, and educators." Marganski and Melander identify several approaches, including better training of healthcare provides to recognize and treat TFVA, education on the nature and consequences of TFVA, clearer legal definitions and education on TFVA offenses, including outlining the harms involved in TFVA, as well as training for legal professionals, to improve victim safety and perpetrator accountability.

Marganski and Melander are clear in their contention that the burden of preventing TFVA should not fall on women and girls who are disproportionately the targets or witnesses of such abuse, but rather we must place the responsibility on the perpetrators, including targeting problematic myths and attitudes that minimize and condone TFVA. This is a key message across many of the chapters in this section, in that it is important for any responses beyond the law to engage with victim–survivors, but not to place the onus on them to be responsible for developing the solution or educating others on the importance of responding to TFVA.

Slupska and Tanczer, for example, argue that existing responses to TFVA often shift the responsibility onto victims and survivors to find ways to protect themselves against such abuse. Likewise, Eva PenzeyMoog and Danielle C. Slakoff suggest that while recognizing the importance of including domestic violence victim–survivors in the development of technology responses to TFVA, there should not be expectations on them to engage in the work, but rather to ensure that they are given the opportunity to be part of the teams creating solutions.

Several chapters also point to the importance of multistakeholder and multi-perspective approaches to TFVA. Discussing their own experiences with multi-stakeholder collaboration through the eQuality Project, for example, Jane Bailey and Raine Liliefeldt explore the benefits and challenges of bringing together industry, civil society, government, and academia to respond to the wicked problem that is TFVA. Highlighting the importance of incorporating a range of perspectives and experiences, and drawing on the specialized knowledge and skills among a variety of stakeholders, Bailey and Liliefeldt consider how working collaborations "can lead to creative co-developed responses where all participants feel invested." Recognizing the challenges inherent in bringing these diverse perspectives together, however, the authors outline eight suggestions to maximize the benefits and recognize the limits of multistakeholder collaborations to address TFVA, which researchers and others can draw on in developing their own collaborative approaches and solutions.

Several of the chapters in this section focus on technology-facilitated domestic violence (TFDV) or technology-facilitated intimate partner violence. Penzey-Moog and Slakoff, for example, expand on the concept of using technology for good, by considering how technology can be used to respond to TFDV. Exploring three specific types of TFDV (financial abuse, targeted smart home devices, and stalking), they argue that building in consideration of how technology may be used to abuse at the design and testing stages of development can help address TFDV and produce "meaningful ways to improve victims' safety." In particular, they urge all tech companies to draw on their six-step "Framework for Inclusive Safety" to reduce the capabilities of technology to be used to abuse.

Slupska and Tanczer's chapter also considers the ways in which technology can be used to address TFDV. In particular, they seek to highlight how and why TFDV requires a collaboration between social and technical responses, and suggest the importance of bringing together IPV and cybersecurity literature to better understand the threats, risks, and responses needed to address TFDV. Slupska and Tanczer present an overview of a hypothetical but prototypical smart lock system that has simple functionality, playing a key role in home security, as one example of an innovative response. In doing so, they seek to showcase how "seemingly neutral design decisions can constrain, shape, and facilitate coercive and controlling behaviors."

Another clear theme within this section is calls for increased corporate and social responsibility in preventing and combatting TFVA. Using examples of image-based sexual abuse, Nicola Henry and Alice Witt argue that existing corporate governance is "inconsistent, reductionist, and ambiguous,"and that there are gaps between "the policy and practice of content regulation." They note that there remains an onus on victims and other users to identify, report, and prevent online abuse. They argue that state-based regulations are needed to improve tech company and website responsibility to protect against TFVA on their platforms, as opposed to being left to govern themselves.

Michael Salter and Elly Hanson expand on the importance of appropriate governance of internet service providers and social media platforms through an exploration of the challenges experienced by individuals, including victims, in reporting and having child sexual exploitation and child sexual abuse material removed from online platforms. They argue that the existing "structure, administration, and regulation of online services and infrastructure have created a highly enabling environment" for child exploitation material to be shared, drawing, for example, on the ways that YouTube normalize and encourage "expressions of sexual interest in children" through its algorithmic recommend function. Salter and Hanson highlight multiple examples of the responsibilization of victims (and other users) to identify and report this abusive material, to the point that even though what they refer to as "pedophile hunting" on social media is not encouraged by authorities, they report that almost half of the prosecutions for grooming in 2018 in the United Kingdom were informed by evidence collected through online vigilante groups.

The vital role of bystanders in shaping social understanding and directly challenging the normalization and downplaying of TFVA perpetration is a key focus of the chapter by Robert D. Lytle, Tabrina M. Bratton, and Heather K. Hydson. They demonstrate how bystander intervention models, specifically the work of Darley and Latané (1968), can be modified to apply to cases of online victimization, using the examples of technology-facilitated suicidality, image-based sexual abuse, and cyberbullying. They argue that bystander intervention models "can be used to reduce bystander apathy, encourage decisions to intervene in emergencies, and perhaps even prevent TFVA by deterring violence." Along the same lines as Marganski and Melander, they call for more research and education on TFVA, including providing guidance or "best practices" to bystanders on how they can safely diffuse or intervene when they witness TFVA online.

Reference

Darley, J. M. & Latané, B. (1968). Bystander intervention in emergencies: Diffusion of responsibility. *Journal of Personality and Social Psychology*, *8*, 377–383.

Chapter 37

Technology-Facilitated Violence Against Women and Girls in Public and Private Spheres: Moving from Enemy to Ally

Alison J. Marganski and Lisa A. Melander

Abstract

While research on digital dangers has been growing, studies on their respective solutions and justice responses have not kept pace. The agathokakological nature of technology demands that we pay attention to not only harms associated with interconnectivity, but also the potential for technology to counter offenses and "do good." This chapter discusses technology as both a weapon and a shield when it comes to violence against women and girls in public spaces and private places. First, we review the complex and varied manifestations of technological gender violence, ranging from the use of technology to exploit, harass, stalk, and otherwise harm women and girls in communal spaces, to offenses that occur behind closed doors. Second, we discuss justice-related responses, underscoring how women and girls have "flipped the script" when their needs are not met. By developing innovative ways to respond to the wrongs committed against them and creating alternate systems that offer a voice, victims/survivors have repurposed technology to redress harms and unite in solidarity with others in an ongoing quest for justice.

Keywords: Gender; technology; technology-facilitated violence; violence against women and girls; justice; technological responses to technology-facilitated violence

The Emerald International Handbook of Technology-Facilitated Violence and Abuse, 623–641

doi:10.1108/978-1-83982-848-520211046

Introduction

Literature on digital dangers has been growing, yet the research on their respective solutions and justice system responses has not kept pace. The agathokakological nature of technology demands that we pay attention to not only harms associated with interconnectivity but also the potential for technology to counter offenses and "do good." The dichotic nature of digital progress in relation to violence against women and girls (VAWG) suggests that much more needs to be done to address and prevent increasingly common episodes of technology-facilitated gender violence, especially for vulnerable and marginalized groups, to exact positive cultural change. Further, we must be concerned with online displays of sexism and misogyny in communal spaces and private technologized violence (i.e., when electronic means are used "behind closed doors" or in exclusive communities as a tool for surveillance) as they may co-occur, and also share commonalities with wider public violations including street harassment and nonpublic violations like family violence.

This chapter reviews VAWG in public spaces and private places, and considers technology as both a weapon against women and girls and a shield for them. We first explore the complex and varied manifestations of technological transgressions, which include the use of technology to harass (e.g., cyberbullying) or nonconsensually record (e.g., "upskirting") women and girls (hereafter referred to as WG), to violate positions of power and authority when electronically tracking them during mediated encounters (e.g., stalking by Uber drivers), and to monitor/control "loved" ones (e.g., home surveillance systems). We then reflect on formal and informal "justice" responses, underscoring the ways by which WG have "flipped the script" when their needs have not been met, to move from victim to survivor, utilizing the very tools that have been misappropriated by others to violate them. Last, we highlight recent, innovative technological approaches to combat online VAWG, closing with comprehensive recommendations on how to better serve victims/survivors of gender-related violence.

Violence against Women and Girls

Despite years of advocacy work, legislative change, and support services, VAWG affects millions across the globe (WHO, 2017), which includes offenses ranging from daily encounters tinged with benevolent sexism (see, e.g., discussion of gender microaggressions in Capodilupo et al., 2010) to less common yet more egregious and hostile events (see, e.g., discussion of mass murder in Marganski, 2019a). One in three women will have experienced an act of physical or sexual violence in her lifetime (WHO, 2013), with rates of physical violence, sexual violence, and stalking higher among bisexual (Walters, Chen, & Breiding, 2013) and transgender (Stotzer, 2009) women, and those belonging to other marginalized groups (e.g., Plummer & Findley, 2012; Rosay, 2016). Further, approximately 50% of women experience intimate partner–perpetrated psychological aggression and/or coercive control in their lifetime (Black et al., 2011). Yet, VAWG has been challenging to study due to definitional and methodological differences that sometimes fail to capture a range of experiences, including street harassment (Vera-Gray, 2017), workplace harassment (Westmarland, 2002), and other offenses (see, e.g., discussion of groping at pubs, clubs, and concert venues in Fileborn, 2016; Fileborn, Wadds, & Tomsen, 2019) by different perpetrators in a variety of settings.

Beyond in-person victimizations, VAWG is also technology-facilitated, consisting of overt and covert behaviors (e.g., aggression and surveillance) where perpetrators need not be present to aggress against their targets. Technology-facilitated VAWG has been defined by the United Nations as "acts of gender-based violence that are committed, abetted or aggravated, in part or fully, by the use of information and communication technologies (ICTs), such as phones, the internet, social media platforms, and email" (APC, 2020, para 1). With internet access being widely available and smart-device ownership overwhelmingly common (Anderson & Jiang, 2018), various social problems seep from the real world into the digital realm.

It is now estimated that three-quarters of WG have experienced or been exposed to online violence (Tandon & Pritchard, 2015), including threats of death or rape, bullying/harassment, and stalking, among other offenses, making this type of victimization more common than any in-person form. Even when these acts are limited to those perpetrated by intimate or dating partners, research indicates most young adults in college (Marganski & Melander, 2018) and youth in schools (Zweig & Dank, 2013; Zweig, Dank, Yahner, & Lachman, 2013) report technology-facilitated relationship violence. These online experiences have been associated with depression, substance use, antisocial behavior (Melander & Marganski, 2020), and increased risk for in-person partner violence victimizations (Marganski & Melander, 2018; NNEDV, 2014).

Technology-facilitated VAWG occurs in public spaces and private places, and it varies between and within groups (e.g., adults and minors, persons of color, those with different abilities, social class, etc.). Younger women, as well as those who are sexual minorities, are at higher risk for technology-facilitated sexual violence victimization, for example, than their counterparts (Henry & Powell, 2018). While the reasons for these patterns are complex, it points to the importance of social location in the study of these contemporary issues. Such violence falls on a continuum of illegal and legal behaviors (see, e.g., Kelly, 1987), and these transgressions threaten the privacy and freedoms of those on the receiving end (Citron, 2014). Further, it is a global phenomenon (see, e.g., Bailey & Steeves, 2015; Tandon & Pritchard, 2015) extending beyond the United States (US), as researchers in Australia (Dragiewicz et al., 2019), the United Kingdom (UK) (Mendes, Ringrose, & Keller, 2019), Canada (Bailey & Mathen, 2019), and elsewhere have noted. In all, technology's abuse, along with associated harms, creates an urgency for investigating VAWG comprehensively so we may derive informed and appropriate solutions.

Technology as a Weapon

Electronically facilitated VAWG has been dubbed an "old behavior in a new guise" (Campbell, 2005). Inherent in the virtual world are larger systems and interactions within those systems that imitate those in the real world; these large-scale structural forces impact power dynamics and abuses in ICTs, including online sexual exploitation and image-based sexual abuse, cyberstalking, and other forms of cyberviolence (Marganski, 2018, 2019b). While WG dominate social media platforms and are more likely to use them than male counterparts (78% vs. 65%[1]), they are not necessarily protected in these spaces and are far more likely to experience certain kinds of victimization, such as technology-facilitated sexual violence and cyberstalking (Flynn & Henry, 2019; Henry & Powell, 2018; Powell, Scott, Henry, & Flynn, 2020). Perpetrators of image-based sexual violence, for example, are commonly ex-husbands and ex-boyfriends who seek out and receive male peer support online that encourages violence against former female lovers (see, e.g., DeKeseredy & Schwartz, 2016; Henry & Flynn, 2019). The reality, then, is that many online harms are gendered in nature.

Some acts of technological VAWG resemble those that occur offline, albeit new offenses have emerged that present novel threats. Such technocrimes include nonconsensual photo/video recordings taken in public or private settings without consent such as "upskirting" and "down-blousing," which sometimes are distributed widely thereafter online (Henry et al., 2020; McGlynn & Downes, 2015; Powell, Henry, Flynn, & Scott, 2019), and cases where persons in power violate positions of trust by electronically tracking victims they meet during the course of their work (see, e.g., discussion of stalking and assaults of passengers by Uber and Lyft drivers in Osterheldt, 2019). Additional examples include, but are not limited to: e-trafficking, cyber-trolling, online impersonation, doxing, swatting, cyber-mob attacks, deep-fakes, and other image-based abuse (Henry & Flynn, 2019).

Similar to in-person VAWG, perpetrators may use technology to objectify, demean, intimidate, and/or control others. In contrast to face-to-face violence, however, perpetrators of technology-facilitated VAWG may be unknown because they may be unseen. They could be strangers, classmates, coworkers, friends, or loved ones (Henry et al., 2020). This may help explain high rates of these transgressions as the veil of anonymity protects and may embolden perpetrators; however, even when perpetrators are known, high rates of aggression still exist (see, e.g., Marganski & Melander, 2018; Melander & Hughes, 2018; Zweig & Dank, 2013).

Individuals have used technologies in invasive and vituperative ways; monitoring, controlling, and punishing others. Domestic and sexual violence programs have reported that technology-facilitated VAWG is a real concern, affecting nearly all who seek their services (NNEDV, 2014). Adolescent girls are also vulnerable to cybervictimization due to the amount of time spent online while navigating through difficult developmental life stages (Chisholm, 2006). Culturally -extolled femininity (Connell, 1987) collides with the normalization of VAWG (Klein, 2006), producing conditions conducive to these events. Girls more than boys experience pressure to sext (Crofts, Lee, McGovern, & Milivojevic, 2015), and those who do may be shamed later on; a by-product of contradictory cultural codes that judge girls on sex appeal while also policing their sexuality. Technology further amplifies harms, permitting perpetrators to reach a much wider audience than ever before, extending those who gaze, shame, and inflict harm. Thus, the ease, accessibility, and speed of our connections holds serious implications and presents unique challenges for not only victims who may experience heightened fear, anger, depression, and/or suicidal ideation (see, e.g., Bates, 2017; Powell, Henry, & Flynn, 2018) but also justice systems whose investigations grow ever more complicated.

Gendered cyberhate has become common in digital spaces, and behaviors comprising it have grown increasingly threatening to recipients (Jane, 2017; Mantilla, 2013). Sexually charged, highly misogynistic content and other forms of vitriol have a strong presence in segments of the Manosphere (see, e.g., discussion of incels, the red pill subreddit, etc. in Center on Extremism, 2018; Ging, 2017; Scaptura & Boyle, 2019; Zimmerman, Ryan, & Duriesmith, 2018), and though there have been challenges to discriminatory language and obscene material in the US (see, e.g., Miller v California, 1973; Pope v Illinois, 1987; Smith v US, 1977), many prejudicial posts have found protection under the guise of free speech. Some online spaces are known to house hostile viewpoints. For example, thousands of insecure men and boys who fail to live up to an ideal (e.g., hegemonic masculinity) have found solace in online communities that call for the subjugation of WG (Woolf, 2014), fostering animosity, violence, and even lethal events. The end result is toxic, as unregulated messages perpetuate myths, misinformation, and hate that influences various kinds of VAWG.

In all, technology-facilitated VAWG comes in many forms and has the potential to result in physical, psychological, behavioral, social, and financial problems. It constitutes legal and moral violations, and it infringes on individuals' active engagement in the digital world, which perpetuates and maintains inequalities that, in turn, continue to breed violence (e.g., Gorman, 2019). This can have devastating consequences on not only the persons targeted but also their families, social networks, and society.

Technology as a Shield

While technology has been used to harm WG, it has also been used to counter transgressions, hold perpetrators accountable for their actions, and protect individuals from future episodes of violence. Far from ideal, justice system responses have fallen short in meeting the justice needs of victims/survivors and, in some cases, contributed to further harms via secondary victimization (Flynn, 2015). WG have been pressured by police, courts, and other social service providers to turn off or alter the settings on their electronic devices, close social media accounts, and change financial and other accounts online, ignoring how difficult, impractical, and silencing/isolating such measures can be (Dragiewicz et al., 2018; Woodlock, McKenzie, Western, & Harris, 2019). When elements fundamental to safety, healing, and recovery are not included in justice practices or otherwise absent from the lives of those who suffer transgressions, the result is untreated, prolonged, and continued suffering. To move forward, it is imperative that structures incorporate trauma-informed care into operating systems and practices to improve users' experiences and set the tone for electronic environments in ways that shape expectations and promote responsible behavior.

For far too long, the burden of stopping or preventing VAWG has disproportionately fallen onto WG who are on the receiving end of violence (and more recently, bystanders, as found in the Mentors for Violence Prevention, Green Dot, etc.[2]), rather than the men and boys perpetrating problematic behaviors. Due to long-standing patriarchal practices, WG who are victims of gender-based violence are often blamed for perpetrator actions or bear the weight of innovating the problem away.

The failure of justice systems to address VAWG online (see, e.g., Dunn, Lalonde, & Bailey, 2017) is symptomatic of larger social failures to treat such violence and discrimination seriously. Feminists have brought light to the issues and absurdities associated with perspectives that blame victims for others' actions, which alleviates the perpetrator – as well as the larger culture – from responsibility and feeds into misbehavior as well as the inability to change. Satire pieces such as "The Rape of Mr. Smith" (n.d.) or "Tips Guaranteed to Prevent Rape" (Tarrant, 2009) highlight unjust practices and the burdens that WG face. Moving from chastity belts to self-defense classes, to antirape technologies that place the onus on potential targets of violence, it seems as though the more things change, the more they stay the same (Flynn, 2015). It should come as no surprise then that our reliance on technology for everyday interactions has led to the proliferation of technological strategies to combat VAWG.

Contemporary "solutions" to VAWG are geared toward potential victims, making rounds on social media as real fixes for large, complex problems. Examples include wearable technologies designed to detect, deter, and even punish violators, including drug detecting nail polish (Zikalala, 2017), wristbands that emit a foul odor to ward off predators (Cuddy, 2019), pepper-spray stilettos (EFE, 2017), internal barbed condoms (Karimi, 2010), and jackets/underwear that deliver powerful jolts of electricity or are nearly impossible to pull off (Euronews, 2013; Kahney, 2003). Noncorporeal technologies also exist including straws to detect spiked drinks (Steffen, 2020), stamps to mark public transit gropers (Koizumi, 2019), and consent condoms that require four hands to open (Cuddy, 2019). When existing patriarchal structures combine with capitalism at a point in history when technology reliance is at an all-time high, we see private companies advertising, marketing, and profiting from strategies that claim to reduce risk, yet ultimately fail to target perpetration and may inadvertently result in target transference or create unexpected harms as a consequence of usage. Further, antirape technologies create a false sense of safety and security, especially considering the plethora of evidence pointing to alcohol as the leading date rape drug (Anderson, Flynn, & Pilgrim, 2017; Hindmarch & Brinkmann, 1999). These technologies, while driven by good intentions, have unanticipated and undesirable effects. They misplace responsibility by targeting victims rather than perpetrators, perpetuate and reinforce rape myths, and undermine victims'/survivors' agency (Bivens & Hasinoff, 2017; White & McMillan, 2019). We would be remiss to overlook this in discussions of effective, evidence-based solutions.

Despite its limitations, technology has been used to counteract women's perceived and actual vulnerability. Cell and mobile phones may be used to connect with others in prearranged calls to avoid "stranger danger," reach emergency services, and document evidence of violations, while Apple watches may activate alarms. Technology can also facilitate the sharing of experiences and access to resources. The SmartSafe+ app, for example, assists with collecting and storing evidence that can be used in criminal justice proceedings (Caneva, 2016), whereas Circle of

6 not only provides immediate access to local and national rape crisis hotlines and resources but also automatically alerts up to six preselected friends that the person either needs help getting home safely, a phone call to interrupt a potentially dangerous situation or to talk immediately, all with the touch of a button (Circle of 6, 2020). EmergenSee and LiveSafe operate in similar ways.

Beyond responding to hazardous circumstances or events, victims/survivors have found support in the aftermath of trauma through digitized social networks, and some have taken action online to have their justice needs at least in some part met while others have advocated more broadly via ICTs (see, e.g., Fascendini & Fialová, 2011). Dissatisfied by formal justice (in)actions, some individuals have sought informal justice online. Referred to as "digital vigilantism," "feminist digilantism," or "DIY justice online" (Jane, 2016; Powell, 2017), women, girls, and allies have taken to technology to fight against online harassment to put perpetrators on notice and hold them accountable for their actions, when the criminal justice system has not (Al-Alosi, 2020). They have explicitly named their rapists online to warn others (Pryor, 2017), responded to unsolicited dick pics with the same kind of content to give perpetrators "a taste of their own medicine" (Hockaday, 2019, para 4), and shared screenshots of misbehavior with perpetrators' mothers, partners, and employers, in the hopes that informal sanctions might follow (e.g., Hawken, 2019; Payton, 2014).

Additionally, victims/survivors have used technology to gain support and organize "speak outs," demonstrations, and "take-back-the-night" rallies (Fileborn, 2014). They have also engaged in hashtag activism through campaigns like #rapedneverreported, #whenIwas, and #NotOkay (Powell & Henry, 2017). Safe spaces such as Women.com, the internet's first women-only social network (Cox, 2014), have also been created, and victims/survivors have collaborated with law enforcement to develop apps like VictimsVoice (Ridley, 2019) to safely collect and store evidence that may later be used to press charges. In rare yet noteworthy instances, institutions have stepped up in solidarity by using positions of power to advocate for victims/survivors while sending a message to perpetrators. For example, *The Bristol Post* posted pictures of the adult men who threatened and harassed teen climate activist, Greta Thunberg, online (Staples, 2020).

In contrast to the dark corners of the web, there are bright ones dedicated to collective resistance, healing, and empowerment. Activism projects and online communities such as Project Unbreakable, Everyday Sexism, Take Back the Tech!, and Hollaback! exist to not only document transgressions but also inform and mobilize victims/survivors of gender-based violence (Mendes et al., 2019; Powell, 2017). As such, WG have become inspired online to discuss experiences in their own words and from their own perspective, which is something traditionally denied through more formal routes. These expressions can be beneficial to victims/survivors, providing them with emotional release and an opportunity to feel validated, help others in similar circumstances, and encourage others to bear the weight of intervention and advocacy (Al-Alosi, 2020). These efforts demonstrate the enormity of VAWG as a broad social problem, drawing attention to the issue in a more public way than could ever be possible through regular, in-person justice routes.

Discussion

In much the same way that offline offenses have not been treated seriously or met with ineffective responses and solutions, online assaults too have been minimized or dismissed, leaving victims/survivors to handle these transgressions with little to no formal support. To counter the inadequacies of criminal justice (in)actions, victims/survivors have taken to technology to pursue their own justice by calling out abuses and collaborating with one another to provide information, education, and support. Although victims of technology-facilitated violence are often without legal recourse, recent news headlines – such as when a judge awarded $13 million to 22 women who were coerced into making sexually explicit videos sold on porn sites without their consent (Grant, 2020) – highlight major victories. Yet challenges remain, as inequalities are evident for groups of people in terms of technology access, ease of use, and overall engagement (Al-Alosi, 2020, 2018; Silver, 2019). Furthermore, some countries restrict or regulate user-generated content or platform access, presenting challenges for victims/survivors, along with researchers, advocates, and others who wish to have their voices heard and address VAWG. This therefore impacts victims'/survivors' options, choices, and pathways to recovery.

Additional issues exist when considering the role of culture in the kinds of transgressions we see, and the tools that render aid. The technology industry and innovations are still male-dominated, male-oriented, and male-controlled, which poses difficulties in meeting WG user needs, and the harms they experience may go unrecognized or be dismissed. Preventing and responding to VAWG therefore requires that we become more inclusive and stretch beyond traditional design to dismantle problematic norms (Bivens & Hasinoff, 2017; Jewkes, Flood, & Lang, 2015). Solutions must engage various actors – including marginalized and oppressed persons – through inclusive collaborations between not only victims/survivors and victim advocates but also tech companies, healthcare providers, legal/criminal justice personnel, and educators to integrate various voices and target the complexity of the issues.

Technology

Technology companies, social networking executives, and software engineers are well poised to make important advances in victim safety and protection. When these powerful institutions and employees combine with advocacy groups, they can better meet the needs of victims/survivors. The Safety Net team at the National Network to End Domestic Violence (NNEDV, 2014) demonstrates the promise these multifaceted collaborations have through its Tech Safety app, which aids individuals in recognizing warning signs of stalking, harassment, and abuse, while offering tips for documentation and resources for support. Beyond education and victim/survivor support, they have targeted perpetration via the Coalition Against Stalkerware (NNEDV, 2019), which advocates for the eradication of spyware due to this tool being used by perpetrators to track victims' locations and activities. Tech entrepreneurs can benefit from education and training on VAWG, which may then influence innovation design in ways that protect users, improve safeguards, lessen perpetration, and provide valuable resources to users, thereby creating a friendlier, sociotechnological space.

Instead of having the ultimate goal of keeping people logged in without consideration of their experience, satisfaction, and well-being, prioritization should be given to "regenerative technology," which refers to healthy online interactions that emphasize having empathy and kindness at the foundation (Zaki, 2019). As such, with any technological advancement, it is important to consider ethics. That is, just because it can be done, does it mean that it should? What are the potential outcomes? Are there ways to offset or respond to harm? It is imperative that those at the helm of these technological innovations, such as software engineers, receive adequate ethics training while reflecting on human rights and the costly consequences of inequality and discrimination that may restrict or impede the digital inclusion and progress of all persons in this era (Beduschi, 2018). Beduschi (2018) warns that the very software engineers who are creating the algorithms behind programs that make our lives easier may also be breaching our rights without even knowing it, invading and recording private conversations, and channeling people into haphazard spaces. Thus, we need to ask technology creators to step up, listen to, and learn from users, including victims/survivors, in order to secure safe digital spaces that maximize experiences and overall connectedness. Tech companies should have clear policies in place for violators, but they should also be willing to work on restorative practices in ways that modify behavior and produce actual change. Further, although much offensive online content enjoys protections, software engineers should be charged with preventing harmful content from being freely shared and finding user-friendly and intuitive ways in which victims/survivors can opt to filter out or limit their exposure to triggering materials. Such collaborations between technology users and designers could prove transformative and reduce initial, repeat, and vicarious victimizations.

Healthcare

Healthcare providers can play vital roles in combating the effects of technology-facilitated VAWG. Physicians, primary care providers, counselors, and others involved in the healthcare system should be educated to recognize the signs and symptoms of tech-related violence, have screening tools available to aid in assessments, and have online and offline treatment plans in place. They may inform parents, as well as their patients, on ways to stay safe online and connect patients with other service providers, such as social workers, to identify sources of local support (Waseem et al., 2017). Much like with other illnesses and injuries, early intervention could be the key in producing more positive outcomes. Physical health, mental health, and wellness services can provide patients with vital services that promote healing and recovery in ways that work best for them. Medical interventions are often quite costly for domestic and sexual violence victims in general, which may deter some from seeking services. As such, it is critical to have online resources such as the Compensation Compass app to alert users of compensation funds to which they may be entitled, which helps alleviate financial strains (Masters, 2019). Such combined efforts signal to the public the serious nature of technological abuse.

Legal/Criminal Justice System

Increasing legislation in the US has been enacted to protect victims of technology-facilitated violence and abuse. There are now 45 laws related to adult cyber-stalking/harassment (Working to Halt Online Abuse, 2020). In the US, there are two federal statutes, the *Interstate Communications Act of 1994* and the *Federal Interstate Stalking Punishment and Prevention Act of 1996*, and many other underutilized statutes that can be used for technology-facilitated violence (Cox, 2014). Recognizing that these offenses can have severe consequences, almost every state in the US has implemented varied laws that criminalize technology-facilitated violence or modify existing law to include cyber-related provisions (Cox, 2014). Nonetheless, there are many challenges and limitations to law.

To prevent technology-facilitated violence and abuse, a clear understanding of specific offenses comprising it (e.g., cyberstalking, online harassment, and image-based sexual abuse) and articulation of what constitutes each type of offense is needed to inform justice systems and personnel. The disseminated information should also include information on the dynamics of these harms, including the cooccurrence of digital and in-person offenses (see, e.g., discussion of nonlethal events in Marganski & Melander, 2018; and lethal events in Todd, Bryce, & Franqueira, 2020). Such training has the potential to improve arrest and prosecution practices that impact victim safety and perpetrator accountability. Importantly, this means taking reports of digital harms seriously. Women's/girls' experiences of technology-facilitated violence have been minimized by law enforcement and others in power, much like in-person experiences of gender violence historically has been (Citron, 2009).

Even when recognition of the problem exists and reports are taken seriously, perpetrators of technology-facilitated crimes continue to evade detection and otherwise fall through the cracks of the justice system. Some cannot be traced; others may be dismissed. Conflicts in law further complicate matters, such as when a perpetrator resides in one jurisdiction while the target resides in another, thereby creating the need for expansion and collaboration when it comes to domestic and international law differences (Flynn & Henry, 2019; Henry, Flynn, & Powell, 2018). The multijurisdictional nature of many crimes calls for federal law enforcement and prosecutors to work in tandem with local agencies and offer resources necessary for investigations (Wilkinson, 2016). Beyond further criminalizing and responding to offenses, however, it is essential that the criminal justice system collaborates with victims' advocates and victims/survivors to outline effective remedies and protect human rights. Effective community responses, therefore, require the convergence of multiple stakeholders to share knowledge and purposively consider lived experiences in contemplating solutions.

Educators

Education on the nature and consequences of technology-facilitated VAWG is crucial and should come from a variety of sources. Teachers at all levels can raise awareness of this social problem. School-based cyberbullying prevention and intervention programs for children and university students, which includes individual-level, multi-level systemic, and universal school approaches, have demonstrable effectiveness in reducing perpetration and victimization (Doane, Kelley, & Pearson, 2016; Gaffney, Farrington, Espelage, & Ttofi, 2019). Cyber harassment programs have also been implemented in the workforce, and it is recommended that not only should there be education/awareness regarding how to respond to specific instances of cyber aggression but also attention to the role of organizational culture in shaping individual behavior (Faucher, Cassidy, & Jackson, 2015). It is imperative that prevention programming includes elements of bystander intervention to reduce these modern transgressions and hold those who may offend to a higher level.

Limitations

Although technology shows promise in addressing VAWG, it has limitations. While it can provide access to much needed services for WG in remote locations, not all women can afford or even know how to operate the latest and greatest technological innovations (Al-Alosi, 2018, 2020). Further, technology is not fail-safe, and routine maintenance, lack of internet access or connections, and other service disruptions can interfere with regular performance, isolating women from sources of support (Al-Alosi, 2020). There are also issues with the corporate model of technology that collects and sells user data, opening users up to privacy risks. As such, overreliance on these devices and platforms may contribute to erroneous conclusions about safety and security that endanger some and contribute to violence. Performance aside, technological advancements may have other unintended consequences, including victim blaming. Similar to asking a woman to switch off her phone if she does not want harassing text messages, it is not inconceivable that a victim would be asked why she did not activate her safety app or gather video evidence of her assault (Henry et al., 2018; Powell, 2017). This modern-day victim blaming may revictimize the woman as she is interrogated about why she did not alter her behavior to prevent the assault (Woodlock et al., 2019). The very technology women may utilize to reach out for help may also be used against them by partners, who may own and control access to their cell and mobile phone accounts, using the same devices and programs to track and monitor activity (Al-Alosi, 2020; Freed et al., 2018). Those who reach out online for community support may also face a different kind of backlash from anonymous strangers who seek to revictimize, shame, and denigrate victims of TFVA.

Nevertheless, technology has much to offer victims of gender violence. Victims/survivors may use digital means aimed at responding to and preventing VAWG, and there are benefits of using technology, including: providing victims access to vital online and in-person resources (e.g., educational materials, service provider support, etc.), warning others of predatory behavior, reducing feelings of isolation through social connections, and giving a voice to those often silenced. More intersectional research, however, is necessary to examine the effectiveness of technology in preventing technology-facilitated VAWG, both in the short and long term, as different groups have varied experiences online (Felmlee, Rodis, & Francisco, 2018; Powell et al., 2020).

Inclusive and culturally appropriate solutions for victims/survivors are necessary. Technological innovations that improve digital device security mechanisms and more accurately assess user patterns to determine that the primary owner is the only permitted user, such as enhanced authentication methods (Freed et al., 2018), and further engagement with online providers to curb harassing activities of their users online (Fascendini & Fialova, 2011; Dragiewicz et al., 2018) are warranted. We should not tell victims to simply stop using social media and electronics. Instead, we should be creating spaces that are safe and empower them to make decisions that promote healing, recovery, and solidarity. We see evidence of gender-based hate, misogyny, and other discriminatory practices in this digital era, which is increasingly recognized and confronted, yet we lag in reactive and proactive solutions. Until we target violence at its source (i.e., perpetrators), technology-facilitated VAWG will continue.

Conclusion

Just as vulnerable communities need a continuum of care that may include mentors, social and recreational activities, and therapy, so too do vulnerable tech users. WG worldwide face real threats to their health and well-being from strangers, classmates, coworkers, intimate partners, and family members, both offline and online. VAWG is a global phenomenon in dire need of attention. Rather than normalizing and dismissing these experiences, we need to collaborate to address perpetration, challenge problematic norms, and offer support to those most marginalized and harmed. Social and structural conditions contribute to technology-facilitated VAWG and allow perpetrators to thrive, perpetuating systemic injustice and maintaining inequalities. By educating and sensitizing various persons to technology-facilitated VAWG, providing safeguards and assistance in digital spaces, and specifying sanctions for law-breaking behavior (Tandon & Pritchard, 2015), toxic behaviors and norms can be diminished. Correcting institutional and systemic responses to address misinformation and propagate promising solutions will shift norms, policies, and practices in informed and responsible ways that exact positive cultural change.

The Anti-Defamation League's Center on Extremism (2018) also articulated specific recommendations for addressing VAWG including: building understanding among law enforcement officers and organizations about the nature of misogynist hate; taking legal and policy actions to recognize modern transgressions as harmful and promote gender equality; incorporating gender-based hate in antidiscrimination educational programming; receiving support from federal and state agencies/leaders for research and services on victims, perpetrators, and communities; forming partnerships between tech and the public; improving and enforcing Terms of Service; filtering out obscene and offensive content; and punitive actions. These proposed measures are an excellent start. However, alternative solutions that address the root causes of these behaviors and work in reintegrative ways are also needed.

Understanding the nature of contemporary technology-facilitated VAWG, along with the unique struggles victims/survivors face can create more compassionate, user-friendly digital spaces (Gjika & Marganski, 2020). By recognizing diverse needs and implementing victim/survivor-centered approaches, larger structures (e.g., media and social media platforms) can help those harmed gain a sense of control and empowerment that allows them to act in their best interests. For too long, victims have been the forgotten persons in our justice systems, and we are witnessing the same apply to the digital world. True justice requires that we work with those who have been injured, and the social forces and norms that permit the continued perpetration of harm, to develop solutions. This requires a systemic understanding of how violence and its regulation affect the tech milieu as a whole. By prioritizing the rights, needs, and wishes of those who are most vulnerable to harm, we can make progress in digital spaces and social interactions.

Notes

1. See, PEW (2017).
2. These programs aim to educate and engage community members such as students, faculty, and staff in bystander intervention strategies, so that individuals may recognize and respond to social problems in constructive ways that simultaneously help create positive cultural change.

References

Al-Alosi, H. (2018, June 17). Technology is both a weapon and a shield for those experiencing domestic violence. *The Conversation*. Retrieved from https://theconversation.com/technology-is-both-a-weapon-and-a-shield-for-those-experiencing-domestic-violence-97776

Al-Alosi, H. (2020). Fighting fire with fire: Exploring the potential of technology to help victims combat intimate partner violence. *Aggression and Violent Behavior*, *52*, 101376.

Anderson, L., Flynn, A., & Pilgrim, L. (2017). A global epidemiological perspective on the toxicology of drug-facilitated sexual assault. *Journal of Forensic and Legal Medicine*, *47*, 46–54.

Anderson, M., & Jiang, J. (2018, May 31). Teens, social media & technology 2018. *PEW Research*. Retrieved from https://www.pewresearch.org/internet/2018/05/31/teens-social-media-technology-2018/

Association for Progressive Communications [APC]. (2020). Understanding technological-related violence against women. Retrieved from https://genderit.org/onlinevaw/faq/. Accessed on March 1, 2020.

Bailey, J., & Mathen, C. (2019). Technologically-facilitated violence against women and girls. *The Canadian Bar Review*, *97*(3), 1–47.

Bailey, J., & Steeves, V. (2015). *egirls, ecitizens*. Ottawa, ON: University of Ottawa Press.

Bates, S. (2017). Revenge porn and mental health: A qualitative analysis of the mental health effects of revenge porn on female survivors. *Feminist Criminology*, *12*, 22–42.

Beduschi, A. (2018, September 26). Technology dominates our lives - that's why we should teach human rights law to software engineers. *The Conversation*. Retrieved from https://theconversation.com/technology-dominates-our-lives-thats-why-we-should-teachhuman-rights-law-to-software-engineers-102530

Bivens, R., & Hasinoff, A. A. (2017). Rape: Is there an app for that? An empirical analysis of the features of anti-rape apps. *Information, Communication & Society*, *21*(8), 1050–1067.

Black, M., Basile, K., Breiding, M., Smith, S., Walters, M., Merrick, M., … Stevens, M. (2011). National intimate partner and sexual violence survey: 2010 summary report. Retrieved from https://www.cdc.gov/violenceprevention/nisvs/summaryreports.html

Campbell, M. A. (2005). Cyber bullying: An old problem in a new guise?. *Journal of Psychologists & Counsellors in Schools*, *15*(1), 68–76.

Caneva, L. (2016, June 30). Family violence app wins inaugural premier's iAward. *Pro Bono Australia*. Retrieved from https://probonoaustralia.com.au/news/2016/06/family-violence-app-winsinaugural-premiers-iaward/

Capodilupo, C. M., Nadal, K. L., Corman, L., Hamit, S., Lyons, O. B., & Weinberg, A. (2010). The manifestation of gender microaggressions. In D. W. Sue (Ed.), *Microaggressions and marginality: Manifestation, dynamics, and impact* (pp. 193–216). Hoboken, NJ: John Wiley & Sons Inc.

Center on Extremism. (2018). *When women are the enemy: The intersection of misogyny and white supremacy*. New York, NY: Anti-defamation League.

Chisholm, J. F. (2006). Cyberspace violence against girls and adolescent females. *Annals of the New York Academy of Sciences*, *1087*(1), 74–89.

Circle of 6. (2020). What: Circle of 6 is for everyone. Retrieved from https://www.circleof6app.com/. Accessed on January 25, 2020.

Citron, D. K. (2009). Law's expressive value in combating cyber gender harassment. *Michigan Law Review*, *108*, 373.

Citron, D. K. (2014). *Hate crimes in cyberspace*. Cambridge, MA: Harvard University Press.

Connell, R. W. (1987). *Gender and power: Society, the person and sexual politics*. Cambridge: Polity Press.

Cox, C. (2014, September 4). Former Facebook employee launches women.com, the Internet's first women-only social network. *The Mary Sue*. Retrieved from https://www.themarysue.com/women-social-network/

Crofts, T., Lee, M., McGovern, A., & Milivojevic, S. (2015). *Sexting and young people*. New York, NY: Palgrave MacMillan.

Cuddy, A. (2019, April 12). 'Consent condoms' and 'anti-rape wristbands': Do they work?. *BBC News*. Retrieved from https://www.bbc.com/news/world-47912200

DeKeseredy, W. S., & Schwartz, M. D. (2016). Thinking sociologically about image-based sexual abuse: The contribution of male peer support theory. *Sexualization, Media, & Society*, *2*(4), 664–696. doi:10.1177/2374623816684692

Doane, A. N., Kelley, M. L., & Pearson, M. R. (2016). Reducing cyberbullying: A theory of reasoned action-based video prevention program for college students. *Aggressive Behavior*, *42*, 136–146.

Dragiewicz, M., Burgess, J., Matamoros-Fernández, A., Salter, M., Suzor, N. P., Woodlock, D., & Harris, B. (2018). Technology facilitated coercive control: Domestic violence and the competing roles of digital media platforms. *Feminist Media Studies*, *18*(4), 609–625.

Dragiewicz, M., Harris, B., Woodlock, D., Salter, M., Easton, H., Lynch, A., … Milne, L. (2019). *Domestic violence and communication technology*. Sydney, NSW: Australian Communications Consumer Action Network.

Dunn, S., Lalonde, J. S., & Bailey, J. (2017). Terms of silence: Weaknesses in corporate and law enforcement responses to cyberviolence against girls. *Girlhood Studies*, *10*(2), 80–96.

EFE. (2017, November 13). High heels with pepper spray, new self-defense weapon for Mexican women. Retrieved from https://www.efe.com/efe/english/life/high-heels-with-pepper-spray-newself-defense-weapon-for-mexican-women/50000263-3436228

Euronews. (2013, May 4). Indian students invent anti-rape electric shock underwear. Retrieved from https://www.euronews.com/2013/04/05/indian-students-invent-anti-rape-electric-shock-underwear

Fascendini, F., & Fialová, K. (2011). *Voices from digital spaces: Technology related violence against women*. Johannesburg: Association for Progressive Communications (APC).

Faucher, C., Cassidy, W., & Jackson, M. (2015). From the sandbox to the inbox: Comparing the acts, impacts, and solutions of bullying in K-12, higher education, and the workplace. *Journal of Education and Training Studies*, *3*(6), 111–125.

Felmlee, D., Rodis, P., & Francisco, S. (2018). What a b!tch!: Cyber aggression toward women of color. *Gender & the Media: Women's Places*, *26*, 105–123.

Fileborn, B. (2014). Online activism and street harassment: Digital justice or shouting into the ether?. *Griffith Journal of Law & Human Dignity*, *2*(1), 32–51.

Fileborn, B. (2016). *Reclaiming the night-time economy: Unwanted sexual attention in pubs and clubs*. London: Palgrave Macmillan.

Fileborn, B., Wadds, P., & Tomsen, S. (2019). Safety, sexual harassment and assault at Australian music festivals: Final report. Retrieved from https://www.researchgate.net/publication/335083604_Safety_sexual_harassment_and_assault_at_Australian_music_festivals_final_report

Flynn, A. (2015). Sexual violence and innovative responses to justice. In A. Powell, N. Henry, & A. Flynn (Eds.), *Rape justice* (pp. 92–111). New York, NY: Palgrave Macmillan.

Flynn, A., & Henry, N. (2019). Image-based sexual abuse: An Australian reflection. *Women & Criminal Justice*, online first. doi:10.1080/08974554.2019.1646190

Freed, D., Palmer, J., Michala, D., Levy, K., Ristenpart, T., & Dell, N. (2018). "A stalker's paradise": How intimate partner abusers exploit technology. In *2018 CHI conference on human factors in computing systems*, Montreal, QC (pp. 1–13).

Gaffney, H., Farrington, D. P., Espelage, D. L., & Ttofi, M. M. (2019). Are cyberbullying intervention and prevention programs effective? A systematic and meta-analytical review. *Aggression and Violent Behavior*, *45*, 134–153.

Ging, D. (2017). Alphas, betas, and incels. *Men and Masculinities*, *20*(1), 1–20.

Gjika, A., & Marganski, A. (2020). Silent voices, hidden stories: A review of sexual assault (non)disclosure literature, emerging issues, & call to action. *International Journal for Crime, Justice, & Social Democracy*, online first. doi:10.5204/ijcjsd.v9i4.1439

Gorman, G. (2019). *Troll hunting: Inside the world of online hate and its human fallout*. Richmond, VIC: Hardie Grant Books.

Grant, H. (2020, January 3). Porn site to pay $12.7m to women who didn't know videos would be posted. *The Guardian*. Retrieved from https://www.theguardian.com/us-news/2020/jan/03/girlsdoporn-site-pay-127m-women-didnt-know-videos-posted

Hawken, L. (2019, August 13). Take a swipe: Scorned mum is exposing Tinder love-rats by forwarding their d**k pics to their wives and girlfriends. *The Sun*. Retrieved from https://www.thesun.co.uk/fabulous/9711373/mum-exposes-tinder-love-rats-forwards-messages-partners/

Henry, N., & Flynn, A. (2019). Image-based sexual abuse: Online distribution channels and illicit communities of support. *Violence Against Women*, online first. doi:10.1177/1077801219863881

Henry, N., Flynn, A., & Powell, A. (2018). Policing image-based sexual abuse: Stakeholder perspectives. *Police Practice and Research: An International Journal*, *19*(6), 565–581.

Henry, N., McGlynn, C., Flynn, A., Johnston, K., Powell, A., & Scott, A. J. (2020). *Image based sexual abuse: A study on the causes and consequences of non-consensual nude or sexual imagery*. London, NY: Routledge.

Henry, N., & Powell, A. (2018). Technology-facilitated sexual violence: A literature review of empirical research. *Trauma, Violence, & Abuse*, *19*(2), 195–208.

Hindmarch, I., & Brinkmann, R. (1999). Trends in the use of alcohol and other drugs in cases of sexual assault. *Human Psychopharmacology: Clinical and Experimental*, *14*(4), 225–231.

Hockaday, J. (2019, September 27). Creep who sent d**k pic to transgender woman gets sent one right back. *Metro UK*. Retrieved from https://metro.co.uk/2019/09/27/creep-sent-dk-pic-transgender-woman-gets-sent-one-right-back-10822491/

Jane, E. A. (2016). Online misogyny and feminist digilantism. *Continuum*, *30*(3), 284–297.

Jane, E. A. (2017). Feminist flight and fight responses to gendered cyberhate. In M. Segrave & L. Vitis (Eds.), *Gender, technology and violence* (pp. 14–27). London: Routledge.

Jewkes, R., Flood, M., & Lang, J. (2015). From work with men and boys to changes of social norms and reduction of inequities in gender relations: A conceptual shift in prevention of violence against women and girls. *The Lancet*, *385*(9977), 1580–1589.

Kahney, L. (2003, May 22). Shocking new jacket hits street. *Wired*. Retrieved from https://www.wired.com/2003/05/shocking-new-jacket-hits-street/

Karimi, F. (2010, June 21). South African doctor invents female condoms with 'teeth' to fight rape. *CNN*. Retrieved from www.cnn.com/2010/WORLD/africa/06/20/south.africa.female.condom/index.html

Kelly, L. (1987). The continuum of sexual violence. In J.Hanmer & M. Maynard (Eds.), *Women, violence and social control. Explorations in sociology (British Sociological Association Conference Volume Series)* (pp. 46–60). London: Palgrave Macmillan.

Klein, J. (2006). An invisible problem: Everyday violence against girls in schools. *Theoretical Criminology*, *10*(2), 147–177.

Koizumi, M. (2019, August 27). Trial run in Japan of anti-groping UV stamps sells out within an hour. Retrieved from https://www.japantimes.co.jp/news/2019/08/27/national/trial-japan-anti-groping-uv-stamp/#.XkmofhNKiu4

Mantilla, K. (2013). Gendertrolling: Misogyny adapts to new media. *Feminist Studies*, *39*(2), 563–570.

Marganski, A. (2018). Feminist theory and technocrime: Examining online harassment, stalking, and gender violence in contemporary society. In K. F. Steinmetz & M. R. Nobles (Eds.), *Technocrime & criminological theory* (pp. 11–34). New York, NY: Routledge/CRC Press.

Marganski, A. (2019a). Making a murderer: The importance of gender and violence against women in mass murder events. *Sociology Compass*, *13*(9), 1–15.

Marganski, A. (2019b). Feminist theory and technological crimes: Examining and responding to modern day misogyny. In T. Holt & A. Bossler (Eds.) *The Palgrave handbook of international cybercrime & cyberdeviance* (pp. 1–29). Cham: Palgrave Macmillan.

Marganski, A., & Melander, L. (2018). Intimate partner violence victimization in the cyber and real world: Examining the extent of cyber aggression experiences and its association with in-person dating violence. *Journal of Interpersonal Violence*, *33*(7), 1071–1095.

Masters, J. (2019, November 22). A new app helps survivors of domestic violence cover the cost of abuse. *Advocate*. Retrieved from https://www.advocate.com/news/2019/11/22/new-app-helps-survivors-domestic-violence-cover-cost-abuse

McGlynn, C., & Downes, J. (2015). Why we need a new law to combat upskirting and downblousing. *Inherently Human*. Retrieved from https://inherentlyhuman.wordpress.com/2015/04/15/we-need-a-new-law-to-combat-upskirting-and-downblousing/

Melander, L., & Hughes, V. (2018). College partner violence in the digital age: Explaining cyber aggression using routine activities theory. *Partner Abuse*, *9*(2), 158–180.

Melander, L. A., & Marganski, A. J. (2020). Cyber and in-person intimate partner violence victimization: Examining maladaptive psychosocial and behavioral correlates. *Cyberpsychology: Journal of Psychosocial Research on Cyberspace*, *14*(1). Article 1.

Mendes, K., Ringrose, J., & Keller, J. (2019). *Digital feminist activism: Girls and women fight back against rape culture*. New York, NY: Oxford University Press.

Miller v. California. (1973). 413 U.S. 15, 24.

National Network to End Domestic Violence [NNEDV]. (2014, April 29). Technology Abuse: Experiences of survivors and victim service agencies. Retrieved from https://nnedv.org/latest_update/technology-abuse-experiences-of-survivors-and-victim-service-agencies/

National Network to End Domestic Violence (NNEDV). (2019, November 19). Making strides to stop stalkerware. Retrieved from https://www.techsafety.org/blog/2019/11/18/making-strides-to-stopstalkerware?eType=EmailBlastContent&eId=f71cf075-f309-43ad-b315-b2bca9e9178c&eType=EmailBlastContent&eId=f71cf075-f309-43ad-b315-b2bca9e9178c&eType=EmailBlastContent&eId=f71cf075-f309-43ad-b315-b2bca9e9178c

Osterheldt, J. (2019, May 7). She ordered an Uber. What she got was a stalker. *Boston Globe*. Retrieved from https://www.bostonglobe.com/metro/2019/05/07/she-ordered-uber-what-she-got-was-stalker/kgOFXxzng3yxTgWw2Df0dJ/story.html

Payton, M. (2014, September 19). Guy's creepy message to girl on Tinder about her breasts completely backfires. *Metro UK*. Retrieved from https://metro.co.uk/2014/09/19/tinder-burn-girl-slams-creep-on-dating-site-4874689/

PEW. (2017, January 11). Social media use by gender. Retrieved from https://www.pewresearch.org/internet/chart/social-media-use-by-gender/

Plummer, S. B., & Findley, P. A. (2012). Women with disabilities' experience with physical and sexual abuse. *Trauma, Violence, & Abuse*, *13*(1), 15–29.

Pope v. Illinois. (1987). 481 U.S. 497.

Powell, A. (2017). Digital justice and feminist activism. In A. Powell & N. Henry (Eds.), *Sexual violence in a digital age* (pp. 271–298). Basingstoke: Palgrave Macmillan.

Powell, A., & Henry, N. (2017). *Sexual violence in a digital age*. London: Palgrave Macmillan.

Powell, A., Henry, N., & Flynn, A. (2018). Image-based sexual abuse. In W. S. DeKeseredy & M. Dragiewicz (Eds.), *Routledge handbook of critical criminology* (2nd ed., pp. 305–315). Abingdon and New York, NY: Routledge.

Powell, A., Henry, N., Flynn, A., & Scott, A. J. (2019). Image-based sexual abuse: The extent, nature, and predictors of perpetration in a community sample of Australian adults. *Computers in Human Behavior*, *9*, 393–402.

Powell, A., Scott, A. J., Henry, N., & Flynn, A. (2020). *Image-based sexual abuse: An international study of victims and perpetrators*. Melbourne, VIC: RMIT University.

Pryor, L. (2017, August 10). Is naming and shaming rapists the only way to bring them to justice?. *The New York Times*. Retrieved from https://www.nytimes.com/2017/08/10/opinion/is-naming-andshaming-rapists-the-only-way-to-bring-them-to-justice.html

Ridley, D. (2019, August 5). New app developed by an N.J. woman will help domestic violence victims file charges against their abusers. Retrieved from https://www.nj.com/mercer/2019/08/2-nj-women-behind-new-app-that-will-help-domestic-violence-victims-file-charges-against-their-abusers.html

Rosay, A. B. (2016). *Violence against American Indian and Alaska native women and men: 2010 findings from the NIPSVS*. National Institute of Justice Research Report. NCJ 249736. Washington, DC: U.S. Department of Justice, National Institute of Justice.

Scaptura, M. N., & Boyle, K. M. (2019). Masculinity threat, "incel" traits, and violent fantasies among heterosexual men in the United States. *Feminist Criminology*, *15*(3), 278–298. doi:10.1177/1557085119896415

Silver, L. (2019, February 5). Smartphone ownership is growing rapidly around the world, but not always equally. *Pew Research*. Retrieved from https://www.pewresearch.org/global/2019/02/05/smartphone-ownership-is-growing-rapidly-around-the-world-but-not-always-equally/

Smith v. United States. (1977). 431 U.S. 291.

Staples, L. (2020, March 2). Newspaper shocks readers by publishing full names and picture of men threatening Greta Thunberg on Facebook. *The Independent*. Retrieved from https://www.indy100.com/article/greta-thunberg-bristol-climate-strike-news-paper-post-abuse-facebook-9369436

Steffen, L. (2020, February 16). Three young girls invent straw to detect date rape drugs. *Intelligent Living*. Retrieved from https://www.intelligentliving.co/three-young-girls-invent-straw-to-detect-date-rape-drugs/

Stotzer, R. L. (2009). Violence against transgender people: A review of United States data. *Aggression and Violent Behavior*, *14*(3), 170–179.

Tandon, N., & Pritchard, S. (2015). *Cyber violence against women and girls: A world-wide wake-up call*. New York, NY: United Nations Broadband Commission for Digital Development.

Tarrant, S. (2009, September 18). Sexual assault prevention tips guaranteed to work!. *Girl w/Pen!*. Retrieved from https://thesocietypages.org/girlwpen/2009/09/18/sex-ual-assault-prevention-tips-guaranteed-to-work/

The Anti-Defamation League's Center on Extremism. (2018). Retrieved from https://www.adl.org/resources/reports/when-women-are-the-enemy-the-intersection-of-misogyny-and-white-supremacy

The rape of Mr. Smith. (n.d.). Retrieved from https://www.newtimesslo.com/files/05_08_14%20Rape%20of%20Mr.%20Smith.pdf

Todd, C., Bryce, J., & Franqueira, V. N. (2020). Technology, cyberstalking and domestic homicide: Informing prevention and response strategies. *Policing and Society*, 1–18.

Vera-Gray, F. (2017). *Men's intrusion, women's embodiment: A critical analysis of street harassment*. Abingdon and New York, NY: Routledge.

Walters, M. L., Chen, J., & Breiding, M. J. (2013). *The national intimate partner and sexual violence survey (NISVS): 2010 findings on victimization by sexual orientation*. Atlanta, GA: National Center for Injury Prevention and Control, Centers for Disease Control and Prevention.

Waseem, M., Paul, A., Schwartz, G., Pauze, D., Eakin, P., Barata, I., … Joseph, M. (2017). Role of pediatric emergency physicians in identifying bullying. *The Journal of Emergency Medicine*, *52*, 246–252.

Westmarland, L. (2002). *Gender and policing*. New York, NY: Routledge.

White, D., & McMillan, L. (2019). Innovating the problem away? A critical study of anti-rape technologies. *Violence Against Women*, *26*(10), 1120–1140. doi:10.1177/1077801219856115

Wilkinson, M. (2016). Cyber misbehavior. *United States Attorney's Bulletin*, *64*(3), 1–63.

Woodlock, D., McKenzie, M., Western, D., & Harris, B. (2019). Technology as a weapon in domestic violence: Responding to digital coercive control. *Australia Social Work*, 1–13.

Woolf, N. (2014, May 30). 'PUAhate' and 'ForeverAlone': Inside Elliot Rodger's online life. *The Guardian*. Retrieved from https://www.theguardian.com/world/2014/may/30/elliot-rodger-puahate-forever-alone-reddit-forums

Working to Halt Online Abuse. (2020). *US laws and other countries*. Retrieved from https://www.haltabuse.org/resources/laws/index.shtml. Accessed on March 1, 2020.

World Health Organization [WHO]. (2013). *Global and regional estimates of violence against women: Prevalence and health effects of intimate partner violence and non-partner sexual violence*. Retrieved from https://www.who.int/reproductivehealth/publications/violence/9789241564625/en/

World Health Organization [WHO]. (2017). *Violence against women*. Retrieved from https://www.who.int/en/news-room/fact-sheets/detail/violence-against-women

Zaki, J. (2019, August 6). The technology of kindness: How social media can rebuild our empathy - and why it must. *Scientific American*. Retrieved from https://www.scientificamerican.com/article/the-technology-of-kindness/

Zikalala, Z. (2017, January 16). This high-tech nail polish can tell if your drink has been spiked. *Women's Health*. Retrieved from https://www.womenshealthsa.co.za/beauty/nail-polish-detects-spiked-drinks/

Zimmerman, S., Ryan, L., & Duriesmith, D. (2018). Recognizing the violent extremist ideology of 'incels'. *Women In International Security*, *9*, 1–5.

Zweig, J. M., & Dank, M. (2013). *Teen dating abuse and harassment in the digital world*. Washington, DC: Urban Institute.

Zweig, J. M., Dank, M., Yahner, J., & Lachman, P. (2013). *The rate of cyber dating abuse among teens and how it relates to other forms of teen dating violence*. Washington, DC: Urban Institute.

Chapter 38

As Technology Evolves, so Does Domestic Violence: Modern-Day Tech Abuse and Possible Solutions

Eva PenzeyMoog and Danielle C. Slakoff

Abstract

The reality of domestic violence does not disappear when people enter the digital world, as abusers may use technology to stalk, exploit, and control their victims. In this chapter, we discuss three unique types of technological abuse: (1) financial abuse via banking websites and apps; (2) abuse via smart home devices (i.e., "Internet of Things" abuse); and (3) stalking via geolocation or GPS. We also argue pregnancy and wellness apps provide an opportunity for meaningful intervention for pregnant victims of domestic violence.

While there is no way to ensure users' safety in all situations, we argue thoughtful considerations while designing and building digital products can result in meaningful contributions to victims' safety. This chapter concludes with PenzeyMoog's (2020) "Framework for Inclusive Safety," which is a roadmap for building technology that increases the safety of domestic violence survivors. This framework includes three key points: (1) the importance of educating technologists about domestic violence; (2) the importance of identifying possible abuse situations and designing against them; and (3) identifying user interactions that might signal abuse and offering safe interventions.

Keywords: Financial abuse; stalking; coercive control; smart home device abuse; pregnancy apps; inclusive safety

The Emerald International Handbook of Technology-Facilitated Violence and Abuse, 643–662

doi:10.1108/978-1-83982-848-520211047

Introduction

People who work in tech define rare instances of user harm as "edge cases." In tech, defining an issue as an "edge case" can be used as an excuse to ignore the issue; it is not worth fixing because only a small number of people will be impacted (Meyer, 2020). Domestic violence is not an "edge case." Globally, 137 women are killed by a member of their household each day (United Nations Office on Drugs and Crime, 2018). In reality, domestic violence is common, and technologists (designers, programmers, project managers, and others who influence the creation of digital products) must acknowledge its reality and plan for it within products.

Domestic violence refers to violence at the hands of a family member, roommate, intimate partner, or someone else in one's domestic setting (United States Department of Justice, n.d.a). Intimate partner violence (IPV) refers to violence at the hands of a current or former intimate partner (World Health Organization, 2017). The World Health Organization (2017) found one-third of women will experience intimate partner violence worldwide, and 90 to 95 percent of IPV involves a male perpetrator and female victim (Belknap & Melton, 2005). Intimate partner violence in the United States (US) cuts across all genders, races, and social classes (Petrosky, Blair, BetzFowler, Jack, & Lyons, 2017) and includes physical, financial, emotional, sexual, and psychological abuse.

The reality of domestic violence does not disappear when people enter the digital world, as abusers may use technology to stalk, exploit, and control their victims. In this chapter, we use vignettes to discuss three types of technological abuse: (1) financial abuse; (2) abuse via smart home devices; and (3) stalking via geo-location or GPS. We also argue pregnancy and wellness apps provide an opportunity for meaningful intervention for pregnant victims of domestic violence.

While there is no way to ensure users' safety in all situations, we argue thoughtful considerations while designing and building digital products can result in meaningful contributions to victims' safety. We also argue that PenzeyMoog's (2020) "Framework for Inclusive Safety," included in this chapter, provides a roadmap for building technology that increases the safety of domestic violence survivors.

As a technologist who speaks at public events, PenzeyMoog is sometimes approached by survivors of technology-related abuse. The scenarios and vignettes in this chapter draw upon the victims' experiences as described in these casual conversations. The vignettes (and all dialog) are *not* word-for-word descriptions of events, but instead serve to illustrate key concepts in the chapter. All conversations occurred between 2017 and 2019, and all identifying information has been removed.

Coercive Control and Technology-Facilitated Intimate Partner Violence: A Brief Summary

"Coercive control" is an aspect of intimate partner violence that includes emotional terrorism and the continued dominance of one person over another person (Stark, 2006, 2007). Coercive control features both implicit and explicit intimidation and threatening behaviors by the perpetrator (Stark, 2006, 2007) and an emphasis on limiting the victim/survivor's independence (Robertson & Murachver, 2011). In the wrong hands, technology can be used to increase a perpetrator's control over a victim/survivor's life by limiting her independence and instilling fear (Douglas, Harris, & Dragiewicz, 2019). Importantly, technology-based domestic abuse is very likely an additional form of abuse perpetrated in the relationship (Harris, 2018; Lyndon, Bonds-Raacke, & Cratty, 2011).

In her seminal study of domestic violence support practitioners in Australia, Woodlock (2013) found almost all (98%) had assisted a survivor of intimate partner violence with technology-based abuse. Moreover, during in-depth interviews with 30 female victims/survivors, George and Harris (2014) discovered each one had experienced some sort of abuse or surveillance through technology. Importantly, instances of technology-related stalking – often featuring unwanted phone calls and surveillance – are a risk factor for domestic homicide (McFarlane, Campbell, & Watson, 2002). Along the same vein, the Queensland Domestic and Family Violence Death Review and Advisory Board (2017) acknowledged that technology-facilitated abuse was "an emerging trend" across cases of domestic homicide (p. 2). Simply stated, technology-facilitated abuse must be taken seriously as a form of oppression and control.

Financial Abuse

Financial abuse is among the most powerful methods abusers have to keep a survivor in a relationship and to diminish their ability to safely leave (National Network to End Domestic Violence, 2014). According to a study of survivors enrolled in a financial literacy program in the United States (Postmus, Plummer, McMahon, Murshid, & Kim, 2012), 94% had experienced some element of financial abuse while in their abusive relationship (see also National Network to End Domestic Violence, 2014). When someone is on an allowance, or when an abuser knows about all the purchases their partner makes, leaving the relationship can seem impossible. Simply put, many survivors do not know how they are going to survive financially if they leave (Hunter, 2006).

Shared or joint bank accounts are normally accounts meant for one person, but two people are given access. Often, a joint account has one login and password both parties use, one email address that receives updates, and one person whose identity gets verified whenever the system detects suspicious activity.

> Helen and Isaac opened a joint bank account. Isaac quickly took control of the pair's money. Each month, he created a budget, paid the bills, and moved their income into various savings accounts.
>
> When Helen logged into the joint account from a new computer or from a new Wifi network, she was faced with identity questions about Isaac, despite having the password. These questions asked about old addresses and house numbers. In order to access the account, she needed to ask Isaac for the answers. One day, he refused to give her the answers, saying he had their finances under control. She tried logging into the banking app on her phone, only to see that the password was changed. She could no longer access her money. (Case study 1)

Helen's experience is common. Often, survivors are not provided or allowed access to their own money (National Network to End Domestic Violence, 2014), and this compounds the survivor's reliance on the abuser. In this way, the survivor's lack of financial independence is yet another means of coercive control.

Importantly, there are some key ways technology design could work to reduce this type of financial abuse. Joint accounts should be accessible by both parties, and each joint account should have two separate logins as well as identity verification questions tied to each individual. Moreover, banks, credit card companies, and other groups who work within the personal finance space, should flag suspicious account activity that could point to financial abuse, such as constantly changing passwords in joint accounts.

When it comes to detecting financial abuse, much can be learned from the existing laws and practices around identifying and supporting victims of elder abuse (Allen, 2000; Chesterman, 2015). According to a memo sent from the Financial Crime Enforcement Network (2011) to members of the United States (US) Treasury, the following are some indicators of elder abuse:

- Changes in typical banking patterns.
- Erratic or unusual banking transactions.
- Frequent large withdrawals.
- Daily maximum currency withdrawals from an ATM.
- Sudden non-sufficient fund activity.
- Uncharacteristic nonpayment for bank or financial services.
- Uncharacteristic attempts to wire large sums of money.
- Closing certificate of deposit or bank accounts without regard to penalties.

These indicators of elder abuse are signs of financial abuse more generally. All customers who display these warning signs warrant some form of outreach. Customers could receive a call from a banker trained in financial abuse detection to discuss the troubling behavior. This communication could assist victims of financial abuse as they may not yet have recognized the abuse, or they may be unsure if the behavior is abnormal and abusive.

Credit card companies could do similar outreach. A common tactic of abusers is ruining the credit of their partner by opening credit cards and/or taking out loans in the name of their partner, which gives the abuser access to funds without the risk of ruining their own credit (Becky's Fund, n.d.). Customers who have been reliable credit card holders but suddenly open multiple accounts or have a lot of unusual account activity could receive a "check-in" call to ensure nothing is amiss. Of course, people in these industries should not make assumptions about whether abuse is occurring. Moreover, a survivor may not be safe enough to discuss it, or they may already be taking steps to safely leave the relationship. These phone calls, however, could be a starting point.

While the ideas above offer a proactive approach, reactive approaches are also important. Two major banks in Australia have created hotlines staffed with trained employees to assist customers experiencing domestic abuse (Commonwealth Bank of Australia, 2020; National Australia Bank Limited, 2020). Although these banks are taking a reactive approach to assisting financial abuse survivors (waiting for the customer to reach out for help), it is an important step other banks should model.

> Vivian, a customer at Australia's Commonwealth Bank reported that, when she told a customer support representative she was disentangling her finances from her soon-to-be ex-husband, the representative, without asking about intimate partner violence directly, asked her questions designed to keep a survivor safe, such as: "Is it safe to receive mail about the changes in banking at home?" and "Do you need assistance finding a new branch?". (Case Study 2)

In all US states except New York, workers at banks and other financial institutions are required to report suspected elder financial abuse to appropriate law enforcement, Elder Care Service providers, and/or human resource workers for the county (Stetson Law, n.d; US Department of Justice, n.d.b); these workers are empowered through training to recognize and support possible victims. This same protocol could be implemented for victims of IPV generally. Most states in the US have laws that define financial abuse of the elderly as a crime (Morton, 2018). However, there is no similar law defining financial abuse of an intimate partner as a crime. In other countries, such as Australia, financial abuse – in the context of family violence – is criminalized federally, as well as in the individual state and territory jurisdictions (see Australia's Family Law Act 1975 [Cth]).

US Senator Patty Murray introduced a bill in 2007 to the 110th Congress that would have strengthened financial protections for survivors of domestic violence, stalking, and sexual assault (GovTrack, 2007). The bill did not make it to a vote before the end of the 110th Congress, which meant that it was cleared from the books (GovTrack, 2007). Murray proposed a similar law in early 2019, and at the time of writing, there still has not been a formal vote on it (S.627 - SAFE Act of 2019). A law focused on the financial abuse of an intimate partner is an essential step toward helping people regain financial control during – or after – an abusive relationship. As it stands, lack of financial security is one of the primary reasons survivors do not leave or quickly return to an abuser (Sharp-Jeffs, 2015). Technologists in the financial sector have a significant opportunity to prevent abuse as well as recognize when it is happening and offer support.

Internet of Things/Smart Home Device Abuse

> Lisa and Ben use an Amazon Echo to connect to their Nest thermostat, Ring doorbell, and touchpad smart lock. Ben installed all of these devices. Lisa is home alone while Ben is traveling when the lights suddenly go out. She uses a phone app to turn them back on – and they go out again. Feeling scared, Lisa leaves the house, hoping that the issue with the lights will be over once she returns.

When she returns home and enters the code into the touchpad on the front door's smart lock, the buttons flash red and the door remains locked. She tries again and, still, it is locked. She calls Ben. "Are you sure you're doing the right code? 1564?" Ben asks.

"The code is 1546," says Lisa. "1564. Write it down. That's always been the code. You know I won't always be available when you forget things," said Ben, exasperated. Lisa is sure she knew the code, but drops it.

Later, while making lunch, Lisa starts sweating. She looks at the Nest thermostat: it is set to 90°F. Suddenly, the phone rings. "Why do you have the temperature set to 90 degrees on the Nest? What the hell are you doing?" "I haven't touched it!" says Lisa. "I'm turning it down," says Ben. "Why can't you figure out these things? It's not that hard." He hangs up.

Lisa is upset about the home device issues and how Ben is treating her. She calls her sister to talk through what's going on, and explains that Ben must be behind some of the issues. The chat is interrupted; Ben is calling again. She answers. Ben asks her how night is going and asks if she'd "talked to her sister lately?". Shocked, Lisa asks, "How did you know?"

"It's just a question. Why are you so paranoid?". (Case Study 3)

Of course, Ben did know Lisa was talking to her sister. He knew because of an Amazon Echo feature that lets him use it as a listening device (Graham, 2019). The "drop in call" feature is useful in some situations. For example, if someone is at home and their phone is dead or in another room, their partner can call them through the drop-in feature. If prior "permission" has been granted, the Amazon Echo simply gives an alert of an incoming call, and the call starts. With the use of an Echo Show (Amazon's tablet), an abuser can create a makeshift home security system that lets you "drop in" on various tablets around the house. This is how Ben monitors Lisa's activity.

Ben was "gaslighting" Lisa by controlling all the smart home devices from apps on his phone. He made Lisa think she was losing touch with reality – she couldn't trust her own experience (Stark, 2019). Gaslighting is a form of psychological abuse where an abuser causes harm and then denies the harm, causing confusion for the victim/survivor (Stark, 2019; Sweet, 2019). Gaslighting is a common form of psychological abuse used against domestic violence victims and reaffirms one person's power over another by causing the victim to feel like they are "going crazy" (Sweet, 2019). Smart home devices gave Ben new opportunities to gaslight Lisa.

According to the research firm Statista (2020), over half of all US households will have at least one smart home device by 2024. As such, abuse through smart home devices is becoming, and will continue to become, increasingly common

(Bowles, 2018). Domestic violence helpline workers polled in 2018 reported an increase in calls focused on smart home devices since 2017, and lawyers are currently working on how to include smart home devices in restraining orders (Bowles, 2018).

Eva Galperin, the Electronic Frontier Foundation's Director of Cybersecurity, explains that abusers often restrict access to necessary apps and choose not to educate their victims about how the product works (Bowles, 2018). She explains: "They're not sure how their abuser is getting in and they're not necessarily able to figure it out because they don't know how the systems work" (as cited in Bowles, 2018, para 24). Sometimes abusers will not set up the necessary app on their victim's phone, or they will withhold passwords in order to ensure control over the product. Victims with knowledge of – and access to – the product are in a better position to stop and recognize the abuse.

Attorney Alexis Moore, a cyberstalking expert, described working with a client whose abuser "would remotely turn on the heat in the survivor's house" during the hottest days of the year, "just to unnerve her and remind her he was in control" (as cited in Kippert, 2019, para 4). Moore described another abuser who would remotely unlock a survivor's home and car doors and then would describe her as an unfit parent for not being able to maintain security (Kippert, 2019). Moore further described abusers listening to their victims through Amazon Alexas and Echos, smart TVs, and home security cameras (Kippert, 2019).

One way to prevent gaslighting and abuse via smart home devices is to include an "activity log" within the user interface. At the time of writing, Nests do not show the user this information. An activity log – which would include what time a user changed the temperature – would provide a timeline of activity to the victim. Moreover, an activity log could help victims explain and prove technological abuse to law enforcement.

Importantly, technologists must explore the potential for abuse in the "activity log" fix. Potentially, abusers could use these logs to keep tabs on victims (e.g., determine their victim's comings-and-goings via the thermostat). While a valid concern, we believe giving the victim the power to fight gaslighting and have "proof" of abuse for police or legal proceedings is an important step. Until all smart home devices show history logs, survivors should make efforts to record smart home abuse details.

Internet of Things devices should also enact basic principles of security, such as requiring strong passwords and two-factor authentication and logging all users out when the password is reset. In 2019, multiple reports described people hacking into Ring cameras (Hanrahan, 2019), often talking to children (Paul, 2019). And while at least one police department has been trying to help survivors by giving them free Ring devices (Eaton, 2019), survivors should use the product with caution. In 2018, Ring did not log out all parties after a password change, a basic safety precaution given abusers may have the old password and would still have access. This protocol has changed, but a test showed it took several hours to log out all logged-in users (Chang, 2018).

Devices should also have phone numbers to support centers on the device itself and within the app, and customer service representatives should understand the realities of abuse enacted through the device and how to support victims. Companies, while likely unable to fully prevent abuse, are responsible for doing everything possible to prevent abuse and to assist those who do experience abuse through their products.

Given the issues with unwanted "drop in" calls on smart devices, we recommend all two-way communication via smart devices follow the standard model of calls to a cell phone, in which the contact number or name is displayed and the call recipient may accept or decline it. Although many use these devices to monitor their own home or to communicate with friends and family, abuse via these devices must be recognized and planned for.

Domestic violence laws must be updated to include abuse via smart home devices. Police officers, who are often on the front lines of survivor support when responding to domestic violence, should be trained on smart home device abuse. Judges should include the termination of abuse through known and unknown smart home devices in civil no-contact orders. And, a large-scale survey about smart home device abuse is desperately needed.

Stalking

> Erica broke up with John due to his controlling behavior. After the break-up, he began to appear where she was; first at a coffee shop, and then at a restaurant. John was stalking Erica, and though she quickly stopped posting her location on social media and changed the password to any accounts he might have access to, the stalking continued. One day, while driving her Land Rover, the air conditioner turned off. She turned it on, only for it to turn off again. After a few failed attempts, she figured the unit was broken. When she returned to her car after work, all the windows were down, though she knew they were left rolled up. Erica realized John must have control over her car. After a call with Land Rover's customer support, she discovered a second person using the Land Rover app to connect with her car. John accompanied her when she purchased the car, so he knew the registration information needed to connect his app. Without Erica knowing, John knew the car's location at all times, and he had power over the temperature, windows, and could remotely start the car. (Case Study 4)

Before digital automobile interfaces, abusive partners could simply check the odometer of the victim's car to see if they had driven any extra miles (Fazzini, 2018). In the modern age of digitized car controls, abusers have new methods of stalking. Woodlock (2013) found abusers use monitoring technology not just for stalking, but to "create a sense of omnipresence" and to isolate, punish, and humiliate victims (p. 5). The Land Rover InControl app is one example of a product that can be subverted for stalking.

Importantly, while some abusers use spyware to stalk victims, it is more common for them to use legal monitoring apps such as parental control apps, Find My, and theft trackers (Levy, 2018). Designed without intimate partner violence in mind, these apps are weaponized by abusers, often without their victims' knowledge (Levy, 2018). Levy (2018) describes how – for victims of technology-facilitated stalking within a domestic violence context – access credentials such as passwords or security questions are ineffective at keeping an intimate partner out of the victim's accounts. Answers to security questions can often be guessed by an intimate partner, and it may be possible to get someone's passwords via threat of violence. Privacy experts must look beyond the "stranger danger" mentality and create solutions for users whose threat comes from inside the home.

As part of a story on technology-facilitated stalking, a *Wired* magazine writer asked his wife to attempt to secretly monitor his location (Greenberg, 2019b). During his shower, she set up a discrete monitoring method on his phone (Greenberg, 2019b). A popular application sends the user emails summarizing who their location has been shared with, which is a positive step in recognizing possible misuse. However, Greenberg (2019b) noted he did not receive an email the first day. Importantly, the app's creator partnered with domestic violence organizations to modify features that abusers weaponized (Newman, 2017). This practice should be standard across all technology companies.

While many abusers stalk their victims through the use of legitimate apps, others turn to specifically designed "stalkerware" products. In 2018, over 200 apps and services catering to would-be stalkers were identified, with features ranging from location tracking to recovering deleted texts from someone's phone (Valentino-Devries, 2018). Many apps are marketed as tools to monitor children's mobile phone use, but can be exploited. While the desire to keep children safe is understandable, evidence shows invasive snooping does more harm than good (Ghosh, Badillo-Urquiola, Guha, LaViola Jr., & Wisniewski, 2018). Indeed, such apps are an invasion of the child's privacy (Lashbrook, 2019) and may be used by abusive parents to surveil their adult or minor children (Ohlheiser, 2019). For example, SMS Tracker is a child safety product aimed at helping parents. In 2013, a man installed the app on his wife's phone days before murdering her (Valentino-Devries, 2018). Company representatives declined to comment on the app's role in the murder (Valentino-Devries, 2018).

Current law prohibits stalking, but it is not illegal to monitor the location of one's child or install tracking software on one's own phone (Lashbrook, 2019). Most tracking software companies tell users to follow local and federal laws while selling products the purchaser can use to break the law. These companies exist in a legal gray area, and current laws are not placing responsibility on these companies for creating products used for intimate partner stalking.

Eva Galperin, Director of Cyber Security for the Electronic Freedom Foundation, calls stalkerware products "spouseware" because of the high prevalence of people using them to spy on their spouses (Greenberg, 2019a, para 2). She is currently pushing antivirus companies to include stalkerware detection in their products. Galperin hopes that, when a user scans their device for malware or viruses using antivirus software, the program will *also* search for tracking apps (Greenberg, 2019a).

We suggest the following design protocol for GPS-connected apps and services: first, any product with a GPS locator must notify the user when GPS is active, and the product should allow the user to see who has access to the device's location. This information should be immediately visible to the user and not buried within a complex user interface. Moreover, a user should be able to quickly remove unwanted users from having access to their location.

Going Further: The Potential for Intervention within Health, Pregnancy, and Wellness Products

Domestic violence victims feel comfortable using phone technologies compared to other forms of technology (Finn & Atkinson, 2009), and we must meet them where they are. While the authors acknowledge real privacy concerns with fitness and wellness apps, specifically with regard to which companies and entities have access to users' inputted information (Lanzing, 2016; Peppet, 2014), we believe these apps have the potential to identify possible survivors and give meaningful help and support to victims.

> Sandra and Jake had been together for five years when she became pregnant. Jake's physical violence had become a standard part of their relationship. Every few months, something small would set him off. Once, it was Sandra going out with friends after work. Another time, it was finding dirty dishes in the sink. Sometimes, Sandra could calm him down before he attacked, but not always. She was hopeful that it would be different now that she was pregnant, and that having a baby would finally mean an end to the violence she'd endured for years. But, she was wrong. (Case Study 5)

Domestic violence against pregnant women is a serious worldwide problem. In the US, 20% of pregnant women experience domestic violence (Parsons, Goodwin, & Peterson, 2000). The World Health Organization (2011) found physical violence rates against pregnant women ranging from 1% (Japan) to 28% (Peru). In Africa, the rate of physical violence against pregnant partners is 23–40% (World Health Organization, 2011). In America, murder is the leading cause of death for pregnant women, with most assailants being intimate partners (Chang, Berg, Saltzman, & Herndon, 2005).

Given an abuser's goal of maintaining control over their victim, the prevalence of violence during pregnancy is not surprising. Indeed, pregnancy marks a turning point in people's lives, and priorities can change. A pregnant person's increased interest in their baby and sometimes diminished physical and emotional availability to their partner can lead an abuser to attempt to regain control via violence (Campo, 2015).

We believe medical professionals remain the most promising point of intervention for pregnant survivors of domestic violence because most women killed during pregnancy "come into contact with the healthcare system before their deaths" (Frye, 2001). In the age of mobile apps acting as supplementary (or surrogate) medical care, we believe medical, health, and wellness-related apps can be designed to provide help or information to pregnant domestic violence victims.

Thankfully, this type of intervention is already happening in an inadvertent way. The fertility app Glow has reported that users frequently post on the message boards describing abuse and seeking advice (Moscatello, 2017). The use of the message boards as a safe space to ask for help is unsurprising, given that online support spaces are sometimes safer (and less obvious to perpetrators) to utilize than in-person services (Finn & Atkinson, 2009). Moreover, abusers who monitor the victim's online activity often look at browser history (Finn & Atkinson, 2009); a fertility app is a much less obvious place to look (Moscatello, 2017).

While pregnant victims seeking out and receiving advice through fertility message boards is a positive development, pregnancy and health app developers should be intentional about supporting survivors, rather than waiting for them to report abuse. Consideration should be given to how the product could recognize potential abuse and offer support.

Apps should offer users a way to record injuries. If a user records an injury, word recognition from the injury description could trigger an automated response related to domestic violence. This message could say, "This injury could be due to interpersonal conflict. Are you safe? Would you like to see some resources that can help?". App developers can include resources such as the National Domestic Violence hotline number, the addresses and phone numbers of local domestic violence shelters, and a summary of safety planning. The message should encourage the user to write down the information and keep it somewhere the abuser could not find it. Moreover, the survivor should be told to use false names if saving a number in their phone.

A second method of assisting pregnant people experiencing abuse is to have products designed to recognize forced pregnancy. Indeed, 8.6% (10.3 million) of women reported having had an intimate partner who tried to get them pregnant when they did not want to (Black et al., 2011). Many fertility/period tracking apps gather information about the user's reason for using the app, and a user may report they are using the app to avoid pregnancy. Then, if the user reported having unprotected sex (a common feature in fertility apps), the app could ask the user to update their goals or provide information about the encounter. Of course, the user may not want to provide the information or may not be in a safe position to do so. Other options within the app might include reporting that the condom broke, that not using a condom was a mistake, or that their partner refused to wear one. Selecting this last option could trigger a message similar to the injury message, giving the user the option to continue on to a list of local resources. In this case, the list should include local family pregnancy crisis centers. A feature like this could also allow period tracking apps to identify if the user has survived a sexual assault, by providing an option that indicates the sexual encounter was not consensual. The resources listed could include nearby emergency rooms, RAINN's National Sexual Assault Telephone Hotline, and contact information for local sexual assault survivor advocacy groups.

Designers should consider the various reasons a user might decline help. One such concern might be that the button to view resources will take them out of the app and into a browser, which the abuser may monitor. A note next to the "yes" button should clearly state the user will stay within the app. This is merely one consideration. The worst case scenario when designing a feature meant to help survivors is to inadvertently alert the abuser that they are researching domestic violence resources, as this can cause further harm and increased monitoring. Given that the rate of both lethal and non-lethal violence soars when a victim leaves the relationship (McGee, 2005), it is essential designers consider how to best hide when a victim is seeking outside help, services, and/or support.

The Framework for Inclusive Safety

In order to combat digital tools being used for abuse, we suggest technologists use PenzeyMoog's (2020) Framework for Inclusive Safety. The Framework's goal is to help technologists uncover ways their product will be misused, design against such misuse, and uncover possible areas where support or intervention might be offered to the user (Fig. 38.1).

The Framework for Inclusive Safety (PenzeyMoog, 2020):

- Includes a domestic violence research lens.
- Creates domestic violence personas.
- Designs for domestic violence personas.
- Identifies areas where user behavior may indicate abuse and how the product might offer support.
- Includes usability test scenarios and stress testing.

Include Survivors of Domestic Violence in Design Research

Design research leads to better design and safer products. It is critical that developers include domestic violence research within their product ecosystem. First, a developer should research similar products and think critically about safety issues that have already been reported. For example, a team building a smart home device should consider how existing devices are used as abuse tools.

Second, when possible, research should include contact with survivors through surveys and interviews. These surveys or interviews should include a question in which the respondent can describe how the product has been (or could be) used for violence. For example, a team creating a banking app might include a survey question such as, "Can you describe a situation – whether personal or not – in which a financial product has been misused in order to exert financial control?" While more pointed questions are typically best practice for user experience research (the area of design that focuses on users and how they interact with a product), a broadly worded question such as this one gives respondents the freedom to safely respond.

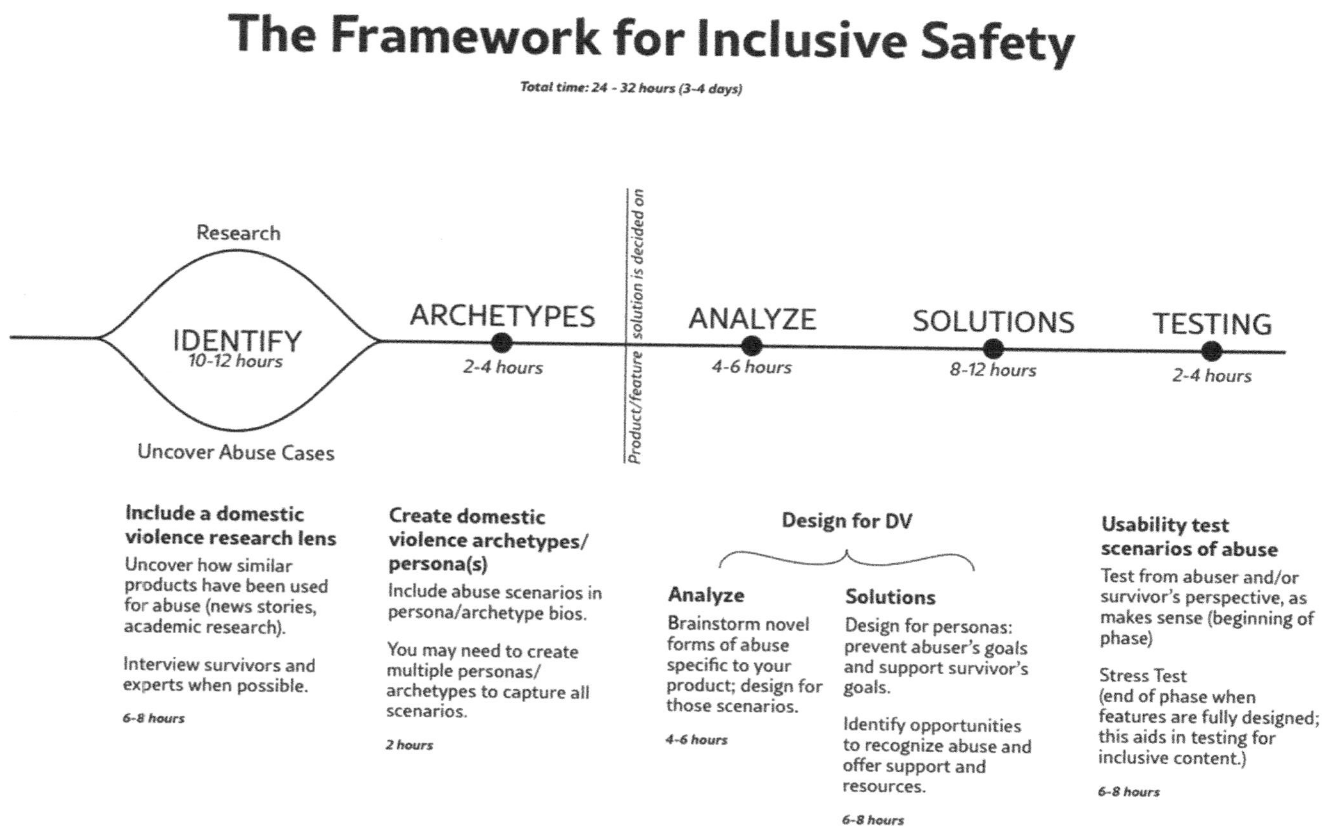

Fig. 38.1. The Framework for Inclusive Safety within the Design Process. *Source:* Reprinted with Permission from Eva PenzeyMoog.

Create Abuser and Survivor Personas

During research synthesis, designers typically identify the types of people the app or product is targeting and create personas for them. In addition to main archetypes, design teams should create two additional personas: an abuser and a survivor. The abuser persona is someone who can use the product to control, monitor, or harass their victim. The survivor persona is someone who can suffer abuse via the product.

Through this process, the design team may realize a survivor can be secretly surveilled via the product. The next step, then, is for the team to consider *how* a survivor could learn the abuse is happening. Alternatively, the survivor may know surveillance is happening but may not be aware of how to stop it. The design team then needs to consider how a survivor can regain control and power over their app use.

Identify and Design Against Abuse Cases

After research and research synthesis (steps one and two) are complete, the design team should include domestic violence abuse cases within their product design. They should draw upon abuse cases identified in their research and should brainstorm novel abuse cases. The three activities that follow are performed during steps three and four of the design process.

During the third step of the design process, we suggest design teams set aside time for a "Black Mirror Brainstorm" (Lewis, 2018). This term – coined by designer Aaron Lewis (2018) – refers to the hit television series *Black Mirror*, a show in which promising technological advancements harm people. A "Black Mirror Brainstorm" session, then, tasks designers with considering the worst ways their products can be (mis)used.

During the final phase of the design process, when the product is being created (either as a prototype or working technology), the design team should do two types of testing:

(1) *Stress Testing:* Stress testing – a term coined by designers Eric Meyer and Sara Watcher-Boettcher (2016) – is a process by which the design team uses their product through the eyes of someone having an extremely bad day (e.g., someone recently fired from a job). The design team should select a scenario, get into the mindset of someone experiencing a terrible day, and use the product. The design team should identify ways the design makes them feel worse – such as sarcastic text that might make a distressed person feel stupid. Once identified, these designs should be modified.
(2) *Abuse Testing:* Design teams should get into the mindset of an abuser, a survivor, or both, depending on which makes the most sense for the product.

When doing this testing, best practice is to find real people who fit the characteristics, have them use the design, and give feedback. However, the ethics of finding someone experiencing their worst day and asking them to test your product are questionable. Similarly, it would be difficult to find a domestic abuser who would willingly product test and discuss how the product facilitates abuse. In these cases, it is acceptable for the design team to role-play and do the testing themselves. However, we do not recommend this approach for other attempts at inclusive design; for example, it would be inappropriate for a white designer to attempt to be in the mindset of Black user to ensure a product is racially inclusive. In this case, the team should hire members of those groups to do testing.

Identify Areas Where User Behavior May Indicate Abuse and How the Product Might Offer Support

If designed properly, financial products, as well as health, wellness, and pregnancy products, could help identify abusive behavior. The design team should conduct a full audit of the product's features and brainstorm what user behavior might indicate abuse. Moreover, they should discuss what resources would be most appropriate to include within the product if a user indicates abuse. Designers should also consider the user's level of safety if the product includes domestic violence resources.

A Final Note on the Importance of Diverse and Inclusive Teams

The importance of diverse, inclusive teams within technology companies is well-documented. Diversity can foster creativity, improve performance, help innovation (Diversity in Tech, 2020; Forbes Technology Council, 2018), and promote empathy (Walter, 2016). Indeed, it is important for technologists to be able to empathize with minority people who are discriminated against by other product users (e.g., when a white Airbnb host refuses to accept a booking from a Black user, as described by Romano, 2016). When people from multiple minority groups belong to a team, there is more open communication about product misuse.

Conclusion

Differences in social location, race, class, (dis)ability status, and the like can produce differential victim experiences with intimate partner violence. Although the scope of this chapter precluded us from an in-depth discussion of intersectionality, the authors want to acknowledge that the intersectional identities of survivors (e.g., their class, race, location, etc.) should also be identified and included during the design process. During the research phase of *any* product, designers should identify who their users are (along multiple dimensions). What designers learn about their users during the research phase should then be utilized during the ideation portion of the design process, with a goal of making the product work for all users.

Within the context of designing against domestic violence, it is imperative that women, who are disproportionately likely to be abuse survivors, are part of the teams creating digital products. However, survivors should *not* be expected to do the emotional work of convincing colleagues as domestic violence is a deadly, common occurrence. Workplace training about technology-based domestic violence can help all colleagues see the importance of designing against domestic violence.

Technology is used to perpetuate domestic abuse (George & Harris, 2014; Woodlock, 2013) and is another mechanism by which abusers exert control and dominance over victims. As described in this chapter, technology can be used by abusers to financially control, stalk, or gaslight victims. Given the role of technology in abuse, coercive control, and stalking, it is vital that designers consider domestic violence when creating new technologies. The Framework for Inclusive Safety (PenzeyMoog, 2020) provides technologists with actionable steps toward making products safer.

While technology is undoubtedly used in ways that are harmful toward victims, technology can also serve as a safe place for victims to receive discreet help and assistance (Finn & Atkinson, 2009). As described in this chapter, we believe health, pregnancy, and wellness products can be designed to provide helpful resources in a safe manner. Ultimately, we recognize the limitations of single solutions used in isolation to stop domestic violence and encourage designers to use multiple techniques in order to ensure digital products are as safe and inclusive as possible. The framework detailed in this chapter provides a starting point.

References

Allen, J. V. (2000). Financial abuse of elders and dependent adults: The FAST (Financial Abuse Specialist Team) approach. *Journal of Elder Abuse & Neglect*, *12*(2), 85–91.

Australia. (1975). Family Law Act 1975 (Cth).

Becky's Fund. (n.d.). Coerced debt. Retrieved from https://beckysfund.org/resources/coerced-debt/

Belknap, J., & Melton, H. (2005). Are heterosexual men also victims of intimate partner abuse? *VAWnet.org: The National Online Resource Center for Violence Against Women*. Retrieved from https://vawnet.org/sites/default/files/materials/files/2016-09/AR_MaleVictims.pdf

Black, M. C., Basile, K. C., Breiding, M. J., Smith, S. G., Walters, M. L., Merrick, M. T., & Stevens, M. R. (2011). The National Intimate Partner and Sexual Violence Survey (NISVS): 2010 summary report. *Centers for Disease Control and Prevention*. Retrieved from https://www.cdc.gov/violenceprevention/pdf/nisvs_report2010-a.pdf

Bowles, N. (2018, June 23). Thermostats, locks and lights: Digital tools of domestic abuse. *The New York Times*. Retrieved from https://www.nytimes.com/2018/06/23/technology/smart-home-devices-domestic-abuse.html

Campo, M. (2015). Domestic and family violence in pregnancy and early parenthood. *The Australian Institute of Family Studies*. Retrieved from https://aifs.gov.au/cfca/publications/domestic-and-family-violence-pregnancy-and-early-parenthood

Chang, L. (2018, May 14). A Ring doorbell vulnerability lets people snoop even after a password change. Retrieved from https://www.digitaltrends.com/home/ring-video-doorbell-security-exploit/

Chang, J., Berg, C. J., Saltzman, L. E., & Herndon, J. (2005). Homicide: A leading cause of injury deaths among pregnant and postpartum women in the United States, 1991–1999. *American Journal of Public Health*, *95*(3), 471–477.

Chesterman, J. (2015). Taking control: Putting older people at the centre of elder abuse response strategies. *Australian Social Work*, *69*(1), 115–124.

Commonwealth Bank of Australia. (2020). Domestic & family violence assistance. Retrieved from https://www.commbank.com.au/support/dv-assistance.html

Diversity in Tech. (2020). The benefits of diversity in tech. Retrieved from https://www.diversityintech.co.uk/the-benefits-of-diversity-in-tech

Douglas, H., Harris, B. A., & Dragiewicz, M. (2019). Technology-facilitated domestic and family violence: Women's experiences. *British Journal of Criminology*, *59*, 551–570.

Eaton, E. (2019, December 29). San Antonio domestic violence victims receive free Ring surveillance devices from local police agencies. *San Antonio Express-News*. Retrieved from https://www.expressnews.com/news/local/article/San-Antonio-domestic-violence-victims-receive-14932616.php

Fazzini, K. (2018, November 5). Secret apps and self-'doxing': How victims of domestic abuse are escaping tech-savvy abusers. *CNBC*. Retrieved from https://www.cnbc.com/2018/11/05/victims-of-domestic-violence-challenged-by-abusers-using-technology.html

Financial Crime Enforcement Network. (2011). Advisory to financial institutions on filing suspicious activity reports regarding elder financial exploitation. Retrieved from https://www.fincen.gov/sites/default/files/advisory/fin-2011-a003.pdf

Finn, J., & Atkinson, T. (2009). Promoting the safe and strategic use of technology for victims of intimate partner violence: Evaluation of the Technology Safety Project. *Journal of Family Violence*, *24*, 53–59.

Forbes Technology Council. (2018). 12 Ways Diversity Makes A Difference In Tech. *Forbes*. Retrieved from https://www.forbes.com/sites/forbestechcouncil/2018/07/12/12-ways-diversity-makes-a-difference-in-tech/#50991c362bc6

Frye, V. (2001). Editorial: Examining homicide's contribution to pregnancy-associated deaths. *Journal of the American Medical Association: The Journal of the American Medical Association*, *285*(11), 1510–1511.

George, A., & Harris, B. (2014). *Landscapes of violence: Women surviving family violence in regional and rural Victoria*. Melbourne, VIC: Deakin University. Retrieved from https://www.deakin.edu.au/__data/assets/pdf_file/0003/287040/Landscapes-of-Violence-online-pdfversion.pdf

Ghosh, A. K., Badillo-Urquiola, K., Guha, S., LaViola, J. J., Jr., & Wisniewski, P. J. (2018). Safety vs. surveillance: What children have to say about mobile apps for parental control. In *Proceedings of the 2018 CHI conference on human factors in computing systems [Paper No. 124]*. doi:10.1145/3173574.3173698

GovTrack. (2007). S. 1136 (110th): Survivors' Empowerment and Economic Security Act. Retrieved from https://www.govtrack.us/congress/bills/110/s1136

Graham, J. (2019, May 14). Alexa Guard can now listen for alarms – or, perhaps, a cheating spouse? *USA Today*. Retrieved from https://www.usatoday.com/story/tech/talkingtech/2019/05/14/alexas-latest-skill-listening-alarms-and-snooping-home-life/1189230001/

Greenberg, A. (2019a, April 3). Hacker Eva Galperin has a plan to eradicate stalkerware. *Wired*. Retrieved from https://www.wired.com/story/eva-galperin-stalkerware-kaspersky-antivirus/

Greenberg, A. (2019b, July 2). The simple way Apple and Google let domestic abusers stalk victims. *Wired*. Retrieved from https://www.wired.com/story/common-apps-domestic-abusers-stalk-victims/

Hanrahan, M. (2019, December 12). Ring security camera hacks see homeowners subjected to racial abuse, ransom demands. *ABC News*. Retrieved from https://abcnews.go.com/US/ring-security-camera-hacks-homeowners-subjected-racial-abuse/story?id=67679790

Harris, B. (2018). Spacelessness, spatiality and intimate partner violence: Technology-facilitated abuse, stalking and justice. In K. Fitz-Gibbon, S. Walklate, J. McCulloch, & J. Maher (Eds.), *Intimate partner violence, risk and security: Securing women's lives in a global world* (pp. 52–70). London: Routledge.

Hunter, R. (2006). Narratives of domestic violence. *Sydney Law Review*, *28*(4), 733.

Kippert, A. (2019). Smart home technology is being used against survivors. Retrieved from https://www.domesticshelters.org/articles/technology/smart-home-technology-is-being-used-against-survivors

Lanzing, M. (2016). The transparent self. *Ethics and Information Technology*, *18*, 9–16.

Lashbrook, A. (2019, September 18). The case against spying on your kids with apps. *OneZero*. Retrieved from https://onezero.medium.com/the-case-against-spying-on-your-kids-with-apps-59760ec780e0

Levy, K. (2018, March 1). No safe haven for victims of digital abuse. *Slate*. Retrieved from https://slate.com/technology/2018/03/apps-cant-stop-exes-who-use-technology-for-stalking.html

Lewis, A. (2018, November 16). In light of the latest FB scandal, here's my proposal for replacing Design Sprints: Black Mirror Brainstorms. A workshop in which you create a Black Mirror episode. The plot must revolve around misuse of your team's product. Pair with @brownorama's idea of "abusability testing" [Tweet]. Retrieved from https://twitter.com/aaronzlewis/status/1063544871472914432

Lyndon, A., Bonds-Raacke, J., & Cratty, A. D. (2011). College students' Facebook stalking of ex-partners. *Cyberpsychology, Behavior, and Social Networking*, *14*, 711–716.

McFarlane, J., Campbell, J. C., & Watson, K. (2002). Intimate partner stalking and femicide: Urgent implications for women's safety. *Behavioral Sciences and the Law*, *20*, 51–68.

McGee, S. G. S. (2005). 20 Reasons why she stays: A guide for those who want to help battered women. Retrieved from http://stopviolence.com/domviol/WhySheSometimesStays.pdf

Meyer, E. (2020). Compassionate design. Retrieved from https://vimeo.com/201986969

Meyer, E. A., & Wachter-Boettcher, S. (2016). *Design for real life*. New York, NY: A Book Apart.

Morton, H. (2018). Combatting elder financial exploitation. *National Conference of State Legislatures*, *26*(20). Retrieved from https://www.ncsl.org/research/financial-services-and-commerce/combatting-elder-financial-exploitation.aspx

Moscatello, C. (2017, September 5). The disturbing conversations women are having on fertility apps. *Elle*. Retrieved from https://www.elle.com/life-love/a12138580/the-disturbing-conversations-women-are-having-on-fertility-apps/

National Australia Bank Limited. (2020). Domestic and family violence support. Retrieved from https://www.nab.com.au/about-us/social-impact/customers/domestic-and-family-violence

National Network to End Domestic Violence. (2014). Join NNEDV & the Allstate Foundation as we say 'no more' to financial abuse this April. Retrieved from https://nnedv.org/latest_update/join-nnedv-the-allstate-foundation-as-we-say-no-more-to-financial-abuse-this-april/

Newman, L. H. (2017, February 1). Tech can do more to help survivors of abuse. Here's where to start. *Wired*. Retrieved from https://www.wired.com/2017/02/tech-can-help-survivors-abuse-heres-start/

Ohlheiser, A. (2019, Oct. 22). 'Don't leave campus': Parents are now using tracking apps to watch their kids at college. *Washington Post*. Retrieved from https://www.washingtonpost.com/technology/2019/10/22/dont-leave-campus-parents-are-now-using-tracking-apps-watch-their-kids-college/

Parsons, L., Goodwin, M. M., & Peterson, R. (2000). Violence against women and reproductive health: Toward defining a role for reproductive health care services. *Maternal and Child Health Journal*, *4*(2), 135–140.

Paul, K. (2019, December 27). Ring sued by man who claims camera was hacked and used to harass his kids. *The Guardian*. Retrieved from https://www.theguardian.com/technology/2019/dec/27/ring-camera-lawsuit-hackers-alabama

PenzeyMoog, E. (2020). The framework for inclusive safety. Retrieved from www.inclusivesafety.com

Peppet, S. R. (2014). Regulating the Internet of Things: First steps toward managing discrimination, privacy, security and consent. *Texas Law Review*, *93*(1), 85–179.

Petrosky, E., Blair, J. M., Betz, J., Fowler, K. A., Jack, S. P. D., & Lyons, B. H. (2017). Racial and ethnic differences in homicides of adult women and the role of intimate partner violence—United States, 2003–2014. *Morbidity and Mortality Weekly Report*, *66*(28), 741–746. Retrieved from https://www.cdc.gov/mmwr/volumes/66/wr/pdfs/mm6628a1.pdf

Postmus, J. L., Plummer, S.-B., McMahon, S., Murshid, N. S., & Kim, M. S. (2012). Understanding economic abuse in the lives of survivors. *Journal of Interpersonal Violence*, *27*, 411–430. doi:10.1177/0886260511421669

Queensland Domestic and Family Violence Death Review and Advisory Board. (2017). Queensland Domestic and Family Violence Death Review and Advisory Board 2016–17 Annual Report. Retrieved from https://www.courts.qld.gov.au/__data/assets/pdf_file/0003/541947/domestic-and-family-violence-death-review-and-advisory-board-annual-report-2016-17.pdf

Robertson, K., & Murachver, T. (2011). Women's and men's use of coercive control in intimate partner violence. *Violence & Victims*, *26*, 208–217.

Romano, A. (2016, May 6). Airbnb has a discrimination problem. Ask anyone who's tried to #Airbnbwhileblack. *Vox*. Retrieved from https://www.vox.com/2016/5/6/11601180/airbnbwhileblack-racism

S. 627: SAFE Act of 2019. (2019). GovTrack. Retrieved from https://www.govtrack.us/congress/bills/116/s627. Accessed on April 2020.

Sharp-Jeffs, N. (2015). A review of research and policy on financial abuse within intimate partner relationships. *Child and Woman Abuse Studies Unit (CWASU)*. Retrieved from https://cwasu.org/wp-content/uploads/2015/12/Review-of-Research-and-Policy-on-Financial-Abuse.pdf

Stark, E. (2006). Commentary on Johnson's "conflict and control": Gender symmetry and asymmetry in domestic violence. *Violence Against Women*, *12*, 1019–1025.

Stark, E. (2007). *Coercive control: How men entrap women in personal life*. New York, NY: Oxford University Press.

Stark, C. A. (2019). Gaslighting, misogyny, and psychological oppression. *The Monist*, *102*, 221–235.

Statista. (2020). Smart home. Retrieved from https://www.statista.com/outlook/279/109/smart-home/united-states

Stetson Law (n.d.). Mandatory reporting statutes for elder abuse, 2016. Retrieved from https://www.stetson.edu/law/academics/elder/home/media/Mandatory-reporting-Statutes-for-elder-abuse-2016.pdf

Sweet, P. L. (2019). The sociology of gaslighting. *American Sociological Review*, *84*(5), 851–875.

United Nations Office on Drugs and Crime. (2018). Global study on homicide - Gender-related killing of women and girls. Retrieved from https://www.unodc.org/documents/data-and-analysis/GSH2018/GSH18_Gender-related_killing_of_women_and_girls.pdf

United States Department of Justice. (n.d.a). Domestic violence. Retrieved from https://www.justice.gov/ovw/domestic-violence

United States Department of Justice. (n.d.b). State elder abuse statutes. Retrieved from https://www.justice.gov/elderjustice/elder-justice-statutes-0

Valentino-Devries, J. (2018, May 19). Hundreds of apps can empower stalkers to track their victims. *The New York Times*. Retrieved from https://www.nytimes.com/2018/05/19/technology/phone-apps-stalking.html

Walter, J. (2016, June 6). Diversity in Tech: The unspoken empathy gap. *Medium*. Retrieved from https://medium.com/tech-diversity-files/diversity-in-tech-the-unspoken-empathy-gap-5b806c83d717

Woodlock, D. (2013). Technology-facilitated stalking: Findings and recommendations from the SmartSafe project. *Domestic Violence Resource Centre*. Retrieved from http://www.dvrcv.org.au/sites/default/files/SmartSafe_0.pdf

World Health Organization. (2011). Intimate partner violence during pregnancy. Retrieved from https://apps.who.int/iris/bitstream/handle/10665/70764/WHO_RHR_11.35_eng.pdf;jsessionid=792A222F6375EF41029EC817F8C9D25F?sequence=1

World Health Organization. (2017). Violence against women. Retrieved from https://www.who.int/news-room/fact-sheets/detail/violence-against-women

Chapter 39

Threat Modeling Intimate Partner Violence: Tech Abuse as a Cybersecurity Challenge in the Internet of Things

Julia Slupska and Leonie Maria Tanczer

Abstract

Technology-facilitated abuse, so-called "tech abuse," through phones, trackers, and other emerging innovations, has a substantial impact on the nature of intimate partner violence (IPV). The current chapter examines the risks and harms posed to IPV victims/survivors from the burgeoning Internet of Things (IoT) environment. IoT systems are understood as "smart" devices such as conventional household appliances that are connected to the internet. Interdependencies between different products together with the devices' enhanced functionalities offer opportunities for coercion and control. Across the chapter, we use the example of IoT to showcase how and why tech abuse is a socio-technological issue and requires not only human-centered (i.e., societal) but also cybersecurity (i.e., technical) responses. We apply the method of "threat modeling," which is a process used to investigate potential cybersecurity attacks, to shift the conventional technical focus from the risks to systems toward risks to people. Through the analysis of a smart lock, we highlight insufficiently designed IoT privacy and security features and uncover how seemingly neutral design decisions can constrain, shape, and facilitate coercive and controlling behaviors.

Keywords: Tech abuse; intimate partner violence; domestic violence; cybersecurity; threat modeling; internet of things

> "I changed the lock on my front door so you can't see me anymore.
>
> And you can't come inside my house, and you can't lie down on my couch.

The Emerald International Handbook of Technology-Facilitated Violence and Abuse, 663–688

doi:10.1108/978-1-83982-848-520211049

I changed the lock on my front door" —Lucinda Williams "Changed the Locks".

Introduction

Technology-facilitated abuse or "tech abuse" through Global Positioning System (GPS) trackers, smartphone apps, or platforms such as *Facebook* has a substantial impact on the nature of intimate partner violence (IPV). The latter encompasses diverse forms of abuse (e.g., physical, sexual, financial) and coercive and controlling behavior by a (current or former) partner or spouse (Bagwell-Gray, Messing, & Baldwin-White, 2015). IPV, and more specifically, domestic abuse[1] globally affects about 1 in 3 (35% of) women in their lifetime (World Health Organization, 2017) and more than 2.4 million UK adults a year (Office for National Statistics, 2019).

Parallel to the widespread deployment of technologies, their misuse, especially in the context of domestic and sexual violence, is increasing. While national figures remain absent (Tanczer, Neira, Parkin, & Danezis, 2018), data points gathered by charities such as Think Social Tech, Snook and SafeLives (2019), and Women's Aid (2018) point to the rising scale as well as the urgency of this issue. According to Refuge (2020), the UK's largest domestic violence charity, more than 72% of their service users experience abuse through technology.

Furthermore, emerging technologies such as smart, internet-connected devices have begun to enter our households. These so-called "Internet of Things" (IoT) range from gadgets such as "smart speakers," as well as embedded infrastructures such as connected thermostats, blinds, or locks. IoT devices open up new avenues to remotely monitor, control, and harass victims/survivors (Parkin, Patel, Lopez-Neira, & Tanczer, 2019).[2] Their interconnectedness and growing level of sophistication make them tools to help facilitate other coercive and controlling offenses, including stalking.

The current chapter sets out to examine the risks and harms[3] that derive from the burgeoning IoT environment. We showcase *how* and *why* tech abuse is a socio-technological issue that requires not only human-centered (i.e., societal), but also cybersecurity (i.e., technical) responses. We thus use the notion of "threat modeling," which is a process that investigates potential cybersecurity attacks to focus on the risks both to *systems* and to *people* (Uzunov & Fernandez, 2014). Through the analysis of a smart lock, we exemplify insufficiently addressed dangers and uncover how seemingly neutral design decisions can constrain, shape, and facilitate coercive and controlling behaviors.

Existing Research

IoT-Enabled Technology-Facilitated Abuse

The proliferation of so-called smart, internet-connected devices poses a new tech abuse challenge. The move toward IoT includes the direct and indirect extension of the internet into a range of physical objects, devices, and products, with a broad range of applications (Tanczer, Brass, Elsden, Carr, & Blackstock, 2019,

p. 37). Previously "offline" and "unrelated" technologies such as conventional household appliances are now being interconnected and become part of a network which allows them to – put simply – "speak" to one another.

While IoT systems range from tiny sensors to large-scale cyber-physical systems such as cars, consumer IoT devices form a dominant focus of ongoing analyses. Consumer IoT describe systems created to be used by "average" end users in a personal capacity and/or within the home setting. Such devices include, for example, smart speakers, wearables, and a range of security systems. In the UK, 31% of the 35–44 age group own three or more connected devices with IoT usage expected to increase significantly over the next decades (Tech UK, 2019).

IoT appliances not only collect reams of information, including personal data, preference settings, and usage patterns, but offer an opportunity to be remotely controlled. Combined with features such as video and audio recording functionalities, IoT devices open up significant exploitative avenues in an IPV context (Leitão, 2019). Society is therefore in urgent need to understand the broader classes of harms IoT systems may cause and conceptualize how these harms could move beyond "conventional" understandings of safety, security, and privacy.

So far, the research on IoT-affiliated tech abuse in the context of IPV is in its infancy. Only a handful of studies have evaluated the tech abuse risks that derive from the deployment of smart devices in the home. Leitão (2018, 2019) examined the potential security and privacy threats that victims/survivors of IPV would face. Strengers, Kennedy, Arcari, Nicholls, and Gregg (2019) conducted an ethnographic study with early IoT adopters. They showed that women need to be able to operate IoT systems safely and securely without exposing themselves or others to additional internal or external threats. Slupska (2019) reviewed 40 smart home security papers and uncovered that the only article that explicitly addressed IPV in their analysis was dismissive of the risk potential and displaced the responsibility of protection onto potential targets of abuse. Besides, the Gender and IoT research project at University College London conducted a usability analysis of the shared device ecosystem (Parkin et al., 2019), exposing, among other findings, that the lack of security and privacy prompts can negatively impact tech abuse victims/survivors. Based on their findings, the research team produced guides and resources for the IPV support sector (Tanczer, Patel, Parkin, & Danezis, 2018, 2019) and briefings for the policy community (Tanczer, Lopez-Neira et al., 2018).

Despite the limited evidence-base on IoT-enabled tech abuse, emerging classes of harms have to be evaluated in light of the dynamics of IPV (Katerndahl, Burge, Ferrer, Becho, & Wood, 2010; de Lucena et al., 2016). For example, Matthews et al. (2017) developed a framework for organizing victims'/survivors' technology practices and challenges into three phases, including: physical control, escape, and life apart (see Fig. 39.1). While their research centered on "conventional" devices such as computers and phones, similar considerations will have to be applied to both the social and technical responses to IoT.

Matthews et al.'s (2017) findings further showcase that tech abuse victims/survivors face high levels of stress and risk, which makes it harder for them to pay

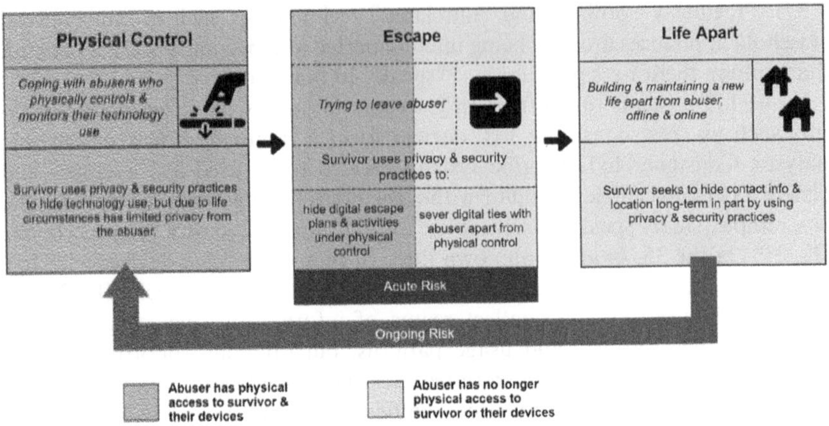

Fig. 39.1. Three Phases of IPV that Affected Technology Use, Focusing on Privacy & Security Practices. *Source:* Adapted from Matthews et al. (2017).

attention to user interface (UI) details. The latter are means by which a user interacts with and regulates a technical system. UI can be graphical controls such as one's home screen or the menu bar, as well as hardware devices such as a remote, switch, or keyboard (Myers, 1989). Victims/survivors are consequently disadvantaged in making use of privacy and security features and struggle to identify, access, and act upon instruction materials (e.g., how to block a phone number, how to set up multi-factor authentication).[4]

Drawing on these insights, Matthews et al. (2017) suggested that technology designers should consider the usability of their inventions and acknowledge the distinct privacy and security requirements of IPV victims/survivors. This focus seems of high relevance looking at the *limited* (i.e., fewer buttons) as well as *dispersed* (i.e., control through the device as well as an app on the phone) interfaces IoT technologies such as smart speakers offer. Yet, as the upcoming section will display, the tech sector has so far ignored the potential challenges that these devices create and failed to implement technical responses to the daily privacy and security trade-offs that IPV victims/survivors must make (Freed et al., 2018; Slupska, 2019).

Cybersecurity Design Shortcomings

The threats and consequent risks deriving from IPV are almost absent in the cybersecurity literature as well as practice and even less of a discussion point in the emerging field of IoT (Slupska, 2019; Tanczer et al., 2018). Instead, the cybersecurity community often focuses on "hard" technical problems posed by remote "external" adversaries who exploit hardware or software vulnerabilities. Yet, as Freed et al. (2018) pointed out, most IPV attacks are technologically unsophisticated. This allows perpetrators to interact with a victim's/survivor's device or account via their standard settings, generic UI, or by simply downloading and installing a ready-made application that facilitates, for instance, the spying on a victim/survivor. Hence, the "typical" tech abuse perpetrators must be thought of as a "UI-bound adversary" (Freed et al., 2018).

This perspective distinguishes IPV perpetrators from the cybercriminals who are the central focal point of cybersecurity research. In fact, perpetrators' lack of technical skill carries the risk that a focus on tech abuse could be dismissed as trivial. However, the socio-technical and interpersonal factors that characterize tech abuse undermine the foundational assumptions under which current digital systems have been designed and built (i.e., insider vs. outsider; legitimate vs. illegitimate user etc.). For example, "safety features" of devices, such as location tracking, are co-opted by abusers for surveillance purposes. This dynamic makes IPV attacks both challenging to technically counteract but also extremely damaging to victims/survivors.

Like most digital products and services, smart home systems are based on an "authentication model." This model implies that features such as passwords and security questions guarantee that an unauthenticated user (i.e., individual without login credentials) cannot access the system. However, IPV perpetrators are often aware of sign-in details, either because they purchased, installed, and maintained the device, or because they convinced or coerced the victim/survivor into sharing the information. Some perpetrators may be able to guess credentials due to personal knowledge they have of victims/survivors. Thus, in many IPV attack scenarios, the abuser is effectively "authenticated" and "authorized."

A possible parallel to the IPV tech abuse problem within the cybersecurity literature is the so-called "insider threat." The latter describes a threat posed to an organization by rogue, disgruntled, or careless employees (Bishop & Gates, 2008; Nurse et al., 2014). Since employees often have access to login details, they are also *authenticated adversaries*. However, insider threats in the context of cybersecurity are almost always conceptualized as actors internal to the company (i.e., rogue employees) rather than internal to the home (i.e., family members). This narrow view of what "insider threat" implies is reflective of the corporate positionality of most cybersecurity research, which we hope to counterbalance in this chapter.

The discussed oversights, including the focus on sophisticated attacks as well as corporate rather than domestic threats, are deficiencies of popular cybersecurity "threat models." Threat models describe a systematic analysis of a probable attacker's profile, the most likely attack vectors, and the assets most desired by an attacker. Threat models, therefore, involve assumptions about likely attackers and can reflect biases and blind spots as seen in the exclusion of IPV perpetrators in cybersecurity practitioners' mental models. Readers may be alerted to the subjective nature of this process. To counter any skewed perspectives, we are arguing in favor of the deployment of thorough procedural methods as well as the inclusion of diverse voices – such as the IPV sector.

So far, existing solutions to the problem of tech abuse have mostly involved the development of guidance to aid victims/survivors as well as support services (Online and Digital Abuse, 2018; Tanczer et al., 2018). Although such tools are useful, they shift responsibility onto victims/survivors. The latter already face significant cognitive, emotional, and financial constraints and are now further burdened having to check settings across a multitude of applications. Harris and Woodlock (2019) describe this additional onus as "safety work." The authors argue that digital coercive control has led to new forms of victim-blaming which manifest itself in women being accused of having inflicted harm upon themselves by choosing to use certain devices and/or platforms. The fact that these systems are frequently victim's/survivor's primary link to their support network is overlooked. Furthermore, possible regional specificities, such as family-internal device sharing practices, are not accounted for (Sambasivan et al., 2019).

Moving beyond these victim/survivor-straining proposals, existing issues associated with tech abuse are closely interlinked with the design of technological systems (Levy & Schneier, 2020). This is exemplified in reported cases of compromised webcams (Anderson, 2013), the repurposing of features such as real-time location sharing via Google Maps (Ashworth, 2018), or the review of victim's/survivor's historical queries and online searches by a perpetrator (Women's Aid, 2018).

A common obstacle to the implementation of better IPV privacy and security measures stems from the fact that IoT's inherent functionalities (e.g., remote control, speech recognition) can equally benefit perpetrators as much as victims/survivors (Parkin et al., 2019). This "dual-use" problem – a term coined to describe the fact that digital systems may be designed for peaceful use but can also be co-opted for malicious purposes and vice versa – has been widely discussed in the cybersecurity literature (Nye, 2018; Riebe & Reuter, 2019). However, it has not yet been modeled onto the context of IPV. For example, a perpetrator may install a smart camera to spy on their partner, while a victim/survivor may install a smart camera to feel in control of their environment. The answer to *who is being empowered* by IoT is consequently dependent on *who has control* over the device and network.

The adjustment of established cybersecurity methods like risk assessments, usability tests, and safety reviews can help tech vendors to consider adversarial users when designing and evaluating UIs (Freed et al., 2018; Parkin et al., 2019). On these grounds, we would like to put forward the idea of designing a dedicated "IPV Threat Model" to explore and document avenues for harming IPV victims/survivors. While not a panacea – as some proposed changes may, in some contexts, benefit perpetrators – such a framework can limit an IoT systems' "abusability" (i.e., its capacity to be abused) and account for the cybersecurity needs of some of the most vulnerable groups in society.

A Method to Threat Model Intimate Partner Violence Tech Abuse

Threat modeling describes a process used to analyze potential attack vectors on a system (Uzunov & Fernandez, 2014). The concept of "threat" is hereby understood as the probable cause of an incident that might result in harm to systems, individuals, and organizations (Sabbagh & Kowalski, 2015), with a "threat actor" being the entity who wishes to cause a – usually negative – impact (Coles & Tarandach, 2020).

While threats may arise from both accidental and deliberate activities of "legitimate users" (the owner/account holder of a device; Omotosho, Haruna, & Olaniyi, 2019), we assume that an IPV threat actor may be a perpetrator who *intentionally abuses* specific technical features to monitor, control, or coerce a victim/survivor. Thus, the perpetrator may be an authorized user yet still abuses the system for illegitimate means.

We acknowledge that the literature on threat modeling can be daunting and full of jargon. It is a field populated by acronyms such as DREAD (i.e., Damage, Reproducibility, Exploitability, Affected User, Discoverability) and STRIDE (i.e., Spoofing, Tampering, Repudiation, Information Disclosure, Denial of Service, Elevation of Privilege), and characterized by debates about the distinction of *threat* and *risk*. Confusingly, the words "threat model" and "threat modeling" are applied in many dissimilar and perhaps incompatible ways. However, for the purpose of this chapter, we will deploy a pragmatic definition and conceptualize threat modeling as the use of abstractions to aid in thinking about threats and risks (for a detailed review, see Shostack, 2014).

There are also various approaches to threat modeling, ranging from: (a) asset-based threat modeling; and (b) system-based threat modeling; to (c) attacker-based threat modeling. These approaches can be applied in conjunction with the attempt to generate: (a) an illustration of the system that is potentially being attacked (e.g., a smart watch); (b) assumptions about the profiles of potential attackers, including their goals, methods, and motives (e.g., an IPV perpetrator); and (c) a catalog of likely threats that may arise (e.g., information disclosure). Threat modeling therefore echoes the risk assessment process currently deployed in the IPV support sector (Nicholls, Pritchard, Reeves, & Hilterman, 2013; van der Put, Gubbels, & Assink, 2019).

Following Shostack's (2014, p. xxvii) suggested system-based approach, threat modeling involves four steps, each answering a deceptively simple question:

(1) What are you (i.e., the tech vendor) building?
(2) What can go wrong with it once it's built?
(3) What should you do about those things that can go wrong?
(4) Did you do a decent job?

Although system-based approaches such as this one are implicitly aimed at tech developers and vendors, we believe it is valuable for anyone studying tech abuse – whether from the perspective of social or computer science – to be comfortable with the conceptual framework of threat modeling. The latter allows researchers to reflect, understand, document, and react to the possible shortcomings of digital devices and services (Sabbagh & Kowalski, 2015; Torr, 2005). By becoming fluent in the language of threat modeling, IPV scholars and practitioners can more effectively critique problematic technology designs.

In the upcoming section, we walk readers through the building blocks of this framework. While it may seem abstract, we hope to showcase the benefit of its adoption in the IPV tech abuse space. Specifically, in the following passages, we will apply Shostack's (2014, p. xxvii) four questions to examine how a hypothetical smart lock IoT system can be breached, leading to the harm of an IPV victim/survivor.

System: What Are You Building?

The threat modeling process begins with collecting necessary information about the relevant components of a device, software program or system (Torr, 2005). This decomposition gives stakeholders an overview of all the different segments, data points, and interactions to effectively identify, understand, and model its makeup (Xiong & Lagerström, 2019). Developers begin by creating simple diagrams and tables to provide an overview of the system being threat modeled. These diagrams can clarify different interdependencies and features of systems, which are particularly important for smart, internet-connected devices (Steven, 2010). For tech designers and vendors, these visual representations form a useful way to abstract all system properties and diagnose what an application does (Coles & Tarandach, 2020).

Threats: What Can Go Wrong with It Once It's Built?

After the exposure of the "anatomy" of a system, tech vendors use the generated diagrams to look at what could go wrong. For example, a brainstorming meeting to determine and enumerate all potential threats could be held. As there are an unlimited number of things which could fail, this second step has the potential to be the most overwhelming. The evaluation of interconnected systems such as IoT technologies creates an additional level of intricacy than the analysis of individual devices and application alone. However, in both cases, tech designers should assess opportunities for abuse across the whole infrastructure (Coles & Tarandach, 2020).

Some approaches start by profiling probable attackers, including their resources, motivations, and capacity (Atzeni, Cameroni, Faily, Lyle, & Flechais, 2011; Little & Rogova, 2006). The identification of an attacker's intentions can assist in the forecasting of an attack's sophistication level, which is particularly useful when examining IPV cases. The threat identification process involves a certain reliance on assumptions as to the nature of a likely perpetrator. These assumptions are often limited and stereotypical (Atzeni et al., 2011), which is – considering the lack of diversity among cybersecurity practitioners, as well as the lack of data on tech abuse – problematic (Lopez-Neira, Patel, Parkin, Danezis, & Tanczer, 2019; Poster, 2018).

Having a diverse team is vital for threat modeling. Institutional and personal life experience shape perceptions of threats. Thus, technologists who specialize in Windows systems will often skew their threat model toward Windows-specific concerns, while web developers will be primarily focused on web-based attacks. Equally, our own biases as authors of this chapter will have influenced the threat actors and attack scenarios we are examining. To mitigate such shortcomings, we want to reiterate that active collaboration with affected groups and communities such as the domestic abuse sector must be sought.

When looking at an attacker's profile, both their opportunities for exploitation and/or their attack motives can be significantly influenced by environmental conditions. For instance, a perpetrator with a background in software development may be far more likely to consider exploiting smart home devices. Nonetheless, an attacker's capacity must be contrasted, considering their potential motivation. Depending on both aspects, one must expect changes to the: (a) intensity; (b) sophistication; and (c) probability of a tech abuse attack taking place; as well as (d) a perpetrator's ability to distort/eliminate forensic evidence (UcedaVelez & Morana, 2015).

Based on the current evidence-base, tech abuse perpetrators are often highly motivated or even obsessed with the desire to monitor, coerce, intimidate, or otherwise harm a victim/survivor. They can, but do not have to, be physically present (Ho et al., 2016). Abusers are also rarely strangers.[5] They often have or had romantic relations with victims/survivors. Nonetheless, tech abuse can also be perpetrated by family members, colleagues, roommates, or acquaintances (Levy, 2015). IPV perpetrators often have intimate knowledge of the victim/survivor, including awareness of their daily habits, history, and login details, or access to personal data like sexually explicit or embarrassing photos and messages (Table 39.1).

In addition to this profiling exercise, it is helpful to account for known attack patterns (UcedaVelez & Morana, 2015). Drawing on Freed et al. (2017) and Leitão (2019), we propose a model of five common tech abuse threats:

Table 39.1. Tech Abuse Threat Model.

Name	Description
Ownership-based access	Being the Owner of a device or account allows a perpetrator to prohibit victims'/survivors' usage or track their location and actions;
Account/device compromise	Guessing or coercing credentials which enables a perpetrator to install spyware, monitor the victim/survivor, steal their data, or lock them out of their account;
Harmful messages	Contacting victims/survivors or their friends, family, employers, etc. without their consent;
Exposure of information	Posting or threatening to post private information or nonconsensual pornography (i.e., image-based sexual abuse);
Gaslighting	Using a device's functionality (e.g., remote changing of temperature) to make a victim/survivor feel as if they are losing their sanity and/or control over their home.

These threats can be connected to the specific features of the device in order to identify which forms of tech abuse are possible/likely (as we do in the following section). The second step ends with documenting as well as rating all diagnosed threats (Meier et al., 2003).

Response: What Should You Do about Those Things that Can Go Wrong?

The third question involves the examination of countermeasures to tackle each threat. Conventionally, responses are (a) to reduce/mitigate threats through the implementation of safeguards and changes to eliminate vulnerabilities or block threats; (b) to assign/transfer threats by placing the cost of the threat onto another entity or organization such as purchasing insurance or outsourcing; or (c) to accept the threat by evaluating if the cost of the countermeasure outweighs the possible cost of loss due to the threat. While the full elimination of threats is generally possible, it would require almost always the removal of features which industry actors may be opposed to (Shostack, 2014).

Mitigations are consequently specific to a device's design goals and limited by a vendor's resources, interests, and capacity. Therefore, this step also involves prioritizing different threats in order to identify which mitigations are most urgent. In the private sector, such assessments are often quantified and based on financial losses. Tech vendors have so far struggled – and often failed – to incorporate more intangible social, emotional, or psychological harms, including damage to reputation or mental health implications. The industry's viewpoint on the importance of economic ramifications disproportionally disregards the broader implications technical innovations may have on different groups of society, which we aspire to alleviate in this chapter.

Validation: Did You Do a Decent Job of Analysis?

The final question involves a critical reflection on the efficacy of the generated threat model. To support this evaluation process, different validation methods can be deployed (Xiong & Lagerström, 2019). What unifies these methods is their attempt to check the model's completeness and accuracy. The scrutiny guarantees that the final model matches the system that is built, addresses all the right and relevant threats, and covers all the decisions that have been made (Shostack, 2014). By this stage, every possible attack scenario should have been considered and accounted for and a planned countermeasure laid out.

A common practice to support this step is the reliance on "test cases" or "case studies" (Shostack, 2014; Xiong & Lagerström, 2019). Another form of explanation and validation includes collecting data on device usage "in the wild." Moreover, data on reported breaches can be helpful, especially if contrasted with initial threat models to understand whether a threat was inadequately addressed or missed entirely. Together with a frequent reiteration of the threat modeling exercise, new and unanticipated threats can be accounted for and timely and effective mitigation strategies implemented.

Threat Modeling a Smart, Internet-Connected Lock

The following section outlines a threat modeling exercise for an IoT consumer device in the context of IPV. We choose the case study of a hypothetical, but prototypical smart lock system because it has relatively simple functionality (i.e., opening and closing a door) and plays a key role in home security (i.e., allowing and preventing access). Furthermore, the adoption and market share of internet-connected locks is expected to grow (PR Newswire, 2019), making it a technology that is, or soon will be, deployed in the home of the "average" end user. We draw on the four questions outlined by Shostack (2014), and use the upcoming passages to

(a) Model the relevant features prevalent in common smart lock systems (what are you building?);
(b) Show how specific features may be abused (what can go wrong?);
(c) Suggest possible mitigation strategies (what should you do about those things that can go wrong?); and
(d) Discuss limitations of the threat model we developed (did you do a good job?).

In the current threat modeling analysis, we are foregrounding the device rather than its user or its interplay with the broader system of interconnected products (i.e., how a smart speaker interacts with the smart lock). We acknowledge that this viewpoint has limitations; as the common security saying goes, "all models are wrong; some models are useful." For one, an IoT system cannot be viewed as a purely "technical" problem. In most cases, social and technical aspects are tightly interwoven, requiring both social and technical countermeasures (Sabbagh & Kowalski, 2015). However, as previous tech abuse mitigation strategies have primarily focused on victims/survivors and support services, our emphasis seems appropriate. For another, investigating a single device over an assembled system allows for vulnerabilities to pass through undetected (J. R. C. Nurse, Creese, & Roure, 2017). While we accept that one must account for the entire IoT "ecosystem" (Aufner, 2020; Omotosho et al., 2019; Seeam, Ogbeh, Guness, & Bellekens, 2019), a broader investigation is beyond the scope of this chapter.

System: What Are You Building?

Our hypothetical "smart lock"[6] is a round knob which attaches to the inside of a standard dead bolt. The smart lock can be physically turned from the inside to open/lock the door. It also allows a user to lock/unlock the door electronically using a mobile application[7] (app) on their smartphone. To do this, the smart lock connects to a user's smartphone using Bluetooth, a wireless technology standard used for exchanging data over short distances (Hadis, Palantei, Ilham, & Hendra, 2018). The smartphone app communicates with the smart lock's company's web servers via Wi-Fi.

Wi-Fi is another wireless technology that uses radio waves to provide high-speed internet and network connections. The company's web servers describe both hardware and software components which store, centralize, and manage the files a user requests when engaging with a company's website or app. The smart lock's setup means that the device itself is not directly connected to the internet. Instead, the smart lock communicates with the smartphone app via Bluetooth. Therefore, for this threat model, the smart lock *system* consists of (a) the smart lock; (b) the smartphone app; and (c) the company's web servers which support the app (see Fig. 39.2).

The smart lock has two "modes" for opening doors: either the user manually opens the smartphone app and presses a large button to open the door or the door is set so that the lock opens the moment the phone is within Bluetooth range. The smart lock device also records which users lock or unlock the door, storing the data on the smartphone app and in the web servers.

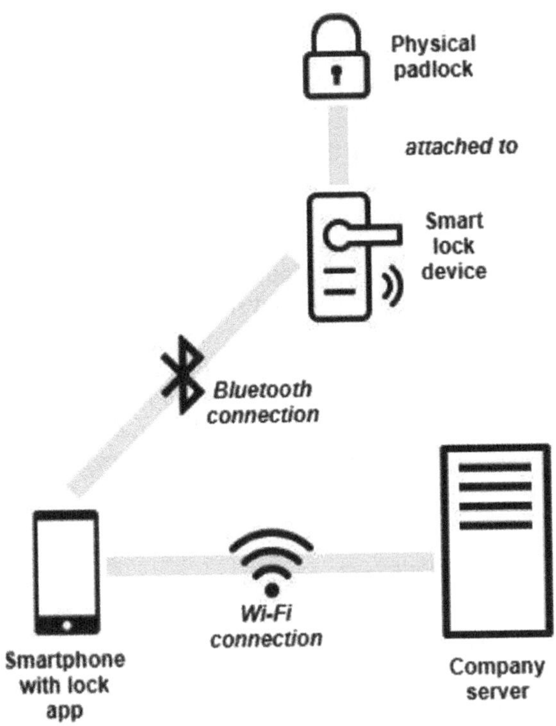

Fig. 39.2. Overview of the Smart Lock System.

Users identify themselves by logging into the smartphone app with their phone number or email address and a corresponding password. There are two different user account types: "Owner" and "Guest." The first and original user is *by default* an Owner. However, the device allows multiple Owners and Guests. The Owner is effectively the administrator of the system. They have more privileges than Guests. For example, an Owner can view the lock's activity log (i.e., past accesses), invite new users to be Owners or Guests, and configure when and for how long Guest users can lock/unlock the door (Ur, Jung, & Schechter, 2013; Table 39.2).

Table 39.2 Account Capabilities.

Capability	Owner	Guest
Lock/unlock door	Yes	Yes
View activity log	Yes	No
Invite new users to be Owner or Guest	Yes	No
Remove Owner or Guest access	Yes	No

Source: Adopted from Ye, Jiang, Yang, & Yan (2017b).

Users cannot access another user's account without having access to a fellow user's credentials. However, the main Owner can remove other users – both Owners and Guests – without having to access (i.e., login) their accounts.[8]

Threats: What Can Go Wrong with It once It's Built?

There are countless possible threats that could apply to a smart lock, some of which have already been explored by cybersecurity researchers (Fernandes, Jung, & Prakash, 2016, p. 636; Pavelić, Lončarić, Vuković, & Kušek, 2018; Ye, Jiang, Yang, & Yan, 2017a).[9] However, our model of IPV threats outlined earlier helps to focus on specific "attack vectors" (i.e., methods by which an adversary may gain access to the lock), followed by eight "threats," (i.e., specific forms of abuse which can occur after a lock has been compromised).

(1) Ownership-based access: Perpetrator has an Owner account and revokes and/or monitors a victim's/survivor's access.
(2) Smartphone compromise: Perpetrator illegitimately accesses the victim's/survivor's phone while within reach of the smart lock, which offers them digital access to the app, as well as physical access to the property.
(3) Account compromise: Perpetrator coerces or guesses victim's/survivor's smartphone app *or* smart lock account details, which allows the perpetrator to log into the victim/survivor's account on the perpetrator's own smartphone or laptop.

(4) Smart lock compromise: Perpetrator physically damages the smart lock making it unusable or causes a power outage which in certain circumstances may restrict residents from entering the house/locking the door.
(5) System compromise: Perpetrator can use default functions of the smart lock as some poorly designed IoT devices allow anyone on the same Wi-Fi home network to control an internet-connected product.

We acknowledge that it is possible to deploy more technically sophisticated attack scenarios (Ye et al., 2017b). However, the attack vectors discussed here showcase the range of relatively simple attack vectors that are available to the "UI-bound adversary." These attack vectors enable some of the following forms of abuse, or "threats":

(1) Restricting access: Perpetrator removes the victim's/survivor's account and/or changes their password, which can restrict the victim's/survivor's access to their account, as well as the shared home. This can be particularly damaging in the context of cohabitation where physical residency can impact decisions on ownership in court settlements.
(2) Gaining access: Perpetrator maliciously gains access to the property even after the victim/survivor attempted to lock them out. This can result in physical or psychological harm to the victim/survivor and/or their family.
(3) Monitoring: Perpetrator monitors the victim/survivor and/or other residents through the account access log. This can facilitate stalking or coercive control by giving the perpetrator the exact times that a victim/survivor and/or other residents enter and exit their home (Ur et al., 2013).
(4) Exposing information: Perpetrator uses the information received from an account compromise to coerce or expose the victim/survivor. This can result in personal information leakage (e.g., address) which threatens the user's privacy.
(5) Impersonating users: Perpetrator compromised the account of another resident and uses these credentials to access the property unnoticed. This engenders the physical safety of the victim/survivor and/or fellow residents.
(6) Gaslighting: Perpetrator unlocks the door just before the victim/survivor arrives home, making it seem like the device is malfunctioning or the door was never locked in the first place. This may result in victims/survivors doubting the functionality and security guarantee of their smart lock.
(7) Contacting victim/survivor: Perpetrator tries to enter the property with an unauthorized smartphone, which leads the victim/survivor to receive a notification (Khalid & Majeed, 2016). This can cause distress and anxiety for the victim/survivor who now has an awareness of the perpetrator's access attempt.
(8) Distracting and deceiving: Perpetrator argues that they had previously physical access to a device such as a victim's/survivor's smartphone which could give them the impression of an attacker having more access than they do. Akin to gaslighting, this can cause a victim/survivor to feel uncertain about their level of security and safety.

The power dynamics inherent to IPV cases add further complications to the scenarios expressed here. Tech abuse stemming from ownership-based access seems particularly likely, as the Owner of a smart home device has an inbuilt advantage in monitoring and controlling other users (i.e., members of the household). Research has demonstrated these gendered aspects of "digital housekeeping," namely that men are more likely to set up and maintain smart home technologies (Kennedy, Nansen, Arnold, Wilken, & Gibbs, 2015; Leitão, 2019; Strengers, Kennedy, Arcari, Nicholls, & Gregg, 2019). Therefore, account ownership may reinforce power inequalities in the household related to gender, technical ability, or finances (as these dictate who purchases devices).

Furthermore, even if a victim/survivor is the authorized Owner of the smart lock, the removal of the perpetrator's account – whether they have had previously held legitimate Guest access or have been detected to have received access to the account illegitimately – can expose the victim/survivor to further risks of violence and abuse. The act of withdrawing a perpetrator's admission can escalate the abuse situation and could cause perpetrators to react (e.g., confront or harm the victim/survivor). For this reason, mitigations to tech abuse – which are discussed hereafter – must be highly context-specific with designers minimizing the risk of abuse independently of the user's ownership status.

Response: What Should You Do About Those Things That Can Go Wrong?

Various research teams have already emphasized possible tech abuse responses industry actors, policymakers, and support services can deploy (Havron et al., 2019; Leitão, 2018; Lopez-Neira et al., 2019; Parkin et al., 2019; Tanczer et al., 2018). However, it is important to stress that technical mitigation strategies will not exhaustively "solve" the problem. As in other attack scenarios, security is never perfect or absolute, and technical solutions need to accompany robust social and legal support for victims/survivors. By the very nature of tech abuse – which includes the notion of the *authenticated adversary* – compromise and security breaches are *always* likely. Thus, one cannot prevent an IPV attacker by simply establishing *conventional* technical barriers (e.g., implementing a firewall, setting up password protections) as there are no trusted "safe zones" victims/survivors can rely on (Weinert et al., 2019).

As seen through our proposed mitigation strategies, many design choices may equally benefit victims/survivors as much as perpetrators. Thus, we are fully aware that an adversary may co-opt our proposed strategies in order to gain access or control victims/survivors further. However, some design decisions can enable harm more easily than others. Consequently, rather than looking to eliminate sources of vulnerability, we believe it is more useful for industry actors to think in terms of beneficial design patterns. The latter are likely to *enable* usability for people experiencing abuse and *hinder* usability for those perpetrating abuse. Tech abuse stemming from the following compromise forms may consequently be mitigated by:

The five attack *vectors* are as follows:
Ownership-based compromise:

(1) Restricting ownership: As preventing ownership-based access is impossible, security designs should give Owners less exhaustive authority over the smart lock system. This may include a security protocol which allows the company to remove an Owner in exceptional circumstances, such as when requested by a domestic abuse court order.[10]
(2) Equalizing account holder rights: Moving away from models where only one user is an account Owner or doing away with an Owner/Guest user distinction.
(3) Consent changes: Shared IoT devices such as smart locks may require all associated users to approve fundamental changes to the settings which prevent Owners from overpowering others.
(4) Customer-facing staff guidance: Akin to the "Assisting Customers Experiencing Domestic and Family Violence Industry Guideline" (Communications Alliance Ltd, 2018), customer-facing staff guidance on how tech vendors can support tech abuse victims/survivors may be developed to assist users in the instance of disputes around who is a legitimate account holder (Tanczer, 2019).

Smartphone Compromise:

(5) Report theft feature: A "report theft" feature could be activated from the victim's/survivor's web account to minimize the access a perpetrator may have over a device such as their smartphone.
(6) Automatic logouts: Users could be automatically logged out of their accounts, requiring them to reauthenticate themselves on timed patterns when using their smartphone to lock/unlock a smart lock. This may prevent unauthorized usage by others should the phone ever get lost.

Account Compromise:

(7) Register of login details: Regular notifications of login locations (i.e., where) and associated timestamps (i.e., when) may be accessible to victim's/survivor's through their account settings (Parkin et al., 2019). Crucially, these should be sufficiently vague so as not to put a victim/survivor in danger should a perpetrator access this information.
(8) New login prompts: Accounts may trigger a notification when a login on a new IoT device is attempted.
(9) Changing of passwords prompts: A new login should be required across all devices if a user changes their password, to ensure that other users do not stay logged in after, for example, a breakup.
(10) Reinstate account ownership: The ability to reinstate access to previously compromised accounts may be mitigated through time-stamped company backups which can allow victims/survivors to regain control over their data (e.g., after a court order).

(11) Multi-factor authentication: Different authentication methods should become part of the IoT design feature and may ensure that accounts are less prone to, for example, password coercion (Leitão, 2018).
(12) Transparency around privileges: Users on lower authorization levels (i.e., Guest accounts) should receive continued reminders of the extent of information they receive in comparison to other account holders, such as "Owners." This may alert victims/survivors to the fewer privileges they hold compared to their partner and remind them that a perpetrator could have access to their activity log.
(13) Access trails: IoT devices could notify other users every time another account holder checks critical settings such as access logs. This may prevent obsessive or routine checking of another user's behavior as the monitoring individual would be informed about this action.

Smart Lock Compromise:

(14) Factory reset: IoT devices should enable a simple mechanism to reset the product to its original state, enabling victims/survivors to restrict access after a compromise or breakup occurred. In the context of IoT, this mechanism needs to be both simple to activate (e.g., through a button) and potentially difficult to pursue from outside the home Wi-Fi network. Once initiated, the device should also send a final "good-bye" message to all users, which would alert them to an illicit factory reset.
(15) Logs: Victims/survivors may need to provide proof that a breach of, for instance, a protection order has occurred. Access logs such as who has accessed, locked, unlocked the door should, therefore, be unchangeable for any account holder.
(16) Disable functionalities: Users should be able to decide if they would like to disable certain functionalities such as the remote closing/opening of a smart lock.

System Compromise:

(17) Connection reminders: Regular prompts reminding users which IoT devices are connected and which accounts are associated with them may flag to victims/survivors if a perpetrator is still linked to their devices (Parkin et al., 2019).
(18) Opt-out: IoT devices should allow users to opt out from distinct data collection measures which are not required for the essential functionality of a connected product. This aligns with data minimization principles.
(19) Actionable advice: Up-to-date guidance on what steps a user should take when they suspect their home network has been compromised must be available to victims/survivors and communicated in a simple and understandable format (Parkin et al., 2019). A dedicated button that says, "I am a victim/survivor of domestic violence" or "I am worried about threats from a former partner or housemate" could automate access to this guidance.

Across this section, we have shown that threat modeling does not need to be complex to be useful. Indeed, our suggested set of mitigations emphasize how such an approach can be both practical and feasible. More research[11] is undoubtedly needed to define, test, and improve our privacy and security propositions – not only to evaluate their effectiveness but to identify further technical response means. Nonetheless, based on the current state of knowledge, we are confident that the above-mentioned design choices could mitigate harms stemming from IPV compromises and further benefit the "average" IoT users whose level of privacy and security is enhanced by these measures.

Validation: Did You Do a Decent Job of Analysis?

Our analysis is by no means flawless. We are conscious of the limitations that underpin our "IPV Threat Model" and the restrictions that derive from our reliance on a single, hypothetic test case (i.e., smart lock). Instead of checking our model for its completeness and accuracy, we consequently hope to have showcased how design features in the context of IoT systems can shape and embed power dynamics and stimulated a discussion which may lead to changes in industrial practices.

To achieve this, future IPV threat modeling exercises must be able to move away from speculative scenarios and involve assumptions and conjectures that are based on facts and quantitative evidence. Our current threat model was built on several qualitative tech abuse studies which compiled the experiences of victims/survivors and support organizations (Dragiewicz et al., 2018; Freed et al., 2018, 2017; Harris & Woodlock, 2019; Leitão, 2018; Lopez-Neira et al., 2019; Parkin et al., 2019; Slupska, 2019). Testimonies of victims/survivors are a critical way to validate a model. This can be done by checking that the model and analysis produced a set of threats that includes what is in the literature, as well as other sources of victim/survivor testimony.

However, it would make for a more robust model, if future threats and attack vectors could be derived from detailed statistical data gathered by statutory and voluntary support organizations, academia, and industry stakeholders. The reliance on multiple data sources will also mitigate potential biases that derive from various forms of victims/survivors under- or non-reporting abuse (Fernández-Fontelo, Cabaña, Joe, Puig, & Moriña, 2019). As scholars such as Tanczer et al. (2018) have highlighted, once more detailed accounts of the frequency, extent, regional specificities, and nature of tech abuse cases have been collated, more targeted mitigations strategies can be developed. The active use of such data will also imply a need to shift away from the "design before attack" paradigm. Thus, the tech sector will have to become comfortable and able to amend and redesign systems after their deployment. In the long run, this will profit not only IPV victims/survivors but also the conventional users who gain from the security and privacy improvements that can be designed and implemented.

Conclusion

This chapter showcased *how* and *why* tech abuse is a socio-technological issue and requires both societal and technical mitigation strategies to tackle the risks and harms that derive from the burgeoning IoT environment. Based on previous qualitative studies, we provided the first exploration of a dedicated IPV tech abuse threat model. The latter describes a systematic approach for identifying threats and improving the security design of technical systems. We tested our model's applicability on the hypothetical case study of a smart lock. The exemplary scenario offered us with a means to demonstrate the difficulty of proposing mitigation strategies, due to certain design choices which may benefit IPV victims/survivors and perpetrators.

We vividly illustrated why IPV research needs to engage with the development of digital devices and keep a tab on emerging technologies such as IoT. While we are hopeful that our framework will probe future research as much as engagements between research, industry, and practice, we are mindful of the limitations of cybersecurity models originally developed for military or business purposes. Despite these concerns, we argue that drawing on established cybersecurity concepts will prove useful. Once these concepts and terminologies are made accessible to the IPV sector and refined to account for victims'/survivors' concerns and needs, they will offer IPV researchers and practitioners a language to advocate for design changes and critique current industry practices.

Our analysis delivers a steppingstone for further cybersecurity-centric evaluations and tackles the potential misuse of technologies from "within." Having outlined a clear set of shortcomings in the existing responses to the problem of tech abuse, our dedicated IPV threat model may guide future technology design, especially among IoT vendors. While we alert readers to the risk of both the over- and underestimation of threats and harms deriving from IoT (Tanczer, 2019), we are optimistic that well-assessed mitigation strategies can slow down the possibility of tech abuse occurring.

Future research may, therefore, draw on our framework and begin to quantitatively assess the frequency, extent, regional specificities, and nature of tech abuse to refine prospective IPV threat models. We are also pointing interested parties to ongoing policy developments such as the UK's IoT Code of Practice (Department for Digital, Culture, Media and Sport, 2018) and the EU's Cybersecurity Act (2019). These advancements can expedite security and privacy improvements in the context of smart technologies, together with other proposals such as the establishment of dedicated IPV cybersecurity clinics (Havron et al., 2019), bodies such as the Australian eSafety Commissioner, and IPV-specific Privacy-Enhancing Technologies (PETs) or Protective Optimization Technologies (POTs). Good reasons to move toward these ideas and pathways are evident. However, it will require incentives – may these be "carrots" and/or "sticks" – to push for further progress in this space.

Notes

1. The term "domestic violence" is used in many countries and organizations to refer to IPV. However, IPV can also include child or elder abuse or abuse by any member of a household, making it more encompassing (World Health Organisation, 2012).
2. The language used to describe people who experience intimate or domestic violence is contested. The commonly used term "victim" has come under criticism for being disempowering. However, the suggested alternative, "survivor" omits murdered victims. To account for both dynamics, this paper will use these terms interchangeably, noting that neither term is ideal or unproblematic.
3. Threat, harm, and risk are interrelated but distinct concepts. *Threat* refers to a person, event, or circumstance (i.e., perpetrator) that results in harm. Thus, *harm* describes the effect and result of the actions/inaction taken by a threat (i.e., perpetrator). *Risk* is a metric used to assess the impact (i.e., extent of harm) of a potential threat.
4. Multi-factor authentication describes processes used in computing to prevent the impersonation of an authorized account holder. Authentication is the process of positively verifying a user's identity by drawing on a piece of information specific to the account holder (e.g., biometrics, such as face recognition or a fingerprint, or a phone number to send a dedicated password to (Velásquez, Caro, & Rodríguez, 2018)).
5. An exception is one form of "sextortion," in which remote hackers extort victims/survivors by threatening to release intimate photos they acquired through hacking online accounts or webcams (Wittes, Poplin, Jurecic, & Spera, 2016).
6. The system is loosely based on the design of an August smart lock (Ye et al., 2017b). The company is an early leader in the smart lock market.
7. Smart door lock control mechanics using biometric solutions such as facial recognition rather than smartphone apps are underway (Krishna Chaithanya, Satish Kumar, & Ramasri, 2019).
8. Additional features such as audio control (i.e., lock/unlock the door via voice) will not be considered in this analysis, but are important to acknowledge in IPV scenarios.
9. For a comprehensive overview of the structure of attacks to the home ecosystem, consult Denning, Kohno, and Levy (2013).
10. We accept that security professionals have traditionally been skeptical of mechanisms which allow external change to account ownership, for fear of creating further vulnerabilities for a cyberattack. Indeed, in some scenarios, it may be challenging to establish a clear perpetrator/survivor division from a company perspective (e.g., in cases where both sides allege abusive behavior). Such situations problematically place companies in the position of arbitrators, which they do not have the experience nor authority to do. Therefore, companies will be (and should be) unwilling to remove ownership-based access easily. However, as IPV situations can and will arise in smart home environments, companies must prepare procedures on how they will manage individual's ownership transfers.
11. "Blue team-red team" exercises where security professionals take on the role of an adversary (i.e., IPV perpetrator) could help to further refine IPV threat models.

References

Anderson, N. (2013, March 11). Meet the men who spy on women through their webcams. *Ars Technica*. Retrieved from https://arstechnica.com/

Ashworth, B. (2018, July 28). The terrible anxiety of location sharing apps. *Wired*. Retrieved from https://www.wired.com/

Atzeni, A., Cameroni, C., Faily, S., Lyle, J., & Flechais, I. (2011). Here's Johnny: A methodology for developing attacker personas. In *Proceedings of the 2011 6th international conference on availability, reliability and security, ARES 2011* (pp. 722–727). Washington, DC: IEEE Computer Society. doi:10.1109/ARES.2011.115

Aufner, P. (2020). The IoT security gap: A look down into the valley between threat models and their implementation. *International Journal of Information Security*, *19*(1), 3–14. doi:10.1007/s10207-019-00445-y

Bagwell-Gray, M. E., Messing, J. T., & Baldwin-White, A. (2015). Intimate partner sexual violence: A review of terms, definitions, and prevalence. *Trauma, Violence, & Abuse*, *16*(3), 316–335. doi:10.1177/1524838014557290

Bishop, M., & Gates, C. (2008). Defining the insider threat. In *Proceedings of the 4th annual workshop on cyber security and information intelligence research: developing strategies to meet the cyber security and information intelligence challenges ahead.* Oak Ridge, TN: Association for Computing Machinery. doi:10.1145/1413140.1413158

Coles, M. J., & Tarandach, I. (2020). *Threat modeling*. O'Reilly Media. Retrieved from https://www.oreilly.com/library/view/threat-modeling/9781492056546/

Communications Alliance Ltd. (2018). G660:2018 assisting customers experiencing domestic and family violence industry guideline. [PDF file]. Retrieved from https://commsalliance.com.au/__data/assets/pdf_file/0003/61527/Communications-Guideline-G660-Assisting-Customers-Experiencing-Domestic-and-Family-Violence.pdf

de Lucena, K. D. T., de Souza Chaves Deininger, L., Coelho, H. F. C., Monteiro, A. C. C., de Toledo Vianna, R. P., & do Nascimento, J. A. (2016). Analysis of the cycle of domestic violence against women. *Journal of Human Growth and Development*, *26*(2), 139–146. doi:10.7322/jhgd.119238

Denning, T., Kohno, T., & Levy, H. M. (2013). Computer security and the modern home. *Communications of the ACM*, *56*(1), 94–103. doi:10.1145/2398356.2398377

Department for Digital, Culture, Media and Sport. (2018). Code of practice for consumer IoT security. Retrieved from https://assets.publishing.service.gov.uk/government/uploads/system/uploads/attachment_data/file/747413/Code_of_Practice_for_Consumer_IoT_Security_October_2018.pdf

Dragiewicz, M., Burgess, J., Matamoros-Fernández, A., Salter, M., Suzor, N. P., Woodlock, D., & Harris, B. (2018). Technology facilitated coercive control: Domestic violence and the competing roles of digital media platforms. *Feminist Media Studies*, *18*(4), 609–625. doi:10.1080/14680777.2018.1447341

Fernandes, E., Jung, J., & Prakash, A. (2016). Security analysis of emerging smart home applications. In *2016 IEEE symposium on security and privacy (SP)*, San Jose, CA (pp. 636–654). doi:10.1109/SP.2016.44

Fernández-Fontelo, A., Cabaña, A., Joe, H., Puig, P., & Moriña, D. (2019). Untangling serially dependent underreported count data for gender-based violence. *Statistics in Medicine*, *38*(22), 4404–4422. doi:10.1002/sim.8306

Freed, D., Palmer, J., Minchala, D. E., Levy, K., Ristenpart, T., & Dell, N. (2017). Digital technologies and intimate partner violence: A qualitative analysis with multiple stakeholders. *Proceedings of the ACM on Human-Computer Interaction, 1*(CSCW), 1–22. doi:10.1145/3134681

Freed, D., Palmer, J., Minchala, D., Levy, K., Ristenpart, T., & Dell, N. (2018). "A Stalker's Paradise": How intimate partner abusers exploit technology. In *Proceedings of the 2018 CHI conference on human factors in computing systems*, 667, 1–13. doi:10.1145/3173574.3174241

Hadis, M. S., Palantei, E., Ilham, A. A., & Hendra, A. (2018). Design of smart lock system for doors with special features using bluetooth technology. In *2018 international conference on information and communications technology (ICOIACT)*, Yogyakarta (pp. 396–400). doi:10.1109/ICOIACT.2018.8350767

Harris, B. A., & Woodlock, D. (2019). Digital coercive control: Insights from two landmark domestic violence studies. *British Journal of Criminology, 59*, 530–550. doi:10.1093/bjc/azy052

Havron, S., Freed, D., Chatterjee, R., McCoy, D., Dell, N., & Ristenpart, T. (2019). Clinical computer security for victims of intimate partner violence. In *28th USENIX security symposium*, Santa Clara, CA (pp. 105–122).

Ho, G., Leung, D., Mishra, P., Hosseini, A., Song, D., & Wagner, D. (2016). Smart locks: Lessons for securing commodity Internet of things devices. In *Proceedings of the 11th ACM on Asia conference on computer and communications security, ASIA CCS 2016*, Xi'an (pp. 461–472). doi:10.1145/2897845.2897886

Katerndahl, D. A., Burge, S. K., Ferrer, R. L., Becho, J., & Wood, R. (2010). Complex dynamics in intimate partner violence: A time series study of 16 women. *Primary Care Companion to The Journal of Clinical Psychiatry, 12*(4). doi:10.4088/PCC.09m00859whi. Retrieved from https://www.ncbi.nlm.nih.gov/pmc/articles/PMC2983457/

Kennedy, J., Nansen, B., Arnold, M., Wilken, R., & Gibbs, M. (2015). Digital housekeepers and domestic expertise in the networked home. *Convergence, 21*(4), 408–422. doi:10.1177/1354856515579848

Khalid, M., & Majeed, S. (2016). A smart visitors' notification system with automatic secure door lock using mobile communication technology. *International Journal of Computer Science and Information Security, 16*(4), 97–101.

Krishna Chaithanya, J., Satish Kumar, G. A. E., & Ramasri, T. (2019). IoT-based embedded smart lock control using face recognition system. In D. Pandian, X. Fernando, Z. Baig, & F. Shi (Eds.), *Proceedings of the international conference on ISMAC in computational vision and bio-engineering 2018 (ISMAC-CVB)* (pp. 1089–1098). Cham: Springer International Publishing. doi:10.1007/978-3-030-00665-5_104

Leitão, R. (2018). Digital technologies and their role in intimate partner violence. In *Extended abstracts of the 2018 CHI conference on human factors in computing systems, SRC11:1–SRC11:6*, New York, NY. doi:10.1145/3170427.3180305

Leitão, R. (2019). Anticipating smart home security and privacy threats with survivors of intimate partner abuse. In *ACM conference on designing interactive systems* (pp. 527–539).

Levy, K. E. C. (2015). Intimate surveillance. *Idaho Law Review, 51*, 679–693. doi:10.3868/s050-004-015-0003-8

Levy, K., & Schneier, B. (2020). Privacy threats in intimate relationships. *Journal of Cybersecurity, 6*(1). Retrieved from https://academic.oup.com/cybersecurity/article/6/1/tyaa006/5849222

Little, E. G., & Rogova, G. L. (2006). An ontological analysis of threat and vulnerability. In *Proceedings of the 9th international conference on information fusion*, Buffalo (pp. 1–8). doi:10.1109/ICIF.2006.301716

Lopez-Neira, I., Patel, T., Parkin, S., Danezis, G., & Tanczer, L. M. (2019). 'Internet of Things': How abuse is getting smarter. *Safe – The Domestic Abuse Quarterly*, *63*, 22–26.

Matthews, T., O'Leary, K., Turner, A., Sleeper, M., Woelfer, J. P., Shelton, M., ... Consolvo, S. (2017). Stories from survivors: Privacy & security practices when coping with intimate partner abuse. In *Proceedings of the 2017 CHI conference on human factors in computing systems*, New York, NY (pp. 2189–2201). doi:10.1145/3025453.3025875

Meier, J. D., Mackman, A., Vasireddy, S., Dunner, M., Escamilla, R., & Murukan, A. (2003). *Improving web application security: Threats and countermeasures* (pp. 1–919). Microsoft Corporation. Retrieved from https://www.microsoft.com/en-gb/download/confirmation.aspx?id=1330

Myers, B. A. (1989). User-interface tools: Introduction and survey. *IEEE Software*, *6*(1), 15–23. doi:10.1109/52.16898

Nicholls, T. L., Pritchard, M. M., Reeves, K. A., & Hilterman, E. (2013). Risk assessment in intimate partner violence: A systematic review of contemporary approaches. *Partner Abuse*, *4*(1), 76–168. doi:10.1891/1946-6560.4.1.76

Nurse, J. R. C., Buckley, O., Legg, P. A., Goldsmith, M., Creese, S., Wright, G. R. T., & Whitty, M. (2014). Understanding insider threat: A framework for characterising attacks. In *Proceedings - IEEE symposium on security and privacy*. doi:10.1109/SPW.2014.38

Nurse, J. R. C., Creese, S., & Roure, D. D. (2017). Security risk assessment in Internet of things systems. *IT Professional*, *19*(5), 20–26. doi:10.1109/MITP.2017.3680959

Nye, J. S., Jr (2018). How will new cybersecurity norms develop?. *Project Syndicate*. Retrieved from https://www.project-syndicate.org/commentary/origin-of-new-cybersecurity-norms-by-joseph-s–nye-2018-03

Office for National Statistics. (2019, November 25). Domestic abuse in England and wales overview: November 2019 [Ons.gov.uk]. *ONS*. Retrieved from https://www.ons.gov.uk/peoplepopulationandcommunity/crimeandjustice/bulletins/domesticabuseinenglandandwales/yearendingmarch2018

Omotosho, A., Haruna, B. A., & Olaniyi, O. M. (2019). Threat modeling of internet of things health devices. *Journal of Applied Security Research*, *14*(1), 106–121. doi:10.1080/19361610.2019.1545278

Online and Digital Abuse. (2018). Women's aid. Retrieved from https://www.womensaid.org.uk/information-support/what-is-domestic-abuse/onlinesafety/

Parkin, S., Patel, T., Lopez-Neira, I., & Tanczer, L. M. (2019). Usability analysis of shared device ecosystem security: Informing support for survivors of IoT-facilitated tech-abuse. In M. Carvalho, W. Pieters, & E. Stobert (Eds.), *Proceedings of the new security paradigms workshop* (pp. 1–15). New York, NY: Association for Computing Machinery (ACM). doi:10.1145/3368860.3368861

Pavelić, M., Lončarić, Z., Vuković, M., & Kušek, M. (2018). Internet of things cyber security: Smart door lock system. In *2018 international conference on smart systems and technologies (SST)* (pp. 227–232). doi:10.1109/SST.2018.8564647

Poster, W. R. (2018). Cybersecurity needs women. *Nature*, *555*, 577–580. doi:10.1038/d41586-018-03327-w

PRNewswire. (2019, May 8). Smart locks market to be worth US$1.01 Bn by 2024. *Bloomberg*. Retrieved from https://www.bloomberg.com/press-releases/2019-05-08/smart-locks-market-to-be-worth-us-1-01-bn-by-2024-growing-use-of-cloud-based-services-augmented-demand-globally-tmr

van der Put, C. E., Gubbels, J., & Assink, M. (2019). Predicting domestic violence: A meta-analysis on the predictive validity of risk assessment tools. *Aggression and Violent Behavior*, *47*, 100–116. doi:10.1016/j.avb.2019.03.008

Refuge. (2020, January 9). 72% of Refuge service users identify experiencing tech abuse. *Refuge Charity - Domestic Violence Help*. Retrieved from https://www.refuge.org.uk/72-of-refuge-service-users-identify-experiencing-tech-abuse/

Riebe, T., & Reuter, C. (2019). Dual-use and dilemmas for cybersecurity, peace and technology assessment. In C. Reuter (Eds), *Information technology for peace and security*. Wiesbaden: Springer Vieweg. doi:10.1007/978-3-658-25652-4_8

Sabbagh, B. A., & Kowalski, S. (2015). A socio-technical framework for threat modeling a software supply chain. *IEEE Security Privacy*, *13*(4), 30–39. doi:10.1109/MSP.2015.72

Sambasivan, N., Consolvo, S., Batool, A., Ahmed, N., Matthews, T., Thomas, K., … Churchill, E. (2019). 'They Don't Leave Us Alone Anywhere We Go': Gender and digital abuse in South Asia. In *Proceedings of the 2019 CHI conference on human factors in computing systems - CHI '19*. doi:10.1145/3290605.3300232

Seeam, A., Ogbeh, O. S., Guness, S., & Bellekens, X. (2019). Threat modeling and security issues for the Internet of things. In *2019 conference on next generation computing applications (NextComp)*, (pp. 1–8). doi:10.1109/NEXTCOMP.2019.8883642

Shostack, A. (2014). *Threat modeling: Designing for security*. Wiley. Retrieved from https://www.wiley.com/en-us/Threat+Modeling%3A+Designing+for+Security-p-9781118809990

Slupska, J. (2019). Safe at home: Towards a feminist critique of cybersecurity. *St. Anthony's St Antony's International Review, Whose Security is Cybersecurity? Authority, Responsibility and Power in Cyberspace*, *15*, 83–100.

Steven, J. (2010). Threat modeling—perhaps it's time. *IEEE Security Privacy*, *8*(3), 83–86. doi:10.1109/MSP.2010.110

Strengers, Y., Kennedy, J., Arcari, P., Nicholls, L., & Gregg, M. (2019). Protection, productivity and pleasure in the smart home emerging expectations and gendered insights from Australian early adopters. In A. Cox, & V. Kostakos (Eds.), *Proceedings of the 2019 CHI conference on human factors in computing systems* (pp. 1–13). New York, NY: Association for Computing Machinery (ACM). doi:10.1145/3290605.3300875

Tanczer, L. M. (2019, October 21). Webinar: "Gender and IoT": The implications of smart technologies on victims and survivors of domestic and sexual violence and abuse. *Internet Society UK*. Retrieved from https://isoc-e.org/webinar-gender-and-iot/

Tanczer, L. M., Brass, I., Elsden, M., Carr, M., & Blackstock, J. (2019). The United Kingdom's emerging internet of things (IoT) policy landscape. In R. Ellis & V. Mohan (Eds.), *Rewired: Cybersecurity governance* (pp. 37–56). Hoboken, NJ: Wiley.

Tanczer, L. M., Lopez-Neira, I., Patel, T., Parkin, S., & Danezis, G. (2018). *Gender and IoT (G-IoT) policy leaflet: Tech abuse – smart, internet-connected devices present new risks for victims of domestic violence & abuse*. London: University College London. Retrieved from https://www.ucl.ac.uk/steapp/sites/steapp/files/giot_policy.pdf

Tanczer, L., Neira, I. L., Parkin, S., Patel, T., & Danezis, G. (2018). Gender and IoT research report technology-facilitated abuse. November.

Tanczer, L. M., Patel, T., Parkin, S., & Danezis, G. (2018). *Gender and IoT (G-IoT) Tech Abuse Guide: How internet-connected devices can affect victims of gender-based domestic and sexual violence and abuse*. London: University College London. Retrieved from https://www.ucl.ac.uk/steapp/research/projects/digital-policy-lab/gender-iot-tech-abuse

Tanczer, L. M., Patel, T., Parkin, S., & Danezis, G. (2019). *Gender and IoT (G-IoT) resource list: How internet-connected devices can affect victims of gender-based domestic and sexual violence and abuse*. London: University College London. Retrieved from https://www.ucl.ac.uk/steapp/research/projects/digital-policy-lab/g-iot-resource-list

Tech UK. (2019). The state of the connected home. Retrieved from http://www.techuk.org/images/assets/Connected_Home/The_State_of_the_Connected_Home_Edition3_Jun19.pdf

Think Social Tech, Snook, & SafeLives. (2019). *Tech vs abuse: Research findings 2019* (pp. 1–39). Comic Relief, The Clothworkers' Foundation, and Esmée Fairbairn Foundation.

Torr, P. (2005). Demystifying the threat modeling process. *IEEE Security Privacy*, *3*(5), 66–70. doi:10.1109/MSP.2005.119

UcedaVelez, T., & Morana, M. M. (2015). *Risk centric threat modeling: Process for attack simulation and threat analysis*. Wiley-Blackwell. Retrieved from https://www.wiley.com/en-gb/Risk+Centric+Threat+Modeling%3A+Process+for+Attack+Simulation+and+Threat+Analysis-p-9780470500965

Ur, B., Jung, J., & Schechter, S. (2013). The current state of access control for smart devices in homes. *Workshop on Home Usable Privacy and Security (HUPS)*, *29*, 209–218.

Uzunov, A. V., & Fernandez, E. B. (2014). An extensible pattern-based library and taxonomy of security threats for distributed systems. *Computer Standards & Interfaces*, *36*(4), 734–747. doi:10.1016/j.csi.2013.12.008

Velásquez, I., Caro, A., & Rodríguez, A. (2018). Authentication schemes and methods: A systematic literature review. *Information and Software Technology*, *94*, 30–37. doi:10.1016/j.infsof.2017.09.012

Weinert, A., Mayfield, P., Costica, Y., O'Donovan, S., Gulati, G., Radhakrishnan, D., … Esibov, A. (2019). *Traditional perimeter-based network defense is obsolete—Transform to a Zero Trust model*. Retrieved from https://www.microsoft.com/security/blog/2019/10/23/perimeter-based-network-defense-transform-zero-trust-model/

Wittes, B., Poplin, C., Jurecic, Q., & Spera, C. (2016). Sextortion: Cybersecurity, teenagers, and remote sexual assault. *Centre for Technology Innovation*. Retrieved from https://www.brookings.edu/research/sextortion-cybersecurity-teenagers-and-remote-sexual-assault/

Women's Aid. (2018). Online and digital abuse. *Women's Aid*. Retrieved from https://www.womensaid.org.uk/information-support/what-is-domestic-abuse/onlinesafety/

World Health Organisation. (2012). Understanding and addressing violence against women (WHO/RHR/12.36; pp. 1–12). WHO. Retrieved from https://apps.who.int/iris/bitstream/handle/10665/77432/WHO_RHR_12.36_eng.pdf;jsessionid=A70EC48CFB8D012BCFAC29B6ED559A4B?sequence=1

World Health Organisation. (2017, November 29). *Violence against women: Key facts*. WHO. Retrieved from https://www.who.int/news-room/fact-sheets/detail/violence-against-women

Xiong, W., & Lagerström, R. (2019). Threat modeling – a systematic literature review. *Computers and Security*, *84*, 53–69. doi:10.1016/j.cose.2019.03.010

Ye, M., Jiang, N., Yang, H., & Yan, Q. (2017a). Security analysis of internet-of-things: A case study of august smart lock. In *2017 IEEE conference on computer communications workshops, INFOCOM WKSHPS 2017*. doi:10.1109/INFCOMW.2017.8116427

Ye, M., Jiang, N., Yang, H., & Yan, Q. (2017b). Security analysis of internet-of-things: A case study of august smart lock. In *2017 IEEE conference on computer communications workshops (INFOCOM WKSHPS)* (pp. 499–504). doi:10.1109/INFCOMW.2017.8116427

Chapter 40

Justice on the Digitized Field: Analyzing Online Responses to Technology-Facilitated Informal Justice through Social Network Analysis

Ella Broadbent and Chrissy Thompson

Abstract

This chapter examines the structure and sentiment of the Twitter response to Nathan Broad's naming as the originator of an image-based sexual abuse incident following the 2017 Australian Football League Grand Final. Employing Social Network Analysis to visualize the hierarchy of Twitter users responding to the incident and Applied Thematic Analysis to trace the diffusion of differing streams of sentiment within this hierarchy, we produced a representation of participatory social media engagement in the context of image-based sexual abuse. Following two streams of findings, a model of social media user engagement was established that hierarchized the interplay between institutional and personal Twitter users. In this model, it was observed that the Broad incident generated sympathetic and compassionate discourses among an articulated network of social media users. This sentiment gradually diffused to institutional Twitter users – or Reference accounts – through the process of intermedia agenda-setting, whereby the narrative of terrestrial media accounts was altered by personal Twitter users over time.

Keywords: Image-based sexual abuse; informal justice; social network analysis; technology facilitated violence; Twitter; digital criminology

The Emerald International Handbook of Technology-Facilitated Violence and Abuse, 689–709

doi:10.1108/978-1-83982-848-520211051

Introduction

On the evening of September 30, 2017, the final siren sounded on the Australian Football League (AFL) season, and the Richmond Football Club (RFC) secured their first Premiership cup in 37 years. In the hours following the evening's celebrations, an image of a young woman with a premiership medal around her neck – her face cropped and breasts exposed – began to circulate through social networking platforms and fan forums. This image was quick to disperse through social media channels, becoming a symbol for the victory celebrations of the young men within the team and their army of supporters. It later emerged that the woman photographed had not consented to having the image shared.

In the month after this incident, a formal police inquiry was conducted at the request of the victim to protect her anonymity, leading to a gradual reduction of the image's appearance within social and terrestrial media. Following the closure of this investigation, the victim's lawyers issued a statement maintaining that while the image had been taken with her consent, she was under the impression that it had been deleted shortly after – and certainly not distributed via social media (Maurice Blackburn Lawyers, 2017). She sought to drop the charges police laid against the accused both to protect her identity and to prevent further distress (SBS, 2017). On 29 October 2017 – almost a month after the image's release – premiership player Nathan Broad was identified as the person responsible for taking and distributing the original image. A press conference was held with Broad and the president of the RFC, Peggy O'Neal, where Broad issued a statement claiming he would take full responsibility for his actions and confirmed he took and distributed the image without consent (Cherny, 2017). The only formal sanction Broad received from the RFC was a three-week suspension at the beginning of the 2018 AFL season (Cherny, 2017).

This incident (henceforth referred to as the "Broad incident")[1] represents a high-profile case of a certain form of technology-facilitated violence (TFV) – image-based sexual abuse (IBSA). Due to police intervention, attempts were made to remove the original image from circulation on social media. While this image can still be located today, its circulation decreased significantly after police attempted to remove it. As a result of these efforts, the ability to analyze the diffusion of the original incident of nonconsensual sexual imagery was limited. However, the subsequent identification in late October 2017 of Nathan Broad as the individual who took the image generated significant social media interest, and produced a body of historical Twitter data that provided a valuable substrate for us to analyze how social media users sought to contest or condone Nathan Broad's naming and sanction.

Incidents such as these hold value for criminological analysis, as they can provide a window into public sentiments on the perpetration of, and institutional responses to, IBSA. Moreover, as criminologists such as Powell, Overington, and Hamilton (2018) have demonstrated, examining responses to high-profile crimes on social media can provide a valuable means of researching the content and diffusion of narratives about crime in the contemporary mediascape. In undertaking such projects, a Social Network Analysis (SNA) methodology provides important insights into the degree of homophily within networks who respond to crimes on social media, and the role of central "nodes" in diffusing narratives about crime and perpetration.[2] Such insights are important given that early work within digital criminology has emphasized the "networked" morphology of contemporary harms – speaking, for example, of "networked misogyny" (Banet-Weiser & Miltner, 2016; Thompson & Wood, 2018, p. 12) – but has yet to examine the structural properties of these networks. To date, criminologists have yet to explore the utility of an SNA approach for examining social media–based responses to IBSA and other criminalized acts. To demonstrate the utility of SNA within this context, this study examined this incident of IBSA in Australia. In addition to answering the questions below, this project was concerned with not only the *what* of the research process but also the *how*. Readers are encouraged to consider the results and analysis as they would a pilot study – wherein qualitative Twitter data and a network of user relations were operationalized to generate an initial framework for understanding how structural analysis of incidents of IBSA can better demarcate the spread of sentiment through a network.

In examining the Broad incident using this methodology, we sought to address the following questions:

(1) What are the structural and intermedia features of Twitter users' responses to IBSA?
(2) In what ways do Twitter users contest and/or condone IBSA?

These questions enabled us to explore user engagement as a process involving both personal and media accounts, and the interactions they share to contest and/ or condone a narrative on an incident of IBSA. Furthermore, our analysis offers a novel approach to analyzing public sentiment toward an incident of IBSA, providing structural and intermedia analysis of the response to the incident.

This chapter is divided into four main sections. In section one, we review the relevant literature relating to online engagement, digital platforms, and IBSA. In the next section, we discuss the methodological contributions of this work and reflect on the utility of the methods used in this research for future studies into TFV and IBSA. In section three, we detail the major findings from this research; drawing on an Applied Thematic Analysis (ATA) we outline the narrative promulgated by both journalist and news media accounts, alongside personal Twitter users, and how interactions between these users generated a reverse-flow of sentiment. This is represented within a hierarchized visual framework characteristic of SNA to outline the flow of information and sentiment between different types of users responding to the Broad incident. This process enabled us to identify three "user roles" – Reference, Mediator, and Listener – with each performing distinct functions in the diffusion and reception of sentiment within the network. These user roles demonstrate how responses to crime on social media may be structured by clear hierarchies, with some users occupying dialogically significant positions within these networks.

Through an ATA of the tweets responding to Broad's naming in the media, we identified an informal justice-seeking response by users to Broad and his actions, alongside a replication of this sentiment within Reference users over time. The counterhegemonic discourses that appeared in response to Broad disrupted the neutral narrative of the Broad incident within Reference accounts and produced a more favorable and balanced consideration of the harms to the victim. Finally, we conclude by reflecting on the implications of this research for online responses to IBSA. We posit that demarcating the connections between social media actors – Mediators, Listeners, and Reference accounts – may enhance our understanding of their specific role in contesting and altering passive narratives of sexual harm online.

Literature Review

This chapter is situated amid a burgeoning literature on the spectatorship of, and engagement with, TFV and IBSA (Henry, McGlynn, Flynn, Johnson, Powell, & Scott, 2020; Henry & Powell, 2018). It is important to note that such spectatorship involves not only individual observation of an incident of IBSA but also their response to this observation. Here, the act of spectatorship is not confined simply to the object and viewer, or "the spectator and the spectacle," but also involves "the association between spectators," or in this instance structural relations between Twitter users (Wood, 2017, p. 9). This grounds our methodology, in seeking to demarcate the connections that shape engagement on social media platforms, a process which is mediated not only by social forces but also the technological (infra)structure of social networking platforms.

Twitter has been described as a "personal public" (Schmidt, 2014, p. 4) – a communicative space framed by the dimensions of software, relations, and rules. The concept of personal publics is not limited to Twitter and operates as a foundation for understanding the mechanics of Web 2.0 and user-generated content and interactions. Within a personal public, information is selected and displayed according to personal relevance criteria such as the social network a user situates themselves within. This is then mediated through ties made explicit by the platform – such as following, retweeting, and liking. Twitter itself can be distinguished from other social networks by the specific articulation of these user relations which are utilized to structure communicative flow – "the nexus of social ties and textual references, based on code-enabled connections" (Schmidt, 2014, p. 6). The foundational concept guiding these Twitter relations is that of "following" users – a unilateral relationship used to subscribe to other users' tweets and calculate user visibility metrics. Replies, retweets, and mentions, function as communicative references that allow for navigation to user profiles. These factors produce a stable and dynamic social networking service consisting of networked and distributed conversations (Schmidt, 2014), which enables potentially exponential public distribution and engagement with nonconsensual sexual imagery such as the image released by Broad.

Researchers have noted that social media platforms such as Twitter have allowed for a redemocratization of the public sphere (Papacharissi, 2002). The assembly of counterpublics (Fraser, 1990) by girls and women on social media to contest social exclusion and subordination has been documented within criminological literature (Khoja-Moolji, 2015). Technology has, for example, allowed victims and their supporters to engage in "name and shame" tactics to ensure that behavior of abusers is not excused, and to contest the inadequacy of institutional responses to sexual violence such as TFV (Powell, 2015; Salter, 2013; Wood, Rose, & Thompson, 2019, p. 3). Considering the inadequacy of existing institutional responses to rape and violence against women in the form of state-sanctioned justice (Powell, 2015), social media–enabled informal justice-seeking plays an important role in the way victims of sexual violence and their supporters can create counterhegemonic discourses online.

Informal justice and contemporary digital activism movements have been conceptualized as an asymmetrical and nonhierarchical endeavor within Powell, Stratton, and Cameron's (2018) theory of rhizomatic justice. Drawing on Deleuze and Guattari's (1988) figuration of the rhizome, Powell, Stratton et al.'s (2018) theory accounts for the diversity of activist behaviors in a digital context, where organizations, groups, and individuals are linked loosely and embody significant diversity (Funke, 2014). The resulting spread of motivations and agendas can lead these forms of activism to both enhance democracy and new forms of bigotry, which may outweigh the original infraction (Powell, Stratton et al., 2018). This is a constructive explanation for the consequences of informal justice-seeking. The utilization of a rhizomatic analogy, however, implies a flattening of hierarchies within these communities, which minimizes the "algorithmically-curated information environment" (Wood, 2019, p. 573) of social media, the in-built architecture that structures social media use. Identifying key nodes and influencers residing within a network who occupy a more significant role in information diffusion (Wood et al., 2019) holds the potential to identify information flow to institutional social media accounts. This chapter compliments the rhizomatic model of informal justice-seeking through an identification of the structural relations that underpinned online users' informal justice response to the Broad incident.

Methodology

Our study utilized a parallel mixed methods research design that combined a quantitative SNA and qualitative ATA (Borgatti, Everett, & Johnson, 2018) to establish a structural understanding of the social media response to the 2017 Broad incident. These methods enabled the assessment of differing components of the phenomenon, enhancing its interpretability. We collected and analyzed these quantitative and qualitative data sources separately before integrating them in the second phase of the project (Creswell & Clark, 2007).

To begin this process, an SNA was conducted to develop a quantitative representation of different user types with a corpus of data relating to an incident of IBSA. SNA enabled the visualization of relational ties between social actors – in this case individual Twitter users, such as journalists, institutional news media accounts, and personal Twitter users. This included interactions such as liking or retweeting user content, and follower/followee relationships. These ties could be typologized through user type differentiation established by Beguerisse-Díaz,

Garduno-Hernández, Vangelov, Yaliraki, and Barahona (2014) in their SNA of the London riots:

> References: Typically, institutional accounts, important sources of content or well-known personalities with many followers who follow few accounts.
> Mediators: Users who interact with … leader categories (i.e., they follow and are followed by high-profile accounts), as well as with nodes in the Listener categories below.
> Listeners: Accounts with few followers (within this network, not necessarily over the whole of Twitter) who follow mostly Reference nodes. Within this particular network, they can be considered as passive recipients of mainstream content (p. 7).

In our model, these roles are established through an observation of the mutual influence of users within different demographics. This can be traced through the direction of their relationships – ingoing or outgoing – to either indicate a follower–following relationship or tweet interaction. For example, a node or user situated within a network who is followed by a large number of users, who follows fewer users, and has high rates of tweet engagement indicated through network edges would be typologized as a Reference user. This position is often occupied by journalists or broadcasters.

SNA is underpinned by the assumption that examining the structure of networks allows for a better understanding of the network members' behavior and beliefs. SNA enables us to examine how relational ties between members of a network provide pathways for the flow of information and sentiment, which may shape members beliefs, perceptions, and actions (Knoke & Yang, 2008). For us, this translated to observing the structure of the network produced within a search term, including the differing demographics of users, their relational ties, and the subnetworks of identified users. Using Gephi, a social network visualization software, alongside data captured using the scraping tool NodeXL, a network of Twitter users appearing within the search term "Nathan Broad" was established.

Structuring analysis and data collection around a singular search term – "Nathan Broad" – occurred as a result of the lack of informal "hashtag" or key phrases associated with the event. Searching Broad's name informally, or other associated terms, generated a large body of irrelevant Twitter content, which was avoided by using the specific search term. Another caveat on project scope was that the online engagement following a local Australian incident of IBSA generated a lower engagement dataset than what would be expected from a study observing an internationally recognized celebrity incident.

These limitations were in part countered through the use of an ATA of every tweet which featured the term "Nathan Broad" from the October 1, 2017 to the November 4, 2017 ($n = 629$). ATA enabled the identification of patterns or themes independent of a specific theoretical framework. The time period the tweets were sampled from encompassed the initial sharing of the image and the media response that followed Nathan Broad's naming. The tweets were procured by copying all data from the complete Twitter search into a text file, representing every tweet within the relevant search criteria. This sample does not represent the full Twitter response to Broad, but instead just those who chose to refer to him by his full name and allowed their tweets to be accessible in Twitter's public search function. Twenty-three tweets were excluded due to irrelevance.[3] The final sample included 629 tweets which were then coded and analyzed using the qualitative data analysis program NVivo.

As noted earlier, this research design provides a new contribution to the current corpus of TFV and IBSA analysis as it specifically demarcates the social phenomenon embedded within electronic infrastructures (Venturini, Bounegru, Gray, & Rogers, 2018), such as Twitter, through the use of a mixed methods research design. To operationalize our considerations of "infrastructures," we attuned our line of inquiry to Twitter's follower–following relationships via Beguerisse-Díaz et al. (2014)'s typology of Twitter users. This allowed us to observe how Twitter as a platform facilitates and structures sentiment diffusion among differing user types in relation to IBSA.

Findings

The Broad incident was unique in its mobilization of a large population of Twitter users who spoke out against Broad and the institutions responsible for his sanction. These counterhegemonic discourses formed the basis of a phenomenon known as online informal justice-seeking – the utilization of social media to contest existing institutional responses to crime (Powell, 2015). In producing a tiered account of the informal justice-seeking response by Twitter users to Broad's naming in the media, we were able to present a unique contribution to TFV and IBSA studies.

Finding One: Structuring Communicative Flows

Our analysis began by first establishing a preliminary understanding of the demographic and sentiment breakdown within the dataset of tweets specific to Nathan Broad from late October to early November 2017. Users were classified into the user types established within Beguirisse-Díaz et al.'s (2014) typology, with a differentiation of users based on their generation and reception of content and information. As this initial analysis was not aided by an automated data scrape differentiating user types, the follower–followee relationship could not be identified at this point in the analysis. Instead, a Listener–Reference dichotomy was utilized based on intuitive coding of screen name, verification status, tweet content, and engagement.[4] Additionally, tweets were coded intuitively based on their sentiment toward Broad's identification and punishment. Tweets that sought to identify Broad as the perpetrator of a sex crime, either literally or through the use of terms denoting shame and humiliation, were coded negatively alongside tweets criticizing institutional responses.[5] Passive observation of the crime and resharing of news media were coded neutrally. Finally, tweets that sought to blame the

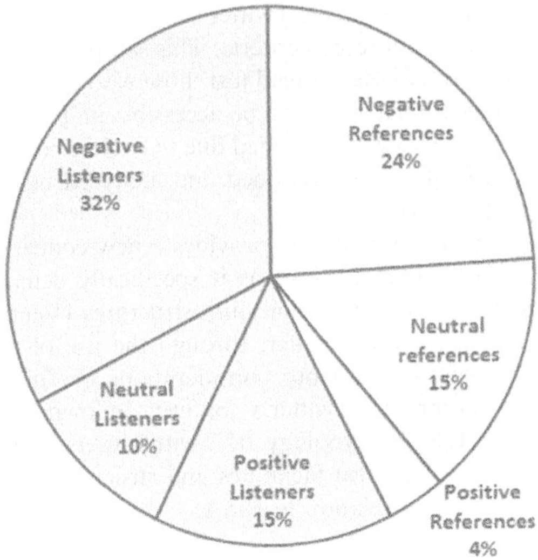

Fig. 40.1. Differentiation in Sentiment and Demographic Responses among Twitter Users within the "Nathan Broad" Search Term.

victim, neutralize the harm of Broad's actions, or minimize Broad's responsibility were coded positively. This allowed for the production of numerical representations of the differing spread of sentiment within the dataset, and which user types they aligned to, as seen in Fig. 40.1.

In Fig. 40.1, Reference accounts made up 43% of the dataset (n = 270), while Listeners made up 56% (n = 352).[6] Use of the search term "Nathan Broad" excluded the acquisition of any tweets that were made about the incident that did not quote Broad's name in full. Consequently, no transferable conclusions can be drawn from the specific ratio of Listeners and Reference users within this dataset. Among Reference users, a shift in sentiment regarding the incident could be observed as time progressed, as reporting and descriptions of the event in the dataset shifted from largely sentiment-neutral to negative, criticizing Broad and his actions. "Reference" media narratives regarding IBSA can be positioned within broader literature on the historical minimization of sexual abuse victims by the media and the institutions aligned with perpetrators (Waterhouse-Watson, 2013). More specifically, Broad's position as an athlete would historically grant him "narrative immunity" within representations of his behavior, a process which seeks to deflect blame from the perpetrators of sexual abuse and alleviate players of responsibility (Waterhouse-Watson, 2013, p. 5). Our findings challenged this, observing a shift from neutral to negative representations of Broad.

The spread of sentiment among Listeners echoed this trend of negative representations of Broad, a sympathetic response to the victim, and an acknowledgment of the harms generated by the image's release. Preliminary themes included frustration at the RFC and the AFL for the lenient sanction Broad received, and confusion over why Broad had not been apprehended by police despite the existence of laws penalizing his behavior within Victoria (Victorian Parliament, 2007). The breadth and depth of this sentiment within this dataset indicates an informal justice-seeking response to the Broad incident by some Twitter users, where the communicative space of Twitter enabled users to project their response to the incident to a wide social media audience (Powell, 2015). This did not occur without victim-blaming and neutralization techniques among 15% of users ($n = 94$), echoing a sentiment that would be expected from some fans and supporters of AFL as an all-male and patriarchal subculture that holds significant power in legitimizing sexual harms against women (DeKeseredy & Schwartz, 2016). Finally, the majority of neutral responses involved individuals resharing neutral news media – an expected product of the retweeting mechanism built into Twitter's platform.

Communication technologies such as social media allow for the production of harms such as IBSA (see Henry, Flynn, & Powell, 2019; Powell, Scott, Flynn, & Henry, 2020). However, they have also enabled users to challenge institutional responses to these crimes through informal justice-seeking (Powell, 2015). Our study sought to identify a structure upon which the flow of sentiment could be observed – to demarcate the way different users produced, directed, and interrupted neutral or sympathetic discourses identified in earlier paragraphs. To do this, we shift our attention to the SNA dataset featuring individual actors engaging with the Broad incident via Twitter.

To ground this process, seven major institutional accounts were identified as Reference users within this network. This occurred on the basis of verification status and follower count (>30,000). These accounts, pseudonymized to accord with ethics requirements,[7] formed the vast majority of incoming edge connectivity within the network – where edges indicate instances of interaction and follower/followee relationship on Twitter. Each node, or user, represented either a prominent institutional account within AFL or a major Australian broadcaster.

Positioning the role of Reference users within this network enabled an identification of Mediator users – "users who interact with … leader categories (i.e., they follow and are followed by high-profile accounts), as well as with nodes in the Listener categories" (Beguerisse-Díaz et al., 2014, p. 7). This process involved an observation of the users within this network, as the primary determinant of a Mediator role was incoming edges from Reference users. These users were identified as the group that was followed by any of the seven identified Reference accounts, rendering their sentiment visible to institutional users. Out of a total 25 outgoing edges among the Reference accounts, nine were identified as "personal" Twitter users. Their identification allowed for a stratified display of each user type situated within the network, as seen in Fig. 40.2.

At this scale, Mediators are seen to permeate varying points of the network and each node was established via a clustering algorithm. Node size relates specifically to their "betweenness centrality" – the number of times each node acts as a bridge along the shortest path in a network, thus allowing for a quantification of the dispersal of information among networked individuals (Freeman, 1977). The six major institutional accounts appear centrally within the network and occupy a

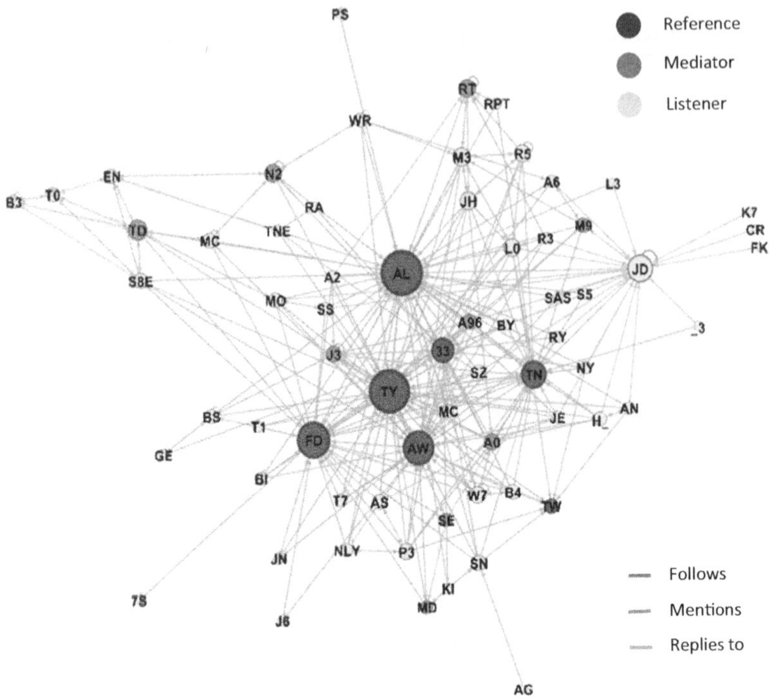

Fig. 40.2. Distribution of References, Mediators, and Listeners within Network. *Note:* Orange edges appearing on certain nodes are an artifact of the data gathering process and should be disregarded.

vast majority of the edge density (201 edges of a total 327).[8] This established stratification between Reference, Mediator, and Listener roles guided the investigation into the specific structure of interactions within this network.

A valuable method for examining the structure of user relations within SNA was through consideration of the subcommunities residing within the larger network. Schmidt (2014) details the role of these groups among Twitter users in developing communities of practice, wherein social rules are produced and upheld. These communities are built by and for the users who utilize Twitter for personal networking and content-sharing – those identified as Listeners in these networks. Having established flows of information between Mediators to Reference accounts, the next step was to consider the differing forms of communication between Listeners and Mediators. These users were not as easily differentiated via follower count, and therefore a consideration of their place within the network beyond the influence of Reference accounts can be seen in Fig. 40.3.

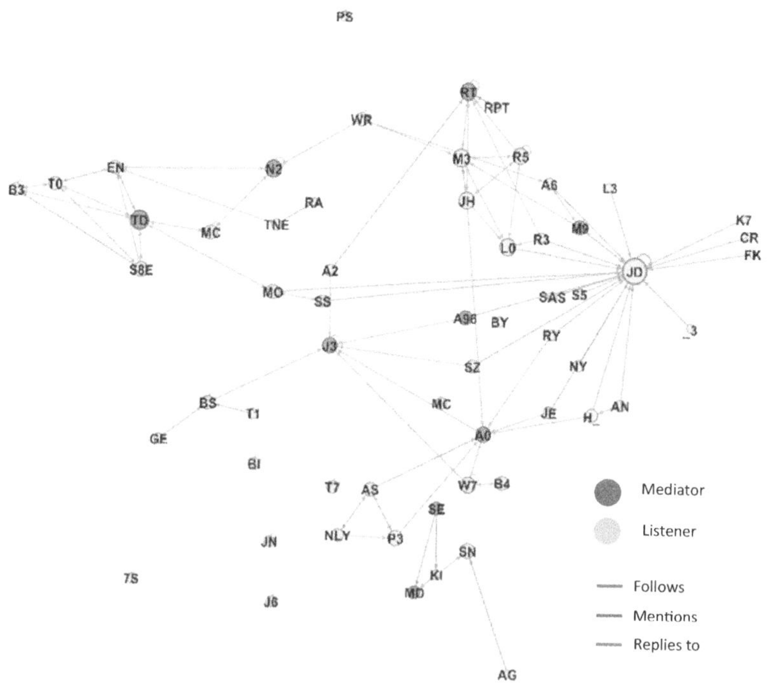

Fig. 40.3. Listener–Mediator Network Prior to Community Detection.

With the vast majority of network edges removed, Fig. 40.3 presents a network of significantly lower global connectivity. However, the modularity ranking of this network tells a different story. Modularity statistics allow for a numerical ranking of the typology of interconnected nodes in a network, and their decomposition into subcommunities with high levels of connectivity (Blondel, Guillaume, Lambiotte, & Lefebvre, 2008). Within the larger social network (inclusive of Reference accounts), the modularity ranking sat at 0.234 (on a scale of 0–1). This is small in comparison to the Mediator network, which had a modularity ranking of 0.603. This Mediator network is illustrated in Fig. 40.4, where a clustering algorithm is applied to reveal five distinct subnetworks contained within the larger network displayed in Fig. 40.3. This network excluded six nodes and the smaller secondary network due to a lack of connectivity to the larger network.

This smaller network solely features people who utilized Twitter purely for personal use, and a number of observations can be drawn from this network based on this composition. Modular subcommunities within networks such as these represented groups wherein "information, interest and influence is propagated, retained and reinforced" (Beguerisse-Díaz et al., 2014, p. 2). Several users

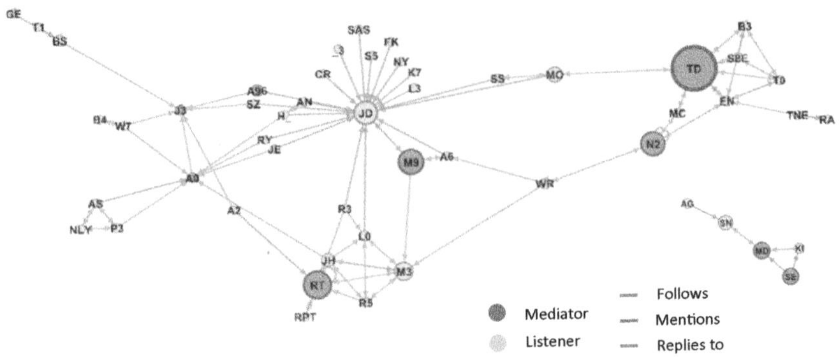

Fig. 40.4. Listener–Mediator Network Following Community Detection via ForceAtlas2 Clustering Algorithm and Size Differentiation Based on Betweenness Centrality. *Note:* Nodes JN, J6, 7S, P5, T7, and BI excluded due to no connection with larger network.

that occupied key positions in these networks – identified by node size (betweenness centrality) – happened to be Mediators. Accounts such as TD and RD appeared centrally within modular subcommunities distinct from the wider network. This smaller network was also unified by the user JD, who shared a tweet which received significant engagement, with many users—both those connected and those disconnected from the wider network—retweeting or mentioning user JD. Multiple Mediator accounts engaged with this tweet, diffusing the sentiment beyond this user both to other subcommunities and to the feeds of Reference accounts.

Several conclusions can be drawn from a structural analysis of this network. The first involves the substantial modularity of the Listener/Mediator subnetwork. The observation of five distinct subcommunities that were only well connected via a general trend of following Reference accounts suggests that prominent institutional media bridged the gap between these groups. The potential for many-to-many communication was also observed as a bridging factor, drawing together multiple distinct subnetworks that reshared and engaged with a prominent tweet from a Listener within the network. Both of these forms of communication operated parallel to one another, producing relationships and interactions that dispersed information through the network.

A second observation concerned the following patterns of Reference accounts. There seemed to be no identifiable characteristic that differentiated Mediator accounts in terms of their strength within the network. This lack of discernible difference means that Mediator accounts permeated a variety of different positions within the larger Twitter network, occupying multiple different subcommunities and interacting with multiple different streams of sentiment.

Drawing from this, we propose that in this network Mediator accounts are utilized by Reference accounts as "sounding boards" upon which public sentiment is observed and acted upon. While these Reference accounts do not explicitly engage with the public, they exist as important sources of content upon which the public rely. Mediator users, and their position between Listeners and References, offer an insight into how Twitter users' responses to an incident of IBSA can be hierarchized. We argue that the identification of these user types provides utility and nuance when conducting thematic analysis of social media responses to an incident of IBSA, as we demonstrate in the following section.

Finding Two: Counterhegemonic Narratives

Above, we established the structural and intermedia features of the Twitter response to the Broad incident. These findings provided a framework to analyze the spread of responses to Broad – both his actions and the sanction he received. A major theme observed within the Twitter responses to Broad was an outpouring of sympathy toward the victim, and a generalized disdain directed toward Broad and the sanction he received from RFC. Viewed collectively, we propose that these tweets made up a counterpublic of individuals seeking to contest the sanction handed down by RFC, and the incident which led to it. Counterpublics provide a space for individuals to challenge the monopoly of speech held by old media, as well as to discuss and challenge incidents of sexual violence contrary to established norms (Salter, 2013). The assignment of blame and guilt was relatively transparent in the Broad incident, a factor that may have contributed to the breadth of sympathetic responses to the victim. Instead of leading to a reduction in responses to the incident due to a "clean case," this straightforwardness instead empowered individuals to voice an array of counterdiscourses criticizing the culture and institutions responsible for the incident, in this case the RFC and AFL. Users expressing this sentiment fell within the "Listener" category – personal Twitter users and passive recipients of mainstream content.

Most notable among these counterdiscourses was an immense frustration at the RFC response to the incident – Broad's three-week sanction at the start of the 2018 AFL season. Numerous tweets suggested that Broad should have been delisted or fired:

> nathan broad retire bitch
>
> 0 replies 1 retweet 6 likes
>
> Richmond Football Club should have fired Nathan Broad, not suspended him. What a slap on the wrist for a sex crime. Disgraceful.
>
> 0 replies 0 retweets 1 like

Some called into question RFC and the AFL's commitment to gender equality following the verdict:

> Replying to @Richmond_FC <https://Twitter.com/Richmond_FC>

> you can't call yourself 'a club committed to gender equality' until nathan broad is fired - what a disgrace
>
> 3 replies 3 retweets 11 likes
>
> What a crock! Nathan Broad gets a 3 game suspension for committing a crime. #AFL disappointingly weak again on respect towards women
>
> 0 replies 0 retweets 2 likes

Users were also persistent in their recognition of the harms of the image and the humiliation faced by the victim:

Nathan Broad from Richmond gets 3 game suspension. Young woman gets smeared for life.

> 0 replies 5 retweets 4 likes
>
> *So very disappointing @AFL #Nathan Broad-3/52, woman-humiliated. poor decision making and Leadership @Richmond_FC* http://www.abc.net.au/news/2017-10-30/richmond-player-nathan-broad-named-over-topless-photo/9098712
>
> 1 reply 0 retweets 1 like

This outcry, the result of a frustrated supporter base disillusioned with the hypocrisy of the RFC's decision, spanned the full breadth of the dataset and was largely unchallenged by other users.

Another notable theme was the acknowledgment of Broad's actions as criminal, warranting intervention by the criminal justice system:

> Since he's admitted to it, I'd have thought Nathan Broad can be arrested now.
>
> 2 replies 9 retweets 38 likes
>
> Nathan Broad: 'I let down a young woman I cared about.'
>
> You committed a CRIME against her.
>
> 1 reply 1 retweet 3 likes

These tweets explicitly associated Broad's actions with laws that criminalize IBSA. The tweets also highlight a confusion at the disjuncture between the existence of laws targeting IBSA and institutions' responsibility to act upon those laws. Preexisting literature has addressed the challenges of prosecuting the distribution and spread of nonconsensual sexual imagery, including the difficulty in proving the originator of the image carried malicious intent, and the diffusion of responsibility to the wider social media audience who shared and reshared the image (Flynn & Henry, 2019; Henry, Flynn, & Powell, 2018; Powell, 2015). In this case, while the victim did not seek to press charges, users were insistent that sex offense charges should have been applied. Instead, the responsibility for punishing Broad was held by his football club, and as noted earlier, some users shared a view that the punishment by RFC should have delivered justice with a harsher sanction.

The discourses circulated by Listeners provide valuable insight into social media users' frustration with inadequate institutional responses to IBSA. They also provided a substrate for operationalizing the Listener/Mediator/Reference user dichotomy established within previous findings. To do this, a framework of intermedia agenda-setting was applied to assess how the responses outlined earlier were mirrored by Reference accounts tweeting about Broad's actions. Sexual misconduct perpetrated by footballers is often represented as an inevitable consequence of a hypermasculine sporting culture (Waterhouse-Watson, 2013). This sentiment is then normalized through the tone and framing utilized by news media to convey reporting on these instances to the public (Henley, Miller, & Beazley, 1995). In early tweets on Broad's identification and sanction on social media, Reference accounts produced tweets that delivered sentiment-neutral or sympathetic representations of Broad and his sanction, as exemplified in the following tweets (identifying information has been redacted):

> Richmond's Nathan Broad: "I'm embarrassed and ashamed.. I deserve to be punished." Suspended for three matches re nude photo. @9NewsMelb
>
> 18 replies 15 retweets 20 likes
>
> BREAKING: Nathan Broad takes "full responsibility" for Tigers nude photo scandal
>
> 3 replies 2 retweets 1 like

Each of these tweets, produced by a major broadcaster or journalist, legitimated Broad's sanction through passive or neutral tone or the inclusion of quotes referencing Broad's regret and shame. The diffusion of neutral and sympathetic responses to Broad throughout Reference responses to his sanction held the potential to reinforce the "narrative immunity" (Waterhouse-Watson, 2013, p. 5) of male athletes who engage in sexual misconduct.

However, as time progressed and the counterpublic narrative among Listeners continued to call out Broad and RFC, Reference account narratives of his actions began to shift. Tweets, again originating from news media accounts and journalists, began to echo the sentiment held by Listener accounts who took a critical and largely unsympathetic view of Broad and made frequent reference to the inadequacy of the sanction:

> Shocked at the Twitter vitriol being directed at the woman in Nathan Broad's photo.. All from men. It's not a crime to pose for a picture.

> 37 replies 16 retweets 194 likes
>
> COMMENT: A longer ban would have been appropriate for Nathan Broad
>
> http://www.theage.com.au/afl/afl-news/nathan-broad-suspension-should-have-been-longer-than-three-matches-20171030-gzaurd …
>
> 16 replies 9 retweets 29 likes

Tweets and news articles also began to appear that specifically referenced the public response to the incident:

> There's been an outcry over a three-match suspension handed to Nathan Broad, at the centre of a topless photo scandal. @AyrtonWoolley #9News
>
> #9News
>
> 9 News Melbourne, nightly at 6.00p.m.
>
> 6 replies 1 retweet 5 likes

Milivojevic and McGovern (2014) documented a similar pattern of news media acknowledging and endorsing social media sentiment in their study of the Jill Meagher case. Reporting that explicitly acknowledges an informal justice-seeking response to incidents of sexual assault represents a determination by news media that such responses are "newsworthy." This ultimately culminated in a vast majority of Reference users reporting on the incident echoing the sentiment of Listeners:

> Catherine Ordway (speaking about Nathan Broad): "Let's have him put his money where his mouth is and actually walk the talk. Go and work with some charities, go and show us that you do respect women." #TheProjectTV
>
> 9 replies 10 retweets 34 likes
>
> Stevie J 6 weeks for public drunkenness. Didak & Shaw last 6 games for lying re crash. M.Stokes 7 for drug charge. Nathan Broad deserved 4+
>
> 60 replies 36 retweets 296 likes

There was a clear, temporal progression in the sentiment shift of Reference accounts responding to the Broad incident over the three days that the story occupied headlines. This shift contrasted significantly with the approach of news media sentiment outlined in preexisting literature to similar incidents (Waterhouse-Watson, 2013). Given Reference accounts in this dataset were prominent broadcasting figures, this process exemplifies the shift in institutional agenda-setting first observed by Milivojevic and McGovern (2014). We suggest that the tweets by Reference accounts of the Broad incident were specifically influenced by social media outcry – a phenomenon that sees media institutions moving away from harmful discourses that minimize sexual harms committed by male athletes (Waterhouse-Watson, 2013).

These findings echo and support the hierarchized model of social media engagement discussed earlier in this chapter. The articulation of Reference accounts within social media networks, and their engagement with Listener subcommunities via Mediator accounts, provides a model of the reverse flow of sentiment enabled by social networking platforms (Sayre, Bode, Shah, Wilcox, & Shah, 2010). In the context of the Broad incident, this model articulates the intervention and disruption of sentiment-neutral discourses by social media users committed to expressing their discontent and frustration at Broad and the institutions that failed to adequately prosecute his behavior.

Conclusion

Studying phenomena such as TFV and IBSA requires innovative methods to attend to the complexities and nuances of justice in the digitized field. This pilot study has sought to bring the mechanics of the technology-enabling TFV and IBSA into focus by visualizing the structural patterns of behavior exhibited by users commenting about the Broad incident on Twitter. This study has illustrated how Twitter facilitated counterhegemonic discourses in relation to Broad's IBSA, and how these discourses disrupted and influenced news media sentiment that initially diminished the harms caused by IBSA. This has important implications for policy makers and practitioners responding to IBSA. It provides a substrate for understanding information diffusion and agenda-setting within the diffuse realm of social media structures, and how these structures impact public engagement with crime and criminality more widely.

The framework and findings discussed in this chapter may also prove helpful for other social media studies concerning responses to harm and crime on social media. The use of SNA is a relatively new and underutilized method within the social sciences (but see, Bright, 2015; Bright & Delaney, 2013; Bright, Greenhill, Ritter, & Morselli, 2015). Fig. 40.5 provides a representation of the ongoing interactions between differing hierarchies of users engaging with the Broad incident. We have highlighted the value of producing a structural representation of informal justice-seeking. This enabled the visualization of links between users, the generation of reverse flows of sentiment, and an analysis of how informal online justice-seeking is mediated by streams of incoming and outgoing information flows within a hierarchy of users.

Given this was a pilot study, it has pointed to avenues for further inquiry on online engagement and IBSA, such as considering user engagement on another platform such as Facebook or Instagram. Further, the production of a larger SNA may provide further detail on the role of Mediator accounts within a wider

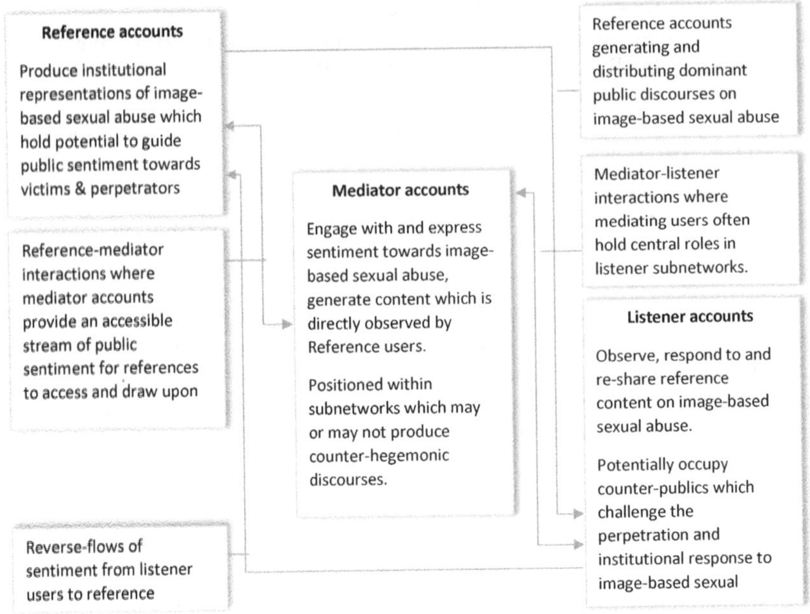

Fig. 40.5. Social Media Spectatorship and Image-Based Sexual Abuse.

network, and their specific position within the diffusion of information between Reference and Listener accounts. A further avenue for inquiry can be drawn from the fact both Broad and the woman he victimized are nonracialized, an important limitation when considering the sympathetic discourses observed in our results. SNA and ATA may prove useful for future studies examining specific media biases toward victims of TFV who are also members of marginalized communities. As social media evolves, so will its ability to enable digital sexual harms, and so we must consider the nature of information diffusion within the structure of online spaces. Methods such as SNA and ATA provide criminological scholars with tools to generate constructive accounts of the structure and flow of discourse surrounding incidents of IBSA and TFV. They offer the opportunity for tentative optimism on the nature of digital justice on social media platforms, and their role in disrupting and intervening in dominant narratives on sexual harm on the digital field.

Notes

1. The framing here is a deliberate choice by the authors to hold the perpetrator in sight and to account.
2. Print readers are encouraged to access the digital version of this paper, or to contact the authors for a digital copy, as figures are not designed to be interpreted in black and white.

3. Irrelevant tweets were bot tweets which aggregated "trending" topics, which provided neither sentiment nor news relevance.
4. Verified users indicate that the user is a legitimate account of public interest – those who may represent journalism, media, government, or other key interest areas.
5. Examples of tweets with negative coding include "Nathan broad is a total scumbag @AFL," whereas neutral coding encompassed sentiment-neutral responses, i.e., "Today, Richmond's Nathan Broad received a 3 week suspension for distributing a nude photo of a woman without her consent."
6. This ratio is the product of the limitations inherent to the scope of what was a small-scale pilot study. A larger study replicating these methods with an internationally recognized celebrity incident would provide greater engagement and thus a larger corpus of public sentiment for analysis.
7. This study received ethics approval through the University of Melbourne Arts HREC in 2018, application ID: 1851376.1.
8. One Reference account was excluded from analysis as it represented a broadcaster not consistently associated with AFL reporting.

References

Banet-Weiser, S., & Miltner, K. M. (2016). #MasculinitySoFragile: Culture, structure and networked misogyny. *Feminist Media Studies*, *16*(1), 171–174.

Beguerisse-Díaz, M., Garduno-Hernández, G., Vangelov, B., Yaliraki, S. N., & Barahona, M. (2014). Interest communities and flow roles in directed networks: The Twitter network of the UK riots. *Journal of The Royal Society Interface*, *11*(101), 1–12.

Blondel, V. D., Guillaume, J. L., Lambiotte, R., & Lefebvre, E. (2008). Fast unfolding of communities in large networks. *Journal of Statistical Mechanics: Theory and Experiment*, *2008*(10), 1–8.

Borgatti, S. P., Everett, M. G., & Johnson, J. C. (2018). *Analyzing social networks*. London: SAGE.

Bright, D. A. (2015). Disrupting and dismantling dark networks: Lessons from social network analysis and computer simulation. In L. Gerdes (Ed.), *Disrupting dark networks* (pp. 39–51). Cambridge: Cambridge University Press.

Bright, D. A., & Delaney, J. J. (2013). Evolution of a drug trafficking network: Mapping changes in network structure and function across time. *Global Crime*, *14*(2–3), 238–260.

Bright, D. A., Greenhill, C., Ritter, A., & Morselli, C. (2015). Networks within networks: Using multiple link types to examine network structure and identify key actors in a drug trafficking operation. *Global Crime*, *16*(3), 219–237.

Cherny, D. (2017). Richmond player Nathan Broad suspended for three games over topless photo scandal. *The Age*. Retrieved from https://www.theage.com.au/sport/afl/richmond-player-nathan-broad-suspended-for-three-games-over-topless-photo-scandal-20171030-gzaqn2.html. Accessed on January 15, 2020.

Creswell, J. W., & Clark, V. L. P. (2007). *Designing and conducting mixed methods research*. Thousand Oaks, CA: SAGE.

DeKeseredy, W. S., & Schwartz, M. D. (2016). Thinking sociologically about image-based sexual abuse: The contribution of male peer support theory. *Sexualization, Media, & Society*, *2*(4), 1–8.

Deleuze, G., & Guattari, F. (1988). *A thousand plateaus*. London: Bloomsbury Publishing.

Flynn, A., & Henry, N. (2019). Image-based sexual abuse: An Australian reflection. *Women & Criminal Justice*. doi:10.1080/08974554.2019.1646190

Fraser, N. (1990). Rethinking the public sphere: A contribution to the critique of actually existing democracy. *Social Text*, 25/26, 56–80.

Freeman, L. C. (1977). A set of measures of centrality based on betweenness. *Sociometry*, *40*(1), 35–41.

Funke, P. N. (2014). Building rhizomatic social movements? Movement-building relays during the current epoch of contention. *Studies in Social Justice*, *8*(1), 27–44.

Henley, N. M., Miller, M., & Beazley, J. A. (1995). Syntax, semantics, and sexual violence: Agency and the passive voice. *Journal of Language and Social Psychology*, *14*(1–2), 60–84.

Henry, N., Flynn, A., & Powell, A. (2018). Policing image-based sexual abuse: Stakeholder perspectives. *Police Practice and Research*, *19*(6), 565–581.

Henry, N., Flynn, A., & Powell, A. (2019). *Responding to revenge pornography: The scope, nature and impact of Australian Criminal Laws: A report to the Criminology Research Council*. Canberra, ACT: Australian Institute of Criminology.

Henry, N., McGlynn, C., Flynn, A., Johnston, K., Powell, A., & Scott, A. J. (2020). *Image-based sexual abuse: A study on the causes and consequences of non-consensual nude or sexual imagery*. London and New York, NY: Routledge.

Henry, N., & Powell, A. (2018). Technology-facilitated sexual violence: A literature review of empirical research. *Trauma, Violence, & Abuse*, *19*(2), 195–208.

Khoja-Moolji, S. (2015). Becoming an "intimate publics": Exploring the affective intensities of hashtag feminism. *Feminist Media Studies*, *15*(2), 347–350.

Knoke, D., & Yang, S. (2008). *Social network analysis*. Thousand Oaks, CA: SAGE.

Maurice Blackburn Lawyers. (2017). Statement regarding premiership media photograph. *Maurice Blackburn Lawyers*. Retrieved from https://www.mauriceblackburn.com.au/about/media-centre/media-statements/2017/statement-regarding-premiership-medal-photograph/. Accessed on April 1, 2018.

Milivojevic, S., & McGovern, A. (2014). The death of Jill Meagher: Crime and punishment on social media. *International Journal for Crime, Justice and Social Democracy*, *3*(3), 22–39.

Papacharissi, Z. (2002). The virtual sphere: The internet as a public sphere. *New Media & Society*, *4*(1), 9–27.

Powell, A. (2015). Seeking rape justice: Formal and informal responses to sexual violence through technosocial counter-publics. *Theoretical Criminology*, *19*(4), 571–588.

Powell, A., Overington, C., & Hamilton, G. (2018). Following# JillMeagher: Collective meaning-making in response to crime events via social media. *Crime, Media, Culture*, *14*(3), 409–428.

Powell, A., Scott, A. J., Flynn, A., & Henry, N. (2020). *Image-based sexual abuse: An international study of victims and perpetrators. Summary Report*. Melbourne, VIC: RMIT University.

Powell, A., Stratton, G., & Cameron, R. (2018). *Digital criminology: Crime and justice in digital society*. London: Routledge.

Salter, M. (2013). Justice and revenge in online counter-publics: Emerging responses to sexual violence in the age of social media. *Crime, Media, Culture*, *9*(3), 225–242.

Sayre, B., Bode, L., Shah, D., Wilcox, D., & Shah, C. (2010). Agenda setting in a digital age: Tracking attention to California Proposition 8 in social media, online news and conventional news. *Policy & Internet*, *2*(2), 7–32.

SBS. (2017). Tigers player said photo had been deleted. *SBS News Australia*, 30 October. Retrieved from https://www.sbs.com.au/news/tigers-player-said-photo-had-been-deleted. Accessed on April 1, 2018.

Schmidt, J. H. (2014). Twitter and the rise of personal publics. In K. Weller, A. Bruns, J. Burgess, M. Mahrt, & C. Puschmann (Eds.), *Twitter & society* (pp. 3–14). New York, NY: Peter Lang Publishing.

Thompson, C., & Wood, M. A. (2018). A media archaeology of the creepshot. *Feminist Media Studies*, *18*(4), 560–574.

Venturini, T., Bounegru, L., Gray, J., & Rogers, R. (2018). A reality check (list) for digital methods. *New Media & Society*, *20*(11), 4195–4217.

Victorian Parliament. (2007). Summary offences Amendment [Upskirting] act 2007 (Vic). *Parliament of Victoria, Victoria*. Retrieved from https://tinyurl.com/y9m6l35u. Last accessed on May 3, 20.

Waterhouse-Watson, D. (2013). *Athletes, sexual assault, and 'trials by media': Narrative immunity*. New York, NY: Routledge.

Wood, M. A. (2017). *Antisocial media: Crime-watching in the internet age*. London: Palgrave Macmillan.

Wood, M. A. (2019). Book review: Anastasia Powell, Gregory Stratton and Robin Cameron, digital criminology: Crime and justice in digital society. *Theoretical Criminology*, *23*(4), 571–574.

Wood, M., Rose, E., & Thompson, C. (2019). Viral justice? Online justice-seeking, intimate partner violence and affective contagion. *Theoretical Criminology*, *23*(3), 375–393.

Powell, A., Stratton, G., & Cameron, R. (2018). *Digital criminology: Crime and justice in digital society*. London: Routledge.
Salter, M. (2018). Justice and revenge in online counter-publics: Emerging responses [illegible]

Chapter 41

Bystander Apathy and Intervention in the Era of Social Media

Robert D. Lytle, Tabrina M. Bratton, and Heather K. Hudson

Abstract

Bystander apathy has been a source of debate for decades. In the past half-century, psychologists developed theoretical frameworks to understand bystander activity, commonly referred to as bystander intervention models (BIMs). More recently, BIMs have been modified to facilitate initiatives to prevent various forms of online victimization. This chapter begins with a review of BIMs and recent applications of bystander intervention research to online environments. We also present several future directions for research along with applications for reducing technology-facilitated violence, including programming recommendations and theoretical development.

Keywords: Bystander apathy; bystander intervention model; prevention; online communities; social media; online victimization

Introduction

If you have visited a metropolitan area, you have likely been present for an incident that could be considered an emergency. This might include walking past an unconscious person on the street one night, a shriek from a child as you walk past a park, or perhaps a heated argument between two adults in the neighboring room. When you perceive these types of stimuli in your environment, you engage in a cognitive process that helps to decide whether or not to act. This process includes a range of cognitive mechanisms wherein we interpret otherwise ambiguous information (e.g., Is the argument between the two adults becoming dangerous?), assess the situation (e.g., Can someone else assist the child in the park?), and consider how best to intervene (e.g., Do you wake the unconscious person and call for help?).

The Emerald International Handbook of Technology-Facilitated Violence and Abuse, 711–728

doi:10.1108/978-1-83982-848-520211052

Though we complete this process quickly, we remain partially paralyzed while resolving the conflict of witnessing a potential emergency.

Social scientists have generated a wealth of literature to explain the process driving bystander action in the presence of a possible emergency (Batson, van Lange, Ahmad, & Lishner, 2007). Much of this research has been built upon the bystander intervention model (BIM) proposed by Latané and Darley (1970) which situates the cognitive processes driving decisions to intervene in ambiguous emergencies within an unpredictable social environment. BIMs have informed applications to promote bystander intervention in emergencies, including violent situations, with some effect (Del Rey, Casas, & Ortega, 2016; Polanin, Espelage, & Pigott, 2012).

Despite this success, society has experienced significant changes in both cognitive processing and environments following the rise of social media. This chapter begins by briefly reviewing the literature on bystander apathy and BIMs, with a special emphasis on developments in bystander theory in light of recent technological advancements. The remainder of the chapter is dedicated to proposed directions for developing theory, methodological considerations for future research, and applying BIMs to understanding and reducing technology-facilitated violence and abuse (TFVA).

The Bystander Intervention Model

In 1968, John Darley and Bibb Latané published a seminal work on an emerging psychological concept referred to as bystander apathy. *Bystander apathy* refers to the phenomenon wherein otherwise moral persons can observe an emergency (e.g., accident, crime) without coming to the aid of those affected by it. Although incidents of bystander apathy were not novel at the time, social commentary grew in the wake of the murder of Kitty Genovese in 1964 (Manning, Levins, & Collins, 2007). Genovese was reportedly murdered while bystanders in the nearby apartments, all aware of the attack, did little to intervene on her behalf. Explanations centered around the moral ambivalence or decay of society at the time. Latané and Darley (1970), however, hypothesized that bystander apathy might emerge from the internal conflict one experiences when confronted with an emergency. In effect, they argued that bystander apathy did not necessarily imply a moral deficiency in the passive bystander; rather, they argued nonintervention could be expected when the situation surrounding the emergency favored nonintervention (Darley & Latané, 1968). After several classic experiments, Latané and Darley (1970) presented their BIM to explain bystander decisions about whether or not to intervene in emergencies.

Latané and Darley's (1970) model holds that people experience internal conflict when observing an emergency, regardless of their desire to assist or intervene in the danger. The BIM consists of five steps that influence whether or not a person will intervene. The first step is to witness the incident. Once a potential emergency has been witnessed, the second step requires the bystander to define the situation as an emergency. If the danger to the bystander or victim is unclear, the bystander may follow others' lead in recognizing whether the ambiguous situation (e.g., smoke, loud sounds) demands a response (Clark & Word, 1972; Darley &

Latané, 1968; Latané & Darley, 1970). This is referred to as *audience inhibition* or *pluralistic ignorance* (Latané & Nida, 1981). This psychological process is so impactful that, even when the situation becomes more clearly threatening, the bystander will remain calm if others witnessing the situation do not react to the threat (Darley & Latané, 1968).

If the bystander defines the situation as an emergency, they then look to the environment for justification to avoid the risk often present in an intervention (e.g., injury, embarrassment) (Latané & Darley, 1970). If a bystander is alone with the victim of an emergency, the responsibility of intervening on the victim's behalf is placed entirely on the bystander. As such, the cost of intervention may not outweigh the moral obligation they feel. However, as the number of other persons capable of intervening increases, the bystander can mentally share the responsibility for providing aid to a victim, which is known as *diffusion of responsibility* (Darley & Latané, 1968; Garcia, Weaver, Moskowitz, & Darley, 2002). As a result, the moral obligation felt by the bystander is attenuated and may not overcome the costs associated with intervention (Darley & Latané, 1968). Scholars often refer to nonintervention facilitated by bystander group size as the "bystander effect" (Levine, Philpot, & Kovalenko, 2020).

Although the BIM has enjoyed the theoretical spotlight for understanding helping behaviors, recent developments have revealed conditions to the initial framework (Fischer et al., 2011). One such development in bystander intervention research has centered around the nature of the emergency. Whereas classic bystander effect studies observed inaction in response to emergencies that posed little to no immediate danger to the participant (Levine & Darley, 1968), more recent research has proposed that dangerous or violent emergencies may be less likely to result in bystander inaction; a phenomenon commonly referred to as *positive bystander effects* (Fischer et al., 2011; Fischer, Greitemeyer, Pollozek, & Frey, 2006). Another relevant development in the bystander intervention literature relevant to understanding online environments involves the group composition of persons surrounding the bystander during the emergency (referred to here as *witnesses*). Based on meta-analyses of bystander intervention research, helping behavior is more likely to occur when a bystander is surrounded by witnesses who are known to one another (Rutkowski, Gruder, & Romer, 1983), share membership in a common social or demographic group (Levine & Crowther, 2008; Levine, Prosser, Evans, & Reicher, 2005), or are simply active observers (Fischer & Greitemeyer, 2013). Relatedly, bystanders who know the victim are also more likely to intervene in an emergency regardless of the size (or composition) of fellow witnesses to the emergency (Palmer, Nicksa, & McMahon, 2018). In this regard, bystander intervention may be similar in online environments. That is, helping behavior is likely dependent on the online relationship between the witness and victim.

Nonetheless, the BIM has demonstrated a moderately weak effect in explaining bystander inaction (Fischer et al., 2011). The utility of this theory can also be observed through its application to various forms of violence reduction and intervention programs, including bullying (Polanin et al., 2012) and campus sexual assault (Banyard, Moynihan, Cares, & Warner, 2014).[1] It has, however, emerged as a helpful tool to combat non-reporting and inaction from persons who observe an emergency, especially incidents that may traditionally have been viewed as "private," such as domestic violence (Levine et al., 2020; McMahon & Banyard, 2012; Palmer et al., 2018).

Bystander Intervention Models in Online Environments

Social interaction has changed significantly since Latané and Darley's (1970) seminal work. In particular, the rise of technological advancements in communication, such as social media, has changed societal norms, behaviors, and social environments. There are numerous benefits to social media, such as widening one's social networks and providing an outlet for communication and knowledge generation. However, the ubiquitous nature of social media today also has the potential to facilitate antisocial online behavior (e.g., Hayes, 2019; Southworth, Finn, Dawson, Fraser, & Tucker, 2007; Woodlock, 2017), including the targeting of minority populations such as racial minorities and members of the LGBTQI communities. Antisocial and cybercrime behaviors like online harassment can have detrimental impacts on the social, mental, and physical wellness of victims (Bates, 2017; Henry et al., 2020; Powell, Scott, Henry, & Flynn, 2020; Powell, Henry, & Flynn, 2018; Tennant, Demaray, Coyle, & Malecki, 2015; Widgerson & Lynch, 2013). These consequences not only lead to stigmatization, they may contribute to psychological distress (Wright, 2016) and suicide (Bauman, Toomey, & Walker, 2013; Sullivan, Annest, Simon, Luo, & Dahlberg, 2015).

Although the emergence of social media has undoubtedly changed the ways and environment in which we communicate with each other, the classic bystander effect may continue to inhibit bystanders from intervening online (Dempsey, Sulkowski, Nichols, & Storch, 2009; Olenik-Shemesh, Heiman, & Eden, 2017; Sticca & Perren, 2013). One possible source of bystander inaction in online environments may be ambiguity in cybervictimization. Cybervictimization, along with the online social environment they occur within, is relatively new. As a result, the norms and values for observing and responding to status updates in social media continue to evolve, which may create uncertainty for witnesses regarding what is and is not acceptable behavior online (Banyard, Plante, & Moynihan, 2005). In much the same way that perpetrators can benefit from anonymity in online environments, bystanders of online victimization may be able to avoid the cognitive conflict that often accompanies witnessing a potential emergency (Dempsey et al., 2009). Intervention may be particularly unlikely when the bystander does not know the victim well (Palmer et al., 2018). Finally, the lack of physical presence can make it complicated for bystanders to intervene in the emergency. This is especially the case when considering a lack of parental socialization toward online defending behavior reported by many adolescents (DeSmet et al., 2014). Witnesses inclined to physically intervene in offline situations (e.g., putting their body in front of a victim) may be uncertain about the best way to intervene in online environments. Despite these differences, however, it appears BIMs apply in both settings (Hayes, 2019).

Much of the research on bystander intervention in online environments has centered around cyberbullying, sexual violence, and intimate partner violence (IPV; Hayes, 2019). This research has generally found that bystander helping behavior, often taking the form of defending the targeted person, can be predicted by a bystander's social group, attitudes, and situational influences. More specifically, research has found that online bystander intervention is most likely to occur when the bystander is female (Allison & Bussey, 2017; Lambe, Della Cioppa, Hong, & Craig, 2019), older (Hayes, 2019; Olenik-Shemesh et al., 2017), and where they enjoy social support or popularity (Lambe et al., 2019; Olenik-Shemesh et al., 2017). Bystanders are less likely to intervene when they hold negative views of the victim (Hayes, 2019) or decline to speak up against prejudice (Moisuc, Brauer, Fonseca, Chaurand, & Greitemeyer, 2018). Finally, the norms and values of a bystander's environment, including those learned from family (DeSmet et al., 2014; Lambe et al., 2019) or school (Allison & Bussey, 2016, 2017), influence bystander intention to defend, as well as actual defending behaviors in cyberbullying events.

Interestingly, though, the ubiquity of social media might also provide a protective effect for victims. For example, victims of cybercrime and online harassment may have more social support than they have offline. To the extent that others might engage in the BIM in online environments, social media may contribute to the prevention of online victimization (e.g., positive bystander effect), as well as curbing the adverse effects of such victimization. Indeed, some scholars have found evidence of a positive bystander effect in online settings (Armstrong & Mahone, 2017). For example, online intervention is more likely, regardless of group size, when witnesses perceive the emergency as being more clearly dangerous or there is a relationship between the bystander and witnesses or victim. This can occur when online bystanders are aware of the dangers associated with online victimization (Armstrong & Mahone, 2017) or share a common identity or group identity (DeSmet et al., 2016; Lambe et al., 2019).

Considerations for Studying Bystander Intervention in Social Media

A variety of complexities arise when applying offline BIMs to online incidents. As BIMs rely heavily on the environment to explain bystander action, it follows that the theoretical pathways used to explain responses to emergencies may differ based on whether they occur offline or online. In this section, we review some of the ways that traditional BIMs may need further examination in research before application to online social environments.

The first step of BIMs is that one must observe the incident (Latané & Darley, 1970). In online settings, especially through social media, it may be difficult to determine when bystanders become aware of potential emergencies (Dillon & Bushman, 2015; McMahon & Banyard, 2012). For example, many social networking sites (SNSs) have a "wall" of posts where comments from followers are brought to the user's attention. SNS walls can be a public "place" used to bully, embarrass, and shame or defend, support, and praise other SNS users. Because of the breadth of information one sees on social media, online bystanders might become aware of incidents days after it occurred (McMahon, Palmer, Banyard, Murphy, & Gidycz, 2017), thereby removing the immediacy of observing the incident from the classic BIM. In light of the asynchronous nature of the online environment, this may be a key consideration for future research.

The second step of the BIM is that the bystander must define the incident as an emergency (Latané & Darley, 1970). As outlined earlier, this process can be influenced by the reactions of others present at the incident (Darley & Latané, 1968). BIMs that apply in the online context may need additional research to clarify the cognitive processes by which bystanders evaluate danger online, including content and other signals for help (Schachter, Greenberg, & Juvonen, 2016).

The keystone of traditional BIMs has been the influence of bystander group size on intervention (Latané & Darley, 1970). Presently, much of the research into online bystander intervention has focused on how diffusion of responsibility affects bystander responses to online emergencies, with a general conclusion being that the presence of online bystanders discourages bystander action (Dempsey et al., 2009; Hayes, 2019; Sticca & Perren, 2013). Although these studies provide an excellent starting point for online bystander intervention research, there remain several important questions for understanding bystander effects online. For example, how do online bystanders become aware of the presence of other bystanders? The anonymity of many online social environments may affect a person's ability to diffuse responsibility if they are not certain others are available to assist the victim. Conversely, anonymity in social media may allow the bystander to rationalize inaction by assuming others are present and observing the same emergency, therefore someone else may step in. Larger bystander group size has been shown to discourage intervention by simply having bystanders think about the presence of other witnesses (Garcia et al., 2002). Therefore, it may be easy for online bystanders to assume the presence of other witnesses regardless of ambiguous evidence.

In addition to applying the classic bystander effect to harassment and violence, research into online bystander intervention should also consider the possibility of positive bystander effects (Fischer et al., 2006). When the victim is in clear danger, such as violence, a larger number of witnesses actually facilitates bystander intervention, regardless of the assumed personal cost to bystanders. This finding has been attributed to both the less ambiguous nature of the threat to a victim in violent encounters (Piliavin, Rodin, & Piliavin, 1969) and the improved chance of successful intervention given the support of other bystanders (Fischer et al., 2011). This makes recognizing danger in online incidents particularly relevant when designing strategies to prevent cybervictimization.

Applications to Technology-Facilitated Violence and Abuse

BIMs can inform the public about TFVA, educate users about how to identify online problems, and provide recommendations for intervention (Moynihan et al., 2015). Evaluations of school-based BIM programs have proved successful in preventing violence in educational settings, especially among high school (Coker, Bush, Brancato, Clear, & Recktenwald, 2019; Polanin et al., 2012) and college students (Banyard, Moynihan, & Plate, 2007). Although most school-based bystander intervention programs do not use all five stages of the BIM, Nickerson, Aloe, Livingston, & Feeley (2014) suggested relying more on BIM to develop school-based, online bystander programs that explicitly teach the five steps of BIMs to decrease online bystander apathy. BIM-driven programs could facilitate the identification of TFVA, interpretation of TFVA as situations requiring intervention, assumption of responsibility for defending the victim, and learning the skills necessary to intervene safely.

Currently, few online bystander intervention programs target TFVA. The BIM can inform strategies to reduce bystander apathy and redirect passive attitudes into acceptable online behavior. Bystander intervention can reduce TFVA by interfering in violent situations before they escalate. Recent research on online bystanders have identified factors that increase the likelihood for intervention such as gender, age, perceived danger, familiarity with the victim, and attitudes (Allison & Bussey, 2016, 2017; Bastiaensens et al., 2014; Hayes, 2019; Olenik-Shemesh et al., 2017). Unfortunately, many of these factors are difficult to implement in programming (i.e., knowing victim, social popularity, and classroom). Furthermore, existing bystander intervention programming, especially with relation to sexual assault prevention, may be difficult to generalize to cases beyond cisgendered, heterosexual male offenders, and female victims (Dunn, Bailey, & Msosa, 2020). Based on existing research, then, intervention training should focus on the factors that can be changed through programming, like helping attitudes and the perceived danger of emergency.

To apply the first step of BIM (Latané & Darley, 1970), observation of the incident can be promoted by raising awareness to TFVA behaviors and warning signs. BIMs could also teach users to identify alarming content and TFVA as an emergency (Step 2). A key decision point to address in online bystander intervention programming will likely be the identification of the situation as an emergency. Recent research has suggested that many forms of TFVA reviewed in this chapter (and beyond), may be perceived by both the offender and witnesses as attempts at humor or "having fun" gone awry (Retter & Shariff, 2012; Shariff & DeMartini, 2016; Shariff, Wiseman, & Crestohl, 2012). Although this research has focused primarily on the motivation of the offender, this finding may also apply to bystander assessments of situations as an emergency. If bystanders believe that some event is a poorly executed joke, or they can quickly rationalize it as such, they can define the situation as a non-emergency and avoid responsibility for action. Multiple strategies may be needed to encourage bystanders to accept responsibility for intervention (Step 3). These strategies should promote social norms that encourage empathy for victims of TFVA (Nickerson et al., 2014), as well as increase self-efficacy for intervention among bystanders (Pöyhönen, Juvonen, & Salmivalli, 2012). Alternatively, online bystander intervention programs should consider how internet users perceive the presence of others to combat diffusion of responsibility and pluralistic ignorance, and identify ways to address these challenges (Darley & Latané, 1968; Latané & Darley, 1970).

Along with recognizing and accepting responsibility for TFVA incidents, BIM holds that bystanders must have a plan for action (Step 4) and be able to intervene (Step 5; Latané & Darley, 1970). Indeed, bystanders who are better trained in how to respond may be better prepared and therefore, more likely to assist in online emergencies effectively and safely (Coker et al., 2011). These strategies should focus on building knowledge and skills regarding how best to act. Although social media may promote opportunities for intervention (such as flagging or reporting TFVA), some aspects of social media like anonymity appear to hinder bystander intervention (Dempsey et al., 2009; Sticca & Perren, 2013). Therefore, programming should present tangible ways to intervene in specific types of TFVA.

Application #1: Technology-Facilitated Suicidality

Suicidality has long garnered attention, but only recently have online presentations of suicidality been considered a path to prevention. Some research suggests that adolescents who have suicidal ideations or engage in self-harm may share their feelings and practices on SNSs (Luxton, June, & Fairall, 2012; Marchant et al., 2017). Moreover, suicidality has been linked to social media use (Mok, Jorm, & Pirkis, 2015) and cybervictimization (Hinduja & Patchin, 2010). Witnesses to suicidal or self-harming posts can escalate self-harm through demeaning comments. As such, bystanders to online suicidal ideation and self-harm represent an opportunity to reduce and prevent suicidality. To observe and intervene in suicidal threats or ideations online, internet users should be trained to identify direct and indirect warning signs (Marchant et al., 2017). For example, programs might include ways to teach users to identify risky hashtags (e.g., #cutting), take them seriously, and respond appropriately.

To accomplish raising the perceived seriousness of online suicidal ideation, programs should incorporate peers into awareness campaigns. For example, peer-facilitators could confront the acceptance of jokes about suicide and rally others to treat all threats seriously. Peer-led bystander intervention exposure has previously been implemented with success in student populations, especially when many students were trained to be peer leaders (Pickering et al., 2018). Even if online suicidal threats are perceived as worthy of intervention, though, BIMs predict that bystanders will be less likely to respond if one can diffuse responsibility with other witnesses (Latané & Darley, 1970). To encourage internet users to accept responsibility, programs can focus on activities that promote empathy for suicidal persons and self-efficacy in intervention, both of which have been shown to discourage diffusion of responsibility online (Nickerson et al., 2014; Pöyhönen et al., 2012).

Even if the witness identifies the situation as an emergency, however, the stress and anxiety produced in individuals intervening in suicidality may create a specific obstacle to bystander action for this form of TFVA (Ting, Jacobson, & Sanders, 2011). In offline settings, the classic bystander apathy effect reverses so that witnesses become less likely to intervene when alone if the emergency poses a danger to the witness (Fischer & Greitemeyer, 2013). Therefore, BIMs intended to address technology-facilitated suicidality might also need to consider ways to help potential interveners process and cope with such anxiety. For example, social media campaigns can educate their users on the importance of intervention despite one's discomfort. In addition, programs to encourage bystander intervention in online environments can include services for interveners should their experience prove to be traumatic.

Peer-facilitators can also role play scenarios to help internet users develop strategies for effective intervention, which can empower bystanders in the face of an emergency. Effective plans for intervention can develop through skills-training, access to effective resources, and education on what works and what worsens the situation. Training programs should guide internet users through scenarios to explore direct and indirect options for intervening. Direct interventions for online suicidality could include approaches to talking to persons threatening self-harm online. Alternatively, bystanders may offer support and resources intended to help suicidal persons (e.g., suicide prevention phone lines or licensed counselors). Indirect measures would include strategies for bringing attention to the suicidal content, such as contacting emergency services in an immediate crisis or reporting alarming content on social media platforms. The benefits for bystander prevention in online suicidality are cumulative in the sense that intervention from one bystander may encourage others to act as well (Darley & Latané, 1968; Latané & Nida, 1981).

Application #2: Image-Based Sexual Abuse

Another source of TFVA that has grown from the ubiquity of social media has been image-based sexual abuse (IBSA). IBSA refers to dissemination of sexualized materials without the subject's consent (Bond & Tyrrell, 2018; Henry & Flynn, 2020). Although still early in its research development, scholars have noted significant health consequences for IBSA that range from symptoms of psychological distress to suicidality (Bates, 2017; Henry, McGlynn, Flynn, Johnson, Powell, & Scott, 2020; Powell et al., 2020; Powell et al., 2018). Despite recognition of the consequences of IBSA for victims, policymakers and police have reported difficulties designing effective responses to IBSA (Bond & Tyrrell, 2018; Henry et al., 2020; Henry, Flynn, & Powell, 2018). This difficulty stems from ambiguity in the definition of IBSA, especially in determining what material should be considered illicit, nonconsensual, and sexual (Bond & Tyrrell, 2018; Flynn & Henry, 2019; Walker & Sleath, 2017).

In light of these limitations, bystander intervention may be useful in discouraging IBSA. IBSA grows in online environments, wherein bystanders not only ignore the victimization but also reward its production (Henry & Flynn, 2020; Walker & Sleath, 2017). In addition, bystanders might assume the sexual material was published consensually and may not accurately recognize it as a form of victimization. Furthermore, if bystanders perceive the IBSA as a "joke" or venting frustration (Shariff & DeMartini, 2016), the situation may be defined as a non-emergency. Consequently, intervention would be perceived to be unnecessary. To the degree that bystander apathy contributes to the proliferation of IBSA, then, we may be able to quell its use, support police efforts to take action, and raise public awareness to the methods and consequences of this form of victimization.

Public education campaigns can help internet users and website administrators recognize and value curbing nonconsensual sexual materials, which could increase intervention on the victim's behalf. Furthermore, BIM programs can train online bystanders on what actions may be best suited to dissuade the spread of IBSA (Powell et al., 2020). For example, the Australian Federal Government has tasked the Office of the eSafety Commissioner with responsibility for addressing IBSA. One such example is that the Office has created a website which provides the public with information on online victimization and services to victims of cybercrime and IBSA, including a portal where victims can report their victimization experiences.[2] As victimization in cyberspace does not take place in a single geography, governments should consider direct action through similar approaches to this initiative implemented in Australia. In addition, social media can publicize "warning signs" and appropriate actions victims and bystanders can use to report potential IBSA to administrators or police. By training bystanders to recognize IBSA, define it as a threat to the victim, take responsibility for action, and make a plan to intervene, BIM programs may offer utility to reduction efforts.

Application #3: Cyberbullying and Online Harassment

BIMs are increasingly common in cyberbullying prevention (Allison & Bussey, 2016). Bullying refers to intentionally aggressive and repetitive acts targeting persons less able to defend themselves (Smith et al., 2008). Cyberbullying involves bullying that occurs online. The prevalence of bystanders in cyberbullying incidents (DeSmet et al., 2016) combined with how easily bystanders might unintentionally support cyberbullies for example, liking a harmful post, sharing a humiliating image (Barlinksa, Szuster, & Winiewski, 2013) make bystander behavior in cyberbullying incidents particularly important. Some scholars have offered recommendations for promoting bystander intervention in cyberbullying contexts, such as defending or comforting the victim (DeSmet et al., 2016). This is especially possible when bystanders empathize with victims and are inclined toward positive bystander behavior (DeSmet et al., 2016).

There have been a number of programs designed to promote bystander intervention in cyberbullying situations (DeSmet et al., 2018). Many of these programs have emphasized the first two stages of the BIM recognizing the situation and defining it as an emergency (Del Rey et al., 2016; DeSmet et al., 2018). More specifically, cyberbullying intervention programs often center around raising participant attention to the signals and dangers of cyberbullying. Furthermore, these programs develop participant empathy toward cyberbullying victims (Allison & Bussey, 2016, 2017).

A central component to BIM programming should be to foster a sense of responsibility for bystanders (DeSmet et al., 2016). This might be accomplished through demonstrations of the bystander effect or role playing scenarios. A more sustained target for promoting bystander responsibility, though, might be social norms regarding internet etiquette and social support. Training teenagers to serve as "active bystanders" in social media environments may influence technological norms for generations. Furthermore, active bystanders can help publicize cyberbullying incidents, rally support to victims, and bring repeated incidents to the attention of authorities (e.g., parents or police).

BIMs may also offer guidance for cyberbullying programs regarding bystander plans for taking action. BIM programs might engage participants in critical thinking exercises to explore potential action plans, including direct, indirect, and distracting interventions. Direct intervention includes actions to help the victim that insert the bystander directly into the cyberbullying incident. For example, a bystander might directly intervene through confrontation, replying with an anti-bullying emoji, or documenting the incident. Indirect intervention would involve bystander actions that help the victim without getting the bystander involved in the incident, such as reporting and flagging content. Bystanders might also use distraction to intervene on the victim's behalf, which serves to "change the topic" away from the cyberbullying content toward something more positive about the victim. Finally, intervention in cyberbullying incidents can also be promoted using BIMs by encouraging participants to develop a plan of action so they are not only prepared to act, but also feel less anxiety about intervention.

Using Bystander Intervention Models to Address Technology-Facilitated Violence and Abuse

BIMs can be used to reduce bystander apathy, encourage decisions to intervene in emergencies, and perhaps even prevent TFVA by deterring violence. The evolving environment surrounding social media and online social interactions makes it difficult to anticipate changes in harmful online activities. However, if more internet users are trained to be active bystanders who recognize the potential danger that various forms of TFVA pose to victims, as well as the need for bystanders to reject the temptation to share responsibility for action, there will be a strong foundation for prevention and intervention efforts.

A goal for researchers moving forward, then, should be to generate "best practices" for online bystander intervention programs. These best practices should build on research in online and offline bystander intervention, including positive bystander intervention effects and perpetrator-victim-bystander relationships. Based on the current state of the literature, bystander intervention programs can facilitate bystander recognition of potentially dangerous situations by presenting, in a publicly translatable manner, changes in the nature, and processes in TFVA. Furthermore, programs should help users to clearly identify the warning signs of online harassment and violence. It is also important for programs to establish the seriousness of TFVA in online environments through public education initiatives, such as public service announcements and awareness campaigns. These efforts may involve developing empathy toward victims of various forms of TFVA, as empathy remains a consistent predictor of positive bystander action in online settings (e.g., DeSmet et al., 2016).

Online bystander intervention programs should also incorporate strategies for discouraging diffusion of responsibility in bystanders witnessing online harassment or violence. Existing research has suggested that online bystanders are susceptible to the same "bystander effect" that has been observed in offline settings. Indeed, some studies have indicated an increased impact of group size on bystander apathy in online situations (Fischer & Greitemeyer, 2013; Levine & Crowther, 2008). Key obstacles to encouraging bystanders to accept responsibility include the anonymity of online witnesses to harassment and violence (Brody & Vangelisti, 2015), ambiguity in the danger posed to the victim in online settings (Schachter et al., 2016), and social norms regulating defending bullying victims (Barlinksa et al., 2013). Finally, BIMs applied to social media would encourage public discourse and education about different options for intervention, highlighting (a) the variety of interventions that can fit the bystander's "intervention style" and (b) the benefit that intervention offers to the victim.

Although these strategies provide a useful first step in promoting online bystander intervention, there remains a significant body of research required to understand the processes by which online bystanders decide to act. One area of research that has received attention in BIMs cyberbullying programming includes positive bystander effects (Fischer & Greitemeyer, 2013; Levine & Crowther, 2008). When bystanders are aware of the danger posed to the victim in the emergency, not only are they more likely to personally intervene but also larger group sizes can serve as support for the bystander to intervene (Fischer et al., 2011; Levine et al., 2005). Processes like these, by which bystander action is heightened offline, may offer useful insight into effective strategies for encouraging bystander intervention online. Furthermore, although their effects will be less immediate, initiatives to change online etiquette and social norms can provide a more sustained contribution to bystander intervention. Indeed, by promoting the defense of persons targeted in TFVA, online bystanders may be primed to confront perpetrators and support victims.

There has also been a noteworthy recent call for BIM research to incorporate an intersectional approach (Dunn et al., 2020). Currently, much of the literature has been based on existing theoretical models that treat bystander apathy as monolithically applied across marginalized groups (e.g., race, ethnicity, gender expression, sexuality, age, ability, etc.; Bang, Kerrick, & Wuthrich, 2017). This unrealistic treatment may pose several threats to the validity of BIMs, however. Many of the current theoretical models have been developed using cisgendered, heterosexual, White populations, often situated with a male offender and female victim (Dunn et al., 2020). Therefore, these models may have limited generalizability for other marginalized groups and offender/victim combinations. For example, bystanders who are persons of color may experience a greater risk for intervening in offenses committed by White men (Wooten, 2017). As scholars work to develop BIM-driven research in online settings, then, there should be efforts made to use samples and programming tailored to such an intersectional approach.

Conclusion

We began this chapter with hypothetical scenarios that would likely be relevant to anyone who has traveled for work or leisure. In the era of social media, though, it may even be more likely for you to have noticed that an active Facebook friend has suddenly desisted from engaging with friends. Or, you may have seen comments on Twitter wherein a friend has increasingly referenced self-harm in online interactions. Although social media can bring people with a common purpose together, it can also serve as a virtual battleground, wherein arguments can evolve into threats and, occasionally, physical or psychological damage. The value of bystander intervention remains as important as it was when Kitty Genovese was brutally attacked in 1964, particularly in the online context. With our attention turned toward often ambiguous online emergencies, then, researchers should not allow the responsibility for further development of BIMs and design for intervention programs to diffuse.

Notes

1. Levine et al. (2020) have recently offered a series of limitations that should be considered when building violence reduction programs out of classic BIM. These recommendations center around programs that apply Latané and Darley's (1970) original model without incorporating recent developments in the research.
2. This website can be found at https://www.esafety.gov.au/about-us/research/image-based-abuse.

References

Allison, K. R., & Bussey, K. (2016). Cyber-by standing in context: A review of the literature on witnesses' responses to cyberbullying. *Children and Youth Services Review*, *65*, 183–194.

Allison, K. R., & Bussey, K. (2017). Individual and collective moral influences on intervention in cyberbullying. *Computers in Human Behavior*, *74*, 7–15.

Armstrong, C. L., & Mahone, J. (2017). "It's on us": The role of social media and rape culture in individual willingness to mobilize against sexual assault. *Mass Communication and Society*, *20*, 92–115.

Bang, A., Kerrick, A., & Wuthrich, C. K. (2017). Examining bystander intervention in the wake of #BlackLivesMatter and #TransLivesMatter. In S. C. Wooten & R. W. Mitchell (Eds.), *Preventing sexual violence on campus: Challenging traditional approaches through program innovation* (pp. 65–80). New York, NY: Routledge.

Banyard, V. L., Moynihan, M. M., Cares, A. C., & Warner, R. (2014). How do we know if it works? Measuring outcomes in bystander-focused abuse prevention on campuses. *Psychology of Violence*, *4*(1), 101–115.

Banyard, V. L., Moynihan, M. M., & Plante, E. G. (2007). Sexual violence prevention through bystander education: An experimental evaluation. *Journal of Community Psychology*, *35*, 463–481.

Banyard, V. L., Plante, E. G., & Moynihan, M. M. (2005). *Rape prevention through bystander education: Bringing a broader community perspective to sexual violence prevention*. Washington, DC: National Institute of Justice. Retrieved from https://www.ncjrs.gov/pdf-files1/nij/grants/208701.pdf

Barlinksa, J., Szuster, A., & Winiewski, M. (2013). Cyberbullying among adolescent bystanders: Role of the communication medium, form of violence, and empathy. *Journal of Community and Applied Social Psychology*, *23*, 37–51.

Bastiaensens, S., Vanderbosch, H., Poels, K., Van Cleemput, K., DeSmet, A., & Bourdeadhuij, I. (2014). Cyberbullying on social network sites: An experimental study into bystanders' behavioural intentions to help the victim or reinforce the bully. *Computers in Human Behavior*, *31*, 259–271.

Bates, S. (2017). Revenge porn and mental health: A qualitative analysis of the mental health effects of revenge porn on female survivors. *Feminist Criminology*, *12*(1), 22–42.

Batson, C. D., van Lange, P. A. M., Ahmad, N., & Lishner, D. A. (2007). Altruism and helping behavior. In M. A. Hogg & J. Cooper (Eds.), *The Sage handbook of social psychology: Concise student edition* (pp. 241–258). Thousand Oaks, CA: Sage.

Bauman, S., Toomey, R. B., & Walker, J. L. (2013). Associations among bullying, cyberbullying, and suicide in high school students. *Journal of Adolescence*, *36*, 341–350.

Bond, E., & Tyrrell, K. (2018). Understanding revenge pornography: A national survey of police officers and staff in England and Wales. *Journal of Interpersonal Violence*. doi:10.1177/0886260518760011

Brody, N., & Vangelisti, A. L. (2015). Bystander intervention in cyberbullying. *Communication Monographs*, *83*(1), 94–116.

Clark, R. D., & Word, L. E. (1972). Why don't bystanders help? Because of ambiguity?. *Journal of Personality and Social Psychology*, *24*, 392–400.

Coker, A. L., Bush, H. N., Brancato, C. J., Clear, E. R., & Recktenwald, E. A. (2019). Bystander program effectiveness to reduce violence acceptance: RCT in high schools. *Journal of Family Violence*, *34*(3), 153–164.

Coker, A. L., Cook-Craig, P. G., Williams, C. M., Fisher, B. S., Clear, E. R., Garcia, L. S., & Hegge, L. M. (2011). Evaluation of green dot: An active bystander intervention to reduce sexual violence on college campuses. *Violence Against Women*, *17*(6), 777–796.

Darley, J. M., & Latané, B. (1968). Bystander intervention in emergencies: Diffusion of responsibility. *Journal of Personality and Social Psychology*, *8*(4), 377–383.

Del Rey, R., Casas, J. A., & Ortega, R. (2016). Impact of the ConRed program on different cyberbullying roles. *Aggressive Behavior*, *42*, 123–135.

Dempsey, A. G., Sulkowski, M. L., Nichols, R., & Storch, E. A. (2009). Differences between peer victimization in cyber and physical settings and associated psychosocial adjustment in early adolescence. *Psychology in the Schools*, *46*, 962–972.

DeSmet, A., Bastiaensens, S., van Cleemput, K., Poels, K., Vandebosch, H., Cardon, G., & de Bourdeaudhuij, I. (2016). Deciding whether to look after them, to like it, or leave it: A multidimensional analysis of predictors of positive and negative bystander behavior in cyberbullying among adolescents. *Computers in Human Behavior*, *57*, 398–415.

DeSmet, A., Bastiaensens, S., van Cleemput, K., Poels, K., Vandebosch, H., Deboutte, G., … de Bourdeaudhuij, I. (2018). The efficacy of Friendly Attac serious digital game to promote prosocial bystander behavior in cyberbullying among young adolescents: A cluster-randomized controlled trial. *Computers in Human Behavior*, *78*, 336–347.

DeSmet, A., Veldeman, C., Poels, K., Bastiaensens, S., van Cleemput, K., Vandebosch, H., & de Bourdeaudhuij, I. (2014). Determinants of self-reported bystander behavior in cyberbullying incidents amongst adolescents. *Cyberpsychology, Behavior, and Social Networking*, *17*(4), 207–215.

Dillon, K. P., & Bushman, B. J. (2015). Unresponsive or un-noticed? Cyberbystander intervention in an experimental cyberbullying context. *Computers in Human Behavior*, *45*, 144–150.

Dunn, S., Bailey, J., & Msosa, Y. (2020). Stand by me: Viewing bystander intervention programming through an intersectional lens. In D. Crocker, J. Minaker, & A. Neuland (Eds.), *Violence interrupted: Confronting sexual violence on university campuses* (pp. 117–140). Montreal, QC: McGill-Queen's University Press.

Fischer, P., & Greitemeyer, T. (2013). The positive bystander effect: Passive bystanders increase helping in situations with high expected negative consequences for the helper. *Journal of Social Psychology*, *153*(1), 1–5.

Fischer, P., Greitemeyer, T., Pollozek, F., & Frey, D. (2006). The unresponsive bystander: Are bystanders more responsive in dangerous emergencies?. *European Journal of Social Psychology*, *36*, 267–278.

Fischer, P., Krueger, J. I., Greitemeyer, T., Vogrincic, C., Kastenmüller, A., Frey, D., … Kainbacher, M. (2011). The bystander-effect: A meta-analytic review on bystander intervention in dangerous and non-dangerous emergencies. *Psychological Bulletin*, *137*(4), 517–537.

Flynn, A., & Henry, N. (2019). Image-based sexual abuse: An Australian reflection. *Women and Criminal Justice*, online first. doi:10.1080/08974554.2019.1646190

Garcia, S. M., Weaver, K., Moskowitz, G. B., & Darley, J. M. (2002). Crowded minds: The implicit bystander effect. *Journal of Personality and Social Psychology*, *83*(4), 843–853.

Hayes, B. E. (2019). Bystander intervention to abusive behavior on social networking websites. *Violence Against Women*, *25*(4), 463–484.

Henry, N., & Flynn, A. (2020). Image-based sexual abuse: Online distribution channels and illicit communities of support. *Violence Against Women*, *26*(16), 1932–1955.

Henry, N., Flynn, A., & Powell, A. (2018). Policing image-based sexual abuse: Stakeholder perspectives. *Police Practice and Research: An International Journal*, *19*(6), 565–581.

Henry, N., McGlynn, C., Flynn, A., Johnston, K., Powell, A., & Scott, A. J. (2020). *Image-based sexual abuse: A study on the causes and consequences of non-consensual nude or sexual imagery*. London and New York, NY: Routledge.

Hinduja, S., & Patchin, J. W. (2010). Bullying, cyberbullying, and suicide. *Archives of Suicide Research*, *14*, 206–221.

Lambe, L. J., Della Cioppa, V., Hong, I. K., & Craig, W. M. (2019). Standing up to bullying: A social ecological review of peer defending in offline and online contexts. *Aggression and Violent Behavior*, *45*, 51–74.

Latané, B., & Darley, J. M. (1968). Group inhibition of bystander intervention. *Journal of Personality and Social Psychology*, *10*, 215–221.

Latané, B., & Darley, J. M. (1970). *The unresponsive bystander: Why doesn't he help?*. New York, NY: Appleton-Century-Crofts.

Latané, B., & Nida, S. (1981). Ten years of research on group size and helping. *Psychological Bulletin*, *89*(2), 308–324.

Levine, M., & Crowther, S. (2008). The responsive bystander: How social group membership and group size can encourage as well as inhibit bystander intervention. *Journal of Personality and Social Psychology*, *95*(6), 1429–1439.

Levine, M., Philpot, R., & Kovalenko, A. G. (2020). Rethinking the bystander effect in violence reduction training programs. *Social Issues and Policy Review*, *14*(1), 273–296.

Levine, M., Prosser, A., Evans, D., & Reicher, S. (2005). Identity and emergency intervention: How social group membership and inclusiveness of group boundaries shape helping behavior. *Personality and Social Psychology Bulletin*, *31*(4), 443–453.

Luxton, D. D., June, J. D., & Fairall, J. M. (2012). Social media and suicide: A public health perspective. *American Journal of Public Health*, *102*(S2), S195–S200.

Manning, R., Levine, M., & Collins, A. (2007). The Kitty Genovese murder and the social psychology of helping: The parable of the 38 witnesses. *American Psychologist*, *62*(5), 555–562.

Marchant, A., Hawton, K., Stewart, A., Montgomery, P., Singaravelu, V., Lloyd, K., … John, A. (2017). A systematic review of the relationship between internet use, self-harm and suicidal behaviour in young people: The good, the bad, and the unknown. *PLoS One*, *12*(8), e0181722. doi:10.1371/journal.pone.0181722

McMahon, S., & Banyard, V. L. (2012). When can I help? A conceptual framework for the prevention of sexual violence through bystander intervention. *Trauma, Violence, and Abuse*, *13*(1), 3–14.

McMahon, S., Palmer, J. E., Banyard, V., Murphy, M., & Gidycz, C. A. (2017). Measuring bystander behavior in the context of sexual violence prevention: Lessons learned and new directions. *Journal of Interpersonal Violence*, *32*(16), 2396–2418.

Moisuc, A., Brauer, M., Fonseca, A., Chaurand, N., & Greitemeyer, T. (2018). Individual differences in social control: Who 'speaks up' when witnessing uncivil, discriminatory, and immoral behaviours?. *British Journal of Social Psychology*, *57*, 524–546.

Mok, K., Jorm, A. F., & Pirkis, J. (2015). Suicide-related internet use: A review. *Australian and New Zealand Journal of Psychiatry*, *49*(8), 697–705.

Moynihan, M. M., Banyard, V. L., Cares, A. C., Williams, L. M., Potter, S. J., & Stapleton, J. G. (2015). Encouraging responses in sexual and relationship violence prevention: What program effects remain one year later?. *Journal of Interpersonal Violence*, *30*, 110–132.

Nickerson, A. B., Aloe, A. M., Livingston, J. A., & Feeley, T. H. (2014). Measurement of the bystander intervention model for bullying and sexual harassment. *Journal of Adolescence*, *37*, 391–400.

Olenik-Shemesh, D., Heiman, T., & Eden, S. (2017). Bystanders' behavior in cyberbullying episodes: Active and passive patterns in the context of personal-socio-emotional factors. *Journal of Interpersonal Violence*, *32*(1), 23–48.

Palmer, J. E., Nicksa, S. C., & McMahon, S. (2018). Does who you know affect how you act? The impact of relationships on bystander intervention in interpersonal violence situations. *Journal of Interpersonal Violence*, *33*(17), 2623–2642.

Pickering, T. A., Wyman, P. A., Schmeelk-Cone, K., Hartley, C., Valente, T. W., Pisani, A. R., … LoMurray, M. (2018). Diffusion of a peer-led suicide preventive intervention through school-based student peer and adult networks. *Frontiers in Psychiatry*, *9*, 598.

Piliavin, I., Rodin, J., & Piliavin, J. (1969). Good Samaritanism: An underground phenomenon?. *Journal of Personality and Social Psychology*, *13*, 289–299.

Polanin, J. R., Espelage, D. L., & Pigott, T. D. (2012). A meta-analysis of school-based bullying prevention programs' effects on bystander intervention behavior. *School Psychology Review*, *41*(1), 47–65.

Powell, A., Henry, N., & Flynn, A. (2018). Image-based sexual abuse. In W. S. DeKeseredy & M. Dragiewicz (Eds.), *Routledge handbook of critical criminology*. (2nd ed., pp. 305–315). Abingdon and New York, NY: Routledge.

Powell, A., Scott, A. J., Henry, N., & Flynn, A. (2020). *Image-based sexual abuse: An international study of victims and perpetrators. Summary report*. Melbourne, VIC: RMIT University.

Pöyhönen, V., Juvonen, J., & Salmivalli, C. (2012). Standing up for the victim, siding with the bully or standing by? Bystander responses in bullying situations. *Social Development*, *21*, 722–741.

Retter, C., & Shariff, S. (2012). A delicate balance: Defining the line between open civil proceedings and the protection of children in the online digital era. *Canadian Journal of Law and Technology*, *10*(2), 232–262.

Rutkowski, G. K., Gruder, C. L., & Romer, D. (1983). Group cohesiveness, social norms, and bystander intervention. *Journal of Personality and Social Psychology*, *44*(3), 545–552.

Schachter, H. L., Greenberg, S., & Juvonen, J. (2016). Who's to blame? The effects of victim disclosure on bystander reactions to cyberbullying. *Computers in Human Behavior*, *57*, 115–121.

Shariff, S., & DeMartini, A. (2016). Cyberbullying and rape culture in universities: Defining the legal lines between fun and intentional harm. In H. Cowie & C.-A. Myers (Eds.), *Bullying among university students: Cross-national perspectives* (pp. 172–190). New York, NY: Routledge.

Shariff, S., Wiseman, A., & Crestohl, L. (2012). Defining the lines between children's vulnerability to cyberbullying and the open court principle: Implications of A.B. v. Bragg. *Communications Inc. Education and Law Journal*, *21*(3), 231–262.

Smith, P. K., Mahdavi, J., Carvalho, M., Fisher, S., Russell, S., & Tippett, N. (2008). Cyberbullying: Its nature and impact in secondary school pupils. *Child Psychology and Psychiatry*, *49*(4), 376–385.

Southworth, C., Finn, J., Dawson, S., Fraser, C., & Tucker, S. (2007). Intimate partner violence, technology, and stalking. *Violence Against Women*, *13*, 842–856.

Sticca, F., & Perren, S. (2013). Is cyberbullying worse than traditional bullying? Examining the differential roles of medium, publicity, and anonymity for the perceived severity of bullying. *Journal of Youth and Adolescence*, *42*, 739–750.

Sullivan, E. M., Annest, J. L., Simon, T. R., Luo, F., & Dahlberg, L. L. (2015). Suicide trends among persons aged 10-24 years United States, 1994-2012. *Centers for Disease Control and Prevention*, *64*(8), 201–205.

Tennant, J. E., Demaray, M. K., Coyle, S., & Malecki, C. K. (2015). The dangers of the web: Cybervictimization, depression, and social support in college students. *Computers in Human Behavior*, *50*, 348–357.

Ting, L., Jacobson, J. M., & Sanders, S. (2011). Current levels of perceived stress among mental health social workers who work with suicidal clients. *Social Work*, *56*(4), 327–336.

Walker, K., & Sleath, E. (2017). A systematic review of the current knowledge regarding revenge pornography and non-consensual sharing of sexually explicit media. *Aggression and Violent Behavior*, *36*, 9–24.

Widgerson, S., & Lynch, M. (2013). Cyber- and traditional peer victimization: Unique relationships with adolescent well-being. *Psychology of Violence*, *3*(4), 297–309.

Woodlock, D. (2017). The abuse of technology in domestic violence and stalking. *Violence Against Women*, *23*, 584–602.

Wooten, S. C. (2017). Revealing a hidden curriculum of Black women's erasure in sexual violence prevention policy. *Gender and Education*, *29*(3), 405–417.

Wright, M. F. (2016). Cyber victimization on college campuses: Longitudinal associations with suicidal ideation, depression, and anxiety. *Criminal Justice Review*, *41*(2), 190–203.

Chapter 42

"I Need You All to Understand How Pervasive This Issue Is": User Efforts to Regulate Child Sexual Offending on Social Media

Michael Salter and Elly Hanson

Abstract

This chapter examines the phenomenon of internet users attempting to report and prevent online child sexual exploitation (CSE) and child sexual abuse material (CSAM) in the absence of adequate intervention by internet service providers, social media platforms, and government. The chapter discusses the history of online CSE, focusing on regulatory stances over time in which online risks to children have been cast as natural and inevitable by the hegemony of a "cyberlibertarian" ideology. We illustrate the success of this ideology, as well as its profound contradictions and ethical failures, by presenting key examples in which internet users have taken decisive action to prevent online CSE and promote the removal of CSAM. Rejecting simplistic characterizations of "vigilante justice," we argue instead that the fact that often young internet users report feeling forced to act against online CSE and CSAM undercuts libertarian claims that internet regulation is impossible, unworkable, and unwanted. Recent shifts toward a more progressive ethos of online harm minimization are promising; however, this ethos risks offering a new legitimizing ideology for online business models that will continue to put children at risk of abuse and exploitation. In conclusion, we suggest ways forward toward an internet built in the interests of children, rather than profit.

The Emerald International Handbook of Technology Facilitated Violence and Abuse, 729–748

doi:10.1108/978-1-83982-848-520211053

Keywords: Sexual abuse; social media; children; sexual exploitation; image-based abuse; justice; self-help

Introduction

The title of this chapter comes from a tweet made by Twitter user @AvriSapir (a pseudonym) on May 1, 2020,[1] in which she describes her efforts to have videos of her own child sexual abuse removed from Twitter. In this chapter, we examine the phenomenon of internet users attempting to report and prevent online child sexual exploitation (CSE) and child sexual abuse material (CSAM) in the absence of adequate intervention by internet service providers, social media platforms, and government. With reports of online CSAM to US authorities increasing by 50% per year for the past 20 years (Bursztein et al., 2019), it is now undeniable that the structure, administration, and regulation of online services and infrastructure have created a highly enabling environment for online CSE. We discuss the history of online CSE, focusing on regulatory stances over time in which online risks to children have been cast as natural and inevitable by the hegemony of a cyberlibertarian ideology that posits a factual and normative order in which it is not only impossible to regulate the internet but where such regulation is inherently authoritarian and unethical (Hanson, 2019). We illustrate the success of this ideology, as well as its profound contradictions and ethical failures, by presenting key examples in which internet users have taken decisive action to prevent online CSE and promote the removal of CSAM. Rejecting simplistic characterizations of "vigilante justice," we argue instead that the fact that often young internet users feel compelled to act against online CSE and CSAM (CBC News, 2018; Pauls & MacIntosh, 2020) undercuts libertarian claims that internet regulation is impossible, unworkable, and unwanted. The chapter argues that scholars of online abuse and policymakers need to pay closer attention to the ways in which exploitative modes of technological design and administration and government inaction have been mystified by cyberlibertarianism and contributed to the contemporary crisis of CSE and CSAM. Recent shifts toward a more progressive ethos of online harm minimization are promising; however, this ethos risks offering a new legitimizing ideology for online business models that will continue to put children at risk of abuse and exploitation. In conclusion, we suggest ways forward toward an internet built in the interests of children, rather than profit.

The History of Online Child Sexual Exploitation

While technology companies have been vocal in their commitment to child protection, the history of online CSE shows that industry has been largely unwilling to prioritize child safety over profits, a posture that has been accepted and, arguably, tacitly endorsed by governments. The authenticity of industry and government expressions of surprise at escalating reports of online CSE and CSAM is undermined by evidence that the use of the internet by pedophiles has been known at the highest levels since the early days of networked computing. In 1986, the US Attorney General noted that the trade in CSAM had shifted online: "recently a significant amount of the exchange has taken place by the use of computer networks through which users of child pornography let each other know about materials they desire or have available" (US Attorney General, 1986, p. 407). Nonetheless, the approach of US legislators to internet regulation has been notoriously lax and oriented toward the growth and profitability of technology companies rather than child protection. This approach is exemplified in the passage of the *Communications Decency Act* (CDA) in 1996, a pivotal moment in the development of the modern internet. Section 230 of the CDA effectively immunized online service providers against legal liability for the content uploaded or provided by their users, paving the way for an internet whose consumer appeal and business model was based on the frictionless circulation of user's preferred content. The alignment of US legislators with the financial interests of the technology sector has created a powerful bloc that has dominated internet governance for a quarter of a century (Carr, 2015).

A pervasive cyberlibertarianism played a major role in legitimizing an anti-regulation ethos within industry and government despite recognition of the likely costs to children. Hanson (2019) defines libertarianism as a "distinct political stance and moral psychology whose guiding principle is the freedom of individuals, in particular from interference by the state" (p. 4), where concern for individual liberty from control and regulation is prioritized over altruistic moral values and responsibility to others. Libertarianism and new technologies emerged from the sociopolitical foment of the 1960s and 1970s as strange but intimate bedfellows and played a formative role in the culture and practices of Silicon Valley. From the 1970s, influential American counterculturalists came to believe that networked technology was the ideal instrument for personal liberation and alternative community building (Turner, 2010). They drew in particular on the libertarian rather than socialist and collectivist strains of the counterculture in ways that framed the developing internet as a transgressive, anarchist space, a new frontier full of possibilities and free of legal regulation. This characterization has been amplified in influential fictional and futurist portrayals of the internet as a parallel disembodied universe or "cyberspace" (Salter, 2017). As the internet and technology industries have taken center stage as global corporate behemoths, their marketing has enthusiastically adopted a countercultural style and promoted the view that their products are conducive to personal and collective freedoms. This view and its encompassing anarchist mystique have been prominent in media coverage and academic analysis of new technologies, promoting an idealized view of the lawlessness of the internet as both antiauthoritarian and radically democratic, despite it being anything but (Dahlberg, 2010). As the following section makes clear, cyberlibertarianism has mystified the monopolistic capture of online technologies by select corporate giants whose platforms closely regulate and manipulate user behavior (Zuboff, 2019, p. 109).

By the late 1990s, it was evident that CSAM and CSE were expanding online at an exponential rate. The prevalence and severity of this material was such that even skeptics such as sociologist Philip Jenkins, whose prior research had argued that community concern over child sexual abuse was characterized by "moral panic" and overreaction, would declare CSAM an escalating and intolerable crisis (Jenkins, 2001). In 2002, as investigations into and prosecutions of CSAM in the United States underscored the seriousness of the problem, then-US Attorney General John Ashcroft held a meeting with the major technology companies calling them to action. In response, they formed an industry body called the Technology Coalition with the stated mission of "eradicating online child sexual exploitation" (Farid, 2017, para. 9). For 5 years, the Technology Coalition did not develop or deploy any effective technological solutions against the spread of CSAM. The Technology Coalition served instead to signal the concerns of technology companies to government and the public in the absence of measurable action or impact.[2] It was during this period of industry abeyance that major social media platforms were established and became the dominant players online. On social media, profit maximization depends on recruiting as many users as possible to circulate content and engage with each other as much as possible; whether this content and engagement is abusive or not does not impact the bottom line. Accordingly, social media platforms have a poor track record of addressing the specific needs and vulnerabilities of children or inhibiting sexual misconduct and coercion.

Social media platforms have sought to elide their responsibilities to users by describing their platforms as neutral, apolitical "facilities," comparable to the water system or electricity grid (Salter, 2017). In this model, the risk of online CSE and the availability of CSAM are positioned as a natural artifact beyond the control of any company or government. It was only in 2008 that Microsoft partnered with Professor Hany Farid to develop PhotoDNA technology, which enables the automatic matching of images against a database of known CSAM (Farid, 2017). This technology was then provided for free to appropriate organizations in order to identify and remove known CSAM. PhotoDNA technology is widely recognized as a major turning point in the fight against CSAM, and the determining factor in the dramatic numbers of CSAM currently being notified to US authorities. PhotoDNA made it possible, for the first time, to screen all images uploaded by users to ensure they were not sharing known CSAM. Nonetheless, it took large companies such as Google as long as five years before they were willing to implement PhotoDNA on their services (Farid, 2017). Furthermore, there has been a lack of significant industry investment in the further development and deployment of the technology. For example, PhotoDNA cannot detect new images of CSAM, nor can it scan video files; a significant drawback as reports of video CSAM are now more common than images (Dance & Keller, 2020). While a new tool, PhotoDNA for Video, was developed around 2018, the extent of its use across the sector is unclear.

In 2018, both Google and Facebook launched technology designed to detect new CSAM images – this is a positive step forward although they still require screening by a human moderator, which is necessarily an expensive proposition for platforms and comes with significant risk of harm and trauma to content moderation teams (Gillespie, 2018).[3] The cost of underinvestment in human moderation is exemplified in the history of Tumblr, the social media platform and blogging site. In November 2018, the Tumblr app was removed from major online stores, effectively preventing new users from joining the platform. It subsequently emerged that the Tumblr app was removed due to the presence of CSAM on the platform (BBC News, 2018). While Tumblr used PhotoDNA to prevent the uploading of known CSAM to the site, an audit of Tumblr content identified that the platform was being used to circulate *new* CSAM that is undetectable to PhotoDNA (Silverstein, 2018). Such material can only be identified through human moderation. In December 2018, Tumblr announced that it was banning all pornographic content from the site, using an algorithm trained to automatically detect and delete photos with nudity (Liao, 2018). Users complained that the algorithm was producing a high level of false positives, with cartoons, dinosaur images, and even pictures of food wrongly flagged as "sensitive" content (Leskin, 2019). Within a year of the ban, Tumblr's unique monthly visitors decreased by more than 20%, and the site was sold in August 2019 for reportedly less than US$3 million, compared to its US$1.1 billion price tag in 2013 (Leskin, 2019).

Some nongovernment organizations have been able to integrate PhotoDNA into highly effective software platforms that proactively detect CSAM and request removal,[4] and other technological developments will make it easier to identify offenders and victims from images. However, these efforts are typically driven by civil society rather than industry. Meanwhile, the public condemnations of online abuse by industry figures too often segue into calls for more parental responsibility and internet safety programs for children, which effectively devolve responsibility for child safety to parents, schools, and children. Necessarily, these strategies are most effective at reaching the least at-risk children, that is, the children with engaged parents who are regularly attending school. Research has consistently shown that the children who are most at risk of online abuse are those who are already vulnerable offline due to disadvantage and prior experiences of abuse and neglect (Jones, Mitchell, & Finkelhor, 2013). Furthermore, a significant proportion of CSAM is, in fact, created by parents and other family members; an inconvenient fact that has been consistently sidestepped by industry and government authorities for decades despite the cumulative evidence (Itzin, 2001; Salter, 2013; Seto, Buckman, Dwyer, & Quayle, 2018). The focus of industry and other voices on "educating" children and parents neglects the children who are most likely to be abused, while deflecting attention from those features of internet services that put children at risk and occluding corporate responsibility for the harms that are facilitated by their online products. Furthermore, this selective focus on education, with its frequent emphasis on the importance of children "keeping themselves safe online," works to blame those who have been victimized (or go on to be) and reinforces the impact and messages of the abuse (Hamilton-Giachritsis, Hanson, Whittle, & Beech, 2017, p. 33). Nonetheless, these strategies remain consistent with the industry's preferred cyberlibertarian approach to CSE with a focus on individual risk and responsibility, even where those individuals are children. This approach is part of a broader rhetorical campaign aimed at responsibilization of targets of many other forms of technology-facilitated violence and abuse (see Henry and Witt, this volume; Marganski and Melander, this volume).

User Regulation of Child Sexual Exploitation on Social Media Platforms

The inevitable result of 30 years of deferring responsibility for online CSAM and CSE has been that, in 2018–2019, US authorities received 70 million reports of suspected CSAM (Dance & Keller, 2020). As of 2018, there was a backlog of millions of suspected CSAM images and videos in need of assessment while police reported being overwhelmed by the increase in cases and the increased volume and severity of CSAM in each case (ECPAT, 2018), and given reported increases in online CSE activity during the pandemic (INTERPOL, 2020) that backlog may well have expanded. While tech and social media companies accumulate billions in profits, CSAM victims and survivors report an almost total lack of access to affordable, effective mental health care or practical assistance with the ongoing impacts of abuse (C3P, 2017; Salter, 2013). As the scale of the crisis has become undeniable, governments are now shifting to a more interventionist posture (see also Henry and Witt, this volume). For example, the UK government has begun developing a legislative regime around "online harms" that aims to hold technology companies directly responsible for social and individual impacts (HM Government, 2019). This move initiated the global drafting and endorsement of a global set of "voluntary principles" to prevent online CSE for industry implementation as a precursor to formal government regulation.[5] In 2018, the United States enacted the Fight Online Sex Trafficking Act (FOSTA, 2017) which removed internet companies' Section 230 protections from liability if they are found to knowingly facilitate sex trafficking, and there is now a further bipartisan proposal to remove these protections from those deemed to be failing to act on online CSE and CSAM (Keller, 2020). Meanwhile, governments such as Australia have been encouraged to move away from a "coregulation" model with industry in recognition of industry failure to comply with internet safety principles (Briggs, 2018). This shift in the tone and approach of governments to the technology industry is also evident in academic scholarship. Over the last 10 years, celebratory academic accounts of the new possibilities of the internet and globalization have given way to more pessimistic assessments of the impact of the internet on inequality, cultural homogenization, and democratic legitimacy. This so-called "techlash" is now interrogating the monopoly power of the technology industries and their role in violating consumer privacy and circulating (and arguably promoting) malicious, deceptive, and illegal content (Hemphill, 2019).

The "techlash" has come to encompass the issue of online CSE as an urgent priority. We are at a critical juncture where the cyberlibertarian posture of industry is being challenged rather than endorsed by governments, some technology companies are themselves asking to be regulated (Bloomberg, 2020), and the prevalence of online CSE and CSAM is such that it has become visible to everyday social media users. No longer the province of secret subcultures, CSAM is prevalent on social media sites, file sharing networks, and free adult pornography "streaming" services (Solon, 2020). The fact that these same sites and services do not have adequate measures in place to prevent CSAM circulation (notwithstanding statements of zero tolerance for CSAM) has never been more evident, leading to increasing expressions of concern about lack of accountability and transparency (Pauls & MacIntosh, 2020) and a rapidly changing policy environment, at both industry and government levels.[6] To illustrate the hypocrisies and contradictions of this historical moment, this section describes the efforts of social media and internet users to police CSAM and CSE on their platforms. In doing so, this section reveals two key facts. First, there are amoral consequences arising from cyberlibertarianism, in which corporate and government responsibility for the prevention of CSE and CSAM has been deferred to the point where internet users themselves are performing this basic civic function. Perhaps the most shocking illustration of this regulatory vacuum is that self-identified CSAM survivors, some only teenagers, are themselves active in seeking out and reporting images and video of their abuse, despite the psychological and legal risks this may entail (C3P, 2020a, pp. 4–5; CBC, 2018; Pauls & MacIntosh, 2020). Second, the section undercuts claims by some in the technology industry, certain privacy advocates, and some in government that the proactive detection of CSAM is difficult or impossible from a practical standpoint. The fact that self-organizing networks of social media users and researchers have (sometimes accidently) identified and interrupted the tactics of online abusers, as indicated in the examples below, suggests that the problem of CSE and CSAM regulation has been at least partially one of political and corporate will.

There are multiple examples in which the efforts of users, rather than platforms, have been efficacious in identifying and publicizing the ways in which CSE is taking place on various services. Frequently, these efforts expose not only the presence and activities of child sexual abusers online but also the shortcomings of platform design that facilitate CSE and make reporting difficult. For example, YouTube is the popular online site in which users can make and upload their own video content. Despite stated policies against child abuse and exploitation, users have uploaded videos to YouTube of children in revealing clothing, and children restrained with ropes, sometimes crying or in distress. Some videos have remained online for years and accumulated millions of views before being removed, only after media reporting and public outcry (Warzel, 2017). In February 2019, YouTube user Matt Watson (who later faced criticism for his tactics and for content that he himself had posted (Alexander, 2019)) uploaded a viral video to YouTube documenting the way in which the YouTube "recommend" system – the machine learning process that automatically suggests and curates videos for users – was linking together self-created videos of young children engaged in activities such as dancing, doing gymnastics, and swimming (Orphanides, 2019).[7] Once YouTube detected a user preferentially seeking out and watching content of young children, the "recommend" system would then generate a playlist of similar content. In doing so, the algorithm was proactively curating videos of scantily clad children for those users who particularly enjoyed such content, that is, pedophiles (Kaiser & Rauchfleisch, 2019; Orphanides, 2019).

In the same month, *WIRED* reported finding videos on YouTube relating to similar kinds of images with high numbers of views and comments seeming to show pedophiles using the "comment" function of YouTube to provide time stamps for parts of the videos where the child may inadvertently expose body parts, posting links to other provocative YouTube videos of children, or exchanging contact details with one another (Orphanides, 2019). *WIRED* reported that these videos had been monetized by YouTube, including preroll and banner advertisements (Orphanides, 2019). After all, the videos themselves were not illegal content; rather, it was the recontextualization of those videos by the YouTube recommend system that generated what Matt Watson[8] called a "soft-core pedophile ring" on the platform (Alexander, 2019). YouTube's initial response to the scandal was to delete accounts and channels of those leaving disturbing comments, report illegal conduct to police, turn off the "comment" function on many videos depicting minors and delete inappropriate comments, while employing an automated comment classifier to detect inappropriate comments with greater speed and accuracy (Wakabayashi & Maheshwari, 2019; see also; YouTube, 2019).

In June 2019, *The New York Times* reported that three researchers from Harvard's Berkman Klein Center for Internet and Society had "stumbled upon" a similar issue while doing research about another topic on YouTube (Fisher & Taub, 2019). In all of these cases, action was seemingly only undertaken in the aftermath of significant reputation damage and the advertiser boycotts that followed the reports (Fisher & Taub, 2019). A critical point here is that this disturbing situation is a direct, though unintended, result of business models like YouTube's which seek to maximize profit by keeping users consuming online content in order to sell ads (Maack, 2019). In order to keep people consuming content, YouTube's algorithmic curation of user preference "promotes, recommends, and disseminates videos in a manner that appears to constantly up the stakes" (Tufekci, 2018, para. 6). Some have characterized this as a "rabbit hole effect" that can sometimes "lead viewers to incrementally more extreme videos or topics which are thought to hook them in" (Fisher & Taub, 2019). YouTube's 2020 Transparency Report provides an update on policies relating to child safety (YouTube, 2020).

TikTok is the hugely popular music-based social media platform with a particular focus on teenage users. While TikTok states that users under the age of 13 are not permitted to use the platform, the app's age verification system can be bypassed by entering a false birthdate (Common Sense Media, 2021). TikTok provides short clips of popular music for users to video themselves miming and dancing to. As a result, the platform features videos of children performing to sexually suggestive or explicit songs. TikTok's default privacy settings had been criticized for being low, with many child users not adjusting these settings to make their accounts private or disallow contact from strangers (Broderick, 2019). As was pointed out, the platform's inherent incentives discourage increased privacy settings which would reduce the number of views and interactions with user content (BBC News, 2020). Journalists have identified an active community of TikTok users who appear to be soliciting nude images from children, while minor users are complaining about repeated solicitation for sexualized images (BBC News, 2020; Cox, 2018). As of 2018, some TikTok user profiles reportedly included open statements of interest in nude images and the exchange of sexual videos, including invitations to trade material via other apps (Cox, 2018). The presence of sex offenders on the app is further evident by reported instances of sexual comments left by men on videos of children (BBC News, 2020; Broderick, 2019). In response, networks of young users have been collecting those usernames who they accuse of sexual misconduct and sharing that information across social media platforms with the aim of shaming offenders and promoting safety on TikTok (Broderick, 2019). Concerned TikTok users have set up social media accounts that focus specifically on "creepy" TikTok interactions, and specific alleged offenders on TikTok have been widely discussed by users on various forums, alongside reports of lax or no response from TikTok to user reports and concerns (BBC News, 2020; Broderick, 2019). The fact that TikTok users are resorting to the self-policing of pedophile activity on the platform raises significant concern about the level of proactive regulation and monitoring of users who seek to engage in the sexual exploitation of children; however, at present, social media platforms are not obliged to publicly report their child protection standards and processes. In 2021, following considerable public pressure, TikTok amended its policies relating to users under 18, which included a change, so that the default setting for accounts created by users aged 13–15 is automatically set to "private" (Peters, 2021).

In 2020, TikTok removed an Australian account that was purporting to "hunt" pedophiles on social media by posing as children and luring men into meetings, which were then filmed (Taylor, 2020). This account was part of a broader pattern of online vigilantes who seek to entrap child sexual abusers by posing as children on social media. This phenomenon has been met with a mixed reception. Australian police have urged people with concerns about online abuse to report to law enforcement (Taylor, 2020) and so have UK police; nonetheless, research by the BBC found that over half of UK prosecutions for grooming in 2018 drew on evidence gathered by online vigilante groups (BBC, 2019). Previous dismissive accounts of online vigilantism have given way to more nuanced analyses of civilian efforts to prevent internet sexual offending, which situate the so-called "pedophile hunting" within an increase in "citizen-led, digitally mediated security initiatives" operating alongside, and often with the cooperation, if not endorsement, of state police and the private sector (Hadjimatheou, 2019, p. 2).

"Pedophile hunting" refers to the proactive luring and entrapment of suspected child abusers using social media (Hadjimatheou, 2019). In the cases described above, social media users are not seeking out sex offenders; they are not "vigilantes" in any meaningful sense. Instead, they are users who are reacting to the ubiquity of sexual misconduct and offending on popularly used platforms, and they are taking action in an attempt to improve their own and others' safety. Unlike "vigilante" groups, who frequently seek police intervention for suspected online misconduct, this form of social media activity tends to rely on social media platforms to take action, and in the absence of a response from platforms, they may seek publicity via online media and mass media. In effect, these users are reacting to the failure of content regulation of which online abuse and exploitation is a symptom, and they are seeking to institute their own mechanisms of regulation where platforms and the state have failed.

In recent years, there has been significant debate over the status of pedophiles and the regulation of CSAM on social media platform Twitter (Gorman, 2020). Twitter is a major social media platform that was launched in 2006 and grew to 330 million monthly active users and 145 million daily users in 2019.[9] Unlike platforms such as Facebook, which aim to connect users with their friends and family, Twitter is famous for its "town hall" approach, in which users "tweet" short public messages which can be commented on by any other user. This focus on interaction between strangers has lent the platform a somewhat alienating and combative online culture that has inhibited its growth. However, it remains one of the most influential platforms among journalists, academics, and policymakers. Twitter is also one of the most libertarian of all social media platforms and was notoriously described as the "free speech wing of the free speech party" by a senior executive in 2012 (Halliday, 2012, para. 1). This enthusiasm for an online "free for all" on Twitter has been tempered over the last decade by the emergence of organized misogyny and far right groups on the platform, and a high prevalence of hate speech, which has directly impacted Twitter's reputation, share price, and investor appeal (Salter, 2018). Twitter has made a number of concessions to its critics, including providing users with more options to limit abuse online.

In a dramatic development, a group of self-identified survivors of CSAM took to Twitter to claim that videos and images of their abuse were circulating on the platform. The most prominent of these survivors is "Avri Sapir" (a pseudonym), who stated on Twitter that she is a teenaged woman who was abused and exploited in CSAM from infancy until the age of 15 (Gorman, 2020).[10] Avri joined Twitter in October 2018 and became increasingly vocal about the presence of her own CSAM on Twitter from early 2020. Along with a group of supportive users, Avri actively sought to police CSAM on the site by identifying and reporting accounts sharing illegal content to Twitter and US authorities. As a self-identified CSAM survivor, Avri received significant abuse and harassment. In a number of "viral" tweets, Avri has provided screenshots of messages she has received on Twitter from CSAM offenders.[11] These include messages from men claiming that they have previously watched her material, and, in one case, a user who described her daily activities in a fashion that indicated he had been following her. She has also provided screenshots of messages from Twitter users asking for links to her abuse material. On February 27, 2020, she stated:

> I have to live with the knowledge that my abuse will never end, and that every second of every day, someone could be – almost certainly is – watching my torture and abuse. Even once I'm dead, my degradation will continue. I will never be able to escape it. This trauma is infinite.
>
> Child porn is not a victimless crime, and it is the worst form of torture a person can be forced to endure. We must wake up to the

> realities of this pervasive and wide-spread abuse, and push past the discomfort of the topic, because I don't have that privilege. We must hold accountable the people, companies, policies, laws, and cultural beliefs that allow this type of abuse to continue and thrive. We must listen to and defend survivors and put an end to the gaslighting, victim-blaming, and excuses that allow this issue to be ignored.[12]

As Avri's prominence on Twitter grew, she began intersecting with and amplifying existing accounts who identified themselves as "antipedophile"; that is, they proactively sought out and reported CSAM and CSE accounts on Twitter to the platform, as well as to authorities such as the National Center for Missing and Exploited Children.[13] A recent report analyzing CSAM reporting options on popular Web platforms concluded that it is "extremely difficult to report content as CSAM on Twitter" (C3P, 2020b, p. 15). When a user encounters a problematic tweet, Twitter offers four categories of "report" options, including that a tweet is "abusive or harmful." However, subsequent options do not allow users to report CSAM. Instead, users have to search to find a separate online form in order to bring CSAM or a CSE issue to the attention of Twitter moderators.[14] One of the key functions of antipedophile Twitter is to increase awareness of this form and encourage followers to mass report identified CSAM abusers. Faced with the significant concerns raised not only by users but also by agencies such as the Internet Watch Foundation (Wright, 2019) and C3P (2020b) regarding CSAM on the site, Twitter's communications team has stated that "Twitter has zero tolerance for any material that features or promotes child sexual exploitation" (de Gallier, 2020, para. 8).

In October 2020, in the face of sustained pressure (Dodds, 2020), Twitter published a significant revision of its CSE policy that explicitly disallowed efforts to normalize or promote pedophilia as a sexual orientation or identity on the platform. The new policy provided expanded detail on the forms of abusive and exploitative behavior that would be considered a breach of terms of service, including the circulation of drawn or computer-generated abuse images and the sharing of links to abuse material (Twitter, 2020). While this is a positive development, the policy contains no information on resourcing or enforcement. As yet, there are no rigorous reporting and transparency requirements that would oblige Twitter to publicly account for their CSAM problem and proposed solutions.

A recent civil suit against Twitter describes another user who, as a young person, struggled to have his abuse material removed from the platform. In the suit, the now 17-year-old complainant alleges that Twitter failed to remove abuse videos of him as a 13 year old boy after he repeatedly notified them of the content. The suit alleges that Twitter only removed the content, five weeks after the first report, once it was escalated by law enforcement (Fonrouge, 2021). It appears that, in the absence of adequate efforts from Twitter, CSAM regulation has become the province of users and, in some cases, victims and survivors themselves. As they identify and report CSAM on Twitter and elsewhere, Avri and other antiabuse activists expose themselves to significant trauma and other risks:

vitriol and attacks from pedophiles and other users on the site, as well as exposure to sexually abusive imagery that carries with it a high likelihood of traumatization. From late 2020, Avri became the subject of a concerted online campaign which attempted to attack her credibility in various ways, including the claim that her narrative had been invented as part of a religiously motivated "antipornography" campaign. This claim was advanced despite Avri's public statements in support of sex workers, in which she made clear distinctions between CSAM and consensual adult content.[15] However, as momentum for online regulation and harm reduction builds apace, due in part to an increasingly vocal CSAM survivor contingent, it is triggering backlash by libertarian activists and coalitions for whom a regulated internet is a censorious one.

Analysis and Reflection

The rhetoric of cyberlibertarianism has powerfully shaped the landscape of the internet, justifying the regulatory stance of technology companies and states in which corporate discretion has been prioritized over user safety. This strategy owes its success to a confluence of factors including the correspondence and mutually reinforcing relationship between cyberlibertarianism and entrenched free-market neoliberalism as well as with some forms of "progressive" identity politics, in which the online proliferation of sexual freedom and self-expression is considered a *prima facie* public good. Nagle (2017) observes the naivete of optimistic academic and media accounts of online transgression as politically emancipatory, pointing to the deeply amoral and nihilistic strains of internet culture that have been facilitated by cyberlibertarianism. However, the catastrophic consequences of cyberlibertarianism for children have been obscured by its often self-interested narration as a bearer of straightforward "goods" such as "freedom of speech," "connection," and "opportunity," and effective use of vagaries and platitudes to hide its contradictions and distasteful aspects. The cyberlibertarian narrative of maximal online freedom with minimal state regulation does not, and cannot, accommodate the categorical differences in vulnerability between children and adults, the moral prerogatives of child protection, or children's internationally recognized and acclaimed human rights. Hence, children, similar to other groups socially marginalized by racism, sexism, homophobia, and other oppressions, are simply *not taken into account* by cyberlibertarianism. During the formative decades of the internet, the core principle of cyberlibertarianism was that it is, by default, the right thing to maximize "online freedom," defined as "freedom from interference" for corporations and individuals alike. The myopic focus on maximal freedom from regulation and oversight was an appealing alternative to the demanding and messy work of adjudicating a plurality of competing interests and even competing freedoms, all of which need to be carefully considered and weighted to achieve a fair and transparent system in which the most egregious harms are prevented.

Few would deny that CSAM survivors' rights to privacy and dignity are violated where images of their abuse are shared online, or where the men who have viewed those images stalk and harass them. However, their assertion of their right to privacy *from other social media users* and *criminal abusers* is considerably broader than the narrow formulation championed by cyberlibertarians, understood solely in terms of freedom from interference from the state. Having lost faith in the willingness of social media platforms to protect them, CSAM survivors and other users instead publicly "name and shame" the platforms who host images and videos of their abuse. They seek external intervention in order to secure their privacy and other basic human rights from the Web 2.0 business model in which abusive and illegal content circulates with de facto impunity. Civil and cyberlibertarians have responded to the prospect of increased state intervention in social media and online content by pointing to the (very real) potential for state and police overreach in the name of child protection; however, they are persistently unwilling or unable to take into account the broader claims to privacy asserted by self-identified CSAM survivors like Avri and others like her. Indeed, the narrow formulation of "online privacy" advanced under cyberlibertarianism continues to justify measures that are in direct conflict with the rights and interests of CSAM victims and survivors. For example, Facebook and Twitter are currently seeking to implement end-to-end encryption on their messenger functions, which would necessarily facilitate CSAM distribution and protect CSAM offenders. It is estimated that Facebook's encryption plans would reduce reports of online CSE in the United States by two-thirds (Valentino-DeVries & Dance, 2019) and reduce arrests for online CSE in the United Kingdom by up to 2,500 per year (Murgia, 2019). Despite ongoing and high-level resistance to Facebook's plans, due to their serious implications for global child protection efforts, Twitter's Head of Product Kayvon Beykpour has stated emphatically that Twitter is also seeking to encrypt its Direct Message (DM) function (Marino, 2019). In this example, the libertarian formulation of privacy in terms of the capability of users to share content (including CSAM) without consequence is prioritized by technology companies over the human rights of CSAM survivors to privacy, dignity, and safety. By (either explicitly or implicitly) adopting the cyberlibertarian narrative, industry, governments, and individuals have effectively given themselves license to see online harms, including child abuse and exploitation, as inevitable "necessary evils" that should be tolerated or ignored given the necessity of "online freedom." This position dovetails with the general societal discomfort with anti-CSAM activists like Avri name, enabling people to remain within their comfort zone, not seeing or recognizing what should be shocking and attention-grabbing levels of child abuse. While the need for greater regulation has been recognized by some governments and other principles for the online environment are now being delineated and asserted, progress, where it happens, is slow (particularly in contrast to the fast speed of innovation for profit), and decisions continue to be made by corporations and states that flow from cyberlibertarianism's fundamentally unethical premises. For example, some technology companies choose not to screen for known CSAM, arguing that this would constitute an invasion of privacy (IICSA, 2020, p. 48), despite their very business model being based around surveillance and the invasion of privacy (Zuboff, 2019). Hypocrite and contradiction loom large, yet are hidden through sleights of hand

and platitudes that remain largely unchallenged. While governments and their inquiries have started to ask pressing questions about the persistent and growing problem of online child abuse, regulation is still seen as a last resort, a regrettable alternative to the supposedly higher plane of "collaboration" with industry. Too often the questions asked are not ambitious enough, they work within, rather than identify and challenge, the overarching cyberlibertarian construction of "online freedom," without critically examining whose "freedom" it is that we are talking about. One consequence of all of this is a situation in which mainstream platforms are beset with CSAM, and users, too often children and/or survivors, are those tasked with its identification and attempts at its removal.

As noted, reports indicating that survivors and other internet users are frequently finding and taking action against CSAM, grooming, and other online pedophilic activity challenges the notions that regulation is unwarranted, unwanted, or unworkable – as well as the alternative argument that adequate safeguards are already in place. While the determination and resourcefulness of these individuals is to be applauded, their efforts should never have been necessary, and the fact that they are points to a deeply troubling state of affairs. The role they are compelled to undertake in the absence of corporate and government action carries numerous personal costs and risks. There is the traumatizing impact of exposure to illegal material, including, in some cases, images of their own abuse, alongside the legal risks involved in following the pathways to it. There is also the risk that speaking out leads to harassment and further abuse of oneself or others, and in particular for survivors, there can be the distressing impact of societal invalidation. Invalidation can be one of the hardest aspects of child sexual abuse to deal with: the message conveyed through the words and actions of the offender(s) that the child's self, agency, and feelings are unimportant (Salter, 2012). When technology companies fail to prevent survivors' CSAM circulating or fail to robustly act when it is brought to their attention (or in other ways fail to take a survivor's abuse seriously), the invalidating message of the original abuse is echoed by "the system." For some survivors, the impact of wider society falling in step with their abuser can be catastrophic, confirming deep-rooted fears about their lack of self-worth and effectively sending them into free fall. It can be the shattering of fragile hopes that the offender(s)' stance toward them did not reflect the truth.

Ways Forward

Continuing technological innovations designed to detect online child abuse, together with recent actions and positions taken by governments, are promising, while the hegemony of cyberlibertarianism has been destabilized and its self-serving rhetoric exposed by multiple colliding world events. Many of the supposed democratic benefits of social media and the internet have been found wanting, and cascading developments have corroded public trust in the technology industry, including the monopolization of the internet by a few mammoth companies, the manipulation of social media to spread disinformation and conspiracy theories, privacy breaches including the Cambridge Analytica scandal, and the use of social media as a surveillance tool by private sector, governments, and police. As conflicts between the public good and the private interests of the technology industries come into focus, civil society and some governments are starting to articulate new, more ethical paradigms of online freedoms that include a duty of care, children's rights, social justice, and an orientation toward human rather than capital ends. These paradigms move beyond libertarian scaremongering in which online privacy is an all-or-nothing proposition, either total freedom from regulation and censorship, or a Big Brother style panopticon of state censorship. Instead, a range of stakeholders are situating online harms within a critique of the ways in which online architecture and administration constitutes its own mode of regulation, albeit one designed for capital rather than public interests.

In many regards, these shifts can be tied toward wider moves toward "progressive capitalism" (Stiglitz, 2019) that seeks to reembed markets within government control and social responsibility. It is undoubtedly the case that a coherent, ethical, and accessible philosophical framework is a necessary basis from which to ask the right questions about online child safety and protection and then set about answering them, and this will surely lead to progress, although it is unclear whether notions of "progressive capitalism" ultimately are up to the task. For example, legislating a statutory "duty of care" may turn corporate attention toward the minimization of potential harms embedded in online services and products but does not directly address the cause of those harms. The current formulation of social media business models generates enabling conditions for abuse and exploitation, structuring user incentives in a way that creates competitive and often alienating hierarchies in an effort to maximize engagement and advertising revenue while harvesting user data (Salter, 2017). In other words, social media companies are invested in maintaining online environments that are conducive to abuse. There is a continuity between an increasingly outmoded cyberlibertarianism and the friendlier face of a "progressive capitalism," in that they both legitimize the exploitation of users (including children) in the interests of profit, albeit the former proposes that such exploitation is natural and inevitable, while the latter seeks to build in basic safeguards. It should, therefore, not be a surprise if sexual exploitation persists on platforms built for user exploitation, regardless of the stipulated corporate philosophy of the platform itself. A more fundamental question is: What would an internet built in the interests of children and other users look like? This is the truly ethical question we need to begin with, journey on from, and keep bringing ourselves back to.

Notes

1. The Twitter account of Avri Sapir remains limited to followers; however, this tweet was made on May 1st at 11.47 a.m. At the time of publication of this book, as with most tweets, no allegation made by Avri has been proven in court.
2. The Technology Coalition has recently announced a "Plan to Combat Online Child Abuse" that includes research and development funds for "technological tools" to prevent online child sexual exploitation (CSE) and the publication of an

annual progress report charting industry efforts, see https://www.technology-coalition.org/2020/05/28/a-plan-to-combat-online-child-sexual-abuse/.

3. Media reports indicate that reliance on human content moderators has been reduced in the context of COVID-19 (Dwoskin, 2020).
4. For example, see Project Arachnid (https://projectarachnid.ca/en/).
5. For example, see Five Country Ministerial. (n.d.). *Voluntary Principles to Counter Online Child Sexual Exploitation and Abuse*. Retrieved from https://static1.squarespace.com/static/5630f48de4b00a75476ecf0a/t/5e6123b6cfea6860596132af/1583424438930/11Voluntary1principles1-1one1page1-1Final.pdf.
6. While we have done our best to reflect changes in this rapidly evolving policy environment, the realities of publication mean that more recent changes may not be incorporated in this chapter.
7. See MattsWhatItIs. (2019, February 17). *Youtube is Facilitating the Sexual Exploitation of Children, and it's Being Monetized (2019)* [Video]. YouTube. Retrieved from https://www.youtube.com/watch?v5O13G5A5w5P0&t55s.
8. See MattsWhatItIs. (2019, February 17). *Youtube is Facilitating the Sexual Exploitation of Children, and it's Being Monetized (2019)* [Video]. YouTube. Retrieved from https://www.youtube.com/watch?v5O13G5A5w5P0&t55s.
9. For example, see Lin, Y. (2019, November 30). 10 Twitter Statistics Every Marketer Should Know in 2020 [Infographic] [Blog post]. Retrieved from https://www.oberlo.com/blog/twitter-statistics.
10. Some of the content of the following section is based on Twitter postings made on a public account @AvriSapir, which is private at the time of publication. Republication of these Twitter postings has been made with the consent of the owner of @AvriSapir.
11. Sapir, A. [@AvriSapir] (2020, 27 February 6.45 a.m.). "This is what it's like to be a survivor of child pornography that was commercially sold, traded, and shared all over the internet" [Tweet].
12. Sapir, A. [@AvriSapir] (2020, 27 February 6.45 a.m.).
13. For example, see this tweet in which Avri requests her followers to report a Twitter account allegedly sharing child sexual abuse material (CSAM) on the platform. Sapir, A. [@AvriSapr] (2020, April 25, 5.35 p.m.) "everyone do me a favor and report (redacted) using Twitter's CSE form do NOT scroll through the account, just report it please" [Tweet].
14. For example, see Twitter. (n.d.). *Report a child sexual exploitation issue* [Online form]. Retrieved from https://help.twitter.com/forms/cse.
15. For example, Avri has publicly objected to policy developments that she feels appropriate notions of "trafficking" to justify the banning of adult pornography or the harmful regulation of adult sex work. Sapir, A. [@AvriSapir] (2021, January 1, 55 a.m.). "If people actually listened to survivors, nonsense like SISEA wouldn't happen. They're not listening to survivors, because this isn't about trafficking – it's about banning pornography under the guise of victim protection. It's offensive" [Tweet].

References

Alexander, J. (2019, February 19). YouTube still can't stop child predators in its comments. *The Verge*. Retrieved from https://www.theverge.com/2019/2/19/18229938/youtube-child-exploitation-recommendation-algorithm-predators

BBC. (2018, November 20). Tumblr removed from Apple app store over abuse images. Retrieved from https://www.bbc.co.uk/news/technology-46275138

BBC. (2019, November 6). Police concerns over rise of 'paedophile hunters'. *BBC*. Retrieved from https://www.bbc.com/news/uk-england-50302912

BBC News. (2020, November 2). TikTok failed to ban flagged 'child predator'. *BBC News*. Retrieved from https://www.bbc.com/news/technology-54773257

Bloomberg. (2020, February 17). Facebook needs, wants, must have regulation, Zuckerberg says. *Los Angeles Times*. Retrieved from https://www.latimes.com/business/technology/story/2020-02-17/facebook-needs-regulation-zuckerberg

Briggs, L. (2018). *Report of the statutory review of the enhancing online safety act 2015 and the review of schedules 5 and 7 to the broadcasting services act 1992 (online content scheme)*. Canberra. Retrieved from https://www.communications.gov.au/publications/report-statutory-review-enhancing-onlinesafety-act-2015-and-review-schedules-5-and-7-broadcasting

Broderick, R. (2019, June 24). TikTok has a predator problem. A network of young women is fighting back. *Buzzfeed*. Retrieved from https://www.buzzfeednews.com/article/ryanhatesthis/tiktok-has-a-predator-problem-young-women-are-fighting-back

Bursztein, E., Clarke, E., DeLaune, M., Elifff, D. M., Hsu, N., Olson, L., … Bright, T. (2019, May 13–17). Rethinking the detection of child sexual abuse imagery on the internet. In Proceedings of the 2019 world wide web conference, WWW '19, San Francisco, CA.

C3P. (2017). *Survivor's survey preliminary report*. Winnipeg, MB: Canadian Centre for Child Protection.

C3P. (2020a). *How we are failing children: Changing the paradigm*. Winnipeg, MB: Canadian Centre for Child Protection. Retrieved from https://www.protectchildren.ca/en/resources-research/child-rights-framework/

C3P. (2020b). *Reviewing child sexual abuse material reporting functions on popular platforms*. Winnipeg, MB: Canadian Centre for Child Protection. Retrieved from https://www.protectchildren.ca/pdfs/C3P_ReviewingCSAMMaterialReporting_en.pdf

Carr, M. (2015). Power plays in global internet governance. *Millennium*, 43(2), 640–659.

CBC News. (2018, August 29). After their child sexual abuse was recorded and spread online, survivors call on governments to take action. *CBC News*. Retrieved from https://www.cbc.ca/news/canada/manitoba/phoenix-11-child-sex-abuse-images-1.4802132

Common Sense Media. (2021). Parents' ultimate guide to TikTok. Retrieved from https://www.commonsensemedia.org/blog/parents-ultimate-guide-to-tiktok

Cox, J. (2018, December 6). TikTok, the app super popular with kids, has a nudes problem. *Motherboard*. Retrieved from https://motherboard.vice.com/en_us/article/j5zbmx/tiktok-the-app-super-popular-with-kids-has-a-nudes-problem?utm_source5mbtwitter

Dahlberg, L. (2010). Cyber-libertarianism 2.0: A discourse theory/critical political economy examination. *Cultural Politics*, 6(3), 331–356.

Dance, G., & Keller, M. H. (2020, February 7). Tech companies detect a surge in online videos of child sexual abuse. *New York Times*. Retrieved from https://www.nytimes.com/2020/2002/2007/us/online-child-sexual-abuse.html

Dodds, L. (2020, January 9). Twitter accused of aiding child abuse by allowing 'explosion' of online paedophile communities. *Telegraph*. Retrieved from https://www.telegraph.co.uk/technology/2020/2001/2009/twitter-accused-aiding-child-abuse-allowing-explosion-online/

Dwoskin, E. (2020, March 24). Stay-home orders test the future of policing online content. *The Washington Post*. Retrieved from https://www.washingtonpost.com/technology/2020/03/23/facebook-moderators-coronavirus/

ECPAT. (2018). *Trends in online child sexual abuse material*. Bangkok: Author.

Farid, H. (2017, September 19). Technology sector should not be shielding sex traffickers online. *The Hill*. Retrieved from https://thehill.com/opinion/technology/351315-technology-sector-should-not-be-shielding-sex-traffickers-online

Fight Online Sex Trafficking Act (FOSTA). (2017). Retrieved from https://www.congress.gov/bill/115th-congress/house-bill/1865/text

Fisher, M., & Taub, A. (2019, June 3). On YouTube's digital playground, an open gate for paedophiles. *New York Times*. Retrieved from https://www.nytimes.com/2019/2006/2003/world/americas/youtube-paedophiles.html

Fonrouge, G. (2021, January 21). Twitter refused to remove child porn because it didn't 'violate policies': Lawsuit. *New York Post*. Retrieved from https://nypost.com/2021/01/21/twitter-sued-for-allegedly-refusing-to-remove-child-porn/

de Gallier, T. (2020, April 7). I make over £20k a month selling nudes online. *BBC*. Retrieved from https://www.bbc.co.uk/bbcthree/article/5e7dad06-c48d-4509-b3e4-6a7a2783ce30

Gillespie, T. (2018). *Custodians of the internet: Platforms, content moderation, and the hidden decisions that shape social media*. New Haven, CT: Yale University Press.

Gorman, G. (2020, December 9). Child abuse victim says porn website Pornhub profited from her child rape. *News.com.au*. Retrieved from https://www.news.com.au/life-style/real-life/news-life/child-abuse-victim-saysporn-website-pornhub-profited-from-her-child-rape/news-story/7e3880aa4a94504acea7675bb8112cff

Hadjimatheou, K. (2019). Citizen-led digital policing and democratic norms: The case of self-styled paedophile hunters. *Criminology & Criminal Justice*. Forthcoming.

Halliday, J. (2012, March 22). Twitter's Tony Wang: 'We are the free speech wing of the free speech party'. *Guardian*. Retrieved from https://www.theguardian.com/media/2012/mar/2022/twitter-tony-wang-free-speech

Hamilton-Giachritsis, C., Hanson, E., Whittle, H., & Beech, A. (2017). *Everyone deserves to be happy and safe. A mixed methods study exploring how online and offline child sexual abuse impact young people and how professionals respond to it*. London: NSPCC.

Hanson, E. (2019). 'Losing track of morality': Understanding online forces and dynamics conducive to child sexual exploitation. In J. Pearce (Ed.), *Child sexual exploitation: Why theory matters* (pp. 87–116). Bristol: Policy Press.

Hemphill, T. A. (2019). 'Techlash', responsible innovation, and the self-regulatory organization. *Journal of Responsible Innovation*, 6, 240–247.

HM Government. (2019). *Online harms white paper*. London: Author.

IICSA. (2020). *The internet: Investigation report*. London: Independent Inquiry into Child Sexual Abuse.

Interpol. (2020, September 7). *INTERPOL report highlights impact of COVID-19 on child sexual abuse*. Lyon: Author. Retrieved from https://www.interpol.int/en/

News-and-Events/News/2020/INTERPOL-report-highlights-impact-of-COVID-19-on-child-sexual-abuse

Itzin, C. (2001). Incest, paedophilia, pornography and prostitution: Making familial abusers more visible as the abusers. *Child Abuse Review*, 10, 35–48.

Jenkins, P. (2001). *Beyond tolerance: Child pornography on the internet*. New York, NY: New York University Press.

Jones, L. M., Mitchell, K. J., & Finkelhor, D. (2013). Online harassment in context: Trends from three youth internet safety surveys (2000, 2005, 2010). *Psychology of Violence*, 3(1), 53–69.

Kaiser, J., & Rauchfleisch, A. (2019). The implications of venturing down the rabbit hole. *Internet Policy Review*, 8(2), 1–22.

Keller, M. H. (2020, March 5). Bill would make tech firms accountable for child sex abuse imagery. *New York Times*. Retrieved from https://www.nytimes.com/2020/2003/2005/us/child-sexual-abuse-legislation.html

Leskin, P. (2019, December 21). A year after Tumblr's porn ban, some users are still struggling to rebuild their communities and sense of belonging. *Business Insider*. Retrieved from https://www.businessinsider.com.au/tumblr-porn-ban-nsfw-flagged-reactions-fandom-art-erotica-communities-2019-2018?r5US&IR5T

Liao, S. (2018, December 3). Tumblr will ban all adult content on December 17th. *Verge*. Retrieved from https://www.theverge.com/2018/2012/2013/18123752/tumblr-adult-content-porn-ban-date-explicit-changes-why-safe-mode

Maack, M. (2019, July 24). 'YouTube recommendations are toxic,' says dev who worked on the algorithm. *Next Web*. Retrieved from https://thenextweb.com/google/2019/06/14/youtube-recommendations-toxicalgorithm-google-ai/

Marino, A. (2019, October 15). Twitter is thinking about how tweets can become more ephemeral. *Verge*. Retrieved from https://www.theverge.com/2019/2010/2015/20913994/podcast-twitter-head-of-product-kayvon-beykpour-interview-auto-delete-tweets-vergecast

Murgia, M. (2019, October 18). Facebook looks to improve child protection over fears encryption will raise risks. *Financial Times*. Retrieved from https://www.ft.com/content/b5480746-f01f-11e9-bfa4-b25f11f42901

Nagle, A. (2017). *Kill all normies: Online culture wars from 4chan and Tumblr to Trump and the alt-right*. Winchester: Zero Books.

Orphanides, K. G. (2019, February 20). On YouTube, a network of paedophiles is hiding in plain site. *Wired*. Retrieved from https://www.wired.co.uk/article/youtube-pedophile-videos-advertising

Pauls, K., & MacIntosh, C. (2020, December 1). Women who spent years scrubbing explicit video from internet urges tech firms to make it easier to remove. *CBC News*. Retrieved from https://www.cbc.ca/news/canada/manitoba/canada-internet-children-abuse-pornography-1.5822042

Peters, T. (2021, January 13). TikTok reveals new privacy settings for kids: What parents should know. *Today*. Retrieved from https://www.today.com/parents/tiktok-changes-privacy-settings-kids-under-18-t205733

Salter, M. (2012). Invalidation: A neglected dimensions of gender-based violence and inequality. *International Journal for Crime, Justice and Social Democracy*, 1(1), 3–13.

Salter, M. (2013). *Organised sexual abuse*. London: Glasshouse/Routledge.

Salter, M. (2017). *Crime, justice and social media*. London; New York, NY: Routledge.

Salter, M. (2018). From geek masculinity to Gamergate: The technological rationality of online abuse. *Crime, Media, Culture*, 14(2), 247–264.

Seto, M., Buckman, C., Dwyer, R., & Quayle, E. (2018). *Production and active trading of child sexual exploitation images depicting identified victims: NCMEC/Thorn research report*. Alexandria, VA: NCMEC.

Silverstein, J. (2018, November 20). Tumblr app disappears from Apple's App Store because of child porn. *CBS News*. Retrieved from https://www.cbsnews.com/news/tumblr-app-disappears-from-apple-app-storebecause-of-child-porn/

Solon, O. (2020, April 23). Child sexual abuse images and online exploitation surge during pandemic. *NBC News*. Retrieved from https://www.nbcnews.com/tech/tech-news/child-sexual-abuse-images-online-exploitation-surge-during-pandemic-n1190506

Stiglitz, J. (2019). *People, power, and profits: Progressive capitalism for an age of discontent*. London: Penguin Books.

Taylor, J. (2020, March 2). TikTok removes Australian account purporting to hunt paedophiles. *Guardian*. Retrieved from https://www.theguardian.com/technology/2020/mar/2002/tiktok-removes-australian-account-purporting-to-hunt-paedophiles

Tufekci, Z. (2018, March 10). YouTube, the great radicalizer. *New York Times*. Retrieved from https://www.nytimes.com/2018/2003/2010/opinion/sunday/you-tube-politics-radical.html

Turner, F. (2010). *From counterculture to cyberculture: Stewart Brand, the whole earth network, and the rise of digital utopianism*. Chicago, IL: University of Chicago Press.

Twitter. (2020). Child sexual exploitation policy. Retrieved from https://help.-twitter.com/en/rules-and-policies/sexual-exploitation-policy

US Attorney General. (1986). *Attorney general's commission on pornography: Final report*. Washington, DC: U.S. Department of Justice.

Valentino-DeVries, J., & Dance, G. (2019, October 2). Facebook encryption eyed in fight against online child sex abuse. *New York Times*. Retrieved from https://www.nyti-mes.com/2019/2010/2002/technology/encryption-online-child-sex-abuse.html

Wakabayashi, D., & Maheshwari, S. (2019, February 21). Advertisers boycott YouTube After pedophiles swarm comments on videos of children. *The New York Times*. Retrieved from https://www.nytimes.com/2019/02/20/technology/youtube-pedophiles.html

Warzel, C. (2017, November 22). YouTube is addressing its massive child exploitation problem. *Buzzfeed*. Retrieved from https://www.buzzfeednews.com/article/charlie-warzel/youtube-is-addressing-its-massive-child-exploitation-problem

Wright, M. (2019, November 11). Twitter responsible for half of child abuse material UK investigators found on web platforms. *Telegraph*. Retrieved from https://www.telegraph.co.uk/news/2019/11/10/twitter-responsible-half-child-abuse-mate-rial-uk-investigators/

YouTube. (2019). An update on our efforts to protect minors and families. Retrieved from https://blog.youtube/news-and-events/an-update-on-our-efforts-to-protect

YouTube. (2020). *Transparency report featured policies: Child safety*. Retrieved from https://transparencyreport.google.com/youtube-policy/featured-policies/child-safety?hl=en&policy_removals=period:2020Q4&lu=policy_removals

Zuboff, S. (2019). *The age of surveillance capitalism: The fight for a human future at the new frontier of power*. London: Profile Books.

Chapter 43

Governing Image-Based Sexual Abuse: Digital Platform Policies, Tools, and Practices

Nicola Henry and Alice Witt

Abstract

The nonconsensual taking or sharing of nude or sexual images, also known as "image-based sexual abuse," is a major social and legal problem in the digital age. In this chapter, we examine the problem of image-based sexual abuse in the context of digital platform governance. Specifically, we focus on two key governance issues: first, the governance of platforms, including the regulatory frameworks that apply to technology companies; and second, the governance by platforms, focusing on their policies, tools, and practices for responding to image-based sexual abuse. After analyzing the policies and practices of a range of digital platforms, we identify four overarching shortcomings: (1) inconsistent, reductionist, and ambiguous language; (2) a stark gap between the policy and practice of content regulation, including transparency deficits; (3) imperfect technology for detecting abuse; and (4) the responsibilization of users to report and prevent abuse. Drawing on a model of corporate social responsibility (CSR), we argue that until platforms better address these problems, they risk failing victim-survivors of image-based sexual abuse and are implicated in the perpetration of such abuse. We conclude by calling for reasonable and proportionate state-based regulation that can help to better align governance by platforms with CSR-initiatives.

Keywords: Digital platforms; platform governance; image-based sexual abuse; nonconsensual pornography; content moderation; corporate social responsibility

The Emerald International Handbook of Technology-Facilitated Violence and Abuse, 749–768

doi:10.1108/978-1-83982-848-520211054

Introduction

The nonconsensual taking or sharing of nude or sexual images, also known as "image-based sexual abuse" (Henry et al., 2020; McGlynn & Rackley, 2017) or "nonconsensual pornography" (Citron & Franks, 2014; Ruvalcaba & Eaton, 2020), is a major social and legal problem in the digital age. With the development of social media and other networked technologies, which enable over three billion users to generate and instantaneously share content on the internet (Kemp, 2020), image-based sexual abuse is not only rapidly increasingly, but also having significant impacts (Henry et al., 2020).

While criminal offenses are an important means to punish perpetrators and provide justice to victim-survivors, criminalization has done little to prevent the scourge of image-based sexual abuse or minimize the harm once images (photographs or videos) are posted online. For example, images can be copied and republished on multiple platforms and devices – in some cases making it virtually impossible to prevent the further spread of images online. Perpetrators are often difficult to identify because of anonymity measures, such as encryption, virtual private networks, and proxy servers that obscure the nature of content, locations of internet traffic, and other information about users and their devices. Moreover, policing for image-based sexual abuse (and cybercrime more generally) is typically resource intensive given that law enforcement agencies often have to work across jurisdictional borders.

In response to the complex challenges raised by harmful online content, governments around the world are introducing new regulatory regimes to attempt to better hold technology companies accountable for hosting harmful content on their platforms. At the same time, technology companies are themselves taking more proactive steps to tackle this problem. In this chapter, we examine the problem of image-based sexual abuse in light of these two forms of governance. In the first section, we focus on the *governance of* digital platforms, examining the introduction of broader governmental and intergovernmental regulatory regimes in a changing landscape, which some have described as a global "techlash" against the major digital platforms (Flew, Martin, & Suzor, 2019, p. 33). In the second section, we examine the *governance by* digital platforms, focusing specifically on the policies, tools, and practices that are being implemented by digital platforms to respond to and prevent image-based sexual abuse.

In the third section, we draw on a model of corporate social responsibility (CSR) to propose ways forward. CSR provides a useful, albeit contested, language to examine the policy and practice of online content moderation or regulation. Although there are different conceptions of CSR, we define it as corporations' social, economic, legal, moral, and ethical responsibilities to address the harmful effects of their activities. Our conception of CSR is embedded within a social justice framework that locates the rationale for action not solely as a profit- or reputation-building exercise, but one that is also contingent on community values and the "common good."

We argue that while many digital platforms are taking proactive steps to detect and address image-based sexual abuse, four main shortcomings are evident in their policy approaches. First, some platforms adopt inconsistent, reductionist, and ambiguous language to describe image-based sexual abuse. Second, although a number of platforms now have an explicit policy position on image-based sexual abuse, there is often a stark gap between the policy and practice of content regulation, as well as a lack of transparency about how decisions are made and what the outcomes of those decisions are. Third, while platforms are increasingly turning to high-tech solutions to either detect or prevent image-based sexual abuse, these are imperfect measures that can be circumvented. And fourth, the onus is predominantly placed on users to find and report image-based sexual abuse to the platforms, which can be retraumatizing and highly stressful.

We contend that because of their governing power, public character, and control of information, digital platforms have an ethical responsibility to detect, address, and prevent image-based sexual abuse on their networks. This is despite the degree of legal immunity that platforms have against harmful content posted by their users under section 230(c) of the United States (US) Communications Decency Act of 1996 (CDA 230). We argue that when platforms govern without sufficient regulatory safeguards in place, such as appeal processes and reason-giving practices (Suzor, 2019), they risk failing victim-survivors of image-based sexual abuse and are implicated in the perpetration of image-based sexual abuse.

Governance of Digital Platforms

Also known as "internet intermediaries," or "online service providers," digital platforms are nonstate, corporate organizations or entities that facilitate transactions, information exchange, or communications between third parties on the internet (see, e.g., Taddeo & Floridi, 2016). According to Gillespie (2018), digital platforms are "sites and services that host public expression, store it on and serve it up from the cloud, organize access to it through search and recommendation, or install it onto mobile devices" (p. 254). Gillespie (2018) explains that what digital platforms share in common is the hosting and organization of "user content for public circulation, without having produced or commissioned it" (p. 254). While digital platforms might appear to be neutral conduits or proxies for the exchange of online content between third parties, they are never neutral, and have been described as the "new governors" or "superpowers" of the digital age (Klonick, 2018; Lee, 2018). Some commentators argue that technology companies are engaged in illicit forms of digital surveillance, plundering the behavioral data of users to sell to business customers (including political advertisers) for economic profit (e.g., Zuboff, 2019), as well as creating the norms and means through which individual users can engage in "performative surveillance" in the form of tracking, monitoring, and observing other users online (e.g., Westlake, 2008).

In addition to potentially illicit forms of surveillance and data harvesting, one of the key ways platforms govern their networks is by moderating user-generated content. As a form of regulation, content moderation encompasses an array of processes through which platform executives and their employees set, maintain, and enforce the bounds of "appropriate" user behaviors (Witt, Suzor, & Huggins, 2019). The norm is for content moderation to be *ex post*, meaning it is undertaken after a user has posted content, and reactive in response to user flags or reports (Klonick, 2018; Roberts, 2019). This means that platforms generally do not proactively screen content, decisions about which are thus predominantly made *after* the material is posted. On some platforms, however, automated systems are increasingly playing a more central role in the detection and removal of harmful online content before anyone has the chance to view or share the material (see further discussion below).

There are significant transparency deficits around the ways that different types of content are moderated in practice (Witt et al., 2019, p. 558). It is often unclear, for instance, what material is signaled for removal, how much content is actually removed, and by what means. It is also impossible to determine precisely who removes content (e.g., a platform content moderator or a user) without access to a platform's internal workings (Witt et al., 2019, p. 572). The secrecy around the inner workings of content moderation is reinforced by the operation of contract law, which governs the platform–user relationship, and powerful legal protections under US law (where many platforms are primarily based). Specifically, CDA 230 protects platforms against liability for content posted by third parties. Consequently, platforms that host or republish content are generally not legally liable for what their users say or do except for illegal content or content that infringes intellectual property regimes. Indeed, technology companies not only exercise "unprecedented power" over "what [users] can see or share" (Suzor, 2019, p. 8), but also have "broad discretion to create and enforce their rules in almost any way they see fit" (Suzor, 2019, p. 106). This means that decisions around content can be based on a range of factors, including public-facing policies like terms of service, community guidelines, prescriptive guidelines that moderators follow behind closed doors, legal obligations, market forces, and cultural norms of use.

Digital platforms are not, however, completely "lawless" (Suzor, 2019, p. 107). Platforms are subject to a range of laws in jurisdictions around the globe, some of which have the potential to threaten the ongoing stability of the CDA 230 safe harbor provisions. Europe has been described as the "world's leading tech watchdog" (Satariano, 2018) especially with European regulators taking an "increasingly activist stance toward… digital platform companies" (Flew et al., 2019, p. 34). The European Union's General Data Protection Regulation (GDPR) and Germany's NetzDG laws, for instance, can result in significant administrative fines for data protection or security infringements (among other punitive consequences for noncompliance) (see Echikson & Knodt, 2018; The European Parliament and the Council of the European Union, 2016/679). There are also many examples of European courts ordering service providers to restrict the types of content users see and how and when they see it (e.g., copyright or defamation lawsuits) (Suzor, 2019, p. 49).

These state-based "regulatory pushbacks" are part of a global "techlash" against the governing powers of digital platforms in recent years (Flew et al., 2019, pp. 33 and 34). At the time of writing this chapter, the United Kingdom had proposed a range of measures in its White Paper on Online Harms, which includes a statutory duty of care that will legally require platforms to stop and prevent harmful material appearing on their networks (Secretary of State for Digital, Culture, Media & Sport and the Secretary of State for the Home Department, 2019). In 2019, Canada released the Digital Charter in Action, which includes 10 key principles designed to ensure the ethical collection, use, and disclosure of data (Innovation, Science and Economic Development Canada, 2019).

Going a step further, after the Christchurch mosque shootings in New Zealand on March 15, 2019, the Australian Federal Government passed the *Criminal Code Amendment (Sharing of Abhorrent Violent Material) Act 2019* (Cth) which gives the Australian eSafety Commissioner powers to issue take-down notices to digital platforms that host abhorrent violent material (AVM). If a service provider fails to remove AVM, they can be subject to prosecution under Australian federal criminal law, among other potential courses of action. Moreover, in 2018, the Australian federal government introduced an innovative civil penalty scheme which prohibits the nonconsensual sharing of intimate images, as well as threatening to share intimate images. Under this scheme, the eSafety Commissioner can issue substantial fines, formal warnings, infringement notices, or take-down notices to individuals and corporations requiring the removal of images within 48 hours.

These domestic and international developments recognize that the decision-making processes of ostensibly "private" digital platforms can have significant impacts on individual users and far-reaching implications for politics, culture, and society (the "public sphere") more broadly. They also suggest that platform immunity from legal liability for both privacy violations and the hosting of harmful content is diminishing – at least in some jurisdictional contexts.

Digital platforms might then not be completely lawless, but do in practice govern, to use Suzor's (2019) term, "in a *lawless* way" (p. 107). Platforms exercise extraordinary power with limited safeguards for users, such as fairness, equality, and certainty, which many Western citizens have come to expect from governing actors (Witt et al., 2019). The result is often a significant gap between platform policies and their governance in practice, as well as a lack of transparency around digital platforms' decision-making processes.

Governance by Digital Platforms

In this section, we explore an array of policies, tools, and practices that are designed to detect, prevent, and respond to image-based sexual abuse on some of the largest digital platforms. Given the rapid pace of innovation in the technology sector, we selected platforms according to their traffic, market dominance, and their capacity to host image-based sexual abuse content. The sites we selected were predominantly the most popular sites as ranked by the analytics company Alexa (Alexa Internet, n.d.). The social media and search engine platforms we examined included Google, YouTube, Facebook, Yahoo!, Reddit, Instagram, Microsoft, Twitter, Flickr, Snapchat, TikTok, and Tumblr. The pornography sites we examined included Pornhub, XVideos, and xHamster. After creating a list of sites, we used the Google search engine to identify each company's policy documents, including their terms of service, community guidelines, reports, and official blogs. Each document was analyzed to identify specific image-based sexual abuse policies, general policies that could be applicable to image-based sexual abuse, and tools for either detecting, reporting, or blocking content, if any. We also searched for any relevant news articles or blogs on platforms' responses to image-based sexual abuse content.

Our approach has four main limitations. The first limitation is that we were only able to examine publicly available policy documents. As such, we were not able to examine the undisclosed guidelines that moderators follow behind closed doors or information about the privatized automated systems that digital platforms might use. Second, we carried out our analysis over a three-month period between January and March 2020 and thus we cannot account for any changes in policies, tools, or practices after this time. Third, we did not examine non-English technology companies, nor did we examine the fringe, "rogue," or underground platforms (e.g., on the Clear Net or Dark Net) where image-based sexual abuse content is being shared and traded (see Henry & Flynn, 2019).

Finally, we did not seek to empirically investigate the experiences or perspectives of either victim-survivors or platform representatives in relation to content removal or platform policies, tools, and practices. Currently there is a pervasive lack of transparency around platform governance and more research is needed to address this gap. The analysis below, however, provides insight into how select platforms are attempting to address and prevent image-based sexual abuse. Here we focus on three key areas of content moderation: platform policies; reporting options and practices; and technological tools.

Platform Policies on Image-Based Sexual Abuse

The term "revenge porn" came into popular usage in 2011 after widespread media attention to the nonconsensual sharing of nude or sexual images of musicians and sportspersons on the website IsAnyoneUp.com and the subsequent criminal trial of its founder Hunter Moore (Martens, 2011). The term, however, is a misnomer because not all perpetrators are motivated by revenge when they share nude or sexual images without consent. Instead they may be motivated for other reasons, such as sexual gratification, monetary gain, social status building, or a desire for power and control (Citron & Franks, 2014; Henry et al., 2020). The term "revenge porn" has been widely criticized as having victim-blaming, harm-minimizing, or salacious connotations. Scholars, activists, victim-survivors, and practitioners also argue that it fails to capture the complexity and diversity of behaviors involving the use and abuse of nonconsensual nude or sexual images by known and unknown persons alike, using diverse means and methods (Henry et al., 2020; McGlynn & Rackley, 2017; Powell, Henry, & Flynn, 2018).

Although a small number of digital platforms continue to refer to "revenge porn" in their terms of service or community guidelines, others have adopted alternative terms, such as "nonconsensual pornography," "involuntary pornography," or "the nonconsensual sharing of intimate images." Tumblr's community guidelines, for instance, state: "Absolutely do not post nonconsensual pornography – that is, private photos or videos taken or posted without the subject's consent" (Tumblr, 2020, Privacy violations, para 1). Other platforms outline prohibitions against broader forms of online content. For instance, Pornhub's terms of service explicitly prohibit, among other behaviors, the impersonation of another person, the posting of copyrighted material, content that depicts a person under the age of 18, and content that is "obscene, illegal, unlawful, defamatory, libellous, harassing, hateful, racially, or ethnically offensive" (Pornhub, 2020, Monitoring and enforcement, para 4). Notably, however, Pornhub does not specify explicit prohibitions against image-based sexual abuse. In their policies, xHamster and XVideos do not specifically mention image-based sexual abuse but instead refer to privacy, abuse, harassment, inappropriate, or illegal content (xHamster, 2020; XVideos, n.d.). TikTok's Community Policy similarly does not mention image-based sexual abuse content and instead tells users that this is "NOT the place to post, share, or promote... harmful or dangerous content" (TikTok, 2019; para 4).

On some platforms, the prohibition of image-based sexual abuse is unclear. For instance, Snapchat states that users should not "take Snaps of people in private spaces – like a bathroom, locker room or a medical facility – without their knowledge and consent" (Snap Inc., 2019, para 4). Although examples are given of what a "private space" might entail, it is unclear whether the nonconsensual sharing of nude or sexual imagery is also prohibited in the context of "public" spaces. Facebook's policy on the sharing of image-based sexual abuse content, on the other hand, is much clearer, allowing the sharing of images to be either "noncommercial" or "private" with an expansive definition of what an "intimate" image includes. Facebook prohibits the nonconsensual sharing of intimate images according to three criteria: the image is noncommercial or produced in a private setting; the person is nude, nearly nude, or engaged in a sexual act or posing in a sexual way; and there is lack of consent indicated by captions, comments, the title of the page, independent sources, or reports from victims or others (Facebook, 2020a). However, the focus on images that are noncommercial, and which are produced in a private setting, appears to deny sex workers or pornographic actors the right to control the dissemination of their images.

There can be significant flow-on effects of ambiguous policy stances on image-based sexual abuse. Platform policies that are open-textured, or which use nondescript terms, can enable ad hoc decision-making in response to business and other pressures (Witt et al., 2019). The lack of consistent language for platforms to name and work through the problems of image-based sexual abuse can make it difficult for stakeholders to discuss the concerns that victim-survivors and other societal actors raise. Moreover, vague guidelines can fundamentally limit the ability of victim-survivors or their authorized representatives to apply platform policies to reporting features or inform users as to the bounds of acceptable behavior.

Given that platforms almost always reserve "broad discretion" to determine what, if any, response will be given to a report of harmful content (Suzor, 2019, p. 106), it is essentially their choice whether or not to impose punitive (or other) measures on users when their terms of service or community guidelines have been violated (some of which have appeals processes in place). While platforms are not able to make arrests or issue warrants, they are able to remove content, limit access to their sites to offending users, issue warnings, disable accounts for specified periods of time, or permanently suspend accounts at their discretion. YouTube, for instance, has implemented a "strikes system" which first entails the removal of content and a warning issued (sent by email) to let the user know the Community Guidelines have been violated with no penalty to the user's channel if it is a first offense (YouTube, 2020, What happens if, para 1). After a first offense, users will be issued a strike against their channel, and once they have received three strikes, their channel will be terminated. Other platforms have similar systems in place. As noted by York and Zuckerman (2019), the suspension of user accounts can act as a "strong disincentive" to post harmful content where social or professional reputation is at stake (p. 144).

Deepfakes

The extent to which platform policies and guidelines explicitly or implicitly cover "deepfakes," including deepfake pornography, is a relatively new governance issue. Deepfakes are a portmanteau of "deep learning," a subfield of narrow artificial intelligence (AI) used to create content and fake images. In December 2017, a Reddit user, who called himself "deepfakes," trained algorithms to swap the faces of actors in pornography videos with the faces of well-known celebrities (see Chesney & Citron, 2019; Franks & Waldman, 2019). Since then, the volume of deepfake videos on the internet has increased exponentially; the vast majority of which are pornographic and disproportionately target women (Ajder, Patrini, Cavalli, & Cullen, 2019).

In early 2020, Facebook, Reddit, Twitter, and YouTube announced new or altered policies prohibiting deepfake content. In order for deepfake content to be removed on Facebook, for instance, it must meet two criteria: first, it must have been "edited or synthesized… in ways that aren't apparent to an average person and would likely mislead someone into thinking that a subject of the video said words that they did not actually say"; and second, it must be the product of AI or machine learning (Facebook, 2020a, Manipulated media, para 3). The narrow scope of these criteria, which appears to be targeting manipulated fake news rather than different types of manipulated media, makes it unclear whether videos with no sound will be covered by the policy – for instance, a person's face that is superimposed onto another person's body in a silent porn video. Moreover, this policy may not cover low-tech, non-AI techniques that are used to alter videos and photographs – also known as "shallowfakes" (see Bose, 2020).

On the other hand, Twitter's new deepfake policy refers to "synthetic or manipulated media that are likely to cause harm" according to three key criteria: first, if the content is synthetic or manipulated; second, if the content was shared in a deceptive manner; and third, if the content is likely to impact public safety or cause serious harm (Twitter, 2020, para 1). The posting of deepfake imagery on Twitter can lead to a number of consequences depending on whether any or all of the three criteria are satisfied. These include applying a label to the content to make it clear that the content is fake; reducing the visibility of the content or preventing it from being recommended; providing a link to additional explanations or clarifications; removing the content; or suspending accounts where there have been repeated or severe violations of the policy (Twitter, 2020).

While specific deepfake policies do not exist on other platforms, some have more general rules relating to "fake/d," "false," "misleading," "digitally manipulated," "lookalike," and/or "aggregate" content, which could result in the take-down of deepfake images. Pornhub (2020) does not mention deepfakes in its Terms of Service; however, in 2018 it did announce a ban on deepfakes (Cole, 2018). Nevertheless, the site continues to host deepfake pornography. When we searched for "deepfakes" using the internal Pornhub search function, no results were found, yet when we searched through Google "deepfakes" and "pornhub," multiple results of fake celebrity videos were returned.

Reporting Harmful Content

Reporting options are another means through which digital platforms can address the problem of image-based sexual abuse. All of the platforms we examined have in place some sort of reporting protocol, including the porn sites, which are supposed to trigger review by human content moderators. On porn sites, for instance, users can report through either a *Digital Millennium Copyright Act of 1998* take-down request, or via a content removal form. Facebook recently announced that image-based sexual abuse content is now triaged alongside self-harm in the content moderation queue (Solon, 2019).

Another important form of content reporting occurs through the "flagging" system where users are enlisted as a "volunteer corps of regulators" to alert platforms about content that violates their policies and community standards (Crawford & Gillespie, 2016, p. 412). Facebook users, for instance, flag around one million pieces of content per day (Buni & Chemaly, 2016). Many companies provide built-in reporting features through which users can report material that potentially violates content policies (Witt et al., 2019, p. 577). For instance, Pornhub allows users to flag videos (using the "Flag this video" link under each video) if it is "illegal, unlawful, harassing, harmful, offensive, or various other reasons," stating that it will remove the content from the site without delay (Pornhub, 2020, Prohibited uses, para 2).

Platform reporting systems predominantly place the onus on victim-survivors or other users to flag or report image-based sexual abuse content. In other words, digital platforms "[responsibilize users] to reduce their own risk of [victimization]" (Salter, Crofts, & Lee, 2018, p. 301). Major online platforms, like Facebook and Instagram, suggest that users take a range of preventive measures, such as unfollowing or blocking those responsible for posting abusive content, reviewing their safety and security settings, and accessing hyperlinked information. Microsoft, for instance, suggests that users should identify the source and/or owner of an image and attempt to have it removed before reporting it as a potential policy violation (Microsoft, 2020). If unsuccessful, victims are encouraged to report content through built-in or other reporting features. Preconditions like this, in many ways, are a "practical solution to the problem of moderating vast amounts of content" (Witt et al., 2019, p. 576). However, while important safety and empowerment messages should be communicated to users, in isolation they can place additional emotional, financial, and other burdens on already vulnerable individuals.

Technological Tools

The third option for enhancing proactive platform action in relation to harmful content is to use technological solutions to prevent users perpetrating further abuse. In 2009, Microsoft and Professor Hany Farid from Dartmouth College developed PhotoDNA, a technology that creates a unique digital signature (also known as a "hash" or "digital fingerprint") of child sexual abuse images, which can then be compared against known images stored in a database curated by the National Center for Missing and Exploited Children in the United States (Langston, 2018, para 13). This technology assists platforms to detect, remove, and block child sexual abuse content on their networks. It is also used by law enforcement to detect, arrest, and prosecute perpetrators, and identify victims.

PhotoDNA technology has led to other technological innovations in regulating harmful online content.[1] In November 2017, Facebook announced a pilot trial in partnership with the Australian Office of the eSafety Commissioner to prevent image-based sexual abuse from occurring on Facebook-owned platforms, which was then expanded to Canada, the United States, and the United Kingdom in May 2018 (Facebook, 2020b). The trial allows people who are concerned that someone might share an image of them to contact the relevant partner agency and complete an online form. The person is then sent an email containing a secure, one-time upload link, where she or he can upload the image. A community operations analyst from Facebook then accesses the image and creates a "hash" of it. If any user in the future attempts to upload or share that same image on the platform, they will be automatically blocked, and the image will not be able to be shared (Facebook, 2020b).

Other companies have adopted similar methods. Pornhub uses a third-party automated audio-visual identification system (called MediaWise®) which first identifies the content using "digital fingerprinting," and then blocks it from being uploaded again in the future (Pornhub, n.d.). To have content digitally fingerprinted, victims are required to email a third-party service to make the request. The victim then receives an email to let them know the content has been fingerprinted and the victim can then report the video by filling out the online form on the site. It is important to note that fingerprinted videos that are blocked can still appear on the site, albeit for a brief time, which can have significant impacts on victim-survivors.

These technological solutions have received significant criticism. The Facebook pilot was widely condemned for asking vulnerable individuals to trust Facebook with their intimate images in the wake of the Cambridge Analytica scandal (see, e.g., Romano, 2018; see also Bailey & Liliefeldt, this volume). More recently, a Motherboard investigation found that Pornhub's fingerprinting system "can be easily and quickly circumvented with minor editing" to change the metadata and therefore prevent the image being matched to the original image stored in the database (Cole & Maiberg, 2020, para 7). The Motherboard investigators, with the consent and cooperation of several women who were featured in nonconsensual pornographic videos, tested Pornhub's content removal system, finding that Pornhub did remove the videos when they reported the content. The investigators also tested the digital fingerprinting system by using editing techniques to alter the videos. They found that after the content had been flagged, removed, and fingerprinted, when they tried to upload the exact same video to Pornhub, the video was removed within an hour. However, they also experimented with using editing techniques to slightly alter a number of videos and found that when they did this, the fingerprinting method did not work and the video was not removed (Cole & Maiberg, 2020). Pornhub's system may be compared with Microsoft's PhotoDNA program where the hashed images are resistant to complex image alterations, including resizing and minor color alterations (Langston, 2018).

In 2019, Facebook introduced a new AI tool that can detect nonconsensually shared "nearly nude" images (Davis, 2019). Using a database of previously confirmed nonconsensual intimate images, the technology works by training the algorithm to recognize language patterns and key words that would suggest those images are not consensual (similar to Google's AI tool for detecting child abuse material). Once the content has been flagged, a member of Facebook's Community Operations team reviews the content and then decides whether the content has violated Facebook's community standards. If they conclude there has been a violation, Facebook will then disable the account or issue a warning to the user (Davis, 2019). This is an important proactive measure for two key reasons. First, it puts the onus back on the platform to find and remove image-based sexual abuse content. Second, it prevents the viewing and/or further sharing of these images. This is crucial since many victim-survivors will not know that images of them are being shared or will only discover their images well after they have been shared online. Nonetheless, it is important to note that this tool is imperfect because in many cases there will be no clear indication that the image has been shared without consent (e.g., clear indications include a victim makes a report, they are underage, or the accompanying text suggest vindictiveness). In cases where there is no clear indication, there is little Facebook and its AI tool can do to determine whether the image has in fact been taken or shared without consent.

Overall, these automated systems are revolutionary, and are helping some platforms to better address and prevent harmful online content. However, end-to-end encryption, where no one (including the platforms) can see the content of sent messages, works to circumvent the use of image hashing systems, thwarting global efforts to reduce the circulation of child sexual abuse or image-based sexual abuse material (see Green, 2019). This is a stark reminder that we cannot and should not rely on technological solutions alone to address the circulation of harmful content online.

Corporate Social Responsibility and Image-Based Sexual Abuse

Having outlined four main shortcomings associated with *governance by* platforms, in this final section we explore how CSR frameworks can provide critical guidance to digital platforms and help to set new norms to ensure that these governing actors take more proactive steps to both address and prevent the circulation of harmful content on their networks. CSR is an "essentially contested" term (Okoye, 2009) because there is little agreement about what it entails and no universally agreed-upon definition (Ihlen, Bartlett, & May 2011). At its broadest, CSR is defined as "the business and society relationship" (Laidlaw, 2017, p. 138), or, at its narrowest, as "social responsibility" that "begins where the law ends" (Davis, 1973, p. 313). There are several justifications for greater social responsibility by platforms; chief among them is the role that these businesses play in facilitating, and in some instances even promoting, harmful content on their networks (Slane & Langlois, 2018, p. 46).

While there is little agreement about the nature and extent of corporations' ethical or moral responsibilities (see Taddeo & Floridi, 2016), companies are increasingly being measured against a set of benchmarks on governance processes and respect for users' privacy and freedom of expression. For instance, the Ranking Digital Rights' (RDR) Corporate Accountability Index (2019) is an industry-level initiative that evaluates 24 of the world's most powerful technology companies according to three key criteria: privacy; freedom of expression; and governance. Other global initiatives, such as the United Nations Guiding Principles (UNGPs) on Business and Human Rights, similarly provide a set of guidelines for transnational corporations, businesses, and states to prevent, address, and remedy human rights violations committed in business operations (see United Nations, 2011). There are, of course, several limitations associated with CSR-initiatives like these. In terms of RDR's Index, only a small number of companies are ranked (none are porn sites) according to 35 broad indicators which measure performance. Unfortunately, they tell us little about how different companies are performing in relation to addressing specific online behaviors, such as image-based sexual abuse. Another concern is that most CSR frameworks, like the UNGPs, impose nonbinding – sometimes described as "blurred," and "soft" – human rights obligations (see Jørgensen, 2017, p. 281; see also Coombs, this volume). Nonetheless, CSR initiatives have led to tangible improvements in the practices of technology companies relating to privacy, freedom of expression, and governance (RDR, 2019, p. 9).

We argue that CSR provides a useful lens through which to examine platform governance. Crane, Matten, and Spence's (2013) conception of CSR comprises six main characteristics: (1) voluntary participation; (2) managing externalities such as impacts on local communities; (3) treating stakeholders as more than just shareholders; (4) aligning social and economic responsibilities; (5) forming business practices and values that address social issues; and (6) moving beyond just philanthropy. These characteristics not only underline what positive action by digital platforms arguably should look like, but they also provide a useful language to identify and work through potential issues. We draw on this conception of CSR in our discussion below by focusing on four key barriers to addressing and preventing image-based sexual abuse on digital platforms. Specifically, we demonstrate the ways in which *governance by* platforms frequently conflicts with these CSR ideals.

Barriers to Corporate Social Responsibility

First, there is reluctance on the part of some companies to voluntarily or proactively intervene to address the problem of harmful online content. This reluctance is understandable from a strict legal perspective when considering the distinction between the responsibilities of digital platforms and the duties and authority of nation states. As mentioned above, CDA 230, for example, does not (with some exceptions) require digital platforms to moderate content (Tushnet, 2008, pp. 1001–1002). For instance, Pornhub's (2020) Terms of Service make clear that they do not have an obligation to review content and do not regularly do so.[2] There are also inherent difficulties in weighing the potentially conflicting demands between freedom of speech and other rights, which form the foundation of some arguments against corporate regulation of content (see Hintz, 2014, p. 349). Moreover, there are well-founded concerns about vesting largely nontransparent and unaccountable regulatory power in private entities, some of which may make mistakes when moderating content by prioritizing commercial interests over ethical issues and community-oriented or social justice goals.

A second related barrier to CSR is economic profit. Platforms are generally focused on attracting more users and thereby generating greater advertising revenue, which can have far-reaching impacts on users' data and privacy. Digital platforms, however, do regularly engage in philanthropic, socially responsible activity, seeking to ostensibly align economic profit with social responsibility. By way of example, in March 2020, in response to the devastation wrought by COVID-19, Pornhub donated surgical masks and some of its proceeds to sex workers affected by the pandemic (Iovine, 2020).

These philanthropic acts stand in stark contrast to a range of nonethical and criminal practices on porn sites like Pornhub. In March 2020, nearly half a million people signed an online petition (started by a group called Exodus Cry) to hold Pornhub accountable for hosting child rape and underage porn videos, some of whom are victims of sex trafficking (Milne, 2020). The petition also claims that Pornhub does not have a reliable system in place to verify the age or consent of those featured in the pornographic content on the site. One key challenge is that on porn sites, nonconsensual content is an extremely profitable enterprise, generating millions of views and attracting millions of dollars of advertising. As such, there may be very little incentive for porn companies to remove image-based sexual abuse content, and little risk that failing to do so will damage their corporate image. Mainstream social media platforms, on the other hand, may have more incentive to address harmful online content because failing to do so could result in significant damage to their corporate reputation.

A third barrier relates to the significant technical, logistical, and emotional challenges that come with attempting to regulate massive volumes of online content (Laidlaw, 2017; Roberts, 2019). This is particularly so on platforms such as Facebook which currently has 2.5 billion active users (Hutchinson, 2020). The sheer scale of content means that not only are there delays in content review and removal processes, but content moderators – many of whom are contracted workers on low-pay – are regularly exposed to violent and harmful content causing some to experience significant vicarious trauma (see Boran, 2020).

Finally, owing to these aforementioned barriers, there is often a gap between the policies on image-based sexual abuse and the actual practice of content review and removal. US lawyer Carrie Goldberg (2019) has commented on Google's lack of action in taking down videos of women who were deceived into performing in porn or sexually assaulted in those videos. According to Goldberg: "If Google decides it will keep linking to a website that contains your nude images, victims are just out of luck. And there's no appellate body. There is no law, only corporate policy, that protects (or fails to protect) victims' most private information" (para 9). Overall, little remains known about the number of images flagged by users, reported by victim-survivors, tagged for review by AI systems, or fingerprinted for future blocking. This in turn makes it difficult for stakeholders to determine how effective platform governance has been in practice for responding to and preventing image-based sexual abuse.

Some technology companies have faced public scrutiny for their opaque content moderation processes (see Hopkins, 2017), leading in some instances to greater transparency by these companies. For instance, Facebook's Transparency Report is a regular reporting system that gives "community visibility" to how Facebook enforces its community standards, protects intellectual property, responds to legal requests for user data or content restrictions, and monitors internet disruptions across its products (Facebook, 2020c, para 1). Facebook also has a companion guide that explains how they write their policies, how they find and review potential violations, and how they measure results (Facebook, 2020d). In relation to the enforcement of its Community Standards, Facebook publicizes metrics on how they are "preventing and taking action on content that goes against these policies" in relation to a number of different issues, such as "adult nudity and sexual activity," "bullying and harassment," "child nudity and sexual exploitation of children," and hate speech (Facebook, 2020c, Community standards enforcement report, para 1 & 4). Regarding "adult nudity and sexual activity," Facebook reports metrics on the prevalence of this content, how much content Facebook took action on, how much content was found by Facebook before it was reported by users, how much content was appealed by users, and how much actioned content was later restored by Facebook (Facebook, 2020c, Community standards enforcement report, para 4). Unfortunately, the Facebook report does not break down the different types of adult nudity and sexual activity – which includes depiction of nudity as well as image-based sexual abuse content. In other words, Facebook does not report specifically on the prevalence of image-based sexual abuse content on their platform nor the actions that Facebook took to remove this content or the consequences for violating users. Nevertheless, Facebook's attempts at greater transparency in relation to content moderation are an example of more accountable forms of CSR, which many other companies have not yet adopted.

Given the barriers to addressing and preventing image-based sexual abuse through CSR-initiatives, as well as the four main shortcomings that we identified with the governance practices of our selected platforms, we argue that governments can and should play a greater role in addressing deficiencies in *governance by* platforms. This is not to suggest that platforms should be held to the same standards as nation states. Top-down, command, and control regulatory responses are generally unsuitable for decentered contexts like the internet and not necessarily desirable for users, lawmakers, and other stakeholders (Witt et al., 2019, p. 593). Rather, we argue what is needed is more state-based regulation (governance *of* platforms) that can help to better align governance *by* platforms with CSR – specifically, initiatives embedded within social justice and human rights frameworks. One positive step forward would be an amendment to CDA 230 so that the safe harbor provision only applies to those platforms that take reasonable steps to review and remove harmful content (see Citron, 2018).

The suggestion to introduce more government regulation is not, in our view, radical. As we have shown in the first section of this chapter, the regulatory landscape around the *governance of* platforms is changing, with many governments around the globe taking steps to hold technology companies responsible for hosting harmful content (Flew et al., 2019). Indeed, in early 2019, Facebook Co-Founder and CEO Mark Zuckerberg acknowledged: "Lawmakers often tell me we have too much power over speech, and frankly I agree. I've come to believe that we shouldn't make so many important decisions about speech on our own" (Zuckerberg, 2019, para 5). We stress, however, that any attempt to regulate platforms must be reasonable, proportionate, and take into account guides to good regulatory design, such as the *Manila Principles on Intermediary Liability* (2015) which seeks to balance user rights to freedom of expression, freedom of association, and the right to privacy. These steps would further propel a new culture of digital platform governance that is predicated not solely on economic profit, but on social justice, community, and ethics.

Conclusion

This chapter has examined the problem of image-based sexual abuse in the context of both the *governance of* and *by* online platforms. In terms of the *governance of* platforms, we paid particular attention to platform protection under CDA 230, which plays an important role in enabling platforms to govern in "lawless" ways (Suzor, 2019). One of the main ways that platforms govern their networks is by moderating user-generated content (Witt et al., 2019, p. 557). Moderation processes, including platform-specific rules around content and the online architecture of platforms themselves, can make it easier or harder for users to undertake certain types of behavior (Suzor, 2019, p. 91). In more recent years, other measures such as reporting options, digital fingerprinting, and other automated detection systems have become an essential part of the repertoire for tackling image-based sexual abuse.

Despite good intentions and significant changes to governance by platforms in recent years, we found that the policies, tools, and practices that are designed to address and prevent image-based sexual abuse are often piecemeal and reactive. Specifically, we identified four main issues: (1) inconsistent, reductionist, and ambiguous language in content policies; (2) a stark gap between the policy and practice of moderating content, including significant transparency deficits; (3) imperfect technology for detecting abuse, given that even where content is removed, images can still appear again on those sites or can be easily circulated on other platforms; and (4) the onus continues to remain predominantly with victim-survivors to report and prevent abuse. Overall, we argued that when platforms fail to address these issues, they risk failing victim-survivors and are implicated in the perpetration of image-based sexual abuse. In response, we called for state-based regulation that can help to better align *governance by* platforms with CSR initiatives.

There are a number of steps that platforms themselves can take to better address the scourge of image-based sexual abuse on their networks: principally, adopting a multifaceted, community-oriented, and social justice-based regulatory approach. Such an approach should include clear and robust policies that specifically prohibit image-based sexual abuse content, with punitive and educative functions clearly attached; architectural modifications, including better systems to reliably verify both the age and consent of those featured in content hosted on platforms; more resources invested into AI and other automated systems for detecting and removing content, with careful attention paid to the shortcomings of these technological solutions; greater multi-stakeholder collaboration and consultation between digital platforms with civil society and government actors to achieve common objectives; and increased public debate about the *governance of* platforms and what CSR should entail. Most importantly, *governance by* platforms should be transparent and accountable, subject to the scrutiny of civil society, and flexible in an ever-changing digital landscape.

Notes

1. The detection of deepfake imagery using machine learning is another technological challenge that requires vigilant testing and refinement to keep up with the rapidly changing development of deepfake technology.
2. Pornhub (2020) also states that it is not responsible for any links to third-party websites that are not owned or controlled by Pornhub, and that it "will not and cannot censor or edit the content of any third-party site" (About our websites, para 2). Indeed, the Pornhub Terms of Service, ad nauseum, claims no liability "for any action or inaction regarding transmissions, communications or Content provided by any user or third party" (Pornhub, 2020, Monitoring and enforcement, para 5). Their Terms of Service also make it clear that users are "solely responsible" for the content and the consequences of posting content (Pornhub, 2020).

References

Ajder, H., Patrini, G., Cavalli, F., & Cullen, L. (2019, September). The state of deepfakes: Landscape, threats, and impact. Retrieved from https://deeptracelabs.com/mapping-the-deepfake-landscape/

Alexa Internet. (n.d.). The top 500 sites on the web. Retrieved from https://www.alexa.com/topsites

Boran, M. (2020, February 27). Life as a Facebook moderator: People are awful. This is what my job has taught me. *The Irish Times*. Retrieved from https://www.irishtimes.com/

Bose, N. (2020, January 9). U.S. lawmakers say Facebook's steps to tackle 'deepfake' videos are not adequate. *Reuters*. Retrieved from https://www.reuters.com/

Buni, C., & Chemaly, S. (2016, April 13). The secret rules of the internet. *The Verge*. Retrieved from https://www.theverge.com

Chesney, D., & Citron, D. (2019). Deep fakes: A looming challenge for privacy, democracy, and national security. *California Law Review*, *107*(6), 1753–1819. doi: 10.15779/Z38RV0D15J

Citron, D. (2018). Section 230's challenge to civil rights and civil liberties. (Legal Studies Research Paper No. 2018–18). Retrieved from https://ssrn.com/abstract=3193214

Citron, D., & Franks, M. (2014). Criminalizing revenge porn. *Wake Forest Law Review*, *49*, 345–391. doi:10.1177/1557085117698752

Cole, S. (2018, February 6). Pornhub is banning AI-generated fake porn videos, says they're nonconsensual. *Vice*. Retrieved from https://www.vice.com

Cole, S., & Maiberg, E. (2020, February 7). Pornhub doesn't care. *Vice*. Retrieved from https://www.vice.com

Crane, A., Matten, D., & Spence, L. J. (2013). Corporate social responsibility in a global context. In A. Crane, D. Matten, & L. J. Spence (Eds.), *Corporate social responsibility: Readings and cases in a global context* (2nd ed., pp. 3–26). Oxon: Routledge.

Crawford, K., & Gillespie, T. (2016). What is a flag for? Social media reporting tools and the vocabulary of complaint. *New Media & Society*, *18*(3), 410–428. doi: 10.1177/1461444814543163

Criminal Code Amendment (Sharing of Abhorrent Violent Material) Act 2019, No. 38. Retrieved from https://www.legislation.gov.au/Details/C2019A00038

Davis, K. (1973). The case for and against business assumption of social responsibilities. *Academy of Management Journal*, *16*(2), 312–322. doi:10.2307/255331

Davis, A. (2019, March 15). Detecting non-consensual intimate images and supporting victims. *Facebook*. Retrieved from https://about.fb.com/news/2019/03/detecting-non-consensual-intimate-images/

Echikson, W., & Knodt, O. (2018, November). Germany's NetzDG: A key test for combatting online hate. (Report No. 2018/09). Retrieved from http://wp.ceps.eu/wp-content/uploads/2018/11/RR%20No2018-09_Germany's%20NetzDG.pdf

The European Parliament and the Council of the European Union. (2016/679). General Data Protection Regulation. Retrieved from https://gdpr-info.eu/

Facebook. (2020a). Community standards. Retrieved from https://www.facebook.com/communitystandards/introduction

Facebook. (2020b). The pilot. Retrieved from https://www.facebook.com/safety/notwithoutmyconsent/pilot

Facebook. (2020c). Facebook Transparency Report. Retrieved from https://transparency.facebook.com/

Facebook. (2020d). Understanding the community standards enforcement report. Retrieved from https://transparency.facebook.com/community-standards-enforcement/guide

Flew, T., Martin, F., & Suzor, N. (2019). Internet regulation as media policy: Rethinking the question of digital communication platform governance. *Journal of Digital Media & Policy*, *10*(1), 33–50. doi:10.1386/jdmp.10.1.33_1

Franks, M. A., & Waldman, A. E. (2019). Sex, lies, and videotape: Deep fakes and free speech delusions. *Maryland Law Review*, *78*(4), 892–898. Retrieved from https://digitalcommons.law.umaryland.edu/cgi/viewcontent.cgi?article=3835&context=mlr

Gillespie, T. (2018). *Custodians of the internet: Platforms, content moderation, and the hidden decisions that shape social media*. New Haven, CT: Yale University Press.

Goldberg, C. (2019, August 17). How Google has destroyed the lives of revenge porn victims. *New York Post*. Retrieved from https://nypost.com

Green, M. (2019). Can end-to-end encrypted systems detect child sexual abuse imagery?. [Blog post]. Retrieved from https://blog.cryptographyengineering.com/2019/12/08/on-client-side-media-scanning/

Henry, N., & Flynn, A. (2019). Image-based sexual abuse: Online distribution channels and illicit communities of support. *Violence Against Women*, *25*(16), 1932–1955. doi:10.1177/1077801219863881

Henry, N., McGlynn, C., Flynn, A., Johnson, K., Powell, A., & Scott, A. J. (2020). *Image-based sexual abuse: A study on the causes and consequences of non-consensual nude or sexual imagery*. London and New York, NY: Routledge.

Hintz, A. (2014). Outsourcing surveillance—privatising policy: Communications regulation by commercial intermediaries. *Birbeck Law Review*, *2*(2), 349–368. Retrieved from http://www.bbklr.org/2-2-10.html

Hopkins, N. (2017, May 22). Revealed: Facebook's internal rulebook on sex, terrorism and violence. *The Guardian*. Retrieved from http://www.theguardian.com

Hutchinson, A. (2020, January 30). Facebook climbs to 2.5 billion monthly active users, but rising costs impede income growth. *Social Media Today*. Retrieved from https://www.socialmediatoday.com

Ihlen, Ø., Bartlett, J., & May, S. (Eds.), (2011). *The handbook of communication and corporate social responsibility*. West Sussex: Wiley-Blackwell.

Innovation, Science and Economic Development Canada. (2019). *Canada's Digital Charter in action: A plan by Canadians for Canadians. (Catalogue no. Iu4-259/2019E-PDF)*. Ottawa, ON: Government of Canada. Retrieved from https://www.ic.gc.ca/eic/site/062.nsf/vwapj/Digitalcharter_Report_EN.pdf/$file/Digitalcharter_Report_EN.pdf

Iovine, A. (2020, March 25). Pornhub Premium is now free for everyone to encourage you to stay home. *Mashable*. Retrieved from https://mashable.com

Jørgensen, R. F. (2017). What platforms means when they talk about human rights. *Policy & Internet*, *9*(3), 280–296. doi:10.1002/poi3.152

Kemp, S. (2020, January 30). Digital 2020: 3.8 billion people use social media. [Blog post]. Retrieved from https://wearesocial.com/blog/2020/01/digital-2020-3-8-billion-people-use-social-media

Klonick, K. (2018). The new governors: The people, rules, and processes governing online speech. *Harvard Law Review*, *131*, 1598–1670. Retrieved from https://harvardlawreview.org/wp-content/uploads/2018/04/1598-1670_Online.pdf

Laidlaw, E. (2017). Myth or promise? The corporate social responsibilities of online service providers for human rights. In M. Taddeo & L. Floridi (Eds.), *The responsibilities of online service providers* (pp. 135–154). Cham: Springer International Publishing.

Langston, J. (2018, September 12). How PhotoDNA for video is being used to fight online child exploitation. *Microsoft*. Retrieved from https://news.microsoft.com

Lee, K. (2018). *AI superpowers: China, Silicon Valley, and the new world order*. Boston, NY: Houghton Mifflin Harcourt.

Manila Principles on Intermediary Liability. (2015). Retrieved from https://www.manilaprinciples.org/

Martens, T. (2011, December 4). Rockers, fully exposed on Is Anyone Up?. *Los Angeles Times*. Retrieved from https://www.latimes.com/entertainment/la-xpm-2011-dec-04-la-ca-pop-nudes-20111204-story.html

McGlynn, C., & Rackley, E. (2017). Image-based sexual abuse. *Oxford Journal of Legal Studies*, *37*(3), 535–561. doi:10.1093/ojls/gqw033

Microsoft. (2020). Non-consensual pornography reporting form. Retrieved from https://www.microsoft.com/en-au/concern/revengeporn

Milne, A. (2020, March 27). Porn site's free service during coronavirus raises sex trafficking fears. *Reuters*. Retrieved from https://www.reuters.com/article/us-britain-women-trafficking-trfn/porn-sites-free-service-during-coronavirus-raises-sex-trafficking-fears-idUSKBN21D3E9

Okoye, A. (2009). Theorising corporate social responsibility as an essentially contested concept: Is a definition necessary?. *Journal of Business Ethics*, *89*, 613–627. doi: 10.1007/s10551-008-0021-9

Pornhub. (2020, March 9). Terms of service. Retrieved from https://www.pornhub.com/information#terms

Pornhub. (n.d.). Content removal request?. Retrieved from https://www.pornhub.com/content-removal

Powell, A., Henry, N., & Flynn, A. (2018). Image-based sexual abuse. In W. DeKeseredy, & M. Dragiewicz (Eds.), *Routledge handbook of critical criminology* (2nd ed., pp. 305–315). Abingdon and New York, NY: Routledge.

Ranking Digital Rights. (2019, May). 2019 Corporate Accountability Index. Retrieved from https://rankingdigitalrights.org/index2019/assets/static/download/RDRindex2019report.pdf

Roberts, S. (2019). *Behind the screen: Content moderation in the shadows of social media*. New Haven, CT: Yale University Press.

Romano, A. (2018, May 24). Facebook's plan to stop revenge porn may be been creepier than revenge porn. *Vox*. Retrieved from https://www.vox.com/

Ruvalcaba, Y., & Eaton, A. A. (2020). Nonconsensual pornography among US adults: A sexual scripts framework on victimization, perpetration, and health correlates for women and men. *Psychology of Violence*, *10*(1), 68–78. doi:10.1037/vio0000233

Salter, M., Crofts, T., & Lee, M. (2018). Beyond criminalisation and responsibilisation: Sexting, gender and young people. *Current Issues in Criminal Justice*, *24*(3), 301–316. doi:10.1080/10345329.2013.12035963

Satariano, A. (2018, May 24). G. D. P. R., a new privacy law, makes Europe world's leading tech watchdog. *New York Times*. Retrieved from https://www.nytimes.com

Secretary of State for Digital, Culture, Media & Sport and the Secretary of State for the Home Department. (2019). Online Harms White Paper. London: HM Government. Retrieved from https://assets.publishing.service.gov.uk/government/uploads/system/uploads/attachment_data/file/793360/Online_Harms_White_Paper.pdf

Slane, A., & Langlois, G. (2018, March). Debunking the myth of "not my bad": Sexual images, consent, and online host responsibilities in Canada. *Canadian Journal of Women and the Law*, *30*(1), 42–81. doi:10.3138/cjwl.30.1.42

Snap Inc. (2019). Community guidelines. Retrieved from https://www.snap.com/en-US/community-guidelines

Solon, O. (2019, November 18). Inside Facebook's efforts to stop revenge porn before it spreads. *NBC News*. Retrieved from https://www.nbcnews.com

Suzor, N. (2019). *Lawless: The secret rules that govern our digital lives*. Cambridge: Cambridge University Press.

Taddeo, M., & Floridi, L. (2016). The debate on the moral responsibilities of online service providers. *Science and Engineering Ethics*, *22*, 1575–1603. doi:10.1007/s11948-015-9734-1

TikTok. (2019, December 12). Understanding our community guidelines. Retrieved from https://newsroom.tiktok.com/understanding-our-community-guidelines/

Tumblr. (2020, January 23). Community guidelines. Retrieved from https://www.tumblr.com/policy/en/community

Tushnet, R. (2008). Power without responsibility: Intermediaries and the First Amendment. *George Washington Law Review*, *76*(4), 986–1016. Retrieved from https://www.gwlr.org/wp-content/uploads/2012/08/76-4-Tushnet.pdf

Twitter. (2020). Synthetic and manipulated media policy. Retrieved from https://help.twitter.com/en/rules-and-policies/manipulated-media

United Nations. (2011). Guiding principles on business and human rights. Retrieved from https://www.ohchr.org/documents/publications/guidingprinciplesbusinesshr_en.pdf

Westlake, E. J. (2008). Friend me if you Facebook: Generation Y and performative surveillance. *TDR/The Drama Review*, *52*(4), 21–40. doi:10.1162/dram.2008.52.4.21

Witt, A., Suzor, N., & Huggins, A. (2019). The rule of law on Instagram: An evaluation of the moderation of images depicting women's bodies. *UNSW Law Journal*, *42*(2), 557–596. Retrieved from http://www.unswlawjournal.unsw.edu.au/wp-content/uploads/2019/06/6-UNSWLJ-422-Witt-Suzor-and-Huggins-Final.pdf

xHamster. (2020, April 22). Terms and conditions: User agreement. Retrieved from https://xhamster.com/info/terms

XVideos. (n.d). XVideos terms of service. Retrieved from https://info.xvideos.com/legal/tos/

York, J. C., & Zuckerman, E. (2019). Moderating the public sphere. In R. F. Jørgensen (Ed.), *Human rights in the age of platforms* (pp. 137–161). Cambridge, MA: The MIT Press.

YouTube. (2020). Nudity and sexual content policies. Retrieved from https://support.google.com/youtube/answer/2802002?hl=en

Zuboff, S. (2019). *The age of surveillance capitalism: The fight for a human future at the new frontier of power*. London: Profile Books.

Zuckerberg, M. (2019, March 30). Mark Zuckerberg: The internet needs new rules. Let's start in these four areas. *Washington Post*. Retrieved from https://washingtonpost.com

Chapter 44

Calling All Stakeholders: An Intersectoral Dialogue about Collaborating to End Tech-Facilitated Violence and Abuse

Jane Bailey and Raine Liliefeldt

Abstract

The emergence of technology-facilitated violence and abuse (TFVA) has led to calls for increased collaboration across and among sectors. Growing recognition of the need for multistakeholder collaboration (MSC) between industry, civil society, government, and academia reflects the number of moving parts involved, the need for specialized knowledge and skills in relation to certain issues, and the importance of recognizing the ways in which interlocking systems of subordination can lead to very different experiences with and impressions of social justice issues (Crenshaw, 1991). Numerous financial, professional, and personal factors incentivize MSC. Notwithstanding growing opportunities and incentives for TFVA-related MSC, collaborative efforts bring with them their own set of challenges. This chapter integrates elements of the literature on MSC, particularly those focusing on risks, benefits, and ways forward, with excerpts from a dialogue between an academic and community organization leader who are collaborating on a research partnership encompassing TFVA against young Canadians.

Keywords: Multistakeholder collaboration; intersectoral cooperation; transdisciplinary initiatives; collaborative models; intersectionality; power imbalance

Introduction

As with other complex social justice issues, the emergence of technology-facilitated violence and abuse (TFVA) has led to calls for increased intersectoral collaboration

The Emerald International Handbook of Technology-Facilitated Violence and Abuse, 769–786

doi:10.1108/978-1-83982-848-520211056

(Canada, 2017, pp. 44–54). This has been particularly true in the context of violent extremist/terrorist content (New Zealand, Ministry of Foreign Affairs Industry and Trade, n.d.), which is emblematic of a call for multistakeholder collaboration (MSC) in the development of internet policy more generally (OECD, 2014, p. 8). Issues such as internet governance and TFVA arguably fall within a broad class of "wicked problems,"[1] like sustainability, that MSC "among industry, government, the public, and researchers is widely acknowledged as a critical success factor" in resolving (Foley, Wiek, Kay, & Rushforth, 2016, p. 2). Those focused on sustainability note that the benefits of MSC include "pooling [the] capacities and resources" (Foley et al., 2016, p. 2) of a wide variety of individuals and organizations with "unique perspectives" in a form of "shared inquiry with others" (Krawchuk, 2013, p. 12). MSC models are touted as enabling "a synergy that no one element could have produced on its own" (Krawchuk, 2013, p. 10). Moreover, stakeholders may be less resistant to implementing changes arising from action plans they were involved in creating (Krawchuk, 2013).

Notwithstanding its promised benefits, MSC is rife with equality-related challenges. These include mistrust and power asymmetry (Foley et al., 2016), as well as ensuring participation of and according an equal voice (Wayne-Nixon, Wragg-Morris, Mishra, Markle, & Kindornay, 2019) to women (Grosser, 2014), young people (Bista, 2016; Livingstone, Byrne, & Bulgar, 2015), and members of other marginalized communities. Such challenges are of particular relevance to TFVA-related MSCs given TFVA's negative effects on communities marginalized by intersecting oppressions such as homophobia (see Dietzel, this volume; and Waldman, this volume), transphobia (see Colliver, this volume), and misogyny (see Gosse, this volume). The stark power imbalances between corporations providing internet platforms and services (Henry & Powell, 2016), governments, and the individuals likely to be targeted by TFVA (and community organizations who support them) add further equality-related complexity to TFVA-related MSCs.

This chapter brings literature on MSC's benefits and challenges into dialogue with excerpts from a discussion about our experiences with TFVA-related MSCs. We connect some of the key issues raised in the literature with our experiences. We begin by introducing ourselves, highlighting our connections with TFVA-related MSC. Next we provide an overview of the literature relating to MSC, focusing on some incentives for and related benefits of such collaboration. Finally, we focus on our experiences with making MSC work on the ground, including considering what "success" looks like, the related issues of power imbalance, legitimacy, accountability, and trust, and how to identify and prioritize the needs of those affected. The conclusion summarizes our recommendations and best practices for TFVA-related MSC.

Who We Are

We are members of *The eQuality Project*, a seven-year research project focused on young people's experiences with privacy and equality in networked spaces, which includes a TFVA-focused stream. The eQuality Project is a collaborative partnership involving academic researchers (from Canada, the United States, Hong

Kong, and Finland) and local, provincial, national, and international community organizations, youth groups, educators, and policymakers. Jane Bailey, who is a Full Professor at the University of Ottawa Faculty of Law, leads the TFVA project stream and co-leads the overall project with Dr. Valerie Steeves, of the University of Ottawa Department of Criminology. Raine Liliefeldt is the Director of Member Services and Development at YWCA Canada, a community organization partner in The eQuality Project. YWCA Canada is a federated organization with member associations across Canada that acts and advocates to "right injustices faced by women and girls in Canada through timely research, responsive projects, pro-active initiatives and relevant advocacy campaigns" (YWCA Canada, 2020).

Our involvement with TFVA arose at different times and through different paths. Over 20 years ago, while a litigation lawyer in Toronto, Jane was part of a team representing a complainant in the first Canadian Human Rights Tribunal proceeding about internet hate speech. Jane's involvement in that case encouraged graduate work and ultimately led to an academic position where she focuses on topics like internet hate propaganda, online child sexual abuse, and the interactions between privacy and equality in networked spaces. About 14 years ago, Raine recognized the need for work around online safety issues after discussing an 18+ (adults only) site, BlackPlanet, with young women at a local YWCA chapter in Toronto. Raine, alongside these young women and a volunteer from TV Ontario, developed a cybersafety workshop with information about blocking your camera and avoiding identifying markers when posting selfies.

We have experience collaborating with individuals and organizations from sectors outside our own and in relation to TFVA. Prior to The eQuality Project, Jane was involved in another collaborative partnership called The eGirls Project, which included MediaSmarts (Canada's leading digital literacy organization), policymakers, and other academics and examined girls' and young women's experiences of TFVA. Jane met Raine while working on The eGirls Project, leading to their collaboration on The eQuality Project. When they met, Raine was leading a YWCA Canada initiative, Project Shift, funded by the Canadian Minister of the Status of Women. Project Shift brought together the justice, academic, and technology/information and communications technology (ICT) sectors, and girls and young women with lived experience of TFVA. Raine has been involved in many other collaborative initiatives over the last 18 years in the nonprofit sector.

In order to prepare this chapter, we met in Toronto on October 16, 2019 and were interviewed for approximately two-and-a-half hours by University of Ottawa law student, Vanessa Ford, about our experiences with TFVA-related MSC. Vanessa's questions were framed around issues arising from her research on MSC, including the meaning of MSC, how to define "success," leveraging diverse resources and expertise from stakeholders, and dealing with differences in stakeholder priorities and power. Our intention was to provide on-the-ground perspectives on making MSC "work" based on differing experiences and standpoints: Jane from the perspective of an academic and Raine from the perspective of a community organization leader. We have incorporated transcribed excerpts from our discussion into the next sections in order to bring our TFVA-related experiences into dialogue with the literature around MSC (which itself does not currently focus on TFVA *per se*).

Multistakeholder Collaboration: Working Definition, Benefits, and Incentives

In this chapter, we define MSC as follows:

> Alliances of individuals and organizations from the nonprofit, government, philanthropic, and business sectors that use their diverse perspectives and resources to jointly solve a societal problem and achieve a shared goal. (Becker & Smith, 2018, p. 2)

MSC is used for different purposes, such as governance (Ansell & Gash, 2008) and planning (Oonk, Gulikers, & Mulder, 2016), as well as in relation to different societal issues, including sustainability (Foley et al., 2016), youth violence (Bista, 2016), and international development (Wayne-Nixon et al., 2019). Prominent among incentives for engaging MSC is the emergence (or at least recognition) of wicked problems, the complexity of which requires "pooling capacities and resources" (Krawchuk, 2013, p. 9) from various sectors representing diverse areas of expertise, knowledge, and experience (see also Foley et al., 2016).

We think TFVA is a compelling example of a wicked problem, as part of a long-standing continuum of violence against women, girls, and members of other marginalized communities involving very *real* spiritual, psychological, emotional, and sometimes physical harms. It can be embroiled in preexisting patterns of domestic violence, but it isn't *just* about individual perpetrators. TFVA also involves technical infrastructures, corporate and law enforcement policies, education and awareness, and broader underlying social structures like misogyny and racism. As Raine put it during our discussion:

> It's the ether. I talk about that often. It's everything that's connected. It's not just one avenue. It's the system, it's the structure, its more than systemic, it's atmospheric.

The potential practical benefits of MSC for addressing this atmospheric problem are numerous. From Raine's perspective:

> It's connecting into different sectors, different pockets of air and so I think that for me, MSC is about recognizing that it takes all of us to solve it.

Further, involving multiple stakeholders with a shared concern about a problem means incorporating a range of perspectives and experiences that can lead to creative codeveloped responses where all participants feel invested. In turn, stakeholder investment in cocreated responses can reduce resistance, and develop a greater commitment to shared plans of action – thus improving the odds of implementation (Krawchuk, 2013).

Individual stakeholders may also benefit in particular ways. Community organizations, for example, may benefit from access to research and syntheses of research that they otherwise would not have the time or money to develop or engage with, as well as through relationships with people/organizations that would otherwise be out of reach. Further, access to funding is increasingly contingent on working collaboratively. In Raine's experience with seeking funding for YWCA Canada initiatives:

> ... more and more what's happening is people, whether funders or corporate or government, they are mandating that organizations work together, that various sectors come together to collaborate.

Similar kinds of financial incentives are evident in academia, including the emergence of the Partnership Grant funding model implemented by Canada's Social Sciences and Humanities Research Council (2019), where funding is contingent on intersectoral collaborative partnerships. Academics are also incentivized to engage with MSC by a renewed emphasis on, as Jane put it, signaling "to the community that it is not just ... med schools that are doing something of relevance to the community: that research *throughout* universities is relevant to the community." Further, MSC, in emphasizing a bottom-up flow of direction and information from marginalized community members affected by TFVA, also offers intrinsic incentives by allowing scholars to use the privilege of academic freedom to connect with what matters to the community.

Working collaboratively also provides opportunities for thinking beyond silos. For Jane, as a law professor, this means, "start[ing] to think about the wide variety of contributions that can be made to address TFVA that don't involve either law or criminalization." Similarly, working in MSCs has made both of us more aware of the in-sector jargon used, which challenges us to avoid or clarify terms that interfere with others receiving our message. For example, Raine learned through engagement with the ICT sector in Project Shift that common nonprofit sector language about "safety and safe spaces ... when ... put in front of engineers and developers [was] a total turn off and no one will pay attention from then on." MSCs have also encouraged us not to presume terms like "safe" or "safety" mean the same thing to everyone. As Jane noted:

> Safety in certain circles is ... tightly associated with criminalization, policing, and surveillance, whereas safety in other circles means respect for diversity and inclusion where you feel safe to participate because you are respected for who you are. Everyone may say we are all for online safety but then the model for online safety that is for securitization is criminal law; it's telling kids do this and don't do that. It's not looking at what kind of an environment we have created in terms of whether everybody feels safe to participate and who is responsible for that environment. It's a very very different kind of response. If you are all on board with "safety" and then all of a sudden you start talking about programming, you are like "oh no, that's not what I meant by safety." So, unpacking terminology is huge in this context.

Financial, personal, and professional incentives for engaging with MSC are also connected with the growth in popularity of more participatory, transdisciplinary (Ayala-Orozco et al., 2018), and community-centered/engaged research models that may better enable equality-based intersectional research and challenge power hierarchies embedded in traditional social science data collection models (Bailey et al., 2019). These include Community-Engaged Research (CER) (Closson & Nelson, 2009), Participatory Action Research (PAR) (Roche, 2011), and Democratic Dialogue (Pruitt & Thomas, 2007). A detailed discussion of these models is beyond the scope of this chapter.[2]

Notwithstanding the positive potential of MSC and the array of incentives for implementation, MSC is replete with equality-related challenges frequently rooted in power imbalances. These challenges are of special significance in the context of addressing a problem such as TFVA, which itself both reflects and is reflective of intransigent forms of structural discrimination within society (Henry et al., 2020; Henry & Powell, 2016). We now move on to discuss several of those challenges.

Making Collaboration Work: Perspectives from the Ground

Defining "Success": Priorities, Measurement, Intersectionality, and Learning from "Failure"

In our experience in the TFVA context, "success" can mean different things to different collaborators. We suggest that a definition of success inclusive of both process and product can be a unifying force in MSC. For Raine, success means:

> That the process is rewarding and it is collegial and respectful and we are working towards the same process and product and that outcome is also reflective of where everyone wanted to go at the beginning because it can be the other way and a real challenge. It is about the process, the ongoing communication, being able to connect to the work, having a real[lly] clear understanding that we are all multiple limbs of one unit moving in the same direction together. Process and product are the success points for me.

Notwithstanding this broad approach to success, however, misalignments in collaborators' priorities can impede actual and/or perceived success. Often, MSC literature focuses on misalignments arising in collaborations involving private sector corporations which are primarily focused on profit (Adam, James, & Wanjira, 2007). This can be challenging in public/private initiatives, since, as Badré (2017) notes, often the interests of these participants:

> … are not immediately aligned and there is suspicion between the two. In most countries in the world, public authorities think that the private sector is willing to reap the reward without taking any

> risk. Vice versa, the private sector believes that the public sector is, in the worst case, corrupt; or is too bureaucratic, too slow, or not reactive enough (para 4).

We have experienced priority misalignments in public/private collaborations. As Jane noted in TFVA-related interactions with government:

> We don't know how to address violence against women and girls to start with and then you add this layer of technology on so you have this intractable problem which means almost inevitably, to me, the solution is long term and progress is not going to be obvious or immediate. [But government works] on election cycles and so often ... what happens ... is they pass some form of criminal legislation, which ... in some circumstances may send an important message, but then it often stops there because that buys them what they need in terms of the electoral impression that the government cares about this issue. ... So to be the academic appearing in front of committees and talking about long term social transformation and smashing the patriarchy, ... there is such a misalignment in terms of priority.

Misalignments in priority, however, are not, in our experience, limited to public/private collaborations. Raine's experience in a collaborative initiative involving nonprofit organizations with different mandates in health, youth, and justice exemplified this:

> [An external funder requested] for these three/four organizations to work together. The challenge lay in the fact that there was a disparity in the size of the organizations, with the one organization having a greater tie to the funder than the others, [and] one having greater community connections across the country, ... but there was never an opportunity for the partners to get together to talk about what success would look like outside of the outcomes and objectives of the project. There were no discussions about what would happen if there was conflict.

From this experience, it became obvious to Raine that:

> Just because non-profit organizations are in the same sector, it doesn't mean we are all working at the same level. We are not all working with a trauma-informed approach or an anti-racism, anti-oppression lens. We are not all connected to our service users in the same way.

In this case, the presumption that same-sector organizations operate similarly meant that mechanisms for resolving disputes and ensuring accountability were never put in place. Having learned from this experience, Raine's team has developed a charter that emphasizes that their

> focus is on respect, integrity, accountability, empathy, compassion, and trust and we say that this is how we are going to work together. We are going to make sure that we are focused on whether we are keeping this at the front of our mind in our communications – not only internally but in our communications with our partners and recognizing that we are working for women and girls, marginalized people, that is at the top of our mind, so that when those priorities and those mandates aren't aligned and we can start sensing it, here's some common language for us to find.

As Raine noted, constating documents can play an important role in addressing misalignments in TFVA-related collaborative initiatives:

> Some challenges arise [where there are differences in organizational values and mandates] and they can be explosive and how you have to deal with it is with the tools you have and the conflict resolution methods that have been entrenched into your agreements or your MOUs [Memoranda of Understanding].

Measuring and proving "success" are two other problems we encountered in our TFVA-related collaborations. As a complex social problem interwoven with long-standing forms of structural discrimination and oppression, meaningful quantifiable measures of "success" arising from MSC can be difficult to identify. Measurability can play an important role in the evaluation of outcomes by external funding agencies. As Jane noted, community partners may especially feel

> pressure ... to have a statistical way of proving success. ... The way that you undo TFVA has to do with undoing violence against women and other vulnerable groups more generally and we all know that doesn't happen by one program or creating a product and then evaluating what people learned from a program even though that might be what a funder would require you to do.

The effects of intersecting forms of oppression also present challenges for measuring success in the context of TFVA-related MSC. For example, a perceived "win" that involves eroding privacy to facilitate improved law enforcement against perpetrators can later backfire by diminishing privacy for TFVA targets. For many TFVA targets, inadequate privacy protections are a critical factor in exposure to abuse in the first place (see, Harris & Woodlock, this volume).

Finally, we recognize that current failures can pave the way to future successes. As Raine recalled:

> I think that through [one failed] collaboration, I learned so much around what not to do. All my future projects with external and internal partners have been modeled on not repeating that. When another opportunity was pushed upon us to work in a similar way, I had all the tools and tricks and understanding to make sure that did not happen again. ... [So that, in another situation where] it was clear to us there wasn't a sense of alignment, we actually pulled out of the opportunity that could have meant a good amount of funding, [because] our values as an organization and as a group of people that work together [were] not matching. ... So we stepped away.

Power Dynamics, Legitimacy, Accountability, and Trust

MSC is imbued with power dynamics (McDonald, Jayasuriya, & Harris, 2012), which affect trust between participants (Foley et al., 2016), as well as their perceptions of process legitimacy and accountability (Global Partnership for the Prevention of Armed Conflict, 2015).

Having greater power often correlates with greater human and financial resources, which in turn can provide greater visibility, credibility, and access to reports, research, and policymakers (Loveridge & Wilson, 2017, p. 28). As noted by Foley et al. (2016), power asymmetry "manifests in instances of withholding information, expertise biases, meeting settings, and exclusive decision making" (p. 9). As a result, those with less resources often have less power to influence or to shift power dynamics in their favor, resulting in underrepresentation of their views and experiences, and sometimes them being abused, overruled, manipulated, or excluded. These realities have led some to argue that marginalized stakeholders should avoid MSC altogether in favor of solidarity networks and social movements (see, e.g., Hiemstra, Brouwer, & Van Vugt, 2012, pp. 5–7).

Power imbalances can also undermine participants' trust in each other. Trust, according to Hiemstra et al. (2012), "is a measure of one party's belief in the honesty, fairness, or benevolence of another party," so if trust is not present, "it has to be created" (p. 15). Meaningful collaboration requires building collaborative processes in which "the fortune of each sector is inextricably linked to the other" (Loveridge & Wilson, 2017, p. 340), and collaborators are held accountable to each other (Badré, 2017) and to any constituencies they are representing. Legitimacy is crucial in these circumstances, and "is usually linked to the credibility of the convener, the participants and the process itself" (Global Partnership for Armed Conflict, 2015, p. 30).

Making MSCs work, therefore, requires attending to power relations (McDonald et al., 2012). Large private sector business players, for example, have to "understand that dialogue in the multi-stakeholder context is different from traditional business negotiation" (Loveridge & Wilson, 2017, p. 640). Space must also be made for naming and recognizing other forms of power (Hiemstra et al., 2012, p. 16), including on-the-ground experience and the trust of individuals/communities directly affected by the issue at hand.

Power, legitimacy, accountability, and trust have all figured heavily in our experiences with TFVA-related MSC. For example, YWCA Canada was engaged in a pilot project, which from Raine's perspective, "wasn't a success because the service providers in shelters were so suspicious of the process." She explained:

> When women came into the shelter having experienced violence, they were asked by the service providers if there is a risk that their abuser might use an intimate image and share it widely online. [A process had been worked out with Facebook] where [the woman targeted] could upload the photo and it would be hashed and digitized and become a thumbnail that can't be shared after the fact. Women were more, and so, concerned about that entire process that they didn't even give up the photo, even if there was one.[3]

Power imbalances in public/private MSCs can lead to situations where those with less resources end up, as Jane put it,

> feeling like you are there for window dressing and the outcome is the outcome of the party with power and now they want to say you've endorsed it because you were along for the ride.

However, our experiences demonstrate that the problem of "window dressing" isn't just associated with private sector players. Academics and nonprofit organizations also enjoy power and privileges when involved in MSCs. These sectors, too, must ensure that TFVA-related collaborations involving young people and others who have experienced violence provide meaningful and respectful opportunities that center their priorities. As Jane recalled:

> One of the things that we've seen in particular working with young people, whose expertise and contributions are often devalued, is to ensure that all participants are adequately resourced, because that signals a respect for knowledge and expertise. Clarity around responsibilities and duties is also a signal of respect to recognize their expertise, including agreements around the form and timing of their contributions. And then also, obviously working with young people in this context, asking them what their needs and priorities are and really making a genuine effort to center those because the minute the project starts to veer off into something young people have told you ten times is not of interest to them, why would they continue to be interested?

Respectful, inclusive, antioppression communication practices that work to recognize and address power asymmetries also involve devoting resources to support meaningful participation by *all* stakeholders. Jane has derived insights on this issue from negative experiences in policymaking forums:

> You're sort of sitting around a table and the policy maker is priding themselves that they're having a MSC and what's immediately clear is that everyone at the table is not the same in terms of power. So you invite some young women from an activist group and a high school and you sit them across from an officer of a giant social media platform and a couple of professors and everybody is not in equal power position[s]. Even if you manage it so everyone gets to say something, people don't come with the same resources. … Even though we know community organizations and individuals are never going to have the lobbying power corporations do, at [a] minimum … we have to address power asymmetries as much as we can in that process.

Mechanisms for addressing power asymmetries include providing financial supports, informational context, and background to those who need it, using plain language, and offering other sorts of capacity-building initiatives (including open access resource materials) to familiarize participants with new settings so their leadership capacities and expertise can be fully realized and applied. This can also include putting members of affected communities in executive positions within MSC, enabling them to hold collaborators accountable. Finally, as discussed above, specifically incorporating protocols for respectful communication and inclusivity within founding MSC documents, as well as dispute resolution mechanisms and off-ramps, can also be a way to minimize the "window dressing" risk. As Jane suggested:

> [Try] to figure out as best you can in the beginning who has what responsibility and what the limits on outcomes are and [have] the capacity at some point to be able to say, "this is the end of the line for us as part of this collaboration [because if this is where things are going], we can't endorse or be a part of that outcome." It's not to say it may not be a functional outcome for other collaborators, [but it may not be for certain individuals or organizations].

In other cases, coping with power asymmetries and differences in mandate and capacities may best be addressed by recognizing that the dial on intransigent social problems can also be moved forward in multiple ways, including through initiatives by subsets of collaborative participants. As Jane put it, recognizing this

> allows for … situations where maybe one partner's values don't align with another's so they don't want, [for example] to do internal work with a private organization, but that doesn't mean that that work can't get done. There are many ways of going about it and different people can bring different kinds of relationships and expertise and limitations on their values and expectations and still be moving forward to produce something without everybody having to participate with everyone else all the time.

Similarly, in Raine's TFVA-related experience, it was important to recognize the meaningful contributions smaller private players made:

> I was always excited about the smaller tech companies that went along with Project Shift and changed their policies and practices along the way. Uken Games started looking at all the issues around user experience and building empathy into their reporting and having a different relationship with the person on the other end. That I think for me was a bigger shift, and they did a big overhaul compared to larger corporations.

Larger corporations can be less nimble so real change may only be incentivized when problems like those involving Cambridge Analytica, that affect mainstream community members (as opposed to marginalized communities), are publicized.

Identifying and Prioritizing What Community Members Need Most

Since TFVA disproportionately affects members of communities whose time and resources are often stretched by the marginalizing effects of structural oppression, TFVA researchers and nonprofit organizations serving these communities often represent the interests of affected individuals/groups in MSCs. In these cases, being an academic or nonprofit sector participant carries special responsibilities. In our TFVA-related work, we have attempted to prioritize representing the perspectives of girls, women, and young people from marginalized communities by insisting not only that organizations (like YWCA Canada) representing girls and women from a variety of social locations be included but also – as we discuss below – that a diverse range of girls and women from marginalized communities who have experienced TFVA be directly included.

Stakeholder inclusion needs to be planned, as opposed to "organically" happening, in order to avoid, as Jane put it:

> [Being in] kind of the filter bubble where you are attracting those who are not just like minded in values, but maybe represent similar communities, not necessarily diverse communities for example, with a connection to intersectionality.

To minimize that risk, as a project begins, YWCA Canada engages in a stakeholder mapping exercise. As Raine described it in relation to Project Shift:

> It was really clear as I started thinking through the issue in the first phase of the project, which was about bringing partners together. I was around looking at who I wanted [to be included] and it's kind of like the user journey,[4] … where I thought if I am someone who's just experienced TFVA and I'm in high school, what am I going to do? And then what am I going to do after that and who am I going to connect with at all those points up until the justice system?

This approach allowed Raine to recognize that there were multiple different connection points – social media platforms, schools, principals, teachers, community organizations, police, mental health organizations – *and* that "these silos understand and address the issue differently." Police, for example, might say, "it's not a thing … off you go," and elected officials and lawyers weren't necessarily clear on the issues either. Centring the experiences on TFVA targets in the analysis broadened the YWCA's understanding of who needed to be at the table in order to meet targets' needs.

From Raine's perspective, taking a user-centered approach also requires directly connecting

> with service users to identify their needs. With Project Shift, it started with a gender-based analysis and needs assessment and it's how we go about doing our research. It's trauma-informed, anti-racist, anti-oppressive, centering the voices of folks with lived experiences. Those are the key pieces, and valuing the contributions and the knowledge of our program workers on the ground in communities who have a really clear understanding of their service users and the issues they are facing.

The eQuality Project also prioritizes engaging with targeted youth from marginalized communities in a respectful way that acknowledges their experience and expertise. This means moving beyond classic data extraction models toward more collaborative and participatory research models, driven by young people from diverse social locations. In addition to standard social science methods like focus groups and interviews, The eQuality Project also employs approaches like art workshops, concept mapping, Q sorting,[5] and deliberative dialogue (Bailey et al., 2019). As Jane noted, it also relies heavily on partnering with trusted and credible organizations "who have their finger on the pulse and are paying attention to constituents' needs as a way of finding out more about … who to talk to or what the issues are."

That said, we both recognize that, as Raine observed, "people aren't going to jump at the opportunity to consult" just because an MSC is dedicated to taking an intersectional approach that prioritizes inclusion of voices from a diverse range of social locations. As Jane noted:

> Number one, a lot of [marginalized] communities are tapped out because you and a thousand other people want their expertise, and number two, maybe they are just not interested in what you're doing. [I can't assume that just because] I think this is so important that it must be on the top of your priority list, too, [especially] when members of marginalized communities are dealing with life and death situations every day.

Although social media companies play a significant role in the TFVA context, it is also important to ensure frontline service providers have the necessary technical information to support clients without relying on corporate actors or actions. As Raine reflected:

> If they feel confident in themselves around the understanding of their data, privacy, and security, then they can have those conversations to say this is something you might want to think about because you may not want to upload your photo to Facebook and have it hashed, but maybe you want to think about turning off your GPS locator. Maybe when you go back you get an escort to your former home, you don't grab your partner's phone and they come find you. It's those kind of conversations I can do something about.

For Raine, addressing reasonable doubts about corporate responses and involvement has also meant supporting TFVA survivors when sharing their lived TFVA experiences with corporate stakeholders (that are amenable to change):

> I think that with the smaller [tech companies], building the empathy, ... I think breaking down that wall and screen between the programmers and their service users essentially, that I think was really successful because, in some cases, having folks hear the impact of something being shared, having a meme created about part of your body and it spreading widely through your school, like the mental trauma that that causes, I think that continues to be the piece that was a bit of the tipping point.

That said, facilitating survivors' telling of their stories carries with it risks that must be addressed. As Raine noted:

> [So] for me it is about making sure that they know that there is an out for them, that this is a leadership opportunity and we are changing something by them telling their story and it's not just a fluff piece. It's not for the sake of re-injuring you. The information you are entrusting me with is going to the right people who can make decisions.

Finally, our experiences have made it clear how important honesty about what can – and cannot – be accomplished through a collaborative initiative, especially when working with those directly affected by TFVA, is expressed. As Raine put it:

> [W]hen people ask for something specific, we need to deliver and if we can't, we have to tell them why.

Conclusion

MSC is becoming a staple approach for responding to complex social problems like TFVA. Numerous financial, professional, and personal incentives provide impetus for the synergistic benefits of bringing together diverse stakeholders with diverse expertise to address atmospheric problems. Incentives and benefits notwithstanding, MSC carries with it challenges, some of which are of special import in relation to problems like TFVA that are underlain by persistent structural inequality. These include how to define and measure success, misaligned priorities between collaborators, how to meaningfully give effect to intersectionality, and how to deal with failed initiatives.

While there is vast literature on MSC and its challenges,[6] our goal has been to discuss how those issues have manifested in our own experiences with TFVA-related MSCs and to derive insights based on them. Our modest suggestions for maximizing the benefits and recognizing the limits of MSCs in order to meaningfully address TFVA are to:

- Employ user-journey tools, needs assessments, and in-person consultations with those directly affected by TFVA to identify participants and priorities for MSC;
- Spend time up front paying close attention to and discussing the development of constating documents, such as MOUs, to ensure they:
  - define the MSC's objectives in terms of both product *and* process, so that success can be measured not just in terms of quantifiable outputs but also whether the collaboration has been carried out in accordance with anti-oppression and intersectional values based on respect for and actualization of diversity and inclusion;
  - set out procedures for addressing and resolving conflicts/disputes;
  - allow for collaboration between subsections of the MSC, subject to group accountability; and
  - provide "off-ramps" that allow collaborators from marginalized communities to leave the MSC when they can no longer agree with its direction and are concerned about becoming "window dressing."
- Schedule relationship-building time into the MSC;
- Measure success at preagreed designated times throughout the MSC and not just by outputs like programs or legal reform, but also by whether the process lived up to articulated commitments to diversity and inclusion, and centered the voices of those with lived experiences of TFVA and their supporters;
- Actualize the MSC's commitment to intersectionality and diversity by:
  - including people and organizations from diverse social locations;
  - providing informational and financial resources and moral supports to promote equal participation of those from marginalized communities; and
  - ensuring diverse representation in executive positions to maximize accountability to affected communities.
- Develop a charter that expresses the core values of your organization, and be prepared to refuse participation in MSCs that don't align with those values or to leave existing MSCs that are not measuring up;

- Use more participatory, community-led models such as PAR and deliberative dialogue to conduct research; and
- Conduct exit interviews with collaborators at the end of the MSC to evaluate what went right, what went wrong, and to identify how those lessons can and will be incorporated into future collaborative initiatives.

As MSC becomes an increasingly favored approach for addressing wicked problems like TFVA, the importance of realistically evaluating its risks and benefits escalates. We hope that sharing lessons learned from our experiences with TFVA-related MSC will contribute meaningfully to that evaluation process.

Notes

1. Krawchuk (2013), adopting the approach of Denning, Dunham, and Brown (2010, p. 315), uses the term "wicked" to describe "issues 'for which there is no consensus on the problem or on the solution and partisan interests [potentially] block collaboration'" (p. 11).
2. CER research is a collaborative process "between the researcher and community partner that creates and disseminates knowledge and creative expression with the goal of contributing to the discipline and strengthening the well-being of the community" (Virginia Commonwealth University, n.d, Community engaged research, para 1). PAR can be thought of both as a community-based research method and as a tool for strengthening community relationships, where "research questions, studies, and evaluation frameworks are developed in partnership with the group or organization under study" (Bailey et al., 2019, p. 9). Democratic (or deliberative) dialogue is a PAR method, a form of "community inquiry" bringing together experts and citizens to create an understanding of issues relevant to policymaking and development (Bailey et al., 2019, p. 9, citing; Escobar, 2014, p. 483).
3. See Henry et al. (2020) for a discussion of this initiative.
4. See Trebble, Hansi, Hydes, Smith, & Baker. (2010) for further discussion of user journey mapping or client/patient-centered approaches.
5. Q sorting and concept mapping "use traditional quantitative methods … to explore the perspectives of individual research participants" and "are effective for examining conceptual spaces that are complex and admit multiple characterizations or are understood from a variety of lived perspectives" (Bailey et al., 2019, p. 7).
6. See, for example: Wayne-Nixon et al. (2019); Foley et al. (2016); Hiemstra, Brouwer, and Van Vugt (2012).

References

Adam, L., James, T., & Wanjira, A. M. (2007). Frequently asked questions about multi-stakeholder partnerships in ICTs for development. [PDF file]. Retrieved from https://www.apc.org/sites/default/files/catia_ms_guide_EN-1.pdf

Ansell, C., & Gash, A. (2008). Collaborative governance in theory and practice. *Journal of Public Administration Research and Theory*, *18*(4), 543–571.

Ayala-Orozco, B., Rosell, J., Merçon, J., Bueno, I., Alatorre-Frenk, G., Langle-Flores, A., & Lobato, A. (2018). Challenges and strategies in place-based multi-stakeholder collaboration for sustainability: Learning from experiences in the Global South. *Sustainability*, *10*(9), 3271.

Badré, B. (2017). To tackle global challenges, the public and private sectors must join forces, here's why. Retrieved from https://www.weforum.org/agenda/2017/02/public-private-cooperation/

Bailey, J., Steeves, V., Burkell, J., Shade, L. R., Regan, P., & Ruparelia, R. (2019). Getting at equality: Research methods informed by the lessons of intersectionality. *International Journal of Qualitative Methods*, *18*(1), 1–13.

Becker, J., & Smith, D. (2018). The need for cross-sector collaboration. *Stanford Social Innovation Review*, *16*(1), C2–C3.

Bista, B. (2016). Youth engage project. [PDF file]. Retrieved from https://www.sfcg.org/wp-content/uploads/2017/06/SFCG_NEP501_YE_Evaluation_Report_FINAL.pdf

Canada, Standing Committee on the Status of Women. (2017). Taking action to end violence against young women and girls in Canada [PDF file]. Retrieved from https://www.ourcommons.ca/Content/Committee/421/FEWO/Reports/RP8823562/feworp07/feworp07-e.pdf

Closson, R., & Nelson, B. (2009). Teaching social justice through community engagement. *International Journal for the Scholarship of Teaching & Learning*, *3*(1), 1–20.

Crenshaw, K. (1991). Mapping the margins: Intersectionality, identity politics, and violence against women of color. *Stanford Law Review*, *43*(6), 1241–1299.

Denning, P., Dunham, R., & Brown, J. S. (2010). *The innovator's way: Essential practices for successful innovation*. Cambridge, MA: MIT Press.

Escobar, O. (2014). Upstream public engagement, downstream policy-making? The brain imaging dialogue as a community of inquiry. *Science and Public Policy*, *41*, 480–492.

Foley, R., Wiek, A., Kay, B., & Rushforth, R. (2016). Ideal and reality of multi-stakeholder collaboration on sustainability problems: A case study on a large-scale industrial contamination in Phoenix, Arizona. *Sustainability Science*, *12*(1), 1–14.

Global Partnership for the Prevention of Armed Conflict. (2015). Multi- stakeholder processes for conflict prevention & peacebuilding. [PDF file]. Retrieved from http://www.mspguide.org/sites/default/files/resource/gppac_mspmanual_interactive_version_final_jan2016_1.pdf

Grosser, K. (2014). Corporate social responsibility and multi-stakeholder governance: Pluralism, feminist perspectives and women's NGOs. *Journal of Business Ethics*, *137*(1), 65–81.

Henry, N., McGlynn, C., Flynn, A., Johnson, K., Powell, A., & Scott, A. J. (2020). *Image-based sexual abuse: A study on the causes and consequences of non-consensual nude or sexual imagery*. London and New York, NY: Routledge.

Henry, N., & Powell, A. (2016). Technology-facilitated sexual violence: A literature review of empirical research. *Trauma, Violence, & Abuse*, *19*(2), 195–208.

Hiemstra, W., Brouwer, H., & Van Vugt, S. (2012). Power dynamics in multistakeholder processes. [PDF file]. Retrieved from https://core.ac.uk/download/pdf/29224523.pdf

Krawchuk, F. (2013). Multi-stakeholder collaboration. [PDF file]. Retrieved from https://oefresearch.org/sites/default/files/documents/publications/msc-digital-final-r.pdf

Livingstone, S., Byrne, J., & Bulgar, M. (2015). Researching children's rights globally in the digital age. [PDF file]. Retrieved from http://eprints.lse.ac.uk/62248/1/__lse.ac.uk_storage_LIBRARY_Secondary_libfile_shared_repository_Content_Livingstone,%20S_Researching%20children's%20rights_2015.pdf

Loveridge, D., & Wilson, N. (2017). Engaging with the private sector through multistakeholder platforms. [PDF file]. Retrieved from https://www.enterprise-development.org/wp-content/uploads/DCED-Platforms-Review.pdf

McDonald, J., Jayasuriya, R., & Harris, M. F. (2012). The influence of power dynamics and trust on multidisciplinary collaboration: A qualitative case study of type 2 diabetes mellitus. *BMC Health Services Research*, *12*(1), 63.

New Zealand, Ministry of Foreign Affairs Industry and Trade. (n.d.). The christchurch call to eliminate terrorist and violent extremist content online. Retrieved from https://www.christchurchcall.com/

Oonk, C., Gulikers, J., & Mulder, M. (2016). Educating collaborative planners: Strengthening evidence for the learning potential of multi-stakeholder regional learning environments. *Planning Practice and Research*, *31*(5), 533–551.

Organization for Economic Co-operation and Development. (2014). OECD principles for internet policy making. [PDF file]. Retrieved from https://www.oecd.org/sti/ieconomy/oecd-principles-for-internet-policy-making.pdf

Pruitt, R., & Thomas, P. (2007). Democratic dialogue –A handbook for practitioners. [PDF file]. Retrieved from https://www.undp.org/content/dam/undp/library/crisis%20prevention/democratic%20_dialogue.pdf

Roche, B. (2011). New directions in community-based research. [PDF file]. Retrieved from https://www.wellesleyinstitute.com/wp-content/uploads/2011/11/newdirectionsincbr.pdf

Social Sciences and Humanities Research Council. (2019). Partnership grants. Retrieved from https://www.sshrc-crsh.gc.ca/funding-financement/programs-programmes/partnership_grants_stage1-subventions_partenariat_etape1-eng.aspx

Trebble, T. M., Hansi, N., Hydes, T., Smith, M. A., & Baker, M. (2010). Process mapping the patient journey: An introduction. *BMJ*, *341*(1), c4078.

Virginia Commonwealth University. (n.d). Center for community engagement and impact. Retrieved from https://community.vcu.edu/faculty-support/

Wayne-Nixon, L., Wragg-Morris, T., Mishra, A., Markle, D., & Kindornay, S. (2019). Effective multi-stakeholder engagement to realize the 2030 Agenda. [PDF file]. Retrieved from https://www.bccic.ca/wp-content/uploads/2019/06/Effective_Engagement_Canada.pdf

YWCA Canada. (2020). Our history. Retrieved from https://ywcacanada.ca/who-are-we/impact-history/

Chapter 45

Pandemics and Systemic Discrimination: Technology-Facilitated Violence and Abuse in an Era of COVID-19 and Antiracist Protest

Jane Bailey, Asher Flynn, and Nicola Henry

Abstract

Technology-facilitated violence and abuse is a truly global problem. As the diverse perspectives and experiences featured in this book have shown, the deep entanglement between technologies, inequality, marginalization, abuse, and violence require multi-faceted and collaborative responses that exist within and beyond the law. When this chapter was written, society was (and continues to be) facing an unprecedented challenge in COVID-19 – a global pandemic. At the same time, a renewed focus on racist police and civilian violence has occurred following the killings of George Floyd, Ahmaud Arbery, and Breonna Taylor in the United States. As we describe in this chapter, these two major moments are ongoing reminders of the profound social inequalities within our global communities, which are grounded in systemically discriminatory oppressions and their intersections. This chapter draws together some thoughts on technology-facilitated violence and abuse in an era of COVID-19 and antiracist protest. It explores these within the context of the book as a whole, highlighting the importance for improved understanding of, and responses to, technology-facilitated violence and abuse as part of a broader push for social justice.

Keywords: Technology-facilitated violence and abuse; COVID-19; racism; pandemic; systemic discrimination and oppression; police violence

The Emerald International Handbook of Technology-Facilitated Violence and Abuse, 787–797

doi:10.1108/978-1-83982-848-520211057

Introduction

The worst and the best of humanity are being graphically showcased on a daily basis as we prepare this manuscript for submission. The global COVID-19 pandemic and renewed focus on racist police and civilian violence following the killings of George Floyd, Ahmaud Arbery, and Breonna Taylor[1] in the United States (US) are ongoing reminders of the lasting and profound social inequalities that plague our global communities. These are social inequalities that are grounded in systemically discriminatory oppressions such as racism, misogyny, colonialism, homophobia, transphobia, ableism, and their intersections. The task of producing a collection about technology-facilitated violence and abuse (TFVA) could easily have been overwhelmed by this unprecedented and chaotic context. We are extremely grateful to our contributors and to those whose intended contributions were rendered impossible by the circumstances that surround us. We deeply appreciate their stalwart efforts and perseverance, which ultimately made this international, intersectional, intersectoral, and interdisciplinary collection happen, notwithstanding the fact that the odds were stacked against it. We say this not simply because we believe in this project but also because we believe that these pandemics of both disease and racist violence render ever more obvious, the deep entanglement between our technologies and ourselves in ways that make the diverse perspectives and experiences of TFVA featured in this book more important than ever.

COVID-19 and Racist Police Violence: Spotlight on Systemic Discrimination

COVID-19 and racist police violence are potent reminders of systemic discrimination and violence. And, like TFVA, while they involve and are experienced by individuals, they are part of a collective, structural context that puts members of marginalized communities at greater risk. Emerging international research on COVID-19 indicates that racialized and immigrant, Indigenous, and low-income populations are disproportionately more likely to contract the disease, to experience a severe case of the illness, and to die from it than their nonracialized and nonimmigrant counterparts (Centers for Disease Control and Prevention, 2020; Public Health Ontario, 2020; UK Office for National Statistics, 2020). The higher risk of exposure to illness and death within these communities reflects a variety of outcomes of systemic discrimination, including: living in densely populated/overcrowded conditions due to neighborhood segregation; living on reservations without adequate water and sanitation facilities; living in areas remote from groceries, medical care, and safe transportation; lack of private means of transportation; overrepresentation in prisons, shelters, and detention centers – which is itself a product of systemic discrimination (Blewett, 2020; Centers for Disease Control and Prevention, 2020) – as well as working in often lower paid public-facing essential services (Blewett, 2020). Further, a number of additional studies indicate that the self-isolation requirements associated with the pandemic have contributed to increased levels of domestic violence reporting (see, e.g., Mohler et al., 2020; Powell & Flynn, 2020; Price, 2020), and escalating violence against women and girls often due to confinement with abusive family members and caregivers, and to reduced access to domestic violence and health services, with disproportionate effects on women and girls "facing multiple forms of discrimination" (UN Women, 2020, p. 1).

As the events of COVID-19 continue to unfold, so too have protests against another pandemic, the "pandemic of racism" that led to the recent highly publicized deaths of Black Americans, George Floyd, Ahmaud Arbery, and Breonna Taylor. Mr. Floyd was killed by a white police officer kneeling on his neck for over 8 minutes, ignoring his pleas that he could not breathe (BBC News, 2020c). At Floyd's memorial service, lawyer Benjamin Crump stated that "it was 'not the coronavirus pandemic that killed George Floyd. It was that other pandemic ... The pandemic of racism and discrimination'" (BBC News, 2020c). Floyd's killing, like the killings of Arbery and Taylor (which occurred earlier in 2020), was captured on videos that were widely circulated online (McLaughlin, 2020), sparking Black Lives Matter protests internationally that aimed not only to raise public awareness of Floyd's death but also to place it, and the deaths of Arbery and Taylor, among others, in the larger and long-standing context of systemic racism and anti-Black policing in countries around the world (Bonhomme, 2020). Tyra Jean (2020) aptly captures the systemic underpinnings of both the differential impacts of COVID-19 and racist police violence as follows:

> Though police brutality and COVID-19 are separate tragedies, they intersect. As with police killings, the COVID-19 death rate is higher among Blacks than the US population overall. The COVID-19 pandemic has shed light on America's deeply rooted structural health inequities. From inadequate access to healthcare to representing a disproportionate share of active frontline essential workers, the U.S. Black population consistently bears the burden of life-threatening consequences due to structural racism and non-inclusive policies throughout multiple institutions.

Public attention is also increasingly being focused on racist police violence against members of other marginalized communities, including Indigenous people in Canada (Britneff, 2020), who are "more than 10 times more likely to have been shot and killed by a police officer in Canada since 2017 than a white person in Canada" (Flanagan, 2020).

The reports relating to the COVID-19 pandemic and racist police violence that are punctuating international headlines as we prepare this manuscript for submission serve as important reminders of the very real impacts of systemic discrimination and violence on the lives of members of marginalized communities. It is important to note that although COVID-19 and racist violence are currently in the news, the systemic discrimination that shapes them is far from new,[2] particularly for members of marginalized communities whose lived realities are affected by it on a daily basis. While the bases of discrimination may vary from nation to nation, as many of the contributions in this volume powerfully demonstrate, preexisting structures of oppression such as misogyny (see, e.g., Chisala-Templehoff & Stevenson; Harris & Woodlock), racism and colonialism (see, e.g., Carlson & Frazer; Bailey & Shayan; Novich & Zduniak), homophobia and transphobia (see, e.g., Colliver), and their intersections, frequently play a pivotal role in TFVA. Just like COVID-19, and racist police and civilian violence, TFVA is experienced by individuals, but is shaped by broader systemic forces that demand not only immediate responses but broader, proactive social change.

COVID-19 and Racist Police Violence: Online/Offline Convergence

The current pandemic and protests against racist police violence also serve to reinforce the deep interconnection between what might previously have been conceived of as the separate "online" and "offline," or "real" and "cyber" worlds – a distinction that many contributions in the book show to be not only untenable, but harmful (see, e.g., Dunn; Gosse). Further, the roles of technology in shaping understandings of, interactions with, and responses to these events helps to highlight the entanglement of technology companies' practices and policies discussed in this book, in this increasingly seamlessly converged reality in which more and more aspects of our lives are made dependent upon digital connectivity (see, e.g., Henry & Witt). As part of this converged reality, just as a number of chapters have noted in relation to technology-facilitated intimate partner violence and image-based sexual abuse (see, e.g., Louie; Ferreira Lopes; Marganski & Melander; Slupska & Tanczer; see also Powell & Flynn, 2020; Price, 2020), we have seen technology used in the pandemic and protest contexts to both respond to and perpetrate violence and abuse in ways that serve to question, as well as to reentrench, the broader systemic forces at play.

COVID-19: (Mis)information, Online Hate, and Other Technological Dimensions

Social media has been a central source of information and misinformation relating to COVID-19, with emerging research suggesting that "top-down misinformation from politicians, celebrities, and other prominent figures," while accounting for only a small fraction of false/inaccurate claims, comprises a significant portion of social media engagement (Brennen, Simon, Howard, & Nielsen, 2020). The spread of misinformation includes false claims about treatments for or prevention of COVID-19 (Ha-Redeye, 2020), inaccurate information about health authorities and their actions (Brennen et al., 2020), conspiracy theories suggesting that a vaccine existed but was being withheld (Oi-Yee Li, Bailey, Huynh, & Chan, 2020), and that COVID-19 is "a leaked bioweapon, a byproduct of 5G wireless technology and a political hoax" (Caulfield, 2020), among many others. Some of the misinformation suggesting drinking bleach and cow urine, for example, presents immediate physical health risks if followed (Caulfield, 2020).

Other misinformation propagated hatred against Chinese people (and to a lesser extent other racial and ethnic minority groups) by using "discriminating and stigmatizing language against Chinese people" that played on preexisting stereotypes about Chinese lifestyle and eating habits, in order to blame Chinese people for the pandemic (Aratani, 2020; Stechemesser, Wenz, & Levermann, 2020). This online hate speech translated to a growth in reported instances of discrimination, aggression, and racism against people of Asian descent in numerous parts of the globe (see, e.g., Aratani, 2020; Gill, 2020; Shimizu, 2020). Some of the online tactics that have been used during the COVID-19 pandemic resemble the sorts of "othering" techniques discussed by Benjamin Colliver and Elina Vaahensalo in their chapters in this book.

At the same time, digital communication technologies have been heralded for enabling the continuation of numerous activities, such as business meetings, classes (Bailey, Burkell, Regan, & Steeves, 2020), medical consultations (Favaro & St Philip, 2020), court hearings (Douglas, 2020), and provision of support services to targets of domestic and sexual violence (see, e.g., Canadian Women's Foundation, 2020; Ottawa Coalition to End Violence Against Women, 2020), without breaking social distancing rules. However, with mass migration of activities to online platforms have emerged new and modified forms of TFVA that often reflect and reentrench preexisting systems of discrimination (Harwell, 2020). Perhaps the most prominent North American example is "Zoombombing" – a practice in which uninvited individuals have exploited security flaws in the Zoom videoconferencing software and/or meeting organizers' lack of awareness of security features in order to make unwelcome interventions in ongoing meetings and classes. Numerous reports indicate that these interventions have included unwanted pornographic, racist, threatening, and/or misogynistic content (see, e.g., Andone, 2020; Redden, 2020). Other forms of TFVA-related content arising in the pandemic context include reported threats and pressures in dating apps for women to break social distancing rules (Iovine, 2020), and expanded accessibility of child sexual abuse material and online sexual exploitation (Europol, 2020).

With the expanded use of digital communications technologies as part of COVID-19, the opportunities for technology companies to collect and make use of data to profile users for the purposes of, among other things, marketing to them, have also expanded (Bailey et al., 2020). Little is known about what exactly is being done with data collected by providers of online videoconferencing software, although information privacy commissioners have expressed concern about these issues (see, e.g., CBC News 2020; Office of the Privacy Commissioner of Canada, 2020). In response to expression of widespread public concern, some platforms have indicated privacy and security are an increasing priority (see, e.g., Zoom, 2020). Even more concerning are reports relating to tracking apps, drones, video surveillance, and other digital technologies being used in countries around the world (including South Korea, Hong Kong, China, and Israel) to, among other things, monitor for compliance with COVID-19 regulations, as well as for indicators of infection (such as elevated body temperature) (Dupont, 2020). While these technologies raise concerns about the possibilities for new forms of state-created TFVA that are of interest to everyone, the historic record of the oversurveillance and profiling of racialized and other marginalized groups in many societies (Gandy, 1993) raises concerning prospects that their privacy-invasive harms will be disproportionately borne by equality-seeking communities.

COVID-19 has also afforded insight into another dimension of the deep entanglement of technology company business models and practices with TFVA. For example, as Nicola Henry and Alice Witt discuss in their chapter, while considerable ink has been spilled on whether social media platforms can and should remove harmful content, technology companies under COVID-19 displayed a remarkable willingness and capacity to act in relation to certain kinds of misinformation (Newton, 2020). Google searches relating to COVID-19 immediately trigger an alert and appear to prioritize content from more reliable sources, including local health authorities (Newton, 2020). As of May 2020, Facebook's misinformation strategy included the use of AI to flag what they deem to be harmful misinformation, and the use of messages warning users to avoid false information any time they interact with flagged content, as well as providing links to the World Health Organization (Brodwin, 2020). While the efforts of both of these companies have been subject to certain criticisms (see, e.g., Brodwin, 2020; Newton, 2020), the very fact that these efforts are being made acknowledges the degree to which platform design and practices can be used to shape user behavior and interaction, raising important questions about whether, and if so, how such techniques could and should be used in response to other forms of TFVA (in this book, see PenzeyMoog & Slakoff; Slupska & Tanczer).

Racist Police Violence: Technological Dimensions

As with COVID-19, digital communications technologies have played significant roles in relation to racist police violence and protest movements responding to them. Some consider the release of the videos of George Floyd's killing, as well as videos of police and civilian killings of other Black Americans, including Ahmaud Arbery and Breonna Taylor, as important catalysts for global protests and expressions of support for Black Lives Matter (see, e.g., Aratani, 2020; Johnson, 2020).[3] Further, use of Twitter hashtags including #BlackLivesMatter and #IdleNoMore have played prominent and important roles in raising public awareness and inspiring calls for justice for racialized and Indigenous communities. These same platforms, however, have been used by far-right extremists for purposes of perpetuating racism, colonialism, and other discriminatory oppressions, often in a bid to radicalize and recruit new members (Townsend, 2020). They have also been used by mainstream politicians, such as Donald Trump, to attack and ridicule calls for racial justice (Wilke, 2020). And while K-pop fans have taken matters into their own hands using "virtual protesting" tactics to "drown out" alt-right commentary by posting videos of their favorite bands on hashtags such as #whitelivesmatter (Schatz, 2020), calls for expanded oversight of platform operations continue in a number of countries (see, e.g., Broadcasting and Telecommunications Legislative Review Panel, 2020, pp. 190–198; Townsend, 2020).

Further, as with COVID-19, surveillance technologies are playing concerning roles in relation to protests against racist police violence. For example, recent reports suggest that facial recognition technologies and drones are being used across US cities to surveil Black Lives Matter protestors (Medium, 2020). Some technology companies, such as IBM, Amazon, and Microsoft have publicly stated they "won't sell or would at least pause police use of their facial recognition technology until there are federal laws on the matter" (Fowler, 2020). However, some have dismissed such statements as publicity stunts, given technology companies' ongoing interference in efforts by civil rights and privacy advocates to have these technologies banned altogether (Fowler, 2020).

Looking to the Future

This Handbook has been incubated and will be born into complex and chaotic times defined by historic global pandemics of disease (COVID-19), racism, and (mis)information. These are times in which the entanglements of social, cultural, economic, political, and technological forces in lived experiences around the globe are undeniable, and where careful attention must be paid to the impacts of discriminatory systems such as misogyny, racism, homophobia, transphobia, colonialism, ableism, classism, and their intersections, as well as to perspectives beyond those of us situated in industrialized nations. Mindful of this context, it is in this spirit that we add this collection to the cacophony of voices calling for improved understanding of, and responses to, TFVA.

Acknowledgment

Thanks to uOttawa JD student Taylor Bain for her research assistance and to the Social Sciences and Humanities Research Council of Canada for funding The eQuality Project, a 7-year initiative co-led by Jane Bailey and Valerie Steeves, which focuses on young people's experiences with privacy and equality in networked environments.

Notes

1. George Floyd was killed by US police officers in Minneapolis on May 25, 2020 (New York Times, 2020). Ahmaud Arbery was shot in Georgia on February 23, 2020 by two white men while jogging (BBC News, 2020a). On March 13, 2020, Breonna Taylor was shot 8 times and killed at home in bed after police officers broke down her apartment door while purportedly "serving a 'no-knock' warrant for a narcotics investigation" (BBC News, 2020b).
2. It is well established that social determinants of health, including race, gender, socioeconomic status, indigeneity, occupation, homelessness, and incarceration have a profound impact on exposure to, contraction and severity of illness, with social and racial inequity having played a proven role in prior pandemics, such as H1N1 (Public Health Ontario, 2020). Similarly, protests against racist policing have been ongoing for decades in the United States and elsewhere, though there is some hope that this time, lasting change will emerge (Chotiner, 2020).
3. It is important, however, not to overstate the role of the public release of such videos, given that prior release of images of racist police violence have not sparked such broad-based and sustained public activism and outrage. Black Lives Matter cofounder, Opal Tometi, has suggested that pandemic conditions may make this

situation different. She has noted that people in the United States are "more tender or sensitive to what is going on," not only in relation to police violence, but with respect to the US government's lack of a "plan of action that is dignified and comprehensive … [and aimed at] the core concerns that the average American has" (Chotiner, 2020).

References

Andone, D. (2020). FBI warns video calls are getting hijacked. It's called 'Zoom-bombing'. *CNN*. Retrieved from https://www.cnn.com/2020/04/02/us/fbi-warning-zoombombing-trnd/index.html

Aratani, L. (2020). 'Coughing while Asian': Living in fear as racism feeds off coronavirus panic. *The Guardian*. Retrieved from https://www.theguardian.com/world/2020/mar/24/coronavirus-us-asian-americans-racism

Bailey, J., Burkell, J., Regan, P., & Steeves, V. (2020). Children's privacy is at risk with rapid shift to online schooling under coronavirus. *The Conversation*. Retrieved from https://theconversation.com/childrens-privacy-is-at-risk-with-rapid-shifts-to-online-schooling-under-coronavirus-135787

BBC News. (2020a). Ahmaud Arbery: What do we know about the case? Retrieved from https://www.bbc.com/news/world-us-canada-52623151

BBC News. (2020b). Breonna Taylor: Louisville officer to be fired for deadly use of force. Retrieved from https://www.bbc.com/news/world-us-canada-53111709

BBC News. (2020c). George Floyd: 'Pandemic of racism' led to his death, memorial told. Retrieved from https://www.bbc.com/news/world-us-canada-52928304

Blewett, T. (2020). Systemic racism, barriers explain higher rates of COVID-19 among immigrant, non-white communities in Ottawa: Experts. *The Ottawa Citizen*. Retrieved from https://ottawacitizen.com/news/local-news/systemic-racism-barriers-explain-higher-rates-of-covid-19-among-immigrant-non-white-communities-in-ottawa-experts/wcm/8c8b3e4a-7b79-48ec-97dd-ca8c9eab1433/

Bonhomme, E. (2020). George Floyd, a survivor's guilt and a global Black Lives Matter. *Aljazeera*. Retrieved from https://www.aljazeera.com/indepth/opinion/george-floyd-survivor-guilt-global-black-lives-matter-200620181544441.html

Brennen, J. S., Simon, F. M., Howard, P. N., & Nielsen, R. K. (2020). Types, sources and claims of COVID-19 misinformation. University of Oxford, Reuters Institute for the Study of Journalism, Oxford Internet Institute, and Oxford Martin School. Retrieved from http://www.primaonline.it/wp-content/uploads/2020/04/COVID-19_reuters.pdf

Britneff, B. (2020). 'Disturbing' police violence against Indigenous people will be investigated: Trudeau. *Global News*. Retrieved from https://globalnews.ca/news/7030052/miller-outraged-police-violence-indigenous-people/

Broadcasting and Telecommunications Legislative Review Panel. (2020). Canada's communications future: Time to act. Retrieved from https://www.ic.gc.ca/eic/site/110.nsf/vwapj/BTLR_Eng-V3.pdf/$file/BTLR_Eng-V3.pdf

Brodwin, E. (2020). Facebook's COVID-19 misinformation campaign is based on research. The authors worry Facebook missed the message. *Stat*. Retrieved from https://www.statnews.com/2020/05/01/facebooks-covid-19-misinformation-campaign-is-based-on-research-the-authors-worry-facebook-missed-the-message/

Canadian Women's Foundation. (2020). *Signal for help*. Toronto, ON: Canadan Women's Foundation. Retrieved from https://canadianwomen.org/signal-for-help/

Caulfield, T. (2020). Pseudoscience and COVID-19 – we've had enough already. *Nature*. doi:10.1038/d41586-020-01266-z

CBC News. (2020). Make sure your virtual meetings are secure says Sask. privacy commissioner. Retrieved from https://www.cbc.ca/news/canada/saskatoon/privacy-virtual-meeting-saskatchewan-1.5545672

Centres for Disease Control and Prevention. (2020). COVID-19 in racial and ethnic minority groups. Retrieved from https://www.cdc.gov/coronavirus/2019-ncov/need-extra-precautions/racial-ethnic-minorities.html

Chotiner, I. (2020). A Black Lives Matter co-founder explains why this time is different. *The New Yorker*. Retrieved from https://www.newyorker.com/news/q-and-a/a-black-lives-matter-co-founder-explains-why-this-time-is-different

Douglas, H. (2020). Changes to our courts: How COVID-19 is changing the landscape. *Slaw*. Retrieved from http://www.slaw.ca/2020/03/31/changes-to-our-courts-how-covid-19-is-changing-the-landscape/

Dupont, B. (2020). Covid-19: Les derives possible de surveillance des données personnelles. *The Conversation*. Retrieved from https://theconversation.com/covid-19-les-derives-possibles-de-surveillance-des-donnees-personnelles-139443

Europol. (2020). Pandemic profiteering: How criminals exploit the COVID-19 crisis. Retrieved from pandemic_profiteering-how_criminals_exploit_the_covid-19_crisis.pdf

Favaro, A., & Philip, E. St. (2020). Ontario implements virtual medical visits in bid to keep doctors, patients safe amid COVID-19. *CTV News*. Retrieved from https://www.ctvnews.ca/health/coronavirus/ontario-implements-virtual-medical-visits-in-bid-to-keep-doctors-patients-safe-amid-covid-19-1.4853436

Flanagan, R. (2020). Why are Indigenous people in Canada so much more likely to be shot and killed by police? *CTV News*. Retrieved from https://www.ctvnews.ca/canada/why-are-indigenous-people-in-canada-so-much-more-likely-to-be-shot-and-killed-by-police-1.4989864

Fowler, G. (2020). Black Lives Matter could change facial recognition forever – If big tech doesn't stand in the way. *Washington Post*. Retrieved from https://www.washingtonpost.com/technology/2020/06/12/facial-recognition-ban/

Gandy, O. (1993). *The panoptic sort: A political economy of personal information*. Boulder, CO: Westview Press

Gill, R. (2020). *Asian communities across Canada report rising racist behaviour during COVID-19. Global News*. Retrieved from https://globalnews.ca/news/7033253/corona-virus-asian-racism-crisis-canada//

Ha-Redeye, O. (2020). False and misleading claims around COVID. *Slaw*. Retrieved from http://www.slaw.ca/2020/05/10/false-and-misleading-claims-around-covid/

Harwell, D. (2020). Everybody seems to be using Zoom. But its security flaws could leave users at risk. *Washington Post*. Retrieved from https://www.washingtonpost.com/technology/2020/04/02/everybody-seems-be-using-zoom-its-security-flaws-could-leave-people-risk/

Iovine, A. (2020). Men are harassing women on dating apps to meet up and break social distancing rules. *Mashable*. Retrieved from https://mashable.com/article/dating-app-meet-harassment-coronavirus-social-distance/

Jean, T. (2020). Black Lives Matter: Police brutality in the era of COVID-19. *Syracuse: Lerner Centre for Public Health Promotion*. Retrieved from https://lernercenter.syr.edu/wp-content/uploads/2020/06/Jean.pdf

Johnson, D. (2020). The George Floyd uprising has brought us hope. Now we must turn protest to policy. *The Guardian*. Retrieved from https://www.theguardian.com/commentisfree/2020/jun/30/black-lives-matter-protests-voting-policy-change

McLaughlin, E. (2020). Three videos piece together the final moments of George Floyd's life. *CNN*. Retrieved from https://www.cnn.com/2020/06/01/us/george-floyd-three-videos-minneapolis/index.html

Medium. (2020). Usage of surveillance drones over Black Lives Matter protests in the USA. *Medium*. Retrieved from https://mediummagazine.nl/usage-of-surveillance-drones-over-black-lives-matter-protests-in-the-usa/

Mohler, G., Bertozzi, A., Carter, J., Short, M. B., Sledge, D., Tita, G. E., … Jeffrey Brantingham, P. (2020). Impact of social distancing during COVID-19 pandemic on crime in Los Angeles and Indianapolis. *Journal of Criminal Justice*, *68*. doi: 10.1016/j.jcrimjus.2020.101692

New York Times. (2020). 8 minutes and 46 seconds: How George Floyd was killed in police custody. *New York Times*. Retrieved from https://www.nytimes.com/2020/05/31/us/george-floyd-investigation.html

Newton, C. (2020). Google has been unusually proactive in fighting COVID-19 misinformation. *Verge*. Retrieved from https://www.theverge.com/interface/2020/3/11/21173135/google-coronavirus-misinformation-youtube-covid-19-twitter-manipulated-media-biden

Office for National Statistics. (2020). Coronavirus (COVID-19) related deaths by ethnic group, England and Wales: 2 March 2020 to 10 April 2020. Retrieved from https://www.ons.gov.uk/peoplepopulationandcommunity/birthsdeathsandmarriages/deaths/articles/coronavirusrelateddeathsbyethnicgroupenglandandwales/2march2020to10april2020

Office of the Privacy Commissioner of Canada. (2020). Privacy tech-know blog: Videoconferencing – Maintain your physical distance, but keep your personal information close. Retrieved from https://www.priv.gc.ca/en/blog/20200501/

Oi-Yee Li, H., Bailey, A., Huynh, D., & Chan, J. (2020). YouTube as a source of information on COVID-19: A pandemic of misinformation? *BMJ Global Health*, *5*(5). Retrieved from https://gh.bmj.com/content/5/5/e002604

Ottawa Coalition to End Violence Against Women. (2020). Where can survivors of violence still access support during the COVID-19 pandemic in Ottawa? Retrieved from https://www.octevaw-cocvff.ca/covid19-services

Powell, A., & Flynn, A. (2020). Reports of 'revenge porn' skyrocket during lockdown: We must stop blaming the victims for it. *The Conversation*. Retrieved from https://theconversation.com/reports-of-revenge-porn-skyrocketed-during-lockdown-we-must-stop-blaming-victims-for-it-139659

Price, H. (2020). Coronavirus 'revenge porn' surge hits helpline. *BBC*. Retrieved from https://www.bbc.com/news/stories-52413994

Public Health Ontario. (2020). COVID-19 – what we know so far about … social determinants of health. Retrieved from https://www.publichealthontario.ca/-/media/documents/ncov/covid-wwksf/2020/05/what-we-know-social-determinants-health.pdf?la=en

Redden, E. (2020). 'Zoombombing' attacks disrupt classes. *Higher Education*. Retrieved from https://www.insidehighered.com/news/2020/03/26/zoombombers-disrupt-online-classes-racist-pornographic-content

Schatz, L. (2020). K-pop fans take over #WhiteLivesMatter and #BlueLivesMatter hashtags. *Cos Entertainment News*. Retrieved from https://consequenceofsound.net/2020/06/k-pop-fans-hashtags-whitelivesmatter-bluelivesmatter/

Shimizu, K. (2020). 2019-nCoV, fake news, and racism. *The Lancet*, *395*, 684–685. doi:10.1016/S0140-6736(20)30359-7

Stechemesser, A., Wenz, L., & Anders, L. (2020). Corona crisis fuels racially profiled hate in social media networks. *EClinical Medicine–The Lancet*, *23*, 100372. doi: 10.1016/j.eclinm.2020.100372

Townsend, M. (2020). Far-right thugs exploit Black Lives Matter movement, warns UK anti-extremism chief. *The Guardian*. Retrieved from https://www.theguardian.com/world/2020/jun/28/far-right-thugs-exploit-black-lives-matter-movement-warns-uk-anti-extremism-chief

UN Women. (2020). Impact of COVID-19 on violence against women and girls and service provision: UN women rapid assessment and findings. Retrieved from https://www.unwomen.org/en/digital-library/publications/2020/05/impact-of-covid-19-on-violence-against-women-and-girls-and-service-provision

Wilke, C. (2020). Trump cranks up attacks on the Black Lives Matter movement for racial justice. *CNBC*. Retrieved from https://www.cnbc.com/2020/06/25/trump-attacks-black-lives-matter-racial-justice-movement.html

Zoom. (2020). Privacy and security. Retrieved from https://zoom.us/docs/en-us/covid19.html#security

Printed and bound by CPI Group (UK) Ltd, Croydon, CR0 4YY
16/09/2026
14963021-0002